American Politics Today

THIRD
EDITION

3e

William T. Bianco

INDIANA UNIVERSITY, BLOOMINGTON

David T. Canon

UNIVERSITY OF WISCONSIN, MADISON

W. W. NORTON & COMPANY · NEW YORK · LONDON

American Politics Today

W. W. Norton & Company has been independent since its founding in 1923, when William Warder Norton and Mary D. Herter Norton first published lectures delivered at the People's Institute, the adult education division of New York City's Cooper Union. The firm soon expanded its program beyond the Institute, publishing books by celebrated academics from America and abroad. By midcentury, the two major pillars of Norton's publishing program—trade books and college texts—were firmly established. In the 1950s, the Norton family transferred control of the company to its employees, and today—with a staff of four hundred and a comparable number of trade, college, and professional titles published each year—W. W. Norton & Company stands as the largest and oldest publishing house owned wholly by its employees.

Editor: Ann Shin

Managing Editor, College: Marian Johnson

Senior Production Manager, College: Benjamin Reynolds

Project Editors: Jack Borrebach, Diane Cipollone, Lory Frenkel

Electronic Media Editor: Peter Lesser

Ancillaries Editor: Lorraine Klimowich

Marketing Manager, Political Science: Sasha Levitt

Editorial Assistant: Sarah Wolf

Editorial Assistant, Media: Kathryn Young

Photo Editor: Michael Fodera

Photo Researcher: Dena Beglio Betz

Permissions Clearing: Bethany Salminen

Text Design: Jillian Burr

Composition: Jouve International—Brattleboro, VT

Manufacturing: R. R. Donnelley & Sons—Jefferson City, MO

Copyright © 2013, 2011, 2009 by W. W. Norton & Company, Inc.

Library of Congress Cataloging-in-Publication Data has been applied for.

ISBN: 978-0-393-91325-5

W. W. Norton & Company, Inc., 500 Fifth Avenue, New York, NY 10110–0017

wwnorton.com

W. W. Norton & Company Ltd., Castle House, 75/76 Wells Street, London W1T 3QT

1 2 3 4 5 6 7 8 9 0

For our families,
Regina, Anna, and Catherine,
Sarah, Neal, Katherine, and Sophia,
who encouraged, empathized, and
helped, with patience,
grace, and love.

ABOUT THE AUTHORS

WILLIAM T. BIANCO

William T. Bianco is professor of political science at Indiana University, Bloomington, and Co-Chair of the Working Group on the Political Economy of Sustainable Democracy at the Workshop in Political Theory and Policy Analysis. He is the author of *Trust: Representatives and Constituents; American Politics: Strategy and Choice*; and numerous articles on American politics. He has received three National Science Foundation grants. He has also served as a consultant to congressional candidates and party campaign committees, as well as to the U.S. Department of Energy, the U.S. Department of Health and Human Services, and other state and local government agencies.

DAVID T. CANON

David T. Canon is professor of political science at the University of Wisconsin, Madison. His teaching and research interests focus on American political institutions, especially Congress, and racial representation. He is the author of *Actors, Athletes, and Astronauts: Political Amateurs in the U.S. Congress; Race, Redistricting, and Representation: The Unintended Consequences of Black Majority Districts* (winner of the Richard F. Fenno Prize); *The Dysfunctional Congress?* (with Kenneth Mayer); and various articles and book chapters. He recently finished a term as the Congress editor of *Legislative Studies Quarterly*. He is an AP consultant and has taught in the University of Wisconsin Summer AP Institute for U.S. Government & Politics since 1997. Professor Canon is the recipient of a University of Wisconsin Chancellor's Distinguished Teaching Award.

CONTENTS IN BRIEF

CONTENTS

9. INTEREST GROUPS 336

PART III: INSTITUTIONS

PART IV: POLICY

14. CIVIL RIGHTS 552

PREFACE

This book is based on three simple premises: politics is conflictual, political process matters, and politics is everywhere. It reflects our belief that politics is explainable, that political outcomes can be understood in terms of decisions made by individuals—and that the average college undergraduate can make sense of the political world in these terms. It focuses on contemporary American politics, the events and outcomes that our students have lived through and know something about. The result, we believe, is a book that provides an accessible but rigorous account of the American political system.

American Politics Today is also the product of our dissatisfaction with existing texts. Twenty-five years ago we were assistant professors at the same university, assigned to teach the introductory class in alternate semesters. While our graduate training was quite different, we found that we shared a deep disappointment with available texts. Their wholesale focus on grand normative concepts such as civic responsibility or their use of analytic themes such as collective action left students with little idea of how American politics really works, how events in Washington affect their everyday lives, and how to piece together all the facts about American politics into a coherent explanation of why things happen as they do. These texts did not engender excitement, fascination, or even passing interest. What they did was put students to sleep.

The first two editions of this book broke new ground in both approach and content. In the Third Edition, our themes continue to embody our belief that it is possible to make sense of American politics—that we can move beyond simply describing what happens in political life to predicting and explaining behavior and outcomes, and, moreover, that this task can be accomplished in the introductory class. In part we wish to counter the widespread belief among students that politics is too complicated, too chaotic, or too secretive to make sense of. More than that, we want to empower our students, to demonstrate that everyday American politics is relevant to their lives. This emphasis is also a response to the typical complaint about American Government textbooks—that they are full of facts but devoid of useful information, and that after students finish reading, they are no better able to answer "why" questions than they were before they cracked the book.

In this edition, we maintain our central focus on conflict and compromise in American politics—identifying what Americans agree and disagree about and assessing how conflict shapes American politics, from campaign platforms to policy outcomes. While this emphasis seems especially timely given the debt ceiling crisis of 2011, the hotly contested presidential election in 2012, and the intense debates in Congress over health care reform, immigration, and budget deficits, our aim is to go beyond these events to identify a fundamental constant in American politics: the reality that much of politics is driven by disagreements over the scope and form of government policy, and that compromise is an essential component of virtually all significant changes in government policy. Indeed, it is impossible to imagine politics without conflict. Conflict was embedded in the American political system by the Founders, who set up a system of checks and balances to make sure that no single group could dominate. The Constitution's division of power guarantees that enacting and implementing laws will involve conflict and compromise. Accordingly, despite the general dislike people have for conflict, our students must recognize that conflict and compromise lie at the heart of politics.

Throughout the text, we emphasize common sense, showing students that politics inside the Beltway is often strikingly similar to the students' own everyday interactions. For example, what sustains policy compromises made by members of Congress? The fact that the members typically have long careers, that they interact frequently with each other, and that they only deal with colleagues who have kept their word in the past. These strategies are not unique to the political world. Rather, they embody rules of thumb that most people follow (or are at least aware of) in their everyday interactions. In short, we try to help students understand American politics by emphasizing how it is not all that different from the world they know.

This focus on common sense is coupled with many references to the political science literature. We believe that contemporary research has something to say about prediction and explanation of events that students care about—and that these insights can be taught without turning students into formal theorists or statisticians. This emphasis has the secondary benefit of tying the introductory course to the wider political science discipline, including the American politics subfield and work on democracies more generally. To this end, in the Second Edition we added a box in each chapter ("What Do Political Scientists Do?") that talks about a specific piece of research, setting out the author's research question and showing how he or she went about answering it. These boxes are augmented by videos in which the authors discuss their research, as well as how they came to be interested in politics and political science. Together, the boxes and videos allow us to offer deeper explanations of political phenomena, as well as reinforce our argument that political science research is both understandable and relevant.

The Third Edition builds on these strengths by improving the book's appeal to students in several ways. First, while adding material in response to reviewers' comments, we have worked to streamline and improve the presentation of text and graphics. The result is a text that is even more accessible to students. We also have improved the pedagogy by adding extensive review and quiz material at the conclusion of every chapter and smart new graphics within the chapters. In the Third Edition, new chapter openers use contemporary stories and examples to highlight the conflict and compromise theme.

We do not frame the text in terms of any one theory or approach. We present the essential insights of contemporary research, motivated by real-world political phenomena and explained using text or simple diagrams. This approach gives students a set of tools for understanding politics, provides an introduction to the political science literature, and matches up well with students' common-sense intuitions about everyday life. Moreover, by showing that academic scholarship is not a blind alley or irrelevant, this approach helps to bridge the gap between an instructor's teaching and his or her research.

While we do not ignore American history, our stress is on contemporary politics—on the debates, actions, and outcomes that most college students are aware of. The text is, as one of us put it, "ruthlessly contemporary." Focusing on recent events emphasizes the utility of the concepts and insights that we develop in the text. It also goes a long way toward establishing the relevance of the intro class.

Finally, our book offers an individual-level perspective on America's government. The essential message is that politics—elections, legislative proceedings, regulatory choices, and everything else we see—is a product of the decisions made by real flesh-and-blood people. This approach grounds our discussion of politics in the real world. Many texts focus on abstractions such as "the eternal debate," "the great questions," or "the pulse of democracy." The problem with these constructs is that they don't explain where the debate, the questions, or even democracy come from. Nor do they help students understand what's going on in Washington and elsewhere, as it's not obvious that the participants care much about these sorts of abstractions—quite the opposite, in fact.

We replace these constructs with a focus on real people and actual choices. The primary goal is to make sense of American politics by understanding why politicians, bureaucrats, judges, and citizens act as they do. That is, we are grounding our description of American politics at the most fundamental level— an individual facing a decision. How, for example, does a voter choose among candidates? Stated that way, it is reasonably easy to talk about where the choice came from, how the individual might evaluate different options, and why one choice might look better than the others. Voters' decisions may be understood by examining the different feasible strategies they employ (issue voting, retrospective evaluations, stereotyping, etc.) and by asking ourselves why some voters use one strategy while others use a different one.

By focusing on individuals and choices, we can place students in the shoes of the decision makers, and in so doing, give them insight into why people act as they do. We can discuss, for example, why a House member might favor enacting wasteful pork-barrel spending, even though a proposal full of such projects will make his constituents economically worse off—and why constituents might reward such behavior, even if they suspect the truth. By taking this approach, we are not trying to let legislators off the hook. Rather, we believe that any real understanding of the political process must begin with a sense of the decisions the participants make and why they make them.

Focusing on individuals also segues naturally into a discussion of consequences, allowing us to move from examining decisions to describing and evaluating outcomes. In this way, we can show students how large-scale outcomes in politics, such as inefficient programs, don't happen by accident or because of malfeasance. Rather, they are the predictable results of choices made by individuals (here, politicians and voters).

The policy chapters—on civil rights in the Core version of the text, and on civil rights, economic policy, social policy, and foreign policy in the Full version—also represent a distinctive feature of this book. The discussion of policy at the end of an intro class often fits awkwardly with the material covered earlier. It is supposed to be a culmination of the semester-long discussion of institutions, politicians, and political behavior, but instead it often becomes an afterthought that gets discarded when time runs out in the last few weeks of class. Our policy chapters explicitly draw on previous chapters' discussions of the actors that shape policy: the president, Congress, the courts, interest groups, and parties. By doing so, these chapters show how all the pieces of the puzzle fit together.

Finally, this book reflects our experience as practicing scholars and teachers, as well as interactions with over fifteen thousand students in introductory classes at several universities. Rather than thinking of the intro class as a service obligation, we believe it offers a unique opportunity for faculty to develop a broader sense of American politics and American political science, while at the same time giving students the tools they need to behave as knowledgeable citizens or enthusiastic political science majors. We hope that it works for you as well as it does for us.

FEATURES OF THE TEXT

THE BOOK'S "THREE KEY IDEAS"—politics is conflictual, political process matters, and politics is everywhere—are fully integrated throughout the text.

▶ **Politics Is Conflictual** and conflict and compromise are a normal, healthy part of politics. The questions debated in elections and the policy options considered by people in government are generally marked by disagreement at all levels. Making policy typically involves important issues on which people disagree, sometimes strongly; so compromise, bargaining, and tough choices about trade-offs are often necessary.

▶ **Political Process Matters** because it is the mechanism we have established to resolve conflicts and achieve compromise. Governmental actions result from conscious choices made by voters, elected officials, and bureaucrats. The media often cover political issues in the same way they do sporting events, and while this makes for entertaining news, it also leads citizens to overlook the institutions, rules, and procedures that have a decisive influence on American life. Politics really is not just a game.

▶ **Politics Is Everywhere** in that the results of the political process affect all aspects of Americans' everyday lives. Politics governs what people can and cannot do, their quality of life, and how they think about events, other people, and situations.

CONFLICT AND COMPROMISE CHAPTER OPENERS

reflect our "politics is conflictual" emphasis. Each chapter begins with an example of conflict in American politics, from debates over what the Constitution means to disagreements within the Democratic and Republican parties. In the Third Edition, all of these openers are new. Within each chapter and especially in the chapter conclusions, we return to the examples, showing how disagreements and efforts to mitigate them shape every area of American politics.

A NEW ORGANIZATION AROUND CHAPTER GOALS

stresses learning objectives and mastery of core material.

▶ **Chapter Goals** appear at the beginning of the chapter and then recur at the start of the relevant sections throughout the chapter to create a more active reading experience that emphasizes important learning objectives.

▶ **NEW: Extensive end-of-chapter review sections organized around the Chapter Goals** include section summaries, practice quiz questions, key terms, and suggested reading lists. Students have everything they need to master the material in each section of the chapter.

BOXED FEATURES reinforce the three key ideas while introducing other important ways to think about American politics.

▶ **NEW "How It Works" infographics** show how the political process works and how it resolves (or fails to resolve) conflicts. These complement the chapter-opening stories, depicting the processes that underlie the conflicts and compromises we see in American politics. Critical-thinking questions ask students to consider the implications of the process and how it affects the outcome.

▶ **"In Comparison" boxes** examine how American political institutions and processes differ from those in other countries, shedding light on how America's distinctive political processes matter.

▶ **"You Decide" boxes** present a controversial issue and encourage students to consider the possible trade-offs involved in proposed solutions. Each box concludes with two critical-thinking questions.

▶ **"What Do Political Scientists Do?" boxes** explain in an engaging, journalistic style how political scientists identify research topics and conduct their studies and what makes this research and analysis important to the lives of ordinary people.

ACKNOWLEDGMENTS

This edition of *American Politics Today* is again dedicated to our families. Our wives, Regina and Sarah, have continued to accommodate our deadlines and schedules and have again served as our most accurate critics and sources of insight and inspiration. Our five children, several of whom are now undergraduates themselves, have again been forced to contend with politics and textbook writing as a perennial topic of conversation and have responded with critiques and insights of their own, which appear throughout the text.

Our colleagues at Indiana University and the University of Wisconsin (and before that, Duke University for both of us) provided many opportunities to talk about American politics and teaching this course.

Bill thanks his colleagues at Indiana University and elsewhere, including Christine Barbour, John Brehm, Ted Carmines, Mike Ensley, Russ Hansen, Jeff Hill, Yanna Krupnikov, Lin Ostrom, Regina Smyth, and Gerry Wright, for sharp insights and encouragement at crucial moments. He is also grateful to the legion of teaching assistants who have helped him organize and teach the intro class at three universities. Finally, he thanks the students at the Higher School of Economics in Moscow, Russia, where he taught the introductory class as a Fulbright Scholar in 2012.

David gives special thanks to Ken Mayer, whose daily "reality checks" and consistently thoughtful professional and personal advice are greatly appreciated. John Coleman, Barry Burden, Charles Franklin, Ken Goldstein, Ben Marquez, Don Moynihan, Ryan Owens, Howard Schweber, Byron Shafer, Dave Weimer, Kathy Walsh, Susan Yackee, and all the great people at Wisconsin have provided a wonderful community within which to teach and research American politics. David would also like to thank the students at the University of Debrecen in Hungary, where he taught American politics as a Fulbright Scholar in 2003–04, and the Eberhard Karls University of Tübingen, Germany, where he taught as a Fulbright Scholar in 2011–12. The Hungarian students' unique perspective on democracy, civil liberties, and the role of government required David to think about American politics in a different way. The German students' views on the role of political parties, campaigns, and the social welfare state also provided a strong contrast to the views of his American students.

Both of us are grateful to the political science faculty at Duke University, who, in addition to providing us with our first academic jobs, worked to construct a hospitable and invigorating place to research and to teach. In particular, Rom Coles, Ruth Grant, John Aldrich, Tom Spragens, Taylor Cole, and David Barber were model colleagues and scholars. We both learned to teach by watching them, and we are the better teachers and scholars for it.

The outstanding people at W. W. Norton made this a much better book than we could have produced on our own. Steve Dunn was responsible for getting the process started and providing good commentary and encouragement from beginning to end. Roby Harrington has been a source of constant encouragement and feedback. We are also extraordinarily grateful for Ann Shin's editorial insights, vision, and judgment, which are reflected in improvements made throughout the text. Once again, Pete Lesser's clear vision for the electronic media and for the textbook itself was a major help, and Lorraine Klimowich ensured order and accuracy in the support materials. Marian Johnson and Jack Borrebach were superb project editors, bringing to the project their talent for clarity of words and visuals. Sarah Wolf and Kathryn Young made sure everyone had the right versions of everything. Dena Betz and Michael Fodera put together an excellent photo program. Bethany Salminen cleared reprint permissions for the figures and tables. Ben Reynolds handled production with efficiency and good humor. Jillian Burr created a beautiful design for the book interior and cover. The entire crew at Norton has been incredibly professional and supportive. We feel very fortunate to work with them.

We are also indebted to the many reviewers who have commented on the text.

FIRST EDITION REVIEWERS

Dave Adler, Idaho State University

Rick Almeida, Francis Marion University

Jim Bailey, Arkansas State University, Mountain Home

Todd Belt, University of Hawaii, Hilo

Scott Buchanan, Columbus State University

Randy Burnside, Southern Illinois University, Carbondale

Carolyn Cocca, SUNY College at Old Westbury

Tom Dolan, Columbus State University

Dave Dulio, Oakland University

Matt Eshbaugh-Soha, University of North Texas

Kevin Esterling, University of California, Riverside

Peter Francia, East Carolina University

Scott Frisch, California State University, Channel Islands

Sarah Fulton, Texas A&M University

Keith Gaddie, University of Oklahoma

Joe Giammo, University of Arkansas, Little Rock

Kate Greene, University of Southern Mississippi

Steven Greene, North Carolina State University

Phil Habel, Southern Illinois University, Carbondale

Charles Hartwig, Arkansas State University, Jonesboro

Ted Jelen, University of Nevada, Las Vegas

Jennifer Jensen, Binghamton University (SUNY)

Terri Johnson, University of Wisconsin, Green Bay

Luke Keele, Ohio State University

Linda Keith, University of Texas, Dallas

Chris Kelley, Miami University

Jason Kirksey, Oklahoma State University

Jeffrey Kraus, Wagner College

Chris Kukk, Western Connecticut State University

Mel Kulbicki, York College

Joel Lieske, Cleveland State University

Steve Light, University of North Dakota

Baodong (Paul) Liu, University of Utah

Ken Long, Saint Joseph College, Connecticut

Michael Lynch, University of Kansas

Cherie Maestas, Florida State University

Tom Marshall, University of Texas, Arlington

Scott McClurg, Southern Illinois University, Carbondale

Jonathan Morris, East Carolina University

Jason Mycoff, University of Delaware

Sean Nicholson-Crotty, University of Missouri, Columbia

Timothy Nokken, Texas Tech University

Sandra O'Brien, Florida Gulf Coast University

John Orman, Fairfield University

L. Marvin Overby, University of Missouri, Columbia

Catherine Paden, Simmons College

Dan Ponder, Drury University

Paul Posner, George Mason University

David Redlawsk, University of Iowa

Russell Renka, Southeast Missouri State University

Travis Ridout, Washington State University

Andy Rudalevige, Dickinson College

Denise Scheberle, University of Wisconsin, Green Bay

Tom Schmeling, Rhode Island College

Pat Sellers, Davidson College

Dan Smith, Northwest Missouri State University

Dale Story, University of Texas, Arlington

John Vile, Middle Tennessee State University

Mike Wagner, University of Nebraska

Dave Wigg, St. Louis Community College

Maggie Zetts, Purdue University

SECOND EDITION REVIEWERS

Danny Adkison, Oklahoma State University

Hunter Bacot, Elon College

Tim Barnett, Jacksonville State University

Robert Bruhl, University of Illinois, Chicago

Daniel Butler, Yale University

Jennifer Byrne, James Madison University

Jason Casellas, University of Texas, Austin

Jeffrey Christiansen, Seminole State College

Richard Conley, University of Florida

Michael Crespin, University of Georgia

Brian DiSarro, California State University, Sacramento

Ryan Emenaker, College of the Redwoods

John Evans, California State University, Northridge

John Fliter, Kansas State University

Jimmy Gleason, Purdue University

Dana Glencross, Oklahoma City Community College

Jeannie Grussendorf, Georgia State University

Phil Habel, Southern Illinois University, Carbondale

Lori Han, Chapman University

Katy Harriger, Wake Forest University

Richard Himelfarb, Hofstra University

Doug Imig, University of Memphis

Daniel Klinghard, College of the Holy Cross

Eddie Meaders, University of North Texas

Kristy Michaud, California State University, Northridge

Kris Miler, University of Illinois, Urbana-Champaign

Melinda Mueller, Eastern Illinois University

Michael Mundt, Oakton Community College

Emily Neff-Sharum, University of North Carolina, Pembroke

David Nice, Washington State University
Tim Nokken, Texas Tech University
Stephen Nuño, Northern Arizona University
Richard Powell, University of Maine, Orono
Travis Ridout, Washington State University
Sara Rinfret, University of Wisconsin, Green Bay
Martin Saiz, California State University, Northridge
Gabriel Ramon Sanchez, University of New Mexico
Charles Shipan, University of Michigan
Dan Smith, Northwest Missouri State University
Rachel Sondheimer, United States Military Academy
Chris Soper, Pepperdine University
Walt Stone, University of California, Davis
Greg Streich, University of Central Missouri
Charles Walcott, Virginia Tech
Rick Waterman, University of Kentucky
Edward Weber, Washington State University
Jack Wright, Ohio State University

THIRD EDITION REVIEWERS

Steve Anthony, Georgia State University
Marcos Arandia, North Lake College
Richard Barberio, SUNY College at Oneonta
Jody Baumgartner, East Carolina University
Brian Berry, University of Texas, Dallas
David Birch, Lone Star College, Tomball
Eileen Burgin, University of Vermont
Randolph Burnside, Southern Illinois University, Carbondale
Kim Casey, Northwest Missouri State University
Christopher Chapp, University of Wisconsin, Whitewater
Daniel Coffey, University of Akron
William Corbett, University of Texas at El Paso
Jonathan Day, Western Illinois University
Rebecca Deen, University of Texas, Arlington
Brian DiSarro, California State University, Sacramento
Nelson Dometrius, Texas Tech University
Stan Dupree, College of the Desert
David Edwards, University of Texas, Austin
Ryan Emenaker, College of the Redwoods
John Evans, University of Wisconsin, Eau Claire
Brandon Franke, Blinn College, Bryan
Rodd Freitag, University of Wisconsin, Eau Claire
Donna Godwin, Trinity Valley Community College
Craig Goodman, Texas Tech University
Amy Gossett, Lincoln University
Tobin Grant, Southern Illinois University

Stephanie Hallock, Harford Community College
Alexander Hogan, Lone Star College, CyFair
Marvin King, University of Mississippi
Timothy LaPira, James Madison University
Mary Linder, Grayson University
Christine Lipsmeyer, Texas A&M University
Michael Lyons, Utah State University
Jill Marshall, University of Texas, Arlington
Thomas Masterson, Butte College
Daniel Matisoff, Georgia Institute of Technology
Jason McDaniel, San Francisco State University
Mark McKenzie, Texas Tech University
Leonard McNeil, Contra Costa College
Melissa Merry, University of Louisville
Ann Mezzell, Lincoln University
Eric Miller, Blinn College, Bryan
Jonathan Morris, East Carolina University
Leah Murray, Weber State University
Farzeen Nasri, Ventura College
Brian Newman, Pepperdine University
David Nice, Washington State University
Stephen Nichols, Cal State University, San Marcos
Tim Nokken, Texas Tech University
Barbara Norrander, University of Arizona
Andrew Reeves, Boston University
Michelle Rodriguez, San Diego Mesa College
Dan Smith, Northwest Missouri State University
Christopher Soper, Pepperdine University
Jim Startin, University of Texas, San Antonio
Jeffrey Stonecash, Syracuse University
Linda Trautman, Ohio University
Kevin Unter, University of Louisiana, Monroe
Michelle Wade, Northwest Missouri State University
Michael Wagner, University of Nebraska, Lincoln
Adam Warber, Clemson University
Wayne Wolf, South Suburban College

It is a humbling experience to have so many smart people helping us find our voice and make our arguments. Their reviews were often critical, but always insightful, and we have been fortunate to have them guide our revisions. Again, they have our profound thanks.

William T. Bianco
David T. Canon
October 2012

American Politics Today

THIRD EDITION

1

Understanding American Politics

PRESIDENT OBAMA CAME INTO conflict with the Republican majority in the House of Representatives over many issues, including the federal debt. In 2011, Obama and House Speaker John Boehner met on numerous occasions, but reaching a compromise on the debt limit and other issues proved difficult. Why?

IN SUMMER 2011, REPUBLICAN MEMBERS OF CONGRESS came into sharp conflict with President Obama and the Democrats over raising the federal government's debt limit. Politicians on both sides of the issue argued that they could not accept the plan proposed by the other side, even if the delay in finding a solution risked harming the economy. Many Americans reported feeling frustrated with Congress and the president, and worried that political conflict was harming the country.

The debate over government debt and the debt limit arose because the federal government's expenditures currently exceed the revenues it collects through taxes and other sources. So the Treasury Department must issue bonds to fund operations. When the government issues bonds, it is effectively borrowing money from the bondholders, who must eventually be paid back, with interest. The total amount of federal borrowing is limited by law, and when Congress authorizes spending that requires more borrowing, it must also enact legislation to raise the debt limit. Most of the time, these increases attract little attention.

However, in 2011, after Congress passed a spending budget that would require an increase in the debt limit, congressional Republicans announced they would not support a debt limit increase without significant spending reductions. Many of the opponents of the increase had been elected in 2010 with the support of Tea Party groups, who were concerned over the size of the federal debt and wanted to reduce spending. President Obama and the Democrats argued that funding the government's current activities and upholding its obligations was necessary, even if it meant borrowing more money. Negotiations dragged out

CONFLICT & COMPROMISE
in American Politics

over several months, as the nation moved closer to the "drop dead date" in early August, when the debt limit would be reached, and the government would have to either refuse to repay bonds that came due or make drastic spending cuts.

At nearly the last minute, a deal was reached that raised the debt limit, implemented cuts in spending, and set up a bipartisan committee to recommend additional cuts, with the threat of automatic spending reductions if the committee's recommendations were not approved. However, the prolonged negotiations contributed to investor jitters and declines in the stock market, as well as the decision by a major bond ratings agency, Standard and Poor's, to lower its ratings on U.S. federal bonds, a move that could increase the costs of future borrowing.

How did this happen? How did politicians decide that the right thing to do was to push debate over the debt limit right to the brink, to the point of doing real harm to the American economy? The episode seems like a classic example of elected officials creating and expanding conflict in order to gain political advantage, ignoring the damage they were doing to the country as a whole.

However, debates over budgets and debt limits are not just about money; they are about determining what government does. How much should the government spend on defense—but also how should America's armed forces be used? How much should be spent on Medicare—but also what are the limits on the government's responsibility to provide health care to senior citizens? How much taxes should people with different incomes pay—and should people get tax breaks for purchasing a home, adopting a child, or other actions? Every disagreement over taxing and spending has in it a disagreement over policies like these. If the debate was only about the size of the federal budget, it might be easy to split the difference between each side's ideal. But since the debate is over policy as well as spending, there is no obvious deal that satisfies everyone. Rather, the two sides have to go back and forth, making multiple offers and counteroffers, before a compromise emerges that gains enough support to be enacted.

Additional insight into the debt limit negotiations can be gained by examining two features of the legislative process. First, the fact that legislation was required to raise the debt limit was not inevitable. Congress could pass a law that allows automatic increases—or enact the increase within the annual budget. Requiring a separate vote gives members an opportunity to oppose increasing the limit and thereby gain favor with constituents who worry about excessive government spending. Members face a trade-off between building political support on the one hand and doing what is necessary to keep the government in business on the other. Second, the fact that America in 2011 had divided government, with Democrats controlling the Senate and the presidency and a Republican majority in the House, meant that a bipartisan compromise was necessary for success. Reaching a compromise required intense negotiation.

This example shows how digging below the surface of political events can help to explain why things happen in American politics—and why raising the debt limit was so difficult in the first place. Our goal is to give you a similar understanding of the entire range of American politics. Much of that understanding will come from the central theme of this book: *politics is about conflict and compromise.* People shy away from conflict in their personal lives and tend to see conflict in politics as a problem. They often view political compromise as "selling out," "caving in," or giving up on core values and principles. However, because Americans disagree about what to do about many issues, conflict is an essential part of politics and compromise is usually needed to enact changes in government policy.

MAKING SENSE OF AMERICAN GOVERNMENT AND POLITICS

DESCRIBE THE BASIC FUNCTIONS OF GOVERNMENT

The premise of this book is simple: *American politics makes sense.* What happens in elections, in Congress, in the White House, and everywhere else in the political process has a logical and often simple explanation.

This claim may seem unrealistic or even naive. On the surface, American politics is full of bewildering complexities, from the enumerated powers in the Constitution to the unwritten rules that govern how Congress works. Many policy questions, from confronting economic crises to deciding what to do about climate change, seem hopelessly intractable. As our chapter opening story suggested, politicians often seem more interested in publicizing their disagreements than in solving them. Election outcomes look random or even chaotic.

Many people, we believe, have given up on American politics because they don't understand the political process, feel helpless to influence election outcomes or policy making, and believe that politics is irrelevant to their lives. As we saw in the case of increasing the debt limit, many people are uncomfortable with the conflict and compromise that are often a part of the political process. Since you are taking a class on American politics, we hope you have not given up on politics entirely. It is *not* our goal to turn you into a political junkie or a policy expert. And it isn't necessary to be completely immersed in politics to make sense of it, but we hope that after finishing this book you will have a basic understanding of the political process.

One goal of this book is to help you take an active role in the political process. A functioning democracy allows citizens to defer complicated policy decisions to

CONFLICTS WITHIN THE GOVERNMENT— say, between the Democrats and Republicans in Congress—often reflect real divisions among American citizens about what government should do about certain issues. Groups on all sides of controversial issues pressure the government to enact their preferred policies.

their elected leaders, but it also requires citizens to monitor what those politicians are doing and to hold them accountable at the voting booth. This book will help you accomplish this important duty by providing the analytical skills you need to make sense of politics, even when it initially appears senseless.

We are not going to spend much time talking about how American politics should be. Rather, our focus will be on explaining American politics as it is. Here are some other questions we will examine:

▶ Why do some people participate in the political system while others do not?

▶ How does the Constitution structure our rights and liberties and the broader political system?

▶ Why do people vote as they do?

▶ Why do so many people mistrust politicians and the political system?

▶ Why do most members of Congress get re-elected?

▶ How do Supreme Court justices decide cases?

▶ Why do presidents sometimes appear all-powerful but look powerless at other times?

▶ How much do the media, interest groups, judges, and bureaucrats influence policy decisions and why?

We will answer these questions and many others by applying three key ideas about the nature of politics: politics is conflictual, political process matters, and politics is everywhere. But first, we begin with an even more basic question: Why do we have a government?

WHY DO WE HAVE A GOVERNMENT?

government The system for implementing decisions made through the political process.

As we prepare to address this question, let's agree on a definition: **government** is the system for implementing decisions made through the political process. All countries have some form of government, which in general serve two broad purposes: to provide order and to promote the general welfare.

FORMS OF GOVERNMENT

The Greek political philosopher Aristotle, writing in the fourth century B.C., developed a classification scheme for governments that is still surprisingly useful today. Aristotle distinguished three pure types of government based on the number of rulers versus the number of people ruled: monarchy (rule by one), aristocracy (rule by the few), and polity (rule by the many—such as the general population).

Additional distinctions can be made within Aristotle's third type, constitutional republican governments, based on how they allocate power among the executive, legislative, and judicial branches. Presidential systems such as we have in the United States tend to follow a separation of power among the three branches, while parliamentary systems such as the one in the United Kingdom elect the chief executive from the legislature, so there is much closer coordination between those two branches.

We can further refine Aristotle's third type by considering the relationships among different levels of the government. In a federal system such as the United

TWO IMPORTANT GOVERNMENT FUNCTIONS described in the Constitution are to "provide for the common defence" and "insure domestic Tranquility." The military and local police are two of the most commonly used forces the government maintains to fulfill those roles.

States, power is shared among the local, state, and national levels of government. In a unitary system, all power is held at the national level. A confederation is a less common form of government in which states retain their sovereignty and autonomy but form a loose association at the national level.

TO PROVIDE ORDER

At a basic level, the answer to the question "Why do we have a government?" seems obvious: without government there would be chaos.

As the seventeenth-century British philosopher Thomas Hobbes said, life in the "state of nature" (that is, without government) would be "solitary, poor, nasty, brutish, and short."[1] Without government there would be no laws—people could do whatever they wanted. Even if people tried to develop informal rules, there would be no way to guarantee enforcement of those rules.

The Founders of the U.S. Constitution noted this crucial role in the document's preamble: two of the central goals of government are to "provide for the common defence" and to "insure domestic Tranquility." The former refers to military protection (by the Army and Navy at the time of the Founding; it now also includes the Marines, Coast Guard, and Air Force) against foreign invasion and the defense of our nation's common security interests. The latter refers to law enforcement within the nation, which today includes the National Guard, Federal Bureau of Investigation (FBI), Department of Homeland Security, state and local police, and courts. So at a minimal level, government is necessary to provide security.

However, there's more to it than that. The Founders also cited the desire to "establish Justice . . . and secure the Blessings of Liberty to ourselves and our Posterity." But do we need government to do these things? It may be obvious that the police power of the state is required to prevent anarchy, but can't people have justice and liberty without government? In a perfect world, maybe, but the Founders had a more realistic view of human nature. As the Founder James Madison said, "But what is government itself, but the greatest of all reflections on human nature? If men were angels, no government would be necessary. If angels were to govern men, neither external nor internal controls on government would be necessary."[2]

Furthermore, Madison continued, people have a variety of interests that have "divided mankind into parties, inflamed them with mutual animosity, and rendered them much more disposed to vex and oppress each other than to co-operate for their common good."[3] That is, without government, we would quickly be headed toward Hobbes's nasty and brutish state of nature.

Madison's view of human nature might sound pessimistic, but it is also realistic. He assumes that people are self-interested: we want what is best for ourselves and for our families, and to satisfy those interests we tend to form groups with like-minded people. Madison saw these groups, which he called **factions**, as being opposed to the public good, and his greatest fear was of tyranny by a faction imposing its will on the rest of the nation. For example, if one group took power and established an official state religion, that faction would be tyrannizing people who practiced a different religion. This type of oppression is precisely why many of the early American colonists fled Europe in the first place.

So government is necessary to avoid the anarchy of the state of nature, and the right kind of government is needed to avoid oppression by whoever controls the policy-making process. As we will discuss in Chapters 2 and 3, America's government seeks to control the effects of factions by dividing government power in three main ways. First, the **separation of powers** divides the government into three branches—judicial, executive, and legislative—and assigns distinct duties to each branch. Second, the system of **checks and balances** gives each branch some power over the other two. (For example, the president can veto legislation passed by Congress; Congress can impeach the president; and the Supreme Court has the power to interpret laws written by Congress to determine whether they are constitutional.) Third, **federalism** divides power yet again by allotting different responsibilities to local, state, and national government. With power divided in this fashion, Madison reasoned, no single faction could dominate the government.

TO PROMOTE THE GENERAL WELFARE

The preamble to the Constitution also states that the federal government exists to "promote the general Welfare." This means tackling the hard problems that Americans cannot solve on their own, such as taking care of the poor, the sick, or the aged, and dealing with global issues like climate change, terrorist threats, and poverty in other countries. However, government is not inevitable—people can decide that these problems aren't worth solving. But if people *do* want to address these large problems, government action is necessary because **public goods** such as these are not efficiently provided by the free market, either because of **collective action problems**, **positive externalities**, or other reasons.

The eighteenth-century Scottish philosopher David Hume explained the problem of collective action:

> *Two neighbours may agree to drain a meadow which they possess in common [so they would be able to use it to grow crops] because 'tis easy for them to know each other's mind and each must perceive that the immediate consequence of his failing in his part is the abandoning the whole project. But 'tis very difficult and indeed impossible that a thousand persons shou'd agree in any such action; it being difficult for them to concert so complicated a design and still more difficult for them to execute it while each seeks a pretext to free himself of the trouble and expence and wou'd lay the whole burden on others. Political society easily remedies both these inconveniences.*[4]

factions Groups of like-minded people who try to influence the government. American government is set up to avoid domination by any one of these groups.

separation of powers The division of government power across the judicial, executive, and legislative branches.

checks and balances A system in which each branch of government has some power over the others.

federalism The division of power across the local, state, and national levels of government.

public goods Services or actions (such as protecting the environment) that, once provided to one person, become available to everyone. Government is typically needed to provide public goods because they will be under-produced by the free market.

collective action problems Situations in which the members of a group would benefit by working together to produce some outcome, but each individual is better off refusing to cooperate and reaping benefits from those who do the work.

positive externalities Benefits created by a public good that are shared by the primary consumer of the good and by society more generally.

That is, it is easy for two people or even a small group to tackle a common problem without the help of government, but a thousand people (to say nothing of the more than 300 million in the United States today) would have a very difficult time. They would suffer from the **free rider problem**: because it is in everyone's interest to "lay the whole burden on others," and because everyone thinks this way, the meadow would never be drained. As Hume notes, "political society"—that is, government—can "remedy those inconveniences" by draining the meadow and providing the desired public good. A government representing 300 million people can provide public goods, such as protecting the environment or defending the nation, that all those people acting on their own would be unable to provide, so they elect leaders and pay taxes to provide those public goods.

A LIGHTHOUSE IS A CLASSIC EXAMPLE of a public good—a service or product that could not be produced by private markets because once the good is provided, anyone can benefit from it without paying. Supplying public goods is one way that the government promotes the public welfare.

Another reason the free market under-produces public goods has to do with what economists call *positive externalities*, which means that the benefits from any public good are shared by the primary consumer of the good and by society at large. Education is a great example. You benefit personally from your college education in terms of the knowledge and experience you gain, and perhaps from the higher salary you will earn because of your college degree. However, society also benefits from your education. Your employer will benefit from your knowledge and skills, as will people you interact with. If education were solely provided by the free market, those who could afford schooling would be educated, but the rest would not, leaving a large segment of society with little or no education and therefore unemployable. So, public education, like many important services, benefits all levels of society and must be provided by the government for the general welfare.

free rider problem The incentive to benefit from others' work without making a contribution, which leads individuals in a collective action situation to refuse to work together.

Now that we understand *why* we have a government, the next question is, *what* does the government do to "insure domestic Tranquility" and "promote the general Welfare"? Many visible components of the government promote these goals, from the police and armed services to the Internal Revenue Service, Post Office, Social Security Administration, National Aeronautics and Space Administration, Department of Education, and Food and Drug Administration. More generally, the government does several things:

▶ It creates and enforces laws and protects private property through the criminal justice system.

▶ It establishes a common currency and regulates commerce among the states and trade with other nations.

▶ It provides public goods that would not be produced or would be undersupplied by the free market, including national defense, an interstate highway system, and national parks.

▶ It regulates the market to promote the general good, specifically by addressing market failures in areas such as environmental pollution and product safety.

▶ It protects individual civil liberties, such as the freedom of speech and the free exercise of religion.

All of these governmental roles engage the interests of political scientists. As you will discover, this book explains how political scientists study American politics to understand what the government, politicians, and citizens do, and why. As you will see, all of these government roles are significant, in the sense that they affect the lives of many Americans. They are controversial, in that Americans disagree about what government should do in each area. Government actions in each area are shaped by process, or the rules that determine who gets to select different policies. And finally, each of these roles is the subject of research by political scientists, research that helps us to understand what government does and why it does it. (See the "What Do Political Scientists Do?" box.)

DEFINE *POLITICS* AND IDENTIFY THREE KEY IDEAS THAT HELP EXPLAIN POLITICS

WHAT IS POLITICS?

politics The process that determines what government does.

We define **politics** as the process that determines what government does. You may consider politics the same thing as government, but we view politics as being much broader; it includes ways of behaving and making decisions that are common in everyday life. Many aspects of our discussion of politics will probably sound familiar because your life involves politics on a regular basis. This may sound a little abstract, but it should become clear in light of the three key ideas of this book.

First, *politics is conflictual.* As the debate over the debt limit illustrates, the questions debated in election campaigns and the options considered by policy makers generally involve disagreement at all levels. The federal government does not spend much time resolving issues that everyone agrees should be decided in a particular way. Rather, making government policy involves issues on which people disagree, sometimes strongly, which makes compromise difficult—and this is a normal, healthy part of politics. Although compromise may be difficult, it is often necessary to produce an outcome that can be enacted and implemented.

Second, *political process matters.* Governmental actions don't happen by accident—they result from conscious choices made by elected officials and bureaucrats. Politics, as the process that determines what governments do, puts certain individuals into positions of power and makes the rules that structure their choices. The media often cover political campaigns the way they would report on a boxing match or the Super Bowl, focusing on the competition, rivalries, and entertaining stories, which can lead people to overlook the institutions, rules, and procedures that have a decisive influence on politics. Indeed, the political process is the mechanism for resolving conflict. The most obvious example is elections, which democracies use to resolve a fundamental conflict in society: deciding who should lead the country.

Third, *politics is everywhere.* Decisions about what government should do or who should be in charge are integral to society, and they influence the everyday lives of all Americans. Politics helps to determine what people can and cannot do, their quality of life, and how they think about events, people, and situations. Moreover, people's political thought and behavior are driven by the same types of calculations and decision-making rules that shape beliefs and actions in other parts of life. For example, deciding which presidential candidate to vote for is similar to deciding which college to attend. In the first instance you might consider issue positions, character, and leadership ability, while in the latter you would weigh which school fits your academic goals, how much tuition you can afford, and where different schools are located. In both cases you are making a decision that will satisfy the criteria most important to you.

DESIGNING AND CONDUCTING RESEARCH

One of the most important facts we want you to get out of this book is that political science research has relevant and compelling things to say about American politics. This claim may come as a surprise. In our classes and our lives outside the university, both of us have found that many people think politics is too random, too complicated, or too subjective to be studied in the same way as atoms, chemicals, or cells.

Research in political science, like research in all sciences, usually starts with an idea—a hypothesis. In their simplest form, hypotheses are statements about how one factor, a dependent variable, is affected by a second factor, an independent variable. (Hypotheses can also have multiple dependent and independent variables.) For example, a scholar interested in explaining election outcomes might develop a hypothesis that explains vote decisions in elections (dependent variable) based on voters' evaluations of the candidates' positions on health care reform (independent variable).

Watch a video clip of William Bianco and David Canon discussing this topic at **wwnorton.com/studyspace**

To develop hypotheses, political scientists draw on theories that make general statements about the motivations and actions of individuals. For example, in the chapter on Congress, we discuss research that assumes legislators have many goals, but that getting re-elected is generally their strongest motivation. In contemporary political science, no one theory of politics has proved to be superior to all others. Accordingly, you will read about many different theories in the chapters to come. Each chapter has a box called What Do Political Scientists Do that describes a piece of political science research and its findings about American politics.

The most common research method in the study of American politics is to gather data on the relevant variables of interest and conduct statistical analysis. So, for example, to explore the impact of health care reform on voting, the researcher could do a survey of 1,500 voters that reveals their views of candidates' positions on health care reform in the 2010 elections. The survey could also ask questions about the voters' background (race, gender, age, and so on), other political variables (such as party affiliation and ideology—are they liberal, conservative, or moderate?), and how they voted in 2010. These responses would be included in a statistical analysis as controls for alternative explanations of how the person voted. That is, we know that someone who is liberal, nonwhite, and a woman is more likely to vote for a Democrat than someone who is conservative, white, and male. The question is whether a candidate's position on health care would influence voting after taking those other explanations into account.

A second approach is to use experiments. Obviously, political scientists cannot conduct different versions of real elections the way that medical researchers can run various real-life trials when they are testing a drug. Instead, political scientists create experimental and control groups either in a laboratory setting, using clever "nat-

Voters line up at a polling station near Lawrence, Kansas. Political scientists use scientific research to study voting and other political processes that matter to Americans' lives.

ural experiments," or with surveys. In each instance, the logic of the experiment is the same: the researcher holds everything constant except for one factor. For example, one could examine the impact of negative advertising on assessments of candidates by exposing one group to negative ads and another group to positive ads.

Another approach is to conduct detailed case studies based on historical analysis of archival documents, "participant observation," or interviews. One of the masters of this approach is political scientist Richard Fenno, who wrote many books based on what he called "soaking and poking."[a] By hanging out with politicians and asking them questions about what they were doing and why, Fenno was able to gain keen insights into politics.

Finally, some American politics scholars are interested in normative questions such as the proper role of the Supreme Court, how politicians *should* represent their constituents, whether political deliberation can create a better understanding of what the public wants, or how the political system can be reformed to better serve the public good. These normative questions are the focus of democratic theory and theories of political representation. Typically there is a division of labor within political science between political philosophers who grapple with these normative questions and researchers who engage in empirical analysis, but empirical work often provides insight into normative questions, and vice versa.

KEY IDEA 1: POLITICS IS CONFLICTUAL

Political scientists have long recognized the central role of conflict in politics. In fact, one prominent theory in the mid-twentieth century saw conflict between interest groups as explaining most outcomes in American politics. The political scientist E. E. Schattschneider argued that the scope of political conflict—that is, how many people are involved in the fight—determines who wins in politics. Others have argued that some conflict is essential for small-group decision making: if nobody challenges a widely shared but flawed view, people may convince themselves that the obvious flaws are not a problem. Bureaucratic politics, congressional politics, elections, and even Supreme Court decision making have all been studied through the lens of political conflict.[5]

Despite the consensus that conflict in politics is essential, most people do not like conflict, either in their personal lives or in politics. You probably have heard people say that the three topics one should not discuss in polite company are money, religion, and politics. Rather than talking about controversial subjects, many people simply avoid them. Indeed, since the 1950s, political scientists have found strong evidence that people avoid discussing politics in order to maintain social harmony.[6]

Many people apply their disdain for conflict to politicians as well. "Why is there so much partisan bickering?" our students frequently ask. "Why can't they just get along?" Many such comments were voiced during negotiations over the debt limit in 2011, and during many other legislative fights in recent years.

This dislike of conflict, and of politics more generally, produces a desire for what political scientists John Hibbing and Elizabeth Theiss-Morse call "stealth democracy"—that is, nondemocratic practices such as running government like a business or taking action without political debate. In essence, this idea reflects the hope that everything would be better if we could just take the politics out of politics. Hibbing and Theiss-Morse argue that we need to do a better job of educating people about conflict and policy differences, and that the failure to do so "is encouraging students to conclude that real democracy is unnecessary and stealth democracy will do just fine."[7] Conflict cannot be avoided in politics; ignoring fundamental disagreements will not make them go away.

CONFLICT IS INHERENT IN AMERICAN politics, a fact that has been driven home by the ongoing national debate over health care reform.

Instead of pretending that we agree on most policies and that conflict is unnecessary, Americans must recognize that political conflict is inevitable because it is rooted in our disagreements on policy questions. It is wrong-headed to claim that there would be no conflict in politics if politicians would just listen to the public—after all, Americans themselves are generally divided on what public policy should look like.

The argument over abortion is a good example. Abortion rights have been a perennial topic of debate since a 1973 Supreme Court decision held that state laws banning abortion were unconstitutional. Surveys about abortion rights show that public support encompasses a wide range of options, with little agreement about which policy is best. (In Chapter 5, Public Opinion, we will examine the political implications of this kind of broad disagreement.) Such conflicts reflect intense differences of opinion that are rooted in self-interest, ideology, and personal beliefs. Moreover, in such situations, no matter what Congress does, many people will be unhappy with the result. You might expect that politicians will ultimately find ways to compromise, but this is not always true. Sometimes the problem is a lack of trade-offs. In many cases, no single policy choice satisfies even a slight majority of elected officials or citizens.

The idea that conflict is nearly always a part of politics should be no surprise. Situations in which everyone (or almost everyone) agrees about what government should be doing are easy to resolve: either a popular new policy is enacted or an unpopular issue is avoided, and the debate moves off the political agenda. However, whereas issues where there is consensus resolve quickly and disappear, conflictual issues remain on the agenda as the winners try to extend their gains and the losers work to roll back policies. Thus, one reason that abortion rights is a perennial issue in campaigns and congressional debates is that there is no national consensus on when to allow abortions, no indication that the issue is becoming less important to citizens or elected officials, and no sign of a compromise policy that would attract widespread support.

An important implication of the inevitable conflicts in American politics is that compromise and bargaining are essential to getting things done. Politicians who bargain with opponents are not necessarily abandoning their principles; striking a deal may be the only way to make some of the policy changes they want. Moreover, agreement sometimes exists even in the midst of controversy. For example, surveys that measure attitudes about abortion find widespread support for measures such as prohibiting government funding for abortions, requiring parental notification when a minor has an abortion, or requiring doctors who perform the procedure to present their patients with information on alternatives such as adoption.

Another implication of conflict is that it is almost impossible to get exactly what you want from the political process. Even when a significant percentage of the population is united behind common goals—such as supporters of Barack Obama after the 2008 election, who favored a broad expansion of the federal government, or Tea Party sympathizers after the 2010 election, who wanted to shrink government and eliminate regulations—these individuals almost always find that they need to accept something short of their ideal to attract enough support to implement policy change. Tea Party sympathizers, for example, had to accept a debt limit deal that did not implement sharp cuts in the size of the federal budget. The

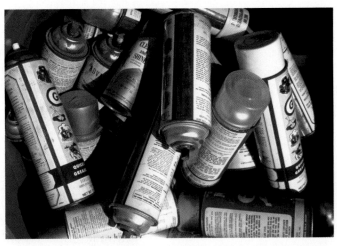

WHEN EVERYONE (OR ALMOST everyone) agrees about what government should do to solve a problem, the issue is generally dealt with quickly and without much conflict. In the 1980s, general consensus was reached on how to deal with chlorofluorocarbons (chemicals once used in aerosol cans), and they were banned. Controversial issues, on the other hand, tend to stay with us and result in more visible political conflict.

need for compromise does not mean that change is impossible, only that what is achievable often falls short of individuals' demands.

Finally, it is important to note that we are not arguing that all conflict is good. For example, the scream fests on cable news and obstruction for the sake of obstruction in Congress do not serve the greater public good. Our point here—as it is throughout this book—is simply that conflict and compromise are inherent parts of politics.

KEY IDEA 2: POLITICAL PROCESS MATTERS

The political process is often described like a sporting event, with a focus on strategies and ultimately on "winning." In fact, a politics news show on CNN has a daily segment titled "The Play of the Day." This focus overlooks an important point: politics is the process that determines what government does, none of which is inevitable. Public policy—everything from defending the nation to spending on Medicare—is up for grabs. And the political process determines these government actions. It is not just a game.

Elections are an excellent example of the importance of the political process. Elections allow voters to give fellow citizens the power to enact laws, write budgets, and appoint senior bureaucrats and federal judges—so it does matter who gets elected. After the 2008 election, when Democrats captured control of Congress and the presidency, they enacted a massive economic stimulus package and new policies for alternative energy, global warming, education, health care, regulation of the mortgage and financial sectors, and the wars in Iraq and Afghanistan. Clearly, political process matters: if the 2008 election had gone the other way, policies in all these important areas would be significantly different. The Republican takeover of the House in the 2010 election and gains in the Senate ended the Democrats' ability to pass similar proposals—unless they can craft them in a way that gains Republican support. Again, elections matter.

POLITICAL PROCESS MATTERED IN THE 2012 presidential election, from determining who the candidates would be, to affecting which states received the most attention from the campaigns.

Yet politics is more than elections. As you will see, many members of the federal bureaucracy have influence over what government does by virtue of their roles in developing and implementing government policies. The same is true for federal judges, who review government actions to see if they are consistent with the Constitution and other federal laws. These individuals' decisions are part of the political process, even though they are not elected to their positions.

Ordinary citizens are also part of politics. They can vote; donate time or money to interest groups, party organizations, or individual candidates; or demand action from these groups or individuals. Such actions can influence government policy, either by determining who holds the power to change policy directly or by signaling to policy makers which options have public support.

THE COMPROMISE THAT DEMOCRATS and Republicans reached regarding the federal debt limit in 2011 involved establishing a budget "Supercommittee" to recommend spending cuts. This process had significant consequences for the Americans who had benefited from each of the programs up for cuts.

Another important element of politics is the web of rules and procedures that determine who has the power to make choices about government policy. These rules range from the requirement that the president must have been born in the United States, to the rules that structure debates and voting in the House and the Senate, to the procedures for approving new federal regulations. Seemingly innocuous rules can have an enormous impact on what can or does happen, which means that choices about these rules are actually choices about outcomes.

Consider the cloture rule for ending debate in the Senate. It states that 60 votes out of 100 are needed to enact a new law, not just a simple majority of 51. During the period of George W. Bush's presidency when Democrats were the minority party in the Senate but the Republican majority fell short of 60 votes, cloture gave the Democrats power over government policy. For the last half of 2009, the Democrats controlled the 60 Senate seats needed to stop a Republican filibuster (a filibuster is a way to extend debate and thereby prevent a vote on a proposal). However, the filibuster-proof majority was short-lived as Republican Scott Brown won a special election in early 2010 to fill the late senator Ted Kennedy's seat in Massachusetts, and Democrats lost additional Senate seats in the 2010 election.

As the cloture example implies, the ability to determine political rules empowers the people who make those choices. To paraphrase a favorite saying of Representative John Dingell, a long-serving Democrat from Michigan, "If you let me decide procedure and I let you decide substance, I'll beat you every time."

KEY IDEA 3: POLITICS IS EVERYWHERE

Even though most Americans have little interest in politics, most of us encounter it every day. When you read the newspaper, watch TV, surf the Web, or listen to the radio, you'll almost surely encounter a political story. When walking down the street you may see billboards, bumper stickers, or T-shirts advertising a candidate, a political party, an interest group, or an issue position. Someone may ask you to sign a petition. You may walk past a homeless person and wonder whether a winning candidate followed through on her promise to help. You may glance at a headline about the war in Afghanistan and wonder whether members of Congress and the president were right to pursue their current policy.

Many people have an interest in putting politics in front of us on a daily basis. Interest groups, political parties, and candidates work to raise public awareness of the political process and to shape what people know and want. Moreover, the news media offer extensive coverage of politics in stories about elections and governing and how government policies affect ordinary Americans. Through efforts like these, politics really is everywhere.

Politics is also a fundamental part of how Americans think about themselves. Virtually all of us can name our party identification (Democrat, Republican, or independent)[8] and can place our views on a continuum between liberal and conservative.[9] Indeed, Americans often see the world through a partisan or ideological lens. For example, surveys conducted after Hurricane Katrina found Democrats more likely than Republicans to give the federal government poor marks for its efforts to help people whose homes were damaged or lost due to the storm.[10] That is, a typical Democrat seeing the same events as a typical Republican would evaluate the situation differently.

Politics is everywhere in another important way, too: actions by the enormous federal government touch virtually every aspect of your life. Figure 1.1 shows a timeline for a typical college student on a typical day. As you can see, from the moment this student wakes up until the end of the day, his or her actions are influenced by federal programs, spending, and regulations. As you will see in later chapters, it's not surprising that the federal government touches your everyday life in so many places. The federal government is extraordinarily large regardless of whether you measure spending (over $3.5 trillion for fiscal year 2012, ending in

THE IDEA THAT "POLITICS IS EVERYWHERE" is evident when government policies influence highly personal decisions, such as those pertaining to marriage, divorce, and abortion. Same-sex marriage has been controversial, and many states have passed laws and constitutional amendments defining marriage as being between a man and a woman.

How It Works

THREE KEY IDEAS FOR UNDERSTANDING POLITICS

POLITICS IS CONFLICTUAL

Conflict and compromise are natural parts of politics.

Political conflict over issues like the national debt, abortion, and health care reflect disagreements among the American people and often require compromises within government.

POLITICAL PROCESS MATTERS

How political conflicts are resolved is important.

Elections determine who represents citizens in government. Rules and procedures determine who has power in Congress and other branches of government.

POLITICS IS EVERYWHERE

What happens in government affects our lives in countless ways.

Policies related to jobs and the economy, food safety and nutrition, student loans, and many other areas shape our everyday lives. We see political information in the news and encounter political situations in many areas of our lives.

POP QUIZ!

1 The rule that the president must receive a majority of votes in the electoral college (not just the most votes from citizens) illustrates the idea that

a politics is conflictual.

b political process matters.

c politics is everywhere.

d the government has police powers.

e the government promotes the general welfare.

2 The fact that virtually no one got exactly what they wanted in the recent health care law (the Affordable Care Act) illustrates the idea that

a politics is conflictual.

b political process matters.

c politics is everywhere.

d the government has police powers.

e the government promotes the general welfare.

October 2012), number of employees (nearly 10 million if you include contractors and the postal service), or new regulations (over 80,000 pages in 2011).[11]

Moreover, the idea that politics is everywhere has a deeper meaning: people's political behavior is similar to their behavior in the rest of their lives. For example, many voters form judgments about candidates by focusing on the candidates' appearance, including ethnic background, gender, or age. Such stereotyping also shapes people's judgments about individuals whom they meet in other areas of life. Also, consider that convincing like-minded individuals to contribute to a group's lobbying efforts is no easy task. Each would-be contributor of time or money also has the opportunity to be a free rider who refuses to participate yet reaps the benefits of others' participation. Because of these difficulties, some groups of people with common goals remain unorganized. College students are a good example: many want more student aid and lower interest rates on government-subsidized student loans, but they fail to organize politically toward those ends.

Similar collective action problems occur when you live with roommates and need to keep common areas neat and clean: everyone has an interest in a clean area, but each person is inclined to let someone else do the work. The same principles help us to understand campus protests of tuition hikes, alcohol bans, or changes in graduation requirements in terms of which kinds of issues and circumstances foster cooperation. In each case, individual free riders acting in their own self-interest may undermine the outcome that most people prefer.

This similarity between behavior in political situations and in the rest of life is no surprise; everything that happens in politics is the result of individuals' choices. And the connections between politics and everyday life mean you already know more about politics than you realize.

FIGURE » 1.1

GOVERNMENT IN A STUDENT'S DAILY LIFE

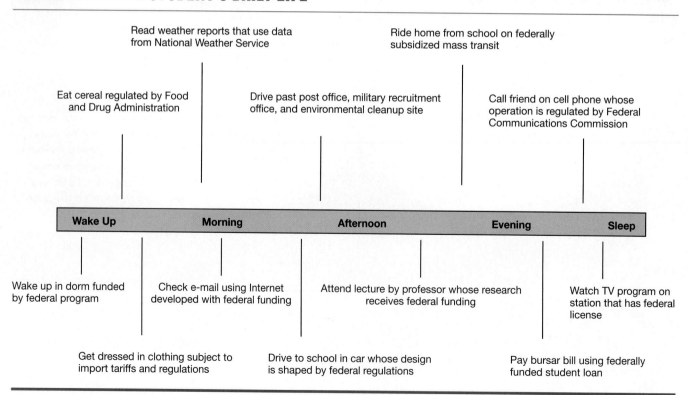

Read weather reports that use data from National Weather Service

Ride home from school on federally subsidized mass transit

Eat cereal regulated by Food and Drug Administration

Drive past post office, military recruitment office, and environmental cleanup site

Call friend on cell phone whose operation is regulated by Federal Communications Commission

| Wake Up | Morning | Afternoon | Evening | Sleep |

Wake up in dorm funded by federal program

Check e-mail using Internet developed with federal funding

Attend lecture by professor whose research receives federal funding

Watch TV program on station that has federal license

Get dressed in clothing subject to import tariffs and regulations

Drive to school in car whose design is shaped by federal regulations

Pay bursar bill using federally funded student loan

issues did not have as much traction in the 2008 elections (they were over-whelmed by economic concerns), but still the politically liberal Barack Obama did not fare well in culturally conservative parts of the country, such as the rural South and Midwest.

Although the precise makeup and impact of "values voters" is still being debated, there is no doubt that many Americans disagree on cultural and moral issues. These include the broad category of "family values" (such as whether and how to regulate pornography, gambling, and media obscenity and violence); whether to supplement the teaching of evolution in public schools with the per-spectives of intelligent design and creationism; gay marriage; abortion; stem cell research; school prayer; the war on drugs; gun control; school vouchers; and religious displays in public places. These are all hot-button issues that interest groups and activists on all sides attempt to keep at the top of the policy agenda.

melting pot The idea that as different racial and ethnic groups come to America, they should assimilate into American culture, leaving their native languages, cus-toms, and traditions behind.

RACIAL, GENDER, AND ETHNIC DIFFERENCES

Many political differences are correlated with racial, ethnic, and gender differ-ences. For example, over the last generation, about 90 percent of African Ameri-cans have been strong supporters of Democratic candidates. Other racial groups have been less cohesive in their voting, with their support for a particular party ranging from 55 to 70 percent. Whites tend to vote Republican; Latinos tend to vote Democratic, with the exception of Cuban Americans, who tend to vote Repub-lican; Asian Americans tend to vote Democratic but less consistently than Latinos. A gender gap in national politics is also evident, with women being somewhat more likely to vote for Democrats and men for Republicans.[14] Because these tendencies are not fixed, however, the political implications of racial, ethnic, and gender dif-ferences can change over time.

One of the enduring debates in American politics concerns whether ethnic and racial differences *should* be tied to political interests. One perspective reflects the **melting pot** image of America, which holds that as different racial and ethnic groups come to this country, they should mostly leave their native languages and customs behind. This perspective focuses on assimilation into American culture, with the belief that while immigrant groups will maintain some native traditions, our common bonds as Americans are more important. Supporters of this view advocate making English the country's official language and oppose bilingual public education.[15]

However, there are varied alternatives to the melting pot view. These range from racial separatists such as the Nation of Islam, whose members see white-dominated society as oppressive and discriminatory, to multiculturalists, who argue that there is strength in diversity.[16] Though debates will continue about the policies best suited to our nation's diverse population, our multira-cial makeup is clear, as Table 1.1 shows. In fact, trends in popula-tion growth suggest that by 2042, whites will no longer constitute a majority of the U.S. population. The extent to which this diversity continues to be a source of political conflict depends on the broader role of race in our society. As long as there are racial differences in employment, education, health, housing, and crime, and as long as

CIVIL AND VOTING RIGHTS POLICIES contributed to the realignment of the South in the second half of the twentieth century, as more whites began supporting the Republican Party, and the Democratic Party came to be seen as the champion of minority rights. Here, blacks and whites in Alabama wait in line together to vote at a city hall after enactment of the 1965 Voting Rights Act.

DEBATE CONTINUES BETWEEN THE advocates of the American cultural "melting pot" and those favoring a multicultural perspective on ethnic heritage. Should our diverse cultures be assimilated into a single, uniquely American identity?

ideology A cohesive set of ideas and beliefs used to organize and evaluate the political world.

conservative One side of the ideological spectrum defined by support for lower taxes, a free market, and a more limited government; generally associated with Republicans.

liberal One side of the ideological spectrum defined by support for stronger government programs and more market regulation; generally associated with Democrats.

libertarians Those who prefer very limited government and therefore tend to be conservative on issues such as welfare policy, environmental policy, and public support for education, but liberal on issues of personal liberty such as free speech, abortion, and the legalization of drugs.

racial discrimination is present in our society, race will continue to matter for politics. The long-running debate over immigration reform is strong evidence that racial and ethnic issues in politics are not going to disappear anytime soon.

Many of the same observations apply to gender and politics. The women's movement is usually viewed as beginning in 1848 at the first Women's Rights Convention at Seneca Falls, New York. The fight for women's suffrage and legal rights dominated the movement through the late nineteenth and early twentieth centuries. In the 1960s and 1970s, feminism and the women's liberation movement highlighted a broad range of issues: workplace issues such as maternity leave, equal pay, and sexual harassment; reproductive rights and abortion; domestic violence; and sexual violence. While progress has occurred on many fronts, gender remains an important source of political disagreement and identity politics.

IDEOLOGY

Another source of differences in interests is **ideology**—which we will define as a cohesive set of ideas and beliefs that allows an individual to organize and evaluate the political world. Ideology may seem most obviously related to political interests through political parties, since Republicans tend to be **conservative** and Democrats tend to be **liberal**. While this is true in a relative sense (most Republicans are more conservative than most Democrats), few Americans consider their own views ideologically extreme.[17]

Ideology shapes specific beliefs. Conservatives promote traditional social practices and favor lower taxes, a free market, and more liited government, whereas liberals support social tolerance, stronger government programs, and more market regulation. However, the picture gets cloudy if we look more closely. **Libertarians**, for example, prefer very limited government providing only national defense and a few other narrowly defined responsibilities. Because they are at the extreme end of the ideological continuum on this issue, libertarians are generally conservative on issues such as social welfare policy, environmental policy, and government funding for education, and generally liberal on issues involving personal liberty such as free speech, abortion, and the legalization of drugs. For libertarians, the consistent ideological theme is limiting the role of government in our lives.

Also, personal ideologies are not always consistent. Someone could be both a fiscal conservative (favoring balanced budgets) and a social liberal (favoring the prochoice position on abortion and marital rights for gay men and lesbians), or a liberal on foreign policy issues (supporting humanitarian aid and opposing the war in Afghanistan) and a conservative on moral issues (being prolife on abortion and opposing stem cell research). Ideology is a significant source of conflict in politics, and it does not always operate in a straightforward manner. In Chapter 5, Public Opinion, we explore whether America is becoming more ideological and polarized, deepening our conflicts and making compromise more difficult.

TABLE » 1.1

THE RACIAL COMPOSITION OF THE UNITED STATES

These census data show the racial diversity of the United States. Only about 75 percent of Americans describe themselves as white. Moreover, the proportion of Hispanics and Latinos in the population is 16.3 percent and rising, although this category contains many distinct subgroups.

RACE	NUMBER	PERCENT
Total U.S. population	**309,349,689**	**100**
White	229,397,472	74.2
Hispanic or Latino (any race)	50,477,594	16.3
Mexican	31,798,258	10.3
Puerto Rican	4,623,716	1.5
Cuban	1,785,547	0.6
Dominican	1,414,703	0.5
Other, Hispanic or Latino	9,163,850	2.5
Black or African American	38,874,625	12.6
Asian	14,728,302	4.7
American Indian and Alaska Native	2,553,566	0.8
Native Hawaiian and Other Pacific Islander	507,916	0.1
Some other race	14,889,440	4.8
Two or more races	8,398,368	2.7

Source: U.S. Census Bureau, 2010 American Community Survey.

You may be surprised to find that the American public has fairly centrist views and that there are relatively few systematic differences between residents of blue states and red states on a broad range of policies. For example, political scientist Morris Fiorina finds that red-state and blue-state residents have very similar views on immigration, English as the official language, environmental policy, school vouchers, affirmative action, equal rights for women, and tolerance of others' views. Although politics is conflictual (a lack of extreme polarization does not mean that reaching agreement on specific policies is easy) and differences are somewhat larger on gay rights, abortion, gun control, and the death penalty, even on these issues Americans' views are not as polarized as you might think. (Out of thirteen issues, only two—gay rights and abortion—showed differences of 10 percent or more between red-state and blue-state respondents).[18]

Figure 1.2 illustrates this finding with data from the 2012 presidential election. The map shows the relative strength by state of Mitt Romney and Barack Obama, with the reddest states showing the strongest Republican support and the bluest states showing the Democratic strongholds. As you can see, most of the country is purple, which indicates a geographic intermixing between the parties and their associated ideological beliefs. One interesting thing about the purple map is that even in very Republican states such as Texas, Mississippi, and Alabama there are very blue areas and in strong Democratic states such as California and New York there are plenty of red counties. Thus, the typical "red and blue" map of the United States that you see on election night is misleading on two levels: the country is much more purple than red or blue and within most states there is a great deal of partisan diversity.

///

CONCLUSION

By understanding that politics is conflictual, that it is rooted in process, and that it is everywhere, you will see that modern American political life makes more sense than you might have thought. Along the way, you will learn important "nuts and bolts" of the American political process as well as some political history. In general, though, your reading in this book will focus on contemporary questions, debates, and examples to illustrate broader points about our nation's political system. After all, American politics in its current form is the politics that will have the greatest impact on your life.

Though you will disagree with some aspects of American politics, and some will make you angry, our goal in this book is to provide you with the tools to understand *why* government operates as it does. We are not arguing that the federal government is perfect or that imperfect responses to policy problems such as the vote on the debt limit are inevitable. Rather, we believe that any attempt to explain these outcomes, or to devise ways to prevent similar problems, requires an understanding of why they happened in the first place. After reading this book, you will have a better sense of how American politics works.

MAKING SENSE OF AMERICAN GOVERNMENT AND POLITICS

▶ Describe the basic functions of government. **Pages 5–10**

SUMMARY

Forms of governments can be characterized by the number of people who hold power (many vs. few) and the number of levels over which power is distributed (national vs. state vs. local). Government exists primarily to provide order, though it must do so while avoiding oppression by the rulers. Government also needs to provide public goods because they will be underprovided by the free market.

KEY TERMS

government (p. 6)

factions (p. 8)

separation of powers (p. 8)

checks and balances (p. 8)

federalism (p. 8)

public goods (p. 8)

collective action problems (p. 8)

positive externalities (p. 8)

free rider problem (p. 9)

ⓢ PRACTICE ONLINE

"Big Think" video exercise: *Self-Government for a Modern Age*

CRITICAL THINKING AND DISCUSSION

What are some examples from your life that illustrate that "politics is everywhere"? How do government policies affect the things you do every day? Can you think of past decisions or experiences that you may not have seen as political, but that illustrate this idea as well?

PRACTICE QUIZ QUESTIONS

1. What did Aristotle call "a government ruled by the many"?
   a) monarchy
   b) aristocracy
   c) polity
   d) unitary system
   e) democracy

2. Which term describes giving each branch of government power over the other two?
   a) separation of powers
   b) checks and balances
   c) federalism
   d) plutocracy
   e) unitary system

3. Which term describes the inability to get individuals to cooperate to achieve a common goal?
   a) positive externality
   b) the Samaritan's dilemma
   c) collective action problem
   d) principal-agent problem
   e) public goods

WHAT IS POLITICS?

▶ Define *politics* and identify three key ideas that help explain politics. **Pages 10–18**

SUMMARY

Conflict cannot be avoided in politics: the American people disagree on nearly every issue on which politicians make policy decisions. Compromise and bargaining are essential to enacting policy, but this means that it is almost impossible to get exactly what you want from the political process. Policy outcomes are also influenced by the policy process itself—different procedures of making policy can lead to different outcomes. Whether it is on the news or influencing most aspects of your life, politics is all around us.

KEY TERMS

politics (p. 10)

CRITICAL THINKING AND DISCUSSION

Consider the observation by Representative John Dingell (D-Mich.) that "If you let me decide procedure and I let you decide substance, I'll beat you every time." Do you think Dingell is right? What are some instances in which process was more important than substance in determining an outcome?

ⓢ PRACTICE ONLINE

"What Do Political Scientists Do?" video exercise: *William Bianco and David Canon discuss how political scientists develop and apply research methods*

PRACTICE QUIZ QUESTIONS

4. What is the main reason why politicians have a hard time resolving the issue of abortion?
    a) Politicians don't listen to the people.
    b) The parties are divided on what abortion policy should look like.
    c) Politicians don't know what their constituents' views are.
    d) The country is divided on what abortion policy should look like.
    e) Abortion is a relatively new issue.

5. Which concept describes the idea that actions by the government touch most aspects of your life?
    a) Politics is understandable.
    b) Politics is conflictual.
    c) Political process matters.
    d) Politics is everywhere.
    e) People have different interests.

6. Rules such as those regulating debate in the Senate, or limiting who can vote in elections, serve as evidence that _____.
    a) politics is understandable
    b) politics is conflictual
    c) political process matters
    d) politics is everywhere
    e) people have different interests

SOURCES OF CONFLICT IN AMERICAN POLITICS

▶ Identify major sources of conflict in American politics. **Pages 19–24**

SUMMARY

Though Americans generally agree on a free market system, there is considerable conflict over how much the government should support tax policies that redistribute wealth. Conflict also arises on cultural grounds, pitting religious "red-state" Americans against the more secular "blue-state" Americans. There is also disagreement on the extent to which racial, ethnic, and gender diversity should be celebrated or minimized. Lastly, though Americans are not as polarized as one would think, liberals and conservatives come into conflict on ideological grounds.

KEY TERMS

free market (p. 19)

economic individualism (p. 19)

redistributive tax policies (p. 19)

culture wars (p. 20)

melting pot (p. 21)

ideology (p. 22)

conservative (p. 22)

liberal (p. 22)

libertarians (p. 22)

CRITICAL THINKING AND DISCUSSION

What are your views on the role of conflict in politics? What types of issues are most likely to be resolved through political conflict and compromise, and which issues are more resistant to compromise?

PRACTICE QUIZ QUESTIONS

7. Democrats tend to favor _____ tax policies and are _____ inclined to regulate industry.
   a) redistributive; more
   b) conservative; more
   c) redistributive; less
   d) conservative; less
   e) regressive; less

8. Which issue is commonly associated with the culture wars?
   a) the national debt
   b) environmental regulation
   c) affirmative action
   d) the tax code
   e) gay marriage

9. An individual who opposes government social welfare policy and supports the legalization of drugs is most likely a _____.
   a) libertarian
   b) socialist
   c) Democrat
   d) Republican
   e) centrist

⑤ PRACTICE ONLINE

"Critical Thinking" exercise: *Polling Report Data on Congressional Job Approval Ratings*

SUGGESTED READING

Dahl, Robert. *On Democracy*. New Haven, CT: Yale University Press, 1998.

Fiorina, Morris P., with Samuel J. Abrams and Jeremy C. Pope. *Culture War? The Myth of a Polarized America*, 2nd ed. New York: Pearson, Longman, 2006.

Gutman, Amy. *Identity in Democracy*. Princeton, NJ: Princeton University Press, 2003.

Schattschneider, E. E. *The Semisovereign People: A Realist's View of Democracy in America*. New York: Holt, Rinehart, and Winston, 1960.

2

The Constitution and the Founding

Signs from the crowd: "DUMP DODD!", "...K INTO BANK!", "I am not your ATM!", "DANGER RUNAWAY GOVERNMENT!", "SAY NO TO TYRANNY!!", "STOP! STOP ENSLAVING AMERICANS ILLEGAL IMMIGRATION CORRUPT POLITICIANS TAKING US TO DEATH", "Taxed Enough Already!"

SUPPORTERS OF THE TEA PARTY movement think the federal government has overstepped the powers granted by the Constitution. Throughout American history, debates over the meaning of the Constitution have persisted.

RECENTLY, THE CONSTITUTION ITSELF HAS BECOME THE FOCUS of political debate and conflict. Starting in the 2010 midterm elections and continuing through the 2012 presidential election, a popular movement known as the Tea Party has supported candidates who endorse a return to the Constitution's founding principles. While the range of views within the Tea Party movement is vast, its supporters generally see the expansion of federal power—which began with Teddy Roosevelt, exploded during the New Deal of the 1930s and Great Society of the 1960s, and continues today with President Obama's health care reform—as constitutional overreach. Many Tea Party supporters see Social Security, Medicare, and the Federal Reserve System as unconstitutional because such policies are not expressly permitted by the Constitution. Jim DeMint, a Republican senator from South Carolina and a leading Tea Partier, recently wrote, "If President Obama's motto is 'Yes, we can,' the Constitution's is 'No, you can't.' . . . Although the Constitution does give some defined powers to the federal government, it is overwhelmingly a document of limits, and those limits must be respected."[1]

To draw more attention to the Constitution, members of Congress took turns reading the document from the floor at the start of the new session of the House of Representatives in 2011. It was the first time in U.S. history that the entire Constitution had been read aloud in Congress. But even this simple gesture proved to be controversial: Representative Jesse Jackson Jr. (D-Ill.) objected to the "whitewashing" of the document that excluded all portions of the Constitution that alluded to slavery.[2]

CONFLICT & COMPROMISE
in American Politics

The Tea Party's efforts to establish constitutional limits on government activity have also met with resistance from those who challenge the Tea Party's take on the Constitution and the Founding. Rather than considering the Constitution a document that created a limited national government and protected state power, these critics argue that it was intended to create a strong national government while limiting state power.[3] Differences of opinion about the Constitution have been part of American politics since the debates between the Federalists and Antifederalists over the ratification of the document. Unfortunately, the Constitution itself provides few definitive answers because its language was intentionally written to be general so it would stand the test of time. Consequently, in every major political debate in our history, both sides have claimed to ground their views in the Constitution. Abolitionists and secessionists during the pre–Civil War period, New Deal supporters and opponents, and civil rights activists and segregationists all claimed to have the Constitution on their side, whether it was a broad or narrow interpretation of the commerce clause, the Fourteenth Amendment, or the Tenth Amendment. Today's vigorous debate about the proper scope of the national government's powers is only the most recent chapter in this perpetual conflict.

One of our graduate students used to carry around a pocket-sized copy of the Constitution. He would whip it out to settle classroom disputes or consult it during political discussions in the student lounge. Though the framers of the Constitution surely did not expect citizens to carry this document at all times, they *did* anticipate (or at least hope) that it would serve as the basis for an enduring government; indeed, the document they created has become the oldest written document that provides the basis for government.

There is a major reason our Constitution has survived so long: since the earliest years of our republic, rather than taking up arms Americans have relied on elections and representative government to settle disputes. Losers of one round of elections know that they have an opportunity to compete in the next election and that their voices can be heard in another part of the government. The peaceful transitions of power and stability in our political system may be attributed to the hallmark characteristic of U.S. constitutional government: the separation of power across the levels of government (national, state, and local) and within government (legislative, executive, and judicial) and the checks and balances of power across the institutions of government.

This stability does not mean that the Constitution *resolves* our political conflicts. The Founders recognized that self-interest and conflict are inherent parts of human nature and cannot be eliminated, so they attempted to control conflict by dispersing power across different parts of government. This means that parts of the political system are always competing with one another in pursuit of various interests: for example Republicans in Congress may want to cut spending to balance the budget while a Democratic president may want a mix of spending cuts and tax increases. This creates a conflictual process that is often criticized as being mired in "gridlock" and "partisan bickering." But that is the system our Founders created. Think about it this way: dictatorships do not have political conflict because dissenters are sent to jail or shot. We have political conflict because there is free and open competition between different interests and ideas.

In addition to guaranteeing that politics is conflictual, the Constitution clearly exemplifies the other two themes of this textbook. The Constitution establishes the basic rules for our institutions of government, prevents the government from doing certain things to citizens (such as denying them freedom of speech), and guarantees specific individual rights. In other words, the Constitution determines the ground rules for the process that guides politics. The sweeping influence of

THE FOUNDERS WANTED TO CREATE a constitution that was general enough to stand the test of time. Their approach succeeded, and the U.S. Constitution is the oldest written constitution still in use today. However, by leaving some passages open to interpretation, they also set the stage for conflict over the meaning of the Constitution.

the Constitution also shows that politics is everywhere. The document shapes every aspect of national politics, which in turn influences many parts of your life. We will return to these themes throughout this chapter.

Finally, the Constitution is highly readable. You do not have to be a lawyer or a political philosopher to understand it. It contains only 4,543 words (about the length of a fifteen-page term paper), and although the writing is somewhat old-fashioned in places, it uses everyday language rather than the legalese that one would confront in a modern document of this type. If you haven't read it recently (or at all), turn to the Appendix and read it now.

THE HISTORICAL CONTEXT OF THE CONSTITUTION

DESCRIBE THE HISTORICAL CIRCUMSTANCES THAT LED TO THE CONSTITUTIONAL CONVENTION OF 1787

The Constitution was created through conflict and compromise, and it is important to understand the historical context within which that process took place. Therefore we focus on the events leading up to the Constitutional Convention, the interests and ideas that were at stake for the framers, and the compromises and decisions they made. Understanding the historical context can help clarify *why* specific choices were made. And exploring the consequences of alternative choices is one way of seeing how politics matters. Key historical events shaped the Constitutional Convention, including the period of British rule over the American colonies, the Revolutionary War, and problems with the first form of government in the United States, the Articles of Confederation.

The first event that led many American colonists to question the fairness of British rule and shape their ideas about self-governance was the Stamp Act of 1765, which imposed a tax on many publications and legal documents in the colonies. The British Parliament enacted the tax to help pay for the French and Indian War (1754–63),

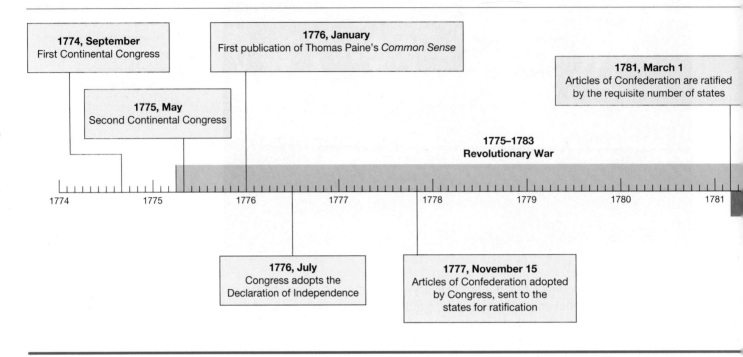

1774, September
First Continental Congress

1776, January
First publication of Thomas Paine's *Common Sense*

1781, March 1
Articles of Confederation are ratified by the requisite number of states

1775, May
Second Continental Congress

1775–1783
Revolutionary War

1776, July
Congress adopts the Declaration of Independence

1777, November 15
Articles of Confederation adopted by Congress, sent to the states for ratification

1774   1775   1776   1777   1778   1779   1780   1781

which they thought was only fair because the American colonists were benefiting from the protection of British troops. Many colonists saw this as unfair "taxation without representation" because they had no say in the passage of the act (they had no representation in the British Parliament). A series of escalating events, including the Tea Act (1773) and the Boston Tea Party later that year, in which colonists dumped tea from the British East Indian Tea Company into the harbor rather than pay the new tax, moved the colonies closer to the inevitable break with Great Britain. The British Parliament responded to the tea party with the Coercive Acts (or Intolerable Acts) of 1774 in a series of moves that were aimed at making sure the colonists paid for the tea they destroyed and to break the pattern of the colonists' resistance to British rule. Attempts at a political solution failed, so the Continental Congress declared independence from Britain on July 4, 1776.[4]

THE ARTICLES OF CONFEDERATION: THE FIRST ATTEMPT AT GOVERNMENT

Throughout the Revolutionary and early post-Revolutionary era, the future of the American colonies was very much in doubt. While many Americans were eager to sever ties with the oppressive British government and establish a new nation that rejected the trappings of royalty, there was still a large contingent of Tories (supporters of the British monarchy) and probably an even larger group of Americans who wished the conflict would just go away. While public opinion on the matter is impossible to know with certainty, John Adams, the second president of the United States, estimated that the Second Continental Congress was about equally

FIGURE » 2.1

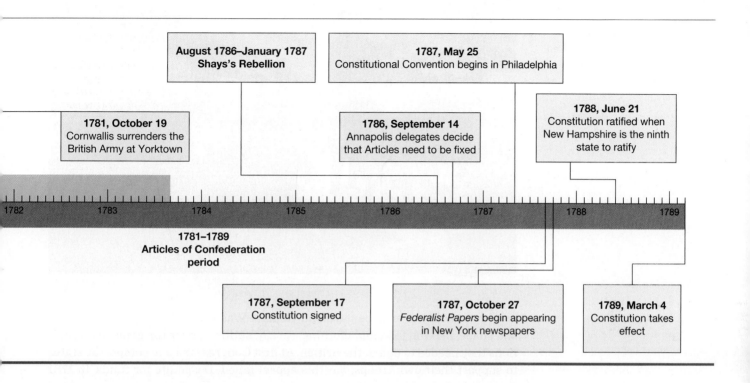

August 1786–January 1787
Shays's Rebellion

1787, May 25
Constitutional Convention begins in Philadelphia

1781, October 19
Cornwallis surrenders the
British Army at Yorktown

1786, September 14
Annapolis delegates decide
that Articles need to be fixed

1788, June 21
Constitution ratified when
New Hampshire is the ninth
state to ratify

1782   1783   1784   1785   1786   1787   1788   1789

1781–1789
Articles of Confederation
period

1787, September 17
Constitution signed

1787, October 27
Federalist Papers begin appearing
in New York newspapers

1789, March 4
Constitution takes
effect

divided between Tories, "true blue" revolutionaries, and "those too cautious or timid to take a position one way or the other."[5] This context of uncertainty and conflict made the Founders' task of creating a lasting republic extremely difficult.

The first attempt to structure an American government, the **Articles of Confederation**, swung too far in the direction of **limited government**. The Articles were written in the summer of 1776 during the Second Continental Congress, which also authorized and approved the Declaration of Independence. The Articles were submitted to all thirteen states in 1777 for approval, but they did not take effect until the last state ratified them in 1781. However, in the absence of any alternative, the Articles of Confederation served as the basis for organizing the government during the Revolutionary War. (See Figure 2.1, "Constitutional Timeline.")

In their zeal to reject monarchy, the authors of the Articles did not even include a president or any other executive leader. Instead, they assigned all national power to a Congress in which each state had a single vote. Members of Congress were elected by state legislatures rather than directly by the people. There was no judicial branch; all legal matters were left to the states, with the exception of disputes among the states, which would be resolved by special panels of judges appointed on an as-needed basis by Congress. In their eagerness to limit the power of government, the authors of the Articles gave each state veto power over any changes to the Articles and required approval from nine of the thirteen states on any legislation. Even more important, the states maintained autonomy and did not sacrifice any significant power to the national government. Powers granted to the national government, such as making treaties and coining money, were not exclusive powers; that is, they were not denied to the states.

Congress also lacked any real authority over the states. For example, Congress could suggest the amount of money each state owed to support the Revolutionary

Articles of Confederation Sent to the states for ratification in 1777, these were the first attempt at a new American government. It was later decided that the Articles restricted national government too much, and they were replaced by the Constitution.

limited government A political system in which the powers of the government are restricted to prevent tyranny by protecting property and individual rights.

army but could not enforce payment. General Washington's troops were in very bad shape, lacking food and clothing—to say nothing about the arms and munitions they needed to defeat the British. At first Congress tried to compel the states to support their own troops, but this appeal failed. Desperate for funds, in 1781 Congress tried to give itself the power to raise taxes, but the measure was vetoed by Rhode Island, which represented less than 2 percent of the nation's population! If France had not come to the aid of the American army with much-needed funds and troops, the weakness of the national government could have led to defeat.[6]

After the Revolutionary War ended with the British surrender at Yorktown in October 1781, the same weaknesses continued to plague Congress. The new government owed millions of dollars in war debts to foreign governments and domestic creditors, so Congress devised a plan to repay the debts over 25 years; but again it had no way to make the states pay their share. Instead, Congress proposed an amendment to the Articles that would allow it to collect import duties—but New York, which had the busiest port in the nation, did not want to share its revenue and vetoed the amendment. Foreign trade also suffered because of the weak national government. If a foreign government negotiated a trade arrangement with Congress, it could be vetoed or amended by a state government, so that a foreign country wanting to conduct business with the United States might have to negotiate separate agreements with Congress and each state legislature.

Disputes with foreign countries about land boundaries also were complex and contentious because of the Articles. When Spain threatened to close trade routes on the Mississippi River and Great Britain disputed the U.S.–Canadian border, it was not clear whether state governments or Congress could resolve the disputes. Even trade among the states was complicated and inefficient: each state could make its own currency, exchange rates varied, and many states charged tolls and fees to export goods across state lines. (Just imagine how difficult interstate commerce would be today if you had to exchange currency at every state line.)

A small group of leaders decided that something had to be done. A group from Virginia urged state legislatures to send delegates to a convention on interstate

COMPARING THE ARTICLES OF CONFEDERATION AND THE CONSTITUTION

Issue	Articles of Confederation	Constitution
Legislature	Unicameral Congress	Bicameral Congress divided into the House of Representatives and the Senate
Members of Congress	Between two and seven per state	Two senators per state; representatives apportioned according to population of each state
Voting in Congress	One vote per state	One vote per representative or senator
Selection of members	Appointed by state legislatures	Representatives elected by popular vote; senators appointed by state legislatures
Executive	None	President
National judiciary	Maritime judiciary established, no general federal courts	Supreme Court; Congress authorized to establish national judiciary
Amendments to the document	When approved by all states	When approved by two-thirds of each house of Congress and three-fourths of the states
Power to coin money	Federal government and the states	Federal government only
Taxes	Apportioned by Congress, collected by the states	Apportioned and collected by Congress
Ratification	Unanimous consent required	Consent of nine states required

commerce in Annapolis, Maryland, in September 1786. Only five sent delegates. However, Alexander Hamilton and James Madison salvaged something from the convention by getting those delegates to agree to convene again in Philadelphia the following May. They also proposed that the next convention examine the defects of the current government and "devise such further provisions as shall appear to them necessary to render the Constitution of the Federal Government adequate to the exigencies of the Union."[7]

The issues that motivated the Annapolis Convention gained new urgency as events unfolded over the next several months. In the years after the war, economic chaos led to a depression, and many farmers lost their land because they could not pay their debts or state taxes. Frustration mounted, and early in 1787 a former captain in the Revolutionary army, Daniel Shays, led a force of a thousand farmers in an attempt to take over the Massachusetts state government arsenal in Springfield. Their goal was to force the state courts to stop prosecuting debtors and taking their land, but the rebels were repelled by a state militia. Similar protests on a smaller scale happened in Pennsylvania and Virginia. Some state legislatures gave in to the debtors' demands, causing national leaders to fear that Shays's Rebellion had exposed fundamental discontent with the new government. The very future of the fledgling nation was at risk.

republican democracy A form of government in which the interests of the people are represented through elected leaders.

monarchy A form of government in which power is held by a single person, or monarch, who comes to power through inheritance rather than election.

republicanism As understood by James Madison and the framers, the belief that a form of government in which the interests of the people are represented through elected leaders is the best form of government.

Although the leaders who gathered in Philadelphia in the summer of 1787 to write the Constitution were chastened by the failure of the Articles of Confederation, they still shared many of the principles that motivated the Revolution. There was still broad consensus on three key principles: (1) popular control of government through a **republican democracy**, (2) a rejection of **monarchy**, and (3) limitations on government power that would protect individual rights and personal property (that is, protect against tyranny).

REPUBLICANISM

First among these principles was rejection of monarchy in favor of a form of government based on self-rule. In its broadest sense, **republicanism** is the ideology of any state that is not a monarchy. As understood by the framers, it is a government in which elected leaders would represent the views of the people. Thomas Paine, an influential political writer of the Revolutionary era, wrote a pamphlet entitled *Common Sense* in 1776 that was a widely read[8] indictment of monarchy and an endorsement of the principles that fueled the Revolution and underpinned the framers' thinking. Paine wrote that a monarchy was the "most bare-faced falsity ever imposed on mankind" and that the common interests of the community should be served by elected representatives.

The Founders' views of republicanism were combined with liberal principles of liberty and individual rights to create their views of the proper form of government. The best expression of these core principles is found in the Declaration of Independence:

> *We hold these truths to be self-evident, that all men are created equal, that they are endowed by their Creator with certain unalienable Rights, that among these are Life, Liberty, and the pursuit of Happiness. That to secure these rights, Governments are instituted among Men, deriving their just powers from the consent of the governed. That whenever any Form of Government becomes destructive of these ends, it is the Right of the People to alter or to abolish it, and to institute new Government.*

"consent of the governed" The idea that government gains its legitimacy through regular elections in which the people living under that government participate to elect their leaders.

natural rights Also known as "unalienable rights," the Declaration of Independence defines them as "Life, Liberty, and the pursuit of Happiness." The Founders believed that upholding these rights should be the government's central purpose.

Three crucial ideas are packed into this passage: equality, self-rule, and natural rights. Equality was not given much attention in the Constitution (in later chapters we discuss how the problem of slavery was handled), but the notion that a government gains its legitimacy from the **"consent of the governed"** and that its central purpose is to uphold the "unalienable" or **natural rights** of the people were central to the framers. The "right of the people to alter or abolish" a government that did not protect these rights served both to justify the revolt against the British and to remind the framers of their continuing obligation to make sure that those needs were met. The leaders who met in Philadelphia thought the Articles of Confederation had become "destructive to those ends" and therefore needed to be altered.

Paine, Jefferson, Madison, and other political thinkers of the American Founding broke new ground in laying out the principles of republican democracy, but they also built on the ideas of political philosophers of their era. As mentioned in Chapter 1, Thomas Hobbes argued that government was necessary to prevent people from living in an anarchic "state of nature" in which life would be "nasty, brutish, and short." However, Hobbes's central conclusion was undemocratic: he believed that a single king must rule because any other form of government would produce warring factions. Another influential seventeenth-century philosopher,

John Locke, took the notion of the consent of the governed in determining a government's legitimacy in a more democratic direction. He discussed many of the ideas that appeared in the Declaration of Independence and the Constitution, including natural rights, property rights, the need for a vigorous executive branch that would be checked by a legislative branch, and self-rule through elections.[9] Baron de Montesquieu, an eighteenth-century political thinker, also influenced the framers. Although he did not use the term *separation of powers*, Montesquieu argued in *The Spirit of the Laws* (1748) that no two, let alone three, functions of government (judicial, legislative, and executive) should be controlled by one branch. He also argued that in order to preserve liberty, one branch of government should be able to check the excesses of the other branches.

HUMAN NATURE AND ITS IMPLICATIONS FOR DEMOCRACY

The most comprehensive statement of the framers' political philosophy and democratic theory was a series of essays written by James Madison, Alexander Hamilton, and John Jay entitled the **Federalist Papers**. These essays explained and justified the framework of government created by the Constitution. They also revealed the framers' view of human nature and its implications for democracy. The framers' view of human nature as basically self-interested led to Madison's assessment that "In framing a government which is to be administered by men over men, the great difficulty lies in this: you must first enable the government to control the governed; and in the next place oblige it to control itself." This analysis, which comes from *Federalist 51*, is often considered the clearest articulation of the need for republican government and a system of separated powers. In *Federalist 10* Madison described the central problem for government as the need to control factions.

Madison argued that governments cannot control the causes of factions, because differences of opinion—based on the fallibility of reason; differences in wealth, property, and native abilities; and attachments to different leaders—are part of human nature. The only way to eliminate factions would be to either remove liberty or try to make everyone the same. The first remedy Madison called "worse than the disease," and the second he found "as impracticable as the first would be unwise." Because people are driven by self-interest, which sometimes conflicts with the common good, government must, however, try to control the effects of factions. This was the task facing the framers at the Constitutional Convention.

SEVENTEENTH-CENTURY POLITICAL philosopher John Locke had a great influence on the Founders. Many ideas discussed in Locke's writing appear in the Declaration of Independence and the Constitution.

Federalist Papers A series of 85 articles written by Alexander Hamilton, James Madison, and John Jay that sought to sway public opinion toward the Federalists' position.

ECONOMIC INTERESTS

Political ideas were central to the framers' thinking at the Constitutional Convention, but economic interests were equally important. Both the economic status of the framers themselves and the broader economic context of the time are relevant here. One constitutional scholar addressed the relative importance of economic interests and political ideas for the framers, noting they "did not promote a new form of government to satisfy an abstract political theory. The framers were men of affairs who sought to advance their fortunes and careers as well as the interests of the states."[10] Charles Beard famously expressed this view nearly 100 years ago in his economic interpretation of the Constitution. He argued that the framers wanted to revise the Articles of Confederation and strengthen the national government largely to protect their own property holdings and investments.[11]

Some undemocratic features of the Constitution probably do reflect the framers' privileged position. However, Beard's argument has been countered by research showing, among other things, that opponents of the Constitution also came from the upper class.[12] Most constitutional scholars now view the Constitution as the product of both ideas and interests. Political scientist David Robertson has summarized this balanced perspective, saying, "The delegates who made the Constitution were first and foremost politicians, not philosophers or real estate investors."[13]

The broader economic context of the American Founding was more important than the delegates' individual interests. First, while there were certainly class differences among Americans in the late eighteenth century, they were insignificant compared to those in Europe. America did not have the history of feudalism that had created tremendous inequality in Europe between landowners and propertyless serfs who worked the land. In contrast, most Americans owned small farms or worked as middle-class artisans and craftsmen. Thus, while political equality did not figure prominently in the Constitution, citizens' relative economic equality did influence the context of debates at the Constitutional Convention.

Second, despite Americans' general economic equality, there were significant regional economic differences. The South was largely agricultural, with cotton and tobacco plantations that depended on slave labor. The South favored free trade because of its export-based economy (bolstered by westward expansion) and the slave trade. The middle Atlantic and northern states, however, had smaller farms and a broad economic base of manufacturing, fishing, and trade. These states favored government-managed trade and commercial development.

Despite these differences, the diverse population favored a stronger national government and reform of the Articles of Confederation. Creditors wanted a government that could pay off its debts to them, southern farmers wanted free trade that could only be efficiently promoted by a central government, and manufacturers and traders wanted a single national currency and uniform interstate commerce regulations. However, there was a deep division between the supporters of empowering the national government and those who still favored strong state governments. These two groups became known as the **Federalists** and the **Antifederalists**. Now the stage was set for a productive but contentious convention.

Federalists Those at the Constitutional Convention who favored a strong national government and a system of separated powers.

Antifederalists Those at the Constitutional Convention who favored strong state governments and feared that a strong national government would be a threat to individual rights.

ANALYZE THE MAJOR ISSUES DEBATED BY THE FRAMERS OF THE CONSTITUTION

THE POLITICS OF COMPROMISE AT THE CONSTITUTIONAL CONVENTION

The central players at the convention were James Madison, Gouverneur Morris, Edmund Randolph, James Wilson, Benjamin Franklin, and George Washington, the unanimous choice to preside over the convention. Several of the important leaders of the Revolution were not present. Patrick "Give me Liberty, or give me Death!" Henry was selected to attend, but he opposed any changes in the Articles, saying he "smelled a rat," and Thomas Jefferson and John Adams were working overseas as U.S. diplomats. Thomas Paine was back in England, and John Hancock and Samuel Adams were not selected to attend. The delegates met in secret to encourage open, uncensored debate.

Although there was broad consensus among the delegates that the Articles of Confederation needed to be changed, there were many tensions over the changes that required political compromise. Among them were the following:

▶ majority rule versus minority rights,

▶ large states versus small states,

▶ legislative power versus executive power (and how to elect the executive),

▶ national power versus state and local power, and

▶ slave states versus nonslave states.

These complex competing interests meant that the delegates had to focus on pragmatic, achievable solutions rather than on proposals that represented particular groups' ideals but could not gain majority support. Robert Dahl, a leading democratic theorist of the twentieth century, argues that it was impossible for the Constitution to "reflect a coherent, unified theory of government" because so much compromising and vote-trading was required to find common ground.[14] Instead, the delegates tackled the problems one at a time, holding lengthy debates and multiple votes on most issues.

MAJORITY RULE VERSUS MINORITY RIGHTS

A central problem for any representative democracy is protecting minority rights within a system ruled by the majority. The framers did not think of this issue in terms of racial and ethnic minorities (as we might today), but in terms of regional and economic minorities. How could the framers be sure that small landowners and poorer people would not impose onerous taxes on the wealthier minority? How could they guarantee that dominant agricultural interests would not impose punitive tariffs on manufacturing while allowing free export of farmed commodities? The answers to these questions can be found in Madison's writings on the problem of factions.

Madison defined a faction as a group motivated by selfish interests against the common good. If these interests prevailed, it could produce the very kind of tyranny that the Americans had fought to escape during the Revolutionary War. Madison was especially concerned about tyranny by majority factions because, in a democracy, minority tyranny would be controlled by the republican principle: the majority could simply vote out the minority faction. If, on the other hand, the majority always rules, majority tyranny could be a real problem. Given the understanding of selfish human nature that Madison so clearly outlined, a populist, majoritarian democracy would not necessarily produce the

JAMES MADISON ARGUED THAT IT is beneficial to put the interests of one group in competition with the interests of other groups, so that no one group can dominate government. He hoped to achieve this through the separation of powers across different branches of the national government and across the national, state, and local levels.

common good. On the other hand, if too many protections were provided to minority and regional interests, the collective interest would not be served because constructive changes could be vetoed too easily, as under the Articles of Confederation.

Madison's solution to this problem provided the justification for our form of government. He argued that to control majority tyranny, factions must be set against one another to counter each other's ambitions and prevent the tyranny of any single majority faction. This was to be accomplished through the "double protection" of the separation of powers within the national government in the form of checks and balances, and also by further dividing power across the levels of state and local governments.

Madison also argued that additional protection against majority tyranny would come from the "size principle." That is, the new nation would be a large and diverse republic in which majority interests would be less likely to organize, and therefore less able to dominate. According to Madison, "Extend the sphere, and you take in a greater variety of parties and interests; you make it less probable that a majority of the whole will have a common motive to invade the rights of other citizens; or if such a common motive exists, it will be more difficult for all who feel it to discover their own strength, and to act in unison with each other."[15] This insight provides the basis for modern **pluralism**, a political theory that makes the same argument about the cross-cutting interests of groups today.

The precise contours of Madison's solution still had to be hammered out at the convention, but the general principle pleased both the Antifederalists and the Federalists. State governments would maintain some autonomy, but the national government would become stronger than it had been under the Articles. The issue was striking the appropriate balance: none of the framers favored a pure populist majoritarian democracy, and few wanted to protect minority rights to the extent that the Articles had.

SMALL STATES VERSUS LARGE STATES

The question of the appropriate balance came to an immediate head in a debate between small states and large states over representation in the national legislature. Under the Articles, every state had a single vote, but this did not seem fair to large states. They were pushing for representation based on population. This proposal, along with other proposals to strengthen the national government, was the **Virginia Plan**. The small states countered with the **New Jersey Plan**, which proposed maintaining equal representation for every state. Rhode Island, the smallest state, was so concerned about small-state power that it boycotted the convention. Tensions were running high; this issue appeared to have all the elements of a deal breaker, and there seemed to be no way to break the impasse.

Just as it appeared that the convention might grind to a halt before it really got started, Connecticut proposed what became known as the **Great Compromise**, or Connecticut Compromise. The plan suggested establishing a Congress with two houses: the Senate would have two senators from each state, and in the House of Representatives each state's number of representatives would be based on its population. Interestingly, Connecticut's population was ranked seventh of the 13 states. It was in a perfect position to offer a compromise because it did not have strong vested interests in the plans offered by either the small states or the large states.

pluralism The idea that having a variety of parties and interests within a government will strengthen the system, ensuring that no group possesses total control.

Virginia Plan A plan proposed by the larger states during the Constitutional Convention that based representation in the national legislature on population. The plan also included a variety of other proposals to strengthen the national government.

New Jersey Plan In response to the Virginia Plan, smaller states at the Constitutional Convention proposed that each state should receive equal representation in the national legislature, regardless of size.

Great Compromise A compromise between the large and small states, proposed by Connecticut, in which Congress would have two houses: a Senate with two legislators per state and a House of Representatives in which each state's representation would be based on population (also known as the Connecticut Compromise).

SMALL STATES, BIG STATES, AND CRAFTING A CONSTITUTION

The European Union (EU) is tackling some of the same issues the Founders faced concerning how to represent states of dramatically different sizes. The EU expanded from 15 to 25 members in May 2004, added two more members in January 2007, and had difficulty creating a new voting structure to incorporate the new members. The first attempt failed when France and the Netherlands rejected the proposed constitution and seven other nations refused to vote on it (ratification was required by all 27 nations). In December 2007, the EU member nations came up with a new draft, the Treaty of Lisbon, that was ratified by member nations and went into effect on December 1, 2009, but the proposed voting system (discussed below) will not be implemented until 2014.

In many ways the EU faces a far more difficult task than the Founders, but the issue of state size is equally vexing. Clearly, tiny states like Luxembourg, with its population of 453,000, cannot receive the same representation on the Council of the European Union as the 82.5 million Germans, just as Delaware and Rhode Island could not demand representation on par with New York and Virginia. However, the current allocation of voting rights favors the small and medium-size EU member states. As the table shows, all nations smaller than Romania receive a disproportionately large share of votes, while large nations—especially Germany—do not receive their fair share.

The Treaty of Lisbon changes this by requiring a "double majority" for most types of measures to pass the Council: legislation requires the support of at least 15 nations (55 percent) that represent at least 65 percent of the EU population (although some issues, including taxation and most foreign policy matters, would require a unanimous vote). This rule would prevent the smaller nations from passing legislation not supported by the larger nations. In fact, the "big four"—United Kingdom, Germany, France, and Italy—would have nearly enough votes between them to block any measure proposed under the new 55/65 rule, while

Poland, Spain, and the other middle-size and smaller countries would lose voting power.

Many other complicated issues had to be resolved, including proposals for a common defense policy, enhancing the powers of the European Parliament, and revamping the European Commission. The sheer length of the rejected constitution is a testament to the complexity of the issues: the failed draft was 69,196 words and about 263 pages long (depending on what language you read it in), compared to the 4,543 words of the U.S. Constitution.[a]

VOTING WEIGHTS IN THE COUNCIL OF THE EUROPEAN UNION

	ACCESSION DATE	POPULATION (MILLIONS)	PERCENTAGE OF EU POP.	PERCENTAGE OF COUNCIL	VOTES
Germany	1957	82	16.7	8.4	29
France	1957	63	12.8	8.4	29
United Kingdom	1973	60	12.3	8.4	29
Italy	1957	59	11.9	8.4	29
Spain	1986	44	8.9	7.8	27
Poland	2004	38	7.7	7.8	27
Romania	2007	22	4.4	4.1	14
Netherlands	1957	16	3.3	3.8	13
Greece	1981	11	2.3	3.5	12
Portugal	1986	11	2.1	3.5	12
Belgium	1957	11	2.1	3.5	12
Czech Republic	2004	10	2.1	3.5	12
Hungary	2004	10	2.0	3.5	12
Sweden	1995	9.0	1.8	2.9	10
Austria	1995	8.3	1.7	2.9	10
Bulgaria	2007	7.7	1.6	2.9	10
Denmark	1973	5.4	1.1	2.0	7
Slovakia	2004	5.4	1.1	2.0	7
Finland	1995	5.3	1.1	2.0	7
Ireland	1973	4.2	0.9	2.0	7
Lithuania	2004	3.4	0.7	2.0	7
Latvia	2004	2.3	0.5	1.2	4
Slovenia	2004	2.0	0.4	1.2	4
Estonia	2004	1.3	0.3	1.2	4
Cyprus	2004	0.77	0.2	1.2	4
Luxembourg	1957	0.46	0.1	1.2	4
Malta	2004	0.40	0.1	0.9	3
EU total		493	100	100	345

Source: The Council of the European Union, http://europa.eu/about-eu/institutions -bodies/council-eu/index_en.htm (accessed 8/14/12).

LEGISLATIVE POWER VERSUS EXECUTIVE POWER

An equally difficult challenge was how to divide power at the national level. Here the central issues revolved around the executive—the president. How much power should the president have relative to the legislative branch? (The courts also figured into the discussions, but they were less central.) And how would the president be elected? One of the central problems was that the convention delegates did not have any positive role models for the executive.

LIMITING PRESIDENTIAL POWER

The delegates knew what they did not want: the king of England and his colonial governors were viewed as tramplers of liberty. But many delegates rejected outright the idea of a single executive because they believed it was impossible to have an executive who would not be oppressive. Edmund Randolph proposed a three-person executive for this reason, arguing that a single executive would be the "fetus of monarchy." The Virginia Plan envisioned a single executive who would share some legislative power with federal judges in a Council of Revision with the power to veto legislation passed by Congress (however, the veto could be overridden by a simple majority vote in Congress). The delegates finally agreed on the single executive because he would have the most "energy, dispatch, and responsibility for the office," but they constrained the president's power through the system of checks and balances. One significant power they granted to the executive was the veto. It could be overridden by Congress, but only with the support of two-thirds of both chambers. This requirement gave the president a significant role in the legislative process.

In addition to Hamilton, the other New Yorkers also favored a strong executive. This was probably because the governorship of New York closely resembled the type of executive that the Constitution envisioned. The governor was elected by the people rather than by the legislature, served for three years, and was eligible for reelection. The New York governor also had a legislative veto power and considerable control over appointments to politically controlled jobs. The arguments the New Yorkers made on behalf of the strong executive relied heavily on the philosophy of John Locke. Locke saw the general superiority of a government of laws created by legislatures, but he also saw the need for an executive with more flexible leadership powers, or what he called "prerogative powers." Legislatures are unable, Locke wrote, "to foresee, and so by laws to provide for all accidents and necessities." They also are, by virtue of their size and unwieldiness, too slow to alter and adapt the law in times of crisis, when the executive could step in to pursue policies in the public's interest.

Although there was support for this view, the Antifederalists were concerned that if such powers were viewed as open-ended, they could give rise to the type of oppressive leader the framers were trying to avoid. Madison attempted to reassure the opponents of executive power, arguing that any prerogative powers would have to be clearly enumerated in the Constitution. In fact, the Constitution explicitly provides only one extraordinary executive power: the right to grant reprieves and pardons, which means that the president can forgive any crimes against the federal government.

SELECTING THE PRESIDENT

The second contentious issue concerning the executive was the method of selecting a president. The way the president was elected incorporated the issues of majority rule and minority rights, state versus national power, and the nature of executive power itself. Would the president be elected by the nation as a whole, by the states, or by coalitions within Congress? If the state-level governments played a central role, would this mean that the president could not speak for national interests? If Congress elected the president, could the executive still provide a check on the legislative branch?

Most Americans do not realize how unique our presidential system is and how close we came to having a parliamentary system, which is the form of government that exists in most other established democracies. In a **parliamentary system**, the executive branch depends on the support of the legislative branch. The Virginia Plan proposed that Congress elect the president, just as Parliament elects the British prime minister. However, facing lingering concerns that the president would be too beholden to Congress, a committee of framers subsequently made the following recommendations: that the president be selected by an electoral college, representation in which would be based on the number of representatives and senators each state has in Congress, and that members of each state's legislature would determine the method for choosing their state's electors.[16] The delegates ultimately approved this recommendation.

Why did the delegates favor this complicated, indirect way of electing the president? One prominent political scientist argues that they had simply run out of alternatives and this was the only widely acceptable solution.[17] As with all good compromises, all sides could claim victory to some extent. Advocates of state power were happy because state legislatures played a central role in presidential elections; those who worried about the direct influence of the people liked the indirect manner of election; and proponents of strong executive power were satisfied that the president would not simply be an agent of Congress.

However, the solution had its flaws and did not work out the way the framers intended. First, if the electoral college was supposed to provide an independent check on the voters, it never played this role because the framers did not anticipate the quick emergence of political parties. Electors became agents of the parties, as they remain today, rather than independent actors who would use their judgment to pick the most qualified candidate for president. Second, the emergence of parties created a serious technical error in the Constitution: the provision that gave each elector two votes and elected the candidate with the most votes as president and the second-place finisher as vice president. With electors acting as agents of parties, they ended up casting one vote each for the presidential and vice-presidential candidate of their own party. This created a tie in the 1800 presidential election when Thomas Jefferson and Aaron Burr each received 73 electoral votes. The problem was easily fixed by the Twelfth Amendment, which required that electors cast separate ballots for president and vice president.

parliamentary system A system of government in which legislative and executive power are closely joined. The legislature (parliament) selects the chief executive (prime minister) who forms the cabinet from members of the parliament.

NATIONAL POWER VERSUS STATE AND LOCAL POWER

Tensions over the balance of power cut across virtually every debate at the convention: presidential versus legislative power, whether the national government could supersede state laws, apportionment in the legislature, slavery, regulation of commerce and taxation, and the amending process. The overall compromise that addressed these tensions was the second of Madison's "double protections," the system of federalism, which divided power between autonomous levels of government that controlled different areas of policy.

Federalism is such an important topic that we devote the entire next chapter to it, but two brief points about it are important here. First, federalism is an example of how careful compromises can alter the Constitution's meaning by changing a single word. The Tenth Amendment, which was added as part of the Bill of Rights shortly after ratification, was a concession to the Antifederalists who were concerned that the national government would gain too much power in the new political system. The Tenth Amendment says, "The powers not delegated to the United States by the Constitution, nor prohibited by it to the States, are reserved to the States respectively, or to the people." This definition of **reserved powers** was viewed as setting outer limits on the reach of national power.

However, the Antifederalists were not happy with this wording because of the removal of a single word; they wanted the Tenth Amendment to read, "The powers not *expressly* delegated to the United States." The new wording would have more explicitly restricted national power. With the word "expressly" removed, the amendment became much more ambiguous and less restrictive of national power. Indeed, the Supreme Court did not use the amendment to strike down an act of Congress until 1871. However, between 1918 and 1937 and then again starting in the 1990s, the Supreme Court has frequently invoked the Tenth Amendment to nullify various laws passed by Congress as unconstitutional intrusions on the reserved powers of the states. (See the discussion in Chapter 3 of the Supreme Court's recent preference for state-centered federalism.)

Second, the **national supremacy clause** of the Constitution (Article VI) says that any national law is the supreme law of the land and takes precedence over any state law that conflicts with it. This is especially important in areas where the national and state governments have overlapping responsibilities for policy.

reserved powers As defined in the Tenth Amendment, powers that are not given to the national government by the Constitution, or not prohibited to the states, are reserved by the states or the people.

national supremacy clause Part of Article VI, Section 2, of the Constitution stating that the Constitution and the laws and treaties of the United States are the "supreme Law of the Land," meaning national laws take precedent over state laws if the two conflict.

SLAVE STATES VERSUS NONSLAVE STATES

Slavery was another nearly insurmountable issue for the delegates. Southern states would not agree to any provisions limiting slavery. Although the nonslave states opposed the practice, they were not willing to scuttle the entire Constitution by taking a principled stand. Even after these basic divisions had been recognized, many unresolved issues remained. Could the importation of slaves be restricted in the future? How would northern states deal with runaway slaves? Most important, how would the slave population be counted for the purpose of slave states' representation in Congress?

The deals that the convention delegates cut on the issue of slavery illustrate the two most common forms of compromise: splitting the difference and logrolling (trading votes). Splitting the difference is familiar to anyone who has haggled over the price of a car or bargained for something at a flea market; you end up meeting halfway, or splitting the difference. Logrolling occurs when politicians trade votes for one another's pet projects.

The delegates went through similar negotiations over how slaves would be counted for purposes of states' congressional representation. The states had been through this debate once before, when they addressed the issue of taxation under the Articles of Confederation. At that point, the slave states had argued that slaves should not be counted because they did not receive the same

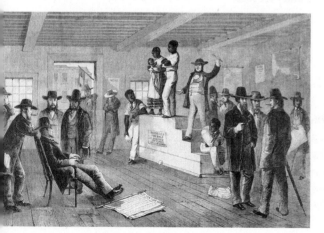

A SLAVE AUCTION IN VIRGINIA. SLAVERY created several problems at the Constitutional Convention: Would there be limits on the importation of slaves? How would runaway slaves be dealt with by nonslave states? And how would slaves be counted for the purposes of congressional representation?

benefits as citizens and were not the same burden to the government. Nonslave states had countered that slaves should be counted the same way as citizens when determining a state's fair share of the tax burden. They had reached a compromise by agreeing that slaves would count as three-fifths of all other persons for purposes of taxation. Now, the arguments over the issue of representation were even more contentious at the Constitutional Convention. Here the positions were reversed, with slave states arguing that slaves should count like everyone else for the purposes of determining the number of House representatives for each state. Once again, both sides managed to agree on the **Three-Fifths Compromise**.

The other two issues, the importation of slaves and dealing with runaway slaves, were handled by logrolling with an element of splitting the difference as well. Logrolling is more likely to occur than splitting the difference when the issue cannot be neatly divided. For example, northern states either would be obligated to return runaway slaves to their southern owners or they would not. There was no way to

Three-Fifths Compromise The states' decision during the Constitutional Convention to count each slave as three-fifths of a person in a state's population for the purposes of determining the number of House members and the distribution of taxes.

2.2 NUTS *& bolts*

MAJOR COMPROMISES AT THE CONSTITUTIONAL CONVENTION

	Position of the Large States	**Position of the Small States**	**Compromise**
Apportionment in Congress	By population	State equality	Great Compromise created the Senate and House
Method of election to Congress	By the people	By the states	House elected by the people; Senate elected by the state legislatures
Electing the executive (president)	By Congress	By the states	By the electoral college
Who decides federal–state conflicts?	Some federal authority	State courts	State courts to decide[a]
	Position of the Slave States	**Position of the Nonslave States**	**Compromise**
Control over commerce	By the states	By Congress	By Congress, but with 20-year exemption for the importation of slaves
Counting slaves toward apportionment	Counted 1:1 like citizens	Not counted	Three-Fifths Compromise
	Position of the Federalists	**Position of the Antifederalists**	**Compromise**
Protection for individual rights	Secured by state constitutions; national Bill of Rights not needed	National Bill of Rights needed	Bill of Rights passed by the 1st Congress; ratified by all states as of December 1791

[a] *This was changed by the Judiciary Act of 1789, which provided for appeals from state to federal courts.*

split the difference. On issues with no clear middle ground, opposing sides will look for other issues on which they can trade votes. The nonslave states wanted more national government control over commerce and trade than under the Articles, a change that the slave states opposed. So a logroll, or vote trade, developed as a way to compromise the competing regional interests of slavery and regulation of commerce. Northern states agreed to return runaway slaves, and southern states agreed to allow Congress to regulate commerce and tax imports with a simple majority vote (rather than the supermajority required under the Articles).

The importation of slaves was included as part of this logroll, along with some split-the-difference negotiating. Northern states wanted to allow future Congresses to ban the importation of slaves; southern states wanted to allow the importation of slaves to continue indefinitely, arguing that slavery was essential to produce their labor-intensive crops. After much negotiation among the states, the final language of the Article resulting from this part of the logroll prevented a constitutional amendment from banning the slave trade until 1808.[18]

From a modern perspective it is difficult to understand how the framers could have taken such a purely political approach to the moral issue of slavery. Many of the delegates believed slavery was immoral, yet they were willing to negotiate for the southern states' support of the Constitution. Some southern delegates were apologetic about slavery, even as they argued for protecting their interests. Many constitutional scholars view the convention's treatment of slavery as its central failure. In fairness to the delegates, it is not clear that they could have done much better if the goal was to create a document that all states would support. However, the delegates' inability to resolve this issue meant that it would simmer below the surface for the next 70 years, finally boiling over into the bloodiest of all American wars, the Civil War.

The convention ended on a relatively harmonious note with Benjamin Franklin moving for adoption. Franklin's motion was worded ambiguously to allow those who still had reservations to sign the Constitution anyway. Franklin's motion was

UNION AND CONFEDERATE TROOPS clash in close combat in the Battle of Cold Harbor, Virginia, in June 1864. The inability of the framers to resolve the issue of slavery allowed tensions over the issue to grow throughout the early nineteenth century, culminating in the Civil War.

in the "following convenient form," "Done in Convention by the unanimous consent of the States present the 17th of September. . . . In Witness whereof we have hereunto subscribed our names." His clever wording meant that the signers were only bearing witness to the approval by the states and therefore could still, in good faith, oppose substantial parts of the document. Franklin's motion passed with 10 ayes, no nays, and one delegation divided. All but three of the remaining delegates signed.

RATIFICATION

CONTRAST THE ARGUMENTS OF THE FEDERALISTS WITH THOSE OF THE ANTIFEDERALISTS

Article VII of the Constitution, which described the process for ratifying the document, was also designed to maximize its chance of success. Only nine states were needed to ratify, rather than the unanimity rule that had applied to changing the Articles of Confederation. Equally important, ratification votes would be taken in state conventions set up specifically for that purpose, bypassing the state legislatures, which would be more likely to resist some of the Constitution's state–federal power-sharing arrangements.

The near-unanimous approval at the Constitutional Convention's end masked the very strong opposition that remained. Many delegates simply left the convention when it became clear that things were not going their way. Rhode Island sent no delegates and refused to appoint a ratification convention; more ominously, New York seemed dead set against the Constitution, and Pennsylvania, Virginia, and Massachusetts were split. The ratifying conventions in each state subjected the Constitution to intense scrutiny, as attendees examined every sentence for possible objections. A national debate raged over the next nine months.

THE ANTIFEDERALISTS' CONCERNS

The Antifederalists were most worried about the role of the president, the transfer of power from the states to the national government, and the lack of specific guarantees of civil liberties. In short, they feared that the national government would become tyrannical. The doubts about the single central executive were expressed by Patrick Henry, a leading Antifederalist. Speaking to the Virginia ratifying convention, Henry was mocking in his indictment, "Your president may easily become a king. . . . There will be no checks, no real balances in this government."[19] Even Thomas Jefferson complained that the president would control the armed forces and could be reelected indefinitely.[20] State power and the ability to regulate commerce were also central concerns. States such as New York would lose substantial revenue if they could no longer charge tariffs on goods that came into their ports. Other states were concerned that they would pay a disproportionate share of national taxes.

The Antifederalists' most important objection was the lack of protections for civil liberties in the new political system. During the last week of the convention,

Elbridge Gerry and George Mason offered a resolution "to prepare a Bill of Rights." However, the resolution was unanimously defeated by the state delegations. Some believed that the national government posed no threat to liberties such as freedom of the press because it did not have the power to restrict them in the first place. Others thought that because it would be impossible to enumerate all rights, it was better to list none at all. Federalists such as Roger Sherman argued that state constitutions, most of which protected freedom of speech, freedom of the press, right to a trial by jury, and other civil liberties, would be sufficient to protect liberty. However, many Antifederalists still wanted assurances that the *national* government would not trample their rights.

THE FEDERALISTS' STRATEGIES

The Federalists counterattacked on several fronts. First, supporters of the Constitution gained the upper hand in the debate by claiming the term *federalist*. It is a common tactic in debates to co-opt a strong point of the opposing side as a positive for your side. The opponents to the Constitution probably had a stronger claim than its supporters to being federalists—that is, those who favor and emphasize the autonomous power of the state governments. Today, for example, the Federalist Society is a conservative group organized around the principles of states' rights and limited government. By calling themselves Federalists, the supporters of the Constitution asserted that they were the true protectors of states' interests, which irritated the Antifederalists to no end. The Antifederalists also had the rhetorical disadvantage of having "anti" attached to their name, thereby being defined in terms of their opponents' position rather than their own. But the problem was more than just rhetorical: the Federalists pointed out that the Antifederalists did not have their own plan to solve the problems created by the Articles.

Second, the Federalists published a series of articles that came to be known as the *Federalist Papers*. Although originally published in New York newspapers, they were widely read throughout the nation. The *Federalist Papers* were essentially one-sided arguments aimed at changing public opinion; the authors downplayed potentially unpopular aspects of the new system, such as the power of the president, while emphasizing points they knew would appeal to the opposition. Despite their biased arguments, the *Federalist Papers* are the best comprehensive discussion of the political theory underlying the Constitution and the framers' interpretations of many of its key provisions.

Third, the Federalists agreed that the new Congress's first order of business would be to add a **Bill of Rights** to the Constitution to protect individual rights and liberties. This promise was essential for securing the support of New York, Massachusetts, and Virginia. The ninth state, New Hampshire, ratified the Constitution on June 21, 1788, but New York and Virginia were still dragging their heels, and their support was viewed as necessary for the legitimacy of the United States, even if it technically was not needed. By the end of the summer, both Virginia and New York finally voted for ratification. Rhode Island and North Carolina refused to ratify until Congress made good on its promise of a Bill of Rights. The 1st Congress submitted 12 amendments to the states, and 10 were ratified by all the states as of December 15, 1791.

Bill of Rights The first 10 amendments to the Constitution; they protect individual rights and liberties.

THE CONSTITUTION: A FRAMEWORK FOR GOVERNMENT

OUTLINE THE MAJOR PROVISIONS OF THE CONSTITUTION

The Constitution certainly has its flaws (some of which have been corrected through amendments), primarily its undemocratic qualities such as the indirect election of senators and the president, the compromises that suppressed the issue of slavery, and the absence of any general statement about citizens' right to vote. However, given the delegates' political context and the various factions that had to be satisfied, the Constitution's accomplishments are substantial.

The document's longevity is testimony to the framers' foresight in crafting a flexible framework for government. Perhaps its most important feature is the system of separation of powers and checks and balances that prevent majority tyranny, while maintaining sufficient flexibility for decisive leadership during times of crisis (such as the Civil War, the Great Depression, and World War II). The system of checks and balances means that each branch of national government has certain exclusive powers, some shared powers, and the ability to check the other two branches (see "How It Works" on page 53).

EXCLUSIVE POWERS

The framers viewed Congress as the "first branch" of government and granted it significant exclusive powers. With the popularly elected House of Representatives and the Senate indirectly elected by state legislatures, Congress was designed to be both the voice of the people and an institution more removed from the people, with a significant role in domestic and foreign policy. Congress was given the power to raise revenue for the federal government through taxes and borrowing, regulate interstate and foreign commerce, coin money, establish post offices and roads, grant patents and copyrights, declare war, "raise and support armies," make rules for the military, and create and maintain a navy. Most important is the so-called power of the purse—control over taxation and spending—given to Congress in Article I, Section 8, of the Constitution: "No money shall be drawn from the Treasury, but in consequence of appropriations made by law." Or as Madison put it, "the legislative department alone has access to the pockets of the people."

Congress's exclusive powers take on additional significance through the **necessary and proper clause**, also known as the elastic clause. It gives Congress the power to "make all Laws which shall be necessary and proper for carrying into Execution the foregoing Powers, and all other Powers vested by this Constitution in the Government of the United States, or in any Department or Officer thereof." This broad grant of power meant that Congress could pass laws

necessary and proper clause
Part of Article I, Section 8, of the Constitution that grants Congress the power to pass all laws related to one of its expressed powers; also known as the elastic clause.

CONGRESS ALONE HAS "THE POWER of the purse" to fund government programs. Although President Bush ordered the invasion of Iraq, the ongoing effort there depended on congressional authorization of funds to pay for the war.

related to any of its exclusive powers. For example, while the Constitution did not explicitly mention Congress's right to compel people to serve in the military, its power to enact a draft was clearly given by the necessary and proper clause, in conjunction with its power to "raise and support armies."

Congress's exclusive powers are more numerous and specific than the limited powers granted to the president. The president is the commander in chief of the armed forces and has power to receive ambassadors and foreign ministers and to issue pardons. The president's most important powers are contained in the executive powers clause that says, "The executive power shall be vested in a President of the United States of America," and in the directive to ensure "that the laws are faithfully executed." As we see later in the chapter, these Article II clauses have given the president most of his power.

The courts did not receive nearly as much attention in the Constitution as either Congress or the president. Alexander Hamilton argued in *Federalist 78* that the Supreme Court would be the "least dangerous branch," because it had "neither the power of the purse nor the sword." The most important positive powers that the framers gave the Supreme Court were lifetime tenure for justices in good behavior and relative independence from the other two branches. The critical negative power of judicial review, the ability to strike down the laws and actions of other branches, will be discussed below.

SHARED POWERS

Along with dividing the exclusive powers between branches, checks and balances designate some shared powers. These are areas where no branch has exclusive control. For example, the president has the power to negotiate treaties and make appointments to the federal courts and other government offices, but these executive actions are to be undertaken with the "advice and consent" of the Senate, which means they were intended to be shared powers. In the twentieth century, these particular powers became executive-centered, with the Senate providing almost no advice to the president and routinely giving its consent (often disapprovingly called "rubber stamping"). However, the Senate can assert its shared power, as shown by the Senate's relatively recent blocking of several of President George W. Bush's and President Obama's lower court nominees.

The war powers, which include decisions about when and how to use military force, were also intended to be shared but have become executive-dominated powers. The framers disagreed about who should control the war powers. Some wanted to keep the arrangement set up by the Articles of Confederation in which nine of the thirteen states had to agree before Congress could declare war. Another group wanted to follow the British system in which the executive branch controlled war powers, while others argued that the president should have the power to repel a sudden attack but that Congress should have the power to declare war. The ultimate compromise that the framers reached shows checks and balances at work, with the president serving as the commander in chief of the armed forces, while Congress has the power to declare war and to appropriate the funds to conduct a war. At the Constitutional Convention, the original proposal gave Congress the power to "make war" rather than "declare war." Clearly this would have been a far more significant grant of power, suggesting an ongoing role for Congress in the conduct of a war.

One other goal of the Founders in making the war powers a shared power was to ensure civilian control of the military. By providing a role for both Congress and the president, the Constitution made it more likely that this important democratic principle would be maintained. One critical step occurred before the Constitution was written when George Washington resigned his commission as commander in chief of the Continental Army. Congress had given Washington complete authority over conduct of the Revolutionary War, and many in Congress wanted him to continue to rule, almost as a king. Washington knew that it was critical for the new nation to have democratically elected leaders control the military. By resigning his commission, he made it clear that any future leadership role he would play (and it was widely assumed by the Founders that he would be the first president) would be as a civilian rather than a general.

Since very early in our nation's history, the president has taken a lead role in the war powers. Presidents have authorized the use of American troops on hundreds of occasions, but Congress has declared war only five times. Of these, Congress debated the merits of entering only one war, the War of 1812. The other "declarations" recognized a state of war that already existed. (For example, after Japan bombed Pearl Harbor, Hawaii, in 1941, Congress's subsequent declaration of war formally recognized what everyone already knew.) Instead, the president usually takes the lead in the decision to use military force. As the 2003 invasion of Iraq demonstrated, if a president is intent on going to war, Congress must go along or get out of the way.

In a few instances, however, Congress wanted to declare war and the president resisted. For example, in 1895 and 1896 when Grover Cleveland was president, tensions mounted in the United States over Cuba's struggle for independence from Spain. Congressional leaders tried to convince Cleveland of the merits of entering the war to help Cuba, but he refused, saying, "I will not mobilize the army. I happen to know that we can buy the Island of Cuba from Spain for $100 million and a war will cost vastly more than that. . . . It would be an outrage to declare war."[21]

Examples such as this are unusual. It would be impossible today for Congress to declare war without a willing commander in chief. However, since the Vietnam War, Congress has tried to redress the imbalance in the war powers in other ways. In 1970, during the Vietnam War, Congress passed a resolution that prevented any funds from supporting ground troops in Laos or Cambodia (nations that bordered Vietnam). In the 1980s, Democrats in Congress prevented President Ronald Reagan from using any appropriated funds to support the Contra rebels in their fight against the Sandinista government in Nicaragua.[22] These examples show that while the president continues to dominate the war powers, Congress can assert its power when it has the will—just as it can by advising the president in treaty negotiations or by withholding approval of the president's nominees for appointed positions.

SONIA SOTOMAYOR IS SWORN IN before the Senate Judiciary Committee at her confirmation hearings to become a justice of the Supreme Court. The president and the Senate share the appointment power to the federal courts: the president makes the nominations, and the Senate provides its "advice and consent."

NEGATIVE OR CHECKING POWERS

The last part of the system of checks and balances is the negative power that the branches have over one another. These powers are especially important to ensure that no single branch dominates the national government.

CONGRESSIONAL CHECKS

impeachment A negative or checking power over the other branches that allows Congress to remove the president, vice president, or other "officers of the United States" (including federal judges) for abuses of power.

power of the purse The constitutional power of Congress to raise and spend money. Congress can use this as a negative or checking power over the other branches by freezing or cutting their funding.

judicial review The Supreme Court's power to strike down a law or executive branch action that it finds unconstitutional.

THE CONSTITUTION ATTEMPTS to strike a balance between protecting our civil liberties from government intrusion and providing for a strong enough government to protect our national security. One consequence of the terrorist attacks of September 11 was more rigorous screening at airports and more widespread surveillance.

Congress has two important negative checks on the other two branches: impeachment and the power of the purse. **Impeachment** was based on the British practice of removing unpopular or corrupt ministers of the king through a vote of no confidence, but the framers made one important change. The president, vice president, or other "officers of the United States" (including federal judges) could not be removed for political reasons, but only for abuses of power—specifically, "Treason, Bribery, or other High Crimes or Misdemeanors." The framers placed this central check with Congress as part of the overall move toward centralizing power at the national level.

Through the **power of the purse,** Congress can punish executive agencies by freezing or cutting their funding or holding hearings on, investigations of, or audits of their operations to make sure money is being spent properly. Congress can also freeze judges' salaries to show displeasure with court decisions, and it has the power to limit the issues that federal courts can consider. Congress can also limit the discretion of judges in other ways, such as by setting federal sentencing guidelines that recommend a range of years in prison that should be served for various crimes. Even today the system of checks and balances is not fixed in stone but evolves according to the changing political climate.

PRESIDENTIAL CHECKS

The framers placed important checks on congressional power as well, and the president's most important check on Congress is the veto. Again there was very little agreement on this topic. The Antifederalists argued that it was "a political error of the greatest magnitude, to allow the executive power a negative, or in fact any kind of control over the proceedings of the legislature." But the Federalists worried that Congress would slowly strip away presidential powers and leave the president too weak. In the end, the Federalist view that the president needed some protections against the "depredations" of the legislature won the day. However, the veto has developed into a major policy-making tool for the president, which is probably broader than the check against "depredations" envisioned by the framers.

The president does not have any formal check on the courts other than the power to appoint judges. However, presidents have, at various times, found unconventional ways to try to influence the courts. For example, Franklin D. Roosevelt tried to "pack the Court" by expanding the size of the Supreme Court with justices who would be sympathetic with his New Deal policies. More recently, George W. Bush attempted to expand the reach of executive power in the War on Terror by taking over some functions within the executive branch that the courts had previously performed. However, the Supreme Court struck down some of these policies as unconstitutional violations of defendants' due process rights. President Obama changed many of Bush's policies, such as harsh interrogation methods and excessive secrecy. But other Bush-era policies were either more difficult to change than Obama anticipated, such as the detainment of enemy combatants in the prison at Guantánamo Bay, or deemed necessary to fight terrorism, such as indefinite detention without trial for suspected terrorists who were arrested outside combat areas.[23] Critics claim that the expansion of executive power in order to fight terrorism has threatened the institutional balance of power by giving the president too much control over functions previously carried out by the courts.[24]

JUDICIAL REVIEW

The Constitution did not provide the Supreme Court with any negative checks on the other two branches. Instead, the practice of **judicial review**, the ability of the

How It Works

CHECKS AND BALANCES

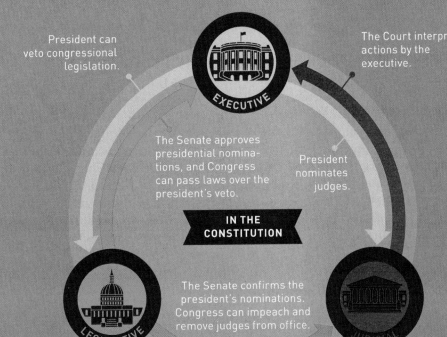

President can veto congressional legislation.

The Court interprets actions by the executive.

The Senate approves presidential nominations, and Congress can pass laws over the president's veto.

President nominates judges.

IN THE CONSTITUTION

The Senate confirms the president's nominations. Congress can impeach and remove judges from office.

EXECUTIVE

LEGISLATIVE

JUDICIAL

IN THE CONSTITUTION

If one branch tries to assert too much power, the other branches have certain key powers that allow them to fight back and restore the balance. (In addition to the powers noted in the diagram, the Congress also can impeach the president and remove him or her from office.)

The Court interprets the laws passed by Congress.

Congress passed an anti-torture law and held hearings.

The Court ruled that the executive violated the rights of suspected terrorists.

AN EXAMPLE

BUSH ADMINISTRATION

CONGRESS

SUPREME COURT

AN EXAMPLE

During the war on terror, concerns arose that President Bush and the executive branch had assumed too much power—especially the unilateral power to disregard due process rights for suspected terrorists. In response, Congress checked the president by passing an anti-torture law and holding hearings to determine if the Department of Justice had acted illegally. The Supreme Court limited the president's power by ruling that the executive branch violated the rights and liberties of suspected terrorists, but the president and Congress responded to limit the scope of the Court's ruling.

POP QUIZ!

1 How can the president (the executive branch) stop Congress (the legislative branch) from asserting too much power?

a by declaring laws unconstitutional

b by impeaching members of Congress

c by vetoing legislation

d by holding hearings

e through nominations

2 How did the Supreme Court "check" the Bush administration in the cases involving the rights of terror suspects?

a by declaring presidential/executive branch acts unconstitutional

b by impeaching the president

c by passing legislation

d through nominations

e through ratification

Answers: 1.c; 2.a

Supreme Court to strike down a law or an executive branch action as unconstitutional, was established by the Court much later, in the landmark decision *Marbury v. Madison* in 1803. According to Madison's notes, nine of the 11 framers who spoke on the topic clearly favored explicitly granting the Supreme Court the power of judicial review, but the issue was not resolved at the convention. In several states, aggressive courts had struck down state laws, and delegates from those states resisted giving an unelected national court similar power over the entire country. While judicial review is not explicitly mentioned in the Constitution, supporters of the practice point to the supremacy clause, which states that the "Constitution, and the Laws of the United States which shall be made in Pursuance thereof . . . shall be the supreme Law of the Land."

As Chief Justice John Marshall argued in *Marbury v. Madison*, in order to enforce the Constitution as the supreme law of the land, the Court must determine which laws are "in pursuance thereof." Critics of judicial review argue that the Constitution is supreme because it gains its legitimacy from the people, and therefore elected officials—Congress and the president—should be the primary interpreters of the Constitution rather than the courts. This dispute may never fully be resolved, but Marshall's bold assertion of judicial review made the Supreme Court an equal partner in the system of separate powers and checks and balances rather than "the least dangerous branch" that the framers described.

EXPLORE HOW THE MEANING OF THE CONSTITUTION HAS EVOLVED

IS THE CONSTITUTION A "LIVING" DOCUMENT?

Recent polls suggest that many Americans are unfamiliar with the Constitution's basic provisions. Indeed, a national poll found that only 42 percent of the public could name the three branches of government, although 73 percent could identify the Three Stooges (Larry, Moe, and Curly). In another survey, 24 percent of the public could not name any First Amendment rights, 52 percent did not know that the Senate has 100 members, and 16 percent thought that the Constitution created a Christian nation.[25]

In the face of such public apathy, can the Constitution provide the blueprint for modern democratic governance? If so, how has it remained relevant after more than 200 years? The answer to the first question, in our opinion, is clearly yes. While the United States falls short on many measures of an ideal democracy, the Constitution remains relevant in part because it embodies many of the central values of American citizens: liberty and freedom, majority rule and minority rights, equal protection for all citizens under the laws, and a division of power across and within levels of government. The Constitution presents a list of substantive values, largely within the Bill of Rights, aimed at legally protecting certain individual rights that we still consider basic and necessary. The Constitution also sets out the institutional framework within which the government operates.

But these observations beg the question of *why* the Constitution remains relevant today. Why does this framework of government still work? How can the framers' values still be meaningful to us? There are at least four reasons that the Constitution continues to be a "living document": a willingness over the years to simply ignore the parts that become irrelevant, ambiguity in central passages that permits flexible interpretation, the amending process, and the document's own designation of multiple interpreters of the Constitution. These factors have allowed the Constitution to evolve with the changing values and norms of the nation.

A LIVING CONSTITUTION?

Debates about how to interpret the Constitution are almost as old as the document itself. One question that dates back to the late nineteenth century is whether the document is a living Constitution—that is, should the Constitution be viewed as a flexible framework or a structural document that has fixed meaning? Those who think the former argue that a dynamic and modern society cannot be bound by ideas rooted in the late eighteenth century. Proponents of the other side of the debate fear that flexibility is a recipe for arbitrary law based on Supreme Court justices' individual preferences and biases. They offer an alternative perspective, called "originalism," that says constitutional interpretation must be based on the original meaning of the document and its amendments.

Political scientists who engage in this debate about the living Constitution are doing a type of research—normative theory—that is different from other work discussed in the "What Do Political Scientists Do?" boxes. Rather than examining empirical questions (what happened and why), they explore normative questions of right and wrong, just and unjust, or in this instance, the proper method for interpreting the Constitution. The method of these scholars is primarily textual analysis: they look at the text of the Constitution, Supreme Court decisions, and relevant historical documents to develop their arguments. For example, supporters of the living Constitution try to argue that their perspective is also consistent with the framers' intent, pointing out that the framers designed the document to be general and flexible so it would be relevant for many generations to come. They point to Edmund Randolph's advice to the Committee on Detail at the Constitutional Convention that it should "insert essential principles only; lest the operations of government should be clogged by rendering those provisions permanent and unalterable, which ought to be accommodated to times and events."[a] That is, essential principles were flexible enough to apply to times and events that could not be foreseen by the framers.

Bruce Ackerman, a law professor and political scientist at Yale University, is one of the most famous defenders of the living Constitution approach. He argues that the Constitution, the "official canon," is not as relevant for understanding the most important issues of the day as the "operational canon" based on landmark statutes and "superprecedents" (important Supreme Court decisions that shape other decisions on that topic). For example, he argues that *Brown v. Board of Education*, the Court decision that desegregated public schools, is more important than the Constitution's reference to a "republican form of government." According to Ackerman, "the living

Watch a video clip of political scientist Mark Graber discussing this topic at **wwnorton.com/studyspace**

There is a vigorous debate among political scientists whether the Constitution is a living document or whether it should be interpreted more strictly according to the original intent of the framers.

Constitution is organized on the basis of an operational canon that does not even assign primacy, much less exclusivity, to the official canon."[b]

Scholars and jurists from the originalist side of the debate strongly disagree. Political scientist Keith E. Whittington argues that "judges should not feel free to pour their own political values and ideals into the Constitution. . . . [T]he constant touchstone of constitutional law should be the purposes and values of those who had the authority to *make* the Constitution—not of those who are charged with governing under it and abiding by it."[c] Whittington goes on to argue that especially when striking down laws passed by Congress, the justification for the Court's decision must be found in an original understanding of the Constitution. Other scholars such as Yale law professor Akhil Reed Amar apply an originalist understanding to interpreting civil liberties.[d] Of course, there is an entirely different approach to this question by empirical scholars of the Supreme Court, such as Jeffrey Segal and Harold Spaeth, who argue that both sides of this debate are expressing basic political attitudes and biases, while hiding behind lofty rhetoric of how best to interpret the Constitution.[e]

Although these normative questions concerning the living Constitution will never be resolved, research by political scientists plays an important role in shaping the debates. Answering the question about how justices *should* interpret the Constitution ultimately depends on one's broader views of the proper role of the Court within a representative democracy, but having the necessary tools and concepts is important for being able to engage that debate.

TURNING A BLIND EYE

Some parts of the Constitution are ignored today because they have no meaning in a modern context. For example, Article I, Section 4, says that "Congress shall assemble at least once in every Year," but the modern Congress is in session throughout the year (with various recesses). Nobody pays attention to this passage anymore because it simply does not matter. Another example is the Third Amendment's prohibition against the quartering of troops in someone's house without their consent. Today the idea that National Guard officers would roll up to your house and ask to sleep on your couch (or worse, kick you out of your bed) is absurd, but this was a real concern when the Constitution was written.

The tendency to ignore (or at least flexibly interpret) relevant passages can have more meaningful applications as well. In the 2000 presidential election, George W. Bush and Dick Cheney nearly ran afoul of part of the Twelfth Amendment, which says that electors in the electoral college shall "vote by ballot for President and Vice-President, one of whom, at least, shall not be an inhabitant of the same state with themselves." This would have stymied the Texas electors because both Bush and Cheney lived in Dallas, but Cheney changed his official state of residence to Wyoming. The courts dismissed legal challenges to this move, allowing the Texas electors to cast their votes for both Bush and Cheney. Whether this example demonstrates the courts' willingness to be flexible in their interpretation of the Constitution or a biased reading of the facts in Cheney's favor depends on your own interpretation.

AMBIGUITY

executive powers clause Part of Article II, Section 1, of the Constitution that states, "The executive Power shall be vested in a President of the United States of America." This broad statement has been used to justify many assertions of presidential power.

commerce clause Part of Article I, Section 8, of the Constitution that gives Congress "the power to regulate Commerce . . . among the several States." The Supreme Court's interpretation of this clause has varied, but today it serves as the basis for much of Congress's legislation.

enumerated powers Powers explicitly granted to Congress, the president, or the Supreme Court in the first three articles of the Constitution. Examples include Congress's power to "raise and support armies" and the president's power as commander in chief.

A more important characteristic of the Constitution that has kept the document relevant is its ambiguity. Key passages were written in very general language, which has allowed the Constitution to evolve along with changing norms, values, and political contexts. This ambiguity was a political necessity: not only were the framers aware that the document would need to survive for generations, but in many instances the language that they chose was simply the only wording that all the framers could agree on.

Three of the most important parts of the Constitution are also among its most ambiguous: the necessary and proper (or elastic) clause, the **executive powers clause**, and the **commerce clause**. As discussed earlier, the necessary and proper clause gives Congress the power to enact laws that are related to its **enumerated powers**, or those that are explicitly granted. But what does "necessary and proper" mean? Congress for the most part gets to answer that question.

The executive powers clause is even more vague: Article II begins with the words "The executive Power shall be vested in a President of the United States of America." This sentence has served to justify a broad range of presidential actions because it does not define any boundaries for the "executive powers" it grants. The vague wording was necessary because the convention delegates could not agree on a definition of executive power. The wording also had the desirable consequence of making the clause flexible enough to serve the country both in times that require strong presidential action (such as the Civil War, the Great Depression, or World War II) and in times when the president was not as central (such as the "golden age of Congress" in the late nineteenth century).

Perhaps the best illustration of the importance of ambiguity in the Constitution is the commerce clause, which gives Congress "the power to regulate commerce . . . among the several States." What is "commerce," and what exactly does "among the states" mean? Different interpretations have reflected prevailing norms of the time. In the nineteenth century, when the national government was relatively weak and more power was held at the state level, the Supreme Court interpreted the clause to mean that Congress could not regulate commerce that was entirely within the boundaries of a single state (intrastate, as opposed to interstate, commerce). Because manufacturing typically occurred within the boundaries of a given state, this ruling led to a distinction between manufacturing and commerce, which had significant implications. For example, Congress could not regulate working hours, worker safety, or child labor given that these were defined as part of manufacturing rather than commerce. In the New Deal era of the mid-1930s, the Court adopted a more expansive interpretation of the commerce clause that largely obliterated the distinction between intrastate and interstate commerce. This view was strengthened in the 1960s when the Supreme Court upheld a civil rights law that, among other things, prevented owners of hotels from discriminating against African Americans. As we discuss more fully in Chapter 3, Federalism, for nearly 60 years this interpretation held. More recently the Supreme Court has tightened the scope of Congress's powers to regulate commerce, but the clause still serves as the basis for most important national legislation. The commerce clause has been unchanged since 1789, and its ambiguous wording has been used to justify or restrict a varying array of legislation.

CHANGING THE CONSTITUTION

The most obvious way that the Constitution keeps up with the times is by allowing for changes to its language. The framers broadly supported the idea behind Article V, which lays out the formal process for amending the Constitution: the people must control their own political system, which included the ability to change it through a regular, nonviolent process. George Washington called constitutional amendments "explicit and authentic acts" and Thomas Jefferson was adamant that each generation needed to have the power to change the Constitution. Toward the end of his life, he wrote in a letter to James Madison:

> *Some men look at constitutions with sanctimonious reverence, and deem them like the ark of the covenant, too sacred to be touched. They ascribe to the men of the preceding age a wisdom more than human, and suppose what they*

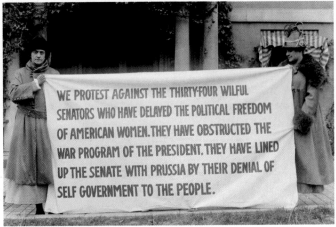

AMENDING THE CONSTITUTION IS DIFFICULT and can be controversial. Some amendments that are widely accepted today, like the Nineteenth Amendment giving women the right to vote, were intensely debated prior to their ratification.

did to be beyond amendment. I knew that age well; I belonged to it and labored with it. . . . It was very like the present. . . . Let us not weakly believe that one generation is not as capable as another of taking care of itself.[26]

PROPOSAL AND RATIFICATION

While there was strong consensus on including in the Constitution a set of provisions for amending it, there was no agreement on how this should be done. The Virginia Plan envisioned a relatively easy process of changing the Constitution "whensoever it shall seem necessary" by means of ratification by the people, while the New Jersey Plan proposed a central role for state governments. Madison suggested the plan that was eventually adopted, which once again accommodated both those who wanted a stronger national government and those who favored the states.

Article V describes the two steps necessary to change the Constitution: proposal and ratification. Congress may *propose* an amendment that has the approval of two-thirds of the members in both houses, or an amendment may be proposed by a national convention that has been called by two-thirds of the states' legislatures. In either case, the amendment must be *ratified* by three-fourths of the states' legislatures or state conventions (see Figure 2.2). A national convention has never been used to propose an amendment, and every amendment except for the Twenty-First, which repealed Prohibition, has been ratified by state legislatures rather than state conventions.

FLAWS IN THE AMENDING PROCESS

Article V was a brilliant compromise that struck a balance between opposing views and made it neither too difficult nor too easy to amend the Constitution. However, the amending process has its flaws. First, one reason that a new constitutional convention has never been called is fear of a "runaway convention." Some scholars argue that nothing in Article V would constrain the convention to consider

FIGURE » 2.2

AMENDING THE CONSTITUTION

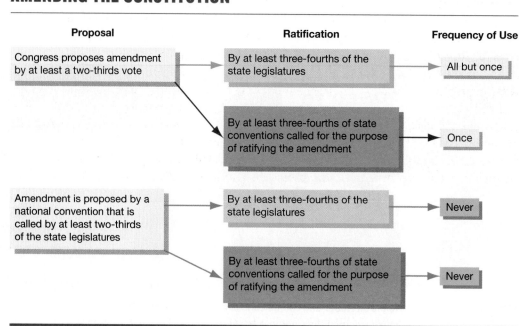

Proposal	Ratification	Frequency of Use
Congress proposes amendment by at least a two-thirds vote	By at least three-fourths of the state legislatures	All but once
	By at least three-fourths of state conventions called for the purpose of ratifying the amendment	Once
Amendment is proposed by a national convention that is called by at least two-thirds of the state legislatures	By at least three-fourths of the state legislatures	Never
	By at least three-fourths of state conventions called for the purpose of ratifying the amendment	Never

only a single issue, so it is possible that the convention could start from scratch, the way the framers did, even proposing a new method of ratification. Others dispute this view, but we have come close to finding out on several occasions. In the 1960s, 35 states—one short of the necessary two-thirds—called for a convention to propose a constitutional amendment that would overturn a Supreme Court decision concerning legislative redistricting. In the late 1970s, 30 states called for a convention to propose an amendment requiring a balanced federal budget.

Even more troubling, Article V also does not specify voting procedures for a constitutional convention. Would votes be apportioned equally so that each state would have one vote (as was true at the 1787 convention), or would the voting power be based on population, or perhaps some mixture of the two, as in the electoral college? Article V is also silent on the mechanism for choosing delegates to attend the state conventions. Thus, there is a wide range in the different states' methods of selection. Delegates may be appointed by the governor, elected by the people, or simply be the current state legislators.

Article V also does not address the question of time limits on amendments; rather, this issue has been left up to Congress. The Eighteenth Amendment (Prohibition) was the first to have a time limit: it had to be ratified within seven years. All amendments before the Eighteenth and some after have been approved by Congress and sent to the states for ratification without time limits. This led to the odd situation surrounding the Twenty-Seventh Amendment, which required that no legislation granting a congressional pay raise could go into effect until after the following election. This amendment was originally proposed in 1789 as part of the original Bill of Rights. It sat unratified for more than 80 years until Ohio ratified it to protest a congressional pay hike; however, no other states followed Ohio's lead. It sat for another 100 years until 1978, when Wyoming ratified the amendment. Then, in the early 1980s, the amendment gained national attention. From 1983 to 1992, enough states ratified the amendment to add it to the Constitution on May 7, 1992, after a lag of more than 202 years!

A RANGE OF AMENDMENTS

Most amendments have been wider reaching than the Twenty-Seventh Amendment, but they have ranged from fairly narrow, technical corrections of errors in the original document (Eleventh and Twelfth Amendments), to important topics such as the abolition of slavery (Thirteenth), mandating equal protection of the laws for all citizens (Fourteenth), providing for the popular election of senators (Seventeenth), giving blacks and then women the right to vote (Fifteenth and Nineteenth), and allowing a national income tax (Sixteenth). Potential constitutional amendments have addressed many other issues, with more than 10,000 proposed; of those, 33 were sent to the states and 27 have made it through the amending process (the first 10 came at once in the Bill of Rights). Table 2.1 shows several amendments that were introduced but not ratified. The "You Decide" box outlines the debate over when it is appropriate to amend the Constitution.

MULTIPLE INTERPRETERS

The final way that the Constitution maintains its relevance is through changing interpretations of the document by multiple interpreters. As we pointed out in the previous discussion of the commerce clause, there have been significant changes

TABLE » 2.1

AMENDMENTS INTRODUCED IN CONGRESS THAT DID NOT PASS

Many proposed constitutional amendments have almost no chance of passing. Indeed, most of those listed here did not even make it to the floor of the House or Senate for a vote. Why do you think a member of Congress would propose an amendment that he or she knew would fail?

112th Congress (2011–12)	Amend the First Amendment to allow limitations on federal campaign contribution and expenditures.
	Protect the right of parents to raise and educate their children without interference from government.
	Require that the federal budget is balanced.
111th Congress (2009–10)	Abolish the electoral college and provide for the direct election of the president and vice president.
	Provide a high-quality education to all citizens of the United States.
	Repeal the Sixteenth Amendment (prohibit an income tax).
110th Congress (2007–08)	Repeal the Twenty-Second Amendment (abolish term limits for the president).
	Provide the right to a clean, safe, and sustainable environment for all persons.
	Permit voluntary school prayer.
	Impose 12-year term limits for the House and Senate.
109th Congress (2005–06)	Make the filibuster in the Senate a part of the Constitution.
	Provide for continuity of government in case of a catastrophic event.
	Prohibit desecration of the U.S. flag.
108th Congress (2003–04)	Include use of the word *God* in the Pledge of Allegiance and the national motto as protected speech.
	Define marriage in all states as a union between a man and a woman.
	Prohibit courts from protecting child pornography.

Source: The U.S. Constitution Online: Some Proposed Amendments, www.usconstitution.net/constamprop.html (accessed 3/22/2012); http://thomas.loc.gov (accessed 3/22/2012).

implied powers Powers supported by the Constitution that are not expressly stated in it.

in the way the Constitution structures the policy-making process, even though the pertinent text of the Constitution has not changed.[27] This point is best understood by examining the concept of **implied powers**—that is, powers that are not explicitly stated in the Constitution but can be inferred from an enumerated power. The Supreme Court often defines the boundaries of implied powers, but Congress, the president, and the public can also play key roles.

Three of the earliest examples of implied powers show the president, the Supreme Court, and Congress each interpreting the Constitution and contributing to its evolving meaning. The first involved the question of how active the president should be in stating national foreign policy principles. In issuing his famous proclamation of neutrality in 1793, George Washington unilaterally set forth a national foreign policy, even though the president's power to do so is not explicitly stated in the Constitution. Alexander Hamilton defended the presidential power to make such a proclamation as implied in both the executive powers clause and the president's explicitly granted powers in the area of foreign policy (receiving ambassadors, negotiating treaties, and serving as commander in chief). Thomas Jefferson, in contrast, thought it was a terrible idea for presidents to have that kind of power. He preferred that such general policy statements be left to Congress.

AMENDING THE CONSTITUTION

In a typical Congress there are between 50 and 100 proposals to amend the Constitution. Some of the proposed amendments reflect efforts to overturn particularly controversial Supreme Court decisions. Recent examples include amendments to prohibit abortion, guarantee the right to obtain an abortion, make flag desecration a crime, and permit prayer in public school. Some amendments are designed to change the government's basic structure and process, such as proposals to replace the electoral college with a direct popular vote, choose presidential electors at the congressional-district level, repeal the Twenty-Second Amendment (which limits presidents to two terms), require a two-thirds congressional vote to raise taxes, impose term limits on representatives and senators, or repeal the Sixteenth Amendment (which permitted a federal income tax). And some proposed amendments would guarantee specific benefits or create new classes of constitutionally guaranteed rights like affordable housing, quality health care, a clean environment, or full employment. The only thing that cannot be changed in the Constitution is the equal apportionment of states' votes in the Senate (two senators per state).[a] Anything short of that is fair game.

One controversial question concerning the amending process is whether it should be used to address specific policy issues such as term limits, balancing the federal budget, burning the flag, the Pledge of Allegiance, or whether a person may be detained for not wearing a seatbelt. The only adopted amendments that fall into this category are Prohibition (which was subsequently repealed with another amendment) and the long-delayed Twenty-Seventh Amendment regarding congressional pay raises. The other amendments address broader policy concerns, expand or protect individual rights and liberties, modify electoral laws and institutions, or address basic concerns about the working of government. Constitutional scholar Kathleen Sullivan is critical of efforts to alter the Constitution. Constitutional principles should not, she concludes, be "up for grabs" or politicized but should be slow to change; amendments should be reserved for setting out the basic structure of government and defining "a few fundamental political ideals."[b] The alternative perspective chides those who "treat the Constitution like an untouchable religious text and the republic's founders as omniscient," and maintains that "meaningful democratic politics requires an aggressive constitutional politics."[c] Many of the recently proposed amendments (see Table 2.1) are clearly policy related, thus many members of Congress view amending the Constitution as a legitimate policy-making tool.

One policy area in the debate over the appropriateness of policy-related constitutional amendments concerns gay marriage. Many states have amended their constitutions to define marriage to exclude same-sex couples. Advocates of this view are pushing for an amendment to the Constitution to define marriage the same way at the national level. Would you support such an amendment? Try to separate your view on the specific issue, gay marriage, from your position on the question of amending the Constitution. If you oppose gay marriage, is it possible that the better path of action would be through the state legislatures?

Some people argue that the Constitution should not be used to make policy, except for broader purposes such as expanding political rights or protecting equality. The Eighteenth Amendment, ratified in 1919, prohibited the consumption of alcohol and is often upheld as an example of a failed policy attempt. In this 1933 photo, a beer distributor readies his first shipment following ratification of the Twenty-First Amendment, which repealed Prohibition.

Critical Thinking Questions

1. What kinds of policies would you favor addressing through constitutional amendments? Do you agree that amendments should be reserved for a "few fundamental political ideas"—things like the right to vote and the structure of government—or that more frequent amendments are necessary for "meaningful democratic politics"?

2. Do you support any of the amendments proposed in Table 2.1? Choose one and explain why a constitutional amendment is (or is not) the best way to address the issue.

The Supreme Court made its mark on the notion of implied powers in a landmark case involving the creation of a national bank. In *McCulloch v. Maryland* (1819) the Court ruled that the federal government had the power to create a national bank and denied the state of Maryland the right to tax a branch of that bank. The Court said it was not necessary for the Constitution to expressly grant Congress the power to create the bank; rather, it was implied in Congress's power over financial matters and from the necessary and proper clause of the Constitution.

Congress got into the act with an early debate over the president's implied power to remove appointed officials. The Constitution clearly gives the president the power to make appointments to cabinet positions and other top executive branch offices, but it is silent on how these people can be removed. This was one of the most difficult issues in the first Congress, and members spent more than a month debating the topic. The record of the debate is the most thorough examination of implied powers ever conducted in Congress. However, Congress ended up not taking any action on the issue, which left the president's removal power implicit in the Constitution.

Issues concerning implied powers continue to surface. The president's appointment powers have recently evolved as the Senate has played a much more aggressive role in providing its "advice and consent" on presidential nominations to the federal courts. As we explore in Chapter 14, in the past 20 years the Senate has blocked court appointments at a significantly higher rate than it did in the first half of the twentieth century. Although this trend reversed when the Democrats gained control of the government and 60 seats in the Senate in 2009, those conditions only held until January 2010 when Republican Scott Brown won the special election to fill the late Ted Kennedy's seat. The relevant language in the Constitution is the same, yet the Senate's understanding of its role in this important process has changed.

Public opinion and social norms also influence the prevailing interpretation of the Constitution, as is evident in the evolving meanings of capital punishment (the death penalty) and freedom of speech. When the Constitution was written, capital punishment was broadly accepted, even for horse thieves. The framers were only concerned that people not be "deprived of life, liberty, or property without the due process of law." Therefore the prohibition in the Eighth Amendment against "cruel and unusual punishment" certainly did not mean to the framers that the death penalty was unconstitutional. However, in 1972 the Supreme Court struck down capital punishment as unconstitutional because it was being applied arbitrarily.[28] Subsequently, after procedural changes were made, the Court once again upheld the practice. However, the Court has since decided that capital punishment for a mentally retarded man constituted cruel and unusual punishment—a decision that reflects modern sensibilities but not the thinking of the framers. Similarly, the text of the First Amendment protections for freedom of speech has never changed, but the Supreme Court has been willing to uphold significant limitations on free speech, especially in wartime. When external threats are less severe, the Court has been more tolerant of controversial speech.

The line between a new interpretation of the Constitution and constitutional change is difficult to define. Clearly not every new direction taken by the Court or new interpretation of the constitutional roles of the president or Congress is comparable to a constitutional amendment. In one respect, a constitutional amendment is much more permanent than a new interpretation by the Court. For example, the Supreme Court could not unilaterally decide that 18- to 20-year-olds, women, and African Americans no longer have the right to vote. Constitutional amendments expanded the right to vote to include these groups, and only further amendments could either expand or restrict the right to vote. However, gradual changes in constitutional interpretation are probably just as important as the amending process in explaining the Constitution's ability to keep pace with the

THE EIGHTH AMENDMENT'S BAN ON "cruel and unusual punishment" is generally viewed as excluding capital punishment, but the execution of juveniles and the mentally retarded has been found unconstitutional. This picture shows the electric chair in the Southern Ohio Correctional Facility in Lucasville, Ohio.

times. Even the large "revolutions" in constitutional change have occurred by both means: the Civil War led to a **constitutional revolution** that was accomplished through three important amendments, whereas the New Deal constitutional revolution happened without changing a single word of the document.

constitutional revolution
A significant change in the Constitution that may be accomplished either through amendments (as after the Civil War) or shifts in the Supreme Court's interpretation of the Constitution (as in the New Deal era).

CONCLUSION

The debate between Tea Party supporters and opponents outlined in the introduction illustrates many of the themes of this chapter: the conflictual nature of politics established by the Constitution, multiple interpreters, and ambiguous language. The separation of powers and the system of checks and balances in our political system divide power to protect against majority tyranny. To Tea Party supporters, we have strayed too far from the limited government roots of the founding. Its opponents claim that the Constitution centralized power in the national government, while moving away from the state-centered Articles of Confederation. Well, which side is right? The rather unsatisfying answer is that both are correct. The Founders *did* create a system of limited government that was intended to protect individual liberty from government tyranny, but at the same time, the Founders wanted a strong and effective government that could overcome the limitations of state-centered government. So clearly a return to founding principles does not mean a return to states' rights; that would be a return to the principles of the Articles of Confederation. But equally clear is that the Founders were concerned about unchecked government power.

Congress, the president, and the Supreme Court all must interpret the Constitution in the normal course of playing their institutional roles. But as the Tea Party debate shows, the public can interpret the Constitution in different ways as well. It is refreshing to see the Constitution thrust to the fore in congressional and presidential candidate debates. Maybe with enough attention, those public opinion polls showing that Americans are more familiar with the Three Stooges than the three branches of government can be reversed. If the public is more informed about the Constitution, they can become an even more important interpreter of the Constitution.

Finally, the general and ambiguous language of the Constitution means that both supporters and opponents of the Tea Party can stake a claim to having views that are informed by the Constitution. When a Tea Party advocate claims that the Federal Reserve is unconstitutional because it is not specifically mentioned in the document, the other side can point out that if that logic is used, then the Air Force is certainly unconstitutional as well (the Constitution mentions Congress's power to support the Army and Navy, but obviously not the Air Force). Furthermore, Tea Party opponents would say, the commerce clause and the necessary and proper clause give Congress all the power it needs.

A leading constitutional scholar, Walter Murphy, addressed the relevance issue this way: "The ideals that it enshrines, the processes it prescribes, and the actions it legitimizes must either help to change its citizenry or, at a minimum, reflect their current values. If a constitution does not articulate at least in general terms, the ideals that form or will reform its people and express the political character they have, it will soon be replaced or atrophy." The Constitution's ability to change with the times and reflect its citizens' values has enabled it to remain relevant and important today. Its flexibility and general language means that there will never be definitive answers to the conflict over its meaning, but it ensures that these debates will be enduring and meaningful.

THE HISTORICAL CONTEXT OF THE CONSTITUTION

▶ Describe the historical circumstances that led to the Constitutional Convention of 1787. **Pages 31–38**

SUMMARY

The U.S. Constitution was shaped by historical events preceding its creation, particularly the period of British rule over the colonies, the Revolutionary War, and the states' experience under the Articles of Confederation. Under British rule, the colonies were relatively independent of one another, and the framers sought to create a strong nation while still maintaining the autonomy of the states in the system. The framers based the Constitution on three key principles: the rejection of a monarchy, popular control of the government, and a limited government that protected against tyranny.

KEY TERMS

Articles of Confederation (p. 33)

limited government (p. 33)

republican democracy (p. 36)

monarchy (p. 36)

republicanism (p. 36)

"consent of the governed" (p. 36)

natural rights (p. 36)

Federalist Papers (p. 37)

Federalists (p. 38)

Antifederalists (p. 38)

PRACTICE QUIZ QUESTIONS

1. How were members of Congress selected under the Articles of Confederation?

a) by the state governor
b) by the state legislature
c) by the state supreme court
d) by popular election
e) by random lot

2. What power did the president have under the Articles of Confederation?

a) power to raise an army
b) power to veto congressional legislation
c) power to negotiate foreign agreements
d) power to nominate federal judges
e) There was no president under the Articles of Confederation.

3. Who is the philosopher that argued that without government, life would be "nasty, brutish and short"?

a) Thomas Hobbes
b) John Locke
c) Baron de Montesquieu
d) Thomas Paine
e) Thomas Jefferson

4. At the American Founding, what is the best way to describe the economic inequality among classes, and the economic inequality among regions?

a) high / high
b) high / low
c) low / high
d) low / low

THE POLITICS OF COMPROMISE AT THE CONSTITUTIONAL CONVENTION

▶ Analyze the major issues debated by the framers of the Constitution. **Pages 38–47**

SUMMARY

While the framers of the Constitution agreed that the Articles of Confederation needed to be changed, there was little consensus otherwise. The Federalists and Antifederalists clashed on several issues, though the most important were (1) balancing majority rule with minority rights, (2) allocating power between large and small states, (3) allocating power between the legislature and executive, (4) allocating power between the national government and the states, and (5) determining how to handle slavery.

KEY TERMS

pluralism (p. 40)

Virginia Plan (p. 40)

New Jersey Plan (p. 40)

Great Compromise (p. 40)

parliamentary system (p. 43)

reserved powers (p. 44)

national supremacy clause (p. 44)

Three-Fifths Compromise (p. 45)

CRITICAL THINKING AND DISCUSSION

If you had been at the Constitutional Convention, which part of the document would you have worked to change? How would you have negotiated a compromise to make that change possible?

ⓢ PRACTICE ONLINE

"Big Think" video exercise: *What Is the Legacy of Slavery in America?*

PRACTICE QUIZ QUESTIONS

5. Madison argued that the best way to prevent the tyranny of factions was to _____.
   a) outlaw political parties
   b) establish a strong national government
   c) have various groups compete against each other in the government
   d) establish strong local governments
   e) try to ensure that all people were equal

6. The Great Compromise provided solutions to which issue?
   a) balancing majority rule with minority rights
   b) allocating power between big and small states
   c) allocating power between the legislature and executive
   d) allocating power between national and state governments
   e) determining how to handle slavery

7. How are executives chosen in most other established democracies?
   a) by popular election
   b) by electoral College
   c) through selection by the judiciary
   d) through selection by the legislature
   e) by the United Nations

8. The outcome of the Three-Fifths Compromise was that slaves counted for three-fifths of a person for the purposes of _____ and _____.
   a) voting; taxation
   b) congressional representation; taxation
   c) voting; congressional representation
   d) taxation; congressional appropriations
   e) congressional representation; agricultural subsidies

RATIFICATION

▶ Contrast the arguments of the Federalists with those of the Antifederalists. **Pages 47–48**

SUMMARY

After the Constitution was written and approved at the Constitutional Convention, it still needed to be ratified by nine states. The Constitution was primarily criticized by the Antifederalists, which gave way to a lengthy public debate over the merits of the proposed framework. Ultimately, the framers had to include the Bill of Rights, which was tailored to protect the rights of states and individuals from the national government, in order to win over the necessary support in the states.

Bill of Rights (p. 48)

PRACTICE QUIZ QUESTIONS

9. What group was concerned about the Constitution's provisions for the strength of the president and the lack of specific guarantees of civil liberties?
   a) Tories
   b) Unionists
   c) Federalists
   d) Antifederalists
   e) Free Soilers

ⓢ PRACTICE ONLINE

"Critical Thinking" exercise: *Politics is Conflictual— The Bill of Rights*

10. James Madison, Alexander Hamilton, and John Jay wrote a series of arguments in support of the Constitution that outlined the political theory behind it. What are their assembled works called?
    a) *Pickwick Papers*
    b) *Federalist Papers*
    c) *Antifederalist Papers*
    d) *Common Sense*
    e) *The Second Treatise of Government*

THE CONSTITUTION: A FRAMEWORK FOR GOVERNMENT

▶ Outline the major provisions of the Constitution. **Pages 49–54**

SUMMARY

The defining feature of the Constitution is its separation of powers while still maintaining flexibility for leadership in times of crisis. The system of checks and balances gives each branch of the federal government some explicit powers, some shared powers, and some ability to limit the power of the other two branches of government.

KEY TERMS

necessary and proper clause (p. 49)

impeachment (p. 52)

power of the purse (p. 52)

judicial review (p. 52)

CRITICAL THINKING AND DISCUSSION

The president has clearly dominated the decision to go to war in the past century, despite the Founders' view that war powers are a shared power. How would a Tea Partier respond to this change? What other areas of the Constitution as a framework for government have evolved?

ⓢ PRACTICE ONLINE

"Critical Thinking" exercise: *Political Process Matters—Impeachment*

PRACTICE QUIZ QUESTIONS

11. The "necessary and proper clause" gives flexibility to which part of government?
    a) the president
    b) the Supreme Court
    c) the bureaucracy
    d) the Congress
    e) interest groups

12. Which branch has the fewest explicit powers?
    a) the president
    b) the Supreme Court
    c) the bureaucracy
    d) the Congress

13. Which of the following negative powers does the president enjoy?
    a) the power to veto legislation
    b) the power to freeze judicial salaries
    c) the power to review the constitutionality of a law
    d) the power to impeach federal justices
    e) the power to dissolve Congress and call new elections

IS THE CONSTITUTION A "LIVING" DOCUMENT?

▶ Explore how the meaning of the Constitution has evolved. **Pages 54–63**

SUMMARY

The Constitution is more than 200 years old, yet it still provides a blueprint for modern governance. It has maintained its relevance due to its ambiguity on several key passages, its ability to be amended rather than entirely rewritten, and the designation of multiple interpreters of the Constitution.

KEY TERMS

executive powers clause (p. 56)

commerce clause (p. 56)

enumerated powers (p. 56)

implied powers (p. 60)

constitutional revolution (p. 63)

Ⓢ PRACTICE ONLINE

"Big Think" video exercise: *The Challenge of Constitutional Interpretation*

CRITICAL THINKING AND DISCUSSION

Should the Constitution be a "living document" that evolves with the values and norms of our society, or should interpretation of the Constitution follow more closely the original intentions of the framers?

PRACTICE QUIZ QUESTIONS

14. Which of the following clauses, central to congressional activity, has been interpreted differently over time though the wording has stayed the same?
   a)   establishment clause
   b)   commerce clause
   c)   enumerated powers clause
   d)   executive powers clause
   e)   prerogative powers clause

15. Which part of government often defines the boundaries of implied powers?
   a)   the president
   b)   the Supreme Court
   c)   the bureaucracy
   d)   the Congress
   e)   the people

SUGGESTED READING

Balkin, Jack M., ed. *The Constitution in 2020*. New York: Oxford University Press, 2009.

Currie, David P. *The Constitution of the United States: A Primer for the People*, 2nd ed. Chicago: University of Chicago Press, 2000.

Dahl, Robert A. *How Democratic Is the American Constitution?* New Haven, CT: Yale University Press, 2001.

Davis, Sue. *Corwin and Peltason's Understanding the Constitution*, 17th ed. Boston: Wadsworth Publishing, 2007.

Hamilton, Alexander, James Madison, and John Jay. *The Federalist Papers*. 1788. Reprint, 2nd ed., edited by Roy P. Fairfield. Baltimore, MD: Johns Hopkins University Press, 1981.

Ketcham, Ralph. *The Anti-Federalist Papers and the Constitutional Convention Debates*. New York: Signet Classics, 2003.

Kurland, Philip B., and Ralph Lerner, eds. *The Founders' Constitution*. Chicago: University of Chicago Press, 1987.

Rossiter, Clinton. *1787: The Grand Convention*. New York: MacMillan, 1966.

Sunstein, Cass R. *Designing Democracy: What Constitutions Do*. New York: Oxford University Press, 2001.

Wood, Gordon S. *The Creation of the American Republic*. New York: Norton, 1969.

3

Federalism

FOLLOWING THE PASSAGE OF THE 2010 AFFORDABLE Care Act (ACA),[1] 26 states sued the national government over the new law. Intended to provide health care coverage to more than 30 million Americans who are currently uninsured, the law was viewed by the attorneys general from these states as an unconstitutional overreach of federal power. David Rivkin, one of the attorneys who filed the suit on behalf of the states, said, "This is one of the most important Constitutional challenges in history. . . . The states' sovereign authority is being trammeled upon by the federal government."[2] In November 2011, Ohio became the tenth state to pass a law or constitutional amendment attempting to limit the application of national health care reform within its borders. "This signifies that state level resistance to federal power is not just an old idea relegated to history books," said Michael Boldin, executive director of the Tenth Amendment Center; "It's something that's alive and well right now."[3]

In their lawsuit against the federal government, the states alleged three instances of constitutional overreach in the ACA: "the individual mandate exceeds Congress's enumerated powers, the Medicaid expansions are unconstitutionally coercive, and the employer mandates impermissibly interfere with state sovereignty."[4]

Supporters of the law argued that standardizing these provisions across all 50 states was crucial to ensuring health care for all Americans because without a national law, millions of Americans would be unable to get health insurance. Some states do an excellent job of providing access to health care (such as

CONFLICT & COMPROMISE
in American Politics

Massachusetts with only 5 percent of its residents uninsured), while others, such as Texas with 26 percent uninsured, do not do as well).[5] Supporters of the ACA insist that access to health care is a basic right that should not depend on which state you live in. As President Obama explained at the signing ceremony for the new legislation, "we have now just enshrined—as soon as I sign this bill—the core principle that everybody should have some basic security when it comes to their health care."[6] Furthermore, the national law gets rid of state-based insurance monopolies that drive up health care costs; competition across state lines through the health insurance exchanges mandated by the ACA will help keep health care costs lower.

The Obama administration and other supporters of the law have rebutted each of the challenges to its constitutionality. The strongest legal challenge is whether Congress can force individuals to buy health insurance under the commerce clause of the Constitution. Opponents of the law say that the decision to *not* buy insurance is not economic activity (but rather is "inactivity") and therefore cannot be regulated by Congress. Supporters point out that everyone participates in the health care system at some point: people who do not buy insurance drive up health care costs for those who do have insurance because the uninsured use emergency rooms when they get sick or injured (which is much more expensive than normal care). Therefore, supporters say, the decision not to buy insurance does have an impact on economic activity. The second point on "coercive federalism" concerns the national government's expanding Medicaid eligibility while shifting more of the costs of Medicaid onto the states. The states complain about this, but supporters of the law say states could always opt out by not accepting the federal money, so they are not forced to do anything. Finally, proponents argue that the Tenth and Eleventh Amendments do not restrain Congress from enacting laws that are "necessary and proper" under its Article I powers.

The Supreme Court largely upheld the ACA, but there were two parts of the decision that accepted the critics' view and have important implications for federalism. First, the basis for upholding the controversial individual mandate was Congress's taxing power, rather than the commerce clause. The Court agreed with critics of the law who argued that Congress's power to regulate interstate commerce does not apply to penalizing economic inactivity (that is, failing to buy health insurance). Second, the Court ruled that the expansion of Medicaid, which would provide health care for an additional 17 million low-income Americans, was unconstitutionally coercive in requiring states to expand Medicaid or lose all their federal funding for the existing Medicaid program. States could still choose to accept the federal funding to expand Medicaid, but they would not lose their other Medicaid funding if they opted out of the expansion (as of this writing, ten states have indicated that they may opt out).

The battles over the ACA illustrate our central theme that politics is about conflict and compromise. Our system of federalism is bound to produce political conflict as the national and state governments often have different ideas about the best direction for a specific policy, as clearly shown by the lawsuit from 26 states over the ACA. Sometimes the policy dispute is resolved when the national government imposes its views on the states. In that instance, there may appear to be little compromise. However, even in the case of health care reform, the states still are having a significant impact on the implementation of the policy.

Federalism also illustrates the other two themes of the book. By dividing power across the levels of government, federalism highlights the importance of

the political process. While the U.S. Congress wrote the law, the 50 states will be implementing it, and this means that the political process of each state will come into play. Federalism also shows that politics is everywhere: decentralizing power across levels of government provides a much broader range of *individual-level* choices than a unitary system. For example, a retiree trying to decide where to live could choose between low-tax, low-service states such as Texas and high-tax, high-service states such as New York. Business owners often decide where to locate a new office or factory by considering the "business climate," which reflects the corporate tax structure, environmental laws, regulatory policy, and levels of education and unionization of the workforce. States differ in these factors because our federal system gives the states autonomy to choose policies that meet their residents' needs.

WHAT IS FEDERALISM AND WHY DOES IT MATTER?

DEFINE FEDERALISM AND EXPLAIN ITS SIGNIFICANCE

Federalism can be defined as a form of government that divides sovereign power across at least two political units. Dividing **sovereign power** simply means that each unit of government (in the U.S. context, the national and state governments) has some degree of authority and autonomy. As discussed in Chapter 2, this division of power across levels of government is central to the system of separated powers in the United States. The concept of dividing power across levels of government seems simple, but as we will see later in this chapter, the political battles over *how* that power is divided have been intense.

federalism The division of power across the local, state, and national governments.

sovereign power The national and state government each have some degree of authority and autonomy.

In practical terms, federalism is about intergovernmental relations: how do the different levels of government interact and how is power divided? But even that may seem a little abstract. Why does federalism matter? On a broad range of issues, the level of government that dictates policy can make a real difference. The conflict over health care reform is the most obvious example, but other recent policies include whether the national government should be able to prevent states from allowing marijuana use for medical purposes, from allowing assisted suicides, or from discriminating against their employees based on age or disability, or be able to compel states to ban guns within or around public schools, have a uniform speed limit on federal highways, integrate schools, or make the drinking age 21. These questions involve defining the disputed boundaries between what the states and national government are allowed to do. Much of U.S. history has been rooted in this struggle to define American federalism.

One other important point concerns the *politics* of federalism: while the states' rights perspective of federalism has traditionally been associated with conservative political causes (most prominently, opposition to civil rights and racial integration in the South in the 1950s and 1960s, and more recently opposition to health care reform and gun control), on many issues such as environmental policy and gay rights the states have been pushing for more progressive policies than the federal government.

Thus federalism influences both the direction of policy outcomes and the politics of the process, but with evolving roles for the national and state governments. Before we consider the changing balance of intergovernmental power in American federalism, we will take a closer look in this section at what federalism means.

LEVELS OF GOVERNMENT AND THEIR DEGREES OF AUTONOMY

A distinguishing feature of federalism is that each level of government has some degree of autonomy from the other levels; that is, each level can carry out some policies that the others may not prefer. In the United States, this means that the national and state governments have distinct powers and responsibilities. The national government, for example, is responsible for national defense and foreign policy. State and local governments have primary responsibility for conducting elections and promoting public safety or **police powers**. In other areas, such as transportation, the different levels of government share responsibilities in the **concurrent powers** (see Nuts and Bolts 3.1). The national government has also taken on additional responsibilities through implied powers that are inferred from the powers explicitly granted in the Constitution (see later discussion in this chapter).

Local governments—cities, towns, school districts, and counties—are not autonomous units of government. They are creatures of the state government. That is, state governments create local governments and control the types of activities they can engage in, by specifying in the state charter either what they *can* do or only what they *cannot* do (that is, they are allowed to do anything not specifically prohibited in the charter). Despite this lack of autonomy, local governments play an important role in providing public education, police and fire departments, and land use policies. They also raise money through property taxes, user fees, and in some cases, local sales taxes. But overall, local governments do not directly share power within our federal system with the state and national governments because of their lack of autonomy.

police powers The power to enforce laws and provide for public safety.

concurrent powers Responsibilities for particular policy areas, such as transportation, that are shared by federal, state, and local governments.

NATIONAL AND STATE RESPONSIBILITIES

National Government Powers	State Government Powers	Concurrent Powers
Print money	Issue licenses	Collect taxes
Regulate interstate commerce and international trade	Regulate intrastate (within the state) businesses	Build roads
Make treaties and conduct foreign policy	Conduct elections	Borrow money
Declare war	Establish local governments	Establish courts
Provide an army and navy	Ratify amendments to the Constitution	Make and enforce laws
Establish post offices	Promote public health and safety	Charter banks and corporations
Make laws necessary and proper to carry out these powers	May exert powers the Constitution does not delegate to the national government or does not prohibit the states from using	Spend money for the general welfare; take private property for public purposes, with just compensation

Powers Denied to the National Government	Powers Denied to State Governments
May not violate the Bill of Rights	May not enter into treaties with other countries
May not impose export taxes among states	May not print money
May not use money from the Treasury without an appropriation from Congress	May not tax imports or exports
May not change state boundaries	May not interfere with contracts
	May not suspend a person's rights without due process

Source: GPO Access: Guide to the U.S. Government, http://bensguide.gpo.gov/3-5/government/federalism.html (accessed 12/5/11).

A COMPARATIVE PERSPECTIVE

It is useful to compare U.S. federalism to forms of government in other countries. Just because a nation is made up of states does not mean that it is a federal system. The key factor is the autonomy of the political subunit. The United Kingdom, for example, comprises England, Scotland, Wales, and Northern Ireland. In 1998, the British Parliament created a new Scottish government and gave it authority in a broad range of areas. However, Parliament retained the right to unilaterally dissolve the Scottish government; therefore the subunit (Scotland) is not autonomous. This type of government in which power is centralized within the national government is a **unitary government**. Unitary governments are the most common in the modern world (about 80 percent); other examples include Israel, Italy, France, Japan, and Sweden. Although federalism is not as common, Australia,

unitary government A system in which the national, centralized government holds ultimate authority. It is the most common form of government in the world.

Austria, Canada, Germany, and Switzerland, among others, share this form of government with the United States (see In Comparison).

confederal government
A form of government in which states hold power over a limited national government.

At the opposite end of the spectrum is a **confederal government**, in which the states have most of the power and often can even veto the actions of the central government. This was the first type of government in the United States under the Articles of Confederation. Because so many problems are associated with having such a weak national government (see Chapter 2), few modern examples exist. The Commonwealth of Independent States (CIS), which formed in 1991 after the breakup of the former Soviet Union, has had some success in coordinating the economic activity and security needs of 12 independent states.[7] Over time, however, rifts among the member states have created problems, and today the CIS is viewed as largely ineffective.

intergovernmental organizations Organizations that seek to coordinate policy across member nations.

Although true confederations are rare, **intergovernmental organizations** have proliferated in recent decades. More than 1,200 multilateral organizations have been created by member nations seeking to coordinate their policies on, for example, economic activity, security, or environmental protection. The United Nations (UN), the International Monetary Fund (IMF), and the North Atlantic Treaty Organization (NATO) are important examples. The European Union is an intergovernmental organization that began as a loose confederation but it is becoming more federalist in its decision-making process and structure. Its relative success, compared to the failure of the CIS, can be explained in part by this move toward a more federal structure, while the CIS maintained its confederal status.

///

BALANCING NATIONAL AND STATE POWER IN THE CONSTITUTION

Although the Founders wanted a national government that was stronger than it had been under the Articles of Confederation, they also wanted to preserve the states' autonomy. These goals are reflected in different parts of the Constitution, which provides ample evidence for advocates of both state-centered and nation-centered federalism. The nation-centered position appears right in the document's preamble, which begins, "We the People of the United States," compared to the Articles of Confederation, which began, "We the undersigned delegates of the States." The Constitution's phrasing emphasizes the nation as a whole over the separate states.

A STRONG NATIONAL GOVERNMENT

Other aspects of the Constitution also support the nation-centered perspective. These reflect the Founders' desire for a strong national government to provide national security and a healthy and efficient economy. In terms of national security, as we saw in Chapter 2, Congress was granted the power to raise and support armies, declare war, and "suppress Insurrections and repel Invasion," while

UNITARY VERSUS FEDERAL SYSTEMS

Unitary systems are about four times more common than federal systems. Why is this the case? The simplest reason is that federal systems are much more complicated and often involve disagreements over the division of power between the central and regional governments (in the United States, these disputes usually must be resolved in the courts). Second, according to some economists, decentralized federal systems undermine prudent financial management, producing slower economic growth and larger budget deficits than unitary systems. However, there is conflicting evidence on the impact of federalism on growth and budget deficits. One study found that if federal systems become more reliant on intergovernmental transfers (that is, grants from the central government to the states) and if states retain the ability to borrow independently, budget deficits tend to be higher. In contrast, if the central government in a federal system imposes borrowing restrictions on the states, or if states have a strong degree of autonomy for both taxing and borrowing, balanced budgets are more common. Unitary systems do not have to worry as much about lower levels of government as a source of national debt because the states have less fiscal autonomy.[a]

Another potential drawback of federalism is that it promotes regional and ethnic separation. The former communist states of Eastern Europe demonstrate this point. Of those nine states, six were unitary and three were federal. The six unitary states have remained intact (in fact, they are now five states because East Germany has reunited with the Federal Republic of Germany), while the three federal states—Yugoslavia, the Soviet Union, and Czechoslovakia—have fractured into 22 independent states! Furthermore, most of the armed conflict in this region has occurred in these states.[b]

On the other hand, federalist systems are a useful tool for dealing with ethnic and national differences within countries. There are many multiethnic countries in the world, but very few of them are democracies—usually the iron fist of totalitarianism keeps these different factions together. In Iraq, for example, the Sunnis, Shiites, and Kurds were held together as one nation by Saddam Hussein's oppressive rule. When he was removed from power, the nation degenerated into sectarian violence as these groups struggled for power. Federalism made the fledgling democracy possible (the Kurds would never have agreed with the constitution without substantial autonomy), but the country may still split apart. There are several success stories of multinational or multiethnic democracies and all are federal: Switzerland, Canada, Belgium, Malaysia, India, and Spain.[c] Federalism allows each group, such as the

Federalism helps democracies deal with ethnic and national differences within their populations. For example, Canada's federal system provides French Canadians with autonomy in Quebec province.

French Canadians in Quebec, to have autonomy while remaining part of the larger country.

Unitary and federal systems may also have varying impacts on environmental policy. On some environmental issues, such as climate change, unitary governments appear to be better suited for taking strong action. In federal systems such as the United States, differences between states such as California and Texas in their approaches to greenhouse gases make it more difficult to have a uniform national policy. However, federal systems may be better suited for policy experimentation and regional implementation of policies that are sensitive to local needs.[d] Overall, in comparing federal to unitary systems, it is clear that there are advantages and disadvantages to each.

the president, as commander in chief of the armed forces, would oversee the conduct of war. Congress's power to regulate interstate commerce promoted economic efficiency and centralized an important economic power at the national level, and many restrictions on state power had similar effects. States were *prohibited* from entering into "any Treaty, Alliance, or Confederation" or keeping troops or "Ships of War" during peacetime. They also could not coin money or impose duties on imports or exports (see Article I, Section 10). These provisions ensured that states would not interfere with the smooth operation of interstate commerce or create problems for national defense. Imagine, for example, that Oklahoma had the power to tax oil produced in other states or that California decided to create its own army. This would create inefficiencies and potential danger for the rest of the country.

The necessary and proper clause (Article I, Section 8) was another broad grant of power to the national government: it gave Congress the power "To make all Laws which shall be necessary and proper for carrying into Execution the foregoing Powers." Similarly, the national supremacy clause (Article VI) says that the Constitution and all laws and treaties that are made under the Constitution shall be the "supreme Law of the Land" and that "the Judges in every State shall be bound thereby, any Thing in the Constitution or Laws of any State to the Contrary notwithstanding." This is perhaps the clearest statement of the nation-centered focus of the Constitution. If any state law or constitution conflicts with national law or the Constitution, the national perspective wins. Thus, the laws passed by states to limit implementation of the ACA will have no effect now that the Supreme Court upheld the central parts of the national law.

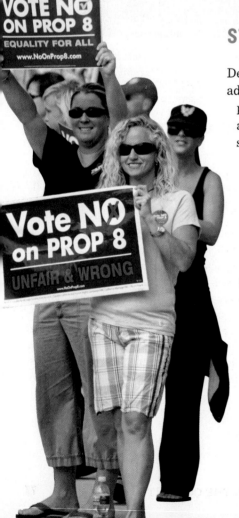

SHOULD SAME-SEX MARRIAGES performed in one state be recognized in another state where such marriages are banned? Here, demonstrators protest against Proposition 8, which was intended to ban gay marriage in California.

STATE POWERS AND LIMITS ON NATIONAL POWER

Despite the Founders' nation-centered bias, many parts of the Constitution also address state powers and limits on national power. Article II gives the states power to choose electors for the electoral college, and Article V grants the states a central role in the process of amending the Constitution. Three-fourths of the states must ratify any constitutional amendment (either through conventions or the state legislatures, as specified by Congress), but the states can also bypass Congress in proposing amendments if two-thirds of the states call for a convention. This route to amending the Constitution has never been used, but the Founders clearly wanted to provide an additional check on national power.

There are also limitations on Congress's authority to regulate interstate commerce. For example, it cannot favor one state over another in regulating commerce, and it cannot impose a tax on any good that is shipped from one state to another. Also, Congress could not prohibit slavery until 1808, but it was allowed to impose a duty of up to $10 per slave.

Article I of the Constitution enumerates many specific powers for Congress, but the list of state powers is much shorter. One could interpret this as more evidence for the nation-centered perspective, but at the time of the Founding, the default position was to keep most power at the state level. Therefore, the federal powers that were exceptions to this rule had to be clearly specified, while state governments received authority over all other matters. The Tenth Amendment supports this view: "The powers not delegated to the United States by the Constitution, nor prohibited by it to the states, are reserved to the states respectively, or to the people."

The Eleventh Amendment, the first one passed after the Bill of Rights, was another important affirmation of state sovereignty. Antifederalists were concerned that the part of Article III that gave the Supreme Court authority over cases involving a "State and Citizens of another State" would undermine state sovereignty by giving the Court too much power over state laws. Federalists assured them this would not happen, but the Supreme Court ruled in *Chisholm v. Georgia* (1793) that citizens of one state could sue the government of another state. The majority opinion ridiculed the "haughty notions of state independence, state sovereignty, and state supremacy." The states struck back by adopting the Eleventh Amendment, which made such lawsuits unconstitutional. While the Supreme Court lost this skirmish over state power, it continued to serve as the umpire in disputes between the national and state governments.

CLAUSES THAT FAVOR BOTH PERSPECTIVES

Article IV of the Constitution has elements that favor both the state-centered and the nation-centered perspectives. For example, its **full faith and credit clause** specifies that states must respect one another's laws, granting citizens the "Full Faith and Credit" of their home state's laws if they go to another state. At the same time, though, the article's **privileges and immunities clause** says that citizens of each state are "entitled to all Privileges and Immunities" of citizens in the other states, which means that states must treat visitors from other states the same as their own residents. This part of the Constitution favors a nation-centered perspective because it was intended to promote free travel and economic activity among the states.

There are many examples of the full faith and credit clause at work today. If you have a New York driver's license and are traveling to California, you do not need to stop at every state line to get a new license; each state will honor your New York license. Similarly, a legal marriage in one state must be honored by another state. (Divorce is more complicated. If a divorce is granted in a state in which the couple does not have a legal residence, their home state does not have to honor that divorce.) Article IV has also fueled the ongoing controversy over same-sex marriage. In 1996, after Hawaii courts gave homosexual marriages most of the same legal rights as heterosexual marriages, many states passed laws saying they would not have to honor those marriages. Congress passed the Defense of Marriage Act, which said that states would not have to recognize same-sex marriages. Hawaii courts have since overturned the decision to recognize same-sex marriages, but as of late 2012 nine states, plus the District of Columbia, allow gay marriages.[8] In 2012 voters in Maine, Maryland, and Washington approved statewide referendums allowing marriage between same-sex couples. This was the first time that voters, rather than courts or legislatures, provided for gay marriages. In addition, five states recognize civil unions between homosexual partners, but not marriage. However, current law holds that the full faith and credit clause does not apply to gay marriage because of the "policy exception."[9]

We can also cite examples of the privileges and immunities clause at work in a modern context. For example, Michigan cannot charge the owner of a lake cabin different property taxes based on whether she lives in Michigan or in another state. Also, states may not deny welfare benefits to new residents or deny police protection to visitors even though they do not pay state taxes. For example, a 1992 law in California limited the cash welfare benefit to new residents to the same level of benefits

full faith and credit clause Part of Article IV of the Constitution requiring that each state's laws be honored by the other states. For example, a legal marriage in one state must be recognized across state lines.

privileges and immunities clause Part of Article IV of the Constitution requiring that states must treat nonstate residents within their borders as they would treat their own residents. This was meant to promote commerce and travel between states.

they had been receiving in the state from which they moved. The law was intended to save California's government some money and also discourage people from moving to California just to get the higher benefit—particularly since California's cash benefit for a mother and one child was $456 a month in 1992, but in the neighboring state of Arizona it was only $275.[10] The Supreme Court ruled that the state law violated the privileges and immunities clause and the right to travel freely between the states.

However, states are allowed to make some distinctions between residents and nonresidents. For example, states do not have to permit nonresidents to vote in state elections, and public colleges and universities may charge out-of-state residents higher tuition than in-state residents. Therefore, the privileges and immunities clause cuts both ways on the question of the balance of power: it allows the states to determine and uphold these laws autonomously, but it also emphasizes that national citizenship is more important than state citizenship.

The Constitution sets the boundaries for the battles over federalism. For example, no state can decide to print its own currency, and the U.S. government cannot take over any public school district in the country. But within those broad boundaries, the balance between national and state power at any given point in history is a political decision, the product of choices made by elected leaders and the courts. Decisions by the Supreme Court have figured prominently in this evolution.

TRACE THE MAJOR SHIFTS IN STATE AND FEDERAL GOVERNMENT POWER OVER TIME

THE EVOLVING CONCEPT OF FEDERALISM

The nature of federalism has changed as the relative positions of the national and state governments have evolved. In the first century of our nation's history, the national government played a relatively limited role and the boundaries between the levels of government were distinct. As the national government took on more power in the twentieth century, intergovernmental relations became more cooperative and the boundaries less distinct. Even within this more cooperative framework, federalism remains a source of conflict within our political system as the levels of government share lawmaking authority (as illustrated by the health care example that opened the chapter).

THE EARLY YEARS

As the United States gained its footing, clashes between the advocates of state-centered and nation-centered federalism evolved into a partisan struggle. The Federalists, the party of George Washington, John Adams, and Alexander Hamilton, controlled the new government for its first 12 years and favored strong national power. Their opponents, the Democratic-Republicans, led by Thomas Jefferson and James Madison, favored state power.

ESTABLISHING NATIONAL SUPREMACY

The first confrontation came when the Federalists established a national bank in 1791, over Jefferson's objections. This controversy did not come to a head until Congress chartered the second national bank in 1816. At that time, the state of

Maryland, which was controlled by the Democratic-Republicans, tried to tax the National Bank's Baltimore branch out of existence, but the head cashier of the bank refused to pay the tax and the case eventually ended up at the Supreme Court. The Court had to decide whether Congress had the power to create the bank, and if it did, whether Maryland had the right to tax the bank.

In the landmark decision *McCulloch v. Maryland* (1819), the Court ruled in favor of the national government on both counts. In deciding whether Congress could create the bank, the Court held that even though the word "bank" does not appear in the Constitution, Congress's power to create one is implied through its enumerated powers—such as the power to coin money, levy taxes, and borrow money. The Court also ruled that Maryland did not have the right to tax the bank because of the Constitution's national supremacy clause. Both the concept of implied powers and the validation of national supremacy were critical for establishing the centrality of the national government.

A few years later, the Supreme Court decided another case that cemented Congress's power to act based on the commerce clause in the Constitution. In *Gibbons v. Ogden* (1824) the Supreme Court held that Congress has broad power to regulate interstate commerce and struck down a New York law that had granted a monopoly to a private company operating steamboats on the Hudson River between New York and New Jersey. By granting this monopoly, the ruling stated, New York was interfering with interstate commerce.

TENSION OVER THE SEDITION ACT

Another early clash over federalism concerned the Sedition Act of 1798, which was passed by a majority-Federalist Congress.[11] The act banned "any false, scandalous writing against the government of the United States." It was a reaction to the rejection of authority and mass political movements that were sweeping through France at that time; the stated purpose of the law was to prevent these from taking hold in the United States. But Jeffersonians argued, rightly, that the law was an

IN THE EARLY 1800s, the Supreme Court confirmed the national government's right to regulate commerce between the states. The state of New York granted a monopoly to a ferry company serving ports in New York and New Jersey, but this was found to interfere with interstate commerce and was therefore subject to federal intervention.

attempt to silence dissent and criticism of the government and was a clear violation of the First Amendment protection of freedom of speech. Indeed, under this law, 10 Democratic-Republican newspaper editors were arrested, fined, and jailed. The issue was important in the 1800 presidential campaign, and when Jefferson was elected he pardoned everyone who had been convicted under the law.

The Sedition Act is important for our purposes because of a political tactic that Jefferson devised to try to overturn the law before he became president. His opponents controlled Congress and the Supreme Court, so he had little hope of using the normal political channels to change the law. Thus, he and Madison circumvented the national government by working through the states: they convinced the Kentucky and Virginia legislatures to pass resolutions challenging the national government's power to pass the Sedition Act through an idea they called the **doctrine of interposition**. Under this doctrine, if the national government passes an unconstitutional law, the people of the states can interpose—or insert—themselves between the law and the national government and declare the law void. This doctrine views the Constitution as a compact among the states. Although the tension over the Sedition Act was defused when Jefferson was elected president in 1800, the approach to federalism he had devised to overthrow the act had important implications for national power.[12]

The idea of interposition soon regained significance as the basis for the southern states' push for broader **states' rights** on issues such as tariffs and slavery. John Calhoun, a South Carolina senator, used the term "nullification" to refer to the same principle, urging South Carolina to ignore a tariff law passed by Congress in 1832. The states' rights perspective was at the center of the dispute between southern and northern states over slavery, and it ultimately led to the secession of the Confederate states and subsequently the Civil War. The stakes were enormous in the battles over federalism: about 528,000 people died in the bloodiest of American wars.[13] As Abraham Lincoln forcefully argued, concepts such as nullification and states' rights, when taken to their logical extremes, were too divisive to be allowed to stand. If states could ignore national laws, the basis of the United States would fall apart.

doctrine of interposition The idea that if the national government passes an unconstitutional law, the people of the states (through their state legislatures) can declare the law void. This idea provided the basis for southern secession and the Civil War.

states' rights The idea that states are entitled to a certain amount of self-government, free of federal government intervention. This became a central issue in the period leading up to the Civil War.

DUAL FEDERALISM

The ideas of states' rights and nullification did not produce the Civil War by themselves. They had some help from the Supreme Court's infamous *Dred Scott* decision; but before explaining the significance of that case, we will look at some key players in the evolution of the Court's approach to federalism. In this section we will discuss the system of dual federalism, which defined intergovernmental relations for nearly the first 150 years of our nation's history. The Supreme Court's narrow interpretation of the Fourteenth Amendment and the commerce clause greatly limited the power of the national government in this period (see Table 3.1).

THE MARSHALL COURT VERSUS THE TANEY COURT

The early to mid-nineteenth century saw incredible stability in the leadership of the Court, because only two chief justices served during this time—John Marshall from 1801 to 1835, and Roger Taney from 1835 to 1864. However, they had very different ideas about federalism. Marshall was a Federalist who opposed states'

TABLE » 3.1

EARLY LANDMARK SUPREME COURT DECISIONS ON FEDERALISM

CASE	HOLDING AND SIGNIFICANCE
Chisholm v. Georgia (1793)	Held that citizens of one state could sue another state; led to the Eleventh Amendment, which prohibited such lawsuits.
McCulloch v. Maryland (1819)	Upheld the national government's right to create a bank and reaffirmed the idea of "national supremacy."
Gibbons v. Ogden (1824)	Held that Congress, rather than the states, has broad power to regulate interstate commerce.
Barron v. Baltimore (1833)	Endorsed a notion of "dual federalism" in which the rights of a U.S. citizen under the Bill of Rights did not apply to that same person under state law.
Dred Scott v. Sandford (1857)	Sided with southern states' view that slaves were property and ruled that the Missouri Compromise violated the Fifth Amendment, since making slavery illegal in some states deprived slave owners of property. Contributed to the start of the Civil War.
National Labor Relations Board v. Jones & Laughlin Steel Corporation (1937)	Upheld the National Labor Relations Act of 1935 as consistent with Congress's commerce clause powers, reversing the Court's more narrow interpretation of that clause.

rights, while Taney was a supporter of states' rights. A series of decisions under Marshall's leadership secured the place of the national government within our federal system; but in the years that followed, Taney was able to limit the reach of the national government through his vision of federalism, which is known as dual federalism.

Under **dual federalism** the national and state governments were viewed as distinct, with little overlap in their activities or the services they provided. In this view, the national government's activities are confined to powers strictly enumerated in the Constitution, despite the necessary and proper clause and the implied powers endorsed in *McCulloch v. Maryland*. While Taney fully developed the idea of dual federalism, one decision toward the end of Marshall's tenure endorsed a notion of "dual citizenship" in which an individual's rights as a U.S. citizen under the Bill of Rights did not apply to the same person under state law. That decision, *Barron v. Baltimore* (1833), held that a man whose wharf in the Baltimore harbor had been ruined by the city's dumping of sand and gravel could not sue the city for violating the Fifth Amendment's prohibition of taking property without due process. The Court ruled that the Fifth Amendment applied only to the U.S. Congress and not to state and local governments, which is a core principle of dual federalism.

Within this framework of distinct national and state powers, the Taney Court expanded the power of the states over commerce in ways that would not be accepted today. For example, this Court gave the mayor of New York City the right to control immigration by requiring shipmasters to post bonds for foreign passengers who might later go on welfare,[14] and it allowed the city of Philadelphia to require ships to use local captains when entering the harbor.[15] Today, these areas of commerce would be regulated by Congress, not local governments.

dual federalism The form of federalism favored by Chief Justice Roger Taney in which national and state governments are seen as distinct entities providing separate services. This model limits the power of the national government.

DRED SCOTT AND CIVIL WAR

The state-centered views of the Taney Court also produced a tragic decision, *Dred Scott v. Sandford* (1857). Dred Scott was a slave who had lived for many years with his owner in the free Wisconsin Territory but was living in Missouri, a slave state, when his master died. Scott petitioned for his freedom under the Missouri Compromise, which said that slavery was illegal in any free state. The majority decision held that slaves were not citizens but private property, and that therefore the Missouri Compromise violated the Fifth Amendment because it deprived people (slave owners) of property without the due process of law. This unfortunate decision contributed to the Civil War, which started four years later, because it indicated that there could not be a political solution to the problem of slavery.

The Civil War ended the dispute over slavery, but it did not resolve basic questions about the balance of power between the national and state systems. Right after the Civil War, the Constitution was amended to ensure that the Union's views on states' rights were the law of the land. The Civil War Amendments banned slavery (the Thirteenth), prohibited states from denying citizens due process or equal protection of the laws (Fourteenth), and gave newly freed male slaves the right to vote (Fifteenth). The Fourteenth Amendment was the most important in terms of federalism because it was the constitutional basis for many of the civil rights laws passed by Congress during Reconstruction.

THE SUPREME COURT AND LIMITED NATIONAL GOVERNMENT

However, the Supreme Court soon stepped in again to limit the power of the national government. In 1873 the Court reinforced the notion of dual federalism, ruling that the Fourteenth Amendment did not change the balance of power between the national and state governments despite its clear language aimed at state action. Endorsing the notion of dual citizenship, the Court ruled that the Fourteenth Amendment right to due process and equal treatment under the law applied to individuals' rights only as citizens of the United States, not to their state citizenship.[16] By extension, freedom of speech, freedom of the press, and the other liberties protected in the Bill of Rights applied only to laws passed by Congress, not to state laws. This distinction between state and national citizenship sounds odd today, partly because the Fourteenth Amendment has long been viewed as the basis for ensuring that states do not violate basic rights.

Ten years later, the Court overturned the 1875 Civil Rights Act, which guaranteed equal treatment in public accommodations. The Court argued that the Fourteenth Amendment did not give Congress the power to regulate private conduct, such as whether a white restaurant owner had to serve a black customer; it affected only the conduct of state governments.[17] This narrow view of the Fourteenth Amendment left the national government powerless to prevent southern states from implementing state and local laws that led to complete segregation of blacks and whites in the South (called Jim Crow laws) and the denial of many basic rights to blacks after northern troops left the South at the end of Reconstruction.

The other area in which the Supreme Court limited the reach of the national government concerned Congress's power to regulate the economy through its **commerce clause powers**. In a series of cases in the late nineteenth and early twentieth centuries, the Supreme Court endorsed a view of laissez-faire capitalism—French for "leave alone"—aimed at protecting business from regulation by the national government. To this end, the Court defined clear boundaries between

commerce clause powers The powers of Congress to regulate the economy granted in Article I, Section 8, of the Constitution.

*inter*state and *intra*state commerce, ruling that Congress could not regulate any economic activity that occurred *within* a state (intrastate). The Supreme Court allowed some national legislation that was connected to interstate commerce, such as limiting monopolies through the Sherman Antitrust Act (1890). However, when the national government tried to use this act to break up a cartel of four sugar companies that controlled 98 percent of the nation's sugar production, the Court ruled that Congress did not have this power.

According to the decision, the commerce clause dealt with the transportation of goods, not their manufacture, and the sugar in question was made within a single state. Even if the sugar was sold throughout the country, this was "incidental" to its manufacture.[18] On the same grounds the Court struck down attempts by Congress to regulate child labor.[19] In some instances, the Court's laissez-faire perspective led the justices to strike down state laws, as in a case that ruled unconstitutional a New York law limiting the working hours of bakers to no more than 60 hours a week or 10 hours a day.[20] Therefore, the limits that the Court placed on Congress during this antiregulation phase did not necessarily tip the balance to the state governments. Rather, big business was the winner over both national and state governments.

COOPERATIVE FEDERALISM

The Progressive Era policies of the early twentieth century and the New Deal policies of the 1930s ushered in a new era of American federalism. Now the national government became much more involved in activities that were formerly reserved for the states, such as education, transportation, civil rights, agriculture, social welfare, and management–labor relations. At first, the Supreme Court resisted this broader reach of national power, clinging to its nineteenth-century conception of

THIS IS ONE RABBIT THAT NEVER FAILED ME!

SPENDING

OLD RELIABLE!

FRANKLIN DELANO ROOSEVELT'S NEW Deal shifted more power than ever to the national government. Through major new programs to address the Great Depression, the federal government expanded its reach, and spent more to pay for these programs.

cooperative federalism A form of federalism in which national and state governments work together to provide services efficiently. This form emerged in the late 1930s, representing a profound shift toward less concrete boundaries of responsibility in national–state relations.

picket fence federalism A more refined and realistic form of cooperative federalism in which policy makers within a particular policy area work together across the levels of government.

dual federalism.[21] But as commerce became more national, the distinction between interstate and intrastate commerce, and between manufacture and transportation, became increasingly difficult to sustain. Starting in 1937 with the landmark ruling *NLRB v. Jones and Laughlin Steel*, the Supreme Court largely discarded these distinctions and gave Congress far more latitude in shaping economic and social policy for the nation.[22]

SHIFTING NATIONAL-STATE RELATIONS

The type of federalism that emerged in the Progressive Era and blossomed in the late 1930s is called **cooperative federalism**, or "marble cake" federalism, as opposed to the "layer cake" model of dual federalism.[23] As the image of a marble cake suggests, the boundaries of state and national responsibilities are not as well defined under cooperative federalism as under dual federalism. With the increasing industrialization and urbanization of the late 1930s and the 1940s, more complex problems arose that could not be solved at one level of government. Cooperative federalism adopted a more practical focus on intergovernmental relations and how to efficiently provide services. State and local governments maintained a level of influence as the implementers of national programs, but the national government played an enhanced role as the initiator of key policies.

Cooperative federalism accurately describes this important shift in national–state relations in the first half of the twentieth century, but it does not begin to capture the complexity of modern federalism. The marble cake metaphor falls short in one important way: the lines of authority and patterns of cooperation are not as messy as implied by the gooey flow of chocolate through white cake. Instead, the 1960s metaphor of **picket fence federalism** is a better description of cooperative federalism in action. As the "How It Works" box shows, each picket of the fence represents a different policy area, and the horizontal boards that hold the pickets together represent the different levels of government. This is a much more orderly image than the marble cake, and it has important implications about how policy is made across levels of government.

The most important point is that activity within the cooperative federal system occurs *within* pickets of the fence—that is, within policy areas. Policy makers within a given policy area will have more in common with others in that area at different levels of government than with people at the same level of government who work on different issues. For example, someone working in a state's education department will have more contact with people working in local school districts and the national Department of Education than with people who also work at the state level but who focus on, say, transportation policy.

Cooperative federalism, then, is likely to emerge within policy areas rather than across them. This may create problems for the chief executives who are trying to run the show (mayors, governors, the president) as rivalries develop among policy areas competing for funds. Also, contact within policy areas is not always cooperative. (Think of detective shows in which the FBI arrives to investigate a local crime and pulls rank on the town sheriff, provoking resentment from local law enforcement officials.) This is the inefficient side of picket fence federalism in action. But overall, this version of federalism provides great opportunities for coordination and the development of expertise within policy areas.

VERSIONS OF FEDERALISM

LAYER CAKE FEDERALISM

No interactions between the levels of government.

NATIONAL
STATE
LOCAL

MARBLE CAKE FEDERALISM

Interactions between the levels of government are common.

NATIONAL
STATE
LOCAL

PICKET FENCE FEDERALISM

Horizontal boards represent levels of government that connect the different policy areas (pickets).

NATIONAL
STATE
LOCAL

AGRICULTURE EDUCATION HIGHWAYS HOUSING ENVIRONMENT MEDICAL CARE TAX POLICY

COERCIVE FEDERALISM

National government uses regulations, mandates, and conditions to pressure states to fall into line with national policy goals.

POP QUIZ!

① Which of the following best describes the system in the United States in the 1800s?

　a layer cake federalism
　b marble cake federalism
　c picket fence federalism
　d coercive federalism
　e none of the above

② Requiring all states to comply with the Motor Voter Act is an example of which version of federalism?

　a layer cake federalism
　b marble cake federalism
　c picket fence federalism
　d coercive federalism
　e none of the above

FEDERALISM TODAY

Federalism today is a complex mix of all the elements our nation's political system has experienced in the past. Our current system is predominantly characterized by cooperative federalism, but it has retained strong elements of national supremacy, dual federalism, and states' rights. Therefore, rather than categorizing types of federalism into neat time periods, the following discussion characterizes the dominant tendency within each period, keeping in mind that competing versions of federalism have always been just below the surface (see Nuts and Bolts 3.2). In the past twenty years, the competing versions are so evident that this period could be considered the "era of balanced federalism."[24]

COOPERATIVE FEDERALISM LIVES ON: FISCAL FEDERALISM

The cooperative relationship between the national and state governments is rooted in the system of transfer payments, or grants from the national government to lower levels of government. This is called **fiscal federalism**. However, just because money flows from Washington does not mean that cooperation by the recipients follows. Depending on how the money is transferred, the national government can either help local and state governments achieve their own goals or use its fiscal power to impose its will. This may sound familiar. When your parents let you use the car or lent you $50, did they expect something in return, such as help with yard work—or was it "no strings attached"? Even in the era of dual federalism this type of issue arose between different levels of government, but far less frequently because the national government provided very little aid to the states.

fiscal federalism A form of federalism in which federal funds are allocated to the lower levels of government through transfer payments or grants.

GRANTS IN AID

Today, most aid to the states comes in one of two forms. **Categorical grants** are for specific purposes—they have strings attached—and therefore we discuss them in the section on coercive federalism. **Block grants** are financial aid to states for use within a specific policy area, but within that area the states have discretion on how to spend the money.

A third type of grant, **general revenue sharing (GRS)**, was tried briefly in the 1970s and 1980s and was popular with the states because it came with *no* strings attached. President Nixon started GRS in 1972 as part of his New Federalism program to return more control over programs to the states. At its peak in 1979, the federal government granted $6.8 billion to the states through this program, which would be more than $25 billion in today's budget. However, the state component of the program was phased out beginning in 1980 and ended in 1986 during a period of large national budget deficits. The political support for GRS was difficult to sustain because of opposition by conservatives who wanted a smaller national government and from liberals who preferred more targeted spending.[25]

Instead, advocates of cooperative federalism promoted block grants as the best way for the levels of government to work together to solve problems: the national government identified problem areas and then provided money to the states to

categorical grants Federal aid to state or local governments that is provided for a specific purpose, such as a mass transit program within the transportation budget or a school lunch program within the education budget.

block grants Federal aid provided to a state government to be spent within a certain policy area, but the state can decide how to spend the money within that area.

general revenue sharing (GRS) A type of grant used in the 1970s and 1980s in which the federal government provided state governments with funds to be spent at each state's discretion. These grants gave states more control over programs.

THE EVOLUTION OF FEDERALISM

Type of Federalism	Period	Characteristics
Dual federalism (layer cake)	1789–1937	The national and state governments were viewed as very distinct with little overlap in their activities or the services they provided. Within this period, federalism could have been state-centered or nation-centered, but relations between levels of government were limited.
Cooperative federalism (marble cake)	1937–present	This indicates greater cooperation and collaboration between the levels of government.
Picket fence federalism	1961–present	This version of cooperative federalism emphasizes that policy makers within a given policy area have more in common with others in their area at different levels of government than with people at the same level of government who work on different issues.
Fiscal federalism	1937–present	This system of transfer payments or grants from the national government to lower-level governments involves varying degrees of national control over how the money is spent: categorical grants give the national government a great deal of control while block grants involve less national control.
New Federalism	1969–present	New federalism attempts to shift power to the states by consolidating categorical grants into block grants and giving the states authority over programs such as welfare.
Coercive federalism	1970s–present	This involves federal preemptions of state and local authority and unfunded mandates on state and local governments to force the states to change their policies to match national goals or policies established by Congress.

help solve them. Between 1966, when the first block grant was created, and 1994, 23 block grants were established.[26] For example, Community Development Block Grants were started in 1974 to help state and local governments revitalize their communities; such grants may support ongoing programs or help with large capital expenditures, such as building a waste treatment plant or a highway. Since the 1970s, grants to the states as a proportion of the size of the national economy (gross domestic product, or GDP) has been relatively constant, while the rate of state and local spending has continued to inch up (see Figure 3.1). Even including those that were part of the 2009 stimulus package, grants to the states were only 4 percent of GDP in 2009.

NEW FEDERALISM

Richard Nixon's New Federalism seemed to be a short-lived experiment in state-centered fiscal federalism, but then it revived during Ronald Reagan's presidency in the 1980s. In his 1981 inaugural address, Reagan emphasized, "All of us need to

FIGURE » 3.1

FEDERAL AND STATE/LOCAL GOVERNMENT SPENDING (INCLUDING GRANTS), 1946–2011

Since the early 1950s, federal spending as a percentage of the overall size of the economy has been flat, while the share of state and local spending has nearly tripled. What does this say about the debates between nation-centered and state-centered federalism?

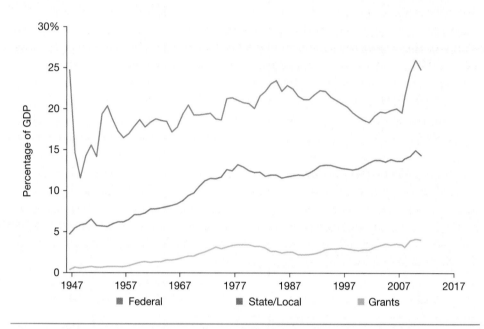

Source: 2012 Statistical Abstract of the United States, Table 4.31, and the Bureau of Economic Analysis, Table 3.2 and Table 3.3 (accessed 8/16/12).

be reminded that the federal government did not create the states. The states created the federal government." This classic statement of the states' rights position is similar to the Antifederalists' position at the Constitutional Convention.

Reagan's goal of returning more power to the states involved consolidating 77 categorical grants into nine general block grants that gave local politicians more control over how money was spent. This change reflected the belief that because state and local politicians were closer to the people, they would know better how to spend the money. However, the increase in state control came with a 25 percent cut in the amount of federal money granted to the states.

The next phase of New Federalism came when Republicans won control of Congress in 1994. Working with President Clinton, a moderate Democrat, Republicans passed several pieces of significant legislation that shifted power toward the states. In 1996 the Personal Responsibility and Work Opportunity Act reformed welfare by creating a block grant to the states, Temporary Assistance to Needy Families (TANF), to replace the largest nationally administered welfare program. Another piece of legislation, the 1996 Prison Litigation Reform

Act, ended federal court supervision of state and local prison systems. And the Unfunded Mandate Reform Act of 1995 made it more difficult for Congress to impose **unfunded mandates** on the states; it required a separate vote on mandates that imposed costs of more than $50 million, and it required a Congressional Budget Office estimate of exactly how much such mandates would cost the states. Although this law could not prevent unfunded mandates, Republicans hoped that bringing more attention to the practice would create political pressure against them.

The shift from categorical grants to block grants was an important part of New Federalism after Reagan, but it has not substantially affected the balance of power between the national and state governments. In fact, the amount of money going to the states through block grants has been surpassed by categorical grants since 1982. We will explore the reason for this later: Congress prefers categorical grants because with them it has more control over how the money is spent.

unfunded mandates Federal laws that require the states to do certain things but do not provide state governments with funding to implement these policies.

THE RISE OF COERCIVE FEDERALISM

Despite the overall shift toward cooperative federalism, strong overtones of national government supremacy remain. Three important characteristics of American politics in the past 40 years have reinforced the role of the national government: (1) reliance on the national government in times of crisis and war, (2) the "rights revolution" of the 1950s and 1960s, as well as the Great Society programs of the 1960s, and (3) the rise of coercive federalism.

CRISIS AND WAR

The first point has always been a characteristic of American politics. Even in the 1800s, during the period of dual federalism and strong state power, the national government's strong actions were needed during the Civil War to hold the nation together. More recently, following the September 11, 2001, terrorist attacks, most Americans expected the national government to improve national security and retaliate for the attacks. Even Republicans, who normally oppose increasing the size of government, largely supported President Bush's proposal to create a cabinet-level Department of Homeland Security. The other major crises of the twentieth century—the Great Depression's New Deal policies, the massive mobilization for World War II, and the response to the banking meltdown of 2008–09—also dramatically shifted the balance of power toward Washington.

THE "RIGHTS REVOLUTION" AND GREAT SOCIETY PROGRAMS

The "rights revolution" created by the Supreme Court, as well as Lyndon Johnson's Great Society programs, contributed to more national control over state policies. Landmark Court decisions thrust the national government into policy areas that had typically been reserved to the states. In the school desegregation and busing cases of the 1950s and 1960s, for example, the Court upheld the national goal of promoting racial equality and fighting discrimination over the earlier norm of local control of school districts.[27] The "one person, one vote" decisions, which required that the populations of legislative districts be equalized when district lines were redrawn, put the federal courts at the center of another policy area that had always been left to the states.[28] The rights revolution also applied to police powers, another area of traditional state control, including protection against self-incrimination and preventing illegally obtained evidence from being used in a criminal trial.[29]

These Court actions were paralleled by a burst of legislation that tackled civil rights, education, the environment, medical care for the poor, and housing. These so-called Great Society policies gave the national government much more leverage over policy areas previously controlled by state and local governments. For example, the 1965 Voting Rights Act sent federal marshals to the South to make sure that African Americans were allowed to vote. Another part of this act required local governments to submit changes in their electoral practices, including the boundaries of voting districts, to the Justice Department to make sure they did not have a discriminatory impact.

During this period, the national government also expanded its reach through an explosion in categorical grants, which the states sorely needed even though the monies came with strings attached. For example, the 1964 Civil Rights Act required nondiscrimination as a condition for receiving any kind of federal grants. The Elementary and Secondary Education Act of 1965 gave the federal government heightened control over public education by attaching certain conditions to federal grant money.

OTHER SHIFTS TOWARD NATIONAL SUPREMACY

coercive federalism A form of federalism in which the federal government pressures the states to change their policies by using regulations, mandates, and conditions (often involving threats to withdraw federal funding).

Categorical grants aimed at a broad national goal have also reinforced national supremacy in recent decades—for example, requiring a state to have a drinking age of 21 before granting it federal highway funds. This policy direction from Washington is part of a trend known as **coercive federalism**. This practice involves the use of federal regulations, mandates, or conditions to force or entice the states to change their policies to match national goals or policies established by Congress. The Clean Air and Water Acts, the Americans with Disabilities Act (which promotes handicapped access to public buildings and commercial facilities), and the "Motor Voter Act" (which requires states to provide voter registration services at

THE AMERICANS WITH DISABILITIES Act of 1990 requires that public accommodations and commercial facilities be handicapped accessible, but recent Supreme Court rulings have held that the law does not apply to most state and local government buildings. Disabled activists are shown in front of the White House lobbying for stronger legislation.

motor vehicle departments) are all laws that forced states to change their policies. The laws most objectionable to the states are unfunded mandates, which require states to do certain things but carry no federal money to pay for them.

Along with these mandates, federal preemption is another method of coercive federalism. Derived from the Constitution's national supremacy clause, **federal preemptions** involve the imposition of national priorities on the states. Many preemptions also include unfunded mandates, making the state and local governments pick up the tab for policies that the national government wants them to implement. The U.S. Conference of Mayors has identified 10 federal mandates that consume 11.3 percent of city budgets, and the National Association of Counties estimates that 12 mandates account for 12.3 percent of county budgets.[30] Many of the most expensive items are environmental laws aimed at goals that a majority of Americans share. However, state and local governments complain that they should not have to shoulder so much of the burden.[31] These are among the most controversial assertions of national power because they impose such high costs on state and local governments.

The presidency of George W. Bush provided strong evidence of this shift toward national power. Beyond the apparent centralization of power associated with fighting terrorism, Bush pushed the national government into more areas that previously had been dominated by the states—including significant mandates and preemptions in education testing, sales tax collection, emergency management, infrastructure, and elections administration. This is particularly noteworthy because it happened at a time when Republicans, who have traditionally supported states' rights, mostly controlled the presidency and Congress.[32]

President Obama continued the shift toward national power with one of the most active domestic policy agendas since the New Deal of the 1930s. A $787 billion economic stimulus package of tax cuts and spending designed to address the financial collapse of 2008–09, a $938 billion health care reform law, efforts to prop up and stimulate the battered housing industry, strengthened regulations of finance and banking, and an expanded jobs program all were on the agenda in Obama's first three years. Health care reform was especially controversial with

federal preemptions Impositions of national priorities on the states through national legislation that is based on the Constitution's supremacy clause.

WITH THE NO CHILD LEFT BEHIND Act, the George W. Bush administration increased the national government's power over education. States are required to test students and meet goals determined by the federal government in order to receive federal funding.

state governments, many of which saw the law as an unwarranted expansion of federal power. This view was supported by the Supreme Court's ruling that states could not be coerced by the federal government into expanding their Medicaid coverage. This Court decision means that there are limits on the scope of coercive federalism. While the overall impact of national health care reform is to centralize more power at the national level, states remain very important in this period of "balanced federalism," as the next section will demonstrate.

THE STATES FIGHT BACK

Most Americans support the national policies that have been imposed on the states: racial equality, clean air and water, a fair legal process, safer highways, and equal access to the voting booth. At the same time, there has always been strong support for state and local governments. In fact, in most national surveys, Americans typically say that they trust state and local government more than the national government, and they believe their tax dollars are spent more efficiently at the lower levels of government. Indeed, the shift in public opinion toward favoring national power after the terrorist attacks of September 11 was temporary, and it appears that state and local governments quickly reasserted their position as the more trusted level of government.

States appear to be reversing their traditional role of resisting change and protecting the status quo. In recent years, states have taken the lead on environmental policy, refusing to accept national pollution standards that are too lenient and a lack of national action on issues such as global warming. Many policies to address climate change—including the development of renewable energy sources, carbon emissions limits, and carbon cap-and-trade programs—have been advocated at the state level. States have been out in front on fighting electronic waste, mercury emissions, and air pollution more generally.[33] States have also taken a lead role on health care policy, immigration, gay marriage, and stem cell research.

However, the willingness of the states to fight back in recent years has not always been for progressive causes. Indeed, with the Republican gains in the 2010 elections and the influence of the Tea Party, many states have been attempting to curb national power and protect their more conservative policies in a broad range of areas, including land use, gun control, immigration, and health care. For example, Alabama, Tennessee, and Washington are considering legislation that would assert local police powers over federal authority, even on federal lands. "There's a tsunami of interest in states' rights and resistance to an overbearing federal government; that's what all these measures indicate," said Gary Marbut, a states' rights activist from Montana.[34] To complicate the ideological picture even more, one of the recent moves by states to resist national power cuts in the liberal direction: Vermont, Rhode Island, and Wisconsin have introduced legislation to require their governors to recall or take control of National Guard troops, arguing that the use of the National Guard by the federal government is unconstitutional (because Article I of the Constitution says that the "militia"—today's National Guard—should be used only for defensive purposes). Many of these state laws will not stand up in federal court, but they are clearly a reflection of state frustration with assertions of federal power.

States have one important advantage over the national government when it comes to experimenting with new policies: their numbers. There are 50 states potentially trying a mix of different policies—another reason that advocates of state-centered federalism see the states as the proper repository of government power. In this view, such a mix of policies produces **competitive federalism**—competition among states to provide the best policies to attract businesses, create jobs, and maintain a healthy social fabric. Supporters point out that competitive federalism is also a check on tyranny because people will "vote with their feet"—that is, move to a different state—if they do not like a given state's policies. One advocate of this view argues that it "disciplines government and forces the states to compete for the citizens' business, talents, and assets," which makes government act more like a free market (see "What Do Political Scientists Do?").[35]

But competitive federalism can also create a "race to the bottom" as states compete in a negative way. Cass Sunstein, head of the Office of Information and Regulatory Affairs in the Obama administration, points out that when states compete for businesses and jobs, they may do so by eliminating more environmental or occupational regulations than would be desirable. Likewise, a priority to keep taxes low may lead to cuts in benefits to those who can least afford it, such as welfare or Medicaid recipients.[36]

There is no doubt that competition among states provides citizens with a broad range of choices about the type of government they prefer. Choices by different state leaders about tax policies, levels of support for public schools and parks, and regulation of business all provide a range of options for businesses in deciding where to locate or expand, and to citizens considering a move. Because different citizens prefer different policies, this is generally viewed as an overall advantage to American democracy.

competitive federalism
A form of federalism in which states compete to attract businesses and jobs through the policies they adopt.

FIGHTING FOR STATES' RIGHTS: THE ROLE OF THE MODERN SUPREME COURT

Just as the Supreme Court played a central role in defining the boundaries of dual federalism in the nineteenth and early twentieth centuries and in opening the door to a more nation-centered cooperative federalism in the late 1930s, today's Court is once again reshaping federalism. But this time the move is decidedly in the direction of state power.

THE TENTH AMENDMENT

On paper, it seems that the Tenth Amendment would be at the center of any resurgence of state power since it ensures that all powers not delegated to the national government are reserved to the states or to the people. In practice, however, the amendment has had little significance except during the early 1930s and quite recently.

Thirty-five years ago, a leading text on the Constitution said that the Tenth Amendment "does not alter the distribution of power between the national and state governments. It adds nothing to the Constitution."[37] To understand why, consider the following example. State and local governments have always controlled their own public schools. Thus, public education is a power reserved to the states under the Tenth Amendment. However, a state law concerning public education is void if it conflicts with the Constitution—as racial segregation conflicted with the equal protection clause of the Fourteenth Amendment—or with a national law that is based on an enumerated power. For example, a state could not compel an

STATES AS LABORATORIES OF DEMOCRACY: THE DIFFUSION OF INNOVATION

One strength of American federalism is the policy innovation that comes from having fifty states simultaneously experimenting to see which policy ideas work best. This feature of American federalism was famously described by Supreme Court Justice Louis Brandeis as the "laboratories of democracy." He wrote, "It is one of the happy incidents of the federal system that a single courageous state may, if its citizens choose, serve as a laboratory; and try novel social and economic experiments without risk to the rest of the country."[a] When states produce innovative policies, they spread across the nation to other states and even the national government, in a process called "policy diffusion." In recent years, policy diffusion has happened in areas such as environmental policy, welfare policy, regulation of electric power, and most recently, health care. The health care reform adopted by the federal government in 2010 was quite similar to a policy enacted by Massachusetts in 2006.

Political scientists Craig Volden and Charles Shipan explain how policies diffuse across state and local government.[b] They identify and conduct a statistical analysis on the incidence of four mechanisms of diffusion–learning, economic competition, imitation, and coercion–for antismoking laws across the 675 largest U.S. cities between 1975 and 2000. *Learning* is the most obvious mechanism and mirrors the "laboratories of democracy" idea: states and cities adopt the policy that works best. *Economic competition* may encourage states and cities to adopt certain policies (or fail to adopt them) in response to economic forces from their neighbors. The most commonly cited example is welfare policy. States fearful of becoming "welfare magnets" will cut their welfare payments to match their neighboring states in a "race to the bottom." The economic competition mechanism for diffusion also applies to policies concerning education, the environment, infrastructure, minimum wage, and antismoking policies. *Imitation* happens when a state or city adopts a policy in an effort to be like another state or city it would like to emulate. Imitation may look like learning, but learning is based on the policy itself (a desire to implement the best policy), while imitation is generally done for other reasons (a city that attracts few tourists, for example, may want to imitate a city that many tourists visit). Finally, *coercion* may lead to diffusion when the national government requires states to adopt certain policies in order to qualify for federal funds, or when states adopt laws that apply to cities.

Volden and Shipan find support for all four mechanisms in the diffusion of smoking policy. The learning mechanism is supported by strong evidence that as more cities within a state adopt smoking restrictions, it becomes likelier that other cities within that state that don't have restrictions will change course and adopt them. They also show that cities are reluctant to adopt antismoking laws if neighboring cities within ten miles do

The manager of a truck stop in Jamestown, North Dakota, smiles after a state ban on indoor smoking went into effect. Political science research suggests that policies may diffuse among states and cities through a variety of mechanisms.

not yet have such laws, which is consistent with the economic competition variable. Bars and taverns are typically the most outspoken critics of the laws. Bar owners make an economic competition argument, saying that they would lose business to surrounding towns if their competitors still allowed smoking. That the likelihood of a city adopting antismoking laws increased when the nearest bigger city had already adopted such a law supports the imitation hypothesis. The coercion mechanism is supported by evidence showing that the adoption of a preemptive state-level law decreases the odds of a local antismoking restriction by 94 percent. In other words, if that state has already placed restrictions on smoking, it is unlikely cities will pass additional restrictions.

This study also has important implications for figuring out which type of policy diffusion is best. Policy adoption based on learning about effective policies is clearly the preferred approach: good policies spread and bad ones die, just as the "laboratories" idea expects. On the other hand, competition can produce bad outcomes if states are forced to change policies that may harm vulnerable populations (a city may decline to restrict smoking because of worries about economic competition and thus fail to reduce its incidence of lung cancer). Imitating other governments may also lead to bad policy choices–simply trying to be like a bigger nearby city is not a valid reason for adopting a policy. Coercion by other governments can produce policy that is in the public interest (such as state-wide bans on smoking), but it also may lead to sub-optimal policies. Understanding how and why policy ideas spread can help encourage better policy making.

18-year-old to attend school if the student had been drafted to serve in the army. Under the Tenth Amendment, the constitutionally enumerated national power to "raise and support armies" would trump the reserved state power to support public education.

This view was validated as recently as 1985 when the Court ruled that Congress had the power to impose a national minimum wage law on state governments, even if this was an area of traditional state power.[38] How times change! With the appointment of three conservative justices who favored a stronger role for the states, the Court started to limit Congress's reach. One technique was to require that Congress provide an unambiguous statement of its intent to overrule state authority. For example, the Court ruled that the Missouri constitution, which requires state judges to retire by age 70, did not violate the Age Discrimination in Employment Act because Congress did not make its intentions "unmistakably clear in the language of the statute."[39] In another case showing that the Tenth Amendment still had some life, the Court ruled that Congress may not "commandeer" state regulatory processes by ordering states to dispose of low-level radioactive waste (under the Low-Level Radioactive Waste Policy Act).[40] The Court also ruled that Congress cannot require local law enforcement officers to perform background checks on prospective handgun purchasers, thus striking down part of the 1993 Brady Handgun Violence Prevention Act (Brady Bill).[41]

A potentially far-reaching decision in 2011 said that individuals, not just states, have the right to challenge the constitutionality of a federal law under the Tenth Amendment. The case involved a woman who was trying to hurt her husband's lover with dangerous chemicals and was prosecuted under a federal law aimed at attempting to limit the spread of chemical weapons. In the majority opinion, Justice Kennedy harkened back to Madison's "double security" in soaring language touting the virtues of federalism in protecting liberty: "Federalism is more than an exercise in setting the boundary between different institutions of government for their own integrity. State sovereignty is not just an end in itself: 'Rather, federalism secures to citizens the liberties that derive from the diffusion of sovereign power.'"[42] The ultimate significance of this ruling remains to be seen, but it does open a new path of challenges to congressional limitations on state power.

THE FOURTEENTH AMENDMENT

The Fourteenth Amendment was intended to give the national government broad control over the potentially discriminatory laws of southern states after the Civil War. Section 1 guarantees that no state shall make or enforce any law depriving any person of "life, liberty, or property, without due process of law," or denying any person the "equal protection of the laws," while Section 5 empowers Congress "to enforce" those guarantees by "appropriate legislation."

The Supreme Court narrowly interpreted the Fourteenth Amendment in the late nineteenth century, severely limiting Congress's ability to affect state policy. However, throughout most of the twentieth century, the Court interpreted Section 5 to give Congress broad discretion to pass legislation to remedy bad state laws. For example, discriminatory application of literacy tests prevented millions of African Americans from voting in the South before the Voting Rights Act was passed in 1965. As part of the federalism revolution of the 1990s, the Court started to chip away at Congress's Fourteenth Amendment powers.

In one important case in 1997 the Supreme Court struck down the Religious Freedom Restoration Act as an overly broad attempt to curtail state-sponsored harassment based on religion. This case established a new standard to justify **remedial legislation**—that is, national legislation that fixes discriminatory state law—under Section 5, saying, "There must be a congruence and proportionality between the injury to be prevented or remedied and the means adopted to that end."[43] Two applications of this logic also applied to the Eleventh Amendment, which originally was interpreted to mean that residents of any state could not sue other (non-home-state) state governments. More recently, the Supreme Court has expanded the reach of the Eleventh Amendment through the concept of **states' sovereign immunity.** States are now immune from a much broader range of lawsuits in state and federal court (see Table 3.2 for some examples). In one application of the new standard for remedial legislation, the Court ruled

TABLE » 3.2

RECENT IMPORTANT SUPREME COURT DECISIONS ON FEDERALISM

CASE	HOLDING AND SIGNIFICANCE
Gregory v. Ashcroft (1991)	The Missouri constitution's requirement that state judges retire by age 70 did not violate the Age Discrimination in Employment Act.
United States v. Lopez (1995)	Carrying a gun in a school did not fall within "interstate commerce," thus Congress could not prohibit the possession of guns on school property.
Seminole Tribe v. Florida (1996)	The Court used the Eleventh Amendment to strengthen states' sovereign immunity, ruling that Congress could not compel a state to negotiate with Indian tribes about gaming and casinos.
Printz v. United States (1997)	The Court struck down part of the Brady Handgun Violence Prevention Act, saying that Congress cannot require local law enforcement officers to perform background checks on prospective handgun purchasers.
City of Boerne v. Flores (1997)	The Court struck down the Religious Freedom Restoration Act as an overly broad attempt to curtail the state-sponsored harassment of religion, saying that national legislation aimed at remedying states' discrimination must be "congruent and proportional" to the harm.
Alden v. Maine (1999)	State employees could not sue the state of Maine for violating the overtime pay provisions of the federal Fair Labor Standards Act.
United States v. Morrison (2000)	The Court struck down part of the Violence against Women Act, saying that Congress did not have the power under the commerce clause to provide a national remedy for gender-based crimes.
Kimel et al. v. Florida Board of Regents (2000)	The Age Discrimination in Employment Act of 1967 could not be applied to state employees because it was not considered "appropriate legislation" under Section 5 of the Fourteenth Amendment.
Alabama v. Garrett (2001)	The Court struck down the portion of the Americans with Disabilities Act that applied to the states, saying that state governments are not required to make special accommodations for the disabled.
Nevada Department of Human Resources v. Hibbs (2003)	The Court upheld Congress's power to apply the 1993 Family Leave Act to state employees as "appropriate legislation" under Section 5 of the Fourteenth Amendment.
United States v. Bond (2011)	The Court upheld individuals' right to challenge the constitutionality of a federal law under the Tenth Amendment.
National Federation of Independent Business v. Sebelius (2012)	The Court upheld most provisions of the Affordable Care Act, but struck down the expansion of Medicaid as an unconstitutional use of coercive federalism (states could voluntarily take the additional funding to cover the expansion, but they would not lose existing funds if they opted out).

that the Age Discrimination in Employment Act of 1967 could not be applied to state employees because it was not "appropriate legislation."[44] The Supreme Court also struck down the portion of the Americans with Disabilities Act (ADA) that applied to the states. Passed in 1990 with nearly unanimous support to protect the 45 million Americans who have some type of disability, the ADA required employers, including state agencies, to make "reasonable accommodations" for a "qualified individual with a disability." However, the majority opinion said that states could refuse to hire people in wheelchairs, or deaf or blind people, as "States are not required . . . to make special accommodations for the disabled."[45] Three years later, the Court made a narrow exception to this ruling, saying that states did need to provide access for the disabled to courthouses.[46]

In another exception to the federalism revolution, the Court upheld Congress's power to apply the 1993 Family Leave Act to state employees as "appropriate legislation" under Section 5 of the Fourteenth Amendment.[47] The key difference between this case and the age or disability cases is that in passing the Family Leave Act, Congress explicitly recognized the gender inequality of family care. That is, when a family member gets sick, the mother or wife typically bears the burden. Constitutional protections for discrimination based on age or disability are much weaker than discrimination based on gender or race.

THE COMMERCE CLAUSE

Another category of cases leading to more state power concerns the commerce clause of the Constitution. The first Court case to limit Congress's commerce powers since the New Deal of the 1930s came in 1995. The case involved the Gun-Free School Zones Act of 1990, which Congress passed in response to the increase in school shootings around the nation. The law made it a federal offense to have a gun within 1,000 feet of a school. Congress assumed that it had the power to pass this legislation, given the Court's expansive interpretation of the commerce clause over the previous 55 years, even though it concerned a traditional area of state power. Although it was a stretch to claim that carrying a gun in or around a school was related to interstate commerce, Congress might have been able to demonstrate the point by showing that most guns are made in one state and sold in another (thus commercially crossing state lines), that crime affects the economy and commerce, and that the quality of education, which is also crucial to the economy, is harmed if students and teachers are worrying about guns in their schools. However, members of Congress did not present this evidence because they did not think it was necessary.

Alfonso Lopez, a senior at Edison High School in San Antonio, Texas, was arrested for carrying a concealed .38 caliber handgun with five bullets in it. Lopez moved to dismiss the charges, arguing that the law was unconstitutional because carrying a gun in a school could not be regulated as "interstate commerce." The Court agreed in *United States v. Lopez*,[48] and the ruling was widely viewed as a warning shot over Congress's bow. If Congress wanted to encroach on the states' turf in the future, it would have to demonstrate that the law in question was a legitimate exercise of the commerce clause powers.

Congress learned its lesson. The next time it passed legislation that affected law enforcement at the state level, it was careful to document the impact on interstate commerce. The Violence against Women Act was passed in 1994 with strong bipartisan

THE *LOPEZ* DECISION STRUCK DOWN the 1990 Gun-Free School Zones Act, ruling that Congress did not have the power to forbid people to carry guns near schools. After the shooting of 12 students and one teacher at Columbine High School in Jefferson County, Colorado, on April 20, 1999, there were renewed calls nationwide for strengthening gun control laws.

support after weeks of testimony and thousands of pages of evidence were entered into the record showing the links between violence against women and commerce. Despite the evidence Congress presented, the Supreme Court ruled that Congress did not have the power under the commerce clause to make a national law that gave victims of gender-motivated violence the right to sue their attackers in federal court (however, the Court struck down only that part of the law; the program funding remained unaffected).[49]

Another far-reaching case that limited Congress's power relative to the states upheld an Alabama law requiring applicants for drivers' licenses to take the written examination in English. This means that individuals who believe they have been subjected to a state law that has a discriminatory effect (rather than one inflicting direct, intentional discrimination) based on race, color, or national origin can no longer sue a state under Title VI of the 1964 Civil Rights Act. Instead, the Court concluded that Congress intended these regulations to be directly enforceable only by the Office for Civil Rights—a political body with very limited resources.

The significance of this line of federalism cases is enormous. Not only has the Supreme Court set new limits on Congress's ability to address national problems (the "congruence and proportionality" test), but it has also clearly stated that the Court alone will determine which rights warrant protection by Congress. The cases have also been quite controversial on the bench. Nearly all of the cases mentioned here were decided by 5–4 margins, with intense and persistent dissents. In many instances the dissenters took the unusual step of reading their opinions from the bench.

Many constitutional experts see these rulings as an important shift of power from the national government to the states. However, it is important to recognize that the Court does not consistently rule against Congress; it often rules against the states because of broader constitutional principles or general public consensus behind a specific issue. For example, the Court struck down Arkansas's three-term limit for members of Congress, ruling that states could not impose any additional limits on the qualifications for being a member of Congress beyond those in the Constitution.[50] The Court has also struck down state laws limiting gay rights as a violation of the equal protection clause of the Fourteenth Amendment,[51] it ruled that the death penalty for those younger than 18 and the mentally retarded is "cruel and unusual punishment" and thus prohibited by the Eighth Amendment,[52] it upheld Congress's power to regulate marijuana over state laws that had allowed its medical use,[53] and while the Court rejected the commerce clause as the constitutional justification for national health care reform, it did uphold the ACA based on Congress's taxing power. [54]

Based on these cases, some would argue that the shift in power toward the states has been relatively marginal. Furthermore, the national government still has the upper hand in the balance of power and has many tools at its disposal to blunt the impact of a Court decision. First, Congress can pass new laws to clarify its legislative intent and overturn any of the Court cases that involved statutory interpretation. Second, Congress can use its financial power to impose its will on the states, as it did with raising the drinking age. So, for example, Congress could pass a law saying that before a state could receive money from the federal government related to the relevant law, it had to agree to abide by the Americans with Disabilities Act or the Age Discrimination in Employment Act. However, as noted above, there are new limits on budgetary coercion. In the health care reform case, the Court ruled that the threat to withhold Medicaid funds was a "gun to the head" of states,[55] meaning states did not have a real choice. This was the first time the Court limited Congress's coercive budgetary power over the states, and the boundaries of the new limits will have to be decided in future cases.

MEDICAL MARIJUANA AND ASSISTED SUICIDE

The debate over devolving power from the national government to the states has grown increasingly complicated in the past several years. The partisan nature of the debate has shifted, the courts have played a larger but inconsistent role, and issues of states' rights increasingly cut across normal ideological and partisan divisions. Since the mid-1990s, the Supreme Court has played a central role in the shift of power to the states, but two recent cases involving medical marijuana (*Gonzales v. Raich*, 2005) and assisted suicide (*Gonzales v. Oregon*, 2006) show how the typical debate between national and state power can change when a moral dimension is introduced.

In both cases, state voters supported liberal policies. In 1996, California voters passed the Compassionate Use Act, by a margin of 56 to 44 percent. This law allowed seriously ill Californians, typically AIDS and cancer patients, to use marijuana as part of their medical treatment with the permission of a doctor. Oregon voters approved the Death with Dignity Act in 1994 by a margin of 51 to 49 percent. This law allows physicians to prescribe a lethal drug dosage for terminally ill patients who wish to end their lives. A court order delayed implementation of the law until 1997, the same year that the matter was put before the voters again, but they rejected repealing the law by a margin of 60 to 40 percent. Both of these states' laws were challenged in federal court in classic confrontations between the states' rights and national power perspectives. Surprisingly, the Supreme Court ruled against medical marijuana and in favor of assisted suicide (this oversimplifies the legal arguments, but these were the bottom-line outcomes).

Should Congress be able to tell a state that it cannot allow the use of medical marijuana? Can the attorney general interpret a congressional law as a prohibition of assisted suicide? Unlike many of the cases discussed in this chapter, the states' rights position in these cases represented the liberal perspective, rather than the conservative position typically associated with state-centered federalism. Social liberals tended to support both the medical marijuana law and the assisted suicide law, while social conservatives tended to oppose them both. However, if you examine these cases in terms of the question of federal versus state power, the traditional liberal and conservative perspectives both look more complex. That is, a national-power liberal and a social conservative would agree that the national government should regulate medical marijuana and assisted suicide. Likewise, states' rights conservatives and social liberals would share the view that the states should decide these issues on their own.

Somewhat surprisingly, there was almost no consistency among the eight justices who voted on both cases (Chief Justice William Rehnquist was replaced by John Roberts between the two cases). Only Justice Sandra Day O'Connor supported the states' rights position in both cases while Justice Antonin Scalia voted as a moral conservative against both laws—and counter to

Federal drug enforcement agents raid a medical marijuana club.

his previously articulated views on national power and federalism. The other six justices mixed their views, voting to uphold one of the laws and to strike down the other. The resulting rulings were inconsistent on the question of federalism as well. In the medical marijuana case, the Court upheld Congress's power to regulate the medical use of marijuana under the Controlled Substances Act. But in the assisted suicide case, the Court said that under that same congressional law, the U.S. attorney general did not have the power to limit the drugs that doctors in Oregon could prescribe for use in an assisted suicide.

Despite the Court's endorsement of Congress's power to regulate medical marijuana, the actual situation is more complex because of the Obama administration's evolving position on enforcing the law. Initially, the Obama administration said it would not enforce the federal law in 19 states that had legalized or decriminalized medical marijuana. But then in 2011 and 2012, the Justice Department shifted course, cracking down on large medical marijuana dispensaries in California, saying that the drug had become widely available for recreational use, not just medical use. The struggle between the national and state governments is likely to continue on this issue in the foreseeable future.

Critical **Thinking Questions**

1. As a matter of policy, should doctors be able to prescribe marijuana to alleviate pain? Should they be able to prescribe lethal drugs to terminally ill patients?

2. Do you tend to support a state-centered or nation-centered perspective on federalism? Now revisit your answers to the first questions. Are your positions more consistent with your views on federalism or with your policy concerns?

ASSESSING FEDERALISM

From Madison's "double security" that protects individual liberty to states as the "laboratories of democracy" in policy innovation, there is much to recommend federalism as a cornerstone of our political system. However, there are disadvantages as well, such as inefficiency in the policy process and inequality in policy outcomes. This section will assess the advantages, disadvantages, and ideological complexities of federalism.

IDEOLOGICAL COMPLEXITIES

Issues concerning federalism seem to break down along traditional liberal and conservative lines. Liberals generally favor strong national power to fight discrimination against women, minorities, disabled people, gay men and lesbians, and the elderly, and they push for progressive national policies on issues such as protecting the environment, providing national health care, and supporting the poor. Conservatives, in contrast, tend to favor limited intrusion from the national government and allowing the states to decide their own mix of social welfare and regulatory policies, including how aggressively they will protect various groups from discrimination.

However, assessing federalism is not so simple. In recent years the tables have turned, and in many cases liberals are suddenly arguing for states' rights while conservatives are advocating the virtues of uniform national laws. On a broad range of new issues, such as medical uses of marijuana, gay marriage, cloning, and assisted suicide, state governments are passing socially liberal legislation.[56] And the Court's earlier, state-centered rulings give it little precedent for striking down these laws. The Court's conservative majority will either have to continue applying its state-centered federalism and uphold these liberal state laws, or strike them down on ideological grounds, which would undermine the Court's credibility.

One potential solution, from a socially conservative perspective, involves passing congressional legislation banning, for example, cloning or gay marriage. This approach would also be difficult for the Court to sustain, however, given its earlier, narrow definition of "economic activity" under the commerce clause. The most interesting of these cases in many ways pertain to the medical use of marijuana and assisted suicide (see "You Decide"). In these cases, political ideology and policy views about the drug laws and the right to die were apparently more important for most of the justices than consistency on questions of federalism.

ADVANTAGES OF A STRONG ROLE FOR THE STATES

In addition to pointing out the ideological complexities of federalism, any assessment of federalism today must consider the advantages and disadvantages for our political system. The advantages of a strong role for the states can be summarized in four main points: states can be laboratories of democracy, state and local government is closer to the people, states provide more access to the political system, and states provide an important check on national power.

The first point refers to the role that states play as the source of policy diversity and innovation. If many states are trying to solve problems creatively, they can complement the efforts of the national government. Successful policies first adopted at the state level often percolate up to the national level. Consider welfare reform. Many states had great success in helping people get off welfare by providing worker training, education assistance, health benefits, and child care. The national government decided that states were doing a better job than it was and, through the TANF block grant mentioned earlier, devolved welfare funding and responsibility to the states. Health care and environmental policy, especially on climate change, are other areas in which states have innovated.

Second, government that is closer to the people encourages participation in the political process. Local politicians know better what their constituents want than further-removed national politicians do. If the voters want higher taxes to pay for more public benefits, such as public parks and better schools, they can enact these changes at the state and local levels. On the other hand, if they prefer lower taxes and fewer services, local politicians can be responsive to those desires. Also, local government provides a broad range of opportunities for direct involvement in politics, from working on local political campaigns to attending school board or city council meetings. When citizens are able to directly affect policies, they are more likely to get involved in the political process.

Third, our federalist system provides more potential paths to address problems. For example, the court system allows citizens to pursue complaints under state or federal law. Likewise, cooperative federalism can draw on the strengths of different levels of government to solve problems. A local government may recognize a need and respond to it more quickly than the national government, but if it needs additional resources to address the problem, it may be able to turn to the state or national government for help.

Finally, federalism can provide a check on national tyranny. Competitive federalism ensures that Americans have a broad range of social policies, levels of taxation and regulation, and public services to choose from (see Figure 3.2). When people "vote with their feet" by deciding whether to move and where to live, they encourage healthy competition among states that would be impossible under a unitary government.

IN THE DEBATE OVER HEALTH CARE Reform and the Affordable Care Act, supporters of nationalized health care argued the federal government could do a better job than the patchwork of state policies to ensure that all Americans receive sufficient care.

DISADVANTAGES OF TOO MUCH STATE POWER

A balanced assessment must acknowledge that there are problems with a federalist system that gives too much power to the states. The disadvantages include unequal distribution of resources across the states, unequal protection for civil rights, and competitive federalism that produces a "race to the bottom." Also, one puzzle (which we will explore in other chapters) is that more people vote in national elections than in state and local elections. Turnout at the local level is often ridiculously low. If people support local government so strongly, why aren't they more interested?

FIGURE » 3.2

TYPES OF SPENDING PER CAPITA BY STATE

Spending varies dramatically by state. What are some of the advantages and disadvantages of living in a low-spending state or in a high-spending state? Which type of state would you rather live in?

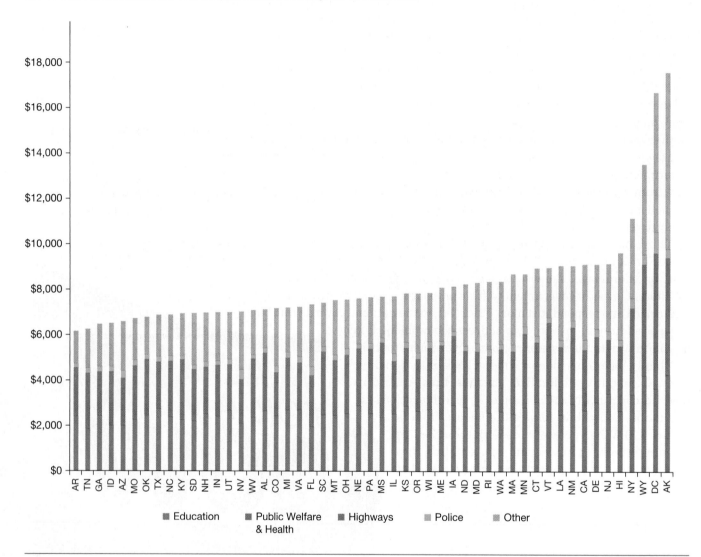

Source: State and Local Government Finance Data Query System, www.taxpolicycenter.org/slf-dqs/pages.cfm (accessed 8/16/12).

One central problem of giving too much responsibility to the states is the huge variation in the distribution of resources. Without federal funding, poor states simply cannot provide an adequate level of benefits because they have the greatest needs (see Figure 3.3a) and the lowest incomes (see Figure 3.3b), which leads to significant disparities in important areas. For example, the wealthiest states spend more than twice as much per capita on education as the poorest states. Citizens of poor states are still citizens of the United States, and one important role for the national government is to ensure that all people have some kind of safety net.

FIGURE » 3.3A

POVERTY RATES BY STATE, 2010

There are huge differences between the wealthiest states and the poorest states in terms of their income levels and poverty rates. What do these disparities imply about the role of the national government in terms of supporting a "social safety net"? How do recent developments in federalism support or undermine the notion of a social safety net?

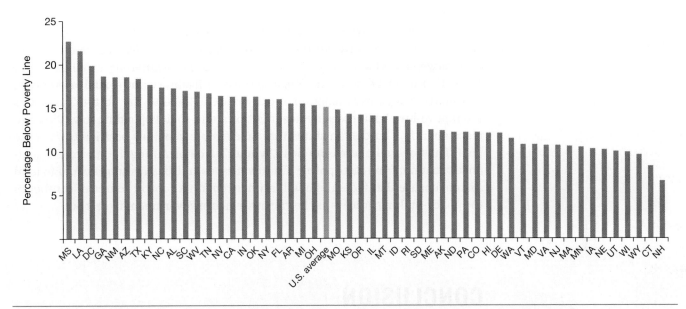

Source: U.S. Census Bureau, Current Population Survey, 2011 Annual Social and Economic Supplement, www.census.gov/hhes/www/cpstables/ 032011/pov/new46_100125_01.htm (accessed 8/17/12).

FIGURE » 3.3B

PER CAPITA INCOME BY STATE, 2010

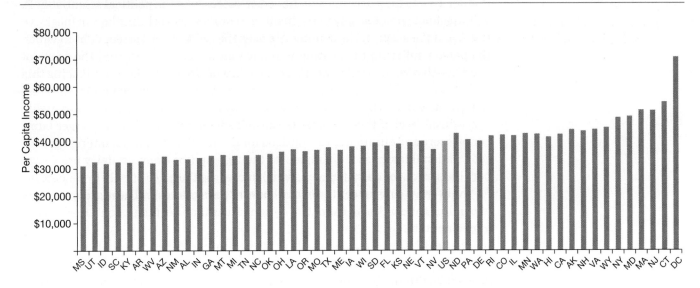

Source: U.S. Department of Commerce, Bureau of Economic Analysis, State Annual Personal Income, August 17, 2012, www.bea.gov/iTable/iTable .cfm?ReqID=99&step=1 (accessed 8/17/12).

The resource problem becomes more acute in dealing with national-level problems that are intractable at the local or state level. For example, pollution spills across state lines, and the deteriorating public infrastructure, like the highway system, crosses state boundaries. In fact, one study estimated that 26 percent of U.S. bridges are structurally deficient or obsolete, 15 percent of highways are in need of repair, and 25 percent of mass transit needs to be updated. Solving these and other infrastructure problems will cost 2.2 trillion dollars, vastly outstripping the resources of state and local governments.[57]

The second problem, unequal civil rights protection, is evident in various federalism cases that have passed before the Supreme Court. These clearly show that states are not uniformly willing to protect the civil liberties and civil rights of their citizens. Without national laws, there will be large differences in the levels of protection against discrimination based on age, disability, and sexual orientation.

Finally, competitive federalism can create a "race to the bottom" as states attempt to lure businesses by keeping taxes and social spending low. This can place an unfair burden on states that take a more generous position toward the poor. Thus, overall, there is no clear "winner" in determining the appropriate balance of national and state power. The advantages and disadvantages of our federal system ensure that federalism will always remain a central source of conflict in the policy-making process as the various levels of government fight it out.

CONCLUSION

Alexis de Tocqueville, a French observer of American politics in the early nineteenth century, noted the tendency of democratic governments to centralize. This is especially true during wartime or times of crisis, as in the aftermath of the September 11 attacks, but it is also true during normal political times.

Powerful interest groups have an incentive to claim national importance for their causes to increase their likelihood of success. As the political scientist E. E. Schattschneider noted, any participant in a conflict who is losing has an incentive to expand the scope of the conflict. He uses the example of a street fight in which the person suffering the beating will have an incentive to expand the scope of conflict—that is, to bring in his three friends who are down the alley. Placing this in the context of federalism, political scientist Michael Greve explains, "Interest groups and parties thrive on redistribution, which is best accomplished at a highly centralized level of government—because it spreads the costs over a larger number of losers and eliminates exit options for them."[58] That is, when interest groups get a national law passed that benefits their group (for example, dairy price support legislation for dairy farmers, which increases the price of milk by 26 percent for the average consumer), the entire country pays the costs. These groups win by expanding the conflict to the entire nation rather than keeping it contained within a specific state.

The health care reform example at the beginning of the chapter also illustrates this point. Passing a single piece of legislation was a much more efficient way to provide health insurance for more than 30 million Americans than attempting to get each state to pass similar legislation. This scenario occurs again and again across a broad range of issues and creates a powerful centralizing force. Within that general pattern of government centralization, however, there have been lengthy periods when states' rights held sway over the national government.

But this evolving balance of power between the national government and the states obscures a broader reality of federalism: we are citizens of several levels of government simultaneously. Martha Derthick, a leading scholar of American federalism, says that the basic question of federalism involves choices about how many communities we will be.[59] If you asked most people in our nation about their primary geopolitical community, they would probably not say, "I am a Montanan" or "I am a Arizonan." Most people would likely say, "I am an American." Yet we have strong attachments to our local communities and state identities. Most Texans would not be caught dead wearing a styrofoam cheese head, but thousands of football fans in Green Bay, Wisconsin, regularly don the funny-looking things to watch their beloved Packers. We are members of multiple communities, a fact that has had an indelible impact on our political system. The beauty of our federal system is that despite its complex and evolving nature, it makes a lot of sense.

ONE OF THE STRENGTHS OF Federalism is that it allows regional diversity to flourish. Green Bay Packers fans proudly wear their cheesehead hats at Lambeau Field, showing that what passes for normal behavior in one part of the country would be viewed differently in other areas.

STUDY *guide*

WHAT IS FEDERALISM AND WHY DOES IT MATTER?

▶ Define federalism and explain its significance. **Pages 71–74**

SUMMARY

A federal system simultaneously allocates power to both the state and federal government, while a confederal system only gives power to the states, and a unitary government only gives power to the federal government.

KEY TERMS

federalism (p. 71)

sovereign power (p. 71)

police powers (p. 72)

concurrent powers (p. 72)

unitary government (p. 73)

confederal government (p. 74)

intergovernmental organizations (p. 74)

PRACTICE QUIZ QUESTIONS

1. What system of government did the Articles of Confederation establish?
    a) unitary
    b) federal
    c) confederal
    d) monarchy
    e) dictatorship

2. Which is an example of a concurrent power?
    a) print money
    b) build roads
    c) conduct elections
    d) declare war
    e) establish post offices

BALANCING NATIONAL AND STATE POWER IN THE CONSTITUTION

▶ Explain what the Constitution says about federalism. **Pages 74–78**

SUMMARY

While the state governments have considerable power in our system, the Founders disproportionately favored the federal government in the Constitution, so that the federal government's interests superseded those of the states in the event of a conflict.

KEY TERMS

full faith and credit clause (p. 77)

privileges and immunities clause (p. 77)

PRACTICE QUIZ QUESTIONS

3. States' rights are protected in the reserve clause, which is found in _____.
    a) the Ninth Amendment
    b) the Tenth Amendment
    c) Article I of the Constitution
    d) Article III of the Constitution
    e) the First Amendment

4. Contemporary conflict over same-sex marriage falls under which constitutional provision?
    a) privileges and immunities clause
    b) exclusionary clause
    c) national supremacy clause
    d) full faith and credit clause
    e) establishment clause

THE EVOLVING CONCEPT OF FEDERALISM

▶ Trace the major shifts in state and federal government power over time. **Pages 78–85**

SUMMARY

The relationship between the state and federal governments has changed dramatically over time. Whereas the federal and state governments traditionally operated with little interaction under the era of dual federalism, the trend over the past 80 years has been one of increasing federal interaction with state governments to address particular policy areas.

KEY TERMS

doctrine of interposition (p. 80)

states' rights (p. 80)

dual federalism (p. 81)

commerce clause powers (p. 82)

cooperative federalism (p. 84)

picket fence federalism (p. 84)

PRACTICE QUIZ QUESTIONS

5. Which analogy best describes the federalism arrangement today?
   a) layer cake federalism
   b) marble cake federalism
   c) picket fence federalism
   d) gumbo federalism
   e) dual federalism

6. Which case bolstered the federal government's power over the states?
   a) *Barron v. Baltimore*
   b) *McCulloch v. Maryland*
   c) *Dred Scott v. Sanford*
   d) *Mapp v. Ohio*
   e) *U. S. v. Lopez*

7. When did the federal government begin cooperating with the states on policy goals?
   a) 1890s
   b) 1930s
   c) 1950s
   d) 1970s
   e) 1990s

Ⓢ **PRACTICE ONLINE**

"Critical Thinking" exercise: *Process Matters—Federal and State Relationships*

FEDERALISM TODAY

Describe the major trends and debates in federalism today. **Pages 86–99**

SUMMARY

Today's federal structure offers a complex mix of all previous components of federalism: some elements of national supremacy combine with states' rights for a varied federal landscape. While the federal and state governments still exercise cooperative federalism to achieve joint policy goals, the federal government has also utilized coercive federalism to impose federal priorities on the states without offering compensation.

KEY TERMS

fiscal federalism (p. 86)

categorical grants (p. 86)

block grants (p. 86)

general revenue sharing (GRS) (p. 86)

unfunded mandates (p. 89)

coercive federalism (p. 90)

federal preemptions (p. 91)

competitive federalism (p. 93)

remedial legislation (p. 96)

states' sovereign immunity (p. 96)

CRITICAL THINKING AND DISCUSSION

On which issues is the national government particularly well suited to serve the people's interests? Which issues are the states better suited to handle? Explain the reasons for your choices.

8. Which form of revenue sharing is given to the states by the federal government with explicit conditions on how it is to be allocated?
   a) block grant
   b) categorical grant
   c) general revenue sharing
   d) federal mandate
   e) tax refund

9. Richard Nixon's plans to increase states' rights led to the increase in _____.
   a) block grants
   b) categorical grants
   c) general revenue sharing
   d) federal mandates
   e) state taxes

10. The imposition of national priorities on the states through congressional legislation and imposition of the national supremacy clause is called _____.
   a) cooperative federalism
   b) dual federalism
   c) competitive federalism
   d) federal preemption
   e) remedial legislation

11. A state would usually challenge the constitutionality of a federal law under which amendment(s)?
   a) Eighth Amendment
   b) Tenth and Eleventh Amendments
   c) Thirteenth Amendment
   d) Fourteenth Amendment
   e) First Amendment

12. The Eleventh Amendment's protections of state sovereign immunity guarantee that _____.
   a) residents of one state cannot sue the government of another state
   b) state governments cannot commit a legal wrong
   c) ambassadors from foreign countries cannot be detained by state governments
   d) state governments can sue the federal government
   e) state governments cannot be sued by anybody

13. The Court has recently overturned a number of Congressional laws rooted in the _____.
   a) national supremacy clause
   b) reserve clause
   c) establishment clause
   d) commerce clause
   e) free exercise clause

Ⓢ **PRACTICE ONLINE**

"Big Think" video exercise: *Improving Government Controls*

ASSESSING FEDERALISM

Analyze the arguments for and against a strong federal government. **Pages 100–104**

SUMMARY

While conservatives have traditionally advocated for states' rights and liberals generally prefer a stronger national government, contemporary issues do not always fit neatly in this scheme. There are several reasons that strong state governments are beneficial for our country, such as the proximity of state and local governments to the citizens; however, there are also some drawbacks to the federal system, such as the vastly disproportionate distribution of resources across states.

CRITICAL THINKING AND DISCUSSION

How would our country be different if it were a unitary system? Do you think we would be better or worse off?

14. Conservatives favor strong _____ rights on gay marriage, and strong _____ rights on providing health care.

   a) states'; states'
   b) states'; federal government
   c) federal government; states'
   d) federal government; federal government
   e) individual; federal government

15. Which of the following is a drawback to strong state power?

   a) State governments are often innovators on policy solutions.
   b) State governments give citizens more access to politicians than the national government.
   c) State governments give citizens several paths to pursue policy reform.
   d) State governments give different civil rights protections to their citizens.
   e) States have an unequal distribution of resources.

⑤ **PRACTICE ONLINE**

"Critical Thinking" exercise: *Politics Is Conflictual—Disparities in State Tax Rates*

SUGGESTED READING

Beer, Samuel. *To Make a Nation: The Rediscovery of American Federalism.* Cambridge, MA: Harvard University Press, 1993.

Conlan, Timothy. *From New Federalism to Devolution: Twenty-Five Years of Intergovernmental Reform.* Washington, DC: Brookings Institution, 1998.

Derthick, Martha. *Keeping the Compound Republic: Essays on American Federalism.* Washington, DC: Brookings Institution, 2001.

Elkins, Stanley, and Eric McKitrick. *The Age of Federalism: The Early American Republic, 1788–1800.* New York: Oxford University Press, 1993.

Grodzins, Martin. *The American System: A New View of Government in the United States.* Chicago: Rand McNally, 1966.

LaCroix, Alison L. *The Ideological Origins of American Federalism.* Cambridge, MA: Harvard University Press, 2010.

Manna, Paul. *School's In: Federalism and the National Education Agenda.* Washington, DC: Georgetown University Press, 2006.

McDonald, Forrest. *States' Rights and the Union: Imperium in Imperia, 1776–1876.* Lawrence: University Press of Kansas, 2000.

Nagel, Robert F. *The Implosion of American Federalism.* New York: Oxford University Press, 2001.

Peterson, Paul E. *The Price of Federalism.* Washington, DC: Brookings Institution, 1995.

Posner, Paul L. *The Politics of Unfunded Mandates: Whither Federalism?* Washington, DC: Georgetown University Press, 1998.

Scheberle, Denise. *Federalism and Environmental Policy: Trust and the Politics of Implementation,* 2nd ed. Washington, DC: Georgetown University Press, 2004.

4

Civil Liberties

SHOULD FREE SPEECH BE protected even when the ideas are offensive? The Supreme Court ruled that the Westboro Baptist Church had a right to protest at military funerals, even though many Americans found their arguments and approach deeply offensive.

SINCE 2005, MEMBERS OF THE WESTBORO BAPTIST Church (WBC) have protested at more than 400 funerals of members of the armed services who were killed in Iraq and Afghanistan. However, these were not typical antiwar protests. Instead, the protesters claimed that the troops' deaths were God's punishment for "the homosexual lifestyle of soul-damning, nation-destroying filth."[1]

The church has drawn strong reactions and counterprotests for their confrontational approach at the military funerals, including their use of signs that say "God Hates Fags," "Thank God for Dead Soldiers," "God Killed Your Sons," and "God Hates America." Critics, including many veterans groups and attorneys general from 48 states, argue that the protests should not be considered protected speech under the First Amendment. The Veterans of Foreign Wars issued a statement saying, "In a time of profound grief and emotional vulnerability, these personal attacks are an affront of the most egregious kind." While recognizing that the First Amendment protects offensive speech, they argued it does not allow "personal attacks targeted at private individuals during a time of mourning."[2] A group of veterans called the Patriot Guard Riders have gathered at the funerals to serve as a buffer for the grieving families by riding motorcycles along the funeral route and singing patriotic songs or revving their engines to drown out the hateful speech.

State legislatures and Congress have also attempted to limit the disruption caused by the WBC. Forty-three states have passed laws limiting protests

CONFLICT & COMPROMISE
in American Politics

civil liberties Basic political freedoms that protect citizens from governmental abuses of power.

at military funerals to a certain distance from the actual services. In 2006, Congress passed the "Respect for Fallen American Heroes Act," that prohibited protests within 300 feet of a federal cemetery one hour before or after a funeral.

When the WBC protested at the funeral of Marine Lance Corporal Matthew Snyder, his father, Albert Synder, sued the church for defamation, intentional infliction of emotional distress, and invasion of privacy. The district federal court ruled in Snyder's favor, awarding $5 million in damages. But the appeals court reversed the ruling, setting up an appeal to the Supreme Court. The case drew extensive attention with 48 states, 42 U.S. senators, and many veterans groups, including the American Legion and Veterans of Foreign Wars, filing briefs on behalf of Snyder, while more than 20 national news organizations filed briefs arguing that the WBC's protests should be protected by the First Amendment.

In their 2011 decision, the Supreme Court ruled 8–1 that the WBC's protests were protected speech. The majority opinion said, "Speech is powerful. It can stir people to action, move them to tears of both joy and sorrow, and—as it did here—inflict great pain. On the facts before us, we cannot react to that pain by punishing the speaker. As a nation we have chosen a different course—to protect even hurtful speech on public issues to ensure that we do not stifle public debate."[3] They said that the speech was not defamation because most of the WBC's signs were related to political issues, such American involvement in wars and the service of gays in the military. They also argued that the Snyder family's privacy rights were not violated because the protesters were 1,000 feet from the funeral. Indeed, the family could only see the tops of the signs on the way to the funeral and did not learn about their content until reading about the protests after the funeral. Justice Samuel Alito, the only dissenter, disagreed, "Our profound national commitment to free and open debate is not a license for the vicious verbal assault that occurred in this case. . . . In order to have a society in which public issues can be openly and vigorously debated, it is not necessary to allow the brutalization of innocent victims."[4]

The Court's strong reaffirmation of the First Amendment's protection of hurtful and unpopular speech is an excellent illustration of our central theme that politics is conflictual. It is difficult to imagine speech that is more conflictual than the WBC's protests. Indeed, the entire purpose of the speech is to generate conflict. But the case also shows that even in such a difficult case, compromise is possible. The "time, manner, and place" restrictions that limit the protests to areas away from the funeral maintain the privacy rights of the families, at least to some extent, while protecting the First Amendment rights of the protesters. While the plaintiffs and their supporters were not happy with this compromise, it represents the outcome of the legislative and judicial process.

The case also illustrates our other two themes. The evolution of the meaning of **civil liberties**, as largely defined by the courts, is a great example that the political process matters. Despite their overwhelmingly unpopular views, the WBC may continue picketing because the legal process endorsed their interpretation of the Constitution. Civil liberties also are an excellent example that politics is everywhere. Freedom of speech, religion, and assembly; privacy rights; and the rights of criminal defendants generate great public interest because they are so central to our political system and our daily lives.

DEFINING CIVIL LIBERTIES

DEFINE WHAT WE MEAN BY
CIVIL LIBERTIES

The terms *civil rights* and *civil liberties* are often used interchangeably, but there are some important differences (see Nuts and Bolts 4.1). To oversimplify a bit, civil liberties are about freedom and civil rights are about equality. Given that civil liberties are rooted in the Bill of Rights, it may have been less confusing if it had been called the "Bill of Liberties." (This distinction is discussed further in Chapter 14, Civil Rights.)

Civil liberties are deeply rooted in our key idea that politics is conflictual and involves trade-offs. When the Supreme Court rules on civil liberties cases, it must balance an individual's freedom with government interests and the public good. In some cases, the Court must not only balance these interests but also "draw a line" between permissible and illegal conduct concerning a specific liberty.

BALANCING INTERESTS

Civil liberties must be balanced against competing interests because when it comes to our freedoms, there are no absolutes. The trade-off between civil liberties and national security in the "war on terrorism" illustrates the point. Many Americans were concerned that our civil liberties were being eroded upon discovering that the government was conducting surveillance of U.S. citizens without court orders, including collecting data from millions of phone calls and e-mail messages; had condoned the abuse of Iraqi prisoners; and was applying a process

HOW CAN CONFLICTS BE RESOLVED between civil liberties and other legitimate interests, such as public safety and public health? Sometimes freedom is forced to give way. Courts have upheld bans on the religious practice of snake handling and laws requiring the Amish to display reflective triangles when driving slow-moving buggies on public roads, despite religious objections to doing so.

DISTINGUISHING CIVIL LIBERTIES FROM CIVIL RIGHTS

Civil Liberties	Civil Rights
Basic freedoms and liberties	Protection from discrimination
Rooted in the Bill of Rights and the "due process" protection of the Fourteenth Amendment	Rooted in laws and the "equal protection" clause of the Fourteenth Amendment
Primarily restrict what the government can do to you ("*Congress* shall make no law . . . abridging the freedom of speech")	Protects you from discrimination both by the government and by individuals

called "extraordinary rendition" in which suspected terrorists were arrested in the United States and taken to a foreign country that is less protective of civil liberties, such as Egypt, Syria, Jordan, or Morocco, to be interrogated through torture.[5] Despite these concerns, even the strongest critic of state-sponsored torture would have to admit that in some instances it might be justified. For example, if a nuclear device were set to detonate in Manhattan in three hours, few would insist on protecting the civil liberties of someone who knew where the bomb was hidden. Once one recognizes that our freedoms are not absolute, it becomes a question of how they are balanced against other interests, such as national security.

Other interests that compete with civil liberties include public safety and public health. For example, in the mid-twentieth century, members of some Christian fundamentalist churches regularly handled dangerous snakes in their services, but many states and cities have laws against "the handling of poisonous reptiles in such manner as to endanger the public health, safety, and welfare." These conflicting interests collided in a 1947 case in which members of a church in North Carolina were each fined $50 for handling a poisonous copperhead snake in a church service. They appealed all the way to the North Carolina Supreme Court, arguing that the local ordinance "impinges on the freedom of religious worship." The court rejected this view, saying that "public safety is superior to religious practice."[6] Similarly, in some states Amish people are forced to place reflective "slow-moving vehicle" triangles on their horse-drawn carriages, even if it violates their religious beliefs, because of the paramount concern for public safety.[7] Yet the Amish are not forced to send their children to public schools despite a state law requiring all children to attend school through age 16. The Court said this law presented "a very real threat of undermining the Amish community and religious practice as it exists today"[8] Similarly, the Court ruled that a Florida town could not prevent animal sacrifice by practitioners of the Santeria religion because the local ordinance was neither neutral nor generally applicable and was targeted at that religion.[9]

These decisions show that balancing interests is never a simple process but involves deciding whether a specific civil liberty or some competing public interest is more compelling in a specific case.

DRAWING LINES

Along with balancing competing interests, court rulings draw the lines defining the limits of permissible conduct by the government or an individual in the context of a specific civil liberty. For example, despite the First Amendment protection of freedom of speech, it is obvious that some speech cannot be permitted; the classic example is falsely yelling "fire!" in a crowded theater. Therefore, the courts must interpret the law to draw the line between protected speech and impermissible speech.

The same applies to other civil liberties such as the establishment of religion, freedom of the press, freedom from illegal searches, or other due process rights. For example, the First Amendment prohibits the government from establishing an official religion, which the Court has carefully interpreted over the years to avoid "excessive entanglement" between any religion and the government. On these grounds, government-sponsored prayer in public schools has been banned since the early 1960s. But sometimes it is difficult to draw the line between acceptable and impermissible government involvement concerning religion in schools. One such ruling allowed taxpayer subsidies to fund parochial schools for buying books but not maps. This odd hair-splitting led the late senator Daniel Patrick Moynihan to quip, "What about atlases?"[10] Another difficult issue is the Fourth Amendment prohibition against "unreasonable searches and seizures" and the role of drug-sniffing dogs. Here the line-drawing involves deciding whether a sniff is a search, and if so, under what circumstances it is reasonable. Search and seizure cases also involve balancing interests: in this case, the individual freedoms of the target of police action and the broader interests in public order and security.

THE ORIGINS OF CIVIL LIBERTIES

> EXPLAIN WHY THE BILL OF RIGHTS WAS ADDED TO THE CONSTITUTION, AND HOW IT CAME TO APPLY TO THE STATES

Courts define the boundaries of civil liberties, but the other branches of government and the public often get involved as well. The earliest debates during the American Founding illustrate the broad public involvement concerning the basic questions of how our civil liberties would be defined: Should government be limited by an explicit statement of individual liberties? Would these limitations apply to the state governments or just the national government? How should these freedoms evolve as our society changes?

ORIGINS OF THE BILL OF RIGHTS

The original Constitution provided only limited protection of civil liberties: a guarantee of habeas corpus rights (a protection against illegal incarceration), a prohibition of bills of attainder (legislation punishing someone for a crime without the benefit of a trial), and ex post facto laws (laws that retroactively change the legal consequences of some behavior). There were a few attempts to include a broader statement of civil liberties, including one by George Mason and Elbridge Gerry five days before the Constitutional Convention adjourned. Mason said, "It would give great quiet to the people; and with the aid of the State

DRAWING LINES AND THE FOURTH AMENDMENT

The Supreme Court has ruled that police do not need a search warrant to have drug-sniffing dogs search luggage at an airport or a car that has been stopped for a traffic violation unrelated to drugs. Lower courts have also ruled that sniffs are not considered searches in a hotel hallway, school locker, outside a passenger train's sleeper compartments, or outside an apartment door. However, lower courts have been split on whether drug-sniffing dogs may be used outside a home without a warrant, due, in part, to a Supreme Court precedent giving homes stronger Fourth Amendment protection than cars, lockers, or other areas. For example, in 2001 the Court ruled that police needed a warrant to use a thermal imaging device outside a home in an attempt to detect marijuana growing under heat lamps inside.

Another case provided an opportunity for the Court to sort out the lower court conflict by determining which precedent from its own decisions was most relevant (the thermal imaging case involving homes or the dog-sniffing cases about airports and cars). The case involved a Houston man, David Smith, who was arrested when a trained dog smelled methamphetamine in his garage. Based on the dog's positive indication, the police obtained a search warrant and found the meth and other evidence of criminal activity. Smith was sentenced to 37 years in prison but has appealed the conviction on the grounds that the evidence against him was illegally obtained. His lawyers argued to the Supreme Court that the thermal imaging case was the relevant precedent and that the charges should be thrown out, saying, "No distinction exists between a thermal imaging device and drug sniffing dog in that they are both sense-enhancing and permit information regarding the interior of a home to be gathered which could not otherwise be obtained without a physical intrusion into a constitutionally protected area." The district attorney, urging the Court to reject the appeal, said the thermal imaging case was not relevant because the Court's ruling in that case was focused on protecting the original meaning of the Fourth Amendment from erosion by new technology. He said that in contrast to thermal imaging devices, "The use of a drug detection dog does not constitute the use of any technology, let alone advanced technology."[a] The Supreme Court declined to hear the case. While this means the conviction stands, it does not imply Court agreement or disagreement with the conviction. Interestingly, in the very same term in which the Court declined to hear this case, they decided the case noted above ruling that using a drug-sniffing dog during a routine traffic stop did not violate the Fourth Amendment.[b]

At the opposite end of the technological spectrum from a drug-sniffing dog are all the new surveillance technologies that are available to law enforcement officials. Video surveillance in public places, cell phones with tracking chips, collection of Wi-Fi data, "E-ZPass" highway toll collection systems, roadside assistance devices, and web traffic data kept by online merchants and social networking sites are some of the more obvi-

Federal agents use a drug-sniffing dog to inspect a car.

ous technologies that could be used by law enforcement officials. Others that are becoming more common or will be used soon include RFIDs (radio frequency identifications), which are the size of a grain of rice and transmit information wirelessly through radio waves; facial recognition software and iris scanners; "smart dust devices"—tiny wireless micromechanical sensors—that can detect light and movement; and drones, which have primarily been used for military purposes but also have vast potential for tracking suspects in any context.

In the context of rapidly changing technology, what is the public's "reasonable expectation" for privacy? Justice Alito raised this question in oral arguments in a Supreme Court case involving a GPS tracking device (we discuss the case later in the chapter). He said, "Technology is changing people's expectations of privacy....Maybe 10 years from now 90 percent of the population will be using social networking sites and they will have on average 500 friends and they will have allowed their friends to monitor their location 24 hours a day, 365 days a year, through the use of their cell phones. Then—what would the expectation of privacy be then?"[c]

Critical **Thinking** Questions

1. If you had to decide the case of the drug-sniffing dog, how would you have ruled? Do you think that homes should have stronger privacy expectations than cars? Even when it concerns illegal drugs?

2. How would you answer Justice Alito's question about the expectation of privacy in an era of rapidly changing technology? When should law enforcement officials have to get a warrant to monitor our behavior?

declarations, a bill might be prepared in a few hours." But their motion to appoint a committee to draft a bill of rights was rejected. Charles Pinckney and Gerry also tried to add a provision to protect the freedom of the press, but that too was rejected.[11]

Mason and Gerry opposed ratification of the Constitution, partly because it did not include a bill of rights, and many Antifederalists echoed this view. In a letter to James Madison, Thomas Jefferson predicted that four states would withhold ratification until a bill of rights was added.[12] Some states ratified the Constitution but urged Congress to draft specific protections for individuals' and states' rights from federal action (they believed protection of civil liberties from state actions should reside in state constitutions). In other states, the Antifederalists who lost the ratification battle continued making their case to the public and Congress. One of the most famous arguments came from the Antifederalists of Pennsylvania, who claimed that a bill of rights was needed to "fundamentally establish those unalienable and personal rights of men, without the full, free, and secure enjoyment of which there can be no liberty, and over which it is not necessary for a good government to have the control."[13] Their statement went on to outline many of those civil liberties that ultimately became the basis for the Bill of Rights.

Madison and other supporters of the Constitution agreed that the first Congress would take up the issue. State conventions submitted 124 amendments for consideration. That list was whittled down to 17 by the House and then to 12 by the Senate. This even dozen was approved by the House and sent to the states, which in 1791 ratified the 10 amendments that became the Bill of Rights.[14]

Despite the profound significance of the Bill of Rights, one point limited its reach: it applied only to the national government and not the states. For example, the First Amendment says that *"Congress* shall make no law" infringing on freedom of religion, speech, and the press, among others. Madison submitted another amendment, which he characterized as "the most valuable of the whole list," requiring states to protect some civil liberties: "The equal rights of conscience, the freedom of speech or of the press, and the right of trial by jury in criminal cases shall not be infringed by any State."[15] But Antifederalists feared another power grab by the Federalists in limiting states' rights, so the proposed amendment was voted down in Congress. This decision proved consequential because the national government was quite weak for the first half of our nation's history. Given that states exercised as much or more power over people's lives than the national government, it would have been more important for the Bill of Rights to limit the states than the federal government, but this did not occur.

CIVIL LIBERTIES BEFORE THE CIVIL WAR

When the Bill of Rights was ratified, the common understanding was that it applied only to the national government. However, Madison and others soon came to believe that these restrictions should also apply to the states.[16] Ultimately, the Supreme Court had to sort this out: In 1833 Chief Justice John Marshall wrote in *Barron v. Baltimore* that indeed the Bill of Rights applied only to the national government and not to the states (see Chapter 3).

In this case, John Barron sued the city of Baltimore when its street-paving project diverted streams and sent sand and gravel into the harbor area he owned, making it impossible for ships to use his once-valuable wharf. Barron claimed that the city owed him the lost value of his property because the Fifth Amendment

THE BILL OF RIGHTS: A STATEMENT OF OUR CIVIL LIBERTIES

First Amendment	Freedom of religion, speech, press, and assembly; the separation of church and state; and the right to petition the government.
Second Amendment	Right to bear arms.
Third Amendment	Protection against the forced quartering of troops in one's home.
Fourth Amendment	Protection from unreasonable searches and seizures; requirement of "probable cause" for search warrants.
Fifth Amendment	Protection from forced self-incrimination or double jeopardy (being tried twice for the same crime); no person can be deprived of life, liberty, or property without due process of law; private property cannot be taken for public use without just compensation; and no person can be tried for a serious crime without the indictment of a grand jury.
Sixth Amendment	Right of the accused to a speedy and public trial by an impartial jury, to an attorney, to confront witnesses, to a compulsory process for obtaining witnesses in his or her favor, and to counsel in all felony cases.
Seventh Amendment	Right to a trial by jury in civil cases involving common law.
Eighth Amendment	Protection from excessive bail, excessive fines, and cruel and unusual punishment.
Ninth Amendment	The enumeration of specific rights in the Constitution shall not be construed to deny other rights retained by the people. This has been interpreted to include a general right to privacy and other fundamental rights.
Tenth Amendment	Powers not delegated by the Constitution to the national government, nor prohibited by it to the states, are reserved to the states or to the people.

says that private property may not be "taken for public use without just compensation." The Maryland state constitution did not have a similar provision, so Barron sued under the U.S. Constitution. He won in district court but lost on appeal. The Supreme Court agreed with the appeals court, saying that the Bill of Rights "demanded security against the apprehended encroachments of the General Government—not against those of the local governments," and "contain no expression indicating an intention to apply them to the state governments."[17]

Thus, the Bill of Rights played a surprisingly small role for more than a century. The Supreme Court used it only once before 1866 to invalidate a federal action—in the infamous *Dred Scott* case that contributed to the Civil War.

SELECTIVE INCORPORATION AND THE FOURTEENTH AMENDMENT

Civil War Amendments
The Thirteenth, Fourteenth, and Fifteenth Amendments to the Constitution, which abolished slavery and granted civil liberties and voting rights to freed slaves after the Civil War.

The significance of the Bill of Rights increased somewhat with the ratification of the Fourteenth Amendment in 1868. It was one of the three **Civil War Amendments** that attempted to guarantee equal rights as citizens of the United States to the newly freed slaves. (The other two Civil War Amendments were the Thirteenth, which abolished slavery, and the Fifteenth, which gave male former slaves the right to vote.) Northern politicians were concerned that southerners would deny basic rights to the former slaves, so the sweeping language of the Fourteenth Amendment was adopted.

Section 1 of the Fourteenth Amendment says:

All persons born or naturalized in the United States, and subject to the juris-diction thereof, are citizens of the United States and of the State wherein they reside. No State shall make or enforce any law which shall abridge the privi-leges or immunities of citizens of the United States; nor shall any State deprive any person of life, liberty, or property, without due process of law; nor deny to any person within its jurisdiction the equal protection of the laws.

This language was intended to make sure that states would not deny newly freed slaves the full protection of the law.[18] The **due process clause**, which forbids any state from denying "life, liberty, or property, without due process of law," led to an especially important expansion of civil liberties because the similar clause of the Fifth Amendment had previously been interpreted by the Court to apply only to the federal government.

EVOLVING INTERPRETATIONS BY THE SUPREME COURT

However, in 1873, in its first opportunity to interpret the Fourteenth Amendment, the Court continued to rule in favor of protection from national government actions only. The case involved a group of butchers and slaughterhouse owners in Louisiana who were about to be run out of business by a law passed by the cor-rupt state legislature, which effectively gave a slaughterhouse monopoly to a single firm. The owners of rival slaughterhouses sued the state under the "privileges and immunities" clause of the Fourteenth Amendment, arguing that the state govern-ment was denying their basic rights.

Despite the clear language of the amendment saying that "no State shall make or enforce any law" limiting citizens' legal "privileges or immunities," the Court embraced the "dual citizenship" idea set forth in *Barron v. Baltimore* and stated that the Fourteenth Amendment protected U.S. citizens against the actions of only the national government, not the state governments. The Court also rejected the plaintiffs' claim that the state was denying them "the equal protection of the laws" on the grounds that the Fourteenth Amendment was intended to strike down laws that discriminated against blacks.[19] One constitutional scholar observed that all that remained of the Fourteenth Amendment after this decision was a vague understanding that it was intended to give citizenship to the newly freed slaves.[20] In other words, all that remained was the first sentence!

Over the next 50 years, a minority of justices tried mightily to strengthen the power of the Fourteenth Amendment and use it to protect civil liberties against state government action. The first step was an 1897 case in which the Court ruled that the Fourteenth Amendment's due process clause forbade the state of Illinois from taking private property without just compensation. However, the decision did not specifically mention the Fifth Amendment's compensation clause.[21] The next step came in a self-incrimination case in which a state judge gave jury instruc-tions that included references to the fact that the accused did not take the stand in his defense. The Supreme Court upheld his conviction but said, "It is possible that some of the personal rights safeguarded in the first eight amendments against National action may also be safeguarded against state action, because a denial of them would be a denial of the due process of law."[22] Thus, in both the property and self-incrimination cases, the Supreme Court started to use the Fourteenth Amendment to prohibit state governments from violating individual rights—but without specific reference to the Bill of Rights.

due process clause Part of the Fourteenth Amendment that forbids states from denying "life, liberty, or property" to any person with-out due process of law. (A nearly identical clause in the Fifth Amend-ment applies only to the national government.)

This progression culminated in the 1925 case *Gitlow v. New York*. Here the Court said for the first time that the Fourteenth Amendment incorporated one of the amendments in the Bill of Rights and applied it to the states. The case involved Benjamin Gitlow, a radical socialist convicted under New York's Criminal Anarchy Act of 1902 for advocating the overthrow of the government. The Court upheld his conviction, arguing that his writings were the "language of direct incitement," but also warned state governments that there were limits on such suppression of speech.

APPLYING CIVIL LIBERTIES TO THE STATES

selective incorporation The process through which the civil liberties granted in the Bill of Rights were applied to the states on a case-by-case basis through the Fourteenth Amendment.

Slowly over the next 50 years, most civil liberties covered in the Bill of Rights were applied to the states on a case-by-case basis through the Fourteenth Amendment (see Table 4.1). However, this process of **selective incorporation** was not smooth and incremental; rather it progressed in surges. The first flurry of activity came in the 1930s when most of the First Amendment was incorporated, requiring the states to allow a free press, the right to assemble, free exercise of religion, and the right to petition. The next flurry came in the 1960s with a series of cases on criminal defendants' rights and due process.

Why the gap of nearly a quarter century (with only two exceptions)?[23] A case involving the double jeopardy clause of the Fifth Amendment determined that some rights were so fundamental that they could not be denied by the states without violating the "due process clause" of the Fourteenth Amendment, while if others were denied (such as being tried twice for the same crime) it would not undermine our sense of "ordered liberty."[24] The example the Court gave of these fundamental rights was the "freedom of thought and speech." By elevating certain rights, this ruling meant that civil liberties would be *selectively* incorporated by the Fourteenth Amendment rather than applied as a group to the states. Thus, for the next 25 years, the Court largely confined selective incorporation to the First Amendment. However, this did not allow the states to ignore the due process of law. By choosing which cases to hear, the Court continued to monitor the states for conduct that, in the words of Justice Felix Frankfurter, "shocked the conscience," or in the blunt language of Justice Oliver Wendell Holmes, "[makes] you vomit."[25]

The second flurry of activity broadly applied the Fourteenth Amendment to the Bill of Rights in a series of cases involving criminal defendants' rights. After another 38-year gap, the incorporation of the Second Amendment's right to bear arms in 2010 meant all the significant amendments now apply to state and local governments. As a result, the Bill of Rights has evolved from the nineteenth century's limitations that affected only national government action to a robust set of protections for freedom and liberty today.

DESCRIBE THE MAJOR FIRST AMENDMENT RIGHTS RELATED TO FREEDOM OF SPEECH

FREEDOM OF SPEECH, ASSEMBLY, AND THE PRESS

The First Amendment's ringing words are the most famous statement of personal freedoms in the Constitution: "Congress shall make no law respecting an establishment of religion, or prohibiting the free exercise thereof; or abridging the freedom of speech, or of the press; or the right of the people peaceably to assemble,

TABLE » 4.1

SELECTIVE INCORPORATION

AMENDMENT	ISSUE	CASE
First Amendment	Freedom of speech	*Gitlow v. New York* (1925)
	Freedom of the press	*Near v. Minnesota* (1931)
	Freedom of assembly	*DeJonge v. Oregon* (1937)
	Right to petition the government	*Hague v. CIO* (1939)
	Free exercise of religion	*Hamilton v. Regents of the University of California* (1934), *Cantwell v. Connecticut* (1940)
	Separation of church and state	*Everson v. Board of Education of Ewing Township* (1947)
Second Amendment	Right to bear arms	*McDonald v. Chicago* (2010)
Fourth Amendment	Protection from unreasonable search and seizure	*Wolf v. Colorado (1949), Mapp v. Ohio* (1961)[a]
Fifth Amendment	Protection from forced self-incrimination	*Malloy v. Hogan* (1964)
	Protection from double jeopardy	*Benton v. Maryland* (1969)
Sixth Amendment	Right to a public trial	*In re Oliver 333 U.S. 257* (1948)
	Right to a fair trial and an attorney in death-penalty cases	*Powell v. Alabama* (1932)
	Right to an attorney in all felony cases	*Gideon v. Wainwright* (1963)
	Right to an attorney in cases involving jail time	*Argersinger v. Hamlin* (1972)
	Right to a jury trial in a criminal case	*Duncan v. Louisiana* (1968)
	Right to cross-examine a witness	*Pointer v. Texas* (1965)
	Right to compel witnesses to testify who are vital for the defendant's case	*Washington v. Texas* (1967)
Eighth Amendment	Protection from cruel and unusual punishment	*Robinson v. California* (1962)[b]
	Protection from excessive bail	*Schilb v. Kuebel* (1971)[c]
Ninth Amendment	Right to privacy and other nonenumerated, fundamental rights	*Griswold v. Connecticut* (1965)[d]

NOT INCORPORATED

AMENDMENT	ISSUE	CASE
Third Amendment	Prohibition against the quartering of troops in private homes	
Fifth Amendment	Right to indictment by a grand jury	
Seventh Amendment	Right to a jury trial in a civil case	
Eighth Amendment	Prohibition against excessive fines	

[a]*Wolf v. Colorado* applied the Fourth Amendment to the states (which meant that states could not engage in unreasonable searches and seizures); *Mapp v. Ohio* applied the exclusionary rule to the states (which excludes the use in a trial of illegally obtained evidence).

[b]Some sources list *Louisiana ex rel. Francis v. Resweber* (1947) as the first case that incorporated the Eighth Amendment. While the decision mentioned the Fifth and Eighth Amendments in the context of the due process clause of the Fourteenth Amendment, this argument was not included in the majority opinion that upheld as constitutional the bizarre double-electrocution of Willie Francis (the electric chair malfunctioned on the first attempt but was successful on the second attempt; see Abraham and Perry, *Freedom and the Court*, pp. 71–72).

[c]Justice Blackmun "assumed" in this case that "the 8th Amendment's proscription of excessive bail [applies] to the states through the 14th Amendment," but later decisions did not seem to share this view. However, Justices Stevens and O'Connor agreed with Blackmun's view in *Browning-Ferris v. Kelco Disposal* (1989). Some sources argue that the excessive bail clause of the Eighth Amendment is unincorporated.

[d]Justice Goldberg argued for explicit incorporation of the Ninth Amendment in a concurring opinion joined by Justices Warren and Brennan. The opinion of the Court referred more generally to a privacy right rooted in five amendments, including the Ninth, but did not explicitly argue for incorporation.

and to petition the Government for a redress of grievances." (The "How It Works" diagram on page 137 illustrates how much is packed into this one amendment.) As we noted earlier, defining the scope of our civil liberties depends on balancing interests and drawing lines. This is especially true of First Amendment freedoms, which can be envisioned on a continuum from most to least protected based on the Supreme Court cases that have tested their limits.

GENERALLY PROTECTED EXPRESSION

Any time you attend a religious service or a political rally, write an article for your student paper, or express a political idea, you are being protected by the First Amendment. However, the nature of this protection is continually evolving due to political forces and shifting constitutional interpretations. For much of our nation's history, the freedom of speech and press were not strongly protected. Only recently have the courts developed a complex continuum ranging from strongly protected political speech to less protected speech.

STANDARDS FOR PROTECTION

The basis for the continuum of protected speech is rooted in the content of the speech. Content-based regulation of speech is typically not allowed by the Court (unless it falls into one of the categories of exceptions we outline later). For example, the Court struck down a local ordinance that banned picketing outside of schools except for labor picketing.[26] This ordinance was content-based regulation because it favored one form of speech (from labor unions) over others. Such regulation is subject to the **strict scrutiny** standard of judicial review, which means the regulation must be narrowly tailored (that is, the least restrictive means) to serve a compelling state interest. In most cases, this means that the speech will be protected and the regulation struck down. If a regulation is content neutral and does not favor any given viewpoint over another, then it is subject to the less demanding **intermediate scrutiny** standard. This means that the government must only demonstrate a substantial interest, that the interest must be unrelated to the content of the speech, and that there are alternative opportunities for communication.[27]

POLITICAL SPEECH

Freedom of speech got off to a rocky start when Congress passed the Alien and Sedition Acts in 1798. The controversial Sedition Act made it a crime to "write, print, utter or publish . . . any false, scandalous and malicious writing or writings against the government of the United States." Supporters of the four acts claimed they were necessary to strengthen the national government in response to the French Revolution, but in reality they were an attempt by the governing Federalist Party to neutralize the opposition Democratic-Republican Party. As many as 25 people, mostly newspaper editors, were tried under the law and 10 were jailed, including Benjamin Franklin's grandson. The outcry against the laws helped propel Thomas Jefferson to the presidency in 1800. Jefferson pardoned the convicted editors, Congress repealed one of the acts in 1802, and the

strict scrutiny The highest level of scrutiny the courts use when determining whether a law is constitutional. To pass this test, the law or policy must be shown to serve a "compelling state interest" or goal, it must be narrowly tailored to achieve that goal, and it must be the least restrictive means of achieving the goal.

intermediate scrutiny The middle level of scrutiny the courts use when determining whether a law is constitutional. To pass this test, the law or policy must further an important government interest in a way that is "substantially related" to that interest. That is, the law must use means that are a close fit to the government's goal and substantially broader than is necessary to accomplish that goal.

others were allowed to expire before the Supreme Court had a chance to rule them unconstitutional.

The next big challenge to freedom of speech came from the states. During the battles over slavery early in the nineteenth century, northern states outlawed positive statements about slavery, while southern states prohibited criticism of slavery. By the end of the nineteenth century, such sedition laws prohibiting behavior considered subversive were quite common at the state level, and hundreds of people had been jailed for criticizing the government and its policies (recall that the First Amendment did not apply to the states in the nineteenth century).

World War I prompted the harshest crackdowns on free speech since the Sedition Act of 1798. The most important case from this period involved the general secretary of the Socialist Party, Charles Schenk, who opposed U.S. involvement in the war. He had printed a leaflet urging young men to resist the draft. Schenk was arrested under the Espionage Act of 1917 that prohibited "interfering with military or naval operations," including the draft. He appealed all the way to the Supreme Court, arguing that the First Amendment permitted him to protest the war and urge others to resist the draft, but the Court sustained his conviction, noting that free speech is not an absolute right:

> *The most stringent protection of free speech would not protect a man in falsely shouting fire in a theatre and causing a panic. . . . The question in every case is whether the words used are used in such circumstances and are of such a nature as to create a clear and present danger that they will bring about the substantive evils that Congress has a right to prevent.*[28]

This **clear and present danger test** meant that the government could suppress speech it thought was dangerous (in this instance, preventing the

clear and present danger test
Established in *Schenk v. United States*, this test allows the government to restrict certain types of speech deemed dangerous.

COMM[UNIST PA]RTY ORGANIZATION U.S.A-FEB. 9, 1950

SENATOR JOSEPH MCCARTHY STANDS in front of a map purporting to show communist activity in the United States. McCarthy was a central figure in the post–World War II Red Scare, during which Americans suspected of supporting communism were persecuted and imprisoned.

direct incitement test Established in *Brandenberg v. Ohio*, this test protects threatening speech under the First Amendment unless that speech aims to and is likely to cause imminent "lawless action."

government from fighting the war). However, critics of the decision argue that Schenk's actions were not dangerous for the country.[29]

While Schenk's actions would have been legal under the current standard for protecting speech, things got worse for supporters of the First Amendment before they got better. Another socialist leader, Eugene V. Debs, was sentenced to federal prison for making a speech in 1918 that condemned U.S. involvement in World War I, and two newspaper publishers were jailed for publishing articles critical of the war. Both high-profile convictions were sustained by the Court.[30] Then Congress passed the more restrictive Sedition Act of 1918, which outlawed any "disloyal, profane, scurrilous, or abusive language about the form of government, the Constitution, soldiers and sailors, flag or uniform of the armed forces" and any words that favored the cause of the German empire or opposed the cause of the United States. In the first test case for the new law, the Court upheld the conviction of six anarchists who supported the cause of the Bolsheviks in Russia and urged the "workers of the world" to strike.

Justice Oliver Wendell Holmes, author of the *Schenk* decision and the clear and present danger test, had had enough. He dissented in the anarchists' case, arguing that the "surreptitious publishing of a silly leaflet by an unknown man" posed no danger to the country. In one of the most famous statements of the importance of the freedom of speech, he touted the "free trade in ideas" saying, "The best test of truth is the power of the thought to get itself accepted in the competition of the market. . . . [W]e should be eternally vigilant against attempts to check the expression of opinion that we loathe and believe to be fraught with death."[31] This notion of the marketplace of ideas in which good ideas triumph over bad is still central to modern defenses of the First Amendment.

Over the next several decades the Court struggled to draw the line between dangerous speech and words that were simply unpopular. During the Red Scare of the late 1940s and early 1950s, the Court had many opportunities to defend unpopular speech, but for the most part they declined. For example, in 1951 the Court upheld the conviction of 11 members of the Communist Party under the Smith Act which banned the advocacy of force or violence against the United States.[32]

In 1969, the Court established a strong protection for free speech that still holds today. This case involved a leader of the Ku Klux Klan who made a threatening speech at a cross-burning rally that was subsequently shown on television. Twelve hooded figures were shown, many with weapons. The speech said that "revengence" [*sic*] might be taken if "our president, our Congress, our Supreme Court continues to suppress the white, Caucasian race." He continued, "We are marching on Congress July the Fourth, four hundred thousand strong." The Klan leader was convicted under the Ohio law banning "sabotage, violence, or unlawful methods of terrorism as a means of accomplishing industrial or political reform," but the Court unanimously reversed his conviction, arguing that threatening speech could not be suppressed just because it sounded dangerous. Specifically, the **direct incitement test** holds that speech is protected "except where such advocacy is directed to inciting or producing imminent lawless action and is likely to incite or produce such action."[33] Under this standard, most, if not all, of the sedition convictions during World War I and the Red Scare would have been overturned.

However, direct incitement is not the only basis for limiting speech that could be viewed as political. One example involved a high school student from Juneau,

Alaska, who was suspended from school for unfurling a banner on a public side-walk that said "Bong Hits 4 Jesus." The incident occurred as the Olympic torch relay passed through Juneau on its way to the 2002 Winter Games in Utah. The student sued the school, claiming his First Amendment rights were violated, but the Supreme Court agreed with the school, saying "It was reasonable for [the principal] to conclude that the banner promoted illegal drug use—and that failing to act would send a powerful message to the students in her charge." Dissenters lamented the invention of "a special First Amendment rule permitting the censorship of any student speech that mentions drugs," based on "a silly, nonsensical banner."[34]

SYMBOLIC SPEECH

The use of signs, symbols, or other unspoken acts or methods to communicate in a political manner—**symbolic speech**—enjoys many of the same protections as regular speech. For example, during the Vietnam War the Court protected the First Amendment right of a war protestor to wear an American flag patch sewn on the seat of his pants,[35] high school students' right to wear an armband to protest the war,[36] and an individual's right to tape a peace symbol on the flag and fly it upside-down outside an apartment window.[37] Lower courts had convicted these protestors under state laws that protected the American flag, or in the armband case, under a school policy that prohibited wearing armbands to protest the Vietnam War. In the flag desecration case involving the peace symbol, the Court stated that protected "speech" need not be verbal: "there can be little doubt that appellant communicated through the use of symbols."[38]

A 1989 case provided the strongest protection for symbolic speech yet. The case involved a man who burned a flag outside the 1984 Republican national convention in Texas, chanting along with other protestors, "America the red, white, and blue, we spit on you. You stand for plunder, you will go under." The Court refrained from critiquing the jingle, but its 5–4 decision overturned the man's conviction under Texas's flag desecration law on the grounds that symbolic political speech is protected by the First Amendment.[39] In response to this unpopular decision, Congress passed the Flag Protection Act of 1989, which the Court also struck down as an unconstitutional infringement on political expression.[40] Congress then attempted to pass a constitutional amendment to overturn the Court decision; the House passed the amendment six times between 1995 and 2005 with the necessary two-thirds vote, but each time the measure failed by a narrow margin in the Senate (by just one vote in 2006).

Although the Court has protected flag burning and other forms of symbolic speech, there are limits, especially when the symbolic speech conflicts with another substantial governmental interest. Here the critical test is whether the action can be regulated for important reasons unrelated to ideas. If so, then the "intermediate scrutiny" standard will apply. For example, Vietnam War protestors who burned their draft cards were not protected by the First Amendment because their actions interfered with Congress's constitutional authority to "raise and support" armies and the purpose of the draft was not to suppress speech.[41]

Spending money in political campaigns may also be protected by the First Amendment since it provides the means for more conventional types of political speech. Here the central question is whether the government can control campaign contributions and spending for a broader public purpose such as controlling

symbolic speech Nonverbal expression, such as the use of signs or symbols. It benefits from many of the same constitutional protections as verbal speech.

THE AMERICAN FLAG IS A POPULAR target for protesters: it has been spat upon, shredded, turned into underwear, and burned, as it was during this 2004 demonstration at the Democratic National Convention in Boston. Despite multiple efforts in Congress to ban flag desecration, these activities remain constitutionally protected symbolic speech.

corruption, or whether such laws violate the First Amendment rights of candidates or their supporters. You probably have heard the old saying "Money talks," which implies that money is speech. Given the importance of advertising in modern campaigns, limitations on raising and spending money could limit the ability of candidates and groups to reach voters with their message. The Court has walked a tightrope on this one, balancing the public interest in honest and ethical elections and the First Amendment rights of candidates and their advocates. The Court has upheld individual candidates' right to spend their own money in federal elections, but presidential candidates give up that right if they accept federal campaign funds (taxpayers' money) in a presidential election. Also, candidates in federal elections are subject to limits on the types and size of contributions they can receive, and they must report all contributions and spending to the Federal Election Commission.[42]

The Bipartisan Campaign Reform Act, which went into effect for the 2004 elections, included a "Millionaires' Amendment" that lifted restrictions on campaign contributions for candidates whose opponent spent more than $350,000 of their own money in the election. This attempt to level the campaign finance playing field was struck down by the Supreme Court in 2008 as a violation of wealthy candidates' First Amendment rights.[43] In 2010, the Court also extended First Amendment rights to corporations and labor unions that want to spend money on campaign ads (these cases are discussed in more detail in Chapter 8). However, the Court upheld a ban on unlimited "soft money" contributions because it was seen by the Court as the type of contribution with the most potential for corruption.[44]

Student fees as a form of symbolic speech came up in a case in 2000 involving student activity fees at the University of Wisconsin. A group of students argued that they should not have to pay fees to fund groups whose activities they opposed, including a student environmental group, a gay and bisexual student center, a community legal office, an AIDS support network, a campus women's center, and the Wisconsin Student Public Interest Research Group. The Court ruled that mandatory student fees could continue to support the full range of groups as long as the process for allocating money was "viewpoint neutral." The Court also said that student referendums that could add or cut money for specific groups violated viewpoint neutrality. The potential for the majority to censor unpopular views was unacceptable to the Court, since "the whole theory of viewpoint neutrality is that minority views are treated with the same respect as are majority views."[45]

HATE SPEECH

Free speech has been a hot topic on many college campuses in the context of **hate speech**. Do people have a right to say things that are offensive or abusive, especially in terms of race, gender, and sexual orientation? By the mid-1990s, more than 350 public colleges and universities said no by regulating some forms of hate speech.[46] One example was a speech code adopted at the University of Michigan that prohibited "any behavior, verbal or physical, that stigmatizes or victimizes an individual on the basis of race, ethnicity, religion, sex, sexual orientation, creed, national origin, ancestry, age, marital status, handicap, or Vietnam veteran status," and "creates an intimidating, hostile, or demeaning environment for educational pursuits, employment or participation in University-sponsored extra-curricular activities."[47] The Supreme Court has yet to rule on this issue, but lower courts struck down the University of Michigan's speech code as well as similar rules at several other universities. If the Court took up any of these cases, they would be likely to strike down the speech codes because they are not "content neutral" regulations and they do not meet the direct incitement test of targeting only expressions that would spur imminent violence.

One final significant issue combines the topics of symbolic speech and hate speech. Can a person who burned a cross on a black family's lawn be convicted under a city ordinance that prohibited conduct "arous[ing] anger, alarm, or resentment in others on the basis of race, color, creed, religion, or gender"? Or is the ordinance an unconstitutional limit on First Amendment rights? The Court said the cross burner could be punished for arson, terrorism, trespassing, or other violations of the law, but he could not be convicted under this St. Paul, Minnesota, ordinance because it was overly broad and vague. The Court said, "Let there be no mistake about our belief that burning a cross in someone's front yard is reprehensible. But St. Paul has sufficient means at its disposal to prevent such behavior without adding the First Amendment to the fire."[48] The city ordinance was unconstitutional because it took selective aim at a disfavored message; it constituted "viewpoint discrimination." However, the Court has since upheld more carefully worded bans of cross burning. Eleven years after the St. Paul case, the Court ruled that Virginia could prohibit cross burning if there was an intent to intimidate. The Court also noted that the law was content neutral because it did not engage in viewpoint discrimination: any burning of a cross in a threatening context was illegal.[49]

ARE LAWS BANNING HATE SPEECH constitutional? Sometimes yes, but the threshold is relatively high. These Ku Klux Klan members are free to hold rallies, preach racism and xenophobia, and burn crosses, as long as they do not directly incite violence or display an "intent to intimidate."

FREEDOM OF ASSEMBLY

The right to assemble peaceably has been consistently protected by the Supreme Court. In an important 1937 case that applied this part of the First Amendment to the states for the first time, the Court upheld the right to teach communist doctrine in public meetings, saying that the right to assemble is "one that cannot be denied without violating those fundamental principles which lie at the base of all civil and political institutions."[50] Peaceful civil rights protestors who were arrested for disturbing the peace had their convictions overturned when the Court said the state of South Carolina could not "make criminal the peaceful expression of unpopular views."[51] Perhaps the most famous assembly case involved a neo-Nazi group that wanted to march in a suburb of Chicago that had 70,000 residents, nearly 60 percent of whom were Jewish, including many Holocaust survivors. The village passed ordinances that effectively banned the group from marching, arguing that residents would be so upset by the Nazi marchers that they might become violent. But the lower courts did not accept this argument, ruling that if "the audience is so offended by the ideas being expressed that it becomes disorderly and attempts to silence the speaker, it is the duty of the police to attempt to protect the speaker, not to silence his speech."[52] Otherwise, the right to assemble would be restricted by a "heckler's veto." The Court elaborated on this responsibility to protect expressions of unpopular views by striking down another town's ordinance that allowed them to charge a higher permit fee to groups whose march would likely require more police protection.[53]

While broad protection is provided for peaceable assemblies, governments may regulate the time, manner, and place of expression as long as the regulation does not favor certain groups or messages over others. For example, antiabortion protestors were not allowed to picket a doctor's home in Brookfield, Wisconsin. The Court ruled that the ordinance banning all residential picketing was content neutral and that there was a government interest in preserving the "sanctity of the home, the one retreat to which men and women can repair to escape from the tribulations of their daily pursuits."[54] "Time, manner, and place" restrictions also may be invoked for practical reasons. If the Ku Klux Klan planned to hold a march around the football stadium on the day of a game, the city council could deny them a permit and suggest they choose another day that would be more convenient. The legal standard for these regulations is that they are "reasonable." While vague, this standard allows the courts to balance the right to assemble against other practical considerations.

FREEDOM OF THE PRESS

The task of balancing interests is central to many First Amendment cases involving freedom of the press. Which is more important, the First Amendment freedom of the press to disclose details about current events or the Sixth Amendment right to a fair trial, which may require keeping important information out of the public eye? When do national security concerns prevail over journalists' right to keep citizens informed? The general issue here is **prior restraint**, the government's right to prevent the media from publishing something. When applied to information concerning an ongoing trial, the prohibition to publish is called a **gag order**.

Prior restraint has never been clearly defined by the Court, but several landmark cases have set a very high bar for applying it. The first involved a Minnesota law that banned "obscene, lewd and lascivious" publications or "malicious, scandalous and defamatory" content. Under this law, the state shut down a racist, bigoted publication that railed against many groups of people. The Court subsequently struck down the law in *Near v. Minnesota*, saying, "The fact that the liberty of the press may be abused by miscreant purveyors of scandal does not make any less necessary the immunity of the press from previous restraint."[55] However, the Court did not specify when prior restraint would be acceptable.

In 1971, the Pentagon Papers case involved disclosure of parts of the top-secret report on internal planning for the Vietnam War. This incredibly divided case had nine separate written opinions! By a 6–3 margin the Court decided that the government could not prevent the publication of the Pentagon Papers, but at least five justices supported the view that, under some circumstances, the government could use prior restraint—though they could not agree on the standard.[56] For some of the justices, a crucial consideration was the papers' revelation that the U.S. government had lied about its involvement in and the progress of the Vietnam War. Justice Hugo Black noted the importance of this point saying, "Only a free and unrestrained press can effectively expose deception in government."[57]

Prior restraint has taken on new significance in the war on terror. The media, especially the *New York Times*, skirmished with the Bush administration over publishing stories on various classified programs, including extraordinary rendition of suspected terrorists, domestic surveillance, and the Terrorist Finance Tracking Program, which monitors all large financial transactions in the international banking system. The sensational leaking of more than 91,000 reports concerning the war in Afghanistan by WikiLeaks ratcheted up the stakes. Some members of

prior restraint A limit on freedom of the press that allows the government to prohibit the media from publishing certain materials.

gag order An aspect of prior restraint that allows the government to prohibit the media from publishing anything related to an ongoing trial.

Congress called the leaks "treason" and urged for prosecution. However, supporters of an unrestrained press point to the Pentagon Papers case as precedent for the role of journalists in holding the government accountable. They argue that the conduct of war and programs such as warrantless wiretapping of U.S. citizens may violate international or domestic law and the public has the right to know about them. The Justice Department investigated leaks from the National Security Administration believed to be the source of some of the *New York Times* stories and promised to prosecute the leakers and the journalists. Congress responded by trying to pass the Free Flow of Information Act, which would have given journalists some protection of confidential sources and information. The bill passed the House in 2007 and 2009 but was killed both times when the Senate failed to get enough votes to prevent a filibuster.

THE PUBLICATION OF THOUSANDS of government documents, including some sensitive reports and communications, raised new questions about press freedom and national security. Here, WikiLeaks founder Julian Assange discusses the leaked documents.

Prior restraint also may be an issue in media coverage of a trial, but gag orders are allowed only when media coverage would make it impossible for the defendant to have a fair trial. In a 1976 case involving a multiple murder in Nebraska, the Court struck down a gag order that prevented the press from describing the facts of the case. The Court said, "The protection against prior restraint should have particular force as applied to reporting of criminal proceedings."[58] Gag orders that prohibit participants in a trial (jury members, witnesses, lawyers, law enforcement officials) from talking to the media operate under more complicated precedents that depend on whether this media contact would undermine a fair trial.[59]

The forms of expression discussed in this section—speech, assembly, and press—all have strong protection from the First Amendment. The strongest protections are for content-based expression; that is, if a regulation is trying to limit *what* can be said, the Court applies the "strict scrutiny" standard and usually strikes down the regulation. However, there are exceptions, such as speech that directly incites an imminent danger. If the regulation is content neutral and does not favor one viewpoint over another, then it is easier to uphold. But even then, the government must have a substantial reason for limiting expression.

LESS PROTECTED SPEECH AND PUBLICATIONS

Some forms of speech do not warrant the same level of protection as political speech because they do not contribute to public debate or express ideas that have important social value. Four categories of speech may be more easily regulated by the government than political speech: fighting words, slander and libel, commercial speech, and obscenity.

FIGHTING WORDS

Governments may regulate **fighting words**, "which by their very utterance inflict injury or tend to incite an immediate breach of the peace."[60] Such laws must be narrowly written; it is not acceptable to ban all foul language, and the prohib-

fighting words Forms of expression that "by their very utterance" can incite violence. These can be regulated by the government but are often difficult to define.

ited speech must target a single person rather than a group. Moreover, the question of whether certain words provoke a backlash depends on the reaction of the targeted person. Inflammatory words directed at Archbishop Emeritus Desmond Tutu would not be fighting words because he would turn the other cheek, whereas the same words yelled at musician Busta Rhymes or actor Sean Penn *would* be fighting words because they would probably deck you. The Court has further clarified the test, based on "what persons of common intelligence would understand to be words likely to cause an average addressee to fight."[61] While this is a more objective test than the previous subjective standard, the fighting words doctrine has still been difficult to apply.

SLANDER AND LIBEL

A more extensive line of cases prohibiting speech concerns **slander**, spoken false statements that damage someone's reputation, and **libel**, written statements that do the same thing. As in many areas of First Amendment law, it is difficult to draw the line between permissible speech and slander or libel. The current legal standard distinguishes between speech about a public figure, such as a politician or celebrity, and about a regular person. In short, public figures must have much thicker skin than the average person because it is much more difficult for them to prove libel. A public figure has to demonstrate that the defamatory statement was made with "actual malice" and "with knowledge that it was false or with reckless disregard of whether it was false or not."[62]

One of the most famous libel cases was brought against *Hustler* magazine by the Reverend Jerry Falwell, a famous televangelist and political activist. Falwell sued *Hustler* for libel and emotional distress after the magazine published a parody of a liquor advertisement depicting him in a "drunken incestuous rendezvous with his mother in an outhouse" (this quote is from the Supreme Court case).[63] The lower court said that the parody wasn't believable, so *Hustler* couldn't be sued for libel, but they awarded Falwell damages for emotional distress. The Court overturned this decision, saying that public figures and public officials have to put up with such things and compared the parody to outrageous political cartoons, which have always been protected by the First Amendment.

COMMERCIAL SPEECH

Commercial speech, which mostly refers to advertising, has evolved from having almost no protection under the First Amendment to enjoying quite strong protection. One early case involved a business owner who distributed leaflets to advertise rides on his submarine that was docked in New York City. Under city ordinances, leafleting was permitted only if it was devoted to "information or a public protest," but not for a commercial purpose. The plaintiff changed the leaflet to have his advertisement on one side and a statement protesting a city policy on the other side (clever guy!). He was arrested anyway, and the Court upheld his conviction, saying that the city council had the right to regulate the distribution of leaflets.[64]

The Court became much more sympathetic to commercial speech in the 1970s when it struck down a law against advertising prescription drug prices and one prohibiting placing newspaper racks on city streets to distribute commercial publications such as real estate guides.[65] The key decision in 1980 established a test that is still central today. The Court ruled that the government may regulate commercial speech if it concerns an illegal activity, if the advertisement is misleading, or if regulating speech directly advances a substantial government interest and the regulation is not excessive. In practice, this test means that commercial speech can be regulated but that the government has to have a very good reason to do it.[66] Even public health concerns have not been allowed to override commercial speech rights. For example, the Court struck down a Massachusetts regulation that limited the content of advertisements aimed at children (the ban on R. J. Reynolds's Joe Camel character is the classic example) in a manner that was more restrictive than federal law.

OBSCENITY

One area in which the press has never experienced complete freedom involves the publication of pornography and material considered obscene. The difficulty arises in deciding where to draw the line. Nearly everyone would agree that child pornography should not be published[67] and that pornography should not be available to minors. However, beyond these points there is not much consensus. For example, some people are offended by nude paintings in art museums, while others enjoy watching hard-core X-rated movies.

Defining obscenity has proven difficult for the courts. In an often-quoted moment of frustration, Justice Potter Stewart wrote that he could not define obscenity, but "I know it when I see it."[68] In its first attempt, the Court ruled that a particular publication could be banned if an "average person, applying contemporary community standards" would find that the material appeals to prurient interests and is "utterly without redeeming social importance." This standard proved unworkable because lower courts differed in their interpretation. The Court took another stab at it in 1973 in a case that gave rise to the **Miller test**, which is still applied today.[69] The test has three standards that must all be met in order for material to be banned as obscene: if it appeals to prurient interests, if it is "patently offensive," and if the work as a whole lacks serious literary, artistic, political, or scientific value. The Court also clarified that *local* community standards were to apply rather than a single national standard, reasoning that what passes for obscenity in Sioux City, Iowa, probably would be considered pretty tame in Las Vegas.

Congress and the president also get in on the act of controlling obscenity. In general, they take a more conservative approach: they seek legislation to limit obscenity. In contrast, the Court focuses on whether certain speech is protected. Furthermore, the Court tends to rein in Congress and the president when they try to limit obscene speech.

Recent efforts have focused on the Internet as a pornography medium. Congress passed the Communications Decency Act in 1996, which criminalized the use of any computer network to display "indecent" material, unless the provider could offer an effective way of screening out potential users under age 18. The Court struck down the law in 1997 because it was overly vague and because limiting access to Web sites based on age is technically impossible. This ruling gives the Internet the same free speech protection as print.[70] But Congress wasn't going to give up without a fight. In 1998 it enacted the Child Online Protection Act, which prohibited commercial Web sites from distributing material that is "harmful to

JOE CAMEL PEDDLES HIS WARES on a New York City billboard. Commercial speech, as a general category, is not as strongly protected by the First Amendment as political speech, but advertising can be limited by the government only in specific circumstances.

Miller test Established in *Miller v. California*, the Supreme Court uses this three-part test to determine whether speech meets the criteria for obscenity. If so, it can be restricted by the government.

minors," using the language of the *Miller* test to specify what this means. The law bounced around in federal courts for six years, twice making it to the Supreme Court, which ultimately struck it down.[71]

The Supreme Court recently addressed an area of the law that it had not touched for more than 30 years: regulating vulgar language that does not rise to the level of obscenity on broadcast television and radio (but not cable or other paid-subscription services). In 1978 the Court ruled that the Federal Communications Commission (FCC) had the power to regulate indecent language, but the FCC had always interpreted that power to only cover repeated use of vulgar words.[72] After the use of vulgar words by Bono during the 2003 Golden Globe Awards and by Cher and Nicole Richie during the 2002 and 2003 Billboard Music Awards, the FCC announced that it would no longer tolerate even "isolated uses of sexual and excretory words."

Fox Television challenged this new rule, but in 2009 the Supreme Court upheld the ban on "fleeting expletives" as "entirely rational" under existing law, while taking a swipe at the "foul-mouthed glitteratae from Hollywood."[73] The Court also ruled the following week that the FCC had not acted capriciously in fining CBS $550,000 for Janet Jackson's infamous "wardrobe malfunction" at the 2004 Super Bowl.[74] However, after sending the cases back to the lower courts and another round of appeals, the Supreme Court ruled that television networks had not had "fair notice" about the changed policy on fleeting expletives, and therefore the regulations were unconstitutionally vague and networks could not be fined. The Court also let stand a lower court ruling that voided the fine against CBS on similar grounds.[75] But the Court did not address the broader constitutional questions, holding open the possibility of stronger First Amendment protections for broadcast radio and television in the future.

Two recent cases made clear that violence in published material could not be regulated in the same way as sexual content. In 2010, the Court struck down a federal law that criminalized depictions "in which a living animal is intentionally maimed, mutilated, tortured, wounded, or killed." The law focused on "crush videos," which show the torture and killing of helpless animals, but also included dog fighting and other forms of animal cruelty. In striking down the law, the Court said the First Amendment protected such depictions, even if the underlying behavior itself could be illegal.[76] In 2011, the Court struck down a California law that banned the sale of violent video games to children, saying, "Like the protected books, plays and movies that preceded them, video games communicate ideas—and even social messages—through many familiar literary devices (such as characters, dialogue, plot and music) and through features distinctive to the medium (such as the player's interaction with the virtual world). That suffices to confer First Amendment protection."

establishment clause Part of the First Amendment that states "Congress shall make no law respecting an establishment of religion," which has been interpreted to mean that Congress cannot sponsor or favor any religion.

free exercise clause Part of the First Amendment that states Congress cannot prohibit or interfere with the practice of religion.

> DESCRIBE THE FIRST AMENDMENT RIGHTS RELATED TO FREEDOM OF RELIGION

FREEDOM OF RELIGION

The First Amendment has two parts that deal with religion: the **establishment clause**, which says that Congress cannot sponsor or endorse any particular religion, and the **free exercise clause**, which states that Congress cannot interfere in the practice of religion. To simplify only slightly, the former says that Congress should not help religion and the latter that it should not hurt religion. The establishment clause is primarily concerned with drawing lines; for example, does a prayer at a public high school football game or a nativity scene on government property constitute state sponsorship of religion? The free exercise clause has more to do with balancing interests; recall the earlier examples of balancing public safety concerns against snake handling in religious services and the use of Amish buggies on highways.

The combination of the establishment and free exercise clauses results in a general policy of noninterference and government neutrality toward religion. As Thomas Jefferson put it in 1802, the First Amendment provides a "wall of eternal separation between church and state." This language continues to be cited in Court cases[77] in which religion and politics intersect. Since both areas carry great moral weight and emotional charge, it's no wonder that vehement debates continue over the appropriateness of the saying "In God We Trust" on our currency, of the White House Christmas tree, and of public schools teaching evolution and "intelligent design." Since politics is everywhere, the boundaries of religious expression remain difficult to draw.

THE ESTABLISHMENT CLAUSE AND SEPARATION OF CHURCH AND STATE

Determining the boundaries between church and state—the central issue of the establishment clause—is very difficult. As a leading text on civil liberties puts it, the words of the establishment clause—"Congress shall make no law respecting an establishment of religion"—are commanding and clear, but their meaning is entirely unclear. What does the clause allow or forbid?[78] We know that the Founders did not want an official state religion nor for the government to favor one religion over another, but beyond that, it's hard to say. Jefferson's "eternal wall of separation" comment has been used in Court decisions that prohibit state aid for religious activities, but lately the Court has been moving toward a more "accommodationist" perspective that sometimes allows religious activity in public institutions.

SCHOOL PRAYER

The prohibition of prayer in public schools has become the most controversial establishment clause issue. It exploded onto the political scene in 1962 when the Court ruled in *Engle v. Vitale* that the following prayer, written by the New York Board of State Regents and read every day in the state's public schools,[79] violated the separation of church and state: "Almighty God, we acknowledge our dependence upon Thee, and we beg Thy blessing upon us, our parents, our teachers, and our country." Banning the prayer caused a huge public outcry protesting the perceived attack on religion.

Over the next 50 years, Congress repeatedly tried, unsuccessfully, to amend the Constitution to allow school prayer. Meanwhile, the Court continued to take a hard line on school-sponsored prayer. In 1985, the Court struck down the practice of observing a one-minute moment of

CAN A CROSS BE DISPLAYED ON federal land? The Supreme Court has ruled that religious displays on government property must be part of larger, secular displays. This cross on federal land in the Mojave Desert was covered up after it became controversial.

silence for "meditation or voluntary prayer" in the Alabama public schools.[80] More recently, the Court said that benedictions or prayers at public school graduations and a school policy that allowed an elected student representative to lead a prayer at a high school football game also violated the establishment clause.[81] Yet the Court has upheld the practice of opening every session of Congress with a prayer and has let stand without comment a lower court ruling that allowed a prayer that was planned and led by students (rather than being school policy) at a high school graduation.[82]

AID TO RELIGIOUS ORGANIZATIONS

The Court has had an even more difficult time coming up with principles to govern aid to religious organizations, either directly, through tax dollars, or indirectly, through the use of public space. One early attempt was known as the **Lemon test**, after one of the parties in a 1971 case involving government support for religious schools (*Lemon v. Kurtzman*). This case said that a practice violated the establishment clause if it (1) did not have a "secular legislative purpose," (2) either advanced or inhibited religion, or (3) fostered "an excessive government entanglement with religion."[83] The third part of the test was later found open to interpretation by lower courts and therefore led to conflicting rulings.

The Court started to move away from the *Lemon* test in a 1984 case involving a crèche owned by the city of Pawtucket, Rhode Island, and displayed in a park owned by a nonprofit corporation. The Court allowed the nativity display, saying, "The Constitution does not require complete separation of church and state; it affirmatively mandates accommodation, not merely tolerance, of all religions, and forbids hostility toward any."[84] This "endorsement test" simply says that government action is unconstitutional if a "reasonable observer" would think that the action either endorses or disapproves of religion. Later rulings upheld similar religious displays, especially if they conformed to what observers have labeled the "three plastic animals rule"—if the baby Jesus is surrounded by Rudolph the red-nosed reindeer and other secular symbols, the overall display is considered sufficiently nonreligious to pass constitutional muster.[85] This picture became more muddled in 2005 when the Court said that the Ten Commandments could not be posted in two Kentucky courthouses but could be displayed on a monument outside the capitol in Austin, Texas. However, there was some consistency between the seemingly contradictory rulings on the commandments and the "three plastic animals rule." Justice Breyer noted that Austin's monument was one of 40 on the capitol grounds, so the display served a "mixed but primarily non-religious purpose," whereas the Kentucky courthouses' displays were clearly religious.[86]

The Court has also applied the accommodationist perspective to funding for religious schools by looking more favorably on providing tax dollars to students' families to subsidize tuition costs rather than funding the parochial schools directly. For example, a 2002 case upheld an Ohio school voucher program that distributed scholarships to needy students so they could attend the Cleveland school of their choice, including private, religious schools. The Court said the program did not violate the establishment clause because it allowed students and their families "to exercise genuine choice among options public and private, secular and religious."[87] Critics of the decision pointed out that 96 percent of the students participating in the scholarship program were enrolled in religiously affiliated schools, which amounted to state-sponsorship of religious education, something that the Court had not previously allowed. In 2011, the Court expanded taxpayer support for religious education when it upheld an Arizona law that provides state tax credits for contributions to organizations that provide tuition for religious schools.[88]

Lemon test The Supreme Court uses this test, established in *Lemon v. Kurtzman*, to determine whether a practice violates the First Amendment's establishment clause.

The Court has also ruled that it is acceptable to use federal funds to buy computers and other educational equipment to be used in public and private schools for "secular, neutral, and nonideological programs"[89] and tax dollars for a sign language interpreter for a deaf student who attended a parochial school.[90]

Another case involved a clash between the First Amendment's free speech and establishment clauses. The University of Virginia declined to support a Christian newspaper because of its religious content (despite funding 118 other student organizations with a range of views), and the editor of the paper sued the university for violating his freedom of speech. The Court ruled that free speech concerns trumped possible establishment issues, so that refusing to fund the Christian paper while funding so many others amounted to "viewpoint discrimination."[91]

THE FREE EXERCISE CLAUSE

While the freedom of belief is absolute, freedom of religious conduct cannot be unrestricted. That is, you can believe whatever you want without government interference, but if you *act* on those beliefs, the government may regulate your behavior. And while the government has restricted religious conduct in dozens of cases, the freedom of religion has been among the most consistently protected civil liberties.

There is one prominent example of the Court restricting the free exercise of religion but then quickly correcting its error. This 1940 case concerned the children in a Jehovah's Witness family who were kicked out of a public school in Minersville, Pennsylvania, for refusing to recite the Pledge of Allegiance.[92] The children cited Exodus 20:3, "you shall have no other Gods before Me," in explaining why they refused to recite the pledge and salute the flag. The Court surprised the experts by siding with the school—until, three years later, the justices reversed course and ruled that the school could not force anyone to say the pledge, especially when it served no important government interest, such as protecting public safety.[93]

LAWYERS FOR TOM GREEN ARGUED that laws against bigamy and polygamy infringed on his religious freedom. Green belonged to a fundamentalist sect of Mormonism that teaches plural marriage. When this photo was taken in 2000, he had five wives and at least 29 children.

Hundreds of cases have come before the Court in the area of the free exercise of religion. Here are some examples of the questions they addressed:[94] May Amish parents be forced to send their children to schools beyond the eighth grade? (no). May religion serve as the basis for attaining "conscientious objector" status and avoiding the draft? (generally yes, but with many qualifications). Is animal sacrifice as part of a religious ceremony protected by the First Amendment? (generally yes). May Mormons have multiple wives? (no). May the Amish be compelled to follow traffic laws and put license plates on their buggies? (yes). May people be forced to work on Friday night and Saturday if those are their days of worship? (no). May a city levy licensing fees that target the selling of religious books? (no). Does the First Amendment protect distributing religious leaflets on public streets? (yes), and religious meetings in public parks? (yes, subject to "time, manner, and place" restrictions). May religious dress be regulated? (generally not, but in some contexts, such as the military, yes). Are all prison inmates entitled to hold religious services? (apparently yes, but this is still an open question). Are religious organizations subject to child labor laws? (yes). Whew! Keep in mind that this list is by no means exhaustive.

A recent case illustrates the need to balance the free exercise of religion against antidiscrimination laws. Could a law school require a student organization, the Christian Legal Society (CLS), to accept all students who wanted to participate in that organization, even if that requirement conflicted with the religious beliefs of the organization? Specifically, to join the CLS, students had to disavow "unrepentant homosexual conduct." The Court ruled that the law school could require the organization to accept all students or lose university funding because the organization was not imposing a viewpoint neutral rule. In a concurring opinion, Justice Stevens said groups that exclude or mistreat homosexuals, Jews, blacks, and women must be tolerated in a free society, but "it need not subsidize them, give them its official imprimatur or grant them equal access to law school facilities."[95]

One case had broad implications that defined the general basis for government restrictions of religious expression. The 1990 case addressed whether the state may deny unemployment benefits to someone who is fired for taking illegal drugs as part of a religious ceremony. The Court ruled that the state of Oregon had not violated the free exercise clause in denying unemployment benefits to the plaintiffs because they were fired from their jobs in a drug rehabilitation clinic for using peyote. The broader significance of the ruling came with the Court's announcement of a new interpretation of the free exercise clause: the government does not need a "compelling interest" in regulating a particular behavior to justify a law that limits a religious practice.[96] In other words, after this decision, it would be easier for the government to limit the exercise of religion because the Court would no longer require a "compelling" reason for the restrictions, just a good one.

Congress responded by passing the Religious Freedom Restoration Act in 1993, reinstating the need to demonstrate a "compelling state interest" before limiting religious freedoms; the act also specified exceptions to the Controlled Substances Act to allow the use of peyote in religious ceremonies. The Court replied in a 1997 decision that Congress could not usurp its power to define the constitutional protections for religion and that the 1993 law did not apply to the states.[97] Congress retaliated in 2000 by passing a more narrowly written law, the Religious Land Use and Institutionalized Persons Act, that only concerned zoning and the religious rights of people in prisons and government-run mental institutions. Under their power to regulate commerce and control spending, Congress told states that if they accepted federal tax dollars, they would have to reinstate the "compelling interest" standard when restricting religious practices in these two areas.

THE FIRST AMENDMENT

Political speech and symbolic speech

FREEDOM OF THE PRESS

Less protected forms of speech

FREE EXERCISE
The government cannot prevent people from practicing their religion.

FREEDOM OF SPEECH

ESTABLISHMENT
The government cannot establish an official state religion or favor one religion over others.

FREEDOM TO PETITION THE GOVERNMENT

FREEDOM OF ASSEMBLY

FREEDOM OF RELIGION

FREEDOM OF EXPRESSION

1ST AMENDMENT
Congress shall make no law respecting an establishment of religion, or prohibiting the free exercise thereof; or abridging the freedom of speech, or of the press; or the right of the people peaceably to assemble, and to petition the Government for a redress of grievances.

POP QUIZ!

1 Which type of speech is strongly protected under the First Amendment?

a political speech

b commercial speech

c obscenity

d libel

e fighting words

2 The First Amendment's "establishment clause" says that the government cannot

a establish categories of speech.

b prevent people from practicing their religion.

c ban offensive speech.

d create an official state religion.

e prevent people from peaceably assembling.

Answers: 1: a; 2: d

The Supreme Court gave partial support to this law in deciding a case involving the religious freedoms of prison inmates in Ohio.[98] The Court also upheld the law in allowing a small religion in New Mexico to use a hallucinogenic tea in its services even though the tea is considered a controlled substance by the federal government. The Court ruled that the government had not demonstrated a compelling interest in barring the sacramental use of the tea, indicating a shift back toward the stricter standard for justifying limits on religious practices.[99]

The struggle between Congress and the Court in defining civil liberties illustrates the importance of the political process. When Congress decides to tackle an important civil liberty such as religious freedom, it can influence outcomes in an area that is usually dominated by the courts.

EXPLORE WHY THE SECOND AMENDMENT'S MEANING ON GUN RIGHTS IS OFTEN DEBATED

THE RIGHT TO BEAR ARMS

Until recently, the right to bear arms was the only civil liberty that the Supreme Court had played a relatively minor role in defining. Between 1791 and 2007, the Court issued only four rulings directly pertaining to the Second Amendment. The federal courts had always interpreted the Second Amendment's awkward phrasing—"A well regulated Militia, being necessary to the security of a free State, the right of the people to keep and bear Arms, shall not be infringed"—as a right to bear arms within the context of serving in a militia, rather than an individual right to own a gun.

Although legal conflict over gun ownership has intensified only recently, battles over guns have always been intense in the broader political realm.[100] Interest groups such as the National Rifle Association have long asserted that the Second Amendment guarantees an individual right to bear arms. Critics of this view emphasize the first clause of the amendment and point to the frequent mentions of state militias in congressional debates at the time the Bill of Rights was adopted. They argue that the Second Amendment was adopted to reassure Antifederalist advocates of states' rights that state militias, not a national standing army, would provide national security. In this view, the national armed forces and the National Guard have made the Second Amendment obsolete.

Before the Court's recent entry into this debate, Congress and state and local lawmakers had largely defined gun ownership and carrying rights, creating significant variation among the states. Wyoming and Montana have virtually no restrictions on gun ownership, for example, whereas California and Connecticut have many. At the national level, Congress tends to respond to crime waves or high-profile assassinations by passing new gun control laws. The broadest one, the Gun Control Act of 1968, was passed in the wake of the assassinations of Robert F. Kennedy and Martin Luther King Jr. The law sets standards for gun dealers, bans the sale of weapons through the mail, and restricts the sale of new machine guns, among other provisions.

Following the assassination attempt on President Reagan in 1981, the push for stronger gun control laws intensified. Spearheading this effort was Sarah Brady, whose husband, James Brady, was Reagan's press secretary and was also shot and disabled in the assassination attempt. It took nearly 13 years for the campaign to bear fruit, but in 1993 Congress passed and President Clinton signed the Brady Bill, which mandates a background check and a five-day waiting period for any handgun purchase.

AFTER A MENTALLY ILL STUDENT shot and killed 32 people at Virginia Tech in 2007, many people called for stricter gun laws.

In 2008, a landmark ruling recognized for the first time an individual right to bear arms for self-defense and hunting.[101] The decision struck down the District of Columbia's ban on handguns, while noting that state and local governments could enforce ownership restrictions, such as preventing felons or the mentally impaired from buying guns. The Court did not apply the Second Amendment to the states in this decision but did so two years later in striking down a gun control ordinance in Chicago, while reaffirming the ownership restrictions noted in the Washington, D.C., case.[102] The dissenters in both strongly divided 5–4 decisions, lamented the Court's activism in reopening a legal question considered settled for 70 years (in 32 instances since a 1939 Court ruling, appeals courts had affirmed the focus on a collective right—in the context of a militia—rather than an individual right to bear arms, and recognized an individual right only twice).[103]

Given the strong public support for gun ownership—there are about 200 million privately owned guns in the United States—and the Supreme Court's endorsement of an individual right to bear arms, stronger gun control at the national level is highly unlikely. However, extensive litigation will be necessary to define the acceptable boundaries of gun control and which state and local restrictions will be allowed to stand. To this point, the verdicts have been mixed, with some lower courts upholding limitations on gun ownership (such as prohibiting felons from owning guns), while others have struck them down. Almost all challenges to gun laws in criminal cases, however, have been unsuccessful.[104]

due process rights The idea that laws and legal proceedings must be fair. The Constitution guarantees that the government cannot take away a person's "life, liberty, or property, without due process of law." Other specific due process rights are found in the Fourth, Fifth, Sixth, and Eighth Amendments, such as protection from self-incrimination and freedom from illegal searches.

LAW, ORDER, AND THE RIGHTS OF CRIMINAL DEFENDANTS

> DESCRIBE THE PROTECTIONS PROVIDED FOR PEOPLE ACCUSED OF A CRIME

Every advanced democracy protects the rights of people who have been accused of a crime. In the United States, the **due process rights** of the Fourth, Fifth, Sixth, and Eighth Amendments include the right to a fair trial, the right to consult a lawyer, freedom from self-incrimination, knowing what crime you are accused of, the right to confront the accuser in court, and freedom from unreasonable police searches.

Difficulties in applying these abstract principles of due process to concrete situations indicate how hard it is to define due process, especially in a way that protects civil liberties without jeopardizing order. The Fifth and Fourteenth Amendments specify that life, liberty, and property may not be denied "without due process of law." In general, this language refers to *procedural* restrictions on what government can do and is based on the idea of fairness and justice. The difficulty comes in defining what is fair or just.

The difference between abstract principles of due process and their specific application also raises difficult *political* questions. Most people endorse the principle of "due process of law" and general ideas such as requiring that police legally obtain any evidence used in court. However, when the Court applies these principles to protect the rights of criminal defendants, there is a public outcry that too many suspects are going free on "legal technicalities," such as having to inform a suspect of his right to talk to an attorney before being questioned by the police. Elected politicians are very vulnerable to such public pressure and have a strong incentive to be "tough on crime," while the courts are left to decide whether a specific case is a legal technicality or a fundamental civil liberty. The first aspect of due process discussed in the next section is a perfect example of the political and legal difficulty of defining and applying due process rights: the Fourth Amendment protection against *unreasonable* searches and seizures.

THE FOURTH AMENDMENT: UNREASONABLE SEARCHES AND SEIZURES

The Fourth Amendment says, "The right of the people to be secure in their persons, houses, papers, and effects, against unreasonable searches and seizures, shall not be violated." Given the abusive practices of the British governors in the colonies, the Founders had strong opinions about this issue, but defining "unreasonable" puts us back in the familiar position of drawing lines and balancing interests.

Over the years, the Court provided strong protections against searches within a person's physical space, typically defined as his or her home. With the introduction of new technology—first telephones and wiretapping, then more sophisticated listening and searching devices—the Court had to confront a broad array of complicated questions. It has attempted to achieve a balance between security and privacy by requiring court approval for search warrants, while carving out limited exceptions to this general rule.

SEARCHES AND WARRANTS

Under most circumstances, a law enforcement official seeking a search warrant must provide the court with "personal knowledge" of a "probable cause" of specific criminal activity and outline the evidence that is the target of the search. Broad, general "fishing expeditions" for evidence are not allowed.

School searches may be permitted with a weaker "reasonable suspicion" (this is because the courts have viewed schools playing the role of surrogate parents, or "in loco parentis," for the students), but there are limits. In 2003, school administrators in Safford, Arizona, responding to a tip that a student was in possession of prescription-strength ibuprofen pills, subjected 13-year-old Savana Redding to a strip search. After searching her backpack and outer clothing and finding nothing, the majority opinion describes what happened next: "Savana was told to pull her bra out and to the side and shake it, and to pull out the elastic on her underpants, thus exposing her breasts and pelvic area to some degree." The Court ruled that this search violated her Fourth Amendment rights because "the content of the suspicion failed to match the degree of intrusion."[105]

Police searches inherently involve a clash between public safety and an individual's private freedom from government intrusions. These issues came to the fore with the passage of the USA PATRIOT Act of 2001 after the terrorist attacks of September 11. (The act's name is an acronym for "Uniting and Strengthening America by Providing Appropriate Tools Required to Intercept and Obstruct Terrorism.") Several of the most controversial parts of the act strengthen police surveillance powers; make it easier to conduct "sneak and peek" searches (the police enter a home with a warrant, look for evidence, and do not tell the suspect of their search until months later); broaden Internet surveillance; increase the government's access to library, banking, and medical records; and permit roving wiretaps for suspected terrorists.

The most common reason for a police search without a warrant is consent of the suspect (and the officers are not required to tell suspects that they may say "no" or request a warrant). Here are examples of other instances when the Court will allow a warrantless search:

CAN THE POLICE SEARCH YOUR HOME without a warrant? After Dollree Mapp was arrested for possession of pornographic material, the case made its way to the Supreme Court and the search was ruled unconstitutional. This case established the "exclusionary rule" for evidence that is obtained without a warrant.

- ▶ Conducting a search at the time of a legal arrest that "is confined to the immediate vicinity of the arrest."

- ▶ Collecting evidence that was not included in the search warrant but is out in the open in plain view.

- ▶ Using a police roadblock to search for information about a crime, at borders, or for sobriety checks (but not for random drug searches or license checks), as long as the roadblock stops all drivers.

- ▶ Searching containers in cars, if the officer has probable cause to suspect criminal activity.

- ▶ Searching the passenger area of a car if the driver has been stopped for a traffic offense—and passengers may also be searched. Automobiles do not have the same Fourth Amendment protections as homes.

- ▶ Searching an area where the officer thinks there is either a crime in progress or an "armed and dangerous" suspect.

- ▶ Searching school lockers, with probable cause.

- ▶ Searching for weapons and/or to prevent the destruction of evidence.[106]

Strip searches after an arrest and before the suspect is put in jail were recently upheld by the Supreme Court even when there was no suspicion of illegal substances. Dissenting justices argued that "the humiliation of a visual strip-search" after being "arrested for driving with a noisy muffler, failing to use a turn signal and riding a bicycle without an audible bell" should not be allowed under the Fourth Amendment.[107]

The Court has generally made it easier for law enforcement officials to conduct searches without warrants, but one important decision in the other direction was a 2012 case that required a warrant to place a GPS tracking device on a vehicle. The FBI suspected Antoine Jones of selling cocaine, so they placed a tracking device on his vehicle without a warrant, monitored his movements for four weeks, and then used the evidence to convict him. Jones was sentenced to life in prison. While the Court required a warrant in this specific case, the basis for the majority's decision was fairly narrow: the placement of the device was a "physical trespass," and the lengthy monitoring of his movement constituted an illegal search.[108] Remote tracking without physical trespass or shorter term monitoring with a GPS device without a warrant may be acceptable to the Court. Additional cases will be required to sort this out.

A second set of cases determines what to do if the police obtain evidence illegally. Here the need to balance security and privacy becomes concrete. Either the evidence is excluded from a criminal trial to protect privacy rights, or it is allowed to support conviction of the suspect.

THE EXCLUSIONARY RULE

exclusionary rule The principle that illegally or unconstitutionally acquired evidence cannot be used in a criminal trial.

In 1961, the Fourth Amendment was incorporated (applied to the states through the Fourteenth Amendment) in a case, *Mapp v. Ohio,* that established the **exclusionary rule** for all courts. Previously, the rule had applied only at the national level.[109] The rule states that illegally obtained evidence cannot be used in a criminal trial.

In the landmark case, police broke into Dollree Mapp's residence without a warrant looking for a suspect thought to be hiding in the house. The officers did not find him, but they did find illegal pornographic material, and Mapp was convicted of possessing it. Her lawyer tried to defend her on First Amendment grounds, claiming she had the right to own the pornography, but instead the Court used the opportunity to apply the Fourth Amendment to the states. The Court threw out Mapp's conviction because the police did not have a search warrant, arguing that applying the Fourth Amendment only to the national government and not the states didn't make any sense: Why should a state's attorney be able to use illegally obtained evidence while a federal prosecutor could not? The justices ruled that for the exclusionary rule to deter illegal searches and seizures, it must apply to law enforcement at both state and national levels.

Subsequent Courts started weakening the exclusionary rule. The public was concerned that too many criminals were being set free because of the limits on obtaining and using evidence, and a majority of justices agreed. In 1974, the Court allowed the use of illegally obtained evidence in grand jury testimony.[110] Several years later it relaxed the general rule to allow the use of evidence if the "totality of circumstances" suggests that the police officer's action was justified.[111] The following year the Court established a "good faith exception" to the exclusionary rule, allowing evidence to be used as long as the officer believed that he or she had conducted a legal search. In the specific case, the officer had a warrant that turned out to have errors on it, such as the wrong address.[112] Yet another case established an exception allowing the use of evidence that was initially obtained in an illegal search but subsequently acquired with a valid warrant.[113] The bottom line is that the exclusionary rule remains in effect, but in the last several decades, the courts have eased the conditions in which prosecutors can use evidence obtained under questionable circumstances.

DRUG TESTING

Another area of Fourth Amendment law concerns drug testing. The clause granting people the right "to be secure in their persons" certainly seems to cover drug testing. However, the courts have long recognized the right of private companies to test their employees for illegal drugs, and in professional sports, testing for performance-enhancing drugs is increasingly common. Tour de France winner

THE TRADE-OFF BETWEEN SECURITY AND CIVIL LIBERTIES

Since the terrorist attacks of 9/11/01, we are regularly reminded of the trade-off between security and civil liberties. With every exposed terror cell and arrested would-be bomber, the nation breathes a collective sigh of relief that we dodged another attack. But heightened airport security and the resultant delays in travel are a regular reminder of the personal costs of the additional security. While nearly everyone is willing to surrender some personal privacy and bear some inconvenience to prevent terrorist attacks, the more difficult question is how to achieve the proper balance between protecting our security and preserving civil liberties.

Specific events sharpen the contours of this debate. The White House–approved domestic surveillance program discussed in the text raised concerns about how much privacy was being sacrificed in the search for terrorists. More recently, the Obama administration's efforts to close the detention facility for suspected terrorists in Guantánamo and to try five suspected terrorists in federal court in New York City have been met with NIMBY politics ("not in my backyard"). Everyone wants to fight terrorism as long as the suspected terrorists are not detained or put to trial in his hometown.

Since September 11, 2001, Americans have been more directly confronted with trade-offs between security and civil liberties.

Watch a video clip of political scientist Howard Schweber discussing this topic at **wwnorton/studyspace.com**

Studying the trade-off between security and civil liberties is a job for political scientists as well as scholars and practitioners in other fields, including law professors and federal judges. Research in this area involves examining relevant court cases and situating the debates within the context of the relevant parts of the Constitution. Two important recent contributions to this debate are by Bruce Ackerman, Yale political scientist and law professor, and Richard Posner, federal appeals court judge and lecturer at the University of Chicago law school.[a]

In a chilling passage from his book *Before the Next Attack: Preserving Civil Liberties in an Age of Terrorism*, Ackerman warns, "The next major attack may kill and maim one hundred thousand innocents, dwarfing the pain and anguish suffered by those who lost family and friends on 9/11. The resulting political panic threatens to leave behind a wave of repressive legislation far more drastic than any imagined by the Patriot Act."[b] While the threat of terrorist attacks is real, according to Ackerman the more serious threat to our freedom comes from within. Terrorist groups do not have the ability to invade and take over our country, therefore, "If anybody destroys our legacy of freedom, it will be us."[c]

Ackerman's advice is to plan ahead so a devastating attack will not produce a police state. He argues that Congress should enact an "emergency constitution" that would be implemented after a terrorist attack. It would contain unilateral presidential power through repeated congressional authorizations, including "escalating supermajorities" in which 60 percent, then

70 percent, and then 80 percent majorities in both houses of Congress would be required to extend emergency powers to the president. Ackerman emphasizes that fighting terrorism is neither a war nor fighting crime, but an emergency. If we deal with terrorism on this basis, the threat to civil liberties will be short term rather than a permanent part of the police state that could be implemented in the wake of a devastating terrorist attack.

Richard Posner is more willing to limit civil liberties to protect the country, at least in the short run. While Posner accepts Ackerman's view that fighting terrorism fits the model of neither a war nor crime, he argues more strongly for limiting the civil liberties of suspected terrorists, and he is not as concerned as Ackerman about concentrating power in the presidency. Posner examines the costs and benefits of different outcomes in cases involving detention, interrogation, radical speech, privacy, and searches based on less than probable cause. He argues that in some cases the president will need to act in an unconstitutional manner to protect the country (similar to Locke's "prerogative powers" discussed in Chapter 2). Posner's solution to this trade-off is that public officials (especially the president) should engage in civil disobedience: "While the term is usually applied to private individuals who deem it their moral duty to disobey positive law, there is no reason why it cannot also be used of public officials who do the same thing."[d] As long as the president was acting in the nation's interest, breaking the law would be justified.

These authors provide contrasting views on how we should balance protecting civil liberties against ensuring national security, while bringing attention to a central debate that is sure to occupy constitutional scholars and politicians for the next generation.

Floyd Landis was stripped of his title in 2006 after testing positive for artificially elevated testosterone levels, and major league baseball has struggled to rein in steroid and human growth hormone use by many of its players, including stars such as Mark McGwire, Manny Ramirez, and Alex Rodriguez.

What about drug testing by the state? The Court has upheld random drug testing for high school athletes and mandatory drug testing for any junior high or high school students involved in extracurricular activities.[114] In the case of athletes, proponents of the policy asserted that safety concerns should preclude a 260-pound lineman or a pitcher with a 90-mile-per-hour fastball from using drugs. However, the same arguments could not be made for members of the choir, band, debate club, social dance, or the chess club, so this decision to include all extracurricular activities was a particularly strong endorsement of schools' antidrug policies.

Federal employees became subject to drug testing in 1986, when President Reagan issued an executive order requiring all employees to refrain from using illegal drugs as a condition of federal employment, and directed each agency to implement drug testing for sensitive positions. Two years later, Congress passed the Drug-Free Workplace Act to apply the same rule to all executive agencies, the uniformed services, and any service providers under contract with the federal government. Despite these prohibitions, drug testing of federal employees is actually limited to people who hold security clearances, carry firearms, or work in public safety or national security. Some employees are subject to random tests; others are tested only when they apply for a job, are involved in a workplace accident, or show signs of drug use. Many states have similar drug-testing policies,[115] and the Court has upheld drug testing of public employees, with one exception. It struck down a Georgia law that would have required all candidates for state office to pass a drug test within 30 days of announcing a run for office because candidates are not public employees.[116] Rather than appealing to the courts, former senator Ernest Hollings of South Carolina had a different approach to avoid drug testing. When his opponent, Representative Tommy Hartnett, challenged him to take a drug test, the senator shot back, "I'll take a drug test if you take an I.Q. test."

THE POST–SEPTEMBER 11 POLITICS OF DOMESTIC SURVEILLANCE

The debate over the trade-off between civil liberties and security intensified in 2005 when a White House–approved domestic surveillance program was revealed (see "What Do Political Scientists Do?"). At the center of this controversy is the National Security Agency (NSA), which was created during the Korean War in 1952 by President Harry Truman. The agency was initially kept so secret that for many years the government even denied its existence. Insiders joked that the NSA stood for "No Such Agency." Today the NSA is responsible for surveillance that is aimed at national security (while the FBI is in charge of spying related to criminal activity, and the CIA oversees foreign intelligence gathering).

Since the terrorist attacks of September 11, 2001, the NSA had been monitoring the phone calls of many U.S. citizens who have had contact with suspected terrorists overseas. These calls were intercepted without the approval of the Foreign Intelligence Surveillance Court (FISC), which Congress created in 1978 specifically for approving the interception of calls. A few months later, another NSA program was revealed—this one aimed at creating a database of every phone call made within the borders of the United States. Phone companies AT&T, Verizon, and BellSouth reportedly turned over records of millions of customers' phone calls to the government.[117]

Critics warn that phone surveillance may be the tip of the iceberg because the government may be monitoring travel, credit card, and banking records more widely than we think. Government agencies have previously skirted the restrictions in the Privacy Act of 1974 and the Fourth Amendment by purchasing this information from businesses, since the Privacy Act requires disclosure of how the government is using personal information only when the government itself collects the data. The Justice Department spent $19 million in 2005 to purchase commercially gathered data about American citizens, according to a report by the Government Accountability Office. These data are then used to search for suspicious patterns of behavior in a process known as data mining.[118]

The debate over domestic surveillance has generated intense disagreement. At one extreme, critics conjure up images of George Orwell's classic novel *1984* in which Big Brother, a reclusive totalitarian ruler, watches the characters' every move. They see the surveillance as a threat to civil liberties and to our system of checks and balances and separation of powers. When the executive branch refuses to obtain warrants through the FISA court, the surveillance programs place too much power in the hands of this branch to determine what is in the nation's interests. But supporters of the program argue that getting a court order may take too long, jeopardizing the surveillance necessary to protect the country. Congress tried to strike a balance between these two positions when it enacted the FISA Amendments Act of 2008. This law continued the ban on monitoring the purely domestic communications of Americans without a court order, gave the government authority to intercept international communications, and provided legal immunity to the telecommunications companies that cooperated in the original wiretapping program. However, the *New York Times* revealed that the NSA had been engaged in "overcollection" of domestic communication between Americans under the new law, including an attempt to wiretap a member of Congress without a court order. Although the Obama administration has vowed to stop purely domestic surveillance without a court order, technical problems make it difficult to distinguish between communications made within the United States and overseas.[119]

IN 2006, CONGRESS HELD HEARINGS on the executive branch's wartime powers and domestic surveillance authority. The goal was to balance security concerns with civil liberties protections.

The idea that politics is everywhere may take on ominous overtones in this case if you are concerned about protecting your civil liberties, or it may provide comforting reassurance if you are more concerned about national security. Either way, this issue will remain significant in your daily life for the foreseeable future.

THE FIFTH AMENDMENT: SELF-INCRIMINATION

The familiar phrase "I plead the fifth" has been part of our criminal justice system since the Bill of Rights was ratified, ensuring that a suspect cannot be compelled to provide court testimony that would cause him or her to be prosecuted for a crime. However, what about outside a court of law? If a police officer coerces a confession out of a suspect, does that amount to self-incrimination?

Such police interrogations were allowed until a landmark case in 1966. Ernesto Miranda had been convicted in an Arizona court of kidnapping and rape, on the basis of a confession extracted after two hours of questioning in which he was not read his rights. The Court overturned the conviction, saying that a police interrogation "is inherently intimidating" and in these circumstances, "no statement

```
DEFENDANT                           LOCATION

SPECIFIC WARNING REGARDING INTERROGATIONS

1. YOU HAVE THE RIGHT TO REMAIN SILENT.

2. ANYTHING YOU SAY CAN AND WILL BE USED AGAINST YOU IN A COURT
   OF LAW.

3. YOU HAVE THE RIGHT TO TALK TO A LAWYER AND HAVE HIM PRESENT
   WITH YOU WHILE YOU ARE BEING QUESTIONED.

4. IF YOU CANNOT AFFORD TO HIRE A LAWYER ONE WILL BE APPOINTED
   TO REPRESENT YOU BEFORE ANY QUESTIONING, IF YOU WISH ONE.

SIGNATURE OF DEFENDANT                        DATE

WITNESS                                       TIME

☐ REFUSED SIGNATURE    SAN FRANCISCO POLICE DEPARTMENT    PR.9.1.4
```

THIS IS A TYPICAL EXAMPLE OF THE
Miranda warning card that police
officers carry with them and read
to a suspect after an arrest.

Miranda **rights** The list of civil
liberties described in the Fifth
Amendment that must be read to a
suspect before anything the suspect
says can be used in a trial.

double jeopardy Being tried
twice for the same crime. This is
prevented by the Fifth Amendment.

obtained from the defendant can truly be the product of his free choice."[120] To make sure a confession is truly a free choice, the Court came up with the well-known ***Miranda rights*** shown here. If police do not read a suspect these rights, nothing the suspect says can be used in court.

The Court has carved out exceptions to the *Miranda* rights requirement because the public has viewed the practice as "coddling criminals" and letting too many people go free on legal technicalities. In one case, police failed to read a suspect his *Miranda* rights until after frisking him, finding an empty holster, and asking him where his gun was. The suspect led police to a gun. The lower court dismissed the charges because the gun had been used as incriminating evidence in the trial, but the Supreme Court reinstated the conviction because "concern for public safety must be paramount to adherence to the literal language of the *Miranda* rule."[121] In 2010, the Court ruled that once a suspect has invoked his or her *Miranda* rights, the prohibition on police questioning is not "eternal." Instead, if the suspect voluntarily has a change of mind, police may resume questioning 14 days after the suspect's release from custody.[122] In another case that same year, a murder suspect in Michigan was read his *Miranda* rights and then remained silent for nearly three hours of police interrogation. Finally, when asked if he believed in God, he said "yes." When asked, "Do you pray to God to forgive you for shooting that boy down?" he also said "yes" and he was convicted based on that confession. The Court ruled that a suspect must explictly invoke the right to remain silent. The dissenters complained that the decision "turned *Miranda* upside down. . . . Criminal suspects must now unambiguously invoke their right to remain silent, which, counterintuitively, requires them to speak."[123]

Although the Court has been willing to carve out limited exceptions to the *Miranda* rule, in 2000 the Court rejected Congress's attempt to overturn *Miranda* by designating all voluntary confessions as legally admissible evidence. The Court ruled that it, and not Congress, has the power to determine constitutional protections for criminal defendants. The justices also affirmed their intent to protect the *Miranda* rule, saying, "*Miranda* has become embedded in routine police practice to the point where the warnings have become part of our national culture."[124]

The Court also strengthened the *Miranda* warning in another case by severely limiting the increasingly common police practice of interrogating a suspect before reading her the *Miranda* warning, getting a confession, then taking a break, then reading the warning, and getting another confession. The Court overturned the conviction of a woman who confessed to a murder in this two-step process, saying that the second-stage confession would be admissible only if the *Miranda* warning and accompanying break are sufficient to give the suspect the reasonable belief that she has the right not to answer any more questions.[125]

Another Fifth Amendment right for defendants is protection against being tried more than once for a particular crime. This circumstance is known as **double jeopardy** because the suspect is "twice put in jeopardy of life or limb" for a single offense. This prohibition was extended to the states in 1969.[126] However, prosecutors can exploit two loopholes in this civil liberty: (1) a suspect may be tried in federal court and state court for the same crime, and (2) if a suspect is found innocent of one set of *criminal* charges brought by the state, he or she may still be found guilty of the same or closely related offenses based on *civil* charges brought by a private individual.

Usually these loopholes are exploited only in high-profile cases in which public or political pressure seeks a conviction. For example, in 1992, four Los Angeles police officers were acquitted of beating Rodney King, a driver they had chased for speeding. Before the trial, a bystander's video of the beating had been widely broadcast; subsequently, at news of the police officers' acquittal, massive and destructive riots broke out that lasted three days. Responding to political pressure, President George H. W. Bush urged federal prosecutors to retry the officers not for the *criminal* use of excessive force but for violating Rodney King's *civil* rights. (Two were ultimately found guilty, and two were acquitted.) A similar pattern of prosecution followed in the trial of football star O. J. Simpson for the murder of his wife and her friend. Simpson was acquitted of first-degree murder but found guilty on civil charges brought by the victims' families.

The final part of the Fifth Amendment is at the heart of a hot legal debate over property rights; the clause says, "nor shall private property be taken for public use, without just compensation." For most of American history, this civil liberty has been noncontroversial. When the government needs private property for a public use such as building a highway or a park, it may force a property owner to sell at a fair market value.

A new, controversial interpretation of the Fifth Amendment's "takings" clause has attempted to expand the principle of just compensation to cover not only "physical takings," but also "regulatory takings." For example, if the Endangered Species Act protects an animal whose habitat is on your land, you would not be able to develop that property. Thus, its market value would probably be lower than if the endangered species did not live on your land. Therefore, the argument goes, because of this law the government has "taken" some of the value of your land by legally protecting the species, so it should compensate you for your loss.

One key Court case decided that if a regulation "deprives a property owner of all beneficial use of his property," the owner must receive compensation. This case involved a man who bought two residential lots on the Isle of Palms, a South Carolina barrier island. His plan was to build single-family homes on the lots, but shortly after his purchase the state legislature enacted a law banning "permanent habitable structures" on this part of the barrier islands to prevent further erosion and destruction of the vulnerable land. The owner sued in state court and won a large monetary judgment, and the Supreme Court upheld this ruling.[127] Another case concerned a takings claim based on a regulation that limited development in a coastal wetlands area in Rhode Island. Here the key legal issue was whether it mattered that the regulation was on the books *before* the plaintiff purchased the land. In a divisive 5–4 ruling, the Court said that a regulatory takings claim could still be made despite the argument that market forces would have already factored in the regulatory loss.[128]

This issue became even more controversial after a case involving a development project in New London, Connecticut. A working-class neighborhood was sold to a private developer to build a waterfront hotel, office space, and higher-end housing, but a home owner sued the city to stop the development. The Court supported the local government, saying that "promoting economic development is a traditional and long accepted function of government" so a "plausible public use" is satisfied. Justice O'Connor wrote a strong dissent, saying that the "specter of condemnation hangs over all property. Nothing is to prevent the State from replacing any Motel 6 with a Ritz-Carlton, any home with a shopping mall, or any farm with a factory."[129] Ironically, after the homes had been moved or bulldozed, the developer failed to get the necessary financing. As of this writing, the waterfront property remains an empty lot.

THE SIXTH AMENDMENT: THE RIGHT TO LEGAL COUNSEL AND A JURY TRIAL

When it comes to criminal law, the right to an attorney is one of the key civil liberties, because the legal system is too complicated for a layperson to navigate. However, at one time, poor people accused of a felony were forced to defend themselves in court because they could not afford a lawyer (except in cases involving the death penalty, for which the state would provide a lawyer).[130] This changed in 1963 with the celebrated case of *Gideon v. Wainwright*. Clarence Gideon was accused of breaking into a pool hall and stealing beer, wine, and money. He could not afford an attorney, so he tried to defend himself. He did a pretty good job—calling witnesses, cross-examining the prosecutor's witnesses, and providing a good summary argument. However, he was convicted and sentenced to five years in jail, based largely on the testimony of the person who turned out to be the guilty party. The Court unanimously overturned his conviction, saying, "In our adversary system of criminal justice, any person hauled into court who is too poor to hire a lawyer cannot be assured a fair trial unless counsel is provided for him."[131]

Unlike the exclusionary rule and the protection against self-incrimination, the right to an attorney has been strengthened over time, through both legislation and subsequent Court rulings. One year after *Gideon*, Congress passed the Criminal Justice Act, which provided better legal representation for criminal defendants in federal court; within two years, 23 states had taken similar action. The Court has defined a general right to *effective* counsel (although the bar is set pretty low in terms of defining "effective") and more recently mandated that defense attorneys must conduct any reasonable investigation into possible lines of defense when presenting evidence that could help the defendant.[132]

The Sixth Amendment also protects an individual's right to a speedy and public trial by an impartial jury in criminal cases. The Court affirmed the right to a speedy trial in 1967,[133] and today under the Federal Speedy Trial Act a trial must begin within 70 days of the defendant's arrest or first appearance in court. This law was strengthened by a recent Court decision stating that a defendant may not waive the right to a speedy trial.[134] The most important legal disputes over the "impartial jury" issue concern the process of jury selection and peremptory challenges, in which lawyers from each side may eliminate certain people from the jury pool without providing any reason. The Court has ruled that race and gender may not be the basis for a peremptory challenge.[135] The Court has also ruled in a series of cases that the right to a trial by a jury limits the way that judges can use sentencing guidelines. The Court has struck down both federal and state sentencing guidelines that require judges to impose sentences based on facts other than those confessed to by the defendant or proved to a jury beyond a reasonable doubt.[136]

THE FIGHT AGAINST TERRORISM HAS raised controversial questions about due process rights. After the United States killed Anwar al-Awlaki—an Al Qaeda leader living in Yemen, and a U.S. citizen—critics argued that his due process rights, such as the right to a fair trial, had been violated.

THE EIGHTH AMENDMENT: CRUEL AND UNUSUAL PUNISHMENT

The Founders would be surprised by the intense debates over whether the Eighth Amendment prohibition against "cruel and unusual punishment" applies to the death penalty. Clearly, the death penalty was accepted in their time (even stealing a horse was a capital offense!), and the language of the Constitution reflects that. Both the Fifth and Fourteenth Amendments say that a person may not be deprived of "life, liberty, or property, without due process of law," which implies that someone *could* be deprived of life as long as the state follows due process. The death penalty remains popular in the United States, with 33 states allowing capital punishment. However, five states have abolished the death penalty since 2007 and dozens of other countries have done so in recent years (see "In Comparison").

SUPREME COURT RULINGS ON THE DEATH PENALTY

The Supreme Court remained silent on this issue for nearly two centuries. But in 1972 the Court ruled that the death penalty was unconstitutional because the process of applying it was too inconsistent. Congress and 35 states rushed to make their laws compliant with the Court decision. The typical fix was to say more explicitly which crimes were punishable by death and to make capital sentencing a two-step process: first the determination of guilt or innocence, and then a sentencing phase if the suspect was found guilty. Four years later, the Court approved these changes and allowed states to bring back the death penalty.[137]

While never again challenging the constitutionality of the death penalty, the Court has been chipping away at its edges for two decades. The Court has struck down state laws that mandated the death penalty in murder cases and another law requiring a death sentence for rape. It has also prohibited the execution of insane prisoners and abolished the death penalty for the mildly retarded (2002), for juveniles under the age of 18 (2005), and for child rapists (2008).[138]

These recent cases have shown that the Court responds to public opinion and political change (this is sometimes called the "living Constitution" perspective, as discussed in Chapters 2 and 13). In his opinion in the juvenile death penalty case, Justice Anthony Kennedy noted that 30 states forbid the death penalty for offenders younger than age 18, which was an increase of five states since the Court upheld the juvenile death penalty in 1989. Similarly, the number of states banning the death penalty for the mildly retarded grew from 14 in 1989 (when the practice was upheld) to 25 in 2002 (when it was struck down).

PROPORTIONALITY

One unsettled area of Eighth Amendment law concerns "proportionality"—the idea that some punishments may be so disproportionate to the crime that they constitute "cruel and unusual punishment." The principle came up in a 1910 case overturning a punishment that required shackling and "hard and painful labor" for the full prison term.[139] Since then, the Court has applied proportionality (disallowed these punishments) in the following situations: taking away citizenship as punishment for a crime,[140] incarceration for drug addiction,[141] beating of prison inmates,[142] and issuing a disproportionate prison sentence.[143] In the last case, the Court ruled that a life sentence without the possibility of parole for a seventh nonviolent felony (cashing a $100 check on a closed account) was unconstitutional.

In 1991, however, the Court began to limit application of the principle to cases with a "gross disproportionality," saying that "the Eighth Amendment contains no proportionality guarantee."[144] More recently, the Court ruled in two cases that California's "three strikes and you're out" law (which mandates very harsh sentences for third felony convictions) did not violate the Eighth Amendment. In the first case, Gary Ewing stole three golf clubs, each valued at $399, and received 25 years to life. In the other case, Leandro Andrade stole nine videotapes valued at $150 from two different K-Marts and received two consecutive terms of 25 years

THE DEATH PENALTY IN THE UNITED STATES AND AROUND THE WORLD

The United States prides itself on its strong protection of individual liberties and freedom, and in many instances that pride is well deserved. Our protections for the freedom of speech, freedom of the press, free exercise of religious beliefs, and criminal defendant rights are among the strongest in the world. So for most civil liberties, we may be different from most countries, but that's a good thing.

However, the United States also differs from its peers when it comes to civil liberties and the death penalty. As of 2010, 96 nations had abolished the death penalty for all crimes, 8 countries have the death penalty only for exceptional crimes such as treason during wartime, and 36 countries have abolished the death penalty in practice (the law is still on the books, but these countries have had no executions in at least 10 years). Japan and South Korea are the only other developed nations that have maintained the death penalty. In contrast, the death penalty is still used in China, Cuba, Liberia, Libya, North Korea, Saudi Arabia, Sudan, Syria, Uganda, Vietnam, and Yemen. This is not a lineup of countries with which the United States is usually associated; indeed, these are some of the worst human rights violators in the world.

In March 2005, the Supreme Court took note of the United States' international standing when it overturned a 16-year-old precedent that allowed the execution of minors. The case involved Christopher Simmons, who, at the age of 17, murdered a woman by tying her up with electrical wire, wrapping her head with duct tape, and throwing her off a bridge into a river. He was tried and sentenced to death as an adult under Missouri law. The Missouri Supreme Court overturned the sentence, and the U.S. Supreme Court upheld the ruling, saying that the decision "finds confirmation in the stark reality that the United States is the only country in the world that continues to give official sanction to the juvenile death penalty."[a] One Court observer noted, "For the Supreme Court itself, perhaps the most significant effect of yesterday's decision is to reaffirm the role of international law in constitutional interpretation."[b] The European Union, human rights lawyers from Great Britain, and several Nobel Peace Prize winners had filed briefs urging the Court to strike down the juvenile death penalty. The majority opinion recognized this expression of international opinion, saying that it "provide[s] respected and significant confirmation for our own conclusions."[c] The three dissenters, led by Justice Antonin Scalia, strongly objected to the role played by international opinion. They criticized the majority for "proclaim[ing] itself sole arbiter of our Nation's moral standards—and in the course of discharging that awesome responsibility purport[ing]

Christopher Simmons was removed from death row when the Supreme Court ruled that executing people who were convicted as juveniles is not permitted under the Eighth Amendment.

to take guidance from the views of foreign courts and legislatures." Scalia also chastised the majority for selectively paying attention to international opinion while ignoring it on other issues (such as abortion). "To invoke alien law when it agrees with one's own thinking, and ignore it otherwise, is not reasoned decisionmaking," he thundered, "but sophistry."[d]

Conservatives in Congress were also outraged that a Court decision would give such weight to international law and opinion, and several have introduced legislation that would ban such practices. Scalia rose to defend his institution, essentially telling Congress to back off. "It's none of your business," he told Congress. "No one is more opposed to the use of foreign law than I am, but I'm darned if I think it's up to Congress to direct the Court how to make its decisions." He went on to say that the proposed legislation "is like telling us not to use certain principles of logic. Let us make our mistakes just as we let you make yours."[e]

Whether the Supreme Court should pay attention to international opinion and law is certainly a matter of debate. What is not open to debate is the importance of "comparing ourselves to others" and being aware of how our civil liberties are similar to and different from those of other nations.

to life (because there were two crimes).[145] In each case, the defendants' previous felony convictions were for nonviolent crimes.

//

PRIVACY RIGHTS

EXPLAIN WHY THE RIGHTS ASSOCIATED WITH PRIVACY ARE OFTEN CONTROVERSIAL

You may be surprised to learn that the word "privacy" does not appear in the Constitution. **Privacy rights** were first developed in a 1965 case that questioned the constitutionality of an 1879 Connecticut law against using birth control. Estelle Griswold, the director of Planned Parenthood in Connecticut, was arrested nine days after opening a clinic that dispensed contraceptives. She was fined $100 and appealed her conviction. Though she lost in state court, she appealed all the way to the Supreme Court, which overturned her conviction.

In a very fractured decision (there were six different opinions), the Court agreed that the law was outdated, but the justices agreed on little else. Even those who based their opinions on an implied constitutional right to privacy cited various constitutional roots. Justice William O. Douglas found privacy implicit in the First Amendment right of association, the Third Amendment's protection against the quartering of troops, the Fourth Amendment's prohibition against unreasonable searches and seizures, the Fifth's protection against self-incrimination, and the Ninth's catchall statement, "The enumeration in the Constitution, of certain rights, shall not be construed to deny or disparage others retained by the people."[146] These all seem like reasonable grounds for implicit privacy rights except the First Amendment right of association—since the Founders clearly meant political association, not an association with your spouse in bed.

The *Griswold* case was significant for establishing the constitutional basis for a right to privacy, but the dissenters in the case were concerned about where this right would lead. Justice Black warned that privacy "is a broad, abstract and ambiguous concept" that can be shrunk or expanded in subsequent decisions. He said that Douglas's argument required judges to determine what is or is not constitutional on the basis of their own appraisal of what laws are unwise or unnecessary. The power to make such decisions belongs of course to a legislative body. Surely it has to be admitted that no provision of the Constitution specifically gives courts blanket power to exercise such a supervisory veto over the wisdom and value of legislative policies and to hold unconstitutional those laws the courts believe to be unwise or dangerous.[147]

privacy rights Liberties protected by several amendments in the Bill of Rights that shield certain personal aspects of citizens' lives from governmental interference, such as the Fourth Amendment's protection against unreasonable searches and seizures.

ABORTION RIGHTS

Justice Black's prediction came true eight years later in *Roe v. Wade*, the landmark ruling that struck down laws in 46 states that limited abortion. Twelve of those states allowed abortions for pregnancies due to rape or incest, to protect the life of the mother, and in cases of severe fetal handicap. The much-criticized trimester analysis in the *Roe* ruling said that states could not limit abortions in the first trimester; in the second trimester, states could regulate abortions in the interests of the health of the mother; and in the third trimester, states could forbid all abortions except those necessary to protect the health or life of the mother. The justices cited a constitutional basis for abortion rights in the general right to privacy outlined in *Griswold*; the concept of "personal liberty" in the Fourteenth Amendment's due process clause; and the "rights reserved to the people" by the Ninth Amendment.[148]

Subsequent decisions have upheld *Roe* but endorsed state restrictions on abortion, such as requiring parental consent, a waiting period, or counseling sessions aimed at convincing the woman not to have an abortion. Most significantly, *Roe's* trimester analysis has been replaced by a focus on the viability of the fetus. When the fetus would be viable (generally at 22 or 23 weeks), states can ban abortions "except where it is necessary, in appropriate medical judgment, for the preservation of the life or health of the mother."[149] Since *Roe*, most political action concerning abortion has been in the courts, but that could change if the Supreme Court overturns this decision. Opponents of abortion are hoping that *Roe* will be overturned, which would shift the politics of abortion back to state legislatures and make it an even more contested political issue. One effort to challenge *Roe* was a "personhood amendment" to the Mississippi constitution that defined life beginning at conception. However, the amendment was soundly defeated in a statewide vote in 2011.[150]

THE RIGHT TO DIE

Privacy rights are also central in debates over the right to die, in which two types of political issues have been hotly debated. The first involves the right of a person who is brain-dead or in a persistent vegetative state to refuse medical treatment so he may die. The second is more complicated: May states allow assisted suicide for people with terminal illnesses, even if that practice conflicts with federal law?

In terms of the first issue, courts have approved living wills in which a person can document his or her wishes in advance about end-of-life medical care. The problem comes when a person who can no longer communicate has not left instructions on how much medical intervention she should receive. Every month thousands of families have to make these decisions during the last few weeks of a patient's life, in consultation with their doctors. Most of the time the decisions are extremely difficult but without legal conflict. The high-profile case of Terri Schiavo illustrated how complicated the situation can get. After a heart failure that resulted in severe brain damage, Schiavo remained in a vegetative state from 1990 though 2005. Her husband said she would not have wanted to be kept alive in that condition, but Schiavo's parents wanted to do everything possible to keep her alive. After the Supreme Court refused to intervene, she was taken off life support at her husband's request. Given this precedent, the courts seem unlikely to get involved in matters traditionally resolved between a family and their doctor.

The second right-to-die issue, involving assisted suicide, applied to a case involving Oregon's Death with Dignity Act (see Chapter 3). This law allows a terminally ill patient to get a prescription from his doctor to end his life. The state's voters approved the law twice. In the law's first 14 years, 596 people ended their lives through this procedure.[151] Oregon, Montana, and Washington are the only states with such a law, and it has been highly controversial; Attorney General John Ashcroft attempted to revoke the medical licenses of doctors who prescribed the drugs. According to Ashcroft's interpretation of the federal Controlled Substances Act, use of prescription drugs in doctor-assisted suicide is not a "legitimate medical purpose" of the drugs and therefore is not allowed under the law. However, the Supreme Court upheld the Oregon law in a recent case, ruling in 2006 that the attorney general should not be given the "extraordinary authority" to "criminalize even the actions of registered physicians, whenever they engage in conduct he deems illegitimate."[152]

GAY RIGHTS

Gay rights have typically been thought of more as a civil right (that is, freedom from discrimination) than a civil liberty. However, a Court ruling in 2003 established very broad privacy rights for sexual behavior. The case involved two Houston men, John Geddes Lawrence and Tyron Garner, who were prosecuted for same-sex sodomy after police entered Lawrence's apartment—upon receiving a false tip about an armed man—and found the two having sex. Under Texas law, sodomy was illegal for gays but not for heterosexuals. In a landmark 6–3 ruling, the Supreme Court said that the liberty guaranteed by the Fourteenth Amendment's due process clause allows homosexuals to have sexual relations. "Freedom presumes an autonomy of self that includes freedom of thought, belief, expression, and certain intimate conduct."[153] This reasoning is rooted in the **substantive due process doctrine** that serves as the basis for the constitutional protections for birth control, abortion, and decisions about how to raise one's children. The decision explicitly overturned *Bowers v. Hardwick*, and the majority opinion had harsh words for that decision, saying it "was not correct when it was decided, and it is not correct today." Five members of the majority signed onto the broad "due process" reasoning of the decision, while Justice O'Connor wrote a concurring opinion in which she agreed that the Texas law was unconstitutional but on narrower grounds. With the broader due process logic, a total of 13 state laws that banned sodomy were struck down.

OPPONENTS OF THE MILITARY'S "DON'T ask, don't tell" policy argued that it infringed on the rights and liberties of gay and lesbian service members, in part because they could be dismissed based on their private sexual behavior. The policy was repealed in 2011.

substantive due process doctrine One interpretation of the due process clause of the Fourteenth Amendment; in this view the Supreme Court has the power to overturn laws that infringe on individual liberties.

CONCLUSION

Every day you are affected by your civil liberties, whether speaking in public, going to church, being searched at an airport, participating in a political demonstration, writing or reading an article in your school newspaper, or being free from illegal police searches in your home. Because civil liberties are defined as those things the government *cannot* do to us, defining civil liberties is a political process. Often this process is confined to the courts; but on many issues—including free speech, freedom of the press, pornography, criminal rights, abortion, and gun control—it take place in the broader political world where defining civil liberties involves balancing competing ideals and interests and drawing lines by interpreting and applying the law. For example, debates over how to balance national security and civil liberties—whether newspapers should publish stories about classified programs that may threaten civil liberties; whether government surveillance powers should be strengthened to fight terrorism—will rage for years. Other cases, such as the opening story of protests at military funerals, illustrate how difficult and politically unpopular it can be to protect our freedoms and liberty. As with all political questions, the evolving nature of our civil liberties is sure to generate more political conflict. But that process affirms the essence of our political system.

STUDY *guide*

DEFINING CIVIL LIBERTIES

▶ Define what we mean by civil liberties. **Pages 113–15**

SUMMARY

Civil liberties are the protections that individuals receive from the government. These are not absolute rights, however, as individual freedoms can become at odds with the public good and government interests. The courts often play the deciding role in determining where to draw the line between individual rights and public safety.

KEY TERMS

civil liberties (p. 112)

CRITICAL THINKING AND DISCUSSION

What is the proper balance between national security and civil liberties? Is it appropriate to restrict civil liberties during a time of war? If so, how much? And if not, why?

PRACTICE QUIZ QUESTIONS

1. Civil liberties are rooted in what document?
a) the Declaration of Independence
b) the Federalist Papers
c) the Magna Carta
d) the Bill of Rights
e) Article I of the Constitution

2. Why are civil liberties not absolute?
a) Equality for a group under the law is hard to define.
b) Individual freedoms may conflict with the public good.
c) Laws are often outdated and don't characterize modern society.
d) The Bill of Rights protections were intentionally weakened by Antifederalists.
e) The Supreme Court generally decides not to hear cases concerning civil liberties.

THE ORIGINS OF CIVIL LIBERTIES

▶ Explain why the Bill of Rights was added to the Constitution, and how it came to apply to the states. **Pages 115–20**

SUMMARY

The Bill of Rights, which lists individual protections from the federal government, was included in the Constitution in response to demands from Antifederalists, who feared a strong national government. For most of the nineteenth century, these individual freedoms were only guaranteed from the *federal* government and did not extend to protections from *state* governments. With the ratification of the Fourteenth Amendment and the process of selective incorporation, federal freedoms have been gradually extended to the state level.

KEY TERMS

Civil War Amendments (p. 118)

due process clause (p. 119)

selective incorporation (p. 120)

PRACTICE QUIZ QUESTIONS

3. The inclusion of the Bill of Rights in the Constitution reflects the _____ concerns that the federal government would be too _____.
a) Antifederalists'; strong
b) Antifederalists'; weak
c) Federalists'; strong
d) Federalists'; weak
e) president's; strong

4. The Bill of Rights originally protected individuals from which level of government?
a) all levels of American government
b) state governments
c) local governments
d) federal government
e) the bureaucracy

5. Which amendment has been used as the basis for selective incorporation?
   a) the Eighth Amendment
   b) the Fourteenth Amendment
   c) the Tenth Amendment
   d) the Nineteenth Amendment
   e) the Fifth Amendment

 PRACTICE ONLINE

"Big Think" video exercise: *Where Do Civil Liberties Come From?*

FREEDOM OF SPEECH, ASSEMBLY, AND THE PRESS

▶ Describe the major First Amendment rights related to freedom of speech. **Pages 120–32**

SUMMARY

The Supreme Court's attempt to balance individual freedoms and public good is reflected in the scope of protections guaranteed by the First Amendment. The Court generally prioritizes protecting individual rights to political speech, hate speech, symbolic speech, the freedom to assemble, and the freedom of the press unless under extreme circumstances (such as speech that directly incites violence). By contrast, the Court regularly places a lower priority on, and affords less protection to, fighting words, slander, libel, and commercial speech.

KEY TERMS

strict scrutiny (p. 122)

intermediate scrutiny (p. 122)

clear and present danger test (p. 123)

direct incitement test (p. 124)

symbolic speech (p. 125)

hate speech (p. 126)

prior restraint (p. 128)

gag order (p. 128)

fighting words (p. 129)

slander (p. 130)

libel (p. 130)

commercial speech (p. 130)

Miller **Test** (p. 131)

CRITICAL THINKING AND DISCUSSION

Do you support complete freedom of speech for the most despicable group you can think of? When should speech be limited, if at all?

PRACTICE QUIZ QUESTIONS

6. Which test does the Court use to determine if speech is considered dangerous and should not be legally protected?
   a) *Lemon* test
   b) clear and present danger test
   c) *Miller* test
   d) direct incitement test
   e) the balancing test

7. Flag burning is an example of _____ that is currently _____ under the First Amendment.
   a) symbolic speech; protected
   b) symbolic speech; not protected
   c) hate speech; protected
   d) hate speech; not protected
   e) offensive slander; not protected

8. Gag orders are limits on what form of expression?
   a) freedom of assembly
   b) freedom of association
   c) freedom of speech
   d) freedom of press
   e) freedom of religion

⑤ PRACTICE ONLINE

"Critical Thinking" exercise: *Politics Is Conflictual— Free Speech and Flag Burning*

FREEDOM OF RELIGION

▶ Describe the First Amendment rights related to freedom of religion. **Pages 132–38**

SUMMARY

Religious freedoms are defined by two clauses in the First Amendment: the establishment clause and the free association clause. Together, they do not allow the government to do anything to benefit any particular religion, nor is it allowed to do anything to hinder religious practice. As is often the case, the Court has struggled to precisely define exactly what constitutes "excessive government entanglement" in religion.

KEY TERMS

establishment clause (p. 132)

free exercise clause (p. 132)

Lemon **test** (p. 134)

CRITICAL THINKING AND DISCUSSION

Has the Supreme Court balanced protection for the free exercise of religion without allowing the state establishment of religion, or has it swung too far in one direction? Which rulings support your conclusion?

PRACTICE QUIZ QUESTIONS

9. The establishment clause is invoked under which of the following circumstances?
    a) allowing "conscientious objectors" to avoid the military draft
    b) outlawing polygamy
    c) prayer in public schools
    d) allowing the Amish to keep children home from school after the eighth grade
    e) banning the handling of snakes in church services

10. Which test does the Supreme Court use to establish whether there has been "excessive government entanglement in religion"?
    a) *Lemon* test
    b) *Kreutz* test
    c) *Miller* test
    d) *Meyer* test
    e) *Brandenburg* test

THE RIGHT TO BEAR ARMS

▶ Explore why the Second Amendment's meaning on gun rights is often debated. **Pages 138–39**

SUMMARY

The Supreme Court has done little to define what freedoms are established in the Second Amendment, largely preferring to allow the national, state, and local governments to make their own laws. The majority of public sentiment appears in favor of continued gun ownership, and limitations on Second Amendment rights appear unlikely.

PRACTICE QUIZ QUESTION

11. Until 2008, the Supreme Court had been _____ in defining Second Amendment laws, and its decisions generally _____ gun rights.
    a) passive; limited
    b) passive; supported
    c) active; limited
    d) active, supported

LAW, ORDER, AND THE RIGHTS OF CRIMINAL DEFENDANTS

▶ Describe the protections provided for people accused of a crime. **Pages 139–51**

SUMMARY

The Fourth, Fifth, Sixth, and Eighth Amendments provide protections to individuals accused of a crime, known as due process rights. Interpreting these general due process rights in specific cases is difficult, however, because specific standards of fairness and justice are very hard to define.

KEY TERMS

due process rights (p. 139)

exclusionary rule (p. 142)

Miranda **rights** (p. 146)

double jeopardy (p. 146)

Do you support due process rights for defendants in criminal cases, even if it means that some potentially guilty people go free? If so, why? If not, are you concerned about convicting innocent people?

PRACTICE QUIZ QUESTIONS

12. Protections from unreasonable searches and seizures are guaranteed by which constitutional amendment?

a) the Third Amendment
b) the Fourth Amendment
c) the Fifth Amendment
d) the Seventh Amendment
e) the Eighth Amendment

13. The *Miranda* rights are protections that fall under which constitutional amendment?

a) the Third Amendment
b) the Fourth Amendment
c) the Fifth Amendment
d) the Seventh Amendment
e) the Eighth Amendment

14. In 1972, the Supreme Court banned the death penalty for what reason?

a) It deprived individuals of their rights to "life, liberty, or property."
b) It was cruel and unusual.
c) It was being inconsistently applied.
d) It was racially biased.
e) It was inconsistent with international law.

PRIVACY RIGHTS

▶ Explain why the rights associated with privacy are often controversial. **Pages 151–53**

SUMMARY

The term "privacy rights" is not found in the Constitution—rather, it was established in a 1965 Supreme Court case—but it may be implied in several amendments in the Bill of Rights. The right to privacy is controversial because of the lack of explicit language in the Constitution, and the lack of consensus on exactly what the right to privacy means.

KEY TERMS

privacy rights (p. 151)

substantive due process doctrine (p. 153)

PRACTICE QUIZ QUESTIONS

15. Which of the following freedoms guaranteed in the Bill of Rights is thought to imply a right to privacy?

a) right to bear arms
b) right to refuse to quarter soldiers
c) right to secure legal counsel
d) right to request a jury trial
e) freedom of speech

16. In what case did the Supreme Court establish the right to privacy?

a) *Roe v. Wade*
b) *Lawrence v. Texas*
c) *Griswold v. Connecticut*
d) *Gonzalez v. Oregon*
e) *Lemon v. Kurtzman*

Ⓢ PRACTICE ONLINE

"Critical Thinking" exercise: *Political Process Matters—Civil Liberties and Privacy*

SUGGESTED READING

Abraham, Henry J., and Barbara A. Perry. *Freedom and the Court: Civil Rights and Liberties in the United States*, 8th ed. Lawrence: University Press of Kansas, 2003.

Amar, Akhil Reed. *The Bill of Rights*. New Haven, CT: Yale University Press, 1998.

Bondenhamer, David J., and James W. Ely, eds. *The Bill of Rights in Modern America*. Bloomington: Indiana University Press, 2008.

Lewis, Anthony. *Gideon's Trumpet*. New York: Random House, 1964.

Moynihan, Daniel Patrick. *Secrecy: The American Experience*. New Haven, CT: Yale University Press, 1998.

Posner, Richard A. *Not a Suicide Pact: The Constitution in a Time of National Emergency*. New York: Oxford University Press, 2006.

Pritchett, C. Herman. *Constitutional Civil Liberties*. Englewood Cliffs, NJ: Prentice Hall, 1984.

Schweber, Howard. *Speech, Conduct, and the First Amendment*. New York: Peter Lang Publishing, 2003.

5

Public Opinion

SHOULD SAME-SEX COUPLES BE allowed to marry? Americans are almost evenly split on this question, making it difficult to find a compromise. However, public opinion also changes over time, so an issue that is sharply divisive today may become easier to resolve as opinions shift.

Americans are sharply divided on the question of whether to allow gay and lesbian couples to marry: a 2012 Pew Trust poll found that 48 percent of Americans support same-sex marriage, while 44 percent are opposed.[1] Moreover, there is a sharp partisan split in opinions, as 65 percent of Democrats are supportive of same-sex marriage rights, while only 24 percent of Republicans feel the same way. Similar divisions can be found in many other areas, from opinions about specific policies such as President Obama's health care reforms to broader questions such as whether America is divided into "haves" and "have nots."[2]

Such polling data gives rise to two questions. First, can common ground be found given the apparently profound disagreements? Some people look at opinion data on issues such as same-sex marriage and see a "culture war" in which Americans are divided into opposing camps across a range of issues, with secular Democrats facing off against religious Republicans.[3] We have said throughout this book that politics is conflictual and that compromise is often necessary to get anything done in Washington, D.C. But if most Americans hold extreme positions on many policy questions and are unwilling to compromise, it is hard to see how politicians can get anything done, unless they are willing to offend large segments of the population—and risk losing their positions in the next election. Moreover, when Americans are divided, as in the case of single-sex marriage, it may be impossible to find a policy option that satisfies even a majority of the population, so no matter what politicians do, majority dissatisfaction is virtually guaranteed.

CONFLICT & COMPROMISE
in American Politics

A second question concerns the quality of public opinion in America. Candidates, political parties, journalists, and political scientists take thousands of polls to determine who is likely to vote; what sorts of arguments, slogans, and platforms would appeal to these voters; and which policies are in demand by the electorate. Yet some scholars have argued that most Americans make up their responses to survey questions on the spot, have no firm opinions about government policy, and are easily swayed by candidates, advocacy groups, or the media. In other words, what do people mean when they say they support marriage rights for gays and lesbians? What does it mean when people say they are opposed?

This chapter shows that Americans hold measurable opinions on a wide range of topics and that these opinions shape their political behavior. The fact that most people can express a wide range of opinions about politics and public policy is one of the strongest pieces of evidence for the idea that politics is everywhere. We examine the sources of public opinion, from everyday events to what politicians say and do, to biological explanations as well as group characteristics such as race, gender, and ethnicity. We consider how politicians take account of public opinion—how their campaign strategies, as well as their actions in office (in particular, their willingness to compromise policy differences), are shaped by information about what the public wants or might want in the future.

The case of gay marriage also illustrates one way that these conflicts are resolved, which is by "generational replacement." Many polls have found a gradual shift in American public opinion over the last generation toward support for single-sex marriage. In the main, this shift is the result of the replacement of older Americans, who tend to oppose gay marriage, by younger Americans, who are much more likely to support this policy. If this trend continues, citizen support for single-sex marriage will gradually increase, leading additional states to adopt legislation or referenda to allow single-sex marriage. These shifts in opinion also make it much less likely that Congress will enact legislation or a constitutional amendment to ban such marriages.

As you will see, process matters in the way individual opinions are formed and the methods used to measure public opinion. These processes shape what people demand from government and how politicians respond to those demands. While most Americans are not policy experts, they tend to think about politics in the same way that they think about most things in their lives. Aside from a few broad principles, such as party identification, that typically form early in life, opinions take form only when they are needed, such as when people vote on Election Day or answer a survey question. In other words, relatively few Americans form concrete opinions about issues such as same-sex marriage until they are asked about the policy in a survey. This process of opinion formation has important consequences for how we should interpret survey results.

Finally, examining American public opinion allows us to identify issues where Americans disagree on policy questions and to better understand the political conflicts they raise. We will also see that although Americans disagree about many important issues, *profound* polarization (such as in current polls on same-sex marriage) is relatively rare, meaning that compromise is sometimes easier to reach than you might think. When polls are designed to tap consensus, they reveal that on wide range of policy questions, most Americans hold opinions that are squarely in the middle of the political spectrum. Thus, there is little evidence of a "culture war" in American politics. Although much of this chapter details how Americans disagree, and the generational and demographic sources of these splits, it is important to remember that disagreement does not always exist, and when it does, acceptable compromises often can be found.

ARE AMERICANS POORLY INFORMED ABOUT POLITICS? One survey found that more Americans could identify characters on *The Simpsons* than could list which liberties the Bill of Rights guarantees, and another found most respondents unable to name any Supreme Court justices.

WHAT IS PUBLIC OPINION?

DEFINE PUBLIC OPINION AND EXPLAIN WHY IT MATTERS IN AMERICAN POLITICS

Public opinion describes what the population thinks about politics and government—what government should be doing, evaluations of what government *is* doing, and judgments about elected officials and others who participate in the political process, as well as the wider set of beliefs that shape these opinions.

Public opinion matters for three reasons. First, citizens' political actions—including voting, contributing to campaigns, writing letters to senators, and other kinds of activism—are driven by their opinions.[4] For example, as we discuss in more detail in Chapter 7, party identification shapes voting decisions. A voter who thinks of herself as a Democrat is more likely to vote for Democratic candidates than a voter who identifies as a Republican.[5] Similarly, a voter who believes in small government would likely oppose new programs such as the health care proposals debated in Congress during 2009 and 2010. Therefore, if we want to explain either an individual's behavior or broader political outcomes, such as who wins an election or the fate of a legislative proposal, we need good data on public opinion.

Second, examining public opinion helps explain the behavior of candidates, political parties, and other political actors. Other chapters in this book (particularly Chapter 8, Elections, and Chapter 10, Congress) show a strong link between citizens' opinions and candidates' campaign strategies and actions in office. Politicians look to public opinion to determine what citizens want them to do and how happy citizens are with their behavior in office. For example, in Chapter 10 we see how congressional representatives are reluctant to cast votes that are inconsistent with their constituents' preferences, especially on issues that constituents consider important. Therefore, to explain a legislator's votes, you need to begin with data on constituents' opinions.

Third, because public opinion is a key to understanding what motivates both citizens and political officials, it can shed light on the reasons for specific policy outcomes. For example, changes in the policy mood—the public's demand for new policies—are linked to changes in government spending.[6] When people want government to do more, spending increases more rapidly; when people want less

public opinion Citizens' views on politics and government actions.

POLITICIANS READ PUBLIC OPINION polls closely to gauge whether their behavior will anger or please constituents. Few politicians always follow survey results—but virtually none would agree with Calvin's father that polls should be ignored entirely.

from the government, spending goes down (or increases more slowly). Thus, to explain what government does and why, we need to measure and understand public opinion.

EARLY THEORIES OF PUBLIC OPINION

Though it may sound strange, early studies of public opinion, based on surveys conducted during the 1950s, found little evidence that the public's political opinions existed at all.[7] The surveys revealed significant inconsistency: many people expressed liberal responses to some questions and conservative responses to others. Responses also varied across time: many people who said in one survey that they favored an activist government switched to favoring a limited government when asked two years later. Few respondents could say why they liked a particular candidate or why they identified as conservative, liberal, or moderate. Americans also had low levels of factual information, such as knowing which party held majorities in the House and Senate. One author estimated that up to 70 percent of survey respondents were either making up their responses—answering more or less at random—or were unable to say anything meaningful. As he put it, "Large portions of the electorate do not have meaningful beliefs, even on issues that have formed the basis for intense political controversy among elites for substantial periods of time."[8] Only a small fraction of the electorate, perhaps 5 percent or less, was categorized as having the highest **level of conceptualization**, which required holding principles and preferences that were consistent with one another and stable over time—for example, an individual who was conservative across issues, favoring higher defense spending and lower spending on social programs, and expressed the same preferences when asked about them years apart.

Some modern studies seem to support these claims. One study found that people are more likely to know the names of characters on *The Simpsons* than to know which individual liberties the Bill of Rights guarantees.[9] Another found that a majority of Americans could not name any members of the Supreme Court.[10] And in a 2007 survey, nearly 20 percent of college students thought that Martin Luther King's 1963 "I have a dream" speech was aimed at abolishing slavery rather than securing voting rights and ending the "separate but equal" system of public accommodations in southern states.[11] If these early studies and modern examples were the last word, there would be little need to study public opinion, because most people would have little to say, many others would make up their responses, and,

level of conceptualization
The amount of complexity in an individual's beliefs about government and policy, and the extent to which those beliefs are consistent with each other and remain consistent over time.

most important, what little public opinion you might discern would have minimal impact on individual behavior or government actions. Contemporary scholarship on public opinion generally takes a different perspective.

THE CONTEMPORARY THEORY OF PUBLIC OPINION

Three arguments forced changes in the early view of public opinion. Some scholars argued that it was no surprise to find that people have trouble talking about politics.[12] After all, even if politics is everywhere, only a few Americans monitor political events or think about politics every day. Another important factor in interpreting survey results is that some survey questions are ambiguous and open to interpretation.[13] As a result, people may have trouble answering even seemingly simple questions about politics or public policy. Finally, the early surveys asked about public opinion in the abstract—in the real world, people are given additional information, such as where the parties or well-known politicians stand on different issues, which can help them to express a consistent set of political opinions.[14]

A second critique focused on the timing of the early public opinion studies of the 1950s. Analysis of surveys taken in the 1960s and afterward found that many opinions remained stable over time.[15] Later surveys also found higher levels of factual knowledge in the American electorate.[16] Both findings suggest that even if the early findings about public opinion were true, at best they described only the American public of the 1950s, not contemporary public opinion.

The third and most important argument was that to capture public opinion accurately, scholars needed to expand their picture of what it might look like. Early surveys sought evidence that citizens' beliefs were internally consistent, stable, and based on a rationale that citizens could explain. In contrast, the new work began with the premise that none of these conditions were necessary and that earlier scholars had failed to find evidence of public opinion because they were looking for the wrong thing, rather than because it didn't exist.[17]

DESCRIBING PUBLIC OPINION

Modern theories of public opinion distinguish between two types of opinions. The first are broad expressions such as how a person thinks about politics, what a citizen wants from government, or principles that apply across a range of issues. These kinds of beliefs typically form early in life and remain stable over time. Some of these beliefs are obviously political, such as party identification, **liberal–conservative ideology**, and judgments about whether elected officials lose touch with citizens. Others, such as beliefs about homosexuality or religion, may seem irrelevant to politics, but their presence on the questionnaire illustrates an important finding: Americans' political opinions are shaped by a wide range of beliefs and ideas, including some that are not inherently political.

Some of these broad beliefs are formed early in life and are relatively stable. Liberal–conservative ideology is a good example of a stable opinion: the best way to predict an American's ideology at age 40 is to assume it will match his ideology at age 20. The same is true for party identification. However, even these

liberal–conservative ideology
A way of describing political beliefs in terms of a position on the spectrum running from liberal to moderate to conservative.

A PERSON'S IDEOLOGICAL PERSPECTIVE is relatively stable over time. People who have a conservative ideology generally oppose increasing government spending and taxes.

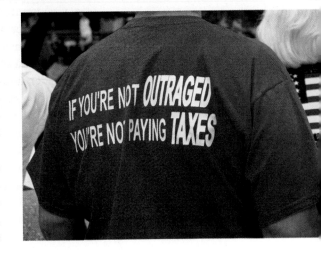

typically stable opinions sometimes change in response to events. For example, although party identification forms during early adulthood and adolescence, and often persists throughout an individual's life, it can change as new issues arise or when candidates' positions contradict a citizen's notion of the differences between parties.[18] In a later section, we look more closely at how such opinions form and why they change.

MANY OPINIONS ARE LATENT

The most important thing to understand about public opinion is that although ideology and party identification are largely consistent over time, they are exceptions to the rule.[19] The average person does not maintain a set of fully formed opinions on all political topics, such as evaluations of all the state- or citywide candidates for office or assessments of the entire range of government programs. Instead, most Americans' political judgments are **latent opinions:** they are constructed only as needed, such as when answering a survey question or deciding just before Election Day how to vote. For example, when an individual is first asked about his opinions on global warming, he will probably not have a specific response in mind. He simply will not have thought much about the question. He might have, at best, some vague ideas about the subject. His opinions on global warming become more concrete only when he is asked to describe them.

People who follow politics closely have more preformed opinions than the average American, whose interest in politics is relatively low. But very few people are so well informed that they have ready opinions on a wide range of political questions. Moreover, even when people do form opinions in advance, they may not remember every factor that influenced their opinions. Thus, an individual may identify as a liberal or a conservative, or as a supporter of a particular party but may be unable to explain the reasons behind these ideological leanings.[20]

latent opinion An opinion formed on the spot, when it is needed (as distinct from a deeply held opinion that is stable over time).

HOW PEOPLE FORM OPINIONS

When people form opinions on the spot, they are based on *considerations*, the pieces of relevant information—such as ideology, party identification, religious beliefs, and personal circumstances—that come to mind when the opinion is requested.[21] The process of forming an opinion usually is not thorough or systematic, since most people don't take into account everything they know about the issue.[22] Rather, they only use considerations that come to mind immediately.[23] Highly informed people who follow politics use this process, as do those with low levels of political interest and knowledge.[24]

Consider how people decide whether they approve of the job the president is doing. Surveys on this topic typically ask respondents whether they approve or disapprove of the president's performance, although the questions' wording can vary. Figure 5.1 shows approval and disapproval percentages for President Obama until just before the 2012 presidential elections. The data show a pattern that is typical for most presidents: initially high approval percentages, then a gradual decline during their first year or two in office. Generally, when a new president takes office, many voters hold high and often contradictory expectations about what he will accomplish during his term. In the case of Obama, some Americans expected a speedy economic recovery and enactment of many new programs, from health care

FIGURE » 5.1

APPROVAL RATINGS FOR PRESIDENT BARACK OBAMA

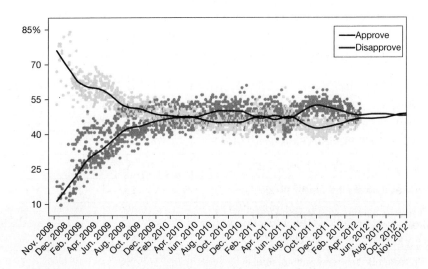

*Data from specific polls are not plotted for May–November 2012. Averages only.

Source: "President Barack Obama Job Approval" http://pollster.com/Obama44JobApprovalr.php (accessed 9/5/12); elections.huffingtonpost.com/pollster/obama-job-approval (accessed 11/9/12).

reform to climate change legislation and repeal of regulations banning homosexuals from military service. Others opposed these initiatives from the beginning, so they never approved of Obama's performance. The downward trend in approval for Obama reflects the fact that some voters switched their positive responses during 2009, 2010, and 2011 as they became disillusioned either with Obama's failure to satisfy their policy demands or the weak state of the American economy.

Many studies of public opinion support the idea that most people form opinions on the spot using a wide range of considerations. Consider the following findings: Attitudes about immigration are shaped by evaluations of the state of the economy.[25] People judge government spending proposals differently depending on whether a Republican or a Democrat made the proposal, using their own party identification as a consideration.[26] Evaluations of affirmative action programs vary depending on whether the survey question reminds respondents that their own personal economic well-being may be hurt by these programs.[27] Voters' party identification and ideology influence their evaluations of candidates.[28] Individuals' willingness to allow protests and other expressions of opinions they disagree with depends on their belief in tolerance.[29] And if people feel obligated to help others in need, they are more likely to support government programs that benefit the poor.[30]

Sometimes competing or contradictory considerations influence the opinion-formation process. In the case of abortion laws, many people believe in protecting human life but also in allowing women to make their own medical decisions.[31] When a survey asks someone with both beliefs for her opinion about abortion laws, her response will depend on which consideration comes to mind and seems most relevant as she is answering the question. Opinions about other morally complex issues such as right-to-die legislation, or about race-related issues such as affirmative action, also often involve competing considerations.[32]

TABLE » 5.1

FEARS OF TERRORIST ATTACK

In this chapter, we argue that opinions are often sensitive to new information or events. Is this true of worries about a future terrorist attack?

	FOLLOWED VERY CLOSELY	VERY WORRIED[a]	
		BEFORE	AFTER
Terrorist attacks in New York and Washington, DC (9/01)	74%	—	28%
Failed shoe bombing on Paris flight (1/02)	20	13	20
Arrest of alleged "dirty bomber" (6/02)	30	20	32
Terrorist bombings in Kenya (12/02)	21	20	31
Terrorist bombings in Madrid (3/04)	34	13	20
Terrorist bombings in London (7/05)	48	17	26
Thwarted British terrorist plot (8/06)[b]	54	17	25
U.S. Special Forces kill Osama Bin Laden (5/11)	50	—	22

[a]Percentage of respondents very worried there will soon be another terrorist attack on the United States. "Before" figures from closest available survey prior to incident; "after" and news interest from closest survey following incident.

[b]"Before" figure from August 9; "after" and news interest from August 10–13.

Source: Pew Research Center, "American Attitudes Hold Steady in Face of Foreign Crises," August 16, 2006, www.people-press.org/reports/display.php3?ReportID=285; "More Optimism about Afghanistan but No Boost in Support for Troop Presence," Pew Research Center, www.people-press.org/2011/05/03/more-optimism-about-afghanistan-but-no-boost-in-support-for-troop-presence/, May 3, 2011 (accessed 4/18/12).

Events can become considerations. Following the September 11 attacks, the Pew Research Center began surveying Americans about their fears of another terrorist attack. As Table 5.1 shows, every time a terrorist attack occurred in the next few years, regardless of its location, the percentage of Americans answering that they were "very worried" about a future attack rose significantly. After the July 2005 bombings in London, the "very worried" segment of the U.S. population increased from 17 to 26 percent, a jump of almost 50 percent.

PERSONAL KNOWLEDGE AND CONSIDERATIONS

Most Americans form legitimate, meaningful opinions when they are needed. Though they don't usually seek out new information or take account of everything they know, their opinions reflect at least some of their knowledge of politics, as well as their bedrock ideological beliefs and their ideas about what they want from government.

One of the most appealing features of this description of public opinions about politics is that it resembles the way most people think about other aspects of their lives. Do you prefer blue or black jeans? Coke or Pepsi? Jon Stewart or Stephen

Colbert? Regular, decaf, or tea? These decisions are probably easy because you face them every day and, as a result, are likely to have highly accessible opinions about which option you prefer. You don't have to think much to form your opinion. Now consider a different question: What kind of house would you like to own? If you are in your late teens or early twenties, you probably have not thought much about this one. New or old? Ranch, split-level, colonial, bungalow, Victorian, or contemporary? Granite counters, slate, Formica, or Corian? Oil, gas, or electric heat—or solar? How do you feel about walkout basements, decks, wall color, floor coverings, and appliances? The list is virtually endless.

If someone asked you to describe your preferred house, you probably could only begin to answer the question. You'd probably base your response on a relatively small set of ideas, using a few mental snapshots of your image of the perfect house and relying on your impressions of the houses you have lived in. You would probably say something very different if you had time to think, were asked on a different day, or were asked when you're ready to buy a house—or after you owned one. This strategy is exactly how most Americans form their opinions about politics. When someone is asked for an opinion on a political question she knows little about, she bases her response on a few general, simple considerations. A question about who should provide health insurance—government or private insurers—may call to mind a fight with an insurance company over a medical claim, recent dealings with government bureaucrats, how a good insurance plan helped a family member survive cancer, or even their views on the president's (or the bureaucracy's) recent performance. These considerations may not lead to the most thoughtful answer, but they may be all that people use to form their opinions.

This description of how most people think about politics explains many of the anomalies in early studies of public opinion. People have trouble expressing their opinions because they often devise them on the spot. Although people often cannot provide a rationale for their beliefs, this doesn't mean their beliefs are made up; rather, they simply may not remember such information. And it makes sense that opinions change over time, as people vary the considerations they use.

Thinking about opinions in terms of considerations implies that it is impossible to measure public opinion once and for all. Even if nothing major happens—no big events, new proposals, or other high-profile political activity—opinions may change as people call up different considerations. Such variation does not mean that people are indecisive or that they do not understand what they are being asked. Rather, it reflects how the average person thinks and develops opinions.

IMAGES OF CONFRONTATION BETWEEN pro-choice and pro-life protesters may conceal the more nuanced considerations that underlie most Americans' opinions about abortion. Most Americans believe that the decision to have an abortion should be left up to the woman but are uncomfortable allowing unrestricted access to the procedure.

WHERE DO OPINIONS COME FROM?

> EXPLAIN HOW PEOPLE FORM POLITICAL ATTITUDES AND OPINIONS

This section describes the sources of public opinion. Some influences come from early life experiences, such as exposure to the beliefs of parents, relatives, or teachers; others result from later life events. Politicians also play a critical role in the opinion-formation process.

SOCIALIZATION: FAMILIES AND COMMUNITIES

political socialization The process by which an individual's political opinions are shaped by other people and the surrounding culture.

Theories of **political socialization** show that many people's political opinions start with what they learned from their parents. These principles include a liberal–conservative ideology, level of trust in others, class identity, and ethnic identity.[33] There is also a high correlation between both the party identification and the liberal–conservative ideology of parents and those of their children.[34] These principles are not necessarily permanent; in fact, people sometimes respond to events by modifying their opinions, even those developed early in life. Even so, for many people, ideas learned during childhood continue to shape their political opinions throughout their lives.[35]

There is also some emerging evidence that biological factors such as genes and personality traits shape how we think about politics. For example, there is some evidence that genes may drive socialization—we think about politics as our parents do, not only because we learned from them but because we have the same genetic makeup, and these genes shape our political thinking.[36] Other research appears to show a relationship between genes and turnout in elections.[37] Similarly, some political psychologists believe that the "Big Five" personality traits including agreeableness (the degree to which someone is modest, altruistic, or trusting) influence behavior—and political scientists have found that these traits correlate with political activity.[38] People with high agreeableness, for example, are more likely to favor economic policies that help the disadvantaged, and are more likely to participate in local politics. However, these findings are on the very frontier of political science research, and much more work will be needed to establish how genes and personality shape public opinion and political behavior.

Beyond these influences, research finds broader aspects of socialization that shape political opinions. People are socialized by their communities, the people they interact with while growing up, such as neighbors, teachers, clergy, and others.[39] Support for democracy as a system of government and for American political institutions is higher for individuals who take a civics class in high school.[40] Growing up in a homogeneous community, one where many people share the same cultural, ethnic, or political beliefs, increases an adult's sense of civic duty—his belief that voting or other forms of political participation are important social obligations.[41] Volunteering in community organizations as a child also shapes political beliefs and participation in later life.[42] Engaging in political activity as a teenager, such as volunteering in a presidential campaign, generates higher levels of political interest as an adult; it also strengthens the belief that people should care about politics and participate in political activities.[43]

CHILDREN TEND TO ADOPT THEIR parents' ideology and party affiliation. Senator Rand Paul (right) and his father, the presidential candidate and House member Ron Paul, are both Republicans and share a libertarian ideology.

EVENTS

Although socialization often influences individuals' fairly stable core beliefs, public opinion is not fixed. All kinds of events—from everyday interactions to traumatic, life-changing disasters—can capture a person's attention and force her to revise her understanding of politics and the role of government. For example, though an individual's initial partisan affiliation likely reflects her parents' leanings, this starting point will change in response to subsequent events such as who runs for office, what platforms they campaign on, and their performance in office.[44]

Some events that shape beliefs are specific, individual experiences. For example, someone who believes that he managed to get a college degree only because of government grants and guaranteed student loans might favor a large, activist government that provides a range of benefits to its citizens. Other events shape the beliefs of large numbers of people in similar ways. Political realignments are a good example. A realignment is a nationwide shift in which many people move from identifying with one political party to identifying with another (see Chapter 7). Beginning in the early 1960s, large numbers of white southerners shifted their party identification from Democratic to Republican. This gradual change was driven by national events, including support of civil rights and voting rights legislation by many Democratic elected officials in Washington.[45]

Recent events have also shaped beliefs. Scholars have shown that after the September 11 terrorist attacks, many citizens became more willing to restrict civil liberties to reduce the chances of future attacks.[46] Support for restrictions increased soon after September 11 and remained elevated even 10 years later, suggesting a long-term change in public opinion. Similarly, many Americans responded to the financial crisis of 2008 by reducing their expectations about future income and changing their spending patterns, becoming less willing to incur debt for new homes, cars, and vacations.[47]

Events hold a similar sway over other opinions, such as presidential approval, which is driven by factors such as changes in the economy. Presidents are more likely to have high approval ratings when economic growth is high and inflation and unemployment are low, whereas their approval ratings fall when growth is negative and unemployment and inflation are high. Many of these factors shape attachments to political parties.[48]

Some events have a greater impact on public opinion than others, and some people are more likely than others to change their views. Political scientist John Zaller has shown that opinion changes generated by an event or some other new information are more likely when an individual considers the event or information to be important and when it is unfamiliar; in such cases, the individual does not have a set of preexisting principles or other considerations with which to interpret the event or information. Changes in opinions are also more likely for people who do not have strong beliefs than for people who hold strong opinions.[49]

Because events matter in shaping opinion, political scientists often find *generational effects,* differences in opinions that vary with respondents' age. For example, in the survey on the 9/11 attacks mentioned at the beginning of this chapter, the percentage of Americans aged 50 and over who believed that luck was the major reason there had not been a major attack since 9/11 was almost double (42% vs. 22%) the percentage of Americans aged 18–29 who expressed the same belief.

Finally, the reaction to events depends on how political information is delivered to people. A study of public opinion on the death penalty found that opposition to the death penalty

ALTHOUGH EVENTS SUCH AS WARS, economic upheavals, and major policy changes certainly influence public opinion, research shows that most Americans acquire some political opinions early in life from parents, friends, teachers, and others in their community.

increased as media coverage of death penalty cases began to deemphasize moral arguments and put more emphasis on the possibility that innocent people were being mistakenly executed.[50] We discuss this phenomenon, known as framing, in the next chapter (Chapter 6, Media).

GROUP IDENTITY

Another influence on an individual's opinions are social categories or groups, such as gender, race, and education level. Political scientists refer to these differences in opinion as *cohort effects*. These characteristics might shape opinions in three ways. First, people learn about politics from the people around them. Therefore, those who live in the same region or who were born in the same era might have similar beliefs because they experienced the same historical events at similar points in their lives or learned political viewpoints from one another. In the United States, opinions on many issues are highly correlated with the state or region where a person grew up. For example, until the 1970s relatively few native white southerners identified with the Republican Party.[51] Even today, native white southerners tend to have distinctly different attitudes about many issues (such as support for affirmative action policies) and hold different attitudes (such as lower support for government involvement in creating racial equality) when compared to people of color and people from different regions of the country.[52]

Individuals also may rely on others who "look like" them as a source of opinions. Political scientists Donald Green, Bradley Palmquist, and Eric Schickler, for example, argue that group identities shape partisanship: when someone is trying to decide between being a Republican or a Democrat, she thinks about which demographic groups are associated with each party and picks the party that has more members from the groups she thinks she is a part of.[53]

One reason for looking at group variations in public opinion is that candidates and political consultants often formulate their campaign strategies in terms of groups. For example, analyses of the 2008 election argued that Obama's presidential win and Democratic gains in the House and Senate were driven by high levels of support from young Americans, African Americans, and people with advanced degrees. Similarly, Democratic losses in 2009 and 2010 special elections were the result of lower turnout among the same groups and strong support for Republican candidates by people who live in suburbs and those with strong religious beliefs.[54]

Table 5.2 reports data on the variation in opinions across different groups of Americans, as measured in the General Social Survey. The table shows group differences on three broad questions: an individual's feelings about the Bible, the role of women in politics, and whether government should redistribute income (that is, tax some people and give the money to others as credits or benefits). These data reveal two important facts about group affiliations and public opinion. First, there are sharp differences among groups on some questions. People of different education levels tend to respond very differently to the question about the Bible: of respondents with a high school education, about a third agree with the statement shown in the table, compared with only 14 percent of respondents with an advanced degree. Similar disparities arise among racial groups on the income redistribution question.

TABLE » 5.2

THE IMPORTANCE OF GROUPS

		"The Bible is the actual Word of God and is to be taken literally, word for word." (percentage who agree)	"Men are better suited [than women] for politics." (percentage who agree)	"Government should reduce the income differences between the rich and the poor." (percentage who strongly agree)
GENDER	Male	28%	32%	17%
	Female	39	31	22
AGE	18–30	31%	27%	18%
	31–40	35	26	18
	41–55	34	39	19
	Over 55	36	42	21
EDUCATION	High school	38%	30%	18%
	Bachelor's degree	17	23	9
	Advanced degree	11	17	11
RACE	White	30%	31%	16%
	African American	56	31	33
	Other	36	31	26
FAMILY INCOME	Less than $15,000	43%	35%	39%
	$15,000–$20,000	37	33	24
	$20,000–$25,000	31	29	49
	More than $25,000	17	25	18
REGION	New England	17%	23%	16%
	Middle Atlantic	31	29	21
	Midwest	32	31	20
	South	52	43	19
	Mountain	29	25	15
	Pacific	23	27	17

Source: Data from 2010 General Social Survey, http://sda.berkeley.edu/archive.htm (accessed 9/5/12).

Second, the data also show a great deal of consensus. There is little variation between men and women on the role of women in politics, although relatively sharp regional and educational differences are apparent. Moreover, no one group holds strong views on all three issues. For example, the table shows that opinions on the Bible vary with a respondent's education level but shows only a weak correlation to opinions about redistribution.

These data indicate that group characteristics can be important predictors of some of an individual's opinions, but they are not the whole story.[55] Americans' opinions are a product of their socialization and life experiences as well as their group characteristics. A person's group characteristics may tell us something

about his opinions on some issues but reveal little about his thoughts on other issues, and these group memberships are only one factor that influences public opinion.

POLITICIANS AND OTHER POLITICAL ACTORS

Opinions and changes in opinion are also subject to influence by politicians and other political actors. The latter group includes political parties and party leaders; interest groups; and leaders of religious, civic, and other large organizations. In part, this link exists because Americans look to these individuals for information based on their presumed expertise. For example, if you do not know what to think about the war in Afghanistan or health care reform, you might seek out someone who knows more about the issues than you do; if that person's opinions seem reasonable, you might adopt them as your own.[56] Of course, people do not search haphazardly for advice; they only take account of an expert's opinions when they generally agree with the expert, perhaps because they are both conservatives, or Democrats, or the individual has some other basis for thinking their preferences are alike.

Politicians and other political actors also work to shape public opinion. Political scientists Lawrence Jacobs and Robert Shapiro argue that politicians describe proposals through arguments and images designed to tap the public's strong opinions, with the goal of winning support for these proposals.[57] These authors argue that public opposition in 1994 to President Bill Clinton's health care reform proposals arose *not* because Americans opposed health care reform or because they disliked what the Clinton plan would do, but because of the way the proposal was described by legislators who opposed it. Their later work shows the same was true for the public's reaction to President Obama's health care proposals.[58] While President Obama and his staff expended much time and effort to promote health care reform, giving dozens of public speeches, holding rallies, and briefing legislators, opponents of the proposal were able to shape the opinions of many Americans by making dire pronouncements of what the proposal might do. While health care reform was eventually enacted in April 2010, these efforts in opposition turned majority public support into a dead heat, and very nearly defeated the proposal.

In sum, public opinion at the individual level is driven by many factors—so many that it is often difficult to explain why an individual holds one belief rather than another. This difficulty helps explain why political scientists often focus on the average opinions for groups or for the entire nation. Even so, the works cited here confirm that our opinions have their roots in life experiences, including current events as we perceive them. The basis for opinions varies across people, but the opinions people hold are very real and influence their behavior.

POLITICIANS ON BOTH SIDES OF THE debate tried to influence public opinion about health care reform. While Obama and the Democrats sought to convince Americans that the new plan was necessary, opponents played up the possible disadvantages, with references to "death panels" and other dangers.

DESCRIBE BASIC SURVEY METHODS AND POTENTIAL ISSUES AFFECTING ACCURACY

MEASURING PUBLIC OPINION

For the most part, information about public opinion comes from **mass surveys**—that is, in-person or phone interviews with hundreds or thousands of individuals. The aim of a mass survey is to measure the attitudes of a particular **population**, or group of people, such as the residents of a particular congressional district, evangelicals, senior citizens, or even the entire adult population in America. For large groups such as these, it would be impossible to survey everyone. So, surveys typically involve **samples** of between a few hundred and several thousand individuals. One of the principal attractions of mass surveys is that they can in theory provide very accurate estimates of public opinion for a large population (such as a state, or even the entire United States) using relatively small samples. This property of surveys is detailed in the Nuts and Bolts Box 5.1. For example, while polls taken early in a presidential campaign (such as a year in advance of the election) are poor predictors of the ultimate outcome, polls taken at the beginning of the campaign, when both party's nominees are known, provide very good predictions of who will win the election and how many votes they will receive.[59]

An alternate technique for measuring public opinion uses focus groups, which are small groups of people interviewed in a group setting. Focus groups allow respondents to answer questions in their own words rather than being restricted to a few options in a survey question, and they can provide deep insights into why people hold the opinions they do. Candidates sometimes use focus groups to test campaign appeals or fine-tune their messages. However, because of their small

mass survey A way to measure public opinion by interviewing a large sample of the population.

population The group of people that a researcher or pollster wants to study, such as evangelicals, senior citizens, or Americans.

sample Within a population, the group of people surveyed in order to gauge the whole population's opinion. Researchers use samples because it would be impossible to interview the entire population.

sampling error A calculation that describes what percentage of the people surveyed may not accurately represent the population being studied. Increasing the number of respondents lowers the sampling error.

5.1 **NUTS** *& bolts*

SAMPLING ERROR IN MASS SURVEYS

The **sampling error** in a survey (the predicted difference between the average opinion expressed by survey respondents and the average opinion in the population, sometimes called the margin of error) using a random sample depends on the sample size. Sampling error is large for small samples of around 100 or less, but decreases rapidly as sample size increases.

The graph shows how the sampling for a random sample decreases as sample size increases. For example, in surveys with 1,000 respondents the sampling error is 2 percent, meaning that 95 percent of the time, the results of a 1,000-person survey will fall within the range of 2 percentage points above or below the actual percentage in the population that holds a particular opinion surveyed. If the sample size was increased to 5,000 people, the sampling error would decline to 0.5 percent.

Sampling errors need to be taken into account in interpreting what a poll says about public opinion. Suppose a 1,000-person survey finds that 60 percent of the sample favor candidate Smith, while 40 percent support candidate Jones. Since the difference in support for the two candidates (20 points) exceeds the sampling error (4 points), it is reasonable to conclude that Smith has more supporters in the population than Jones and should be considered the favorite to win the election.

In contrast, suppose the poll found a narrow 51 to 49 percent split slightly favoring Smith over Jones. Since the difference in support is smaller than the sampling error, it would be

a mistake to conclude that Smith is the likely winner. Even though Smith is ahead among the sample, Jones may have more supporters in the population. Put another way, given the sampling error, the survey results tell us that there is a 95 percent chance that Smith's support in the population is between 49 and 53 percent, and Jones is between 47 and 51 percent. In other words, when a poll shows a difference in support smaller than the sampling error, the only thing that poll tells us is that neither candidate is the clear favorite.

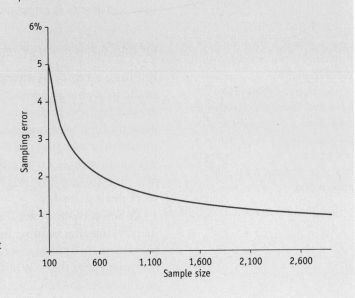

size, focus groups cannot be used to draw conclusions about public opinion across the entire country.

Large-scale surveys such as the American National Election Study (ANES), which is conducted every election year, use various types of questions to measure citizens' opinions. In presidential election years, participants in the ANES are first asked whether they voted for president. If they say they did, they are asked which candidate they voted for: a major party candidate (Barack Obama or John McCain in 2008), an independent candidate, or some other candidate.

Another kind of survey question measures people's preferences using an *issue scale*. For a range of topics, two opposing statements are given, and respondents are asked to agree with the one that comes closest to their views, including options in the middle of the two extremes. As we discuss later, on questions such as these, most Americans pick positions in the middle of these scales.

A typical survey will ask a hundred or so of these issue and candidate evaluation questions, along with questions that elicit personal information such as a respondent's age, education, marital status, and other factors. Some surveys conducted by candidates or political parties are shorter, focusing on voter evaluations of the candidates and the reasons for these evaluations. In the main, the length of a survey reflects the fact that interviewing people is expensive, so there is a trade-off between learning more about each respondent's opinions and maximizing the number of individuals in the survey—the fewer questions asked, the more people can be interviewed.

PROBLEMS IN MEASURING PUBLIC OPINION

While measuring public opinion seems an easy task—just find some people and ask them questions—it is actually very complicated. The problems begin with gathering an appropriate sample and are compounded with issues such as the wording of questions and the very nature of public opinion itself. As a result, survey results must be read carefully, taking into account who is being surveyed, what opinions people are being asked, when they are being surveyed, and what mechanism is used to ask survey questions.

ISSUES WITH SURVEY METHODS

random sample A subsection of a population chosen to participate in a survey through a selection process in which every member of the population has an equal chance of being chosen. This kind of sampling improves the accuracy of public opinion data.

Building a **random sample** of individuals is not an easy task. One standard tactic is to choose households at random from census data and send interviewers out for face-to-face meetings, or contact people by telephone using random digit dialing, which allows surveyors to find people who have unlisted phone numbers or who just use a cell phone. While each technique in theory produces a random sample, in practice they both may deviate from this ideal. For example, face-to-face interviewing risks losing households in which both adults work during the day

To keep costs down, many organizations use other strategies. These may include Internet polling, in which volunteer respondents log on to a Web site to participate in a survey, or robo-polls, in which a computer program phones people and interviews them. While these techniques are less expensive, there are serious doubts about the randomness of the samples they produce.[60] (Push polls, in which a campaign uses biased survey questions as a way of driving support away from an

TABLE » 5.3

QUESTION WORDING AND OPINIONS ABOUT GAYS IN THE MILITARY

POLL	QUESTION	RESPONSES
ABC News/Wash. Post Poll, Dec. 9-12, 2010	"Do you think gays and lesbians who do NOT publicly disclose their sexual orientation should be allowed to serve in the military or not?"	Allowed: 83% Not Allowed: 14% Unsure: 4%
	"Do you think gays and lesbians who DO publicly disclose their sexual orientation should be allowed to serve in the military or not?"	Allowed: 77% Not Allowed: 21% Unsure: 4%
Quinnipiac University Poll, Nov. 8-15, 2010	"Federal law currently prohibits openly gay men and women from serving in the military. Do you think this law should be repealed or not?"	Should be: 58% Should Not be: 34% Unsure: 8%
McClatchy-Marist Poll. Nov. 15-18, 2010	"Do you think the current Democratic Congress should repeal the 'Don't Ask, Don't Tell' policy and allow gay men and women to serve openly in the military or do you think they should not repeal it so they continue to serve but not openly?"	Should Repeal: 47% Should not Repeal: 48% Unsure: 5%

For additional details on these polls, see www.pollingreport.com/civil.htm (accessed 9/5/12).

opponent, are not really polls because they are not designed to measure opinion—they are designed to shape it. See Chapter 8.)

Question wording can also influence survey results. Table 5.3 shows four different questions asked during late 2010 to measure opinions about the change in government policy to allow gays and lesbians to serve openly (disclose their sexual orientation) in the U.S. military. As you see, support for this change depends on whether a question mentions serving openly versus keeping their orientation private, whether the policy change is described in terms of repealing a law, or whether the repeal is tied to action by the then-Democratic Congress. Depending on how the question is worded, support for repeal can be almost cut in half, from 83 percent to 47 percent.

The very act of asking people their opinions can shape their responses. Typically, surveys include details about the policies that respondents are asked about, to make sure the respondents understand the questions. However, Jennifer Jerit and Jason Barabas found that people respond to this information differently from the way they would if they had read the same information in a newspaper, perhaps because they assume that the information is true, or because they spend more time thinking about it because they know they are going to be asked for their opinion in the survey.[61] Either way, how people respond to information in a survey may be very different from how they would respond in the real world.

UNRELIABLE RESPONDENTS

Moreover, people are sometimes reluctant to reveal their opinions. Rather than speaking truthfully, they often give socially acceptable answers or the ones they believe interviewers want to hear. In the case of voter turnout in elections, up to one-fourth of respondents who say they voted when surveyed actually did not vote at all.[62] Political scientists refer to this behavior as the social desirability bias, meaning that people were less willing admit to actions or express opinions such as racial prejudice that they believed their neighbors or society at large would disapprove of.[63]

Pollsters use various techniques to address this problem. One approach is to verify answers whenever possible, such as checking with County Boards of Election to see if respondents who said they voted had actually gone to the polls. When there is concern that respondents will try to hide their prejudices, pollsters sometimes frame a question in terms of the entire country rather than the respondent's own beliefs. For example, during the 2012 presidential primaries, rather than asking respondents whether they were willing to vote for a Mormon candidate (such as Republicans Mitt Romney or John Huntsman), some pollsters posed the question indirectly, asking whether a respondent believed that the country was ready for a Mormon president.

Opinion researchers also have to contend with the opinion-formation process discussed earlier. Since many people develop their opinions on the fly, their answers will depend on the considerations that come to mind at the moment they are asked. As a result, the answer a person gives may change a day, a week, or a month later. This problem often arises in polls taken early in a presidential campaign; results vary from week to week not necessarily because of what the candidates have done but because opinions are based on relatively little information and can shift according to very small changes in what people know.[64]

THE ACCURACY OF PUBLIC OPINION

As noted earlier, early theories of public opinion held that the average American's opinions about politics were incomplete at best and wildly inaccurate at worst. Modern theories have revised these conclusions. It is true that many Americans have significant gaps in factual information, such as which party controls the House or the Senate.[65] Americans also routinely overestimate the amount of federal money spent on government programs such as foreign aid. However, rather than reflecting ignorance, these misperceptions often result from poor survey design or respondents' misinterpretation of survey questions.

In some cases, inaccurate or outlandish survey returns result because some people don't take surveys seriously. They agree to participate but are not interested in explaining their beliefs to a stranger. Faced with a long list of questions, they give quick, thoughtless responses so as to end the interview as quickly as possible. Misperceptions may also result from respondents forming opinions on the basis of whatever considerations come to mind. This strategy causes many respondents to exclude important pieces of information from their opinion-formation process.

Consider claims about health care reform. In a 2009 survey, the Pew Research Center found that 86 percent of respondents had heard that reform legislation would create so-called death panels. (The question asked about "government organizations that will make decisions about who will and will not receive health services when they are critically ill.")[66] Moreover, 30 percent of these respondents believed these claims, even though no such provision was included in any of the proposals offered by President Obama or members of Congress.

How can these findings be squared with our earlier statement that Americans generally hold opinions that have some basis in reality? For one thing, many respondents have not thought about these questions in detail—probably only a very

MEASURING WHAT A NATION OF 300 MILLION THINKS: A CHECKLIST

A RANDOM SAMPLE

Were the people who participated in the survey selected randomly, such that any member of the population had an equal chance of being selected?

SAMPLE SIZE

How many people do researchers need to survey to know what 300 million Americans think? Major national surveys usually use a sample of 1,000–2,000 respondents.

SAMPLE ERROR

As Nuts and Bolts 5.1 explains, for a group of any size (even 300 million), a survey of 1,000 randomly selected respondents will measure the average opinion in a population within 2%, 95% of the time. Reputable surveys will usually give the sampling error (sometimes also called "margin of error").

QUESTION WORDING

Did the way the question was worded influence the results? Scientific surveys try to phrase questions in a neutral way, but even in reputable polls, differences in question wording can make a difference.

RELIABLE RESPONDENTS

Respondents often give socially acceptable answers rather than truthful ones—or invent opinions on the spot. Is there a reason to think people may not have answered this survey honestly and thoughtfully?

POP QUIZ!

1 To measure public opinion, most reputable national surveys use a sample of

a 300 million people.

b 2–5% of the population.

c at least 10,000 people.

d 1,000–2,000 people.

e none of the above

2 Which of the following means that each individual in the population has an equal chance of being selected?

a random sample

b reliable respondents

c sampling error

d sample size

e none of the above

Answers: 1.d; 2.a

few had read through all the health care reform proposals, which were hundreds of pages long. When asked for an opinion as part of a survey, respondents had no time to do research or think things through, so they guessed. Thus, it's no surprise that a significant percentage of respondents said that death panels were part of the bill: some people who guess an answer say yes, and some say no.

Incomplete or inaccurate responses to survey questions may also reflect respondents' unwillingness to admit they don't know about something. There is good evidence that survey participants sometimes make up responses to avoid appearing ill-informed.[67] Thus, when asked about death panels and health care reform, respondents might affirm that a link existed even if they know little or nothing about the situation. In the main, people are more likely to express sensible, thoughtful, and accurate opinions when an issue or topic is *salient*, or important to them.

Moreover, opinions about health care proposals are subject to influence by politicians and others. While health care was under debate, some Republican politicians claimed that death panels *were* part of reform proposals or that reform might lead to future death panels. Thus, when survey respondents mention death panels, their response might reflect opinions formed after hearing these public figures. (The fact that Republican respondents were more likely to say that claims about death panels were true supports this conclusion—after all, Republican legislators were the more vocal proponents of this claim.)

Finally, many supposed facts are actually "contested truths," meaning that it is reasonable for individuals to hold a range of views.[68] In the case of death panels, respondents might know that the proposals did not contain this provision but answer in the affirmative because they think that reforms might lead to such panels at some future time. Since it is impossible to be sure either way, we cannot say that such respondents are mistaken in their beliefs.

Such problems do not arise in all areas of public opinion. Studies show that respondents' ability to express specific opinions, as well as the accuracy of their opinions, rises if the survey questions have something to do with their everyday life.[69] Thus, the average American would be more likely to have an accurate sense of the state of the economy or their personal economic condition than of the situation in Afghanistan. Everyday life gives us information about the economy; we learn about Afghanistan only if we take time to gather information. These effects are magnified insofar as the respondent considers the economy the more salient issue of the two.

HOW USEFUL ARE SURVEYS?

Survey results are most likely to be accurate when they are based on a simple, easily understood question about a topic familiar to most Americans, such as their evaluation of the president, and when the designers have worked to construct a random sample of their target population. You can be even more confident if multiple surveys addressing the same topic in different ways and at different times produce similar findings. If a single survey asks about a complex, unfamiliar topic—replacing the income tax with a national sales tax, for example—then the results may not provide much insight into public opinion. The same is true if a survey poses a hypothetical question or tries to elicit unpopular or immoral opinions. For all of these reasons, while mass surveys are a powerful tool for measuring public opinion, their results must be interpreted carefully—and sometimes largely ignored.

CHARACTERISTICS OF AMERICAN PUBLIC OPINION

PRESENT FINDINGS ON WHAT AMERICANS THINK ABOUT MAJOR POLITICAL ISSUES

Here we describe American public opinion in detail, including what people think of the federal government, their ideological beliefs, and their positions on public policy questions such as abortion rights and global warming. These opinions drive public demands for government action, from spending to regulation and other types of policy. So, in order to understand what America's national government does and why, we have to determine what Americans ask of it. The other priority is to describe the differences of opinion that divide Americans, from specific questions of policy to general statements of belief.

IDEOLOGICAL POLARIZATION

We begin by examining liberal–conservative ideology and party identification to see whether historical data show evidence of polarization. Are there fewer moderates and more strong liberals and conservatives today than a generation ago? Figure 5.2 shows data from the General Social Survey (GSS) on Americans' ideological opinions from the 1970s to 2010, aggregated (grouped) by decade. The liberals category in the figure combines people who said they were either "extremely liberal" or "liberal." Similarly, the group of conservatives includes respondents calling themselves either "extremely conservative" or "conservative." Moderates said they were either "moderate," "slightly liberal," or "slightly conservative."

The plots in Figure 5.2 show no evidence of **ideological polarization**—or a culture war that expresses itself in Americans' ideology. Over the last several

ideological polarization The effect on public opinion when many citizens move away from moderate positions and toward either end of the political spectrum, identifying themselves as either liberals or conservatives.

FIGURE » 5.2

LIBERAL–CONSERVATIVE IDEOLOGY IN AMERICA

Many commentators describe politics in America as highly conflictual, with most Americans holding either liberal or conservative points of view and very few people in between. Do opinion data confirm or disprove this description?

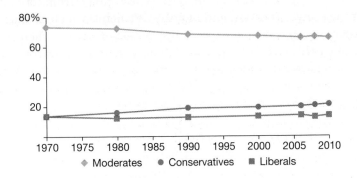

Source: Data from General Social Survey, http://sda.berkeley.edu/archive.htm (accessed 9/5/12).

FIGURE » 5.3

PARTY IDENTIFICATION IN AMERICA, 1970–2010

Party identification is another place to look for evidence of an increasingly polarized America. Do these data show evidence of polarization?

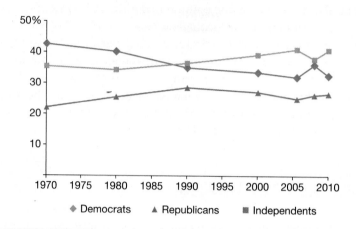

Source: Data from General Social Survey, http://sda.berkeley.edu/archive.htm (accessed 9/5/12).

decades, a strong majority of Americans have continued to say they are moderates, with fewer than 40 percent saying they are liberal or conservative. There is also no evidence that ideological polarization has increased; in fact, the percentage of liberals and of conservatives has remained relatively constant.[70]

Figure 5.3 shows decade-by-decade data about how citizens describe their party identification. The figure uses General Social Survey data and combines "strong Democrats" with "Democrats," "strong Republicans" with "Republicans," and classifies everyone else as independent. Here again, there is little evidence of polarization. Since 1970, the percentage of Republicans has increased slightly, while the percentage of Democrats has declined significantly, with some increase in 2008. The number of independents (people who have no strong attachment to either party) also increased. As with the plots for ideology, the long-term trend for party identification is toward moderation and no strong attachments to parties.

Looking more closely at opinion polarization, Table 5.4 shows responses to questions that tap important principles. These range from foreign policy to domestic issues, civil liberties, and morality. Principles such as these form the basis for opinions that people express in surveys or act on when they vote or engage in other political behavior. Although the responses show considerable disagreement, supporting the idea that a culture war really exists in America, it is important to point out that this particular survey was *designed* to divide people into categories based on what they believe and what they want from government. Moreover, on each principle, the survey asked respondents to choose between two reasonable points of view described in neutral language, and all the questions tapped subjects of impassioned debate during recent political campaigns. Like most surveys, this one did not ask about noncontroversial issues in American politics.

TABLE » 5.4

MEASURING AMERICAN PUBLIC OPINION: EXAMPLES OF PRINCIPLES

If polarization is not evident in ideological or party identification, perhaps it can be found in responses to specific questions about principles. Do responses to these questions show consistent evidence of polarization? Why might opinion surveys overstate the amount of polarization in the population?

	STRONGLY AGREE	AGREE	NEITHER, DON'T KNOW	AGREE	STRONGLY AGREE	
Government regulation of business is necessary to protect the public interest.	33%	14%	8%	10%	35%	Government regulation of business usually does more harm than good.
This country should do whatever it takes to protect the environment.	59	14	5	7	17	This country has gone too far in its efforts to protect the environment.
Racial discrimination is the main reason why many black people can't get ahead these days.	17	9	14	15	45	Blacks who can't get ahead in this country are mostly responsible for their own condition.
The growing number of newcomers from other countries threatens traditional American values and customs.	30	9	9	16	36	The growing number of newcomers from other countries strengthens American society.
Homosexuality is a way of life that should be accepted by society.	45	13	8	5	28	Homosexuality is a way of life that should be discouraged by society.
We should all be willing to fight for our country, whether it is right or wrong.	36	9	7	9	39	It's acceptable to refuse to fight in war if you believe it is morally wrong.
Americans need to be willing to give up more privacy and freedom in order to be safe from terrorism.	26	17	6	11	57	Americans shouldn't have to give up privacy and freedom in order to be safe from terrorism.

Source: Pew Research Center, "Beyond Red and Blue: the Political Topology," May 4, 2011, www.people-press.org/2011/05/04/beyond-red-vs-blue -the-political-typology/ (accessed 9/15/12).

Until 1998, the GSS asked whether respondents believed that "women should take care of home, not country."[71] In 1974, more than a third of respondents agreed; but by 1998, agreement had declined to only about 15 percent, which is why the question has been dropped. There is no reason to gather data on issues about which the vast majority of Americans hold the same opinion. Around the same time, the GSS also stopped asking whether respondents believed that white people had the right to a segregated neighborhood—not out of moral considerations, but because public opinion data showed an almost universally antisegregation perspective, whether everyone truly thought that way or not.

WHAT DO CITIZENS IN OTHER COUNTRIES THINK ABOUT AMERICAN DEMOCRACY?

Americans may not be happy with their government, but they stand by the idea of democracy. Even though many Americans don't bother to vote and few people pay attention to politics on a daily or even weekly basis, support for our democratic system of government is nearly universal, to the extent that most surveys have stopped asking the question. Most Americans consider the advantages of democracy obvious.

Of course, Americans' enthusiasm for democracy does not imply that people elsewhere feel the same way. Many of us were born into this democracy and have known no other system of government. For us, support for democracy may be more a matter of habit or socialization than a firm, informed preference. People who have not experienced free and fair elections, or the slow, conflictual process of policy making by elected officials, may have very different views on the merits and disadvantages of a democratic system.

In 2003, the Pew Charitable Trust funded a survey of public opinion in more than 40 countries to find out what people elsewhere thought about some of the values generally associated with American democracy. In particular, respondents were asked whether it was "very important" to live in a country that permitted citizens to freely criticize the government, had a trustworthy two-party system, and allowed the media to report without censorship. The table below shows that there is majority support in these regions for all three elements of democracy. Importantly, the differences between predominantly Muslim countries and others in the sample are fairly small. Even among those countries, few of which have strong, stable democracies or a tradition of democratic elections, nearly seven in ten respondents see freedom of speech and honest elections as critical. Of course, put another way, about a third of the population in those nations does not see these factors as very important.

It is also important not to over-read these survey findings. The respondents who favor these particular democratic institutions are not expressing support for America or American-style democracy, and a substantial fraction of the respondents are not strong supporters of democracy in any form. Thus, it would be a mistake for Americans to believe that everyone in

OPINIONS ABOUT DEMOCRACY IN OTHER NATIONS

Surveys of Americans show strong support for democracy and civil liberties. Is this support something unique to established democracies such as the United States or is it shared by people throughout the world?

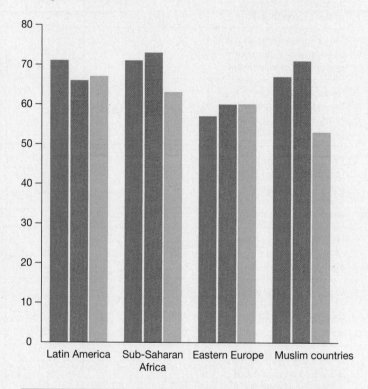

Source: Pew Research Center. "World Publies Welcome Global Trade—But not Immigration." Pew Global Attitudes Project www.pewglobal.org/reports/pdf/258.pdf (accessed 4/18/12).

other countries wants to copy the American model of democracy or that other countries would either accept the imposition of democracy or express gratitude for American attempts to change their political system.

TABLE » 5.5

MEASURING AMERICAN PUBLIC OPINION: BELIEFS ABOUT GOVERNMENT

Surveys show that Americans generally like their elected representatives in Congress. Presidents are sometimes extremely popular. Do Americans have positive feelings about government itself?

	STRONGLY AGREE	AGREE	NEITHER, DON'T KNOW	AGREE	STRONGLY AGREE	
Government is almost always wasteful and inefficient.	46%	9%	6%	12%	27%	Government often does a better job than people give it credit for.
Too much power is concentrated in the hands of a few large companies.	66	12	6	7	9	The largest companies do not have too much power.
Elected officials in Washington lose touch with the people pretty quickly.	60	12	5	8	14	Elected officials in Washington try hard to stay in touch with voters back home.
Most elected officials care about what people like me think.	15	11	5	60	10	Most elected officials don't care about what people like me think.

Source: Pew Research Center, "Beyond Red and Blue: the Political Topology," May 4, 2010, www.people-press.org/2011/05/04/beyond-red-vs-blue-the-political-typology (accessed 9/15/12).

Finally, survey responses that reveal conflict over broad principles do not tell us whether these differences translate into conflicts over specific policy questions. As we have seen, opinions have many sources, some of which, such as the reaction to well-publicized events, may lead to consensus rather than conflict.

EVALUATIONS OF GOVERNMENT AND OFFICEHOLDERS

Another set of opinions that are important for American politics address how people view their government: how well or poorly they think government is doing, whether they trust the government, and their evaluations of individual politicians, notably their own representatives in Congress. These opinions matter for several reasons. A citizen's judgments about the government's overall performance may shape his evaluations of specific policies, especially if he does not know much about the program.[72] Evaluations of specific policies may also be shaped by how much a citizen trusts the government; more trust brings higher evaluations.[73] Trust in government and overall evaluations might also influence a citizen's willingness to vote for incumbent congressional representatives or a president seeking re-election.[74]

Table 5.5 reveals that the average American is fairly disenchanted with the government. A majority believes that elected officials lose touch with the people and don't care what average people think, and that corporations have too much power. A near-majority believes that government is almost always wasteful and

TRUST IN GOVERNMENT REACHED A low point during the mid-1970s. The decline partly reflected the economic downturn and conflict over the Vietnam War, but opinions were also shaped by the discovery that President Richard Nixon lied about the Watergate scandal. Here, Nixon resigns from office to avoid impeachment.

inefficient. These evaluations are nothing new; many surveys over the last two generations show similar responses.[75]

This impression of a disenchanted and disapproving public is amplified by Figure 5.4, which shows declining levels of trust in government since the 1960s. All-time lows in trust were recorded in the mid-1970s during the Watergate scandal and impeachment of then-president Nixon, and in the early 1990s during an economic downturn. Levels of trust have approached these lows during the recent financial crisis. As noted earlier, many scholars have argued that low levels of trust make it harder for elected officials to enact new policies, especially those that require large expenditures.[76] On a more profound level, some scholars argue that low levels of trust raise questions about the future of democracy in America.[77] How can we say that American democracy is a good or popular form of government when so many people are unhappy with the performance of elected officials and bureaucrats?

One important response is that although Americans don't like their government in general, they tend to be far happier with their own representatives in Washington (see Chapter 10). One possibility is that putting a human face on government by asking about specific individuals improves respondents' evaluations because it calls to mind different considerations. Asking about "the government" may call to mind a vast room of bureaucrats pushing paperwork from one desk to another, whereas asking about "your representative" may lead people to think of someone working on their behalf.

FIGURE » 5.4

TRUST IN GOVERNMENT

In America, trust in government varies widely over time. What factors drive these changes?

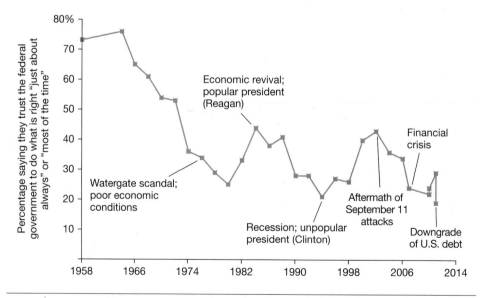

Source: Pew Research Center, "Obama Leadership Image Takes a Hit, GOP Ratings Decline," Pew Research Center, August 25, 2011, www.people-press.org/files/legacy-pdf/8-25-11%20Political%20Release.pdf (accessed 9/5/12).

In addition, members of Congress work hard to convince their constituents that they are doing everything possible to satisfy constituents' demands. Sometimes members blame the institution of Congress and the government bureaucracy for shortcomings, portraying themselves as standing between their constituents and an inept, inefficient government. As one scholar put it, "House members run for Congress by running against Congress."[78] In fact, members who deviate from this strategy while running for re-election by trying to convince their constituents that Congress does a good job are more likely to be defeated—not because they do a worse job than their colleagues, but because their statements call to mind unfavorable impressions of government that constituents consider when deciding how to vote.[79]

POLICY PREFERENCES

In a diverse country of more than 300 million, people care about a wide range of government policies. One useful measure of Americans' policy preferences is the **policy mood,** mentioned earlier, which captures the public's collective demands for government action on domestic policies.[80] Policy mood measures are constructed from surveys that ask about opinions on a wide range of policy questions.[81]

Changes in the policy mood in America have led to changes in defense spending, environmental policy, and race-related policies, among others—and have influenced elections.[82] Figure 5.5 shows that when the policy mood leans in a

policy mood The level of public support for expanding the government's role in society; whether the public wants government action on a specific issue.

POLICY MOOD

As the labels in the figure indicate, sharp changes in the policy mood often precede changes in the composition of Congress or the party that holds the presidency. Could you have used the recent policy mood data to predict the outcomes of the 2012 presidential and congressional elections?

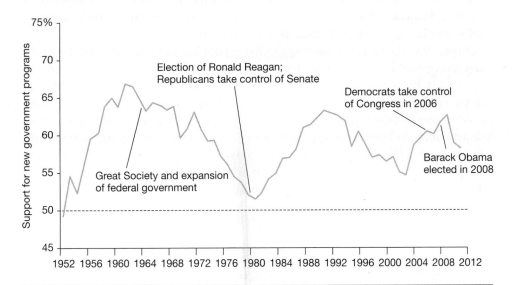

Source: James Stimson, University of North Carolina, Chapel Hill, www.unc.edu/~jstimson (accessed 9/5/12).

liberal direction, such as in the early 1960s, conditions are ripe for an expansion of the federal government involving more spending and new programs. In contrast, when the policy mood leans toward the conservative, such as in the late 1970s and early 1980s, elected officials are likely to enact smaller increases in government spending and fewer new programs.

Turning to specific issues, surveys conducted in the past few years show that most Americans focus on the same set of issues: the wars in Iraq and Afghanistan, economic conditions, energy policy, health care, immigration, global warming, abortion, and gay rights.[83] The remainder of this section presents opinion data on these issues. Some show significant levels of conflict, with large numbers of people on all sides of the question. In other cases, either most people hold similar opinions or the level of conflict depends on how the question is asked, meaning that most people's opinions are not very strong.

IRAQ AND AFGHANISTAN

The wars in Iraq and Afghanistan have influenced American politics since U.S. troops invaded these countries in March 2003 and October 2001, respectively. And public opinion on both conflicts has changed profoundly since the wars began. Given the pessimistic tone of public opinion at the time of the 2006 midterm elections, it makes sense that the wars were a central issue in many congressional campaigns and that Democratic candidates, who generally took antiwar positions, gained support. By the 2008 election, with public opinion on these conflicts being less negative and many Americans worrying about the economy, candidates' positions on the wars were not a decisive factor in most races.

Trends in opinion concerning the wars in Iraq and Afghanistan reveal a lot about where public opinion comes from and how best to interpret it. Consider Figure 5.6, which shows the percentage of respondents in surveys from 2007 to 2011 who believed that the wars in Iraq or Afghanistan were going well or very well for the United States. The first thing to note, particularly in 2008 and 2009, is that the percentages are very different for the two wars. By late 2008, about 50 percent more people believed that the war in Iraq was going well compared to the percentage for Afghanistan. Thus, when forming opinions, most people weren't just making an automatic response based on their feelings about wars in general; they were distinguishing between the two conflicts.

Second, the data reveal the complexity of political calculations about America's involvement in Afghanistan. Clearly, in 2009, with a majority of respondents believing that the war was not going well, public support for sending additional troops was limited. Thus, when the Obama administration debated sending additional troops to Afghanistan, it worked hard to explain the decision to the public, because officials knew that support for this move would not be automatic. Subsequent events, including a series of successful drone attacks on Taliban and Al Qaeda targets and the death of Osama Bin Laden, contributed to a modest increase in the percentage of people who believed the war was going well.

ECONOMIC CONDITIONS

It is no exaggeration to say that Americans are always worried about the economy. Even when other pressing issues, such as the war in Iraq or terrorism, surpass the economy as the most important problem to Americans, the economy is typically listed second or third.

WHAT TIES OPINIONS TOGETHER?

Our description of public opinion suggests that respondents come up with opinions only when these are needed, using whatever considerations (facts, ideas, other opinions, etc.) they happen to call to mind at the time. One interpretation of this claim is that public opinion is wildly variable—opinions and the information used to construct them vary dramatically across people. For example, if we were looking at trust in government, one person might form opinions based on recent scandals, while another might recall a candidate's promises. If people behaved this way, it would be hard to interpret public opinion—people holding the same opinions might be doing so for very different reasons.

However, work by political scientist James Stimson shows that in many cases, people use similar or the same considerations.[a] In fact, a small set of considerations, most notably the economy, shapes a wide range of disparate evaluations of politicians and government itself. Stimson's analysis begins by showing how approval ratings for the president, Congress, senators, and governors, as well as the average level of trust in government varied over a 25-year period, as shown in the first figure. The line for presidential approval gives the average approval rating for whoever was president at the time the survey was taken, the line for Congress gives the average rating for the institution over time, and the rating for senators and governors is the average for all the individuals who happened to hold these offices.

These data suggest two things. First, for each kind of opinion, the average evaluations move up and down largely in uni-

Watch a video clip of James Stimson discussing this topic at **wwnorton.com/studyspace**

GENERIC APPROVAL AND CONSUMER SENTIMENT

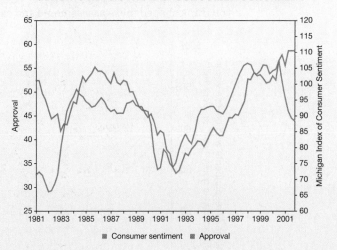

■ Consumer sentiment   ■ Approval

son, suggesting that many people are using the same or similar considerations. Stimson's analysis identifies this critical consideration as evaluations of economic conditions.

The second figure compares the average opinion line from the first figure with a measure of consumer sentiment (the Michigan Index of Consumer Sentiment) that asks whether people think economic conditions are good or bad. As you see, the two lines move up and down virtually in unison. In other words, one consideration—evaluations of economic conditions—plays a critical role in shaping a wide range of opinions.

Stimson's analysis tells us three critical things about public opinion. First, when evaluating politicians and government performance, most people rely at least in part on the same consideration, the state of the economy. Thus, the process of opinion formation helps to make democracy work—it connects the performance of people in government (as measured by the state of the economy), evaluations of their performance (as measured by approval ratings), and their prospects for re-election (since approval shapes vote decisions).

This research also indicates that incumbents are to some extent the beneficiaries or victims of factors that are beyond their control. An individual governor or senator, for example, may be unable to do much about the economy. Even so, the electoral fate of these individuals rests to some extent on economic conditions.

Finally, Stimson's work helps us to interpret data on trust in government. Low levels of trust are often seen as a signal that Americans are weary of gridlock in Washington or upset about scandals. However, in the main, trust in government appears to be driven by what people think about the economy. If so, attempts to restore trust by establishing new ethics requirements or making government more open and transparent may have little impact on trust.

APPROVAL OF ELECTED OFFICIALS AND TRUST IN GOVERNMENT

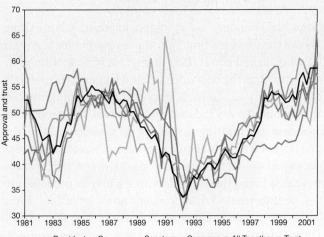

■ President   ■ Governors   ■ Senators   ■ Congress   ■ All Together   ■ Trust

FIGURE » 5.6

PERCEPTIONS OF THE WARS IN IRAQ AND AFGHANISTAN

Assessments of the wars in Iraq and Afghanistan have varied considerably over time. What factors do you think shaped these assessments and caused them to change?

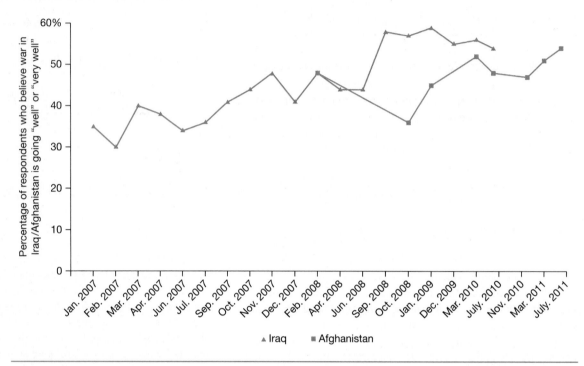

Sources: "Obama's Ratings Little Affected by Recent Turmoil," Pew Research Center, www.people-press.org/2010/06/24/obamas-ratings-little-affected-by-recent-turmoil/, June 24, 2010. "Record Number Favors Removing U.S. Troops from Afghanistan," Pew Research Center, www.people-press.org/2011/06/21/record-number-favors-removing-u-s-troops-from-afghanistan/, June 21, 2011 (accessed 9/5/12).

Recent history shows evidence of this pattern. Throughout 2006 and 2007, more than one-third of Americans rated the wars in Iraq and Afghanistan as the most important problem, while the economy ranked a distant second.[84] However, conditions changed in 2007 and worsened severely in 2008: a collapse in housing prices and the near meltdown of the global financial system, along with improving conditions in Iraq, led many Americans to revise their opinions.

Not everyone who mentions "the economy" as a problem means the same thing. Consider Table 5.6, which shows the answers that Pew survey respondents gave in January 2008 and May 2011 when asked about their diagnoses of economic problems. Looking across the two surveys, as the economic crisis deepened, the percentage of respondents citing the economy as the most important problem increased. Moreover, respondents in the second survey focused on job losses, budget deficits, and general economic conditions as the main symptoms of economic hard times.

These data make sense, given what we know about the opinion-formation process. Most Americans base their judgments about the economy on whatever considerations come to mind when the survey takes place; these considerations may be personal circumstances, long-held values, or information from a recent news broadcast. Since individual considerations vary, so do people's judgments about the economy and their diagnoses of the problems. Only in extreme situations do most Americans see events in the same way. These differences in opinion have an important policy implication: policies designed to improve economic conditions may prove widely unpopular if they do not address the considerations that lead individuals to worry.

HEALTH CARE

Health care is another important concern for Americans. Surveys from 2008 and 2009 showed that many Americans worried about losing their health coverage and complained about the high cost of health care. This raises a puzzling question: if a majority of Americans were unhappy with the health care system, why had it stayed in place, despite many reform proposals?[85] A 2009 Pew Research Center survey shows that these fears do not translate into strong support for reforms to America's health care system. Respondents were asked whether they supported different elements of various health care reform proposals, then whether they supported the various reform proposals being debated in Congress at the time. As Table 5.7 shows, although majorities supported the specific provisions, only about a third approved of the reform proposals—proposals that include some or all of the specific reforms that respondents were asked about. One month after the Obama proposal was enacted, opinion was almost evenly split, with many survey respondents remaining uncertain.

How can we explain the apparently anomalous responses in the early survey? Respondents might have believed that the reform proposals included other provisions, such as the "death panels" mentioned earlier. Or the respondents might have known that the provisions they supported were in the proposals but believed that enacting them would lead to other problems, such as increased health care costs.

In any case, these data explain the difficulties that politicians faced in 2009 and 2010 when trying to build support for health care reform—and the persistent calls for reform in 2011 and 2012. The obvious strategy was to emphasize the specific reforms in the proposals—particularly those that attracted strong support, such as requiring coverage for preexisting conditions, which more than 80 percent of survey respondents supported. But many respondents who knew that this reform was in the congressional proposals opposed them anyway, which means that providing this information might not change anyone's mind. As a result, these efforts had only modest effects.

IMMIGRATION

Immigration is a good example of an issue on which the level of conflict among elected officials is much higher than among the general public. Recently many immigration reform proposals have been debated in Congress but none enacted, as representatives and senators could not compromise on a proposal.[86] However, there is broad consensus among the American public for specific reforms. In a recent survey, more than two-thirds of respondents favored allowing illegal immigrants to become citizens after several years—with similar support for fining businesses that hired illegal workers. So why has immigration reform been stymied in

TABLE » 5.6

AMERICANS' DIAGNOSES OF THE MOST IMPORTANT ECONOMIC PROBLEMS

Opinion data from early 2008 show little consensus about the most important economic problems facing the country. By mid 2011 polls showed more agreement. What might explain this change?

	MAY 2011	JANUARY 2008
Economy (general)	28%	20%
Unemployment	26%	5%
Budget Deficit	10%	0%
Health Care	6%	10%
Other Economic Issue	22%	20%
Non-Economic Issues	19%	36%
Don't Know	7%	9%

Source: Pew Research Center, "Views of Middle East Unchanged by Recent Events," June 10, 2011, www.people-press.org/2011/06/10/views-of-middle-east-unchanged-by-recent-events/ (accessed 9/5/12).

TABLE » 5.7

PUBLIC OPINION ON HEALTH CARE REFORM, 2009–2010

The table shows that close to a majority of Americans opposed congressional health care reforms in 2009, even as strong majorities supported many of the provisions included in these reforms. By the time the program was enacted, support had increased but only slightly. How are these patterns explained by the theories of opinion formation described in the chapter?

PROPOSALS IN CONGRESS	OCTOBER 2009	APRIL 2010
Generally favor	34%	40%
Generally oppose	47	44
Don't know	19	16
PERCENTAGE WHO FAVOR . . .	**OCTOBER 2009**	
Requiring insurance companies to cover preexisting conditions	82%	
Requiring all to have insurance; government aid for those unable to afford	66	
Requiring employers to provide or pay into a government fund	59	
Raising taxes on high-income families to fund health overhaul	58	
Government health insurance to compete with private plans	55	

Source: Pew Research Center, "Support for Health Care Principles, Opposition to Package," October 8, 2009, www.people-press.org/reports/pdf/551.pdf (accessed 11/11/09); Pew Research Center, "Distrust, Discontent, Anger and Partisan Rancor," April 18, 2010, www.people-press.org/reports/pdf/606.pdf (accessed 6/21/10).

Congress? The problem is not partisan divisions in the electorate. Data suggest that the failure to reform immigration laws may have more to do with conflict within Congress, pressures from a small number of voters who have intense preferences, or the fact that recent economic concerns have overshadowed immigration for most Americans.

GAY RIGHTS

Social issues are among the most divisive in American politics. Typically they involve the question of whether the government should restrict an individual's behavior in line with a particular moral code. Good examples are opinions concerning gay rights, where support for gay rights depends on how the question is asked. A majority of Americans favor allowing gay couples to form civil unions (partnerships that confer the same legal standing as marriage), but somewhat less support allowing gay couples to marry.[87] Table 5.8 shows that the conflict splits Americans in partisan terms, with a majority of Republicans opposing gay marriage and a majority of Democrats favoring marriage rights. Thus, while the data show high levels of conflict, they suggest that disagreements over gay rights may be driven by partisan identification. The data on opinions by age show that support for gay marriage and civil unions is higher for younger voters than older voters. If these differences persist, support for both policy changes should increase significantly in coming years.

RESPONDING TO PUBLIC OPINION ON GAYS AND LESBIANS IN THE MILITARY

As we discuss in Chapter 10, elected officials in America work hard to cast votes and take other actions that their constituents will like. At first glance, this behavior seems easy. All a politician needs to do is take a poll, measure public opinion in her state or district, and comply with the demands expressed in the survey responses.

Actually, it is not easy for a representative to find out what her constituents want, because public opinion is hard to measure. Everything you have learned in this chapter suggests that taking a poll doesn't necessarily tell the whole story. Poll results need interpretation and may not provide clear guidance to elected officials.

Consider public opinion on allowing gays and lesbians to serve in the military. Suppose a member of the House represents a district where public opinion on this issue is the same as the national data in Table 5.3 (see p. 175). Also assume that this representative wants to mirror district opinion to gain political support and stay in office. What sort of guide does the survey data provide to the representative?

The first problem is that the survey provides different guidance depending on which question the representative looks at. As we discuss throughout the chapter, small differences in question wording can produce large changes in responses. Our representative could find data showing support for several different interpretations—that her district is sharply divided or that it is in favor of changing the policy.

These data reveal two problems with reading public opinion for guidance. In many cases, opinions are sensitive to question wording, so a representative cannot be sure that survey results are indicative of actual feelings or are an artifact of how the questions were asked. Moreover, since opinions are typically formed on the spot, based on relatively little information, even if the survey questions were not changed, opinions might look very different if a survey was taken a day, a month, or a year later, as people take account of new or different information. The problem is not that the people who conduct surveys try to bias their results—rather, the difficulty in measuring public opinion stems from how Americans think about politics and respond to survey questions.

For these reasons, voting in line with polls may not be politically advantageous. A representative who did so might find later that the poll's results were shaped by question wording, and that her constituents actually preferred a different policy and a different vote—or that opinions shifted between the time she voted and the next election because people changed how they formed their opinions on the issue. And, as we discussed earlier, when opinions are changing, as they are in the case of

Polls on the military's "Don't Ask Don't Tell" policy reported very different findings, making it difficult to know what the public really thought.

gay marriage, a poll taken at one point in time may not be a good guide to public opinion a short time afterward.

These findings create a quandary for elected officials: even if they want to vote in accordance with constituent opinion, these opinions are hard to measure and may change over time for a variety of reasons. But representatives must vote, even when they are not sure what their constituents want. How should they vote? You decide.

Critical Thinking Questions

1. Looking though this chapter, do you see cases where you think opinion surveys provide an accurate picture of public opinion?

2. What advice would you give representatives on the limits of polling and how to read survey findings?

TABLE » 5.8

GENERATIONAL AND PARTISAN DIFFERENCES ON GAY RIGHTS

	GAY MARRIAGE		
	FAVOR	OPPOSE	DON'T KNOW
Total	48%	44%	6%
Age 18–29	64	30	6
Age 30–49	50	42	8
Age 50–64	42	48	7
Age 65+	32	56	12
Conservative Republican	11	84	4
Moderate/liberal Republican	28	66	7
Independent	37	53	11
Conservative/moderate Democrat	30	59	10
Liberal Democrat	66	27	7

Source: Pew Research Center, "Two-Thirds of Democrats Now Support Gay Marriage," July 31, 2012, www.pewforum.org/Politics-and-Elections/2012-opinions-on-for-gay-marriage-unchanged-after -obamas-announcement.aspx (accessed 9/5/12).

CLIMATE CHANGE

Although most Americans agree that global warming is happening, the public is split on its causes. On this issue, grouping respondents by their partisanship reveals sharp differences in opinion, as shown in Table 5.9. Democrats are much more likely to believe that global warming is real and being caused by humans; Republicans are more likely to believe that global warming isn't happening, or if it is, that it is a natural phenomenon that humans have no decisive role in influencing. Given this split and the decline since 2006 in the overall percentage of people who see "solid evidence" of global warming, it is no surprise that members of Congress and the president have been unable to agree on policies to combat climate change.

SUMMARY

These examples show conflict in American politics. In fact, it is hard to find an issue where nearly everyone agrees about what should be done. Of course, in a country that is as large and diverse as the United States, this finding is no surprise. What is surprising is the potential for policy compromise in these data—a finding that argues against describing American politics in terms of a culture war. Questions that ask about ideology or party identification find that most Americans are moderates. While Americans in 2010 and 2011 disagreed on the source of economic hard times, they agreed that the economy is the most important problem. And questions on issues such as immigration and gay rights find strong major-

TABLE » 5.9

THE PARTISAN SPLIT OVER GLOBAL WARMING

The data reveal sharp position splits in voter attitudes on global warming. To what extent are these divisions reflected in congressional consideration of measures to fight global warming?

	SOLID EVIDENCE OF WARMING	BECAUSE OF HUMAN ACTIVITY	BECAUSE OF NATURAL PATTERNS	NO WARMING	DON'T KNOW/ MIXED
Republicans	38%	16%	18%	53%	3%
Democrats	79	53	18	14	8
Independents	56	32	17	31	7

Source: Pew Research Center, "Little Change in Opinions about Global Warming," October 27, 2010, www.people-press.org/files/legacy-pdf/ 669.pdf (accessed 10/24/11).

ity support for some policy changes. Thus, while disagreement is a fact of life in American politics, in many areas it does not appear to be so profound as to eliminate the possibility for compromise.

DOES PUBLIC OPINION MATTER?

EVALUATE THE RELATIONSHIP BETWEEN PUBLIC OPINION AND WHAT GOVERNMENT DOES

As we mentioned earlier, some observers of American politics argue that most Americans have no real opinions about candidates, policies, or anything else. Others claim that these opinions exist but that government officials ignore them. Having described what political scientists know about American public opinion, we can now analyze these claims.

PUBLIC OPINION IS RELEVANT

We can say with confidence that public opinion remains highly relevant in American politics today. Key evidence is the amount of time and effort politicians, journalists, and political scientists spend trying to find out what Americans think. If people were just making up their opinions, there would be no point in conducting elaborate public opinion surveys. The intense effort to find out what people think, as well as the importance given to these data by candidates, party leaders, and political strategists, provide the best evidence that these opinions matter.

Of course, it is easy to find examples in which the political process appears to ignore public opinion because policy has stayed the same despite a majority supporting change. In other cases, new policies have been enacted even though a majority preferred the status quo. But these examples do not mean that public opinion is irrelevant. Rather, they reflect the complexities of the policy-making process. It's not always possible to please a majority of citizens; politicians' willingness to do so depends on whether the majority is organized into interest groups, how much they care about the issue (and the intensity of the opposition), whether their demands are shared by elected officials—and how important the majority considers the issue to be. Moreover, the checks and balances among branches of government make it hard to change most government policies.

Many arguments about the irrelevance of public opinion hinge on the misreading of poll results. Indeed, an individual's support for a particular policy option hinges on how survey questions are worded. For example, the percentage of survey respondents who say they favor allowing gays to serve in the military depends on whether the question describes the motivations for the procedure. Thus, depending on which poll results we use, the results of a particular policy can look either closely aligned with, or completely contradictory to, the opinions of a majority of Americans.

Most people's opinions are not predetermined, firm ideas. Shifts in opinion mean that it is often difficult to connect aggregate-level opinions (what Americans think as a group) with outcomes such as who wins an election or whether Congress enacts proposed legislation. In trying to connect outcomes to opinions, we are aiming at a moving target.

PUBLIC OPINION CAN INFLUENCE GOVERNMENT

PUBLIC OPINION INFLUENCES government at election time, when voters' opinions about incumbent politicians and the party in power influence voters' decisions at the polls. In 2012, voters' evaluations of President Obama and the Democrats were an important influence on the election outcome.

Despite all the difficulties described, public opinion exerts conspicuous influence in widespread areas of government. We mention this broad influence repeatedly throughout this book. For example, our preceding discussion noted that significant policy mood changes have often been followed by changes in government policy. In Chapter 10, Congress, we describe how legislators endeavor to determine what their constituents want and how constituents will respond to different actions. In Chapter 8, Elections, we see how voters use retrospective evaluations to form opinions about whom to vote for and how candidates incorporate the public's views into campaign platforms that will attract widespread support. And in Chapter 7, Political Parties, we discuss how voters use candidates' party affiliations like brand names to determine how candidates will behave if elected.

Many political scientists have found evidence that congressional outcomes and government policy reflect public opinion. Scholars have found that congressional actions on a wide range of issues, from votes on defense policy to the confirmation of Supreme Court nominees, are shaped by constituent opinion.[88] Moreover, careful analysis of the link between opinions and actions shows that this linkage does not exist because politicians are able to shape public opinion in line with what they want to do; rather, constituents' opinions, at least in the short run, are fixed. Politicians behave in line with them because to do otherwise would place them in jeopardy of losing the next election.[89]

Of course, all politicians, particularly those with a national audience such as the president, work to shape public opinion. In the main, however, these efforts serve to publicize opinions that people already hold, as a way of influencing the behavior of other elected officials, rather than change what citizens believe.[90]

Recent events also speak to the influence of public opinion. In the case of the war in Iraq, as long as public support remained high, members of Congress voiced few criticisms of military strategy or reconstruction efforts. However, as public support waned, more House members and senators from both parties began to express reservations, disagree with President Bush's claims that conditions were improving, and suggest that Congress revise the war policy.[91] These comments no doubt reinforced the downward trend in public support for the war and may have influenced the pro-Democratic shift in the 2006 and 2008 elections (see Chapter 8). The ebbing of combat operations in late 2009 and the continued reductions in troop levels in 2010 and 2011 were also consistent with public opinion during this time period.

In fact, it is hard to find a major policy change that did not have majority support at the time it was made. Consider 2011. From the U.S. intervention in Libya to the budget reduction agreements and establishment of the debt Supercommittee, all of these efforts reflected the demands of a majority of Americans. This is exactly what we should expect if public opinion is real and relevant to what happens in politics.

CONCLUSION

Public opinion is real, and it matters. Americans have ideas about what they want government to do, and they use these ideas to guide their political choices. While public opinion often shows considerable disagreement among Americans in many areas, it also shows agreement on some issues—and areas where compromise is possible. In a country as large and diverse as the United States, disagreement over government policy is inevitable. However, as we have shown in this chapter, disagreement does not make compromise impossible—and it does not support the idea that Americans are engaged in a culture war. In many areas, people disagree, but their opinions reflect a willingness to accept compromise.

The role of public opinion in shaping the policy response to the recent financial crisis or the various deficit reduction deals is an example of how much public opinion matters in American politics. The average American is not an expert on government policies and knows relatively little about possible alternatives. But even a small amount of information is enough to inform beliefs about what policies should be enacted. Politicians, moreover, generally take care to behave in accordance with these demands. And the changes in the last few years in government policy, politicians' statements, and election outcomes all reflect changes in the policy mood.

Likewise, very few Americans are experts about gay rights, health care reform, or economic stimulus policies. Their responses to questions about these issues may vary from day to day, but most Americans know enough to decide what they want government to do about these problems—and to act on these opinions. Politicians, in turn, take public opinion very seriously, as it provides the yardstick that measures citizens' judgments of their behavior in office.

WHAT IS PUBLIC OPINION?

▶ Define public opinion and explain why it matters in American politics. **Pages 161–67**

SUMMARY

What the population thinks about politics and government matters for three reasons: people's political actions are driven by their opinions; there is a strong linkage between people's opinions and political actors' behavior; and public opinion helps us understand how specific policy outcomes are achieved. While early research was skeptical that people held meaningful opinions, current research shows that people have real and meaningful policy positions.

KEY TERMS

public opinion (p. 161)

level of conceptualization (p. 162)

liberal-conservative ideology (p. 163)

latent opinion (p. 164)

CRITICAL THINKING AND DISCUSSION

Given that many Americans cannot answer basic political questions and many of the opinions they express vary from day to day without anything changing in the political world, how can we say that public opinion exists?

PRACTICE QUIZ QUESTIONS

1. What does it mean that most political judgments are latent opinions?
a) Most Americans have preformed opinions.
b) Most Americans have well-thought-out reasons for preferring a policy.
c) Most Americans do not have any meaningful political attitudes.
d) Most Americans form their opinions only as needed.
e) Most opinions are not accurate.

2. Which of the following is *not* true regarding considerations?
a) Well-informed and poorly informed people use them in forming opinions.
b) Opinions on morally complex issues do not involve considerations.
c) Political events can become considerations.
d) They may be contradictory.
e) Party identification is often used in considerations.

WHERE DO OPINIONS COME FROM?

▶ Explain how people form political attitudes and opinions. **Pages 167–72**

SUMMARY

Political opinions are influenced by a number of factors. The belief systems of parents and relatives influence our opinions early on, and our social groups influence our perspectives later in life. Personal events such as attending college or moving to a new city may influence how we think about politics, as do national events such as the September 11, 2001, attacks or the decision to go to war. Even debates among political elites and party leaders shape our political attitudes.

KEY TERMS

political socialization (p. 168)

3. The theory of political socialization says that people's opinions are influenced most by _____.
   a) what they learned from their parents
   b) the way political parties change over time
   c) genetic and biological factors
   d) their personality traits
   e) politicians

4. An event or some other new information is most likely to change an individual's opinion when _____.
   a) the individual is highly informed about the issue
   b) the individual holds strong opinions
   c) the individual is strongly partisan
   d) the individual does not have a set of preexisting principles
   e) the individual does not watch the news

5. The idea that individuals will rely on others who "look like" them for opinions relates to _____.
   a) party indentification
   b) political socialization
   c) group identity
   d) political events
   e) generational effects

6. Which phrase best completes the following statement regarding the sources of public opinion? "Politicians and other political actors work to _____ public opinion."
   a) respond to
   b) ignore
   c) disregard
   d) stabilize
   e) shape

ⓢ PRACTICE ONLINE

"Critical Thinking" exercise: *Politics Is Everywhere— State Opinions and the Election*

MEASURING PUBLIC OPINION

▶ Describe basic survey methods and potential issues affecting accuracy. **Pages 172–78**

SUMMARY

While most information on public opinion comes from mass surveys where thousands of people respond, some information comes from focus groups where small groups of people are interviewed together. Despite a number of limitations, most research on public opinion focuses on large surveys, as they can be used to draw broad conclusions about the country.

KEY TERMS

mass survey (p. 173)

population (p. 173)

sample (p. 173)

sampling error (p. 173)

random sample (p. 174)

CRITICAL THINKING AND DISCUSSION

In light of the many problems with measuring public opinion, how should you read survey results?

PRACTICE QUIZ QUESTIONS

7. Why are focus groups helpful in understanding public opinion?
   a) They provide deep insights into why people hold the views that they do.
   b) They provide a representative sample of the population.
   c) They use a small number of respondents to draw conclusions about the country.
   d) It's impossible to understand someone's partisanship based on a survey.
   e) They restrict respondents to a few answer choices.

8. Which of the following is *not* a random sampling technique?
   a) random digit dialing
   b) face-to-face interviewing
   c) Internet polling
   d) push polls
   e) robo-polling

9. Why is it important to get a random survey sample?
   a) to keep costs down
   b) to provide deep insights into why people hold their opinions
   c) to help candidates fine tune their campaign messages
   d) to be able to generalize about the broad population
   e) to prevent question wording from biasing survey results

10. Which of the following is *not* a problem with survey data?
    a) It's impossible to get a random sample.
    b) People often give the socially desirable answer to a question.

   c) People often don't take surveys very seriously.
   d) Question wording can influence survey responses.
   e) People may invent responses to avoid appearing uninformed.

⑤ **PRACTICE ONLINE**

"Big Think" video exercise: *Why Does Polling Matter?*

CHARACTERISTICS OF AMERICAN PUBLIC OPINION

▶ Present findings on what Americans think about major political issues. **Pages 179–93**

SUMMARY

As a whole, the American electorate is ideologically moderate, with relatively little ideological polarization. Moreover, there is considerable agreement on the most important problems in the country, and potential for compromise on most policy areas. Paradoxically, while trust in the government has declined steadily since the 1960s, people are still generally happy with their own representatives in Washington, D.C.

KEY TERMS

ideological polarization (p. 179)

policy mood (p. 185)

CRITICAL THINKING AND DISCUSSION

How much conflict is there in American public opinion?

PRACTICE QUIZ QUESTIONS

11. In the 1970s, the majority of Americans identified themselves as ideologically _____; in the 2000s, most Americans identified as _____.
    a) moderate; conservative
    b) moderate; moderate
    c) moderate; liberal
    d) conservative; moderate
    e) conservative; conservative

12. What is policy mood?
    a) public support for Congress
    b) presidential approval rating
    c) trust in government
    d) public demand for government action on domestic policies
    e) public demand for government action on international policies

13. Which policy area is always near the top of Americans' concerns?
    a) economic conditions
    b) health care
    c) gay rights
    d) immigration
    e) the environment

14. Americans generally _____ of the government and generally _____ of their own representatives.
    a) approve; approve
    b) approve; disapprove
    c) disapprove; approve
    d) disapprove; disapprove

⑤ **PRACTICE ONLINE**

"Critical Thinking" exercise: *Politics Is Conflictual— Public Opinion and Health Care*

DOES PUBLIC OPINION MATTER?

▶ Evaluate the relationship between public opinion and what government does. **Pages 193–95**

SUMMARY

While it can be difficult to determine exactly what the American public wants, public opinion is still quite relevant in American politics. Government policy and congressional outcomes are responsive to changes in public mood, and most policy decisions reflect the demands of a majority of Americans.

PRACTICE QUIZ QUESTION

15. When the government enacts policies even though a majority of Americans prefer the status quo, it serves as evidence that _____.
   a) public opinion is irrelevant
   b) the policy-making process is complex
   c) politicians don't listen to what their constituents want
   d) the government is not trustworthy
   e) public opinion is stable

Ⓢ PRACTICE ONLINE

"Big Think" video exercise: *Does Public Opinion Influence Your Decisions as a Judge?*

SUGGESTED READING

Alvarez, R. Michael, and John Brehm. *Hard Choices, Easy Answers*. Princeton, NJ: Princeton University Press, 2002.

Campbell, David. *Why We Vote: How Schools and Communities Shape Our Civic Life*. Princeton, NJ: Princeton University Press, 2006.

Carmines, Edward G., and James A. Stimson. *Issue Evolution: Race and the Transformation of American Politics*. Princeton, NJ: Princeton University Press, 1990.

Converse, Phillip E. "The Nature of Belief Systems in Mass Publics." In *Ideology and Discontent*, edited by David E. Apter, 206–61. Glencoe, IL: Free Press of Glencoe, 1964.

Delli Carpini, Michael X., and Scott Keeter. *What Americans Know about Politics and Why It Matters*. New Haven, CT: Yale University Press, 1997.

Green, Donald P., Bradley Palmquist, and Eric Schickler. *Partisan Hearts and Minds*. New Haven, CT: Yale University Press, 2002.

Hibbing, John R., and Elizabeth Theiss-Morse. *Congress as Public Enemy: Public Attitudes toward American Political Institutions*. New York: Cambridge University Press, 1995.

Jacobs, Lawrence R., and Robert Y. Shapiro. *Politicians Don't Pander: Political Manipulation and the Loss of Democratic Responsiveness*. Chicago: University of Chicago Press, 2000.

Lupia, Arthur, and Mathew D. McCubbins. *The Democratic Dilemma*. New York: Cambridge University Press, 1998.

Marcus, George E., John L. Sullivan, Elizabeth Theiss-Morse, and Sandra L. Wood. *With Malice toward Some: How People Make Civil Liberties Judgments*. New York: Cambridge University Press, 1995.

Peffley, Mark, and Jon Hurwitz. *Justice in America: The Separate Realities of Blacks and Whites*. New York: Cambridge University Press, 2010.

Zaller, John. *The Nature and Origins of Mass Opinion*. New York: Cambridge University Press, 1992.

6

The Media

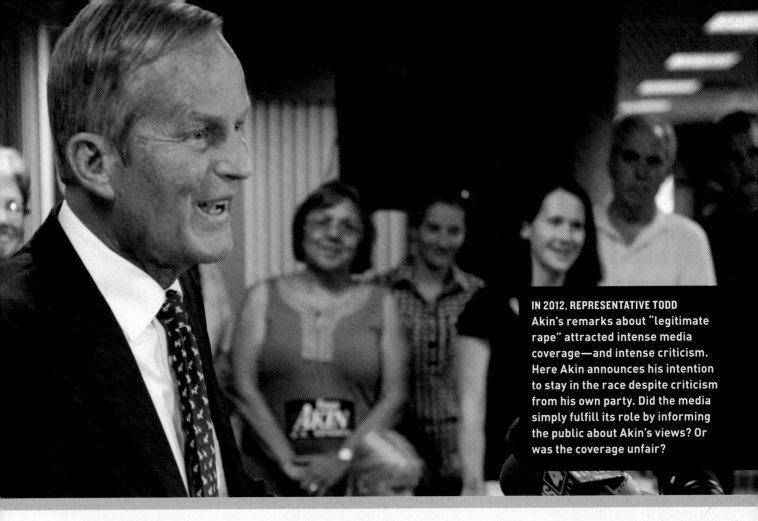

IN 2012, REPRESENTATIVE TODD Akin's remarks about "legitimate rape" attracted intense media coverage—and intense criticism. Here Akin announces his intention to stay in the race despite criticism from his own party. Did the media simply fulfill its role by informing the public about Akin's views? Or was the coverage unfair?

TO UNDERSTAND WHAT THE MEDIA DOES IN AMERICAN POLITICS AND WHY they are so often criticized, consider how the media covered the campaign of Todd Akin, a Republican member of the House of Representatives who ran for a Senate seat in Missouri in 2012.

In the beginning, Akin's candidacy attracted little attention beyond his home state. After he won the Republican primary, some stories in the national media noted that he managed to do so despite the fact that one of his opponents spent more than five times what Akin did. Other stories argued that he had an excellent chance of defeating incumbent Democrat Claire McCaskill in the general election, but for the most part, Akin's candidacy was not a focus of the national media.

However, when responding to a question about abortion rights during an interview with a local TV station in August 2012, Akin argued that women who were victims of "legitimate rape" rarely get pregnant. The remark received widespread press coverage, especially after many Democratic politicians and some Republicans, including presidential nominee Mitt Romney, denounced it and called on Akin to withdraw from the race. Akin refused, although he did issue an apology.

In the days and weeks that followed, Akin's supporters, including former Republican presidential contender Mike Huckabee, argued that media coverage of Akin was unfair, as it focused on Akin's original remarks and paid little attention to his apology and his record in Congress. Such coverage, they believed, presented a biased picture of Akin that would make it impossible for him to win.

While Akin stayed in the race, his remarks continued to receive considerable media coverage both nationally and in Missouri. National party organizations

CONFLICT & COMPROMISE

in American Politics

and many interest groups refused to contribute to Akin's campaign or run ads supporting his candidacy, even though McCaskill was seen as one of the most vulnerable Democratic senators running for re-election. Ultimately, Akin was defeated by McCaskill in the November 2012 general election.

As the coverage of Todd Akin illustrates, the role of the media in a democracy is to inform the public about politics and government, including the qualifications of candidates running for political office. Such information allows citizens to determine which candidates and which policy proposals best reflect their views on what they want government to do.

Given that conflicts involving candidates and policy options are natural parts of American politics, complaints about media coverage are no surprise. Akin's supporters wanted favorable coverage of his campaign because they knew that media reports would influence what people thought about Akin and thereby affect his chances of winning the election. While there is no evidence that reporters were motivated by a desire to scuttle Akin's candidacy, their reports were an important factor in his defeat. Thus, Akin's opponents were happy about the media attention to Akin's comments, just as his supporters were outraged.

However, complaints about how the media cover politics go beyond evaluations based on a preference for a candidate or a program. For democracy to work, citizens need to have a clear sense of which candidates and policy options are consistent with their goals—not that everyone has to be an expert, but that people have to meet a minimum standard of knowing which direction they would like government policy to go and which candidates would work toward this goal if elected.

While studies show that Americans learn a great deal from media coverage,[1] many observers blame the media for gaps in Americans' political knowledge, low levels of civic engagement, and distrust of the federal government.[2] These observers want coverage that gives Americans a detailed appreciation of the policy questions facing elected officials and bureaucrats. Critics also argue that the media should provide coverage that holds elected officials accountable for their campaign promises and behavior in office—rather than a steady stream of scandals, failures, and poll results.[3] Why do the media fail to fulfill this important role in American politics?

Media coverage shapes what people think about candidates and policy options and, ultimately, election outcomes and government policy. To say that everything Americans know about Todd Akin or other aspects of American politics comes from the media is an exaggeration. But there is no doubt that the media is an important source.

Not only does the content of many news stories influence politics, but political processes and outcomes also influence the news industry. Coverage is shaped by federal regulations that affect what journalists can print or broadcast, as well as by the structure and ownership of media corporations, most of which need to make a profit to survive. These political influences on the media can, in turn, affect how Americans view officeholders, candidates, and events.

Our discussion of the news media addresses these arguments about the nature of and forces behind media coverage of American politics. Who are the media, and how do they cover politics? Who determines which stories make the news and they way they are reported? Is media coverage politically biased? Where do people get their political information? How are Internet-based information sources affecting both the traditional media business and what Americans know about politics?

THE NEWS MEDIA IN AMERICA

TRACE HOW THE AMERICAN MASS MEDIA HAVE EVOLVED OVER TIME, AND DESCRIBE THE MAJOR TYPES OF NEWS SOURCES TODAY

This section describes the **mass media**, the many sources of political information available to Americans. It also describes the dramatic changes occurring in new forms of media and the way these changes affect not only the amount of political information available and how it is delivered, but also how people use this information.

HISTORICAL OVERVIEW

The role of the media as an information source and the controversy over how the media report about politics are nothing new. Since the Founding, politicians have understood that Americans learn about politics largely from the media; and they have complained about coverage and sought to influence both the media's selection of stories and the way they report on them.

THE EARLY DAYS

Long before there was a United States, the news media were active in colonial America. Ben Franklin published one of the earliest newspapers, the *Pennsylvania Gazette*, beginning in 1729. For the most part, newspapers had relatively low circulations, due partly to their cost and partly because they were available only in major cities.[4] During the Revolutionary War and afterward, many newspapers chronicled the conflict and became a venue for debates over the proposed federal government.[5]

Despite the guarantee of freedom of the press included in the First Amendment of the Constitution, in 1798, Congress and President John Adams enacted the Alien and Sedition Acts, which made it a crime to criticize the president or Congress.[6] While these press restrictions were later repealed or allowed to expire, they serve as a reminder that the American media have never been free of government regulation, both in terms of what is published and who can own a newspaper or other media source.

THE PENNY PRESS, YELLOW JOURNALISM, AND MUCKRAKERS

Beginning in the 1830s, a combination of new technologies, entrepreneurs, and political ambition transformed the news media. In 1833, the *New York Sun* began selling papers for a penny a copy rather than the standard price of six cents—thus earning the label the **penny press**. The price reduction, which was facilitated by cheaper, faster printing presses, made the newspaper available to the mass public for the first time, and this increase in circulation made it possible, even with the lower price, to hire larger staffs of reporters.[7] The development of the telegraph also aided newspapers by enabling reporters on assignment throughout the country to quickly send stories back home for publication. The Associated Press, the first **wire service**, was formed in the 1840s by a group of newspapers in New York to share the benefits and costs of this new technology.[8]

mass media Sources that provide information to the average citizen, such as newspapers, television networks, radio stations, and websites.

penny press Newspapers sold for one cent in the 1830s, when more efficient printing presses made reduced-price newspapers available to a larger segment of the population.

wire service An organization that gathers news and sells it to other media outlets. The invention of the telegraph in the early 1800s made this type of service possible.

THE RISE OF DIGITAL MEDIA HAS transformed the media industry, as an increasing number of Americans get news and other information online. How does this change affect the media's role in politics?

Other inexpensive newspapers soon appeared. Many were unabashedly partisan, using their coverage of events to support a particular political party or position. Some were even published by party organizations. For example, the *New York Tribune* was strongly antislavery. By 1860, the *Tribune*'s circulation was larger than that of any other newspaper in the world, and its articles "helped to add fuel to the fires of slavery and sectionalism that divided North and South."[9]

The period after the Civil War saw the beginning of **yellow journalism**. This new type of newspaper reporting appealed to a wider audience by using bold headlines, illustrations, and sensational stories (the name came from the yellow paper they were printed on). The best example was the *New York Journal*, published by William Randolph Hearst. During the months before the Spanish-American War, Hearst's reporter in Cuba cabled that there were no signs of war and asked whether he should return home. Hearst cabled back, "Please remain. You furnish the pictures and I'll furnish the war."[10] Of course, America did not fight the Spanish-American War just because of the articles in Hearst's newspaper—but it appears that the paper had a significant impact on public opinion.

At the same time, other authors and reporters used newspapers and books to call for reforms to federal, state, and local governments. These **investigative journalists**, known as muckrakers, included Lincoln Steffens, who criticized corruption in municipal governments, and Upton Sinclair, who raised concerns about food safety and public health.[11] The year 1896 saw the purchase of a small New York newspaper by Adolph Ochs, who wanted to rebuild it around the goal of journalistic impartiality, accuracy, and complete coverage of events. He gave the *New York Times* a new motto: "All the News That's Fit to Print."[12]

NEW TECHNOLOGIES AND FEDERAL REGULATION

After World War I, new communications technology made it possible to broadcast programs over radio—and for many Americans to buy radios to hear these programs.[13] During the 1920s, hundreds of small, local stations appeared, along with some larger stations that could broadcast countrywide, eventually leading to the development of networks, groups of local radio (and later, TV) stations owned by one company that broadcast a common set of programs.

The Communications Act of 1934 authorized the **Federal Communications Commission (FCC)** to regulate **broadcast media**, which at the time meant radio stations and subsequently included television stations, cable TV, and other communications technologies. FCC regulations reflected the assumption that the airways were public property, so no one had an inherent right to operate a radio or TV station. Rather, station owners were expected to serve the public interest, as defined by the FCC.

A central concern of the FCC was that one company or organization might buy enough stations to dominate the airwaves in an area, so that only one set of programs or point of view would be available. Over the next two generations, the FCC developed regulations to limit the number of radio and TV stations a company could own in a community and the total nationwide audience that a company's TV stations could reach.[14]

The 1940s saw the rise of TV as Americans' primary news source. Television made it possible to report on stories using instantly accessible visual footage rather than printed words—

---

yellow journalism A style of newspaper popular in the late 1800s that featured sensationalized stories, bold headlines, and illustrations to increase readership.

investigative journalists Reporters who dig deeply into a particular topic of public concern, often targeting government failures and inefficiencies.

Federal Communications Commission (FCC) A government agency created in 1934 to regulate American radio stations and later expanded to regulate television, wireless communications technologies, and other broadcast media.

broadcast media Communications technologies, such as television and radio, that transmit information over airwaves.

WITH THE DEVELOPMENT OF NATIONAL radio networks in the 1920s and 1930s, Americans throughout the nation could hear coverage of important events as they occurred.

a crucial distinction, given that many citizens are not highly motivated to learn about political events and issues. In fact, decades later, a frequent argument about public opinion during the Vietnam War was that declining public support for the war arose at the first time in American history that stories depicting the war's horror firsthand were a staple on nightly news broadcasts.[15] Such images were not new (previous wars had produced graphic photos in magazines and many newsreels), but they became commonplace with the advent of television.

In the late 1940s, the FCC also developed the **fairness doctrine** which required TV and radio stations to offer a variety of political views in their programming.[16] As a result of this rule, stations offered debates and presentations supporting different political positions as part of their news programs, as well as talk shows and interviews featuring a wide range of political figures. The FCC also created the **equal time provision**, which states that if a radio or television station gives air time to a candidate outside its news coverage—such as during an entertainment show or a cooking program—it has to give equal time to other candidates running for the same office. TV satirist Stephen Colbert's brief (and sarcastic) presidential candidacy in 2007 raised the question of whether *The Colbert Report* was subject to the equal time provision, since news and interview shows are normally exempted but comedy shows are not. The issue became moot when Colbert withdrew from the race.

fairness doctrine An FCC regulation requiring broadcast media to present several points of view to ensure balanced coverage. It was created in the late 1940s and eliminated in 1987.

equal time provision An FCC regulation requiring broadcast media to provide equal airtime on any non-news programming to all candidates running for an office.

DEREGULATION

The FCC's limits on ownership and content assumed that radio and TV stations were public trustees with a responsibility to provide full, fair, and unbiased coverage of political events. This assumption changed with the development of new communications technologies such as cable TV, satellite TV, and the Internet. After all, with so many sources of information, if one broadcaster ignored a candidate, issue or viewpoint, citizens could still find out what they wanted to know from another source. Pressure for deregulation also came from the owners of media companies, who wanted to buy more TV, radio, and cable stations, as well as from book and magazine publishers, Internet service providers, and newspapers, in order to increase efficiencies and profits.[17] After much debate, Congress enacted the Telecommunications Act of 1996, which gave the FCC the power to revise all ownership and content restrictions enacted over the last two generations; since then, the FCC has abolished most ownership restrictions. (The equal time provision is still in place, but the fairness doctrine was eliminated in 1987.)[18]

These regulatory changes accelerated two trends in American news media. The first is **concentration**, which involves one company owning more than one media source in a town or community. For example, Clear Channel Communications owns multiple AM and FM radio stations in more than thirty cities. The second trend is **cross-ownership**, which involves one company owning several different kinds of media outlets, often in the same community. The Tribune Company in Chicago owns the WGN radio station, the WGN TV station, and the *Chicago Tribune* daily newspaper. These trends have given rise to **media conglomerates**, companies that control a wide range of news sources.[19] Today, all four major television networks (ABC, NBC, CBS, and Fox) are part of larger companies that each own many other broadcast and cable stations, movie production and distribution companies, radio stations, newspapers, and other media outlets. Nuts and Bolts 6.1 shows the diverse holdings of one such company, News Corporation.

One FCC commissioner argued for deregulation, saying, "Democracy and civic discourse were not dead in America when there were only three to four stations in

concentration The trend toward single-company ownership of several media sources in one area.

cross-ownership The trend toward single-company ownership of several kinds of media outlets.

media conglomerates Companies that control a large number of media sources across several types of media outlets.

6.1 NUTS & bolts

HOLDINGS OF NEWS CORPORATION

News Corporation is an example of a media conglomerate, a company that controls a variety of different media outlets throughout the world. It owns cable television networks, TV and radio stations, newspapers, movie production companies, magazines, and even sports teams. This structure allows the company to operate more efficiently, as it can rebroadcast or reprint stories in different outlets, but opponents are concerned that conglomerates might expand to control most or even all of the sources that are available to the average citizen, making it impossible to access alternate points of view.

Fox Television Stations	Film Companies	Books and Magazines
27 U.S. stations	20th Century Fox	*The Weekly Standard*
	Fox Searchlight Pictures	*TV Guide* (partial)
	Fox Television Studios	3 other magazines
	Blue Sky Studios	45 book publishers worldwide
	11 other film companies	

Satellite and Cable Holdings	Newspapers	Other Holdings
DirecTV	*New York Post*	Los Angeles Kings (40 percent ownership)
Fox News Channel	*Wall Street Journal*	Los Angeles Lakers (10 percent ownership)
46 other cable channels worldwide	4 UK newspapers	Hulu.com (32 percent ownership)
		18 news and entertainment websites
	20 Australian newspapers	15 other businesses
	24 local U.S. newspapers	

most markets in the 1960s and 1970s, and they will surely not be dead in this century when there are, at a minimum, four to six independent broadcasters in most markets, plus hundreds of cable channels and unlimited Internet voices."[20] Other commissioners disagreed, arguing that concentration would limit citizens' choices and force programming to become increasingly homogenized. As one commissioner put it, "As big media companies get bigger, they're likely to broadcast even more homogenized programming that increasingly appeals to the lowest common denominator. If [television] is [like] the toaster with pictures, soon only Wonder Bread will pop out."[21] As of now, it is not clear which viewpoint is correct, although, as we show later, there is no sign that the increased number of sources is leading to a better-informed population—or that media concentration in some markets is having the opposite effect.

MEDIA SOURCES

There are many sources of political information—both from **mainstream media** such as newspapers, TV and radio stations, books, and magazines, and from countless Internet-based sources. In this section we will consider each major type of media before taking a deeper look, in the following sections, at how the rise of the Internet is changing the way Americans experience politics through the media.

mainstream media Media sources that predate the Internet, such as newspapers, magazines, television, and radio.

NEWSPAPERS AND MAGAZINES

National newspapers, such as the *New York Times, Washington Post, Los Angeles Times,* and *Wall Street Journal,* cover American politics using a large worldwide staff. Foreign publications such as the United Kingdom's *Financial Times* also cover American politics. Smaller regional and local papers serve medium- to large-sized cities and smaller towns. Recent years have seen significant declines in newspaper readership. Companies that once owned newspapers in Chicago, Philadelphia, and Minneapolis have gone bankrupt, and one major U.S. city, Seattle, now has no hometown daily newspaper. It is too early to say that newspapers are "dead," but decreases in both circulation and advertising revenues are forcing many newspapers to cut foreign bureaus, some local reporters, and the amount of news in every edition.[22]

Of the many magazines that cover politics, national weeklies such as *Time* often feature political events as front-page news. Many other magazines, such as *Reader's Digest, GQ,* and *Ladies' Home Journal,* sometimes run an article about political issues or a profile of a politician. A small number of magazines offer extensive coverage of political events, including the *National Journal, The New Republic, The Nation,* and *The National Review.* Many books with political content are published each year.

prime time Evening hours when television viewership is at its highest and networks often schedule news programs.

news cycle The time between the release of information and its publication, like the twenty-four hours between issues of a daily newspaper.

TELEVISION

The four major national TV networks (ABC, CBS, Fox, and NBC) and many cable channels, such as CNN, offer nightly news as well as **prime time** news programs. Some cable stations offer news coverage throughout the day and night, creating the twenty-four-hour **news cycle**. Local TV stations also cover some

AS THESE STARK IMAGES FROM
Vietnam and Iraq illustrate, photos and televised images of war have the potential to capture attention and shape public opinion.

local political events in addition to running the national networks' programming. News coverage varies from the "talking head" format of a person behind a desk reading copy to the camera, to investigative reporting that involves reporters and camera crews gathering information in the field and assembling it for broadcast, to talk shows that air interviews with political figures. Some programs combine these formats; one example is *The O'Reilly Factor*, a nightly show on the Fox News Network hosted by conservative commentator Bill O'Reilly. In a typical episode, O'Reilly reports news stories, offers political commentary, and interviews elected officials, party officials, journalists, and other prominent people in the news.

RADIO

The major radio networks, such as ABC, CBS, and Clear Channel Communications, offer brief news programs throughout the day; but most political content on the radio consists of talk radio programs that include a host discussing politics with listeners who phone in. The major nationwide talk radio shows, such as *The Rush Limbaugh Show*, generally offer a politically conservative point of view—and openly advertise this orientation.[23] Liberal talk radio programs also are broadcast, but their audience is a small fraction of the size of conservative programs' audience. Other political programs air on National Public Radio, an organization funded by the government and private donations. Overall, there are more than 13,000 radio stations in America. Just as with other media sources, only a fraction focus on delivering news or political coverage.

THE INTERNET

Over the last two decades, the Internet has emerged as a major source of information about American politics. Some Internet sources are electronic versions of sources that originate in other kinds of media; for example, you can read the *New York Times* on its website, and listen to Rush Limbaugh's radio program. Other sources exist only in cyberspace, such as the source that revealed sexual harassment complaints against Herman Cain, Politico.com, as well as many blogs authored by political scientists, political consultants, and elected officials. Video sites such as YouTube offer coverage of congressional proceedings, campaign events, speeches by major political figures, and many other political topics.

Another new information source on the Internet is social media sites, including Facebook, Twitter, and many sites that offer forums, chat rooms, and other venues for interaction. Virtually every political organization in America uses some or all of these tools for keeping in touch with supporters and offering their own point of view on the issues they care about. For example, during the Occupy Wall Street protests, organizers used Facebook and Twitter to keep supporters informed about upcoming protests and to post pictures of protests, including the police response in different cities. These tools also created a venue for supporters to exchange ideas about what the goals of the movement should be, to report on local activities that other media might have missed, and to compare notes about successful protest tactics.

ARE ALL MEDIA THE SAME?

From how they look to how they cover the news, media sources are not the same. One difference is timeliness. Newspapers in particular are prisoners of the news cycle because they publish only once per day. Publishing a book can take months or years from the time writing begins to the day it's available for sale. Radio and TV coverage is somewhat easier to produce on short notice, but Internet sites are even faster. Just write some new content, upload pictures, and the information is out.

A second difference is breadth. Nightly news programs on the major networks have only 30 minutes to deliver their report (23 minutes excluding commercials). As a result, even an important political event like the president's State of the Union address receives only a brief discussion. Many radio programs face similar constraints, although some, such as NPR's *All Things Considered* and many talk radio programs, run for several hours every day, allowing them to spend more time on in-depth coverage. Newspapers may have more flexibility in depth of coverage, although they aim to print a set number of pages per section and per issue. Internet outlets are the least constrained.

A final difference is resources. Major newspapers and television networks have offices and reporters stationed throughout the world. Local TV and radio stations, most newspapers, and many Internet sites depend on stories first published elsewhere, or they hire freelance reporters from different regions as needed. Similarly, during a presidential campaign, reporters from the major newspapers and TV networks accompany the candidates throughout the campaign, while smaller newspapers and local TV stations generally rely on stories, photos, and video generated by others.

These differences mean that media sources are not interchangeable—what you learn about politics depends on where you look. People who get their political information exclusively from the nightly local news learn less about politics than people who thoroughly read a major paper such as the *New York Times*.

WHAT DIFFERENCE DOES THE INTERNET MAKE?

The evolution of the Internet has made new kinds of political information available to the average citizen. Many sites offer the full text of government reports and analyses; for example, anyone can download the president's annual budget request, new regulations published in the *Federal Register*, or evaluations of government programs released by the Government Accountability Office.[24] Twenty years ago, these documents were available only at major libraries.

The Internet also makes available a wealth of analytic information. During the 2011 debate over reducing the federal deficit, many websites—including the authoritative Congressional Budget Office—offered detailed analyses of how people would be affected by different budget cutting plans. While analyses like these existed before the Internet, they were generally circulated only among a few scholars and policy makers. Similarly, the proliferation of videos on the Internet allows average Americans to see politics at first hand. For example, you can watch online videos of the Occupy Wall Street protests or just about any other political event of significance.

A RANGE OF ONLINE SOURCES

Political and analytic information abounds in a wide range of electronic sources. For example, some Internet sites collect links to political information. The Center for Responsive Politics offers a searchable database of contributions to candidates and political organizations.[25] The Pollster site collects and analyzes public opinion surveys, including presidential election polls, and offers interpretations of the results as well as discussions of possible sources of bias.[26] Other websites offer less useful but entertaining political information. For example, when then–U.S. Senator Larry Craig was arrested in 2007 for lewd conduct in an airport restroom, The Smoking Gun published his police mug shot.[27]

Most American newspapers, television networks, radio stations, and cable stations offer free access to most or all of their daily news via Internet sites as well as providing some web-only information. They also post blogs written by their reporters. One of the most influential conservative weekly magazines, *National Review*, has a web version, National Review Online, where many of the magazine's reporters publish web-exclusive stories.[28] And most major newspapers use Twitter feeds to announce new articles or photos, especially about emerging or time-critical events.

Other Internet-only news providers, such as Politico's Playbook, offer collections of links to daily political coverage throughout the nation or a preview of upcoming political events in Washington.[29] SCOTUS-blog (Supreme Court of the United States blog) analyzes Supreme Court decisions, judicial nominations, and other legal questions.[30] And many blogs such as The Monkey Cage use political science research to explain contemporary American politics.[31]

Another Internet site that concentrates on political coverage is Slate.[32] Some news sites are expressly partisan—Salon and The Huffington Post lean in the liberal direction, while Power Line and Town Hall offer a conservative viewpoint.[33] Finally, an enormous amount of professional and amateur video coverage of politics is available on YouTube and many other websites. Various political organizations and candidates use Facebook, Twitter, and other social networking sites to recruit and organize supporters.

SEXUAL HARASSMENT COMPLAINTS against 2012 presidential candidate Herman Cain were first revealed on the Politico website. The story was then picked up by other websites and the mainstream media, eventually leading to Cain's withdrawal from the race.

LOWERED BARRIERS TO PUBLICATION

The Internet also has lowered the barriers to publication. A generation ago, it was all but impossible for average citizens to report on what they knew or present their analyses to the general public.[34] The Internet has created more opportunities for home-grown media, allowing a would-be political reporter to easily set up a website or Facebook page. For example, thousands of active-duty and retired military personnel have used blogs to chronicle their service in Iraq and Afghanistan, a phenomenon known as milblogging.[35] Many interest groups use Facebook to keep supporters informed about issues and events. One of the major Tea Party organizations, Tea Party Patriots, had nearly a million followers on their Facebook page as of late 2011.

Similarly, YouTube has videos of campaign events and campaign ads, many prepared by people with no official connections to the candidates. These videos have the potential to change elections: in the 2006 Virginia Senate race, a volunteer for challenger James Webb recorded incumbent George Allen using a Tunisian racial slur, "macaca," to refer to the volunteer, who was of Indian descent.[36] The episode, which mainstream media later picked up, dogged Allen for the entire campaign. After initially seeming a shoo-in for re-election, Allen lost by more than 9,000 votes.

The Internet creates new opportunities for two-way interaction between citizens, reporters, and government officials. Many reporters respond to comments posted by readers or host live chat sessions, allowing people to ask follow-up questions about published stories.[37] Politicians do the same: in April 2011, President Obama used Facebook for a "town hall meeting," where he responded to questions posted online.[38]

Finally, the Internet enables ordinary citizens to report on events as they happen. For example, when New York City police arrested Occupy Wall Street protesters on the Brooklyn Bridge in October 2011, the first reports and videos of the event appeared as Twitter posts. Politicians must now assume that

THE INTERNET MAKES IT EASIER TO share political information. Most political groups now have websites or Facebook pages. Here, the founders of a local Tea Party group in Massachusetts check the group's Facebook page.

THE INTERNET ALLOWS ORDINARY citizens to report on events as they happen. During the Occupy Wall Street protests, photos of police arresting mostly peaceful protesters were shared on Twitter and then circulated widely.

THIS FABRICATED PHOTO SHOWS President Obama apparently talking into a telephone he is holding upside down. The easy availability of doctored photos of many elected officials on the Internet highlights the dangers of relying on unvetted websites as a primary source of political information.

anything they say or do (good or bad) will be instantly publicized using the same technology.

BUT DO WE HAVE A BETTER-INFORMED CITIZENRY?

How much difference does all this Internet information make? Some pundits argue that the Internet will transform American politics, leading to a better-informed, more politically active citizenry.[39] And it may—someday. Some studies show that Internet usage is associated with higher levels of political participation, yet others show no such association.[40] Moreover, there is no clear evidence that surfing the web makes people more politically informed.[41]

Why hasn't the Internet created a better-informed citizenry? While the percentage of people who routinely use the Internet is very high, access is only the first step in becoming informed. One problem is that finding information on the Internet still requires doing your own research. Despite search engines, it is not always obvious where to look for political information. Suppose you wanted to learn more about the conflict in Afghanistan. A Google search in late 2012 on the terms "America," "Afghanistan," and "war" returned over 200 million web pages, from reports on America's military strategy to pictures of Afghan civilian casualties. Thus, the problem is not in finding information, but in deciding which of the millions of pages will help you learn about the conflict.

Second, some of the vast quantity of information on the Internet is of questionable reliability. For example, it is easy to find fake photographs of President Barack Obama on the phone while holding the receiver upside down, or a fake photo of a deceased Osama Bin Laden. Some websites identify these pictures as the fabrications that they are, but others do not. In a world where websites come and go, and when citizens do not take the time to investigate what they see or read, false information may easily be accepted as true.

Another problem is that most people do not consult a wide range of media sources, instead focusing on sites with views on political events that are compatible with their own—thus, Democrats look for sites that favor Democratic policies, conservatives look for websites run by conservative individuals or organizations, and so on.[42] The use of information supplied by political blogs shows the same pattern.[43]

In short, despite the Internet's wealth of information, there is no guarantee that people will sit down, search for what they want or need to know, distinguish truth from falsehood, and assemble their findings into coherent conclusions. In fact, people may prefer to focus on events that catch their attention, such as a new celebrity scandal or viral video, and avoid "boring" stories such as current events in politics.[44]

DESCRIBE WHERE REPORTERS AND OTHERS IN THE NEWS MEDIA GET POLITICAL INFORMATION

POLITICAL REPORTING: SOURCES, LEAKS, AND SHIELD LAWS

Because media coverage of politics influences what citizens know as well as their vote decisions, their evaluations of government programs, and the demands they place on elected officials or bureaucrats, the reality of reporting on politics is that many people involved in the political process don't want the public to know everything they are doing—or want only their own version of events to be publicized.

DO MORE NEWS SOURCES IMPROVE POLITICAL KNOWLEDGE?

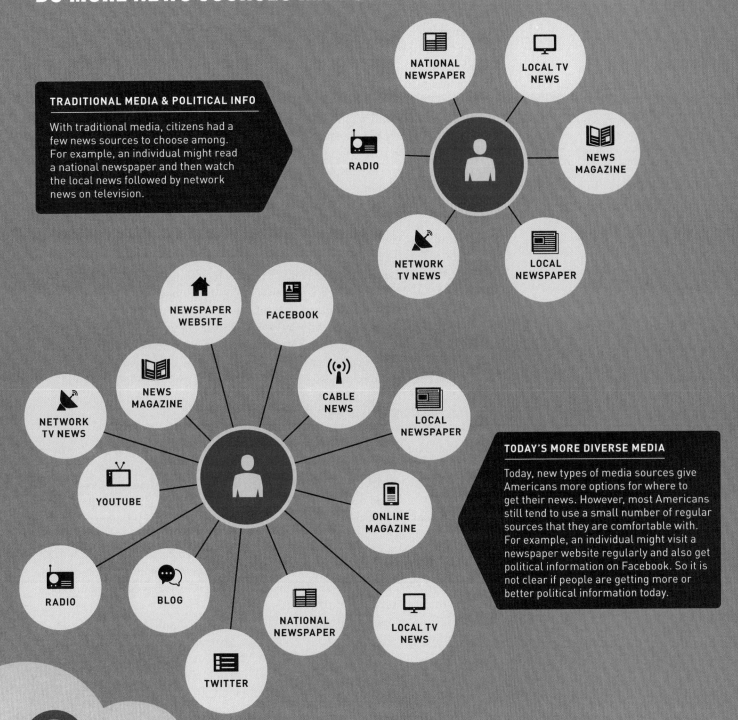

TRADITIONAL MEDIA & POLITICAL INFO

With traditional media, citizens had a few news sources to choose among. For example, an individual might read a national newspaper and then watch the local news followed by network news on television.

NATIONAL NEWSPAPER

LOCAL TV NEWS

NEWS MAGAZINE

RADIO

NETWORK TV NEWS

LOCAL NEWSPAPER

NEWSPAPER WEBSITE

FACEBOOK

NEWS MAGAZINE

CABLE NEWS

LOCAL NEWSPAPER

NETWORK TV NEWS

YOUTUBE

ONLINE MAGAZINE

RADIO

BLOG

NATIONAL NEWSPAPER

LOCAL TV NEWS

TWITTER

TODAY'S MORE DIVERSE MEDIA

Today, new types of media sources give Americans more options for where to get their news. However, most Americans still tend to use a small number of regular sources that they are comfortable with. For example, an individual might visit a newspaper website regularly and also get political information on Facebook. So it is not clear if people are getting more or better political information today.

POP QUIZ!

1 As compared with 20 years ago, Americans have _____ sources of political information.

a many more
b a couple more
c the same number of
d slightly fewer
e far fewer

2 According to the chapter, one advantage of new media is that

a people spend more time learning about politics.
b individuals use a larger number of sources than in the past.
c online information is more authoritative.
d it is always easy to navigate.
e it allows ordinary citizens to share information and opinions.

Politicians want media coverage that highlights their achievements in order to build public support and secure election (or re-election), bureaucrats want favorable attention for their programs, and interest groups want publicity to further their causes. Thus, coverage of American politics reflects trade-offs between reporters who want complete, accurate information and sources who want favorable coverage.

Reporters also face legal hurdles as they research stories. Notwithstanding the freedom of the press guaranteed in the Bill of Rights, reporters are subject to legal limitations, including the clear and present danger test and prior restraint. If the government can convince a judge that publication of a particular story would lead to immediate harm to a person or persons, a judge can halt publication; this action is called prior restraint. But the clear and present danger test sets the bar extremely high for stopping publication of a story. As we discussed in Chapter 4, most attempts to prevent publication have been unsuccessful.

To appreciate the issues surrounding classified information and prior restraint, consider the organization WikiLeaks. In 2010, WikiLeaks approached several major publications across the world, including the *New York Times*, to offer access to a collection of classified State Department cables that reported on the international events, profiles of foreign leaders (including embarrassing details about their personal lives), assessments of the state of the war in Afghanistan, and other matters.[45] The pessimistic tone of many of the latter documents contrasted with the relatively optimistic perspective of the Obama and Bush administrations' public comments. These documents were leaked to WikiLeaks by Bradley Manning, an American soldier whose job gave him access to classified information. (WikiLeaks had previously released documents on the Iraq War and the American prison for terror suspects in Guantánamo Bay, Cuba, as well as videos showing an American attack in Iraq that caused civilian casualties.)

After spending several months verifying the legitimacy of the documents and holding discussions with the U.S. government over what information could be released without harming national security or placing confidential sources in jeopardy, the *Times* and other media sources published a series of articles based on the WikiLeaks information. While some government officials mentioned the possibility of invoking the prior restraint prohibition, no attempts were made to do so; the information in the cables was embarrassing, and arguably sensitive, but the government stood little chance of stopping publication in court. In any case, even if the *Times* could be deterred from publication, the information would soon appear in stories published by other outlets.

The WikiLeaks episode illustrates how government officials work to deter leaks or influence the media's coverage of a story without resorting to prior restraint. First, there are laws prohibiting the disclosure of classified information. In the case of WikiLeaks, the American who provided the information, Bradley Manning, faces a court-martial and possibly a long jail sentence. Second, government officials try to persuade reporters and editors to voluntarily refrain from publishing sensitive stories. In the case of WikiLeaks, the *New York Times* sat on the story for a full year, publishing only when it was rumored that another paper planned to release its own version of the story. Moreover, *Times* reporters and editors agreed to keep certain information out of their stories, such as the names of Afghans who were working for the U.S. military or acting as confidential informants—this restriction later became moot, after WikiLeaks published all of the cables on their website without editing out all these names.

PRIOR RESTRAINT OF SECRET INFORMATION

The conflict between reporters and government officials is particularly sharp in the case of confidential information. Consider the diplomatic cables that were released to the public by WikiLeaks in 2010 and 2011. Some of the information is simply embarrassing—such as reports of a foreign leader's mistress. But other information contained in these documents was more serious, such as the identities of confidential informants. As Porter Goss, former director of the CIA, argued, if someone living abroad is found to be an employee of the CIA, that person's ability to gather information will surely be compromised; in some places, the person's life might be in danger.[a]

Publishing confidential analyses is still a problem even if sources are removed. The leaked reports revealed, for example that the United States had little confidence that the Afghan government could win support from its citizens, suggesting that if the Taliban forces could hold out until U.S. forces left the country, they could topple the government and return to power.

These concerns speak to the need for prior restraint, which gives the government the power to keep the details of secret operations and the names of covert operatives out of the newspapers and other media sources. But as we discussed in Chapter 4, attempts to invoke prior restraint are almost never successful. In this case, the U.S. government could not stop WikiLeaks from releasing the information since it is located outside the country. But the government could have gone to court to prevent the *New York Times* from publishing analyses based on the WikiLeaks information. Even if the information would eventually be released, restraining the *Times* would help to minimize the damage. Why isn't keeping secrets an easy call?

The problem is accountability. If the media are restrained from publication, then there is a risk that government officials will be able to do whatever they want, because the public, and most elected officials, will not find out. Put another way, without media watchdogs, the small number of unelected bureaucrats who make decisions about secret operations will never have to answer for those decisions to the public or to elected representatives. Moreover, these same bureaucrats would decide which operations would be considered secret in the first place. In some cases, the ability to keep operations secret has allowed intelligence agencies to carry out programs that might have been prohibited had they been publicized from the start, such as the network of CIA prisons in Eastern Europe that was revealed in 2005.

The situation is somewhat different for individuals who leak classified information to the press. Bradley Manning, the source for WikiLeaks, violated a series of criminal statutes and Army regulations that prohibit the unauthorized release of classified information. The Manning case is notable because of the size of the leak and because Manning is being prosecuted. Often, the source of a leak is never identified. Even if a lead can be traced back to an individual, in many cases criminal charges are not

Bradley Manning (center), whose job in the U.S. military gave him access to classified information, downloaded thousands of classified videos, diplomatic cables, reports, and other information and gave them to the website WikiLeaks.

brought, although a leaker may be fired, face disciplinary proceedings, or have no chance of being promoted—the threat of which discourages people from leaking information in the first place. Of course, without leaks, many government failures and embarrassing incidents will not come to light, which further weakens accountability.

In sum, decisions about prior restraint are difficult, precisely because they involve balancing two important goals: allowing the government to carry out covert operations, and informing the public about government actions so that citizens can evaluate and respond to them.

Critical **Thinking** Questions

1. If you had to evaluate an intelligence agency's request for prior restraint, what criteria would you use to decide whether to grant the request?

2. Should individuals such as Bradley Manning who leak classified information to the press be punished or praised for their actions? What circumstances or specifics would lead you to decide one way or the other?

Why do reporters and publishers restrain their stories? Sometimes they agree that keeping secrets is in the national interest. Other times, reporters are rewarded for cooperating—they may get information about another government policy or future access to officials. Alternately, reporters may be coerced to back down from a story through threats, such as the possibility of losing access to people in government for future stories or even going to jail.

STAGING THE NEWS

People inside the federal government, from the president to the large numbers of bureaucrats, work to shape media coverage to suit their personal goals. President Reagan's press secretary had a sign in his office that said, "You don't tell us how to stage the news, and we won't tell you how to cover it."

Politicians and others in government try to influence coverage by providing select information to reporters. Sometimes they hold **press conferences** when they take questions from the media. Other times, they speak to single reporters or to a group **on background** or **off the record**, meaning that the reporter can use the information but cannot attribute it to the politician by name. Another strategy is to hold events aimed at securing favorable press coverage. In October 2007, officials at the Federal Emergency Management Agency (FEMA) held a press conference to detail its response to massive wildfires outside San Diego, California. The conference was attended only by television camera crews; FEMA allowed reporters to listen to the conference by phone, but they could not ask questions. So, who asked the questions? Other FEMA employees. Clearly, the event was designed to showcase the scope and effectiveness of FEMA's relief efforts, but the effort collapsed when the circumstances of the press conference came to light. A variation on this approach occurred at a press conference in 2009, when President Obama's staff apparently coordinated with a Huffington Post reporter to ask a specific question on Iran—and made sure that the reporter was able to ask the question early in the press conference.[46]

Some scholars argue that these examples illustrate a more general pattern: that elected officials use the media to shape public opinion, doling out information to reward reporters who write stories that support the officials' points of view.[47] However, while there is no doubt that elected officials would like to receive sympathetic media coverage and are sometimes successful, news reports on American politics reflect a multitude of sources and information. If nothing else, the fact that conflict is endemic to American politics means that one official's attempt to shape coverage may be negated by another's efforts to promote a different point of view. The result is that different sources cover the same events differently; if you are interested in different points of view, they are generally not hard to find.

press conference An event at which a politician speaks to journalists and, in most cases, answers their questions afterward.

on background or **off the record** Comments a politician makes to the press on the condition that they can be reported only if they are not attributed to that politician.

REVEALING SOURCES

Reporters covering important or controversial stories often promise their sources that they will remain anonymous in any coverage based on the information they provide. These assurances are an important factor in the decision to leak information, especially classified information. However, this assurance is not absolute. Reporters and their editors can, under certain circumstances, be compelled by a court to reveal the sources for their stories. While some states have **shield laws** that allow reporters to refuse to name their sources, there is no such law at the federal level. As a result, federal prosecutors can ask a judge to force reporters to name their sources, on the grounds that the source's identity is fundamental to their case. If the judge agrees, the reporter can be jailed for contempt for an indefinite period unless he or she provides the information. For example, in 2005, *Times* reporter Judith Miller was jailed for refusing to name the Bush administration official who gave her the identity of a clandestine CIA employee whose husband had written a report discrediting the administration's claim that Iraq was developing nuclear weapons. After three months in prison, Miller's source agreed to let her release his name: I. Lewis Libby, then–Vice President Dick Cheney's deputy chief of staff. Libby was later convicted of lying to a grand jury about his actions.

The complex relationship between reporters and their sources highlights three important influences on media coverage of politics. A reporter's desire to tell the whole story about a political event may be trumped by, first, his or her concerns over jeopardizing national security—or, second, the often equally strong concern with maintaining good relationships with government sources. Third, since many political events are shaped by the goal of generating favorable press coverage, reporters and citizens alike must consider whether what they are seeing or reading represents the truth or an attempt to shape public opinion.

shield laws Legislation, which exists in some states but not at the federal level, that gives reporters the right to refuse to name the sources of their information.

HOW DO AMERICANS USE THE MEDIA TO LEARN ABOUT POLITICS?

ANALYZE WHO USES WHICH NEWS SOURCES AND WHETHER IT MATTERS

Americans now have many more ways to learn about politics than they did a generation or two ago. Imagine yourself in the 1940s. Suppose you want to learn about President Truman's State of the Union speech. You can't go to Washington to hear it in person. Where do you get your information? If you live in a big city, the speech will probably be covered in tomorrow's newspaper. If you live in a small town, your local paper may or may not have a story, and if it doesn't, you will need a subscription to either a big-city paper (arriving a week later) or a weekly or monthly news magazine, or a radio that can pick up a station broadcasting the speech.

Now consider the modern era in which major political events saturate the media. You can tune in to one of the four major television networks, numerous cable news channels, public TV stations, or radio stations, or listen to live streaming of the speech on the Internet. Most TV stations will feature pundits' commentary on the speech and will interview prominent politicians and commentators about it. Jay Leno and David Letterman will make jokes about the speech in their opening monologues on late-night TV, and Jon Stewart and Stephen Colbert will skewer it on their shows. Tomorrow the speech will be front-page news, and larger papers will publish the full text. Countless Internet sites will offer information and analyses. And you will be able to watch a video of the speech on YouTube and many other sites.

The fact that there are many sources of political information in the modern era does not imply that the average American uses most of them. For the most part,

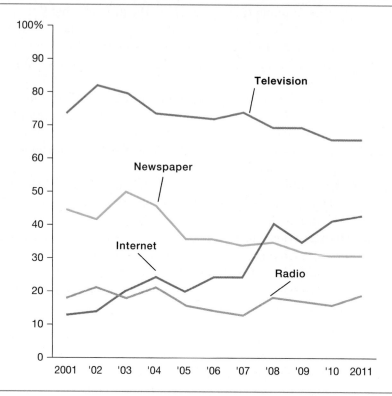

FIGURE » 6.1

MAIN SOURCE OF NATIONAL AND INTERNATIONAL NEWS

Source: "Press Widely Criticized, but Trusted More Than Other Information Sources." Pew Research Center, www.people-press.org/2011/09/22/press-widely-criticized-but-trusted-more-than-other-institutions/, September 22, 2011 (accessed 8/28/12).

by-product theory The idea that many Americans acquire political information unintentionally rather than by seeking it out.

Americans learn about politics in the same way they become aware of other things, through a process that the **by-product theory** explains.[48] This theory posits that many Americans acquire political information accidentally. They read a newspaper's sports pages and glance at front-page stories along the way. They watch *The Daily Show* and learn about politics while laughing at Jon Stewart's reports. They read a story on a political blog or Internet news site because the title catches their eye as they're looking for something else. Thus, while the sexual harassment complaints against Herman Cain were originally published on Politico.com, a website that relatively few people read on a regular basis, most people learned about the matter from the many other print, TV, radio, and Internet sites that picked up the story and issued their own reports.

After encountering new information, whether an individual either remembers that information later or uses it to modify her thoughts about politicians or policies depends on her level of interest. John Zaller's work on information processing shows that highly interested people are unlikely to change their minds when they learn something new, as they have already decided what they think. Other people who are uninterested in politics are less likely to encounter new political information in the first place. Thus, media coverage is most likely to affect the beliefs of people who take a moderate interest in politics.[49]

MEDIA USAGE TRENDS

Even though there are many news sources, none of them suits everyone. Figure 6.1 highlights some important trends in media usage.[50] The percentage of people who read newspapers declined by almost a third over the last decade; the percentage watching TV news also declined. Use of online sources including blogs and social media has tripled and will likely continue to increase. Table 6.1, which shows data on respondents' main news source, shows that all age groups use Internet-based sources, but usage is most prevalent among younger Americans, as is the decline in traditional sources such as newspapers.

These generational differences have important implications for the survival of different media organizations. One question is whether additional young Americans will start to read newspapers or watch TV news as they grow older—if they don't, many of these media sources will cease operations as their audience disappears. Moreover, if Americans rely more and more on the Internet as an information source, new websites and social media outlets are likely to emerge in response to this demand.

DOES THE SOURCE MATTER?

People acquire different kinds of information in different formats from each type of media source. A newspaper can report on a Taliban attack in Afghanistan in a fair amount of detail and may have a few pictures—whereas a TV news show can include footage of the attack and the aftermath, even in a less detailed story. Do people who rely on different kinds of media sources learn different things about politics? And do most people tend to accumulate broad, general political knowledge, or information about specific topics?

TABLE » 6.1

TRADITIONAL NEWS SOURCES FACE STIFF COMPETITION

Older Americans grew up without cable channels, the Internet, or even color TV. Are there generational differences in the use of different media sources?

	AGE 18–29	30–49	50–64	65+
NEWS YESTERDAY . . .				
Watched TV news	52%	63%	71%	79%
Read a newspaper	21	22	38	47
Listened to radio news	15	19	34	13
Got news online	65	48	15	14

Source: Pew Research Center, "Internet Gains on Television as Public's Main News Source," January 4, 2011 17, 2008, www.people-press.org/2011/01/04/internet-gains-on-television-as-publics-main-news -source/ (accessed 8/28/12).

In 2007, the Pew Trust asked survey respondents 23 questions about contemporary politics, defining "high-knowledge" individuals as those who answered 15 or more questions correctly. The researchers then divided respondents according to their principal source of political information, and calculated the percentage of high-knowledge people who used each news source. Table 6.2 shows the results. For each source, the table also gives the percentage of respondents who answered four of the survey's specific political questions correctly. Regardless of the type of news source, the percentage of high-knowledge people rarely creeps above 50 percent, and the same is true for the percentage who answered all four questions correctly. In other words, Americans are learning from news coverage, but very few learn enough to be considered current-events experts.

TABLE » 6.2

KNOWLEDGE LEVELS BY NEWS SOURCE

One of the most important questions about media usage is whether people who know a lot about politics get their information from different sources than those used by people who don't know as much. Does this table show differences between high-information and low-information?

	PERCENTAGE WHO COULD . . .				
	HIGH-KNOWLEDGE GROUP	IDENTIFY SUNNIS	IDENTIFY LIBBY	IDENTIFY PUTIN	APPROXIMATE U.S. DEATHS IN IRAQ
Nationwide	35%	32%	29%	36%	55%
THE AUDIENCE OF . . .					
The Daily Show/The Colbert Report	54%	50%	44%	52%	59%
Major newspaper websites	54	52	42	58	64
NewsHour	53	46	45	54	67
The O'Reilly Factor	51	43	44	53	64
National Public Radio	51	49	43	51	66
The Rush Limbaugh Show	50	40	42	52	70
Local daily newspaper	43	36	35	43	60
News from Google, Yahoo, etc.	41	44	33	44	60
CNN	41	38	36	41	60
Network evening news	38	31	33	37	61
Online news discussion blogs	37	35	32	36	57
Fox News Channel	35	32	29	38	58
Local TV news	35	30	30	35	57
Network morning shows	34	30	30	35	57

Entries show the percentage of regular viewers, readers, or listeners of each outlet who fall in the high-knowledge group (correctly answered at least 15 of 23 questions about politics and world affairs) and the percentage who correctly answered some of the individual questions on the test.

Source: Pew Research Center, "What Americans Know: 1989–2007," April 15, 2007, www.people-press.org/reports/pdf/319.pdf (accessed 8/30/12).

Table 6.2 also shows differences in the percentage of high-knowledge people who use the different media sources. *The Daily Show* and *The Colbert Report*, along with major online news sites, *NewsHour* (a PBS nightly newscast), *The O'Reilly Factor*, National Public Radio, and *The Rush Limbaugh Show* were among those drawing the highest percentages of high-knowledge individuals. At the other extreme were groups who get their information from network evening news, blogs, the Fox News Channel, local TV news and, at the bottom, network morning news.

It would be a mistake to infer from these data that the way to become informed about politics is to listen to Rush Limbaugh and NPR during the day, and watch Jon Stewart and Stephen Colbert at night—and avoid network news, blogs, and the other sources mentioned by low-information respondents. A deeper look at the data shows that high-information individuals are exposed to many more sources than individuals with low information. Thus, while it is true that some sources provide more information than others, it is difficult to pin down which ones are better than others. What is clear is the value of getting news from a wide range of sources.

MEDIA EFFECTS ON AMERICAN CITIZENS AND GOVERNMENT POLICY

> EXPLAIN THE WAYS IN WHICH THE MEDIA MAY INFLUENCE POLITICS

The study of **media effects** explores whether exposure to media coverage of politics changes what people think or do. There is considerable evidence that media coverage influences its audience. However, much of the impact stems not from what such stories contain but from what they leave out, how they present information, or even whether a story is reported at all. Political scientists label these mechanisms priming, filtering (also called agenda-setting), slant, and framing.[51]

media effects The influence of media coverage on average citizens' opinions and actions.

Among the first wave of scholars studying the media's impact on public opinion, there was little doubt of the media's power. Writing in the 1920s, Walter Lippmann argued that by reading or listening to news coverage, Americans learned which issues they should care about, what government could do about these concerns, and the consequences of different policy choices.[52] This certainty was reversed beginning in the 1950s, when scholars started testing claims about media effects using survey data. The early studies yielded extremely negative results—media effects appeared to have little influence on what Americans knew about politics or their political behavior.[53] By the 1980s, however, other researchers claimed that these findings about the nonexistence of media effects were incorrect: the result of poorly designed surveys, inadequate statistics, and a narrow conception of what media effects would look like.[54]

MODERN THEORIES OF MEDIA INFLUENCE

Modern theories of media influence distinguish various ways in which coverage can affect media consumers' beliefs. The most obvious mechanism is the use of the media as a forum for persuasion, in which an overt effort seeks to persuade people to change their minds about a candidate or an issue. However, people are not

THE WAY A STORY IS REPORTED—which information is included in an article or which images are used—makes a big difference in what people learn from it. A story about the Palestinian-Israeli conflict, for example, might emphasize the hardships faced by poor Palestinians (left) or suicide bombings by Palestinians in Israel (right).

filtering The influence on public opinion that results from journalists' and editors' decisions about which of many potential news stories to report.

slant The imbalance in a story that covers one candidate or policy favorably without providing similar coverage of the other side.

priming The influence on the public's general impressions caused by positive or negative coverage of a candidate or issue.

framing The influence on public opinion caused by the way a story is presented or covered, including the details, explanations, and context offered in the report.

always conscious of the ways media reports shape their beliefs. Theorists describe four media effects that work largely without consumers' awareness.

▶ **Filtering** results from journalists' and editors' decisions about which of many potential news stories to report.

▶ **Slant** in a story gives favorable coverage to one candidate or policy without providing "balanced" favorable coverage of other sides.

▶ **Priming** occurs when media coverage of a story affects the importance people place on the issues or events mentioned in the coverage

▶ **Framing** refers to how the description or presentation of a story, including the details, explanations, and context, changes the reaction people have to the information.

The existence of these media effects does not imply that reporters or editors try to mislead the public or sway public opinion to conform to their own ideas. If you read an article about a particular issue and decide to change your position, this doesn't suggest that the story was inaccurate or biased. Your decision may well be justified by the facts of the situation. Similarly, when slanted campaign coverage praises one candidate and dismisses another as unqualified, you might conclude that the author agrees with the first candidate's positions and wrote the story to help that candidate get elected. But what if the first candidate is actually the most qualified? If so, then slanted coverage of the campaign might be objective.

The same is true for other media effects. Space limitations mean that some filtering is inevitable as reporters and editors decide which stories to cover. Similar decisions about what to report and how to present the information lead to priming and framing effects. Even if everyone in the political media adhered to the highest standards of accuracy, these influences would still exist.

James Druckman and Michael Parkin's 2005 study of a Senate race in Minnesota exemplifies the modern conception of media effects. The researchers found that different newspapers covered the candidates differently, both in the amount of coverage for each candidate and the percentage of positive versus negative stories. Druckman and Parkin showed that a given paper's slant in coverage was correlated with endorsements, such that papers gave more coverage and more positive coverage to the candidates they endorsed. Voters who were regular readers of a paper that endorsed a particular candidate were more likely to hold a positive opinion of that candidate and more likely to vote for him.[55]

MEASURING MEDIA EFFECTS

One of the biggest problems with measuring media effects is that it is hard to determine causality—to be sure that exposure to a story, image, or website actually led people to change their minds about some issue. One solution is to develop an experiment in which the experimenters first measure the political beliefs of their subjects, expose the subjects to different versions of a political story, and then measure their beliefs again, to see if different stories caused different beliefs. This is the strategy used by Thomas Nelson, Rosalee Clawson, and Zoe Oxley for their study on media effects.[a]

The authors focused on one kind of media effect, framing. They recruited a group of people who live in Columbus, Ohio, divided them randomly into two groups, and had the members of each group watch one of two television news stories that had run on two different local TV stations. The viewing took place in a lab facility on the campus of The Ohio State University.

Watch a video clip of Zoe Oxley discussing this topic at **wwnorton.com/studyspace**

Both news stories described a rally that a local chapter of the Ku Klux Klan planned to hold in a nearby town. The first version of the story emphasized the threat to public safety posed by the rally—that members of the Klan might incite others to violence, or that there might be fights between Klan members and counter-protesters. The second story was almost identical except it omitted safety concerns, focusing instead on the free speech issues raised by the rally—that constitutional rights of free speech allow the expression of beliefs and attitudes that a majority finds hateful and distasteful.

After watching one of the two stories, people answered a series of questions that measured their tolerance for the rally, as well as how important they considered free speech and public order. The authors' hypothesis was that the group who viewed the story emphasizing the threat to safety would give a higher priority to public order over free speech, and that the ordering would be reversed for the group who had viewed the story that emphasized the importance of free speech. Moreover, the safety-story group was also expected to have a lower tolerance for the rally.

The results for the two groups, shown in the second table, provided clear evidence of framing. The group who saw the story that emphasized free speech had a far greater tolerance for the rally and speeches than the people who saw the safety-focused story; they also placed a higher importance on free speech and a lower importance on public order. Both of these effects were measured using surveys that were given to respondents before and after they watched the television stories.

Additional research shows that frames work most effectively at shaping what people think when the frames are simple and easy to understand and when a citizen is exposed to only one account of a particular political event and therefore doesn't see competing frames.[b] In particular, news stories on television, which are short and simple and present strong visual images, can have especially significant framing effects on their viewers, effects that are larger than what might be observed for an equivalent story in a newspaper or on a web page.[c]

These findings do not necessarily imply that real-world stories on TV or elsewhere have strong framing effects, or if they do, that the effects are long-lasting. It may be that the media try to present balanced coverage or that even when they present stories that have framing effects, viewers soon forget whatever they might have learned. Even so, the important contribution of this study is to show that framing effects can really occur—that how events are reported can change evaluations and opinions related to the events. Having established this point, the next step is to measure the extent and longevity of framing effects in the real world.

Experiments are not a perfect way to measure media effects, because it is impossible to be sure that subjects will respond to real-world stories in the same way they do in an experiment. After all, because they are in an experiment and not watching TV at home, people may pay closer attention than they might otherwise. Moreover, knowing their responses are being analyzed, subjects may be reluctant to give what they perceive to be a "wrong" response, such as refusing to support free speech in this example. People who agree to participate in an experiment may interpret a story differently than people who refuse to participate. However, because experiments allow researchers to measure how individuals respond to a carefully specified dose of information, they remain a valuable tool for studying media effects as well as many other political phenomena.

MEASURING FRAMING EFFECTS

	PUBLIC ORDER FRAME	FREE SPEECH FRAME
Tolerance for rallies	3.31	3.96
Tolerance for speeches	3.54	4.17
Importance of free speech	5.25	5.49
Importance of public order	5.43	4.75
Higher numbers indicate greater tolerance.		

Source: Thomas E. Nelson, Rosalee A. Clawson, and Zoe M. Oxley, "Media Framing of a Civil Liberties Conflict and Its Effect on Tolerance," *American Political Science Review* 91 (1997): 567–83.

A study of priming by Jon Krosnick and Laura Brannon found that exposure to press coverage of the Persian Gulf War in 1990 and 1991 moved citizens to evaluate then-president George H. W. Bush on the basis of his effectiveness in managing the war rather than on other factors such as the state of the economy.[56] Such priming is more likely when citizens are politically knowledgeable about the issues being discussed and trust the authors of the related news stories.[57]

The concept of filtering is illustrated by Project Censored's annual list of Top Censored Stories.[58] The group's list for 2012 included stories about the U.S. military's use of social media for recruitment, and the government's plans for weather modification. The group's point is not that the government forces reporters to keep quiet; rather, the claim is that reporters and their editors decide against covering these stories, sometimes for self-serving reasons, such as beliefs about what their audience wants to see or read. Of course, everyone can think of stories that they believe deserve more attention. However, because no media source can report on everything—due to lack of space, time, and staff—some events or problems fall through the cracks, receiving little or no attention despite their significance.

For an example of framing, consider a comparison of polling questions used to measure support for President Obama's economic stimulus package that was enacted in early 2009 (Table 6.3). Looking across the three poll questions, it appears that including Obama's name reduced support for the package, whereas

TABLE » 6.3

HOW FRAMING WORKS: ALTERNATIVE QUESTIONS ABOUT ECONOMIC STIMULUS

News stories sometimes exhibit framing effects: the way they describe a political event shapes the judgments formed by citizens, even though the story presents the same facts it otherwise would and the author has no conscious or unconscious bias. These data illustrate framing by showing how responses to poll questions vary with the specific wording of the question.

	FAVOR	OPPOSE	UNSURE
RASMUSSEN REPORTS			
Do you favor or oppose the economic recovery package proposed by Barack Obama?	45%	34%	21%
GALLUP			
Do you favor or oppose Congress passing a new $775 billion economic stimulus program as soon as possible after Barack Obama takes office?	53	36	11
ABC NEWS/*WASHINGTON POST*			
Would you support or oppose new federal spending of about $800 billion on tax cuts, construction projects, energy, education, and health care to try to stimulate the economy?	70	27	3

Source: Mark Blumenthal, "Economic Stimulus and the Many Faces of 'Public Opinion,'" January 27, 2009, www.pollster.com/blogs/economic_stimulus_and_the_many.php (accessed 11/20/09).

adding details about how the money would be spent and omitting mention of Obama yielded increased support. Presumably, the inferences that respondents drew from stories about the stimulus package—and their judgments about whether they supported the package or opposed it—depended on which details the stories emphasized.

In sum, these studies show that the details of media coverage affect what citizens know about politics and government policy, how they evaluate officeholders and government programs, how they vote, and what demands they put on elected officials. Confirmation of this linkage between media coverage on the one hand and election outcomes and public policy on the other comes from how people in government work to shape media coverage and respond to unfavorable coverage. For example, early in the Iraq war, the Department of Defense implemented a new plan of "embedding" news reporters with military units, allowing reporters to view military operations firsthand. Though this practice seems designed to give the media maximum leeway, in fact it imposed new constraints on coverage by filtering what events reporters were exposed to. Whereas during the Vietnam War, for example, reporters had been able to travel freely and make their own choices about which stories to investigate, embedded reporters in Iraq and Afghanistan traveled with a particular unit and could be steered away from embarrassing or sensitive stories.

Along the same lines, the government's response to damage caused by Hurricane Katrina in 2005 increased significantly after early media coverage emphasized foot-dragging by the Federal Emergency Management Agency (FEMA)—put another way, framing the story in terms of government incompetence led to a more aggressive policy response. And recent efforts by politicians and bureaucrats to put limits on the compensation of senior Wall Street executives were probably a response to stories primed by public opinion to focus on how firms receiving bailout funding from the federal government were granting large bonuses to senior management.

ASSESSING MEDIA COVERAGE OF AMERICAN POLITICS

> ASSESS WHETHER THE MEDIA FULFILL THEIR ROLE IN AMERICAN DEMOCRACY

In a democracy, the media's job is to provide citizens with information about politicians, government actions, and policy debates. Here we examine some of the arguments about how the media fall short, the evidence pro and con, why journalists and editors make the choices they do, and what the impact is of those decisions on coverage and on what Americans know.

MEDIA BIAS

Surveys of the American electorate routinely find that Democrats generally think the media favors Republicans, while Republicans have the opposite belief.[59] Conservative critics point to surveys which show that most reporters identify themselves as liberals; liberal critics respond that most pundits, especially on radio and

TV, offer conservative points of view—and many media sources are owned by large corporations, which leads to underreporting of some stories, such as those offering a favorable portrayal of labor unions.[60] The common thread is that media coverage of American politics falls short of some ideal of objective, full coverage.

In the main, most Americans, regardless of their party affiliation, do not have great confidence in the mainstream media, as Table 6.4 shows, with Republicans showing lower levels of confidence for all sources except Fox News. However, while people do not have a great deal of confidence in the media as a group, they have more confidence in the sources they regularly consult for information—and most people can find several sources that they consider reliable.[61]

It is easy to find examples of suspicious decisions by reporters and their editors that suggest some sort of overt bias in coverage. In fall 2009, editors at Fox News used video footage of a 2008 presidential campaign rally to illustrate a story about a book-signing event by former vice-presidential candidate Sarah Palin. The story as broadcast gave the impression that Palin's book event had attracted much larger crowds than it actually did. Although Fox attributed the mix-up to an honest mistake, critics charged that the campaign footage was spliced in as part of a deliberate effort to support Palin because of Fox's presumed preference for Republicans.[62]

Many journalists and commentators admit that they take an ideological or partisan perspective. The talk show host Rush Limbaugh, for example, describes himself as a strong conservative. And many commentators on the Fox News Channel make no secret of their conservative viewpoint. Similarly, the political news maga-

TABLE » 6.4

PARTISANSHIP AND NEWS SOURCE CREDIBILITY

Do Americans consider all media sources equally reliable for learning about politics? Are there partisan differences in the sources people choose?

BELIEVE ALL OR MOST OF WHAT ORGANIZATION SAYS	REPUBLICANS	DEMOCRATS	GAP
Fox News Channel	41%	21%	+20
USA Today	16	20	-4
Network news (average)	17	30	-13
New York Times	14	31	-17
60 Minutes	25	42	-17
CNN	19	40	-21
National Public Radio	16	37	-21
MSNBC	13	34	-21

Percentages are based on those who could rate each.

Source: Pew Research Center, "Americans Spending More Time Following the News," September 12, 2010, www.people-press.org/2010/09/12/americans-spending-more-time-following-the-news/ (accessed 8/29/12).

zine *The Nation* describes itself as "a weekly journal of left/liberal opinion, covering national and international affairs as well as the arts."[63] These journalists' and organizations' points of view are well known and easy to see. Some people might even find the bias useful. A liberal, for example, could use *The Nation*'s endorsements as a guide to which candidates to support, and a conservative might listen to Rush Limbaugh to get similar information.

Leaving aside these obvious gaffes and clear statements of points of view, claims about overt media bias make strong assumptions about what fair coverage would look like. For example, during 2005 and 2006, many media critics agued that reports on the Iraq war overemphasized negative events and failed to report on positive developments. Suppose these clams are true, in the sense that media coverage gave a pessimistic sense of what was happening in Iraq? However, during this time, thousands of American troops and large numbers of civilians were killed or wounded; there were thousands of bombings, kidnappings, and other attacks by insurgent forces; and most economic indicators revealed a country in deep crisis.[64] In other words, if the expectation is that the media should give an accurate picture of what's happening in Iraq, it is not clear that optimism was appropriate in 2005 and 2006. Also, as the situation improved in Iraq during 2007 and 2008, media coverage changed in a more positive direction.

It is hard to find a scholarly study that presents strong evidence of systematic media bias in a liberal or conservative direction. Part of the problem is that it is hard to measure media bias. For example, one study found that when the Fox News network began broadcasting in a community, voting for Republican candidates in the next election increased significantly.[65] Does this mean that some viewers became pro-Republican after listening to allegedly pro-Republican broadcasts on Fox News? Perhaps, but the study did not directly measure the behavior of individuals in these communities, so there is no way to be sure that new Republican supporters were actually Fox News viewers. Even if they are, it may be that watching Fox News has no effect on voting, but that Fox News executives look for communities that are trending Republican when deciding which new markets to enter. Untangling these effects is a complex task.

An alternate strategy for measuring media bias is to focus on content. Political scientist Timothy Groseclose analyzed whether there was a liberal or conservative bias to coverage of American politics by counting the number of times that media reports cited work by different think tanks and policy groups.[66] His conclusion was that there was a strong liberal bias. However, the accuracy of this finding hinges on correctly classifying think tanks and policy groups as expressing liberal or conservative views—and critics of Groseclose's work have argued that when groups are classified correctly, the bias findings disappear.[67]

OTHER NEGATIVE ASPECTS

Even if media coverage is not openly biased in one direction or another, there are many ways in which it fails to provide essential information about politics to the American public. As political scientist and journalism professor Andrew Cline puts it, there are many ways in which media coverage of politics is biased—meaning influenced—in one direction or another by various forces.[68] Various aspects of content and slant affect the media's performance in covering politics. For example, scholars such as Thomas Patterson have documented the rise of **attack journalism**, in which "bad news makes for good news," "the mere whiff of a controversy or scandal is grounds for a story," and "public officials are [portrayed as] an ineffective and untrustworthy lot."[69] Other researchers have argued that campaign coverage overemphasizes the **horse race** aspects, such as which candidates are ahead and which are falling behind, rather than offering a complete description of each candidate's promises and an analysis of how they are likely to behave in office.[70] Similarly, coverage of debates over public policy often focus on personalities and predictions about who is likely to achieve his or her goals. In all of these cases, coverage of how these events might shape government policy often gets ignored until after the scandal, election, or policy debate is over.[71] Such practices virtually guarantee incomplete coverage of any news story, particularly at the time when people are actually paying attention.

Media coverage of politics also emphasizes **soft news** (stories that are sensational or entertaining) over **hard news** (stories that focus on important issues and emphasize facts and figures).[72] At the same time, talk shows and those focused on entertainment have increased their political coverage mainly by reporting on scandals, personalities, and other topics that attract an audience rather than presenting hard facts.[73] A truism about local TV news is that "if it bleeds, it leads." An overemphasis on crime stories, coupled with a focus on the victims of crimes rather than on the causes and context of criminal events, leads people to overestimate the chances of being the victim of a violent crime.[74]

Moreover, citizens' perceptions of government may mirror press coverage. Many authors have suggested that citizens' low level of trust in government, as well as high levels of disapproval and dissatisfaction, may have more to do with how the media report on American politics than with how government actually works.[75] The lack of hard information in much political coverage also fails to address the profound ignorance that many Americans have about the structure of the federal government, particular government policies, and decision-making processes.

attack journalism A type of increasingly popular media coverage focused on political scandals and controversies, which causes a negative public opinion of political figures.

horse race A description of the type of election coverage that focuses more on poll results and speculation about a likely winner than on substantive differences between the candidates.

soft news Media coverage that aims to entertain or shock, often through sensationalized reporting or by focusing on a candidate or politician's personality.

hard news Media coverage focused on facts and important issues surrounding a campaign.

FIGURE » 6.2

HOW JOURNALISTS VIEW THEIR PROFESSION

Many observers complain about the quality of reporting on American politics. Do journalists share these concerns?

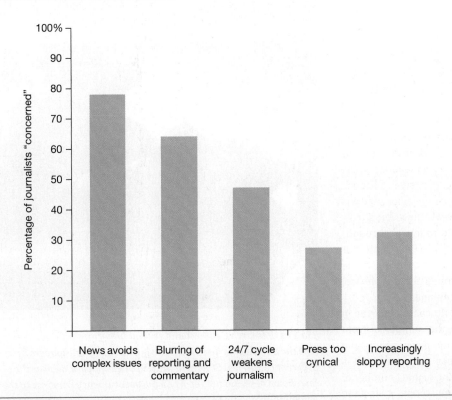

Source: Pew Research Center, "Financial Woes Now Overshadow All Other Concerns for Journalists," March 17, 2008, www.people-press.org/reports/pdf/403.pdf (accessed 9/14/12).

Many journalists agree with these criticisms of their field. Figure 6.2 shows that a majority of journalists believe the media avoid complex stories and are too timid, and that the line between reporting and commentary is becoming blurred. Similarly, a 2000 survey of journalists found that 53 percent avoided stories that they thought were too complex for their target audience and over 70 percent avoided stories that they believed were "important but dull."[76]

THE EFFECT OF MARKET FORCES

A deeper question about the American media's coverage of politics is *why* there is so much attack journalism, soft news, sensationalism, and scandal. If journalists are aware of the problem, why don't they take their role as political watchdogs for the public interest more seriously? One response is that journalists may feel the

JOURNALISM THROUGHOUT THE WORLD

One of the central themes in this chapter is that much of the media's coverage of political events is driven by the demands of the people who consume this coverage. A significant amount of political coverage tends to be somewhat shallow, focusing on scandals, horse races, and lurid events at the expense of detailed, dispassionate analyses. Yet, for all that Americans complain about this type of coverage, it is what the average American is drawn to when searching for something to read or watch.

One of the interesting questions about this pattern is whether it holds in media coverage in other countries. Do journalists in other countries provide dispassionate coverage, or are they driven to be as sensationalistic as their colleagues in the United States? This is not an easy question to answer, because events tend to be local to a particular country or region, and it is hard to compare coverage of the same event. However, a truly global story broke in the spring of 2009, as countries throughout the world faced the swine flu epidemic. The Pew Center for Excellence in Journalism looked at newspaper coverage of the epidemic across seven countries: the United States, Mexico, Canada, Spain, France, China, and New Zealand.[a]

The table shows the number of swine flu cases reported in each country during April and May 2009, the number of front page stories about swine flu in the major newspapers, and the ratio of cases to stories. Looking across the numbers, it is clear that although the United States had the highest number of cases and the highest number of front page stories, it also had the lowest ratio of cases to stories. In other words, newspapers in other countries made more (in terms of front page coverage) of a relatively smaller number of cases.

U.S. newspaper coverage also compared well in terms of its content. The Pew researchers found that U.S. reporting covered "every angle" of the epidemic, including the spread of the

The Pew Research Center found several important differences in how the 2009 swine flu epidemic was covered by newspapers in different countries. Stories in Mexican newspapers, such as the one shown here, did not report on the government's response to the epidemic, while American newspapers were more likely to cover all aspects of the story.

disease throughout the world, how governments were reacting, the role played by international organizations, and how people could lower their chances of getting the disease. In contrast, coverage by Mexican newspapers focused on the impact of the epidemic on business and the economy as well as work and school closings but said nothing about the government's response. The state-controlled Chinese media gave full coverage to the aid that their government sent to Mexico but did not mention the quarantine that the Chinese government imposed on foreign tourists in China. Coverage in all of the other countries had similar lapses.

Of course, swine flu is only one case, and the Pew researchers did not compare other forms of media coverage. Nor did the study claim that the U.S. newspapers' coverage of the epidemic was perfect. But it does appear that in this case, American newspapers did a noticeably better job than their counterparts.

HOW NEWSPAPERS IN DIFFERENT COUNTRIES COVERED SWINE FLU			
COUNTRY	CASES OF SWINE FLU	FRONT-PAGE STORIES	STORIES PER CASE
United States	2,254	31	1:225
Mexico	1,626	20	1:81
Canada	240	6	1:47
Spain	93	7	1:13
France	12	2	1:6
New Zealand	7	6	1:1
China	1	9	9:1

need to demonstrate their independence from politicians and government interests, and perhaps counter or prevent claims of media bias. The result can be overly aggressive questioning of elected officials and cynical stories about the political process.[77]

The more significant explanation for the soft, sensationalistic nature of much political coverage is that reporters and their editors are in a competitive business to attract a paying audience. Describing the media as an information source for citizens makes sense in terms of how American politics works, but this description does not capture the sometimes contradictory incentives that journalists face. Most American media outlets are for-profit enterprises. Because they need to produce coverage that attracts an audience, they often seek to create stories that consumers want and that are consistent with how members of their target audience think about politics. For example, many Americans hold dismal evaluations of the Republican and Democratic parties, of Congress, and of the American political system in general. Given these perceptions, the prevalence of attack journalism is no surprise; journalists provide coverage that fits the public's preconceptions. Americans are not changing what they think in response to attack stories and soft news. Rather, the way journalists cover politics reflects the tone of American public opinion.[78]

Although journalists can and do shape public opinion—as the discussion of media effects showed—media coverage is also substantially shaped by the need to attract an audience. The shift in the tone and content of political coverage also reflects expansion in the number of media sources and competition among them for a finite audience. As longtime ABC reporter Sam Donaldson put it,

> *We're trying desperately to hold onto an ever-shrinking audience, as far as the big commercial networks are concerned. . . . We're reaching out more and more for people who believe there are three-headed cows. . . . I'm part of the process of trying to find a larger audience of people who never really cared about news. . . . And to get them, we have to do things we didn't ever used to do before.*[79]

The same factors can lead to an emphasis on stories about Americans and America over coverage of events in other countries. Coverage may even be shaped by a reporter's background—for example, someone who grew up in a middle-class neighborhood may have difficulty understanding or reporting accurately on the problems of the poor.[80]

Even if reporters tried to explain how government works, especially the need for compromise, it is unlikely that citizens would respond favorably. As researchers John Hibbing and Elizabeth Theiss-Morse discovered, "Citizens . . . dislike being exposed to processes endemic to democratic government. People do not wish to see uncertainty, conflicting options, long debate, competing interests, confusion, bargaining, and compromised, imperfect solutions."[81] In other words, coverage that offers exclusively hard news, policy details, and sober analysis rather than at least some soft news, cynicism, scandals, and attack journalism would probably not find much of an audience.

Market forces also explain other aspects of the political media. The focus on campaigns as horse races, for example, reflects the kind of stories that the average voter finds interesting: who's ahead in the race, rather than details of the candidates' campaign promises.[82] Similarly, the trend toward political coverage by soft news programs reflects the expectation that viewers want to find out about the personalities rather than the facts.[83]

HOW WELL DO THE MEDIA DO THEIR JOB?

As this section illustrates, there are many situations in which media coverage of American politics falls short of the ideals mentioned in the introduction. However, there are also many explanations for why the media cover American politics as they do. Reporters move beyond "just the facts" for many different reasons, one of which being that much of what happens in American politics requires interpretation. They must choose what to report because so many things happen every day, and they must decide how to report staged news, whether to reveal secrets, and which sources to rely on. Thus, filtering and framing of the news are inevitable. You may disagree with the decisions of a particular reporter or publication, but there is no such thing as completely objective journalism; your preferred coverage would just involve a different frame, a different filter, and different kinds of priming.

For example, consider media coverage of the events surrounding the 2011 debate in Wisconsin over a proposal by Republican governor David Walker to sharply curtail collective bargaining rights for state employees. Media scholar George Lakoff argued that coverage framed the implications of Walker's proposal in terms of how it would reduce the ability of state employees in Wisconsin to demand higher wages and better benefits.[84] However, Lakoff argued, the articles could have been framed around the wider implications of the change, including how they might affect the ability of unions to organize to support their favored candidates to state and federal offices. Lakoff argued that if this alternate frame was used, people might make different judgments about the controversy. Lakoff may be right. However, it is hard to say that one kind of coverage is better than the other—unless you favor one outcome over the other, and want to see media coverage that is favorable to your point of view. Thus, in a world where conflict is so endemic to politics, complaints about media coverage are all but inevitable.

If Americans were unaware that media coverage could be incomplete or clearly biased, then it would be right to worry about how these effects shaped media coverage—people might get an incomplete or biased view of a story depending on which media sources they consulted. However, Americans are well aware of these problems. For example, the finding that people focus on sources they consider reliable, or sources whose ideological leanings appear to be compatible with their own, is exactly what we would expect to see if people wanted to make sure that they were not misled by incomplete coverage. There are also indications that media sources are more likely to offer alternate points of view and to be more conscious of possible gaps or biases in their coverage when multiple sources report on the same event.[85] In that case, the expansion of news sources that has occurred over the last generation may help citizens to avoid being misled, because there are more sources to consult, and because the increased number of sources motivates reporters and editors to offer balanced coverage.

///

CONCLUSION

News media are the primary source of public information about American politics and policy. The considerable controversy about how well the media fulfill this role reflects both the importance of the task and the interest many people have in shaping political coverage. The news media landscape is undergoing a massive transition, as the Internet supports an ever-growing variety of new information sources and fewer people rely on newspapers or television for news. Even so, these traditional sources remain the most popular for political information. Their coverage of politics is nowhere near perfect, but their imperfections are generally not the product of reporters and editors working to color coverage with biased views.

Stories about Todd Akin's Senate campaign illustrate the causes and consequences of media coverage of American politics. In running story after story on Akin's comments about rape and pregnancy, media sources are largely responding to public demand for dramatic coverage. Americans might be better informed if the media ignored sensational stories and focused on the details of public policy, but lurid stories help attract and keep the audience that media companies need to stay in business.

The average American consults only a tiny fraction of the information provided by the media. Americans tend to learn about politics as a by-product of other activities and focus on exciting stories regardless of their importance. This process can lead people to some peculiar conclusions, even about well-reported events. Such shortcomings do not constitute an indictment of the news media or of the average American. In the case of Todd Akin, for example, even a small amount of research using different sources would produce a detailed understanding about his background, policy proposals, and the complaints against him. We cannot blame people for refusing to become well informed; but at the same time, we cannot blame the media for citizens' refusal to consider what is placed before them.

THE NEWS MEDIA IN AMERICA

▶ Trace how the American mass media have evolved over time, and describe the major types of news sources today.
Pages 203–12

SUMMARY

The media have been the primary sources of political information in America since the Founding, though the forms of media have changed considerably over time. In the early days, media sources were very partisan and sensationalistic, but journalistic integrity standards became commonplace in the twentieth century. While the term "media" traditionally only referred to print sources, technological advances allowed political information to be spread through radio, TV, and now the Internet.

KEY TERMS

mass media (p. 203)

penny press (p. 203)

wire service (p. 203)

yellow journalism (p. 204)

investigative journalists (p. 204)

Federal Communications Commission (FCC) (p. 204)

broadcast media (p. 204)

fairness doctrine (p. 205)

equal time provision (p. 205)

concentration (p. 206)

cross-ownership (p. 206)

media conglomerates (p. 206)

mainstream media (p. 207)

prime time (p. 207)

news cycle (p. 207)

CRITICAL THINKING AND DISCUSSION

One argument against deregulating the media is that consolidation and the formation of media conglomerates would reduce the number of independent sources of information that are available to the average American. Based on the media sources that you and your friends use, do you agree or disagree with this argument? Why?

PRACTICE QUIZ QUESTIONS

1. What is the fairness doctrine?
    a) TV and radio stations must offer a variety of political views in programs.
    b) TV and radio stations must give equal time to candidates running advertisements.
    c) News anchors cannot slander political candidates.
    d) Radio station owners cannot also own TV and print media outlets.
    e) Journalists must investigate challengers as well as incumbents.

2. The deregulation of the media has resulted in _____.
    a) increasing enforcement of the equal time provision
    b) increasing enforcement of the fairness doctrine
    c) increasing use of the Internet
    d) increasing scrutiny of media concentration
    e) increasing frequency of cross-ownership

3. Why aren't media sources interchangeable?
    a) They all are able to diffuse information on the same time frame.
    b) Local news stations depend on major news sources for most of their content.
    c) They are all able to spend the same amount of time covering an event.
    d) They have similar access to campaigns and political offices throughout the country.
    e) Newspapers offer very brief content.

4. Which is the result of the decreased barriers to publication on the Internet?
  a) Few opportunities exist for citizens to interact with reporters or government officials.
  b) People with no official connection to candidates can have a significant influence on elections.
  c) The accuracy of political information has improved.
  d) Few average citizens report on events as they happen.
  e) Like-minded political supporters have difficulty organizing and staying informed on issues.

5. Why hasn't the Internet increased citizens' political knowledge?
  a) It can be hard to find political news on the Internet.
  b) Most people do not have access to the Internet.
  c) Most people read content from a wide range of balanced media sources.
  d) Most people only focus on websites that reinforce their own views.
  e) Search engines don't include political topics.

Ⓢ **PRACTICE ONLINE**

"Critical Thinking" exercise: *Politics Is Conflictual—Political Blogs*

POLITICAL REPORTING: SOURCES, LEAKS, AND SHIELD LAWS

▶ Describe where reporters and others in the news media get political information. **Pages 212–17**

SUMMARY

Coverage of politics requires that the reporter makes a trade-off between cultivating sources with favorable stories and providing complete and accurate information. One of the best ways reporters can cover political events is to get information "off the record." To maintain this information resource, the confidentiality of sources must be protected, though reporters can be compelled to reveal them in court.

KEY TERMS

press conference (p. 216)

on background (p. 216)

off the record (p. 216)

shield laws (p. 217)

PRACTICE QUIZ QUESTIONS

6. "Staging the news" refers to _____.
  a) the media's attempts to frame public opinion
  b) sources' attempts to remain confidential

  c) newspaper editors determining which story to put on the front page
  d) politicians attempting to influence coverage by providing select information
  e) reporters' choices to delay a story

7. Shield laws _____.
  a) allow editors to protect their reporters from vengeful politicians
  b) allow politicians to protect reporters who provide favorable coverage
  c) protect politicians from slander
  d) allow reporters to protect confidential sources
  e) protect reporters from being sued for slander

Ⓢ **PRACTICE ONLINE**

"Critical Thinking" exercise: *Political Process Matters—Access to Politicians*

HOW DO AMERICANS USE THE MEDIA TO LEARN ABOUT POLITICS?

▶ Analyze who uses which news sources and whether it matters. **Pages 217–21**

SUMMARY

Whereas most Americans in the 1940s would learn about political events from a small subset of media sources, today we enjoy a variety of ways to stay informed about politics. However, the average American does not use very many of these resources, and learns about politics indirectly. Most studies find that the more sources an individual gets their news from, the better informed they are.

KEY TERM

by-product theory (p. 218)

CRITICAL THINKING AND DISCUSSION

What advice would you give to someone who wants to learn about American politics? What types of media sources should they seek out, which ones should they avoid, and why?

PRACTICE QUIZ QUESTIONS

8. What is the by-product theory of political information?
   a) Local media sources often rely on major sources for their national news coverage.
   b) Most Americans learn about politics accidentally.
   c) Reporters often learn about a political story while working on a different story.
   d) Bloggers typically do not produce news; rather, they comment on news gathered secondhand.
   e) News coverage often influences policy decisions.

9. Which news source has the greatest proportion of high-knowledge viewers?
   a) a network morning news show
   b) Fox News Channel
   c) a network evening news show
   d) *The Colbert Report*
   e) local news shows

ⓢ PRACTICE ONLINE

"Big Think" video exercise: *How Does Political Journalism Affect Voters?*

MEDIA EFFECTS ON AMERICAN CITIZENS AND GOVERNMENT POLICY

▶ Explain the ways in which the media may influence politics. **Pages 221–25**

SUMMARY

Nearly all modern research finds that the media have significant effects on both government policy and American citizens. By determining which stories to cover, how a story is written, or how many stories to write on a given topic, media sources influence the way that citizens think about politics.

KEY TERMS

media effects (p. 221)

filtering (p. 222)

slant (p. 222)

priming (p. 222)

framing (p. 222)

PRACTICE QUIZ QUESTIONS

10. What is priming?
    a) a journalist's decision about which story to report on, and which story to skip

   b) a journalist giving favorable coverage to one candidate without providing balanced coverage of the opponent
   c) when a journalist's story affects the importance people place on the issue being covered
   d) the particular way that a journalist decides to present and describe a story
   e) the decision to prioritize one story over another

11. Space limitations mean that some _____ is inevitable.
    a) filtering
    b) slant
    c) priming
    d) framing
    e) soft news

ⓢ PRACTICE ONLINE

"What Do Political Scientists Do?" video exercise: *Issue Framing*

ASSESSING MEDIA COVERAGE OF AMERICAN POLITICS

▶ Assess whether the media fulfill their role in American democracy. **Pages 225–32**

SUMMARY

In a democracy, the media's job is to provide citizens with information about politicians, government action, and policy debates. While the media often fall short of this ideal, there are many reasons for this failure. In particular, the effects of filtering and framing are simply unavoidable given limited resources.

KEY TERMS

attack journalism (p. 228)

horse race (p. 228)

soft news (p. 228)

hard news (p. 228)

CRITICAL THINKING AND DISCUSSION

To what extent are journalists, editors, and the owners of media businesses to blame for the fact that the average American is often uninformed about and uninterested in politics?

PRACTICE QUIZ QUESTIONS

12. What is one problem with research on media bias?
    a) Few scholars are interested in studying media bias.
    b) It is difficult to measure bias.
    c) No journalist will admit that bias exists.
    d) There's little chance that media sources are biased.
    e) There are not enough media sources to create a sample.

13. Which is an example of "soft news"?
    a) CNN showing coverage of a White House press conference
    b) ABC airing coverage of the president's State of the Union address
    c) NPR reporting on the details of the debt-ceiling debate
    d) CBS coverage of election results
    e) a CNN story about a member of Congress posting risqué photos of himself to his Twitter account

14. Which of the following statements best characterizes soft news?
    a) Soft news stories sell far better than hard news stories.
    b) Journalists aren't interested in writing hard news, and would prefer to write soft news pieces.
    c) Hard news and policy analysis articles tend to sell better than soft news.
    d) Most citizens have several sources of hard news, and they have to search to find soft news stories.
    e) Soft news was popular in the past but is now declining.

15. Why do reporters move beyond "just the facts" reporting?
    a) Politicians are corrupt, and people need to know about it.
    b) Americans don't realize the media are not always objective.
    c) Readers have already interpreted the news themselves.
    d) Politics is complicated and often requires some interpretation.
    e) They have a strong personal bias and can't write strictly factual stories.

SUGGESTED READING

Baum, Matthew A. *Soft News Goes to War: Public Opinion and American Foreign Policy in the New Media Age.* Princeton, NJ: Princeton University Press, 2003.

Braestrup, Peter. *How the American Press and Television Reported and Interpreted the Crisis of Tet 1968 in Vietnam.* New Haven, CT: Yale University Press, 1983.

Cappella, J. N., and K. H. Jamieson. *Spiral of Cynicism: The Press and the Public Good.* New York: Oxford University Press, 1997.

Davenport, Christian. *Media Bias, Perspective, and State Repression: The Black Panther Party.* New York: Cambridge University Press, 2010.

Iyengar, Shanto. *Is Anyone Responsible? How Television Frames Political Issues.* Chicago: University of Chicago Press, 1991.

Kuklinski, James H., and Lee Sigelman. "When Objectivity Is Not Objective." *The Journal of Politics* 54:3 (1992): 810–33.

Lippmann, Walter. *Public Opinion.* 1922. Reprint, New York: Free Press, 1997.

Nelson, Thomas E., Rosalee A. Clawson, and Zoe M. Oxley. "Media Framing of a Civil Liberties Conflict and Its Effect on Tolerance." *American Political Science Review* 91 (1997): 567–83.

Norris, Pippa. *A Virtuous Circle? Political Communications in Post-Industrial Democracies.* New York: Cambridge University Press, 2000.

Patterson, Thomas. *Out of Order.* New York: Knopf, 1993.

Prior, Markus. *Post-Broadcast Democracy: How Media Choice Increases Inequality in Political Involvement and Polarizes Elections.* New York: Cambridge University Press, 2007.

Political Parties

BEGINNING IN 2009, GROUPS AFFILIATED WITH the Tea Party movement began encouraging candidates sympathetic to their goals to run for office in 2010. The Tea Party movement encompasses numerous groups that organized in opposition to a broad range of developments in 2009 and 2010, including federal economic stimulus spending; bailouts of banks, auto companies, and other businesses; health care reform; immigration reform; affirmative action; and other issues. These groups, ranging from the Tea Party Patriots to the Tea Party in Space, have attracted a wide range of citizens to their rallies, used face-to-face meetings and social networks to discuss issues, and recruited candidates.

Their recruitment efforts bore fruit in the 2010 midterm elections, when nearly 150 candidates ran for Congress with the endorsement of one or more Tea Party groups. About a third were elected. These candidates ran as Republicans or independents. Some won the Republican nomination with little or no opposition, but others defeated candidates who were supported by the state or local Republican Party organization. One Tea Party candidate in Utah defeated an incumbent Republican senator for the nomination; another in Delaware won the Republican Senate nomination by defeating a well-known Republican House member who had the support of most state and local party officials.

As we will see repeatedly throughout this textbook, political parties are often at the center of conflicts in American politics. The two main American political parties, the Republicans and the Democrats, come into conflict over what

CONFLICT & COMPROMISE
in American Politics

government should do and how to do it. But even within parties, groups of party members (both in Washington and throughout the nation) often squabble over what the party stands for. In this way, conflict in American politics occurs within as well as between the Democratic and Republican parties—both in Congress and throughout the nation. For example, the rise of the Tea Party movement as a force within the Republican Party caused the party to confront conflicting points of view and forge compromises among its members.

During the 112th Congress (2011–12), candidates who won with support from Tea Party groups formed a Tea Party Caucus, comprising over 70 Republican House and Senate members. These legislators were among the most vocal in demanding cuts in federal spending; they were also the focus of intense lobbying efforts by Republican Party leaders during negotiations over enacting the annual federal budget, raising the federal debt limit, and crafting a deficit-reduction package. Many of the details of these packages, including cuts in federal programs and a vote on a constitutional amendment requiring a balanced federal budget, were added in order to reach a compromise between Tea Party members and other Republicans.

The rise of the Tea Party movement highlights the enduring conflict in American politics over the proper role of government in society. While Tea Party groups differ on the specifics, in the main they are unified around the goal of reducing the size of the federal government and its regulation of individuals, groups, and corporations. (Members do, however, disagree somewhat on other issues.) As we will see in this chapter, the Tea Party movement is not generally considered a political party, but it has played an important role in influencing the priorities of the Republican Party.

In a broader perspective, American political parties have been at the center of debates over the role of government ever since the Founding. By competing for control of the presidency, House, and Senate, as well as state and local offices, and by offering different visions of what government should do, parties and their candidates embody some of the most fundamental conflicts that underlie American politics. Parties help shape the way Americans think about candidates, policies, and vote decisions. Parties also impact elections by recruiting candidates, paying for campaign ads, and mobilizing supporters. After elections, the winning party's candidates implement their vision, while the losers try to derail these efforts and develop an alternative vision that will attract support in the next election. In so doing, parties unify and mobilize disparate groups, simplify the choices that voters face, and bring efficiency and coherence to government policy making. The Tea Party organizations, for all their impact on American politics, have fulfilled some—but not all—of this job description.

Why do parties play these roles in American politics? The emergence of the Tea Party movement, along with periodic conflicts within the Democratic and Republican parties, illustrates that the question "Why parties?"[1] does not have an obvious answer. Although American political parties often have an impact on elections and policy, the same organizations can seem inept and irrelevant in other situations. A good answer to "Why parties?" must explain this variation. Why are American political parties sometimes powerful and sometimes powerless? The answer developed in this chapter rests on the notion that political process matters: understanding what parties do (and cannot do) requires an appreciation of how they are organized, as well as the rules and regulations that shape the behavior of party leaders, politicians, and citizens.

AMERICAN POLITICAL PARTIES have three largely separate components: the party organization, represented here by Debbie Wasserman Schultz, chair of the Democratic National Committee; the party in government, represented by House minority leader Nancy Pelosi and her leadership team; and the party in the electorate, exemplified by the crowd at a rally for Barack Obama.

WHAT ARE POLITICAL PARTIES?

DEFINE POLITICAL PARTIES AND THE THREE MAJOR ASPECTS OF AMERICAN PARTIES

Political parties are organizations that run candidates for political office and coordinate the actions of officials elected under the party banner. Looking around the world, we find many different kinds of parties. In many western European countries, the major political parties have millions of dues-paying members, and party leaders control what their elected officials do. In contrast, in many new democracies, candidates run as representatives of a party, but party leaders have no control over what candidates say during the campaign or how they act in office. America's major political parties, the Republicans and the Democrats, lie somewhere between these extremes. Many Americans have a deep, enduring connection to one of these parties, and these organizations' actions affect both election returns and policy outcomes.

However, rather than being unified organizations with party leaders at the top, candidates and party workers in the middle, and citizen-members at the bottom, American political parties are decentralized, a loose network of organizations, groups, and individuals who share a party label but are under no obligation to work together.[2] For example, the Speaker of the House of Representatives, John Boehner, is the leader of House members from his party, the Republicans, but he works independently of the party's national organization, the Republican National Committee (RNC); neither one is in charge of the other. Boehner is also not in charge of other Republican groups in Congress, such as the Tea Party Caucus—while Caucus members may listen to Boehner's arguments, they are under no obligation to do what he asks. Similarly, the RNC cannot command state and local Republican Party organizations to take some actions and not others. Moreover, while many Americans think of themselves as members of a political party, neither the Republicans nor the Democrats have formal membership. Someone who identifies with the Republican Party does not have to work for or give money to the party, or vote for its candidates.

party organization A specific political party's leaders and workers at the national, state, and local levels.

party in government The group of officeholders who belong to a specific political party and were elected as candidates of that party.

party in the electorate The group of citizens who identify with a specific political party.

In light of this defining characteristic of American political parties, scholars describe these organizations as comprising three separate and largely independent pieces:[3] The **party organization** involves the structure of national, state, and local parties, including party leaders and workers. The **party in government** is made up of the politicians who were elected as candidates of the party. And the **party in the electorate** includes all the citizens who identify with the party. As you will see, organization matters: the fact that American political parties are split into three parts has important implications for what they do and for their impact on the nation's politics.

SHOW HOW AMERICAN POLITICAL PARTIES AND PARTY SYSTEMS HAVE EVOLVED OVER TIME

HISTORY OF AMERICAN POLITICAL PARTIES

The Republican and Democratic parties have existed for a long time—the Republicans since 1854 and the Democrats since even earlier in the 1800s. The nickname for the Republican Party is the G.O.P., or "Grand Old Party," a play on G.A.R., the Grand Army of the Republic, which refers to the Union Army in the Civil War. The symbol for the Republicans is an elephant; for the Democrats, a donkey. This section shows that at certain points in history both major American political parties have looked and acted very differently from the way they do today and that the contemporary parties do not resemble their historical counterparts.

party system A period in which the names of the major political parties, their supporters, and the issues dividing them remain relatively stable.

Political scientists use the term **party system** to describe periods in which the major parties' names, their groups of supporters, and the issues dividing them have all been constant. As Table 7.1 shows, there have been six party systems in

TABLE » 7.1

AMERICAN PARTY SYSTEMS

PARTY SYSTEM	MAJOR PARTIES (DOMINANT PARTY IN BOLDFACE)	KEY ISSUES
First (1789–1828)	**Federalists**, Democratic-Republicans	Location of the capital, financial issues (e.g., national bank)
Second (1829–56)	**Democrats**, Whigs	Tariffs (farmers vs. merchants), slavery
Third (1857–96)	Democrats, **Republicans**	Slavery (pre–Civil War), Reconstruction (post–Civil War), industrialization
Fourth (1897–1932)	Democrats, **Republicans**	Industrialization, immigration
Fifth (1933–68)	**Democrats**, Republicans	Size and scope of the federal government
Sixth (1969–present)	Democrats, Republicans (neither party is dominant)	Size and scope of the federal government, civil rights, social issues, foreign policy

America.[4] For each party system, the table gives the names of the two major parties, indicates which party dominated (won the most presidential elections or controlled Congress), and describes the principal issues dividing the parties.

THE FIRST PARTY SYSTEM, 1789–1828

Political parties formed soon after the Founding of the United States. While many of the Founders expressed their dislike of political parties, most affiliated with a party soon after the first elections. The first American parties, the Federalists and the Democratic-Republicans, were primarily parties in government. As political scientist John Aldrich put it, members of Congress had ideas about what the new government should look like and what it should do, but they needed votes to translate these ideas into concrete policies.[5] The first parties comprised like-minded legislators: Federalists wanted a strong central government and a national bank, and they favored assumption of state war debts by the national government; Democratic-Republicans took the opposite positions based on their preference for concentrating power at the state level. These political parties were quite different from their modern counterparts. In particular, there were no national party organizations, few citizens thought of themselves as party members, and candidates for office did not campaign as representatives of a political party.

THE SECOND PARTY SYSTEM, 1829–56

The second American party system began with the disintegration of the Federalist Party. Many Federalist legislators had opposed the War of 1812 and supported a politically unpopular pay raise for members of Congress.[6] Ultimately, Federalist politicians were either defeated for re-election or switched their party affiliation, eliminating the Federalist Party as a political force in American politics.

The demise of the Federalists gave way to the Era of Good Feelings, a period when there was only one political party, the Democratic-Republicans. Following the election of President Andrew Jackson in 1828, the organization that elected Jackson was transformed by him and by then-senator (later president) Martin Van Buren into the Democratic Party, the ancestor of the modern-day organization. At the same time, another new party, the Whigs, was formed, and the Democratic-Republican Party dissolved, with most of its politicians becoming Democrats.

The new Democratic Party embodied two important innovations. First, it cultivated electoral support as a way of strengthening the party's hold on power in Washington. The party built organizations at the state and local levels to mobilize citizens to support its

FOLLOWING HIS ELECTION IN 1828, President Andrew Jackson strengthened the Democratic Party by encouraging party organizations at the state and local levels and by creating the spoils system to reward loyal party members. Here, Jackson makes a speech while on his way to Washington to take office.

party principle The idea that a political party exists as an organization distinct from its elected officials or party leaders.

spoils system The practice of rewarding party supporters with benefits like federal government positions.

candidates. These efforts helped to bind citizens to the party, encouraging them to think of themselves as party members and creating the first American party in the electorate. The Democrats' second innovation was what Van Buren called the **party principle**, the idea that a party is not just a group of elected officials but an organization that exists apart from its candidates.[7] Jackson and Van Buren also created the **spoils system**, whereby individuals who worked for the party were rewarded with benefits such as federal government jobs.

THE THIRD PARTY SYSTEM, 1857–96

The issue of slavery split the second party system. Most Democratic politicians and party officials either supported slavery outright or wanted to avoid debating the issue.[8] The Whig Party was split between politicians who agreed with the Democrats and abolitionists who wanted to end slavery. Ultimately, antislavery Whigs left the party and formed a new organization, the Republican Party, which also attracted antislavery Democrats. As the remaining Whig candidates began to have difficulty winning office against both Republican and Democratic opponents, Whig officeholders left the party and joined one of these two more powerful parties. This move divided the country into a largely Republican Northeast, a largely Democratic South, and politically split midwestern and border states.[9]

The demise of the Whigs and the rise of the Republican Party illustrate that parties exist only because elites, politicians, party leaders, and activists want them to. The Republican Party was created by people such as Abraham Lincoln who wanted to abolish slavery, and many other politicians subsequently joined the party because of ambition: they each believed their chances of winning political office were higher as a Republican than as a Whig or a Democrat.

THE FOURTH PARTY SYSTEM, 1897–1932

Although the Civil War settled the issue of slavery, it did not change the identity of the major American parties. In the postwar era, the Republicans and the Democrats remained the two prominent, national parties, and the same regional split persisted between these organizations. Slavery was no longer an issue, but the parties were divided on related concerns such as the withdrawal of the Union Army from southern states. At about the same time, the rapid growth of American cities and increased immigration raised new debate over the size and scope of the federal government: should it help farmers and rural residents, inhabitants of rapidly expanding cities, or neither group? A related concern was whether the federal government should regulate America's rapidly growing industrial base.

The political parties took opposing positions on this issue, leading to a new party system. Democrats, led by three-time presidential candidate William Jennings Bryan, attempted to build a coalition of rural and urban voters by proposing a larger, more active federal government and other policies that would help these groups. Although Bryan was never elected president, the issues he stood for divided the major parties and defined the debate in Washington for more than a generation.

The move from the third to the fourth party system shows how American political parties reflect the basic divisions in society over what government should do. In the third party system, the parties were divided over slavery and, after the Civil War, the pace of Reconstruction. Once these issues were settled, politicians and party leaders found new issues to campaign on—partly because they cared about these issues and partly because taking these positions helped to attract votes and other support to themselves and to their party.

THE FIFTH PARTY SYSTEM, 1933-68

The fifth party system was born out of the Great Depression, a worldwide economic collapse. With millions unemployed, prices declining, and ever-growing soup lines of those unable to afford food becoming a common sight in major American cities, the critical question was what the federal government should do to get things moving again.

Many Republican politicians, especially President Herbert Hoover, argued that conditions would improve over time and that government intervention would be costly and do little good. Democratic challenger Franklin Delano Roosevelt proposed new government programs that would help people in need and spur economic growth. Roosevelt won the 1932 presidential election, and voters also elected many new Democrats to Congress. Together, the president and Congress enacted the New Deal, a series of federal programs designed to stimulate the national economy, help needy people, and impose a variety of new regulations.

Debate over the New Deal brought together the **New Deal Coalition** of African Americans, Catholics, Jewish people, union members, and white southerners, who became strong supporters of Democratic candidates over the next generation.[10] This transformation also established the basic division between the Republican and Democratic parties that persists to the present day: Democrats generally favor a large federal government that takes an active role in managing the economy and regulating individual and corporate behavior, and Republicans believe that many such programs should either be provided by state and local governments or be kept entirely separate from government.

DEBATE OVER ROOSEVELT'S NEW DEAL programs established the basic divide between Democrats and Republicans that continues to this day: Democrats favor a strong federal government that takes an active role in the economy; Republicans prefer a smaller federal government and fewer programs and regulations.

New Deal Coalition The assemblage of groups who aligned with and supported the Democratic Party in support of New Deal policies during the fifth party system, including African Americans, Catholics, Jewish people, union members, and white southerners.

THE SIXTH PARTY SYSTEM, 1969-PRESENT

The move from the fifth to the sixth party system was marked by issue expansion: the introduction of new political questions and debates that divided the parties.[11] Beginning in the late 1940s, and more decisively during the 1960s, many Democratic candidates and party leaders, particularly outside the South, came out against the "separate but equal" system of racial discrimination in southern states and in favor of programs designed to ensure equal opportunity for minority citizens throughout the nation.

At the same time, Democratic politicians, particularly President Lyndon Johnson, argued for expanding the federal government into health care funding (in the form of the Medicare and Medicaid programs), antipoverty programs, education, and public works. Johnson called his plan the Great Society. Although some Republican politicians supported portions of the Great Society, particularly the civil rights reforms, there was considerable Republican opposition to expanding the role of government in society.

This division on civil rights—along with differences on other issues such as foreign policy and social issues including abortion rights, and continuing disagreement over the size and scope of government—produced a gradual but significant shift in the groups that identified with each party. White southerners and some Catholics gradually moved to the Republican Party, and minorities, particularly African Americans, started identifying more strongly as Democrats. Candidates (particularly those entering politics) either chose or changed their party affiliations to reflect the new party coalitions. By the late 1980s, all three elements of the Republican and Democratic parties (organization, government, and electorate) were much more like-minded than they had been a generation earlier.

The sixth party system also brought changes in the party organizations. Both the Republican and the Democratic parties became "parties in service", increasing their involvement in recruiting, training, conducting fund-raising, and campaigning for their party's congressional and presidential candidates.[12] Just as in the first party system, the parties in government became more involved in elections as a way of electing like-minded colleagues who would vote with them to enact their preferred policies. At the same time, the parties in government began to play a larger role in building policy compromises within and across the parties and in working to shape legislative proceedings to enact these compromises into law.

REALIGNMENTS

realignment A change in the size or composition of the party coalitions or in the nature of the issues that divide the parties. Realignments typically occur within an election cycle or two, but they can also occur gradually over the course of a decade or longer.

Each party system is separated from the next by a **realignment**, a change in one or more of the factors that define a party system, including the issues that divide supporters and candidates from each party, the nature and function of the party organizations, the composition of the party coalitions, and the specifics of government policy.

In some cases, a realignment begins with the emergence of a new question or issue debate that captures the attention of large numbers of ordinary citizens, activists, and politicians.[13] To spur a realignment, the issue has to be crosscutting, meaning that within each party coalition, people disagree on what government should do.

In the case of the second party system (1829–56), the new issue was slavery.[14] Although most Democratic Party leaders and elected officials supported keeping slavery legal, the Whig Party was split between proslavery and abolitionist members. The result was the formation of a new political party, the Republicans, by antislavery Whigs and some Democrats. Within a few years, citizens and politicians moved to whichever party reflected their feelings about slavery, resulting in the realignment that yielded the third party system.

A realignment between the fifth party system (1933–68) and the sixth (1969–present) produced the division between modern-day Republicans and Democrats.[15] The fifth party system was born during the Great Depression, when the parties were primarily divided by their positions on the appropriate size of the federal government and how much it should control the behavior of individuals and corporations. In the sixth party system, new issues such as civil rights emerged to divide the parties and their supporters. In the electorate, these changes split the New Deal Coalition, with white southerners and evangelicals moving to the Republican Party, and African American voters becoming even stronger Democratic identifiers.[16] By the 1980s, the changes in party coalitions and election outcomes were apparent, with control of Congress and the presidency divided between the two parties. Republicans gained House and Senate seats in southern states, and Democrats gained seats in the Northeast, West, and Southwest.[17] By early 2010, Republicans controlled only four Senate seats in the Northeast, with three of these held by the least conservative Republicans in the Senate.

While issues appear to be the driving force behind realignment and the move from one party system to another, other factors contribute to the separation between party systems. For example, one important factor that separated the fifth from the sixth party system was the introduction of new technologies such as television and the ability to measure public opinion using mass surveys, which enabled candidates to win political office without the help of a party organization. Moreover, the changes between the fifth and sixth party systems were to some extent the result of changes in the party coalitions, as white southerners moved to the Republican Party—not just because of civil rights, but because they shared the views of the party on a wide range of issues.

We've seen that from the beginning, political parties have been a central feature of American politics. The next steps are to examine the different aspects (the party organization, the party in government, and the party in the electorate) of American political parties, describe the role they play in elections and in government, and compare their behavior in practice to the job description presented in the introduction.

//

MODERN AMERICAN POLITICAL PARTIES

DESCRIBE THE MAIN CHARACTERISTICS OF AMERICAN PARTIES AS ORGANIZATIONS, IN THE GOVERNMENT, AND IN THE ELECTORATE

In this section, we examine the contemporary Democratic and Republican parties in terms of their party organization, party in government, and party in the electorate. In doing so, we convey basic information about the parties, show how their three distinct parts work, and consider some implications of this three-part structure.

THE PARTY ORGANIZATION

The principal body in each party organization is the **national committee**, which consists of representatives from state party organizations, usually one man and one woman per state. The state party organizations in turn are made up of professional staff plus thousands of party organizations at the county, city, and town levels. The job of these organizations is to run the party's day-to-day operations, recruit candidates and supporters, raise money for future campaigns, and work to build a consensus on major issues. (Of course, other groups in the party, as well as individual politicians, carry out similar tasks at the same time and not always in agreement with the national or state committees.)

national committee An American political party's principal organization, comprising party representatives from each state.

PARTY ORGANIZATIONS AT THE LOCAL level coordinate support for the party's candidates, but they don't necessarily have to follow the lead of the national party organization.

political action committee (PAC) An interest group or a division of an interest group that can raise money to contribute to campaigns or to spend on ads in support of candidates. The amount a PAC can receive from each of its donors and the amount it can spend on federal electioneering are strictly limited.

527 organization A tax-exempt group formed primarily to influence elections through voter mobilization efforts and issue ads that do not directly endorse or oppose a candidate. Unlike political action committees, they are not subject to contribution limits and spending caps.

Both parties also include a number of constituency groups (the Democrats' term) or teams (the Republicans' term). These organizations within the party work to attract the support of demographic groups considered likely to share the party's issue concerns—such as African Americans, Hispanics, people with strong religious beliefs, senior citizens, women, and many others—and assist in fund-raising.[18] In some cases, they also attempt to win over groups typically identified with the other party. For example, African Americans have long been strong supporters of Democratic candidates. Accordingly, the Democratic Party has a constituency group that informs African Americans about the party's candidates and works to convince these citizens to vote on Election Day. The Republican Party's corresponding constituency team works toward the opposite goal, trying to convince African Americans that Republican policies and candidates would better serve their interests.

Each party organization also includes groups designed to build support for or coordinate the efforts of particular individuals or politicians. These include the Democratic and the Republican Governors' Associations, the Young Democrats, the Young Republicans, and more specialized groups such as the Republican Lawyers' Organization or the Democratic Leadership Council (DLC), an organization of moderate Democratic politicians.[19] The parties use their college and youth organizations to motivate politically minded students to work for the party and its candidates. Groups such as the Governors' Associations and the DLC hold meetings where elected officials discuss solutions to common problems and try to formulate joint strategies. People who work for a party organization carry out a wide range of tasks, from recruiting candidates and formulating political strategies to mobilizing citizens, conducting fund-raising, filling out campaign finance reports, researching opposing candidates and parties, and developing websites for the party and its candidates.

Many other groups, such as **political action committees (PACs)** or **527 organizations**, labor unions, and other interest groups and organizations, are loosely affiliated with one of the major parties. For example, the organization MoveOn.org typically supports Democratic candidates. Similar organizations on the Republican side include the Club for Growth and many evangelical groups. Other organizations such as Americans for Job Security take advantage of a loophole in a provision of the IRS code to legally solicit large, anonymous donations from corporate and individual contributors. Though these groups often favor one party over the other, they are not part of the party organization and do not always agree with the party's positions or support its candidates—in fact, many have to operate independently of the parties and their candidates to preserve their tax-exempt status. (For more details on campaign finance, see Chapter 8, Elections, and Chapter 9, Interest Groups.)

While the Tea Party organizations use the word "party" in their name, in function and appearance they more closely resemble these loosely affiliated organizations. The Tea Party organizations do not run candidates on their own; rather, they endorse and give contributions to candidates (almost always Republicans) who are running for a major party nomination. As of 2012, there is no unified national organization with the Tea Party label—rather, there are a large number of organizations of varying size and activity that share a common name and some policy preferences, but that generally do not work together to elect candidates or shape government policy.

As this description suggests, the party organization has a fluid structure rather than a rigid hierarchy.[20] Individuals and groups work with a party's leaders and candidates when they share the same goals, but unless they are paid party employees, they are under no obligation to do so (even paid party workers can, of course, quit rather than work for a candidate or a cause they oppose).

PARTY BRAND NAMES

The Republican and Democratic Party organizations have well-established brand names. Because the parties stand for different things, both in terms of their preferred government policies and their ideological leanings, the party names themselves become a shorthand way of providing information to voters about the parties' candidates.[21] Hearing the term "Democrat" or "Republican" calls to mind ideas about what kinds of positions the members of each party support, what kinds of candidates each party runs, and how these candidates will probably behave in office. Citizens can use these brand names as a cue to decide whom to vote for in an election. (See Chapter 8 for more information on voting cues.)

Figure 7.1 provides a general guide to the Democratic and Republican brand names. The figure reports voters' impressions of the two parties, measured on a liberal–conservative scale (1 = most liberal, 7 = most conservative). The average American sees significant differences between the parties, placing the Demo-

FIGURE » 7.1

REPUBLICAN AND DEMOCRATIC BRAND NAMES

Over the last generation, Americans have consistently rated the Republican Party as more conservative than the Democratic Party. How might these perceptions shape candidates' decisions about which party to join and how to campaign?

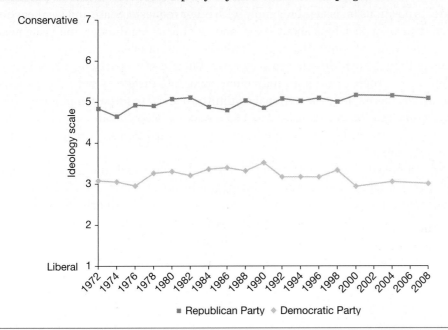

■ Republican Party ◆ Democratic Party

Source: Calculated from the 1948–2008 American National Election Studies Cumulative Data File, available at www.electionstudies.org/studypages/cdf/cdf.htm (accessed 8/31/12).

cratic Party toward the liberal end of the ideological spectrum and the Republican Party toward the conservative end. The specific positions vary over the years, but the parties are always far apart in the average American's mind. Moreover, as we show later, these differences in brand names reflect actual differences between Democratic and Republican politicians.

These data do not mean that the issue positions of American political parties are always distinct. Consider three of the biggest issues of President Barack Obama's first term in office: health care reform, the war in Afghanistan, and economic stimulus. People in all three sections of the party—organization, government, and electorate—held a variety of positions on these matters. As a result, it would be difficult to say exactly where "the party" stood on these issues.

THE LIMITS OF THE PARTY ORGANIZATION

The critical thing to understand about the Democratic and Republican party organizations is that they are not hierarchies. No one person or group in charge determines what either organization does. Because the Republican National Committee (RNC) and Democratic National Committee (DNC) are organized in the same way, we can consider the example of Tim Kaine, chair of the DNC as of 2012. He has enormous influence over who works at the DNC. However, the party organization's issue positions are set not by Kaine's employees but by DNC members from all 50 states. Since individual committee members are appointed by their state party organizations, they do not owe their jobs to Kaine—in fact, they can remove him from office if they like. If Kaine and the committee disagree, he can't force the committee members to do what he wants. In many cases, from civil rights proposals in the 1950s to health care reform in 2009, the Democratic Party has been internally divided, but party leaders have been unable to force a consensus. The Republican Party is likewise subject to the same limitations.

The national party organization is also unable to force state and local parties to share its positions on issues or comply with other requests. State and local parties make their own decisions about state- and local-level candidates and issue positions. The national committee can ask nicely, cajole, or even threaten to withhold funds (although such threats are very rare). But if a state party organization, an independent group, or even an individual candidate disagrees with the national committee, there's little the national committee can do to force compliance. Similarly, while Tea Party organizations often endorse Republican candidates, they operate independently of the Republican Party organization and are not subject to orders or control.

An example of friction between the national committees and their respective state party organizations occurred during the spring and summer of 2007. At that time, many state parties moved their states' presidential primaries and caucuses to dates earlier in the primary season, such that one month into the five-month primary season, most states' delegates to the parties' presidential nominating conventions would already be committed to a candidate.[22] The Republican and Democratic national committees preferred a drawn-out process, in which many populous states with large numbers of delegates would not hold their primary or caucus until May or June. Both party organizations penalized states that held their primaries early without authorization by halving those states' convention delegations. But they were powerless to stop state party organizations from changing their primary dates in the first place.

POLITICAL MACHINES

A **political machine** is a party organization built around the goal of gaining political power to enrich party leaders, party workers, and citizen supporters.[23] Political machines give government services to citizens, government jobs to party workers, and government contracts to higher-level party officials and contributors. In return, the recipients of these benefits are expected to help by campaigning for machine candidates, contributing to the party, and voting for the machine's candidates.

Such patronage used to be common in American politics. One classic example of a political machine was Tammany Hall, an organization of Democratic Party politicians in New York City who were especially powerful during the late 1800s and early 1900s.[24] One of the most famous Tammany Hall politicians, George Washington Plunkitt, argued that political machines did not reduce the quality or increase the costs of local government but just made sure that people who worked for the party would receive a disproportionate share of government money, a practice he labeled "honest graft."[25] This practice is the same as the spoils system discussed earlier. At first glance, honest graft or the spoils system is not obviously hurtful—if party workers are just as qualified as applicants outside the party to receive a job or contract, then the spoils system looks a lot like giving a preference to former members of one's college fraternity or sorority under the same conditions. Of course, there are numerous cases where the graft was not honest, where people who worked for the machine were incompetent or received no-show jobs or contracts at inflated prices.

Although political machines were once common in cities and towns, they declined as a result of several factors: civil service legislation enacted in the 1890s, and the expansion of government services to the poor and lower-middle class. American political parties at the national level have never operated as political machines. Major party leaders do not control anywhere near the amount of resources they would need if they wanted to use a machine-like system to attract large numbers of workers to their organizations or to win support for candidates by providing services to citizens.

"THAT'S WHAT'S THE MATTER."

Boss Tweed. "As long as I count the Votes, what are you going to do about it? say?"

THE TAMMANY HALL POLITICAL machine, depicted here as a rotund version of one of its leaders, William "Boss" Tweed, controlled New York City politics for most of the nineteenth and early twentieth centuries. Its strategy was "honest graft," rewarding party workers, contributors, and voters for their efforts to keep the machine's candidates in office.

political machine An unofficial patronage system within a political party that seeks to gain political power and government contracts, jobs, and other benefits for party leaders, workers, and supporters.

THE PARTY IN GOVERNMENT

The party in government consists of elected officials holding national, state, and local offices who took office as candidates of a particular party. They are the public face of the party, somewhat like the players on a sports team. Though players are only one part of a sports franchise—along with owners, coaches, trainers, and support staff—their identities are what most people call to mind when they think of the team. Because the party in government is made up of officeholders, it has a direct impact on government policy. Members of the party organization can recruit candidates, write platforms, and pay for campaign ads, but only those who win elections—the party in government—serve as members of Congress or as executive officials and actually propose, debate, vote on, and sign the legislation that determines what government does.

The party in government is largely independent of the party organization. Some elected officials or former elected officials serve as members of their party's national committee or hold a position in a state or local organization, but most

PARTY ORGANIZATIONS IN OTHER COUNTRIES

Our description of American political parties highlights their lack of control over what their candidates say and do in government and in elections. Most American politicians—and nearly all officeholders—run as the candidate of a political party, but the major-party organizations have little power to determine who gets their nominations.

The situation is very different in many other democracies. In most western European countries and others such as Israel, the leaders of political parties can force candidates from their party to run on the party platform and, if elected, to vote according to the wishes of party leaders.[a] Where do they get this power? For one thing, the party organizations can determine which politicians are nominated to run for office. In some countries, party organizations routinely move candidates from one district to another, a practice known as parachuting. The national party organizations may also control most of the campaign resources. Finally, after the election, the leaders of the party that won the election often get to decide which of the elected politicians from their party will serve in the winning candidate's cabinet and wield policy-making power. This combination of incentives and threats makes most politicians in these countries highly loyal to their party organization.

What are the consequences of these differences? Legislatures in western Europe show high levels of party discipline—elected officials generally vote according to party leaders' instructions. Elections in these countries focus on party platforms rather than the promises made by individual candidates; instead of comparing candidates, citizens compare parties and their platforms when deciding how to vote.

Strong parties also lead candidates to focus on doing things that help their party win elections and enact legislation, for their ability to win re-election depends on their party's performance in office. Without strong parties, candidates change their focus to cultivating what's called their *personal vote*—behaving in accordance with their constituents' demands rather than their party's agenda, and working to deliver government benefits to their districts.

Research on the personal vote demonstrates how party strength and the details of elections make it more or less likely that candidates will work to build their personal vote. To show this pattern, the table below lists five countries—Israel, Ireland, Mexico, Australia, and the United States—and three variables describing how legislative candidates are elected: type of district (proportional representation, single member districts, or one candidate elected per district, multi-member districts or more than one candidate elected per district, or a mix), whether party leaders control who can run as a candidate for the party (this is a good measure of party strength), and whether ballots allow citizens to vote for one candidate only or for multiple candidates (first place, second place, etc.). The last variable is blank for Israel because citizens there vote for parties, not can-

ELECTORAL SYSTEMS AND PARTIES IN SELECTED COUNTRIES

COUNTRY	TYPE OF DISTRICTS	DO PARTIES CONTROL BALLOT ACCESS?	DO CITIZENS VOTE FOR MULTIPLE CANDIDATES?	MAGNITUDE OF PERSONAL VOTE (1-10)
Israel	Proportional Representation	Yes	-	1
Ireland	Mix	Yes	No	4
Mexico	Multi-Member Districts	Yes	No	6
Australia	Single-Member Districts	No	Yes	8
USA	Single-Member Districts	No	No	10

Source: Joel W. Johnson and Jessica S. Wallack, "Electoral Systems and the Personal Vote," http://hdl.handle.net/1902.1/17901 (accessed 10/17/12).

didates. The last column is the amount of effort that legislators in each country make to cultivate a personal vote with their constituents, measured on a 10-point scale (1 = low, 10 = high).

The table shows that the U.S. political system of single-member districts, open ballot access, and voting for one candidate creates the largest incentive for candidates to cultivate a personal vote. Conversely, the lowest incentive is for Israel's system of proportional representation, which is also used in many Western European democracies. In between, the amount of personal vote depends on the districting system in their country, whether party leaders control nominations, and the kinds of votes citizens cast.

These findings show that the amount of attention legislators pay to their constituents' concerns depends on the details of their political system. Put another way, by changing these factors through constitutional reform or legislation, we could change the behavior of politicians in our system.

Which system is better? It depends on what you think is important. The organization of Western European parties helps them devise meaningful platforms and coordinate the activities of their elected officials, and gives citizens a specific organization to hold accountable for government performance. However, precisely because candidates in these systems campaign as party members rather than as individuals, they cannot tailor their appeals to the specific demands of voters in their district or state—and, as a result, their personal vote is generally lower than in systems such as the United States. As a result, Western European voters in some areas may find that none of the candidates they see in an election is addressing the issues that matter to them.

American politicians go through their entire political careers without holding a position in their party organization.

CAUCUSES AND CONFERENCES

The Democratic and Republican parties in government in the House and Senate are organized around working groups—Democrats call theirs a **caucus**, and Republicans have a **conference**. The party caucus or conference serves as a forum for debate, compromise, and strategizing among a party's elected officials. For example, throughout 2009, members of the House Democratic Caucus held numerous meetings to decide their group's position on health care reform.[26] The Democrats' strategy for addressing these proposals reflected the consensus reached in the caucus.

Each party's caucus or conference also meets to decide legislative committee assignments, leadership positions on committees, and leadership positions within the caucus or conference.[27] Caucus or conference leaders also serve as spokespeople for their respective parties, particularly when the president is from the other party. The party in government also contains groups that recruit and support candidates for political office, the Democratic Congressional Campaign Committee (DCCC), the Democratic Senatorial Campaign Committee (DSCC), the National Republican Senatorial Committee (NRSC), and the National Republican Congressional Committee (NRCC).

caucus (congressional) The organization of Democrats within the House and Senate that meets to discuss and debate the party's positions on various issues in order to reach a consensus and to assign leadership positions.

conference The organization of Republicans within the House and Senate that meets to discuss and debate the party's positions on various issues in order to reach a consensus and to assign leadership positions.

POLARIZATION AND HETEROGENEITY

The modern Congress is polarized: in both the House and the Senate, Republicans and Democrats hold different views on government policy. Figure 7.2 compares legislators on the basis of their ideology, or their general feelings about government policy, as measured by a liberal–conservative scale. The data reflect two House sessions: the contemporary 112th House (served 2011–12) and the 83rd House of almost 60 years ago (served 1953–55).

These graphs tell us two things. First, over the last 60 years, the magnitude of ideological differences between the parties in Congress has increased. In the 83rd House, there was some overlap between the positions of Democrats and Republicans, but it had disappeared by the 112th House.[28] (For more details, see the "What Do Political Scientists Do?" box later in this chapter.) Of course, because Democrats and Republicans in Congress often disagree does not mean that compromise is impossible. In 2009, for example, even as the parties clashed over health care, the wars in Afghanistan and Iraq, and economic policy, they managed to agree on legislation that placed limits on fees and interest rates charged by credit card issuers and loosened rules on carrying concealed firearms in national parks.[29]

The second fact that Figure 7.2 reveals is that both parties in government include a heterogeneous mixture of ideologies, not a homogenous or uniform consensus opinion. In the 83rd House plot, for example, Democrats vary from the relatively liberal left end of the scale to the moderate (middle) and even somewhat conservative right side. Democrats in the 112th House were, on average, more liberal than their colleagues were in the 83rd, but a wide range of ideologies were still represented in the Democratic caucus. The same is true for Republicans, who leaned in the conservative direction in both the 112th and the 83rd Houses.

The heterogeneity of the party in government can create situations where a caucus or conference is divided on a policy question. Compromise within a party

FIGURE » 7.2

IDEOLOGY OF THE PARTIES IN GOVERNMENT: HOUSE OF REPRESENTATIVES, 1952 AND 2010

Over the last several decades, ideological differences between Democrats and Republicans in Congress have increased significantly. However, even in the 112th House, both parties still included a wide range of views. In light of these data, would you expect more or less partisan conflict in the modern Congress than there was in the early 1950s? According to these data, would you expect House members in each party to agree on what policies to pursue?

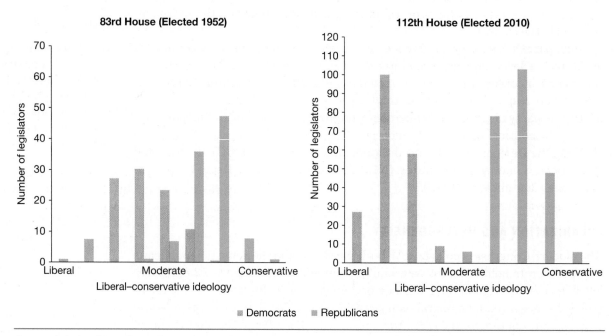

Source: Calculated from Royce Carroll, Jeff Lewis, James Lo, Nolan McCarty, Keith Poole, and Howard Rosenthal, "DW-NOMINATE Scores with Bootstrapped Standard Errors," January 23, 2009, www.voteview.com/dwnomin.htm (accessed 8/31/12).

caucus is not inevitable—even though legislators share a party label, they may not be able to find common ground. In the last few years, congressional Democrats have been divided on issues such as funding for the wars in Iraq and Afghanistan, health care reform, immigration reform, and plans for economic stimulus. These issues have also divided congressional Republicans, although they usually voted as a block against Democratic-sponsored proposals. On the Republican side, divisions arose in 2011 over the need for tax increases in deficit-reduction packages.[30]

While there is a Tea Party Caucus in Congress, its activities and powers fall far short of the Republican and Democratic caucuses and conferences. As we discuss here and in Chapter 10, the major parties are active in organizing Congress, recruiting and supporting candidates, and building legislative coalitions. Members of the Tea Party Coalition meet to discuss legislation, but have little direct influence on the legislative process.

"SOMETHING'S HAPPENING HERE"

Most college students reading this book have grown up in a partisan era, with Republicans and Democrats in Congress disagreeing on many issues and continuously battling each other to determine government policy. Accordingly, this chapter focuses on the parties in government and their policy disagreements. You may be surprised to learn, then, that a generation ago most political scientists saw the Republican and Democratic parties as being almost irrelevant organizations. As one put it in 1974, "No theoretical treatment of the United States Congress that posits parties as analytic units will go very far."[a] Most studies of Congress focused on individual members. The parties in government existed, but their influence was thought to be limited and party leaders were seen as powerless servants of their caucus. One of the principal explanations for these patterns was the split in the Democratic caucus between relatively liberal northern Democrats and conservative southern Democrats. Because these legislators could agree on little, neither group wanted to let the party have the power to encourage or even force a compromise.

Although this view was accurate for political parties in Congress as they existed in the 1950s and 1960s, we now know that somewhere in the late 1970s, things began to change. The first scholar to document these changes was political scientist David Rohde, then a professor at Michigan State University and now at Duke University. He knew that his results would be surprising to many political scientists, so he chose the title of his 1986 paper carefully: "'Something's Happening Here, What It Is Ain't Exactly Clear': Southern Democrats in the House of Representatives."[b]

Watch a video clip of David Rohde discussing this topic at **wwnorton.com/studyspace**

Looking at data from the early 1980s, Rohde found a sharp increase in the percentage of House votes that were party unity votes (a vote in which a majority of Democrats are on one side and a majority of Republicans are on the other). The percentage of party unity votes increased from 37 percent in 1981 to 55 percent in 1986. Moreover, Democrats (who were the majority party in the House at the time) were more and more likely to win on party unity votes. In other words, over this short period, the parties were increasingly likely to disagree on legislative proposals, and Democrats were more likely to win these disagreements.

Rohde's analysis also revealed an important change in the Democratic Caucus: the long-standing divide between northern and southern Democrats in Congress was disappearing. As the figure shows, northern Democrats always had high party unity scores. For southern Democrats, the pattern was different. In 1969, the average southern Democrat voted with his or her party on a party unity vote only 47 percent of the time. By 1985,

however, southern Democrats had a much higher average party unity score of 76, not much different from the average score for northern Democrats of 90.

To congressional scholars, these differences were a clear signal that the old descriptions of the parties in Congress were no longer accurate. Northern and southern Democrats were more likely to vote together, suggested that Democratic Party leaders were having an easier time finding compromises that could unite their caucus, and using their powers to make sure these proposals came to a vote and were enacted.

In the 25 years since Rohde's work, congressional scholars have confirmed virtually all of the elements of Rohde's argument. We now know that the trends he identified were occurring because voters throughout the country (but especially in the South) were sorting themselves by party, so that liberals became Democrats and conservatives became Republicans. Politicians, in turn, sorted themselves in the same way. The result was that the party caucuses in Congress became more and more distinct from each other, creating a polarized Congress where lawmakers from the same party cooperate to shape policy outcomes. (See the "What Do Political Scientists Do?" box in Chapter 10 for more on current research into polarization in Congress.)

Rohde's work tells us that the disagreements between the parties in the modern Congress reflect sincere disagreements between Republican and Democratic legislators about what government should be doing—disagreements that arise from the policy concerns held by individual members and their constituents. Moreover, strong congressional parties are not inevitable. After all, a generation ago, these cross-party differences did not exist. But once Democrats and Republicans began to disagree, they naturally turned to the parties in government as the vehicles to achieve their policy goals.

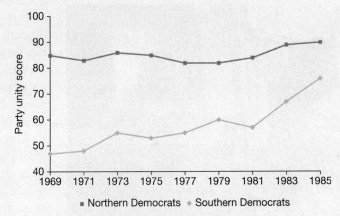

DEMOCRATIC PARTY UNITY BY REGION, 1969–85

■ Northern Democrats ◆ Southern Democrats

Source: Rohde, "'Something's Happening Here.'"

THE PARTY IN THE ELECTORATE

The party in the electorate consists of citizens who identify with a particular political party. Most Americans say they are either Democrats or Republicans, although the percentage has declined over the last two generations. Party identification is a critical variable in understanding votes and other forms of political participation.

PARTY IDENTIFICATION

Party identification (party ID) is different from formal membership in a political party. Although the Republicans and the Democrats have websites where people can sign up to receive e-mail alerts and to contribute to party causes, joining a party does not give a citizen any direct influence over what the party does. It is the party leaders and the candidates themselves who make the day-to-day decisions. These individuals often heed citizens' demands, but there is no requirement that they do so. Real participation in party operations is open to citizens who become activists by working for a party organization or one of its candidates. Activists' contributions vary from stuffing envelopes to helping out with a phone bank, being a delegate to a party convention, attending campaign rallies, or campaigning door-to-door. Relatively few Americans are activists, only a small percentage of the population.

Early theories of party identification described it as a deep attachment to a party that was acquired early in life from parents, friends, and political events and was generally unaffected by subsequent events.[31] Further work showed that party ID is a running tally, or an evaluation that takes account of new information.[32] Thus, when someone says he identifies with the Republican Party, he is saying that based on what he has seen in American politics, he prefers the positions suggested by the Republicans' brand name or how Republicans behave in office. New information tends to reinforce existing loyalties, which is why party identification is generally stable (see Chapter 5, Public Opinion). However, citizens can revise their party identification when circumstances warrant.

Figure 7.3 gives data on party identification in America over the last 60 years. The first plot shows that the Democratic Party had a considerable advantage in terms of the number of citizens identifying with the party from the 1930s until the late 1980s. During the 1970s, nearly half of adults identified with the Democratic Party, and only about 20 percent identified with the Republicans. During the 1990s, the percentage of Democratic identifiers decreased significantly and the percentage of Republican identifiers increased slightly, to the point that in 2002 the parties had roughly the same percentage of identifiers.[33] However, beginning in 2003 the Democrats again opened up a significant advantage in terms of identifiers, although the difference has largely disappeared in recent years. The two lines in Figure 7.3 do not add up to 100 percent, and the difference represents the percentage of independent voters who do not identify with either party. Just like the percentages of Republican and Democratic identifiers, the percentage of independents fluctuates over time.

Here again, the Tea Party falls short of being a formal party organization—while some Americans express sympathy for the issue stands taken by various Tea Party organizations, when people are asked about their party affiliation, they don't say they belong to the Tea Party; either they affiliate with the Republicans, the Democrats, or, occasionally a minor party.

ACTIVIST VOLUNTEERS UNDERTAKE most of the one-on-one efforts to mobilize support for a party and its candidates.

FIGURE » 7.3

PARTY IDENTIFICATION TRENDS AMONG AMERICAN VOTERS

In terms of party identification, the parties have moved from rough parity in the 1930s and 1940s, to a period of Democratic advantage that lasted from the 1950s to the 1980s. Beginning in 2003, Democrats appeared to be opening up another advantage, although this change has eroded in recent years. What events might have caused these changes in party identification?

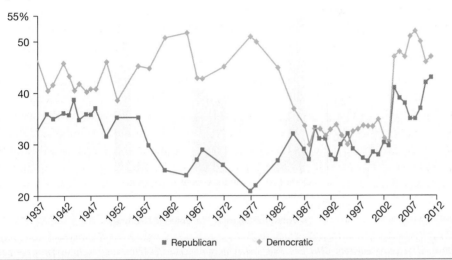

Source: Pew Research Center, "GOP Makes Big Gains among White Voters," July 22, 2011, www.people -press.org/2011/07/22/gop-makes-big-gains-among-white-voters/ (accessed 9/17/12).

INDEPENDENTS

Some early analyses concluded that independents were unaffiliated with a party because they were in the process of shifting their identification from one party to the other.[34] Others saw independents as evidence that more and more people regard the parties as irrelevant to their view of politics and their vote decisions.[35] The rise in the number of independents was also seen as an indication that Americans were becoming more politically savvy, learning more about candidates and not always blindly voting for the same party.[36]

More recent work has modified these findings. The percentage of independent voters has remained relatively constant over the last 20 years, and many independents actually have some weak attachment to one of the major political parties.[37] Although some independents are angry about or alienated from politics, most of them simply do not find the parties attractive enough to identify with either of them.[38] In any case, independents are not necessarily better informed about candidates, parties, or government policy than party identifiers. One of the few differences is that independents' vote decisions are more sensitive to things that happen during political campaigns.[39]

With a closer look at vote decisions, Figure 7.4 shows how Democrats, Republicans, and independents voted in the 2012 presidential election. Almost all Democrats voted for Barack Obama, the Democratic nominee, and almost all Republicans voted for Mitt Romney, the Republican nominee. Independent voters slightly favored Romney, but Obama won because Democrats are the largest group in the electorate. Simply put, if you are trying to predict how someone will vote, the most

FIGURE » 7.4

THE IMPACT OF PARTY IDENTIFICATION ON VOTE DECISIONS IN THE 2012 PRESIDENTIAL ELECTION

Americans are much more likely to vote for candidates who share their party affiliation. What does this relationship tell us about the impact of campaign events (including speeches, debates, and gaffes) on vote decisions?

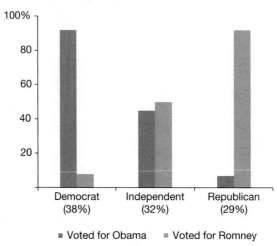

Source: Data compiled from CNN Exit Poll, www.cnn.com/election/2012/results/race/president#exit-polls (accessed 11/7/12).

important thing to know is his or her party identification.[40] Party ID also influences other kinds of political behavior; for example, people whose identification is strong are more likely to work for the party or to make a contribution than people with weak party identification.[41]

PARTY COALITIONS

party coalitions The groups that identify with a political party, usually described in demographic terms such as African American Democrats or evangelical Republicans.

Data on party identifications allow scholars to identify the **party coalitions**, or groups of citizens who identify with each party. Table 7.2 shows the contemporary Democratic and Republican party coalitions. As you can see, some groups are disproportionately likely to identify as Democrats (African Americans), some are disproportionately likely to be Republicans (white evangelicals), and other groups have no clear favorite party (people with some college education).

The Republican and Democratic party coalitions differ systematically in terms of their policy preferences—what they want government to do—as shown in Table 7.3. The second and third columns give the percentages of Republican and Democratic identifiers who considered each item a priority. The fourth column shows the differences between the Republican and Democratic party coalitions, which disagree about the relative importance of issues like providing health insurance to the uninsured, dealing with global warming, and strengthening the military. On only a few issues are the percentages in both parties who consider the matter a priority nearly the same, such as reducing the budget deficit. These data demonstrate that party labels are meaningful: if you know someone is a Republican (or a Democrat), this information tells you something about what that person probably wants government to do, and how he or she will likely vote in the next election.

TABLE » 7.2

THE PARTY COALITIONS

Many groups, such as African Americans and white evangelicals, are much more likely to affiliate with one party than the other. What are the implications of these differences for the positions taken by each party's candidates?

		DEMOCRATIC/LEAN DEMOCRATIC	REPUBLICAN/LEAN REPUBLICAN
GENDER	Male	43%	47%
	Female	52	42
AGE	18–29	52%	39%
	30+	45	47
RACE	White	39%	52%
	African American	86	8
REGION	Northeast	45%	41%
	Midwest	38	50
	South	35	57
	West	41	50
EDUCATION	No college	48%	44%
	Some college	46	45
	College graduate	59	41
RELIGION	White evangelical	32%	60%
	White mainline Protestant	40	49
	White Catholic	40	50

Source: Pew Research Center, "GOP Makes Big Gains among White Voters," July 22, 2011, www.people-press.org/2011/07/22/gop-makes-big-gains-among-white-voters/ (accessed 9/17/12).

TABLE » 7.3

ISSUE DIFFERENCES BETWEEN THE REPUBLICAN AND DEMOCRATIC PARTIES IN THE ELECTORATE

The Republican and Democratic Party coalitions have different priorities on many issues, from health care reform to strengthening the military—and on a few issues their differences are small, such as trade and the budget deficit. Do these differences make sense in light of each party's "brand name"?

PERCENTAGE CONSIDERING EACH AS A "TOP PRIORITY"	REPUBLICANS	DEMOCRATS	REPUBLICAN–DEMOCRATIC DIFFERENCE
Providing health insurance to uninsured	26%	75%	−49
Dealing with global warming	11	43	−32
Dealing with problems of poor	40	67	−27
Protecting the environment	34	60	−26
Reducing health care costs	48	71	−23
Improving educational system	54	75	−21
Securing Medicare	54	72	−18
Dealing with U.S. energy problem	43	56	−13
Improving job situation	80	90	−10
Reducing crime	46	55	−9
Securing Social Security	62	68	−6
Strengthening nation's economy	81	87	−6
Dealing with global trade	32	37	−5
Reducing middle-class taxes	45	45	0
Reducing budget deficit	61	60	+1
Dealing with moral breakdown	52	45	+7
Defending U.S. against terrorism	89	80	+9
Reducing influence of lobbyists	45	27	+18
Dealing with illegal immigration	49	30	+19
Strengthening the military	64	44	+20

Source: Pew Research Center, "Energy Concerns Fall, Deficit Concerns Rise," January 25, 2010, www.people-press.org/files/legacy-pdf/584.pdf (accessed 9/17/12).

THE ROLE OF POLITICAL PARTIES IN AMERICAN POLITICS

EXPLAIN THE IMPORTANT FUNCTIONS PARTIES PERFORM IN THE POLITICAL SYSTEM

Political parties play an important role in American politics, from contesting elections to building consensus across branches of government. However, these activities are not necessarily coordinated. Candidates and groups at different levels of a party organization may work together, refuse to cooperate, or even actively oppose one another's efforts.

CONTESTING ELECTIONS

In modern American politics, virtually everyone elected to a state or national political office is either a Republican or a Democrat. In the 111th Congress, elected in 2008, there were only two independent senators and no independent House members. In fall 2010, 49 of 50 states' governors were either Democrats or Republicans, and of more than 7,300 state legislators, very few were independents or minor-party candidates, including those elected with Tea Party support.

RECRUITING AND NOMINATING CANDIDATES

Actions taken inside party organizations shape citizens' choices on Election Day. Historically, the recruitment of candidates was left up to local party organizations. But the process has become much more systematic, with national party leaders playing a central role in finding and recruiting candidates—and often promising those candidates help in assembling a staff, organizing a campaign, and raising money.[42]

After the 2008 election, for example, members of the Republican House and Senate Campaign Committees believed that the party could win seats in the 2010 midterms by running candidates, particularly political outsiders with business experience, minorities, and women, who would take strong positions against many of President Obama's policy priorities, including health care reform. They began a two-year process of persuading these individuals to run, and training them in the art of campaigning.[43] Their efforts were one reason that Republican congressional candidates did so well in the 2010 midterms.

For all of these efforts, though, parties do not control who runs in House or Senate races. In most states, candidates for these offices are selected in a **primary election** or a **caucus,** in which they compete for a particular party's spot on the ballot. (Most states use primaries; a few state parties use conventions to select candidates.) Nuts and Bolts 7.1 further explains these different ways that the parties select candidates.

Running as a party's nominee is almost always the easiest way to get on the general election ballot. Some states give the Republican and Democratic nominees an automatic spot on the ballot; even in states that don't automatically allocate ballot slots this way, the requirements for the major parties to get a candidate on the ballot are much less onerous than those for minor parties and independents. For example, in California, a party and its candidates automatically qualify for a

primary election A ballot vote in which citizens select a party's nominee for the general election.

caucus (electoral) A local meeting in which party members select a party's nominee for the general election.

TYPES OF PRIMARIES AND CAUCUSES

PRIMARY ELECTION	An election in which voters choose the major party nominees for political office, who subsequently compete in a general election.
Closed primary	A primary election system in which only registered party members can vote in their party's primary.
Nonpartisan primary	A primary election system in which candidates from both parties are listed on the same primary ballot. Following a nonpartisan primary, the two candidates who receive the most votes in the primary compete in the general election, even if they are from the same party.
Open ("crossover") primary	A primary election system in which any registered voter can participate in either party's primary, regardless of the voter's party affiliation.
Semi-closed Primary	A primary election system where voters registered as party members must vote in their party's primary, but registered independents can vote in either party's primary.
CAUCUS ELECTION	A series of local meetings at which registered voters select a particular candidate's supporters as delegates who will vote for the candidate in a later, state-level convention. (In national elections, the state-convention delegates select delegates to the national convention.) Caucuses are used in some states to select delegates to the major parties' presidential nominating conventions. Some states' caucuses are open to members of any party, while others are closed.

position on the ballot if any of the party's candidates for statewide office received more than 2 percent of the vote in the previous election. In contrast, independent candidates need to file petitions with more than 150,000 signatures to get on the ballot without a major-party label—an expensive, time-consuming task.[44] These advantages help explain why virtually all prominent candidates for Congress and the presidency run as Democrats or Republicans—including many congressional candidates who ran with Tea Party support in 2010 and 2012.

National parties also manage the nomination process for presidential candidates. This process involves a series of primaries and caucuses held over a six-month period beginning in January of a presidential election year. The type of election (primary or caucus; about two-thirds of states use primaries) and its date are determined by state legislatures, although national party committees can limit the allowable dates, using their control over seating delegates at the party conventions to motivate compliance. Voters in these primaries and caucuses don't directly select the parties' nominees. Instead, citizens' votes are used to determine how many of each candidate's supporters become delegates to the party's national **nominating convention**, where delegates vote to choose the party's presidential and vice-presidential nominees. The national party organizations determine how many delegates each state sends to the convention based on factors such as state population, the number of votes the party's candidate received in each state in the last presidential election, and the number of House members and senators from the party that each state elected.

nominating convention A meeting held by each party every four years at which states' delegates select the party's presidential and vice-presidential nominees and approve the party platform.

CAMPAIGN ASSISTANCE

One of the most visible ways that the political parties support candidates is by contributing to and spending money on campaign activities. By and large, federal law mandates that these funds be spent by the organization that raised them—the

NOMINATING PRESIDENTIAL CANDIDATES

OPEN PRIMARIES
Open to voters from any political party and independents

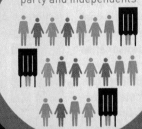

CLOSED PRIMARIES
Only voters registered with party vote

CAUCUSES
Party members meet in groups to select delegates

SELECT DELEGATES TO NATIONAL CONVENTION

Republican Party
States can divide delegates or give all to the winning candidate.

Democratic Party
The state's delegates are divided up proportionately.

NATIONAL NOMINATING CONVENTIONS

Delegates from all states attend the national convention, where they vote for the party's presidential and vice presidential nominees, based on the primary and caucus results. Superdelegates—important party leaders—also vote at the convention.

POP QUIZ!

1 In an open primary
- **a** only voters from that party vote.
- **b** members of any party and independents may vote.
- **c** party members meet in groups.
- **d** voters select more than one candidate for each office.
- **e** delegates are not selected.

2 Primary elections and caucuses select
- **a** delegates, who support a specific candidate at the national convention.
- **b** superdelegates, who support a specific candidate at the national convention.
- **c** state party leaders.
- **d** the president and vice president.
- **e** members of the electoral college.

SHOULD PARTIES CHOOSE THEIR CANDIDATES?

One of the facts of life for the leaders of the Democratic and Republican parties is that they cannot determine who runs as their party's candidate for political office. They can encourage some candidates to run and attempt to discourage others by endorsing their favorites and funneling money, staff support, and other forms of assistance to the candidates they prefer. But in the end, congressional candidates get on the ballot by winning a primary or a vote at a state party convention; presidential candidates compete in a series of primaries and caucuses.

Political parties don't always get the nominees that their leaders want. In the 2010 election cycle, for example, insurgent (and Tea Party–backed) candidates Christine O'Donnell in Delaware and Joe Miller in Alaska captured their party's nominations for U.S. Senate seats. In Alaska, Miller defeated incumbent Lisa Murkowski; in Delaware, O'Donnell won an open seat contest against a veteran House member, Mike Castle. After their primary victories, both candidates struggled to justify extreme positions they had taken in the past. These problems came as no surprise to Delaware and Alaska Republican state party leaders, virtually all of whom had favored the losing candidates, based on the calculation that they were more likely to win in the general election. The expectations of the state party leaders proved correct, as Miller lost in the general election to a write-in campaign by Murkowski and O'Donnell was defeated by a little-known Democratic opponent. However, because both state parties chose their nominees in primaries, state party leaders had to accept whoever won the primary, even if they preferred another candidate.

Party leaders cannot force candidates out of a race. In spring 2008, many Democratic Party leaders wanted Hillary Clinton to end her presidential candidacy as it became increasingly clear that Barack Obama would win the nomination. Clinton stayed in the race until the primaries ended, forcing Obama to campaign aggressively, spend additional campaign funds, and respond to attacks from the Clinton campaign.

Why not let party leaders pick their candidates? Many scholars have argued that doing so would increase the chances of getting experienced, talented candidates on the ballot.[a] After all, party leaders probably know more than the average primary voter about who would make a good candidate or elected official. Plus, party leaders have a strong incentive to find good candidates and convince them to run—their party's influence over government policy increases with the number of people they can elect to political office.

Why, then, do voters in America get to pick party nominees in primaries? Direct primaries were introduced in American politics during the late 1800s and early 1900s.[b] The goal was explicit: reform-minded party activists wanted to take the choice of nominees out of the hands of party leaders and give it to the electorate, with the assumption that voters should be

In 2012, some Republicans worried that the fierce fight in the primary elections turned off voters, divided the party, and depleted campaign funds that would be better spent campaigning against Obama in the general election.

able to influence the choice of candidates for the general election. Moreover, reformers believed that this goal outweighed the expertise held by party leaders.

Here is the trade-off: if party leaders selected nominees, they would likely choose electable candidates who share the policy goals held by party leaders. If voters choose nominees, they can pick whoever they want, using whatever criteria they like—but there is no guarantee that these candidates will be skilled general-election campaigners or effective in office.

Of course, our system of primary elections is unlikely to go away. However, it would be possible to increase the influence that party leaders have over the process. One option would be to change campaign finance laws to increase the importance of the parties as a source of campaign funds. Another is to create a mechanism such as a state or district-level convention where party leaders could select candidates for a primary—and making it harder for candidates to get on the ballot without the leaders' endorsement.

Critical **Thinking Questions**

1. Would a system that gave additional power to party leaders in selecting nominees generally help incumbents more than challengers or the reverse?

2. What kind of nomination procedure would be favored by insurgent groups such as the various Tea Party organizations?

national party, for example, is limited in the amount of money it can contribute to congressional and presidential candidates or to state party organizations. As we discuss in Chapter 8, however, party organizations that raise campaign funds can use them to help candidates get elected through independent expenditures—running their own ads in a candidate's district or state.

Figure 7.5 shows the amount of money raised by the top groups within the Republican and Democratic parties for the 2012 election (through November 2). The final figures show that the parties and their various committes raised nearly a billion dollars each. The Democratic and Republican national committees (DNC and RNC) raised the most money, but the congressional campaign committees also raised significant sums. Congressional Democratic committees outraised their Republican counterparts. And state and local party committees also raised large sums in the 2012 elections.[45]

ONE OF THE MOST IMPORTANT WAYS parties help candidates is by raising money to fund campaigns. In 2012, the DNC raised nearly a billion dollars to help re-elect Obama and to support other Democratic candidates. The RNC raised a similar amount.

Along with supplying campaign funds, party organizations give candidates other assistance, ranging from offering campaign advice (on which issues to emphasize, how to deal with the press, and the like) to conducting polls. Party organizations at all levels also undertake get-out-the-vote activities, encouraging supporters to get to the polls. During the last few elections, the Republican Party has organized a "72-Hour Task Force" of volunteers to spend the days just before the election staffing phone banks and going door-to-door campaigning for candidates in close races.

PARTY PLATFORMS

The **party platform** is a set of promises explaining what candidates from the party will do if elected. The most visible party platform is the one approved at each party's presidential nominating convention, but the party organizations in the House and Senate also release platforms, as do other groups in the major parties. Party platforms generally reflect the brand name differences between the parties discussed earlier. For example, in the case of abortion rights, the 2012 Republican presidential platform favored a total ban on abortions, while the Democratic presidential platform expressed support for a woman's right to choose, meaning that abortion would be legal under a wider range of conditions.

party platform A set of objectives outlining the party's issue positions and priorities. Candidates are not required to support their party's platform.

In theory, party platforms describe differences between the major parties, capture each party's diagnosis of the problems facing the country, and give the party's plan for solving those problems. In this way, party platforms give citizens an easy way to evaluate candidates. However, candidates are not obligated to support their party's platform, and many take divergent stances on some issues. For example, notwithstanding the consistently strong pro-choice position on abortion in the Democratic Party's presidential platforms over the last generation, some Democratic congressional candidates, such as Pennsylvania senator Robert Casey, have promised to vote to restrict abortions if elected—a position closer to the Republican platform.[46] For some of these candidates, this position reflected personal or religious beliefs; for others, it was driven by the desire to reflect the opinion of voters in their district or state.

Notwithstanding these exceptions, party platforms are important documents. To the extent that there is conflict in American politics, is it likely to be revealed in differences between the platforms of the major parties. Moreover, political

FIGURE » 7.5

DEMOCRATIC AND REPUBLICAN FUND-RAISING IN THE 2011–12 ELECTION CYCLE

In the 2011–12 election cycle, party committees raised more than $1.7 billion in campaign funds. Although most of this money was raised by the national committees, the state, local, and candidate committees also raised significant sums. To what extent might these funds allow the national committees to force candidates to run on the party platform?

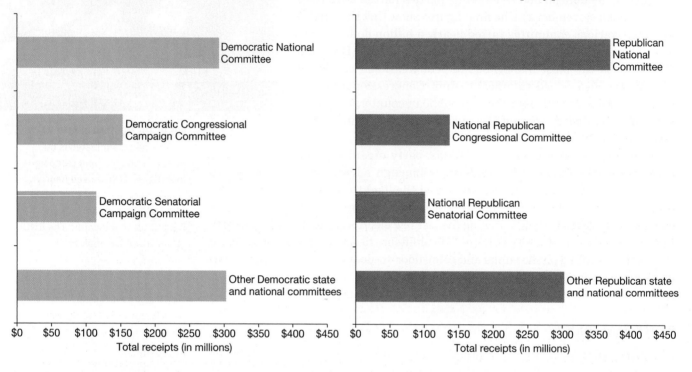

Source: www.opensecrets.org/parties/index.php, based on data released by the Federal Election Commission on 11/2/12 (accessed 11/2/12).

scientist John Geering's research shows that platforms provide a general guide for voters about the issues and issue positions that separate the major parties, and what sorts of policies winning candidates are likely to vote for if elected—while some candidates may ignore or run against their party's platform, most candidates will support the platform because they agree with it, or because they believe it is popular among their constituents.[47]

COOPERATION IN GOVERNMENT

conditional party government The theory that lawmakers from the same party will cooperate to develop policy proposals.

The theory of **conditional party government** states that as policy differences between the parties in government increase in number and intensity, the parties in government will become increasingly active as a forum for like-minded legislators to develop policy plans and as a source for legislative strategies to enact these proposals. This theory explains what has happened in Congress over the last 50 years. Although conditional party government has led to the enactment of many important proposals, there is no guarantee that party members will cooperate. Party leaders in the modern Congress work to find agreements that are attractive to their members, but in many recent instances these efforts have failed. And if the party in government can't reach agreement, it will stay on the sidelines.

AGENDA SETTING

Throughout the year, the parties in government meet to devise strategies for legislative action—that is, to set agendas. What proposals should they offer, and in what order should they be considered? Should they try to make a deal with the president or with legislators from the other party? For example, after the 2008 election, Democratic congressional leaders met with president-elect Barack Obama and his staff to discuss priorities for the 2009–10 legislative term, including climate change legislation, health care reform, and an economic stimulus package. Some of these efforts were highly successful. Less than a month after Obama took office, Congress passed a $787 billion stimulus plan, which Democrats passed with no Republican support in the House and only three Republican votes in the Senate, with landmark health care reform legislation enacted with no Republican votes a year later.

WITHIN THE GOVERNMENT, politicians from the same party work together to develop an agenda and try to get it enacted. Here, President Obama meets with Democratic leaders from the Senate.

Similarly, after Republicans gained control of the House after the 2010 mid-terms, the House Republican Conference used its control of the chamber to shape negotiations with President Obama over deficit reduction. Their efforts ensured that the package enacted in April 2011 with an increase in the federal debt limit contained no tax increases and established a congressional "Supercommittee" to recommend additional reductions.

However, the party in government can act collectively this way only when its members can agree on what they want. Such agreement is not always possible or may require extensive negotiation and compromise. For example, health care legislation was enacted only after protracted negotiations with Democratic senators and the granting of concessions in return for their support. Similarly, in 2006, House Republicans, who were in the majority, were split on immigration reform. Some members favored a proposal that created a path to citizenship for illegal immigrants while others opposed amnesty and wanted to stiffen criminal penalties against these immigrants. Ultimately, they never reached an agreement, and no reform measure came to a vote.[48]

The defeat on immigration reform is noteworthy because the Republicans held majorities in both houses of Congress. In other words, if President Bush could have convinced Republican legislators to support his immigration proposals, he would have carried the day, because the Republicans in the House and Senate had enough votes to enact the proposals without support from Democrats. House Republicans now face similar problems: while they have a majority in the chamber, there are significant disagreements in their ranks about legislative priorities on issues such as budget cuts and immigration.

COORDINATION

Political parties play an important role in coordinating the actions taken in different branches of government. Such coordination is extremely important for enacting new laws, because unless supporters in Congress can amass a two-thirds majority to override a veto, they need the president's support. Similarly, the president needs congressional support to enact the proposals he favors. To these ends, the president routinely meets with congressional leaders from his party and occasionally meets with the entire caucus or conference. Various members of the president's staff also meet with House and Senate members to present the president's proposals and hear what members of Congress from both parties want to enact.

During 2009, President Obama held many meetings with Democratic members of Congress to lobby them to support his proposals for health care reform. Although many congressional Democrats supported Obama's proposals, enactment was nearly derailed by several Democratic representatives and senators who demanded amendments to restrict government payment for abortions. Obama opposed these efforts but was powerless to stop them. In fact, getting the last few votes needed for enactment required Obama to promise to issue an executive order that had essentially the same effect as the proposed amendments.

Coordination can also occur between caucuses or conferences in the House and Senate. At the same time President Obama and Democrats in Congress were negotiating over health care reform, congressional Republicans were devising strategies for delaying and defeating these proposals. Although their efforts did not prevent the enactment of reform legislation, their strong opposition required the president and congressional leaders to accept many changes favored by moderate and conservative Democrats in order to enact the legislation without Republican support.

FOCUSING ON PARTIES CAN MAKE it easier for voters to issue rewards and punishments. In 2011, Republicans in Congress (including Senate minority leader Mitch McConnell, shown here) held numerous press conferences to contrast their position on the budget and the national debt with the Democrats' position.

Such coordination efforts require real work and compromise, as party leaders in the House and the Senate do not have authority over each other or over the elected members of their party. Nor can the president order a House member or senator to do anything, even if the legislator is from the president's own party. In 2010, for example, President Obama and congressional leaders needed the votes of several antiabortion Democrats, including Congressman Bart Stupak, to pass health care legislation through the House of Representatives. The leaders and the president held repeated meetings with Stupak and his allies, offering various promises and enticements to secure their votes. Ultimately, these legislators voted for the proposal, but neither the president nor party leaders could have forced them to support it.

ACCOUNTABILITY

One of the most important roles of political parties in a democracy is giving citizens identifiable groups to reward or punish for government actions, thereby providing a means for voters to focus their desire for accountability. By rewarding and punishing elected officials, often based on their party affiliation and other party members' behavior in office, voters use the party system to hold officials accountable for outcomes such as the state of the economy or America's relations with other nations.

During periods of **unified government**, when one party holds majorities in both the House and the Senate *and* controls the presidency, that party is the party in power. It has enough votes to enact policies in Congress and a good chance of having them signed into law by the president. During times of **divided government**, when one party controls Congress but not the presidency, or when different parties control the House and Senate, the president's party is considered the party in power. Focusing on parties makes it easy for a citizen to issue rewards and punishments. Is the economy doing well? Then that citizen will vote for the candidates from the party in power. But if the economy is doing poorly, or if the citizen feels that government is wasting tax money or enacting bad policies, she can vote for candidates from the party that is currently out of power. When citizens behave this way, they strengthen the incentive for elected officials from the party in power to work together to develop policies that address voters' concerns—on the premise that if they do, voters will reward them with another term in office. Consider the 2010 midterm elections, when many Americans voted against Democratic candidates because of poor economic conditions. While Democrats lost seats in both the House and the Senate, most Democratic incumbents were returned to office. Why? Some were elected from states or districts dominated by Democratic identifiers. But many others were re-elected because they campaigned on a platform of changing policy or because of their efforts to help local businesses, saying in effect, "Instead of punishing me for my party affiliation, reward me for working on your behalf."

Some political scientists have argued that legislators from the same party should be forced to work as a team—to run on the same campaign platform, work together in Washington to enact their platform, and be collectively held accountable in elections for whether their proposals worked or not. Political organizations that function this way are called responsible parties,[49] and they have never existed in American politics. If American parties worked this way, it is likely that more people would hold the party in power and its officeholders directly accountable for the state of the economy and other national-level outcomes.

In contrast to the responsible party model, the three-part structure of contemporary American parties complicates decisions about accountability. Suppose, for example, a legislator from the party in power opposed the policies enacted by her party. If so, it may not make sense for a voter to reward this legislator for good outcomes of those policies or punish her for bad outcomes. Even though she is from the party in power, she did not cause the outcomes that the voter cares about. What should a voter do in this case?

In the end, re-electing members of the party in power despite a poor economy or other troubles makes sense given how American political parties are organized and their lack of control over individual officeholders. Of course, insofar as incumbent members of the party in power present themselves as loyal party members and cast votes in accordance with the wishes of party leaders, they will increase the chances that their constituents will take account of their party label when casting their votes—which will help them get re-elected in good times, but will increase the chances of defeat when conditions turn against their party.

unified government A situation in which one party holds a majority of seats in the House and Senate and the president is a member of that same party.

divided government A situation in which the House, Senate, and presidency are not controlled by the same party, such as if Democrats hold the majority of House and Senate seats, and the president is a Republican.

CONSIDER THE ROLE OF
MINOR PARTIES IN A
SYSTEM DOMINATED BY
TWO MAJOR PARTIES

MINOR PARTIES

So far, this chapter has focused on the major American political parties, the Republicans and the Democrats, and paid less attention to other party organizations. The reason is that minor political parties in America are *so* minor that they are generally not significant players on the political stage. Many such parties exist, but few run candidates in more than a handful of races, and very few minor-party candidates win political office. Few Americans identify with minor parties, and most of these parties exist for only a relatively short period.

Even so, you may think we're giving minor parties too little attention. Consider Ralph Nader, who ran as the Green Party nominee for president in 2000, winning almost 5 percent of the vote. In some states, the number of votes Nader received exceeded the margin separating Democrat Al Gore from Republican George Bush. In particular, in Florida, where Bush won by only a few hundred votes after a disputed recount, Nader received almost 100,000 votes—enough to swing the state, and the election, to Gore.

However, the outcome of Nader's 2000 presidential campaign doesn't so much highlight the importance of minor parties as it illustrates the closeness of the 2000 presidential election. If Nader had not run, Gore might have received enough additional support to win. But given that Bush's margin of victory in Florida was so small, any number of seemingly minor events (a polling station closing early, or rain in some areas and sunshine in others) could have changed the outcome.

MINOR PARTY PRESIDENTIAL candidates, such as Ralph Nader in 2000, sometimes attract considerable press attention because of their distinctive, often extreme policy preferences—but they rarely affect election outcomes. Nader ran again, as an independent, in 2004 and 2008.

EFFECTS ON ELECTION OUTCOMES

Minor parties did not play a decisive role in the 2008 presidential election, but in several swing states they received more votes than the margin of difference between Obama and McCain. The most successful were the Independent Party (661,000 votes) and the Libertarian Party (491,000), while others like the Boston Tea Party and the U.S. Pacifist Party received far fewer votes (2,305 and 97, respectively). Minor parties won about 1.5 million votes in the 2008 presidential race, whereas the two major parties received 121 million votes.

Even in terms of lower offices, minor-party candidates typically attract only meager support. The Libertarian Party claimed to have more than 154 officeholders as of 2011. However, many of these officials held unelected positions such as seats on county planning boards or ran unopposed for relatively minor offices such as justice of the peace.[50]

Looking back in history, some minor-party candidates for president have attracted a substantial percentage of citizens' votes. George Wallace ran as the candidate of the American Independent Party in 1968, receiving about 13 percent of the popular vote nationwide. Ross Perot, the Reform Party candidate for president in 1996, won 8.4 percent of the popular vote. Perot also ran as an independent in 1992, winning 18.2 percent of the popular vote.

As we have already discussed, as of 2012 the Tea Party does not qualify as a minor party because of the lack of an organization or position on the ballot. It may be that over time, the organizations that make up the Tea Party will unite and work together to formulate a joint platform, get their candidates on the ballot, and, ultimately, win elections to state and national offices. If they do, the new organization would likely look like one of these minor parties discussed here, unless and until it managed to elect a significant number of its candidates.

UNIQUE ISSUES FACING MINOR PARTIES

The differences between major and minor political parties in contemporary American politics grow even more substantial when considered in terms other than election outcomes. For most minor parties, the party in government does not exist, as few of their candidates win office. Many minor parties have virtually no organization beyond a small party headquarters and a website. Some minor parties, such as the Green Party, the Libertarian Party, and the Reform Party, have local chapters that meet on a regular basis. But these modest efforts pale in comparison to the nationwide network of offices, thousands of workers, and millions of dollars deployed by Republican and Democratic party organizations.

Research shows that people vote for minor-party candidates because they find these candidates' positions more attractive than those of the major parties and also because they believe that neither major party can govern effectively.[51] In 2008, for example, presidential candidate Ralph Nader advocated an immediate withdrawal of American troops from Iraq, as well as deep cuts in defense spending. To vote for Nader, a citizen would have had to like Nader's issue stands and believe that neither of the major parties could effectively address these problems.

The issues and issue positions taken by minor parties and their candidates are almost always very different from those espoused by the major parties. The Constitution Party, for example, advocates an end to government civil service regulations; a ban on compulsory school attendance laws; withdrawal of the United States from the United Nations and all international trade agreements; abolishing foreign aid, the income tax, the Internal Revenue Service, and all federal welfare programs; and repealing all campaign finance legislation, the Endangered Species Act, and federal firearms regulations. These positions are extreme, not in the sense of being silly or dangerous, but in the sense that relatively few Americans feel the same way.

The basic structure of the American political system also works against minor political parties. This principle is summed up by **Duverger's law**, which states that in a democracy that has **single-member districts** and **plurality voting** (as in contemporary American politics, although the law mandating single-member districts was not passed until the 1950s), there will be only two political parties that elect a significant number of candidates to political office. Given these electoral institutions (see Chapter 8), many people consider a vote for a minor-party candidate to be a wasted vote, as there is no chance that the candidate will win office. As a result, well-qualified candidates are driven to affiliate with one of the major political parties because they know that running as a minor-party nominee will put them at a considerable disadvantage. These decisions reinforce citizens' expectations that minor-party candidates have no chance of winning elections and that a vote for them is a wasted vote. Although there is no evidence that the Founders wanted to choose electoral institutions that made it hard for minor parties and their candidates, there is no doubt that the rules of the American electoral game have these effects.

Duverger's law The principle that in a democracy with single-member districts and plurality voting, like the United States, only two parties' candidates will have a realistic chance of winning political office.

single-member districts An electoral system in which every elected official represents a geographically defined area, such as a state or congressional district, and each area elects one representative.

plurality voting A voting system in which the candidate who receives the most votes within a geographic area wins the election, regardless of whether that candidate wins a majority (more than half) of the votes.

WHAT KIND OF DEMOCRACY DO AMERICAN POLITICAL PARTIES CREATE?

Parties help political activists, party leaders, and citizens who identify with the party to pursue their policy goals by focusing collective efforts on electing people who share their priorities. For politicians, parties provide ballot access, a brand name, campaign assistance, and a group of like-minded colleagues with whom they can coordinate, compromise, and strategize. For citizens, political parties provide information and a means of holding specific individuals accountable for what government does.

The question of whether political parties are good or bad for democracy depends on how individual party members and officials carry out these tasks. Political parties can help democracy by filling the ballot with well-qualified candidates, helping them get elected, offering citizens clear choices about government policies, informing citizens about platforms and candidates, motivating citizens to vote, and, after the election, helping elected officials enact the party platform. The problem is that the people who make up American political parties are not primarily interested in democracy; they are interested in their own careers, policy goals, and winning political office. These goals often lead them away from actions that would improve American democracy.

RECRUITING GOOD CANDIDATES

One of the most important things the Republican and Democratic parties can do for democracy is to recruit candidates for national political offices who can run effective campaigns and responsibly uphold their elected positions. After all, a citizen's choices as a voter are limited to the people on the ballot. If good candidates decide against running or are prevented from doing so, citizens will be dissatisfied no matter who wins the election.

As we discussed, the Republican and Democratic parties work to find good candidates and persuade them to run. However, the potential candidates have to decide for themselves whether their chances of winning justify the enormous investment of time and money needed to run a campaign. When a party is unpopular, the best potential candidates may decide to wait until the next election to run, leaving the already disadvantaged party with a less competitive set of candidates.[52] And even when a party does not face economic or other headwinds, state- or district-level factors may deter good candidates from running under the party's banner. As a result, insofar as conditions favor one party's candidates over those from the other party, the disadvantaged party may find it difficult to offer citizens a compelling candidate to vote for on Election Day.

WORKING TOGETHER IN CAMPAIGNS

Parties can also work to simplify voters' choices by trying to get candidates to emphasize the same issues or to take similar issue positions. That way, citizens know that when they vote for, say, a Democrat, they are getting someone whose policy positions are likely to differ from those held by Republicans. The problem is that members of the party organization and the party in government do not always agree. Sometimes the differences within the parties reflect genuine differences of opinion. Other times, candidates are trying to match the preferences of citizens in their state or district. Either way, the simple fact is that political parties in America generally speak with many voices, not one.

Why don't party leaders simply order their candidates to support the party platform or to work together in campaigns? As we have discussed, party leaders actually have very little power over candidates.[53] They can't kick a candidate off the ballot because candidates win the nomination in a primary election or at a convention. Even though parties have a lot of campaign money to dispense, their contributions typically make up only a fraction of what a candidate spends on a campaign. And incumbent candidates, who generally hold an advantage over challengers when seeking re-election, are even less beholden to party leaders. Even if party leaders could somehow prevent an incumbent from running for re-election, they would have to find another candidate to take the incumbent's place, which would mean losing the incumbent's popularity and reputation and reducing the party's chances of holding the seat.

WORKING TOGETHER IN OFFICE

Because candidates are not required to support their party's platform, there is no guarantee that they will be able to work together with other members of the party in office. Sometimes, as with the Democrats and the economic stimulus plan, the members of a party can compromise to resolve their differences. However, there are also many examples of issues that split a party wide open, such as Democrats and health care reform or Republicans and immigration reform. Sometimes party members can compromise their differences, as in the case of Democrats and health care reform, but at other times, such as the Republicans' immigration proposals, compromise may be impossible. And of course, even if the members of a party can find common groups, they may fail at building the bipartisan coalitions that are often necessary to enact major legislation, such as deficit reduction proposals.

The fact that American political parties are heterogeneous means that elected members of the party may not agree on spending, policy, or anything else. In that sense, voters can't expect that putting one party in power will result in specific policy changes. Instead, policy outcomes depend on how (and whether) individual officeholders from the party can resolve their differences. Institutions such as the party caucuses or conferences provide a forum in which elected officials can meet and seek common ground, but there is no guarantee that they will find acceptable compromises.

Moreover, concerted action by members of a party in government may be aimed at political rather than policy goals. For example, during the last several years, Republicans in the House and Senate uniformly opposed many Democratic initiatives. Moreover, legislators from both parties failed to find common ground in the Supercommittee negotiations around deficit reduction. For many legislators, opposition was based on their policy goals. But for others, their opposition reflected a political calculation—that this strategy was their party's best bet for gaining seats in the 2012 elections. In this way, American political parties can work against the enactment of effective responses to public problems and increase, rather than decrease, the amount of conflict in American politics.

PROVIDING ACCOUNTABILITY

The final task for a party is to serve as an accountability mechanism that gives citizens an identifiable group to reward when policies work well and to punish when policies fail. However, individual legislators also work to build a reputation with voters that is independent of their party label. They are happy to emphasize their party affiliation when it brings them support, but they choose not to mention it when the party is associated with unpopular policies or outcomes. Republican legislators, for example, highlighted their party identification in the 2002 and 2004 elections, as many voters held the party in high regard.[54] However, by 2006, with voter evaluations of the party and President Bush at all-time lows, many Republican candidates deemphasized their con-

VOTERS MAY PUNISH THE PARTY in power if they are unhappy with its policies. In 2010, frustration with many of President Obama's policies worked against Democrats and helped Republicans. Senator Marco Rubio of Florida was one of the new Republican members elected to Congress that year.

nection to the party.[55] The same was true for many Democratic candidates in 2010 and 2012: given the unpopularity of many of President Obama's policies and low voter evaluations of the party in power, these candidates' best bet for re-election was to emphasize their efforts to respond to district concerns and downplay their party affiliation or past support for the president.

When politicians work to secure their own political future in this way, they make it harder for voters to use party labels to decide who should be rewarded and who should be punished for government performance. The result is that legislators are held accountable for their own performance in office, such as how they voted—but no one in Congress is accountable for large-scale outcomes such as the state of the economy or for foreign policy. Of course, some voters hold legislators accountable based on whether they are members of the party in power, which is why Republicans lost House and Senate seats in 2006 and 2008 and Democrats lost seats in 2010. Even so, most Republicans and Democrats in Congress managed to survive these elections, which suggests that party-based accountability is rather weak in contemporary American politics.

CITIZENS' BEHAVIOR

As we have seen, most Americans identify as either Republican or Democrat, and many citizens use party labels to cue their vote decisions. However, citizens are under no obligation to give money or time to the party they identify with or to any of its candidates. They don't have to vote for its candidates or even vote at all. All these actions would strengthen party organizations, but citizens do not have to take them even if they strongly identify with a party.

Here again, citizens are free to choose how to participate in American politics, including the option of not participating. But many of the things citizens do—such as not contributing to campaigns or party organizations, voting for candidates from separate parties to hold different offices, or ignoring party affiliation in their retrospective evaluations—weaken party organizations and make it harder for them to operate as a team to enact policies and oversee the bureaucracy.

CONCLUSION

American political parties help organize elections, unify disparate social groups, simplify the choices facing voters, and build compromises around party members' shared policy concerns. A close look at how parties operate demonstrates that groups such as the various Tea Party organizations, for all their activities and press attention, fall far short of what it takes to make a political party.

However, in all these activities the success of political parties depends on whether individual party members—candidates, citizens, and party leaders—are willing to take the actions necessary to achieve these goals. Sometimes they are, but at other times they decide that their own interests, or those of their constituents, are best served by ignoring or working against party priorities. And when party members refuse to cooperate, political parties may be unable to do the things that help American democracy work well.

The case of the Democratic Party from 2006 to 2012 illustrates these limits. It was an easy choice for Democratic candidates to emphasize their party affiliation in the 2006 and 2008 elections, but the brand name was valuable during these contests only because of the unpopularity of then-president Bush and the Republicans in the House and Senate. Those individuals were seen as being responsible for the poor state of the economy and the unpopular wars in Iraq and Afghanistan.

After the 2008 election, however, divisions within the Democratic Party in government soon became apparent. Though Democrats were able to unite to enact an economic stimulus package, building consensus around health care reform legislation took considerable time and required jettisoning provisions that many Democratic legislators supported. Despite having strong majorities in both houses of Congress, Democratic leaders had to worry as much about keeping their own members in line as they did about thwarting Republican opposition.

And in the 2010 mid-terms and 2012 presidential elections, with Democrats seen as the party responsible for poor economic conditions, many Democratic candidates tried to disassociate themselves from the party and campaigned on their personal accomplishments.

Of course, these difficulties do not reflect a problem with Democrats per se. Republicans did little better when they controlled the House, Senate, and presidency, and they may have similar problems given the additional seats their candidates won in 2010. Rather, the difficulties show that the individuals who make up American political parties often do not have an incentive to behave in the interests of their party or as theories of democracy suggest they should.

WHAT ARE POLITICAL PARTIES?

▶ Define political parties and the three major aspects of American parties. **Pages 241–42**

SUMMARY

Political parties are organizations that run candidates for political office and coordinate the actions of officials elected under the party banner. Here in the United States parties are relatively decentralized, with a loose configuration of candidates who share a party label but don't necessarily work together. The parties are composed of three semi-autonomous units: the party organization; the party in government; and the party in electorate.

KEY TERMS

party organization (p. 242)

party in government (p. 242)

party in the electorate (p. 242)

PRACTICE QUIZ QUESTION

1. Which statement best characterizes the American political parties?
   a) Parties in the electorate pay dues to the party organization; leaders in the party organization tell elected officials what to do.
   b) Candidates run as representatives of the party; leaders have no influence on how candidates campaign or govern.
   c) Candidates are generally autonomous of the party organization, though they do receive support from the party organization.
   d) Parties only help candidates after they are elected.
   e) Parties handle 90 percent of fundraising for candidates.

HISTORY OF AMERICAN POLITICAL PARTIES

▶ Show how American political parties and party systems have evolved over time. **Pages 242–47**

SUMMARY

Political parties are a central feature of American politics, though they look and act very differently today than they have over time. Political scientists use the term *party system* to refer to a period of party stability; in all, there have been six different party systems in the country's history. Party systems are broken up by realignments, which occur when some of the defining factors of the party system are changed or specified, and rifts in the group develop because of these changes.

KEY TERMS

party system (p. 242)

party principle (p. 244)

spoils system (p. 244)

New Deal Coalition (p. 245)

realignment (p. 246)

CRITICAL THINKING AND DISCUSSION

Is the spoils system a good idea or a bad idea? Why?

PRACTICE QUIZ QUESTIONS

2. Which were the first well-known parties in the United States?
   a) Federalists and Democratic-Republicans
   b) Democrats and Republicans
   c) Whigs and Federalists
   d) Democratics and Whigs
   e) Whigs and Republicans

3. The idea that a party is not just a group, but an organization that exists apart from its candidate, is called the _____.
  a) party system
  b) spoils system
  c) conditional party government
  d) patrty identification
  e) party principle

4. The Third Party System was broken up by which issue?
  a) creation of a national bank
  b) size and regulatory power of government
  c) the admission of California to the Union
  d) the adoption of the greenback
  e) the New Deal

5. In order for an issue to trigger a party realignment, it has to be _____.
  a) important
  b) controversial
  c) economic
  d) cross-cutting
  e) salient

⑤ PRACTICE ONLINE

"What Do Political Scientists Do?" video exercise: *Divisions in Political Parties*

MODERN AMERICAN POLITICAL PARTIES

▶ Describe the main characteristics of American parties as organizations, in the government, and in the electorate.
Pages 247–60

SUMMARY

The modern party is composed of three parts. The party organization is a loosely defined group of individuals and organizations that are focused on supporting political candidates when they share the same policy goals. The party in the government consists of elected officials who are the members of a particular party. The party in the electorate consists of citizens who identify with a particular political party.

KEY TERMS

national committee (p. 247)

political action committee (PAC) (p. 248)

527 organization (p. 248)

political machine (p. 251)

caucus (congressional) (p. 253)

conference (p. 253)

party identification (party ID) (p. 256)

party coalitions (p. 258)

CRITICAL THINKING AND DISCUSSION

How would we know that a realignment is taking place in American politics?

PRACTICE QUIZ QUESTIONS

6. The Democratic and Republican party organizations _____ hierarchical; they are _____ to force state and local parties to share their positions on issues.
  a) are not; able
  b) are not; unable
  c) are; able
  d) are; unable
  e) are; sometimes able

7. A group of elected officials of the same party who come together to organize and strategize is called a _____.
  a) cabal
  b) conditional party government
  c) primary
  d) political action committee
  e) caucus

8. The modern Congress is _____; the distance between the parties has _____ over the past 60 years.
  a) polarized; increased
  b) polarized; stayed the same
  c) not polarized; decreased
  d) not polarized; stayed the same
  e) not polarized; increased

9. What has recent analysis of political independents concluded?
   a) They are in the process of changing parties.
   b) More and more people regard parties as irrelevant.
   c) Americans are politically savvy and do not blindly follow party lines.
   d) The number of independents has grown substantially in the past 20 years.
   e) Independents are not better informed on candidates, parties, or policy.

⑤ **PRACTICE ONLINE**

"Critical Thinking" exercise: *Politics Is Everywhere— Party Identification*

THE ROLE OF POLITICAL PARTIES IN AMERICAN POLITICS

▶ Explain the important functions parties perform in the political system. **Pages 261–69**

SUMMARY

Political parties serve two major roles in the political system. First, they contest elections by recruiting and nominating candidates and supporting candidate campaigns. Second, they facilitate cooperation in government by providing a framework for agenda setting, coordination, and accountability among members of the same party.

KEY TERMS

primary election (p. 261)

caucus (electoral) (p. 261)

nominating convention (p. 262)

party platform (p. 265)

conditional party government (p. 266)

unified government (p. 269)

divided government (p. 269)

CRITICAL THINKING AND DISCUSSION

Suppose you are the leader of your party's caucus or conference in the House of Representatives. Why would you want to convince your party's elected officials to support the party's position on an issue? Why might you want to let them vote as they think best?

PRACTICE QUIZ QUESTIONS

10. Which is *not* one of the ways political party organizations support candidates?
    a) by controlling who runs in House and Senate races
    b) by contributing money to campaign activities
    c) by offering advice on how to deal with the press
    d) by organizing get-out-the-vote activities
    e) by offering advice on which issues to emphasize

11. Why do most candidates support their party platforms?
    a) because candidates are required to support the platforms
    b) because all candidates vote on the platforms that are written
    c) because candidates get kicked out of the party for not doing so
    d) because both major parties' platforms are essentially the same
    e) because most candidates and their constituents generally agree with the platform

12. Which of the following options best defines the theory of conditional party government?
    "As policy differences between the parties in government _____, the parties in government will be _____ important in helping legislators develop policy plans and strategies."
    a) increase; less
    b) increase; more
    c) decrease; less
    d) decrease; more
    e) decrease; equally

13. When the president, House, and Senate are controlled by the same party, this is called:
    a) party in government
    b) responsible party government
    c) unified government
    d) divided government
    e) conditional party government

MINOR PARTIES

▶ Consider the role of minor parties in a system dominated by two major parties. **Pages 270–71**

SUMMARY

There are many different minor political parties, and while they rarely make a significant impact on the political stage, they do occasionally influence election outcomes. The two big issues facing minor parties are that their platforms do not appeal to a large portion of Americans, and that the electoral system makes it hard for minor parties to win elections.

KEY TERMS

Duverger's law (p. 271)

single-member districts (p. 271)

plurality voting (p. 271)

PRACTICE QUIZ QUESTION

14. The principle that single-member districts and plurality voting will support only two political parties is
_____.
    a) Condorcet's theorem
    b) Pascal's paradox
    c) Duverger's law
    d) Fermat's theorem
    e) Conditional party government

Ⓢ PRACTICE ONLINE

"Big Think" video exercise: *Are Two Parties Enough?*

WHAT KIND OF DEMOCRACY DO AMERICAN POLITICAL PARTIES CREATE?

▶ Evaluate the benefits and possible problems of the American party system. **Pages 272–74**

SUMMARY

Political parties do a number of things that are important to facilitate good democracy: they generally recruit good candidates, simplify voters' choices, encourage candidates to work together in office, and provide a mechanism for holding politicians accountable. Nonetheless, there are limits to the extent to which parties are able to achieve these goals, partially due to the fact that the people who make up the parties are primarily interested in their own careers.

PRACTICE QUIZ QUESTION

15. Which feature of political parties is undermined by legislators who build a reputation with voters independent of the party label?
    a) the recruitment of good candidates
    b) the provision of ballot access
    c) the simplification of voter choices
    d) the encouragement of policy cooperation
    e) the provision of electoral accountability

SUGGESTED READING

Aldrich, John. *Why Parties?* Chicago: University of Chicago Press, 1995.

Carmines, Edward G., and James A. Stimson. *Issue Evolution: Race and the Transformation of American Politics.* Princeton, NJ: Princeton University Press, 1989.

Cohen, Marty, David Karol, Hans Noel, and John Zaller. *The Party Decides: Presidential Nominations Before and After Reform.* Chicago: University of Chicago Press, 2008.

Cox, Gary, and Mathew McCubbins. *Setting the Agenda: Party Government in the U.S. House of Representatives.* New York: Cambridge University Press, 2005.

Fiorina, Morris. *Retrospective Voting in American National Elections.* New Haven, CT: Yale University Press, 1981.

Green, Donald, Bradley Palmquist, and Eric Schickler. *Partisan Hearts and Minds.* New Haven, CT: Yale University Press, 2004.

Key, V. O. *Politics, Parties, and Pressure Groups.* New York: Crowell, 1956.

Polsby, Nelson. *Consequences of Party Reform.* New York: Oxford University Press, 1983.

Rohde, David. *Parties and Leaders in the Post-Reform House.* Chicago: University of Chicago Press, 1991.

Schattschneider, E. E. *Party Government.* New York: McGraw-Hill, 1942.

Schlesinger, Joseph. *Political Parties and the Winning of Office.* Ann Arbor: University of Michigan Press, 1994.

Sundquist, James L. *Dynamics of the Party System.* Rev. ed. Washington, DC: Brookings Institution, 1983.

8

Elections

IN THE 2012 ELECTION, BARACK Obama and Mitt Romney offered Americans a choice between two distinct visions of government. Throughout the campaigns, and especially during their three debates, the candidates competed to appeal to voters.

A MERICAN NATIONAL ELECTIONS ARE ABOUT CONFLICT—they are contests in which candidates compete for political office, offering voters a choice between different backgrounds, records, and promises. In the 2012 presidential election, Democrat Barack Obama and Republican Mitt Romney gave the electorate two distinct, competing visions of what the federal government should do, from what the tax code should look like to how this money should be spent and what regulations should be imposed on individuals and corporations. One of the central themes of this chapter is that elections matter; what government does depends on who wins these political contests. Some policies remain the same no matter who wins—but there is no doubt that a President Romney would make many different choices if he was in office, from defense spending to Medicare, alternative energy, corporate regulations, and Supreme Court nominees.

The same is true in House and Senate elections. As we have seen over the last two years, the policies emerging from a Republican-led House of Representatives look very different than those enacted when the Democrats were in the majority. And if the Senate had switched from a Democratic to a Republican majority in 2012, the policies emerging from that chamber would be very different as well. Even at the level of individual House and Senate seats, elections determine who represents a given state or district—which policies they fight for, whose demands they consider when deciding what to do, and which party agenda they will support in Congress.

The presence of conflict in American elections is no surprise: as we discussed in Chapter 5 on public opinion, Americans often disagree about what

CONFLICT & COMPROMISE
in American Politics

government should do. These differences are reflected among the candidates for the House, Senate, and presidency—both in the promises they make during campaigns and in the actions they take in office. Even when candidates largely agree on policy questions, which occasionally happens in House and Senate races, elections are still conflictual, as debate centers on which one is better-qualified to make the choices he or she will face if elected.

Elections are also about compromise. Some of the voters who supported Mitt Romney during the Republican nomination process did so not because he was their most-preferred candidate, but because he was good enough in their view, and they believed that he had the best chance of beating Barack Obama. Similarly, as Romney's rivals, including Herman Cain, Newt Gingrich, and Rick Santorum, dropped out of the race, they endorsed Romney and campaigned for him. While each would have preferred to be the nominee rather than Romney, their endorsement reflected the fact that they would rather see Romney win than have four more years of Obama in office.

On the Democratic side, after Obama won the presidency in 2008, he named his principal rival for the Democratic nomination, Hillary Clinton, as his secretary of state. Obama's vice president, Joe Biden, had also competed for the democratic nomination. While Clinton's and Biden's policy views differed from Obama's in some areas, their interest in Obama succeeding in office was enough to overcome their disagreements. And, while there was some conflict within the Democratic Party over some decisions Obama made in his first term in office, most dissenters supported Obama because they believed he was the best candidate the party could put forth. As these examples illustrate, compromise is often an essential ingredient in a winning electoral strategy, both for voters and for candidates.

Elections also demonstrate that political process matters. Candidates in American elections compete for a wide variety of offices. They are elected for different periods of time to represent districts, states, or the entire nation—places that vary tremendously in terms of what constituents want from government. A variety of rules determine who can run, who can vote, and how candidates can campaign. Even ballot layouts and how votes are cast and counted vary across states. Elections also differ in the amount of media coverage they receive, the level of involvement of political parties and other organizations, and the amount of attention citizens pay to the contests. All these aspects of the election process—who runs, how they campaign, and how voters respond—shape outcomes.

Elections, as prominent public forums that give Americans the opportunity to debate policy preferences, provide further evidence that politics is everywhere. During election season, campaign coverage and ads for candidates become almost impossible to avoid. Even so, one of the most important tasks all campaigns face is getting citizens' attention and convincing them to listen to the candidate's appeals.

Our goal in this chapter is to explain how American elections work. By making the election process more comprehensible and by focusing on the promises candidates make in campaigns, we aim to demonstrate how and why elections matter. We show that there are real differences between candidates and that these differences have profound implications for public policy. We show that the actions candidates take during campaigns shape citizens' perceptions and their vote decisions. And we show that despite Americans' general detachment from politics, their votes reflect both their policy preferences and considerable insight into candidates' promises and performance.

HOW DO AMERICAN ELECTIONS WORK?

PRESENT THE MAJOR RULES AND PROCEDURES OF AMERICAN ELECTIONS

The American political system is a representative democracy: Americans do not make policy choices themselves, but they vote for individuals who make these choices on their behalf. This section describes the rules and procedures that define American national elections. Our working assumption for explaining these processes as well as the behavior of candidates and voters is that these rules and actions are tied directly to what elections do: select representatives, give citizens the ability to influence the direction of government policy, and give citizens the opportunity to reward and punish officeholders seeking re-election.

SELECTING REPRESENTATIVES

The most visible function of American national elections is the selection of officeholders: members of the House and Senate, and the president and vice president. Candidates can be **incumbents** or challengers. America has a representative democracy, which means that by voting in elections, Americans have an indirect effect on government policy. Though citizens do not make policy choices themselves, they determine which individuals get to make these choices. In this way, elections are supposed to connect citizen preferences and government actions.

incumbent A politician running for re-election to the office he or she currently holds.

Most congressional elections are *normal elections*, where a high percentage of incumbents are re-elected, and the party ratios in the House and Senate do not change significantly. These elections turn largely on district- or state-level factors and high re-election rates for both parties.[1] Some congressional elections, such as those in 2006, 2008, and 2010, do not fit this description, however. In these cases, known as *nationalized elections*, the turnover is much higher, and re-election rates are significantly lower for one party's incumbents. Nationalized elections typically involve a change in party control of one or both houses of Congress or the presidency, and these changes can profoundly affect what government does.

AMERICAN CANDIDATES, SUCH AS California House member Tom McClintock, shown here, compete for different offices under a complex set of regulations. At the national level, their large campaign organizations often spend millions. Even so, elections are best understood in individual terms: one candidate trying to win one citizen's vote.

SHAPING POLICY

The fundamental choice in an election is between two or more candidates running for some political office—a seat in the House or the Senate, or the presidency. In part, voters choose between candidates, deciding which individual they would prefer to see in office. But elections also involve a choice between candidates' policy platforms, the set of things they promise to do if elected. By investigating candidates' platforms, citizens learn about the range of options for government policy. Moreover, their vote decisions, which lead to the election of some candidates and the defeat of others, determine who gets to make choices about future government policy, and thereby shapes government policy itself. These effects are easiest to see in a nationalized election, but even in a normal election, some incumbents retire or are defeated, leading to a different set of people in Congress making choices that shape government policy.

PROMOTING ACCOUNTABILITY

The election process also creates a way to hold incumbents accountable. When citizens choose between voting for an incumbent or a challenger, they can make a retrospective evaluation. They consider the incumbent's performance, asking, "Has she done a good job on the issues I care about?"[2] Citizens who answer yes typically vote for the incumbent, and those who say no typically vote for the challenger.

Retrospective evaluations are significant because they make incumbents responsive to their constituents' demands.[3] If an elected official anticipates that some constituents will make retrospective evaluations, he will try to take actions that these constituents will like. If an incumbent ignores the possibility of voters' retrospective evaluations, voters can opt to remove him from office because they disapprove of his performance. Retrospective evaluations can also form the basis for prospective judgments—voters' beliefs about how the country will fare if different candidates win. This provides an additional reason for incumbents to be responsive to citizen demands.

Many Americans use retrospective evaluations to judge members of Congress and the president. One of the important differences between normal and nationalized elections is that in nationalized elections, voters' overall evaluations of Congress and the president are much more negative, leading more voters to vote against incumbents from the party in power.

TWO STAGES OF ELECTIONS

House and Senate candidates face a two-step procedure. First, if the prospective candidate wants to run on behalf of a political party, she must win the party's nomination in a primary election. If the would-be candidate wants to run as an independent, she needs to gather signatures on a petition to secure a spot on the ballot. Different states hold either **open primaries** or **closed primaries**, and state law sets the timing of these elections. A few states hold single primaries, where there is one election involving candidates from both parties, with the top two finalists (regardless of party) receiving nominations to the general election.

The second step in the election process, the **general election**, is held throughout the nation on the first Tuesday after the first Monday in November, which federal law designates as Election Day. General elections determine who wins elected positions in government. The offices at stake vary depending on the year. Presidential elections occur every four years (2008, 2012, . . .). In a presidential election year, Americans elect the entire House of Representatives, one-third of the Senate, and a president and vice president. During midterm elections (2006, 2010, . . .), there is no presidential contest, but the entire House and a third of the Senate are up for election.

The Constitution limits voting rights to American citizens who are at least 18 years old. There are also numerous restrictions on voter eligibility that vary across states, including residency requirements (usually 30 days), and whether people convicted of a major crime can vote. A new development in American elections is an increase in the practice of early voting, or casting a general election vote prior to Election Day.[4] This has always been an option for voters who show that they cannot vote on Election Day because of travel, illness, religious obligations, or

open primary A primary election in which any registered voter can participate in the contest, regardless of party affiliation.

closed primary A primary election in which only registered members of a particular political party can vote.

general election The election in which voters cast ballots for House members, senators, and (every four years) a president and vice president.

AMERICANS VOTE IN ALL SORTS OF places—even private homes. Here, people vote in a garage in Stockton, California, during the 2008 general elections.

similar reasons. These voters may cast an absentee ballot, typically by mailing it to a designated location. Recently, many states have established no-excuse-required absentee ballots or simply allowed voters to vote early by mail or at polling stations. Oregon votes entirely by mail, and over 98 percent of voters in Washington vote by mail. Though many Americans vote early (about 33 percent in 2010) and studies show that early voters are likely to have strong party identification, it is not clear whether early voting has changed election outcomes.[5] If enough people vote early in future elections, it could have a significant impact on campaign tactics; for example, candidates would have to begin campaign advertising earlier to ensure that early voters see these appeals.

CONSTITUENCIES: WHO CHOOSES REPRESENTATIVES?

Another critical feature of American elections is that officeholders are elected in single-member districts in which only the winner of the most votes takes office. (Although each state's senators both represent the whole state, they are elected separately; they are not the first- and second-place election winners.) Senate candidates compete at the state level; House candidates compete in congressional districts. In most states, congressional district lines are drawn by state legislatures. In a few states, nonpartisan commissions or committees of judges perform this function. Although redistricting can happen at any time, in general the district lines are revised after each national census to make sure the boundary lines reflect shifts in population across and within states. (For details on redistricting, see Chapter 10.)

Because members of the House and Senate are elected from specific geographic areas, they often represent very different kinds of people. These constituents differ in terms of age, race, income level, occupation, and political leaning, including party affiliation and ideology. Therefore, legislators from different areas of the country face highly diverse demands from their constituents—leading them to pursue very dissimilar kinds of policies.

For example, Democratic senator John Kerry, elected from Massachusetts, represents a fairly liberal state where gay marriage is legal, while Republican senator Orrin Hatch is from the conservative state of Utah. Suppose the Senate votes on a measure to ban gay marriage nationwide. Kerry knows that most of his constituents would probably want him to vote against the proposal, and Hatch knows that most of his constituents would probably want him to vote for it. This example illustrates that congressional conflicts over policy often reflect differences in constituents' demands. Kerry and Hatch themselves may hold different views on a gay marriage ban, but even if they agreed, their constituents' distinct demands would likely ensure that as legislators they voted differently.

DETERMINING WHO WINS

plurality voting A voting system in which the candidate who receives the most votes within a geographic area wins the election, regardless of whether that candidate wins a majority (more than half) of the votes.

majority voting A voting system in which a candidate must win more than 50 percent of votes to win the election. If no candidate wins enough votes to take office, a runoff election is held between the top two vote-getters.

runoff election Under a majority voting system, a second election held only if no candidate wins a majority of the votes in the first general election. Only the top two vote-getters in the first election compete in the runoff.

Most House and Senate contests involve **plurality voting**: the candidate who gets the most votes wins. However, some states use **majority voting,** meaning that a candidate needs a majority (more than 50 percent of the vote) to win. If no candidate has a majority, a **runoff election** takes place between the top two finishers. Some candidates have lost runoff elections even though they received the most votes in the first contest.

The two-step process of primary and general elections can have a similar effect on the election's outcome. Sometimes the winner of a primary is not a party's best candidate for the general election. For example, in the 2010 Alaska Senate Republican primary, politically inexperienced challenger Joe Miller defeated incumbent Lisa Murkowski. Murkowski won the general election as a write-in candidate.[6]

Americans vote using a wide range of machines and ballots.[7] Some counties use paper keypunch ballots, on which voters use a stylus to punch out holes in a ballot card next to the names of their preferred candidates. These ballots are then scanned, although they can also be hand-counted. Other counties use mechanical voting machines that require voters to pull a lever next to the name of their preferred candidates. A few localities still use paper ballots on which voters mark their preferred candidate with an "X." Touch-screen voting machines are becoming increasingly popular, but this type of voting is controversial because of its cost, the potential for delays on Election Day (since voters often take longer to cast their votes using this technology), and because of concerns that machines could be manipulated to change election outcomes.[8] One solution is to have optical machines generate a paper receipt that citizens can inspect after they vote and then put into a secure box, in order to enable manual recounts. Of course, earlier technologies aren't perfect either; vote totals in lever machines can also be manipulated, and paper ballots can be lost or altered. Moreover, the widespread use of touch screens in recent elections has occurred without major problems.[9]

Different voting methods show different rates of undervotes. These can happen when a voter casts an unmarked ballot, votes in some races on the ballot but not others, or casts a ballot that cannot be counted for some reason. The confusion that surrounded the 2000 presidential election outcome in Palm Beach County,

PROPORTIONAL REPRESENTATION

The Congress and state legislatures in the United States are elected using single-member districts, but many other countries, particularly most West European countries, use proportional representation.[a] Under this system, there are no districts or other geographic units that elect their own representatives. Instead, there is a single nationwide campaign in which each party runs a list of as many candidates as there are seats in the legislature. On Election Day, citizens vote for a party, not a candidate. Votes are then counted nationwide for each party, and the parties receive the number of seats in the legislature proportional to the percentage of the nation's votes it received.

As an example, suppose America had used proportional representation in the 1996 presidential election and that people cast party votes in accordance with the votes they cast for presidential candidates. In this election Republican Bob Dole received 40.7 percent of the popular vote, Democrat Bill Clinton received 49.2 percent, and Reform Party candidate Ross Perot received 8.4 percent. The 435 House seats would then be allocated proportionately to these results: the Republican Party would hold 177 seats (40.7 percent of 435), the Democrats would hold 214 seats, and the Reform Party would hold 39 seats.

One country that uses proportional representation is Israel. The figure below shows the number of seats won by Israeli political parties in the 120-seat Knesset in the last election. As you see, a total of 12 parties won seats, with the largest, Kadima, winning only 29 seats, or about a fourth of the total.

This example illustrates the pros and cons of proportional representation. By counting votes nationwide rather than district

In countries such as Germany, elections sometimes produce coalition governments in which multiple parties (such as the Social Democratic Party) share control.

by district, proportional representation enhances the political power of small interests that are organized into a political party. Under the system of single-member districts and the electoral college, the Reform Party was a failure; its congressional candidates never won a House or Senate seat, and its presidential candidates never won any electoral votes. Under proportional representation, the Reform Party would be a force to be reckoned with. Its candidates would hold nearly 10 percent of House seats. More important, under proportional representation in an election such as this one, the smaller party would hold the balance of power between the Republicans and the Democrats. Neither major party would hold enough seats to enact legislation on its own. Thus, to get anything done, they would both be forced to find common ground with Reform legislators.

Some scholars have proposed proportional representation in America as a way to increase the political power of minority groups or to give small ideological groups the opportunity to elect representatives to Congress.[b] However, because proportional representation enhances the power of small groups, countries that use this system tend to have many political parties, each of which elects some people to the legislature, with none of the parties even approaching holding a majority of seats—Israel is a good example of both patterns. As a result, enacting new policies requires complex negotiations among many competing interests represented in the legislature. In Israel, for example, it can take weeks or even months to build a majority coalition in the Knesset to form a government and select a prime minister. The implication is that enhancing representation for small groups through proportional representation comes at a price: the ability to get things done in the resulting legislature.

SEATS WON BY ISRAELI PARTIES, 2009

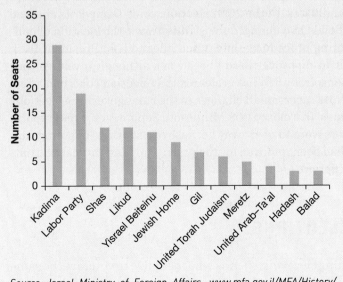

Source: Israel Ministry of Foreign Affairs, www.mfa.gov.il/MFA/History/Modern+History/Historic+Events/Elections_in_Israel_Feburary_2009.htm (accessed 9/20/12).

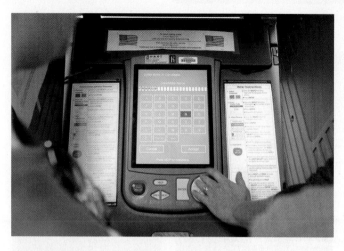

MANY DIFFERENT MECHANISMS are used to record votes in American elections, including paper keypunch ballots and computerized, electronic machines (above).

Florida, showed what a difference the ballot structure can make. Palm Beach County residents voted on punch cards in combination with a device called a butterfly ballot. This type of ballot lists the candidates on both sides of a center column, and voters indicate their preference by pressing down with a stylus on the circle in the center column that corresponds to the name of their preferred candidate. A punch card inserted underneath the ballot records the stylus marks, and votes are counted by tallying holes in the punch cards.

While punch-card ballots are generally regarded as a good technique—the technology is relatively cheap, the paper ballots are a permanent record of voting, and it is easy to manually recount ballots if needed—the butterfly ballot structure appears to have caused some supporters of Al Gore in Palm Beach County to mistakenly vote for Pat Buchanan. As the picture shows, Gore's name and Buchanan's were on facing pages at about the same level, so it would be easy for a voter to press down on the wrong circle. Analyses suggested that the butterfly ballot cost Gore several thousand Palm Beach County votes—enough to change the results of the election in Florida, and thus the outcome of the 2000 presidential election.[10] However, the butterfly ballot in Palm Beach County is only one example of the influence of a voting method on election results. We don't know whether ballots used in other counties and states favored Gore or some other candidates. But it is clear that choices about how ballots are structured can affect who wins elections.

Ballot counting adds more complexities. Most states have laws that allow vote recounts if a race is sufficiently close (within 1 percent or less). Even when a recount occurs, it may be impossible to definitively determine who won a particular election, as the statutes that determine which ballots are valid are often open to interpretation. More significant is that when an election is close, the question of which candidate wins may depend on how ballots are structured and votes counted. The problem is not that election officials are dishonest; rather, close elections inherently tend to produce ambiguous outcomes.

Claims are often made that officials manipulate election rules to guarantee wins for their favored candidates. In the 2004 election, some Democrats charged that Republican local officials had changed registration laws, the location of polling stations, ballot-counting procedures, and other rules to help President Bush win Ohio.[11] It is difficult to disprove these allegations, although investigations found no evidence of a conspiracy.[12] What is clear is that election rules can affect results. Particularly in close races, small changes in the rules governing elections can easily change outcomes. In a close 2008 Minnesota Senate race, press reports suggested that some voters were turned away because of a shortage of voting supplies. If polling stations had been required to stock extra supplies, the election outcome might have been different.

PRESIDENTIAL ELECTIONS

Many of the rules governing elections, such as who is eligible to vote, are the same for both presidential and congressional elections. However, presidential contests have several unique rules regarding how nominees are determined and how votes

8.1 NUTS &bolts

CONSTITUTIONAL REQUIREMENTS FOR CANDIDATES

Office	Minimum Age	Residency Requirement	Term of Office
President	35	Born in the United States	Four years
Senator	30	Resident of state; U.S. citizen for at least 9 years	Six years
Representative	25	Resident of state; U.S. citizen for at least 7 years	Two years

are counted. The constitutional requirements for presidential candidates are also somewhat stricter than those for congressional candidates (see Nuts and Bolts 8.1).

THE NOMINATION: PRIMARIES AND CAUCUSES

Presidential nominees from the Democratic and Republican parties are determined by state-level **primaries** and **caucuses** over a five-month period beginning in January of an election year.[13] These elections select delegates to attend the nominating conventions that take place during the summer. There, the delegates cast the votes that determine their party's presidential and vice-presidential nominees. The format of these elections, including their timing and the number of delegates selected per state, is determined on a state-by-state basis by the state and national party organizations.[14] In some states, each candidate preselects a list of delegates who will attend the convention if the candidate wins sufficient votes in the primary or caucus. In other states, candidates select delegates from a list developed by party leaders. In both cases, a candidate's principal goal is to win as many delegates as possible—and to select delegates who will be reliable supporters at the convention. Surprisingly, neither party requires delegates to support the candidate who selected them, but there is an expectation that they will do so.

The details of translating primary and caucus votes into convention delegates vary from state to state, but some general rules apply. All Democratic primaries and caucuses use **proportional allocation** to divide each state's delegate seats among the candidates; thus, if a candidate receives 40 percent of the votes in a state's primary, the candidate gets roughly 40 percent of the convention delegates from that state. Some Republican contests use proportional allocation, but others are **winner-take-all**. In these, the candidate who receives the most votes gets all of the state's convention delegates. While these rules were not significant in 2012, they had a significant effect on the 2008 Republican nomination. John McCain's early victories in winner-take-all primaries helped him build a large lead in delegates that caused some other candidates to drop out. Overall, McCain won only 47 percent of the primary and caucus vote but claimed 72 percent of the delegates. If Republicans used only proportional allocation, McCain would have faced tougher opposition through additional contests and might not have won the nomination. In

primary A ballot vote in which citizens select a party's nominee for the general election.

caucus A local meeting in which party members select a party's nominee for the general election.

proportional allocation During the presidential primaries, the practice of determining the number of convention delegates allotted to each candidate based on the percentage of the popular vote cast for each candidate. All Democratic primaries and caucuses use this system, as do some states' Republican primaries and caucuses.

winner-take-all During the presidential primaries, the practice of assigning all of a given state's delegates to the candidate who receives the most popular votes. Some states' Republican primaries and caucuses use this system.

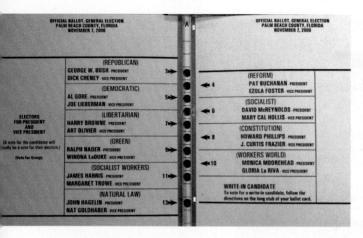

THE DESIGN OF THE INFAMOUS
Palm Beach County, Florida, butterfly ballot, used in the 2000 presidential election, inadvertently led some people who intended to vote for Democrat Al Gore to select Reform Party candidate Patrick Buchanan.

contrast, in 2012, with fewer states using winner-take-all, candidates' delegate totals more closely matched the total votes they received. However, states are free to move back to using winner-take-all, which might advantage certain candidates in a future contest.

The ordering of state primaries and caucuses is important because many candidacies do not survive beyond the early contests.[15] Most presidential candidates pour everything they have into the first few elections. Candidates who do well attract contributions, campaign workers, endorsements, and additional media coverage, all of which enable them to move on to subsequent primaries or caucuses. But for candidates who do poorly in the first contests, contributions and coverage dry up, and these candidates usually drop out. Thus, the candidate who leads after the first several primaries and caucuses generally wins the nomination.[16] However, when the first few contests do not yield a clear favorite, the race can continue until the last states have voted, or even until the convention.

If a sitting president runs for re-election, as Barack Obama did in 2012, he typically faces little opposition for the party's general-election nomination—not because challengers defer to the president, but because most presidents are popular enough among their own party's faithful supporters that they can win the nomination without too much trouble. Only presidents with particularly low approval ratings have faced serious opposition in their nomination bids.

Among the states, the presidential nomination process is always changing.[17] There has been a trend toward regional primaries, when all the states in a geographic area elect delegates on the same day, as well as frontloading, when states schedule their primaries to take place earlier in the process. For many years, Iowa and New Hampshire have held the first presidential nomination contests in January, with the Iowa caucus held a week before the New Hampshire primary. These states' position at the beginning of the process is largely a historical accident, but it is often controversial. State party officials from other states often complain about the media attention given to these contests and their disproportionate influence in winnowing the candidate pool, but there is no consensus around an alternate schedule. As a result, the 2012 nomination process was roughly the same as in previous years, with Iowa and New Hampshire holding the initial contests, in early January 2012, followed by primaries in South Carolina and Florida later in the month, and the remaining contests beginning in February and continuing to June.

The national committees can issue rules and requirements about the timing of state presidential primaries, but state law sets the election dates, meaning that a committee's directives may not be followed. Indeed, the changes described above have prompted many state legislatures to frontload their states' primaries and caucuses. In 2008, for example, the Michigan and Florida state legislatures moved their primaries to mid- and late January, respectively, prompting Iowa and New Hampshire to hold their contests even earlier than usual in an effort to keep their privileged position. As a result of these and related changes, significant numbers of both parties' convention delegates were selected by early February, about one month into the nomination process. On the Republican side in 2008, these changes helped John McCain become the presumptive nominee by mid-February. However, on the Democratic side, both Hillary Clinton and Barack

Obama emerged from early primaries and caucuses with roughly equal delegate counts and continued to fight for the nomination until the end of the primary process in early June.

Another recent change that distinguishes the parties' candidate selection processes is that about one-fifth of delegates to the Democratic Convention are not supporters of a particular candidate, chosen to attend the convention through primary and caucus results. Rather, they are elected officials and party officials whom their colleagues select to serve as superdelegates. Most are automatically seated at the convention regardless of primary and caucus results, and they are free to support any candidate for the nomination. By forcing candidates to court support from superdelegates, the party aims to ensure that the nominee is someone these officials believe can win the general election and whom they can work with if elected.[18]

THE NATIONAL CONVENTION

Presidential nominating conventions happen late in the summer of an election year. Their main task is to select the party's presidential election nominee, although for the most part the vote at the convention is a formality; in all recent contests, one candidate has emerged from the nomination process with a clear majority of delegates and wins the nomination on the first ballot.[19] To get the nomination, a candidate needs the support of a majority of the delegates. If no candidate receives a majority after the first round of voting at the convention, the voting continues until someone does.

After the convention delegates nominate a presidential candidate, they select a vice-presidential nominee. The presidential nominee gets to choose his or her running mate, and the delegates almost always ratify this choice without much debate. Delegates also vote on the party platform, which describes what the party stands for and what kinds of policies its candidates will supposedly seek to enact if they are elected.

The final purpose of a convention is to attract public attention to the party and its nominees. Public figures give speeches during the evening sessions when all major television networks have live coverage. At some recent conventions, both parties have drawn press attention by recruiting speakers who support their political goals despite being associated with the opposing party.

Once presidential candidates are nominated, the general election campaign officially begins—though it often unofficially starts much earlier, as soon as the presumptive nominees are known. We say more about presidential campaigns in a later section.

COUNTING PRESIDENTIAL VOTES

Even though in the voting booth you choose between the candidates by name, you actually don't vote directly for a presidential candidate. Rather, when you select your preferred candidate's name, you are choosing that person's slate of pledged supporters from your state to serve as electors, who will then vote to elect the president.

The number of electors for each state equals the state's number of House members (which varies by state population) plus the number of senators (two per state). Altogether, the electors chosen by the citizens of each state constitute the **electoral college**, the body that formally selects the president. Small-population states, therefore, have few electoral votes—Delaware and Montana each have only three—while the highest-population state, California, has 55 (see "How It Works"). In most states, electoral votes are allocated on a winner-take-all basis: the candidate who receives the most votes from a given state's citizens gets all of that state's electoral votes. Two states, Maine and Nebraska, allocate most of their electoral votes at the congressional district level: in those states, the candidate who wins the most votes in each congressional district wins that district's single electoral vote. Then, the remaining two electoral votes go to the candidate who gets the most votes statewide.[20]

The winner-take-all method of allocating most states' electoral votes makes candidates focus their attention on two kinds of states: high-population states with lots of electoral votes to be gained, and, more important, swing states where the contest is relatively close. It's better for a candidate to spend a day campaigning in California, with its 55 electoral votes, than in Montana, where only three electoral votes are at stake. However, if one candidate is sure to win a particular state, both candidates will direct their efforts elsewhere. For example, in the last days of the 2012 campaign, Mitt Romney's campaign bought additional TV time in Pennsylvania and Ohio, but not Nevada and Iowa, believing that the first two states might be winnable but that the other two were probably out of reach. The Obama campaign responded with additional advertising in Ohio and Pennsylvania and in Florida. The result: Obama won all three of the contested states.

Nuts and Bolts 8.2 divides states based on their electoral vote and whether they are swing states—defined as a state that each party won at least once in 2000, 2004, and 2008. The chart explains why both campaigns in 2012 spent so much time and campaign funds on states such as Virginia, Ohio, and Florida (swing states with large electoral votes)—and why they largely ignored the District of Columbia and other states in the small-state, one-party dominant category.

After citizens' votes are counted in each state, the slates of electors meet in December in the state capitals. At their meetings, the electors almost always vote for the presidential candidate they have pledged to support. After the votes

electoral college The body that votes to select America's president and vice president based on the popular vote in each state. Each candidate nominates a slate of electors who are selected to attend the meeting of the college if their candidate wins the most votes in a state or district.

THE ELECTORAL COLLEGE

538 TOTAL ELECTORS

ELECTORAL VOTES PER STATE

The number of electors from each state equals the state's number of House members (which varies based on state population) plus the number of senators (two per state). Each elector has one vote in the electoral college.

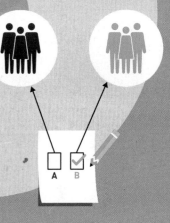

A B

WHO ARE THE ELECTORS?

Candidates to be electors are nominated by their political parties. They pledge to support a certain candidate if they are elected to the electoral college. When you cast your vote for a presidential candidate, you are in fact voting for the slate of potential electors who support that candidate.

100% OF ELECTORAL VOTES GO TO WINNER

37%

61%

WINNING A STATE

Most states give all of their electoral college votes to the candidate who wins the most votes from citizens in the state. So, even if a candidate only gets 51% of the vote in the state, his or her entire slate of electors is elected, and he or she gets all of the state's votes in the electoral college.

POP QUIZ!

1 The number of electors that each state has in the electoral college is based on

  a voter turnout in the previous election.

  b an equal number for all states.

  c the number of parties in the state.

  d the date the state joined the Union.

  e population.

2 When you cast your vote in a presidential general election, you are actually voting for

  a a political party.

  b delegates who pledge to support a specific candidate at the party's national convention.

  c electors who pledge to support a specific candidate in the electoral college.

  d whoever gets the most votes in the state.

  e a slate of presidential candidates.

Answers: 1.e; 2.c

ELECTORAL VOTES AND SWING STATES

Presidential campaigns focus their attention on states with high electoral votes and swing states, those where each candidate has a good chance of winning. In this box, we group states into categories based on their number of electoral votes, and on whether one party always won the state in the 2000, 2004, and 2008 presidential elections.

		One Party Dominates in Recent Elections	
		Yes	No
Electoral Votes (2012 Election)	3–5	D.C., Delaware, Alaska, Montana, North Dakota, South Dakota, Vermont, Wyoming, Hawaii, Maine, Rhode Island, Idaho, Nebraska, West Virginia	New Hampshire, New Mexico
	6–10	Arkansas, Kansas, Utah, Connecticut, Oregon, Oklahoma, Kentucky, Louisiana, Alabama, South Carolina, Wisconsin, Maryland, Missouri	Mississippi, Iowa, Nevada, Colorado, Minnesota
	More than 10	Massachusetts, Arizona, Tennessee, Washington, New Jersey, Michigan, Georgia, Illinois, Pennsylvania, New York, Texas, California	Indiana, Virginia, North Carolina, Ohio, Florida

are certified by a joint session of Congress, the candidate who wins a majority of the nation's electoral votes (at least 270) is the new president. One peculiarity of the electoral college is that in a majority of states it is legal for an elector to either (1) vote for a candidate he or she is not pledged to support, or (2) abstain from voting.[21] Such events are uncommon for the simple reason that electors are selected by the presidential candidates with an eye toward reliable support—and many states have laws prohibiting such behavior.

If no candidate receives a majority of the electoral college votes, the members of the House of Representatives choose the winner. They follow a procedure in which the members from each state decide which candidate to support and then cast one collective vote per state, with the winner needing a majority of these state-level votes to win. This procedure has not been used since 1824, although it might be required if a third-party candidate wins a significant number of electoral votes or if a state's electors refuse to cast their votes.[22]

A presidential candidate can win the electoral college vote, and thus the election, without receiving a majority of the votes cast by citizens—particularly if the vote is divided between more than two candidates. When a third-party candidate for president receives a substantial number of votes, the election winner can easily end up receiving more votes than any other candidate without winning a majority of the **popular vote**. Bill Clinton, for example, won a substantial

popular vote The votes cast by citizens in an election.

FIGURE » 8.1

POPULAR VOTE vs. ELECTORAL VOTE, 2000–2012

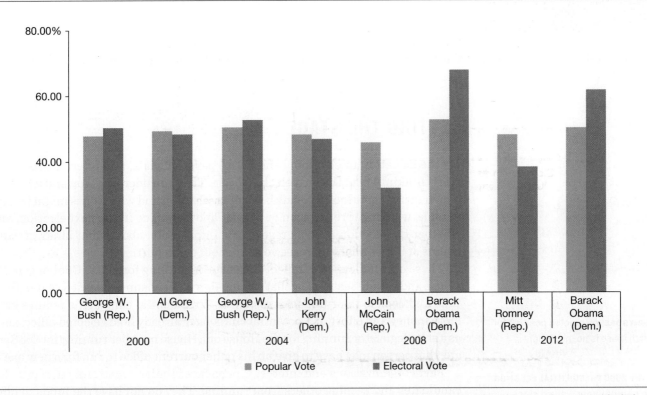

Source: U.S. National Archives and Records Administration, www.archives.gov/federal-register/electoral-college/historical.html (accessed 11/12/12).

electoral college majority in 1992, while receiving only 43 percent of the popular vote. This was because Ross Perot, running as a third-party candidate, received almost 19 percent of the national popular vote but not enough support in any one state to win **electoral votes**. Even in a race where no third-party candidate wins a significant percentage of the vote, the electoral college magnifies the winning candidate's vote percentage.

However, because of the way popular votes translate into electoral votes, a candidate can receive a majority of the electoral vote even though another candidate wins more popular votes. As Figure 8.1 shows, in 2012, for example, Barack Obama received about 50 percent of the popular vote, but nearly 62 percent of the electoral votes. When the popular vote is very close, as in 2004, the winner's advantage in the electoral college is smaller but still exists. It is also possible for a candidate who loses the popular vote to receive the majority of electoral votes and win the election. Thus, George Bush, the winner of the 2000 election, received about 540,000 fewer votes than his main rival, Al Gore. Other presidents who won the electoral college vote but lost the popular vote were John Quincy Adams in 1824, Rutherford B. Hayes in 1876, and Benjamin Harrison in 1888—and this almost occurred in 2004, when George W. Bush was re-elected.

electoral votes Votes cast by members of the electoral college; after a presidential candidate wins the popular vote in a given state, that candidate's slate of electors cast electoral votes for the candidate on behalf of that state.

ELECTORAL CAMPAIGNS

election cycle The two-year period between general elections.

This section explores the campaign process and what candidates do to convince people to vote for them on Election Day. Our emphasis is on things that candidates do regardless of the office they are running for, across the entire **election cycle**, the two-year period between general elections.

SETTING THE STAGE

On the day after an election, candidates, party officials, and interest groups all start thinking about the next election cycle. They consider who won and who lost, which incumbents look like safe bets for re-election and which ones might be vulnerable, who might retire soon or run for another office in the next election, and whether the election returns reveal new information about what kinds of campaigns or issues might increase voter turnout or support.

These calculations also reflect the costs of running for office. Challengers for House and Senate seats know that a campaign will consume at least a year of their time and deplete their financial resources. Presidential campaigns require even more money and effort. If a potential challenger already holds elected office, such as a state legislator running for the House or a House member running for the Senate, that person may have to give up his or her current office to run for a new one.[23]

open seat An elected position for which there is no incumbent.

IN THE 2000 PRESIDENTIAL ELECTION, the popular vote was so close in Florida that individual ballots were examined to make sure every last vote was counted accurately before Florida's electoral votes were all given to the winner. In the end, all of Florida's electoral votes went to George W. Bush, giving him the additional electoral votes he needed to win the presidency.

Party organizations and interest groups face similar constraints in recruiting candidates and keeping others from running. They do not have the funds to offer significant support to candidates in all 435 congressional districts, 33 or 34 Senate races, and a presidential contest.[24] So which races draw their attention? The answer depends on many factors, such as how well incumbents did in the last election and how much money those who won have on hand for the next election, whether party affiliation in the state or district favors Republicans or Democrats (and by how much), and whether the newly elected officeholders are likely to run for re-election.

For example, in the year before the 2012 election, many reports noted the poor re-election prospects of Nebraska Democratic senator Ben Nelson. While Nelson was usually classified as a moderate Democrat, he was elected from a relatively conservative state. Many polls showed that Nelson would have a tough time getting re-elected. Faced with dismal prospects, Nelson announced his retirement in mid-2011, creating a wide-open race for his Senate seat.

Party committees and candidates also consider the likelihood that incumbents might retire, thereby creating an **open seat**. In the run-up to the 2010 election, many Democratic House members from moderate and conservative-leaning districts announced their retirements, believing that they would face a tough fight in the next election. Open seats are of special interest to potential candidates and other political actors because incumbents generally hold an election advantage.[25] So, when a seat opens, candidates from the party that does not control the seat know that they may have a better chance to win because they will not have to run against an incumbent. Consequently, the incumbent's party leaders have to recruit an especially strong candidate in order to hold the seat. Interest groups watch all these decisions with an eye toward deciding whom to endorse or support with campaign donations and advertisements.

Presidential campaigns work the same way. Virtually all first-term presidents run for re-election. So, potential challengers in the opposing party study the results of the last election to see how many votes the president received and how this support was distributed across the states to determine their own chances of winning against the president. Candidates in the president's party make the same calculations, although no sitting president in the twentieth century was denied renomination. Some presidents (Harry Truman in 1952, Lyndon Johnson in 1968) retired because their chances of being renominated were not good, while others (Gerald Ford in 1976, Jimmy Carter in 1980) faced tough primary contests.[26]

BEFORE THE CAMPAIGN

Most incumbent House members, senators, and presidents work throughout the election cycle to secure their re-election. Political scientists label this activity the permanent campaign.[27] To stay in office, incumbents have to do two things: keep their constituents happy, and raise money for their campaign. As we see in Chapter 10, congressional incumbents try to keep their constituents happy by taking actions that ensure the voters can identify something good that the incumbent has done. This, in turn, boosts voters' retrospective evaluations at election time.[28]

Incumbent presidents make the same kinds of calculations. During Barack Obama's first months in office, many of his advisers argued that he had to offer an economic stimulus plan in light of polls showing the economy was an overriding concern to most Americans. Obama did so—a decision driven by political as well as policy concerns. Of course, many presidential actions are taken in response to events rather than being initiated to gain voter support. Particularly in the case of wars and other conflicts, it is far-fetched to say that presidents initiate hostilities for political gain. Even so, presidents, just like other politicians, are keenly aware of the political consequences of their actions and the need to build a record they can run on in the next election.

SOME CANDIDATES RUN FOR OFFICE to gain publicity for causes they support. During the 2008 and 2012 presidential campaigns, Representative Ron Paul of Texas ran for the Republican presidential nomination. Although Paul knew that he had little chance of winning the party's nomination, his goal was to garner press and public attention for his libertarian ideology.

political business cycle

Attempts by elected officials to manipulate the economy before elections by increasing economic growth and reducing unemployment and inflation, with the goal of improving evaluations of their performance in office.

Presidents can also use the federal bureaucracy to their own advantage and to help members of their party. For example, some scholars have argued that presidents try to increase economic growth in the months prior to elections, with the aim of increasing support for themselves (if they are eligible to run for re-election) and for their party's candidates, a phenomenon called the **political business cycle**.[29] Given the size and complexity of the U.S. economy, and the fact that the independent Federal Reserve System controls monetary policy, it is unlikely that such efforts could have much success. Even so, out of a desire to stay in office and help their party's candidates, it seems clear that presidents would want to be seen as having a positive impact on the economy.

Candidates for all offices, incumbents and challengers alike, also devote considerable time before the campaign to raising campaign funds. Fund-raising helps an incumbent in two ways.[30] First, it ensures that if the incumbent faces a strong opponent, she or he will have enough money to run an aggressive campaign. Second, successful fund-raising deters opposition. Potential challengers are less likely to run against an incumbent if that individual is well funded with a sizable campaign war chest.[31]

The other thing candidates do before the campaign is build their campaign organization.[32] Just like fund-raising, the success or failure of these efforts is a signal of a candidate's prospects. If experienced, well-respected people agree to work in a candidate's campaign, observers conclude that the candidate's prospects for being elected are probably good.

Skilled campaign consultants are among the most sought-after campaign staff. These consultants plan strategies, run public opinion polls, assemble ads and buy television time, and talk with members of the media on the candidate's behalf, among other things. For many consultants, electioneering is a full-time, year-round position. Many concentrate on electing candidates from one party, although some work for whoever will pay them.

Almost all campaigns have paid and volunteer staff, ranging from the dozen or so people who work for a typical House candidate to the thousands needed to run a major-party candidate's presidential campaign. Some campaign staff work full-time for an incumbent's campaign committee or are on the incumbent's con-

MOST OFFICEHOLDERS ARE ALWAYS campaigning—traveling around their states or districts, talking with constituents, and explaining their actions in office—all in the hope of winning and keeping support for the next election. Here, Republican representative Sam Graves greets constituents during a 2008 parade in Kearney, Missouri.

gressional or presidential staff. With some exceptions for senior presidential staff, federal law prohibits government employees from engaging in campaign activities during work hours or with congressional resources.[33] As a result, many congressional staffers take a leave of absence from their government jobs to work on their bosses' re-election campaigns during the last few months of the election cycle, then return to working for the government after the election—assuming the incumbent is re-elected.

It's hard to separate what candidates do at election time from what they do between elections—incumbents are *always* campaigning, which is part of the reason they are so likely to win re-election. In many cases, incumbent House members and senators also wind up running against poorly funded, inexperienced candidates. Stronger challengers see that the incumbent has been working hard to solidify a hold on the constituency, and they decide to wait until the incumbent retires, when they can run for the open seat. Thus, incumbents are not automatically favored for re-election, but they often win by large margins because of all the things they do while holding office in between elections.[34]

THE GENERAL ELECTION CAMPAIGN

General election campaigns begin in early September. By this point, both parties have chosen their presidential nominees and their congressional candidates. Interest groups, candidates, and party committees have raised most of the funds they will use or donate in the campaign. The race is on.

Having made numerous trips to the first primary and caucus states, presidential campaigns shift focus once the primaries and caucuses start. Now the campaigns emphasize wholesale politics, in which candidates contact voters indirectly, such as through media coverage and campaign advertising. At this point, presidential campaign events generally involve large numbers of citizens, or if they are smaller events or one-on-one encounters, they are designed to generate media coverage and thereby reach a larger audience. In contrast, some campaigns for the House and even a few Senate races are more likely to stress direct contact with voters, or retail politics. At the same time, average citizens start to pay more attention to the various campaigns. This combination of increased voter attention and a shift in campaign tactics means that pre-election polls can show sharp shifts in support for different candidates as the campaign gets under way.

BASIC CAMPAIGN STRATEGIES

One of the most fundamental campaign strategies, particularly in congressional campaigns, is to build name recognition. Since many citizens tend not to be well informed about congressional candidates, efforts to increase a candidate's name recognition in these races can deliver a few extra percentage points of support—enough to turn a close defeat into a victory. (Practically all voters can identify the major party presidential candidates, so name recognition efforts are not as central to these elections.)

A second basic strategy is mobilization. Turnout is not automatic: just because a citizen supports a candidate does not mean that he or she will actually vote. Candidates have to make sure that their supporters go to the polls and vote. Moreover, focusing on getting supporters to the polls is a relatively efficient use of candidates' resources. Given that most people don't pay much attention to politics, it's much easier to get a supporter to go to the polls than it is to convert an opponent into a supporter.

Campaign professionals refer to voter mobilization efforts as **GOTV ("get out the vote")** or the **ground game**.[35] Most campaigns for Congress or the presidency use extensive door-to-door canvassing, as well as phone banks and e-mail. Both Republican and Democratic campaigns use sophisticated databases, combining voter registration data with demographics and even purchasing data to determine who their potential supporters are and how best to reach them.[36] There is clear evidence that these efforts boost a candidate's electoral support.[37]

GOTV ("get out the vote") or the **ground game** A campaign's efforts to "get out the vote" or make sure their supporters vote on Election Day.

Sometimes candidates also try to decrease support and turnout for their opponent. One tactic is push polling, in which a candidate or a group that supports a candidate conducts a voter "survey," typically by phone, that isn't actually designed to measure opinions so much as to influence them. Campaigns use these so-called polls to spread false or misleading information about another candidate by including this (mis)information in questions posed to large numbers of citizens.[38]

The availability of the Internet and social media sites has important implications for how campaigns are run. In part, these technologies help candidates do things that they always have done, such as recruiting supporters and informing them about a candidate's appearances and issue positions. A generation ago,

AMERICAN PRESIDENTIAL CAMPAIGNS depend on thousands of paid and volunteer staff. Here, workers for Republican candidate Mitt Romney contact potential supporters.

this information might have been disseminated using a phone bank, flyers, or volunteers going door-to-door. Now, candidates get the word out using e-mail, Twitter, a Facebook update, or similar tools. Social media sites are especially useful for organizing large numbers of volunteers—in 2008, for example, Barack Obama's campaign ran extensive GOTV operations during the nomination process and the general election using the Internet as the primary point of contact between the campaign and the volunteers.

The Internet also allows candidates to do things that were impossible a generation ago. For example, many candidates prepare Internet-only campaign ads, counting on media attention to spread the word about the ad's content. Particularly for campaigns with low budgets, this strategy can be a useful form of advertising.

However, just as we saw in the Chapter 6 discussion of how the Internet has changed what voters know about politics, it is hard to say how the Internet has changed the essentials of campaigning for political office in contemporary America. The essential goal of a campaign is to convince people to support a candidate, and to motivate them to vote on Election Day. The Internet provides new ways to contact supporters and potential supporters, and creates some new strategies for campaign advertising, but the problems candidates face in winning office remain largely unchanged.

PROMISES AND PLATFORMS

Another set of campaign decisions involves the candidate's campaign platform, which includes stances on issues and promises about how the candidate will act in office. Given that few voters are well informed about public policy or inclined to learn, candidates do not win elections by trying to educate the electorate or making complex promises. What works is making promises and taking positions that are simple and consistent with what the average voter believes, even if these beliefs are inconsistent with reality. For example, many people believe that interest groups have too much power in Washington, although their influence is far less powerful than most Americans believe (see Chapter 9). Even so, many candidates accuse their opponents of being beholden to interest groups. These claims may be far-fetched, but they work well politically because they play to citizens' perceptions.

In writing their platform, candidates may be constrained by positions they have taken in the past or by their party affiliation. Chapter 7 showed that the parties have strong brand identities that lead many citizens to associate Democrats with liberal policies and Republicans with conservative ones. Candidates often find it difficult to make campaign promises that contradict these perceptions. In 2006, many Republican candidates tried to avoid talking about the unpopular war in Iraq, even though polls suggested that most voters were focused on this issue.[39] Why avoid the topic? Because most Republican incumbents had previously supported the war, so voters might not see a newly adopted antiwar position as credible. Moreover, taking a strong stand against the war would place them at odds with Republican president George Bush. The war was much less important for platforms in the 2008 contest. With American casualties decreasing, voters were more concerned about candidates' positions on the economy, energy, and health care.

Another influence on a candidate's positions are demands from potential supporters. In a state or district with many conservative or Republican voters, opposition to health care reform legislation or to amnesty for illegal immigrants might be a winning electoral strategy—just as support for these proposals would generally be helpful for candidates running in states or districts where most voters are moderate to liberal or Democrats.

The two-step electoral process in American elections also influences candidate positions. To win office, candidates have to campaign twice, first in a primary and then in a general election. Voters in primary elections generally hold more extreme views than the average voter in a general election. As a result, in the typical congressional district, Republican candidates win primaries by taking conservative positions, while Democratic candidates win primaries by upholding liberal views. However, a position or promise that attracts votes in a primary election might not work so well in the general election, or vice versa. For example, during debates before the 2012 Iowa caucuses, some Republican presidential candidates cited their religious beliefs as an influence on their personal lives and political stands—a useful strategy given the large number of religious conservatives expected to attend the Iowa caucuses, but a less useful strategy given the lower proportion of such voters across the entire nation.

For all these reasons, different parties' candidates for the same office often make some similar campaign promises even though they disagree on other matters. During the 2008 North Carolina Senate race, candidates Elizabeth Dole and Kay Hagan held roughly the same positions on issues such as immigration, the Iraq War, and the government's bailout of financial firms. As a result, the race turned on other issues, such as Dole's low effectiveness ranking in a survey of Senate staff.

Table 8.1 lists part of the campaign platforms of the 2012 presidential candidates and shows the similarities and differences in five issue areas that received considerable attention during the campaign: abortion rights, same-sex marriage, Medicare, Social Security, and defense spending. In all of these areas, Romney and Obama offered sharply different ideas of what government should do. However, there were some similarities between the two candidates' platforms. In the case of energy policy, for example, their positions were essentially identical, differing only in the details of their proposals.

Issues matter in American elections. A candidate's issue positions help to mobilize supporters and attract volunteers, activists, interest-group endorsements, and contributions. Issue positions also define what government will do differently

TABLE » 8.1

PRESIDENTIAL CANDIDATES' ISSUE POSITIONS (SELECTED), 2012

ISSUE	BARACK OBAMA	MITT ROMNEY
ABORTION RIGHTS	Supports *Roe v. Wade* and a woman's right to make decisions regarding pregnancy	Believes unborn children have a right to life that cannot be infringed
SAME-SEX MARRIAGE	Supports marriage equality and equal treatment under the law for same-sex couples	Supports a constitutional amendment that defines marriage as between one man and one woman
MEDICARE	Opposes privatization or voucher program	Favors transition to a voucher program
SOCIAL SECURITY	Opposes changes that would eliminate guaranteed benefits	Favors changes to give Americans more control over how their contributions are invested
DEFENSE SPENDING	Favors reduction in defense spending as part of deficit reduction	Opposes automatic cuts in defense spending

depending on who gets elected. And as we see later in this chapter, some citizens vote based on candidates' issue positions. Even so, there is considerable evidence that many voters do not know much about candidates' issue positions, particularly for House and Senate races. As a result, when a candidate wins a race or a party wins seats across the country, it is risky to read the outcome as a sign that the winners had the most popular set of issue positions.

CONFRONTING OTHER CANDIDATES

Candidates often contrast their own records or positions with those of opposing candidates or make claims designed to lower citizens' opinions of their opponents. Sometimes these interactions occur during a formal debate. Most congressional campaigns involve debates in front of an audience of likely voters, a group of reporters, or the editorial board of a local newspaper. Typically candidates take questions from reporters, although sometimes candidates question each other or answer questions from the audience.

Presidential campaigns involve multiple debates during the primary and caucus season. During the months before the first primaries and caucuses, each party's candidates gather for many single-party debates using a variety of formats. During the general election, the Republican and Democratic nominees meet for several debates. (The number and format are negotiated by the campaigns and the Commission on Presidential Debates, an organization that hosts the debates.)[40] The 2012 presidential campaign featured three debates between the presidential nominees and one between the vice-presidential nominees.

The debates not only give candidates a chance to present themselves to the electorate, but they also offer valuable free exposure. Given a relatively uninterested electorate, candidates must figure out how to present themselves to voters in a way that captures their attention and gains their support. Thus, in the 2004 presidential debates, George Bush's first remarks emphasized the September 11 attacks, arguing that the overthrow of the Taliban in Afghanistan and the invasion of Iraq had reduced the chances of another terrorist attack in America.[41] This argument was politically advantageous given that many Americans saw preventing a terrorist attack as a top priority—and at the time, they gave Bush high marks for his performance on September 11.

Candidates also attempt to win support by emphasizing their understanding of citizens' concerns and their willingness to address them. In fact, many campaign events are designed to reinforce the impression that candidates share voters' concerns and values. Ideally, they have reporters watching in order to gain wide coverage. Just before the 2008 Democratic primaries in Indiana and Pennsylvania, Barack Obama visited a Pennsylvania bowling alley, where he bowled a game before a few startled patrons—and the reporters following his campaign.[42] A week later, rival Hillary Clinton visited a bar in Indiana, where she joined patrons in a round of beers and whiskey shots as reporters documented the event.[43] Although these efforts don't always work as intended, there is no doubt about what candidates are trying to do: convince voters that they are "just like them."

Candidates also try to raise doubts about their opponents by citing politically damaging statements or unpopular past behavior. In conducting opposition research, candidates and interest groups dig into an opponent's past for embarrassing incidents or personal indiscretions, either by the candidate or by a member of the candidate's family or staff. Campaigns may then leak this information to the media or release it on their own. Candidates, parties, and interest groups also routinely use trackers, staff who attend their opponents' events with video cameras in the hopes of recording embarrassing behavior or statements. The resulting videos may be posted on the Internet, given to the press, or used in a campaign ad.

The spread of trackers' sometimes unflattering videos shows just one effect of how much easier the Internet makes distributing information about candidates. Virtually all congressional nominees in 2010 had websites and Facebook pages.[44] Many candidates now routinely hold political events over the Internet. Debates and campaign ads are available on YouTube; in 2008, CNN ran presidential debates in which citizens submitted questions for the candidates in the form of YouTube videos. Many candidates also contend with Internet distribution of their past interviews or public appearances, some made long before they got into politics. Delaware Republican senatorial candidate Christine O'Donnell, for example, was unable to escape negative publicity from a several-years-old TV appearance in which she claimed to have attended several Wiccan events—even though she began one campaign ad by stating "I'm not a witch."

Candidates who are behind in the polls sometimes resort to attack ads, campaign ads that criticize the opponent. Many such ads stretch the truth (or break it outright), trying to get voters to stop and think—or to get the opposing candidate to spend time and money denying the ads' claims. In the 2010 campaign, various candidates were accused of "wanting to gas house pets, inject young girls with dangerous drugs, let men beat their wives, and assist child molesters, whether by buying them Viagra or protecting their privacy."[45]

One of the realities of modern American electoral campaigns is that they are conducted largely through campaign advertising. Candidates, party committees, and interest groups spend more than several billion dollars during each election cycle on campaign-related activities by all candidates for federal office. Most of that money is spent on campaign advertising, usually as 30-second television spots. Campaign advertising is critical because candidates cannot assume that citizens will take the time to learn from other sources about the candidates, their qualifications, and their issue positions.

WHAT DO THE ADS INVOLVE?

Campaign advertising has evolved considerably over the last generation.[46] During the early years of television, many campaign ads consisted of speeches by candidates or endorsements from supporters, and they ran several minutes in length. In the 1964 presidential race, Lyndon Johnson's campaign ran a five-minute ad titled "Confessions of a Republican," featuring an actor talking about why he didn't want to vote for Republican Barry Goldwater.[47] Johnson's campaign also ran a one-minute ad, titled "Peace, Little Girl" and nicknamed "Daisy," which featured a child counting the petals she is pulling from a daisy one by one, interspersed with a voice-over of a military countdown and images of the detonation of a nuclear bomb.[48] The implication was that electing Goldwater would increase the chances of a future conflict involving nuclear weapons. The ad remains one of the most iconic pieces of campaign advertising.

Much like the "Daisy" ad, modern campaign ads are short, with arresting images, and often use photo montages and bold text to engage a distracted citizenry. Content varies depending on who is running the ads. Table 8.2 gives data from the 2000 and 2004 presidential elections showing that campaigns, parties, and interest groups run a mix of positive ads extolling a candidate's record, background, or campaign promises, and negative ads citing an opponent's shortcomings or failures. An interesting feature of Table 8.2 is that of all the groups that run campaign ads, candidates themselves run the highest percentage of positive ads. In contrast, in the 2000 election the authors of the study could not find a single positive ad run by an advocacy group. Analyses of more recent campaigns showed little change: advocacy ads in the primaries and the general election were overwhelmingly negative.

All kinds of political organizations run campaign ads. Table 8.3 shows the number of ads run by interest groups during the 2004 general election campaign for the presidency. Liberal groups ran the most ads in this campaign, although many ads came from all categories. (The proportion of ads from different sources varies; in the 2000 election, business groups ran more than half of the total.) The total number of ads is concentrated among a few organizations: in 2004, the Media Fund ran more than a quarter of the total.

DO CAMPAIGN ADS WORK?

One critical question about campaign advertising is whether the ads work—whether they shape what people know or influence

THE "DAISY" AD FROM THE
1964 presidential campaign interspersed images of a child in a field of flowers and footage of a nuclear detonation. It was broadcast only once but caused much controversy—and helped to crystallize doubts about Republican candidate Barry Goldwater.

TABLE » 8.2

PERCENTAGE OF POSITIVE CAMPAIGN ADS IN THE 2000 AND 2004 PRESIDENTIAL ELECTIONS

As this study shows, candidates are most likely to run positive ads, and parties and especially interest groups run mostly negative ads. Why would candidates want to avoid "going negative" against their opponents?

AD SPONSOR	2000	2004
Candidate	64.8%	43.6%
Party	37.2	8.6
Interest groups	0	7.5
Overall	46.2	31.5

Source: Robert Boatright, Michael Malbin, Mark Rozell, and Clyde Wilcox, "Interest Groups and Advocacy Organizations after BCRA," in The Election after Reform, *ed. Michael Malbin (Washington, DC: Rowman and Littlefield, 2006), pp. 112–82.*

their vote decisions or other forms of participation. Some observers have complained that campaign ads depress voter turnout and reinforce citizens' negative perceptions of government.[49] Many of these arguments focus on attack ads or negative campaigning. During the 2010 campaign, one candidate's ad showed the opponent as an evil blimp hovering over Washington; another used video of a kindergarten while talking about the need to reduce conflict in Congress.[50] These ads seek to catch voters' attention, to get them to focus on a race long enough to consider the candidates and their real messages.

What do Americans learn from campaign ads? Do they simply believe what they are told, or are they discerning about what they infer? Analyses suggest that Americans are reasonably thoughtful when assessing campaign ads. In 2008, an ad run by incumbent North Carolina senator Elizabeth Dole against her Democratic challenger, Kay Hagan, claimed that Hagan had taken "godless money" from the Godless Americans PAC. What, the ad asked, had she promised in return? The ad ended with a voice similar to Hagan's saying, "There is no God." In response, Hagan held a press conference with the minister of her church, who confirmed that she was a regular attendee and elder. Hagan also ran a counterattack ad accusing Dole of "bearing false witness against a fellow Christian." Exit polls suggested that Dole's initial ad backfired badly.

Evidence suggests that campaign advertising has several beneficial effects. Scholars have found that people who are exposed to campaign ads tend to be more interested in the campaign and know more about the candidates.[51] Moreover, many campaign ads highlight real differences between the candidates and the parties.[52] Even so, average citizens know that they cannot believe everything they see on television, so campaign advertising typically captures their attention without necessarily changing their minds.[53]

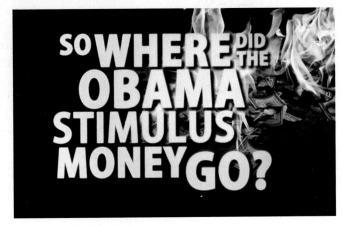

IN THE 2012 PRESIDENTIAL RACE, many of the ads aired by the Romney campaign and Republican groups criticized President Obama, blaming him for the nation's ongoing economic problems.

TABLE » 8.3

CAMPAIGN ADVERTISING BY INTEREST GROUPS, 2004

ORGANIZATION	NUMBER OF ADS RUN
LIBERAL GROUPS, TOTAL	146,615
Media Fund	74,915
MoveOn.org	43,143
New Democratic Network	10,609
Citizens for a Strong Senate	3,830
League of Conservation Voters	3,182
Municipal Employees	2,111
EMILY's List	2,399
Others	6,426
CONSERVATIVE GROUPS, TOTAL	43,810
Progress for America	23,354
Swift Vets and POWs for Truth	8,690
Club for Growth	8,151
Americans United to Preserve Marriage	705
National Rifle Association	1,083
Others	1,827
LABOR GROUPS, TOTAL	24,502
AFL-CIO	10,962
National Education Association	5,238
United Auto Workers	2,664
Service Employees International Union	2,213
Association of Federal, State, County, and Municipal Employees	2,111
Others	1,314
BUSINESS GROUPS, TOTAL	11,114
Americans for Job Security	5,279
United Seniors Association	2,291
National Association of Realtors	1,701
American Medical Association	1,109
Others	734

Source: Robert Boatright, Michael Malbin, Mark Rozell, and Clyde Wilcox, "Interest Groups and Advocacy Organizations after BCRA," in The Election after Reform, ed. Michael Malbin (Washington, DC: Rowman and Littlefield, 2006), pp. 112–82.

With regard to negative campaigning, early evidence suggested that attack ads depressed voter turnout, but later studies have shown that they do not have much of an effect.[54] However, negative ads run by a candidate's campaign can backfire, driving away supporters from the candidate who runs them. As a result, candidates often rely on party committees and interest groups to run negative ads; then the candidates themselves can run more positive ads (recall Table 8.2). However, because negative ads can backfire, candidates sometimes try to disassociate themselves from groups running negative ads against their opponents, fearing that citizens may see the ads and think they come from the candidates' organization.

In the end, despite all the money and effort poured into campaign advertising, these messages must be designed to capture the attention of citizens whose interest in politics is minimal, delivering a message that can be understood without too much interpretation. In this way, campaign advertising reflects an old political saying, that most things candidates do in campaigns are wasted efforts that have little impact on the election. The problem is that candidates don't know which of their actions will amount to wasted efforts and which will help them win, so they try them all.

CAMPAIGN FINANCE

Campaign finance refers to money collected for and spent on campaigns and elections by candidates, political parties, and other organizations and individuals. The **Federal Election Commission** is in charge of administering election laws, including the complex regulations pertaining to how campaigns can spend money. The most recent changes in campaign finance rules, which were passed as the Bipartisan Campaign Reform Act (BCRA), took effect after the 2002 elections and have been modified by subsequent Supreme Court decisions. (In particular, the decision in *Citizens United v. Federal Election Commission* removes all restrictions on independent efforts funded by corporations and labor unions. We will note the implications of this act throughout our discussion.)

Federal Election Commission The government agency that enforces and regulates election laws; made up of six presidential appointees, of whom no more than three can be members of the same party.

TYPES OF FUNDING ORGANIZATIONS

The limits on campaign contributions in the BCRA—also known as the McCain–Feingold Act—vary depending on whether contributions are made by an individual or a group, and by the type of group, as shown in Table 8.4. For example, during the 2012 elections, individuals could contribute up to $2,500 to a candidate per election (donations to the primary and general elections count separately), $28,500 to a political party, $10,000 to a state party, and $5,000 to a PAC, with an overall limit of about $100,000. Individuals and corporations can also make unlimited contributions to 527 organizations, which can use the money for voter mobilization efforts or issue advocacy as long as they do not directly support or oppose a particular candidate, and can spend unlimited amounts on independent expenditures, which are efforts not connected to a particular candidate, party, or committee.

Political action committees (PACs) are groups that aim to elect or defeat particular candidates or political parties. A company or organization can form a PAC and solicit contributions from employees or group members. As Table 8.4 shows, the amount PACs can give to each candidate in an election is limited, but these limits pertain only to **hard money**, which means they restrict only the

hard money Donations that are used to help elect or defeat a specific candidate.

TABLE » 8.4

CONTRIBUTION LIMITS IN THE 2012 ELECTIONS

	INDIVIDUAL CANDIDATES	NATIONAL PARTY COMMITTEE	STATE PARTY	POLITICAL ACTION COMMITTEE	LIMIT ON TOTAL CONTRIBUTIONS
Individuals	$2,500	$30,800	—	—	$46,200 to candidates, $70,800 to organizations
Political action committees	$5,000	$15,000	$5,000	$5,000	—
National party committee	$5,000	—	Unlimited transfers	$5,000	—
State and local party committees	$5,000	Unlimited transfers	Unlimited transfers	$5,000	—

Source: Federal Election Commission "Contribution Limits for 2011–2012," www.fec.gov/info/contriblimits1112 .pdf (accessed 11/12/12).

soft money Contributions that can be used for voter mobilization or to promote a policy proposal or point of view as long as these efforts are not tied to supporting or opposing a particular candidate.

funds given directly to a candidate. PACs can also form what are known as 527 organizations, which can then accept unlimited amounts of **soft money**, which can be used to mobilize voters or advocate a particular issue as long as these efforts are not tied to or controlled by a specific candidate or candidates.

As discussed in Chapter 7, political party committees are entities within the Republican and Democratic parties. Both major parties have a national committee and a campaign committee in each house of Congress. Party committees are limited in the amount of hard money they can give to a candidate's campaign and in the amount they can spend on behalf of the candidate as a coordinated expenditure. However, a party committee (and, after the *Citizens United* decision, corporations and labor unions) can spend an unlimited amount in independent expenditures to elect a candidate or candidates. To be considered independent (not coordinated), expenditures must not be controlled, directed, or approved by any candidate's campaign. Independent expenditures can pay for campaign advertising, either to promote a party's candidate or to attack an opponent, but the candidate or candidates cannot be consulted on the specific messages.

The 527 organizations (named after the provision of the Internal Revenue Code that allows them) can raise unlimited soft money from individuals for voter mobilization and for issue advocacy, but these expenditures must not be coordinated with a candidate or a party. Ads by 527s cannot advocate the election or defeat of a particular candidate or political party; any phrases in an ad that do so—and thereby change the ways the ad can be funded—are termed magic words.[55] Another type of organization, again described using the IRS code as a 501(c)(4), played a major role in the 2010 campaign. The principal difference between 527s and 501(c)(4)s is that the latter type of organization does not have to disclose the names of its contributors. Chapter 9 looks more closely at PACs, 527s, and 501(c)(4)s.

Presidential campaigns have different financing rules. During the primary process, the federal government provides matching funds to candidates who raise $5,000 in each of at least 20 states in contributions of $250 or less. Once a candidate passes this fund-raising threshold, the government matches the first $250 of each subsequent contribution. To receive these funds, candidates must agree to an overall cap on the amount they will spend during the nomination process ($42.05 million in 2008), and to spending caps for each primary or caucus of 67 cents per voting-age person in the state. If candidates forgo the federal matching funds, they can ignore these spending caps—a strategy followed by all of the major presidential candidates in 2008 and all in 2012.

During the general election, presidential candidates can receive federal funding for their campaigns: $84.1 million in 2008, along with an extra $16.4 million for the nominating convention. Candidates do not have to accept this funding, although every major party nominee did so between 1976, when the law took effect, and 2008, when Democrat Barack Obama became the first candidate to opt out—he continued to do so in 2012. Funds are also given to minor political parties if their candidate received more than 5 percent of the vote in the previous election. Only two candidates have passed this threshold: John Anderson, who ran as an independent in 1980, and Ross Perot, who ran in 1992 and 1996 (the second time, his party, the Reform Party, received federal funds).

These federal funds are generated, in part, by money that taxpayers voluntarily allocate out of the taxes they pay to the federal government by checking off a particular box on their federal tax return form. In recent years, the amount of money an individual taxpayer can choose to put to this use is $3. (This donation does not reduce an individual's refund or increase that person's taxes.) When this voluntary check-off procedure has not allocated sufficient funds to pay for candidates' public funding, the rest has been taken from general government revenues.

These complex campaign finance regulations reflect two simple truths. First, any limits on campaign activities involve balancing the right to free speech about candidates and issues with the idea that rich people or well-funded organizations should not be allowed to dominate what voters hear during the campaign. Second, an enormous amount of money is spent on American elections. Table 8.5 shows the amount raised by candidates, political parties, and others in 2006, 2008, 2010, and 2012. More than $5 billion was raised for the 2008 election, nearly $3 billion in 2010, and over $6 billion in 2012. The amount of midterm election independent expenditures (spending by other than candidates and party groups) increased sharply from about $60 million in 2006 to over $294 million in 2010. Moreover, campaign spending is concentrated among a relatively small number of organizations with sizable electioneering budgets. In each of the last several election cycles, the largest organizations have spent more than $100 million.

The principal concern about all this campaign cash is that the amount of money spent on a candidate's campaign might matter more than the candidate's qualifications or issue positions. That is, a candidate—in particular, a wealthy candidate who could self-fund his or her campaign—could get elected regardless of how good a job he would do, simply because he has more money than competing candidates to pay for campaign ads, polls, a large staff, and mobilization efforts. Another concern is that individuals and organizations or corporations that can afford to make large contributions (or to fund their own electioneering efforts)

CAMPAIGN FINANCE REGULATIONS

Campaign finance regulations place restrictions on what Americans can do to influence election outcomes. Suppose you are a wealthy person or the head of a corporation with deep pockets. Under current law, you and your corporation can only donate about $15,000 to a candidate's campaign; corporations have to form a political action committee to do so and cannot pay for the contribution with business revenues. You can also form an organization called a 527 that can run campaign ads designed to help elect your preferred candidates or donate to an existing 527. You can also spend unlimited amounts on independent expenditures, efforts that help a particular candidate, as long as the candidate or campaign has no control over these expenditures. But if your goal is to help your favorite candidate directly, whether by a cash contribution or an ad linked to the campaign, you face serious limits.

These limits on campaign spending arguably conflict with fundamental tenets of American democracy. The Bill of Rights states that Congress cannot abridge "freedom of speech, or of the press; or the right of the people peaceably to assemble, and to petition the Government for a redress of grievances." One interpretation of the First Amendment is that people should be free to spend whatever they want on contesting elections—excluding bribes, threats, and other illegal actions, of course. Thus, ending limits on campaign contributions would support free speech rights, although in practice it would affect only a small number of individuals, those who had large sums of money to spend.

The principal argument for restricting campaign contributions is that money conveys political power. That is, if we let rich people spend as much as they want on electioneering, they could control election outcomes by giving their favored candidates enough money to win regardless of who ran against them. This argument implies that removing contribution restrictions would result in election outcomes driven purely by campaign spending rather than by voters' preferences. (Of course, the lack of limits on independent expenditures works against this logic.)

However, even with unlimited funds, it is hard to get voters' attention—and harder still to change their minds. There are many examples of candidates who lost despite outspending their opponents. And there is no evidence in the corporate world that a company that spends enough on advertising can dominate its market and put its competitors out of business.

Even so, because money for ads is a necessary component of a political campaign, the possibility remains that a rich donor could change election outcomes by giving large sums to challengers in congressional elections. Many challengers never find out how voters would respond to their platforms because they lack the funds to run a full-blown campaign, including paying for an extensive ad campaign. Though most poorly funded challengers would stand no chance of beating their incumbent opponents even with an unlimited advertising budget, some might. And in close races, giving a candidate extra funds to

In a 2010 decision, the Supreme Court ruled that the Citizens United group (whose leader David Bossie is shown here) should have been allowed to release the film Hillary: The Movie *during the 2008 presidential campaigns. This decision opened the door to more campaign spending by groups and corporations.*

increase his or her get-out-the-vote efforts or to run additional campaign ads might be enough to change the outcome.

Critical **Thinking** Questions

1. Limits on individual campaign contributions guard against allowing wealthy people to dominate elections. What are some of the possible drawbacks of such regulations?

2. Since the *Citizens United* decision in 2010, corporations and unions (not just individuals) are allowed unlimited political expenditures as long as they are independent of a candidate's campaign organization. Why do you think independent expenditures are less regulated than direct contributions to campaigns?

TABLE » 8.5

CANDIDATE, PARTY, AND INTEREST GROUP ELECTION FUND-RAISING, 2006–2012

Candidates and political parties raise and spend a great deal of money in their campaigns. Do these numbers help to explain the high re-election rates for members of Congress?

	2006	2008	2010	2012
PRESIDENTIAL CANDIDATES*				
Republican	—	(McCain) $360,000,000	—	(Romney) $989,652, 023
Democrat	—	(Obama) $639,000,000	—	(Obama) $928,497, 835
CONGRESSIONAL CANDIDATES				
House incumbents	$198,137,808	$539,879,135	$481,226,815	$631,553,983
House challengers	$27,680,023	$193,381,140	$256,639,703	$198,720,761
House open seat candidates	$16,453,309	$150,938,532	$141,773,031	$163,615,546
Senate incumbents	$190,492,258	$361,183,002	$186,563,786	$282,484,082
Senate challengers	$44,307,619	$100,188,001	$129,210,379	$162,483,481
Senate open seat candidates	$18,382,257	$59,328,470	$320,664,118	$265,825,062
POLITICAL PARTIES				
Republicans	$598,127,532	$1,228,025,068	$497,570,243	$906,957,839
Democrats	$493,311,599	$1,210,831,060	$559,585,362	$859,745,655
INDEPENDENT EXPENDITURES	$59,861,371	$286,459,718	$294,379,276	$977,495,372
TOTALS	$1,881,827,402	$5,268,316,289	$2,867,612,713	$6,367,026,932

*Presidential spending includes federal matching funds for the general election.
Source: Data compiled from the Center for Responsive Politics, www.opensecrets.org (accessed 11/2/12).

might be able to dictate election outcomes or, by funding campaigns, garner a disproportionate amount of influence over the subsequent behavior of elected officials. In the main, these concerns affect soft money contributions and independent expenditures because the current law places no limits on how much soft money a party can collect, or the size of a group's independent expenditures.

MAKING SENSE OF CAMPAIGN FINANCE

Campaign finance records are amazingly transparent. It is easy to find which individuals or organizations gave money to a candidate, political party, or other organization.[56] Thus, if you are worried that a particular organization is using campaign contributions to influence elected officials, you can learn which officeholders have received the group's donations. In fact, campaign finance records are so readily available that it is generally easy to identify fraudulent organizations.

When you look at campaign finance data, the first thing you will see is that a lot of money is spent trying to win elections. However, the raw data do not always tell the whole story. For example, the huge amounts make more sense when you consider what is at stake during each election cycle: control of the federal government, with a budget of about $3 trillion a year, and the power to start wars and regulate many aspects of citizens' lives. It is also important to recognize that the total amount spent on electioneering represents the sum of all funding for the 435 House contests, 33 or 34 Senate races, and a presidential election. Moreover, consider the cost of television advertising. Nearly 80 percent of campaign expenditures are for television time. In major media markets, a 30-second ad on a major television network can cost tens or hundreds of thousands of dollars.[57] Given that even House campaigns may run hundreds of ads, and presidential campaigns run tens of thousands, it is easy to see why campaign costs pile up so quickly.

One way to put campaign expenses in context is to consider what major corporations pay in advertising expenses. A retail chain such as Wal-Mart, Target, or Best Buy pays billions of dollars every year for newspaper, magazine, and television ads.[58] When you consider how much these companies spend in advertising, it's not surprising that American political campaigns are so expensive. After all, retail chains want to contact average people and get their attention, just as candidates and other political organizations do. And corporations and candidates also use the same media, such as television ads, to deliver their messages. More important is to recognize that although money certainly matters in political campaigns, it cannot work miracles. Candidates for national political office need significant funding to have a realistic chance of winning, but money does not ensure success.

For political actors, such as parties, PACs, and 527s, it is important to distinguish between the amount of money an organization collects and the amount it actually spends on electioneering. Consider EMILY's List, a political action committee that supports pro-choice, Democratic female candidates. It collected more than $30 million during the 2012 election cycle.[59] Less than a third of this total was used for donations, advertising, phone banks, and other campaign activities. The rest was spent on the organization's payroll, office rent, and the direct mail operations that solicited the contributions.

There is also little evidence that campaign contributions alter legislators' behavior, or that contributors are rewarded with votes supporting their causes or favorable policies. Research suggests that most contributions are intended to help elect politicians whom contributors already like, with no expectation that these officials will do anything differently because they received a contribution.[60] Contributions may help contributors gain access, getting the contributor an appointment to present arguments to a politician or her staff. But people and organizations that contribute are already friendly with the politicians they support, and the politicians would likely hear their arguments in any case.

In sum, although money helps shape elections, claims about the power of large contributors and big spenders are typically overstated. Much of the campaign spending in American elections is funded by average Americans making small donations. Moreover, no candidate, political organization, or corporation has the ability to dominate the airwaves and crowd out other voices. In the end, citizens are exposed to campaign advertising from a variety of sources, and they must decide which arguments to take seriously—just like they do with all the other information they receive during the campaign.

HOW DO VOTERS DECIDE?

EXPLAIN THE KEY FACTORS THAT INFLUENCE VOTERS' CHOICES

All the electoral activities we have considered so far are directed at citizens: making sure they are registered to vote, influencing their vote decisions, and getting them to the polls. In this section, we examine how citizens respond to these influences. The first thing to understand is that the high level of attention, commitment, and energy exhibited by candidates and other campaign actors is not matched by ordinary citizens. We have seen throughout this chapter and others that politics is everywhere, and we have described elections as the primary mechanism citizens have to control the federal government. Even so, only a minority of citizens report high levels of interest in campaigns, many people know little about the candidates or the issues, and many people do not vote.[61]

THE DECISION TO VOTE

Politics is everywhere, but getting involved is your choice; voting and other forms of political participation are optional. Surprisingly, even a strong preference between two candidates may not drive a citizen to the polls because each citizen's vote is just one of many.[62] The only time a vote "counts," in the sense that it changes the outcome, is when the other votes are split evenly so that one vote breaks the tie. Moreover, voting involves costs. Even if you don't learn about the candidates but vote anyway, you still have to get to the polls on Election Day. Thus, the **paradox of voting** is this: why does anyone vote, given that voting is costly and the chances of affecting the outcome are small?

Figure 8.2 shows that among Americans, the percentage of registered voters who actually voted has been, in recent presidential elections, around 60 percent, although the turnout has been close to 50 percent. (Voter turnout is calculated based on the whole voting age population, including people who didn't vote because they opted not to register or were ineligible to register because of a felony conviction or other factors.)[63] As the figure shows, turnout is significantly higher in presidential elections than in midterm elections. Turnout is even lower in

paradox of voting The question of why citizens vote even though their individual votes stand little chance of changing the election outcome.

VOTING IS COSTLY IN TERMS OF TIME and effort. After registering and informing themselves about the election, voters have to take the time to go to the polls and possibly wait in line.

FIGURE » 8.2

TURNOUT IN PRESIDENTIAL AND MIDTERM ELECTIONS, 1992–2012

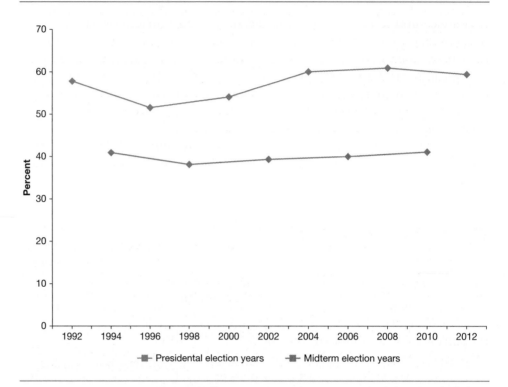

-■- Presidental election years   -■- Midterm election years

Source: United States Election Project, http://elections.gmu.edu/voter_turnout.htm (accessed 11/12/12).

primaries and caucuses: in the 2012 presidential primaries, some states reported turnout exceeding 30 percent, which were regarded as unusually high. For caucuses, which require individuals to spend several hours voting, turnout is generally only a few percentage points.

In the main, turnout is higher for whites than nonwhites, and for older Americans than younger cohorts, and for college graduates than people with a high school education or less. Men and women, however, say they vote at roughly the same rate. Many factors explain variation in turnout. People who vote regularly are more likely to consider going to the polls an obligation of citizenship, to feel guilty when they do not vote, and to think that the elections matter. In contrast, turnout is much lower among those who are angry with the government, think that government actions do not affect them, or think that voting will have no impact on government policy. Citizens who hold these beliefs are unlikely to care about the outcome of the election and are unlikely to feel guilty for abstaining or to see voting as an obligation.[64]

These findings demonstrate the importance of mobilization in elections. As we discussed earlier, many candidates for political office spend at least as much time trying to convince their supporters to vote as they do attempting to persuade others to become supporters in the first place. Because many Americans either do not vote or vote only sporadically, mobilization is a vital strategy for winning elections.

The reasons nonvoters abstain can suggest what kinds of arguments might convince them to change their minds and go to the polls. If a campaign can make nonvoters think that the election matters and that it is their duty to vote, the chances that they will go to the polls on Election Day may increase. However, making people angry at Washington—perhaps with negative campaign ads—could lower turnout.

The turnout data provide another example of how the rules of the political process can shape outcomes. Among people who have moved within the last two years, turnout is extremely low, at least partly because moving often requires citizens to re-register at their new address and to locate their new polling place. Since passage of the Motor Voter Act in 1993, people have been able to register at the Department of Motor Vehicles at the same time they renew their driver's license, which has increased turnout by a few percentage points.[65]

HOW DO PEOPLE VOTE?

The image of the average citizen as uninterested in the details of politics still holds, even among those who decide to vote. Some **issue voters** are highly interested in politics, collect all the information they can about the candidates, and vote based on this information.[66] However, most citizens are not interested enough in politics to spend their time that way, and they aren't so concerned with voting for the candidates that come closest to their preferences. Reliable information about candidates is also often difficult to find. Although candidates, parties, and other organizations produce a blizzard of endorsements, reports, and press releases throughout the campaign, much of this information may be difficult to interpret. It is a daunting task, even for the rare, highly motivated voter.

This combination of a lack of interest and a relatively complex task leads the majority of American voters to base their vote decision on easily interpretable pieces of information, or **voting cues**.[67] Voters in American national elections use many kinds of cues, including these:

▶ *Incumbency:* Vote for the incumbent candidate.[68]

▶ *Partisanship:* Vote for the candidate whose party affiliation matches your own.[69]

▶ *Personal vote:* Vote for the incumbent if he or she has helped you get assistance from a government agency or has helped your community benefit from desirable government projects.[70]

▶ *Personal characteristics:* Vote for the candidate whose personal characteristics (age, race, gender, ethnicity, or religious beliefs) match your own or suggest you have common values, ideologies, or policy preferences.[71]

▶ *Retrospective evaluations:* Focus on a small set of votes the incumbent has cast while in office or other duties of the office that you care about, and vote for the incumbent if he or she has behaved the way you want in these circumstances.[72]

▶ *For (or against) the party in power:* Vote for a candidate based on a comparison of that candidate's party with an assessment of the party in power (the party that controls the presidency and has majorities in the House and Senate).[73]

Cues give people a low-cost way to cast what political scientist and campaign consultant Samuel Popkin called a reasonable vote—a vote that, more likely than not, is consistent with the voter's true preference among candidates.[74] Studies have

issue voters People who are well informed about their own policy preferences and knowledgeable about the candidates, and who use all of this information when they decide how to vote.

voting cues Pieces of information about a candidate that are readily available, easy to interpret, and lead a citizen to decide to vote for a particular candidate.

DO INDEPENDENTS REALLY VOTE INDEPENDENTLY?

Many news stories about contemporary politics focus on independent voters—people who say they do not belong to a political party. We are told that independents are the largest political group in America (and getting larger), that independents evaluate candidates in terms of their qualifications and policy views rather than blindly voting on the basis of their party identification, and that understanding how independents think is necessary to make sense of American politics or predict future election outcomes.

For example, an increase in the number of independents might signal that Americans are rejecting the Republican and Democratic parties and might be attracted to a new political organization. Moreover, if more and more people become independents, it seems that it will be much harder to predict how these individuals will vote in elections, making it more difficult to predict the outcomes of these elections.

Watch a video clip of John Sides discussing this topic further at **wwnorton.com/studyspace**

One of the best responses to these assumptions was presented by John Sides, a professor at George Washington University who specializes in voting behavior and elections, on a blog called the Monkey Cage that he runs along with some other political scientists.[a] His fundamental insight was to note that in studies showing a high and ever-increasing percentage of independents, pollsters generally ask one question about partisanship that usually looks like this: "Are you a Republican, Democrat, or Independent?" The problem with this question is that it gives people only three options and forces them to pick one. For example, someone who does not think of herself as a Democrat, but who usually votes for Democratic candidates, would probably say she is an independent, similar to someone who votes for Republicans but who does not identify as a Republican. The result is that one-question surveys lump these Democratic or Republican leaners in the same category as "pure" independents, voters who have no connection with either party and who are just as likely to vote for Democrats as Republicans.

Most academic surveys, such as the American National Election Study (ANES), use a series of questions to measure an individual's partisanship. In his blog post, Sides used ANES data to show how the percentage of pure independents compares to the percentage of Republican and Democratic leaners, and how this percentage has varied over the last 50 years, as shown in the first figure. The data reveal that the increase in the percentage of independent voters over the last generation consists entirely of partisan leaners; the percentage of pure independents has, if anything, declined a bit. But even if the new

independents are leaners, don't they behave more like independents than partisans? The answer, Sides's analysis shows, is that independent leaners vote a lot like partisans. Over the last two generations, the probability that an independent leaner votes for his party's presidential candidate is only a little lower than it is for strong partisans (see the graph below).

The take-away point from Sides's analysis is that pundits who focus on the rise of independent voters in contemporary American politics may be focusing on the wrong kinds of data. As Sides noted, "90% of the public is partisan and about 80–90% of those voters vote for their party's candidate." To put it another way, party identification remains an important influence on vote decisions and an important determinant of elections.

It may seem exciting to talk about an America where partisan ties are weak and where people vote based on their assessments of the candidates. In such a world, campaigns would matter more than they do now, precisely because candidates could not count on support from a large number of partisans in their electorate. They would have to campaign with the goal of converting a large number of independents into supporters. However, for better or worse, American elections do not fit this description. Party identification plays a central role in modern elections, just as it has in elections for at least the last two generations.

PERCENTAGE VOTING FOR OWN OR PREFERRED PARTY'S PRESIDENTIAL CANDIDATE

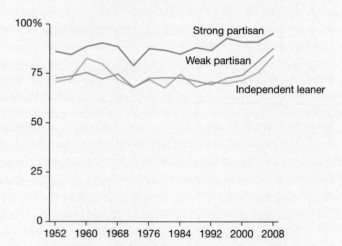

Source: Data compiled from the American National Election Study by John Sides, "Three Myths about Political Independents," The Monkey Cage, December 17, 2009, www.themonkeycage.org/2009/12/three_myths_about _political_in.html (accessed 10/18/12).

found that citizens who use cues and are politically well informed are more likely to cast a reasonable vote than those who use cues but are otherwise relatively politically ignorant. In essence, information helps people to select the right cue.[75]

Consider the partisanship cue. As discussed earlier, Republican and Democratic candidates usually hold different positions on many important issues. Thus, a candidate's party affiliation tells a voter something about how the candidate is likely to behave if elected. The signal is not foolproof: a Republican voter who is pro–gay rights might have used a partisan cue to vote for George Bush because he was the Republican nominee, even though more investigation would have revealed that Bush's position on gay rights is the opposite of her own. Even so, because partisan cues are so easy to employ, they are a favorite voting strategy in American elections.

A candidate's personal characteristics also play a crucial role in vote decisions. As we saw in Chapter 5, information about race, ethnicity, gender, religion, or age provides a fairly solid basis for predictions about some of a person's ideological beliefs. Thus, when voters choose a candidate who "looks like them," they are not necessarily behaving irrationally. Rather, they may be using a cue that suggests they share the candidate's priorities. Exit polls in the 2008 election suggested that Americans with strong religious beliefs were more likely to vote for the McCain–Palin ticket, partly because of Sarah Palin's membership in a charismatic Christian church.

Cues can also involve retrospective evaluations. A citizen can vote for or against a House member or senator based on how that person voted on a specific issue or on judgments about an incumbent's honesty or qualifications, willingness to do casework to help constituents, or success at attracting government spending to the constituents' area. Although none of these factors tells the whole story about an incumbent's performance, each provides a rationale for deciding whether an incumbent deserves another term.[76] Similarly, a voter might use the state of the economy to decide whether the president deserves another term in office. In fact, economic conditions such as rates of growth, inflation, and unemployment are very good predictors of how many people will vote for a president running for re-election.[77] Conversely, it is also possible to vote prospectively, based on expectations of how any of these indicators will change over the next few years after the election.

Table 8.6, based on surveys of voters in congressional elections, shows how incumbent-based cues shape vote decisions. People were more likely to vote for a House or a Senate incumbent if they felt that the incumbent had done a good job keeping in touch with constituents, had responded well to requests for casework, and had voted (or would vote) in line with the respondent's preferences.

Some Americans also look to the candidates' backgrounds and life experiences. Table 8.7 offers some details on what these voters are looking for. Military service is an asset, as is being a governor and having business experience. However, many Americans tend not to want a candidate who is an atheist, has had an extramarital affair, or is homosexual. The benefits or drawbacks of certain characteristics vary across states and districts according to beliefs held by voters.

These data are a reminder that even though the average American spends little effort to learn about the candidates in congressional or presidential elections, information about the candidates still matters. If voters happen to learn about a candidate's life experiences or beliefs from media coverage or an opponent's ads, this information can have an enormous impact on their willingness to support the candidate.

TABLE » 8.6

VOTE DECISIONS IN CONGRESSIONAL ELECTIONS: CANDIDATE CUES

Americans are much more likely to vote for candidates who keep in touch, respond to contacts, vote as their constituents prefer, and do a good job on important problems. If you were a member of Congress who wanted to stay in office, what sorts of actions would you take to secure re-election?

QUESTION	RESPONSE	PERCENTAGE VOTING FOR INCUMBENT	
		HOUSE	SENATE
How good a job does the incumbent do keeping in touch with people?	Very good	88%	87%
	Very poor	24	21
Level of satisfaction with incumbent's response to voter-initiated contact?	Very satisfied	90%	90%
	Not at all satisfied	13	26
Agreed or disagreed with incumbent's vote on particular bill?	Agreed	93%	—
	Disagreed	43	—
Which candidate would do a better job on the most important problem?	Incumbent	97%	—
	Challenger	11	—

Note: Latter questions were not asked in Senate survey.

Source: Gary Jacobson, The Politics of Congressional Elections, *6th ed. (New York: Pearson Longman, 2004), Table 5.11.*

VOTING IN NORMAL AND NATIONALIZED ELECTIONS

coattails The idea that a popular president can generate additional support for candidates affiliated with his party. Coattails are weak or nonexistent in most American elections.

split ticket A ballot on which a voter selects candidates from more than one political party.

straight ticket A ballot on which a voter selects candidates from only one political party.

All the strategies discussed so far for making vote decisions are used to some extent in every election. However, in normal elections, when congressional re-election rates are high and the seat shift between the parties is small, voters generally use cues that focus on the candidates themselves, such as incumbency, partisanship, a personal connection to a candidate, the candidate's personal characteristics, or retrospective evaluations. This behavior is consistent with what Tip O'Neill, Speaker of the House from 1977 to 1987, meant when he said that "all politics is local": congressional elections are independent, local contests in which a candidate's chances of winning depend on what voters think of the candidate in particular—not the president, Congress, or national issues. It also explains why electoral **coattails** are typically very weak in American elections, and why so many Americans cast **split tickets** rather than **straight tickets**. In the main, vote decisions in presidential and congressional elections are made independently of each other.

Nationalized elections generally occur when a large number of voters switch to using the anti-party-in-power cue, which leads them to vote against candidates

TABLE » 8.7

CANDIDATE TRAITS AND VOTE CHOICE

Likelihood of supporting a candidate who . . .

	MORE LIKELY	LESS LIKELY	WOULDN'T MATTER
Has served in the military	49	4	47
Has been a governor	37	5	55
Has been a business executive	35	14	49
Has been an elected official in Washington for many years	26	25	46
Is a woman	14	7	77
Is Hispanic	8	11	80
Is black	7	3	89
Is Mormon	5	25	68
Does not believe in God	5	61	33
Has used marijuana in the past	5	24	69
Has been divorced	3	11	85
Is homosexual	3	33	62
Had an extramarital affair in the past	2	46	49

Source: "Republican Candidates Stir Little Enthusiasm" Pew Research Center, www.people-press
.org/2011/06/02/republican-candidates-stir-little-enthusiasm/, June 2, 2011 (accessed 9/5/12).

from the president's party. Typically this kind of shift happens when many voters become highly concerned about a national issue such as the state of the economy or an international conflict. In 1980, the crucial issue for many voters was the poor state of the economy. Economic concerns were salient again in 1994, along with disapproval of President Clinton and a recent tax increase. In 2006, many voters rated the war in Iraq as the most important issue, and they generally disapproved of how the war was being conducted.[78] And in 2010, economic concerns again returned to the fore, with many voters disapproving of economic conditions in general as well as corporate bailouts, economic stimulus legislation, and health care reform.

National-level concerns such as these cause citizens to lower their evaluations of the president and of Congress, and to use different cues to guide their voting decisions.[79] Specifically, many voters look for someone to blame, focusing on members of Congress from the party in power. They then vote against these members, either as a protest vote, because they disapprove of their performance, or because they want to put different individuals in charge in the hope that new members will bring about improved conditions. Whether viewed in terms of voting against one party's incumbents or for the other party's challengers, these motivations lead to the same voting behavior; the difference is a matter of voters' attitudes and emphases.

Even in nationalized elections, re-election rates for members of Congress (the percentage of incumbents who successfully ran for re-election) are generally high, as Figure 8.3 shows. Over the last generation, neither party has a House re-election rate less than 80 percent—even in 2006, when 100 percent of Democratic House incumbents running for re-election won, the re-election rate for House Republican incumbents was almost 90 percent. Re-election rates for senators are somewhat lower, but still quite high. In nationalized elections such as those in 2006 and 2010, one party's re-election rate is significantly higher than that of the other party; in normal elections such as the ones in 2000 and 2002, the rates are similar and approach 100 percent. (Re-election rates for Senate incumbents are somewhat lower but show the same patterns.)

Re-election rates for members of Congress are so high because the members work to insulate themselves from electoral challenges through tactics we discussed in this chapter and in Chapter 10 (Congress). They raise large sums of campaign cash well in advance of upcoming elections, use redistricting to give themselves a safe district populated by supporters, and enact pork-barrel legislation that provides government benefits and programs to their constituents. Even so, congressional incumbents are not necessarily safe from electoral defeat. Rather, their high re-election rates result from the actions they take every day, which are calculated to win favor with their constituents. In normal elections, these strategies are generally enough to ensure re-election. In nationalized elections, however, they are not enough to for some legislators from the disadvantaged party, such as Democrats in 2010.

As we have seen throughout this chapter, nationalized elections like 2006 and 2010 can produce sharp shifts in Washington, and exit polls showed that all pol-

FIGURE » 8.3

INCUMBENTS RE-ELECTED

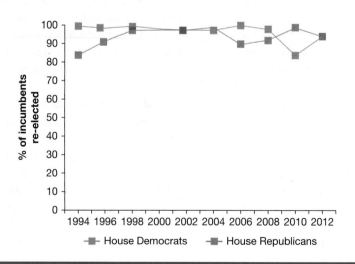

TABLE » 8.8

ISSUES AND VOTING IN THE 2012 ELECTION

In the 2012 election, many Americans appear to have based their vote on their feelings about tax increases, the state of the economy, evaluations of health care legislation enacted in 2010, and evaluations of President Obama. How can you explain the sharp divisions in the table given the relatively high re-election rates for incumbents in 2012?

ISSUE	OPINION	VOTE IN HOUSE RACE	
		DEMOCRAT	REPUBLICAN
Should taxes be raised to cut the deficit	Yes	74	23
	No	38	60
Condition of the U.S. economy	Excellent or good	89	10
	Not so good or poor	39	58
Health care law	Expand	88	9
	No change	78	21
	Repeal	19	81
President Barack Obama	Approve	86	12
	Disapprove	7	91

Source: http://elections.msnbc.msn.com/ns/politics/2012/all/house (accessed 11/7/12).

itics was *not* local in these elections. In 2006, the shift toward the Democratic Party was born out of national-level issues. Many voters strongly opposed the war in Iraq, felt that Congress was bedeviled by ethical lapses and corruption, and disapproved of President Bush's performance in office.[80] Similarly, in 2012, some voters blamed Democratic House members and senators for the state of the economy, for the enactment of unpopular health care legislation, and for their support of tax increases for deficit reduction. As Table 8.8 shows, voters who had these concerns, or who disapproved of President Obama, were much more likely to vote for Republican candidates in 2012.

Despite the sequence of three nationalized elections in 2006, 2008, and 2010, nationalized elections are relatively rare because most of the time, relatively few citizens are highly concerned about national issues or hold strong opinions of the president, Congress, or the overall state of the nation. Congressional incumbents also work hard to focus attention on the good things they have done for their constituents. And it is important to remember that even in nationalized elections, some voters still use the incumbent-centered cues described earlier. In a nationalized election, voters don't suddenly become better informed about politics. Rather, some of them just switch to a different set of voting cues depending on the circumstances of the election.

UNDERSTANDING THE 2012 ELECTIONS

In contrast to the previous three elections, the 2012 elections might have seemed much less dramatic: Democrats held on to their majority in the Senate, Republicans continued to control the House, and President Obama was re-elected, albeit by a narrow margin. There appeared to be no major changes in the balance of power in the national government.

Despite this stability, the 2012 elections confirmed that politics is conflictual. The two presidential candidates, Democrat Barack Obama and Republican Mitt Romney, along with the congressional candidates from each party, offered very different ideas about the size and scope of the federal government in areas ranging from deficit reduction to social issues. Obama's re-election combined with the congressional results will lead to very different policies than would have arisen from a Romney victory and Republican control of both houses of Congress.

The 2012 elections also illustrate the idea that process matters. For example, one reason that Republican losses in the House were small was that Republican legislators in many states drew voting districts that favored their Republican colleagues in the House of Representatives. And the Supreme Court's *Citizens United* decision resulted in a wave of so-called independent spending that helped both presidential campaigns in their efforts to win close races in Ohio, Virginia, Florida, and other swing states.

Finally, the 2012 returns also confirm our argument that focusing on the general election campaign ignores many important factors outside this narrow window of time. Accordingly, we begin our discussion of the 2012 elections by reviewing what happened in the 2008 and 2010 elections.

ALTHOUGH THE 2012 ELECTIONS confirmed the status quo, with President Obama re-elected and control of the House and Senate remaining the same, Americans and the major parties were sharply divided on many issues. In his 2012 acceptance speech, Obama alluded to these conflicts and the need for compromise in the coming months and years.

THE PATH TO 2012: THE 2008 AND 2010 ELECTIONS

The 2008 and 2010 elections were very different contests. In 2008, Barack Obama defeated John McCain with 365 electoral votes and nearly 53 percent of the popular vote. Democrats gained 8 seats in the Senate and 21 in the House. In contrast, Republicans dominated the 2010 midterms, gaining 63 House seats and control of the chamber, and they narrowed the Democrats' advantage in the Senate. In the end, the two elections illustrate the findings that Americans are sharply divided on many issues and that short-term factors such as the state of the economy or international conflicts can produce large changes from election to election.

THE 2008 ELECTION

Some characteristics of the 2008 contest distinguished it from all previous American elections. For the first time, an African American was elected president. The election also included the first female candidate to have a significant chance of winning a major party's nomination, Democrat Hillary Clinton, and only the second female vice-presidential nominee, Alaska governor Sarah Palin. For the first time since 2001, the wars in Iraq and Afghanistan were not central issues. And the American economy was faltering due to high energy prices, the failure of several large financial firms, the collapse of house prices, and banks' unwillingness to lend money, even to well-established, secure firms.

The 2008 contest was also shaped by the rules and procedures governing the process. One explanation for Republican losses was that a disproportionate number of Republican officeholders retired rather than face two more years in the minority, which enabled Democrats to pick up open seats. Of course, given voters' propensity in 2008 to blame President Bush and the Republicans for the poor state of the American economy, Republicans faced an uphill fight from the start. Nevertheless, these structural factors certainly increased their troubles.

In the general election, Obama's get-out-the-vote operation was far more elaborate than McCain's. The Obama campaign did all the usual things, from knocking on doors to organizing shuttle vans to drive voters to the polls, but their operation was one of the largest and most effective ever seen in a presidential race. Similar efforts were crucial to Obama's success in the 2012 contest.

There were real differences in 2008 between Republican and Democratic candidates on issues such as how to address economic problems, how to reform health care, and what to do in Iraq and Afghanistan. Exit poll data showed that a clear majority of voters cited the economy as the most important issue and that Obama was the favorite among people who wanted the government to address the economy.

THE 2010 MIDTERM ELECTION

In the two years following the 2008 election, Democrats managed to enact significant portions of the party's policy agenda. However, debate over these policies exposed deep divisions within the House and Senate Democratic caucuses, as well as strong differences of opinion among voters. More important, Republicans regained the initiative, offering proposals for sharp changes in government policy, while most Democratic candidates seemed to avoid talking about their party's policy accomplishments. Many who supported Democratic candidates in 2008 switched to become equally strong supporters of Republican candidates in 2010.

While some explanations of the 2010 contest focus on Obama's declining popularity, the flood of independent spending, or the rise of the Tea Party, perhaps a better explanation for Republican successes in 2010 lies in two of our central themes. First, politics is conflictual. The previous two years had shown what a president with united congressional majorities can accomplish. But they also reminded Americans of their policy disagreements, and, in doing so, gave Republicans a ready-made constituency of people who opposed some or all of Obama's achievements or who favored the Democratic party's overall goals but disagreed with their implementation.

Moreover, in 2010, the procedural advantages were on the Republican side. For example, Democratic gains in the 2006 and 2008 House elections meant that as many as 50 to 60 incumbent Democrats were running in pro-Republican districts. These seats were winnable for Democrats as long as Republicans were tagged with an extremely unpopular war (as in 2006) or an economy in freefall (as in 2008). But in 2010, Republican candidates in these districts were free of these burdens for the first time in six years, giving them a decided advantage.

THE STATE OF THE COUNTRY IN 2012

As in 2008 and 2010, the economy was the central issue in the 2012 campaign. Unemployment remained relatively high throughout the primary and general election contests, dipping below 8 percent nationally only in the final month before the general election. Economic growth was relatively low as well, holding steady at about 1.5 percent per year.

At first glance, the economic data appeared to pose a serious threat to President Obama's re-election chances—historically, a poor economy dooms a president's chance of re-election. In Obama's case, though, many Americans seemed to hold him only partially responsible for the economy, believing that he inherited many of the problems from previous administrations. The result was that at the national level, Obama's economic policies, including the economic stimulus legislation, did not hinder his chances of re-election, although they did not help much either. However, in some crucial states such as Ohio, declining unemployment and policies such as the government's financial assistance to the automobile industry generated support for Obama and other Democrats, such as Ohio Democratic senator Sherrod Brown.

Many Republican candidates ran on platforms emphasizing the need to reduce government spending and regulations, generally citing the repeal of President Obama's health care reforms as a central priority. Most Democrats either championed the health care reforms or, in swing districts and states, talked about them as little as possible. Given the strong divisions in the country over these issues, as discussed in Chapter 5 (Public Opinion) and Chapter 15 (Economic Policy), the Republicans' positions were useful primarily to mobilize GOP voters and get them to the polls, rather than persuading Democratic or undecided voters. In the main, Democratic candidates, including President Obama, supported immigration reform that gave illegal immigrants a path to residency status, while Republicans generally opposed such measures.

Debates about the federal budget deficit were also significant. As we discussed at the beginning of this book, the failure to achieve a deficit reduction agreement in 2011 meant that large automatic cuts in military and domestic spending would take place in early 2013, along with tax increases resulting from the scheduled end

of the Bush-era tax cuts and the temporary reduction in the taxes Americans pay to fund Social Security. Nonaction on these issues was often mentioned in surveys as a prime example of gridlock in Washington, as reflected in Americans' low ratings of Congress (see Chapter 10).

However, while virtually all candidates argued that something needed to be done to avoid this so-called fiscal cliff, very few were willing to commit to the painful policy changes that would be needed to deal with the problem. The only consensus was that the problem would have to be dealt with during a lame-duck session of Congress after the election or (more likely) by the new Congress elected in 2012.

Social issues such as gay marriage were not often mentioned during the campaign—although this may have been due to poll results that show a solid majority of Americans are not opposed to changes that would give gay and lesbian couples some form of marriage rights. President Obama's support of marriage equality for gays and lesbians and abortion rights was well-known.

One difference between 2012 and the previous few elections was that international conflicts were not central issues in the campaign, both because of the withdrawal of American ground forces from Iraq and the gradual drawdown of forces from Afghanistan and because of the Obama administration's successes in the war on terror and the NATO operation in Libya. Differences between Republicans and Democrats centered on details, such as whether the United States should firmly commit to a withdrawal from Afghanistan by 2014 (the Obama policy) or use this date simply as a goal (the position of many Republicans, including presidential nominee Mitt Romney). Republicans also criticized the Obama administration for its handling of an attack by militants on an American consulate in Libya and the trade deficit with China. In the end, however, these issues did not move many voters.

In sum, while many issues arose during the 2012 campaign, none of them gave Republican or Democratic candidates a solid advantage. Instead, victory or defeat hinged on candidates' personal characteristics, their campaign promises, and, for incumbents, their record in office.

THE PRESIDENTIAL NOMINATION PROCESS AND CONVENTIONS

The Republican and Democratic presidential nomination campaigns were very different. On the Republican side, Mitt Romney was the front-runner from the beginning of the race to the end, although he faced serious opposition for most of the primary season from several candidates, including former senator Rick Santorum, former House Speaker Newt Gingrich, and businessman Herman Cain.

The most notable thing about the Republican nomination process was that many seemingly viable candidates opted to stay out the race, including New Jersey governor Chris Christie, Indiana governor Mitch Daniels, former Florida governor Jeb Bush, and former vice presidential candidate Sarah Palin. Some of these candidates may have been influenced by personal concerns or a belief that they would not appeal to the mostly conservative Republican primary electorate. But in all of their minds, the difficulty of defeating an incumbent president, even given a mediocre economy, was almost surely an important factor.

Even if these candidates had run, Romney's winning the nomination would not have been a surprise. He was experienced, having run for president in 2008 and served as governor of Massachusetts. His record as a businessman appealed to voters who thought that government should be run more efficiently. He was conservative but had not taken many controversial stands, such as calling for a total ban on abortion, although he did say that he would sign such a measure if Congress enacted it. He also opposed gay marriage. So, while Romney was not a perfect candidate—some voters disliked him because of his Mormon faith and his personal fortune, which together suggested to some that he was unfamiliar with the conditions facing average Americans—he was well-positioned to win the Republican nomination. Doubts about whether he was sufficiently conservative were muted after he selected conservative representative Paul Ryan of Wisconsin as his vice presidential candidate.

In contrast to Romney and the Republicans, President Obama won renomination with no significant opposition, as is usual for incumbent presidents. His team spent the primary campaign raising money and developing an extensive network of field offices and volunteers.

Both parties officially announced their nominees for president and vice president at their national conventions in late summer. The message at the Republican convention, articulated by Romney, Ryan, and others, was that President Obama should be blamed for poor economic conditions and pay the price for his support of programs such as health care reform that expanded the role of government in society. The Republicans promised significant change that would lead to a smaller, more efficient federal government. Democrats, in turn, emphasized how bad the economy was when Obama came into office and noted the many policy successes of Obama's first term.

THE GENERAL ELECTION: OBAMA VS. ROMNEY

Early in the general election campaign, Obama appeared to be opening up a significant lead over Romney, after a Democratic convention that was perceived to have made an effective case for his re-election. With most states squarely in one candidate's camp or the other, attention focused on nine swing states where neither candidate was significantly ahead: North Carolina, Ohio, Virginia, Florida, New Hampshire, Nevada, Wisconsin, Colorado, and Iowa. The candidate who did well in a majority of these states would almost surely win the election.

THE DEBATES

The presidential debates in 2012 were an exception to the rule that debates have little influence on voter preferences: Obama's poor performance in the first debate, coupled with a strong performance by Romney, shifted the electorate two or three points toward Romney, which made the race effectively tied at the national level and extremely close in the swing states. The impact of the first debate was magnified by the fact that the two candidates were so close in the polls that even a small shift in voter sentiment made a large difference. Obama recovered in the second and third debates, responding effectively to Romney's criticisms and winning back a significant portion of the ground he lost in the first debate.

Afterward, the polls settled back close to where they were before the convention, with the candidates roughly tied in national polls, but Obama favored to win enough swing states to gain the electoral votes needed for another term.

WERE VOTERS' DECISIONS IN 2012 driven by any one event during the campaign, such as a debate or a specific remark? Possibly, but more often elections are decided by broadly held perceptions that develop over time and are difficult to change.

CAMPAIGN STRATEGY

While both candidates refused federal funding and spent over a billion dollars each on the campaign (along with an equal amount spent by outside groups), as we have seen in other campaigns, there is little evidence that spending had much impact on the outcome. Part of the problem, as we have seen in earlier chapters, is that many Americans pay relatively little attention to politics, so even a large amount of campaign advertising may not get the message heard. Moreover, in the presidential race, polls showed that most Americans had largely made up their minds fairly early in the campaign, and few were open to persuasion.

Under these conditions, voter mobilization played a crucial role—and Obama's campaign was much better organized to get people to the polls, both for early voting and on Election Day. Many Democrats also went to court to contest laws that required voters to show picture ID at the polls, believing that this requirement would lower turnout by their supporters.

OBAMA'S VICTORY

Obama also gained an unexpected advantage in the last week of the campaign as the Northeast was hit by an extremely large storm, Hurricane Sandy. Effective relief efforts by the Federal Emergency Management Agency (FEMA) as well as Obama's well-publicized tour of storm-damaged coastal towns with Republican New Jersey governor Chris Christie (and Christie's enthusiastic thank you to Obama) countered Romney's closing arguments that bipartisanship was lacking under Obama and that government under Obama was ineffective. In the last days of the campaign, polls showed a small but significant shift in support toward Obama.

FIGURE » 8.4

THE 2012 PRESIDENTIAL ELECTION: STATE-BY-STATE

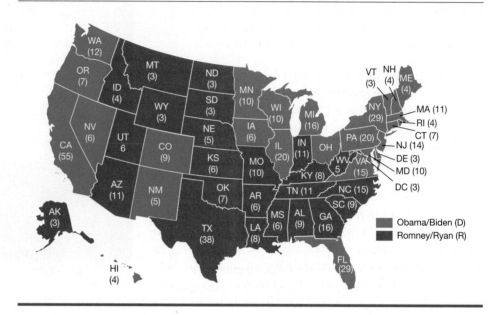

In the end, Obama's record and campaign organization were just enough: he defeated Romney by a slight margin in the popular vote and a somewhat larger margin in the electoral college. Figure 8.4 displays the state-by-state results, showing Obama's strength in the Northeast, Midwest, and West Coast states, and Romney's dominance of western and southern states.

CONGRESSIONAL RACES

At the beginning of the 2012 campaigns, many political scientists believed that the Democrats would lose seats in both the House and the Senate regardless of the outcome of the presidential election. In the House, the expectation was that Republican-controlled state legislatures would use redistricting to put Democratic incumbents in vulnerable districts. Moreover, Democrats controlled 23 (including 2 independents who caucus with Democrats) of the 33 seats that were contested in the campaign and had several vulnerable incumbents, including Jon Tester of Montana and Claire McCaskill of Missouri, who had won their seats during the Democratic surge in the 2006 election, but who represented states where Republican candidates normally did well.

Surprisingly, Democrats won one additional Senate seat (counting 2 independents expected to caucus with Democrats) and gained 8 House seats. Their success was due to two factors. First, Republicans' control of redistricting was limited by the fact that in some states, redistricting is determined by nonpartisan commissions, while in others, Democratic governors had to approve districting schemes. In some cases, Republicans were able to use the redistricting process to their advantage. In North Carolina, Democratic representative Brad Miller retired rather than face his colleague Democrat David Price in a primary—a Republican-controlled redistricting had transformed Miller's formerly Democratic-leaning district into a safe Republican district and placed Miller's home in Price's district.

Republican prospects were also constrained by their large gains in the 2010 election. There were not that many vulnerable Democratic incumbents in 2012 because many such candidates had been defeated or had retired in 2010. Conversely, Republicans faced the problem of securing their gains from that election, helping a large class of freshmen House members get re-elected.

Moreover, while there were vulnerable Democratic senators in 2012, some Republican senators were vulnerable as well, most notably Scott Brown of Massachusetts, who won a special election in 2009 in a state that typically sends Democrats to Congress. Maine senator Olympia Snowe's decision to retire unexpectedly placed a Republican seat in play in a state where Democrats were competitive, although the seat was ultimately won by an independent, former governor Angus King.

Democrats benefited from some surprise primary election outcomes. In several states, Republican incumbents faced challenges from candidates backed by Tea Party organizations. In some cases, these efforts failed—Utah senator Orrin Hatch, for example, won his primary against a well-funded Tea Party opponent. However, Tea Party candidates won other Senate nomination contests, including Indiana, where longtime Republican moderate Richard Lugar lost a primary to the state treasurer, Richard Mourdock, and Missouri, where Representative Todd Akin defeated three other candidates despite being outspent by a large margin. These primary upsets translated into Democratic gains, as both candidates proved to be too conservative to win their general election contests.

Democrats also benefited from campaign gaffes by Republican candidates. For example, Akin's prospects were severely harmed by his claim during an interview that it was nearly impossible for a woman to become pregnant from a rape. After this remark produced a nationwide firestorm of protest, many organizations, including the Republican National Committee and Senate Campaign Committee, refused to support his candidacy. His opponent, Claire McCaskill, who was regarded as one of the most vulnerable Democratic incumbents, gained support after the controversy and ultimately won re-election.

SENATOR CLAIRE MCCASKILL OF Missouri—shown here canvassing for votes in the state—was one of several Democratic incumbents considered vulnerable in 2012. However, McCaskill prevailed after her opponent Todd Akin's remarks about rape drew wide criticism.

ANALYZING THE 2012 ELECTIONS

It is always easy to attribute an election outcome to a single event or factor. We might say that Mitt Romney lost the presidential election because he was a Mormon or because of his remarks at a campaign event that 47 percent of Americans want to be dependent on government. If Obama had lost, we could attribute it to a poor performance in the first debate, dissatisfaction with his health care or economic stimulus proposals, or the September 11, 2012, attack on the U.S. Consulate in Bengazi, Libya, which killed the American ambassador and three others.

TABLE » 8.9

GROUPS AND VOTES IN THE 2012 PRESIDENTIAL ELECTION

		PERCENT VOTE FOR	
		OBAMA	ROMNEY
Gender	Male	48%	53%
	Female	55	45
Age	18–29	60	40
	30–44	52	48
	45–64	51	49
	65 and over	44	56
Race/Ethnicity	White	41	59
	Black	93	7
	Hispanic	71	29
	Asian	73	27
Income	Under 30K	63	37
	30–49K	57	43
	50–100K	53	47
	100K or more	46	54

Source: Exit poll data at http://elections.nytimes.com/2012/results/president/exit-polls (accessed 11/7/12).

Sometimes campaigns do turn on a single event or decision. Todd Akin probably lost his Senate race in Missouri because of his comments about rape and pregnancy. Richard Lugar's defeat in the Indiana Senate primary was not due to his age or the Tea Party's efforts against him, but to the perception that he had lost touch with his constituents—a perception that became especially strong after it was discovered that he no longer had a residence in Indiana. After the candidate who defeated him, Richard Mourdock, commented during a debate that a pregnancy resulting from rape was something "God intended to happen," Mourdock's narrow lead turned into a sizable deficit, giving Democrat Joe Donnelly victory in the election.

More commonly, however, elections are decided by broadly held perceptions that develop over time and are hard to change. Obama's appeal was based on his economic stimulus programs, health care reform, ending of the wars in Iraq and Afghanistan, promises of immigration reform, and positions on social issues such as gay marriage and abortion rights. Romney's campaign emphasized opposition to the stimulus and health care reforms and promised to roll back regulations, promote a more aggressive foreign policy, and champion more conservative stands on social policy. These differences are reflected in the kinds of voters that supported each candidate, as shown in Table 8.9.

Table 8.9 shows that Obama's coalition was younger, more female, more diverse, and had lower incomes than those supporting Romney. These differences make sense given the issue positions and records of the two candidates and the opinions and preferences held by these groups, as discussed in Chapter 5.

Why, then, was the presidential contest so close—even at the end? For one thing, as we discuss in this chapter, presidents who win overwhelming victories either have a strong economy to talk about or an opponent who can be criticized for a weak performance or empty promises. Obama had neither of these things; nor did Romney. Moreover, as we discuss throughout this book, we are at a moment in American politics where the country is divided almost evenly on several major issues, from health care to social policy. Under these conditions, it is extraordinarily hard for any candidate to take issue positions that generate a large supporting coalition—positions that attract some votes will drive others away. As long as these conflicts persist, it is likely that we will continue to see close presidential elections.

CONCLUSION

Candidates in American national elections compete for different offices using a variety of rules that determine who can run for office, who can vote, and how ballots are counted and winners determined. Election outcomes are shaped by who runs for office and how they campaign, who decides to vote, and how they decide whom to support, but also by the rules that govern electoral competition.

It is easy to complain about American elections. Citizens are not experts about public policy. They often know little about the candidates running for office. Candidates sensationalize, attack, and dissemble rather than giving details about who they are and what they would do if elected. Even so, there are clear, systematic differences between Democratic and Republican candidates that translate into different government policies depending on who holds office. Moreover, the criteria that average Americans use to make vote decisions reflect these differences.

In addition, many examples of seemingly strange behavior in American elections make more sense once you examine them. It makes sense that so few Americans are issue voters and that many people decide to abstain. It also makes sense that candidates seeking the attention of distracted voters tend to emphasize sensationalism over sober discussion of policies. The outcome of the election is the result of all these individual-level choices added together. In that sense, election outcomes reflect the preferences of the American people.

American elections are not perfect, but it is impossible to say that they are irrelevant. By determining who holds political office, elections determine what government does. The 2010 and 2012 elections illustrate this point. After Republicans gained control of the House and won additional Senate seats in 2010, congressional Democrats and President Obama had to scale back plans for new policy initiatives. The last two years have also seen extended deadlock over deficit reduction and government spending, reflecting the divided control of government. The 2012 elections, which preserved this outcome, are likely to produce deadlock on many issues as well.

HOW DO AMERICAN ELECTIONS WORK?

▶ Present the major rules and procedures of American elections. **Pages 283–95**

SUMMARY

Elections in America generally have two steps. Primary elections select candidates for each party, and general elections determine who wins the office. Some of the rules for presidential elections differ from other elections; notably, the electoral college system determines the winner of the general election.

KEY TERMS

incumbent (p. 283)

open primary (p. 284)

closed primary (p. 284)

general election (p. 284)

plurality voting (p. 286)

majority voting (p. 286)

runoff election (p. 286)

primary (p. 289)

caucus (p. 289)

proportional allocation (p. 289)

winner-take-all (p. 289)

electoral college (p. 292)

popular vote (p. 294)

electoral votes (p. 295)

PRACTICE QUIZ QUESTIONS

1. Runoff elections only occur in states that use
   _____.
   a) majority voting
   b) primary elections
   c) plurality voting
   d) absentee ballots
   e) proportional allocation

2. The recent trend in the presidential nomination process has been to _____.
   a) schedule primary elections later in the process
   b) schedule primary elections earlier in the process
   c) replace primaries with caucuses
   d) break up primaries so that they are not held in the same region at the same time
   e) limit the influence of third party candidates

3. What are superdelegates?
   a) Democratic party officials who are free to support any candidate for nomination
   b) Democratic party officials who are constrained to support a particular candidate's nomination
   c) Republican party officials who are free to support any candidate for nomination
   d) Republican party officials who are constrained to support a particular candidate's nomination
   e) Officials from either party who have the power to veto a candidate's nomination

4. The winner-take-all method of allocating most states' electoral votes results in candidates focusing on _____ states and _____ states.
   a) low population; safe
   b) high population; safe
   c) low population; swing
   d) high population; swing
   e) safe; swing

Ⓢ PRACTICE ONLINE

"Big Think" video exercise: *Abolish the Electoral College?*

ELECTORAL CAMPAIGNS

▶ Describe the features and strategies of campaigns for federal office. **Pages 296–313**

SUMMARY

Party organizations and candidates begin preparing for the next election the day after the last election ends. They focus on fund-raising and determining which races are likely to be competitive. Incumbents work throughout the election cycle to maintain their good standing among the voters and secure their re-election bids. During a campaign, candidates work hard, particularly through the use of advertisements, to increase their name recognition and mobilize their supporters.

KEY TERMS

election cycle (p. 296)

open seat (p. 296)

political business cycle (p. 298)

GOTV ("get out the vote") or the **ground game** (p. 299)

Federal Election Commission (p. 307)

hard money (p. 308)

soft money (p. 308)

CRITICAL THINKING AND DISCUSSION

What kinds of candidates are helped by limits on campaign contributions by individuals and organizations such as PACs? What kinds of candidates do these restrictions hurt? Why do such limits affect these types of candidates differently?

PRACTICE QUIZ QUESTIONS

5. An open-seat election is one where _____.
   a) there is no challenger in the race
   b) there is no incumbent in the race
   c) an incumbent loses his/her seat due to redistricting
   d) an incumbent faces a challenger in his/her own primary
   e) an incumbent faces a challenger in the general election

6. What effect does fund-raising have for incumbents?
   a) It ensures the potential for an aggressive campaign, but it has no effect on opposition.
   b) It ensures the potential for an aggressive campaign, and it deters opposition.
   c) It ensures the potential for an aggressive campaign, and it encourages opposition.
   d) It has no effect on the potential for an aggressive campaign, but it does deter opposition.
   e) It has no effect on the potential for an aggressive campaign, nor does it deter opposition.

7. GOTV and "ground game" refer to a candidate's attempts to _____.
   a) boost name recognition
   b) mobilize supporters
   c) increase fundraising
   d) deter opposition
   e) win endorsements

8. Research shows that modern campaign ads are likely to _____.
   a) change voters' minds
   b) feature speeches by the candidate
   c) have beneficial effects, such as informing voters
   d) run several minutes in length
   e) increase turnout

9. What is soft money?
   a) money that can be given directly to a candidate
   b) money that is given by members of the opposing party
   c) money that can be spent to mobilize voters for a specific candidate
   d) money that candidates spend to boost the party's reputation
   e) money that is not tied to a specific candidate

Ⓢ PRACTICE ONLINE

"Critical Thinking" exercise: *Politics Is Conflictual—Campaign Ads*

HOW DO VOTERS DECIDE?

▶ Explain the key factors that influence voters' choices. **Pages 313–21**

SUMMARY

Despite the fact that politics is everywhere, ordinary voters don't pay much attention to politics. Turnout rates are modest, and people know relatively little about the candidates and their positions. While some voters are highly interested in politics and collect all the information they can about the candidates, most voters make their decision based on voting cues. Most elections are determined by local-level politics, but occasionally national issues come to the fore.

KEY TERMS

paradox of voting (p. 313)

issue voters (p. 315)

voting cues (p. 315)

coattails (p. 318)

split ticket (p. 318)

straight ticket (p. 318)

CRITICAL THINKING AND DISCUSSION

Using cues to make vote decisions lowers the cost of voting, in terms of the time and effort involved in a voter's decision. Under what conditions will cues help a voter make the right choice in an election, defined as the same choice that would result from having complete information about the candidates? Under what conditions will cues lead a voter to make the wrong choice?

PRACTICE QUIZ QUESTIONS

10. What is the paradox of voting?
   a) Voting is costly and the chances of affecting the election outcome are small.
   b) Voting is costly and approval for government is high.
   c) Voting is easy and the chances of affecting the election outcome are large.
   d) Voting is easy but informing yourself about the candidates takes time.
   e) Approval for government is low, but voter turnout rates are high.

11. Voters who rely on voting cues to determine their vote choice are _____.
   a) likely to cast a reasonable vote, regardless of their information level
   b) unlikely to cast a reasonable vote, regardless of their information level
   c) likely to cast a reasonable vote, and more so if they are informed
   d) unlikely to cast a reasonable vote, and less so if they are informed
   e) neither more nor less likely to cast a reasonable vote than voters who ignore cues.

12. Weak coattails and split tickets serve as indicators that _____.
   a) most voters don't know anything about the candidates
   b) most elections are determined by local issues
   c) most elections are determined by national issues
   d) most voters use political parties as their dominant voting cue
   e) most voters use incumbency as their dominant voting cue

> ## ⓢ PRACTICE ONLINE
>
> "What Do Political Scientists Do?" video exercise:
> *Party Identification and Independent Voters*

UNDERSTANDING THE 2012 ELECTIONS

▶ Analyze the issues and outcomes in the 2012 elections. **Pages 322–31**

The 2012 elections preserved the status quo, with a Republican House, a Democratic Senate, and the re-election of President Obama. With the nation divided on many questions and a lackluster national economy, the presidential campaigns focused on a small number of swing states, including Ohio, Florida, and Virginia. President Obama's victory owed much to his campaign's extensive mobilization efforts and success at portraying Republican Mitt Romney as out of touch with the concerns of average Americans.

PRACTICE QUIZ QUESTIONS

13. What is the most accurate statement about the role of economic conditions in the 2012 election?
    a) Looking across the entire nation, economic conditions did not strongly favor either candidate.
    b) The Obama campaign's mobilization efforts offset the loss of support from a weak economy.
    c) Mitt Romney's campaign avoided talking about the economy.
    d) Economic conditions did not matter because most Americans based their vote on other issues.
    e) The Obama campaign convinced voters that Republican Senate leaders were to blame for the poor economy.

14. What role did the question of marriage rights for gays and lesbians play in the 2012 election?
    a) Surveys showed that President Obama gained many votes because of his continued opposition to allowing gays to marry.
    b) Neither campaign emphasized this issue.
    c) Mitt Romney did not talk about this issue because of his Mormon religious beliefs.
    d) In contrast to 2010, more voters saw the issue as important.
    e) Both candidates supported a constitutional amendment to allow gays and lesbians to marry.

15. Why was congressional turnover so low in 2012?
    a) Incumbents used the redistricting process to build safe districts.
    b) Spending on campaign ads by outside groups favored House and Senate incumbents.
    c) Neither party could find enough qualified challengers to run in House and Senate races.
    d) Too many House members and senators lost primary elections.
    e) Most vulnerable House members and senators had already lost in 2008 and 2010.

SUGGESTED READING

Abramson, Paul, John Aldrich, and David Rohde. *Change and Continuity in the 2004 and 2006 Elections.* Washington, DC: CQ Press, 2007.

Bartels, Larry. *Presidential Primaries and the Dynamics of Public Choice.* Princeton, NJ: Princeton University Press, 1988.

Cramer, Richard Ben. *What It Takes: The Way to the White House.* New York: Vintage, 1993.

Donovan, Todd, and Shaun Bowler. *Reforming the Republic: Democratic Institutions for the New America.* New York: Pearson, 2007.

Fiorina, Morris P. *Retrospective Voting in American National Elections.* New Haven, CT: Yale University Press, 1981.

Hellemann, John, and Mark Halpern. *Game Change: Obama and the Clintons, McCain and Palin, and the Race of a Lifetime.* New York: Random House, 2009.

Jacobson, Gary. *The Politics of Congressional Elections,* 6th ed. New York: Pearson Longman, 2004.

Key, V. O. *The Responsible Electorate.* New York: Vintage, 1966.

Museum of the Moving Image, "The Living Room Candidate: Presidential Campaign Commercials, 1952–2004," online exhibit at http://livingroomcandidate.movingimage.us.

Niemi, Richard G., and Herbert F. Weisberg. *Controversies in Voting Behavior,* 4th ed. Washington, DC: CQ Press, 2001.

Popkin, Samuel. *The Reasoning Voter.* Chicago: University of Chicago Press, 1991.

9

Interest Groups

THE GROUPS INVOLVED IN THE OCCUPY Wall Street movement argued that the government showered benefits on wealthy corporations and individuals, while ordinary Americans ("the 99%") struggled. They claimed that lobbying efforts by corporations influenced government policy.

DESPITE DISAGREEING ABOUT MANY ASPECTS OF AMERICAN politics and public policy, one thing that the groups involved in the Occupy Wall Street movement generally opposed was the federal government's bailout in 2008 and 2009 of major banks and financial institutions. The federal bailouts, they argued, rewarded the same firms whose actions had caused widespread economic distress—distress that made the bailouts crucial to the firms' survival. These groups also agreed on why the bailout occurred: lobbying efforts by the corporations that stood to gain from a bailout. In their view, lobbying together and separately allowed these firms to achieve a change in government policy that made them vastly better off—in some cases, saved them from going bankrupt—at the expense of the great majority of the American public, many of whom lost their jobs or saw their home values plummet, but received no special government help.

At first glance, there is evidence to support these claims. An analysis conducted by the Center for Responsive Politics (CRP) argued that a firm's success in getting funds from the government's principal bailout program, the Troubled Assets Relief Program (TARP), hinged on its lobbying efforts. Twenty-five firms spent a total of $114 million on lobbying in 2008 and received a total of $295 billion from TARP. Many of the firms that spent a lot on lobbying, such as AIG, Citigroup, and Bank of America, received some of the higher TARP allocations. As the head of the CRP put it, "Even in the best economic times, you won't find an investment with a greater payoff than what these companies

CONFLICT & COMPROMISE
in American Politics

have been getting. Some of the companies and industries that have received payments may now consider their contributions and lobbying to be the smartest investments they've made in years."[1] Looking at the same evidence, one member of Congress claimed that "Wall Street owns Washington."[2]

With examples like these, it is not surprising that Americans are suspicious of interest groups and worry about their ability to dominate the political process. What do these companies get from lobbying? How can average Americans change government policy when they are fighting against organizations that have millions of dollars and extensive connections on their side? Even if individuals try to form new groups to advance their policy goals, their battle against well-entrenched groups does not seem like a fair fight. Moreover, despite the proliferation of interest groups and lobbyists in America, some large groups of like-minded Americans have no identifiable interest group fighting for their policy concerns. Where, for example, are the groups that lobby for what college students want? And how can debates over policy be considered a fair fight when some groups are unrepresented in the process?

This chapter surveys the wide range of interest groups in American politics, from large, powerful groups such as the National Rifle Association (NRA) to small organizations that lobby on issues that concern only a few Americans. In part, our discussion will confirm the conventional wisdom: conflicts over government policy are the driving force behind interest group activities. For example, the NRA fights to maintain and extend Americans' ability to own and carry firearms, while other groups, such as Handgun Control, work to impose restrictions on these rights. Government policy reflects, at least in part, the actions taken by these groups.

However, interest groups are not only the tools of the rich and powerful. Virtually all Americans belong to interest groups or have groups that lobby on their behalf. And many of the clubs, groups, and organizations to which Americans belong have little known yet extensive lobbying arms. Moreover, policy victories do not always go to the organization that spends the most money or has hired the most expensive talent. Groups can succeed by mobilizing their members, forming alliances with other groups, becoming sources of political or policy expertise, or using the courts to fight policy battles. Thus, although people are correct to understand interest groups in terms of conflict, they are wrong in thinking that these groups invariably work against the interests of average Americans. Moreover, groups often serve as a source of compromise in the policy process, either in the proposals they offer or their efforts to work together with other groups.

You will also see that many of the claims about the vast influence of interest groups are not supported by evidence. In the case of TARP, for example, some firms received relatively little in bailout funds even though they lobbied a lot— General Motors (GM), for example, spent the most of any firm on lobbying but received far less than the top TARP recipients. One bank, Wells Fargo, spent only a tenth of what GM did on lobbying but received more than twice the TARP allocation. Other firms, such as E*Trade, spent considerable amounts on lobbying but were denied TARP funding.

In the end, the example of TARP does not reveal that interest groups are all-powerful in American politics. Rather, it shows how America's political institutions provide many opportunities for groups to influence policy making. Thus, while it is surely wrong to say that interest groups are irrelevant—in many cases, their efforts have an important impact on public policy—it is equally wrong to say that they are the dominant force in the policy process.

THE INTEREST GROUP UNIVERSE

DEFINE INTEREST GROUPS AND DESCRIBE THE CHARACTERISTICS OF DIFFERENT TYPES OF GROUPS

Interest groups are organizations that seek to influence government policy by helping to elect candidates who support their policy goals and by **lobbying** elected officials and bureaucrats. In its most basic form, lobbying involves persuasion—using reports, protests, informal meetings, or other techniques to convince an elected official or bureaucrat to help enact a law, craft a regulation, or do something else that a group wants. The members of an interest group can be individual citizens, local governments, businesses, foundations or nonprofit organizations, churches, or virtually any other entity. An interest group's employees or members may lobby on the group's behalf, or a group may hire a lobbyist or lobbying firm to do the work for it. Groups may lobby on their own, or work with other groups to enact compromise proposals. Nuts and Bolts 9.1 gives some examples of the types of interest groups found in contemporary American politics.

In general, lobbying is anti-majoritarian, in the sense that groups often lobby for policy changes that will help a small fraction of the population at the expense of everyone else. To some extent, this characteristic of lobbying is inevitable—policy changes that benefit majorities are already likely to be enacted due to strong public support, making lobbying irrelevant. However, the anti-majoritarian feature of lobbying raises an important question: on balance, looking across the entire range of interest groups, does lobbying benefit everyone, or are some people and groups left out, either because no interest group exists to fight for what they want, or because lobbying efforts on their behalf were unsuccessful? In the case of TARP, for example, one claim is that the banks and other recipients of bailouts had strong lobbying operations, while ordinary citizens had no one fighting on their behalf.

Interest groups and political parties both hope to change what government does, but there are three critical differences between these organizations. First, political parties focus on running candidates for office and coordinating the activities of elected officials. Some interest groups do these things, but they do not have an official position on electoral ballots to offer their candidates. Moreover many interest groups do not get involved in elections at all. Second, the major political parties hold certain legal advantages over even the largest interest groups when it comes to influencing policy (one such advantage is having guaranteed positions on electoral ballots). Third, the elected members of political parties have a direct influence over government activity: they propose, debate, and vote on policies. In contrast, interest groups have, at best, an indirect influence: they must either persuade elected officials to support their point of view or help elect candidates who already share their goals.

Sometimes interest groups are primarily political organizations. One such group is Public Citizen, which conducts research projects, lobbies legislators and bureaucrats, and tries to rally public opinion on a range of environmental, health, and energy issues. Usually, though, lobbying is only one part of what an organization does. The NRA, for example,

interest group An organization of people who share common political interests and aim to influence public policy by electioneering and lobbying.

lobbying Efforts to influence public policy through contact with public officials on behalf of an interest group.

MORE THAN 4 MILLION INDIVIDUALS belong to the National Rifle Association, one of the most powerful interest groups in America. At their national convention, shown here, members can attend a gun show and meetings where they debate the group's goals and select leaders.

TYPES OF INTEREST GROUPS

Scholars often divide interest groups into categories based on who their members are or the number or kinds of things they lobby for. While it's important to not take these categories too literally—very few groups, for example, lobby on only one issue—the categories explain what kinds of interest groups exist and what they lobby for.

▶ *Economic groups* include corporations, trade associations, labor groups, and professional organizations. Economic interest groups aim to influence policy in ways that will bring their members economic—that is, monetary—benefits. Many corporations such as Microsoft, Exxon, or Boeing have lobbying operations that petition government for contracts or favorable regulations of their firm or industry.

▶ *Labor organizations* are another kind of economic group. The American Federation of Labor and Congress of Industrial Organizations (AFL-CIO) lobbies for regulations that make it easy for workers to form labor unions, and a range of other policies. Professional organizations, a third type of economic group, lobby for government policies that financially benefit their members.

▶ The second interest group category is *citizen groups*, or public interest groups. This category captures a range of organizations, from those with mass membership (such as the Sierra Club) to those that have no members but claim to speak for large segments of the population. One such group is the Family Research Council, which describes itself as "promoting the Judeo-Christian worldview as the basis for a just, free, and stable society." This group lobbies for a range of policies, from legislation that defines marriage as between a man and a woman to legislation that would eliminate estate taxes.

▶ The third category of interest group is the *single-issue groups*. These groups focus on a narrow range of topics or a single government program or piece of legislation. Examples include the National Right to Life Committee, which lobbies for restrictions on abortion rights, and NumbersUSA, which lobbies against guest worker programs for noncitizens.

endorses candidates, contributes to campaigns, and lobbies elected officials. But it also runs gun safety classes, holds competitions, and sells gun accessories to its members. In other cases, interest group activity is almost hidden within an organization. For example, most drivers know the AAA (formerly the Automobile Association of America) as a provider of emergency roadside service and maps, but AAA is also an interest group that lobbies for increased funding for highways and less for mass transit.

As these descriptions suggest, interest groups and lobbying are ubiquitous in American politics. Many organizations have lobbying operations or hire lobbyists to work on their behalf. You may think that you don't belong to a group that lobbies the federal government, but the odds are that you do.

In fact, one important view of American politics, pluralism, identifies interest groups as America's fundamental political actors.[3] Pluralists argue that most Americans participate in politics through their membership in interest groups like Public Citizen, the NRA, or even AAA. These groups lobby, try to elect candidates who share their views, and negotiate among themselves to encourage legislators to pursue policies that benefit their members. Others describe America as an **interest group state**, meaning that these groups are involved whenever policy is made.[4]

interest group state A government in which most policy decisions are determined by the influence of interest groups.

THE BUSINESS OF LOBBYING

Interest group lobbying is heavily regulated.[5] Lobbying firms must file annual reports identifying their clients and specifying how much each client paid. Similarly,

INTEREST GROUPS IN OTHER NATIONS

Just as in America, people all over the world have ideas about what they would like government to do, and they organize to shape policies in line with their preferences, making interest groups a fundamental component of democracy.[a] Studies have even found that the longer a country has been a democracy, the more interest groups it has.[b] Interest groups in other countries are also structured similarly to those that operate in America. They are often either affiliated with or part of larger organizations, such as labor unions, ethnic associations, or religious groups. Citizens often belong to several interest groups.

While many more data are available about lobbying in the United States than for other countries, the sheer number and types of groups appears to be much the same. For example, one study categorized the kinds of organizations that lobbied the European Union (EU) in 2008, as shown in the figure.[c] As you see, the vast majority of these organizations are interest groups, although corporations, trade associations, and even a few labor unions lobbied the EU as well.

Comparing countries also reveals three important differences in how interest groups lobby. First, the targets of their lobbying vary. As discussed in Chapter 7, political parties are often stronger in many European countries than they are in America. When parties are strong, individual politicians have to follow the orders of party leaders or risk being removed from office or prevented from running in the first place.[d] As a result, interest groups in these countries focus on lobbying party lead-

Interest groups are active in almost every democracy. In 2011 and 2012, labor groups in Greece helped organize protests intended to influence the Greek government and the European Union.

ers rather than individual legislators, who ultimately have to do what party leaders demand.

Interest groups in other nations are also typically subject to stringent campaign finance restrictions.[e] In Great Britain, for example, interest groups cannot contribute to the campaigns of individual candidates for Parliament. In many other European countries, interest groups can run campaign ads but must cease doing so during the last days of the electoral campaign.

Differences in governmental institutions also change how interest groups lobby.[f] Consider parliamentary systems, where the party controlling the legislature selects not only the prime minister, who serves as the head of the government, but also the ministers who control specific organizations within the government. In the American system, the branches of government are often controlled by different political parties, so interest groups face a choice. Should they lobby the executive branch to seek a regulation that suits their purposes, or should they lobby Congress for a budget request or new legislation? In a parliamentary system, this choice does not exist: interest groups can only lobby the party in power.

A final difference in the way interest groups abroad lobby has to do with the influence of the European Union.[g] Interest groups in the member states that want a change in policy can lobby either their own government or the legislators and bureaucrats in the EU government for policies that would apply to all member states.

LOBBYING THE EU

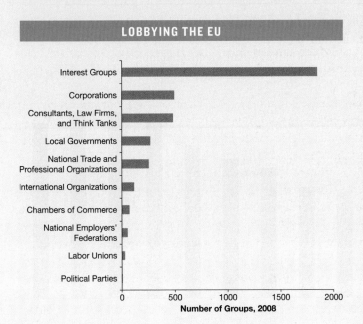

Number of Groups, 2008

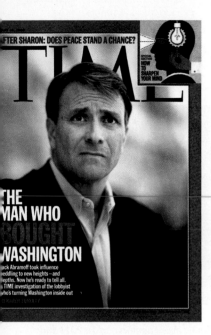

interest groups and corporations must file reports listing staff members who spent more than 20 percent of their time lobbying Congress, and detailing expenditures to lobbying firms. Also, most executive or legislative branch employees who take lobbying jobs are legally required to refrain from lobbying people in their former office or agency for one year; elected officials who become lobbyists must wait two years.

Today, lobbying involves billions of dollars a year. Figure 9.1 presents annual lobbying expenditures for 2000 through 2011. As the figure shows, a total of $3.27 billion was spent on lobbying in 2011. Figure 9.2 indicates that a multitude of groups and organizations lobby the federal government. The amount spent as well as the number of groups lobbying government has increased significantly over the last decade.

Why are there so many interest groups and registered lobbyists, and why are their numbers increasing? Figure 9.2 suggests that this proliferation is related to the large size and widespread influence of the federal government. People get involved and lobby because they have a stake in what the government does. They want their company to get a government contract, or they want a new regulation to favor their business sector. They want the government to either limit what citizens can do or relax restrictions on behavior. Simply put, the federal government does so many things and spends so much money that many individuals, organizations, and corporations have strong incentives for lobbying. Studies of Washington-based lobbying operations confirm this: interest groups are more likely to form around issues that have high levels of government involvement, or when new programs or changes in government policy are likely.[6] Moreover, as groups form on one side of a policy question and start to lobby, people who oppose them may form their own interest groups and start lobbying as well, either separately or in concert.[7]

FIGURE » 9.1

TOTAL SPENDING ON LOBBYING, 2000–2011

These data show that in recent years, interest groups have spent several billion dollars lobbying the federal government—and their spending is steadily increasing. Does this amount seem surprisingly large or surprisingly small, given what lobbyists do?

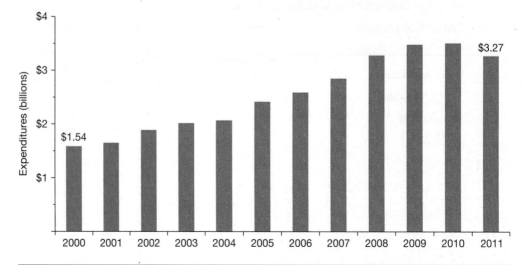

Source: Center for Responsive Politics, "Total Lobbying Spending," www.opensecrets.org/lobby/index.php; "Lobbying Database," *www.opensecrets.org/lobby/index.php (accessed 1/30/12).*

FIGURE » 9.2

GROWTH IN FEDERAL SPENDING AND IN LOBBYING

In general, as the federal government has grown, so has the number of lobbyists. One explanation is that lobbyists get the government to spend money that it otherwise would not. Can you think of a different explanation that is consistent with the data?

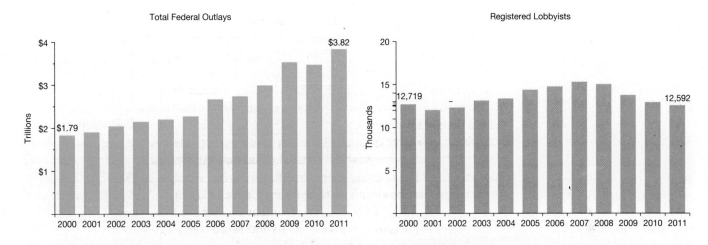

Source: Center for Responsive Politics, "Lobbying Database," www.opensecrets.org/lobby/index.php (accessed 1/30/12); GPO Access, Budget of the United States Government, Historical Table 1.1 (FY 2012), available at www.gpoaccess.gov/usbudget/fy09/hist.html (accessed 1/30/12).

The pressure of lobbying is especially strong when large new policy initiatives are under consideration, such as President Obama's health care reforms.[8]

Changes in communication technology may also contribute to the increasing numbers of interest groups and lobbyists.[9] Television and the Internet make it easier for people to discover their common interests, and cell phones, e-mail, social networking, and other forms of electronic communication enable geographically dispersed groups to organize and implement lobbying strategies. Even so, many like-minded groups in America remain **latent** or unorganized, without a group to represent them, suggesting that some people still opt not to participate.

The expenditures shown in Figure 9.1 pay for many things. For example, beginning in 2003, lobbyists for the Boeing Corporation were working to secure a government contract with the U.S. military for Boeing to build tanker aircraft (planes that can refuel other planes in midair). A Boeing memo detailed the effort: along with meetings between Boeing employees and Department of Defense staff to negotiate the contact, Boeing's lobbyists and employees were meeting with members of Congress, congressional staff, senior members of President Bush's staff, and the leaders of labor unions whose members worked for Boeing.[10] Boeing also ran ads in Washington newspapers promoting its tanker proposal. Thus, in pursuing the contract, Boeing paid the salaries of its employees who planned and executed the lobbying effort, paid for outside lobbyists and their meetings on Capitol Hill, and spent money on broader publicity efforts. Despite this campaign, Boeing did not win the contract, nor did any other company. The Air Force decided to initiate a new competition in 2010, in part because Boeing argued that the first competition was unfair to its proposal. Ultimately, Boeing won the contract.

latent A group of politically like-minded people that is not represented by any interest group.

TABLE » 9.1

TOP 20 SPENDERS ON LOBBYING, 1998–2012

U.S. Chamber of Commerce	$885,975,680
General Electric	$274,100,000
American Medical Association	$274,017,500
American Hospital Association	$225,269,136
Pharmaceutical Research & Manufacturers of America	$224,263,920
AARP	$217,612,064
National Association of Realtors	$194,515,133
Blue Cross/Blue Shield	$191,452,052
Northrop Grumman	$180,565,253
Exxon Mobil	$176,362,742
Verizon Communications	$167,546,543
Edison Electric Institute	$165,566,789
Boeing Company	$164,139,310
Business Roundtable	$162,910,000
Lockheed Martin	$158,350,688
AT&T, Inc.	$145,529,336
Southern Company	$138,680,694
National Cable & Telecommunications Association	$132,340,000
General Motors	$131,704,170
Pfizer, Inc.	$126,227,268

Source: "Top Spenders," www.opensecrets.org/lobby/top.php?indexType=s (accessed 9/11/12).

The disclosure data in Table 9.1 also reveal the big spenders. Dominating the list are corporations like General Electric (GE) and business groups such as the Chamber of Commerce. Two exceptions are the American Medical Association and AARP (formerly the American Association of Retired Persons). Of General Electric's $11.4 million spent on lobbying in 2006, more than $8 million was spent on GE employees, and the remaining $3 million paid for the services of fourteen lobbying firms.[11]

Most interest groups or corporations spend much less on lobbying efforts. The Sierra Club, for example, spent less than $100,000 on lobbying in 2006.[12] All of these funds helped pay the salaries of Sierra Club employees whose jobs include lobbying. Many other groups spend even less, barely scraping together enough cash to send someone to plead their case in Washington.

Other companies lobby through their membership in **trade associations**. Consider the National Beer Wholesalers Association (NBWA), a nationwide group of local businesses that buy beer from brewers and resell it to stores and

trade association An interest group composed of companies in the same business or industry (the same "trade") that lobbies for policies that benefit members of the group.

RESTRICTIONS ON INTEREST GROUP LOBBYING

In 2005, a major lobbyist, Jack Abramoff, was accused of using "golf junkets, meals at his restaurant, seats at sporting events, and, in some cases, old-fashioned cash" to lobby members of Congress.[a] Abramoff was convicted in 2006 of conspiracy, fraud, and tax evasion. Representative Bob Ney (R-Ohio) and several aides and high-ranking bureaucrats were also convicted of accepting Abramoff's bribes or making false statements about their relationship with him.[b] The case suggests that some interest groups and lobbying firms are not playing by the rules. Rather than just making their case to officials, they are offering money and other inducements in return for policy change.

It seems that to solve this problem, interest groups and lobbying firms should be regulated to ensure that they cannot unfairly dominate the policy process by buying support from members of Congress and bureaucrats. This proposal raises two questions. First, would new regulations prevent abuses of power? Second, are such abuses of power commonplace enough to justify a new regulation?

Consider the six-point lobbying reform proposal offered after the Abramoff scandal by a coalition of six public interest groups.[c]

1. Place low limits on interest groups' contributions to candidates.

2. Ban interest groups from providing subsidized travel to people in government.

3. Ban gifts from interest groups and their staff to members of Congress and congressional staff.

4. Establish an independent ethics review board to oversee interactions between lobbyists and both Congress and the bureaucracy, and increase penalties for ethics violations.

5. Ban former members of Congress, legislative staff, and bureaucrats from lobbying for two years after leaving office.

6. Require electronic filing of lobbying registration forms and congresspersons' financial disclosure forms.

Most of these proposals seem unobjectionable. Even so, there are three fundamental problems with these restrictions. First, some of them violate freedoms that many Americans value. The campaign finance restrictions in point one would make it harder for people to organize to influence elections. For example, the amount that groups such as the NRA or AARP contribute to political campaigns would be severely limited compared to the current rules. A second problem is that it is difficult to tell whether these regulations would work as intended. As discussed in this chapter, interest groups are already highly regulated in terms of who can lobby, how they can lobby, and what kinds of gifts and assistance they can offer to government officials. Giv-

This cartoon summarizes public assumptions about lobbying and its impact on members of Congress. In reality, Jack Abramoff's conduct is the exception rather than the rule among lobbyists

ing legislators, staffers, or bureaucrats gifts in return for policy changes is already against the law, and if those laws aren't working, it is hard to see how new, similar laws will solve the problem.

Finally, this chapter shows that these reforms are, to some extent, based on a misunderstanding of how interest groups operate. The case of Jack Abramoff is interesting precisely *because* it is a glaring exception. Most interest groups are small and have such limited resources that they couldn't offer gifts or threaten to withhold large campaign donations even if they wanted to. Moreover, interest groups tend to focus on offering advice and information to people in government who already support their goals. None of the reforms described here would change anything about those practices, except to add some additional reporting requirements and further limit their (already restricted) ability to hire people who used to work in government. (Moreover, additional restrictions on electioneering might not be possible given the *Citizens United* decision discussed in Chapter 8.)

Critical **Thinking** Questions

1. To what extent do you think these laws will curb illegal behavior by interest groups—especially in light of the fact that existing laws do not?

2. Are these laws aimed at exceptional cases or average interest groups?

restaurants. The NBWA's principal lobbying goal is to ensure that laws remain in place requiring middlemen between beer producers and the stores, bars, and restaurants that sell beer to consumers. If the rules change to allow beer producers to deal with the end-sellers directly, then the NBWA's members are out of a job.

Although the amount of money spent on lobbying by interest groups may seem like a lot, it is small compared to how much is at stake.[13] The federal government now spends more than $3 trillion every year. In recent years, spending by interest groups and by the lobbying arms of organizations and corporations amounts to $3 billion every year. That's a lot of money, but it's still only about 0.1 percent of total federal spending. This difference raises a critical question: if interest groups could control policy choices by spending money on lobbying, why aren't they spending more?

ORGANIZATIONAL STRUCTURES

centralized groups Interest groups that have a headquarters, usually in Washington, D.C., as well as members and field offices throughout the country. In general, these groups' lobbying decisions are made at headquarters by the group leaders.

confederations Interest groups made up of several independent, local organizations that provide much of their funding and hold most of the power.

There are two main models of interest group structure. Most large, well-known organizations like AARP and the NRA are **centralized groups**. These national organizations typically have headquarters in Washington, D.C., field offices in large state capitals, and members nationwide. Their defining feature is that the organization's leadership is concentrated in its headquarters. These leaders have the responsibility to determine the group's lobbying goals and tactics. The other structural model is a **confederation**, which comprises largely independent, local organizations. For example, the National Independent Automobile Dealers Association (NADA) is made up of fifty state-level organizations that provide most of the membership benefits to car dealers who join the organization, and raise much of the money that NADA contributes to candidates running for political office (several million dollars in recent elections).

Both organizational structures have advantages and disadvantages. A centralized organization controls all of the group's resources and can deploy them efficiently, but it can be challenging for these groups to find out what their members want. Confederations have the advantage of maintaining independent chapters at the state and local levels, so it is easier for the national headquarters to learn

CENTRALIZED INTEREST GROUPS in America often have an office in Washington, D.C., which helps them to stay in touch with members of Congress, bureaucrats, and the president and his staff. It also provides a venue for attracting press coverage of the group's concerns. This 2009 town hall meeting on health care held at the Washington headquarters of AARP was attended by President Obama.

what their members want—all they have to do is contact their local groups. But this strength is closely related to a weakness. State and local chapters mostly function independently of the national headquarters, since they attract members and raise money largely on their own. The national headquarters depends on the local organizations for funds to pay its staff and make campaign contributions. Thus, in most confederated organizations, when local chapters send money to headquarters to be used for campaign contributions, they also specify which candidates they want to receive it.[14] As a result, confederated groups often are beset with conflict, as different local chapters disagree over what to lobby for and which candidates to support.

Two sets of organizations that are hard to categorize are the Tea Party movement discussed in Chapter 7 and the Occupy Wall Street groups mentioned in the introduction to this chapter. The organizations that make up both of these movements are very diverse. Some hold meetings or public protests, some endorse candidates, and some are simply a website run by one or two people. The issues that motivate each organization also vary widely, from opposition to or support for President Obama to calls for radical changes in government. Virtually all lack formal dues-paying members, a headquarters, or a formal organizational structure, and few engage in the wide range of lobbying activities that we describe later in this chapter. Moreover, it is unclear whether many of these organizations will survive more than a few months or years. For all these reasons, very few of the organizations that identify themselves as part of the Tea Party or Occupy movements are interest groups as we describe them here, although some may evolve into formal interest groups in the future.

STAFF

Interest group staff falls into two categories: experts on the group's main policy areas, and people with useful government connections and knowledge of procedures. The first group includes scientists, engineers, and others with advanced degrees; the second is dominated by people who have worked inside government as elected officials, bureaucrats, or legislative staff.[15] Sometimes these former members of government are also policy experts, but their unique contribution is their knowledge of how government works and their relationships with officeholders and other former coworkers.

The practice of moving from a government position to one with an interest group or lobbying firm, or transitioning from lobbyist to officeholder, is often called the **revolving door**.[16] A 2005 study found that from 1998 to 2005, more than 40 percent of members leaving the House or Senate joined a lobbying firm after their departure.[17] A separate study in 2006 found that more than two-thirds of the Department of Homeland Security's original senior staff left their positions to work for corporations or lobbying firms.[18] Examples such as these were behind President Obama's policy to bar people who served in his administration from lobbying the government after they left their position, and to prevent registered lobbyists who are appointed to government positions from administering policies or agencies that they once lobbied.[19]

The Obama policy highlights the dilemma of the revolving door. On one hand, people who have worked in industry or as lobbyists know a particular field and the relevant laws, making them well qualified to work in this area for the executive branch. Similarly, former officeholders, congressional staff, and bureaucrats are attractive to lobbying firms, as they have firsthand knowledge of how policies are made and enjoy established relationships with people in government.

revolving door The movement of individuals from government positions to jobs with interest groups or lobbying firms, and vice versa.

MANY INTEREST GROUPS SPEAK FOR large numbers of Americans, but some lobby for changes that would benefit only a few people or a single corporation. The Coalition for Luggage Security, for example, has only one member: a company that specializes in shipping travelers' baggage, which would gain considerable business if the coalition's lobbying efforts succeeded.

mass associations Interest groups that have a large number of dues-paying individuals as members.

peak associations Interest groups whose members are businesses or other organizations rather than individuals.

Thus, although Obama's policy was well intentioned, it may lead to a shortage of experienced candidates for government positions. On the other hand, the problem with the revolving door is that people in government may try to help particular firms and interest groups in return for a well-paid position after they leave government service. Or, when the influence works in the opposite direction, lobbyists-turned-lawmakers may favor the firms and organizations that once employed them. It is very hard to craft restrictions that avoid these problems.

MEMBERSHIP

Interest groups can also be distinguished by the size of their membership and the members' role in the group's activities. Some are **mass associations** with many dues-paying members. One example is the Sierra Club, which has more than 750,000 members who each pay annual dues of about $30. Besides keeping its members informed about the making of environmental policy in Washington, D.C., the Sierra Club endorses judicial nominees and candidates for elected positions, and works with members of Congress to develop legislative proposals. The group's members elect the organization's board of directors.

However, not all mass associations give members a say in selecting a group's leaders or determining its mission. To join AARP, which has more than 35 million members, you have to be at least 50 years old and pay dues of about $16 per year. Members get discounts on insurance, car rentals, and hotels, as well as driver safety courses and help doing their taxes. AARP claims to lobby for policies its members favor, but members actually have no control over which legislative causes the group chooses. Moreover, AARP does not poll members to determine its issue positions, nor do members pick AARP leadership.

Peak associations have a different type of membership,[20] exemplified by the Business-Industry Political Action Committee (BIPAC). This association of several hundred businesses and trade associations aims to elect "pro-business individuals" to Congress.[21] Individuals cannot join peak associations—they may work for member companies or organizations, but they cannot become dues-paying members on their own.

RESOURCES

The resources that interest groups use to support their lobbying efforts are people, money, and expertise. We examine interest group strategies in a later section; here we emphasize that a group's resources influence its available lobbying strategies. Some groups have sufficient funding and staff to pursue a wide range of strategies, while smaller groups with fewer resources have only a few lobbying options.

PEOPLE

A crucial resource for most interest groups is the membership. Group members can write to or meet with elected officials, travel to Washington for demonstrations, and even offer expertise or advice to their leaders. When the "members" of a group are corporations, as is the case with trade associations, CEOs and other corporate staff can help with the group's lobbying efforts.

Many mass organizations try to get their members involved in the lobbying process. MoveOn.org, for example, has a web page that helps people send letters to the editors of various national and local newspapers. MoveOn hopes to bring public attention to its political priorities by getting these web-generated letters printed. Using the organization's site, you provide your address, choose from a list of papers to contact, and compose a message—using MoveOn's "talking points," which cover a wide range of issues—if you choose. The page automatically imports your message into correctly addressed e-mails to your selected newspapers.[22] Other groups have similar pages that send e-mails to members of Congress or to the president.

Interest groups' ability to use people as a resource faces two major challenges. First, it requires having members, but recruiting new members can be difficult and expensive. The second challenge is motivating members to participate, especially since those who don't participate will reap the same policy benefits as those who do if the group succeeds. As we discuss later, although some interest groups have managed to change government policy by persuading their members to write to and visit elected officials, the more common situation is that interest groups ask for members' help but receive little response.[23]

MONEY

Virtually everything interest groups do, from meeting with elected officials to fighting for what they want in court, can be purchased as services. Money can also go toward campaign contributions or developing and running campaign ads. And, of course, money is necessary to fund interest groups' everyday operations.

Well-funded interest groups have a considerable advantage in the lobbying process. If they need an expert, a lobbyist, or a lawyer, they can hire one. They can pay for campaign ads and make campaign contributions, while groups with less cash cannot use these strategies. The importance of money for interest group operations is evident in their funding appeals to members. For example, the donations page from the Sierra Club's website shows that supporters can give a membership as a gift, join as a life member, or pay dues monthly. They can make commemorative or memorial gifts, set up a planned giving scheme, or donate stock. The group even offers gift-giving plans for non-U.S. residents and a Spanish-language version of its donations page.

For many groups, spending on lobbying is sensitive to economic conditions. For example, many banking and financial firms slashed lobbying expenditures during early 2009, even though they faced government proposals to limit top executives' pay and to impose restrictions on many transactions. Because these firms were facing huge losses and declining revenues, they cut expenses across the board, including amounts spent on lobbying. As these companies' balance sheets improved later in 2009, their lobbying expenses increased to previous levels.

Still, groups can be effective without spending much. They can rely on members to lobby for them, hire staff willing to work for low pay because they share the group's goals, or cite published research rather than funding their own studies to bolster their case for policy change. Moreover, the fact that a group has lots of money is no guarantee that its lobbying efforts will succeed (recall the Boeing example from earlier in this chapter).

INTEREST GROUPS USE A VARIETY of tactics to draw attention to their concerns, including events designed to generate media coverage. Jon Davids, a Public Interest Research Group staffer, traveled nearly 20,000 miles across America with an 18-foot inflatable largemouth bass named Freddie to publicize the dangers of mercury pollution in lakes and streams.

EXPERTISE

Expertise takes many forms. Some interest group leaders know a lot about their members' preferences or about what people in a community, congressional district, or state want.[24] Other groups can offer information to elected officials and bureaucrats that ranges from reports on policy questions to concrete legislative proposals. Group leaders can use this information to negotiate with officials or bureaucrats as part of a trade to get what the group wants. Expertise can also involve knowledge of political factors, such as what kinds of policies party caucuses or individual legislators support, or information about the constitutionality of proposed laws. Lobbying firms that employ former members of Congress and bureaucrats are a good source of such information.

Consider AARP, whose website offers a vast array of research and analyses. Included is information about seniors' part-time employment and how people invest their 401(k) retirement accounts, and a comparison of long-term care policies in Europe and the United States.[25] AARP's lobbyists use this research when arguing for policy changes in their public testimony and in private meetings with members of Congress and congressional staff.

Not all interest groups have such expertise. Some groups focus on mobilizing people outside government. However, particularly for groups headquartered in Washington or state capitals, expertise often comes naturally. In the course of their jobs, most interest group staff become well versed in the details of current policies and policy options. When they talk with members of Congress and bureaucrats on a daily basis, they learn who their friends are—and how to change enemies into friends. Expertise can also help a group gain access to congressional or bureaucratic offices—getting in the door does not ensure that the group will get what it wants, but it at least will be able to present its argument.

GETTING ORGANIZED

EXPLAIN HOW SUCCESSFUL INTEREST GROUPS OVERCOME COLLECTIVE ACTION PROBLEMS

A new interest group's first priority is to get organized, which involves raising the money needed to hire staff, renting an office, setting up a website, and formulating policy goals and a lobbying strategy. In some cases, a lobbying firm is hired to perform these jobs. Once organized, the group must continue to attract funds for ongoing operations. These tasks are not easy. Even if a group of people (or corporations) shares the same goals, the challenge is to persuade them to donate time or money to a lobbying operation.

THE LOGIC OF COLLECTIVE ACTION

Research has found that a problem arises when a group of individuals (or corporations) has an opportunity to make itself better off through the provision of public goods. (For interest groups, the public good would be a change in government policy desired by group members.) Scholars refer to these situations as involving collective action. As Nuts and Bolts 9.2 explains, even when all members of a group agree on the desirability of a public good and the costs of producing the good are negligible, cooperation is neither easy nor automatic. This problem is illustrated with the classic example of a **collective action problem**, the **Prisoner's Dilemma**.

The logic of collective action provides insights into how interest groups are organized and how they make lobbying decisions. First, the logic of collective action tells us that group formation is not automatic. Even when a number of citizens want the same things from government, their common interest may not lead them to

collective action problem A situation in which the members of a group would benefit by working together to produce some outcome, but each individual is better off refusing to cooperate and reaping benefits from those who do the work.

Prisoner's Dilemma A simple two-person game that illustrates how actions that are in a player's individual self-interest may lead to outcomes that all players consider inferior.

9.2 **NUTS** *& bolts*

COLLECTIVE ACTION PROBLEMS

Collective action refers to situations in which a group of individuals can work together to provide themselves with public goods. For example, changes in government policy (such as those lobbied for by interest groups) are public goods: if the government changes policy, such as increasing the size of college tuition grants, everyone who is eligible for the grants benefits from the increase. These circumstances make it hard to motivate people to contribute to collective efforts, because each would-be member can see that his contribution would be only a minuscule portion of what the group needs to succeed. This is known as a collective action problem. Regardless of how many other people join, an individual is better off free riding—refusing to join but still being able to enjoy the benefits of any successes the group might have. But if everyone acts on this calculation, no one will join the group and the organization will be unable to lobby for tuition grants or anything else.

One class of real-world collective action problems involve

situations where people can exploit a renewable natural resource, such as a forest or fishery. The problem is that each participant can maximize her profits by taking as much as she can from the resource area without worrying about whether the area can sustain this activity. However, if everyone behaves this way, the common resource will be destroyed—all the fish will be caught or all the trees will be cut down.

The same kinds of problems arise in everyday life. As a college student, you may live in some sort of group housing situation, either a dormitory or an off-campus apartment or house. Anyone who has ever lived in such a situation knows that one constant problem is sharing the responsibility for common living spaces. Everyone typically agrees that these areas should be kept clean, but each resident sees an opportunity to free ride by leaving his mess for someone else to take care of. But if everyone follows this incentive, common living spaces will remain messy if not uninhabitable.

organize. Some groups remain latent, which explains why certain debates in Washington feature well-organized groups on one side of the issue but few on the other.

The logic of collective action offers clues about how interest groups operate. Unless people can easily see benefits from participating, which does not happen often, group leaders must worry about finding the right strategies to get people to join. Thus, given the logic of collective action, attracting members is just as important for a group's success as its lobbying strategy.

Society is full of groups of like-minded people (such as college students) who do not organize to lobby or who choose to **free ride** and enjoy the benefits of organizations without participating. Most organizations develop mechanisms to promote cooperation in such situations. These solutions fall into three categories: benefits from participation, coercion, and selective incentives.

Studies of political parties and interest groups find that some individuals volunteer out of a sense of duty or because they enjoy working together toward a common goal. Scholars refer to these benefits of participation as either **solidary benefits**, which come from working with like-minded people, or **purposive benefits**, which come from working to achieve a desired policy goal.[26] If most people were spurred to political action because of participation benefits, the free rider problem wouldn't exist. However, when these benefits are not enough, groups try other measures in order to organize.

A second way to solve the free rider problem is through **coercion**, or requiring participation. Consider labor unions. They provide public goods to workers by negotiating with management on behalf of worker-members over pay and work requirements. Why don't union members free ride? Because in many cases, they have to join the union: union shop laws require them to pay union dues as a condition of their employment. These laws are critical to unions; states with laws that make union membership optional typically have weak unions—if any.

Finally, **selective incentives** (also called material incentives) are benefits given only to the members of an interest group. These incentives are not public goods; an individual can receive a selective incentive only by joining the group. Thus interest groups offer selective incentives in the hope of providing a new reason to participate. One of the most interesting cases of selective incentives provided by an interest group involves AAA. Members with car trouble can call AAA at any time for emergency service. AAA also provides annotated maps and travel guides to its members, a travel agency, a car-buying service, discounts at hotels and restaurants, and other benefits. These services mask the interest group role of AAA. For example, its Foundation for Traffic Safety delivers research reports to legislators on topics ranging from lowering the blood alcohol level threshold that legally defines drunk driving to increasing the restrictions on driving by senior citizens.[27] It's unlikely that many AAA members—who join for the selective incentives—are aware of the organization's lobbying efforts. The inducements drive membership, which funds the organization's lobbying operation.

APPLYING THE THEORY OF COLLECTIVE ACTION

The variety of recruitment strategies just described suggests that the motivations of interest group members for joining may be very different from those of the group's leaders. Often members join because of coercion, selective incentives, or the enjoyment they get from being part of the group. In some cases, these members may not know or care about their group's lobbying efforts. Leaders, in contrast, determine what their group lobbies for, so policy goals may drive their participation.

free riding The practice of relying on others to contribute to a collective effort while failing to participate on one's own behalf, yet still benefiting from the group's successes.

solidary benefits Satisfaction derived from the experience of working with like-minded people, even if the group's efforts do not achieve the desired impact.

purposive benefits Satisfaction derived from the experience of working toward a desired policy goal, even if the goal is not achieved.

coercion A method of eliminating nonparticipation or free riding by potential group members by requiring participation, as in many labor unions.

selective incentives Benefits that can motivate participation in a group effort because they are available only to those who participate, such as member services offered by interest groups.

The theory of collective action also explains why economic groups, such as trade associations, have historically been easier to form than citizen groups. Because economic groups often involve a small number of corporations or individuals, the costs of free riding are relatively high: one actor's efforts or contributions can boost the likelihood of success, and one member's failure to contribute can compromise the group's efforts. (When groups are small, the logic of free riding is much less likely to apply—the benefits are smaller and costs higher.) Thus, economic groups can often form on the strength of their shared policy or monetary goals, without the need for coercion, selective incentives, or solidary benefits. In contrast, citizen groups, with many more potential members, typically need to use at least one of these methods to solve their collective action problems.

The logic also explains why some interest groups have no members at all. Sometimes a single wealthy company or individual funds an interest group. Or groups raise money from foundations or corporate donors.[28] Why not try to attract members? They can be surprisingly hard to find, and it takes even more time and money to convince them to participate.

Finally, the logic of collective action highlights the crucial role of leaders or interest group entrepreneurs in successful collective action. Of course, all groups have a leader who oversees the day-to-day activities. But more important, interest groups need someone to make the case for the group, define its mission, identify goals, and develop a strategy for achieving them.[29]

Why would someone want this job? Many people who help to organize and run interest groups have strong policy goals—they sincerely believe in the group's mission. In effect, these individuals offer potential group members a trade: if the members join the group, the leaders will get the group organized, formulate its lobbying strategy, and manage its work to change government policy.[30] Moreover, leaders may have considerable freedom to determine what to lobby for: in many mass interest groups, members have no influence over their group's lobbying efforts. And in organizations such as AAA, whose members join to get selective incentives and whose lobbying efforts are not well known, lobby decisions may be completely unconstrained by member preferences.

For the leaders, organizing and operating the group is also a form of goal-directed political participation: by doing this work, they increase the chances that their policy preferences will become reality. Many interest group leaders, such as Ralph Nader of Public Citizen, fit this description. In some cases, however, the people who organize and operate interest groups are driven by strictly financial considerations: members get the benefits of the group's lobbying efforts, and the leader gets a salary.[31]

THE AAA (FORMERLY THE AUTOMOBILE Association of America) is a well-known provider of emergency road service, yet few people are aware of its role as an interest group that lobbies for a wide range of policy changes.

inside strategies The tactics employed within Washington, D.C., by interest groups seeking to achieve their policy goals.

outside strategies The tactics employed outside Washington, D.C., by interest groups seeking to achieve their policy goals.

INTEREST GROUP STRATEGIES

EXPLORE THE WAYS INTEREST GROUPS TRY TO INFLUENCE GOVERNMENT POLICIES

Once a group has organized and determined its goals, the next step is to decide how to lobby. There are two types of possible tactics: **inside strategies**, which are actions taken in Washington, and **outside strategies**, which involve actions taken outside Washington.[32] Generally, these strategies involve a single group, working on their own, sometimes opposed by another group or groups. However, as we discuss later, interest groups sometimes work together toward common legislative goals.

INSIDE STRATEGIES

Inside strategies involve some form of contact with elected officials or bureaucrats. Thus, inside strategies require a group to establish an office in Washington or hire a lobbying firm to act on its behalf.

DIRECT LOBBYING

direct lobbying Attempts by interest group staff to influence policy by speaking with elected officials or bureaucrats.

When interest group staff meet with officeholders or bureaucrats, they plead their case through **direct lobbying**, asking government officials to change policy in line with the group's goals.[33] Such contacts are very common. A search of disclosure data maintained by Congress found that more than 66,000 groups and individuals lobbied members of Congress in 2011.[34]

Direct lobbying is generally aimed at officials and bureaucrats who are sympathetic to the group's goals.[35] In these efforts, interest groups and their representatives do not try to convert opponents into supporters; rather, they help like-minded legislators secure policy changes that they both want. Their help can range from sharing information about the proposed changes, to providing lists of legislators who might be persuadable, to drafting legislative proposals or regulations.

These efforts usually are not part of a trade, in which the group expects legislative action in return for its help. Rather, the group's efforts function more like a subsidy, a way of helping a legislator to enact policies that she prefers—and that the group prefers as well.[36] The legislator knows that a like-minded group has no reason to misrepresent its policy information. In fact, the member and her staff will be happy to meet with the group's representatives, as their information may be vital to the legislator's efforts to enact legislation, manage the bureaucracy, or keep the support of constituents back home in the district.[37]

Interest groups also contact legislators who disagree with their goals, as well as fence sitters (legislators who are not supporters or opponents), with the goal of converting them into supporters. These efforts are less extensive than the lobbying of supporters, because opponents are unlikely to change their minds unless a group can provide new information that causes them to rethink their position. However, lobbying opponents may be useful if it forces opposing interest groups to use some of their limited resources in lobbying their own supporters to make sure that they do not change their position.[38]

As these descriptions indicate, groups place a high priority on maintaining access to their lobbying targets, on being able to present their arguments, regardless of whether they expect to get what they want. Of course, groups want to achieve their policy goals, but access is the necessary first step that makes persuasion possible. Therefore, many interest groups try to keep their efforts low-key, providing information to friends and opponents alike, avoiding threats or harsh words, in the hope that they will leave a favorable impression and be able to gain access the next time they want to lobby. After all—people who are opposed to a group's current priorities one day may agree with them on some future issue.

Who do these groups contact for direct lobbying? Analysis of lobbyists' annual disclosure forms shows that they contact people throughout the federal government: elected officials, members of the president's staff, and bureaucrats in the executive branch. They seek this wide range of contacts because different officials play distinct roles in the policy-making process and thus have various types of influence. Members of Congress shape legislation and budgets; members of the president's staff influence the formation of new policies and obtain presidential consent for new laws; and executive branch bureaucrats change the ways regulations are written and policies are implemented.

DRAFTING LEGISLATION AND REGULATIONS

Interest groups sometimes draft legislative proposals and regulations, which they deliver to legislators and bureaucrats as part of their lobbying efforts.[39] Surveys of interest groups found that more than three-quarters reported drafting proposals for members of Congress.[40]

Interest groups don't give proposals to just anyone. As with direct lobbying, they seek out legislators who already support their cause and who have significant influence within Congress. A lobbying effort aimed at cutting interest rates on student loans would target supporters of this change who are also members of the congressional committee with jurisdiction over student loan programs—preferably someone who chairs the committee or one of its subcommittees.[41] Interest groups also lobby bureaucrats to influence the details of new regulations.[42] If the types of regulations involved can go into effect without congressional approval, then lobbying can give groups what they want directly. But even if new regulations require approval by Congress or White House staff, interest groups can increase their chances of success by getting involved in the initial drafting.

THE AMERICAN CIVIL LIBERTIES Union is an interest group that often uses litigation strategies in its efforts to change government policy. Here, an ACLU attorney describes the group's efforts to limit the Department of Homeland Security's use of "no fly lists" to screen airline passengers.

RESEARCH

Interest groups often prepare research reports on topics of interest to the group. For example, Public Citizen recently featured on its website a series of research reports on topics such as medical malpractice, the house building industry, toy safety, and international trade.[43] Such reports serve multiple purposes. They may sway public opinion or help persuade elected officials or bureaucrats, and are another source of access. They also help interest group staff claim expertise on some aspect of public policy. Members of Congress are more likely to accept a group's legislative proposal if they think that the group's staff have research to back up their claims. Journalists are also more likely to respond to an interest group's requests for publicity if they think that the group's staff has evidence supporting their claims.

HEARINGS

Interest group staff often testify before congressional committees. In part, this activity is aimed at informing members of Congress about issues that matter to the group. For example, the NRA's website shows that its staff have testified in favor of "right to carry" laws as well as laws that would grant immunity to gun manufacturers for harm committed with weapons they produced.[44]

LITIGATION

Another inside strategy involves taking the government to court. In bringing their case, groups can argue that the government's actions are not consistent with the Constitution or that the government has misinterpreted the existing law.[45] Groups can bring these actions via lawyers on their staff, a hired law firm, or lawyers who will work for no fees. Groups can also become involved in an existing case by filing amicus curiae ("friend of the court") briefs, documents that offer judges the group's rationale for how the case should be decided. The drawback of litigation is that it is costly and time-consuming—cases can take years to work through the federal courts system. At a minimum, groups that use the litigation strategy generally combine it with direct lobbying or other strategies.

WORKING TOGETHER

To increase their chances for success, interest groups can work together in their lobbying efforts, formulating a common strategy and future plans. Generally these are short-term efforts focused on achieving a specific outcome, like supporting or opposing the confirmation of judicial and cabinet nominees.[46] Similarly, one of the larger groups active during the recent debate over health care reform was Better Health Care Together, a coalition of labor unions, large corporations, and Washington-based think tanks, including the Service Employees International Union (SEIU), Wal-Mart, and the Center for American Progress.

Why do groups work together? The most obvious reason is the power of large numbers: legislators are more likely to respond, or at least provide access, when many groups with large or diverse memberships are all asking for the same thing.[47] The groups involved may also have different kinds of resources to contribute. In the case of Better Health Care Together, the unions generated the grassroots support, while the think tanks provided research and contacts inside Congress and the government. Moreover, members of Congress are likely to listen to a labor union lobbyist if there are large numbers of union members in their district, or to a corporation that employs many of their constituents.

The problem with working together is that groups may agree on general goals but disagree on specifics, thereby requiring negotiation. If differences cannot be bridged, groups may undertake separate and possibly conflicting lobbying efforts or decide against lobbying entirely. For example, during the 2009 debate over climate change legislation, many environmental interest groups sat on the sidelines despite having pressed for such legislation for more than a decade. The problem? The groups disagreed on which policies should be implemented, who should pay for them, and whether the government should aid companies that would be forced to purchase new antipollution equipment. Lacking agreement and unwilling to act alone, many groups took no position at all on the legislation.[48] And, as we noted earlier, many Tea Party organizations agreed with many Occupy groups about their opposition to bank and other corporate bailouts. However, the fragmented nature of these organizations made all but impossible the development of a united lobbying effort, to prohibit future bailouts or punish legislators who supported them.

OUTSIDE STRATEGIES

Outside strategies involve things that groups do across the country rather than in Washington. Again, these activities can be orchestrated by the group or be organized by a firm hired by the group.

GRASSROOTS LOBBYING

grassroots lobbying A lobbying strategy that relies on participation by group members, such as a protest or a letter-writing campaign.

Directly involving interest group members in lobbying efforts is called **grassroots lobbying**. Members may send letters, make telephone calls, participate in a protest, or express their demands in other ways. Many groups encourage grassroots lobbying. For example, AARP's website has a page where members can find contact information for their representatives in Congress.[49] Other links allow members to e-mail or fax their representatives letters that are prewritten by AARP to express the group's positions on various proposals, such as pension protection legislation and proposals to curb identity theft. AARP also organizes district meetings with elected officials and encourages its members to attend.

Mass protests are another form of grassroots lobbying. In addition to trying to capture the attention of government officials, mass protests also seek to draw media attention, with the idea of publicizing the group's goals and perhaps gaining new members or financial support. Three months into President Obama's term, groups opposed to his economic stimulus proposals held "tea parties" on April 15 (the deadline for filing income tax returns) to mobilize public opinion against the proposals. Later, some of the same groups worked to get people to attend congressional town hall meetings to express opposition to congressional health care reform proposals, while other groups worked to get supporters of the reform to the same meetings. (As discussed earlier, the Tea Party movement is hard to classify as a defined interest group, but it has used some classic strategies such as mass protests).[50] The various Occupy groups that were organized during the winter of 2011, including the most famous, Occupy Wall Street, also focused their efforts on mass protests—although just as with the Tea Party movement, these groups do not meet our definition of an interest group.

Grassroots strategies are useful because elected officials are loath to act against a large group of citizens who care enough about an issue to express their position.[51] These officials may not agree with the group's goals, but they are likely to at least arrange a meeting with its staff, so that they appear willing to learn about their

MASS PROTESTS, SUCH AS THIS April 4, 2009, Tea Party rally in California, attract media attention and demonstrate the depth of public support for a group's goals.

constituents' demands.[52] However, these member-based strategies work only for a small set of interest groups. To take advantage of them, groups first need a large number of members. Legislators begin to pay attention to a letter-writing campaign only when they receive several thousand pieces of mail. (Remember, congressional districts contain roughly 700,000 citizens.)

In addition, for grassroots lobbying to be effective, the letters or other efforts have to come from a member's own constituents. For example, a representative who opposes increases in student aid is not going to worry about a letter-writing campaign if most of the letters come from people outside his district. The effectiveness of grassroots lobbying also depends on perceptions of how much a group has done to motivate participation. Suppose a representative gets 10,000 e-mails demanding an increase in student aid. However, virtually all the messages contain the same appeal because they were generated and sent from a group's website. People in Washington sometimes refer to these efforts as **astroturf lobbying**.[53] Given the similarity of the letters, the representative may discount the effort, believing that it says more about the group's ability to make campaign participation accessible than it does about the number of district residents who strongly support an increase in student aid. Even so, politicians are sometimes reluctant to completely dismiss astroturf efforts—the fact that so many people participated, even with facilitation by an interest group, means that their demands must at least be considered.

The evolution of the Internet has important implications for grassroots lobbying. As noted earlier, one argument is that technological developments such as blogs and e-mail make grassroots lobbying easier: they lower the costs of encouraging the members and would-be members of an interest group to get involved by writing a letter, sending an e-mail, making a phone call, or showing up for a protest. Certainly the Internet makes it easier to contact people and lowers the cost of getting involved in some kinds of lobbying efforts. However, if Internet-driven grassroots lobbying looks like astroturf lobbying, it may be less likely to achieve its goal of influencing elected officials and bureaucrats.

MOBILIZING PUBLIC OPINION

One strategy related to grassroots lobbying involves trying to change what the public thinks about an issue. The goal is not to get citizens to do anything, but to influence public opinion in the hope that elected officials will see this change and respond by enacting (or opposing) new laws or regulations to keep their constituents happy. Virtually all groups try to influence opinion. Most maintain a web page that presents their message and write press releases to get media coverage. Any contact with citizens, whether to encourage them to join the group, contribute money, or engage in grassroots lobbying, also involves elements of persuasion—trying to transform citizens into supporters, and supporters into true believers.

A focused mobilization effort involves contacting large numbers of potential supporters through e-mail, phone calls, direct mail, television advertising, print media, and websites. In order to get legislators to respond, a group has to persuade large numbers of people to get involved. One example of mobilization occurs during congressional hearings on nominees to the Supreme Court or other federal judgeships. One study found that about one-third of the groups that lobbied for or against these nominees also deployed direct mail and leaflets, and ran phone banks to influence public opinion.[54] Similarly, a study of lobbying on health care policy found that interest groups and lobbyists from business, consumer groups, and other organizations routinely work to shape public opinion so as to build congressional support for their preferred outcomes.[55]

astroturf lobbying Any lobbying method initiated by an interest group that is designed to look like the spontaneous, independent participation of many individuals.

LOBBYING THE FEDERAL GOVERNMENT: INSIDE AND OUTSIDE STRATEGIES

INSIDE STRATEGIES

Groups lobby government officials directly in Washington, D.C.

Examples: meeting with lawmakers, drafting legislation, providing research and testimony, taking the government to court.

OUTSIDE STRATEGIES

Groups use public pressure, elections, and the media to influence government.

Examples: grassroots email, letter, or phone campaigns; contributing to election campaigns; getting media coverage of their cause.

POP QUIZ!

1 Which of the following is an example of outside lobbying?

  a providing research to lawmakers

  b suing the government

  c working with bureaucrats

  d making campaign contributions

  e meeting with lawmakers

2 When officials in Washington, D.C., work with lobbyists, it is typically because

  a officials are afraid of being sued.

  b officials are hoping to benefit personally.

  c lobbyists are good at "converting" politicians to their cause.

  d lobbyists provide valuable information.

  e lobbyists threaten them with negative publicity.

ELECTIONEERING

Interest groups get involved in elections by making contributions to candidates, mobilizing people (including their staff) to help in a campaign, endorsing candidates, funding campaign ads, or mobilizing a candidate's or party's supporters. All these efforts seek to influence who gets elected, with the expectation that changing who gets elected will affect what government does.

Federal laws limit groups' electioneering and lobbying efforts. Nuts and Bolts 9.3 provides information on what different types of organizations can and cannot do. For example, most private organizations and associations in America are organized as **501(c)(3) organizations**, a designation based on their Internal Revenue Service classification, which means that donations to the group are tax deductible. However, 501(c)(3)s are not allowed to engage in any political activities or lobbying (other than certain voter education programs or voter registration drives that are conducted in a nonpartisan manner). Groups that want to engage in lobbying or electioneering can incorporate under other IRS designations and operate as a **political action committee (PAC)**, a **527 organization**, or a 501(c)(4). While contributions to these organizations are not tax-deductible, they have fewer restrictions on the size of contributions or how money can be spent: 527 organizations, for example, have no contribution or spending limits.

In 2012, federally focused 527 organizations spent more than $300 million on electioneering, and PACs spent nearly $375 million.[56] Table 9.2 reports campaign spending for the top ten 527 organizations. The top-spending 527, ActBlue, spent almost $12 million in 2012, and even the tenth-ranked organization, the International Brotherhood of Electrical Workers, spent nearly $3 million, which was more than the largest PAC. The box also shows that most of the large 527 organizations are strongly tied to one of the major parties. Indeed, the literature from these organizations leaves no doubt about their partisan leanings. Though some 527s spend a lot on electioneering, the average is lower than you might think. In the 2012 election, the 576 active 527 organizations that participated in the campaign spent an average of about $486,000 each. In other words, although some 527s run substantial national ad campaigns, the average 527 gets involved in only a few races.

The data on the top ten PACs in 2012 are shown in Table 9.3. The largest PAC contributed just under $3 million to candidates in the 2012 election, and the tenth largest slightly less than $2 million. These organizations donating millions of dollars are the exception by a significant margin: in the 2008 election, the average PAC gave only $100,000 in contributions. Part of the reason for this lower spending is that PACs' direct contributions to candidates are capped at $5,000 per candidate, and their contributions to party committees are also strictly limited.

Two new options for electioneering for interest groups emerged in the 2010 election: "Super PACs" and 501(c)(4) organizations. The former was a consequence of the *Citizens United* Supreme Court decision that authorized unlimited independent spending by corporations and labor unions in federal elections. Many groups set up new political action committees to take advantage of these new rules—the "super" label reflects the fact that these groups take in and spend much more money than the typical PAC. For example, President Bush's former political strategist Karl Rove set up the Super PAC American Crossroads to help elect Republicans in 2010. However, many businesses preferred that their contributions remain secret because they were afraid of angering shareholders

---

501(c)(3) organization A tax code classification that applies to most interest groups; this designation makes donations to the group tax-deductible but limits the group's political activities.

political action committee (PAC) An interest group or a division of an interest group that can raise money to contribute to campaigns or to spend on ads in support of candidates. The amount a PAC can receive from each of its donors and the amount it can spend on federal campaigning are strictly limited.

527 organization A tax-exempt group formed primarily to influence elections through voter mobilization efforts and issue ads that do not directly endorse or oppose a candidate. Unlike political action committees, 527s are not subject to contribution limits and spending caps.

SUPER PACS, SUCH AS THE American Conservative Union Foundation, have been influential in recent elections. Here, Senator Jim DeMint of South Carolina addresses the group's Conservative Political Action Conference in 2012.

TABLE » 9.2

BIG SPENDERS IN THE 2012 ELECTION: 527 ORGANIZATIONS

This table shows the amount of money spent on electioneering by the top ten 527 organizations. Does this information support claims of interest groups having a disproportionate influence over election outcomes, especially in light of the high costs of campaigning described in chapter 8?

ORGANIZATION	GENERALLY SUPPORTS	TOTAL EXPENDITURES
ActBlue	Democrats	$11,648,124
College Republican National Committee	Republicans	$9,172,430
Citizens United	Republicans	$8,120,525
EMILY's List	Democrats	$7,716,027
Service Employees International Union	Democrats	$6,191,200
Plumbers / Pipefitters Union	Democrats	$4,700,542
Gay & Lesbian Victory Fund	Democrats	$3,792,865
GOPAC	Republicans	$3,303,261
New Conservative Coalition	Republicans	$3,030,479
International Brotherhood of Electrical Workers	Democrats	$2,838,540

Source: Center for Responsive Politics, "527 Committees: Top Fifty Federally Focused Organizations," available at www.opensecrets.org/527s/527cmtes.php. Based on data released by the Federal Election Commission on November 2, 2012.

and customers who might have disagreed with their political spending. Rove also established a 501(c)(4), Crossroads GPS, for businesses that did not want to have their contributions disclosed. Rove's two groups spent more than $100 million in the 2012 elections. Overall, there were over a thousand Super PACs active in the 2012 election, spending well over $600 million during the campaign—however, here again, most of these organizations are small, with the average spending just over $500,000 in 2012.

These data highlight a sharp difference in electioneering strategies between the very few large, well-funded interest groups and everyone else. A few 527s, Super PACs, 501(c)(4)s, and PACs have the money to deploy massive advertising and mobilizing efforts for a candidate or issue they like or against those they don't. There are also some mass associations that can persuade large numbers of members to work for and vote for candidates the group supports or against candidates the group wants to defeat. But these strategies are not available to the vast majority of interest groups, which simply don't have the resources. For the most part, they hope to give modest help to candidates who are sympathetic to the group's goals, and to generate access. That is, they donate to a campaign in the hope that once elected, the officeholder will remember their contribution when the group asks for a meeting. Some groups give money to both candidates in a race (as long as neither candidate actively opposes the group's position), figuring that regardless of who wins, they will be able to meet with the winner.[57] A few groups wait until

TABLE » 9.3

BIG SPENDERS IN THE 2012 ELECTION: POLITICAL ACTION COMMITTEES

Do the largest PACs disproportionately support Republican or Democratic candidates, or is there no clear pattern?

ORGANIZATION	GENERALLY SUPPORTS	TOTAL CONTRIBUTIONS
National Association of Realtors	Mixed	$2,886,331
National Beer Wholesalers Association	Mixed	$2,721,000
Honeywell International	Republicans	$2,671,659
Operating Engineers Union	Democrats	$2,486,110
Intl Brotherhood of Electrical Workers	Democrats	$2,298,850
American Association for Justice	Democrats	$2,264,000
AT&T Inc.	Republicans	$2,235,050
American Bankers Association	Republicans	$2,217,950
Plumbers/Pipefitters Union	Democrats	$2,007,000
Northrop Grumman	Republicans	$1,984,400

Note: Support is mixed if fewer than 60 percent of contributions are given to one party.

Source: Center for Responsive Politics, "Top PACs," available at www.opensecrets.org/pacs/toppacs .php. Based on data released by the Federal Election Commission on November 2, 2012.

taking the late train An interest group strategy that involves donating money to the winning candidate after an election in hopes of securing a meeting with that person when he or she takes office.

after the election to make their contribution to the winning candidate—a strategy known as **taking the late train**.

It is important to remember that electioneering is only one strategy available to interest groups. Some groups do not do any electioneering at all, either because they lack sufficient funds, want to avoid making enemies because of whom they support or whom they don't, or because other strategies are more promising because of the resources available to these groups. Many groups opt for quiet lobbying efforts that utilize their expertise or undertake grassroots efforts to build public support for their policy goals. Massive electioneering operations by interest groups are relatively rare.

CULTIVATING MEDIA CONTACTS

Media coverage helps a group publicize its concerns without spending any money. Thus, most interest group leaders talk often with journalists to suggest news stories that pertain to the group's issues and to pursue favorable coverage. Such attention may mobilize public opinion indirectly, by getting people to join the group, contribute money, or demand that elected officials support the group's agenda. Favorable media coverage also helps a group's leaders assure members that they are actively working on members' concerns.

DOES CAMPAIGN SPENDING BUY POLICY OUTCOMES?

Many Americans are deeply suspicious of the impact that money plays in congressional elections, believing that contributions are often made as an explicit trade—candidates get money to fund their campaigns, then pay their contributors back by voting as requested on legislative proposals.

At first glance, this claim about the role of money in elections should be easy to test. After all, groups are required to file reports detailing virtually all the contributions they make, and members of Congress generally cast recorded votes on significant proposals. The only task would be to tie contributions to votes in order to show how one is influenced by the other.

However, it turns out that linking campaign contributions to congressional voting behavior is an extraordinarily difficult task. The problem is that there are many other factors that might produce a link between contributions and votes, even when congressional members and their contributors make no deals of any kind. For example, suppose that contributors do not expect anything in return for their contributions but simply give money to legislators who happen to share their views on government policy, and further, that legislators ignore contributions when deciding how to vote, instead making their decision based on their personal evaluation of each proposal. If so, you would see a positive link between contributions and votes, because legislators who receive contributions from a like-minded group are more likely to support proposals favored by the group, even though contributions were made without the expectation of anything in return.

Three scholars, Stephen Ansolabehere, John de Figueiredo, and James Snyder, published an analysis that provides insights into the relationship between campaign contributions and policy outcomes.[a] To begin with, the authors aggregated the results of all previous studies of this phenomenon that have appeared in scholarly journals—nearly forty in all. Of these, they found only a few that show any link between contributions and outcomes. Moreover, of those that do, three out of four found a negative relationship—in other words, receiving a contribution makes a legislator less likely to vote in line with the wishes of the group that made the contribution. All in all, there is simply no evidence of money buying policy outcomes.

Next, the scholars looked at the growth in campaign spending over time. Their data, which adjusted campaign spending for inflation in order to facilitate comparisons across years, is shown in the figure. The vertical line in the mid-1970s shows when candidates were required to file campaign spending reports with the Federal Election Commission; before that, the only data they have is for presidential campaigns, and it is based on estimates developed by other scholars. Simply put, the data show that campaign spending is not increasing—which, in light of the increase in the number of interest groups, we would expect to see if campaign contributions helped to secure policy outcome.

The authors identified other evidence that is consistent with their aggregate analysis. Essentially, they asked, what if money really does buy policy outcomes in ways that previous analyses have not uncovered? If this is the case, what kinds of contribution patterns would we expect to see? Among other predictions, they argued that we would find that most campaign contributions had been made by political action committees, or PACs (which is the only way corporations can make contributions to candidates), that most if not all major corporations would have a PAC, and that PACs would generally make the largest possible contribution to a candidate in order to maximize their influence over the candidate's future voting behavior. Their analysis of campaign finance data from the 1990s shows that none of this happened.

Ultimately, Ansolabehere, de Figueiredo, and Snyder concluded that contributions may in some cases help interest groups or corporations gain access to members of Congress and their staff, but they have little impact beyond this modest effect. Ultimately, the authors concluded that rather than buying votes and outcomes, contributions fit the alternative explanation mentioned earlier: groups give money to legislators who share their policy views, with no expectation that the member will do anything different because of the contribution. This prediction is consistent with work that shows contributions are directed to members who are experts in issue areas that interest groups care about.[b] Put another way, although there is a great deal of money in American politics, there is no evidence to support the alarmist view that contributions are eroding the foundation of democracy in America.

Watch a video clip of Stephen Ansolabehere discussing this topic at **wwnorton.com/studyspace**

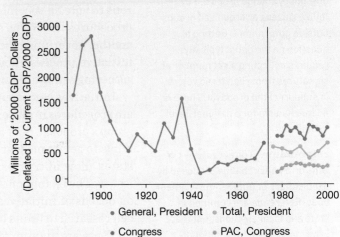

CAMPAIGN SPENDING

- General, President
- Total, President
- Congress
- PAC, Congress

INTEREST GROUPS AND ELECTIONEERING: TYPES OF ORGANIZATIONS

The ability of an interest group to engage in electioneering depends on how it is organized—what section of the IRS code applies to the organization. The table below gives details on four common organizations: 501(c) organizations, 527 organizations, political action committees (PACs), and so-called Super PACs.

Therefore, many chose to contribute money to nonprofits organized as 501(c)(4) groups, which can lobby and engage in electioneering as long as their "primary activity" (at least half of their overall activity) is not political.

Type of Organization	Advantages	Disadvantages
501(c)(3)	Contributions tax-deductible	Cannot engage in political activities or lobbying, only voter education and mobilization
527	Can spend unlimited amounts on issue advocacy and voter mobilization	Cannot make contributions to candidates or coordinate efforts with candidates or parties
501(c)(4)	Can spend unlimited amounts on electioneering, do not have to disclose contributors	At least half of their activities must be nonpolitical, cannot coordinate efforts with candidates or parties
PACs	Can contribute directly to candidates and parties	Strict limits on direct contributions
Super PACs	Can spend unlimited amounts on electioneering, can support or oppose specific candidates	Cannot make contributions to candidates or coordinate efforts with candidates or parties

Journalists listen when interest groups call if they feel that the group's story will catch their readers' attention or address their concerns. Smart interest group leaders make it easy for journalists to cover their cause, holding events that produce intriguing news stories. These stories may not change anyone's mind, but the media coverage provides free publicity for the groups' policy agendas.

BYPASSING GOVERNMENT: THE INITIATIVE PROCESS

A final outside strategy for interest groups bypasses government entirely: a group can work to get its proposed policy change voted on by the public in a general election through an **initiative** or a **referendum**. Referenda and initiatives allow citizens to vote on specific proposed changes in policy. The difference between these procedures lies in the source of the proposal. In a referendum, the legislature or another government body proposes the question that is put to a vote, whereas the initiative process allows citizens to put questions on the ballot, typically after gathering signatures of registered voters on a petition.

Initiatives can occur only in states and municipalities that have the appropriate procedures in place; there is no mechanism for a nationwide vote on an interest group's proposal. So if a group wants to use this process to effect national change, it has to get its measure on the ballot in one state at a time. Moreover, only some states allow initiatives; others permit this kind of vote only on a narrow range of issues. The champion state for initiatives is California, whose citizens often vote on dozens of initiatives in each general election, ranging from funding for stem cell research to limits on taxation and spending.[58]

There are many examples of groups using the initiative process to change government policy. Most notably, advocates of term limits on state legislatures have

initiative A direct vote by citizens on a policy change proposed by fellow citizens or organized groups outside government. Getting a question on the ballot typically requires collecting a set number of signatures from registered voters in support of the proposal. There is no mechanism for a national-level initiative.

referendum A direct vote by citizens on a policy change proposed by a legislature or another government body. Referenda are common in state and local elections, but there is no mechanism for a national-level referendum.

used the initiative process to establish limits in twenty-one states, though some have since been overturned by legislative action or subsequent initiatives.[59]

One of the principal concerns about the initiative process is that it favors well-funded groups that can advertise heavily in support of their proposals and mobilize supporters to vote on Election Day.[60] However, money often is not enough: even groups with substantial resources have sometimes been unable to reform policy through the initiative process.[61]

CHOOSING STRATEGIES

Most groups give testimony, do research, contact elected officials and bureaucrats, talk with journalists, and develop legislative and regulatory proposals.[62] In fact, as Table 9.4 shows, most groups use more than one of these strategies. Some groups do not contact legislators and bureaucrats at all, and only a bare majority of interest groups engage in grassroots lobbying. Relatively few groups organize protests, endorse candidates, or provide campaign workers.

A particular group's decisions about which strategies to use depend partly on its resources and partly on what approach the group believes will be most effective in promoting its particular issues. Some strategies that work well for one group's agenda might not be appropriate for another's. The Humane Society is an organization that lobbies to prevent abuse and neglect of animals. It has 10 million members and a $120 million annual budget but only a small Washington office.[63] This is because the group focuses on grassroots lobbying and electioneering. During 2009, the Humane Society organized grassroots efforts on behalf of legislation allowing wild horses to graze on government land, as well as to ban the importation of so-called exotic pets such as pythons.[64]

Other interest groups have few members and not much money, but they can use other resources to attract attention to their cause. For example, during the 2011–12 congressional debate over the Stop Online Piracy Act (SOPA), many Internet firms and websites organized viral campaigns to get users to contact their representatives and tell them to oppose the proposals.[65] Several sites, including Wikipedia, even went off-line on January 18, 2012, to emphasize the seriousness of their concerns. While SOPA had already attracted opposition, these protests attracted considerable media attention and were one factor that led to modification of the proposals.

HOW MUCH POWER DO INTEREST GROUPS HAVE?

EVALUATE INTEREST GROUP INFLUENCE

In April 2005, Jeffrey Birnbaum, a reporter for the *Washington Post*, criticized elected officials for focusing on what he saw as minor issues, such as appointing federal judges, while ignoring problems such as the rise in Americans' health care costs and major international issues such as poverty and AIDS. The problem, Birnbaum argued, is that elected officials let interest groups define their agenda:

> *Like it or not, we increasingly live in a stage-managed democracy where highly orchestrated interests filter our priorities for us. These groups don't have*

TABLE » 9.4

INTEREST GROUP TACTICS

Most groups use both inside and outside strategies, and virtually all groups utilize a wide variety of inside strategies. Several outside strategies (advertising, endorsements, and protests) are used by relatively few groups. How might groups' resources drive these lobbying strategies?

TACTIC	PERCENTAGE USING
INSIDE STRATEGIES	
Contacting journalists	72%
Direct lobbying	84
Drafting new legislation	78
Drafting new regulations	85
Litigation	60
Research reports	81
Testimony at Hearings	95
OUTSIDE STRATEGIES	
ELECTIONEERING	
Campaign workers or advertising	24%
Candidate endorsements	22
Campaign contributions	58
GRASSROOTS LOBBYING	
Organizing protests	20%
Soliciting letters or e-mails	68

SOURCE: After Table 8.1 in Frank Baumgartner and Beth Leech, Basic Interests: The Importance of Groups in Politics and in Political Science (Princeton, NJ: Princeton University Press, 1998), p. 152.

absolute power, of course. In the nation's capital, home to 30,000 registered lobbyists, hundreds of elected politicians, thousands of journalists, and untold numbers of entrenched bureaucrats, no one's in charge. But long-established entities like the AARP, the Family Research Council, and the U.S. Chamber of Commerce mold our collective thinking and regularly dictate the language and tenor of our civil debates.[66]

Other critics echo Birnbaum's arguments. For example, the website of the Alliance for Retired Americans includes detailed critiques of the Medicare Prescription Drug Benefit, arguing that key elements of the program, including the ban on importing cheaper prescription drugs from abroad, resulted from health care industry lobbying. As the Alliance sees it, drug companies got what they wanted; the rest of us did not. Interest groups are also thought to have enormous influence over the actions of unelected bureaucrats. Their claims are an example of the theory of bureaucratic capture, which posits that agencies are vulnerable to being "captured," or having their policy goals displaced by the aims of the individuals and corporations they are supposed to regulate. When this happens, bureaucrats become more interested in catering to interest groups than in implementing policies that are good for the general population.[67] (See Chapter 12 for further discussion of bureaucratic capture.) Such outcomes would be an example of the anti-majoritarian impact of interest groups.

The evidence on interest group influence does not support these claims. Interest group scholars Frank Baumgartner and Beth Leech reviewed all the studies of interest group influence published in major political science journals and concluded that the literature was a "maze of contradictions."[68] Half the studies they analyzed found that interest group lobbying had some impact on policy, while the other half found the influence to be marginal or nonexistent.[69] Some interest groups get what they want from government some of the time, but that success can prove elusive even for groups with many members and large budgets. More important, there is no correlation between the amount of money spent on lobbying and a group's success at achieving its policy goals.[70]

This conclusion makes sense in light of four truths about interest group influence. First, interest groups lobby their friends in government rather than their enemies and usually moderate their demands in the face of resistance. A high success rate for an interest group's efforts may reflect these kinds of calculations rather than supporting the case that they are extremely powerful. For example, the NRA leadership would probably favor a new federal law that made it legal to carry a concealed handgun throughout the nation, since the NRA has lobbied for these laws at the state level and sent its representatives to testify at congressional hearings.[71] Why doesn't the NRA demand federal legislation? Because there is no sign that Congress would enact this proposal. A proposal that would force states to honor concealed carry permits issued by other states has been introduced in Congress several times but never brought up for debate or a vote.[72] Thus, the NRA's decision to forgo lobbying for a federal concealed carry law shows the limits of the organization's power.

Second, some complaints about the power of interest groups come from the losing side in the political process. Consider the Alliance for Retired Americans and its claims about the Medicare Prescription Drug Benefit just mentioned. The Alliance lobbied against the Medicare legislation just as the drug companies lobbied for it. However, the Alliance was on the losing side, and many of the provisions the group favored were not enacted, making it more prone to complain about the influence of "special interests."

Third, many interest groups claim responsibility for policies and election outcomes regardless of whether their lobbying made the difference. Consider former senator Elizabeth Dole (R-NC), who was defeated in her 2008 reelection bid. Many interest groups funded ads criticizing Dole or contributed to her opponent's campaign. The ads may have helped defeat Dole, but she was also hurt by strong Democratic Party support for her opponent, as well as by the popularity of President Obama in Dole's home state. In particular, the leaders of interest groups have a considerable incentive to make strong claims about their group's influence and impact, as these claims help them attract members and keep their jobs.[73] But much of what groups

WHILE MANY OBSERVERS CREDIT lobbying by the pharmaceutical industry for policies such as the Medicare Prescription Drug Benefit (and its ban on importing medicines), favorable public opinion, the efforts of AARP, and bureaucrats' independent judgments probably had greater influence on passing the Drug Benefit.

do—issuing reports, testifying, sending out appeals, talking with journalists—has little direct impact on policy. Publicizing these activities may reflect a leader's desire to build support for himself, but they say little about the group's influence.

Fourth, arguments about the impact of interest groups on election outcomes, such as Dole's defeat in 2008, ignore the fact that groups are almost always active on both sides of an election campaign. Although Dole was the target of attack ads funded by interest groups, and although many groups gave contributions to her opponent, Dole also received support from interest groups in the form of campaign contributions and independent ads. Thus, it doesn't make sense to attribute Dole's defeat to actions taken by one set of groups without asking why similar efforts on Dole's behalf had no effect. You can't conclude that interest groups are all-powerful without explaining why Dole's supporters were unable to save her seat.

WHAT DETERMINES WHEN INTEREST GROUPS SUCCEED?

Rather than asking why interest groups are so powerful, it makes more sense to ask when they are powerful.[74] Two related factors determine the success of lobbying efforts. The first is salience: How many Americans care about what a group is trying to do? The second is conflict: To what extent do other groups or the public oppose the policy change?

SALIENCE

salience The level of familiarity with an interest group's goals among the general population.

Interest groups are more likely to succeed when their request has low **salience**, or attracts little public attention.[75] When the average voter does not know or care about a group's request, legislators and bureaucrats do not have to worry about the political consequences of giving the group what it wants—there is no cost to allowing access or complying with a group's demands. The only question is whether the officials themselves favor the request or can be convinced that the group's desired change is worthwhile. In contrast, when salience is high, a legislator's response to lobbying will hinge on her judgment of constituent opinion: Do voters favor what the group wants? After all, the average legislator has a strong interest in reelection and is unlikely to act against her constituents' wishes. As a result, lobbying may count for nothing in the face of public opposition or be superfluous when the group's position already has public support.[76]

Many policies that are the focus of lobbying efforts are not at all salient. Consider the National Turkey Federation, an association of turkey farmers and processors. The Federation sponsors the annual ritual of presenting the president with a live Thanksgiving turkey, which is officially "pardoned" by the president and sent to a local petting zoo. In 2002, the Federation persuaded federal bureaucrats to change federally funded school lunch program regulations in a way that increased the allowable amount of turkey in various entrees. The policy change resulting from the Federation's lobbying efforts attracted no publicity, which is precisely the point. When few people know or care about a policy change, interest groups are able to dominate the policy-making process.

Low-salience issues are surprisingly common. The idea of interest group lobbying probably brings to mind titanic struggles on controversial issues, such as gun control, abortion rights, or judicial nominations, over which groups try to capture public attention as a way of pressuring people in government. And in fact, many groups are active for or against these issues. However, the typical issue attracts much less activity. One analysis of lobbying disclosure forms found that 5 percent of issues attracted more than 50 percent of lobbying activity, and 50 percent of issues attracted less than 3 percent.[77] Thus, the typical issue debated by members of Congress may involve relatively little interest group activity, and a group's request may generate little or no opposition from other groups. On these noncontroversial issues, getting access to legislators is probably easy to obtain; and all a group needs to do is persuade the legislator that its demands have merit.

CONFLICT

Lobbying is subject to two kinds of conflict. One involves disagreements between interest groups: some prefer spending more on a given program, some less. The other involves differences between what a particular interest group wants and the preferences of the general public. Both kinds of conflict can exist over the same issue, and both work against the success of a lobbying effort.[78]

In the case of the National Turkey Federation, for example, virtually no one in the general public knew about its proposal, and no interest group lobbied against it. In essence, bureaucrats heard one group asking for something, and, hearing no opposition, decided the policy change was worth making. The situation might have been very different if another group—perhaps the American Pork Producers or the American Cattlemen—had lobbied against the Turkey Federation. If so, satisfying one group would have required displeasing at least one other group. Faced with this no-win situation, bureaucrats or legislators would be less likely to give the group what it wanted. At a minimum, they would have had to measure the Turkey Federation's arguments against those made by the other groups.

As the analysis mentioned earlier suggests, many cases of interest group influence look a lot like the Turkey Federation's request: a group asks for something, there is relatively little opposition, and Congress or the bureaucracy responds with appropriate policy changes. These cases are examples of true interest group influence, because a group asks for something and gets it. However, one of the primary reasons for the group's success is that its efforts are essentially unopposed.

You may be wondering, if conflict is fundamental to politics, shouldn't there be at least one group opposing every lobbying effort? The answer is, not necessarily. Potential opponents may remain latent (unorganized) or decide against lobbying to concentrate their efforts on other matters. Many policy questions are just not that important to many people. Thus, the obstacles to a group's goals may not be the other groups that oppose its request; rather, the obstacles may be the groups that are asking for something completely different, because members of Congress and bureaucrats have time to make only so many policy changes in any year.

Interest group influence is much less apparent on conflictual issues—those over which public opinion is split and groups are typically active on both sides of the question. Consider a high-salience issue such as health care reform. The 2009–10 debate over health care reform attracted many well-funded interest groups and coalitions, which supported different versions of reform or wanted no change at all. There was no consensus either among members of Congress, interest groups, or the American public about which policy changes were needed. Under these conditions, access doesn't count for very much—legislators have a keen sense of the political costs of accommodating a group's demands. Moreover, policy changes are

IF YOU HAVE EVER HEARD OF THE National Turkey Federation, it's probably because of their participation in the annual presidential "pardoning" of a turkey before Thanksgiving. The Federation's relative anonymity has been beneficial: its effort to increase the amount of turkey served in federally funded school lunches was aided by most Americans' lack of awareness of the proposal.

likely to reflect a complex process of bargaining and compromise, with no groups getting exactly what they want—which is what happened with health care reform. In such cases, it is hard to say whether a particular group won or lost, or to attribute any aspect of the final bargain to a particular group's efforts.

The case of health care reform illustrates that being large or well funded often does not help an interest group convince government officials to comply with its requests. As mentioned earlier, many people worry that well-funded interest groups will use their financial resources to dominate the policy-making process, even if public opinion is against them; but these fears are largely unfounded. The conditions that are ripe for well-funded interest groups to become involved in a policy debate typically ensure that there will be well-funded groups on all sides of a question. Under these conditions, no group is likely to get everything it wants, and no group's lobbying efforts are likely to be decisive. Some groups may not get anything.

WHEN CONGRESS CONSIDERED VARIOUS forms of health care legislation in 2010, the health insurance and pharmaceutical industries lobbied for laws that would benefit them. Here, two top executives from the health insurance company Wellpoint testify before Congress.

HOW GROUPS SUCCEED

Even when issues are highly salient, interest groups can still be influential. Research and testimony may help members of Congress develop legislative proposals and give them arguments to use in the bargaining process. Grassroots and media efforts may mobilize public opinion, pressuring members to vote for options favored by their constituents. If a particular group decided against doing these things, and no other group took its place, then groups on the other side of the debate might be more likely to carry the day. But interest group leaders are well aware of the potentially dire consequences of not getting involved and are unlikely to be inactive on questions that matter to them and the members of their group—even if a full-fledged lobbying effort is unlikely to produce many identifiable benefits, given the opposition by other groups.

Even on high-salience issues, lobbying efforts may produce identifiable benefits when they are focused on relatively small details of a policy change. However, groups are successful in these efforts precisely because they seek relatively modest policy changes, which are nonetheless important to their members but generate minimal opposition. Particularly when policy questions are complex, groups may focus their attention on achieving seemingly minor policy changes that have large benefits for their members.

Another measure of the limits of lobbying on conflictual questions is evident in groups' decisions about which issues to refrain from lobbying on. Think about one of the most powerful interest groups, the NRA, and its advocacy of concealed carry laws. There is little doubt that the NRA's leaders and most of its members favor the passage of such laws, but its efforts are unlikely to be successful given public opinion and well-funded opposition. As a result, the NRA chooses to lobby on other matters—policy questions with which it might succeed or where its efforts are necessary to prevent other groups from succeeding in changing policies in ways that the NRA opposes.

Thus, being large or well funded often does not help an interest group convince government officials to comply with its requests. It all depends on what the group is asking for, and in particular, whether there is significant opposition in the form of opposing groups or public opinion. As mentioned earlier, many Americans worry that well-funded interest groups will use their financial resources to dominate the policy-making process, even if public opinion is against them. It would be a considerable overstatement to say that interest groups have no power and lobbying makes no difference, because, if nothing else, groups may lobby to prevent the policy changes that would occur if they stayed inactive. And interest groups often succeed in efforts to change low-salience policies or small details of salient proposals. But when large, powerful groups seek controversial changes, their resources are matched by the difficulty of the task. These groups can send staff to lobby officeholders, commission research reports, testify, bring lawsuits, and encourage grassroots activity, but such tactics are unlikely to prevail in the face of public opposition or counteractive lobbying by other groups. Fears of large groups dominating the policy-making process to the exclusion of public opinion are largely unfounded.

CONCLUSION

The number of American interest groups and the amount those groups spend on lobbying have increased rapidly in recent years, bringing a larger variety of organizations and lobbying tactics. Contrary to the image of interest groups as powerful manipulators, one of the biggest challenges for these organizations is galvanizing their members to participate in their efforts. Interest groups are more likely to get what they want when their demands attract little public attention and no opposition from other groups. When a group asks for a large or controversial policy change, it stands little chance of success, even if the group has many members, a large lobbying budget, or an influential leader directing its operation. Moreover, because interest groups are more likely to succeed when they work together, and because many of their tactics help to inform members of Congress and bureaucrats about the details of public policy and the shape of public opinion, interest group lobbying can be a force for compromise in American politics as well as a source of conflict.

The 2008 and 2009 bailouts of large banks and corporations exemplifies all of these findings. While most of the corporations that received bailout funds had significant lobbying operations, the bailout legislation was high-salience and controversial; consequently, legislators' vote decisions were unlikely to be affected by lobbying or other interest group strategies such as electioneering. These lobbying efforts may have helped to inform members about the details of the proposal or the impact that a bailout would have on employment in their districts, but there is no evidence that support for these proposals was shaped by lobbying.

In sum, while individual lobbying efforts are often anti-majoritarian, in that they reflect the efforts of small groups to achieve favored policy outcomes at the expense of the majority, looking across the entire range of interest group activities, a different picture emerges: in the main, interest groups reflect the conflictual nature of American politics, and the resulting drive of individuals, groups, and corporations to shape American public policy in line with their policy goals.

STUDY*guide*

THE INTEREST GROUP UNIVERSE

▶ Define interest groups and describe the characteristics of different types of groups. **Pages 339–50**

SUMMARY

Interest groups are organizations that seek to influence government policy by helping elect candidates who support their policy goals, and by lobbying elected officials and bureaucrats. Though they are generally viewed with disdain, interest groups are ubiquitous—most organizations have lobbyists working on their behalf—and under the theory of pluralism, are regarded as fundamental actors in American politics.

KEY TERMS

interest group (p. 339)

lobbying (p. 339)

interest group state (p. 340)

latent (p. 343)

trade association (p. 344)

centralized groups (p. 346)

confederations (p. 346)

revolving door (p. 347)

mass associations (p. 348)

peak associations (p. 348)

PRACTICE QUIZ QUESTIONS

1. In contrast to political parties, interest groups can _____.
   a) run candidates for office
   b) coordinate the activities of elected officials
   c) guarantee positions on electoral ballots
   d) directly influence government activity
   e) indirectly influence government activity

2. Why is the number of lobbyists increasing?
   a) The federal government is growing in size and influence.
   b) Lobbying is not closely regulated.
   c) Citizens are now more supportive of special interests.
   d) Politicians can concurrently serve their terms and work as lobbyists.
   e) Interest groups have more money to spend.

3. In contrast to a confederation, a centralized interest group _____.
   a) maintains lots of independent chapters
   b) often has local chapters competing over resources
   c) deploys the group's resources more efficiently
   d) is able to find out what its members want
   e) has no weaknesses

4. The practice of moving from government positions to working for interest groups is called

   _____.
   a) interest-group capture
   b) the revolving door
   c) an iron triangle
   d) escalator politics
   e) the spoils system

ⓈPRACTICE ONLINE

"Critical Thinking" exercise: *Politics Is Everywhere—Whom Do 527 Organizations Represent?*

GETTING ORGANIZED

▶ Explain how successful interest groups overcome collective action problems. **Pages 351–53**

SUMMARY

A primary challenge in operating an interest group is getting members to coordinate with one another. Interest groups have a number of different ways of overcoming the problem of collective action, with varying degrees of success.

KEY TERMS

collective action problem (p. 351)

Prisoner's Dilemma (p. 351)

free riding (p. 352)

solidary benefits (p. 352)

purposive benefits (p. 352)

coercion (p. 352)

selective incentives (p. 352)

CRITICAL THINKING AND DISCUSSION

As described in this chapter, college students are a latent group in American politics. Based on the logic of collective action, what would an interest group entrepreneur have to do to organize this group?

PRACTICE QUIZ QUESTIONS

5. The logic of collective action says that when people _____ on policy priorities, and the costs are _____, cooperation is not easy.
   a) agree; high
   b) agree; covered by one person
   c) disagree; low
   d) disagree; high
   e) disagree; low

6. Purposive benefits come from _____; while solidary benefits come from _____.
   a) working with like-minded people; working to achieve a desired policy goal
   b) receiving material goods; working with like-minded people
   c) receiving material goods; working to achieve a desired policy goal
   d) working to achieve a desired policy goal; receiving material goods
   e) working to achieve a desired policy goal; working with like-minded people

7. The logic of collective action implies that economic groups are _____ to form (as/than) citizen groups.
   a) easier
   b) just as easy
   c) harder

8. Labor unions and trade associations are generally able to overcome the collective action problem through the use of _____.
   a) solidary benefits
   b) purposive benefits
   c) coercion
   d) selective incentives
   e) recruitment

Ⓢ **PRACTICE ONLINE**

"Big Think" video exercise: *How Do You Lobby?*

INTEREST GROUP STRATEGIES

▶ Explore the ways interest groups try to influence government policies. **Pages 353–65**

SUMMARY

Interest groups have two types of tactics for lobbying elected officials. They can attempt to influence politics by taking action in Washington, or they can take action elsewhere. The decision to pursue an inside or outside strategy comes down to the interest group's resources, and which strategy members think will be most effective.

KEY TERMS

inside strategies (p. 353)

outside strategies (p. 353)

direct lobbying (p. 354)

grassroots lobbying (p. 356)

astroturf lobbying (p. 358)

501(c)(3) organization (p. 360)

political action committee (PAC) (p. 360)

527 organization (p. 360)

taking the late train (p. 362)

initiative (p. 364)

referendum (p. 364)

CRITICAL THINKING AND DISCUSSION

The chapter describes the last few decades' significant increases in the number of interest groups and lobbyists, and in the amount spent on lobbying. What factors could cause this increase to level off or even reverse?

PRACTICE QUIZ QUESTIONS

9. Asking government officials to change policy in line with the group's goals is _____.
   a) revolving door lobbying
   b) astroturf lobbying
   c) direct lobbying
   d) indirect lobbying
   e) outside lobbying

10. Interest groups generally _____ draft legislation; they generally _____ provide testimony before committees.
    a) do; do
    b) do not; do
    c) do; do not
    d) do not; do not

11. Directly involving interest group members in lobbying efforts is called _____.
    a) astroturf lobbying
    b) grassroots lobbying
    c) democratic lobbying
    d) lobbying through referendum
    e) inside lobbying

12. For indirect lobbying to be effective, _____.
    a) only a few pieces of mail are necessary
    b) mail must come from all over the country
    c) all messages have to have exactly the same appeal
    d) letters have to come from constituents
    e) letters have to come from prominent officials

13. "Taking the late train" refers to interest groups who _____.
    a) sway the tie-breaking vote
    b) target the way regulations are written
    c) wait until the general election to make a contribution
    d) wait until after an election to make a contribution
    e) avoid electioneering efforts altogether

ⓢ PRACTICE ONLINE

"Big Think" video exercise: *What Distinguishes the Israel Lobby from Other Special Interest Groups?*

HOW MUCH POWER DO INTEREST GROUPS HAVE?

▶ Evaluate interest group influence. **Pages 365–71**

SUMMARY

It is commonly argued that elected officials are letting interest groups define their agenda. However, the evidence on interest groups does not support these claims: there is no correlation between the amount of money spent on lobbying and a group's success, nor is there conclusive evidence that group lobbying influences policy. Groups are generally most influential when the issues attract little public attention, and when an issue does not have organized opposition.

KEY TERM

salience (p. 368)

CRITICAL THINKING AND DISCUSSION

A friend complains to you about the enormous power of organized interests in American politics, citing a group's recent victory in getting members of Congress to approve its policy proposal. Present three other possible explanations for this victory that do not involve the political power of the interest group.

14. Interest groups generally lobby _____ in government.

a) their opponents
b) their friends
c) the undecided
d) the newly elected
e) the less informed

15. Interest groups are more likely to succeed when their request has _____ salience; and when it has _____ conflict.

a) low; little
b) high; little
c) low; high
d) high; high
e) high; zero

Ⓢ PRACTICE ONLINE

"Big Think" video exercise: *How Do Lobbies Affect the Way We Eat?*

SUGGESTED READING

Ainsworth, Scott. *Analyzing Interest Groups: Group Influence on People and Policies.* New York: Norton, 2002.

Baumgartner, Jeffrey, M. Berry, Marie Hojnacki, David C. Kimball, and Beth L. Leech. *Lobbying and Policy Change: Who Wins, Who Loses, and Why.* Chicago: University of Chicago Press, 2009.

Carpenter, Daniel. *The Forging of Bureaucratic Autonomy: Reputations, Networks, and Policy Innovation in Executive Agencies, 1862–1928.* Princeton, NJ: Princeton University Press, 2002.

Kollman, Kenneth. *Outside Lobbying: Public Opinion and Interest Group Strategies.* Princeton, NJ: Princeton University Press, 1998.

Lowi, Theodore. *The End of Liberalism: The Second Republic of the United States.* New York: Norton, 1979.

Olson, Mancur. *The Logic of Collective Action,* 2nd ed. Cambridge, MA: Harvard University Press, 1971.

Schattschneider, E. E. *The Semi-Sovereign People.* New York: Harper and Row, 1959.

Schlozman, Kay Lehman, and John Tierney. *Organized Interests and American Democracy.* New York: HarperCollins, 1986.

Stigerwalt, Amy. *The Battle over the Bench: Senators, Interest Groups, and Lower Court Confirmations.* Charlottesville: University of Virginia Press, 2010.

Verba, Sidney, Kay Lehman Schlozman, and Henry Brady. *Voice and Equality: Civic Participation in America.* Cambridge, MA: Harvard University Press, 1995.

Walker, Jack. *Mobilizing Interest Groups in America.* Ann Arbor: University of Michigan Press, 1991.

10

Congress

DEMOCRATS GIVE A STANDING OVATION while Republicans sit silently during a speech by President Obama to a joint session of Congress. Is Congress hopelessly divided, or is compromise still possible?

A s the dust settled from the 2012 elections, Congress and the nation faced a problem that came to be known as the "fiscal cliff." This term referred to the $100 billion in spending cuts and the $500 billion in tax increases scheduled to occur in 2013 because the "Supercommittee" formed in 2011 to decide how to reduce the deficit failed to reach an agreement (see Chapter 1). Half the cuts triggered by the Supercommittee's failure would come from military spending and half from domestic spending, and taxes would increase as the Bush-era income tax cuts expired. If Congress did not act, it was feared that the spending cuts and tax increases would send the economy back into a recession in 2013.

Democrats and Republicans in Congress had very different ideas on how to proceed. Nobody wanted deep cuts in defense spending or tax increases on 98 percent of Americans. However, Republicans wanted to extend tax cuts to everyone, while Democrats wanted to raise taxes on the wealthiest 2 percent of Americans back to the levels they were at in the 1990s. Democrats offered to accept 2.5 dollars in spending cuts for every dollar in tax increases, but Republicans wanted much deeper cuts in spending. Another point of contention was that Republicans only wanted to raise revenue by limiting deductions and closing loopholes, while Democrats wanted to raise the top tax rate on the wealthy. Many observers worried that if a compromise wasn't reached the nation would end up hurtling off the fiscal cliff. As of late 2012, both sides were playing tough, but it seemed likely the Congress would agree on a "bridge" solution that

CONFLICT & COMPROMISE
in American Politics

would postpone the changes until after the new Congress took over in January, allowing legislators more time to work out a compromise.

The essential nature of conflict and compromise in the legislative process is not very well understood by the general public. Americans often view the type of wheeling and dealing that is necessary to reach compromises as improper and wonder why there is so much conflict; a typical sentiment is, "Why does there have to be so much partisan bickering? Can't they just implement the best solutions to our problems?" Many don't even attempt to understand the legislative process and the nature of conflict and compromise because it seems hopelessly complex. Anyone who has watched congressional debates on C-SPAN knows that legislative maneuvers can make your head spin, and the discussions can seem mind-numbing. Certainly the legislative details of the bill to address the fiscal cliff would be too complicated for more than a small handful of experts to comprehend.

In this chapter, we show that the basic characteristics of Congress are straightforward and that the motivations that guide members' behavior and the way that Congress works are transparent. This chapter argues that members' behavior is driven by their desire to respond to constituent interests (and the closely related goal of re-election) and constrained by the institutional structures within which they operate (such as the committee system, parties, and leadership). At the same time, members try to be responsible for the broader national interests, which are often at odds with constituent interests and the goal of re-election.

This tension between being responsible and responsive is a source of conflict and requires members of Congress to make tough decisions, often involving political trade-offs and compromises. Should a House member vote for dairy price supports for her local farmers even if it means higher milk prices for families around the nation? Should a senator vote to subsidize the production of tobacco, the biggest cash crop in his state, despite the tremendous health costs it imposes on millions of Americans? Should a member vote to close a military base, as requested by the Pentagon, even if it means the loss of thousands of jobs back home? These are difficult questions. On a complex issue such as the fiscal cliff there is no obvious "responsible" solution: Republicans favor spending cuts with no changes in tax rates while Democrats want both tax increases on the wealthy and spending cuts to reduce the deficit, which obviously leads to conflict.

The tension between responsibility and responsiveness illustrates the other two themes of this book as well. Members of Congress regularly make decisions that affect our everyday lives. Indeed, they spend much of their time trying to respond to our desires, which means that many laws are relevant for our interests, such as government support for education, transportation, tax laws, and energy policy. The idea that political process matters is probably more evident in this chapter than any other. By controlling the legislative agenda, determining which amendments will be allowed on a given bill, or stacking an important committee with sympathetic partisans, the legislative process affects political outcomes.

This chapter begins by examining the constitutional underpinnings of the representational tensions Congress must address. After exploring different ways of understanding representation, we describe Congress's image problem, the incumbency advantage, and Congress's central institutional features. We conclude by considering some potential reforms that might make Congress work better.

CONGRESS'S PLACE IN OUR CONSTITUTIONAL SYSTEM

Congress was the "first branch" in the early decades of our nation's history. The Constitution gave Congress the lead role in a vast array of enumerated powers, including regulating commerce, coining money, raising and supporting armies, creating the courts, establishing post offices and roads, declaring war, and levying taxes (see Article I, Section 8, of the Constitution in the Appendix). The president, in contrast, was given few explicit powers and played a much less prominent role early in our history. Many of Congress's extensive powers come from its implicit powers rooted in the elastic clause of Article I, which gives Congress the power "to make all Laws which shall be necessary and proper for carrying into Execution the foregoing Powers."

As noted in Chapter 2, the compromises that gave rise to Congress's initial structure reflected an attempt to reconcile the competing interests of the day (large vs. small states, northern vs. southern interests, and proponents of strong national power vs. state power). These compromises included establishing a **bicameral** (two-chambered) institution made up of a popularly elected House and a Senate chosen by state legislatures, allowing slaves to count as three-fifths of a person for purposes of apportionment for the House, and setting longer terms for senators (six years) than for House members (two years). But these compromises also laid the foundation for the split loyalties that members of Congress have between their local constituencies and the nation's interests. Although the Founders hoped that Congress would pass legislation that emphasized the national good over local interests, they also recognized the importance of local constituencies. Thus, the two-year House term was intended to tie legislators to public sentiment.

At the same time, the *Federalist Papers* made it clear that the new government was by no means a direct democracy that would put all policy questions to the public. In *Federalist 57*, Madison asserted that "the aim of every political constitution is, or ought to be, first to obtain for rulers men who possess most wisdom to discern, and most virtue to pursue, the common good of society." This common good may often conflict with local concerns, such that members are expected to both "refine and enlarge the debate" to encompass the common good *and* represent their local constituents.

In general, the Founders viewed the Senate as the more likely institution to enlarge the debate and speak for the national interests; it was intended to check the more responsive and passionate House. Because senators were indirectly elected and served longer terms than House members, the Senate was more insulated from the people. A famous (though maybe fictional) story that points out the differences between the House and Senate involves an argument between George Washington and Thomas Jefferson. Jefferson did not think the Senate was necessary, while Washington supported having two chambers. During the argument, Jefferson poured some coffee he was drinking into his saucer. Washington asked him why he had done so. "To cool it," replied Jefferson. "Even so," said Washington, "we pour legislation into the senatorial saucer to cool it."

bicameralism The system of having two chambers within one legislative body, like the House and Senate in the U.S. Congress.

THE FOUNDERS VIEWED THE HOUSE as more passionate than the Senate, or as the "hot coffee" that needed to be cooled in the "saucer" of the Senate. This perception probably did not include coming to blows over differences in policy as Congressmen Albert G. Brown and John A. Wilcox did in 1851 about whether Mississippi should secede from the Union.

This idea of a more responsible Senate survived well into the twentieth century, even after the Seventeenth Amendment in 1913 allowed the direct, popular election of senators. Today the Senate is still more insulated than the House. Because of the six-year term, only one-third of the 100 Senate seats are contested in each election, while all 435 House members are elected every two years. However, differences between the representational roles of the House and the Senate have become muted as senators seem to campaign for re-election 365 days a year, every year, just like House members.[1] This "permanent campaign" means that senators are less insulated from electoral forces than they were earlier.

The relationship between the president and Congress has also evolved significantly. Congress's roots in geographic constituencies made it well suited for the politics of the nineteenth century. Early in U.S. history, several great presidents left their mark on national politics (George Washington, Andrew Jackson, and Abraham Lincoln, among others), but Congress dominated much of the day-to-day politics, which revolved around issues such as the tariff (taxes on imported or exported goods), slavery, and internal improvements such as building roads and canals. Given the tendency to address these issues with patronage and the **pork barrel** (that is, jobs and policies targeted to benefit specific constituents), Congress was better suited for the task than the president was.

Beginning around the turn of the twentieth century and accelerating with the New Deal of the 1930s (which established modern social welfare and regulatory policies), the scope of national policy expanded and politics became more centered in Washington. With this nationalization of politics and the increasing importance of national security issues concerning World War II; the Cold War; wars in Korea, Vietnam, and Iraq; and the War on Terror, the president has assumed a more central policy-making role. However, the central tensions between representing local versus national interests remain key in understanding the legislative process and the relationship between members of Congress and their constituents.

pork barrel Legislative appropriations that benefit specific constituents, created with the aim of helping local representatives win re-election.

EXPLAIN HOW MEMBERS OF CONGRESS REPRESENT THEIR CONSTITUENTS AND HOW ELECTIONS HOLD MEMBERS ACCOUNTABLE

CONGRESS AND THE PEOPLE

Americans have a love-hate relationship with Congress; that is, we love our own member of Congress, but we hate the Congress as a whole. Well, "hate" is a strong word, but as we show later in this section, members of Congress routinely have approval ratings 30 to 40 points higher than the institution's. Before explaining that puzzling pattern and Congress's more general image problem, we'll explore the nature of representation in Congress. What are the linkages between members of Congress and their constituents? How are congressional districts formed? And what do we really think about our members of Congress?

REPRESENTATION AND THE CONSTITUENCY

TYPES OF REPRESENTATION

First let's examine the two basic components of the relationship between a constituency and its member of Congress: descriptive representation and substantive representation. The former is rooted in the politician's side of the relationship.

Does the member of Congress "look like" the constituents in demographic terms—for example, African American, Latino, or white; male or female; Catholic, Protestant, or some other religion? Many people believe that such **descriptive representation** is a distinct value in itself. Having positive role models for various demographic groups helps create greater trust in the system, and there are benefits in being represented by someone who shares something as basic as skin color with constituents.

Descriptive representation is also related to the perceived responsiveness of a member of Congress. In general, constituents report higher levels of satisfaction with representatives who are of the same racial or ethnic background as the constituents themselves. Thus, descriptively represented constituents are more likely to assume that their interests are being represented than those who are not.[2] If you doubt that descriptive representation makes a difference, ask yourself whether it would be fair if all 435 House members and 100 senators were white, male Protestants. Although the demographics of Congress are considerably more diverse than this, the legislature does not come close to "looking like us" on a nationwide scale (see Figures 10.1A and B). This is especially true in the Senate, where only three African Americans and eight Latinos have been elected in the history of the institution (no African Americans and three Latinos currently are in the Senate as of 2013).[3]

Although descriptive representation is important, it goes only so far. More important than a member's race, gender, or religion, many argue, is the *substance*

descriptive representation
When a member of Congress shares the characteristics (such as gender, race, religion, or ethnicity) of his or her constituents.

FIGURE » 10.1A

WOMEN IN CONGRESS, 1933–2013

While Congress still does not have gender parity, there have been substantial gains in recent years (with the exception of 2011, when the number of women in the House dropped for the first time in thirty years). What difference does it make for policy to have more women in Congress?

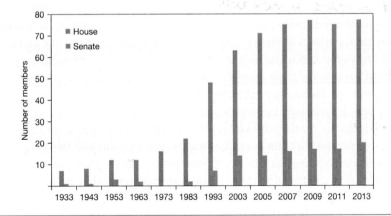

Source: Jennifer E. Manning and Colleen J. Shogan, "Women in the United States Congress: 1917–2009," Congressional Research Service Report RL30261, December 23, 2009, www.senate.gov/CRSReports /crs-publish.cfm?pid=%270E%2C*PLS%3D%22%40%20%20%0A (accessed 1/4/10). Source for 2009 and 2011, CQ Roll Call, Guide to the New Congress, November 4, 2010, pp. 14–15, http://innovation.cq.com /newmember/2010elexnguide.pdf (accessed 4/10/12). Source for 2013: Roll Call, "Meet the New Members of the 113th Congress," November 9, 2012, http://atr.rollcall.com/meet-the-new-members-of-the-113th -Congress (accessed 11/9/12).

FIGURE » 10.1B

MINORITIES IN THE HOUSE, 1933–2013

Hispanics now comprise the largest ethnic minority in the United States, yet they still lag behind African Americans in terms of representation in the House. What do you think explains this difference? How might it affect policy?

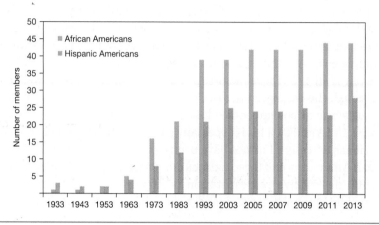

Source: Compiled from Mildred L. Amer, "Black Members of the United States Congress: 1870–2005," Congressional Research Service Report RL30378, August 4, 2005; Government Printing Office, Hispanic Americans in Congress, 1822–1995. 1995, www.loc.gov/rr/hispanic/congress/(accessed 1/4/10). Source for 2009 and 2011, CQ Roll Call, Guide to the New Congress, November 4, 2010, pp. 14–15, http://innovation.cq.com/newmember/2010elexnguide.pdf (accessed 4/10/12). Source for 2013: Roll Call, "Meet the New Members of the 113th Congress," November 9, 2012, http://atr.rollcall.com/meet-the-new-members-of-the-113th-congress (accessed 11/9/12).

substantive representation
When a member of Congress represents constituents' interests and policy concerns.

trustee A member of Congress who represents constituents' interests while also taking into account national, collective, and moral concerns that sometimes cause the member to vote against the preference of a majority of constituents.

delegate (congressional role) A member of Congress who loyally represents constituents' direct interests.

of what that person does. Merely because a representative shares some characteristics with you does not necessarily mean that he or she will represent your interests. **Substantive representation** moves beyond appearances to specify how the member serves constituents' interests. Two long-standing models are (1) the **trustee**, who represents the interests of constituents from a distance, weighing numerous national, collective, local, and moral concerns; and (2) the **delegate**, who carries out the direct desires of the voters. In a sense, trustees are more concerned with being responsible and delegates are more interested in being responsive.

One of the most famous examples of a representative acting as a trustee was Marjorie Margolies-Mezvinsky (D-Penn.) in a crucial 1993 vote on President Clinton's budget, which included controversial tax increases and spending cuts to balance the budget. Hours before the vote, she told reporters that she would vote against the budget, in accordance with her constituents' wishes. But she had also promised Clinton she would support the bill if her vote was needed. As she cast the critical vote in the 218–216 cliffhanger (in which she fulfilled her promise to the president), she did what she thought was in the best long-term interests of her constituents and the nation, even though it meant voting against their wishes and thereby leading to her defeat in the next election. More recently, bipartisan majorities in the House and Senate voted for the hugely unpopular Troubled Asset Relief Program (TARP, or as its critics called it, "the Wall Street bailout") because President Bush and congressional leaders convinced them it was necessary to prevent a complete economic meltdown.

A delegate, in contrast, does not have to worry about angering voters because he or she simply does what they want. Examples are so numerous it is pointless to single out one member for attention: when it comes to tax cuts, agricultural subsidies, increases in Medicare payments, or new highway projects, hundreds of representatives act as delegates for their districts' interests.

Truth be told, the trustee/delegate distinction is mostly important as a theoretical point of departure for talking about representation roles. Nearly all members act like trustees in some circumstances and like delegates in others. The third model of representation is the **politico**, who is more likely to act as a delegate on issues that are highly salient to the constituency (such as immigration reform), but to be a trustee on less salient or very complex issues (such as some foreign policies). Therefore, the crucial component of representation is the nature of the constituency and how the member of Congress attempts to balance and represent constituents' conflicting needs and desires.

politico A member of Congress who acts as a delegate on issues that constituents care about (such as immigration reform) and as a trustee on more complex or less salient issues (some foreign policy or regulatory matters).

THE ROLE OF THE CONSTITUENCY

Our characterization of the representative–constituency relationship raises numerous questions. How much do voters monitor their representatives' behavior? Can representation work if voters are not paying attention? The most demanding theory of representation, known as policy responsiveness, requires that voters express basic policy preferences, representatives respond to those desires, and then voters monitor and assess the politicians' behavior. However, those conditions rarely play out because most constituents do not follow congressional politics.

Despite this lack of attention, representational links remain strong through indirect mechanisms. Members of Congress behave as if voters were paying attention, even when constituents are inattentive. Incumbents know that at election time, challengers may raise issues that become salient after the public thinks about them, so they try to deter challengers by anticipating what the constituents would want *if they were fully informed*.[4] For example, the public didn't know much about the "fiscal cliff" that the nation could fall from in January 2013, until it became a big issue in the 2012 elections. Savvy incumbents would have tried to preempt vulnerability on that issue *before* a strong challenger raised the issue in a campaign by staking out a position consistent with what the voters would want once they knew more about the issue. Richard Fenno points out that some segments of the constituency are more attentive and more important for a member's re-election than others (see Figure 10.2).[5]

Another way to examine the representative–constituency relationship is to look at differences across districts. How do districts vary? First, they differ in size: Senate "districts" (that is, states) vary in terms of area and population. House districts all have about 700,000 people, but they vary tremendously in geographic size. Districts also differ in terms of who lives there and what they want from government. Some districts are located in poor city neighborhoods, where voters' concerns are economic development, crime control, antipoverty programs, and looser immigration regulations. Some are wealthy and urban, where citizens are more supportive of

FIGURE » 10.2

FENNO'S CONCENTRIC CIRCLES

The concentric circles of a congressional constituency illustrate the various parts of a district a member represents: personal (advisers, friends, and family), primary (strongest supporters), re-election (those who vote for the member), and geographic (the entire district). Can you think of an issue on which a House member would be more responsive to her re-election constituency than to her geographic constituency?

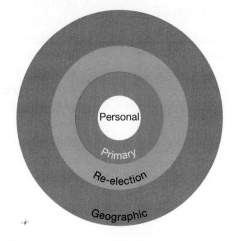

Personal
Primary
Re-election
Geographic

Source: Based on Richard F. Fenno, Home Style: House Members in Their Districts *(Boston: Little, Brown, 1978).*

MEMBERS OF CONGRESS SPEND a good deal of time in their districts, developing relationships with constituents. Here, Representative Jason Chaffetz of Utah meets constituents after a town hall meeting.

casework Assistance provided by members of Congress to their constituents in solving problems with the federal bureaucracy or addressing other specific concerns.

foreign aid and higher taxes. Some are suburban, where funding for education and transportation are critical issues. Some are conservative and rural, where agricultural policies, gun rights, and support for tax cuts dominate. Districts vary from the religious to the secular, from domination by one industry to a diversified corporate base to no industry at all. Some consider government a force for good, while others argue that government should get off the people's backs. And some districts are a mixture of all these things.

Because districts are so multifaceted, the legislators they elect differ from one another as well. Regardless of the office, most voters want to elect someone whose policy positions are close to theirs. As a result, legislators tend to reflect the central tendencies of their districts. At one level, electing a legislature that "thinks like America" sounds good: if legislators act and think like their districts, then the legislature will contain a good mixture of the interests representing the country or state. But finding an acceptable compromise is not easy. We elect legislators to get things done, but they may be unable to agree on anything because their disagreements are too fundamental to bridge. Consider abortion rights. The country is sharply divided on this issue, as are the House, the Senate, and most state legislatures. The fact that legislators have not come to a decision on this issue is no surprise: just as citizens disagree, so do their elected representatives.

Despite the vast differences between congressional constituencies, voters want many of the same things: a healthy economy, a safe country (in terms of national defense and local crime), good schools, and effective health care. Figure 10.3 reports responses to a survey about the importance of three aspects of a legislator's job: dealing with national issues, making sure that his or her district receives its fair share of federal support, and helping individual constituents interact with government. The survey showed strong support for our recurring theme concerning tensions between local and national concerns. Citizens clearly want their elected officials to get them a fair share of the federal pie and do **casework** for the district. But respondents showed little interest in having the representatives "work in Congress concerning national bills." Thus, responsibilities for national

FIGURE » 10.3

THE JOB OF A MEMBER OF CONGRESS

Congress is often criticized for passing pork-barrel policies that benefit specific districts. Yet this survey clearly shows that people want their "fair share" and are less concerned with whether their representative works on "national bills." Why do you think that is?

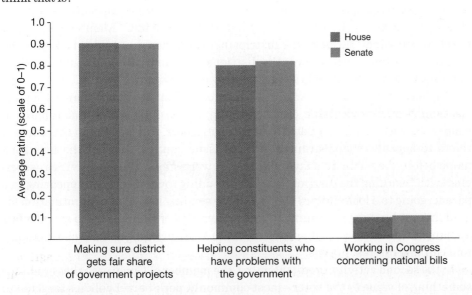

Source: Adapted from Paul Gronke, The Electorate, the Campaign, and the Office: A Unified Approach to Senate and House Elections *(Ann Arbor: University of Michigan Press, 2001), Table 6.5.*

interests may be more difficult for members of Congress to explain to their constituents.

THE ELECTORAL CONNECTION

Members' relationship to their constituents also must be understood within the context of their desire to be re-elected. Political scientist David Mayhew argues in *Congress: The Electoral Connection* that re-election must come first.[6] Members certainly hold multiple goals, including making good policy, but if they cannot maintain their seats, then they cannot attain other goals in office.

After assuming that re-election is central, Mayhew asks this question: "Members of Congress may be electorally motivated, but are they in a position to do anything about it?"[7] Although individual members of Congress cannot do much to alter national economic or political forces, they can control their own activities in the House or Senate. The importance of the **electoral connection** in explaining the behavior of members of Congress seems especially clear for marginal incumbents who are constantly trying to shore up their electoral base. But for those from safe districts, why should they worry?

electoral connection The idea that congressional behavior is centrally motivated by members' desire for re-election.

INCUMBENTS WORK TOWARD RE-ELECTION

Objectively, it looks as though about 90 percent of House members (and a large proportion of senators) are absolutely safe, but incumbents realize that this security is not guaranteed. Even in elections with relatively low turnover, many incumbents are "running scared"; in every election, a few supposedly safe incumbents are unexpectedly defeated, and members tend to think that it could be them the next time around. Mayhew warns, "When we say 'Congressman Smith is unbeatable,' we do not mean that there is nothing he could do that would lose him his seat." As we noted in Chapter 8, this actually means, "Congressman Smith is unbeatable as long as he continues to do the things that he is doing."[8] Members recognize that becoming inattentive to the district, being on the wrong side of a key string of votes, or failing to bring home the district's share of pork could cost them their seat. A potential challenger is always waiting in the wings.

Mayhew outlines three ways that members promote their chances for re-election: through advertising, credit claiming, and position taking. Each approach shapes the way members relate to their constituents. Advertising in this context refers to appeals or appearances without issue content that get the member's name before the public in a favorable way. Advertising includes activities associated with "working the district," such as attending town meetings, appearing in a parade, going to a local Rotary Club lunch, or sending letters of congratulation for graduations, birthdays, or anniversaries. Members of Congress also spend a fair amount of time meeting with constituents in Washington, such as school groups, tourists, and interest groups.

In the second activity, credit claiming, the member of Congress takes credit for something of value to the voter—most commonly, pork-barrel policies targeted to specific constituents or the district. The goods must be specific and small scale enough that the member of Congress may believably claim credit. In other words, it is far less credible to take credit for a national drop in violent crime or an increase in SAT scores than for the renovations at a local veterans' hospital or a highway improvement grant. The other main source of credit claiming is casework for individual constituents who request help with tasks such as tracking down a lost Social Security check or expediting the processing of a passport. This activity, like advertising, has both district-based and Washington-based components.

Position taking refers to any public statement—such as a roll call vote, speech, editorial, or position paper—about a topic of interest to constituents or interest groups. This may be the toughest aspect of a member's job because, on many issues, the member is likely to alienate a certain segment of the population no matter what position she takes. Members try to appeal to specific audiences within their district. For example, while speaking to the Veterans of Foreign Wars, a member might emphasize his support for a particular new weapons program, but in a meeting with college students, he might highlight his opposition to the war in Afghanistan.

The focus on re-election has some costs. We'll identify five common ones here. (1) There is a perception that Congress has granted itself too many special privileges aimed at securing re-election (such as funding for large staffs and the franking privilege of sending mail at no cost). This perception has led to harsh criticism of Congress in recent years. (2) Evidence suggests that some voters question the value of pork-barrel spending, even when it is targeted to their district.[9] (3) Members' desire to please means that Congress has a difficult time refusing any group's demands, which may lead to passage of contradictory policies. (4) Given that most members are experts at getting re-elected, they achieve a certain level of independence from the party leadership; that is, they do not depend on party leaders for their re-election. This fact contributes to the fragmentation of Congress and creates difficulties for congressional leaders as they attempt to shepherd policies through the legislative maze. (5) Time spent actively campaigning takes time away from the responsibilities of enacting laws and overseeing their implementation.

NATIONAL FORCES IN CONGRESSIONAL ELECTIONS

There is also another consequence of the electoral connection. Because congressional politics tends to be local, voters generally are not strongly influenced by the president or the national parties (although the president can play a role in congressional elections). Also, the national economy can have both direct and indirect influences on congressional races. However, the fact that most incumbents can insulate themselves from national forces makes it more difficult to hold the government accountable and may reduce the responsiveness of the political system.

Many House and Senate candidates distance themselves from the national party. For example, in the 2010 West Virginia Senate race, Democratic candidate Joe Manchin made his opposition to the Democratic Party's energy policy very clear with an ad in which he shoots a mock version of the bill with a rifle. However, in nationalized midterm elections, national issues can overwhelm incumbents' attempts to insulate themselves. In 2006, many House Republicans tried to distance themselves from President Bush and the unpopular war in Iraq, but more than twenty were defeated. In the 2010 midterms, the same thing happened to moderate Democrats who were ousted by voters who believed the government had gone too far in its response to the recession and health care. These national forces led to a loss of at least sixty House seats and six Senate seats for Democrats in 2010.

National forces in congressional elections also may be evident in presidential years. In 2008, Republicans faced a backlash against Bush, whose approval ratings had hit record lows. Republican members of Congress avoided being seen with him, and Democrats highlighted their opponents' earlier support for the president. The 2012 congressional elections ratified the status quo; despite Obama's solid win, the Republicans retained control of the House and the Democrats increased their majority in the Senate only slightly. Overall, the localized nature of congressional elections and the incumbency advantage promotes congressional stability in the face of presidential change. This has profound implications for governance because it increases the likelihood that different parties will control the presidency and Congress. This kind of divided government complicates accountability because the president and Congress have become adept at blaming each other when things go wrong.

SOME DEMOCRATS WHO WERE successful in the 2010 elections had to distance themselves from the party. Although Joe Manchin of West Virginia received support from prominent Democrats, including former president Bill Clinton, he won by emphasizing his willingness to go against his party.

REDISTRICTING

To understand the context of legislative constituencies, we also must consider their physical boundaries. District boundaries determine who is eligible to vote in any given congressional race, and these boundaries are redrawn every ten years, after each national census. **Redistricting** is the task of state legislatures. Its

redistricting Redrawing the geographic boundaries of legislative districts. This happens every ten years to ensure that districts remain roughly equal in population.

official purpose is to ensure that districts are roughly equal in population, which in turn ensures that every vote counts equally in determining the composition of the legislature.

apportionment The process of assigning the 435 seats in the House to the states based on increases or decreases in state population.

District populations vary over time as people move from state to state or from one part of a state to another. At the national level, states gain or lose legislative seats after each census through a process called **apportionment** as the fixed number of House seats (435) is divided among the states. (States growing the fastest gain seats, and those that are not growing as fast lose seats.) The one legislature in America that is not redistricted is the U.S. Senate, which elects two legislators per state, thus giving voters in small states more influence than those in large states.

CRITERIA FOR REDISTRICTING

In theory, redistricting proceeds from a set of principles that define what districts should look like. One criterion is that districts should be roughly equal in population. They should also capture "communities of interest," grouping like-minded voters into the same district. There are also technical criteria, including compactness (districts should not have extremely bizarre shapes) and contiguity (one part of a district cannot be completely separated from the rest of the district). Mapmakers also try to respect traditional natural boundaries, avoid splitting municipalities, preserve existing districts, and avoid diluting the voting power of racial minorities.

PARTISAN REDISTRICTING

Although these principles are important, they are not the driving force in the redistricting process. Just as war is "diplomacy by other means," redistricting is electioneering by other means. Suppose a Democrat holds a state assembly seat from an urban district populated mainly by citizens with strong Democratic Party ties. After a census, the Republican-dominated state legislature develops a new plan that extends the representative's district into the suburbs, claiming that the change counteracts population declines within the city by adding suburban voters. However, these suburban voters will likely be Republicans, increasing the chance that the Democrat will face strong opposition in future elections and maybe lose her seat. Such changes have an important impact on voters as well. Voters who are "moved" to a new district by a change in boundaries may be unable to vote for the incumbent they have supported for years, instead getting a representative who doesn't share their views.

In congressional redistricting, a reduction in the number of seats allocated to a state can lead to districting plans that put two incumbents in the same district, forcing them to run against each other. Incumbents from one party use these opportunities to defeat incumbents from the other party. Both parties use this technique and other tools of creative cartography to gain partisan advantage. In the 2012 redistricting cycle Illinois drew the most egregious map in favor of Democrats, including one district in Chicago that looks like a pair of earmuffs, while Pennsylvania drew a "group of Rorschach-inkblot districts" that turned a state that normally tilts Democratic to one in which twelve of eighteen districts lean Republican.[10] The most dramatic recent example of redistricting for partisan purposes was in Texas. Deviating from the standard practice of redrawing district lines only once every decade, Republicans decided to change the district boundaries that had been in effect for only one election. Democratic legislators were outraged by the partisan power grab and fled the state (they hid out in Oklahoma) to prevent the special session of the legislature from convening. Eventually Republicans were able to implement their plan and gain five House seats in the 2004 elections. The U.S. Supreme Court upheld the Texas plan, saying that even when partisan advantage is the only motivation for redistricting, this does not make the resulting plan unconstitutional.[11]

These attempts to use the redistricting process for political advantage are called **gerrymandering**. The term is named after Elbridge Gerry, a Massachusetts House member and governor, vice president under James Madison, and author of one of the original partisan redistricting plans (including a district with a thin, winding shape resembling a salamander). In addition to the partisan gerrymanders discussed here, see Nuts and Bolts 10.1 for descriptions of several other types.

gerrymandering Attempting to use the process of redrawing district boundaries to benefit a political party, protect incumbents, or change the proportion of minority voters in a district.

RACIAL REDISTRICTING

Redistricting may yield boundaries that look highly unusual. During the 1992 redistricting in North Carolina, the Justice Department told state legislators that they needed to create two districts with majority populations of minority voters (called majority-minority districts). Figure 10.4 shows the plan they enacted, in which the district boundaries look like a pattern of spider webs and ink blots. Moreover, one of the districts had parts that ended up being only as wide as interstate I-85, following the highway off an exit ramp, over a bridge, and down the entrance ramp on the other side. This move prevented the I-85 district from bisecting the district it

10.1 NUTS & bolts

TYPES OF GERRYMANDERS

Partisan gerrymanders: Elected officials from one party draw district lines that benefit candidates from their party and hurt candidates from other parties. This usually occurs when one party has majorities in both houses of the state legislature and occupies the governorship, and can therefore enact redistricting legislation without votes from the minority party.

Incumbent gerrymanders: Lines are drawn to benefit the current group of incumbents. This usually occurs when control of state government is divided between parties and support from both parties is required to enact a districting plan, or when plans must be approved by judges or bipartisan panels.

Racial gerrymanders: Redistricting is used to help or hurt the chances of minority legislative candidates. The Voting Rights Act (VRA) of 1965 mandated that districting plans for many parts of the South be approved by the U.S. Department of Justice or a Washington, D.C., district court. Subsequent interpretation of the 1982 VRA amendments and Supreme Court decisions led to the creation of districts in which racial minorities are in the majority. The original aim of these majority-minority districts was to raise the percentage of African American and Latino elected officials. However, Republicans in some southern states have used this requirement to enact plans that elect minorities (who tend to be Democrats) in some districts but favor Republicans in adjoining districts.

Candidate gerrymanders: District plans that favor certain individuals, particularly state legislators planning to run for the U.S. House. For example, a Republican state legislator would want to construct a congressional district with a high percentage of Republican voters and as many of his current constituents as possible.

FIGURE » 10.4

NORTH CAROLINA REDISTRICTING, 1992

This set of House districts was the subject of the landmark Supreme Court ruling *Shaw v. Reno* (1993), in which the Court said that "appearances matter" when drawing district lines. Do you agree? Should other factors such as race, party, and competitiveness play a greater role than district shape?

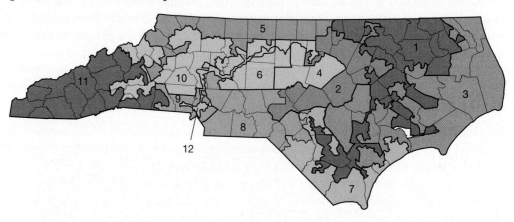

Source: North Carolina General Assembly, 1992 Congressional Base Plan No. 10, http://ncga.state.nc.us/GIS/ Download/ReferenceDocs/2011/NC%20Congressional%20Districts%20-%20Historical%20Plans%20-%201941 -1992.pdf (accessed 10/26/12).

was traveling through, which would have violated the state law requiring contiguous districts.

The North Carolina example shows how convoluted redistricting plans can become. Part of the complexity is due to the availability of census databases that allow line-drawers to divide voters as closely as they want, moving neighborhood by neighborhood, even house by house. Why bother with this level of detail? Because redistricting influences who gets elected; it is active politicking in its most fundamental form. The North Carolina plan was ultimately declared unconstitutional by the U.S. Supreme Court—a ruling that opened the door for dozens of lawsuits about racial redistricting. The current legal standard is that race cannot be the predominant factor in drawing congressional district lines, but it may be a factor. However, there is still plenty of room to create districts that have profound political consequences. The obvious political implications of redistricting often lead to demands that district plans be prepared or approved by nonpartisan committees or by panels of judges who are theoretically immune from political pressure. Such a process, as in Iowa, often produces more competitive districts.

CONGRESS'S IMAGE PROBLEM

Despite members' strong links to their constituents, efforts to secure re-election, and districts that are designed in their favor, public approval of Congress is generally very low. Bashing Congress has long been a favorite national pastime.

Mark Twain said, "It could probably be shown by facts and figures that there is no distinctly native criminal class except Congress." He also said, "Assume you are a fool. Now assume you are a member of Congress . . . but I repeat myself."

Many Americans seem to agree with Twain. Approval of Congress rarely tops 50 percent (a recent exception was following the terrorist attacks of September 11, 2001). Through most of 2012, approval for Congress hovered in the low teens and was only 16 percent before Election Day in November. And the public's cynical view of Congress runs deep. Well over half of all Americans agree with statements such as "The government is pretty much run by a few big interests looking out for themselves." A poll conducted by Fox News asked, "In general, which of the following do you think better describes most senators and representatives on Capitol Hill these days? (a) Statesmen doing service for their country; (b) Petty politicians fighting for personal gain." Only 17 percent answered "statesmen," and 63 percent said "petty politicians" (the rest said "mixed" or "unsure"). Another poll found that members of Congress landed fifth from the bottom in a ranking of twenty-six professions in terms of perceived honesty and ethical standards.[12]

Why does Congress have such an image problem? Some of the abuse heaped on Congress is self-inflicted. Although political corruption for personal gain is rare in Congress (only four members have been indicted on bribery charges since 1981), there are periodic scandals such as the "check bouncing" incident involving members' accounts at the House bank and the misuse of House post office funds in the early 1990s.[13] Several members of Congress, Democrats and Republicans alike, were implicated in the scandal surrounding lobbyist Jack Abramoff (see Chapter 9). Mark Foley (R-Fla.) brought more shame on the House when his steamy e-mails to sixteen-year-old House pages were revealed. Foley quickly resigned when his inappropriate behavior was exposed. Other sex scandals involved Senator Larry Craig (R-Ida.), who pled guilty to a "disorderly conduct" charge for an apparent attempt to solicit sex in a men's bathroom in the Minneapolis airport; Senator John Ensign (R-Nev.), who had an affair with a campaign staffer who was the wife of Ensign's administrative assistant; and Representative Anthony Weiner (D-N.Y.), who resigned after sending lewd pictures of himself on Twitter. The two most serious recent cases involved bribery. In one, representative William Jefferson (D-La.) was found guilty of soliciting bribes, money laundering, and using his office as a racketeering enterprise. Jefferson was infamous for being caught with $90,000 in marked bills hidden in his freezer that the FBI said were to be used to bribe Nigerian officials. Yet, despite such scandals, most members of Congress are dedicated public servants who work hard for their constituents.

UNFORTUNATELY, MEMBERS OF Congress do include some of the "criminal class" noted by Mark Twain. Former representatives Randy "Duke" Cunningham (R-Calif.), shown with his wife Nancy, and William Jefferson (D-La.) are both serving time in federal prison for corruption. The bottom photo shows cash found in Jefferson's freezer.

MEDIA INFLUENCES

Although politicians traditionally blame the media for their poor standing in the polls, in this instance there is some basis for the complaints. One study examined stories on Congress in various national newspapers and magazines during ten political periods between 1946 and 1992 and concluded that coverage of Congress has always been somewhat superficial and negative: "press coverage of Congress focuses on scandal, partisan rivalry, and interbranch conflict rather than the more complex subjects such as policy, process, and institutional concerns."[14]

From this perspective, the professional context of journalism, with its short news cycle and the need to produce a salable product, creates pressure for superficial

coverage that perpetuates Congress's image problem. Burdett Loomis, a congressional scholar, bets his students every year that they cannot find a post-1970 political cartoon that depicts Congress in an unambiguously positive light. In more than ten years, no student has been able to collect on the bet.[15] However, a recent study using more than 8,000 newspaper stories on members of Congress over a two-year period found that 70 percent of news stories were neutral, and of the 30 percent that had some spin, positive stories outnumbered negative stories five to one. Letters to the editor and editorials or opinion pieces were evenly balanced between negative and positive viewpoints.[16]

THE RESPONSIBILITY–RESPONSIVENESS DILEMMA

Congress's image problem isn't simply a matter of negative media coverage or a cynical public. It is rooted in the basic representational conflicts that arise from Congress's dual roles: responsibility for national policy making and responsiveness to local constituencies.[17] This duality may make members of Congress appear to be simultaneously small-minded seekers of meaningless symbolic legislation and great leaders who debate important issues. Indeed, the range of issues that Congress must address is vast, from taxes and health care reform to overseeing the classification of black-eyed peas; from authorizing the war with Afghanistan and expanding free trade to declaring a National Cholesterol Education Month. Part of the national frustration with Congress arises because we want our representatives to be responsible *and* responsive; we want them to be great national leaders *and* take care of our local and, at times, personal concerns.

But often it is impossible to satisfy both of these demands at the same time—difficult choices have to be made between being responsive or responsible. Rather than understanding these issues as inherent in the legislative process, we often accuse members of **gridlock** and partisan bickering when our conflicting demands are not met. For example, public opinion polls routinely show that the public wants lower taxes; more spending in education, the environment, and health care; and balanced budgets, but those three things cannot happen simultaneously. We often expect the impossible from Congress and then are frustrated when it doesn't happen.

The responsibility–responsiveness dilemma brings us back to the puzzle we posed at the beginning of this section: Why is there a persistent 30 percent to 40 percent gap between approval ratings for individual members and for the institution? As one of the leading congressional scholars of the twentieth century, Richard Fenno, put it, "If Congress is the 'broken branch,' how come we love our congressman so much?"[18] The answer may simply be that members of Congress tend to respond more to their constituents' demands than they take on the responsibility of solving national problems. And when Congress becomes embroiled in debates about constituencies' conflicting demands, the institution may appear ineffectual. But as long as members keep the "folks back home" happy, their individual popularity will remain high. The next section describes how members use this and other techniques to cultivate an incumbency advantage.

gridlock An inability to enact legislation because of partisan conflict within Congress or between Congress and the president.

MEMBERS OF CONGRESS TRY to keep the "folks back home" happy with projects like this groundbreaking ceremony in New Jersey for an $8.7 billion tunnel. (The project was later canceled.)

THE INCUMBENCY ADVANTAGE AND ITS SOURCES

ANALYZE THE FACTORS THAT HELP MEMBERS OF CONGRESS GET RE-ELECTED

The desire to be re-elected influences House members' and senators' behavior both in the district and in Congress. Consider the early career of Representative Tammy Baldwin (D-Wis.). In 1998 she became the first woman from Wisconsin and the first openly gay person ever elected to a freshman term in Congress.[19] In her first two elections, she won with the overwhelming support of liberal voters in Madison but lost the surrounding rural areas and suburbs, narrowly winning districtwide. Baldwin recognized that she needed to shore up support outside Madison and spent time over the next several years meeting with constituents in the rural and suburban parts of her district. She also explored issues important to these voters, such as the dairy price support program and the problem of chronic wasting disease in Wisconsin deer. Having shored up her electoral base (and having benefited from favorable redistricting in 2002), she cruised to victories in her next two elections winning nearly two-thirds of the vote.

As this story plays out across the country, members' success at pleasing constituents produces large election rewards. As Figures 10.5A and 10.5B show, very few members are defeated in their re-election races. One way that political scientists have documented the growth of **incumbency advantage** is to examine the electoral margins in House elections. If a member is elected with less than 55 percent of the vote, he or she is said to hold a marginal seat. Since the late 1960s, the number of marginal districts has been declining. Having fewer marginal districts does

incumbency advantage The relative infrequency with which members of Congress are defeated in their attempts for re-election.

FIGURE » 10.5A

HOUSE INCUMBENCY RE-ELECTION RATES, 1948–2012

The rate of defeat for incumbent House members is very low, typically in the 5 percent to 10 percent range, while total turnover is quite a bit higher. Which data are more central for debates about the importance of term limits? Which data are more central to discussions of electoral accountability?

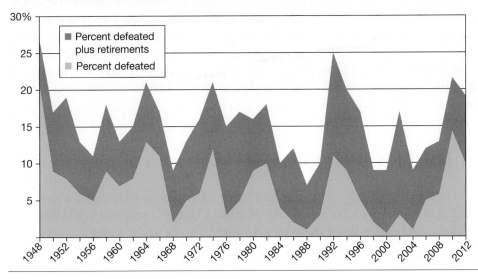

FIGURE » 10.5B

SENATE INCUMBENCY RE-ELECTION RATES, 1948–2012*

Incumbency re-election rates are noticeably more volatile in the Senate than in the House. What implications does this have for the Founders' belief that the Senate should be more insulated from popular control than the House? Does the Senate's six-year term help provide that insulation?

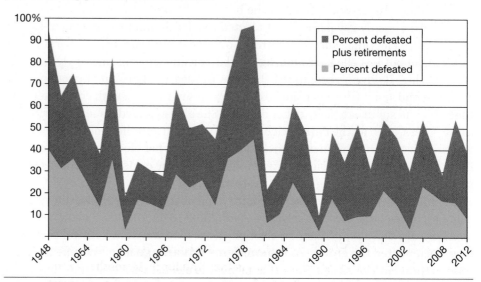

*Percentage for the Senate is of those up for re-election.

Sources for 10.5A and B: Compiled from Center for Responsive Politics, Re-election Rates over the Years, www.opensecrets.org/bigpicture/reelect.php; and Norman J. Ornstein, Thomas E. Mann, and Michael J. Malbin, Vital Statistics on Congress: 1999–2000 (Washington, DC: CQ Press, 2000), pp. 60–63; 2010 and 2012 percentages calculated from election results, http://elections.nytimes.com (accessed 11/10/12).

not necessarily translate into fewer incumbent defeats, but in the past two decades, incumbent re-election rates have been near record-high levels, with 95 to 98 percent of House incumbents winning in many years.[20]

In 2008, in an election that many called "transformational," 95 percent of House incumbents were re-elected. Although the Democrats picked up some seats in the Senate, re-election remained the norm there as well. Even in the "tsunami" election of 2010, in which Republicans made the largest gains in the House since 1948 in picking up at least 60 seats, 86 percent of incumbents were re-elected. Why are incumbents so successful? Scholars have offered several reasons for this increase in incumbency advantage.

IN THE DISTRICT: HOME STYLE

One explanation for increasing incumbency advantage is rooted in the diversity of congressional districts and states. Members typically respond to the diversity in their districts by developing an appropriate home style: a way of relating to the district.[21] A home style shapes the way members allocate resources, the way incumbents present themselves to others, and the way they explain their policy positions.

Given the variation among districts, members' home styles vary as well. In some rural districts it is important for representatives to have local roots, and voters expect extensive contact with members. Urban districts expect a different kind of style. They have a more mobile population, so it is not crucial to be home-grown. Voters expect less direct contact and place more emphasis on how members explain their policy positions. Incumbency advantage may be explained in part by the skill with which members have cultivated their individual home styles in the last two decades. Members are spending more time at home and less time in Washington than was true a generation ago. This familiarity with the voters has helped them remain in office.

Table 10.1 shows how one member, Representative Tammy Baldwin, spends her time in Washington and in her district. In general, a legislator's workday in the Capitol is split between committee meetings, briefings, staff meetings, meetings with constituents, and various dinners and fund-raisers with interest groups and other organizations, punctuated by dashes to the floor of the House or Senate to vote. Days in the district are spent meeting with constituents to explain what is happening in Washington and listen to voters' concerns.

CAMPAIGN FUND-RAISING

Raising money is also key to staying in office. Thomas "Tip" O'Neill, Speaker of the House in the 1970s and 1980s, used to say that "money is the mother's milk of politics." Incumbents need money to pay for campaign staff, travel, and advertising. It takes at least $1 million to make a credible challenge to an incumbent in most districts, and in many areas with expensive media markets the minimum price tag is $2 million or more. Few challengers can raise that much money. The gap between incumbent and challenger spending has grown dramatically in the past decade, and incumbents now spend about three times as much, on average, as challengers. Incumbents have far greater potential to raise vast sums of money, in part because political action committees (PACs) are unwilling to risk alienating an incumbent by donating to challengers. (For more on campaign finance, see Chapters 8 and 9).

Money also functions as a deterrent to potential challengers. A sizable re-election fund signals that an incumbent knows how to raise money and will run a strong campaign. The aim is to convince would-be challengers that they have a slim chance of beating the incumbent—and to convince contributors and party organizations that there's no point in trying to find or support a challenger.

This last point is crucial in explaining incumbency advantage because it is nearly impossible to beat an incumbent with a weak challenger. Consider that only 10 percent to 15 percent of challengers in a typical election year have any previous elective experience; when such a high proportion of challengers are amateurs, it is not surprising so many incumbents win.

CONSTITUENCY SERVICE

Another thing incumbents do to get re-elected is "work their districts," taking every opportunity to meet with constituents, listen to their concerns, and perform case-work (helping constituents interact with government programs or agencies). Most

TABLE » 10.1

TYPICAL WORK DAYS FOR REPRESENTATIVE TAMMY BALDWIN (D-WIS.)

IN WASHINGTON, D.C.
(Votes scheduled throughout the day)

9:15–9:45	Office time
9:45–10:00	Caucus, Democratic members, Subcommittee on Energy and Environment on markup legislation
10:00–12:00	Markup H.R. 3276, H.R. 3258, H.R. 2868, Subcommittee on Energy and Environment
11:30–11:45	Step outside markup to meet with constituents on specifics of health care reform legislation
12:00–12:15	Travel to Department of Justice
12:15–1:15	Lunch with Attorney General Eric Holder
1:30–1:45	Meet with health care CEO on specifics of health care reform legislation
2:00–3:00	Meet with members who support single-payer health care amendment
3:00–4:30	Markup H.R. 3792, Subcommittee on Health
4:30–5:30	Office time
5:30–6:00	Caucus, Democratic members, Energy and Commerce Committee on financial services bill
6:00–6:30	Meet with legislative staff
6:30–7:00	Meet with chief of staff
7:00–7:50	Office time
8:00–10:00	Dinner with chief of staff and political adviser

IN THE DISTRICT

7:00 ET–8:00 CT	Fly from Washington, D.C., to Madison, WI
8:15–10:30	Free time at home
10:30–10:40	Phone interview with area radio station on constituent survey, health care reform, and upcoming listening session
12:15–12:25	Travel to office
12:25–1:05	Office time, edit/sign correspondence
1:00–1:20	Travel to Madison West High School
1:30–1:55	Remarks at school plaza dedication ceremony
2:00–2:30	Travel to Stoughton, WI
2:45–5:00	Listening session (originally scheduled for one hour but continued until all present could speak)
5:00–5:40	Travel home
5:15–5:20	Phone interview with University of Wisconsin student radio station
6:15–6:45	Travel to Middleton, WI
7:00–8:00	Attend and give brief remarks at NAACP annual banquet
8:05–8:25	Travel home

Note: The authors would like to thank Representative Tammy Baldwin and her press secretary, Jerilyn Goodman, for sharing this information. Ms. Goodman emphasized that there really isn't a "typical day" for the member but said that these two days illustrate the work load.

legislators travel around their districts or states with several staffers whose job is to talk to people who meet the incumbent, and write down contact information and what the incumbent has promised to do. High levels of constituency service may help explain why some incumbents have become electorally secure.

Members of Congress love doing constituency service because it is an easy way to make voters happy. If a member can help a constituent solve a problem, that person will be more likely to support the member in the future.[22] Many voters might give the incumbent some credit simply for being willing to listen. Therefore, most members devote a significant portion of their staff to constituency service, publish newsletters that tout their good deeds on behalf of constituents, and solicit citizens' requests for help through their newsletters and websites. Most House members have a "How can I help?" type of link on their home page that connects to information on government agencies, grants, internships, service academies, and visiting Washington, D.C.

Most House members work their districts to an extreme; they are said to be in the "Tuesday to Thursday Club," meaning they are in Washington only during the middle of the week, spending the rest of their time at home in their districts. These members go to diners and coffee shops on Saturday mornings to chat over coffee, spend the day at public events in their "Meet Your Representative" RV, then hit the bowling alleys at night to meet a few more people. One member has even joked that his wife has given up sending him out for groceries because he spends three hours talking with people while getting a loaf of bread.

This combination of factors gives incumbents substantial advantages over candidates who might run against them. By virtue of their position, they can help constituents who have problems with an agency or program. They attract media attention because of their actions in office; small local newspapers will even reprint members' press releases verbatim because they do not have the resources to do their own reporting. Members can use the money and other resources associated with their position for casework and contact with voters (trips home to their district and the salaries of their staffers who do constituency service are taxpayer-funded). And they use their official position as a platform for raising campaign cash. A contributor who donates as a way to gain access to the policy-making process will be inclined to give to someone already in office. Finally, most incumbents represent states or districts whose partisan balance (the number of likely supporters of their party versus the number likely to prefer the other party) is skewed in their favor—if it wasn't, they probably wouldn't have won the seat in the first place.

SENATOR ROY BLUNT (R-MO.) spoke on the Senate floor in September of 2011 about the need for disaster relief funding for Missourians.

THE STRUCTURE OF CONGRESS

EXAMINE HOW PARTIES, THE COMMITTEE SYSTEM, AND STAFFERS ENABLE CONGRESS TO FUNCTION

Much of the structure of Congress is set up to meet the electoral needs of its members. David Mayhew's key observation supporting this idea is that very little of what it takes to get re-elected involves zero-sum processes, in which one person's gain is another's loss.[23] For example, it would be possible for the majority party to shut out the minority party when it came to allocating discretionary resources. Veterans hospitals, federal government offices, and grants to universities could be located in majority party members' districts. If the institution were more zero-sum, then there would be more competition and rivalry. Instead, norms of universalism and reciprocity still dominate, so resources are shared more broadly. There are several aspects of the structure of Congress that facilitate members' re-election, including informal structures (norms) and formal structures (staff, the committee system, parties, and the leadership).

Despite the importance of the electoral connection, the goal of being re-elected cannot explain everything about members' behavior and the congressional structure. This section examines some other explanations for the way Congress is set up: the policy motivations of members, the partisan basis for congressional institutions, and the informational advantages of the committee system.

INFORMAL STRUCTURES

Various norms provide an informal structure for the way Congress works. Universalism is a norm stating that when benefits are being divided up, as many districts and states as possible should benefit. Thus, when it comes to handing out federal highway dollars or expenditures for the Pentagon's weapons programs, the benefits are broadly distributed across the entire country, which means that votes in support of these bills tend to be very lopsided. For example, the $662 billion 2012 defense appropriations bill contained some spending in every part of the country and passed by an 86-to-13 vote in the Senate and a 286-to-136 margin in the House.[24]

Another norm, reciprocity, reinforces universalism with the idea that "if you scratch my back, I'll scratch yours." This norm (also called logrolling) leads members of Congress to support bills that they otherwise might not vote for in exchange for another member's vote on a bill that is very important to them. For example, a House member from a dairy state might vote for tobacco price supports even if there are no tobacco farmers in his state, and in return he would expect a member from the tobacco state to vote for the dairy price support bill. This norm can produce wasteful pork-barrel spending. For example, in 2011 a $1.1 trillion omnibus appropriations bill contained more than 6,488 **earmarks** worth $8.3 billion, so nearly everyone gained something by passing it. The 2012 omnibus appropriations bill did not include any traditional earmarks, following congressional efforts to limit the practice; however, there was still $3.5 billion in unauthorized spending on defense alone.[25] The "You Decide" box describes some of the fierce debates in Congress and among political commentators about the merit of this type of spending.[26]

The norm of specialization is also important, both for the efficient operation of Congress and for members' re-election. By specializing and becoming expert on a given issue, members provide valuable information to the institution as a whole and also create a basis for credit claiming. This norm is stronger in the House, where members often develop a few areas of expertise, whereas senators tend to be policy generalists. For example, Representative Henry Waxman (D-Calif.) has dedicated much of his decades-long House career to the issue of health care, while Senator John McCain (R-Ariz.) has had his hand in a variety of issues, including

earmarks Federally funded local projects attached to bills passed through Congress.

campaign finance and lobbying reform, tax policy, telecommunications and aviation issues, national defense, foreign policy, and immigration policy.

The **seniority** norm also serves individual and institutional purposes. This norm holds that the member with the longest service on a committee will chair the committee. Although there have been numerous violations of the norm in the past thirty years, whereby the most senior member is passed over for someone whom the party leaders favor instead, the norm benefits the institution by ensuring orderly succession in committee leadership.[27] The norm also benefits members by providing a tangible reason that voters should return them to Congress year after year. Many members of Congress make this point when campaigning, and the issue is more than just posturing. Committee chairs *are* better able to "bring home the bacon" than a junior member who is still learning the ropes. For example, Don Young, the former Transportation Committee chair in the House, was able to secure funding for the infamous "bridge to nowhere," a $435 million project to connect Ketchikan, Alaska, with a barely inhabited island. (The project was canceled after it became a symbol of pork-barrel spending.)

seniority The informal congressional norm of choosing the member who has served the longest on a particular committee to be the committee chair.

FORMAL STRUCTURES

Formal structures also shape member behavior in Congress. Political parties, party leadership, the committee system, and staff provide the context within which members of Congress make policy and represent their constituents.

PARTIES AND PARTY LEADERS

Political parties are important for allocating power in Congress. Party leaders are always elected on straight party-line votes, and committee leadership, the division of seats on committees, and the allocation of committee resources are all determined by the majority party. Parties in Congress also become more important when opposing parties control the two chambers. This was the case between 1981 and 1987 when Republicans controlled the Senate and Democrats

PARTY LEADERSHIP IS CENTRAL in the legislative process. Following the overwhelming victory in the 2010 midterm elections that swept their party to power, Republicans Eric Cantor (R-Va.) and John Boehner (R-Ohio) met to talk about strategy for the upcoming Congress. Boehner became the Speaker and Cantor the House majority leader in January 2011.

controlled the House, and in part of 2001 and 2002 and 2011–12 when the opposite was true.

A leading theory of congressional organization points to the importance of parties in solving collective action problems in Congress. Without parties, the legislative process would be much more fractured and decentralized because members would be autonomous agents in battle with each other. Parties provide a team framework that allows members to work together for broadly beneficial goals. Just think how difficult it would be for a member of Congress to get a bill passed if she had to build a coalition from scratch every time. Instead, parties provide a solid base from which coalition building may begin. As discussed in Chapter 7, political parties provide the collective good of brand name recognition for members.

Speaker of the House The elected leader of the House of Representatives.

The top party leader in the House—and the only House leader mentioned in the Constitution—is the **Speaker of the House**, who is the head of the majority party and influences the legislative agenda, committee assignments, scheduling, and overall party strategy. The Democratic Party made history in January 2007 when its representatives elected Nancy Pelosi as the first woman to serve as Speaker. John Boehner was elected Speaker in 2011 after Republicans retook control of the House in the 2010 midterm elections. The Speaker is aided by the **majority leader**, the majority whip, and the caucus chair (in addition to many other lower-level party positions). The majority leader is one of the national spokespersons for the party and also helps with the day-to-day operation of the legislative process. The majority whip oversees the extensive **whip system**, which has three functions: information gathering, information dissemination, and coalition building. The whips meet regularly to discuss legislative strategy and scheduling. The whips then pass along this information to colleagues in their respective parties and indicate the party's position on a given bill. Whips also take a headcount of party members in the House on specific votes and communicate this information to the party leaders.

majority leader The elected head of the party holding the majority of seats in the House or Senate.

whip system An organization of House leaders who work to disseminate information and promote party unity in voting on legislation.

If a vote looks close, whips try to persuade members to support the party's position ("whip" comes from the term "whipper-in" from English fox hunts, the person who keeps the hounds from wandering too far from the pack; similarly, party whips try to ensure that members do not stray too far from the party position). The conference chair (or caucus chair for the Democrats) runs the party meetings to elect floor leaders, make committee assignments, and set legislative agendas. The minority party in the House has a parallel structure: its leader is the **minority leader,** and the second in command is the minority whip.

minority leader The elected head of the party holding the minority of seats in the House or Senate.

The Senate leadership does not have as much power as the leadership of the House, mostly because individual senators have more power than House members due to the Senate's rule of unlimited debate. The majority leader and minority leader are the leaders of their respective parties, and second in command to them are the assistant majority and minority leaders. The Senate also has a whip system, but it is not as developed as the House system. Republicans have a separate position for the conference chair, while the Democratic leader serves also as conference chair. The country's vice president is officially the president of the Senate, but he appears in the chamber only when needed to cast a tie-breaking vote. The Constitution also mentions the **president pro tempore** of the Senate, whose formal duties involve presiding over the Senate when the vice president is not there. This is typically the most senior member of the majority party, and the position does not have any real power. (In fact, the actual president pro tempore rarely presides over the Senate, and the task is typically given to a more junior senator.)

president pro tempore A largely symbolic position usually held by the most senior member of the majority party in the Senate.

POLARIZATION IN CONGRESS

The evidence that parties in Congress have become increasingly polarized over the past forty years is not in dispute. What *is* in dispute are the *reasons* this is the case.

The debate over the causes of polarization in Congress is a good example of an important thing political scientists do: test rival explanations and offer alternatives that seem to explain things better. The first work on this topic was David Rohde's finding of a shift in the behavior of southern Democrats. This work became the basis for electorally grounded explanations for increased polarization in Congress. Rohde's initial insights are true, but subsequent work provided a more complete explanation.

The evolution of this topic shows the two distinct phases that most research questions go through: political scientists build on some original work (such as Rohde's) and then begin to offer challenges (often these two phases happen simultaneously rather than sequentially). Researchers have built on the electorally based explanations for polarization by offering three main reasons that Congress has become more polarized: ideological sorting, redistricting, and the nomination process. The first refers to the natural sorting of voters into purer partisan enclaves, which happens when people want to live with others who think like they do. For example, wealthy suburban communities tend to vote Republican; urban, racially diverse communities tend to vote Democratic. There is good evidence that this "big sort" has produced ideological polarization.[a] Redistricting initially seems to be another appealing explanation for why Congress is more polarized, but evidence suggests this is not the case. Finally, increasing party influence over the nomination process may produce more polarizing candidates with parties implementing a "purity test" that filters out more moderate nominees.

Watch a videoclip of Sean Theriault discussing this topic at **wwnorton.com/studyspace**

All of these strands of research provide some support for Rohde's initial claim, but recent work by University of Texas political scientist Sean Theriault suggests there may be more to the story. He argues that if increased polarization is caused only by electoral forces, polarization should be evident only in those districts that have become more homogeneous in partisan and ideological terms. However, he finds that polarization is also evident in moderate, competitive districts.[b]

So why are House members in competitive districts more polarized now than they were forty years ago and why is the Senate, which is less affected by the "big sort" and completely unaffected by redistricting, also more polarized today? Theriault offers compelling evidence that much of the increased polarization in Congress is due to the larger proportion of procedural votes on legislative process (as opposed to final votes on legislation) in the past three decades. Procedural

Senate Minority Leader Mitch McConnell (R-Ky.) and Senate Majority Leader Harry Reid (D-Nev.) in a rare moment of comity. Why has polarization in Congress increased?

votes in the House include votes on motions to recommit and on the rules of debate; and in the Senate, on whether amendments will be allowed or on cloture. These votes tend to be much more polarized than votes on final passage because, as we have argued, process in Congress is a powerful force for determining winners and losers. For example, the motion to recommit gives the minority party their last shot at changing a bill. Those votes tend to break down along party lines. If that vote fails, then members of the minority party must either vote for or against the existing bill, and often there is enough they like about the bill that they vote for it, even if they voted against it in the procedural vote. Thus, votes on final passage are often less polarized than procedural votes.

In subsequent work, Theriault examines the co-sponsorship of legislation in the House on 968 bills. If the polarization of Congress is due to substantive differences between the parties, polarization should be evident in co-sponsorship (Democrats co-sponsor Democratic bills and Republicans co-sponsor Republican bills). Indeed, the polarization of co-sponsors has increased since the 1970s (thus about 80 percent of co-sponsors are from the same party), but that increase is about 25 percent less than the increase in member polarization, which means that procedural polarization probably accounts for the difference.[c]

This important new work should be viewed as a complementary explanation to the previous electorally based arguments. As Theriault says, "Only when the changes within the constituency interact with the legislative process does the complete picture of party polarization in the U.S. Congress come into clearer focus."

THE ROLE OF PARTIES AND CONDITIONAL PARTY GOVERNMENT

Political parties in Congress also reflect the individualism of the institution. Compared to parliamentary systems, U.S. congressional parties are very weak (see Comparing Ourselves to Others). They do not impose a party line or penalize members who vote against the party. Indeed, they have virtually no ability to impose electoral restrictions (such as denying the party's nomination) on renegade members. Thus, from the perspective of a member seeking re-election, parties are more useful for what they are not—they do not force members to vote with the party—than for what they are. Though there are significant party differences on many issues, on about half of all **roll call votes**, majorities of both parties are on the same side.

Although still weaker than their overseas counterparts, parties in Congress have greatly strengthened since the 1960s (see Figure 10.6). Partisanship—evident when party members stick together in opposition to the other party—reached its highest levels in the post–World War II era in the mid-1990s. About 70 percent of all roll call votes were **party votes**, in which a majority of one party opposed a majority of the other party. The proportion of party votes has since fallen but remains between 50 and 60 percent. The *Congressional Quarterly* created the measure in 1953, and since that time, the high in the Senate was reached in 2009 at 72 percent and 75.8 percent in the House in 2011. **Party unity**, the percentage of party members voting together on party votes, soared during this period as well, especially in the House.

The Democratic Party has become much more cohesive as southern Democrats have started to vote more like their northern counterparts, partly because of the increasing importance of African American voters in the South and because increasing Republican strength in the South means that remaining Democratic districts are more liberal. Similarly, there are fewer moderates within the Republican Party, as most regions of the country that used to elect them are now electing Democrats.[28] Another way to examine these developments is the ideological

roll call vote A recorded vote on legislation; members may vote yes, no, abstain, or present.

party vote A vote in which the majority of one party opposes the position of the majority of the other party.

party unity The extent to which members of Congress in the same party vote together on party votes.

FIGURE » 10.6A

PARTY VOTES IN CONGRESS, 1962–2011

These graphs make two important points. First, partisanship has increased in the last two decades, both in terms of the proportion of party votes and the level of party unity. Second, despite these increased levels of partisanship, only about half of all votes in the House and Senate divide the two parties. Given these potentially conflicting observations, how would you assess the argument that partisanship in Congress is far too intense?

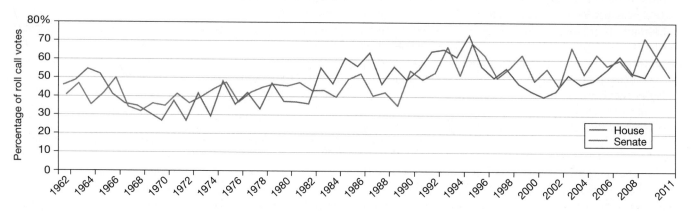

FIGURE » 10.6B

PARTY UNITY IN CONGRESS, 1962–2011

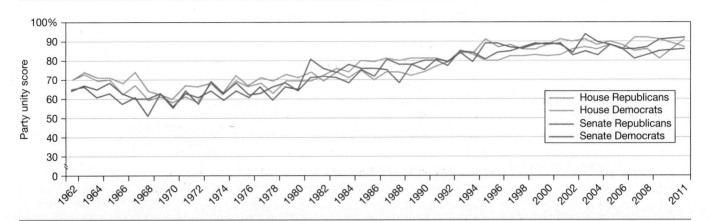

Sources for 10.6A and 10.6B: Data from Norman J. Ornstein, Thomas E. Mann, and Michael J. Malbin, Vital Statistics on Congress: 1999–2000 *(Washington, DC: CQ Press, 2000), pp. 201–3, and more recent editions of* Congressional Quarterly Almanac.

distribution of members of Congress (see Figure 10.7). In the 1970s, there was considerable overlap between the Democratic and Republican parties, but in the most recent Congress, the two parties are almost completely separated. That is, only a few Democrats are more conservative than the most liberal Republican. (See the What Do Political Scientists Do? box for an explanation of increasing partisan polarization.)

This greater cohesiveness within parties and separation across parties means that conditional party government (see Chapter 7) may be in play; that is, strong party leadership is possible in Congress, but it is conditional on the consent of party members.[29] That consent is more likely if there are strong differences between the parties and homogeneity within parties. Leaders' primary responsibility is to get their party's legislative agenda through Congress, but their negative powers are quite limited. The positive powers they have mostly take the form of agenda control and persuasion. Leaders' success largely depends on personal skills, communicative abilities, and trust. Some of the most successful leaders, such as Lyndon Johnson (D-Tex.), majority leader of the Senate from 1955 to 1961, and Sam Rayburn (D-Tex.), Speaker of the House for more than seventeen years, kept in touch with key members on a daily basis.

Leaders also must have the ability to bargain and compromise. One observer noted, "To Senator Johnson, public policy evidently was an inexhaustibly bargainable product."[30] Such leaders find solutions where none appear possible. Leaders also do favors for members (such as making campaign appearances, helping with fund-raising, contributing to campaigns, helping them get desired committee assignments, or guiding pet projects through the legislative process) to engender a feeling of personal obligation to the leadership when it needs a key vote.

The party's most powerful positive incentives are in the area of campaign finance. In recent years the congressional campaign committees of both parties and the national party organizations have been supplying candidates with money and resources in an attempt to gain more influence in the electoral process. Party leaders may also help arrange a campaign stop or a fund-raiser for a candidate with

FIGURE » 10.7

IDEOLOGICAL DISTRIBUTION OF MEMBERS

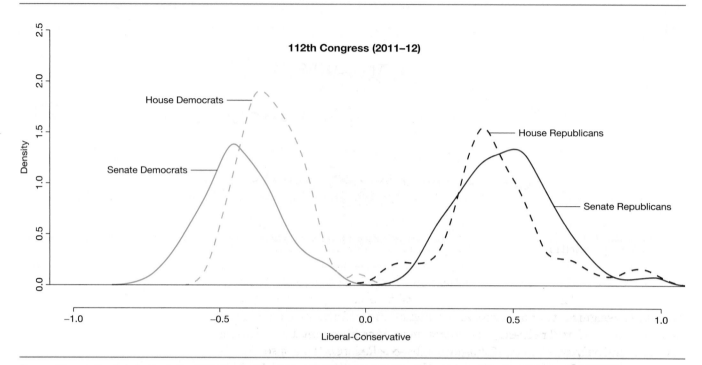

Source: "Forecasting Polarization in the 113th Senate," September 10, 2012, voteview, http://voteview.com/blog/?p=567 (accessed 9/19/12).

party leaders or the president. For example, President Obama held dozens of fund-raisers for Democrats in 2010, earning him the label of "Fundraiser-in-Chief" from CBS News.[31] Such events typically raise $500,000 to more than $1 million.

Despite these positive reinforcements, members' desire for re-election always comes before party concerns, and leadership rarely tries to force a member to vote against his or her constituents' interests. For example, Democrats from rural areas, where most constituents support gun ownership and many are hunters, would not be expected to vote the party line favoring a gun-control bill. To be disciplined by the party, a member of Congress must do something much more extreme than not supporting them on roll call votes, such as supporting the opposing party's candidate for Speaker or passing strategic information to the opposition.

Two recent examples show that party leaders have limits in terms of how much they will tolerate. Former representative James Traficant of Ohio was a true maverick in the Democratic Party. He often took to the floor to give outrageous speeches, occasionally looking up to the ceiling, holding up his arms, and blurting out, "Beam me up Scottie." In April 2002, Traficant was convicted and eventually jailed for bribery, racketeering, and tax evasion. When the House Ethics Committee was investigating him, his closing statement was,

> I want you to disregard all the opposing counsel has said. I think they are delu-sionary. I think they've had something funny for lunch in their meal. I think they should be handcuffed to a chain-link fence, flogged, and all of their hearsay evidence should be thrown the hell out. And if they lie again, I am going to go over and kick them in the crotch. Thank you very much.[32]

While he was still fighting the investigation, he voted for the Republican candidate for Speaker. The Democratic Party leadership promptly stripped him of his committee assignments and let him know that he was no longer welcome in the party. Soon after that, Traficant became only the second representative since the Civil War (and only the fifth in U.S. history) to be expelled from the House.

Former senator Jim Jeffords (I-Vt.) also felt the pinch of party power. In 2001, when Jeffords left the Republican Party to become an independent, he became a hero to the Democratic Party, as his switch gave them control of the Senate. However, when Republicans retook control of the Senate in November 2002, they were in no mood to do any favors for Jeffords (such as allowing him to keep his committee chair).

Despite these occasional strong-arm tactics, party leaders have moved toward a service-oriented leadership, recognizing that their power is only as strong as the leeway granted by the rank-and-file membership. Within this context, however, leaders can gain a fair amount of power. This is demonstrated by Newt Gingrich's reign as Speaker between 1995 and 1999 and Tom DeLay's service as whip and majority leader between 1995 and 2005. Gingrich largely engineered the Republican takeover of the House in 1994, placed his loyalists in top leadership positions, and then tried to push through his Contract with America (promises to the American people about what Republicans would do if they became the majority party). DeLay, nicknamed "The Hammer," was a fund-raising and election-strategy genius who tried to make Republicans the majority party for the next generation. However, he was forced to step down as majority leader late in 2005 when he was indicted for his fund-raising activities in Texas.

The Democratic Party's success in the 2006 midterm elections was attributable in part to voters' reaction against this "culture of corruption." Although House Minority Leader Pelosi and Senate Majority Leader Reid do not have the same reputation for the strong-arm leadership of Gingrich and DeLay, in 2009 and 2010 they were effective in holding together Democratic majorities in the face of nearly unified Republican opposition on many important pieces of legislation. When Republicans retook control of the House in 2010, gridlock returned to Congress as the Democratic Senate and Republican House were unable to agree on numerous pressing issues. Republicans blamed the gridlock on Reid, while Democrats blamed Speaker John Boehner and the Tea Party coalition in the House.

THE POLITICS OF PORK

The infamous "bridge to nowhere" in Ketchikan, Alaska, mentioned earlier in this chapter, is one of the most famous examples of wasteful pork-barrel spending, but it is unusual only in its scale rather than its kind. It is also unusual because the outcry over the bridge prompted Alaska to pull the plug on the project, whereas most pork-barrel spending survives. Pork typically takes the form of earmarked funding for a specific project that is not subjected to standard, neutral spending formulas or a competitive process.

One tactic legislators often use to win approval for pork is to insert it into emergency spending bills that are expected to pass, such as disaster relief for flood and hurricane victims, spending for national security after the September 11 attacks, or funding for the wars in Iraq and Afghanistan. For example, the $636.3 billion 2010 defense appropriations bill included $128.3 billion for the wars in Iraq and Afghanistan and was stuffed with 1,719 earmarks worth $7.6 billion.[a] One controversial earmark was $2.5 billion for ten C-17 transport planes that had not been requested by the Pentagon. Senator John McCain (R-Ariz.) opposed the earmark, saying that the bill would "fund the purchase of new aircraft that we neither need nor can afford. . . . That would have a significant impact on our ability to provide the day-to-day operational funding that our servicemen and women and their families deserve." Other earmarks in that bill included $23 million for the Hawaii Healthcare Network, $18.9 million for the Edward M. Kennedy Institute for the Senate, and $20 million for the National World War II museum in New Orleans.

Some broader definitions of pork include any benefit targeted to a particular political constituency (typically an important business in a member's district or a generous campaign contributor), even if the benefit is part of a stand-alone bill. Examples of this type of targeted federal largesse include the bill that provided federal support to the airlines after the September 11 attacks, which sailed through Congress without much debate, and the lucrative contracts to rebuild Iraq that were awarded to politically well-connected businesses.

Pork has plenty of critics. Citizens against Government Waste, one of the most outspoken groups to tackle pork-barrel spending, compiles each year's federal pork-barrel projects into their annual *Pig Book* to draw attention to pork. Representative Dave Obey (D-Wis.) and Senator John McCain (R-Ariz.), among others, have been trying to get Congress to cut back on earmarks. The ban on earmarks imposed by House Republicans in 2011 has helped a great deal, but committee and informal earmarks are still pervasive. The arguments against pork are especially urgent during a time of massive budget deficits. According to this view, the national interest in a balanced budget should take priority over localized projects.

However, some argue that pork is the "glue of legislating," because these small side payments secure the passage of larger bills. If it takes a little pork for the home district or state

Surrounded by members of Congress, President Obama signs the National Defense Authorization Act for 2010. The law included 1,719 earmarks worth $7.6 billion.

in order to get important legislation through Congress, so be it. The motives of budget reform groups that call for greater fiscal discipline in Congress may also be questioned, since many of these groups oppose government spending in general—not just on pork. In some cases, policies they identify as pork have significant national implications: military readiness, road improvements to support economic infrastructure, or the development of new agricultural and food products. National interests can be served, in other words, by allowing local interests to take a dip into the pork barrel. Put another way, "pork is in the eye of the beholder," or one person's pork is another person's essential spending. Finally, defenders of pork point out that even according to the critics' own definition, pork spending constitutes about one-half of 1 percent of the total federal budget.

Critical Thinking Questions

1. If you were a member of Congress, would you work hard to deliver pork to your district or work to eliminate as much pork as you could from the budget?

2. Why is it so difficult to ban earmarks even in the face of massive budget deficits?

THE COMMITTEE SYSTEM

The committee system in the House and Senate is another crucial part of the legislative structure. There are four types of committees: standing, select, joint, and conference. **Standing committees**, which have ongoing membership and jurisdictions, are where most of the work of Congress gets done. These committees draft legislation and oversee the implementation of the laws they pass. For example, The Agriculture Committee in the House and the one in the Senate have jurisdiction over farm programs such as commodity price supports, crop insurance, and soil conservation. But they also create and oversee policy for rural electrification and development, the food stamp and nutrition programs, and the inspection of livestock, poultry, seafood, and meat products. Many committees share jurisdiction on policy: for example, the House Natural Resources committee oversees the National Forest Service and forests on federally owned lands and the Agriculture Committee oversees policy for forests on privately owned lands.

Select committees typically address a specific topic for one or two terms, such as the Select Committee on Energy Independence and Global Warming that operated from 2007 to 2010. These committees do not have the same legislative authority as standing committees but mostly serve to collect information, provide policy options, and draw attention to a given issue. **Joint committees** are made up of members of both the House and the Senate, and they rarely have legislative authority. The Joint Committee on Taxation, for example, does not have authority to send legislation concerning tax policy to the floor of the House or Senate. Instead, it gathers information and provides estimates of the consequences of proposed tax legislation. Joint Committees may also be temporary, such as the "Supercommittee" (officially the Joint Select Committee on Deficit Reduction) discussed in the chapter opener. **Conference committees** are formed to resolve specific differences between House and Senate versions of legislation that passes each chamber. These committees mostly comprise standing committee members from each chamber who worked on the bill. Table 10.2 shows the policy areas covered by each type of committee.

The committee system creates a division of labor that helps re-election by supporting members' specialization and credit claiming. For example, a chair of the Agriculture Committee or of a key agricultural subcommittee may reasonably take credit for passing an important bill for the farmers back home, such as the Cottonseed Payment Program that provides assistance to cottonseed farmers who lost crops due to hurricanes. The number of members who could make these credible claims expanded dramatically in the 1970s with the proliferation of subcommittees (there are 108 in the House and 73 in the Senate). One observer of Congress suggested, with some exaggeration, that if you ever forget a member's name, you can simply refer to him or her as "Mr. or Ms. Chairman" and you will be right about half the time. This view of congressional committees is based on the **distributive theory**, which is rooted in the norm of reciprocity and the incentive to provide benefits for the district. The theory holds that members will seek committee assignments to best serve their district's interests, the leadership will accommodate those requests, and the floor will respect the views of the committees in a big institution-level logroll (that is, committee members will support each other's legislation). This means that members tend to have an interest in and support the policies produced by the committees they serve on. For example, members from farm states will serve on the Agriculture Committee and members with a lot of military bases or defense contractors in their districts would want to be on the Armed Services Committee.

standing committees Committees that are a permanent part of the House or Senate structure, holding more importance and authority than other committees.

select committees Committees in the House or Senate created to address a specific issue for one or two terms.

joint committees Committees that contain members of both the House and Senate but have limited authority.

conference committees Temporary committees created to negotiate differences between the House and Senate versions of a piece of legislation that has passed through both chambers.

distributive theory The idea that members of Congress will join committees that best serve the interests of their district and that committee members will support each other's legislation.

TABLE » 10.2

CONGRESSIONAL COMMITTEES

Equivalent or similar committees in both chambers are listed across from each other.

HOUSE COMMITTEES	SENATE COMMITTEES	JOINT COMMITTEES
Agriculture	Agriculture, Nutrition, and Forestry	Joint Economic Committee
Appropriations	Appropriations	Joint Committee on the Library
Armed Services	Armed Services	Joint Committee on Printing
Budget	Budget	Joint Committee on Taxation
Education and Workforce	Health, Education, Labor, and Pensions	
Energy and Commerce	Commerce, Science, and Transportation	
Ethics	Select Committee on Ethics	
Financial Services	Banking, Housing, and Urban Affairs	
Foreign Affairs	Foreign Relations	
Homeland Security	Homeland Security and Governmental Affairs	
House Administration	Rules and Administration	
Select Committee on Intelligence	Select Committee on Intelligence	
Judiciary	Judiciary	
Natural Resources	Energy and Natural Resources	
Small Business	Small Business and Entrepreneurship	
Transportation and Infrastructure	Environment and Public Works	
Veterans' Affairs	Veterans Affairs	
Ways and Means	Finance	
The committees below are specific to one chamber.	*Specific to one chamber*	
Oversight and Government Reform	Special Committee on Aging	
Rules	Indian Affairs	
Science, Space, and Technology		

informational theory The idea that having committees in Congress made up of experts on specific policy areas helps to ensure well-informed policy decisions.

However, the committee system does not exist simply to further members' electoral goals. It is also a *corrective* to individualism because the structure of committees creates more expertise than if the policy process were more ad hoc.[33] This expertise, according to the **informational theory**, provides collective benefits to the rest of the members because it helps reduce uncertainty about policy outcomes. By deferring to expert committees, members are able to achieve beneficial outcomes while using their time more efficiently. This informational theory is also consistent with the argument made by Richard Fenno forty years ago that members will serve on committees for reasons other than simply trying to achieve reelection (which is implied by the distributive theory). Fenno argued that members also were interested in achieving power within the institution and making good policy.[34] Others argue that goals vary from bill to bill, and all members pursue reelection advantage, institutional power, and effective policy in different circumstances.[35] Thus, the committee system does not exist only to further members' electoral goals, but it often serves that purpose.

Committees also serve the policy needs of the majority party, largely because it controls a majority of seats on every committee. The party ratios on each committee generally reflect the partisan distribution in the overall chamber, but the majority party gives itself somewhat larger majorities on the important committees such as Ways and Means (which controls tax policy), Appropriations, and Rules. This is especially true for the Rules Committee where the majority party controls nine of the thirteen seats. The Rules Committee is important to the majority party because it structures the nature of debate in the House by setting the length of debate and the type and number of amendments to a bill that will be allowed. These decisions are called "rules" and must be approved by a majority of the House floor. The Rules Committee has become an arm of the majority party leadership, and in many instances it provides rules that support the party's policy agenda or protect its members from having to take controversial positions. For example, the Rules Committee prevented many amendments on the 2010 health care reform bill; if they had come to a vote, they would have divided the Democratic Party. Majority members are expected to support their party on votes on rules, even if they end up voting against the related legislation.

CONGRESSIONAL STAFF

The final component of the formal structure of Congress is congressional staff. The size of personal and committee staff exploded in the 1970s and 1980s and has since leveled off. The total number of congressional staff is more than four times as large as it was fifty years ago. Part of the motivation for this growth was to reduce the gap between the policy-making capability of Congress and the president, especially with regard to fiscal policy. The larger committee staffs gave members of Congress independent sources of information and expertise with which to challenge the president. The other primary motivation was electoral. By increasing the size of their personal staff, members were able to open multiple district offices and expand the opportunities for casework. When the Republicans took control of Congress in 1994, they vowed to cut the waste in the internal operation of the institution, in part by cutting committee staff. However, although they reduced committee staff by nearly a third, they made no cuts in personal staff.

The structure of Congress generally serves its members' needs. The norms of the institution and its formal structure facilitate members' electoral and policy goals. If any aspect of this structure were to hinder Congress's goals, it is within members' power to change that aspect of the institution.

HOW A BILL BECOMES A LAW

TRACE THE STEPS IN THE LEGISLATIVE PROCESS

Every introductory textbook on American politics has an obligatory section, including the neat little diagram, that describes how a bill becomes a law. This book is no exception; however, we provide an important truth-in-advertising disclosure: many important laws do not follow this orderly path. In fact, Barbara Sinclair's book *Unorthodox Lawmaking* argues that "the legislative process for major legislation is now less likely to conform to the textbook model than to unorthodox lawmaking."[36] After presenting the standard view, we describe the most important deviations from that path.

TYPES OF LEGISLATION

Bill: A legislative proposal that becomes law if it is passed by both the House and the Senate in identical form and approved by the president. Each is assigned a bill number, with "HR" indicating bills that originated in the House and "S" denoting bills that originated in the Senate. Private bills are concerned with a specific individual or organization and often address immigration or naturalization issues. Public bills affect the general public if enacted into law.

Simple resolution: Legislation used to express the sense of the House or Senate, designated by "H.Res." or "S.Res." Simple resolutions only affect the chamber passing the resolution, are not signed by the president, and cannot become public law. Resolutions are often used for symbolic legislation, such as congratulating sports teams (see Figure 10.8).

Concurrent resolution: Legislation used to express the position of both chambers on a nonlegislative matter to set the annual budget, or to fix adjournment dates, designated by "H.Con.Res" or "S.Con.Res." Concurrent resolutions are not signed by the president and therefore do not carry the weight of law.

Joint resolution: Legislation that has few practical differences from a bill unless it proposes a constitutional amendment. In that case, a two-thirds majority of those present and voting in both the House and the Senate, and ratification by three-fourths of the states, are required for the amendment to be adopted.

THE CONVENTIONAL PROCESS

The details of the legislative process can be incredibly complex, but its basic aspects are fairly simple (see "How It Works"). The most important thing to understand about the process is that before a piece of legislation can become a law it must be passed *in identical form* by both the House and the Senate and signed by the president. If the president vetoes the bill, it can still be passed with a two-thirds vote in each chamber. Here are the basic steps of the process:

1. A member of Congress introduces the bill.
2. A subcommittee and committee craft the bill.
3. Floor action on the bill takes place in the first chamber (House or Senate).
4. Committee and floor action takes place in the second chamber.
5. The conference committee works out any differences between the House and Senate versions of the bill. (If the two chambers pass the same version, steps 5 and 6 are not necessary.)
6. The conference committee version is given final approval on the floor of each chamber.
7. The president either signs or vetoes the final version.
8. If the bill is vetoed, both chambers can attempt to override the veto.

The first part of the process, unchanged from the earliest Congresses, is the introduction of the bill. Only members of Congress can introduce the bill, either by dropping it into the "hopper," a wooden box at the front of the chamber in the House, or by presenting it to one of the clerks at the presiding officer's desk in the Senate. Even the president would need to have a House member or senator introduce his bill. Each bill has one or more sponsors and often many co-sponsors (see Nuts and Bolts 10.2 for a description of the different types of bills). Members may introduce bills on any topic they choose, but often the bills are related to a specific constituency interest. For example, House Resolution 544 was introduced by Representative Steven R. Rothman of New Jersey to congratulate the New York Giants on winning Super Bowl XLVI (Figure 10.8). Obviously, most legislation is more substantive, but members of Congress are always attentive to issues their constituents care about.

The next step is to send the bill to the relevant committee. House and Senate rules specify committee jurisdictions (there are more than 200 categories), and the bill is matched with the committee that best fits its subject matter. In the House, major legislation may be sent to more than one committee in a practice known as multiple referral, but one of them is designated the primary committee, and the bill is reviewed by different committees sequentially or in parts. The practice is less common in the Senate, partly because senators have more opportunities to amend legislation on the floor. However, there were three committees in the House and two in the Senate that simultaneously worked on health care reform in 2009.

Once the bill goes to a committee, the chair refers it to the relevant subcommittee where much of the legislative work is done. The subcommittee holds hearings, calls witnesses, and gathers the information necessary to rewrite, amend, and edit the bill. The final language of the bill is determined in a collaborative process known as the **markup**. During this meeting, members debate aspects of the

markup One of the steps through which a bill becomes a law, in which the final wording of the bill is determined.

FIGURE » 10.8

TAKING CARE OF THE FANS

H. Res. 544

In the House of Representatives
February 8, 2012

Congratulating the National Football League champion New York Giants for winning Super Bowl XLVI.

Whereas, on February 5, 2012, in Indianapolis, Indiana, the New York Giants defeated the New England Patriots by a score of 21 to 17 in Super Bowl XLVI to win the National Football League Championship; [...]

Whereas the Giants have been the model of resilience this season by overcoming both injury and adversity, having to place 13 players on injured reserve and becoming the first team to win the Super Bowl after losing 7 games in the regular season;

Whereas quarterback Elisha Nelson 'Eli' Manning [...] was voted the winner of the pete Rozelle Trophy, awarded to the Most Valuable Player of the Super Bowl, becoming the first Giants player to win the award more than once and only the fifth player to do so in National Football League history, proving that he is truly one of the game's elite quarterbacks; [...]

Whereas the Giants organization is one of the most successful in National Football League history, boasting 15 Hall of Fame players, 28 postseason appearances, more than 600 wins, 18 National Football League divisional championships, and 8 National Football League championships [...] that captivated fans in New York, in New Jersey, and around the country; [...]

Whereas the entire Giants franchise has become a model of professionalism, teamwork, and community service in representing the entire New York and New Jersey metropolitan area: Now therefore, be it

Resolved, That the House of Representatives congratulates the National Football League champion New York Giants for winning Super Bowl XLVI.

Source: Excerpted from H. Res. 544, 112th Congress, Second Session (February 8, 2012), http://thomas .loc.gov/cgi-bin/query/z?c112:H.RES.544 (accessed 7/16/12).

issue and offer amendments to change the language or content of the bill. After all amendments have been considered, a final vote is taken on whether to send the bill to the full committee. If it is sent, the full committee then considers whether to pass it along to the floor. This committee also has the option of amending the bill, passing it as-is, or tabling it (which kills the bill). Every bill sent to the floor by a committee is accompanied by a report and full documentation of all the hearings. These documents constitute the bill's legislative history, which the courts, executive departments, and the public use to determine the purpose and meaning of the law.

When the bill makes it to the floor, it is placed on one of the various legislative calendars. Bills are removed from the calendar to be considered by the floor under a broad range of possible rules. (Some of the most important rules are discussed later, when we outline certain differences between the House and Senate; but most of the technical details are not central to the basic story.) When the bill reaches the floor, the majority party and minority party each designate a bill manager who is responsible for guiding the debate on the floor. In the House, debate proceeds according to tight time limits and rules governing the nature of amendments. Senate debate is much more open and unlimited in most circumstances (unless all the senators agree to a limit). If you have ever watched C-SPAN, you know that often there are very few people on the floor during debates. Typically only the small number of people who are most interested in the bill (usually members of the committee that produced it) actively participate and offer amendments.

When debate is completed and all amendments have been considered, the presiding officer calls for a voice vote, with those in favor saying "aye," and those opposed "no." If it is unclear which side has won, any member may call for a "division vote," which requires members on each side to stand and be counted. At that point any member may call for a recorded vote (there is no way of recording members' positions on voice votes and division votes). If at least twenty-five members agree that a recorded vote is desired, buzzers go off in the office buildings and committee rooms, calling members to the floor for the vote. Once they reach the floor, members vote by an electronic system in which they insert ATM-like cards into slots and each vote is recorded on a big board at the front of the House or Senate chamber.

If the bill passes the House and the Senate in different forms, the discrepancies have to be resolved. On many minor bills, one chamber may simply accept the other chamber's version to solve the problem. On other minor bills and some major bills, differences are resolved through a process known as amendments between the chambers. In this case, one chamber modifies a bill passed by the other chamber and sends it back. These modifications can go back and forth several times before both houses agree on an identical bill. A complicated version of this approach was used to pass health care reform in 2010.

The most common way to resolve differences on major legislation is through a conference committee comprising key players in the House and the Senate. About three-fourths of major bills go to a conference committee, but only 12 percent of all bills go this route.[37] Sometimes the conferees split the difference between the House and Senate versions, but at other times the House and Senate approaches are so different that one must be chosen—an especially tricky prospect when different parties control the two chambers. Sometimes the conference cannot resolve differences and the bill dies. If the conference committee can agree on changes, each chamber must pass the final version, the conference report, by a majority vote and neither chamber is allowed to amend it.

How It Works

PASSING LEGISLATION: THE CONVENTIONAL METHOD

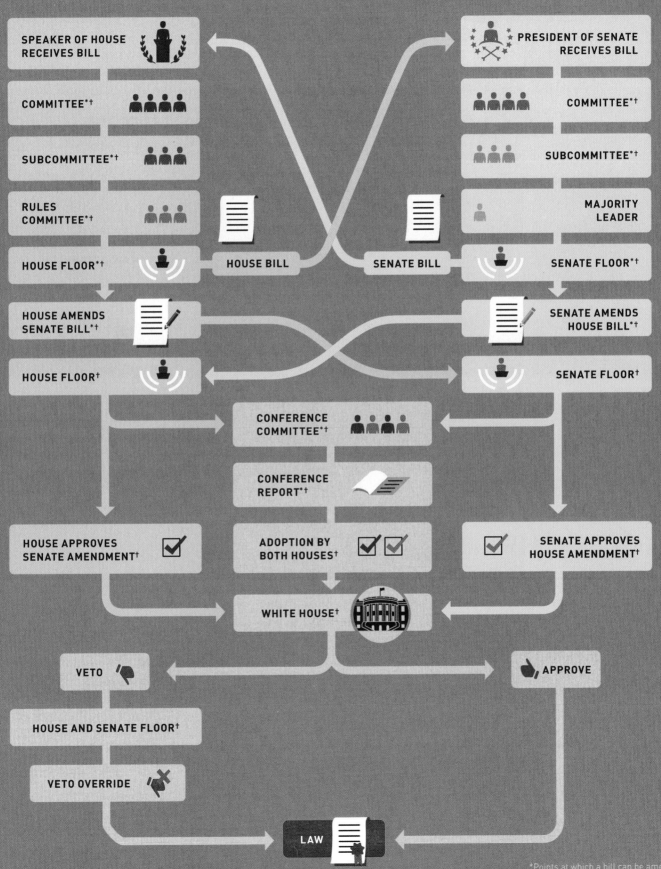

SPEAKER OF HOUSE RECEIVES BILL

COMMITTEE*†

SUBCOMMITTEE*†

RULES COMMITTEE*†

HOUSE FLOOR*†

HOUSE BILL

SENATE BILL

PRESIDENT OF SENATE RECEIVES BILL

COMMITTEE*†

SUBCOMMITTEE*†

MAJORITY LEADER

SENATE FLOOR*†

HOUSE AMENDS SENATE BILL*†

SENATE AMENDS HOUSE BILL*†

HOUSE FLOOR†

SENATE FLOOR†

CONFERENCE COMMITTEE*†

CONFERENCE REPORT*†

HOUSE APPROVES SENATE AMENDMENT†

ADOPTION BY BOTH HOUSES†

SENATE APPROVES HOUSE AMENDMENT†

WHITE HOUSE†

VETO

APPROVE

HOUSE AND SENATE FLOOR†

VETO OVERRIDE

LAW

*Points at which a bill can be amended.
†Points at which a bill can die.

DEVIATIONS FROM THE CONVENTIONAL METHOD: AN EXAMPLE

CONVENTIONAL STEPS after a bill is introduced. (See the preceding page.)

THE 2010 AFFORDABLE CARE ACT (ACA) provides an example of how passing legislation often deviates from the conventional method.

A committee and a subcommittee revise the bill

In the House, **3 committees** crafted the bill.

5 committees worked on the Senate version.

Speaker Nancy Pelosi assumed a central role in shaping the final bill, adding things that weren't in the committee version.

After a deadlock between two committees, Majority Leader Harry Reid pushed through a merged version of the bill, adding things that weren't in the committee version.

President Obama was intensely involved. The White House held daily meetings with the committees.

Floor action

Floor action

Floor action

Conference committee reconciles House and Senate versions.

No conference committee. Instead, committee leaders, White House staff, and party leadership negotiated the details of the bill.

Adoption of final bill by both House and Senate

The Senate version of the bill was passed by the House, but then the House also passed a separate reconciliation bill that included many amendments to the Senate version.

That reconciliation bill was then passed by the Senate.

President signs bill into law.

President Obama signed the ACA into law.

POP QUIZ!

1 A conference committee's job is to

  a draft an original bill.

  b determine whether a bill should be considered by Congress.

  c determine whether a bill is constitutional.

  d reconcile differences between House and Senate versions of a bill.

  e convince the president to sign the bill.

2 One way the passage of the ACA differed from the conventional process is that

  a committees were not involved.

  b President Obama and party leaders were directly involved in shaping the bill.

  c no floor action took place.

  d only one house voted on the bill.

  e the president signed it into law.

Answers: 1.d; 2.b

The bill is then sent to the president. If he approves and signs the measure within ten days (not counting Sundays), it becomes law. If the president objects to the bill, he may **veto** it within ten days, sending it back to the chamber where it originated, along with a statement of objections. Unless both the House and the Senate vote to override the veto by a two-thirds majority, the bill dies. If the president does not act within ten days and Congress is in session, the bill becomes law without the president's approval. If Congress is not in session, the measure dies through what is known as a **pocket veto**. Each Congress is made up of two one-year sessions, and there is some dispute about whether pocket vetoes between sessions of Congress are legitimate, or whether they must happen at the end of the second session. Recent presidents have claimed that pocket vetoes between sessions are legitimate, but both Congress and the Washington, D.C., Appeals Court disagreed. The Supreme Court has not offered a definitive ruling on this matter.[38]

One final point on how a bill becomes a law is important: any bill that appropriates money must pass through the two-step process of authorization and appropriation. In the authorization process, members debate the merits of the bill, determine its language, and limit the amount that can be spent on the bill. The appropriations process involves both the Budget Committees in the House and the Senate, which set the overall guidelines for the national budget, and the Appropriations Committees in the two chambers, which determine the actual amounts of money that will be spent. In recent years Congress has been unable to pass its appropriations bills in time for the start of the new fiscal year, so it ends up having to pass "continuing resolutions" that spend money at the last year's levels in order to keep the government open. Congress passed four continuing resolutions for the 2012 fiscal year. That may sound like a lot, but the record is twenty-one for the 2001 fiscal year.[39]

veto The president's rejection of a bill that has been passed by Congress. A veto can be overridden by a two-thirds vote in both the House and Senate.

pocket veto The automatic death of a bill passed by the House and Senate when the president fails to sign the bill in the last ten days of a legislative session.

DEVIATIONS FROM THE CONVENTIONAL PROCESS

There are many ways in which legislation may not follow the typical path. First, in some congresses up to 20 percent of *major* bills bypass the committee system. This may be done by a discharge petition, in which a majority of the members force a bill out of its assigned committee, or by a special rule in the House. In some cases, a bill may go to the relevant committee, but then party leadership may impose its version of the bill later in the process. For example, the PATRIOT Act, which was passed in the wake of the terrorist attacks of 9/11 to give the government stronger surveillance powers, was unanimously reported by the Judiciary Committee after five days of hard bipartisan work. But a few days later, according to committee member Representative Jerrold Nadler (D-N.Y.), "Then the bill just disappeared. And we had a new several hundred page bill revealed from the Rules Committee" that had to be voted on the next day. Most members of Congress did not have a chance to read it.[40] The Affordable Care Act passed in 2010 also deviated from the standard path (see "How It Works"). Second, about one-third of major bills are adjusted post-committee and before the legislation reaches the floor by supporters of the bill to increase the chances of passage. Sometimes the bill goes back to the committee after these changes, and sometimes it does not. Thus, although most of the legislative work is accomplished in committees, a significant amount of legislation bypasses committee review.

Third, summit meetings between the president and congressional leaders may bypass or jump-start the normal legislative process. For example, rather than

THE LEGISLATURE IN THE POLITICAL PROCESS

The U.S. Congress is quite different from many other legislatures around the world in terms of how its members are elected, its relations to the executive, and its internal operations. Congressional representation is based on geographically determined single-member districts that hold plurality, winner-take-all elections, whereas (as discussed in Chapter 8) most other legislatures are elected using party lists and some version of proportional representation. In an election with party lists, each party makes a list of people who would serve in the legislature. Using proportional representation with party lists means that the number of people from each party's list who actually serve as legislators depends on how much support the party receives in the election. For example, if there are 100 seats in the legislature and a party wins 40 percent of the vote, in a strictly proportional system the party would make the first 40 people from their list the legislators from that party. Legislatures that are elected from national party lists are much more likely to concern themselves with national rather than parochial interests. There are no incentives to "bring home the pork" to your district if you are not elected from a district.

Examining the 2010 parliamentary election in Iraq highlights the significance of these differences. Iraqi voters may select candidates or parties in an "open party list" system in which the nation's 325 legislators are chosen based on the proportion of votes each party receives. This means that even relatively small factions can elect a few people to the legislature as long as they muster a small percentage of the national vote. This has the virtue of creating more proportional representation, but it also fractures political power more broadly. Eighty-six parties competed and nine won representation. Party lists also allow more descriptive representation. Twenty-six percent of Iraqi legislators are women because the law mandates that every third person on the party lists has to be a woman (only about 17 percent of members of the U.S. Congress are women).

There are too many other differences among legislatures to describe them all in detail. Briefly, relations with the executive are much stronger in a parliamentary system than in a presidential system because the prime minister is elected from the legislature. Indeed, the lines between executive and legislative power are much more blurred in a parliamentary system. Parties tend to be highly unified in parliamentary systems and less so in presidential systems. Oversight powers, legislative capacity (ratifying treaties, amending constitutions, approving

The Iraqi parliament in session.

executive appointments, and impeachment power), the number of votes and how they are recorded, tenure and re-election rates, and the relative power of committees in the institution also vary tremendously.[a]

One other important difference between the U.S. Congress and many other legislatures around the world is the veto. The power of the president to veto congressional legislation is an important part of our system of checks and balances, but many other nations do not have a comparable veto power. In the Westminster system and other constitutional monarchies, the power to "withhold the Royal Assent" is rarely used. For example, the last time this veto was used in the United Kingdom was in 1707 by Queen Anne with the Scottish Militia Bill. Ten European parliamentary republics, including France, Portugal, Ireland, Italy, and Hungary, have some form of executive veto, but it tends to be a more limited veto than under the U.S. Constitution. For example, in Italy and France, the president may call for a reconsideration of a bill that has been passed by Parliament, but this weak form of the veto may be overridden by a simple majority vote.[b]

going through the Budget Committees to set budgetary targets, the president may meet with top leaders from both parties and hammer out a compromise that is presented to Congress as a done deal. This technique is especially important on delicate budget negotiations or when the president is threatening to use the veto. Often the congressional rank-and-file go along with the end product of the summit meeting, but occasionally they reject it—as happened in December 2011, when House Republicans balked at a two-month extension for the payroll tax cuts that had been passed by the Senate and agreed to by House leadership.

Fourth, **omnibus legislation**—massive bills that run hundreds of pages long and cover many different subjects and programs—often requires creative approaches by the leadership to guide the bill through the legislative maze. Leadership task forces may be used in the place of committees, and alternatives to the conference committee may be devised to resolve differences between the two chambers. In addition, the massive legislation often carries riders—extraneous legislation attached to the "must pass" bill to secure approval for pet projects that would otherwise fail. This is a form of pork-barrel legislation and another mechanism used in the quest for re-election.

omnibus legislation Large bills that often cover several topics and may contain extraneous, or pork-barrel, projects.

DIFFERENCES IN THE HOUSE AND SENATE LEGISLATIVE PROCESSES

There are three central differences in the legislative processes of the House and the Senate: (1) the continuity of the membership and the impact this has on the rules, (2) the way in which bills get to the floor, and (3) the structure of the floor process, including debate and amendments. First, as discussed earlier, the Senate is a continuing body, with two-thirds of its members returning to the next session without facing re-election (because of the six-year term), whereas all House members are up for re-election every two years. This has an important impact on the rules of the two chambers: there has been much greater stability in the rules of the Senate than the House. Whereas the House adopts its rules anew at the start of each new session (sometimes with major changes, sometimes with only minor modifications), the Senate has not had a general reaffirmation of its rules since 1789. However, the Senate rules can be changed at the beginning of a session to meet the needs of the new members.

The other two differences between the House and Senate are even more important. The process by which a bill gets to the floor is much more complicated in the House than the Senate. In the House, when a bill is reported from a committee it goes to the bottom of the legislative calendar. However, the leadership can move a bill to the top of the agenda in several ways. One mechanism is to have the bill considered under **suspension of the rules**, which is mostly used for noncontroversial legislation. Debate is limited to forty minutes, no amendments are allowed, and bills must pass by a two-thirds vote. Another mechanism used for major legislation is for the Rules Committee to make a special rule that, if approved by a majority vote of the House, moves the bill to the top of the list for immediate consideration.

suspension of the rules One way of moving a piece of legislation to the top of the agenda in the House: debate on the bill is limited to forty minutes, amendments are not allowed, and the bill must pass by a two-thirds vote.

The procedure is much easier in the Senate. As in the House, certain bills have privileged status over others, such as conference reports and vetoed bills on which Congress will attempt an override. Because they are in the final stages of the process, they are promoted to the top of the list so they don't have to wait in line with newer bills. Other than privileging these bills, the Senate does not use special rules

IN 2010 SENATOR BERNARD SANDERS of Vermont spoke on the Senate floor for 8 hours and 37 minutes to draw attention to his concerns about a proposed tax plan. However, Sanders's long speech wasn't technically a filibuster because it didn't prevent Senate business from proceeding (none was scheduled for that day).

cloture A procedure through which the Senate can limit the amount of time spent debating a bill (cutting off a filibuster), if a supermajority of 60 senators agree.

filibuster A tactic used by senators to block a bill by continuing to hold the floor and speak—under the Senate rule of unlimited debate—until the bill's supporters back down.

hold An objection to considering a measure on the Senate floor.

or various calendars. If the majority leader wants action on a given bill, he simply puts it on the legislative agenda, either through a motion or by unanimous consent.

The floor process is also much simpler and less structured in the Senate than in the House. In part, this is due to the relative size of the two chambers: the House with its 435 members needs to have more rules than the 100-person Senate. Ironically, however, the floor process is actually much easier to navigate in the House because of its structure. Since the adoption of Reeds Rules in 1890, the House is a very majoritarian body (that is, a majority of House members can almost always have its way). Named after Speaker Thomas Reed, the rules were an implementation of his view that "the best system is to have one party govern and the other party watch." In contrast, the Senate has always been a much more individualistic body. Former majority leader Howard Baker compared leading the Senate to "herding cats," saying it was difficult "trying to make ninety-nine independent souls act in concert under rules that encourage polite anarchy and embolden people who find majority rule a dubious proposition at best."[41] Part of this difficulty is rooted in the Senate's unlimited debate and very open amendment process. Unless restricted by a unanimous consent agreement, senators can speak as long as they want and offer any amendment to a bill, even if it isn't germane (that is, directly related to the underlying bill). Debate may be cut off only if a supermajority of 60 senators agrees in a process known as invoking **cloture**. Therefore, one senator can stop any bill by threatening to talk the bill to death if forty of his or her colleagues agree. This practice is known as a **filibuster.**

The filibuster strengthens the hand of the minority party in the Senate, giving it veto power over legislation unless the majority party has sixty senators who unanimously support a bill. The filibuster has played a critical role in congressional policy making in recent years, especially after Republican Scott Brown won Ted Kennedy's seat in January 2010 (which gave the Republicans forty-one seats). Republicans filibustered the health care reform bill, which could have killed it if Democratic leaders had not used the reconciliation process to pass the legislation (reconciliation is used in the budget process, typically as a budget-cutting device, and is not subject to the filibuster).

Before the 1960s, senators really did hold the floor for hours by reading from the phone book or reciting recipes. The late Strom Thurmond, the senator from South Carolina who was the longest serving and oldest senator until his retirement in January 2003 (at 100 years old and after forty-eight years in the Senate), holds the record of twenty-four hours and eighteen minutes of continuous talking. Today it is rare for a filibuster to tie up Senate business, since a senator's threat to filibuster a bill is often enough to take the bill off the legislative agenda. If the bill is actually filibustered, it goes on a separate legislative track so it does not bring the rest of the business of the Senate to a halt. Alternatively, if supporters of the bill think they have enough votes, they can invoke cloture to stop the filibuster and bring the bill to the floor for a vote.

Because of the practice of unlimited debate in the Senate, much of its business is conducted under unanimous consent agreements by which senators agree to adhere to time limits on debate and amendments. However, because these are literally *unanimous* agreements, a single senator can obstruct the business of the chamber by issuing a **hold** on the bill or presidential nomination. This practice is often a bargaining tool to extract concessions from the bill's supporters, but sometimes, especially late in a session when time gets tight, a hold can actually kill a bill by removing it from the active agenda.

In contrast, the House is a more orderly, if complex, institution. The Rules Committee exerts great control over the legislative process, especially on major legislation, through special rules that govern the nature of debate on a bill. There are three general types of rules: **closed rules** do not allow any amendments to the bill, **open rules** allow any germane amendments, and **modified rules** allow some specific amendments but not others. Once a special rule is adopted and the Committee of the Whole convenes, general debate is tightly controlled by the floor managers. All amendments are considered under a five-minute rule, but this rule is routinely bent as members offer phantom "pro forma" amendments to, for example, "strike the last word" or "strike the requisite number of words." This means that the member is not really offering an amendment but is simply going through the formal procedure of offering one in order to get an additional five minutes to talk about the amendment.

These descriptions of the two chambers shows that although the Senate is formally committed to unlimited debate, senators often voluntarily place limits on themselves through unanimous consent, which makes them operate much more like the House. Similarly, though the House has very strict rules concerning debate and amendments, there are ways of bending those rules to make the House operate a bit more like the potentially free-wheeling Senate.

closed rules Conditions placed on a legislative debate by the House Rules Committee prohibiting amendments to a bill.

open rules Conditions placed on a legislative debate by the House Rules Committee allowing relevant amendments to a bill.

modified rules Conditions placed on a legislative debate by the House Rules Committee allowing certain amendments to a bill while barring others.

OVERSIGHT

> DESCRIBE HOW CONGRESS ENSURES THAT THE BUREAUCRACY IMPLEMENTS POLICIES CORRECTLY

Once a bill becomes a law, Congress plays another crucial role by overseeing the implementation of the law to make sure the bureaucracy interprets it as Congress intended. Other motivations drive the oversight process as well, such as the desire to gain publicity that may help in the re-election quest or to embarrass the president if he is of the opposite party. For example, in President Bush's last two years, Democrats investigated fraud and cost overruns in Defense Department contracts to rebuild Iraq that went to corporations with close Republican Party ties. In 2011, Republicans used their oversight powers to call attention to policy failures in the Obama administration such as "Operation Fast and Furious" (a Justice Department program to sell guns to drug dealers that could then be tracked to Mexican drug lords; the program went horribly awry when hundreds of the guns could not be tracked and two of the guns were found where a Border Patrol agent was killed).[42] However, the basic motivation for oversight is to ensure that laws are implemented properly.

There are several mechanisms that Congress may use to accomplish this goal; we address these in detail in Chapter 12 but briefly describe them here. First, the bluntest instrument is the power of the purse. If members of Congress think an agency is not properly implementing their programs, they can simply cut off the funds to that agency. However, this approach to punishment is rarely used because it often cuts good aspects of the agency along with the bad.

Second, Congress may hold hearings and investigations. By summoning administration officials and agency heads to a public hearing, Congress can use the media spotlight to focus attention on problems within the bureaucracy or on issues that have been overlooked. For example, the economic meltdown of 2008–09 produced dozens of hearings on topics ranging from the bailout of the auto industry (and subsequent bankruptcy of General Motors) to the use of TARP money by financial institutions, executive pay in the financial sector, the housing market and subprime mortgage crises, and accountability of the Federal Reserve.

THE CEOs OF GENERAL MOTORS, Ford, and Chrysler testify before the Senate Banking, Housing and Urban Affairs Committee about a proposed $34 billion federal bailout for the auto industry. When members of Congress took this extraordinary step in 2009, they wanted to make sure that taxpayers' money would be wisely spent.

legislative veto A form of oversight in which Congress overturns bureaucratic decisions.

National security issues continue to produce oversight hearings on a broad range of topics as well. The attempted bombing of a Northwest Airlines jet on Christmas Day 2009 prompted a new round of congressional hearings focusing on airport security and the sharing of intelligence across government agencies. This type of oversight is known as fire alarm oversight—that is, members wait until there is a crisis before they spring to action.[43] This is in contrast to police patrol oversight, which involves constant vigilance in overseeing the bureaucracy. For example, the Oversight and Government Reform Committee held several hearings to make sure that stimulus money from the Recovery Act was being spent as intended. Of the two, fire alarm oversight is far more common because Congress does not have the resources to constantly monitor the entire bureaucracy.

Third, Congress may use **legislative vetoes**, which resemble fire alarm oversight in being a reactive rather than a proactive form of oversight. In writing laws, Congress often gives the bureaucracy broad discretion over how to implement policies because it is impossible for Congress to foresee every scenario that might arise. However, Congress is reluctant to give full control to the implementing agencies. Legislative vetoes resolve this dilemma by allowing Congress to overturn bureaucratic decisions. There are one-house, two-house, and committee versions of legislative vetoes. In 1983, the Supreme Court ruled that many forms of legislative vetoes are unconstitutional.[44] Despite this ruling, however, Congress has enacted more than 400 new legislative vetoes since 1983, mostly of the committee and subcommittee type.[45]

Finally, the Senate exercises specific control over other executive functions through its constitutional responsibilities to provide "advice and consent" on presidential appointments and approval of treaties. The Senate typically defers to the president on these matters, but it may assert its power, especially when constituent interests are involved. One current example would be the Senate's increasing skepticism about free trade agreements negotiated by the president's trade representatives and holds on presidential nominations.

The ultimate in congressional oversight is the process of removing the president, vice president, other civil officers, or federal judges through impeachment. The House and Senate share this power: the House issues articles of impeachment, which outline the charges against the official, and the Senate conducts the trial of the impeached officials. Two presidents have been impeached: Andrew Johnson in the controversy over Reconstruction after the Civil War, and Bill Clinton over the scandal involving White House intern Monica Lewinsky. However, neither president was convicted and removed by the Senate.

> **EVALUATE ARGUMENTS FOR MAKING CONGRESS MORE ACCOUNTABLE**

CONGRESSIONAL REFORM

The pork-laden 2010 defense appropriations bill is a good example of why many Americans are convinced that the entire political system is dysfunctional (see "You Decide"). This deep cynicism is rooted in the perception that government is not serving the public interest. Attempts to reform Congress address either Congress's external image or internal "quality of life" concerns. The former, which attempt to tackle the absence of institutional leadership and accountability, are difficult to address through congressional reforms. The only way to achieve complete accountability is through responsible party government (see Chapter 7), though this is an elusive goal at best, even when the same party controls Congress and the presidency. However, in a decentralized, individualistic institution such as Congress, the only force for collective responsibility is the majority party.

Specific reform proposals seeking to take advantage of this force include giving the Speaker more power over committee assignments, strengthening the role of the party caucus, reforming the filibuster in the Senate to give the majority party more control, and requiring the leadership to play a larger role in agenda setting. The latter could be accomplished in three ways: through an annual "state of the Congress" address by congressional leaders, the creation of a specific agenda, and increased activism by the leadership in pushing the agenda. Unfortunately, providing the potential for stronger parties in Congress will not ensure that leaders use their new powers effectively. Some leaders may be reluctant to encroach on committees' turf. For example, Newt Gingrich, the strong Speaker during the mid-1990s, was much more willing to push committees to work with his agenda than was his successor, Dennis Hastert. The relationship of Nancy Pelosi and John Boehner with committee chairs is somewhere between the style of these two extremes.

Proposals aimed at improving the quality of life in Congress attempt to expand the time available to members for legislative work and reduce some of the external pressures. Specific proposals that address quality of life concerns include revoking some of the "sunshine reforms" of the 1970s, which opened up committee hearings to the general public. By closing more of these meetings, members would be more insulated from interest group pressure. Other proposals include having fewer recorded votes, reducing the number of committee and subcommittee assignments, providing public financing of congressional elections, giving serious consideration to the minority party's grievances, and creating an ombudsman (a person who investigates complaints) office to handle most constituency requests rather than having the members' staff do it.

Unfortunately, the two reform agendas are at odds with each other. Most steps that would improve the quality of life in Congress, such as insulating members from outside pressure, would not enhance its image; most people would see this as a way of shielding Congress from public accountability. And strengthening parties in Congress could come at the expense of more partisan in-fighting. The minority party typically prefers weaker party leadership, while the majority party is willing to tolerate strong leadership while maintaining a solid base in committee power. Efforts to truly strengthen party leadership often encounter howls of protest from the minority party and sometimes from junior members of the majority party, thus exacerbating quality of life concerns.

The one exception to this trade-off is campaign finance reform, which would both free up time for members (if public financing is adopted) and enhance Congress's image if the public accepts it as true reform. After a decade-long battle, Congress passed the Bipartisan Campaign Reform Act, also called the McCain–Feingold Act after two of its primary sponsors, banning so-called soft money and limiting issue ads. However, in 2010 the Supreme Court struck down part of the law, allowing corporations and unions to spend directly on issue ads and other political ads without limitations. (See Chapter 8 for a discussion of this case and campaign finance more generally.)

There have been some incremental congressional reforms, however. When Democrats regained majority control in 2007, they implemented several important reforms, including bans on gifts and meals paid for by lobbyists, restrictions on travel paid for by lobbyists, strong disclosure rules on earmarks, and a two-year "revolving door" ban on lawmakers becoming lobbyists after leaving Congress. The House established a new independent Office of Congressional Ethics (which fell short of the hopes of reformers because it does not have subpoena power). House Republicans implemented a complete ban on earmarks when they took control of the House in 2011. While this ban has not been entirely effective (as noted, committee earmarks remained in the 2012 omnibus appropriations bill), earmarks are down substantially since their peak.

One other topic that continues to receive attention from congressional critics and reformers is term limits. Critics complain that incumbents are too entrenched and there is not enough turnover. They note that more than 95 percent of the House incumbents who ran for re-election between 1984 and 2010 were returned to office (however, only 86 percent were re-elected in 2010). As a reaction to incumbency advantage, a grassroots movement to limit terms started in 1990 and reached a fever pitch in 1992, as voters in ten states passed term limits for state legislators. Currently fifteen states limit terms for state legislators, but the movement appears to be losing steam. Twenty states had passed congressional term limits before the 5–4 Supreme Court decision in *U.S. Term Limits v. Thornton* (1995) ruled that term limits on Congress could be accomplished only by constitutional amendment. Then in 1999, Mississippi voters rejected a state referendum that would have imposed term limits for their state legislature. Four state supreme courts have struck down term limits. In 2002, Idaho became the first state to have its legislature repeal term limits, and Utah followed suit in 2003.

There are two interesting ironies associated with the term limits movement. First, the Founders feared that the House would be an unstable body with excessive turnover and a lack of professionalism. Technically it *is* possible that 435 new members of Congress could be elected every two years, but obviously the opposite has happened. Second, as noted earlier, while the public is critical of Congress as an institution, most voters do not feel this way about their own individual representative. One bumper sticker opposing term limits succinctly captures this irony: "Stop me before I vote again." Thus, while many people claim to support term limits, they don't want to vote out their own members of Congress.

CONCLUSION

Though the details of the legislative process and the institutions of Congress can be complicated, the basic explanations for member behavior are quite straightforward when viewed in terms of the trade-off between responsiveness and responsibility. Members of Congress want to be re-elected, so they are generally quite responsive to constituents' interests. They spend considerable time on casework, meeting with people in the district, and delivering benefits for the district. At the same time, members are motivated to be responsible—to rise above local interests and attend to the nation's best interests. The conflict between these two impulses can create contradictory policies that contribute to Congress's image problem. For example, we subsidize tobacco farming at the same time that we spend billions of dollars to treat the health problems tobacco use creates. We have laws on water rights that encourage farmers to irrigate the desert at the same time that we pay farmers to leave parts of their land unplanted in areas of the country that are well suited for agriculture. These policies, and others, can be explained by the desire to serve local interests and by the norms of reciprocity and universalism.

Considering members' motivations is crucial to understanding how Congress functions, but their behavior is also constrained by the institutions in which they operate. The committee system is an important source of expertise and information, and it provides a platform from which members can take positions and claim credit. Parties in Congress provide coherence to the legislative agenda and help structure voting patterns on bills. Rules and norms constrain the nature of debate and the legislative process. Although these institutions shape members' behavior, it is important to remember that members can also change those rules and institutions. Therefore, Congress has the ability to evolve with changing national conditions and demands from voters, groups, and the president.

In this context, much of what Congress does can be understood in terms of the conflicts inherent in politics. How can members act responsibly without sacrificing responsiveness? Can Congress be structured in a way that allows members to be responsive (and therefore have a better chance of getting re-elected) without losing the ability to make unpopular decisions when needed, like cutting budget deficits? The example discussed in the chapter introduction concerning the "fiscal cliff" shows that partisan conflict in Congress makes it difficult to resolve basic disputes over taxes and spending. But ultimately both sides have to give up something and compromise if we are going to solve the nation's budget problems.

This chapter also shed light on some of the ways that political process matters. With a better understanding of how Congress operates, you are better able to assess the outputs of government. For example, this chapter provided a closer look at party leaders and pork-barrel spending: party leaders in Congress help members solve their collective action problems rather than causing gridlock and policy failure, as is commonly assumed. Some pork may be wasteful, but in other cases it is important for the districts that receive the benefits and may serve broader collective interests as well. Congress does not always live up to the expectations of being the "first branch" of government, but it often does an admirable job of balancing the conflicting pressures it faces.

MEMBERS OF CONGRESS WANT TO be re-elected, and this goal explains much of their behavior. In 2010, New York senator Kirsten Gillibrand participated in the Dominican Day parade, an important event for many Dominican Americans in New York City. However, members must balance local interests with the good of the nation as a whole.

STUDY *guide*

CONGRESS'S PLACE IN OUR CONSTITUTIONAL SYSTEM

▶ Describe how the Founders envisioned Congress's role. **Pages 379–80**

SUMMARY

The Constitution gave Congress vast enumerated powers, making it the "first branch" of government. The bicameral structure represented a number of compromises between competing interests among the Founders—notably the differences in constituency size, election mechanisms, and length of terms. While Congress has long dominated day-to-day politics, the president has become considerably more powerful over time.

KEY TERMS

bicameralism (p. 379)

pork barrel (p. 380)

PRACTICE QUIZ QUESTIONS

1. What did the Seventeenth Amendment do?
a) repeal Prohibition
b) grant women's suffrage
c) give senators six-year terms
d) allow for direct election of senators
e) lower the voting age to 18

2. Why do senators have longer terms than members of the House of Representatives?
a) to reduce the number of candidates in each election
b) to make sure that senators were tied to the public sentiment
c) to provide more opportunities for pork barrel legislation
d) to make elections easier to administer
e) to make sure that senators were somewhat insulated from the people

CONGRESS AND THE PEOPLE

▶ Explain how members of Congress represent their constituents and how elections hold members accountable. **Pages 380–92**

SUMMARY

Despite the low approval ratings for Congress itself, most voters like their members of Congress. Members of Congress work hard to strike a balance between responding to what constituents want, and what is in the constituency's best interest. In the balance, however, they prioritize district interests over national policy.

KEY TERMS

descriptive representation (p. 381)

substantive representation (p. 382)

trustee (p. 382)

delegate (congressional role) (p. 382)

politico (p. 383)

casework (p. 384)

electoral connection (p. 385)

redistricting (p. 387)

apportionment (p. 388)

gerrymandering (p. 389)

gridlock (p. 392)

PRACTICE QUIZ QUESTIONS

3. How would most members of Congress classify their representation style?
a) trustee
b) politico

c) delegate

d) consulate

e) advisor

4. Most constituents are _____; most members of Congress act as if the constituency _____ paying attention.

a) inattentive; is not

b) inattentive; is

c) attentive; is not

d) attentive; is

e) selectively attentive; is not

5. Members of Congress generally hold multiple goals. Which goal comes first?

a) getting re-elected

b) passing good policy

c) serving their political party

d) blocking the opposing party

e) serving special interests

6. What is apportionment?

a) determining presidential primary election winners

b) determining whether the state legislature or courts will redraw district lines

c) determining which states win/lose seats in the Senate

d) determining which states win/lose seats in the House

e) determining how many seats a party has in Congress

ⓢ PRACTICE ONLINE

"Critical Thinking" exercise: *Process Matters—Gerrymandering*

THE INCUMBENCY ADVANTAGE AND ITS SOURCES

▶ Analyze the factors that help members of Congress get re-elected. **Pages 393–97**

SUMMARY

Very few members of Congress are defeated in their re-election bids. Incumbents are successful because they are able to relate to their constituents well, they are generally successful in raising money for their political campaigns, and because they perform lots of constituency service.

KEY TERM

incumbency advantage (p. 393)

CRITICAL THINKING AND DISCUSSION

What types of activities do members of Congress undertake to work toward re-election? How do they structure the institutions of Congress to help themselves achieve this goal? Do these behaviors and institutions serve broader public interests as well as the narrower goal of re-election?

PRACTICE QUIZ QUESTIONS

7. A home style shapes the way members of Congress _____.

a) work with party leaders

b) vote in Congress

c) write legislation in committees

d) present themselves to their district

e) spend campaign money

8. On average, incumbents spend _____ times as much as challengers.

a) one and half

b) three

c) five

d) ten

e) twenty

ⓢ PRACTICE ONLINE

"Critical Thinking" exercise: *Politics Is Conflictual–Congressional and Presidential Fund-Raising*

THE STRUCTURE OF CONGRESS

▶ Examine how parties, the committee system, and staffers enable Congress to function. **Pages 397–409**

SUMMARY

Many aspects of Congress are set up to meet the needs of its members. The norms of universalism and reciprocity still dominate, meaning that members of Congress share resources more broadly than partisan politics would dictate.

earmarks (p. 398)

seniority (p. 399)

Speaker of the House (p. 400)

majority leader (p. 400)

whip system (p. 400)

minority leader (p. 400)

president pro tempore (p. 400)

roll call vote (p. 402)

party vote (p. 402)

party unity (p. 402)

standing committees (p. 407)

select committees (p. 407)

joint committees (p. 407)

conference committees (p. 407)

distributive theory (p. 407)

informational theory (p. 408)

CRITICAL THINKING AND DISCUSSION

If you were in charge of the Commission on Congressional Reform, what proposals would you make to change how Congress operates? Would your proposals have a chance of being implemented?

PRACTICE QUIZ QUESTIONS

9. The norm of _____ says that federal highway dollars are likely to be divided up so that many districts benefit.
   a) reciprocity
   b) seniority

HOW A BILL BECOMES A LAW

▶ Trace the steps in the legislative process. **Pages 409–19**

SUMMARY

Most bills become law in a conventional manner, but major pieces of legislation generally deviate considerably from this path. The legislative process differs for the House and Senate, sometimes making it difficult to reconcile differences between bills.

KEY TERMS

markup (p. 411)

veto (p. 415)

pocket veto (p. 415)

omnibus legislation (p. 417)

suspension of the rules (p. 417)

cloture (p. 418)

   c) party unity
   d) universalism
   e) specialization

10. Committee leadership, division of seats on committee, and allocation of committee resources are determined by _____.
   a) the majority party
   b) the size of the election margin
   c) unanimous consent
   d) seniority
   e) the president pro tempore

11. The Senate leadership is _____ the House leadership.
   a) more powerful than
   b) as powerful as
   c) less powerful than

12. Party leaders have the power to _____.
   a) force members of Congress to vote a particular way
   b) keep a member of Congress off the ballot in the next election
   c) force their members to share their campaign money
   d) exclude a member from a roll call vote
   e) help their members get favorable committee assignments

⑤ PRACTICE ONLINE

"Critical Thinking" exercise: *Politics Is Everywhere–Earmarks*

filibuster (p. 418)

hold (p. 418)

closed rules (p. 419)

open rules (p. 419)

modified rules (p. 419)

PRACTICE QUIZ QUESTION

13. Compared to the Senate, the floor process in the House is very _____ and _____.
   a) unstructured; majoritarian
   b) structured; majoritarian
   c) unstructured; individualistic
   d) structured; individualistic
   e) individualistic; majoritarian

OVERSIGHT

▶ Describe how Congress ensures that the bureaucracy implements policies correctly. **Pages 419–20**

SUMMARY

After passing bills into law, Congress oversees the bureaucracy in its implementation of the law, making sure it fits Congress's intentions. Though controlling funding is the most powerful mechanism for this, Congress has a number of other mechanisms for achieving bureaucratic fidelity. Generally, Congress does not actively patrol the bureaucracy, but waits to act until a crisis emerges.

KEY TERM

legislative veto (p. 420)

CRITICAL THINKING AND DISCUSSION

If you had to choose between having a responsive or responsible member of Congress, which would you choose and why? Would your answer depend on how other members of Congress were behaving?

PRACTICE QUIZ QUESTION

14. Waiting for a crisis to emerge before taking action is called _____.
    a) police patrol oversight
    b) fire alarm oversight
    c) emergency room oversight
    d) reactionary oversight
    e) bureaucratic oversight

> ## ⑤ PRACTICE ONLINE
>
> "Big Think" video exercise: *Senator George Mitchell on Congress and Bureaucracy*

CONGRESSIONAL REFORM

▶ Evaluate arguments for making Congress more accountable. **Pages 420–22**

SUMMARY

Despite the general perception that the government does not serve the public interest, congressional reforms are relatively rare. Generally, reform attempts either address Congress's external image, or internally improve the efficiency of lawmaking, and a trade-off exists between the external and internal concerns.

PRACTICE QUIZ QUESTION

15. The McCain-Feingold Act is an example of a reform that _____ Congress's image and _____ the internal efficiency.
    a) improved; improved
    b) improved; reduced
    c) reduced; improved
    d) reduced; reduced
    e) reduced; had no effect on

> ## ⑤ PRACTICE ONLINE
>
> "Big Think" video exercise: *How Has Washington Changed?*

SUGGESTED READING

Bianco, William T. *Trust: Representatives and Constituents.* Ann Arbor: University of Michigan Press, 1994.

Canon, David T. *Race, Redistricting and Representation: The Unintended Consequences of Black Majority Districts.* Chicago: University of Chicago Press, 1999.

Fenno, Richard F. *Congressmen in Committees.* Boston: Little, Brown, 1973.

Hall, Richard L. *Participation in Congress.* New Haven, CT: Yale University Press, 1996.

Jacobson, Gary C. *The Politics of Congressional Elections,* 5th ed. New York: Addison-Wesley, 2001.

Mayhew, David R. *Congress: The Electoral Connection.* New Haven, CT: Yale University Press, 1974.

Theriault, Sean. *Party Polarization in Congress.* New York: Cambridge University Press, 2008.

11

The Presidency

PRESIDENTIAL DECISIONS, SUCH as President Obama's choice to use drones for attacks on enemy targets in Afghanistan and elsewhere, are often controversial. Here, Obama discusses military and defense strategy in 2012.

ONE OF THE CORE ELEMENTS OF President Barack Obama's strategy to fight terrorist groups has been the increased use of drones—small, unmanned aircraft that fly into foreign airspace, monitor the activities of terror suspects on the ground, and, once the identities of suspects have been verified and the president's approval received, launch missles to attack these suspects and their facilities. Over the last four years, drone attacks in countries such as Afghanistan, Yemen, and Pakistan have decimated the leadership and infrastructure of terrorist groups and inflicted significant casualties on lower-level fighters. Drones also played a key role in identifying the safe house in Pakistan where Al Qaeda leader Osama bin Laden was located, making possible the helicopter attack by U.S. Special Forces that resulted in bin's Laden's death in 2011.

Decisions involving military force provide an example of presidential power and how it may be controversial. In the case of using drones, virtually all Americans support the idea of fighting back against terror groups such as Al Qaeda. The controversy arises because some Americans favor a more aggressive approach that would involve sending ground forces to fight terrorist strongholds rather than attacking from the air. Others are uncomfortable with the use of drones because of the difficulty of being absolutely sure that the people being attacked are all terrorists. Finally, some observers have criticized the Obama administration drone strategy on the grounds that it is motivated by politics rather than a judgment about the most effective approach. They worry that Obama and his advisors favor unmanned attacks in order to minimize American casualties, which would be politically unpopular even if they were part of a more effective strategy.

CONFLICT & COMPROMISE
in American Politics

These dissenting opinions reflect the fact that the reliance on unmanned drones is actually a compromise among different strategies for fighting the war on terror—between aggressive strategies that rely on ground forces and more defensive approaches that focus on preventing attacks against Americans. Drone attacks are an intermediate option, allowing attacks on terrorist groups without putting U.S. troops in harm's way. This compromise helps the president obtain the support of Congress and the American public. While such support is not necessary to order individual attacks, in the long run presidents generally need congressional and public support in order to carry out their decisions.

The president's power to order American forces into combat is only one example of presidential power. As we discuss in this chapter, America's presidents have considerable power over foreign and domestic policy and have used this power to make real, significant changes in government policy that have had real consequences for the lives of ordinary Americans. For example, Barack Obama's first term in office was marked by the enactment of landmark health care legislation, new financial regulations, economic stimulus, and the appointment of two Supreme Court justices. Accomplishments such as these are often cited as evidence that presidential power has gotten out of control—that presidents are virtual dictators, able to do almost whatever they want without congressional consent or judicial review.

This chapter offers a different interpretation of presidential power. U.S. presidents face decisions that are highly conflictual, with many people holding strong opinions on both sides of the question. Although some Americans approved of Obama's accomplishments, many others were opposed. Success for presidents is not automatic; they face the problem of reaching their own policy goals while at the same time trying to satisfy the demands of their supporters in Congress and among the American people—and seeking to avoid alienating people who disagree with presidential decisions.

To put it another way, while presidents are powerful, they are not dictators: in most cases, their actions either require congressional consent to take effect or can be undone by subsequent congressional action. Presidents must also cultivate public opinion in order to get re-elected or to elect members of Congress from their party, and must monitor the bureaucracy to make sure that their decisions are faithfully implemented. And sometimes, as with health care reform for Obama or George W. Bush's failed 2005 Social Security reform initiative, presidents must decide whether to scale back their proposals in an effort to get them enacted or risk completely failing to accomplish their goals.

Accordingly, one of the fundamental questions we ask in this chapter is, what are the limits of presidential power? When are presidents able to prevail in the face of conflict in the country, in Congress, or in the bureaucracy? Has presidential power grown over time? How does conflict affect the decisions that presidents make and the ways they try to implement their policy goals?

The second fundamental question we ask is, what are the sources of presidential power? The answer lies in the idea that political process matters. In some situations, the powers allocated in the Constitution enable the president to change government policy unilaterally. However, there are limits on this power. Congress and the Supreme Court can and at times do overturn presidential actions. Moreover, many policy changes require explicit congressional approval. This chapter shows that all presidents face opportunities and constraints, and their success in office depends on the particular challenges that arise, their personal policy goals, and their skill at using the power of the presidency.

AMERICA'S PRESIDENTS

TRACE THE EVOLUTION OF PRESIDENTIAL POWER OVER TIME

As we consider the histories of America's 44 presidents, three facts stand out. First, presidents get their power from a variety of sources, from provisions of the Constitution to their administration of the executive branch of government. Second, presidential power has increased over time, not because of changes in the Constitution, but because of America's growth as a nation, its emergence as a dominant actor in international politics, the expansion of the federal government, and various acts of legislation that gave new authority to the president. Third, there are sharp limits to presidential power. Presidents are often forced to compromise in the face of public, congressional, or foreign opposition.

EARLY YEARS THROUGH WORLD WAR I

Since the early years of the Republic, presidents' actions have had profound consequences for the nation. Presidents George Washington, John Adams, and Thomas Jefferson forged compromises on issues such as choosing a permanent location for the nation's capital, establishing the federal courts, and devising a system for financing the government.[1] Presidents Andrew Jackson and Martin Van Buren were instrumental in forming the Democratic Party and its local party organizations.

Early presidents also made important foreign policy decisions. For example, the Monroe Doctrine issued by President James Monroe in 1823 stated that America would remain neutral in wars involving European nations and that these nations must cease attempts to colonize or occupy areas in North and South America.[2] Presidents John Tyler and James Polk oversaw the admission of the huge territory of Texas into the Union following the Mexican-American War. Polk also negotiated the Oregon Treaty with Britain, which led to acquisition of land that later became Oregon, Washington, Idaho, and parts of Montana and Wyoming.[3]

Several presidents sought compromise on slavery prior to the Civil War and to the prosecution of the war itself. President Millard Fillmore's support helped to enact the Compromise of 1850, which limited slavery in California, and Franklin Pierce supported the Kansas-Nebraska Act, which regulated slavery in these territories. Abraham Lincoln, who helped form the Republican Party in the 1850s, played a transformative role in setting policy as president during the Civil War. His orders raised the huge Union Army, and as commander in chief he directed the conduct of the bloody war that kept the southern states from seceding permanently. Lincoln issued the Emancipation Proclamation, which freed the slaves in the South, and temporarily suspended the writ of habeas corpus, allowing the government to imprison people without filing charges against them.[4]

During the late 1800s and early 1900s, presidents were instrumental in federal responses to the nation's rapid expansion and industrialization.[5] The country's growing size and economy generated conflict over which services the federal government should provide to citizens and how much the government should regulate individual and corporate behavior.[6] Various acts of legislation created new federal agencies and, in doing so, also created new presidential powers

GEORGE WASHINGTON REMAINS, FOR many Americans, the presidential ideal—a leader whose crucial domestic and foreign policy decisions shaped the growth of America's democracy.

and responsibilities. For example, Republican president Theodore Roosevelt used the Sherman Antitrust Act to break up the Northern Securities Company, a mammoth nationwide railroad trust. He increased the power of the Interstate Commerce Commission to regulate businesses and expanded federal conservation programs. Democrat Woodrow Wilson further increased the government's role in managing the economy through his support of the Clayton Antitrust Act, the Federal Reserve Act, the first federal income tax, and legislation banning child labor.[7]

As these examples illustrate, presidential power has grown over time as the president and members of the executive branch have obtained new regulatory powers over corporations and individual Americans, and as presidents have responded to shifts in public opinion by proposing new policies. Essentially, because the president is the head of the bureaucracy, as the number of agencies and bureaucrats grows, so does presidential power.

At the same time, Wilson's foreign policy activities illustrate the limits of presidential power. While he campaigned in the 1916 election on a promise to keep America out of World War I, he ultimately ordered American troops to fight on the side of the Allies. After the war, Wilson offered a peace plan that proposed reshaping the borders of European countries in order to mitigate future conflicts; creating an international organization, the League of Nations, to prevent future conflicts; and taking other measures to encourage free trade and democracy.[8] However, America's allies rejected most of Wilson's proposals, and the Senate refused to allow American participation in the League of Nations.

THE GREAT DEPRESSION THROUGH THE PRESENT

PRESIDENT FRANKLIN DELANO Roosevelt called on the public to support his New Deal programs and other policies. Here, he delivers one of his "fireside chat" radio broadcasts, designed to communicate his arguments to the American people and win their support.

Presidential actions defined the government's response to the Great Depression, a worldwide economic collapse in the late 1920s and 1930s marked by high unemployment, huge stock market declines, and bank failures. Republican president Herbert Hoover favored only modest government actions in response, arguing that more substantial efforts would be of little use.[9] After Hoover lost the 1932 election, Democrat Franklin Roosevelt and his staff began reshaping American government. Roosevelt's New Deal reforms created many federal agencies that helped individual Americans and imposed many new corporate regulations.[10] This expansion continued under Roosevelt's successors. Even Republican Dwight Eisenhower, whose party had initially opposed many New Deal reforms, presided over the creation of new agencies and the building of the interstate highway system.[11]

Presidents were instrumental in the civil rights reforms and expansion of the federal government in the 1960s. Democrat John Kennedy established the Peace Corps and began bargaining with members of Congress over legislation that would guarantee voting rights and civil rights for African Americans. Democrat Lyndon Johnson, who assumed the presidency after Kennedy's assassination, campaigned for re-election on his proposals for the Great Society and a War on Poverty. Johnson's administration created a wide range of domestic programs, such as the Department of Housing and Urban Development, Medicare, Medicaid, and federal funding for schools, and finished the job of enacting voting rights and civil rights legislation. Again, this expansion of the federal government through legislation added to presidential power.

Both Johnson and his successor, Richard Nixon, directed America's involvement in the Vietnam War, with the goal of forcing the North Vietnamese to abandon their plans to unify North and South Vietnam. Here again, presidential efforts did not meet with success: despite enormous deployments of American forces and more than 58,000 American soldiers killed, Nixon eventually signed an agreement that allowed American troops to leave but did not end the conflict, which concluded only after a North Vietnamese victory in 1975.

The two presidents after Nixon, Republican Gerald Ford and Democrat Jimmy Carter, faced the worst economic conditions since the Great Depression, largely due to increased energy prices. Both presidents offered plans to reduce unemployment and inflation, restore economic growth, and enhance domestic energy sources. However, their efforts were largely unsuccessful, and this became a critical factor in their failed re-election bids.

In the last generation, the political and policy importance of presidential actions has only increased. Republican Ronald Reagan's popular campaign platform of tax cuts, fewer regulations, smaller government, and a tougher stand against the Soviet Union helped Republicans gain majority control of the Senate in 1980 and attract many new voters to the party. Reagan and his staff negotiated important arms control agreements with the Soviet Union, efforts that accelerated under Reagan's successor, George H. W. Bush. Bush led American and international participation in the Persian Gulf War during 1990 and 1991, which succeeded in removing Iraqi forces from Kuwait with minimal American casualties.

Democrat Bill Clinton's presidency was marked by passage of the North American Free Trade Agreement, welfare reform, arms control agreements, successful peacekeeping efforts by U.S. troops in Haiti and the Balkans, one of the longest periods of economic growth in U.S. history, and the first balanced budgets since the 1960s. However, despite efforts to drum up public support for health care reform, congressional and public opposition doomed Clinton's proposals. The same factors delayed peacekeeping efforts in Bosnia and Kosovo, and deterred American efforts to stop the massive genocide from civil war in Rwanda. President Obama to date has secured several notable changes in foreign and domestic policy, such as the enactment of health insurance reform. However, he had to compromise on many of these questions, and in other cases, such as his efforts to enact comprehensive immigration reform, he was completely unsuccessful. In this chapter, we examine these and other instances of presidential successes and failures in order to understand the limits of presidential power.

THE PRESIDENT PLAYS A PREDOMINANT role in American foreign policy. In the 1980s, President Ronald Reagan negotiated numerous arms agreements with the Soviet Union. Here, Reagan and Soviet leader Mikhail Gorbachev sign a treaty eliminating certain types of nuclear missiles.

constitutional authority Powers derived from the provisions of the Constitution that outline the president's role in government.

THE PRESIDENT'S JOB DESCRIPTION

DESCRIBE THE CONSTITUTIONAL AND STATUTORY POWERS OF THE PRESIDENT TODAY

This section describes both the president's **constitutional authority**, derived from the provisions of the Constitution that describe the president's governmental role, and his **statutory authority**, which comes from laws that give the president additional responsibilities. These powers are summarized in Nuts and Bolts 11.1. As the box indicates, some presidential powers arise from one source, such as the Constitution, while others derive from a combination of constitutional and statutory authority. Our aim is to show how these provisions operate in modern-day American politics: what kinds of opportunities and constraints they create for the current president and future holders of the office.

statutory authority (presidential) Powers derived from laws enacted by Congress that add to the powers given to the president in the Constitution.

PRESIDENTIAL POWERS

Constitutional Authority	Statutory Authority	Other
Head of Government, Head of State (Vesting Clause)		Executive Privilege
Implementation of Laws ("faithful execution")	Implementation of Laws (as directed in statutes)	Recommend Annual Federal Budget and other Legislative initiatives
Executive Orders and similar directives (rare)	Executive Orders and similar directives	
Administer Executive Branch		
Nominations and appointments to Executive Branch and Judiciary	Nominations and appointments to Executive Branch and Judiciary	
Commander in Chief of Armed Forces		
Negotiation of Treaties and Executive Agreements	Negotiation of Treaties and Executive Agreements	
Veto of Congressional Actions		
Presidential Pardons		
Other Ceremonial powers		

HEAD OF THE EXECUTIVE BRANCH

The president's job description begins with the list of constitutional responsibilities of the office. The Constitution's **vesting clause,** "The executive Power shall be vested in a President of the United States of America," makes the president the **head of government**, granting authority over the executive branch, as well as **head of state**, or the symbolic and political representative of the country. The precise meaning of the vesting clause has been debated for more than 200 years. Presidents and their supporters argue for an expansive meaning; their opponents counter that the clause is so vague as to be meaningless. These debates are an important clue that a president's power is only partially due to the specific grants of power in the Constitution—some of it comes from interpretations of less concrete statements such as the vesting clause.

The Constitution also places the president in charge of the implementation of laws, saying, "he shall take Care that the Laws be faithfully executed." Sometimes the implementation of a law is nearly automatic, as was the case with a 2010 law that extended tax cuts originally enacted during the presidency of George W. Bush. In that case, all the president needed to do to implement the law was to ensure that bureaucrats in the Internal Revenue Service notified employers to adjust tax withholding for their employees.

vesting clause Article II, Section 1, of the Constitution, which states that "executive Power shall be vested in a President of the United States of America," making the president both the head of government and the head of state.

head of government One role of the president, through which he or she has authority over the executive branch.

head of state One role of the president, through which he or she represents the country symbolically and politically.

THE PRESIDENT AS HEAD OF THE EXECUTIVE BRANCH

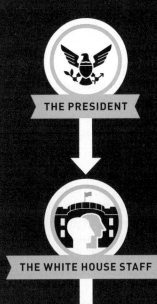

THE PRESIDENT

THE WHITE HOUSE STAFF

White House Office
Office of Management & Budget
Council of Economic Advisers
National Security Council
Office of National Drug Control Policy
Office of the U.S. Trade Representative

Council on Environmental Quality
Office of Science & Tech. Policy
Office of Policy Development
Office of Administration
Vice President

**EXECUTIVE OFFICE
OF THE PRESIDENT**

Examples:
Federal Election Commission
Federal Trade Commission
Social Security Administration
National Transportation Safety Board

**INDEPENDENT
AGENCIES & GOV.
CORPORATIONS**

THE CABINET

Dept. of Housing & Urban Development
Dept. of the Interior
Dept. of Commerce
Dept. of Labor
Dept. of Education
Dept. of Transportation
Dept. of Energy
Dept. of Veterans Affairs
Dept. of Justice
Dept. of Defense
Dept. of State
Dept. of Homeland Security
Dept. of Health & Human Services
Dept. of the Treasury
Dept. of Agriculture

POP QUIZ!

1 The president has direct control over the cabinet departments, but his control of _____ is more limited.

a the White House staff

b the Executive Office of the President

c the Cabinet

d the independent agencies

e the vice president

2 Officials who serve on the National Security Council and the Council of Economic Advisers are part of the

a White House staff.

b Executive Office of the President.

c Cabinet.

d independent agencies.

e government corporations.

AFTER CONGRESS FAILED TO PASS the DREAM Act, President Obama issued an executive order to stop the deportation of some young illegal immigrants in 2012. People under age 30 who came to the United States as children, had been successful students or served in the military, and posed no security threat were given a two-year deferral.

More commonly, the president's authority to implement the law requires his using judgment to translate legislative goals into programs, budgets, and regulations. For example, the bank bailout legislation of late 2008 gave bureaucrats in the Bush (and later Obama) administration funds to help banks and other companies in financial distress but let the bureaucrats decide who would receive the money, how much, and under what terms.[12] Similarly, the Military Commissions Act of 2006 established the goal of using military tribunals to review evidence against terror suspects but allowed President Bush and his appointees to determine the procedures of those tribunals, such as whether defendants could see classified information that was part of the evidence against them and whether evidence obtained through coercive interrogation could be used in the trials.[13] Presidents and their staff can also delay implementation of a law, either to avoid putting in place policies they disapprove of or to gain time to lobby Congress to reverse the decision.

Finally, the president's control of the executive branch allows him to issue orders to government agencies that make significant policy changes. For example, in April 2010 President Obama directed the Department of Health and Human Services to prohibit discrimination against gay and lesbian couples in hospital visitation rules.[14] While this order could be overturned by Congress, the president's ability to act unilaterally conveys significant power—unless opponents in Congress can organize, write legislation, shepherd it through the House and Senate, and override a presidential veto, the president's decision will prevail. In this sense, the ability to act unilaterally allows the president to impose outcomes and avoid the need to compromise with opponents in Congress.

APPOINTMENTS

The president appoints ambassadors, senior bureaucrats, and members of the federal judiciary, including Supreme Court justices.[15] As the head of the executive branch, the president controls about 8,000 positions, ranging from high-profile jobs such as secretary of state to mundane administrative and secretarial positions. About 1,200 of these appointments—generally high-level positions such as cabinet secretaries—require Senate confirmation. In the main, the Senate approves the majority of the president's nominees without much debate or controversy, with exceptions concentrated in defense, intelligence, and justice positions.

In addition, presidents make nominations to the federal courts; Presidents Bill Clinton and George W. Bush each appointed more than 400 judges. Because federal judgeships are lifetime appointments, they enable the president to put people into positions of power who will remain after he leaves office. For example, President George W. Bush appointed two conservative justices to the Supreme Court, John Roberts and Samuel Alito, whose impact was immediately apparent in a series of Court decisions released in 2007 on issues such as abortion rights, gun control, and affirmative action.[16] As of late 2012, Obama's two Supreme Court appointments, Sonya Sotomayor and Elena Kagen, have not had as dramatic an impact. Even so, the effects of lifetime appointments, along with the many other judicial appointments that Obama has made or will make, will not be fully apparent for years to come.

The Senate approves the vast majority of the president's nominees without much controversy, but the need for Senate confirmation of his appointments fundamentally limits this presidential power. Rather than demanding that the Senate vote on every nomination, presidents have often compromised and withdrawn the most controversial names and found other candidates who are more satisfactory to the Senate. For example, President Obama's nominee for secretary of health and human services, former senator Tom Daschle, withdrew his name from consideration after it was revealed that he had to pay more than $100,000 in back taxes for the use of a car and driver while he was a lobbyist.[17]

One way the president can temporarily dodge the need for Senate approval is to make a **recess appointment** during a period that Congress is not in session. These appointments, however, are temporary, lasting only for the rest of the legislative term. By making recess appointments, the president can fill vacant ambassadorships or designate heads of cabinet departments without waiting for a Senate vote. This provision was included in the Constitution because it was expected Congress would not be in session much of the year, but in the modern era, when Congress is in session almost continuously, recess appointments are sometimes used to bypass the confirmation process for controversial nominees. President Obama used this strategy in July 2010 to name Donald Berwick to head the Centers for Medicare and Medicaid Services.[18] Berwick had been nominated in April 2010 but faced significant Senate opposition. Obama's appointment was notable because at the time, the Senate was scheduled to be in recess for less than two weeks. While Berwick's appointment was never confirmed by the Senate, he remained in his position until almost the end of the next session of Congress, until his resignation in November 2011.

EXECUTIVE ORDERS

Presidents have the power to issue **executive orders**, proclamations that unilaterally change government policy without subsequent congressional consent.[19] (Presidents can also issue other kinds of orders that change policy, such as National Security Presidential Directives and Presidential Findings.)

One executive order issued by President Obama on December 17, 2009, gave federal employees a half-day off on Christmas Eve. Another order issued on December 29 changed the guidelines for classified information, declaring that "if there is significant doubt about the need to classify information, it should not be classified." A third executive order, issued on January 17, 2010, mobilized some reserve military personnel to participate in relief operations after the earthquake in Haiti.

Political scientists Kenneth Mayer and Kevin Price estimated that more than 1,000 executive orders issued between 1949 and 1999 were the subject of press coverage, congressional hearings, litigation, scholarly articles, or presidential public statements.[20] Most dealt with relatively minor matters. However, some executive orders, such as the one about classifying information, make significant policy changes.

Executive orders may appear to give the president authority to do whatever he wants, even in the face of strong opposition from Congress. However, a president's power to issue executive orders is limited. In many cases, Congress enacts a law giving presidents the authority to issue an executive order on a particular question. Moreover, regardless of the authority used to issue an order, if members had objected to the policy changes, they could have passed a law overturning any executive orders or deny funding to implement them—although they would need support from two-thirds of both houses to override the expected presidential veto. The threat of congressional response often influences the specifics of executive orders, so that they reflect a compromise between what the president wants and what members of Congress are willing to tolerate.

The president can, in theory, cite the Constitution as the sole source of his authority to issue an executive order, although this strategy is uncommon. If this

recess appointment Selection by the president of a person to be an ambassador or the head of a department while the Senate is not in session, thereby bypassing Senate approval. Unless approved by a subsequent Senate vote, recess appointees serve only to the end of the congressional term.

executive orders Proclamations made by the president that change government policy without congressional approval.

EXECUTIVE ORDERS, PRESIDENTIAL APPROVAL, AND PRESIDENTIAL POWER

One of the central arguments about presidential power in this chapter is that much of a president's ability to shape public policy comes from his ability to take unilateral actions—to implement policy changes that remain in place unless members of Congress reverse them. However, the examples cited here do not tell us the extent of a president's unilateral power: Is it something he does every day or rarely? What factors make the exercise of unilateral power more or less likely? One place to analyze the extent of presidents' unilateral power is the executive orders they issue during their time in office. As we discuss elsewhere in this chapter, executive orders implement changes in government policy without explicit congressional consent. Members of Congress can reverse these decisions only by passing a resolution and either gaining the president's support (unlikely, given that the president issued the order) or by putting together a coalition large enough to override a presidential veto. So a further question is, to what extent do executive orders make significant changes in policy? If all they do is make minor, non-controversial changes, they are hardly an example of presidential power.

Watch a video clip of Kenneth Mayer discussing this topic at **wwnorton.com/studyspace**

These questions were addressed by Professor Kenneth Mayer of the University of Wisconsin–Madison and one of his graduate students, Kevin Price.[a] Their study focused on executive orders that were "significant," meaning that they resulted in major policy changes or were controversial. For example, President Obama's early 2009 order to limit harsh interrogation of terror suspects would be categorized as significant, whereas another order issued in 2009 that allowed federal employees to leave work early on Christmas Eve was much less so. A high rate of significant executive orders means that a president frequently exercises unilateral powers in the form of significant executive orders in ways that matter, and a low rate suggests that, for whatever reasons, this exercise is rare. However, a low rate of significant orders may not signal a lack of presidential power: a president who has a loyal legislative majority may opt to pursue policy changes through legislation rather than by executive order because he is confident of congressional support.

Mayer and Price first determined that about 7,500 executive orders had been issued between 1936 and 2000. They analyzed a sample of 1,028 orders and defined a significant order as one that satisfied one or more of the following criteria: there was some press coverage of the order, members of Congress held committee hearings to discuss the order, scholarly work referenced the order, the president who issued the order also issued subsequent statements that referred to the order, there was litigation involving the order, or the order created a new governmental agency. Although these criteria are arbitrary—it may be that some insignificant orders received press coverage or provoked hearings—it makes sense to assume that orders satisfying none of these criteria are truly insignificant, meaning they do not reflect real presidential power.

Mayer and Price found that 146 out of 1,028 (about 15 percent) of executive orders met their criteria for significance. This finding confirms that many executive orders deal with relatively trivial matters. However, given that presidents issue hundreds of executive orders every year, the data also tells us that a substantial number do involve important policy questions.

The authors also used their data to identify the conditions under which presidents issue significant executive orders. They hypothesized that popularity would influence whether a president would enact a policy change through legislation rather than with an executive order. As a president's popularity increases, he could be more confident that public pressure would lead to congressional support for his desired policy change, but as his popularity decreases, a president would be more likely to use an executive order to change policy rather than risk his proposal being rejected.

This expectation was confirmed. For example, the probability that a president with a 30 percent approval rating issues at least one significant executive order in a year is .705; but the probability that a president with 70 percent approval issues at least one significant order is only .165—in other words, popular presidents issue fewer significant executive orders, which is consistent with the study's hypothesis.

These findings show that American presidents exercise their unilateral powers on a regular basis. Moreover, they show how political factors, such as a president's approval rating, influence the decision to issue executive orders. Although unilateral power is not unlimited, it is clearly a significant asset for presidents.

PRESIDENTIAL APPROVAL AND SIGNIFICANT EXECUTIVE ORDERS	
APPROVAL RATING	PROBABILITY OF ONE OR MORE SIGNIFICANT ORDERS
30%	.705
50	.503
70	.165

Source: Adapted from Kenneth R. Mayer and Kevin Price, "Unilateral Presidential Powers: Significant Executive Orders, 1949–99," *Presidential Studies Quarterly* 32:2 (2002): 367–86.

happens, Congress can pass a law overturning the order, but the president could potentially refuse to abide by the new law, arguing that the constitutional grant of power can be changed only by amending the Constitution itself. Such a disagreement would likely end up before the Supreme Court. If the Court disagreed with the president, its ruling would void the order.

COMMANDER IN CHIEF

The Constitution makes the president the commander in chief of America's military forces but gives Congress the power to declare war. These provisions are potentially contradictory, and the Constitution leaves open the broader question of who controls the military.[21] In practice, however, the president controls day-to-day military operations through the Department of Defense and has the power to order troops into action without explicit congressional approval. This happened in 2002, when President George W. Bush deployed more than 100,000 troops, hundreds of aircraft, and dozens of warships in anticipation of action against Iraq. Although Congress eventually passed a resolution authorizing combat operations against Iraq, this happened after the deployments had occurred. (Subsequent deployments of troops to Iraq and Afghanistan have also occurred without further congressional approval.)

Congress has the power to declare war, but this power by itself does not constrain the president. In fact, even though the United States has been involved in hundreds of military conflicts since the Founding, there have been only five declarations of war: the War of 1812, the Mexican-American War (1846), the Spanish-American War (1898), World War I (1917), and World War II (1941). However, especially in recent years, members of Congress have used other methods to try to constrain presidential war-making powers.

In particular, Congress enacted the War Powers Resolution in 1973 (see Nuts and Bolts 11.2). However, a 2004 report by the Congressional Research Service found that between 1975 and 2003, despite dozens of U.S. military actions—ranging from embassy evacuations to large-scale operations, including the 1991 Persian Gulf War and the invasions of Iraq and Afghanistan—the War Powers Resolution

11.2 NUTS & bolts

THE WAR POWERS RESOLUTION OF 1973

1. The president is required to report to Congress any introduction of U.S. forces into hostilities or imminent hostilities.

2. The use of force must be terminated within 60 days unless Congress approves of the deployment. The time limit can be extended to 90 days if the president certifies that additional time is needed to safely withdraw American forces.

3. The president is required whenever possible to consult with Congress before introducing American forces into hostilities or imminent hostilities.

4. Any congressional resolution authorizing the continued deployment of American forces will be considered under expedited procedures.

Source: Richard F. Grimmett, "The War Powers Resolution: After Thirty Years," Congressional Research Service Report RL32267, March 11, 2004.

has been invoked only once.[22] Moreover, despite being in effect for nearly 40 years, it has never faced Supreme Court review. Some scholars have even argued that the resolution actually expands presidential power because it gives the president essentially unlimited control for the first 90 days of a military operation.[23]

Despite its limitations, the War Powers Resolution has forced presidents to gain congressional approval, in the form of congressional resolutions, for large-scale military actions such as the invasion of Iraq, as well as for lesser operations such as the deployments of peacekeeping forces in Bosnia during the 1990s. Members of Congress can also curb a president's war-making powers through budget restrictions, legislative prohibitions, and, ultimately, impeachment.[24]

TREATY MAKING AND FOREIGN POLICY

Treaty-making power is shared between Congress and the president: presidents and their staff negotiate treaties, which are then sent to the Senate for approval, which requires the support of a two-thirds majority. In the case of treaties negotiated under **fast-track authority**, both the House and Senate vote on the treaty, with majority support in each chamber required for approval. However, the president has a **first-mover advantage** in the treaty-making process. Congress considers treaties only after negotiations have ended; there is no way for members of Congress to force the president to negotiate a treaty. However, the need for congressional approval often leads presidents to take account of senators' preferences when negotiating treaties, leading again to significant compromise between the two branches.

Presidents have two strategies for avoiding a congressional treaty vote. One is to announce that the United States will voluntarily abide by a treaty without ratifying it. President Clinton used this tactic to implement the 1997 Kyoto Protocol, an agreement that set limits on carbon emissions by industrialized nations.[25] It is also possible to structure a deal as an **executive agreement** between the executive branch and a foreign government, which does not require Senate approval. Relative to a ratified treaty, which remains in force after the president who negotiated it leaves office, both voluntary compliance and executive agreements have the disadvantage that a subsequent president can simply undo the action, as President George W. Bush did in the case of compliance with the Kyoto Protocol.

The president also serves as the principal representative of the United States in foreign affairs other than treaty negotiations. These duties include communicating with foreign leaders, nongovernmental organizations, and even ordinary citizens to persuade them to act in what the president believes is in the United States' interest. For example, in June 2009, President Obama gave a speech in Cairo, Egypt, aimed at "convincing people throughout the Middle East of America's sympathy to their concerns, such as the creation of a Palestinian state."[26]

The amount of time the president devotes to foreign policy is subject to world events and therefore not entirely under his control. George W. Bush campaigned on the priorities of tax cuts and education reform[27] and against nation building abroad. Nonetheless, in response to the September 11 attacks, he initiated efforts to build stable democracies in Afghanistan and Iraq.[28] Similarly, Barack Obama campaigned on a largely domestic agenda but spent considerable time reformulating American policy in Iraq and Afganistan, as well as on trips and speeches such as the trip to the Middle East mentioned earlier.

fast-track authority An expedited system for passing treaties under which support from a simple majority, rather than a two-thirds majority, is needed in both the House and Senate, and no amendments are allowed.

first-mover advantage The president's power to initiate treaty negotiations. Congress cannot initiate treaties and can only consider them once they have been negotiated.

executive agreement An agreement between the executive branch and a foreign government, which acts as a treaty but does not require Senate approval.

AS HEAD OF STATE, THE PRESIDENT often negotiates agreements with other countries. In 2009, President Obama visited China and met with Chinese president Hu Jintao and other officials to discuss a number of issues, including exchange rates, human rights, and cooperation on sanctions against Iran.

WHO LEADS OTHER COUNTRIES?

The American president serves as both head of state and head of government, an arrangement that gives the president an enormous opportunity to shape what government does. However, these responsibilities create a huge workload for the president, even with the help of appointees to manage the federal government. How common is this arrangement among the world's democracies?

Scholars of comparative politics have identified three ways to structure a democracy. First, in a presidential system (or presidential republic), such as the United States, a single chief executive, who is elected separately from legislators, serves as both head of state and head of government.

Second, in a parliamentary system (or parliamentary monarchy), a member of the legislature—usually the leader of the majority party—serves as the head of government. Some of these countries do not have a head of state, and in those that do, the position is usually held by a king or queen whose role is largely ceremonial. For example, David Cameron is Great Britain's prime minister, or head of government, and the country's head of state is Queen Elizabeth II. The queen delivers the annual message of the government to Parliament, which is the equivalent of the president's State of the Union address, but the speech is written by the prime minister and his staff; the queen simply reads the text.

Countries with a semipresidential system, like France, have a head of government (prime minister) and a separate head of state (president). In France, Prime Minister Jean-Marc Ayrault (front right) focuses on domestic policy, while President François Hollande (front left) has primary responsibility for foreign policy.

The third type of democracy is a semi-presidential system, which resembles a parliamentary system in that the head of government is chosen from the members of the legislature. Unlike a parliamentary system, however, a semi-presidential system also has a separately elected head of state or president. The powers of this chief executive vary widely among countries. In France the president largely focuses on foreign policy, while the prime minister generally handles domestic policy, but in some other countries, such as Germany and Israel, the president's job is largely ceremonial.

The graph below reports the distribution of these three systems. The most common form of government worldwide is a mixed republic with a separate head of government and head of state. There are also a substantial number of parliamentary monarchies. However, most of the semi-presidential systems listed in the table actually work much like parliamentary systems. In these countries, the chief executive has relatively little power, just like the monarch in a parliamentary monarchy.

Moreover, although America is not alone in having a presidential system, most other countries that use this system are new, relatively small democracies in Central or South America or in Africa, such as Nicaragua, Argentina, Nigeria, and South Africa. Among democracies in the developed world, America's presidential system is highly unusual.

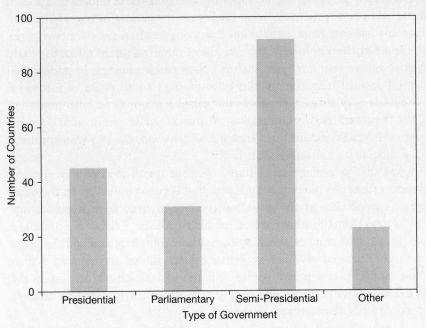

TYPES OF GOVERNMENT, 2008

Source: Pippa Norris, Driving Democracy *(New York: Cambridge University Press, 2008).*

Looking at presidential actions since World War II, some scholars have argued that there are "two presidencies," one dealing with domestic policy, the other foreign policy. This theory contrasts high levels of citizen, interest group, and legislator interest in domestic concerns such as taxation, spending, or regulation of industries, with low levels of interest in many foreign policy questions, such as minor treaties or outcomes that affect only people in other countries.[29] As a result, these scholars argued, presidents may prefer to focus on foreign policy because they can often act without congressional consent or public scrutiny. Although this thesis still makes some sense, the increasing connection between domestic and foreign policy in areas such as trade or environmental protection, as well as the increasing significance of international conflicts such as the wars in Iraq or Afghanistan, mean that more often, presidential actions are inherently conflictual regardless of whether they fall into the category of domestic policy, foreign policy, or something in between.

LEGISLATIVE POWER

State of the Union An annual speech in which the president addresses Congress to report on the condition of the country and recommend policies.

The Constitution establishes lawmaking as a shared power between the president and Congress, meaning that compromise is fundamental to this activity.[30] The president can recommend policies to Congress, notably in the annual **State of the Union** address. The president and his staff also work with members of Congress to develop legislative proposals, and although the president cannot formally introduce legislation, it is typically easy to find a member of Congress willing to sponsor a presidential proposal.[31] Presidents and their legislative staff also spend considerable time lobbying members of Congress to support their proposals and negotiating with legislative leaders over policy details.

The president's legislative power also stems from the ability to veto legislation (see Chapter 10). Once both chambers of Congress have passed a bill by simple majority, the president must decide within two weeks of congressional action whether to sign it or issue a veto. Signed bills become law, but vetoed bills return to the House and Senate for a vote to override the veto. If both chambers enact the bill again with at least two-thirds majorities, the bill becomes law; otherwise, it is defeated. If Congress adjourns before the president has made his decision, the president can pocket veto the proposal by not responding to it. Pocket vetoes cannot be overridden, but congressional leaders can avoid them by keeping Congress in session for two weeks after a bill is enacted, thereby forcing the president either to sign the bill or to veto it.

Presidential vetoes can have significant policy consequences. President Bill Clinton vetoed several bills that would have banned some types of late-term abortion. Supporters of these measures comprised a majority in both houses of Congress, but they could not amass the two-thirds majority required to override Clinton's veto.[32] After President Bush took office, however, the ban was approved by the House and Senate and signed into law.

Studies show that vetoes are most likely to occur under divided government, when a president from one party faces a House and Senate controlled by the other party.[33] Under these conditions, the veto allows the president to block proposals supported by legislators from the other party, producing gridlock.[34] Vetoes are much less likely under unified government, when one party controls Congress and the presidency, because the chances are much higher that the president and legislators from his party hold similar policy priorities. By vetoing legislation, presidents gain raw power over the legislative process and can stop a proposal dead in its tracks unless it has strong support in both houses of Congress.

Democratic president Bill Clinton faced divided government, working with a Republican-controlled Congress for all but the first two years of his eight years in office. Republican president George W. Bush, in contrast, had divided government with Democratic control of the Senate during most of his first two years, unified government for the middle four years, and divided government once again when the Democrats took control of Congress in the 2006 midterms. Clinton issued almost 40 vetoes in his eight years in office, whereas Bush vetoed only 11 pieces of legislation in the same time. Bush's low number of vetoes was a consequence of the more unified government he enjoyed while in office. As of late 2012, President Obama had vetoed only two pieces of legislation, reflecting unified government during his first two years in office, and little legislation of consequence passed during the second half of his first term.

A president's threats to veto legislation provide an additional source of power: they allow the president to specify what kinds of proposals he is willing or unwilling to accept from Congress. Legislators then know that they need to write a proposal that attracts two-thirds support in both houses or accede to a president's demands. For example, during the 2007 debate over funding for the war in Iraq, then-president Bush said he would veto any legislation that included a timetable for troop withdrawal. Whether Bush was willing to follow through with his threat is unclear, but the threat worked. The funding bill that ultimately passed Congress did not include any sort of timetable. In this sense, the veto power can facilitate compromise between presidents and members of Congress—compromises that favor the president's point of view.

While the veto is useful to block legislation or issue a threat that encourages legislators to negotiate before casting their votes, it cannot force members of Congress to enact a proposal they oppose.[35] The president and his staff bargain with legislators, trying to craft proposals that a majority will support and sometimes offering inducements to individual lawmakers, such as presidential support for other favored policies. House members and senators from the president's party may feel obligated to help him, but it is very hard for a president to win over opponents in Congress, especially if helping the president will anger a legislator's constituents. Under these conditions, compromises are likely to favor congressional preferences.

For example, one of President Obama's greatest domestic priorities in 2009 was enactment of health care legislation. Obama made speeches on the subject, held meetings with the public, attended bargaining sessions with legislators from both parties, and dispatched aides to lobby members of Congress in favor of proposals that would reduce the number of uninsured individuals, end the ability of insurance companies to deny coverage for preexisting conditions, and, in theory, reduce the rate of increase in health care costs. However, although Obama's goals were popular, his proposals were not. As public opposition increased, congressional support even among Democrats began to waver, and Republicans were unified in their opposition. Although Obama ultimately prevailed and health care legislation was enacted in March 2010, the president had to make significant compromises to win support from reluctant Democrats—and was unable to bridge the conflict with congressional Republicans. So although enactment of health care reform is rightly cited as an example of presidential power, it also illustrates the limits of this power.

In sum, by using a combination of their proposal power, lobbying, issuing vetoes and veto threats, and the other powers discussed in this section, presidents have considerable—but not unlimited—influence over legislative outcomes.

OTHER DUTIES AND POWERS

The Constitution gives the president several additional powers, including the authority to pardon people convicted of federal crimes or commute their sentences.

The only limit on this power is that a president cannot pardon anyone who has been impeached and convicted by Congress. (Thus, if a president is removed from office via impeachment, he can neither pardon himself nor be pardoned when his vice president assumes the presidency.)

Although most presidential pardons attract little attention, some have been extremely controversial. Presidents have pardoned their own appointees for crimes committed while serving in their administrations, as well as campaign contributors and personal friends. In July 2007, President Bush commuted a 30-month jail term given to Lewis "Scooter" Libby, Vice President Dick Cheney's former aide. Libby had been convicted of lying to a grand jury about his role in leaking the name of Valerie Plame, a covert CIA agent, to several journalists.

The president's power to pardon raises the concern that pardons could become part of a tacit bargain between a president and his subordinates. That is, the possibility of a presidential pardon could allow executive branch employees to pursue the president's objectives with impunity, even if it meant breaking the law. Similarly, pardons granted to campaign contributors, such as President Clinton's pardon of contributor Marc Rich, who had been convicted of tax evasion, could become a way to trade money for leniency. (There is, however, no evidence that Clinton made such a bargain.) Nonetheless, even when a pardon is controversial, there is no way to reverse a president's decision.

The Constitution also gives the president a number of largely ceremonial powers, such as the power to convene Congress or to adjourn it if legislators cannot agree on an adjournment date. This provision gave the president real power during the early days of the Republic, when Congress was in session for only a few months every year. Now that Congress is in session for most of the year and party leaders set dates for the beginning and end of legislative sessions well in advance, this power is irrelevant. Similarly, the Constitution gives the president the responsibility for receiving ambassadors from other nations by officially recognizing that they speak on behalf of their countries' rulers. The president also signs commissions to formally appoint military officers.

EXECUTIVE PRIVILEGE

Finally, although this power is not formally set out in the Constitution or a statute, all presidents have claimed to hold the power of **executive privilege**. This refers to the ability to shield themselves and their subordinates from revealing White House discussions, decisions, or documents (including e-mails) to members of the legislative or judicial branches of government.[36] The nature of executive privilege—exactly what it protects versus what Congress can force the president to release—is an unsettled question. Some constitutional scholars even argue that in legal terms, executive privilege doesn't exist.[37]

Although claims of executive privilege have been made since the ratification of the Constitution in 1789, it is still not clear exactly what falls under the privilege and what does not. In the 1974 case *United States v. Nixon*, a special prosecutor appointed by the Justice Department to investigate the Watergate scandal challenged President Nixon's claims of executive privilege to force him to hand over tapes of potentially incriminating Oval Office conversations involving Nixon and his senior aides. The Supreme Court ruled unanimously that executive privilege does exist, but that the privilege is not absolute. The Court's decision required Nixon to release the tapes, which proved his involvement with attempts to cover up the scandal—but the ruling did not clearly state the conditions under which a future president could withhold such information.[38]

President Clinton invoked executive privilege 13 times on matters such as an investigation of Secretary of Agriculture Mike Espy, the firing of employees in the White House Travel Office, and the investigation of his own conduct with White House intern Monica Lewinsky.[39] In all of these cases, however, federal courts ordered the documents to be released.

Claims of executive privilege present a dilemma. On the one hand, members of Congress need to know what is happening in the executive branch. In the case of President Nixon and the Watergate scandal, claims of executive privilege allowed the Watergate cover-up to continue for more than a year and would have kept this information secret permanently if the Court had ruled in Nixon's favor.[40] Claims of executive privilege can also weaken accountability to the public, as restricting information may leave the average voter unaware of what an administration is doing. On the other hand, the president and his staff need to be able to communicate freely, discussing alternative strategies and hypothetical situations or national security secrets without fearing that they will be forced to reveal conversations that could become politically embarrassing or costly. (Suppose the discussions included political strategies for the next election or a sarcastic remark about jailing their opponents.) Moreover, allowing aides to testify before Congress is enormously time-consuming and can be costly for the aides if they hire lawyers.

Even when executive privilege does not apply (if Congress has not issued a subpoena), presidents can and do refuse to provide information to the media, Congress, or the general public. For example, despite President Obama's promises to increase the transparency of government, his administration did not disclose the specifics of White House negotiations over health care reform, announcing the details of the deal only after it was carried out. However, this reluctance is no surprise given the conflict over heath care reform. Disclosure of what participants said in meetings and what they were willing to trade away would be politically embarrassing. In this sense, some confidentiality may be necessary for a president to arrive at the compromises needed to change government policy.

THE PRESIDENT AS POLITICIAN

As the head of the executive branch, the president has considerable influence over policy. However, much of what presidents do (or want to do) requires support from legislators, bureaucrats, and average citizens. As a result, the presidency is an inherently political office. The president has to take into account the political consequences of his decisions—both for his own re-election prospects and for the re-election of legislators from his party. He must also contend with the reality that achieving his policy goals often requires bargaining and compromising with others, both inside and outside government.

Presidents try to deliver on their campaign promises not only because they believe in them but also because fulfilling them is politically advantageous. For example, one of President Obama's central campaign promises was to restore economic growth, a promise partly fulfilled by the enactment of economic stimulus legislation in February 2010. While these measures did not restore robust economic growth by the 2012 elections, Obama gained support from voters who believed that the measures had prevented a more extreme economic downturn. Obama also benefited from the positive impact of the stimulus in swing states such as Ohio.

THE LIMITS OF EXECUTIVE PRIVILEGE

Deciding which information a president can be compelled to release to the public or to other branches of government and what he can keep confidential requires confronting fundamentally political questions. There are no right answers, and the limits of executive privilege remain unclear. On the one hand, members of Congress need facts, predictions, and estimates from the executive branch to make good public policy. More important, members need to be able to weigh the pros and cons of a range of policy alternatives.

Consider the controversy over the Obama administration's grant of federal loan gaurantees to the Solyndra Corporation.[a] These loan guarantees were supposed to allow Solyndra to bring cheaper, more efficient solar power panels to market. However, the company's efforts were unsuccessful and it declared bankruptcy in August 2011, at a cost to taxpayers exceeding $500 million. Republican critics in Congress charged that a high-level Obama appointee in the Department of Energy whose wife did legal work for Solyndra had pushed for the loans and that the Obama administration had ignored warnings because they wanted to claim credit for a "green energy" program. There were several congressional investigations during 2011 and 2012, and numerous congressional subpoenas for documents—some of which were challenged by the Obama administration on grounds of executive privilege.

The Solyndra case may seem like a situation in which executive privilege does not apply. Shouldn't the American people know the reasons the loan guarantees were made? If the Energy Department staff did nothing wrong, why wouldn't the Obama administration comply with congressional subpoenas and make their staff available for congressional hearings?

The problem is that testifying before Congress, or even releasing documents in response to a congressional request, is enormously time-consuming and can be surprisingly expensive. Presidential appointees who have testified before Congress have faced personal legal bills of $100,000 or more. If members of Congress could require information and testimony of executive branch employees whenever they wanted, it would be hard for the executive bureaucracy to get anything done—and hard to convince anyone to work there.

Of course, there are two sides to this story. Republicans opposed the loan guarantees on policy grounds, believing that the free market rather than the government should decide which new companies get funded. And of course, the investigations did help to publicize the fact that the Obama administration's decision to lend money to Solyndra was, at least in retrospect, a mistake. But even leaving these concerns aside, it is not surprising that the administration invoked executive privilege, as the costs of complying with the supoenas in terms of time, effort, and a loss of confidentiality were substantial.

The Obama administration refused to have some energy department staffers testify before Congress about loans to the Solyndra Corporation, claiming executive privilege.

In sum, although being able to get information from a president can help members of Congress make better policy choices, there are situations in which confidentiality helps the president and his staff make good choices as well. However, executive privilege can also be used to hide crimes or questionable political tactics, or to prevent members of Congress from embarrassing the president by publicizing his mistakes or private comments. Should presidents have an executive privilege? What limits should apply to congressional requests for information and testimony? You decide.

Critical Thinking Questions

1. Decisions about executive privilege involve a tradeoff between informing the public and members of Congress about executive branch deliberations, and facilitating the free exchange of information between a president and his or her aides. What criteria or decision rules should determine whether claims of executive privilege are upheld or dismissed?

2. In the case of the Solyndra program, would you allow President Obama to claim executive privilege or force him to release all of the information requested by members of Congress? Would your answer be different if Obama were a Republican?

The president also typically keeps a close eye on the **presidential approval rating**, a survey-based measurement of the percentage of the public who thinks he is doing a good job in office. Particularly during his first term, one of the president's primary concerns is to build a record that will get him re-elected, and keeping approval levels as high as possible is a crucial part of this strategy. Figure 11.1, which shows the presidential approval ratings for the last six presidents who ran for re-election, reveals that first-term presidents with less than 50 percent approval are in real trouble. No recent president has been re-elected with less than a 50 percent approval rating. We will say more about presidential approval later in this chapter.

presidential approval rating
The percentage of Americans who feel that the president is doing a good job in office.

THE PRESIDENT AS PARTY LEADER

The president is the unofficial head of his political party and generally picks the day-to-day leadership of the party, or at least has considerable influence over the selection. This process begins when a presidential candidate captures the party's nomination. For example, soon after Barack Obama became the presumptive Democratic Party nominee by amassing a majority of convention delegates, some of his senior aides and advisers took on leadership positions in the Democratic Party organization.[41]

The president's connection to the party reflects the intertwining of their interests. The president needs support from his party members in Congress to enact

FIGURE » 11.1

PRESIDENTIAL POPULARITY AND RE-ELECTION

This figure shows the pre-election year average approval ratings for recent presidents who ran for re-election. It shows that a president's chances of winning re-election are related to his popularity. At what level of approval would you say that an incumbent president is likely to be re-elected?

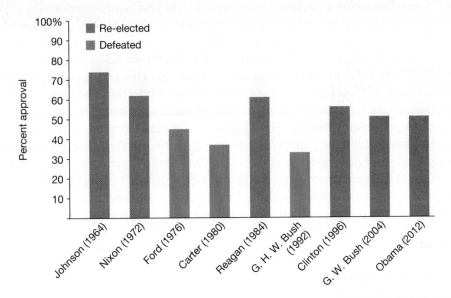

Source: Approval data from the Roper Center for Public Opinion Research, University of Connecticut, "Data Access: Presidential Approval," http://webapps.ropercenter.uconn.edu/CFIDE/roper/presidential/ webroot/ presidential_rating.cfm (accessed 10/26/12).

THE PRESIDENT IS THE UNOFFICIAL head of his party and works with fellow party members in government. In 2011, President Obama and the Democrats met with congressional Republicans to try to resolve the conflict between the two parties over the deficit and the national debt.

legislation, and the party and its candidates need the president to compile a record of policy achievements that reflect well on the party and to help raise the funds needed for the next election. Therefore, party leaders generally defer to a presidential candidate's (or a president's) staffing requests, and most presidents and presidential candidates take time to meet with national party leaders and the congressional leadership from their party to plan legislative strategies, make joint campaign appearances, and raise funds for the party's candidates.

When presidential approval ratings drop to low levels, most members of Congress see no political advantage to campaigning with the president or supporting his proposals, and they may become increasingly reluctant to comply with his requests. In the 2002 and 2004 elections, Republican legislators stressed their connection to President Bush and gladly accepted offers of joint campaign appearances. In 2006 and 2008, however, many Republican candidates deemphasized their connection to Bush and did not ask him to campaign with them.[42] A similar phenomenon arose in the 2010 midterms for Democratic candidates and President Obama: in many districts, incumbents believed that campaigning with Obama would reduce their chances of re-election, as it would remind voters of unpopular proposals championed by Obama, such as health care reform and the economic stimulus legislation, both enacted in 2009.

GOING PUBLIC

The president would appear to be in an excellent position to communicate with the American people because of his prominent role and the extensive media coverage devoted to anything he says to the nation. Broadcast and cable networks even give the president prime time slots for his State of the Union speech and other major addresses. The media attention that comes with the presidency provides the president with a unique strategy for shaping government policy: the ability to **go public**, or appeal directly to American citizens.[43] Presidential appeals are partly designed to persuade, but they also serve to bring an issue that the president considers important to the attention of citizens who already share his views, in the hope that they will pressure members of the House and Senate to support the president's requests. For example, in 1981 Ronald Reagan used televised speeches to build support for his tax cut proposals, which received a warm welcome from many Americans.

The problem for most presidents is that going public is often counterproductive: while it may energize supporters, it has a similar effect on opponents.[44] Thus, rather than facilitating compromise (or a wholesale presidential victory), publicizing an issue often deepens existing conflicts. Presidents are often better off keeping quiet and focusing on trying to negotiate a compromise with opponents in Congress. As examples, in 2006 and 2007, as public approval for the war in Iraq declined, President Bush gave several televised speeches in an attempt to regain support for the conflict, but these efforts had little effect.[45] Similarly, President Obama's speeches aimed at building support for health care reform had minimal effects on public opinion. More generally, studies suggest that most of the time, most Americans ignore or reject a president's attempts to go public. Thus, while presidents might want to shape public opinion in this way, in general they find it hard to be successful.[46] Going public may also have political consequences for the president. It can

go public A president's use of speeches and other public communications to appeal directly to citizens about issues the president would like the House and Senate to act on.

alienate members of Congress, as it represents an attempt to go over legislators' heads to reach the American people directly, thereby getting Congress to agree with the president without the benefit of the usual bargaining and negotiations.[47]

President Obama's experiences illustrate the limits and possibilities of this strategy. During the campaign, his organization made excellent use of social networking sites and e-mail to stay in contact with millions of supporters.[48] This crucial mobilization network helped Obama win the nomination by dominating caucus elections where turnout is low and candidates need to get supporters to the polls. The network proved less useful as a way to lobby Congress in favor of Obama's proposals, such as health care, although some Democrats in Congress cited letters and e-mails from supporters as one reason for their vote in favor of the president's proposals.

PRESIDENTIAL SUCCESSION

Under the Constitution, presidents are limited to two full terms in office. A vice president who becomes president in between elections can, if re-elected, serve two more full terms if he or she takes over during the first half of the predecessor's term; otherwise this individual can serve only one additional term. Under the Twenty-Fifth Amendment, a vice president can also temporarily take over as president, a procedure used in 2007 when President George W. Bush had a medical procedure requiring anesthesia.[49]

If both the president and the vice president were to die or become incapacitated, the Speaker of the House of Representatives would become president. Next in line is the president pro tempore of the Senate, and then a list of cabinet secretaries in the order shown in Table 11.1. Whenever the entire cabinet and Congress gather in one place, such as at the annual State of the Union address, at least one member of the cabinet is assigned to be somewhere else, so that in the event of a catastrophe someone in the line of succession would survive to assume the presidency.

In the event that the vice president must be replaced due to resignation, impeachment, or incapacity, the Twenty-Fifth Amendment allows the president to nominate a new vice president, who must be confirmed by majority votes in the House and the Senate. This procedure was used twice in the 1970s, first to make Gerald Ford vice president under Richard Nixon (replacing Spiro Agnew), then, after Nixon's resignation, to make Nelson Rockefeller vice president under Ford.[50]

THE EXECUTIVE BRANCH

EXPLAIN HOW THE EXECUTIVE OFFICE OF THE PRESIDENT, THE VICE PRESIDENT, AND THE CABINET HELP THE PRESIDENT

As head of the executive branch, the president runs a huge, complex organization with hundreds of thousands of employees. This section describes the organizations and staff who help the president exercise his vast responsibilities, from managing disaster-response efforts to implementing policy changes.[51] Among these employees are appointees who hold senior positions in the government. These individuals serve as the president's eyes and ears in the bureaucracy, making sure that bureaucrats are following presidential directives.

TABLE » 11.1

PRESIDENTIAL SUCCESSION

The order of presidential succession is set out in the Constitution. Why do you think the Founders put the vice president first, congressional leaders second, and cabinet secretaries third?

1. THE VICE PRESIDENT

2. LEGISLATIVE BRANCH LEADERS

   The Speaker of the House

   The President Pro Tempore of the Senate

3. CABINET SECRETARIES (IN THE ORDER OF THEIR DEPARTMENT'S CREATION)

   A. Secretary of State

   B. Secretary of the Treasury

   C. Secretary of Defense

   D. Attorney General

   E. Secretary of the Interior

   F. Secretary of Agriculture

   G. Secretary of Commerce

   H. Secretary of Labor

   I. Secretary of Health and Human Services

   J. Secretary of Housing and Urban Development

   K. Secretary of Transportation

   L. Secretary of Energy

   M. Secretary of Education

   N. Secretary of Veterans Affairs

   O. Secretary of Homeland Security

Many other executive branch employees work within the Executive Office of the President, which has employed about 1,800 people in recent administrations. About one-third of these employees are concentrated in two offices: the Office of Management and Budget, which develops the president's budget proposals and monitors spending by government agencies, and the Office of the United States Trade Representative, which negotiates trade agreements with other nations.[52]

THE EXECUTIVE OFFICE OF THE PRESIDENT

Executive Office of the President (EOP) The group of policy-related offices that serves as support staff to the president.

Nuts and Bolts 11.3 lists the organizations that make up the **Executive Office of the President (EOP)** and one of its main components, the White House Office. Both include offices that have clear policy-related or political missions.

One of the most important duties of EOP staff is helping the president and candidates from his party achieve their policy goals and get re-elected. Consider the Office of National Drug Control Policy (ONDCP). During 2006, representatives from the office traveled throughout the country to hold joint press conferences with Republican and Democratic members of Congress to announce federal grants for drug abuse prevention programs. However, three months before that year's midterm elections, with Republicans in danger of losing majority control of the House and Senate, ONDCP officials began holding press conferences exclusively with Republican legislators.[53] An e-mail from the head of the office revealed that this strategy was an attempt to help vulnerable Republican candidates. In other words, people in the ONDCP did not abandon their official duties, but they also did everything they could to help Republicans in the 2006 election.

Even the lower-level offices within the White House Office play political roles as they carry out their official responsibilities. One office that fulfills such a dual role is the Photo Office, whose official job is to "photographically document and maintain an archive of official events of the president, the first lady, the vice president, and his wife."[54] The office also photographs the president with political supporters, providing pictures that can be used to thank them for their contributions or other efforts.

The most influential EOP staff occupy the offices in the West Wing of the White House. The West Wing contains the president's office, known as the Oval Office, and space for the president's chief aide and personal secretary, as well as senior aides such as the vice president, the president's press secretary, and the chief of staff, who coordinates White House operations. Many recent chiefs of staff have been central in the development of policy proposals and negotiations with members of Congress. However, the chief of staff serves as the agent of the president—what matters is what the president wants, not a chief of staff's policy preferences.

Most EOP staff members are presidential appointees who retain their positions only as long as the president who appointed them remains in office. These individuals are often drawn to government service out of loyalty to the president or

11.3 NUTS & bolts

THE EXECUTIVE OFFICE OF THE PRESIDENT

Council of Economic Advisers

Council on Environmental Quality

National Security Council

Office of Administration

Office of Management and Budget

Office of National Drug Control Policy

Office of Science and Technology Policy

Office of United States Trade Representative

President's Foreign Intelligence Advisory Board

White House Office

White House Office

Domestic Policy Council

Homeland Security Council

National Economic Council

Office of Faith-Based and Community Initiatives

Office of the First Lady

Office of National AIDS Policy

Privacy and Civil Liberties Oversight Board

USA Freedom Corps

White House Fellows Office

White House Military Office

THE PRESIDENT'S CLOSEST ADVISERS are chosen for their loyalty to the president and his policy goals. For example, President Obama's senior adviser David Axelrod (left) had served as the chief strategist for Obama's 2008 campaign, and also held that role in 2012.

because they share his policy goals. However, most leave their positions after a year or two to escape the pressures of the job, the long hours, and the relatively low government salaries.[55] Despite the fairly frequent turnover in many EOP positions, some EOP offices—such as the Office of Management and Budget, the Office of the United States Trade Representative, and the National Security Council—also have a significant number of permanent staff analysts and experts.[56]

When the president appoints people to EOP positions, his primary expectation of them is loyalty rather than a concern for the general public or policy expertise.[57] (Exceptions to the loyalty rule for appointees are individuals who received their jobs because of their expertise, their connections to the president's political party as opposed to the president himself, or links to an important group outside the government.) Why is loyalty so important? Put yourself in the position of a president whose packed day begins with an intelligence briefing and ends with a state dinner. All the while, crucial decisions about public policy are being made throughout the federal government. You have no time to make these decisions yourself or to supervise those who make them, so you need staff who understand what you want the government to do and who will dedicate themselves to implementing your vision.[58]

The emphasis on loyalty in presidential appointments also has an obvious drawback: appointees may not know much about the jobs they are given and may not be very effective at managing the agencies they are supposed to control. As we discuss in Chapter 12, The Bureaucracy, many observers believe that delays in providing federal disaster relief after Hurricane Katrina resulted partly because many of the senior positions in the Federal Emergency Management Agency were held by political appointees who knew little about its operations.[59]

TODAY, VICE PRESIDENTS ARE MORE influential than they were in the past. President Obama drew on Vice President Joseph Biden's foreign policy expertise and entrusted him with numerous important initiatives.

THE VICE PRESIDENT

As set out in the Constitution, the vice president's job is to preside over Senate proceedings. This largely ceremonial job is usually delegated to the president pro tempore of the Senate, who in turn typically gives the duty to a more junior member. The vice president also has the power to cast tie-breaking votes in the Senate. As mentioned earlier, the vice president's other formal responsibility is to become president if the current president dies, becomes incapacitated, resigns, or is impeached. Of the 44 people who have become president, nine were vice presidents who became president in midterm.

These rather limited official duties of the vice president pale in comparison to the influential role played by recent vice presidents. Vice President Dick Cheney, who served with President George W. Bush, exerted a significant influence over many policy decisions, including the rights of terror suspects, tax and spending policy, environmental decisions, and the writing of new government regulations.[60] Many critics claimed that Cheney had too much power, and some even described him as a co-president.[61]

Although Cheney's level of influence was unique, other recent vice presidents have also had real power. For example, Vice President Al Gore was an important adviser to President Bill Clinton. And Barack Obama's vice president, Joe Biden, also appears to play an important role, attending all significant meetings and serving as the last person the president talks to before making a decision.

The vice president's role as a senior adviser and trusted confidant is a recent development. Before this change, vice presidents were often chosen to provide political or regional balance to a presidential candidate's electoral appeal. For example, Dwight Eisenhower chose then-senator Richard Nixon as his vice president in order to appeal to conservative groups in the Republican Party (but then Eisenhower excluded Nixon from many meetings once in office). The expansion of the federal government beginning in the 1960s appears to have led recent presidents to look beyond political or regional factors when choosing a vice president to find a like-minded individual who can help them manage the bureaucracy and achieve their policy goals. Barack Obama's choice of Joe Biden reflected these priorities, as Biden's foreign policy expertise was expected to offset Obama's relative inexperience in this area.

THE PRESIDENT'S CABINET

The president's **Cabinet** is composed of the heads of the 15 executive departments in the federal government, along with other appointees given cabinet rank by the president. Nuts and Bolts 11.4 lists the cabinet positions. The cabinet members' principal job is to be the frontline implementers of the president's agenda in their executive departments. As we discuss in more detail in Chapter 12, they monitor the actions of the lower-level bureaucrats who retain their jobs regardless of who is president and are not necessarily sympathetic to the president's priorities.

Cabinet The group of 15 executive department heads who implement the president's agenda in their respective positions.

11.4 NUTS & bolts

CABINET POSITIONS

The president's Cabinet is composed of the heads of the 15 Executive Departments along with other appointees given cabinet rank by the president.

Secretary of Agriculture	Secretary of the Treasury
Secretary of Commerce	Secretary of Transportation
Secretary of Defense	Secretary of Veterans Affairs
Secretary of Education	Vice President
Secretary of Energy	White House Chief of Staff
Secretary of Health and Human Services	Attorney General
Secretary of Homeland Security	Head of the Environmental Protection Agency
Secretary of Housing and Urban Development	Head of the Office of Management and Budget
Secretary of the Interior	Head of the Office of National Drug Control Policy
Secretary of Labor	United States Trade Representative
Secretary of State	

Like other presidential appointees, cabinet members are chosen for a combination of loyalty to the president and expertise. Barack Obama's secretary of transportation, Ray LaHood, a former moderate Republican congressman, had served on the Transportation and Infrastructure Committee while a member of the House of Representatives, so he had a good working knowledge of federal transportation programs. And Secretary of Energy Steven Chu was a Nobel Prize–winning physicist who had directed a major energy research laboratory.

EXPLAIN HOW AMERICANS EVALUATE PRESIDENTS

THE AMERICAN PUBLIC AND THE PRESIDENT

As we have described, presidents need to cultivate public support to get re-elected and to enact their policy proposals. Thus, to understand the kinds of policy goals presidents set and how they seek to come across to the public, it is important to consider what Americans want from their presidents and which characteristics they associate with a successful president.

Table 11.2 shows survey results about the qualities Americans want in a president. Large majorities want the president to have good judgment and to be ethical and compassionate; smaller majorities want a president who says what he believes, holds consistent positions, and is forceful and decisive. A third or fewer want the president to be willing to compromise, to have political experience and savvy, to have Washington experience, or to be loyal to his party. Relatively few Americans consider military experience an important presidential asset.

The interesting part of this table lies in the comparison of items that received strong support (consistency, forcefulness, and decisiveness) with those that fewer people found appealing (compromise, political experience, political savvy, Washington experience, and party loyalty). We have seen that American politics is conflictual, which means that compromising and bargaining are fundamental parts of what successful politicians do. However, it seems that most Americans are not looking for a president who has the traits and experiences that facilitate negotiating and deal making. Moreover, presidents may face tough decisions between building a public reputation for firmness and making the compromises necessary to change or implement policies.

GAUGING PRESIDENTIAL POPULARITY

Various factors shape presidential popularity. In general, any issue that is at the top of the public's list of most important problems is likely to be reflected in presidential popularity. For example, the slow decline in public support for the war in Iraq and the increase in the number of people who saw the war as the most important problem was reflected in a systematic decline in then-president Bush's popularity in 2006 and 2007. When the war dropped from the top of the most important problem list, it was replaced by the economy, which did not help Bush's approval ratings because most people were dissatisfied with economic conditions and blamed it on Bush's administration. The slow recovery from poor economic condi-

TABLE » 11.2

CITIZEN DEMANDS ON THE PRESIDENT

These data show that many Americans want the president to stick to his principles, say what he believes, and be forceful and decisive. Fewer consider political experience and willingness to compromise essential presidential qualities. How might the political necessity for bargaining and compromise affect a president's ability to satisfy citizens' expectations?

ESSENTIAL QUALITIES	1995	1999	2003
Sound judgment	76%	78%	76%
High ethical standards	67	63	67
Compassion	64	63	63
Saying what one believes	59	57	56
Consistent positions	51	50	52
Forcefulness and decisiveness	50	46	49
Willingness to compromise	34	33	38
Experience in public office	30	38	37
Political savvy	31	–	36
Experience in Washington	21	27	32
Party loyalty	25	33	30
Military experience	–	–	16

Source: Pew Research Center, "Bush Reelect Margin Narrows to 45%–43%," news release, September 25, 2003, www.people-press.org/reports/pdf/194.pdf (accessed 9/20/12).

tions also contributed to President Obama's relatively low approval ratings during his first term in office.

As this example indicates, presidential approval is mostly about outcomes, not a president's policies or actions. Approval doesn't arise from voters learning about a president's programs and voicing their support or opposition. Rather, most people look at the world around them, decide whether they like what they see, and express approval or disapproval accordingly. In this sense, presidential approval is to some extent out of a president's control. Bill Clinton enjoyed relatively high approval ratings during most of his eight years in office due to a strong domestic economy, but this economic strength probably had less to do with Clinton's policies and more to do with macroeconomic factors that were well out of Clinton's control. In contrast, Presidents Carter and Ford had the misfortune to be in office at a time when macroeconomic conditions were relatively weak and largely out of their control. In this sense, presidential popularity is to some extent a matter of luck.

On the other hand, the public is generally forgiving of scandal. President Clinton's affair with a White House intern had only a modest impact on his approval numbers. In fact, you have to go back to the 1970s and the Watergate scandal, which

PRESIDENTIAL APPROVAL IS influenced by international events that concern Americans, such as the taking of American hostages by militant Iranian students in 1979. President Jimmy Carter initially saw his approval ratings increase, but they declined steadily as the crisis continued into 1980.

resulted in the resignation of President Nixon (and all-time low approval numbers), to find a scandal that had a sustained impact on a president's popularity.

All presidents have staff and consultants who regularly poll the public to discern its feelings about the president and find out what actions might increase approval. These findings influence but do not determine presidential actions. For example, poll results probably played no role in President Obama's decision to send additional troops to Afghanistan in 2010 or the gradual drawdown that began in 2012. Although these moves received majority support, Obama likely would have made the same decision even if he had faced much stronger public opposition. However, some legislators' tepid support for Obama's proposed health care reform proposals was driven, at least in part, by an absence of public enthusiasm for the proposal.

Political considerations matter somewhat less to a second-term president (since running for re-election is not an option), but politics still matters in the second term. Members of Congress are more likely to support policy initiatives proposed by a popular president, believing that this popularity reflects public support for the president's goals. Conversely, an unpopular president, such as President Bush in 2007 and 2008, finds it much harder to build support for new programs. For example, when Bush called on members of Congress to end the practice of earmarking federal funds for specific projects to benefit their own constituents, even members of Bush's party in the House and Senate ignored the proposal.[62]

As these examples indicate, presidential popularity is more than just a measure of opinion—it is a resource that presidents can draw on to advance their policy agendas. However, high popularity doesn't allow presidents to do whatever they want, nor does low popularity make it impossible to do anything. Moreover, presidential popularity is shaped by factors such as the state of the economy that are only partly under a president's control.

IN 2012, MANY AMERICANS BLAMED President Obama for high unemployment rates. Here, job seekers line up hoping to find work at a job fair in New York. Although people tend to hold the president responsible for economic conditions, the president's influence over the economy is limited.

EXPLAINING PRESIDENTIAL APPROVAL

Mass surveys have asked questions about the public's approval of the president ever since Franklin Roosevelt was president. Figure 11.2 reports presidential approval data for the three most recent presidents: Bill Clinton, George W. Bush, and Barack Obama. The data for Clinton show a relatively rare pattern of steady improvement throughout his time in office. In contrast, George W. Bush's popularity steadily declined following the sharp spike upward after the September 11 attacks. Popularity figures for President Obama show gradual decline during the initial part of his term, and a slight increase during the second part.

What explains this variation? Presidential approval generally spikes during national crises, such as the Iranian Hostage Crisis during Jimmy Carter's term, the Persian Gulf War during George H. W. Bush's term, or the September 11 attacks during George W. Bush's first term. This phenomenon has been called the "rally 'round the flag" effect,[63] comparing the electorate to troops gathering around a flag during a battle.

There are no such spikes in the chart for Bill Clinton, reflecting the lack of national crises during his time in office. In such relatively calm times, presidential approval

FIGURE » 11.2

PRESIDENTIAL APPROVAL RATINGS FOR RECENT PRESIDENTS

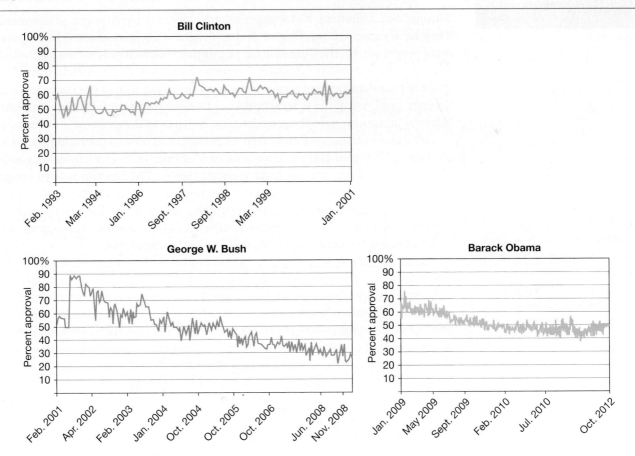

Source: Approval data from the Roper Center for Public Opinion Research, University of Connecticut, "Data Access: Presidential Approval," http://webapps.ropercenter.uconn.edu/CFIDE/roper/presidential/webroot/presidential_rating.cfm (accessed 11/11/12).

reflects the overall state of the nation, including citizens' perceptions of economic conditions and national security. In Clinton's case, economic conditions steadily improved throughout his presidency, generating the increase in his approval ratings. Even when Clinton was being impeached in 1998 and 1999, his popularity did not suffer. This finding may suggest that even if Americans want an ethical president, they forgive a president's misdeeds if his performance is good on the issues they care about, such as the economy. In contrast, during George W. Bush's two terms in office, he presided over an increasingly unpopular war in Iraq, along with a deteriorating economy, particularly during his last two years in office. Both of these factors contributed to the steady decline in Bush's approval ratings.

Similarly, while President Obama's first term in office has been largely free of scandal, and Obama has enacted a substantial portion of his campaign agenda, such as health care reform, withdrawal of American combat forces from Iraq, and financial stimulus legislation, his lackluster poll numbers suggest that most Americans are focused on the mediocre state of the economy—and that Obama's popularity will increase significantly only if the economy improves.

ANALYZE WHY PRESIDENTS HAVE BECOME MUCH MORE POWERFUL SINCE THE FOUNDING

ASSESSING PRESIDENTIAL POWER

Throughout American history, presidents have realized major achievements. They have expanded the United States, fought wars, and enacted large government programs. Yet the Constitution grants the president only rather limited powers. Assessing presidential power requires examining this contradiction. Saying that the presidents gained power because of the expansion of the United States or the increased size of the federal budget or bureaucracy tells only part of the story. Why did this power go to the presidents rather than to Congress or to bureaucrats?

Debates over the source and extent of presidential powers have a long history. In the 1790s, Alexander Hamilton and James Madison, writing anonymously as Helvidius and Pacificus, argued about whether George Washington needed congressional approval to declare the United States neutral in the war between Britain and France.[64] Even after more than two centuries, many of the limits to presidential powers—including which executive actions require congressional approval and which ones can be reversed by Congress—are not well defined.

These constitutional ambiguities are mirrored by the unwritten nature of many presidential powers. Recall our discussion of the president's ability to influence the legislative process. In the Constitution, the president's powers are limited to a vague reference to advising Congress on the state of the union and the power to veto legislation, subject to congressional override. But presidents often have very real influence at all points in the legislative process. One classic work in presidential studies argues that this influence comes from a president's power to persuade legislators to accept the president's point of view—presidents can offer a variety of small inducements like visits to the Oval Office and campaign assistance, and can draw on the natural respect that most people (including members of Congress) feel for the presidency regardless of who holds the office, thereby securing compromises that achieve the president's policy goals.[65] The relatively high presidential success scores noted earlier suggest that most presidents have considerable success in their persuasion efforts.

The very ambiguity of the Constitution also creates opportunities for the exercise of presidential power. Recall the case of the president's war-making powers: the

Constitution makes the president military commander in chief but gives Congress the power to declare war and to raise and support armies, without specifying which branch of government is in charge of the military. Thus, at least part of presidential authority must be derived or assumed from what the Constitution *does not say*—ways in which it fails to define or delineate presidential power or grants inherent power to the president.[66]

PRESIDENTS AND UNILATERAL ACTION

Presidency scholars Terry Moe and William Howell argue that constitutional ambiguities about presidential power have enabled presidents to take **unilateral action**, changing policy on their own without consulting Congress or anyone else. Although Congress could, in theory, undo unilateral actions through legislation, court proceedings, or impeachment, Moe and Howell argue that the costs of doing so, in terms of time, effort, and public perceptions, are often prohibitive. The result is that presidents can take unilateral action despite congressional opposition, knowing their actions stand little chance of being reversed. Of course, unilateral action may not lead to policy change—presidents and their staffs have to monitor subsequent actions by bureaucrats to make sure they are implementing the president's decision.

The 2007 debate over funding the war in Iraq provides a good example of how constitutional ambiguities create opportunities for unilateral actions. During the debate, many Democrats in Congress wanted to cut off war funding to force the withdrawal of American forces from Iraq, but supporters of the Bush administration responded with what they called the **unitary executive theory**. They argued that the Constitution's vesting clause allows the president to issue orders and policy directives that members of Congress cannot undo unless the Constitution explicitly gives them this power. In the case of funding the Iraq war, they maintained that the Constitution's description of the president as commander in chief of America's armed forces meant that even if Congress refused to appropriate funds for the war, the president could order American forces to stay in Iraq and order the Department of the Treasury to spend any funds necessary to continue operations. Ultimately, members of Congress approved a funding resolution. (If they hadn't and the president had refused to withdraw American forces, the disagreement likely would have required resolution by the Supreme Court.)

Many unilateral actions occurred throughout the Bush presidency. President Bush acted unilaterally when he restricted the legal rights of terror suspects, made strategic decisions about the wars in Iraq and Afghanistan, froze the financial assets of members of Al Qaeda and other terrorist organizations, reorganized America's intelligence agencies to create the Department of Homeland Security, and relaxed environmental regulations. Bush unilaterally withdrew the United States from the Anti-Ballistic Missile Treaty that limited U.S. and Russian defensive missile installations, and he authorized wiretaps of Americans' international phone conversations without gaining warrants from the Foreign Intelligence Surveillance Court, a special federal court created to approve such requests.[67]

It is important to understand that Bush was not the only president to take (or threaten to take) broad, unilateral actions. President Obama, for example,

THE CONSTITUTION MAKES THE president commander in chief but limits that power by giving Congress the power to raise and support armies. When President Obama ordered a "surge" in the number of American troops in Afghanistan in 2009, he needed Congress to approve the $30 billion it was estimated to cost. The day after announcing the decision, Obama made the case for the "surge" in a speech at West Point.

unilateral action (presidential) Any policy decision made and acted upon by the president and his staff without the explicit approval or consent of Congress.

unitary executive theory The idea that the vesting clause of the Constitution gives the president the authority to issue orders and policy directives that cannot be undone by Congress.

unilaterally issued executive orders limiting how terror suspects could be interrogated and strengthening driver safety rules for federal employees and for commercial truck drivers.[68] Moreover, Moe and Howell cite many historical examples of unilateral presidential actions, such as the annexation of Texas, the freeing of slaves in the Emancipation Proclamation, the desegregation of the U.S. military, the initiation of affirmative action programs, and the creation of major agencies such as the Peace Corps.[69] Other studies found that the majority of federal administrative agencies had been created by unilateral presidential actions and that more than 90 percent of American agreements with other nations since the 1940s were concluded as executive agreements between the president and a foreign government, rather than as treaties requiring ratification by Congress.[70]

CONTROL OVER THE INTERPRETATION AND IMPLEMENTATION OF LAWS

signing statement A document issued by the president when signing a bill into law explaining his interpretation of the law, which often differs from the interpretation of Congress, in an attempt to influence how the law will be implemented.

Most presidents have tried to control the interpretation and implementation of laws by issuing a **signing statement** when signing a bill into law. These documents, which explain the president's interpretation of the new law, are issued most often when the president disagrees with the interpretation of members of Congress who supported the legislation but still wishes to approve the bill. Presidents issue signing statements so that if the courts have to resolve uncertainties about the bill's intent, judges can take into account not only the views expressed during congressional debates about the bill, but also the president's interpretation of it.[71] The president can also influence the implementation of a law through a signing statement, essentially telling the bureaucracy to follow his interpretation of the law rather than Congress's. (The same end can be achieved by giving bureaucrats internal instructions about how to implement a law.)

In some cases, presidents have found loopholes in laws designed to restrict their power. An analysis of several pieces of legislation designed to curb presidential power that were enacted in the 1970s (including the War Powers Resolution, the Ethics in Government Act, and measures dealing with budgets and intelligence agencies) found that subsequent presidents have actually used these laws to justify unilateral actions—the opposite of what was intended.[72] For example, current law requires the president to give congressional leaders "timely notification" of secret intelligence operations. During the Reagan administration, senior officials did not reveal the existence of ongoing operations for several months. When these operations were eventually discovered, officials claimed they were within the letter of the law because it did not specify a time limit for notification.[73]

Unilateral actions are especially likely in the last days of a presidency, especially if the next president is from the other party, as the outgoing president tries to influence as many important policies as possible before leaving office.[74] For example, in January 2001, President Clinton finalized regulations that would lower the amount of arsenic allowed in drinking water by 2006. When President George W. Bush took office, he and his staff debated whether to rescind the regulations, believing they imposed too many economic costs, but decided against it. They did not want to publicly oppose a regulation that made water safer to drink. However, President Obama issued an executive order in 2009 that reversed a Bush-era order that prevented California from implementing gas mileage standards that were higher than existing federal regulations.

CONGRESSIONAL RESPONSES TO UNILATERAL ACTION

In theory, members of Congress can undo a president's unilateral action by enacting a law to overturn it, but this is harder than it may sound.[75] Some members of Congress may approve of what the president has done or be indifferent to it, or may give a higher priority to other policies. Still, reversals do happen: after Obama announced plans to close the Guantánamo Bay detention center for terrorist suspects, the House and Senate added an amendment to a spending bill stating that the prison could not be closed until the administration released plans explaining where the prisoners would be sent.

Members of Congress can also write laws in a way that limits the president's authority over their implementation.[76] The problem with this approach is that members of Congress delegate authority to the president or the executive branch bureaucracy for good reasons—either because it is difficult for legislators to predict how a policy should be implemented, or because they cannot agree among themselves on an implementation plan.[77] Members of Congress from the president's party may also want him to have the authority because they hold similar policy goals and would therefore benefit from the exercise of unilateral power.

Even if members of Congress tried to use these strategies to limit the president's authority, the president could still argue—along the lines of the unitary executive theory—that Congress could not overturn his actions because the Constitution did not explicitly give the legislature this power. The only option for members of Congress would be to take the president to court (probably all the way to the Supreme Court) to demonstrate that he overstepped his constitutional authority, which is not a very practical or expedient option. Aside from the fact that the Court might not side with Congress, these legal proceedings could take years.

For example, in May 2010, executives from British Petroleum (BP) agreed to President Obama's request that they set up a $20 billion fund to compensate people whose homes or businesses were harmed by the oil spilled from BP's Deepwater Horizon oil well in the Gulf of Mexico. While several members of Congress opposed Obama's action, they could not muster enough votes to reverse it; moreover, they could not mount a court challenge because BP had *voluntarily* agreed to set up the fund. Even so, opponents of some unilateral actions have used court decisions to limit presidential power. In 1952, when steel mill workers were planning to go on strike, President Truman argued that federal control of the steel mills was necessary to sustain the United States' efforts in the Korean War. Ninety minutes before the strike was to begin, President Truman went on national television to announce that the U.S. government would seize the nation's steel mills to keep them operating. However, the Supreme Court's ruling in *Youngstown Sheet and Tube v. Sawyer* reversed President Truman's actions.[78] More recently, in the 2006 case *Hamdan v. Rumsfeld* and the 2008 case *Boumediene v. Bush,* the Supreme Court reversed the Bush administration's actions that had denied terror suspects access to federal courts.[79]

Congress also has the power to remove the president or vice president from office through the **impeachment** process. However, removing a president is much more difficult than passing a law to undo a unilateral action. First, House members must impeach (indict) the president by majority vote, which accuses him of a crime

impeachment A negative or checking power over the other branches that allows Congress to remove the president, vice president, or other "officers of the United States" (including federal judges) for abuses of power.

CONGRESS HAS THE POWER TO BLOCK most types of presidential action, if it chooses. For example, in 2009, President Obama ordered the closure of the detention center for terror suspects at Guantánamo Bay, Cuba, but Congress passed legislation preventing the closure until the Obama administration developed detailed plans for relocating the prisoners.

FEDERAL COURTS CAN UNDO unilateral presidential actions. A series of Supreme Court rulings forced the George W. Bush administration to allow terror suspects such as Salim Hamdan, an Al Qaeda member captured in Afghanistan, to challenge their imprisonment. This courtroom sketch from the U.S. naval base in Guantánamo, Cuba, shows Hamdan (far left) and his legal team.

or breach of his sworn duties. Then senators hold a trial, followed by a vote—in which a two-thirds majority is required to remove the president from office.

These procedures are rarely used; only two presidents have faced an impeachment vote: Andrew Johnson in 1866 and Bill Clinton in 1999. Johnson was involved in a political dispute over administration of the southern states after the Civil War; Clinton was alleged to have lied under oath in a sexual harassment lawsuit. Though both of these presidents were impeached by the House, they were not convicted by the Senate, so they stayed in office. One reason impeachment is difficult is that members of Congress who are upset about certain presidential actions might nevertheless oppose removing the president from office. They might approve of his other initiatives, want to prevent the vice president from becoming president, or have concerns about the political backlash that impeachment could generate against them or their party.

In sum, ambiguities in the Constitution create opportunities for unilateral presidential action. These actions are subject to reversal through legislation, court decisions, and impeachment, but members of Congress face significant costs if they undertake any of these options. As long as the president is careful to limit exercise of unilateral power to actions that do not generate intense opposition in Congress, he can implement a wide range of policy goals without official congressional consent—provided that bureaucrats go along with the president's wishes, a question we take up in the next chapter. Thus, presidential power has important consequences for government policy—but it is not unlimited.

CONCLUSION

A president's power over government policy is derived from constitutional authority, statutory authority, and ambiguities within these official grants of power that give the president a substantial ability to act unilaterally. Even so, presidential power is limited. The president shares many powers with Congress, including lawmaking, treaty-making, and war-making powers. Moreover, presidents are politicians who need public support, both to win re-election and to persuade members of Congress to approve their policy initiatives. The public evaluates the president based on how he handles issues that are a priority for many Americans, such as the economy, health care, and national security.

These factors suggest a very different explanation for the seemingly expansive power of President Barack Obama, which we discussed at the beginning of this chapter. For one thing, Obama's successes, from the War on Terror to the enactment of health care reform, are not unusual. Many presidents have similar records of accomplishment. Moreover, although Obama enjoyed notable successes, he was forced to compromise in many areas in order to win congressional support. Also, many of Obama's (and other presidents') successful unilateral actions concerned policy areas in which members of Congress and the public either favored their proposals or had no strong feelings about them. Thus, the president remains an important figure in American politics but is clearly not solely responsible for setting government policy.

STUDY *guide*

THE PRESIDENT'S JOB DESCRIPTION

▶ Describe the constitutional and statutory powers of the president today. **Pages 431–49**

SUMMARY

The president's formal powers arise from a combination of constitutional provisions and additional laws that give him additional responsibilities. The president has many duties, but his primary responsibilities are to oversee the executive branch and implement laws passed by Congress. While presidents have the authority to focus on both domestic and foreign policy, most tend to focus on one aspect.

KEY TERMS

constitutional authority (p. 433)

statutory authority (presidential) (p. 433)

vesting clause (p. 434)

head of government (p. 434)

head of state (p. 434)

recess appointment (p. 437)

executive orders (p. 437)

fast-track authority (p. 440)

first-mover advantage (p. 440)

executive agreement (p. 440)

State of the Union (p. 442)

executive privilege (p. 444)

presidential approval rating (p. 447)

go public (p. 448)

PRACTICE QUIZ QUESTIONS

1. Presidents use recess appointments when they are trying to _____.
   a) fill a judicial vacancy outside the scheduled period
   b) fill a vacant seat in Congress
   c) temporarily dodge the need for Senate approval
   d) temporarily dodge the need for House approval
   e) fill vacancies with a permanent replacement

2. A presidential proclamation that unilaterally changes government policy without congressional consent is called _____.
   a) an executive privilege
   b) a fast-track authority
   c) an executive agreement
   d) an executive order
   e) statutory authority

3. The War Powers Resolution has effectively expanded the power of _____.
   a) the president
   b) Congress
   c) the Supreme Court
   d) the Department of Defense
   e) the State Department

4. The first-mover advantage refers to the president's negotiating advantage over _____.
   a) foreign leaders
   b) governors
   c) the bureaucracy
   d) Congress
   e) international organizations

5. For most presidents, the problem in going public is that _____.
   a) the public is more focused on Congress
   b) they are not very persuasive
   c) they energize their opponents
   d) they generally address unimportant issues
   e) they do not reach their target audience

Ⓢ PRACTICE ONLINE

"What Do Political Scientists Do?" video exercise: *Ken Mayer on presidential power and the use of executive orders*

THE EXECUTIVE BRANCH

▶ Explain how the Executive Office, the vice president, and the Cabinet help the president. **Pages 449–54**

SUMMARY

The executive branch is a huge, complex organization that helps the president exercise his vast responsibilities. Presidential appointees to the branch serve as his eyes and ears on the bureaucracy. Most positions turn over with new administrations.

KEY TERMS

Executive Office of the President (EOP) (p. 450)

Cabinet (p. 453)

CRITICAL THINKING AND DISCUSSION

Why might bureaucrats who are not presidential appointees be more responsive to congressional mandates and demands than to the president's orders, even though the president heads the executive branch?

PRACTICE QUIZ QUESTIONS

6. In most appointments to EOP positions, presidents generally emphasize _____.
    a) experience
    b) expertise
    c) effectiveness
    d) public opinion
    e) loyalty

7. Recent vice presidents have had _____ official duties; and/but _____ been influential in their role.
    a) no; have not
    b) limited; have
    c) limited; have not
    d) extensive; have
    e) extensive; have not

THE AMERICAN PUBLIC AND THE PRESIDENT

▶ Explain how Americans evaluate presidents. **Pages 454–58**

SUMMARY

Popularity is critical for presidents to get re-elected and enact their policy proposals. Nonetheless, presidential popularity itself is affected by factors that may not actually be influenced by the president himself.

CRITICAL THINKING AND DISCUSSION

Why do you think Americans often hold the president more accountable than Congress for the state of the economy?

PRACTICE QUIZ QUESTIONS

8. Most Americans want a president who is _____; while few Americans want a president who is _____.
    a) consistent; decisive
    b) consistent; politically savvy
    c) politically savvy; decisive
    d) politically savvy; consistent
    e) decisive; consistent

9. Presidential approval is generally based on _____.

    a) policy outcomes
    b) policy positions
    c) presidential actions
    d) presidential appointments
    e) an absence of scandals

10. Presidential popularity generally _____ over time; and it _____ during national crises.
    a) declines; drops
    b) increases; drops
    c) declines; spikes
    d) increases; spikes
    e) remains even; spikes

ⓢ PRACTICE ONLINE

"Critical Thinking" exercise : *Politics Is Conflictual–Presidential Approval Ratings*

ASSESSING PRESIDENTIAL POWER

▶ Analyze why presidents have become much more powerful since the Founding. **Pages 458–62**

SUMMARY

While presidents have gained power over time, the Constitution grants the president rather limited powers. The growth of presidential power is closely related to the fact that most limits on it are not well-defined, and presidents have succeeded in taking advantage of these ambiguities.

KEY TERMS

unilateral action (presidential) (p. 459)

unitary executive theory (p. 459)

signing statement (p. 460)

impeachment (p. 461)

CRITICAL THINKING AND DISCUSSION

What can members of Congress do to stop a president from changing policy unilaterally? Which of these methods seems most effective, and why?

PRACTICE QUIZ QUESTIONS

11. The _____ was used by the George W. Bush administration to argue in favor of the power to station American forces in Iraq.
    a) principal-agent theory
    b) unitary executive theory
    c) unilateral agreement theory
    d) dual presidency theory
    e) signing statement power

12. Most presidents use the _____ to control the interpretation and implementation of laws.
    a) line item veto
    b) recess appointment
    c) executive order
    d) signing statement
    e) pocket veto

13. Unilateral actions are most likely _____.
    a) at the end of a president's term
    b) at the beginning of a president's term
    c) in the middle of the term
    d) soon after re-election
    e) under unified government

14. Congressional challenges to presidential authority are _____ used and are generally _____ at constraining presidential power.
    a) rarely; successful
    b) rarely; unsuccessful
    c) commonly; successful
    d) commonly; unsuccessful

ⓢ PRACTICE ONLINE

"Big Think" video exercise: *What Is the Case for a Strong Executive?*

SUGGESTED READING

Alter, Jonathan. *The Promise: President Obama, Year One*. New York: Simon and Schuster, 2010.

Canes-Wrone, Brandice. *Who Leads Whom? Presidents, Policy, and the Public*. Chicago: University of Chicago Press, 2006.

Howell, William G. *Power without Persuasion: The Politics of Direct Presidential Action*. Princeton, NJ: Princeton University Press, 2003.

Lewis, David E. *Presidents and the Politics of Agency Design*. Palo Alto, CA: Stanford University Press, 2003.

Mayer, Kenneth. *With the Stroke of a Pen: Executive Orders and Presidential Power*. Princeton, NJ: Princeton University Press, 2001.

Neustadt, Richard E. *Presidential Power and the Modern Presidents: The Politics of Leadership from Roosevelt to Reagan*. New York: Free Press, 1990.

Rudalevige, Andrew. *Managing the President's Program: Presidential Leadership and Legislative Policy Formation*. Princeton, NJ: Princeton University Press, 2002.

Skowronek, Stephen. *The Politics Presidents Make: Leadership from John Adams to Bill Clinton*. Cambridge, MA: Harvard University Press, 1997.

12

The Bureaucracy

THE FEDERAL HOUSING FINANCE AGENCY (FHFA) supervises corporations responsible for the mortgages on millions of American homes. In 2011, the FHFA came into conflict with the Obama administration over a plan to help homeowners who were unable to make their mortgage payments and risked losing their homes to the bank.

MILLIONS OF AMERICANS WORK IN THE FEDERAL BUREAUCRACY. Most of the time, their work days are filled with routine actions that attract little attention from elected officials or the general public. However, even professional bureaucrats who were hired for their technical expertise—rather than their connections to a politician or party—can find themselves at the center of political conflict. Consider the case of Edward DeMarco, acting director of the Federal Housing Finance Agency (FHFA) in 2011.[1]

One of the primary roles of DeMarco's agency is to supervise two federally sponsored corporations, the Federal National Mortgage Association and the Federal Home Loan Mortgage Corporation (also known as Fannie Mae and Freddie Mac), that own trillions of dollars of home mortgages—if you or your parents own a home with a mortgage, chances are good that your monthly payment goes to one of these agencies. After the sharp declines of housing prices in 2007–08, Fannie Mae and Freddie Mac required federal bailouts totaling over $170 billion, and they now face uncertain futures.

The conflict DeMarco faced involved the Obama administration's attempts in 2010 and 2011 to help homeowners whose mortgages were "underwater"—meaning their homes were worth less than what they owed on their mortgages. Obama proposed new regulations that would encourage corporations that held these mortgages to reduce the amount owed, cutting monthly payments and making it easier for homeowners to continue paying their mortgages rather than abandoning their homes to foreclosure.

CONFLICT & COMPROMISE
in American Politics

These programs could be implemented only if DeMarco certified that they would be "loss minimizing" for Fannie Mae and Freddie Mac—that the two corporations would be better off because mortgages that had been reduced were more likely to be repaid. Based on his assessment of the programs, DeMarco refused. His decision did not appear to reflect political considerations or opposition to the Obama administration's initiatives. Rather, DeMarco was following the legal mandate of the FHFA as he interpreted it and trying to do what was best for the agency. This is not to say that the Obama administration didn't want what was best for Fannie Mae and Freddie Mac; rather, the situation was one where reasonable people could disagree about the consequences of the proposed policy.

The Obama administration attempted to sidestep DeMarco by finding a new permanent head of the FHFA, or by removing DeMarco in favor of a different acting director, who presumably would be more sympathetic to their initiatives. However, these efforts were blocked by congressional disapproval and by regulations that make it hard to remove bureaucrats from their positions. Ultimately, the Obama plan was rewritten to eliminate the aspects that DeMarco objected to. As of summer 2012, DeMarco remained in his position at the FHFA.

The case of Edward DeMarco and the FHFA highlights just one instance of conflict and compromise within the federal bureaucracy. It also illustrates the impact of bureaucratic agencies on life in America. The bureaucracy, it seems, is everywhere. Americans encounter the work of government employees every day: when they sort through mail delivered by the Postal Service, drive on highways funded by the Department of Transportation, or purchase food inspected by the Food and Drug Administration. The prices Americans pay to surf the web, watch television, or use a cell phone are influenced by regulations issued by the Federal Communications Commission. When they go on vacation, their bags are inspected by the Transportation Security Administration, the aircraft and pilots are scrutinized by the Federal Aviation Administration, and the beaches may be maintained by the Army Corps of Engineers.

While many federal bureaucrats work diligently to serve the American public, examination of what they do and how they do it reveals a paradox: the same organization that accomplishes so many big tasks also does things that are inefficient, wasteful, and downright dumb. Do these shortcomings result from inevitable accidents—or are they the consequences of deliberate actions? And if so, why were agencies designed to fail or to do things that look a lot like failure?

Consider the recent financial meltdown in the American economy and the sharp decline in housing prices. What role was played by bureaucrats tasked with regulating and monitoring banks and other financial firms? Did they do the best job they could, or was their inability to prevent the meltdown the result of bureaucratic incompetence or malfeasance?

In this chapter, we show that many bureaucratic failures can be explained by the bureaucracy's procedures for making decisions, including the complexity of the tasks it undertakes, and by the political conflicts that ensue when elected officials and interest groups attempt to control bureaucrats' actions. These conflicts are at the root of many seemingly inexplicable bureaucratic actions and outcomes. For example, the need to monitor bureaucrats to ensure that they carry out congressional mandates often leads to the use of rigid procedures that make it impossible for bureaucrats to shift policies in light of changing circumstances or local conditions. In many cases, these structures reflect compromises among lawmakers holding different ideas of what they would like bureaucrats to do. In this sense, the bureaucracy is just like Congress, multinational corporations, or other large enterprises that have many employees and undertake complex tasks. As the recent economic crisis suggests, managers in large corporations can be just as fallible as government bureaucrats.

This chapter also shows that the public's disdain for bureaucrats is not uniform. Most Americans award higher ratings to government agencies and offices with which they have personal experience. Similarly, most bureaucrats believe deeply in their agency's mission and work hard to achieve its goals.

bureaucracy The system of civil servants and political appointees who implement congressional or presidential decisions; also known as the administrative state.

civil servants Employees of bureaucratic agencies within the government.

WHAT IS THE FEDERAL BUREAUCRACY?

DEFINE BUREAUCRACY AND EXPLAIN ITS MAJOR FUNCTIONS

The federal **bureaucracy** that makes up the government's executive branch is composed of millions of **civil servants**, who work for the government in permanent positions, and thousands of **political appointees** holding short-term, usually senior positions, who are appointed by the president. Another name for the bureaucracy is the administrative state, which refers to the role bureaucrats play in administering government policies.[2] Most constitutional scholars agree that the president is nominally in charge of the bureaucracy—although in most cases he shares this power with members of Congress.

political appointees People selected by an elected leader, such as the president, to hold a government position.

WHAT DO BUREAUCRATS DO?

The task of the bureaucracy is to implement policies established by congressional acts or presidential decisions. These tasks are summarized in Nuts and Bolts 12.1. Sometimes the tasks associated with putting these laws and resolutions into effect are very specific. For example, in the appropriations bill for fiscal year 2010, Congress mandated a 3.4 percent pay increase for military personnel and funds for specific new military equipment.[3] These provisions required no discretion on the part of the bureaucrats who implement them. Their tasks were limited to making the administrative changes necessary to raise military pay and following through with the purchase of specified equipment.

More commonly, however, legislation determines only the general guidelines for meeting governmental goals, allowing bureaucrats to develop specific policies and programs. In these cases, bureaucrats' actions determine the essence of government action, deciding "who gets what, when, and how."[4] For example, the 1938 Federal Food, Drug, and Cosmetic Act gave the Food and Drug Administration (FDA) the job of determining which drugs are safe and effective, but it allowed FDA bureaucrats to develop their own procedures for making these determinations.[5]

WHILE THE TERM "BUREAUCRACY" MAY suggest workers sitting behind desks in offices, the agencies of the federal bureaucracy perform a wide range of tasks. Following the explosion of BP's *Deepwater Horizon* oil rig in 2010, the Coast Guard—a government agency— responded to try to put out the fire.

Currently the FDA requires that drug manufacturers first test new drugs for safety, then conduct further trials to determine their effectiveness. An FDA advisory board of scientists and doctors reviews the results of these tests. Then FDA bureaucrats decide whether to allow the manufacturer to market the drug.

In general, the job of the federal bureaucracy includes a wide range of activities, from regulating the behavior of individuals and corporations to buying everything from pencils to jet fighters. These activities are inherently political and often conflictual: ordinary citizens, elected officials, and bureaucrats themselves often disagree about aspects of these activities, and they work to influence bureaucratic actions to suit their own goals.

REGULATIONS

regulation A rule that allows the government to exercise control over individuals and corporations by restricting certain behaviors.

A **regulation** is a government rule that affects the choices that individuals or corporations make. It does so by either allowing or prohibiting behavior, setting out the conditions under which certain behaviors can occur, or assessing costs or granting benefits based on behavior. For example, in the case of deepwater offshore drilling, which became an issue in 2010 after an explosion at a British Petroleum (BP) oil well in the Gulf of Mexico created a massive oil spill, attention focused on a government agency known as the Minerals Management Service; this agency regulated every aspect of the drilling process—from how many lifeboats should be on a rig to what kinds of hardware should be used to drill and maintain the well site on the ocean floor. Bureaucrats gain the authority to write regulations by the statute that sets up their agency or by a subsequent act of Congress.

notice and comment procedure A step in the rule-making process in which proposed rules are published in the Federal Register and made available for debate by the general public.

Regulations are developed according to the **notice and comment procedure.**[6] Before a new regulation can take effect, it must be published in the *Federal Register,* an official publication that includes rules, proposed rules, and other types of government documents. Individuals and companies that will be affected by the regulation can then respond to the agency that proposed it, either supporting or opposing it, and offering different versions for consideration. Those potentially affected can also appeal to members of Congress or to the president's staff for help in getting the proposed rule revised. The agency then issues a final regulation, incorporating changes based on the comments. This final regulation is also published in the *Federal Register* and then put into effect.

The process of devising or modifying regulations is often political. Members of Congress and the president usually have strong opinions about how new regulations should look—and even when they don't, they may still get involved on behalf of a constituent or interest group. Bureaucrats take account of these pressures from elected officials for two reasons. First, the bureaucrats' policy-making power may derive from a statute that members of Congress could overturn if they disapprove of bureaucrats' actions. Second, bureaucrats need congressional support to get larger budgets and more important tasks for their agency, and to prevent budget cuts. Thus, despite bureaucrats' power to implement policies, their agencies' budgets, appointed leaders, and overall missions are subject to elected officials' oversight.

Many regulations are issued each year. Lately the *Federal Register* has contained more than 22,000 pages and about 4,000 new regulations a year.[7] Although nearly all government agencies issue regulations, most come from a few agencies, including the Federal Trade Commission, which regulates commerce; the Federal Communications Commission, which regulates media companies that create content as well as telecommunications companies that transmit information; and the FDA, which regulates drugs, medical products, food, and cosmetics.

Federal regulations affect every aspect of everyday life. They influence the gas mileage of cars sold in the United States, the materials used to build roads, and the price of gasoline. They determine the amounts that doctors can charge senior citizens for medical procedures; the hours that medical residents can work; and the criteria used to determine who gets a heart, lung, or kidney transplant. Regulations set the eligibility criteria for student loans, limit how the military can recruit on college campuses, determine who can get a home mortgage and what their interest rate will be, and describe what constitutes equal funding for men's and women's college sports teams. Regulations also shape contribution limits and spending decisions in political campaigns.

Some regulations can have a life-or-death impact. In 2007 the Centers for Medicare and Medicaid Services established criteria that hospitals performing organ transplants must meet for their transplant procedures to qualify for Medicare reimbursement. These regulations determine which hospitals senior citizens on Medicare can use if they need a transplant. To qualify for reimbursement, a hospital must perform a set number of transplants per year, meet minimum success rates for those operations, manage its patient waiting lists according to certain criteria, and provide particular services to transplant recipients and their families.[8]

Regulations are often controversial because they involve trade-offs between incompatible goals, as well as decisions made under uncertain circumstances. For example, the FDA drug approval process prioritizes the goal of preventing harmful drugs from coming to market.[9] As a result, patients sometimes cannot get access to experimental treatments because FDA approval has not been granted, even when those treatments are the patients' only remaining option.[10] Advocates for patients have argued that people with dire prognoses should be allowed to use an experimental treatment as a potentially life-saving last resort.[11] However, current FDA regulations prevent them from doing so except under very special circumstances, arguing that unapproved treatments may do more harm than good and that allowing wider access to these drugs may tempt manufacturers to market new drugs without adequate testing.

FEDERAL REGULATIONS INFLUENCE many aspects of everyday life that would not seem likely to be affected by government action. The increase in the number of women's intercollegiate athletic teams is partly due to regulations that require equal funding for men's and women's teams.

PROCUREMENT

Bureaucrats also handle government purchases, buying everything from pencils to aircraft carriers. The General Services Administration (GSA) manages 8,600 buildings owned or leased by the government and a fleet of 208,000 vehicles, and provides government agencies with most of their supplies.[12]

Procurement seems a straightforward task: agencies determine what they need, find out who can supply it, and choose the lowest-cost provider. However, procurement for the federal government can be surprisingly complicated. Consider the purchase of a new model of fighter plane or an attack submarine. Bureaucrats must devise criteria for choosing between designs with very different strengths and weaknesses. Procurement decisions are also shaped by congressional and executive mandates. For example, when the GSA searches for suppliers of a particular product, it often has to give preference to small businesses or firms owned by minorities or veterans. These guidelines are the result of the political process, as elected officials try to shape government actions to suit their own policy goals.

Just about every president has tried to reform the procurement process. President Obama, for example, has proposed an end to cost-plus and no-bid contracts. (Under cost-plus, contractors are paid whatever it costs to provide a service plus a percentage of costs as their profit; under no-bid contracts, contracts are awarded without a competitive bidding process.) Although these practices may seem wasteful, the government may be forced to use them because of the complex and unique goods and services it needs to buy.

PROVIDING SERVICES

Street-level bureaucrats provide services to help ordinary Americans.[13] These services include certain job-training programs and disaster assistance. In addition, federal employees manage tourist attractions from the National Zoo to the Statue of Liberty to Mount Rushmore. They inspect passenger baggage at airports, monitor aircraft maintenance, and direct aircraft in flight.

RESEARCH AND DEVELOPMENT

Government scientists work in areas from medicine to astronomy to agriculture. Sometimes they do basic research, such as working for the National Institutes of Health to discover mechanisms that govern cell reproduction and death. Government scientists also do applied research, from developing new cancer drugs to improving crop management techniques. Federal funds support research in many universities and corporations that examines similar issues.

MANAGING AND DIRECTING

Some bureaucrats supervise actions taken by people outside government. For example, the Department of Defense uses civilian contractors to provide support services in Afghanistan, from doing laundry to performing maintenance work on planes, trucks, and ships. Many workers at government facilities and public works projects are employees of private corporations working on government contracts.

street-level bureaucrats
Agency employees who directly provide services to the public, such as those who provide job-training services.

AFTER NEWS OF AN $800,000 GSA conference at a Las Vegas resort came to light in 2012, Congress held hearings on the agency's practices. Here, Representative John Mica criticizes the apparent misuse of taxpayer money.

Mr. MICA

BUREAUCRATIC EXPERTISE AND ITS CONSEQUENCES

Bureaucrats are experts. Even compared to most members of Congress or presidential appointees, the average bureaucrat is a specialist in a certain policy area, with a better grasp of his or her agency's mission. For example, people who hold scientific or management positions in the FDA usually know more about the benefits and risks of new drugs than people outside the agency do. Their decision to deny unapproved drugs to seriously ill patients may seem cruel, but it may also reflect a thoughtful balancing of two incompatible goals: preventing harmful drugs from reaching the market, and allowing people who have exhausted all other treatments access to risky, experimental products. A bureaucracy of experts is an important part of what political scientists call **state capacity**—the knowledge, personnel, and institutions needed to implement policies that change society.[14]

RED TAPE AND STANDARD OPERATING PROCEDURES

Despite bureaucrats' policy expertise, their decisions often appear to take too much time, rely on arbitrary judgments of what is important, and have unintended consequences—to the point that actions designed to solve one problem may create worse ones. Many critics cite the abundance of **red tape**, which refers to unnecessarily complex procedures, or **standard operating procedures**, which are the rules that lower-level bureaucrats must follow when implementing policies regardless of whether they are applicable. The performance of the Federal Emergency Management Agency (FEMA) after Hurricane Katrina in 2008 is a classic example: while many observers criticized FEMA for taking several days to fully implement disaster relief, FEMA employees were following long-established plans that had been approved by FEMA managers and members of Congress.

There have been many attempts to make the bureaucracy operate more effectively by mandating that bureaucrats make decisions using specific procedures or criteria. These efforts have added many acronyms to the language of Washington bureaucrats: PPBS, MBO, ZBB, PBB, and REGO.[15] Though each of these efforts can claim modest success, none have fundamentally changed the way the government does business. The lesson seems to be that examples of poor performance by America's bureaucracy have little to do with the bureaucracy itself. Otherwise, one of these reform packages would have solved these problems, resulting in a well-functioning bureaucracy.

Cases of bureaucratic ineptitude and failed reform efforts raise a critical question: How can an organization full of experts develop such dysfunctional ways of doing business? Bureaucrats are neither clueless nor malevolent. What, then, explains red tape and counterproductive standard operating procedures? The answer is the very strength of the American bureaucracy: its expertise.

Because bureaucrats know things that elected officials do not and because bureaucrats have their own policy goals, it is hard for elected officials to evaluate what bureaucrats are doing. For example, FEMA was criticized for using a cruise ship to house relief workers after Hurricane Katrina, which cost more than it would have to send these employees on a Caribbean cruise. While the contract was expensive, the FEMA staffer who signed

state capacity The knowledge, personnel, and institutions that the government requires to effectively implement policies.

red tape Excessive or unnecessarily complex regulations imposed by the bureaucracy.

standard operating procedures Rules that lower-level bureaucrats must follow when implementing policies.

DESPITE THEIR POLICY EXPERTISE, bureaucrats still make mistakes. When the Medicare program implemented the Prescription Drug Benefit in 2006, information about the coverage was available on an easy-to-read website, but the agency soon learned that many seniors who needed the information did not know how to use a web browser.

the contract may have found that all other options were more expensive or simply impossible. Similarly, the Minerals Management Service's decision to skimp on routine safety inspections on oil rigs in the Gulf of Mexico may have been the result of laziness—but it may also have reflected a decision to focus on what then seemed to be more serious concerns. Without looking deeper into these issues, it is impossible to be sure.

Of course, sometimes bureaucrats simply make mistakes. For example, the FDA has delayed helpful drugs from reaching the market or has approved drugs that were later found to have harmful side effects. However, these decisions may have been justified based on the information available to bureaucrats at the time. Here again, it is hard to say that bureaucrats are at fault for such decisions.

THE PROBLEM OF CONTROL

Political scientists refer to the difficulty that elected officials and their staff face when they try to interpret or influence bureaucratic actions as the **problem of control**.[16] A classic example is the **principal–agent game**. The principal–agent game describes an interaction that involves an individual or group (an "agent") acting on behalf of another (the "principal"). In the federal government, for example, the president and Congress are principals, and bureaucrats are agents. An agent may not want to work, or may prefer outcomes that the principal does not like. Moreover, because the agent is an expert at the task he has been given, he has private information inaccessible to the principal. The problem for the principal, then, is this: giving the agent very specific orders prevents the agent from acting based on expertise; but if the principal gives the agent the freedom to make decisions based on expertise, the principal has less control over the agent's actions.

For example, suppose Congress and the president direct the FDA to shorten its drug approval process. FDA officials might have mandated a lengthy process based on their expert assessment of the best way to screen out harmful drugs. By giving orders that supersede the FDA officials' screening process, elected officials would be sacrificing the valuable bureaucratic expertise behind the policy and risking the hasty approval of unsafe drugs. On the other hand, if Congress and the president allow FDA bureaucrats to devise their own procedures and regulations, there is a chance that the FDA could use this freedom to pursue goals that have nothing to do with drug safety. For example, critics of the FDA's procedures have asserted that a drawn-out approval process is designed to favor large companies that already have drugs on the market over smaller companies trying to get approval for drugs that would compete with existing products.

The principal-agent game can also be framed in terms of citizens. Figure 12.1 shows that a majority of survey respondents agreed that the federal government is typically inefficient and wasteful—although the percentage agreeing with this assessment declined from its peak in 1992 until recent years, where it again increased. A survey conducted in 1999 found similar results. Only 8 percent of respondents believed that the federal government has had a large number of policy successes, whereas a near majority could not name a single government success.[17] These opinions give citizens a strong motivation to demand that elected officials control the bureaucracy—to reduce the waste and inefficiency that many see as commonplace.

Members of Congress and citizens are sometimes right to question the motives of members of the bureaucracy. Sometimes bureaucratic actions are the result of **regulatory capture**, which occurs when bureaucrats cater to a small group of

FIGURE » 12.1

HOW AMERICANS VIEW THE FEDERAL BUREAUCRACY

Many Americans believe the bureaucracy is wasteful and inefficient. Note, however, that the magnitude of negative feelings varies over time. Consider the time frame represented on the graph. What happened during these years that might explain the changes in citizens' opinions about the government?

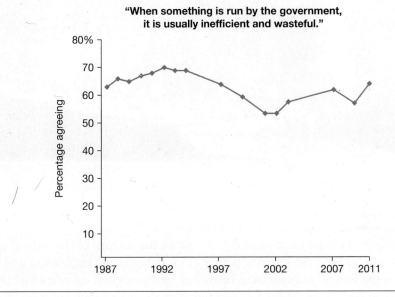

"When something is run by the government, it is usually inefficient and wasteful."

Source: Pew Research Center, "The Generation Gap and the 2012 Elections," Pew Research Center, November 1, 2011, www.people-press.org/files/legacy-pdf/11-3-11%20Generations%20Release.pdf (accessed 9/22/12).

individuals or corporations regardless of the impact of these actions on public welfare. In the case of the Minerals Management Service, press reports documented that agency employees accepted meals, gifts, and sporting trips from companies they were regulating. Several employees even used drugs and had sex with industry employees. More significant, the agency's mission changed from regulating with an eye on safety to encouraging as much drilling as possible—an ideal scenario for profit-minded energy companies.[18]

You might think that the problem of control isn't too difficult to solve as long as bureaucrats act as impartial experts and set aside their own policy goals. Many studies of bureaucracies, beginning with the work of the early political theorist Max Weber, argue for **neutral competence**, the idea that bureaucrats should provide information and expertise, and avoid taking sides on policy questions or being swayed by elected officials, people outside government, or their own policy goals.[19] However, bureaucrats' behavior doesn't always fit Weber's vision. Many enter the bureaucracy with their own ideas about what government should do, and they make decisions in line with those goals. Bureaucrats may also be tempted to favor interest groups or corporations to secure a better-paying job after they leave government service. However, even if bureaucrats wanted to remain completely dispassionate, they would face a government in which many other people with their own policy goals attempted to influence their behavior. Members of Congress or the president

neutral competence The idea, credited to theorist Max Weber, that suggests bureaucrats should provide expertise without the influence of elected officials, interest groups, or their own political agendas.

sometimes try to use the bureaucracy to implement policies that reflect their personal preferences or reward their political supporters.[20]

The problem of control has existed throughout the history of the federal government. It affects both the kinds of policies that bureaucrats implement and the structure of the federal bureaucracy, including the number of agencies and their missions, staff, and tasks. Moreover, elected officials use a variety of methods to solve the problem of control, including making it easier for people outside government to learn about agency actions before they take effect. However, all these tactics are at best partial solutions to the problem of control. The trade-off between expertise and control remains.

HISTORY OF THE AMERICAN BUREAUCRACY

TRACE THE EXPANSION OF THE FEDERAL BUREAUCRACY OVER TIME

The evolution of America's federal bureaucracy was not steady or smooth. Most of its important developments occurred during three short periods: the late 1890s and early 1900s, the 1930s, and the 1960s.[21] In all three periods, the driving force was a combination of demands from citizens for enhanced government services and the desire of people in government to either respond to these demands or increase the size and scope of the federal government in line with their own policy goals.

THE BEGINNING OF AMERICA'S BUREAUCRACY

From the beginning of the United States until the election of Andrew Jackson in 1828, the staff of the entire federal bureaucracy numbered at most in the low thousands. There were only three executive departments (State, Treasury, and War), along with a Postmaster General.[22] The early federal government also performed a narrow range of tasks. It collected taxes on imports and exports and delivered the mail. The national army consisted of a small Corps of Engineers and a few frontier patrols. The attorney general was a private attorney who had the federal government as one of his clients. Members of Congress outnumbered civil servants in Washington; the president had very little staff at all.[23]

The small size of the federal government during those years reflected Americans' deep suspicion of government, especially unelected officials. In the Declaration of Independence, one of the charges against King George III was that he had "erected a multitude of new offices and sent hither swarms of officers to harass our people and eat out their substance."[24] Executive branch offices were formed only when absolutely necessary. Nonetheless, conflicts soon arose around control of the bureaucracy. The legislation that established the departments of State, Treasury, and War allowed the president to nominate the people in charge of these departments but made these appointments subject to Senate approval. (The same is true today for the heads of all executive departments and many other presidential appointments.)

The election of Andrew Jackson in 1828 brought the first large-scale use of the spoils system, in which people who had worked in Jackson's campaign were rewarded with new positions in the federal government (usually working as local postmasters).[25] The spoils system was extremely useful to party organizations, as it gave them a powerful incentive with which to convince people to work for the party—a particularly important tool for Jackson, as his campaign organization was at that time the largest ever organized.

The challenge facing the spoils system was ensuring that these government employees, who often lacked experience in their new fields, could actually carry out their jobs. The solution was to develop procedures for these employees, so that they knew exactly what to do even if they had little or no experience or training.[26] These instructions became one of the earliest uses of standard operating procedures. They ensured that the government could function even if large numbers of employees had been hired in reward for political work rather than because of their qualifications.[27]

As America expanded in size, so did the federal government, which saw an almost eightfold increase in the bureaucracy between 1816 and the beginning of the Civil War in 1861. This growth did not reflect a fundamental change in what the government did; in fact, much of the increase came in areas such as the Post Office, which needed to serve a geographically larger nation—and, of course, to provide "spoils" for party workers in the form of government jobs.[28] Even by the end of the Civil War, the federal government still had very little involvement in the lives of ordinary Americans. State and local governments provided services such as education, public works, and welfare benefits, if they were provided at all. The federal government's role in daily life was limited to mail delivery, collecting import and export taxes, and a few other areas.

BUILDING A NEW AMERICAN STATE: THE PROGRESSIVE ERA

Changes in the second half of the nineteenth century transformed America's bureaucracy.[29] This transformation began after the Civil War, but the most significant changes occurred during the Progressive Era, 1890–1920. Many laws

THIS CARTOON OF A MONUMENT TO President Andrew Jackson riding a pig decries his involvement in the spoils system, which allowed politicians to dole out government service jobs in return for political support.

and executive actions increased the government's regulatory power during this period, including the Sherman Antitrust Act of 1890, the Pure Food and Drug Act of 1906, the Meat Inspection Act, expansion of the Interstate Commerce Commission, and various conservation measures.[30] Now the federal government was no longer simply a deliverer of mail and a defender of borders; rather, it had an indirect impact on several aspects of everyday life. When Americans bought food or other products, went to work, or traveled on vacation, the choices available to them were shaped by the actions of federal bureaucrats in Washington and elsewhere.

These developments were matched by a fundamental change in the federal bureaucracy following passage of the 1883 Pendleton Civil Service Act. This measure created the **federal civil service**, in which the merit system (qualifications, not political connections) would be the basis for hiring and promoting bureaucrats.[31] In other words, when a new president took office, he could not replace members of the civil service with his own campaign workers. Initially, only about 13,000 federal jobs acquired civil service protections, but over the next two decades many additional positions were incorporated into the civil service, to the point that in the modern era virtually all full-time, permanent government employees have civil service protection. In some cases, presidents gave civil service protections to people who had been hired under the spoils system to prevent the next president from replacing these bureaucrats with their own loyalists.

Over time, these reforms created a bureaucracy in which people were hired for their expertise and allowed to build a career in government without having to fear being fired when a new president or Congress took office.[32] These changes also attracted government employees who were motivated primarily by their interest in shaping government policy. Studies of this transformation have found that one of the driving forces behind the changes was a shift in citizens' demands. People wanted a greater role for government, both in regulating the behavior of large corporations and in delivering more services to citizens.[33]

When civil service reforms were adopted, their impact on party organizations was well understood. As one New York City machine politician, George Washington Plunkitt, put it, "This civil service law is the biggest fraud of the age. It is the curse of the nation. . . . How are you going to interest our young men in their country if you have no offices to give them when they work for their party?"[34] Plunkitt meant that without the spoils system, organizations like his would be in serious danger of losing their hold on government, as they would be unable to use the promise of a government job to motivate people to help elect the machine's candidates. Members of Congress, some of whom were members of spoils-based organizations, enacted civil service legislation because of strong public pressure to reform the bureaucracy—and because the protections would apply to current federal workers, some of whom had received their position in return for partisan work.[35]

Increased bureaucratic activity during the Progressive Era also highlights another interesting feature of government regulation: under some conditions, the targets of new regulation welcome government intervention. For example, early efforts to regulate the food production industry were supported by some very large producers that wanted a level playing field against smaller competitors who skimped on sanitation and safety requirements. More recently, some auto companies have lobbied the federal government for more stringent gas mileage and pollution standards not because they are enthusiastic about the new rules but because they want to preempt the imposition of even stiffer requirements by states such as California.

federal civil service A system created by the 1883 Pendleton Civil Service Act in which bureaucrats are hired on the basis of merit rather than political connections.

THE NEW DEAL, THE GREAT SOCIETY, AND THE REAGAN REVOLUTION

Dramatic expansion of the federal bureaucracy occurred during the New Deal period in the 1930s and during the mid-1960s Great Society era. In both cases, the changes were driven by a combination of citizen demands and the preferences of elected officials who favored an increased role of government in society. This expansion was only marginally curtailed during the Reagan Revolution of the 1980s.

THE NEW DEAL

The New Deal refers to the government programs implemented during Franklin Roosevelt's first term as president in the 1930s. At one level, these programs were a response to the Great Depression and the inability of local governments and private charities to respond to this economic crisis. Many advocates of the New Deal also favored an expanded role for government in American society, regardless of the immediate need for intervention.[36] Roosevelt's programs included reforms to the financial industry as well as efforts to help people directly and to stimulate employment, economic growth, and the formation of labor unions. The Social Security Act, the first federally funded pension program for all Americans, was also passed as part of the New Deal.[37]

These reforms represented a vast increase in the size, responsibilities, and capacity of the bureaucracy, as well as a large transfer of power to bureaucrats and to the president.[38] While the Progressive Era reforms created an independent bureaucracy and increased its state capacity, the New Deal reforms increased the range of policy areas in which this capacity could be applied. Before the New Deal, the federal government influenced citizens' choices through activities such as regulating industries and workplace conditions. Afterward, the federal government took on the role of delivering a wide range of benefits and services directly to individuals, from jobs to electricity, as well as increased regulation of many industries, including the banking and financial industries.

The expansion of the federal government and the subsequent delegation of power to bureaucrats and to the president were controversial changes, both when they were enacted and as they were implemented in subsequent years.[39] Many Republicans opposed New Deal reforms because they believed that the federal government could not deliver services efficiently and that an expanded federal bureaucracy would create a modern spoils system. Many southerners worried that the federal government's increased involvement in everyday life would endanger the system of racial segregation in southern states.[40] Even so, Democratic supporters of the New Deal, aided by public support, carried the day.

THE GREAT SOCIETY

The Great Society was a further expansion in the size, capacity, and activities of the bureaucracy that occurred during Lyndon Johnson's presidency (1963–69). During these years, Johnson proposed and Congress enacted programs that funded bilingual education, loans and grants for college students, special education, preschools, construction of elementary and secondary schools, mass transit programs in many cities, health care for seniors and poor people, job training and urban renewal, enhanced voting rights and civil rights for minorities, environmental protection, and funding for the arts and cultural activities.[41]

Members of Congress frequently attempted to control these new programs, with the goal of delivering valuable benefits to their own constituents. In the case

UNDER PRESIDENT GEORGE W. BUSH, the federal bureaucracy continued to expand. Programs like No Child Left Behind increased the role of government in society.

of the Model Cities Program, which was designed to fund efforts to revitalize decaying urban areas, members of Congress demanded expansion of the program from a small set of experimental projects to a nationwide, 150-city effort. In return for this congressional support of the agencies associated with the program, members of Congress forced bureaucrats to fund lucrative projects in their districts.[42]

The Great Society programs had mixed success. Voting rights and civil rights reforms ended the "separate but equal" system of social order in southern states and dramatically increased political participation by African Americans.[43] At the same time, many antipoverty programs were dismal failures. Poverty rates among most groups remained relatively constant, and other indicators, such as the rate of teen pregnancies, actually increased.[44] In retrospect, the people who designed and implemented these programs did not realize the complexities of the problems they were trying to address.[45] For example, many antipoverty programs were built on the assumption that most people receiving welfare needed job training programs in order to transition from welfare to permanent, paid employment. However, additional data that were available a decade later showed that most people receiving welfare do so for short periods because of divorce or medical hardship—problems that the Great Society programs did not touch.[46] Despite these shortcomings, the expansion of the federal government during the New Deal and Great Society has remained in place over the last generation.

THE REAGAN REVOLUTION

The election of Ronald Reagan to the presidency in 1980, along with a Republican takeover of the Senate and significant Republican gains in the House of Representatives, created an opportunity for conservatives to roll back the size and scope of the federal government. However, after eight years of Reagan in office followed by four years of George H. W. Bush, and Republican control of Congress during most of Democrat Bill Clinton's presidency as well as during most of the presidency of Republican George W. Bush, the growth of the federal government did not slow. Few programs were eliminated, and the federal budget steadily increased.[47]

Conservative presidents and members of Congress have enacted programs and regulations that increased the impact of government on society. For example, George W. Bush's administration added the No Child Left Behind education reforms, which imposed many new requirements on local schools; the Medicare Prescription Drug Benefit, which was the biggest new health care program since the 1960s; the Sarbanes–Oxley Act, which increased financial reporting requirements for corporations; and a host of other regulations, from specifications on backyard play sets to inspections of baggage on commercial aircraft.[48] The trend toward increased federal regulation continued in the Obama administration, especially with health care and financial industry reforms enacted in Obama's first term.

> DESCRIBE THE SIZE AND STRUCTURE OF THE EXECUTIVE BRANCH TODAY

THE MODERN FEDERAL BUREAUCRACY

The size and scope of the modern federal bureaucracy reflects the expansion of the federal government over the last half-century and its increased role in the lives of everyday Americans. The structure of the bureaucracy also reflects ongoing attempts by presidents, members of Congress, and others to control bureaucratic actions in line with their policy goals.

THE STRUCTURE OF THE FEDERAL GOVERNMENT

Figure 12.2 shows the structure of the executive branch of the federal government. As discussed in Chapter 11, the Executive Office of the President (EOP) contains organizations that support the president and implement presidential policy initiatives—individuals working in these organizations are part of the administrative presidency that works to ensure that bureaucrats implement the president's policy priorities, bringing the actions of bureaucrats (agents) in line with the president's (principal's) preferences.[49] Among its many offices, the EOP contains the **Office of Management and Budget**, which prepares the president's annual budget proposal, and monitors government spending and the development of new regulations. Below the EOP are the fifteen executive departments, from the Department of Agriculture to the Department of Veterans Affairs, which constitute the major divisions within the executive branch. The heads of these fifteen organizations make up the president's cabinet.

Each executive department contains many smaller organizations. Figure 12.3 shows the organizational chart for the Department of Agriculture. As you can see, Agriculture includes offices that help farmers produce and sell their crops, as well as offices that ensure food safety, but it also houses the Forest Service and offices

Office of Management and Budget An office within the Executive Office of the President that is responsible for creating the president's annual budget proposal to Congress, reviewing proposed rules, and other budget-related tasks.

FIGURE » 12.2

THE EXECUTIVE BRANCH OF THE FEDERAL GOVERNMENT

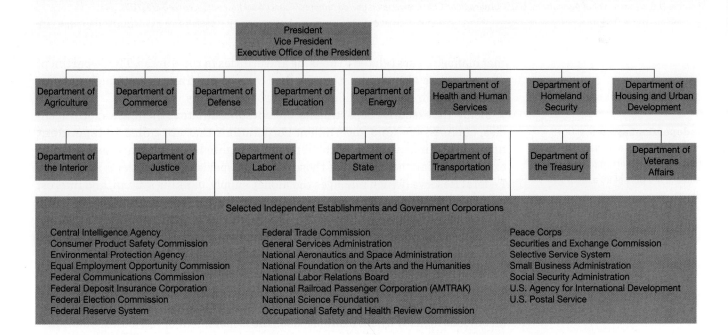

Source: Based on GPO Access: Guide to the U.S. Government, http://bensguide.gpo.gov/files/gov_chart.pdf (accessed 9/22/12).

FIGURE » 12.3

THE STRUCTURE OF THE DEPARTMENT OF AGRICULTURE

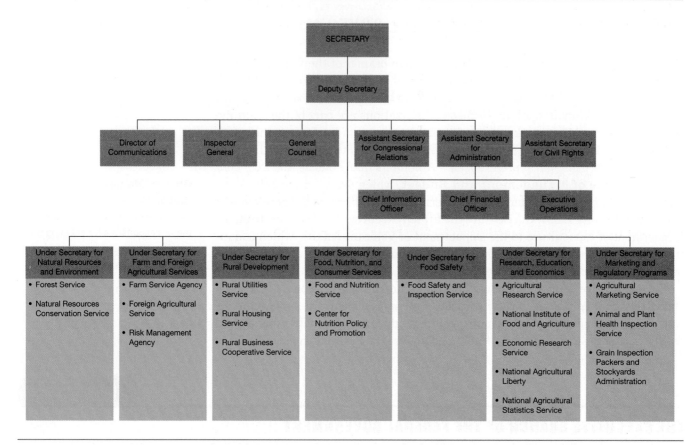

Source: U.S. Department of Agriculture, USDA Organization Chart, www.usda.gov/documents/AgencyWorkflow.pdf (accessed 4/23/10).

independent agencies Government offices or organizations that provide government services and are not part of an executive department.

that manage issues related to housing and utilities in rural areas. The Department of Agriculture also administers the food stamps program, even though the program has no direct connection to farming or food safety.

Below the executive departments, but not subordinate to them, are a set of agencies, commissions, and government corporations that are called **independent agencies**, or independent establishments, to highlight that they are not part of an executive department. Most of these carry out specialized functions, such as the Federal Reserve (which manages the money supply, banking system, and interest rates) and the Federal Deposit Insurance Corporation (which regulates the banking industry and during 2008–10 closed or merged several hundred banks that had lost money as a result of increased mortgage foreclosures). The figure only includes some noteworthy or well-known agencies; there are many more.

There are two important lessons to draw from these charts. First, the federal government serves an enormous range of functions. Second, the division of activities among executive departments and independent agencies does not always have an obvious logic. Why, for example, does the Department of Agriculture administer rural utilities programs and food stamps? Similarly, it is not always clear why certain tasks are handled by an independent agency while others fall within the scope of an executive department.[50] Why is the Federal Reserve an independent agency rather than part of the Department of the Treasury?

Organizational decisions like these often reflect elected officials' attempts to shape agency behavior—and the extent to which political process matters. Part of the difference between independent agencies and the organizations contained within executive departments has to do with the president's ability to control these organizations' activities. Organizations that fall within an executive department, such as the Internal Revenue Service, can be controlled by the president (to some extent) through his appointees.[51] In contrast, independent agencies have more freedom from oversight and control by the president and Congress. For example, the president nominates governors of the Federal Reserve, who (if the Senate confirms them) serve for fourteen years. Outside the nomination and confirmation process, the president and Congress have very little control over the Federal Reserve's policies; the organization is self-financing, and its governors can be removed from office only if Congress takes the extreme step of impeaching them.

These details about the hiring and firing of bureaucrats and the location of agencies in the structure of the federal government matter because they determine the amount of political control that other parts of the government can exercise over an agency, as well as who gets to exercise this power. As political scientist Terry Moe puts it, "The bureaucracy rises out of politics, and its design reflects the interests, strategies, and compromises of those who exercise political power."[52]

An extreme example of bureaucratic structure being driven by political concerns rather than efficiency or effectiveness comes from the use of intelligence agencies by the Bush administration in the months before the Iraq War. At the time, there was a spirited debate within the administration about the justification for war. Central Intelligence Agency (CIA) reports expressed strong doubts about purported links between Al Qaeda and Iraq, and they believed that Iraq was nowhere near having an operational nuclear weapon.[53] Both of these conclusions weakened the case for war. In response, senior leaders in the Bush administration set up the Office of Special Plans (OSP) within the Department of Defense to develop an alternate view on Iraq's nuclear program, placing a bureaucrat who favored war with Iraq at its head.[54] The OSP relied on raw intelligence reports—including information from defectors—rather than summaries and interpretations of this information prepared by the CIA and other agencies. The resulting reports made a strong case for invading Iraq, based on links between the country's leadership and terrorist organizations and the claim that the country had developed weapons of mass destruction—conclusions that later proved almost completely false. In retrospect, it is clear that the OSP was created and staffed to make the case for war that other agencies were unwilling to make based on the available evidence.

THE SIZE OF THE FEDERAL GOVERNMENT

The federal government employs millions of people. Table 12.1 reports the number of employees in each executive department and selected independent agencies. The Department of Defense is the largest cabinet department, with more than 600,000 civilian personnel. The Department of Education is the smallest, with only 4,000. Many departments are on the small side: five cabinet departments have fewer than 20,000 employees. Many independent agencies also have relatively modest numbers of employees. The General Services Administration, for

TABLE » 12.1

EMPLOYMENT IN SELECTED FEDERAL ORGANIZATIONS

ORGANIZATION	TOTAL EMPLOYEES
CABINET DEPARTMENTS	
Defense (civilian only)	652,000
Veterans Affairs	280,000
Homeland Security	171,000
Justice	108,000
Treasury	88,000
Agriculture	82,000
Interior	67,000
Health and Human Services	64,000
Transportation	55,000
Commerce	39,000
Labor	16,000
Energy	15,000
State	15,000
Housing and Urban Development	9,000
Education	4,000
INDEPENDENT AGENCIES	
Social Security Administration	64,000
National Aeronautics and Space Administration	18,000
Environmental Protection Agency	18,000
General Services Administration	12,000
Federal Deposit Insurance Corporation	5,000
Smithsonian Institution	4,000

Source: U.S. Bureau of Labor Statistics, Career Guide to Industries, "Federal Government, Excluding the Postal Service," Table 1, March 2012, www.bls.gov/oco/cg/cgs041.htm (accessed 9/22/12).

example, has only 12,000 employees. The remaining independent agencies generally have only a few thousand employees each. Millions of additional people work for the government as members of the armed forces, as employees of the Postal Service, for civilian companies that contract with the government, or as recipients of federal grant money.

Figure 12.4 shows the size of the federal budget since 1968. Clearly, the budget has steadily increased, to the point that annual spending in recent years tops

FIGURE » 12.4

THE SIZE OF THE FEDERAL BUDGET

The graph on the left shows that federal spending has increased sharply since the 1960s. However, the one on the right shows that as a percentage of gross domestic product (GDP), which measures the size of the American economy, the increase is much smaller, except for the financial bailout and economic stimulus programs enacted in 2008 and 2009. What might these figures suggest about the increase in government spending?

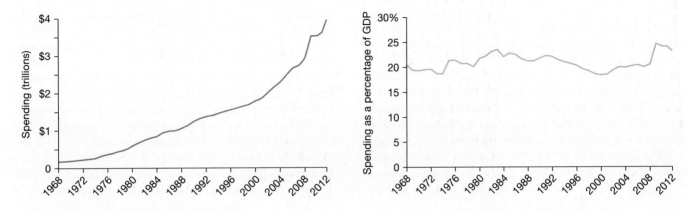

Sources: Congressional Budget Office, Historical Budget Data, "Revenues, Outlays, Deficits, Surpluses, and Debt Held by the Public," www.cbo.gov/budget/data/historical.shtml; "CBO's 2011 Long-Term Budget Outlook," http://cbo.gov/publication/41486 (accessed 3/21/12).

$3 trillion per year. The best explanation for the size of the federal government is the size of America itself—more than 300 million people spread out over an area more than twice the size of the European Union—coupled with America's position as the most powerful nation in the world. However, some observers argue that the real explanation has to do with bureaucrats themselves. This view suggests that the government is so large because bureaucrats are **budget maximizers** who never pass up a chance to increase their own funding, regardless of whether the new spending is worthwhile.[55]

This argument misses some important points. First, the increase in total federal spending masks the fact that many agencies see their budgets shrink.[56] Particularly in recent administrations, one of the principal missions of presidential appointees, both in agencies and in the Executive Office of the President, has been to scrutinize budget requests with an eye to cutting spending as much as possible.[57] And every year, some government agencies are eliminated.[58]

Moreover, public opinion data provide an explanation for the overall growth in government: the American public's demand for services.[59] Despite complaints about the federal bureaucracy, polls find little evidence of demands for less government. When the Harris Poll asked people in 2007 to decide which two programs should have their spending cut as a way of reducing the budget deficit, a majority favored cutting relatively small programs: 52 percent picked the space program and 79 percent picked foreign economic aid (see Table 12.2). Far fewer people favored cuts in the programs that account for the overwhelming majority of federal spending: defense, health care spending, and Social Security. In other words, while in the abstract Americans might want a smaller government that is

budget maximizers Bureaucrats who seek to increase funding for their agency whether or not that additional spending is worthwhile.

THE SIZE OF AMERICA'S GOVERNMENT

Many Americans believe that taxes are too high and that the federal government is wasteful and inefficient. These complaints raise the question of how U.S. government spending compares to spending by other countries. Although the extent of the services provided by different governments varies considerably, generally speaking the United States provides a much narrower range of benefits to its citizens compared to other developed nations, such as the industrialized democracies of western Europe. Many other countries offer benefits such as government-funded universal health care, a free or low-cost college education, and more generous old-age pensions. Thus, if the United States spends more than these countries, this would suggest that the federal government really is wasteful and inefficient—spending more and delivering less.

The Organization for Economic Cooperation and Development (OECD) collects a large variety of economic statistics about its thirty-three member nations, which include the United States and most other advanced democracies. The figure reports government spending in some of these countries, measured as a percentage of gross domestic product (GDP), which includes the value of all the goods and services produced in an economy over a set period—usually one year. (Note that much of recent U.S. spending on the wars in Iraq and Afghanistan is excluded from the figure.) We report government spending relative to the country's GDP because these countries differ greatly in terms of the overall size of their economies and populations. That is, a country that spends more than others in absolute terms might simply be richer or have a larger population than most. Considering spending as a percentage of GDP allows us to factor in the size of each country's population and economy to compare more accurately. (The data do not account for spending by state and local governments, which is significantly higher in America than elsewhere. On the other hand, the U.S. federal government spends more on defense, which offsets the difference in terms of social services.)

The data show that compared to other countries, the United States has one of the lowest levels of government spending. In fact, in some countries, such as Sweden, spending is almost double the level of spending in the United States. Of course, this doesn't imply that Swedish bureaucrats are doubly wasteful; rather, it reflects the many services that the Swedish government provides to its citizens, such as health care, child care, and unemployment compensation—services that the U.S. government either does not provide or provides at lower levels.

No one likes to pay taxes. It is important to consider what Americans get from government for their contributions and whether additional spending on new programs is warranted. It is also important to explore other ways of delivering services, such as substituting private companies for government operations. However, the fact that many Americans believe the government is too large does not mean it is inherently wasteful or harmful to the nation's economy. Also, as these data show, the U.S. government is actually small relative to other Western democracies.

THE SIZE OF AMERICA'S GOVERNMENT COMPARED TO THOSE OF OTHER NATIONS

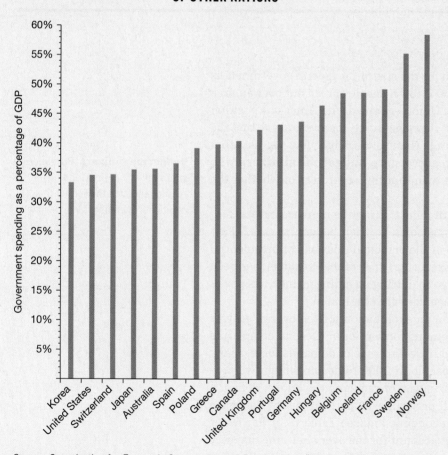

Source: Organization for Economic Cooperation and Development. "OECD in Figures, 2009," www.oecd.org/infigures (accessed 9/22/12).

TABLE » 12.2

PUBLIC PREFERENCES FOR SPENDING CUTS

Many Americans complain about the size of the federal government. However, their complaints do not translate into support for cuts in specific programs that could significantly reduce spending. Based on these data, are there any kinds of proposals for significantly reducing the size of the federal government that might attract widespread support?

PROGRAM	PERCENTAGE FAVORING CUTS
Foreign economic aid	79%
Space program	52
Welfare	52
Defense spending	42
Farm subsidies	42
Pollution control	37
Health care	22
Social Security	12

Source: Harris Poll, "Cutting Government Spending May Be Popular But Majorities of the Public Oppose Cuts in Many Big Ticket Items in the Budget," March 1, 2012, www.harrisinteractive.com/NewsRoom/HarrisPolls/tabid/447/ctl/ReadCustom%20Default/mid/1508/ArticleId/972/Default.aspx (accessed 9/22/12).

less involved in everyday life, they do not support the large-scale budget cuts that would be necessary to achieve this goal. The public's desire for more government services is often encouraged by elected officials, who create new government programs (and expand existing ones in response to constituent demands) as a way of building support and improving their chances of re-election.

THE HUMAN FACE OF THE BUREAUCRACY

DESCRIBE WHO BUREAUCRATS ARE AND THE REGULATIONS THAT GOVERN THEIR EMPLOYMENT

The term "bureaucrat" applies to a wide range of people with different qualifications and job descriptions. Nuts and Bolts 12.2 shows data on the range of jobs that federal workers do. There are a lot of managers (680,000 people) and administrative support staff (273,000), but there are also 670,000 professionals such as scientists and 8,000 people whose positions involve farming, fishing, and forestry. The federal government includes so many different kinds of jobs because of the vast array of services it provides. This section describes who these people are and the terms of their government employment.

While complaints are often heard about the efficiency or motivations of federal bureaucrats, survey data show that many have a strong interest in public service.

TYPES OF FEDERAL WORKERS

Occupation	Employees	Percentage of Federal Work Force
Management, business, and financial jobs (e.g., purchasing agents, accountants, tax collectors)	680,000	34%
Professional and related jobs (e.g., scientists, engineers, computer specialists, lawyers, doctors, nurses)	670,000	33
Office and administrative support jobs (e.g., secretaries, record clerks)	273,000	14
Service jobs (e.g., jailers, police officers, detectives)	161,000	8
Installation, maintenance, and repair jobs (e.g., mechanics, electricians)	101,000	5
Transportation and moving jobs (e.g., air traffic controllers, transportation inspectors)	61,000	3
Farming, fishing, and forestry jobs (e.g., agricultural inspectors, farmworkers, loggers)	8,000	0.4

Source: Based on the U.S. Bureau of Labor Statistics, "Career Guide to Industries, 2010–2011 Edition," Table 3, available at www.bls.gov/oco/cg/cgs041.htm (accessed 2/4/10).

Figure 12.5 describes a 2003 survey that asked bureaucrats and people working for private firms whether their primary interest was job security or the desire to help the public.[60] The bars on the left show that a large majority of federal employees mentioned salary and benefits as prime motivations. Even so, about one-third reported that their main incentive was an interest in public service or in what government does. The right side of Figure 12.5 shows that federal employees' motivations closely parallel those expressed by people working outside government. Like everyone else, the average federal employee's work-related decisions are often driven by self-interest. However, just like people who work outside government, many federal employees have other motivations, including the desire to do a good job.[61]

CIVIL SERVICE REGULATIONS

A key characteristic of most jobs in the federal bureaucracy is that they are subject to the civil service regulations mentioned earlier.[62] The current civil service system sets out a job description and pay ranges for all federal jobs.[63] People with less than a college degree are generally eligible for clerical and low-level technical jobs. As in the private sector, a college degree or an advanced degree and work experience qualify an individual for higher-level positions. Federal salaries are supposed to be comparable to what people earn in similar, private sector positions, and salaries are increased somewhat for federal employees who work in areas with a high cost of living.

FIGURE » 12.5

MOTIVATIONS FOR EMPLOYMENT: COMPARING BUREAUCRATS AND PRIVATE SECTOR EMPLOYEES

This chart shows that the motivations of federal employees are much the same as those of private sector workers for pursuing particular jobs. Some join the bureaucracy for the pay and benefits, but a substantial proportion work for the government because of policy goals—they want to help people or make a difference in how government works.

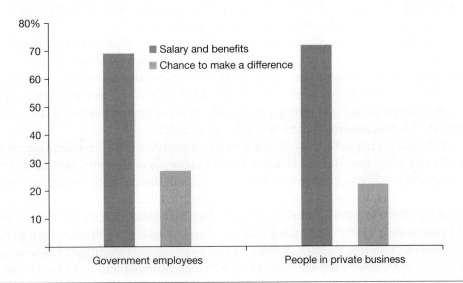

Source: Data from Paul Light, "The Content of Their Character: The State of the Nonprofit Workforce," The Nonprofit Quarterly (Fall 2002): 6–16.

The civil service system also establishes tests that determine who is hired for low-level clerical and secretarial positions. The people who receive the highest scores are hired as vacancies arise. A similar system applies for Postal Service employees and for federal air traffic controllers. Hiring for higher-level jobs involves comparing the qualifications and experience of candidates who meet the educational requirements for the position. Seniority, or the amount of time a person has worked for the government or at a particular type of position, also determines which employees receive promotions.

Civil service regulations provide job security. After three years of satisfactory performance, employees cannot be fired except "for cause," meaning that the firing agency must cite a reason. Civil service regulations set out a multistep procedure for firing someone, beginning with low performance evaluations, then warning letters given to the employee, followed by a lengthy appeals process before a firing takes place. In simple terms, it is very hard to fire someone from the federal bureaucracy as long as he or she shows up for work. One study found that only about 11,000 civil servants are fired in a given year.[64] A subpar performer may be assigned other duties, transferred to another office, or even given nothing to do in the hope that the person will leave voluntarily out of boredom.

Despite the difficulties associated with firing an individual underperforming bureaucrat, it is possible to reduce the size of the federal workforce through reductions in force (RIF), which occasionally occur when an entire office or program is terminated. Employees who have been laid off due to an RIF can apply for civil service positions in other parts of government. Another strategy for reducing the federal workforce is simply not to replace employees who decide to leave government service, or to hire contractors, who lack civil service protections and can be terminated at will.

If you think civil service regulations sound extraordinarily cumbersome, you're right.[65] The hiring criteria remove a manager's discretion to hire someone who would do an excellent job but lacks the education or work experience that the regulations specify as necessary for the position. The firing requirements make it extremely difficult to remove poor performers. The salary and promotion restrictions create problems with rewarding excellent performance or promoting the best employees rather than those with the most seniority.

Why do civil service requirements exist? Recall that the aim of these regulations was to separate politics from policy. The mechanism for achieving this goal was a set of rules and requirements that made it hard for elected officials to control the hiring and firing of government employees to further their own political goals. In effect, even though civil service regulations have obvious drawbacks, they also provide this less apparent but very important benefit.

Although loyalty to the president is a widely accepted criterion for hiring agency heads and other presidential appointees, professionals with permanent civil service positions are supposed to be hired on the basis of their qualifications, not their political beliefs. In fact, it is illegal to bring politics into these hiring decisions. However, there are well-documented cases in which administrations have made political beliefs a priority in hiring mid-level bureaucrats. For example, during the presidency of George W. Bush, Justice Department officials admitted to screening job applicants based on their ideological leanings. Membership in a liberal organization such as Greenpeace listed on a candidate's resumé reduced the likelihood of the person's being hired, while membership in a conservative organization such as the Federalist Society boosted an applicant's chances.[66] Though the Bush administration is the most severe known recent example of this practice, it is likely that other administrations have behaved similarly.

LIMITS ON POLITICAL ACTIVITY

Federal employees are limited in their political activities. The Hatch Act, enacted in 1939 and amended in 1940, prohibited federal employees from engaging in organized political activities.[67] Under the act, employees could vote and contribute to candidates but could not work for candidates or for political parties. These restrictions were modified in the 1993 Federal Employees Political Activities Act, allowing federal employees to undertake a wider range of political activities, including fund-raising and serving as an officer of a political party.

Senior members of the president's White House staff and political appointees are exempt from most of these restrictions, though they cannot use government resources for political activities. This became an issue early in the 2006 election campaign when, at a NASA awards ceremony, NASA administrator Michael Griffin referred to Congressman Tom DeLay, whose district contained NASA's Johnson Space Center, by saying, "The space program has had no better friend in its entire existence than Tom DeLay. He's still with us and we need to keep him there."[68] The problem was not what Griffin said; he was a political appointee and could endorse DeLay if he wanted to. Rather, the problem was that Griffin had flown to Texas for the NASA ceremony on a government aircraft, which, because of the endorsement, could be construed as using government resources for political purposes.

These regulations make life especially difficult for presidential appointees whose job duties often mix government service with politics, such as helping the president they work for get re-elected. In order to comply with Hatch Act restrictions, these officials need to carry separate cell phones to make calls related to their political activities and maintain separate e-mail accounts—usually provided by the party or campaign committee—for their political communications. Inevitably, some messages are sent using the wrong system. During the Bush administration, various political appointees used the Republican Party e-mail system to send messages relating to the controversial dismissal of several U.S. attorneys.[69]

It is not completely clear which activities are allowed or prohibited by these laws. For example, in spring 2007, congressional Democrats complained that Karl Rove, deputy White House chief of staff and a close political adviser to President George W. Bush, had given briefings to senior political appointees on Republican losses in the 2006 midterm elections and plans for the 2008 campaign. Although these meetings had been approved as legal by the White House counsel, their political content is obvious. During one briefing, the head of the General Services Administration asked how her agency could help elect Republican candidates in 2008.[70] As a senior member of the White House staff, Rove was exempt from the Hatch Act's prohibitions, but the more junior White House staff involved in the briefings probably were not. While ultimately no action was taken against Rove or his aides, this example illustrates the ambiguities inherent in separating the political and policy role of federal bureaucrats, especially those who work in the White House.

FEDERAL LAW PROHIBITS the use of government money, facilities, or services for political activities. Here, former Republican representative Tom DeLay (left), whose Texas district included NASA's Johnson Space Center, attends an awards ceremony with NASA administrator Michael Griffin. Although Griffin flew to Houston on a government plane primarily to present awards to NASA employees, his trip was cited as an illegal use of funds because his speech praised DeLay, who was running for re-election.

POLITICAL APPOINTEES AND THE SENIOR EXECUTIVE SERVICE

Not every federal employee is a member of the civil service. The president appoints over 7,000 individuals to senior positions in the executive branch that are not subject to civil service regulations, such as the leaders of executive departments and independent agencies, as well as members of the Executive Office of the President. (In some cases, the Senate must confirm these nominees.) Some of these presidential appointees get their jobs as a reward for working on the campaign staff, contributing substantial funds, or raising money from other donors. These individuals may not be given positions with real decision-making power. Some government agencies have the reputation of being **"turkey farms,"** places where campaign stalwarts can be appointed without the risk that their lack of experience will lead to bad policy.[71]

The majority of a president's appointees act as the president's eyes, ears, and hands throughout the executive branch. They hold positions of power within government agencies, serving as secretaries of executive departments, agency heads, or senior deputies. Their jobs involve finding out what the president wants from their agency and ordering, persuading, or cajoling their subordinates to implement presidential directives.

"turkey farms" Agencies where campaign workers and donors can be appointed to reward them for their service because it is unlikely that their lack of qualifications will lead to bad policy.

In many agencies, people in the top positions are members of the Senior Executive Service (SES), who are also exempt from civil service restrictions.[72] As of 2010, there were a few thousand SES members, most of whom were career government employees who held relatively high-level agency positions before moving to the SES. This change of employment status costs them their civil service protections but allows them to apply for senior leadership positions in the bureaucracy. Some political appointees are also given SES positions, although most do not have the experience or expertise held by career bureaucrats who typically move to the SES.

The president's ability to appoint bureaucrats in many different agencies helps him control the bureaucracy. By selecting people who are loyal or like-minded, a president can attempt to control the actions of lower-level bureaucrats and implement his policy agenda. The SES also gives civil servants an incentive to do their jobs well, as good performance in an agency position can help build a career that might allow them to transfer to the SES.

EXPLAIN HOW CONGRESS AND THE PRESIDENT OVERSEE THE EXECUTIVE BRANCH

CONTROLLING THE BUREAUCRACY

As the expert implementers of legislation and presidential directives, bureaucrats hold significant power to influence government policy. This situation creates the problem of political control illustrated by the principal–agent game: elected officials must figure out how to reap the benefits of bureaucratic expertise without simply giving bureaucrats free rein to do whatever they want.

One strategy is to take away discretion entirely and give bureaucrats simple, direct orders. One such case came to light in summer 2007 when outgoing surgeon general Richard Carmona revealed in a congressional hearing that he had been ordered to mention President Bush's name at least three times on every page of his speeches and to refrain from criticizing administration policies in the controversial areas of stem cell research, abstinence-only sex education programs, and the "morning-after pill" method of birth control called Plan B.[73]

Similarly, after NASA scientist James Hansen gave a speech in 2006 calling for policies to combat global warming that did not reflect the Bush administration's preferences, he was told to submit all future papers, lectures, and interview requests to NASA political appointees for review.[74] In this case, NASA reversed the order after it received press attention, and the agency's head released a statement supporting scientific openness.[75] Soon after this episode, however, NASA's official mission statement was modified to exclude studies of Earth, thereby choking off its studies of climate change entirely.[76]

Attempts such as these to control the bureaucracy are common. At the same hearing that featured Bush's outgoing surgeon general, David Satcher, who was surgeon general during the Clinton administration, testified that he had been ordered not to release a report on sexuality and public health in order to avoid embarrassing President Clinton, who was then being accused of having an affair with White House intern Monica Lewinsky.

The problem with eliminating bureaucrats' discretion is that it limits the positive influence of their expertise. Particularly when new policies are being developed, taking away bureaucratic discretion is costly for legislators or presidential appointees, as it forces them to work out the policy details themselves—and may

IS POLITICAL CONTROL OF THE BUREAUCRACY BENEFICIAL?

When working with bureaucrats, elected officials face the problem of political control: Should they allow bureaucrats to exercise judgment when implementing policies or give them specific, narrow directives? Letting bureaucrats set policy allows them to base decisions on their expertise or private information, but it also gives them the freedom to ignore elected officials' policy goals and preferences in favor of their own. While this exercise of expertise sounds like a good idea—shouldn't we let government policy be formulated by the most-knowledgeable people—in practice it remains a difficult decision.

Consider the case of America's involvement in the Libyan Civil War in 2011. The United States, along with its allies in NATO, provided the Libyan rebels with weapons and other supplies, and conducted manned and drone airstrikes on the government's military bases and infrastructure. After some initial strikes, the U.S. involvement was limited to drone missions, refueling of NATO aircraft, and logistics support. However, by the provisions of the War Powers Act (see Chapter 11), after sixty days the president was obligated to determine whether U.S. involvement constituted "hostilities," and, if it did, to inform members of Congress, who could vote on whether to continue the mission or end it.

While the final decision about whether an operation constitutes hostilities rests with the president, typically presidents have relied on the judgment of lawyers in the State Department to make this determination. In the case of Libya, these lawyers argued that the Libyan mission constituted hostilities. However, the president ignored this advice and relied on the judgment of his advisers in the Executive Office of the President, who came to the opposite conclusion, meaning that there was no need to ask Congress to pass judgment on the operation.

Many observers criticized the president's decision to overrule the judgment of his legal experts. As Speaker of the House Republican John Boehner put in, "The White House says there are no hostilities taking place. Yet we've got *drone attacks* under way. We're spending $10 million a day. We're part of an effort to drop bombs on Qaddafi's compounds. It just doesn't pass the straight-face test, in my view, that we're not in the midst of hostilities." Even leaving politics aside—the Libya operation was opposed by many Republicans, including Boehner—the episode raises an important question: If bureaucrats are experts, why shouldn't they make policy decisions, rather than leaving them up to politicians, who may know far less about the decisions they face?

The problem with bureaucratic discretion is that it cuts both ways. Allowing bureaucrats to act as they think best means that they can disregard the stated goals of legislation or the preferences of elected officials and simply implement the policies they favor. Even bureaucrats' public statements can have policy consequences—they may influence public opinion and in turn shape government policy. If experts in the bureaucracy sound

While legal experts in the State Department said that U.S. involvement in Libya in 2011 constituted "hostilities" and was therefore subject to a possible vote in Congress, the Obama administration chose to ignore the experts and follow their own plan.

the alarm, people outside government may listen and even take action in the form of protests, legal action, or other organized attempts to overturn the decision inside government. Even if their efforts are unsuccessful, the president and the people working for him or her may spend considerable time responding to public pressure.

Another down side that comes with bureaucratic discretion is that bureaucrats are unelected and most are very difficult to fire because of their civil service protections. Moreover, if bureaucrats are given a great deal of leeway to use their judgment in policy making, it becomes very difficult to determine the criteria for judging whether their removal is warranted or not. How much discretion should elected officials allow bureaucrats to use? You decide.

Critical **Thinking** Questions

1. It's easy to see why opponents of the president's policies would like to reduce political control of the bureaucracy. However, there are situations where even a president might want to reduce his or her control over bureaucratic actions. Why?

2. The benefits and costs of political control vary across the different agencies and departments that make up the bureaucracy. Where do you think the benefits are high, and where do you think they are low? What about costs?

still produce less effective policies than those constructed by bureaucrats with specialized knowledge.[77] Moreover, preventing bureaucrats from using their judgment makes it impossible for them to craft policies that take into account new developments or unforeseen circumstances.[78] Directives may also make it impossible for bureaucrats to develop and implement policies incrementally, meaning a process where new rules and regulations are developed and put in place over time as opposed to all at once.[79] Incrementalism is a good strategy to follow when policies are complex and no one is sure what the impact of new regulations will be—but directives from elected officials to develop and implement regulations as fast as possible can make this strategy impossible.

bureaucratic drift Bureaucrats' tendency to implement policies in a way that favors their own political objectives rather than following the original intentions of the legislation.

For all these reasons, elected officials must find ways to reduce or eliminate **bureaucratic drift**—that is, bureaucrats pursuing their own goals rather than their assignments from officeholders or appointees—while still reaping the benefits of bureaucratic expertise. This section describes two common strategies: changing the way agencies are organized and staffed, and using standardized procedures for monitoring agency actions. In both cases, the aim is to set up the agency so that bureaucrats can use their expertise, while making sure their actions are consistent with elected officials' wishes.[80] These measures mitigate—but do not eliminate—the problem of control discussed earlier.

AGENCY ORGANIZATION

Over the last twenty years, political scientists have shown how agencies can be organized to minimize bureaucratic drift.[81] Specifically, when an agency is set up or given new responsibilities, the officials who initiated the change don't simply tell the agency what to do. To make sure that they get the policies they want, they also determine where the agency is located within the federal government structure and who runs it. These efforts may occur solely within Congress, involve both Congress and the president, or be arranged by presidential actions.[82]

For example, when legislation was written to form the Department of Homeland Security in 2002, the Bush administration pushed to have the Coast Guard transferred out of the Department of Transportation and into the new department. This move was designed to change the Coast Guard's priorities from search and rescue operations and routine patrol to a focus on port security, without increasing its budget. The shift worked: over the next few years, the amount of effort expended by Coast Guard personnel on port security increased from a small percentage of total effort to nearly 50 percent, with a corresponding decrease in other activities.[83]

Another strategy is to impose limits on who is allowed to run the agency. In the case of the Federal Communications Commission, elected officials were concerned that the organization would adopt regulations on political advertising that favored one political party over the other. To prevent this, the legislation that created the agency mandates that it will be run by five commissioners, all of whom are nominated by the president and confirmed by the Senate.[84] However, no more than three of the commissioners can be from the same political party. As a result, if a partisan majority on the commission tries to enact laws that favor one party, opponents only need to convince one supporter to switch positions in order to block the measure. The same rule is used to select commissioners for other agencies. The Federal Election Commission has six commissioners, three Democrats and three Republicans, to guard against one party gaining control of the agency and making biased decisions.[85] In many cases, commissioners are also prohibited from having a business relationship (as a consultant, stockholder, or otherwise) with any company that is subject to their agency's rulings.

Delegation of rule-making power to an agency can also allow federal courts to review agency action.[86] One study of rule making by the Federal Communications Commission, which regulates television, radio, and other broadcasting firms, found that relying on the courts reduced the uncertainties faced by members of Congress, because they have more faith in the impartiality of federal judges than of bureaucrats or other members of Congress.

MONITORING

One of the most important ways elected officials prevent bureaucratic drift is to know what bureaucrats are doing or planning to do. Information gathering by members of Congress about bureaucratic actions is termed **oversight**. Congressional committees often hold hearings to question agency heads, secretaries of executive departments, or senior agency staff. Similarly, one of the primary responsibilities of presidential appointees is to monitor how bureaucrats are responding to presidential directives. The problem is that presidential appointees may be unable to fulfill this role. Because they are chosen for their loyalty to the president, they may lack the experience needed to fully understand what bureaucrats in their agency are doing. Moreover, given that appointees typically hold their position for only a year or two, they have little time to learn the details of agency operations.

oversight Congressional efforts to make sure that laws are implemented correctly by the bureaucracy after they have been passed.

ADVANCE WARNING

Members of Congress, the president, and his staff gain advance knowledge of bureaucratic actions through the notice and comment procedure described earlier in the chapter, which requires bureaucrats to disclose proposed changes before they take effect.[87] This delay gives opponents the opportunity to register complaints with their congressional representatives, and it allows these legislators time either to pressure the agency to revise the regulation or even to enact another law undoing or modifying the agency action.

INVESTIGATIONS: POLICE PATROLS AND FIRE ALARMS

Investigations involve Congress, legislative staff, or presidential appointees selecting some government program or office and scrutinizing the organization, its expenditures, and its activities. The two types of oversight, police patrols and fire alarms, are described in Nuts and Bolts Box 12.3. Ideally, every agency would be investigated as often as possible, with agencies that had large budgets or carried out important functions being investigated more frequently. These investigations may involve fact-finding trips to local offices, interviews with senior personnel, audits of agency accounts, and calls to the agency to see how it responds to citizens' requests. This method of investigation is called **police patrol oversight**.[88] Think of a police officer walking her beat, rattling doors to see if they are locked, checking out broken windows, and looking down alleys for suspicious behavior.

police patrol oversight A method of oversight in which members of Congress constantly monitor the bureaucracy to make sure that laws are implemented correctly.

The disadvantage of police patrol oversight is that it is costly in terms of money and staff time. Moreover, these investigations often find that agencies are doing what they should. Because of these drawbacks, Congress and the president also look outside government for information on what bureaucrats are doing. Rather than undertaking a series of investigations, they wait until they receive a complaint about bureaucratic actions, then focus investigative efforts on those cases, a practice labeled **fire alarm oversight**.[89]

fire alarm oversight A method of oversight in which members of Congress respond to complaints about the bureaucracy or problems of implementation only as they arise rather than exercising constant vigilance.

The so-called fire alarm can take many different forms. Representatives and their staff meet frequently with constituents, who may let them know of a problem with the bureaucracy. Similarly, the president and his staff are often contacted by lobbyists, corporate executives, and ordinary citizens with complaints about bureaucratic actions. Newspaper reporters and Internet bloggers also provide information on what bureaucrats are doing. Some agencies have advisory committees that not only help make agency decisions but also serve to keep Congress and the president informed about them.[90]

The case of NASA climate change scientist James Hansen described earlier provides a clear example of fire alarm oversight. The order requiring that Hansen submit all his public statements and work for review became known when it was reported by the *New York Times* and other newspapers. The resulting firestorm of protest from members of Congress forced NASA head Michael Griffin to rescind the order.

These fire alarms provide exactly the sort of information that Congress and the president often lack about how bureaucrats are implementing laws and directives, including cases when bureaucrats are doing (or planning to do) something that contradicts their mandate. Such communications tell Congress and the president where to focus their efforts to monitor the bureaucracy, drawing their attention to agencies or programs where problems have been reported, rather than trying to oversee the entire government at once.

CORRECTING VIOLATIONS

When members of Congress or the president find a case of bureaucratic drift, they can take steps to influence the bureaucrats' actions. Many tactics can be used to bring a wayward agency into line. Legislation or an executive order can send a clear directive to an agency or remove its discretion, tasks and programs can be moved to an agency more closely aligned with elected officials' goals, political appointees at an agency can be replaced, and agencies can be reorganized. For example, in the wake of the BP oil spill, there were numerous congressional hearings about proposals to reorganize the Minerals Management Service, expand its staff and budget, and refocus its mission on safety and preventing spills. In extreme situations, members of Congress can even fail to renew an agency's statutory authority, in effect putting the agency out of business.

One of the most significant difficulties in dealing with bureaucratic drift is disagreement between members of Congress and the president about whether an agency is doing the right thing—regardless of whether the agency is following its original orders. Most of the tactics discussed earlier require joint action by the president and congressional majorities. Without presidential support, members of Congress need a two-thirds majority to impose corrections. Without congressional support, the president can only threaten to cut an agency's proposed budget, change its home within the federal bureaucracy, or set up a new agency to do what

CONTROLLING THE BUREAUCRACY

▶ Explain how Congress and the president oversee the executive branch. **Pages 492–99**

SUMMARY

With their expertise, bureaucrats have the power to significantly influence government policy. This creates a dilemma for elected officials, who want to enjoy the benefits of the expertise while retaining control of the bureaucracy. Lawmakers can generally organize agencies and monitor their behavior to reduce, but not eliminate, bureaucratic drift.

KEY TERMS

bureaucratic drift (p. 494)

oversight (p. 495)

police patrol oversight (p. 495)

fire alarm oversight (p. 496)

CRITICAL THINKING AND DISCUSSION

Why might bureaucrats pay more attention to orders and directives from members of Congress than those from the president or his political appointees?

PRACTICE QUIZ QUESTIONS

13. When bureaucrats pursue their own goals rather than their assignments from officeholders, this is called

_____.

a) an iron triangle
b) regulatory capture
c) problem of control
d) turkey farming
e) bureaucratic drift

14. Giving direct orders to bureaucrats _____ the influence of their policy expertise and _____ the potential for incrementalism.

a) limits; reduces
b) increases; reduces
c) limits; increases
d) increases; increases
e) limits; had no effect on

15. While police patrol oversight has the advantage of being _____, it has the drawback of being

_____.

a) affordable; unresponsive
b) responsive; costly
c) affordable; generally unnecessary
d) responsive; unpopular
e) affordable; ineffective

Ⓢ PRACTICE ONLINE

"Big Think" video exercise: *Sen. George Mitchell on Congress and Bureaucracy*

SUGGESTED READING

Aaron, Henry J. *Politics and the Professors: The Great Society in Perspective*. Washington, DC: Brookings Institution Press, 1978.

Brehm, John, and Scott Gates. *Working, Shirking and Sabotage*. Ann Arbor: University of Michigan Press, 1998.

Carpenter, Daniel P. *The Forging of Bureaucratic Autonomy: Reputations, Networks, and Policy Innovation in Executive Agencies, 1862–1928*. Princeton, NJ: Princeton University Press, 2001.

Epstein, David, and Sharyn O'Halloran. *Delegating Powers: A Transaction Cost Politics Approach to Policy Making under Separate Powers*. New York: Cambridge University Press, 1999.

Huber, John D., and Charles R. Shipan. *Deliberate Discretion? The Institutional Foundations of Bureaucratic Autonomy*. New York: Cambridge University Press, 2002.

Lewis, David E. *The Politics of Presidential Appointments: Political Control and Bureaucratic Performance*. Princeton, NJ: Princeton University Press, 2010.

Light, Paul. *A Government Well-Executed: Public Service and Public Performance*. Washington, DC: Brookings Institution Press, 2003.

McCubbins, Mathew D., Roger G. Noll, and Barry R. Weingast. "Structure and Process as Solutions to the Politician's Principal–Agency Problem," *Virginia Law Review* 74 (1989): 431–82.

Miller, Gary. *Managerial Dilemmas: The Political Economy of Hierarchy*. New York: Cambridge University Press, 1987.

Moe, Terry M. "Political Control and the Power of the Agent." *Journal of Law, Economics, and Organization* 22 (2006): 1–21.

Nelson, Michael. "A Short, Ironic History of American National Bureaucracy." *Journal of Politics* 44 (1982): 747–78.

Skowronek, Stephen. *Building a New American State: The Expansion of National Administrative Capacities, 1877–1920*. New York: Cambridge University Press, 1982.

Wilson, James Q. *Bureaucracy: What Government Agencies Do and Why They Do It*. 2nd ed. New York: Basic Books, 2000.

13

The Courts

IN 2012, THE SUPREME COURT RULED on a controversial immigration law passed by the state of Arizona. Conflict surrounded the issue, but the Court's decision also reflected a compromise between national power and states' rights.

I N JUNE 2012, THE SUPREME COURT thrust itself into the middle of election-year politics by deciding two cases—one concerning health care reform (see Chapters 3 and 16) and one on immigration policy—that had important political implications. In the 2012–13 term, the Court was slated to hear cases on politically controversial topics, including affirmative action in higher education, same-sex marriage, and the Voting Rights Act. Scholars of the Court had to reach back to 1936 and the battles between the Court and President Franklin Roosevelt to find a comparable period in which the Court was so involved with the central political debates of the day.

In the 2012 health care and immigration cases, the Supreme Court largely ruled in favor of national power, disappointing conservatives who had hoped the Court would strike down the national laws that were involved. The Court's decision about which path to take in a given case is often very political, involving conflict, tradeoffs, and compromise, much like decision-making in Congress. That the Supreme Court is a policy-making and political institution may seem inappropriate. After all, the guiding principles of the "rule of law" in the American political system—embodied in the words carved above the entrance to the Supreme Court ("equal justice under the law") and the statue of Justice represented as a blindfolded women holding a set of scales—seem to contradict the view of a political Supreme Court. We normally think of the courts as objectively applying the law and interpreting the Constitution for each case. But the immigration and health care cases clearly represented compromises. The

CONFLICT & COMPROMISE
in American Politics

507

health care case upheld the most important part of the Affordable Care Act—the so-called individual mandate, requiring people to obtain insurance—but did so on narrower constitutional grounds than liberals wanted, while striking down the expansion of Medicaid as an unfair example of coercive federalism, which made conservatives happy. The immigration case struck down three parts of Arizona's immigration law while upholding the most controversial "show your papers" part of the law, allowing both liberals and conservatives to claim victory in the case. Politics is an inherent part of the judiciary, and a single set of objective standards is not always available for a given case.

Although we certainly expect them to be fair and objective, judges have their own political views and opinions, and these often shape their views of cases, in part *because* there are usually multiple legal justifications for any case. For example, there is no simple or clear-cut way to determine objectively the relative legal merits of Justice Scalia's dissenting view in the immigration case that "the federal executive's refusal to enforce the nation's immigration laws" opens the door for states to enforce the law or the majority view that Congress has the power to dictate immigration policy because of the supremacy clause of the Constitution. To a large extent, this depends on the justices' views of whether the supremacy clause applies in this context.

For those who resist the view that the courts are a policy-making institution, at least in the same way that Congress is, the theme "political process matters" may not seem to apply in this chapter. However, the courts often *do* make policy, and the manner in which they make decisions has an impact on outcomes. To see how political process matters for the courts, it is important to answer the following questions: What are the different roles of the courts? What is the structure of the judicial system? How do court decisions shape policy? In a nutshell, what is the nature of judicial decision making?

The role of the Supreme Court as a policy-making and political institution also illustrates the third theme of this book. On the one hand, the courts seem to resist our characterization that politics is everywhere. There is an aura of mystery and prestige to the courts that seems to isolate them from the rest of the political process. However, most Americans will come into contact with the court system at some point in their lives, whether it is to contest a traffic ticket, fight a local zoning change, or serve on a jury (we assume that you will not be on the "wrong side" of the law). The relevance of the courts in national politics is similarly self-evident. Dramatic moments, such as the *Bush v. Gore* decision that determined the 2000 presidential election and the health care reform case, are the most obvious examples of the relevance (and political nature!) of the courts. Less visible decisions that are handed down every day in the federal courts affect the lives of millions of Americans across a broad range of areas, including environmental policy, employment law, tax policy, civil rights, and civil liberties. In fact, some critics of the courts complain about an "imperial judiciary" that has become *too* powerful in the political system. This chapter examines the issues centered on the proper place of the courts within our political system. How much power should unelected judges have? Are they a necessary check on the other branches of government or a source of unaccountable power that contradicts core principles of democracy? How do the courts interact with the other branches? Before addressing these questions, we discuss how the Founders viewed the judicial system.

THE DEVELOPMENT OF AN INDEPENDENT AND POWERFUL FEDERAL JUDICIARY

> EXPLAIN HOW THE POWER OF JUDICIAL REVIEW WAS ESTABLISHED

The role of the courts in American politics and the Supreme Court's authority as the ultimate interpreter of the Constitution were not definitively established in the Constitution. The powers of the Supreme Court evolved over time, and debates about its proper role continue to this day.

THE FOUNDERS' VIEWS OF THE COURTS: THE WEAKEST BRANCH?

The Federalists and Antifederalists did not see eye-to-eye on much, and the judiciary was no exception. Alexander Hamilton, writing in *Federalist 78*, said that the Supreme Court would be "beyond comparison the weakest of the three departments of power." In contrast, the author of the *Antifederalist Papers* wrote, "The supreme court under this constitution would be exalted above all other power in the government and subjected to no control."[1] Hmmm, which is it, weakest or strongest? While the framers could not agree on the likely relative power of the Court, there was surprisingly little debate at the Constitutional Convention about the judiciary. Article III of the Constitution created one Supreme Court and gave the courts independence by providing federal judges with lifetime terms (assuming "good behavior").

The main disagreements about the judiciary had to do with how independent the courts should be vis-à-vis the other branches of government and how much power to give the courts. Some of the framers feared a tyrannical Congress and wanted to create a judicial and executive branch that could check this power. Others argued for making the executive and judicial branches more closely related so they would be better able to balance Congress. A central debate was whether to give the judiciary some "revisionary power" over Congress, similar to the president's veto power. This idea of judicial review would have given the Supreme Court the power to strike down laws passed by Congress that violated the Constitution. The framers could not agree on judicial review, so the Constitution remained silent on the matter. As the power of judicial review has evolved, it has become a central part of the system of checks and balances (see Chapter 2).

Many details about the Supreme Court were left up to Congress, including its size, the time and place it would meet, and its internal organization. These details, and the system of lower federal courts, were outlined in the **Judiciary Act of 1789**. This law set the number of justices at six (one chief justice and five associates). The number of justices gradually increased to ten by the end of the Civil War and was then restricted to seven under Reconstruction policies. The number was set at nine in 1869, where it has remained since.[2] The 1789 Act also created a system of federal courts, which included thirteen **district courts** and three circuit courts—the intermediate-level courts that heard appeals from the district courts. The district courts each had one judge; the circuits comprised two Supreme Court justices and one district judge. This odd arrangement for staffing the circuit courts remained in place for more than 100 years, over the objections of the justices who resented having to "ride circuit" in difficult traveling conditions.[3] Today, separate judges are appointed to fill the circuit courts (what we call "appeals courts"). Furthermore, the act refined the jurisdiction of the federal courts. One controversial provision was Section 25, which expanded the Court's **appellate jurisdiction** (cases heard on appeal from lower courts) to include state supreme court cases involving conflicts between state law and federal law or treaties or the U.S. Constitution.

The Supreme Court had a rough start. Indeed, it seemed determined to prove Alexander Hamilton right that it was the weakest branch. Of the six original justices appointed by George Washington, one declined to serve and another never showed up for a formal session. The Court's first sessions lasted only a few days because it did not have much business. In fact, the Court did not decide a single case in 1791 or 1792. When Justice Rutledge resigned in 1791 to take a state court position, two potential appointees turned down the job in order to keep their positions in their state legislatures! Such career decisions would be unimaginable today, when serving on the Supreme Court is considered the pinnacle of a legal career.[4]

Judiciary Act of 1789 The law in which Congress laid out the organization of the federal judiciary. The law refined and clarified federal court jurisdiction and set the original number of justices at six. It also created the Office of the Attorney General and established the lower federal courts.

district courts Lower-level trial courts of the federal judicial system that handle most U.S. federal cases.

appellate jurisdiction The authority of a court to hear appeals from lower courts and change or uphold the decision.

JUDICIAL REVIEW AND *MARBURY V. MADISON*

The Court started to gain more power when John Marshall was appointed chief justice in 1801. Marshall single-handedly transformed the Court into an equal partner in the system of checks and balances. The most important step was the decision *Marbury v. Madison* (1803), which gave the Supreme Court the power of **judicial review**. As noted earlier, the framers were split on the wisdom of giving

judicial review The Supreme Court's power to strike down a law or executive branch action that it finds unconstitutional.

the Court the power to strike down laws passed by Congress; therefore the Constitution does not explicitly address the issue. However, historians have established that a majority of the framers, including the most influential ones, favored judicial review. Given the silence of the Constitution, Marshall simply asserted that the Supreme Court had the power to determine when a law was unconstitutional.

The facts and legal reasoning behind *Marbury* are worth explaining because this is one of the most important court cases in American history. The Federalists had just lost the election of 1800 to Thomas Jefferson and the Democratic-Republicans. In a last-minute power grab, the Federalist-controlled lame-duck Congress gave outgoing President Adams an opportunity to appoint forty-two new justices of the peace for the District of Columbia and Alexandria, Virginia. Adams made the appointments, and the Senate confirmed them, but time ran out before the new administration took over, and the secretary of state, John Marshall, did not ensure that all legal documents concerning the appointments were delivered by midnight (the same Marshall who had just been confirmed as chief justice). When President Jefferson assumed office, his secretary of state, James Madison, ordered that several of the documents not be delivered because of partisan differences with the outgoing administration. William Marbury was one of the people who did not receive his commission, so he asked the Supreme Court to issue an order giving him the position.

As leading figures in opposing parties, Chief Justice Marshall and President Jefferson did not like each other. This put Marshall in a difficult position. He was concerned that if he issued the order that Marbury wanted (giving Marbury his job), Jefferson probably would ignore it (technically, Secretary of State Madison was the other party in the lawsuit, but Jefferson was calling the shots). Given the weakness of the Court, having such an order disregarded by the president could have been a final blow to its position in the national government. However, if the Court did not issue the order, it would be giving in to Jefferson despite the merits of Marbury's case—he really had been cheated out of his job. It appeared that the Court would lose whether it issued the order or not.

To get out of the mess, Marshall established the idea of judicial review. Although the idea was not original to Marshall (as noted, the framers debated the issue and Hamilton endorsed it in some detail in *Federalist 78*), the Court had never exercised its authority to rule on the constitutionality of a federal law. Marshall's reasoning was quite clever: the Court's opinion said that Marbury was due his commission, but the Court did not have the power to give him his job because the part of the Judiciary Act of 1789 that gave it that power was unconstitutional! The core issue was Section 13 of the act, which gave the Court the power to issue orders (writs of mandamus) to anyone holding federal office. This section expanded the **original jurisdiction** of the Supreme Court, and that was where Congress overstepped its bounds, according to Marshall. The original jurisdiction of the Court is clearly specified in the Constitution, so any attempt by Congress to change that jurisdiction through legislation would be unconstitutional; the only way to change original jurisdiction would be through a constitutional amendment.[5] Marshall writes, "It is emphatically the province and duty of the judicial department to say what the law is. . . . If two laws conflict with each other, the courts must decide on the operation of each. So if a law be in opposition to the Constitution . . . the courts must determine which of these conflicting rules governs the case. This is of the very essence of judicial duty."[6]

original jurisdiction The authority of a court to handle a case first, as in the Supreme Court's authority to initially hear disputes between two states. However, original jurisdiction for the Supreme Court is not exclusive; it may assign such a case to a lower court.

CHIEF JUSTICE JOHN MARSHALL favored the idea of judicial review and claimed this power for the Court in the *Marbury v. Madison* decision.

JURISDICTION OF THE FEDERAL COURTS AS DEFINED IN ARTICLE III OF THE CONSTITUTION

JURISDICTION OF LOWER FEDERAL COURTS

▶ Cases involving the U.S. Constitution, federal laws, and treaties.

▶ Controversies between two or more states. (Congress passed a law giving the Supreme Court exclusive jurisdiction over these cases.)

▶ Controversies between citizens of different states.

▶ Controversies between a state and citizens of another state. (The Eleventh Amendment removed federal jurisdiction in these cases.)

▶ Controversies between a state or its citizens and any foreign states, citizens, or subjects.

▶ Cases affecting ambassadors, public ministers, and consuls.

▶ Cases of admiralty and maritime jurisdictions.

▶ Controversies between citizens of the same state claiming lands under grants of different states.

JURISDICTION OF THE SUPREME COURT

Original Jurisdiction[a]

▶ Cases involving ambassadors, public ministers, and consuls.

▶ Cases to which a state is a party.

Appellate Jurisdiction

▶ Cases falling under the jurisdiction of the lower federal courts, "with such exceptions, and under such Regulations as the Congress shall make."

[a]*This does not imply exclusive jurisdiction. For example, the Supreme Court may refer to a district court a case involving an ambassador (the more likely outcome).*

Source: Lee Epstein and Thomas G. Walker, Constitutional Law for a Changing America: Institutional Powers and Constraints, *5th ed. (Washington, DC: CQ Press, 2004), p. 65.*

JUDICIAL REVIEW IN PRACTICE

Chief Justice Marshall lost the battle—poor Mr. Marbury never did get his job, and Jefferson appointed the people he wanted to be justices of the peace—but the Supreme Court won the war. By asserting its power to review the constitutionality of laws passed by Congress, the Court became an equal partner in the institutional balance of power. Although it would be more than fifty years until the Court would use judicial review again to strike down a law passed by Congress (in the unfortunate 1857 *Dred Scott* case concerning slavery that basically led to the Civil War), the reasoning behind *Marbury* has never been challenged by subsequent presidents or Congresses.[7]

Interpreting federal laws may be seem a logical responsibility for the Supreme Court, but what about state laws? Should the Supreme Court have final say over them as well? The Constitution does not answer this question. However, the supremacy clause requires that the Constitution and national laws take precedence over state constitutions and state laws when they conflict. The Judiciary Act of 1789 made it clear that the Supreme Court would rule on these matters.

It didn't take long for the Court to assert its power in this area. In 1796 the Court heard a case concerning a British creditor who was trying to collect a debt from the state of Virginia. The state had passed a law canceling all debts owed by Virginians (or the state) to British subjects. However, the Treaty of Paris, which ended the Revolutionary War and recognized American independence, ensured the collection of such debts. This conflict was resolved when the Court struck down the state law and upheld Americans' commitments under the treaty.[8] Advocates of states' rights were not happy with this development, but it was crucial for the national government that the Constitution be applied uniformly rather than be subject to different interpretations by every state.

The contours of the relationship between the national government and the states were largely defined by how active the Supreme Court was in asserting judicial review and how willing it was to intervene in matters of state law. For much of the nineteenth century the Court embraced dual federalism, in which the national government and the states operated on two separate levels (see Chapter 3). Later the Court involved itself more in state law as it moved toward a more active role for the national government in regulating interstate commerce and using the Fourteenth Amendment to selectively incorporate the amendments that constitute the Bill of Rights (see Chapter 4).

All in all, the Court has struck down more than 170 acts of Congress and about 1,400 state laws. This sounds like a lot, but Congress passed more than 60,000 laws in its first 220 years, so only about one-quarter of 1 percent have been struck down by the Court. The number of state laws passed throughout history is more difficult to measure, but the percentage of state laws that have been struck down is also quite small. Over time the Court has ruled on state laws in many important areas, including civil liberties, desegregation and civil rights, abortion, privacy, redistricting, labor laws, employment and discrimination, and business and environmental regulation.

When the Supreme Court strikes down a congressional or state law, it engages in **constitutional interpretation**—that is, it determines that the law is unconstitutional. But the Supreme Court also engages in **statutory interpretation**—that is, it applies national and state laws to particular cases (statutes are laws that are passed by legislatures). Often the language of a statute may be unclear, and the Court must interpret how to apply the law. For example, should the protection of endangered species prevent economic development that may destroy the species' habitat? How does one determine if an employer is responsible for sexual harassment in the workplace? How should the voting rights of minorities be protected? In each case, the Court must interpret the relevant statutes to determine what Congress really meant. In addition, the Court is sometimes required to assess the appropriateness of statutory interpretation by federal agencies that are responsible for implementing the laws. Often, this involves the controversial practice of consulting legislative histories—floor debates, congressional hearings, and so on—to determine legislative intent. Justice Antonin Scalia argues that such searches are inherently subjective and that justices should only interpret the actual statutory text.

Although politicians and other political actors accept judicial review as a central part of the political system, critics are concerned about its antidemocratic nature. Why, for example, do we give nine unelected justices such awesome power over our elected representatives? Debates about the proper role for the Court will

constitutional interpretation The process of determining whether a piece of legislation or governmental action is supported by the Constitution.

statutory interpretation The various methods and tests used by the courts for determining the meaning of a law and applying it to specific situations. Congress may overturn the courts' interpretation by writing a new law; thus it also engages in statutory interpretation.

THE USE OF JUDICIAL REVIEW

From the time the ancient Greek philosopher Plato examined the various rules of Greek city-states to come up with his ideal legal institutions, scholars and philosophers have described and categorized judicial systems. However, the practice of judicial review is a much more recent development. The early precursor to judicial review goes as far back as 1180 in the old German Reich, where judicial bodies dealt with disputes between individual rulers. However, the modern practice of judicial review, in which a high court strikes down a law of the national government, was first used by the U.S. Supreme Court with *Marbury v. Madison* in 1803.

The practice was slow to take hold in the rest of the democratic world. One exception was Latin America. When the Spanish colonies gained independence, many adopted judicial review based on the U.S. example.[a] A recent study of judicial review explains why European nations did not go this route, with this summary of British thinking on the subject: "Parliament had the 'right to make or unmake any law whatever; and further, that no person or body is recognized by the law of England as having a right to override or set aside the legislation of Parliament.'"[b] This thinking dominated Europe through the nineteenth and early twentieth centuries, as legislatures were seen as the truest expression of the will of the people. Today Great Britain remains one of the few democracies in which courts do not have judicial review of national legislation (though the House of Lords and the European Court of Justice can review the laws of Parliament).

Norway, Denmark, Greece, Austria, and Switzerland implemented versions of judicial review in the late nineteenth century, and then between the world wars several other European nations adopted the Austrian model.[c] Following World War II, more European nations began to view the Constitution as supreme rather than the Parliament and adopted the European (or "continental") version of judicial review. There are several important differences between the American and European models of judicial review. Rather than integrating judicial review within the court system, the European model has a separate, specialized constitutional court. The European constitutional court may act preemptively before a law has taken effect, it does not have to respond to a specific concrete case, and a much broader range of parties can ask for a constitutional review, including politicians and the other courts (even if they would not have standing in the American model).[d]

Judicial review has spread dramatically during the "third wave" of democracy. Unlike our hybrid system of checks and balances and separation of powers, which has been largely shunned by established and emerging democracies in favor of the parliamentary form of government, judicial review has become an important American export. As one scholar put it, "the world seems to have been seized by a craze for constitutionalization and judicial review."[e] Of the seventy nations that became democratic between 1986 and 2000,

Pakistani lawyers and party activists hold portraits of the deposed chief justice of the Supreme Court in May 2008. Then-president Pervez Musharraf sacked forty-one judges because of challenges to his controversial reelection, sparking a nationwide protest and demands for an independent judiciary. The controversy contributed to Musharraf's decision to resign in August 2008.

twenty-nine have some form of judicial review by the courts, adopting a mix of the American and European models (in eight of those nations, judicial review is shared with another special body), twenty-four have judicial review by a special body, and only seventeen have limitations on judicial review.[f] Of course, many of these nations have judicial review in name only, as the courts are largely compliant with the dominant regime. Nonetheless, the idea of a court that can check the power of the elected branches of government, especially to protect the political rights of the minority, has become an increasingly important component of democratic governance.

continue as long as it is involved in controversial decisions. We take up this question later in the chapter when we address the concepts of judicial activism and judicial restraint.

THE AMERICAN LEGAL AND JUDICIAL SYSTEM

OUTLINE THE STRUCTURE OF THE COURT SYSTEM

Two sets of considerations are necessary to understand the overall nature of our judicial system: the fundamentals of the legal system that apply to all courts in the United States, and the structure of the court system within our system of federalism.

COURT FUNDAMENTALS

The general characteristics of the court system begin with the people who are in the courtroom. The **plaintiff** brings the case, and the **defendant** is the person or party who is being sued or charged with a crime. If the case is appealed, the petitioner is the person bringing the appeal, and the respondent is on the other side of the case. In a civil case, the plaintiff sues to determine who is right or wrong and to gain something of value, such as monetary damages, the right to vote, or admission to a university. For example, imagine that your neighbor accidentally backs his car into the fence that divides your property, destroying a large section of it. The neighbor does not have adequate insurance to cover the damages and refuses to pay for the repairs. You do not want to pay the $1,000 deductible on your insurance policy, so you (the plaintiff) sue your neighbor (the defendant) to see whether your neighbor has to pay for the repairs. In a criminal case, the plaintiff is the government, and the prosecutor attempts to prove the guilt of the defendant (the person accused of the crime).

Many, but not all, civil and criminal cases are heard before a jury that decides the outcome in the case, which is called the verdict. Often cases get settled before they go to trial (or even in the middle of the trial) in a process known as **plea bargaining**. In a civil case, this would mean that the plaintiff and defendant agree on a monetary settlement and admission of guilt (or not; in some cases the defendant may agree to pay a fine or damages but not to admit guilt). In a criminal case, the defendant may agree to plead guilty in exchange for receiving a shorter sentence or being charged with a lesser crime. Plea bargaining is an excellent example of how legal conflict between two parties can be resolved through a compromise that is satisfactory to both sides.

plaintiff The person or party who brings a case to court.

defendant The person or party against whom a case is brought.

plea bargain An agreement between a plaintiff and defendant to settle a case before it goes to trial or the verdict is decided. In a civil case this usually involves an admission of guilt and an agreement on monetary damages; in a criminal case it often involves an admission of guilt in return for a reduced charge or sentence.

DIFFERENCES BETWEEN CIVIL AND CRIMINAL CASES

There are important differences between civil and criminal cases. One is the standard of proof that serves to determine the outcome of the case. In civil cases the jury has to determine whether the "preponderance of evidence"—that is, a majority

O. J. SIMPSON DONS A PAIR OF GLOVES during testimony in his double-murder trial in Los Angeles in June 1995. The jury was not convinced of his guilt "beyond all reasonable doubt" and thus acquitted Simpson in this criminal trial. However, a subsequent civil trial found that a "preponderance of evidence" was against him.

class-action lawsuit A case brought by a group of individuals on behalf of themselves and others in the general public who are in similar circumstances.

common law Law based on the precedent of previous court rulings rather than on legislation. It is used in all federal courts and forty-nine of the fifty state courts.

precedent A legal norm established in court cases that is then applied to future cases dealing with the same legal questions.

of the evidence—proves that the plaintiff wins. In a criminal case, a much stiffer burden must be met—"beyond all reasonable doubt."

Another difference is where the burden of proof lies. In criminal cases there is a presumption of "innocent until proven guilty." That is, the state must prove the guilt of the defendant. However, in civil cases the burden of proof may be on the plaintiff or the defendant, depending on the law that governs the case. Even more complicated, in civil cases the plaintiff may have to prove certain points and the defendant other points. For example, in certain race-based voting rights cases, the plaintiff would have to prove that race was the predominant motivation for creating a black-majority congressional district. If that point is demonstrated, then the burden of proof shifts to the defendant to show that there was some "compelling state interest" to justify the use of race as a predominant factor.

One type of civil suit is the **class-action lawsuit**, a case brought by a group of individuals on behalf of themselves and others in similar circumstances. The target may be a corporation that produced hazardous or defective products, or that engaged in illegal behavior that harmed a particular group. For example, 1.5 million current and former female Wal-Mart employees sued the retailing giant for sex discrimination, claiming that the store has paid women less than men for the same work and has promoted fewer women than men.[9] Suits are often filed on behalf of shareholders of companies that have lost value because of fraud committed by corporate leaders. Cases like these are a very important mechanism for providing accountability and justice in our economic system. Federal regulators do not have the ability to ensure the complete safety of food, drugs, and consumer products or to continually monitor all potential business fraud. Therefore, consumers rely on the legal system and class-action lawsuits to ensure that businesses act fairly and produce safe products.

COMMON ELEMENTS OF THE JUDICIAL SYSTEM

Several characteristics of the judicial system apply to all cases. First, ours is an adversarial system in which lawyers on both sides have an opportunity to present their case, challenge the testimony of the opposing side, and try to convince the court that their version of the events is true. The process of "discovery," in which both sides share the information that will be presented in court, ensures a fair process and few last-minute surprises. Second, forty-nine of the fifty states and the federal courts operate under a system of **common law**, which means that legal decisions build from precedent established in previous cases and apply commonly throughout the jurisdiction of the court. The alternative, which is practiced only in Louisiana, is the civil law tradition that is based on a detailed codification of the law that is applied to each specific case. Common law is the most general way of describing how judges make their decisions and encompasses the three main areas of American law: constitutional, statutory, and administrative. The first two were described earlier and administrative law refers to court decisions concerning the administrative agencies that implement policy.

The notion of **precedent** (or stare decisis—"let the decision stand") deserves special attention. Precedent is a previously decided case or set of decisions that serves as a guide for future cases on the same topic. Lower courts are bound by Supreme Court decisions when there is a clear precedent that is relevant for a given case. In many cases, following precedent is not clear-cut because several precedents may seem relevant. The lower courts have considerable discretion in sorting out which precedents are the most important. The Supreme Court tries to follow its own precedents, but in the past fifty years justices have been willing to deviate from earlier decisions when they think that the precedent is flawed. As Table 13.1 shows, the Court has overruled more than twice as many decisions since 1953 than in the previous 164 years. Part of this can be explained by the relatively small number of precedents that *could* have been overturned in the first few decades of our nation's history. But even accounting for the natural accumulation of more precedents to potentially overturn, recent courts have been much more willing to deviate from precedent than previous courts. As this record indicates, precedent is not a rule the Court must follow but a norm that constrains its behavior.

TABLE » 13.1

SUPREME COURT CASES OVERRULING PRECEDENT AND ACTS OF CONGRESS, 1789–2011

The Supreme Court has overruled precedent in a far higher proportion of cases in the past 60 years than it did during the first 160 years of U.S. history. More acts of Congress have also been struck down in recent years—but even in some earlier periods, the Court has played an activist role. What do these data say about the role of the Supreme Court within our constitutional system?

COURT (CHIEF JUSTICE)	YEARS	CASES OVERRULING PRECEDENT	PRECEDENTS OVERRULED	CASES OVERRULING ACTS OF CONGRESS	ACTS OVERRULED PER YEAR
Jay Court	1789–1795	0	0	0	0
Rutledge Court	1795	0	0	0	0
Ellsworth Court	1796–1800	0	0	0	0
Marshall Court	1801–1836	1	1	1	0.03
Taney Court	1836–1864	2	3	1	0.03
Chase Court	1864–1874	1	1	8	0.8
Waite Court	1874–1888	9	11	7	0.5
Fuller Court	1888–1910	3	4	13	0.52
White Court	1910–1921	4	4	10	1.1
Taft Court	1921–1930	5	6	13	1.44
Hughes Court	1930–1941	15	22	15	1.36
Stone Court	1941–1946	8	11	1	0.20
Vinson Court	1946–1953	6	11	2	0.28
Warren Court	1953–1969	37	53	23	1.44
Burger Court	1969–1986	46	62	31	1.82
Rehnquist Court	1986–2005	38	44	35	1.84
Roberts Court	2005–present	8	n.a.	8	1.3

Note: This table includes only cases in which the reversal of precedent is clearly stated in the Court decision. A single case can overrule more than one precedent.

Source: For 1789–2003, David G. Savage, Guide to the Supreme Court, 4th ed. (Washington, DC: CQ Press, 2004), pp. 320, 1192–1204. For 2004–2011, The Supreme Court Database, Washington University, http://scdb.wustl.edu (accessed 10/2/12).

standing Legitimate justification for bringing a civil case to court.

Two more points must be considered before a case is filed. First, the person bringing the case must have **standing** to sue in a civil case, which means that the person has a legitimate basis for bringing the case. This usually means that the individual has suffered some direct and personal harm from the action addressed in the court case. Standing is easy to establish for private parties—for example, if your neighbor destroys your fence, you have been harmed. However, it gets more interesting when the government is a party. For example, when an environmental group challenged the Interior Department's interpretation of the Endangered Species Act, the Court ruled that it did not have standing because it did not demonstrate that the government's policy would cause "imminent" injury to the group.[10] Similarly the Court has ruled that thirty-one members of Congress did not have standing to challenge American bombing in Kosovo and that taxpayers do not have standing to sue the government if they disagree with a specific policy.[11] Depending on your politics, you may not want your hard-earned cash going to buy school lunches for poor children or to fund the war in Afghanistan. However, your status as a taxpayer does not give you enough of a personal stake in these policies to challenge them in court. You would not have standing. As we discuss below in the section on how cases get to the Supreme Court, justices have some leeway in defining standing.

jurisdiction The sphere of a court's legal authority to hear and decide cases.

The final general characteristic of the legal system is the **jurisdiction** of the court—when bringing a case before the court, you must choose a court that actually has the power to hear your case. A simple example: if you want to contest a speeding ticket, you would not file your case in the state supreme court or the federal district court, but in your local traffic court. What if you believed you were the victim of discrimination in the workplace? Would you sue in state or federal court? You probably could do either, but the decision would be based on which set of laws would provide you more protection from discrimination. This varies by state, so the proper jurisdiction for a given case is often a judgment call based on specific legal questions (this practice of seeking the best court for your case is called "venue shopping").

STRUCTURE OF THE COURT AND FEDERALISM

The structure of the court system is like the rest of the political system: it is divided within and across levels of government. Across the levels of government, the court system operates on two parallel tracks within the state and local courts and the national courts. Within each level of government, both tracks include courts of original jurisdiction, appeals courts, and courts of special jurisdiction. As shown in the "How It Works" diagram, the state courts are entirely separate from the federal courts, with the exception of the small proportion of cases that are appealed from a state supreme court to the U.S. Supreme Court. There is much variation in the structure of state courts in terms of their names and the number of levels of courts. However, they all follow the same general pattern of trial courts with limited and general original jurisdiction and appeals courts (either one or two levels, depending on the state).

DISTRICT COURTS

The Judiciary Act of 1789 created the lower federal courts. Workhorses of the federal system, the district courts handle more than a quarter of a million filings a year. There are eighty-nine districts in the fifty states, with at least one district court for each state. There are also district courts in Puerto Rico, the Virgin Islands, the District of Columbia, Guam, and the Northern Mariana Islands

THE COURT SYSTEM

If federal question

FINAL APPEALS COURTS

State Supreme Courts
About 85,000 cases in 50 courts.

United States Supreme Court
Received 7,857 filings for the 2010–11 term; 86 cases argued; 83 disposed of in 75 signed opinions.*

INTERMEDIATE APPEALS COURTS

Courts of Appeals
300,000 cases in the 38 states with courts of appeals.

U.S. Courts of Appeals
12 regional courts and the U.S. Court of Appeals for the Federal Circuit; decided 55,126 cases in 2010–11.

TRIAL COURTS

TRIAL COURTS OF LIMITED AND SPECIAL JURISDICTION

Examples: Juvenile Court, Traffic Court, Small Claims Court, Justice of the Peace, Family Court.

TRIAL COURTS OF GENERAL AND ORIGINAL JURISDICTION

District Courts, County Courts, Municipal Courts
About 90 million filing in state and local courts of original jurisdiction.

TRIAL COURTS OF GENERAL AND ORIGINAL JURISDICTION

94 District Courts
Decided 289,252 civil cases and 78,440 criminal cases in 2010–11.

TRIAL COURTS OF LIMITED AND SPECIAL JURISDICTION

Examples: Federal Claims Court, Tax Court, Court of International Trade, Court of Veterans Appeals.

STATE AND LOCAL COURTS

FEDERAL COURTS

*Data on federal courts are from the U.S. Supreme Court, "2011 Year-End Report on the Federal Judiciary," www.supremecourt.gov/publicinfo/year-end/2011year-endreport.pdf (accessed 9/5/12).

POP QUIZ!

1 If you are convicted in a U.S. district court and want to appeal the ruling, with which court would you file an appeal?

 a the state supreme court

 b the state court of appeals

 c the U.S. court of appeals for your region

 d the U.S. Supreme Court

 e none of the above

2 If your case is heard by your state supreme court and you want to appeal the decision, with which court would you file an appeal?

 a the trial court of original jurisdiction

 b the state court of appeals

 c the U.S. court of appeals for your region

 d the U.S. Supreme Court (if the case involves a federal question)

 e none of the above

to bring the total to ninety-four districts with 678 judges.[12] There are two limited jurisdiction district courts: the Court of International Trade, which addresses cases involving international trade and customs issues, and the U.S. Court of Federal Claims, which handles most claims for money damages against the United States, disputes over federal contracts, unlawful "takings" of private property by the federal government, and other claims against the United States.

APPEALS COURTS

appeals courts The intermediate level of federal courts that hear appeals from district courts. More generally, an appeals court is any court with appellate jurisdiction.

The **appeals courts** (called "circuit courts" until 1948) are the intermediate courts of appeals, but in practice they are the final court for most federal cases that are appealed from the lower courts. The losing side in a federal case can appeal to the Supreme Court, but given that the highest court in the land hears so few cases, the appeals courts usually get the final word. Appeals courts did not always have this much power; in fact, through much of the nineteenth century they had very limited appellate jurisdiction and did not hear many significant cases.

The only real effort to create an independent set of federal appellate courts in the first 100 years of our nation's history was the aborted effort by the outgoing Adams administration in 1800. As part of the Federalists' plan to stack the federal courts (recall the maneuver with the justice of peace positions that led to *Marbury v. Madison*), the Federalists created eighteen appeals court judgeships that were filled at the last minute by President Adams and a sympathetic Senate. Rather than allow the Federalists to have that much power over the federal courts, the incoming Jefferson administration and the Democratic-Republican Congress simply abolished these courts the next year. (The move may have been in violation of the constitutional mandate of life tenure for federal judges, but that was a fight that Chief Justice Marshall did not want to take on.)

In 1869 the circuit courts finally were given some of their own judges rather than being staffed entirely by district court judges and Supreme Court justices.[13] The Judiciary Act of 1891 created nine regional circuit courts and expanded their appellate jurisdiction to include most cases from the district courts. This process of expanding the power of the appeals courts was largely completed in the 1925 Judiciary Act.[14] Today the only appeals of district court cases that go directly to the Supreme Court and bypass the appeals court are cases that concern legislative reapportionment and redistricting, voting rights, and some issues related to the 1964 Civil Rights Act.[15]

The number of appeals courts slowly expanded as the workload grew, to the current twelve regional courts (the eleven numbered districts shown in Figure 13.1, plus the appeals court for the District of Columbia) and the Court of Appeals for the Federal Circuit, which handles specialized cases from all over the country. The smallest of the regional appeals courts is the First Circuit, which has six judges, and the largest is the Ninth Circuit with twenty-nine judges.[16] In 2011, there were 179 appeals court judges and 92 "senior judges" (these numbers include the twelve judges and five senior judges of the appeals court for the federal circuit).[17] Senior judges are semi-retired judges who hear certain cases to help out with the overall federal court system workload; they typically handle about 15 percent of the workload for the federal court system.

THE SUPREME COURT

The Supreme Court sits at the top of the federal court system. The rest of this chapter outlines many important aspects of the Court, including how cases get to the Court, nominations, decision making, and relations with the other branches.

FIGURE » 13.1

MAP OF THE FEDERAL APPEALS COURTS

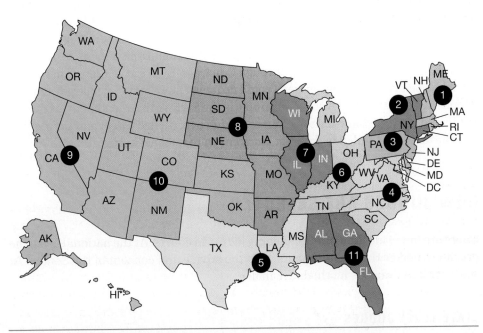

Source: U.S. Courts, Circuit Map, www.uscourts.gov/courtlinks (accessed 10/5/12).

The immediate discussion concerns the Court's place within the judicial system and its relationship to the other courts.

The Supreme Court is the "court of last resort" for cases coming from both the state and the federal courts. One important function of the Court is to ensure that the application and interpretation of the Constitution is consistent nationwide by resolving conflicts between lower courts, or between a state law and federal law, or between the states. For example, before the Court took up the issue of affirmative action in higher education, there were several conflicting lower court decisions, which meant that affirmative action was legal in certain parts of the country and unconstitutional in other parts. A district court or appeals court ruling is applicable only for the specific region of that court, whereas Supreme Court rulings apply to the entire country.

Although the Supreme Court is the most important interpreter of the Constitution, the president and Congress also interpret the Constitution on a regular basis. This means that the Supreme Court does not always have the final say. For example, if the Court strikes down a federal law for being overly vague, Congress can rewrite the law to clarify the offending passage. When this happens, Congress may have the final word. For example, Congress overturned *Ledbetter v. Goodyear Tire and Rubber* (2007) when it passed the "Lilly Ledbetter Fair Pay Act" in 2009. The law said that the Supreme Court had misinterpreted the 1964 Civil Rights Act when it ruled that Ledbetter would have had to file her pay discrimination suit within 180 days of being hired.[18]

Even on matters of constitutional interpretation rather than statutory interpretation, Congress can fight back by passing a constitutional amendment. However, this is a difficult and time-consuming process; hundreds of amendments are proposed every year, but very few even get a hearing or come to a vote in Congress, and even fewer are passed and submitted to the states for ratification (see Chapter 2). Nevertheless, that option is available as a way of overturning an unpopular Court decision. Perhaps the best example of this is the very first major case ever decided by the Supreme Court—*Chisholm v. Georgia* (1793). This case upheld the right of a citizen of one state to sue another state in federal court. The states were shocked by this challenge to their sovereignty, and a constitutional amendment to overturn the decision quickly made its way through Congress. By 1795 the Eleventh Amendment had been ratified, and citizens could no longer sue a state (in federal court) in which they did not live.[19] Another example is the Sixteenth Amendment, authorizing income taxes from whatever source, which overturned a decision saying that income taxes on dividends, interest, and rent were unconstitutional.[20]

HOW JUDGES ARE SELECTED

There are many mechanisms for placing judges in courts. At the national level, the president makes the appointments with the advice and consent of the Senate. At the state level, various methods are in use.

STATE-LEVEL JUDGES

At the state level judges are selected for trial courts in five different ways: appointment by the governor (two states), appointment by the state legislature (two states), partisan elections (nine states), nonpartisan elections (seventeen states), and the system called the Missouri Plan in which the governor makes appointments from a list compiled by a nonpartisan screening committee (seventeen states; four more states use the Missouri Plan for some courts and another means for other courts).[21] With this last method, the appointed judge usually has to run in a retention election within several years of the appointment, making this system a hybrid of the political nomination and popular election routes to the court.

There is some controversy over the wisdom of electing judges. They may undermine the courts' role as the protector of unpopular minority rights, and even in states where judicial elections are officially nonpartisan, it is clear who the liberal and conservative candidates are, so judicial elections can be very partisan. Interest groups often get involved by making endorsements or running their own advertisements for or against the judicial candidates. Electing judges also raises the potential for conflicts of interest if campaign contributors have cases before the court (see, for example, the case involving the West Virginia state supreme court and $3 million in campaign spending by a coal company which had a case pending before the court).[22] On the other hand, elected judges will be more responsive to public opinion, especially on salient issues such as the death penalty[23] and abortion.[24] Furthermore, the alternative to elections—appointing judges—has been criticized as elitist by giving power over nominations to lawyers and for claiming that the process is "merit-based" without much evidence.[25]

FEDERAL JUDGES

The Constitution does not specify requirements for serving on the federal courts, unlike the detailed stipulations for Congress and the president. Federal judges don't even have to have a law degree! (This is probably due to the limited number of law schools at the time of the Founding; someone who wanted to be a lawyer usually would have served as an apprentice to learn the trade.) The president appoints federal judges with the "advice and consent" of the Senate (the Senate must approve the nominees with a majority vote).

Nomination battles for federal judges can be intense because the stakes are high. As the discussion of judicial review made clear, the Supreme Court plays a central role in the policy process, and because a justice has life tenure, a justice's impact can outlive the president and Senate who put him or her on the Court. The justices often serve for decades, much longer than the people who appoint them.

THE ROLE OF THE PRESIDENT

Given the Constitution's silence on the qualification of federal judges, presidents have broad discretion over whom to nominate. Presidents have always tried to influence the direction of the federal courts and especially the Supreme Court by picking people who share their views. Because the Senate often has different ideas about the proper direction for the Court, nomination disputes end up being a combination of debates over the merit of a nominee and of partisan battles about the ideological composition of the Court.

Although presidents would *like* to influence the direction of the Court, it is not always possible to predict how judges will behave once they are on the Court. Earl Warren is a good example. He was appointed by Republican president Dwight Eisenhower and had been the Republican governor of California, yet he turned out to be one of the most liberal chief justices in the last century. Eisenhower called Warren's nomination the biggest mistake he ever made.[26] Former justices Brennan, Souter, and Stevens were nominated by Republican presidents but regularly voted with the liberal bloc.

The president can make a good guess about how a justice is likely to vote based on the nominee's party affiliation and the nature of his or her legal writings and decisions (if the nominee has prior judicial experience). Not surprisingly, 98 of 108 justices who have served on the Court have shared the president's party (just over 90 percent). Overall, more than 90 percent of the lower court judges appointed by presidents in the twentieth century have also belonged to the same party as the president.

The most partisan move to influence the Court was President Franklin Delano Roosevelt's infamous plan to pack the Court. FDR was frustrated because the Court had struck down several pieces of important New Deal legislation, so to get a more sympathetic Court he proposed nominating a new justice for every justice who was over seventy years old. Six justices were over seventy, so this would have increased the size of the Court to fifteen. This effort to disguise the partisan power play as a humanitarian gesture (to help the old-timers with their workload) didn't fool anyone. The plan to pack the Court ran into opposition, but in the so-called switch in time that saved nine, the Court started ruling in favor of the New Deal legislation, so the plan was dropped. In addition to the ideological considerations about whom to nominate, the president also considers the individual's reputation as a legal scholar and his personal relationship to the candidate, as well as the candidate's ethical standards, gender, and race (see Table 13.2 for data on the latter two points).

PRESIDENTS CAN INFLUENCE THE direction of the federal courts by selecting judges who share their views. In his first term, President Obama had the opportunity to nominate two justices to the Supreme Court: Sonia Sotomayor and Elena Kagan (shown here).

TABLE » 13.2

THE DEMOGRAPHICS OF THE FEDERAL BENCH

All presidents try to appoint qualified candidates to the federal courts; however, there is variation in the types of people they nominate. Identify some characteristics common to most judges and some that vary across presidents. Which traits vary by the president's party?

	OBAMA[a]		G. W. BUSH		CLINTON		BUSH		REAGAN	
Experience[b]										
Judicial	61%	(36)	52%	(136)	52%	(159)	47%	(69)	46%	(134)
Prosecutorial	54	(32)	47	(123)	41	(126)	39	(58)	44	(128)
Neither	24	(14)	25	(65)	29	(88)	32	(47)	29	(83)
Average age at nomination	51		49.1		49.5		48.2		48.6	
Law school education										
Public	39%	(23)	49%	(128)	40%	(121)	53%	(78)	45%	(130)
Private	37	(22)	39	(102)	41	(124)	33	(49)	43	(126)
Ivy League	24	(14)	12	(31)	20	(60)	14	(21)	12	(34)
Gender										
Male	51%	(30)	79%	(207)	72%	(218)	80%	(119)	92%	(226)
Female	49	(29)	21	(54)	29	(87)	20	(29)	8	(24)
Ethnicity/race										
White	56%	(33)	82%	(213)	75%	(229)	89%	(132)	92%	(268)
African American	27	(16)	7	(18)	17	(53)	7	(10)	2	(6)
Hispanic	7	(4)	10	(26)	6	(18)	4	(6)	5	(14)
Asian	10	(6)	1	4	1.3	(4)	–	–	0.7	(2)
Native American	–		–	–	0.3	(1)	–	–	–	–
Percentage white male	30	(18)	67	(176)	52	(160)	73	(108)	85	(246)
Political identification										
Democrat	90%	(53)	8%	(21)	88%	(267)	6%	(9)	5%	(14)
Republican	–		83	(217)	6	(19)	89	(131)	92	(266)
Other	–		–	–	0.3	(1)	–	–	–	–
None	10	(6)	9	(23)	6	(18)	5	(8)	3	(10)
Net worth										
Under $200,000	3%	(2)	5%	(13)	13%	(41)	10%	(15)	18%	(52)
$200–499,999	7	(6)	18	(47)	22	(66)	31	(46)	38	(109)
$500–999,999	20	(12)	22	(57)	27	(82)	26	(39)	22	(63)
$1 million+	66	(39)	55	(144)	38	(116)	32	(48)	23	(66)
Total number of appointees		59		261		305		148		290

a. Through 2010.

b. Percentages sum to more than 100 because some appointees have both judicial and prosecutorial experience.

Source: Sheldon Goldman, Sara Schiavoni, and Elliot Slotnick, "Obama's Judiciary at Midterm," Judicature 94:6 (May–June 2011): 296–97.

THE ROLE OF THE SENATE

The other half of the equation to determine the composition of the federal courts is the Senate. The Senate has shifted from a very active role in providing "advice and consent" on court appointments to a passive role and then back to an active role. One constant is that the Senate rarely rejects nominees because of their qualifications, but rather for political reasons. Of twenty-eight nominees rejected by the Senate in the history of the United States, only two were turned down because they were seen as unqualified: George Williams in 1873 and G. Harold Carswell in 1970. Serious questions were also raised about a third, current justice Clarence Thomas, who had served for only eighteen months as a federal judge before being nominated to the Court. Thomas also was accused of sexual harassment by a former colleague. Thomas ultimately won confirmation by a 52-to-48 vote, the second narrowest successful margin in history. The other twenty-six nominees were rejected for political reasons. Most commonly, when a "lame duck" president makes a nomination and the Senate is controlled by the opposing party, the Senate will kill the nomination, hoping that its party will win the presidency and nominate a justice more to its liking.

SENATE HEARINGS ON SUPREME Court nominations have been more conflictual since the 1960s. Although Sonia Sotomayor was confirmed by a 68-to-31 vote in 2009, Senate Republicans challenged her to explain and defend her views on several issues.

Throughout the nineteenth century the Senate was very willing to turn down Court nominations for political reasons. In fact, twenty-one nominees were not confirmed by the Senate from 1793 through 1894 (about a third of the total number of nominees). Then in the first half of the twentieth century the Senate allowed presidents to appoint whom they wanted. Between 1894 and 1968, the Senate did not even require nominees to testify and only one nominee was rejected.

A rethinking of this passive role occurred in the late 1960s. President Nixon vowed to move the Court back from the "liberal excesses" of the Warren Court, but the Senate stiffened its spine and rejected two nominees in a row in 1969 (Clement Haynsworth) and 1970 (Harold Carswell). For Haynsworth there were ethical problems involving his participation in cases in which he had a financial interest. Carswell had a mediocre judicial record, and civil rights groups raised questions about his commitment to enforcing antidiscrimination laws. Nixon must have thought that the Senate wouldn't reject his choice twice in a row! The most recent Senate rejection was of Judge Robert Bork, a brilliant, very conservative and controversial figure. Liberal interest groups mobilized against him, and the Senate rejected him by the widest margin of any nominee since 1846 (the vote was 42 to 58), giving the English language a new verb: to get "borked" means to have your character and record challenged in a very public way.

However, not all recent Supreme Court nominations have been controversial. President Bill Clinton's two Supreme Court picks were judicial moderates who were overwhelmingly confirmed—Ruth Bader Ginsburg by a 96-to-3 vote and Stephen Breyer by an 87-to-9 margin. George W. Bush's nominees, John Roberts and Samuel Alito, were confirmed by comfortable margins; the former by a 78-to-22 vote, with half of the Democrats supporting him, and the latter by a 58-to-42 margin. President Obama appointed the first Hispanic to serve on the Supreme Court, Sonia Sotomayor, who was confirmed by a 68-to-31 vote. Elena Kagan's confirmation by a 63-to-37 vote in 2010 meant that three women are serving on the Court for the first time.

The contentious battles between the president and the Senate over nominees to the federal bench and the Supreme Court have recently expanded to include nominees to the district and appeals courts. For much of the nation's history the president did not play a very active role in the nomination process for district courts, instead deferring to the home-state senator of the president's party to suggest candidates—a norm called **senatorial courtesy**. If there was no senator of the president's party from the relevant state, the president would consult House members and other high-ranking party members from the state. The president typically has shown more interest in appeals court nominations. The Justice Department plays a key role in screening candidates, but the local senators of the president's party remain active as well through the "blue slip" process: home state senators record their support or opposition to nominees on blue slips of paper. Some committee chairs have allowed a single home-state senator to use the blue slip to veto a nominee, but others have not followed the process so strictly.

Recently, the process has become much more contentious. The confirmation rate for federal judges has gone from between 80 percent and 100 percent to less than 50 percent in recent years. When Republicans took control of the Senate in 1995, they stopped more than sixty of President Clinton's nominees to the lower federal courts. The average length of delay from nomination to confirmation has increased from a little over 50 days in the 1980s to over 200 days in recent years (see Figure 13.2). The situation has intensified in recent years (see "You Decide"). Democrats blocked thirty-nine of President Bush's nominees between 2001 and 2009,[27] and Republicans have been returning the favor since then, blocking twenty of President Obama's nominees, including two filibusters of appeals court nominees Goodwin Liu and Caitlin Halligan.[28] The partisan battle over nominations means that about 10 percent of all federal judgeships remain vacant, which increases the workload for current judges and creates a growing backlog of cases.

Although there is no definitive answer as to how active the Senate should be in giving "advice and consent"—especially how much power a minority of forty-one senators should have—it is clear that the Founders intended the Senate to play an active role. The first draft of the Constitution gave the Senate the sole power to appoint Supreme Court justices. However, the final version made appointment a shared power with the goal of promoting responsibility through the president's role and "security" through the Senate's. It was not expected that the Senate would compete with the president over whom to nominate, but it *was* assumed that the

FIGURE » 13.2

CONFIRMATION DELAY FOR FEDERAL JUDGES, 1981–2012

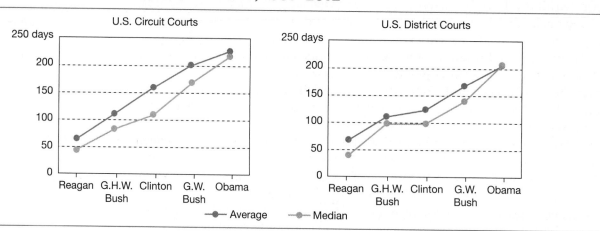

Source: "Length of Time from Nomination to Confirmation for 'Uncontroversial' U.S. Circuit and District Court Nominees: Detailed Analysis," Barry J. McMillion, Congressional Research Service, September 18, 2012, www.fas.org/gsp/crs/misc/R42732.pdf (accessed 10/2/12).

ADVICE AND CONSENT: PRINCIPLED OPPOSITION OR OBSTRUCTIONISM?

The use of the filibuster to stop presidential nominations to the federal courts has been the source of intense partisan battles in the past fifteen years (recall that forty-one senators can stop action on any bill or nomination through a filibuster). However, the positions in those battles are determined by which party controls the Senate and the presidency. Democrats who railed against Republican obstruction when Clinton was president used the same tactics when they were in the minority party and Bush was president. Now the tables are turned again and some of the strongest Republican critics of Democratic filibusters, such as Jeff Sessions, led the first filibuster against an Obama appeals court nominee (which failed).

The partisan struggles have led to serious discussion about limiting the use of the filibuster for court nominations. In Bush's first term, Senate Democrats stopped lower court nominees through the filibuster. After winning reelection in 2004, President Bush resubmitted seven nominees who had been rejected in the previous Senate (and thirteen more who were nominated in the previous term but did not come up for a vote). After Democrats indicated that they were not going to abandon the filibusters, the Republican leadership in the Senate considered implementing the "nuclear option," which would have prevented filibusters on judicial nominations (this plan gets its name because Democrats threatened to essentially shut down the Senate if they lost the filibuster). This crisis was defused when the "Gang of 14"—seven moderate Republicans and seven moderate Democrats—agreed to a compromise that preserved the Democrats' right to filibuster but only in the most extreme cases. The compromise was not put to a critical test (both of Bush's Supreme Court nominees were confirmed without filibusters), and Republicans have pursued an approach of delaying nominations through holds in the Judiciary Committee and on the floor.

Let's do a thought experiment to try to strip partisanship from this issue and figure out if you support the principle of filibustering judicial nominations. Put yourself in the place of a Democratic senator on the Judiciary Committee during the Bush years. President Bush has nominated a candidate for an appeals court position whom you believe is unqualified. Should you support a filibuster to stop the nomination even if it means that the Republican leadership might take away the filibuster? Now put yourself in the place of a Republican senator. You strongly favor President Bush's right to nominate whom he wants to the federal courts, and you support his policy positions, especially on abortion and the regulation of the free market. However, the Democrats are opposed and threatening to filibuster. You have to decide whether to support the "nuclear

When they are the minority party in the Senate, both Democrats and Republicans have been willing to use the filibuster to block judicial nominees.

option" to take away the Democrats' right to filibuster the nomination. There are at least fifty-six votes in favor of the nominee but not the sixty needed to cut off the filibuster. On the one hand, you don't think it is fair that Democrats are obstructing the vote. On the other hand, you were in the Senate back when the Republicans were in the minority, and you remember how important the filibuster was to protect the views of the minority party. You are worried that supporting the "nuclear option" would seriously damage the institution that you value and respect as the world's greatest deliberative body. What is the best option? You decide.

Critical Thinking Questions

1. What would you do in the situation just described? Why?

2. Now to complete the thought experiment, flip the positions of the senators for an Obama nominee to the appeals court. Is your position still the same?

Senate would exercise independent judgment as to the suitability of the president's nominees. Furthermore, the Founders did not expect that the process would be free of politics or that the Senate would be an essentially passive and subordinate player in a nominally joint enterprise. Even George Washington had two of his nominations turned down by the Senate for political reasons! Therefore, politics will continue to play an important role in deciding who serves on the federal bench.

DESCRIBE HOW CASES REACH THE SUPREME COURT

ACCESS TO THE SUPREME COURT

It is extremely difficult to have a case heard by the Supreme Court. Currently the Court hears about 1 percent of the cases submitted (roughly 85 of about 8,000 cases). This section explains how the Court decides which cases to hear. When a case is submitted, the clerk of the Court assigns it a number and places it on the docket, which is the schedule of cases.

THE COURT'S WORKLOAD

Statistics on the Supreme Court's workload initially suggest that the size of the docket has increased dramatically since the 1970s (see Figure 13.3). However, a majority of cases are frivolous and are dismissed after limited review. The Court has become increasingly impatient with these frivolous petitions and has moved to prevent "frequent filers" from harassing the Court. One often-cited case involved Michael Sindram, who asked the Court to order the Maryland courts to remove a $35 traffic ticket from his record. Our favorite example concerned a wealthy drug dealer, Frederick W. Bauer, who was convicted on ten counts of dealing drugs (seven counts involved a total of 4,100 pounds of marijuana, two counts for nearly 250 pounds of cocaine, and one count for six gallons of hashish oil and a package of black gum hashish) and repeatedly petitioned the Court. In his initial trial he applied for a court-appointed attorney (which is supplied for people who cannot afford their own legal counsel) but was turned down because a court hearing revealed that he had "unencumbered assets [that] totaled almost $500,000." The court found the petitioner's testimony that he was poor "ambiguous, evasive and in many respects completely incredible."[29] Bauer petitioned the Court twelve times on various issues, and finally the justices had had enough. They ruled that "Bauer has repeatedly abused this Court's certiorari and extraordinary writ processes" and directed "the Clerk not to accept any further petitions for certiorari or petitions for extraordinary writs from Bauer in noncriminal matters" unless he paid his docketing fees. They concluded that the order will "allow this Court to devote its limited resources to the claims of petitioners who have not abused our processes."[30]

Though the increase in workload is not as significant as it appears due to the high number of frivolous cases, another change is more important: the number of opinions issued by the Court has fallen by more than half in the past twenty years. The Court heard about 150 cases a year through the 1980s, but this number has fallen to only 75 to 85 in recent years (see Figure 13.3).[31] The change is even more dramatic when one considers that the Court has reduced the number of "summary decisions" it issues (cases that do not receive a full hearing, but the Court rules on

FIGURE » 13.3

THE COURT SEES MORE OPPORTUNITIES . . . BUT HEARS FEWER CASES

The Supreme Court's workload appears to be headed in two directions: the Court is receiving more cases but hearing fewer of them. What are the implications of having the Supreme Court hear fewer cases? Should something be done to try to get the Court to hear more cases?

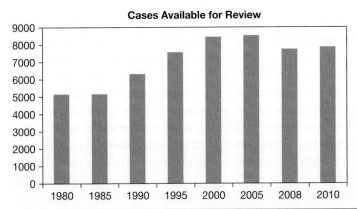

Cases Available for Review

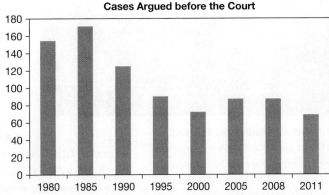

Cases Argued before the Court

Sources: Data compiled from "Chief Justice's Year-End Reports on the Federal Judiciary," www.supremecourtus.gov/publicinfo/year-end/2011year-endreport.html, and Kedar Bhatia, "Final Term 2011 Stat Pack and Summary Memo," SCOTUSblog, June 30, 2012, www.scotusblog.com/2012/06/final-October-term-2011-stat-pack-and-summary-memo/ (accessed 10/2/12).

the merits of the case) from 150 a year in the 1970s to a handful today. The number of summary judgments declined when Congress gave the Court more control over its docket and dramatically reduced the number of cases that it was *required* to hear on appeal. However, there is no good explanation for why the Court issues half as many opinions as it used to, other than that the chief justices have decided that the Court shouldn't issue so many opinions.[32]

RULES OF ACCESS

With the smaller number of cases being heard, it is even more important to understand how the Court decides which cases to hear. There are four paths that a case may take to get to the Supreme Court. First, Article III of the Constitution specifies that the Court has original jurisdiction in cases involving foreign ambassadors, foreign countries, or cases in which a state is a party. As a practical matter, the Court shares jurisdiction with the lower courts on these issues.

In recent years, the Court has invoked original jurisdiction only in cases involving disputes between two or more states over territorial or natural resource issues. For example, New Jersey and New York had a disagreement about which state should control about twenty-five acres of filled land that the federal government had added around Ellis Island. Another case involved a dispute between Kansas and Colorado over who should have access to water from the Arkansas River (recent disputes often concern water rights).[33] If original jurisdiction is granted and there are factual issues to be resolved, the Court will appoint a "special master" (usually a retired federal judge) to hold a hearing, gather evidence, and make a

ON RARE OCCASIONS THE SUPREME Court serves as a court of original jurisdiction. One of those unusual times is when there is a dispute between two states, such as when the Court had to settle a disagreement between New York and New Jersey over Ellis Island.

writ of certiorari The most common way for a case to reach the Supreme Court, in which at least four of the nine justices agree to hear a case that has reached them via an appeal from the losing party in a lower court's ruling.

recommendation to the Court. This process is necessary because the Supreme Court is not a trial court. The "special master" arrangement allows the Court to function in its normal capacity as an appeals court by treating the master's recommendation as a lower court decision, even if technically the Court is a trial court in these original jurisdiction cases. In the history of our nation, only about 175 cases have made it to the Court through this path, an average of less than one per year, and typically these cases do not have any broader significance beyond the parties involved.[34]

The other three routes to the Court are all on appeal: as a matter of right (usually called "on appeal"), through certification, or through the writ of certiorari. Cases "on appeal" are those that Congress has determined to be so important that the Supreme Court must hear them. Before 1988 these cases constituted a larger share of the Court's docket, and they included (1) cases in which a lower court declared a state or federal law unconstitutional, or (2) cases in which a state court upheld a state law that had been challenged as unconstitutional under the U.S. Constitution. Lately Congress has given the Court much more discretion on these cases; the only ones that the Court is still compelled to take on appeal are some voting rights and redistricting cases.

A writ of certification occurs when an appeals court asks the Court to clarify a new point of federal law in a specific case. The Court can agree to hear the case, but given that appeals court and state supreme court judges are the only people who can make these requests, this path to the Court is very rare. (In fact, since 1982 the Court has not taken up a certified question from one of the appeals courts and has certified only five cases from state supreme courts.)[35]

The third path is the most common: at least 95 percent of the cases in most sessions arrive through a **writ of certiorari** (from the Latin "to be informed"). In these cases, a litigant who lost in lower court can file a petition to the Supreme Court explaining why it should hear the case. If four justices agree, the case will get a full hearing (this is called, reasonably enough, the "Rule of Four"). This process may sound simple, but sifting through the 8,000 or so cases that the Court receives every year and deciding which eighty-five of them will be heard is daunting. Former justice William O. Douglas said that this winnowing process is "in many respects the most important and interesting of all our functions."[36]

THE COURT'S CRITERIA

How does the Court decide which cases to hear? Several factors come into play, including the specific characteristics of the case and the broader politics surrounding it. Although several criteria generally must be met before the Court will hear the case, justices still have leeway in defining the boundaries of these conditions.

COLLUSION, STANDING, MOOTNESS, AND RIPENESS

First, there are the constitutional guidelines, which are sparse. The Constitution limits the Court to hearing actual "cases and controversies," which has been interpreted to mean that the Court cannot offer advisory opinions about hypothetical situations but must deal with actual cases. The term "actual controversy" also includes several other concepts that limit whether a case will be heard: collusion, standing, mootness, and ripeness. Collusion simply means that the litigants in the case cannot want the same outcome and cannot be testing the law without an actual dispute between the two parties.[37]

Standing is the most general criteria; as we noted earlier it means that the party bringing the case must have a personal stake in the outcome. The Court has discretion in defining standing: it may hear cases that it thinks are important even when the plaintiff may not have standing, as traditionally understood, or duck cases that may be politically sensitive on the grounds that there is no standing. For example, the Court decided several important racial redistricting cases even when the white plaintiffs had not suffered any personal harm by being in the black-majority districts.[38] On the other hand, in a politically sensitive case involving the pledge of allegiance and the First Amendment, the Court decided not to hear the case, saying the father of the student who brought the case did not have standing because he did not have sufficient custody over his daughter (he was divorced and the mother had primary custody).[39] Clearly the Court was more eager to voice its views on redistricting than the pledge of allegiance because it could have just as easily ducked the former case by saying the plaintiffs did not have standing and ruled on the merits of the latter case.

Mootness means that the controversy must still be relevant when the Court hears the case. For example, a student sued a law school for reverse discrimination, saying that he had not been admitted because of the university's affirmative action policy. A lower court agreed and ordered that the student be admitted. The appeals court reversed the decision, but the student was allowed to remain enrolled while the case was appealed to the Supreme Court. By the time the Court received the case, the student was in his last semester of law school and the university said that he would graduate no matter the outcome of the case. Therefore, the Court refused to hear the case because it was moot.[40] However, there have to be exceptions to this principle because some types of cases would always be moot by the time they got to the Supreme Court. For example, exceptions have been made for abortion cases because a pregnancy lasts only nine months, and for a case to get from district court, to the appeals court, to the Supreme Court is always a longer time than that.

Ripeness can be considered the opposite of mootness. With mootness the controversy is already over; with ripeness the controversy has not started yet. Just as you wouldn't want to eat a piece of fruit before it is ripe, the Court doesn't want to hear a case until it is ripe. Sometimes ripeness can affect standing. One example is the line-item veto, which Congress gave to President Clinton at the start of his second term. Almost immediately some members of Congress challenged the constitutionality of the law because they believed that the president should not be able to veto part of a bill. A district court agreed and ruled that the law was unconstitutional. The case was appealed to the Supreme Court, but the justices refused to hear it: because the issue was not ripe, the members of Congress did not have standing. That is, President Clinton had not yet used the line-item veto, so there was no controversy and the members had not been harmed. Two months later, Clinton used the veto, another case was filed, and the Court eventually struck down the law.[41]

Thousands of cases every year meet the basic criteria. One very simple guideline eliminates the largest number of cases: if a case does not involve a "substantial federal question," it will not be heard. This essentially means that the Court does not have to hear a case if the justices do not think the case is important enough. Of course, the "federal" part of this standard is also important: if a case is governed by state law rather than federal law, the Court would decline to hear the case. The "political question doctrine," discussed later, is another basis upon

mootness The irrelevance of a case by the time it is received by a federal court, causing the court to decline to hear the case.

ripeness A criterion that federal courts use to decide whether a case is ready to be heard. A case's ripeness is based on whether its central issue or controversy has actually taken place.

which the Court may decide not to hear a case. This still leaves about 20 percent to 30 percent of the cases that are winnowed to the final list with the more specific guidance of Rule 10 in the Supreme Court rules (see Nuts and Bolts 13.2). Of the criteria listed in Rule 10, conflict between appeals court decisions is most likely to produce a Supreme Court hearing.

INTERNAL POLITICS

Not much is known about the actual discussions that determine which cases will be heard. The justices meet in conference with no staff or clerk. Leaks are rare, but a few insider accounts and the papers of retired justices provided some insights. First, since the late 1970s most justices have used a **cert pool**, whereby their law clerks take a first cut at the cases (law clerks to the justices are top graduates of elite law schools who help justices with background research at several stages of the process). Clerks write joint memos about groups of cases, providing their recommendations about which cases should be heard. The ultimate decisions are up to the justices, but clerks have significant power to help shape the agenda.

Second, the chief justice has an important agenda-setting power: he decides the "discuss list" for a given day. Any justice can add a case to the list, but there is no systematic evidence on how often this happens. Only 20 percent to 30 percent of the cases are discussed in conference, which means that about three-quarters of the cases that are submitted to the Supreme Court are never even discussed by the Court. In most cases this is justified because of the high proportion of frivolous suits submitted to the Court.[42]

Many factors outside the legal requirements or internal processes of the Court influence access to the Court and which cases will be heard. Cases that have generated a lot of activity from interest groups or other governmental parties, such as the solicitor general, are more likely to be heard. The **solicitor general** is a presidential appointee who works in the Justice Department and supervises the litigation of the executive branch. In cases in which the federal government is a party, the solicitor general or someone else from that office will represent the government in court. The Court accepts about 70 percent to 80 percent of cases in which the U.S. government is a party compared to about 1 percent overall.[43]

cert pool A system initiated in the Supreme Court in the 1970s in which law clerks screen cases that come to the Supreme Court and recommend to the justices which cases should be heard.

solicitor general A presidential appointee in the Department of Justice who conducts all litigation on behalf of the federal government before the Supreme Court and supervises litigation in the federal appellate courts.

13.2 NUTS & bolts

DECIDING TO HEAR A CASE IN THE SUPREME COURT

Rule 10 of the *Rules of the U.S. Supreme Court* says that a case is more likely to be heard when

- ▶ there is conflict between appeals court opinions,
- ▶ there is conflict between a federal appeals court and a state supreme court on a substantial federal question,
- ▶ a lower court decision has "departed from the accepted and usual course of judicial proceedings,"
- ▶ a state court or appeals court has ruled on a substantial federal question that has not yet been addressed by the Court, or
- ▶ a state supreme court or appeals court ruling conflicts with Supreme Court precedent.

Rule 10 also states that certiorari is unlikely to be granted when "the asserted error consists of erroneous factual findings or the misapplication of a properly stated rule of law."

Source: U.S. Supreme Court, Rules of the U.S. Supreme Court, *adopted January 27, 2003, effective May 1, 2003, www .supremecourtus.gov/ctrules/rulesofthecourt.pdf (accessed 11/5/12).*

Even with these influences, the Court has a great deal of discretion on which cases it hears. Well-established practices such as standing, ripeness, and mootness may be ignored (or modified) if the Court wants to hear a specific case. However, one final point is important: although the justices may pick and choose their cases, they cannot set their own agenda. They can only select from the cases that come to them.

HEARING CASES BEFORE THE SUPREME COURT

DESCRIBE THE SUPREME COURT'S PROCEDURES FOR HEARING A CASE

A surprisingly small proportion of the Court's time is actually spent hearing cases—only 40 days in the 2012–13 term. The Court is in session from the first Monday in October through the end of June or early July. It hears cases on Mondays through Wednesdays in alternating two-week cycles in which it is in session from 10 A.M. to 3 P.M. with a one-hour break for lunch. In the other two weeks of the cycle when it is not in session, justices review briefs, write opinions, and sift through the next batch of petitions. On most Fridays when the Court is in session the justices meet in conference to discuss cases that have been argued and decide which cases they will hear. Opinions are released throughout the term, but the bulk of them come in May and June.[44]

The Court is in recess from July through September. Justices may take some vacation, but they mostly use the time for study, reading, writing, and preparing for the next term. During the summer the Court also considers emergency petitions (such as stays of execution) and occasionally hears important cases. For example, during the Watergate scandal of Richard Nixon's presidency, the Court was asked to decide whether the president had to hand over tapes of conversations that had been secretly recorded in the White House. In a unanimous ruling on July 24, 1974, the Court said that Nixon had to release the tapes. Two weeks later Nixon resigned.[45] More recently, on September 9, 2009 (nearly a month before the fall session started), the Court heard a challenge to the Bipartisan Campaign Reform Act, more commonly known as the McCain–Feingold Act after its two principal sponsors. Congress urged the Court to give the law a speedy review given its importance for the upcoming 2010 elections. In the blockbuster case *Citizens United v. Federal Election Commission*, the Supreme Court decided that independent spending in campaigns by corporations and labor unions is protected by the First Amendment (see Chapter 8).

BRIEFS

During the regular sessions, the Court follows rigidly set routines. The justices prepare for a case by reading the briefs that both parties submit. Because the Supreme Court hears only appeals, it does not call witnesses or gather new evidence. Instead, in structured briefs of no more than fifty pages, the parties present their arguments about why they either support the lower court decision or believe the case was improperly decided. Interest groups often submit **amicus curiae** ("friend of the court") briefs that convey their opinions to the Court; in fact, 85 percent of cases before the Supreme Court have at least one amicus brief.[46] The federal government

amicus curiae Latin for "friend of the court," referring to an interested group or person who shares relevant information about a case to help the Court reach a decision.

also files amici curiae on important issues such as school busing, school prayer, abortion, reapportionment of legislative districts, job discrimination against women, and affirmative action in higher education.

It is difficult to determine the impact of amici curiae on the outcome of a case, but those that are filed early in the process increase the chances that the case will be heard. Interestingly, even amici curiae that are filed *against* a case increase the chances that the case will be heard.[47] Given the limited information that justices have about any given case, interest group involvement can be a strong signal about the importance of a case.

CAMERAS ARE NOT ALLOWED IN the Supreme Court, so artists' sketches are the only images of oral arguments. This sketch shows solicitor general Donald Verrilli arguing for the Affordable Care Act in 2012, as justices Antonin Scalia and John Roberts listen.

oral arguments Spoken presentations made in person by the lawyers of each party to a judge or appellate court outlining the legal reasons their side should prevail.

ORAL ARGUMENT

Once the briefs are filed and have been reviewed by the justices, cases are scheduled for **oral arguments**. Except in unusual circumstances, each case gets one hour, which is divided evenly between the two parties. In especially important cases, extra time may be granted. Usually there is only one lawyer for each side who presents the case, but parties who have filed amicus briefs may participate if their arguments "would provide assistance to the Court not otherwise available." Given the tight time pressures, the Court is usually unwilling to extend the allotted time to allow "friends of the court" to testify.[48] The relevant party can share part of its thirty minutes if it wants, but that doesn't happen often. Therefore, the participation of friends of the court is usually limited to written briefs rather than oral arguments.

The Court is strict about its time limits and uses a system of three lights to show the lawyers how much time is left. A green light goes on when the speaker's time begins, a white light provides a five-minute warning, and a red light means to stop. Most textbooks cite well-known examples of justices cutting people off in midsentence or walking out of the courtroom as the lawyer drones on. One source implies that these anecdotes are generally revealing of Court procedure, saying, "Anecdotes probably tell as much about the proceeding of the Court during oral argument as does any careful study of the rules and procedures."[49]

However, having a preference for "careful study" over anecdotes, we were curious about how common it was for justices to strictly impose the time limits. Initially we examined forty-two cases from the 2004–05 term, using the online transcripts on the Court's website.[50] We found that most lawyers did not use all their allotted time, with 62 percent of the cases coming in under sixty minutes, 17 percent exactly an hour, and 21 percent over an hour. One-sixth of the lawyers still had at least five minutes left on the clock. We found only two instances in which a justice cut someone off in midsentence after the person had gone over the half-hour limit. We updated the analysis for the Roberts Court, examining all seventy-four cases argued in the 2009 calendar year. Roberts was not much of a stickler for adhering to the time limits: nearly 60 percent of oral arguments went past their allotted time (most by only a minute or two), 13.5 percent were exactly an hour, and 27 percent were under an hour. Again, only two of the seventy-four oral arguments ended with an attorney being cut off in midsentence by the chief justice. Thus, while the Court tries to stay within its time limits, it is not as draconian as some anecdotes imply.

Some lawyers may not use all of their time because their train of thought is interrupted by aggressive questioning. Transcripts reveal that justices jump in with questions almost immediately, and some attorneys never regain their footing. The frequency and pointedness of the questions vary by justice, with Justices Scalia, Breyer, Kagan, and Sotomayor being the most aggressive on the current Court, while Justice Thomas has gone more than six years without asking a single question.[51] Cameras are not allowed in the courtroom, so most Americans have never seen the Court in action—though a small live audience is admitted every morning the Court is in session. If you are curious about oral arguments, audio recordings of every case since 1995 are available at www.oyez.org.

CONFERENCE

After oral arguments, the justices meet in conference to discuss and then vote on the cases. As with the initial conferences, these meetings are conducted in secret. We know, based on notes in the personal papers of retired justices, that the conferences are orderly and structured but can become quite heated. The justices take turns discussing the cases and outlining the reasons for their positions. Justice Thurgood Marshall described the decision-making process in conference and the need for secrecy as

> a continuing conversation among nine distinct individuals on dozens of issues simultaneously. The exchanges are serious, sometimes scholarly, occasionally brash and personalized, but generally well-reasoned and most often cast in understated, genteel language. . . . In other cases, a majority of justices start down one path, only to reverse direction. . . . This is the kind of internal debate that the justices have argued should remain confidential, taking the position that only their final opinions have legal authority. They have expressed concern that premature disclosure of their private debates and doubts may undermine the court's credibility and inhibit their exchange of ideas.[52]

OPINION WRITING

After the justices indicate how they are likely to vote on a case, if the chief justice is in the majority (which is most of the time), he decides who will write the majority opinion. For example, Warren Burger assigned 1,891 of the 2,201 opinions (about 86 percent) when he was chief justice in the 1970s and 1980s.[53] Otherwise, the most senior justice in the majority assigns the opinion. Many considerations determine how a case will be assigned. First, the chief justice will try to ensure the smooth operation of the Court. Along these lines, in 1989, Chief Justice Rehnquist announced a change in how he assigned opinions. In his first three terms, he tried to give each justice the same number of cases, but he recognized that "this policy does not take into consideration the difficulty of the opinion assigned or the amount of work that the 'assignee' may currently have backed up in his chambers. . . . It only makes sense in the assignment of additional work to give some preference to those who are 'current' with respect to past work."[54] A second factor is the justices' individual areas of expertise. For example, Justice Blackmun had developed expertise in medical law when he was in private practice. This experience played a role in Chief Justice Burger's decision to assign Blackmun the majority opinion in the landmark abortion decision

Roe v. Wade (1973). Likewise, Justice O'Connor developed expertise in racial redistricting cases and authored most of those decisions in the 1990s.

The final set of factors is more strategic: it includes the Court's external relations, internal relations, and the personal policy goals of the opinion assigner. The Court must be sensitive to how others might respond to its decisions because it must rely on the other branches of government to enforce its decisions. One famous example of this consideration in an opinion assignment came in a case from the 1940s that struck down a practice that had prevented African Americans from voting in Democratic primaries.[55] Originally, the opinion was assigned to Justice Felix Frankfurter, but Justice Robert Jackson wrote a memo suggesting that it might be unwise to have a liberal, politically independent Jew from the Northeast write an opinion that was sure to be controversial in the South. Chief Justice Harlan Fiske Stone agreed and reassigned the opinion to Justice Stanley Reed, a Protestant and Democrat from Kentucky.[56] It may not seem that the Court is sensitive to public opinion, but these kinds of considerations happen fairly frequently in important cases. Internal considerations occasionally cause justices to vote strategically—different from the justice's sincere preference—in order to be in the majority so the justice can assign the opinion (often to himself or herself).

Justices may also assign opinions to help achieve their personal policy goals. The most obvious strategy is for the chief justice to assign opinions to justices who are closest to his position. Obviously, this practice is constrained by the first point—ensuring the smooth operation of the Court. If the chief justice assigned all the opinions to the justices who are closest to him ideologically, then justices with other ideological leanings would get a chance to write opinions only in the 15 percent to 20 percent of cases in which the chief is in the minority. That wouldn't work. Charles Hughes, chief justice from 1930 to 1941, sometimes assigned opinions on liberal decisions to conservative justices and cases with conservative outcomes to liberal justices in order to downplay the importance of ideology on the Court.[57]

After the opinions are assigned, the justices work on writing a draft opinion. Law clerks typically help with this process. Some justices insist on writing all of their opinions, while others allow a clerk to write the first draft. The drafts are circulated to the other justices for comment and reactions. Some bargaining may occur, in which a justice says he or she will withdraw support unless a provision is changed. Justices may join the majority opinion, may write a separate concurring opinion, or may dissent (see Nuts and Bolts 13.3 for details on the types of opinions).

Two final points about the process of writing and issuing opinions are important. First, until the 1940s there was a premium placed on unanimous decisions. John Marshall, who was chief justice from 1800 to 1835, started this practice. Through the 1930s, about 80 percent to 90 percent of decisions were unanimous. This changed dramatically in the 1940s, when most cases had at least one dissent. In recent decades, about two-thirds of cases have a dissent. Second, dissents serve an important purpose. Not only do they allow the minority view to be expressed, but they also often provide the basis for reversing a poorly reasoned case. When justices strongly oppose the majority opinion, they may take the unusual step of reading a portion of the dissent from the bench.

Majority opinion: The core decision of the Court that must be agreed upon by at least five justices. The majority opinion presents the legal reasoning for the Court's decision.

Concurring opinion: Written by a justice who agrees with the outcome of the case but not with the legal reasoning. Concurring opinions may be joined by other justices. A justice may sign on to the majority opinion and write a separate concurring opinion.

Plurality opinion: Occurs when a majority cannot agree on the legal reasoning in a case. The plurality opinion is the one that has the most agreement (usually three or four justices). Because of the fractured nature of these opinions, they typically are not viewed as having as much clout as majority opinions.

Dissent: Submitted by a justice who disagrees with the outcome of the case. Other justices can sign on to a dissent or write their own, so there can be as many as four dissents. Justices can also sign on to part of a dissent but not the entire opinion.

Per curiam opinion: (Latin for "by the court") An unsigned opinion of the Court or a decision written by the entire Court. However, this is not the same as a unanimous decision that is signed by the entire Court. Per curiam opinions are usually very short opinions on noncontroversial issues, but not always. For example, *Bush v. Gore*, which decided the outcome of the 2000 presidential election, was a per curiam opinion. Per curiam decisions may also have dissents.

SUPREME COURT DECISION MAKING

ANALYZE THE FACTORS THAT INFLUENCE SUPREME COURT DECISIONS

There are many different influences on judicial decision making. The two main categories are legal and political. Legal factors include the precedent of earlier cases and norms that justices must follow the language of the Constitution. Political influences include the justices' preferences or ideologies, their stances on whether the Court should take a restrained or activist role with respect to the elected branches, and external factors such as public opinion and interest group involvement. Some scholars argue that all court behavior is political and that the use of legal factors is just a smoke screen for hiding personal preferences.

LEGAL FACTORS

Those who put forward the legal view usually present their position in normative terms; that is, justices *should* follow precedent and the words of the Constitution. Advocates of this view recognize that justices often stray from these legal norms, but they criticize the interjection of personal preferences as a harmful politicization of the courts. Our view is that legal factors are often used as justification for political positions on the Court, but they also independently influence judicial decision making on a broad range of cases.

PRECEDENT

The most basic legal factor is stare decisis, or precedent, discussed earlier. Precedent does not determine the outcome of any given case, because every case has a range of precedents that can serve to justify a justice's decision. The "easy" cases, in which settled law makes the outcome obvious, are less likely to be heard by the Court because of the justices' desire to focus on the more controversial areas of unsettled law. However, there are areas of the law—such as free speech, the death penalty, and search and seizure—in which precedent is an important explanation for how the justices decide a case.

THE LANGUAGE OF THE CONSTITUTION

The various perspectives that emphasize the language of the Constitution all fall under the heading of **strict construction**. The most basic of these is the literalist view of the Constitution. Sometimes this view is called a textualist position because it sees the text of the document as determining the outcome of any given case. Literalists argue that justices need to look no further than the actual words of the Constitution.

Justice Hugo Black was one of the most famous advocates of the literalist position. When the First Amendment says that "Congress shall make no law . . . abridging the freedom of speech," that literally means *no* law. Justice Black said, "My view is, without deviation, without exception, without any ifs, buts, or whereases, that freedom of speech means that government shall not do anything to people . . . either for the views they have or the views they express or the words they speak or write."[58] While that may be clear enough with regard to political speech, how about pornography, Internet speech, or symbolic speech, such as burning an American flag or wearing an armband to protest the Vietnam War? A literal interpretation of the Constitution does not necessarily help determine whether these forms of speech should be restricted. (Indeed, Black was one of the two dissenters in a case that upheld students' right to wear armbands as a form of symbolic speech. Black believed that school officials should be allowed to decide whether a symbolic protest would be too disruptive in the classroom and argued that only spoken and written speech should be afforded the strongest protection of the First Amendment. So much for "without deviation, without exception" concerning restricting expression of the "views [people] have"!)

Critics of strict construction also point out that the Constitution is silent on many important points (such as a right to privacy) and could not have anticipated the changes in technology in the twentieth and twenty-first centuries that have many legal implications, such as eavesdropping devices, cloning, and the Internet. Also, though the language of the First Amendment is relatively clear when it comes to political speech, other equally important words of the Constitution such as "necessary and proper," "executive power," "equal protection," and "due process" are open-ended and vague. Some strict constructionists respond by arguing that if the words of the Constitution are not clear, the justices should be guided by what the Founders *intended*, a perspective called the **original intent** or originalist perspective. Clarence Thomas is the current justice who is most influenced by this view, especially on issues of federalism.

Justice Antonin Scalia has a similar view, arguing that the text of the Constitution should be closely followed and if the text is ambiguous, justices should figure out what the words generally meant to people at the time they were written. This view leads Scalia to some unpopular positions, such as his view that the Sixth Amendment provision that "in all criminal prosecutions the accused shall enjoy the right . . . to be confronted with the witnesses against him" applies even in the case of an accused child molester. The majority of the Court disagreed and held that it was acceptable to have the child testify in front of the prosecutor and

strict construction A way of interpreting the Constitution based on its language alone.

original intent The theory that justices should surmise the intentions of the Founders when the language of the Constitution is unclear.

MARY BETH TINKER AND TWO OTHER students in the Des Moines, Iowa, public schools were suspended for wearing armbands to protest the Vietnam War. The Supreme Court ruled that the First Amendment protected symbolic political speech, even in public schools. Mary Beth is shown here with her mother at the trial.

defense attorney, with the judge, jury, and the accused viewing from another room over closed-circuit television because of the potential trauma the child would experience by having to confront the defendant face-to-face.[59]

Critics of the strict constructionist view are often described as supporting a **living Constitution** perspective on the document (see Chapter 2). They argue that originalism or other versions of strict construction can "make a nation the prisoner of its past, and reject any constitutional development save constitutional amendment."[60] If the justices are bound to follow the literal words of the Constitution, *with the meaning they had when the document was written,* we certainly could be legally frozen in time. The option of amending the Constitution is a long and difficult process, so that is not always a viable way for the Constitution to reflect changing norms and values. Justice William Brennan, a critic of originalism, also argued it was "arrogance cloaked in humility" to presume to know what the Framers intended. According to this view, interpreting the Constitution is always somewhat subjective and it is misleading to claim otherwise.[61]

living Constitution A way of interpreting the Constitution that takes into account evolving national attitudes and circumstances rather than the text alone.

POLITICAL FACTORS

The living Constitution perspective points to the second set of influences on Supreme Court decision making: political factors. Indeed, many people are uncomfortable thinking about the Court in political terms and prefer to think of the image of "blind justice," in which constitutional principles are fairly applied. However, political influences are clearly evident in the Court—maybe less than in Congress or the presidency, but they are certainly present. This means that the courts respond to and shape politics in ways that often involve compromise, both within the courts themselves and in the broader political system.

POLITICAL IDEOLOGY AND ATTITUDES

The most important political factor is the justice's ideology or attitudes about various issues (this is often called the **attitudinalist approach** to understanding Supreme Court decision making). Liberal judges are strong defenders of individual civil liberties (including defendants' rights), tend to be prochoice on abortion, support regulatory policy to protect the environment and workers, support national intervention in the states, and favor race-conscious policies such as affirmative action. Conservative judges favor state regulation of private conduct (especially on moral issues), support prosecutors over defendants, tend to be pro-life on abortion, and support the free market and property rights over the environment and workers, states' rights over national intervention, and a color-blind policy on race.

attitudinalist approach A way of understanding decisions of the Supreme Court based on the political ideologies of the justices.

These are, of course, just general tendencies. However, they do provide a strong basis for explaining patterns of decisions, especially on some types of cases. For example, there were dramatic differences in the chief justices' rulings on civil liberties cases from 1953 to 2001: Earl Warren took the liberal position on 79 percent of the 771 cases he participated in, Warren Burger took the liberal position on 30 percent of 1,429 cases, and William Rehnquist took the liberal position on only 22 percent of his 2,127 cases.[62] If justices were neutrally applying the law, there would not be such dramatic differences.

Proponents of the attitudinalist view also argue that justices who *claim* to be strict constructionists or originalists are really driven by ideology because they selectively use the text of the Constitution. For example, Justice Thomas voted

judicial restraint The idea that the Supreme Court should defer to the democratically elected executive and legislative branches of government rather than contradicting existing laws.

judicial activism The idea that the Supreme Court should assert its interpretation of the law even if it overrules the elected executive and legislative branches of government.

against the University of Michigan's affirmative action program without considering whether the authors of the Fourteenth Amendment supported the practice (the historical record shows that they supported similar policies for the newly freed slaves). Therefore, if Justice Thomas had been true to his originalist perspective, he would have supported affirmative action, but his ideology led him to oppose the policy. The example of Hugo Black's contradictory position on free speech rights cited earlier demonstrates that a liberal textualist view may also be inconsistently applied.

THE STRATEGIC MODEL

A strategic approach to understanding Supreme Court decision making focuses on justices' calculations about the preferences of the other justices, the president, and Congress; the choices that other justices are likely to make; and the institutional context within which they operate. After all, justices do not operate alone: at a minimum they need the votes of four of their colleagues if they want their position to prevail. Therefore, it makes sense to focus on the strategic interactions that take place to build coalitions.

The median voter on the Court—the one in the middle when the justices are arrayed from the most liberal to the most conservative—has an especially influential role in the strategic model. For many years the median justice was Sandra Day O'Connor; when Samuel Alito replaced her, Anthony Kennedy became the new median (see Figure 13.4). The four conservatives to his right (Thomas, Scalia, Roberts, and Alito) and the four liberals to his left (Breyer, Ginsberg, Souter, and Stevens) all wanted to attract his vote. When Justice Sotomayor replaced Justice Souter and when Justice Kagan replaced Justice Stevens, Kennedy remained the median voter on the Court (because Souter, Sotomayor, Stevens, and Kagan are all to his left). Research shows that at least one justice switches his or her vote at some stage in the process (from the initial conference to oral arguments to the final vote) on at least half of the cases, so strategic bargaining appears to be fairly common.[63] Our earlier discussion of opinion assignment and writing opinions to attract the support of a specific justice is more evidence in support of the strategic model.

SEPARATION OF POWERS

Another political influence on justices' decision making is their view of the place of the Court with respect to the democratically elected institutions (Congress and the president). Specifically, do they favor an activist or a restrained role for the Court? Advocates of **judicial restraint** argue that judges should defer to the elected branches and not strike down their laws or other actions. In contrast, advocates of **judicial activism** argue that the Court must play an active role in interpreting the Constitution to protect minority rights even if it means overturning the actions of the elected branches. Yet another approach says that these normative arguments about how restraint or activism ought to work don't really matter because the Court usually follows public opinion and rarely plays a lead role in promoting policy change. One scholar found that three-fifths to two-thirds of Supreme Court decisions are consistent with public opinion when the public has a clear preference on an issue.[64] However, there are plenty of examples of when the Court has stood up for unpopular views, such as banning prayer in schools, allowing flag burning, and protecting criminal defendants' rights.

Often, assessments of the Court's role vary with the views of a specific line of cases. A political conservative may favor "activist" decisions striking down environmental laws or workplace regulations but oppose activist decisions that defend flag burning or defendants' rights. Political liberals may be the opposite—calling for judicial restraint on the first set of cases but activism in protecting civil liberties. Sometimes, the popular media mistakenly assert that liberal justices are more activist than conservative justices. In fact, though, that is not always the case. The current Court is quite conservative, but it is also activist.[65] Two conservatives, Justice Kennedy and Justice Thomas, have voted to overturn laws passed by Congress 93 percent and 81 percent of the time, respectively, whereas two of the most liberal justices, Breyer and Ginsburg, have taken the activist position in only 42 percent and 48 percent of the cases.[66] The 1930s Court that struck down much of the New Deal legislation was also conservative and activist, but the Warren Court of the late 1950s and early 1960s was liberal and activist (see Table 13.1).

A prominent legal journalist observed that the way the popular media describe activism and restraint typically boils down to ideology: if you like a decision, it is restrained; if you do not like a decision, it is activist. For example, *Bush v. Gore*, the decision that decided the outcome of the 2000 presidential election, shows that "most conservatives tie themselves in knots to defend judicial activism when they like the results and to denounce it when they do not. As the reaction to *Lawrence* [the recent gay sex case] and, earlier, *Roe* [the landmark abortion case] has shown, liberals have been no less selective in their outrage at judicial adventurousness."[67] However, there are instances in which restraint reflects more than ideology and preferences. Justice O'Connor, for example, took restrained positions on abortion and affirmative action, despite her personal views against these policies. The most dramatic example of this was the health care reform decision noted in the introduction to his chapter. In a classical statement of judicial restraint, the chief justice said that some decisions "are entrusted to our nation's elected leaders, who can be thrown out of office if the people disagree with them." However, despite providing the pivotal vote to uphold central provisions of the law, he made his personal views clear. "It is not our job," he said, "to protect the people from the consequences of their political choices."[68]

It is important to define activism and restraint in terms of the Court's role in our nation's system of separated powers: Does it check the elected branches by overturning their decisions through judicial review? This is the only objective way to define activism and restraint.

OUTSIDE INFLUENCES: INTEREST GROUPS AND PUBLIC OPINION

Finally, there are external influences on the Court, such as public opinion and interest groups. We have already talked about the role of interest groups in filing amicus briefs. This is the only avenue of influence open to interest groups; other tactics such as lobbying or fund-raising are either inappropriate or irrelevant

FIGURE » 13.4

IDEOLOGY OF SUPREME COURT JUSTICES, 2010

Notice that the estimates of the justices' ideology vary in their precision. What might explain the relatively tight distribution for Breyer or Kennedy, compared to the broad distribution for Sotomayor?

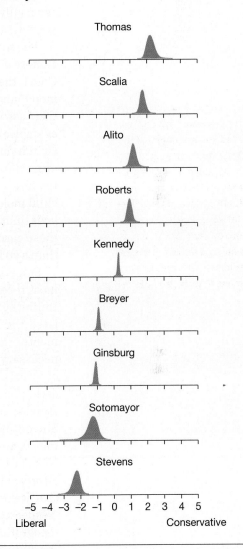

Source: Alexander Tahk and Stephen Jessee, Supreme Court Ideology Project, http://sct.tahk.us/current.html (accessed 10/2/12).

(because justices are not elected). The role of public opinion is more complex. Obviously, justices do not consult public opinion polls the way elected officials do. However, the Court expresses the public's preferences in several indirect ways.

The first was most colorfully expressed by Mr. Dooley, a fictional Irish American bartender whom newspaper satirist Finley Peter Dunne created at the turn of the nineteenth century. Mr. Dooley offered keen insights on politics and general social criticism, including this gem on the relationship between the Supreme Court and the public: "th' supreme coort always follows th' iliction returns."[69] That is, the public elects the president and the Senate, who appoint and confirm the justices. Therefore, sooner or later, the Court should reflect the views of the public. Subsequent work by political scientists has confirmed this to be largely the case,[70] especially in recent years when Supreme Court nominations have become more political and more important to the public.[71]

The second mechanism through which public opinion may influence the Court is more direct: when the public has a clear position on an issue that is before the Court, the Court tends to agree with the public. One study found that the "public mood" and Court opinions correlated very highly between 1956 and 1981, but that their association was weaker through the rest of the 1980s.[72] Several high-profile examples support the idea that the Court is sensitive to public opinion: the Court's switch during the New Deal in the 1930s to support Roosevelt's policy agenda after standing in the way for four years, giving in to wartime opinion to support the internment of Japanese Americans during World War II, limiting an accused child molester's right to confront his accuser in a court room, and declaring that laws limiting sex between consenting gay adults were unconstitutional. In each of these cases the justices reflected the current public opinion of the nation rather than a strict reading of the Constitution or the Founders' intent.

Sometimes the Court may shift its views to reflect *international* opinion. The most recent example struck down the death penalty for minors in twelve states. Ruling by a 5–4 margin that the execution of sixteen- or seventeen-year-olds violated the Eighth Amendment's prohibition against "cruel and unusual punishments," the majority opinion overturned a 1989 case and said the new decision was necessary to reflect the "evolving standards of decency" concerning the definition of "cruel and unusual punishments." Justice Kennedy, who voted on the other side of this issue sixteen years earlier, wrote, "It is fair to say that the United States now stands alone in a world that has turned its face against the juvenile death penalty." Since 1990, he noted, only seven other countries have executed people for crimes they committed as juveniles, and all seven—Iran, Pakistan, Saudi Arabia, Yemen, Nigeria, China, and Congo—no longer execute minors. Justice Kennedy said that although the Court was not obligated to follow foreign developments, "it is proper that we acknowledge the overwhelming weight of international opinion" for its "respected and significant confirmation for our own conclusions." This explicit recognition of the role of public opinion firmly placed a majority of the Court on the side of the "living Constitution" perspective on this issue, while rejecting the strict constructionist view of the dissenters.

Another way that the Court may consider the public mood is to shift the timing of a decision. The best example here is the landmark school desegregation case, *Brown v. Board of Education* (1954), that the Court sat on for more than two years— until after the 1952 presidential election—because it didn't think the public was ready for its bombshell ruling.[73] Others have argued that the Court rarely *changes* its views to reflect public opinion,[74] but at a minimum the evidence supports the notion that the Court is usually in step with the public.

THE ROLE OF THE COURT AS A POLICY MAKER

We conclude with the topic addressed early in the chapter—the place of the Court within the political system. Is the Court the "weakest branch"? As Alexander Hamilton pointed out, the Court has "neither the power of the purse nor the sword." Therefore, it is not clear how it can enforce decisions. In some instances the Court can force its views on the other branches; in other cases it needs their support to enforce its decisions. (See "What Do Political Scientists Do?")

COMPLIANCE AND IMPLEMENTATION

To gain compliance with its decisions, the Court can rely only on its reputation and on the actions of Congress and the president to back them up. If the other branches don't support the Court, there isn't much it can do. The extreme example was the result of an ongoing feud between Chief Justice John Marshall and President Andrew Jackson in the 1830s. The case concerned a missionary, Samuel Worcester, who was arrested on Cherokee land in Georgia because he did not have the proper license to be there. Worcester claimed that the U.S. government, not the state of Georgia, should have control over the Cherokee Nation, and that therefore Georgia had no right to arrest him under its laws. The Supreme Court agreed.[75] After the decision, Jackson remarked, "John Marshall has made his decision. Now let him enforce it if he can." Georgia instead enforced its laws and ignored the Court—Worcester remained in jail for another year.

At the other extreme, some decisions are nearly self-enforcing because of their visibility and narrow application. If the decision primarily affects one party, the attention and focus on the case compels compliance. For example, in 1974 Richard Nixon knew that he had to go along with the Court ruling forcing him to give up his secret tapes for the Watergate investigation or he would have been impeached. But even cases that seem to have narrow application (such as *Bush v. Gore* in 2000) often see broad application by lower courts and future litigants. If the Court knows it is likely to face resistance, it can attempt to get a unanimous vote, since even one dissent can provide a rationale for resisting a Court ruling.

The Court's lack of enforcement power is especially evident when a ruling applies broadly to millions of people who care deeply about the issue. Consider school prayer, which still exists in hundreds of public schools nationwide despite having been ruled unconstitutional more than forty years ago. It is impossible to enforce the ban unless someone in a school complains and is willing to bring a lawsuit.

In most cases that involve a broad policy, the Court depends on the president for enforcement. After *Brown v. Board of Education* (1954), the landmark school desegregation case, presidents Eisenhower and Kennedy had to send in the National Guard to desegregate public schools and universities. However, presidential foot-dragging can have a big impact on how the law is enforced. President Nixon attempted to lessen the impact of a school busing decision in 1971 that forced the integration of public schools by interpreting it very narrowly. Republican presidents who oppose abortion have limited the scope of *Roe v. Wade*, which legalized abortion in 1973, by

HIGH SCHOOL STUDENTS IN MAIZE, Kansas, join hands around a flagpole at the annual nationwide event calling Christian youth to preclass schoolyard prayer at the start of the new school year. Enforcing the prohibition of school prayer and drawing the line between permissible and impermissible prayer have both been difficult for the Court.

CAN THE SUPREME COURT BE AN AGENT OF CHANGE?

Ever since Chief Justice Earl Warren led the liberal Supreme Court in the 1950s and 1960s, many political observers have assumed that the Supreme Court can bring about social change. On a range of topics that include school desegregation, criminal defendants' rights, school prayer, one-person-one-vote requirements in legislative redistricting, the right to privacy and family planning, and the freedom of speech, the Supreme Court has been ahead of public opinion and seemed to lead the elected branches.

However, in his book *The Hollow Hope*, political scientist Gerald Rosenberg argues that courts can almost never produce significant social reform. He says, "At best, they can second the social reform acts of the other branches of government."[a] In his conclusion, entitled "The Fly Paper Court," Rosenberg warns that social reformers may be seduced by the "lure of litigation," wasting their time in the courts when they could be using their resources more effectively elsewhere. He argues that the American political system inherently limits the effectiveness of the courts through three structural constraints: (1) the limited nature of constitutional rights (for example, there is no constitutional right to "housing, adequate levels of welfare, a job, or a clean environment," all goals of social reformers), (2) Congress's constraints on judicial independence through the nomination process and statutory interpretation, and (3) the judiciary's limited enforcement powers. These constraints can be overcome only when there is adequate legal precedent for change, when there is support for legal change from Congress and the president, when there is either strong support from some citizens or weak opposition from all citizens, and when conditions otherwise support compliance with the judicial decision.

Rosenberg then looked at the evidence of whether these constraints can be overcome and the Court can be an agent for social change. Rosenberg tackled the instances in which most people have assumed that the Court *did* produce change: civil rights, abortion and women's rights, the environment, legislative reapportionment, criminal law, and gay marriage. But in each instance, Rosenberg argues, this was not the case. For example, although the *Brown v. Board of Education* (1954) decision officially desegregated schools in the South, no real progress was made until after the 1964 Civil Rights Act was passed. In the 1964–65 school year, the last year before the Civil Rights Act would have had any impact, only 2.3 percent of black children in the South attended elementary or secondary school with white children. By 1972–73, that figure was 91.3 percent. Similarly, the 1965 Voting Rights Act had a much bigger impact on black voter registration in the South than the series of court cases on voting rights in the 1950s and 1960s.

Watch a video clip of political scientist Michael McCann discussing this topic at **wwnorton.com/studyspace**

Earl Warren served as chief justice of the Supreme Court from 1953 to 1969. Decisions during his tenure on racial segregation, civil rights, and criminal defendants' rights raised expectations that the Court would be an agent of social change.

Legislative apportionment appears to be one of the strongest examples of the impact of the courts. *Baker v. Carr* (1962) and subsequent cases mandated that legislative districts be of equal population ("one person, one vote"). Indeed, by the end of the 1960s, nearly every state legislative district and U.S. House district was in compliance with the Court decisions. However, as Rosenberg points out, for the social reformers, getting legislative districts to be equal in size was only a means to an end, and that end was not achieved: reformers were concerned that rural interests were overrepresented in legislatures, which skewed policy away from the interests of urban residents; however, most studies of the impact of population equalization in legislative districts show little to no impact on policy.

The responses to Rosenberg's argument range from, "What's the big deal? Since Alexander Hamilton pointed it out in *Federalist 78*, we have known that the Court depends on the other branches to enforce its decisions" to those who argue that Rosenberg is using an improper causal model for determining the impact of Supreme Court decisions—rather than a unitary actor that influences the behavior of other institutions through its decisions, the Court must be viewed within our system of separated and shared powers. That is, the Court cannot produce change by itself, but this is not a realistic expectation, given our system of government. Furthermore, the Court may be a catalyst for change by helping create the climate in which it is possible for the other branches of government to act.[b]

The Hollow Hope is an excellent example of how empirical evidence can be brought to bear on an important question and produce novel and provocative arguments. The twenty years of debate produced by the book is strong testimony to the continued disagreements over the role of the Court within our political system.

denying federal support for abortions for Medicaid recipients, banning abortions on military bases, and preventing doctors from mentioning abortion as an option during pregnancy counseling. The Court must rely on its reputation and prestige to compel the president and Congress not to stray too far from its decisions.

RELATIONS WITH THE OTHER BRANCHES

The Court's relations with the other branches of government may be strained as it has to rule on fundamental questions about institutional power. The Court has limited the power of the president in several high-profile cases, including Lincoln's suspension of the writ of habeas corpus during the Civil War, Truman's use of the National Guard to open steel mills that had been shut down by a labor dispute during the Korean War, Nixon's attempt to suppress information about the Vietnam War, and George W. Bush's suspension of civil liberties for "enemy combatants" during the War on Terror.[76] Yet the Court has consistently upheld the president's broader war-making power, including Lincoln's blockade of southern ports when Congress was out of session in 1861 and various other presidents' unilateral military actions in Vietnam, El Salvador, Grenada, Panama, the Persian Gulf, and Iraq.

RESISTANCE FROM THE OTHER BRANCHES

The president and Congress often fight back when they think the Court is exerting too much influence, which can limit the Court's power as a policy-making institution. For the president, this can escalate to open conflict. Examples include the battle between Jackson and Marshall over jurisdiction within the Cherokee Nation; the conflict between Jefferson and Marshall, which included the impeachment of a Supreme Court justice for political reasons (although the Senate acquitted the justice on all charges), and the repeal of the 1801 Judiciary Act; FDR's court-packing scheme, which was his response to the obstructionist New Deal Court; and President Obama's calling out the Supreme Court in his 2010 State of the Union message for a decision he disagreed with. When Obama said that the Supreme Court's ruling in *Citizens United v. Federal Election Commission* (2010) had opened the floodgates for corporate spending—including foreign corporations—in elections, Justice Alito was caught on camera mouthing the words "not true." Washington was abuzz for days about whether the president's comment or Alito's response was out of line. Chief Justice Roberts added fuel to the fire a few weeks later when he said he found the president's comment and the partisan atmosphere of the speech "very troubling," and he indicated that justices may not attend State of the Union addresses in the future.

The president can counter the Court's influence in a more restrained way by failing to enforce a decision vigorously. Congress can try to control the Court by blocking appointments it disagrees with (however, this often involves a disagreement with the president more than the Court), limiting the jurisdiction of the federal courts, changing the size of the Court, or even impeaching a judge. The latter three options are rarely used, but Congress often threatens to take these drastic steps. The most common way for Congress to respond to a Court decision that it disagrees with is simply to pass legislation that overturns the decision (if the case concerns the interpretation of a law). Sometimes these disputes last for a while, as with the recent flap over sentencing guidelines. Congress wanted the federal courts to get tougher on criminals, so it passed a law telling federal judges the range of sentences that they had to give for specific crimes. Chief Justice Rehnquist was upset that Congress passed the law without input from the judiciary, and the Court struck back by invalidating the sentencing guidelines as an unfair imposition on the judiciary. The Roberts Court is deeply involved in this issue as well.

SELF-IMPOSED RESTRAINT

In general, the Court avoids stepping on the toes of the other branches unless it is absolutely necessary. The Court often exercises self-imposed restraint and refuses to act on "political questions"—issues that are outside the judicial domain and should be decided by elected officials. One of the earliest applications was an 1804 dispute over whether a piece of land by the Mississippi River belonged to Spain or the United States. The Court observed, "A question like this, respecting the boundaries of nations, is . . . more a political than a legal question, and in its discussion, the courts of every country must respect the pronounced will of the legislature."[77]

A more recent application of the doctrine was a 1948 case in which the Court refused to review orders of the Civil Aeronautics Board granting or denying applications by citizen carriers to engage in overseas and foreign air transportation. The Court's reasons to avoid this issue show its deference to the elected branches on foreign policy:

> The very nature of executive decisions as to foreign policy is political, not judicial. Such decisions are wholly confided by our Constitution on the political departments of government, executive and legislative. They are delicate, complex, and involve large elements of prophecy. They are and should be undertaken only by those directly responsible to the people whose welfare they advance or imperil. They are decisions of a kind for which the Judiciary has neither aptitude, facilities, nor responsibility and which has long been held to belong in the domain of political power not subject to judicial instrument or inquiry.[78]

Though this self-imposed limitation on judicial power is important, one must also recognize that the Court reserves the right to decide what a political question is. Therefore, one could argue that this is not much of a limit on judicial power after all. For example, for many decades the Court avoided the topic of legislative redistricting, saying that it did not want to enter that "political thicket." However, it changed its position in the 1960s in a series of cases that imposed the idea of "one person, one vote" on the redistricting process and it has been intimately involved in redistricting ever since. The Court's ability to define the boundaries of political questions is an important source of its policy-making power.

THE COURT'S MULTIFACETED ROLE

This "big picture" question about the relationship of the Court to the other branches boils down to this: Does the judiciary constrain the other branches, or does it defer to their wishes? Given the responsiveness of the elected branches to the will of the people, this question can alternatively be stated: Does the Court operate in a countermajoritarian way as a protector of minority interests, or does it defer to the popular will? The evidence on this is mixed.

The judicial branch as a whole contains a basic paradox: it may be simultaneously seen as the least democratic and most democratic branch.[79] The least democratic part is obvious: federal judges and many state and local judges are unelected and are not accountable to the voters (except indirectly through the elected leaders who appoint them). But the courts can also be seen as the most democratic branch. Cases that are brought to the courts come from the people and as long as the legal criteria for bringing a case are met, the courts must hear those cases. While people have the right to petition "the government for a redress of grievances," there is no guarantee that

Congress or the executive branch will listen to them. Of course, only a small fraction of the cases brought to the Supreme Court are heard, so the antidemocratic charge carries more weight at the top. However, the court system as a whole may be seen as providing an important outlet for participation in our political system.

The countermajoritarian nature of the Supreme Court is also a complicated question to sort out. The Court is activist on many issues, exercising judicial review, but on many other issues it defers to the elected institutions. Sometimes an activist Court defends minority interests on issues such as criminal defendants' rights, school prayer, gay rights, and flag burning, but that is not always the case. Is the Court acting undemocratically when it exercises its power of judicial review (or, as critics would say, "legislates from the bench")? Or is it playing its vital role in our constitutional system as a check on the other branches?

The answers depend somewhat on one's political views. Conservatives would generally applaud the activism of the Rehnquist and Roberts Courts, while liberals would see it as an unwarranted check on the elected branches. Moreover, the Court's role has varied throughout history: in some instances it defended unpopular views and strongly protected minority rights; in other cases it followed majority opinion and declined to play that important role. Clearly the Court has the *potential* to play an important policy-making role in our system of checks and balances; whether it actually plays that role depends on the political, personal, and legal factors outlined in this chapter.

THE COURTS HAVE BEEN AN IMPORTANT protector of minority rights, including in the civil rights era. But at other times the courts have supported the will of the majority.

CONCLUSION

The courts demonstrate that politics is conflictual. Although plenty of unanimous Supreme Court decisions do not involve much conflict among the justices, many landmark cases deeply divide the Court on constitutional interpretation and how to balance those competing interpretations against other values and interests. These conflicts in the Court often reveal deeper fault lines in the broader political system.

It shouldn't be surprising that political process matters in the courts. The rules of courtroom procedures, including discovery and how evidence is presented, can have an important impact on outcomes. Political process is also important for selecting judges and determining which cases the Supreme Court hears.

Politics is indeed everywhere, even in the courts, where you would least expect to see it. Despite the idealized image of Justice as a blindfolded woman holding a set of scales, politics affects everything from the selection of judges to the decisions they make. Some characteristics of the federal courts (most important being judges' lifetime tenure) insulate the system from politics. However, courts are subject to influence by judges' ideologies, interest groups, and the president and Senate, who try to shape their composition through the nomination process.

Returning to the example that opened this chapter demonstrates the important role that the courts play in the political system. The Supreme Court endorsed the national government's dominant role in shaping immigration policy, but also recognized the states' right to enforce the federal law. The federal courts may serve as a referee between the other branches, and between the national and state government, defining the boundaries of permissible conduct.

THE DEVELOPMENT OF AN INDEPENDENT AND POWERFUL FEDERAL JUDICIARY

▶ Explain how the power of judicial review was established. **Pages 509–15**

SUMMARY

In contrast to other branches of government, the Constitution offers few specifics on the organization of the judiciary. In fact, most of the details on the arrangement of the judiciary do not come from the Constitution at all, but from congressional action. In addition, the Supreme Court's strongest power—judicial review—is not even mentioned in the Constitution, but was established in the *Marbury v. Madison* decision.

KEY TERMS

Judiciary Act of 1789 (p. 510)

district courts (p. 510)

appellate jurisdiction (p. 510)

judicial review (p. 510)

original jurisdiction (p. 511)

constitutional interpretation (p. 513)

statutory interpretation (p. 513)

CRITICAL THINKING AND DISCUSSION

What do recent decisions on immigration and health care reform reveal about the role of the Supreme Court in our political system? Did the Founders approve of the practice of judicial review?

PRACTICE QUIZ QUESTIONS

1. Most of the details about the Supreme Court were established in _____.
   a) the Judiciary Act of 1789
   b) Article I of the Constitution
   c) Article II of the Constitution
   d) *The Federalist Papers*
   e) *Marbury v. Madison*

2. *Marbury v. Madison* is significant because it _____.
   a) established the Supreme Court
   b) introduced the process of selective incorporation
   c) changed the manner of judicial selection
   d) established judicial review
   e) gave Supreme Court justices lifetime appointments

3. Judicial review enables the Supreme Court to _____.
   a) submit legislation to Congress
   b) strike down laws passed by Congress
   c) revise laws passed by Congress
   d) oversee presidential appointments to the bureaucracy
   e) approve judicial appointments to lower courts

4. The Court's application of national and state laws to particular cases is called _____.
   a) constitutional interpretation
   b) judicial restraint
   c) judicial activism
   d) original jurisdiction
   e) statutory interpretation

THE AMERICAN LEGAL AND JUDICIAL SYSTEM

Outline the structure of the court system. **Pages 515–28**

SUMMARY

All courts within the United States have a similar set of fundamental attributes, such as the distinction between civil and criminal cases and the reliance on legal precedent. The judicial system is divided between state and federal courts, and within each level of government, there are courts of original jurisdiction and appeals courts.

KEY TERMS

plaintiff (p. 515)

defendant (p. 515)

plea bargain (p. 515)

class-action lawsuit (p. 516)

common law (p. 516)

precedent (p. 516)

standing (p. 518)

jurisdiction (p. 518)

appeals courts (p. 520)

senatorial courtesy (p. 526)

CRITICAL THINKING AND DISCUSSION

What is the proper role for the Senate in providing "advice and consent" on the selection of federal judges? Should the Senate play the role of an equal partner to the president or simply approve most of the president's choices?

PRACTICE QUIZ QUESTIONS

5. A system of _____ relies on legal decisions that build on precedent established in previous cases.
   a) common law
   b) civil law
   c) statutory law
   d) stare decisis
   e) plea bargaining

6. When one has suffered direct and personal harm from the action addressed in a case, it is called
   _____.
   a) precedent
   b) appellant
   c) plea bargaining
   d) jurisdiction
   e) standing

7. The president appoints federal judges with the "advice and consent" of the _____.
   a) House of Representatives
   b) Senate
   c) Supreme Court
   d) attorney general
   e) vice president

ⓢ PRACTICE ONLINE

"Critical Thinking" exercise: *Political Process Matters—Senatorial Approval and the Nomination Process*

ACCESS TO THE SUPREME COURT

Describe how cases reach the Supreme Court. **Pages 528–33**

SUMMARY

The Supreme Court hears only about 1 percent of the cases that are brought to it. To help decide which cases to hear, the Court generally uses four factors: collusion, standing, mootness, ripeness. Ultimately, the justices have a great deal of discretion in deciding to hear a case, but they can only hear cases that come to them.

KEY TERMS

writ of certiorari (p. 530)

mootness (p. 531)

ripeness (p. 531)

cert pool (p. 532)

solicitor general (p. 532)

8. When a litigant who lost in a lower court files a petition, the case reaches the Supreme Court _____

a) as a matter of right
b) through a writ of certification
c) through a writ of certiorari
d) as a matter of original jurisdiction
e) through senatorial courtesy

9. _____ means that the controversy is not relevant when the Court hears the case.

a) Mootness
b) Ripeness

c) Collusion
d) Standing
e) Precedent

10. Most justices _____ in initially deciding which cases should be heard.

a) personally review all cases
b) personally review a random sample of cases
c) follow the recommendations of the chief justice
d) use a random selection process
e) use a cert pool

HEARING CASES BEFORE THE SUPREME COURT

Describe the Supreme Court's procedures for hearing a case. **Pages 533–37**

SUMMARY

When hearing a case, the justices prepare by reading briefs before they hear the oral arguments. After oral arguments, the justices meet in conference to discuss and vote on the cases. The majority opinion explains the rationale for how a decision is reached, though justices can also write dissenting and concurring opinions.

KEY TERMS

amicus curiae (p. 533)

oral arguments (p. 534)

PRACTICE QUIZ QUESTIONS

11. Oral arguments generally last _____, and justices _____ wait until the end of the arguments to ask questions.

a) one hour; will
b) one hour; do not

c) one day; will
d) one week; will
e) one week; do not

12. Generally, the chief justice or the _____ justice decides who writes the majority opinion; justices' individual areas of expertise _____ a factor in making this assignment.

a) most junior; are not
b) most junior; are
c) most senior; are not
d) most senior; are
e) dissenting; does not

⑤ **PRACTICE ONLINE**

"Critical Thinking" exercise: *Politics Is Conflictual— Sandra Day O'Connor on* The Daily Show

SUPREME COURT DECISION MAKING

Analyze the factors that influence Supreme Court decisions. **Pages 537–42**

SUMMARY

The Court makes decisions based on legal factors such as precedent and informal norms, and political factors such as the justices' own ideologies and positions on the role that the Court plays in government. Though the Court does not consult public opinion the way elected officials do, most decisions generally stay in step with the public.

KEY TERMS

strict construction (p. 538)

original intent (p. 538)

living Constitution (p. 539)

attitudinalist approach (p. 539)

judicial restraint (p. 540)

judicial activism (p. 540)

Should unelected judges have the ability to overturn laws passed by the elected branches? If so, should there be any mechanism for *political* accountability?

PRACTICE QUIZ QUESTIONS

13. The perspective that when the Constitution is not clear, the justices should be guided by what the Founders wanted is called _____.
    a) judicial activism
    b) strict construction
    c) original intent
    d) attitudinalist approach
    e) interpretive statute

14. Advocates of _____ argue that the Court must defer to the elected branches and not strike down their laws.
    a) judicial restraint
    b) judicial activism
    c) judicial limitation
    d) legal maximization
    e) the strategic model

Ⓢ PRACTICE ONLINE

"Big Think" video exercise: *The Challenge of Constitutional Interpretation*

THE ROLE OF THE COURT AS A POLICY MAKER

Assess the Supreme Court's power in the political system. **Pages 543–47**

SUMMARY

Given the constitutional weakness of the Court, it is unclear how it is able to enforce its decisions. Depending on context, the Court is occasionally able to force its views on the elected branches, though more often it requires their support.

PRACTICE QUIZ QUESTION

15. In general, the Court _____ challenges with the elected branches and often _____ to act on "political questions."
    a) avoids; agrees
    b) avoids; refuses
    c) pursues; agrees
    d) pursues; refuses

Ⓢ PRACTICE ONLINE

"What Do Political Scientists Do?" video exercise: *The Impact of Litigation and Courts in American Politics*

SUGGESTED READING

Baum, Lawrence. *Judges and Their Audiences: A Perspective on Judicial Behavior.* Princeton, NJ: Princeton University Press, 2006.

Cornell University Law School, Supreme Court Collection, http://supct/law.cornell.edu/supct.

Eisgruber, Christopher L. *Constitutional Self-Government.* Cambridge, MA: Harvard University Press, 2001.

Hansford, Thomas G., and James F. Spriggs II. *The Politics of Precedent on the U.S. Supreme Court.* Princeton, NJ: Princeton University Press, 2006.

Northwestern University, Oyez: Supreme Court Multimedia, www.oyez.org.

O'Brien, David M. *Storm Center: The Supreme Court in American Politics.* 9th ed. New York: Norton, 2011.

Rosen, Jeffrey. *The Most Democratic Branch: How the Courts Serve America.* New York: Oxford University Press, 2006.

Sunstein, Cass R., David Schkade, Lisa M. Ellman, and Andres Sawicki. *Are Judges Political? An Empirical Analysis of the Federal Judiciary.* Washington, DC: Brookings Institution Press, 2006.

Tushnet, Mark. *A Court Divided: The Rehnquist Court and the Future of Constitutional Law.* New York: Norton, 2006.

U.S. Supreme Court website, www.supremecourt.gov.

14

Civil Rights

Have your papers ready—
Racial profiling just ahead.

Cuéntame   paid for by Brave New Foundation

CRITICS OF A 2010 IMMIGRATION law in Arizona worried that it would subject Latinos to racial profiling. One group opposing the law sponsored this billboard in Phoenix to draw attention to their concerns. Supporters of the law, such as Phoenix sheriff Joe Arpaio, argued that strong measures were necessary to discourage illegal immigration.

JOE ARPAIO OF PHOENIX, ARIZONA, is the self-described "toughest sheriff in America." He was also the target of a four-year investigation by the U.S. Justice Department of discriminatory practices in the enforcement of immigration laws. He is either a hero or villain, depending on one's views concerning illegal immigration. His supporters see him as a courageous and tireless fighter who is enforcing the law that the federal government seems incapable or unwilling to do. His critics see him as a bigoted publicity hound who abuses the civil rights of people who are nonwhite and live in Maricopa County.

In a report it issued in December 2011, the Justice Department concluded that Sheriff Arpaio's office has "a pervasive culture of discriminatory bias against Latinos . . . that violates the Constitution and federal law."[1] The expert who conducted the analysis noted that Latino drivers were four to nine times more likely to be stopped than non-Latino drivers, calling this practice "the most egregious racial profiling he had ever seen."[2] Sheriff's deputies would use minor traffic violations, such as failure to signal a lane change, to pull over Latinos and ask for their documents. One incident that drew international attention was a neighborhood sweep of a town of about 6,000 Yaqui Indians and Latinos outside of Phoenix. Over a period of two days, more than 100 deputies conducted hundreds of searches, netting nine undocumented immigrants. Residents have sued the county and one critical report said, "The community was so scarred by the event that families are still terrified to leave their homes when they see the Sheriff's patrol cars."[3] While the federal abuse of power

**CONFLICT &
COMPROMISE**
in American Politics

investigation was closed without criminal charges being brought against Arpaio, a class action civil suit is still in the courts as of early 2013.

Sheriff Arpaio defended his office, saying, "We are proud of the work we have done to fight illegal immigration." He was upset that the Justice Department would no longer provide the immigration status of suspects held in his custody (given the report's findings of discrimination), saying that the move "was tantamount to setting up a neon welcome sign for illegal immigrants."[4]

Enforcing immigration law is an extremely conflictual issue. Hardliners on immigration, such as Sheriff Arpaio, see illegal immigrants as a threat to the country and want to make securing our borders as the top priority of immigration policy (while deporting all illegal immigrants). The alternative perspective emphasizes controlling illegal immigration, while protecting the civil rights of citizens and legal residents, and providing a path to citizenship for illegal residents who are productive and law-abiding. It would seem that such a conflictual issue would not be very amenable to compromise. Indeed, President Bush tried and failed to enact comprehensive immigration reform, and President Obama has not fared much better in his first term. Frustrated with Congress's inactivity on the Dream Act, which would have given legal status to young immigrants who came to the United States as children, Obama issued an executive order halting their deportation for two years. However, nearly everyone agrees that the current immigration system is broken and Obama is determined to enact reforms in his second term. Any reform that secures our borders while protecting the civil rights of law-abiding people will involve compromise.

Civil rights policy encompasses much more than immigration policy. Indeed it is one of the best examples of the idea that politics is everywhere: policies concerning discrimination in the workplace and in housing, and against women, minorities, gays, and the disabled affect millions of Americans every day. To see how civil rights policy may affect you, consider the following scenarios. You are driving home one night with a few of your friends after a party. It is late at night, but you have not had anything to drink and you are following all traffic laws. Your heart sinks as you see the red flashing lights of a squad car signaling you to pull over. As the police officer approaches your car, you wonder if you have been pulled over because you and your friends are African Americans driving in an all-white neighborhood. Have your civil rights been violated? Change the scene to a car full of white teenagers with all the other facts the same. Can an officer pull you over just because he thinks that teenagers are more likely to be engaging in criminal activity than older people?

Scenario two: you are a twenty-one-year-old Asian American woman applying for your first job out of college. After being turned down for the job at an engineering firm, you suspect that you didn't get the job because you are a woman and would not fit in with the "good ol' boy" atmosphere of the firm. Have your civil rights been violated?

Scenario three: you and your gay partner are told that "your kind" are not welcome in the apartment complex that you wanted to live in. Should you call a lawyer?

Scenario four: you are a white male graduating from high school. You have just received a letter of rejection from the college that was first on your list. You are very disappointed, but then you get angry when a friend tells you that one of your classmates got into the same school even though he had virtually the same grades as you and his SAT scores were a bit lower. Your friend says that it is probably because of the school's affirmative action policy—the classmate who was accepted is Latino. Are you a victim of "reverse discrimination"? Have your civil rights been violated?

A GROUP OF TEENAGERS IS DETAINED and questioned by police. When is a police stop legitimate? How do we know if it might be a violation of civil rights?

All of these scenarios would seem to be civil rights violations. However, some of them are, some are not, and some depend on additional considerations (we will return to these examples in the conclusion). Applying civil rights law can be very complex, but a central goal of this chapter is to provide a better understanding of the origins of specific civil rights by examining the policy-making process. This chapter will also focus on the theme that political process matters by highlighting how the enforcement of civil rights has varied, both over time and across institutions. That is, sometimes the Supreme Court is a strong defender of civil rights and Congress is not. At other points in history, the reverse has been true.

THE CONTEXT OF CIVIL RIGHTS

DESCRIBE THE HISTORICAL STRUGGLES GROUPS HAVE FACED IN WINNING CIVIL RIGHTS

We begin by examining the context of civil rights: we define civil rights, explore how racial and ethnic categories have changed, and then provide a historical overview of the struggle for civil rights.

In general, **civil rights** is the right to be free from discrimination. A more specific understanding of the term comes from the mission statement of the U.S. Commission on Civil Rights, a bipartisan, independent, federal commission that was established by the 1957 Civil Rights Act.[5] Its mission is to "appraise federal laws and policies," investigate complaints, and collect information with regard to citizens who are "being deprived of their right to vote," discriminated against, or being denied the "equal protection of the laws under the Constitution because of race, color, religion, sex, age, disability, or national origin." It investigates government actions, such as allegations of racial discrimination in elections, and the actions of individuals in the workplace, commerce, housing, and education.

civil rights Rights that guarantee individuals freedom from discrimination. These rights are generally grounded in the equal protection clause of the Fourteenth Amendment and more specifically laid out in laws passed by Congress, such as the 1964 Civil Rights Act.

This definition seems straightforward enough, but some confusion may arise when comparing the terms civil rights and *civil liberties.* They are often used interchangeably, but there are important differences. Civil liberties refer to the freedoms guaranteed in the Bill of Rights, such as the freedom of speech, religious expression, and the press, as well as the "due process" protection of the Fourteenth Amendment. In contrast, civil rights protect all persons from discrimination and are rooted in laws and the equal protection clause of the Fourteenth Amendment. Moreover, civil liberties primarily limit what the government can do to you ("*Congress* shall make no law . . . abridging the freedom of speech"), whereas civil rights protect you from discrimination both by the government and by individuals. To oversimplify, civil liberties are about freedom, and civil rights are about equality.

Neither civil liberties nor civil rights figured prominently at the Constitutional Convention. Equality is not even mentioned in the Constitution or the Bill of Rights. The Bill of Rights is centrally concerned with freedom, but it was not added to the Constitution until the Antifederalists made it a condition for ratification, as discussed in Chapter 2. However, equality was very much on the Founders' minds, as is evident in this ringing passage from the Declaration of Independence: "We hold these truths to be self evident, that all men are created equal, that they are endowed by the Creator with certain unalienable rights, that among these are life, liberty, and the pursuit of happiness." Despite the broad language, this was a limited conception of equality. The reference to "men" was an intentional oversight of the other half of the population: women had no political or economic rights in the late eighteenth century. Similarly, equality did not apply to slaves or to Native Americans. Even propertyless white men did not have full political rights until several decades after the Constitution was ratified. Therefore, equality and civil rights in the United States have been a continually evolving work in progress.

One way to gauge the awareness of different racial and ethnic groups is to track the changes in U.S. Census categories. The census is taken every ten years to measure the size and characteristics of the U.S. population. In 1860, Native Americans became the second ethnic minority group to be acknowledged on the census (after African Americans); however, those living on reservations or in the Indian Territories were not counted in the U.S. population for purposes of congressional apportionment until 1890. The Chinese were first listed as a separate group in 1860 only in California and then more generally in 1870; the Japanese were added in 1890; and Asian and Pacific Islander categories (including Hindu, Korean, and Filipino) were added in 1910. Although "Mexican" was designated as a race in the 1930 census and data had been collected previously on mother tongue and Spanish surnames, the first comprehensive attempt to identify Hispanics was in 1970.

The method for collecting information about race has also changed over the years. Before 1960, census takers identified a person's race according to Census Bureau guidelines. In 1960 and 1970, a combination of direct interview and self-identification was used, and since 1980 people have identified their own race on census forms. In 2000, for the first time, people were allowed to check more than one racial category to reflect the growing reality of a multiracial population. This evolution of census practices shows that even though different racial groups have always been present in the United States, the way they are classified and counted varies depending on the policies of a bureaucratic agency.

AFRICAN AMERICANS

From the early nineteenth century, with the abolitionists' efforts, until the mid-twentieth century and the civil rights movement, the central focus of civil rights was on the experiences of African Americans. Other groups received attention more gradually. Starting in the mid-nineteenth century, women began their fight for equal rights, and over the next century the civil rights movement expanded to include other groups such as Native Americans, Latinos, and Asian Americans. Most recently, attention has turned to the elderly, the disabled, and LGBTs (lesbian, gay, bisexual, and transgender people). The most divisive civil rights issue with the greatest long-term impact, however, has been slavery and its legacy.

Slavery was part of the American economy from nearly the beginning of the nation's history. Dutch traders brought twenty slaves to Jamestown, Virginia, in 1619, a year before the Puritans came to Plymouth Rock. The number of slaves remained fairly small until the late seventeenth century, when three developments spurred the demand for slaves from Africa. First, the growth of the southern plantation system and the increased importance of tobacco as a cash crop created a need for labor. Second, the supply of indentured servants decreased rapidly.[6] Then, just as the demand for slaves started to wane, Eli Whitney patented the cotton gin in 1794, which created greater demand. From 1619 to 1808, after which year the importation of slaves was banned, about 600,000 to 650,000 slaves were forcibly brought from Africa to the United States (and about 75,000 to 100,000 more were brought from Africa but died in transit).[7]

SLAVERY WAS PART OF THE AMERICAN economy from the 1600s until the Civil War in 1861. The system of slavery in the South created a highly unequal society in which African Americans were denied virtually all rights.

It is impossible to overstate the importance of slaves to the southern economy. The 1860 census shows that there were 2.3 million slaves in the Deep South, constituting 47 percent of its population, and there were nearly 4 million slaves overall. Most slaves worked on plantations, but others labored as shipyard workers, carpenters, bakers, stone masons, millers, spinners, weavers, and domestic servants. In the states that later seceded from the Union, 30.8 percent of households owned slaves. The economic benefits of slavery for the owners were clear. By 1860, the per capita income for whites in the South was $3,978; in the North it was $2,040. The South had only 30 percent of the nation's free population, but it had 60 percent of the wealthiest men.[8]

Abolitionists worked to rid the nation of slavery as its importance to the South grew, setting the nation on a collision course that would not be resolved until the Civil War. The Founders largely ducked the issue (see Chapter 2), and subsequent legislatures and courts did not fare much better. The **Missouri Compromise** of 1820, which limited the expansion of slavery and kept the overall balance between slave states and free states, eased tensions for a while, but the issue persisted. Slave owners became increasingly frustrated with the success of the Underground Railroad, which helped some slaves escape to the North. The debate over admitting California as a free state or a slave state (or making it half free and half slave) threatened to split the nation once again. Southern states agreed to admit California as a free state, but only if Congress passed the Fugitive Slave Act, which required northern states to treat escaped slaves as property and return them to their owners. Soon after, Congress enacted the Compromise of 1850, which overturned the Missouri Compromise and allowed each new state to decide for itself whether to be a slave state or a free state.

All possibility of further compromise on the issue ended with the misguided *Dred Scott v. Sandford* decision in 1857. The Supreme Court ruled that states could not be prevented from allowing slavery. It also held that slaves were property rather than citizens and had no legal rights. With Abraham Lincoln's victory in the 1860 presidential election, the southern states believed that slavery was in jeopardy, so they seceded from the Union and formed the Confederacy.

The outcome of the Civil War restored national unity and ended slavery, but the price was very high. About 528,000 Americans died in the war, with an astonishingly high casualty rate of 25 percent among combatants.[9] Republicans moved quickly to ensure that the changes accomplished by the war could not be easily undone: they promptly adopted the Civil War Amendments to the Constitution. The Thirteenth Amendment banned slavery, the Fourteenth guaranteed that states could not deny newly freed slaves the equal protection of the laws and provided citizenship to anyone born in the United States, and the Fifteenth gave African American men the right to vote. These amendments were ratified within five years of the war, although southern states resisted giving freed slaves "equal protection of the laws" over the next 100 years.

During Reconstruction (1866–77), blacks in the South gained political power through institutions such as the Freedmen's Bureau and the Union League. With the protection of the occupying northern army, blacks were able to vote and even hold public office. When federal troops withdrew and the Republican Party abandoned the South, blacks were almost completely **disenfranchised** through the imposition of residency requirements, poll taxes, literacy tests, the **grandfather clause**, physical intimidation, and other forms of disqualification. Later the practice known as the "white primary" allowed only whites to vote in Democratic primary elections; given that the Republican Party did not exist in most southern states, blacks were effectively disenfranchised. Although most of these provisions

Missouri Compromise An agreement between pro- and antislavery groups passed by Congress in 1820 in an attempt to ease tensions by limiting the expansion of slavery while also maintaining a balance between slave states and free states.

disenfranchised To have been denied the ability to exercise a right, such as the right to vote.

grandfather clause A type of law enacted in several southern states to allow those who were permitted to vote before the Civil War, and their descendants, to bypass literacy tests and other obstacles to voting, thereby exempting whites from these tests while continuing to disenfranchise African Americans and other people of color.

claimed to be race neutral, their impact fell disproportionately on black voters. For example, the grandfather clause enabled illiterate whites to avoid the literacy test.[10] Many states also had "understanding" or "good character" exceptions to the literacy tests, which gave election officials substantial discretion over who would be allowed to vote.

The collective impact of these obstacles virtually eliminated black voting. For example, only 6 percent of blacks were registered to vote in Mississippi in 1890, and only 2 percent were registered in Alabama in 1906. After the last post-Reconstruction black congressman left the House in 1901, seventy-two years passed before another black represented a southern district in Congress. In Mississippi, one county in 1947 had 13,000 blacks who were eligible to vote, but only six were registered. Despite the constitutional guarantees of the Fourteenth and Fifteenth Amendments, blacks had little access to the political system in the South, and they had little success in winning office at any level in the rest of the nation.[11]

The social and economic position of blacks in the South followed a path similar to their political fortunes. Soon after the Civil War ended, sympathetic Republicans passed the Civil Rights Acts of 1866 and 1875, which aimed to outlaw segregation and provide equal opportunity for blacks. However, there were no enforcement provisions, and when Reconstruction ended in 1877 the southern states enacted "black codes," or **Jim Crow laws**, that led to complete segregation of the races. Then in 1883 the Supreme Court ruled that the 1875 Civil Rights Act was unconstitutional because Congress did not have the power to forbid racial discrimination in private business. Southern states interpreted this decision as a signal that the national government was unconcerned about protecting the rights of blacks.

Jim Crow laws forbade interracial marriage and mandated the complete separation of the races in neighborhoods, hotels, apartments, hospitals, schools, restrooms, drinking fountains, restaurants, elevators, and even cemetery plots. In cases where it would have been inconvenient to completely separate the races, as in public transportation, blacks had to sit in the back of the bus or in separate cars on the train and give up their seats to whites if asked. The Supreme Court validated these practices in *Plessy v. Ferguson* (1896) in establishing the **"separate but equal"** doctrine, officially permitting segregation as long as blacks had equal facilities.

In the first several decades after Reconstruction, the rest of the nation mostly ignored the status of blacks because 90 percent of all African Americans lived in the South. But blacks' northward migration to urban areas throughout the first half of the twentieth century transformed the nation's demographic profile and its racial politics. America's "race problem" was no longer a southern problem. Although conditions for blacks were generally better outside the South, they still faced discrimination and lived largely segregated lives throughout the nation. In World Wars I and II, black soldiers fought and died for their country in segregated units. Professional sports teams were segregated, and black musicians and artists could not perform in many of the nation's leading theaters. Blacks largely were hired for the lowest-paying, menial jobs.

Progress began in the 1940s. The Supreme Court struck down the white primary in 1944, Jackie Robinson broke the color line in major league baseball in 1947, and President Harry Truman issued an executive order integrating the U.S. armed services in 1948. Then came the landmark decision *Brown v. Board of Education* (1954), which rejected the "separate but equal" doctrine, followed by *Brown II* (1955), which ordered that public schools be desegregated "with all deliberate speed." These events set the stage for the growing success of the civil rights movement, discussed later in this chapter.

Jim Crow laws State and local laws that mandated racial segregation in all public facilities in the South, many border states, and some northern communities between 1876 and 1964.

"separate but equal" The idea that racial segregation was acceptable as long as the separate facilities were of equal quality; supported by *Plessy v. Ferguson* and struck down by *Brown v. Board of Education*.

NATIVE AMERICANS, ASIANS, AND LATINOS

The legacy of slavery and racial segregation in the South has been the dominant focus of U.S. civil rights policies, but many other groups as well have fought for equal rights. Their history of interactions with the majority white population includes the following: eradication and removal of Native Americans from huge parts of the East and Midwest, battles with and discrimination against Mexicans in the Southwest, and poor treatment of Asian Americans on the West Coast and then their internment during World War II. This historical review is necessary to understand today's civil rights policies, which were created, at least in part, in response to historical events and current conditions.

Native Americans were the first group to confront the European immigrants. Though initial relations were good in many places, the settlers' appetite for more land and their insensitivity to Native American culture soon led to continual conflict. The Native Americans were systematically pushed from their land and placed on reservations. The most infamous example was the removal of 46,000 members of the "Five Civilized Tribes" from the southeastern United States following the enactment of the Indian Removal Act in 1830. Thousands of Native Americans died on the "trail of tears" on their way to reservations in Oklahoma.[12] Native Americans had no political rights; indeed, through much of the nineteenth century they were considered "savages" to be eliminated. They did not gain the universal right to vote until 1924, just after women and well after black men. Although the U.S. government signed treaties with them that regarded their tribes as sovereign nations (not foreign nations but "domestic dependent nations"),[13] in practice the government ignored most of the agreements. Only in recent decades has it started to uphold its obligations, though compliance remains spotty. Native Americans have struggled to maintain their cultural history and autonomy in the face of widespread poverty and unemployment.

Latinos also have struggled for political and economic equality. The early history is rooted in the Mexican-American War (1846–48) and the conquest by the United States of much of the territory that today makes up most of the southwestern states.

IN THE 1960S AND 1970S, CESAR Chavez and the United Farm Workers union successfully organized mostly Mexican American farm workers, first in California and then in other parts of the country. Here, Chavez speaks to a group in Texas.

Since that time, Mexicans have resided in large numbers in the Southwest. One of their first major political successes was Cesar Chavez's effort to organize farmworkers in the 1960s and 1970s. He established the United Farm Workers union and forced growers to bargain with 50,000 mostly Mexican American field-workers in California and Florida. While many Mexican Americans have roots that go back hundreds of years, a majority of Latinos have been in the United States for less than two generations. Consequently, they have become a political force only recently, despite the fact that they now are the nation's largest minority.

Latinos' relative lack of political clout when compared to African Americans can be explained by two factors. First, Latinos vote at a much lower rate than African Americans because many have language barriers and about one-third of Latinos are not U.S. citizens (which is a requirement for voting in national elections). Second, unlike African Americans, Latinos are a relatively diverse group politically. They include Mexican Americans, Cuban Americans, Puerto Ricans, Dominicans, and people from many other Latin American nations. Most Latino voters are loyal to the Democratic Party, but a majority of Cuban Americans are strong Republicans. Although this diversity means that Latino voters do not speak with one voice, it brings opportunity for increased political clout in the future. The diversity of partisan attachments among Latinos and their relatively low levels of political involvement mean that both parties are eager to attract them as new voters.

THROUGHOUT AMERICAN HISTORY, immigrant groups have been crucial to the nation's growth, but they have often faced discrimination. Today, debates over the rights of immigrants continue.

In addition to the internment of Japanese Americans during World War II (discussed later in this chapter), Asian Americans experienced discrimination beginning with their arrival in the United States in the nineteenth century. The first wave of Chinese immigrants came with the 1848 California gold rush. Initially foreign miners, including the Chinese, were able to stake out their claims along with Americans. However, by 1850, when the easy-to-find gold was gone, Americans tried to drive out the Chinese through violence and the Foreign Miners Tax. Subsequently, Chinese immigrants played a crucial role in building the intercontinental railroad between 1865 and 1869; but since they were given the more dangerous jobs, many lost their lives. After the railroad was completed, Chinese workers returned to the West Coast, where they experienced increasing discrimination and violence. Following several race riots, Congress passed the Chinese Exclusion Act of 1882, which prevented Chinese already in the United States from becoming U.S. citizens. (The Supreme Court later granted their American-born children automatic citizenship under the Fourteenth Amendment.)[14] The Chinese Exclusion Act also barred virtually all immigration from China—the first time in U.S. history that a specific ethnic group was singled out in this way. In recent decades a much broader range of Asians has emigrated to the United States, including Koreans, Filipinos, Hmong, Vietnamese, and Asian Indians. This diversity in national heritage, culture, and language means that Asian Americans are quite heterogeneous in their political views, partisan affiliation, and voting patterns.

WOMEN AND CIVIL RIGHTS

When John Adams attended the Constitutional Convention in 1787, his wife, Abigail, advised him not to "put such unlimited power in the hands of the husbands.

Remember, all men would be tyrants if they could. . . . If particular care and attention is not paid to the ladies, we . . . will not hold ourselves bound by any laws in which we have no voice or representation."[15] John Adams did not listen to his wife. The Constitution did not give women the right to vote, and they were not guaranteed that civil right until the Nineteenth Amendment was ratified in 1920—though sixteen states allowed women to vote before then. Until the early twentieth century, women in most parts of the country could not hold office, serve on juries, bring lawsuits in their own name, own property, or serve as legal guardians for their children. A woman's identity was so closely tied to her husband that if she married a noncitizen, she automatically gave up her citizenship!

protectionism The idea under which some people have tried to rationalize discriminatory policies by claiming that some groups, like women or African Americans, should be denied certain rights for their own safety or well-being.

The rationale for these policies was called **protectionism**. The argument was that women were too frail to compete in the business world and that they needed to be protected by men. This rationale served in many court cases to deny women equal rights. For example, in 1869 Myra Bradwell requested admission to the Illinois bar to practice law. She was the first woman to graduate from law school in Illinois, the editor of *Chicago Legal News*, and held all the qualifications to be a lawyer in the state except for one—she was a woman. Her request was denied, and she sued all the way to the Supreme Court. It ruled in 1873 that the prohibition against women lawyers did not violate the Fourteenth Amendment's privileges and immunities clause because there was no constitutional right to be an attorney. If the Court had stopped there, the decision would have been unremarkable for its time. But Justice Joseph Bradley went on to provide a classic example of protectionism:

> *The civil law as well as nature itself has always recognized a wide difference in the respective spheres and destinies to man and woman. Man is, or should be, women's protector and defender. The natural and proper timidity and delicacy which belongs to the female sex evidently unfits it for many of the occupations of civil life. The constitution of the family organization which is founded in the divine ordinance, as well as the nature of things, indicates the domestic sphere as that which properly belongs to the domains and functions of womanhood.[16]*

THE PROTECTIONIST VIEW THAT women are weaker and unfit for some occupations was one reason women were excluded from the military for most of the nation's history. In 2008, Specialist Monica Brown became the second woman to receive the Silver Star medal for valor in the face of the enemy.

While protectionist sentiment on the Court had waned by the mid-twentieth century, as recently as 1961 a court upheld a Florida law that automatically exempted women, but not men, from compulsory jury duty. The case involved a woman who killed her husband with a baseball bat after he admitted that he was having an affair and wanted to end the marriage. The woman argued that her conviction by an all-male jury violated her Fourteenth Amendment guarantee of "equal protection of the laws" and that a jury panel containing some women would have been more sympathetic to her "temporary insanity" defense. The court rejected this argument, ruling that the Florida law excluding women from jury duty was reasonable because "despite the enlightened emancipation of women from the restrictions and protections of bygone years, and their entry into many parts of community life formerly considered to be reserved to men, woman still is regarded as the center of home and family life."[17] Apparently it was unthinkable to the all-male court that a man might have to stay home from work and take care of the kids while his wife served on a jury. Later in this chapter we will describe how the Supreme Court has moved away from this discriminatory position and rejected protectionist thinking.

GAYS AND LESBIANS

The most recent group in the struggle for civil rights is the LGBT community. For most of American history gays and lesbians lived secret lives and were subject to abuse and discrimination if they came out, or openly acknowledged their sexual preferences. The critical moment that spurred the gay rights movement occurred on June 28, 1969, during a routine police raid on the Stonewall Inn in New York City. (Police often raided gay bars to harass patrons and selectively enforce liquor laws.)[18] This time, rather than submitting to the arrests, the customers fought back, throwing stones and beer bottles, breaking windows, and starting small fires. A crowd of several hundred people gathered, and the fighting raged for three nights. The Stonewall Rebellion was a galvanizing event for the gay community by demonstrating the power of collective action.

Since Stonewall, the gay rights movement has made steady progress through a combination of political mobilization and protest, legislative action, and legal action. Public support for gay rights has increased dramatically in recent years. Between two-thirds and three-fourths of Americans (depending on the poll) agree with the new national policy that gays may openly serve in the military, whereas a majority of Americans opposed this policy when it was first proposed by President Clinton in 1993. A CBS News poll showed that only 25 percent of Americans believe that gays and lesbians should have no legal recognition of their relationships, whereas 40 percent support gay marriage and 30 percent support civil unions (between 51 and 56 percent approve of gay marriage when presented without the civil union option). Sixty-three percent believe that same-sex couples should be entitled to the same benefits as heterosexual couples, whereas only 32 percent think they should not.[19] In May 2012, President Obama endorsed same-sex marriage for the first time, completing his gradual evolution on the issue. Thus, while the gay rights movement is still in its relatively early stages, public support for equal rights based on sexual orientation is growing.

A COLOR-BLIND SOCIETY?

Why does this history matter for politics today? There are two main responses. First, the effects of slavery and Jim Crow laws are still quite evident: legal racial segregation ended less than fifty years ago, and its legacy—especially in the relative quality of education available to most whites and blacks—remains. As noted, other racial and ethnic minorities have also faced exclusion and discrimination. Second, active discrimination based on race, gender, and sexual orientation is still evident in our society. Given the importance of race in the everyday lives of millions of Americans and in gaining an understanding of American politics, a grasp of the history that got us to where we are today is an important starting point (this section will focus on race, but the struggle for civil rights applies to the other groups discussed in this chapter).

Martin Luther King Jr. presented the vision for a color-blind society in his "I Have a Dream" speech, which he delivered before 250,000 people at the March on Washington in August 1963. He said, "I have a dream that my four little children will one day live in a nation where they will not be judged by the color of their skin but by the content of their character." Most Americans share this dream, but there are differences of opinion about how close we are to that goal. Those who

CIVIL RIGHTS LEADER MARTIN LUTHER King Jr. waves to supporters from the steps of the Lincoln Memorial on August 28, 1963, in Washington, D.C. The March on Washington drew an estimated 250,000 people who heard King deliver his famous "I Have a Dream" speech.

feel that we must "move beyond race" argue that we already have achieved a level playing field on which all people have equal opportunities to succeed. Furthermore, they argue, efforts to make up for past discrimination or to create additional opportunities for racial minorities through affirmative action perpetuate discrimination by classifying people based on race. Others feel that discrimination is still an all-too-real part of life for racial minorities.

To see if you think we have reached King's color-blind ideal, consider what you notice when you meet people for the first time. Do you notice their hair color, height, body type, or whether they wear glasses? Do you notice their skin color? If you have met a person once or twice, you may not remember her hair color or whether she had glasses. But you probably would remember her skin color as a defining feature. In a truly a color-blind society, race will be as unimportant for forming an opinion about someone as whether he wears glasses or, say, has a beard. That is, awareness of race will not affect our opinions or our actions. However, considerable research shows that awareness of race still influences many people's opinions and behavior (see "What Do Political Scientists Do?").[20] Some people engage in racial stereotyping without being aware of it.[20] Others intentionally discriminate based on race.

In addition to research data, personal anecdotes can be informative. Let's consider two examples from a liberal, northern midwestern city that prides itself on being tolerant. The first example represents unintentional stereotyping; the second, racial discrimination. One morning one of the authors was at the checkout line at a local grocery store, and the cashier was giving the lady ahead of him a hard time. The woman had a large basket of groceries, and her bill was well over $100. She wanted to pay for some of the groceries with food stamps and the rest with a personal check. The cashier wanted to see a driver's license or two other forms of photo ID, and the lady did not have them. The author couldn't see exactly what was going on, but the woman had some type of ID that was not adequate. After calling over the store manager and a lot of hemming and hawing, the cashier finally accepted her check. Then the author unloaded his similarly sized cart of groceries and paid by check, which the cashier accepted without hesitation—and with no identification. In fact, he has never been asked for identification when paying by check in that store, despite not being personally known by any of the cashiers. It was hard not to conclude that the woman and the author were treated differently because she was black and using food stamps and he is white.

The second example involved a former graduate student in our department who is white and whose wife is black. They wanted to rent a bigger apartment, so they searched the want ads and made appointments to see some apartments. One landlord told them to meet him in front of the apartment at a specific time. They waited where they were told, but the landlord didn't show up. Later, they remembered seeing a car that slowed down and almost stopped but then sped away. They wondered if this was a case of a "drive-by landlord"—one who checks out potential tenants' race from a distance; if they are not white, he or she skips the appointment and tells them it is rented if they ask. This is exactly what happened. They called the landlord, asked what had happened, and were told the apartment was already rented. To check their suspicions they had some friends ask about the apartment, and the friends were told it was available. Their friends (both white) made an appointment to meet the landlord, and this time the same car slowed down but pulled up and stopped. The landlord showed them the apartment and was very friendly. The next day the graduate student filed a racial discrimination lawsuit.

These kinds of stories, ranging from irritating and demeaning to a serious violation of the law, are familiar to nearly every racial minority, woman, and gay person in the United States. Consider the well-dressed businessman who cannot get a cab in a major city because he is black, the woman who is sexually harassed by her boss but hesitates to say anything for fear of losing her job, the teenage Latino who is shadowed in the music store by a clerk, the Arab American who endures taunts about her head covering, or the lesbian couple who cannot find an apartment. Combined with the research results described in the "What Do Political Scientists Do?" box, such evidence of continuing discrimination indicates that we have not yet achieved a color-blind (or gender- and sexual orientation–neutral) society.

THE RACIAL DIVIDE TODAY

ANALYZE INEQUALITY AMONG RACIAL, ETHNIC, AND SOCIAL GROUPS TODAY

In addition to the unequal treatment of racial minorities, women, and gays and lesbians, a gulf remains between the objective condition of minorities and that of whites and the political views that they hold. Although substantial progress has been made in bridging that gulf, inequalities in political, social, and economic conditions remain.

DIFFERENCES IN VOTING ACCESS

The political divide is mostly evident in lower levels of voter turnout among racial minorities relative to whites. Different rates of voter turnout can mostly be accounted for by education and income—especially between blacks and whites—but there are many examples of practices and institutions that depress minority turnout. And many of these are intentional. They include moving and reducing the number of polling places in minority-majority areas, changing from district-based to at-large elections, redistricting that dilutes minority voting power, withholding information about registration and voting procedures from blacks, and "causing or taking advantage of election day irregularities."[21]

Consider the 2000 presidential election in Florida, where the U.S. Commission on Civil Rights investigated dozens of complaints from minorities who were not allowed to vote. One target of the investigation was the "voter purge list" that the state had created to remove voters from the registration list. Most people on the list were supposed to be felons, who are not allowed to vote under Florida state law. However, the list was compiled without cross-checking that the people listed were indeed felons. In fact, thousands of people on the list had not committed any crime, including a disproportionate number of minorities, and they had to clear their names before being allowed to vote. Many did not realize the problem until Election Day, and most attempts to clear up the confusion failed. In addition, the commission described the use of police roadblocks close to voting places in predominantly minority neighborhoods as another practice that depressed minority voter turnout. Finally, the high incidence in

DESPITE THE REMOVAL OF MOST formal barriers to voting, Latinos are less likely to vote and participate in politics than whites, blacks, and Asian Americans. Groups like Voto Latino (represented here by Rosario Dawson and John Leguizamo) have tried to mobilize Latino voters in recent elections.

EVIDENCE OF SUBTLE RACISM AND ITS POLITICAL IMPACT

One important role of government in civil rights policy is to enforce antidiscrimination laws to provide an equality of opportunity. However, racial discrimination may be very subtle and not easily detected by those enforcing the law, which raises the question, "How can we best measure discrimination?" Because discrimination today is less likely to be overt, those who study this topic must be clever in designing their research to see if more subtle forms of discrimination still exist. One method to try to define the extent of discrimination is through experiments that simulate real-world situations. Here we discuss two such examples that attempted to measure racially motivated behavior: one in hiring decisions and the other in political advertising.

Our first example comes from the field of economics (economists are interested in racial discrimination because of its impact on labor markets), but the approach described could be used by political scientists or any other type of social scientist. Two economists examined how a person's race could influence his or her chances of getting a job interview. In their experiment, they created resumés for job applicants—some were well qualified and others were not as well qualified for a particular job. They then assigned names to their fictitious applicants that are common among blacks and whites (based on the ratio of black newborns and white newborns that are given specific names). For example, African American names included Lakisha and Tyrone and white names included Allison and Brad. Four resumés (high and low qualification for each race) were then sent for actual job openings in Boston and Chicago in sales, administrative support, clerical, and customer service jobs. The study found that resumés with white names received 50 percent more calls for interviews than resumés with black names. In addition, 8.4 percent of the employers contacted at least one more white applicant than black applicants, whereas only 3.5 percent of employers contacted at least one more black applicant than white applicants. The value of a high-quality resumé also varied between the two races. White resumés of high quality received 27 percent more calls than those of low quality, but for black resumés, the difference was only 8 percent in favor of the high-quality ones.[a] This type of controlled experiment reveals that a person's race still matters for something as important as getting a job interview.

An experiment by political scientists Nicholas Valentino, Vincent Hutchings, and Ismail White examined another subtle influence of race on behavior: Do political ads prime racial attitudes during campaigns? Subjects watched different versions of the same presidential campaign ad for George W. Bush featuring a discussion of government spending, tax cuts, and health care reform. The ads had the same narrative, but

Research on campaign commercials has shown that images of African Americans counting money can prime negative racial attitudes.

Watch a video clip of Vincent Hutchings discussing this topic at **wwnorton.com/studyspace**

the visual cues changed: some were neutral; some compared whites and blacks; some depicted "undeserving blacks." The neutral version showed images of the Statue of Liberty, George Bush sitting on a couch, a neighborhood with no people on the street, and hospital workers in surgical garb (so their race could not be determined). The race comparison ad showed many of those same images but also an African American counting money at the point the narrator says, "Democrats want to spend your tax dollars on wasteful government programs." As the narrator noted that Bush supports tax cuts "because you know best how to spend the money you earn," positive white images appeared. The "undeserving black" version was the same as the comparison version but without the images of white people.

After seeing the "undeserving" ad, viewers were more likely to express negative attitudes toward African Americans and toward government policies they believed would benefit African Americans than they were after seeing the "neutral" ad. Viewers of the "comparison" ad were also more likely to express negative attitudes toward African Americans. The authors concluded, "Far from being a spent force, the impact of race and racism in America can emerge from some of the most common political messages that mainstream candidates rely upon as their stock-in-trade."[b] However, they also found that when ads present blacks in a favorable light, the impact of racial attitudes declines.

These two studies suggest that the influence of race on behavior may be subtle and not readily detected if one is only looking for obviously racist behavior. However, even if one accepts the findings of these studies (and there are alternative views),[c] the policy implications are still open to debate.

minority areas of "spoiled ballots" that could not be counted was not accounted for by differences in voters' income or education levels.[22] Given that the outcome of the 2000 presidential election (George W. Bush became president) was decided by a few hundred votes in Florida, and given that large majorities of African American voters supported Al Gore, these efforts to depress minority turnout had an important impact. Florida was not the only state to experience such allegations. New Jersey, Missouri, Arkansas, and Louisiana also were accused of efforts to depress minority turnout in recent elections.[23]

In the 2008 elections, numerous practices were identified that likely led to voter suppression and intimidation. Some were based on race. Three states removed voters from the voting rolls if there wasn't an identical match between the name the voter used when registering to vote and the name as it appeared in another state database (often the database of driver's license information). States also used voter purges (seven states), voter challenges targeted at minority voters (five states), technical barriers to voter registration and voting (six states), student voting barriers (seven states), voter registration access (a number of states did not comply with the law that requires voter registration services at social services offices), voter intimidation and deceptive practices (fourteen states), and poor ballot design (three states).[24]

SOCIOECONOMIC INDICATORS

The racial divide is also evident in social and economic terms. Nearly three times as many black families are below the poverty line as white families: 27.6 percent compared to 9.8 percent in 2011. The poverty rate of 25.3 percent for Hispanic families in 2009 was similar to that of black families.[25] Furthermore, while black median household income in 2011 was $32,229 (only 58.2 percent of white family income), the gap in overall wealth is much more dramatic. The average white household has more than six times the assets of the typical nonwhite family. In 2010 the median household net worth was $130,600 for whites and $20,400 for nonwhites. Figures for Hispanics are somewhat better, but the gaps are still large. Hispanic household income was 69.7 percent of white income, $38,626 compared to $55,412.[26] Poverty is not distributed equally throughout the United States but rather is concentrated in areas where the minority population is the highest (see Figures 14.1A and 14.1B).

Other indicators show similar patterns. The rate of black, adult male unemployment has been about twice as high as that of white adult males for the past forty-five years. In August 2012, the unemployment rate among blacks was 14.1 percent compared to 6.8 percent for whites and 10.2 percent for Latinos.[27] Moreover, slightly more than 37.7 percent of black children lived in two-parent households in 2011, compared to 77.2 percent of white children and 66.9 percent of Latino children.[28] Also, blacks are significantly more likely than whites to be victimized by crime. A black male between the ages of eighteen and twenty-four is 10.5 times as likely to be murdered as a white male in the same age range.[29]

On every measure of health—life expectancy, infectious diseases, infant mortality, cancer rates, heart disease, and strokes—the gaps between whites and blacks are large and, in many cases, increasing. For example, life expectancy for blacks is about five years shorter than for whites (73.6 years compared to 78.4), the infant mortality rate is more than double for blacks (13.69 deaths per 100,000 births compared to 5.76

FIGURE » 14.1A

PERCENTAGE OF PEOPLE IN POVERTY, 2010

Together, these maps show that the poverty rate in the United States is closely related to the minority population. How do you think these patterns might affect the politics of civil rights policies that are aimed at reducing discrimination in the workplace or housing?

FIGURE » 14.1B

PERCENTAGE OF THE POPULATION THAT IS WHITE, 2010

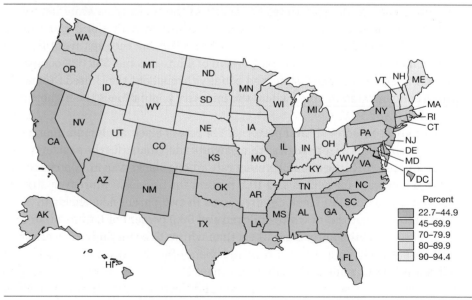

Source: Poverty data from U.S. Census Bureau, "Poverty: 2010 and 2011 American Community Surveys," September 2010, www.census.gov/acs; race data from U.S. Census Bureau, 2012 Statistical Abstract, Population Table 18, "Resident Population by Hispanic Origin and State: 2010," www.census.gov/compendia/statab/2012/tables/12s0018.pdf (accessed 11/3/12).

for whites), and maternal mortality is more than quadruple (24.9 deaths per 100,000 births for blacks compared to 5.6 for whites). Similar gaps exist for incidence of cancer, diabetes, strokes, and heart attacks.[30]

CRIMINAL JUSTICE AND HATE CRIMES

The greatest disparity between racial minorities and whites may be in the criminal justice system. Racial profiling subjects many innocent blacks to intrusive searches. Nick Cannon, the rapper and host of *America's Got Talent*, has complained about constantly being stopped for "driving while black." He said, "Now in LA I get pulled over like once a week. Honestly, I think it's because I'm a black man in a nice car."[31] Studies have shown that blacks are not only more likely than whites to be convicted for the same crimes, but also more likely to serve longer sentences.[32] In many large American cities, tensions between police departments and minority communities periodically boil over. The largest race riots since the 1960s were in Los Angeles in 1992 following the acquittal of four white police officers who had been videotaped brutally beating a black man, Rodney King. The riots left fifty-four people dead and more than 2,000 injured and caused more than $1 billion in damage. In 1999 New York police killed Amadou Diallo, a law-abiding African immigrant, in a hail of forty-one bullets as he was standing in his own doorway. The officers were looking for a black suspect, and when Diallo reached for his wallet they assumed it was a gun. Ultimately the officers were acquitted, which outraged the African American community. A similar killing of an unarmed black man, nineteen-year-old Timothy Thomas, by police in Cincinnati in 2001 led to three days of rioting. The officer in this case was also acquitted. More recent cases include James Dennis, who was killed by Norfolk police in 2007, and Sean Bell, who was shot dead in 2006 in New York City hours before his wedding. In July 2010, residents of Oakland rioted after a white transit officer was convicted only of voluntary manslaughter (rather than second-degree murder) for shooting Oscar Grant in the back as he lay facedown and unarmed on a subway platform. Civil rights advocates point out that such incidents are not rare.

African Americans and other minorities are also subjected to hate crimes much more frequently than whites. A murder that received national attention in 1998 involved a black man, James Byrd Jr., who was chained to the back of a pickup truck by three white men and dragged to his death. Two of the murderers were sentenced to death, and the other received life in prison. According to the FBI's hate crime statistics, of the 6,624 hate crimes in 2010, 47.3 percent were race related. Of these, nearly 70 percent were "anti-black" and only 18 percent were "anti-white," which means that the rate of anti-black hate crimes is more than five times what would be expected based on the percentage of African Americans in the United States, while the rate of anti-white hate crimes is about one-fourth as high as would be expected.[33]

This backdrop of racial inequality, discrimination, and violence drives civil rights activists to push their agenda in the three branches of government: legislative, executive, and judicial. In some instances, activists work in several arenas simultaneously; in others, they seek redress in one arena after exhausting alternatives. The civil rights movement, which was crucial in the early policy successes, also continues to mobilize the grass roots.

JAMES BYRD JR. WAS MURDERED in Jasper, Texas, by three white supremacists who chained him to a pickup truck and dragged him down a road until he was decapitated. According to FBI statistics, in 2008 nearly three-quarters of race-related hate crimes in the United States were "anti-black."

THE POLICY-MAKING PROCESS AND CIVIL RIGHTS

Our system of separated and shared powers almost ensures that each of the three branches has some say in making policy. Each branch has played a central role at different points in history, depending on the political context. For example, in the 1940s and the 1950s the courts were considered the most sympathetic branch for advancing the civil rights agenda because segregationist southern Democrats controlled key congressional committees and none of the presidents of this era made civil rights a top priority. Then, in the mid-1960s, Congress took the lead role by passing landmark legislation.

The policy-making process in the area of civil rights also provides insight into the importance of federalism. To promote African Americans' civil rights, the national government required the southern states to desegregate schools, allow blacks to vote, and generally dismantle the system of segregation, thus demonstrating the importance of nation-centered federalism. However, in terms of gay rights, state and local governments have taken the lead role. Congress, in contrast, has taken steps to restrict gay rights, especially gay marriage (although with a few important exceptions, such as the service of gays in the military). In terms of women's rights, both the national and state governments have taken important actions.

CIVIL RIGHTS TIMELINE

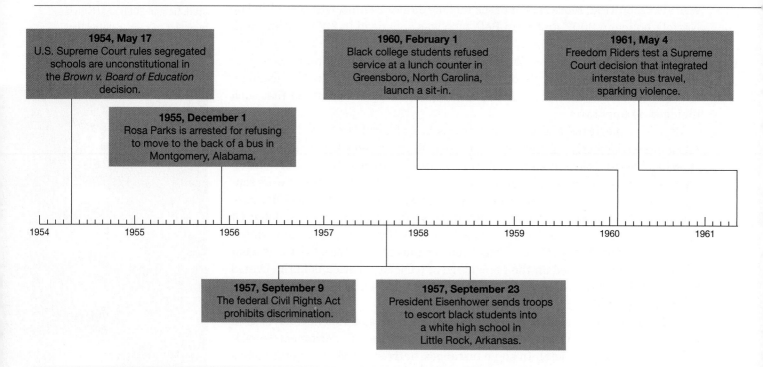

1954, May 17
U.S. Supreme Court rules segregated schools are unconstitutional in the *Brown v. Board of Education* decision.

1955, December 1
Rosa Parks is arrested for refusing to move to the back of a bus in Montgomery, Alabama.

1960, February 1
Black college students refused service at a lunch counter in Greensboro, North Carolina, launch a sit-in.

1961, May 4
Freedom Riders test a Supreme Court decision that integrated interstate bus travel, sparking violence.

1957, September 9
The federal Civil Rights Act prohibits discrimination.

1957, September 23
President Eisenhower sends troops to escort black students into a white high school in Little Rock, Arkansas.

| 1954 | 1955 | 1956 | 1957 | 1958 | 1959 | 1960 | 1961 |

Source: Adapted from "Key Moments in Civil Rights History," Ann Arbor News, January 11, 2004, www.mlive.com/news/aanews/index.ssf?/base/features-0/1073819921106320.xml.

SOCIAL MOVEMENTS

Much of our discussion of civil rights focuses on the governmental policy-making process, but we must also note the importance of social movements. From the early women's rights movement and abolitionists of the nineteenth century to the gay rights and civil rights movements of the mid-twentieth century, activists have pressured the political system to change civil rights policies. Through collective action, these social movements have made sure that such controversial issues remained on the policy agenda.

Women started to push for the right to vote at a convention in 1848 at Seneca Falls, New York. Subsequently, a constitutional amendment to give women the right to vote was regularly introduced in Congress between 1878 and 1913 but never was passed, despite the efforts of women such as Susan B. Anthony and Elizabeth Cady Stanton. After a parallel movement at the state level had some success, the constitutional amendment finally passed in 1919 and was ratified in 1920.

The civil rights movement of the 1950s and 1960s, aimed at ending segregation and gaining equal political and social rights for blacks, is the most famous example of a successful social movement (see Figure 14.2). Although the *Brown v. Board of Education* decision, which struck down segregation in public schools, gave the movement a boost, most southern blacks saw little change in their daily lives. As white school boards and local governments resisted integration, black leaders became convinced that the courts would not effect change because of resistance to their decisions. The only way to change the laws was to get the public, both black and white, to demand change.

FIGURE » 14.2

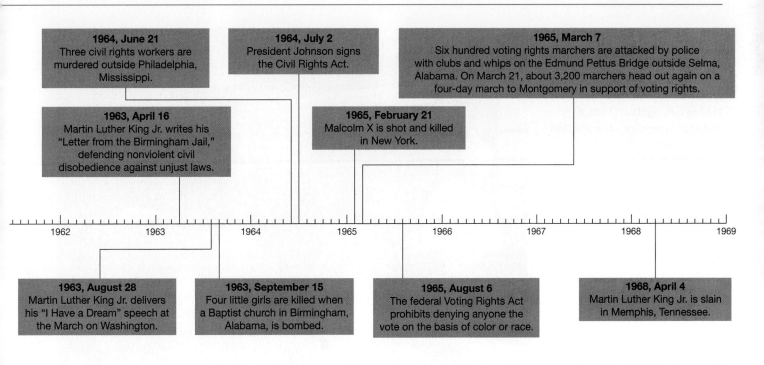

1964, June 21
Three civil rights workers are murdered outside Philadelphia, Mississippi.

1964, July 2
President Johnson signs the Civil Rights Act.

1965, March 7
Six hundred voting rights marchers are attacked by police with clubs and whips on the Edmund Pettus Bridge outside Selma, Alabama. On March 21, about 3,200 marchers head out again on a four-day march to Montgomery in support of voting rights.

1963, April 16
Martin Luther King Jr. writes his "Letter from the Birmingham Jail," defending nonviolent civil disobedience against unjust laws.

1965, February 21
Malcolm X is shot and killed in New York.

1963, August 28
Martin Luther King Jr. delivers his "I Have a Dream" speech at the March on Washington.

1963, September 15
Four little girls are killed when a Baptist church in Birmingham, Alabama, is bombed.

1965, August 6
The federal Voting Rights Act prohibits denying anyone the vote on the basis of color or race.

1968, April 4
Martin Luther King Jr. is slain in Memphis, Tennessee.

1962   1963   1964   1965   1966   1967   1968   1969

The spark came on December 1, 1955, in Montgomery, Alabama, when a woman named Rosa Parks refused to give up her seat on a bus to a white person, as she was required to do by law. Parks is often described as a seamstress who was tired after a long day's work and simply did not want to give up her seat. That is true, but there is more to the story. Local civil rights leaders had been waiting for years for an opportunity to boycott the local bus company because of its segregation policy. They needed a perfect test case—someone who would help draw attention to the cause.

Rosa Parks was just that person. She was a well-educated, law-abiding citizen who had been active in local civil rights organizations. In her book, *My Story*, Parks says, "I was . . . no more tired than I usually was at the end of a working day. . . . No, the only tired I was, was tired of giving in."[34] When she was arrested for refusing to give up her seat, local civil rights leaders organized a boycott of the bus company that lasted more than a year. Whites in Montgomery tried to stop the boycott, including arresting and fining blacks who arranged a car pooling system to get to work: people waiting for a car to pick them up were arrested for loitering, and car pool drivers were arrested for lacking appropriate insurance or having too many people in their car. Martin Luther King Jr. was elected leader of the group, and he was subjected to harassment and violence—his house was firebombed, and he was arrested several times. Finally a federal district court ruled that the segregation policy was unconstitutional, and the Supreme Court upheld the ruling.

NONVIOLENT PROTEST

On February 1, 1960, four black students in Greensboro, North Carolina, went to a segregated lunch counter at a local Woolworth's and asked to be served. They sat there for an hour without being served and had to leave when the store closed.

FOUR AFRICAN AMERICAN COLLEGE students protest at a whites-only lunch counter in Greensboro, North Carolina. These sit-ins spread throughout the South in 1960 as civil rights activists were able to put pressure on businesses to integrate through their nonviolent protests.

When twenty students returned the next day, national wire services picked up the story. Within two weeks the sit-ins spread to eleven cities. In some cases the students were met with violence; in others they were simply arrested. However, the students continued to respond with passive resistance, and succeeding waves of protesters replaced those who were arrested. The Student Nonviolent Coordinating Committee (SNCC) was created to coordinate the protests. The Greensboro Woolworth's was integrated on July 26, 1961, but the protests continued in other cities. By August 1961, the sit-ins had 70,000 participants and 3,000 arrests.[35] The sit-ins marked an important shift in the tactics of the civil rights movement away from the court-based approach and toward the nonviolent civil disobedience that had been successful in Montgomery.

Another important event during this period was the effort by Freedom Riders to get President Kennedy to enforce two Supreme Court decisions that banned segregation in interstate travel, including bus terminals, waiting rooms, restaurants, and other public facilities related to interstate travel.[36] On May 4, 1961, a group of whites and blacks boarded two buses in Washington, D.C., headed for New Orleans. The whites and blacks sat together and went into segregated areas of bus stations. The trip was uneventful until Rock Hill, South Carolina, where several Riders were beaten. Then in Anniston, Alabama, one bus had its tires slashed and was firebombed. The Riders were beaten as they fled the burning bus. The second group encountered an angry mob at the bus station in Birmingham and was severely beaten with baseball bats and iron pipes. When it became clear that police protection would not be forthcoming, the Riders abandoned the trip and regrouped in Nashville. After much internal debate, they decided to continue the rides.

Following more violence in Montgomery, President Kennedy intervened, and his brother, Robert Kennedy, the attorney general, worked out a deal: the Riders would receive police protection, federal troops would not intervene, and the Riders would face the local courts upon their arrest for "disturbing the peace." The Freedom Rides continued throughout the summer. They successfully drew national attention to the continuing resistance in the South to desegregation rulings, forced the Kennedy administration to take a stand on this issue, and led to a stronger Interstate Commerce Commission ruling banning segregation in interstate travel.[37]

THE LETTER FROM THE BIRMINGHAM JAIL

The next significant events occurred in Birmingham, Alabama, in 1963. Birmingham had more racial violence than any southern city, with eighteen unsolved bombings of black churches and homes in a six-year period. The city had closed its parks and golf courses rather than integrate them, and there was no progress on integrating the local schools. A leading supporter of integration had been castrated to intimidate other blacks who might advocate the policy. The city's police chief, "Bull" Connor, was a strong segregationist who had allowed the attacks on the Freedom Riders. During a peaceful protest in April 1963, Martin Luther King Jr. and many others were arrested. While in solitary confinement, King wrote his now-famous "Letter from the Birmingham Jail," an eloquent statement of the principles of nonviolent civil disobedience.

The letter was a response to white religious leaders who had told King in a newspaper ad that his actions were "unwise and untimely" and that "when rights are consistently denied, a cause should be pressed in the courts and in negotiations among local leaders, and not in the streets." King responded with a justification for civil disobedience, writing that everyone had an obligation to follow just

A FIFTEEN-YEAR-OLD CIVIL RIGHTS
demonstrator, defying an anti-parade ordinance, is attacked by a police dog in Birmingham, Alabama, on May 3, 1963. The next day, during a meeting at the White House, President Kennedy discussed this photo, which had appeared on the front page of the *New York Times*. Reaction against this police brutality helped spur Congress and the president to enact civil rights legislation.

laws but an equal obligation to break unjust laws, which he defined in two ways. First, "[a] just law is a man-made code that squares with the moral law of the law of God. An unjust law is a code that is out of harmony with moral law." Second, an unjust law is "a code that a majority inflicts on a minority that is not binding on itself" or "a code that a majority inflicted upon a minority which that minority had no part in enacting or creating because they did not have the unhampered right to vote." This second component of defining an unjust law is very similar to the rationale that Thomas Jefferson laid out in the Declaration of Independence for resisting British rule. The cry of "no taxation without representation" was heard from the colonists who dumped British tea in the Boston harbor because they viewed the tax on tea as unjust.

King also laid out the four steps of nonviolent campaigns: (1) collection of the facts to determine whether injustices are alive; (2) negotiation with white leaders to change the injustices; (3) self-purification, which involved training to make sure that the civil rights protesters would be able to endure the abuse that they would receive; and (4) direct action to create the environment where change will be able to happen (such as sit-ins and marches), but always in a nonviolent manner. By following these steps, civil rights protesters ensured that their social movement would draw attention to their cause while turning public opinion against their opponents' violent tactics.

Following King's release from jail, the situation escalated. The protest leaders decided to use children in the next round of demonstrations. After more than 1,000 children were arrested and the jails were overflowing, the police turned fire hoses and police dogs on children who were trying to continue their march. Media coverage of the incident turned the tide of public opinion in favor of the marchers as the country expressed outrage over the violence in Birmingham. Similar protests occurred throughout the South, with more than 1,000 actions in over 100 different southern cities and more than 20,000 people arrested throughout the summer.

On June 11, 1963, President Kennedy called on Congress to take action. The next day Medgar Evers, a civil rights leader in Mississippi, was shot and killed in his driveway. A week later Kennedy sent a comprehensive civil rights bill to Congress that would guarantee equal social and political rights to blacks. On August 28, King delivered his "I Have a Dream" speech to a crowd that represented the largest political protest in the country's history up to that point. Two weeks later four African American girls were killed when a Birmingham church was bombed. President Kennedy was assassinated before his legislation could be passed, but the activists' concerted efforts over two decades played a key role in pressuring Congress to pass meaningful legislation. (For details of the legislation, see "The Legislative Arena," later in this chapter.)

With the passage of this landmark legislation, large-scale activity for civil rights for African Americans started to decline. However, mass protest became the preferred tool of many other social movements. Vietnam War protesters marched on Washington by the hundreds of thousands in the late 1960s and early 1970s. The women's rights, gay rights, and environmental movements have staged many mass demonstrations in Washington and other major cities.

Most recently, large-scale demonstrations against Wall Street and international organizations, such as the International Monetary Fund and the World

Trade Organization have swept the nation. The "Occupy Wall Street" movement, which started in September 2011, has spread to more than 1,500 cities in eighty-two nations. Rooted in the nonviolent protests of the civil rights era, protestors occupy public spaces to make their views known. The Occupy movement's slogan "We are the 99%" has drawn attention to income inequality and helped set the tone for the 2012 presidential election. Conservative activists, such as those in the pro-life movement, have also used nonviolent protest, sit-ins, and mass demonstrations. Protests against President Obama's policies early in 2009 evolved into the "Tea Party" movement (evoking the Boston Tea Party of the American Revolution). Rooted in an opposition to high taxes and activist government, the Tea Party movement organized protests on Tax Day (April 15) that drew more than 300,000 people in 346 cities.[38] Clearly, the legacy of the civil rights movement has been not only to help change unjust laws but also to provide a new tool for political action across a broad range of policy areas.

THE JUDICIAL ARENA

Early in the civil rights movement in the 1930s and 1940s, the Supreme Court provided most of the successes, especially in voting rights and desegregation. Later the Court's attention turned to discrimination cases in employment (in addition to cases in voting rights), and here its record was more mixed from the perspective of civil rights supporters. In two early voting rights cases, the Court struck down the grandfather clause in 1915 and the white primary in 1944.[39] Both devices had prevented blacks from voting.

CHALLENGING "SEPARATE BUT EQUAL" IN EDUCATION

The National Association for the Advancement of Colored People (NAACP), which fights for equal rights for blacks, started a concerted effort to nibble away at the "separate but equal" doctrine. Rather than tackle segregation head-on, the NAACP challenged an aspect of segregation that would be familiar to the Supreme Court justices: the ways in which states kept blacks out of all-white law schools. Another strategy was to challenge admission practices in law schools outside the Deep South to demonstrate that segregation was not just a "southern problem" and to raise the chances for compliance with favorable Court decisions. A young attorney named Thurgood Marshall (who later became the first African American Supreme Court justice) argued the NAACP's first successful case in 1936. This suit challenged the University of Maryland's practice of sending black students to an out-of-state law school rather than admitting them to the university's all-white law school. (The state gave black students a $200 scholarship, which did not cover the costs of tuition and travel and was not available to all black students who wanted to attend law school.) The Maryland appeals court rejected this arrangement and ordered that black students be admitted to the University of Maryland law school.[40]

The Supreme Court's first ruling in this area came two years later in a similar case from Missouri. Here, the state paid the black students' tuition to attend an out-of-state school, while white students attended the in-state school tuition-free. The state defended the practice under the separate but equal doctrine, pointing out that the law schools in adjacent states were as good as the Missouri law school and had essentially the same curriculum. The state also distinguished its case from Maryland's by arguing that Missouri had a provision for creating a law school at Lincoln University, the state school for African Americans. The Court rejected both arguments and expressed skepticism that the state would ever create a black law school that was equal in quality to the white school. The bottom line was that white students could attend law school in the state and similarly qualified black students could not, which violated the Fourteenth Amendment's equal protection of the laws.[41]

In 1948 the Court ruled that a black student had to be admitted to the state law school in Oklahoma rather than having to wait until a "separate but equal" black law school was constructed, or, alternatively, that no white students could be admitted to law school until the equal school was available.[42] Another case from Oklahoma found that black students had to be fully integrated into a graduate program rather than being required to sit in a separate row in the classroom and at separate tables in the library and cafeteria.[43] Although these cases were incremental steps toward eliminating segregation, the basic doctrine of "separate but equal" remained intact.

The next case chipped away at the principle itself. In 1950 Texas had a separate law school for black students, but it was not equal to the law school for whites. When the lawsuit was brought, the law school for black students had only four part-time faculty, none of whom had offices at the school; no librarian in the law library; and a library with few of the promised books. The situation started to improve after the case was under way; the Court observed, "[The black law school] is apparently on the road to full accreditation. It has a faculty of five full-time professors; a student body of 23; a library of some 16,500 volumes serviced by a full-time staff; a practice court and legal aid association; and one alumnus who has become a member of the Texas Bar." However, in a crucial move, the Court ruled that *this was not good enough*. There were more intangible aspects of the quality of law school that could not be measured by the number of books or faculty, such as the school's reputation, the "position and influence of the alumni," and "traditions and prestige." This came very close to saying that "separate but equal" was a contradiction in terms, but the Court stopped just short of reaching that conclusion.[44]

After these victories there was a debate within the NAACP whether to continue the case-by-case approach against the separate but equal doctrine, or to directly challenge the principle itself. The latter approach was risky because it was unclear if the Court was ready to take this bold step and because defeat in the Court would set back the movement. However, the signals increasingly indicated that the Supreme Court was ready to strike down the separate but equal doctrine. In addition to the law school cases, in 1948 the Court ruled that "restrictive covenants"—clauses in real estate contracts that prevented a property owner from selling to an African American—could not be enforced by state or local courts because of the Fourteenth Amendment's prohibition against a state denying blacks the "equal protection of the laws."

This application of the Fourteenth Amendment was expanded in the landmark ruling *Brown v. Board of Education*. The case arrived on the Court's docket in 1951, was postponed for argument until after the 1952 elections, and then was reargued in December 1953. The ruling was postponed for so long because the Court was keenly aware of the firestorm that would ensue. In its unanimous decision the Court ruled, "In the field of public education, the doctrine of separate but equal has no place. Separate educational facilities are inherently unequal, depriving the plaintiffs of the equal protection of the laws. Segregated facilities may generate in black children a feeling of inferiority that may affect their hearts and minds in a way unlikely ever to be undone."[45] The case was significant not only because it required all public schools in the United States to desegregate but also because it used the equal protection clause of the Fourteenth Amendment in a way that had potentially far-reaching consequences.

However, the decision was limited by focusing on segregation in schools rather than segregation more generally, and by focusing on the psychological damage done to black schoolchildren because of segregation rather than on the broader claim that racial classification itself was not allowed by the Constitution. Chief Justice Earl Warren wanted a unanimous vote and knew that two justices would not support a broader ruling that would overturn *Plessy v. Ferguson* and rule segregation unconstitutional in all contexts. Even if segregation in other public places still was legal, the *Brown* ruling provided an important boost to the civil rights movement. (However, see "What Do Political Scientists Do?" in Chapter 13 for an argument that the courts cannot be agents of social change.)

BUSING STUDENTS FROM ONE school district to another in the interest of desegration has been controversial since the 1960s. In 2007, the Supreme Court invalidated a voluntary desegration plans in Louisville and Seattle school districts.

THE PUSH TO DESEGREGATE SCHOOLS

In 1955, *Brown v. Board of Education II* addressed the implementation of desegregation and required the states to "desegregate with all deliberate speed."[46] The odd choice of words, "all deliberate speed," was read as a signal by southerners that they could take their time with desegregation. The phrase does seem to be contradictory: being deliberate does not usually involve being speedy. Southern states engaged in "massive resistance" to the desegregation order, as articulated by segregationist Virginia senator Harry F. Byrd. In some cases they even closed public schools rather than integrate them—and then reopened the schools as "private," segregated schools for which the white students received government vouchers. However, Maryland, Kentucky, Tennessee, Missouri, and the District of Columbia desegregated their schools within two years.

Eight years after *Brown I*, little had changed in the Deep South: fewer than 1 percent of black children attended school with white children.[47] The Supreme Court became frustrated with the lack of progress in desegregating the schools, saying there was "too much deliberation and not enough speed."[48] Through the 1960s the courts had to battle against the continued resistance. In 1971 the Court shifted its focus from **de jure** segregation (segregation mandated by law) to **de facto** segregation (segregation that existed because of segregated housing patterns) and approved school busing as a tool to integrate schools.[49] This approach was extremely controversial. The Court almost immediately limited the application of busing by ruling in a Detroit case that busing could not go beyond the boundaries of a city's school district; that is, students did not have to be bused from suburbs to cities unless it could be shown that the school district's lines were drawn in an intentionally discriminatory way.[50] This rule encouraged "white flight" from the cities to the suburbs in response to court-ordered busing.

The Supreme Court retreated further from enforcing desegregation in 1991 when it ruled that a school district could be released from a court-ordered desegregation plan if the district had taken "all practicable steps" to desegregate. Furthermore, districts do not have to address segregation in public schools that is caused by segregated housing.[51] The Court ruled in 1995 that low minority achievement scores are not evidence of a district's failure to desegregate, and said that school districts cannot be forced by the courts to spend money to establish magnet schools with special programs that could attract white students from the suburbs.[52]

de jure Relating to actions or circumstances that occur "by law," such as the legally enforced segregation of schools in the American South before the 1960s.

de facto Relating to actions or circumstances that occur outside the law or "by fact," such as the segregation of schools that resulted from housing patterns and other factors rather than from laws.

In perhaps the most important decision on race in education since *Brown*, in 2007 the Court invalidated voluntary desegregation plans implemented by public school districts in Seattle and Louisville. Both districts set goals for racial diversity and denied assignment requests if they tipped the racial balance above or below certain thresholds. In a ringing endorsement of the color-blind approach, the majority opinion said, "The way to stop discrimination on the basis of race is to stop discriminating on the basis of race." In this case, the discrimination was against white students who wanted to be in schools with few minority students rather than black students who wanted to be in integrated schools. However, it was not immediately clear how race would factor into school desegregation plans in the future, because only four justices signed on to the strict color-blind view. Justice Anthony Kennedy articulated a position between the conservatives' view, that race may not be used to classify students, and the liberals' view, that racial considerations are necessary to achieve integrated schools.[53]

EXPANDING CIVIL RIGHTS

Other significant rulings struck down state laws that forbade interracial marriages (sixteen states had such laws), upheld all significant parts of the Civil Rights Act, and upheld and expanded the scope of the Voting Rights Act. The central cases ruled that Congress had the power to eliminate segregation in public places, such as restaurants and hotels, under the commerce clause of the Constitution.

The first case involved a hotel in Atlanta that was close to an interstate highway, advertised extensively on the highway, and had a clientele that was about 75 percent from out of state. The Court ruled that this establishment was clearly engaging in interstate commerce, so Congress had the right to regulate it.[54] Ironically, the white hotel owner objected that his Thirteenth Amendment rights were violated by Congress forcing him to serve black people (he claimed to have been forced into "involuntary servitude"), but the Court rejected that argument. In the second case, "almost all, if not all" of the patrons of Ollie's Barbeque in Birmingham, Alabama, were local. However, the Court pointed out that meat purchased for the restaurant came from out of state, and this constituted 46 percent of the total amount spent on supplies. Therefore, the practice of segregation would place significant burdens on "the interstate flow of food and upon the movement on products generally."[55]

The next important area of cases was in employment law. In 1971 the Court ruled that employment tests, such as written exams or general aptitude tests, that are not related to job performance and that discriminate against blacks violate the 1964 Civil Rights Act.[56] The burden of proof was on the employer to show that the test was a "reasonable measure of job performance" and not simply an excuse to exclude African Americans from certain jobs. Another important aspect of this **disparate impact standard** of discrimination is that the *intent* of the company or person who is discriminating does not matter; whether the practice has an adverse *effect* on a racial group is the key point. This decision had a tremendous impact on integrating the workplace. In 1989, however, the Supreme Court reversed itself and placed the burden of proof on the employee to show that the discriminatory practice did not result from a business necessity.[57] This ruling made it much more difficult to prove workplace discrimination, and Congress subsequently overruled the Court on the issue, as discussed later. (See Nuts and Bolts 14.1 for the legal definition of race-based workplace discrimination.)

disparate impact standard The idea that discrimination exists if a practice has a negative effect on a specific group, whether or not this effect was intentional.

RACE-RELATED DISCRIMINATION AS DEFINED BY THE EQUAL EMPLOYMENT OPPORTUNITY COMMISSION

Below are excerpts from the U.S. Equal Employment Opportunity Commission's publication defining race/color discrimination.

Race/Color Discrimination

Race discrimination involves treating someone (an applicant or employee) unfavorably because he/she is of a certain race or because of personal characteristics associated with race (such as hair texture, skin color, or certain facial features). Color discrimination involves treating someone unfavorably because of skin color complexion. . . . Discrimination can occur when the victim and the person who inflicted the discrimination are the same race or color.

Race/Color Discrimination & Work Situations

The law forbids discrimination when it comes to any aspect of employment, including hiring, firing, pay, job assignments, promotions, layoff, training, fringe benefits, and any other term or condition of employment.

Race/Color Discrimination & Harassment

It is unlawful to harass a person because of that person's race or color. Harassment can include, for example, racial slurs, offensive or derogatory remarks about a person's race or color, or the display of racially-offensive symbols. Although the law doesn't prohibit simple teasing, offhand comments, or isolated incidents that are not very serious, harassment is illegal when it is so frequent or severe that it creates a hostile or offensive work environment or when it results in an adverse employment decision (such as the victim being fired or demoted). The harasser can be the victim's supervisor, a supervisor in another area, a co-worker, or someone who is not an employee of the employer, such as a client or customer.

Race/Color Discrimination & Employment Policies/Practices

An employment policy or practice that applies to everyone, regardless of race or color, can be illegal if it has a negative impact on the employment of people of a particular race or color and is not job-related and necessary to the operation of the business.

Source: U.S. Equal Employment Opportunity Commission, "Race/Color Discrimination," www.eeoc.gov/laws/types/race_color.cfm (accessed 10/4/12).

THE COLOR-BLIND COURT AND JUDICIAL ACTIVISM

The Roberts and Rehnquist Courts of the past two decades have been gradually imposing a "color-blind jurisprudence" over a range of issues. One significant area was the 1992 racial redistricting in which fifteen new U.S. House districts were drawn to help elect African Americans and ten districts were drawn to help elect Latino members. The resulting dramatic change in the number of minorities in Congress (an increase greater than 50 percent) was rooted in the 1982 amendments to the Voting Rights Act. Instead of mandating a fair *process*, this law and subsequent interpretation by the Supreme Court mandated that minorities be able to "elect representatives of their choice" when their numbers and configuration permit. As a result, the legislative redistricting process now had to avoid discriminatory *results* rather than being concerned only with discriminatory *intent*.

However, in a series of decisions starting with the 1993 landmark case *Shaw v. Reno,* the Supreme Court's adherence to a color-blind jurisprudence has thrown the constitutionality of black-majority districts into doubt. The Court has ruled that black-majority districts are legal as long as they are "done right,"[58] but it has consistently held that if race is the predominant factor in drawing district lines, the districts are unconstitutional because they violate the equal protection clause of the Fourteenth Amendment. This line of cases struck down black-majority districts in North Carolina, Georgia, Louisiana, Virginia, Texas, and Florida. The most recent case, in 2001, upheld the redrawn Twelfth District in North Carolina, which no longer was black majority, arguing that when race and partisanship are so intertwined—as they are when 90 percent of African Americans vote for the Democratic candidate—plaintiffs cannot assume that African Americans were placed together for racial reasons. This ruling opens the door for a greater consideration of race than had been allowed in the previous cases. However, racial redistricting is an unsettled area of the law, and many other countries have used more aggressive policies such as quotas to ensure more equal representation for minorities and women (see "In Comparison").[59]

The racial redistricting cases illustrate that the Supreme Court is increasingly activist in civil rights. It is generally unwilling to defer to any other branch of government that disagrees with its view of discrimination and equal protection (see Chapter 13 for a discussion of judicial activism). In some periods, judicial activism may serve to further civil rights, as in the 1950s and 1960s, or to limit them, as in the recent period.

WOMEN'S RIGHTS

The Supreme Court has also been central in determining women's civil rights. Until relatively recently the Court did not apply the Constitution to women, despite the Fourteenth Amendment's language that states may not deny any *person* the equal protection of the laws. Apparently, women were not regarded as people when it came to political and economic rights in the nineteenth and early twentieth centuries. These protectionist notions were finally rejected in three cases between 1971 and 1976, when the Court made it much more difficult for states to treat men and women differently.

The first case involved an Idaho state law that gave a man priority over a woman when they were otherwise equally entitled to execute a person's estate. This law was justified on the "reasonable" grounds that it reduced the state courts' workload by having an automatic rule that would limit challenges. However, the Court ruled that the law was arbitrary, did not meet the "reasonableness" test, and therefore violated the woman's equal protection rights under the Fourteenth Amendment.[60] The second case involved a female Air Force officer who wanted to count her husband as a dependent for purposes of health and housing benefits. Under the current law a military man could automatically count his wife as a dependent, but a woman could claim her husband only if she brought in more than half the family income. The Court struck down this practice, saying protectionist laws "in practical effect, put women not on a pedestal, but in a cage."[61]

These two cases still relied on the **rational basis test** for discrimination between men and women. It wasn't until 1976 that the Court established the **intermediate scrutiny test** in a case involving the drinking age. In the early 1970s some states had a lower drinking age for women than for men on the "rational basis" that eighteen- to twenty-year-old women are more mature than men of that age (states argued that women were less likely to be drunk drivers and less likely to abuse alcohol than men). The new

rational basis test The use of evidence to suggest that differences in the behavior of two groups can rationalize unequal treatment of these groups.

intermediate scrutiny test The middle level of scrutiny the courts use when determining whether a law is constitutional. To pass this test, the law or policy must further an important government interest in a way that is "substantially related" to that interest. This means that the law uses means that are a close fit to the government's objective and not substantially broader than necessary to accomplish that important objective.

BETTY DUKES, A PLAINTIFF IN A sexual discrimination lawsuit—the largest in the nation's history—filed against Wal-Mart, leaves a San Francisco courthouse with her attorney. Wal-Mart lost its appeal to remove the class-action status for plaintiffs and will face billions of dollars in damages if it loses the case.

REPRESENTATION OF WOMEN AND MINORITIES

A central problem for representative democracy is to provide a voice for minority interests in a system that is dominated by the votes of the majority. The legitimacy and stability of any democracy depends, in part, on its ability to accomplish that difficult aim. The recent experiences in nation building in Iraq, Afghanistan, and Sudan provide dramatic evidence for this point: if minorities are excluded from the political process, they often resort to violence and terrorism to gain a seat at the table. The American experiment in nation building in Philadelphia in 1787 faced similar, if less severe, divisions. The Founders' institutional solution of the separation of powers within and across levels of government provided multiple points of access for various interests and some assurance that no single interest would dominate government for extended periods. Majority tyranny was prevented by a pluralist politics in which "minorities rule," to use Robert Dahl's famous phrase. However, for at least forty years, scholars and politicians have recognized that our system did not provide adequate representation for certain groups in society, especially racial minorities and women (even if women are a numerical majority in most countries, they do not control the majority of political power).[a] Our pluralist system does not deal very well with specific racial, ethnic, or gender-based interests because our electoral system is based on single-member, winner-take-all (WTA) districts where the majority (or at least the plurality) clearly rule. Some U.S. communities are experimenting with different electoral mechanisms to enhance minority representation, but many other countries have better formal representation of racial minorities and women than the United States (which, for example, ranks seventy-first in the world in the representation of women in national legislatures).

Nations that have proportional representation are more likely to represent minority interests than those with WTA systems. Usually there is a threshold that a party must meet (often 5 percent) before it is represented in a national legislature. Therefore, any racial or ethnic group with a strong common identity could conceivably gain representation in the national legislature with as little as 5 percent of the population. Some nations, such as Germany, Denmark, and Poland, even waive the threshold if the party is representing an ethnic minority. The strongest provision for the representation of racial, ethnic, and gender-based interests in legislatures is known as "reserved communal seats." For example, Jordan reserves eighteen of its eighty seats for Christians, Circassians, and Bedouins, while Taiwan reserves eight of its 225 seats for Aboriginals. Overall, at least seventeen countries use this mechanism to promote equal representation of racial and ethnic minorities and seventeen use it for gender equity for their national legislature.[b] This system of reserved seats, which is a form of quotas, was explicitly rejected in the 1982 Voting Rights Act amendments that provided minority voters in the United States an equal opportunity to elect candidates of their choice but said that the new law should not be seen as endorsing proportional representation or quotas.

Another mechanism that is commonly used to enhance representation for women but less so for racial and ethnic minorities is requiring that a certain percentage of candidates on the party list are women. In Iraq, for example, where women did not serve in public office under the previous regime, the Iraqi constitution requires that at least 25 percent of the seats in parliament are held by women. As it turned out, in the March 2010 elections, 25.5 percent of the seats in the new parliament went to women. Fifty nations have party list requirements for women ranging from 50 percent to 5 percent. Seventeen of the top twenty nations in terms of representing women have some form of gender quotas. Ensuring representation of different racial and ethnic groups can also be an important mechanism for bringing peace to war-torn areas: Bosnia, Cyprus, Rwanda, Fiji, Sri Lanka, Zimbabwe, Kosovo, Macedonia, Afghanistan, and Iraq have all produced power-sharing settlements that require a certain number of seats for the various factions within their nations.

Finally, it is important to note that WTA systems can incorporate reserved seats into their system of district elections. India, Pakistan, and Samoa, among others, provide representation for minority interests through reserved seats even if they have single-member-district WTA elections. As the United States continues to struggle with issues of how to best represent its increasingly diverse electorate, it may learn some valuable lessons from other nations that have used a variety of techniques for many decades.

WOMEN IN LEGISLATURE	
Nordic Countries	42%
Americas	24%
Europe	22.9%
Sub-Saharan Africa	20.3%
Asia	18%
United States	15.2%
Pacific	15.2%
Arab States	13%

Source: Inter-Parliamentary Union, "Women in National Parliaments, www.ipu.org/wmn-e/world.htm (accessed 11/5/12).

intermediate scrutiny standard meant that the government's policy must be "substantially related" to an "important government objective" to justify the unequal treatment of men and women, so the law was struck down.[62]

Before this case, only two standards served to apply the Fourteenth Amendment to different categories of people: the reasonable basis test and the strict scrutiny test. Racial minorities received the strongest protection as the "suspect classification" where the **strict scrutiny test** is applied. Under this test there must be a "compelling state interest" to discriminate among people if race is involved. The suspect classification was first used in a case involving the internment of Japanese Americans during World War II. It is one of the few instances in which racial classification has survived strict scrutiny. In a controversial ruling, the Court said that the internment camps were justified on national security grounds.[63] The only other test before the new intermediate one said that it was acceptable to discriminate against a group of people as long as there was a "rational basis" for that state law. Today, for example, states can pass a twenty-one-year-old drinking law on the grounds that traffic fatalities will be lower with that drinking age rather than with a law that allows eighteen-year-olds to drink.

The intermediate scrutiny test gives women stronger protections than the reasonable basis test, but it is not as strong as strict scrutiny. To use the legal jargon, the gender distinction would have to serve an "important government objective," but not a "compelling state interest," in order to withstand intermediate scrutiny. Some distinctions between men and women are still allowed. For example, in 1981 the Supreme Court said that gender differences influence combat roles and military needs and therefore justify male-only draft registration. This issue has not been relevant recently because of the all-volunteer armed services, but it would become relevant again if the draft were reinstated.[64]

In many instances, as with the Idaho case, the rights of women were strengthened by the new standard of equal protection. However, in other instances, women may actually be worse off by being treated the same as men. For example, in the drinking age case, instead of dropping the drinking age for men to eighteen, states raised the age for women to twenty-one. Similarly, the Court struck down an

strict scrutiny test The highest level of scrutiny the courts use when determining whether a law is constitutional. To pass this test, the law or policy must be shown to serve a "compelling state interest" or goal, it must be narrowly tailored to achieve that goal, and it must be the least restrictive means of achieving the goal.

14.2 **NUTS** *& bolts*

LEVELS OF SCRUTINY IN DISCRIMINATION LAWSUITS

When deciding a lawsuit, federal judges use different levels of scrutiny to determine whether discrimination is allowed, based on the status of the plaintiff.

Rational Basis Test The use of evidence to suggest that differences in the behavior of two groups can rationalize unequal treatment of these groups, such as charging sixteen- to twenty-one-year-olds higher prices for auto insurance than people over twenty-one because younger people have higher accident rates.

Intermediate Scrutiny Test The middle level of scrutiny the courts use when determining whether unequal treatment is justified by the effect of a law; this is the standard used for gender-based discrimination cases and for many cases based on sexual orientation.

Strict Scrutiny Test The highest level of scrutiny the courts use when determining whether unequal treatment is justified by the effect of a law. It is applied in all cases involving race. Laws rarely pass the strict scrutiny standard; a law that discriminates based on race must be shown to serve some "compelling state interest" in order to be upheld.

DETERMINING IF DISCRIMINATION IS LEGAL

CASES INVOLVING "SUSPECT CLASSIFICATION" (race, ethnicity, creed, or national origin)

STRICT SCRUTINY TEST

1. Is unequal treatment justified by a "compelling state interest"?
2. Is unequal treatment the "least restrictive" option?

YES If yes to both, discrimination is legal. However, very few cases meet this standard.

NO If not, discrimination is illegal.

CASES INVOLVING SEX OR GENDER EQUALITY

INTERMEDIATE SCRUTINY TEST

1. Is the discriminatory policy "substantially related" to an "important government objective"?
2. Is the discrimination "no greater than necessary" to achieve this objective?

YES If yes to both, discrimination is legal. Some discrimination based on gender is permitted, but this test is harder to pass than the rational basis test applied to gender cases in the past.

NO If not, discrimination is illegal.

CASES INVOLVING AGE, ECONOMIC STATUS, OR OTHER CRITERIA

RATIONAL BASIS TEST

1. Is the law rationally related to furthering a legitimate government interest?
2. Does the policy avoid "arbitrary, capricious, or deliberate" discrimination?

YES If yes to both, discrimination is legal. This is the easiest hurdle for a law or policy to pass.

NO If not, discrimination is illegal.

POP QUIZ!

1 Unequal treatment based on race is typically subject to

a strict scrutiny by the courts.

b intermediate scrutiny by the courts.

c rational basis test by the courts.

d First Amendment protections.

e majority preferences.

2 An example of unequal treatment that would pass the rational basis test is

a affirmative action programs.

b hiring whites only.

c banning Jews from certain government positions.

d systematically paying men more than women.

e banning people under a certain age from driving.

Answers: 1.a; 2.e

Alabama divorce law in which husbands but not wives could be ordered to pay alimony.[65] Arguably women would have been better off in these two specific instances under the old discriminatory laws (because they could drink at eighteen instead of twenty-one and did not have to pay alimony in some states). However, the more aggressive application of the Fourteenth Amendment for women was an important step in providing them the equal protection of the laws, as clearly shown in a Court decision that struck down the Virginia Military Institute's (VMI) male-only admission policy. The majority opinion stated that VMI violated the Fourteenth Amendment's equal protection clause because it failed to show an "exceedingly persuasive justification" for its sex-biased admissions policy.[66]

Two other areas where the Supreme Court helped advance women's rights were affirmative action and protection against sexual harassment. In 1987 the Court approved affirmative action in a case involving a woman who was promoted over a man despite the fact that he scored slightly higher than she did on a test. The Court ruled that this was acceptable to make up for past discrimination.[67] The Court made it easier to sue employers for sexual harassment in 1993, saying that a woman did not have to reach the point of a nervous breakdown before claiming that she was harassed; it was enough to demonstrate a pattern of "repeated and unwanted" behavior that created a "hostile workplace environment."[68] Later rulings stated that if a single act is flagrant, the conduct did not have to be repeated to create a hostile environment.

As with civil rights for minorities, the Court has also restricted the rights of women in some instances. In 1984 the Court ruled that Title IX of the Education Amendments of 1972, which prohibits sex discrimination in "any education program or activity receiving Federal financial assistance," applied to private colleges and universities in which students received federal financial aid. However, in a blow to equal treatment for women, the Court said that only the program receiving federal funds could not discriminate, rather than the institution as a whole. This ruling released many athletic programs from their obligation to provide equal opportunity for women athletes.[69] Congress overturned the ruling with the Civil Rights Restoration Act in 1988.

More recently, Lilly Ledbetter sued Goodyear Tire and Rubber Company for receiving lower pay than men for the same work over a twenty-year period, which she claimed was gender discrimination. However, the Court rejected her claim, saying that she did not meet the time limit required by the law, as the discrimination must have occurred within 180 days of the claim. Dissenters pointed out that pay discrimination usually occurs in small increments over long periods, so it would be impossible to recognize the discrimination within 180 days. Furthermore, workers do not have access to information about fellow workers' pay, so it would be almost impossible to meet the standard set by the Court. The longstanding policy of the Equal Employment Opportunity Commission (EEOC) was that each new paycheck restarted the 180-day clock as a new act of discrimination, but the Court overturned that policy, making it almost impossible to sue for discriminatory pay based on gender or race under the Civil Rights Act.[70] Congress overturned this decision and restored the old standard in January 2009 by passing the Lilly Ledbetter Fair Pay Act. As Figure 14.3 shows, significant pay disparities between men and women remain throughout much of the United States.

Recent verdicts won by the EEOC include a $19 million settlement that Outback Steakhouse agreed to pay in a sex discrimination and "glass ceiling" lawsuit. Thousands of female employees at hundreds of restaurants alleged they were

FIGURE » 14.3

WOMEN'S EARNINGS AS A PERCENTAGE OF MEN'S EARNINGS, 2007

There is a substantial difference between women's and men's earnings in the United States. What could account for this variation? How much do you think it has to do with levels of discrimination and how much with differences in the nature of the jobs that men and women hold?

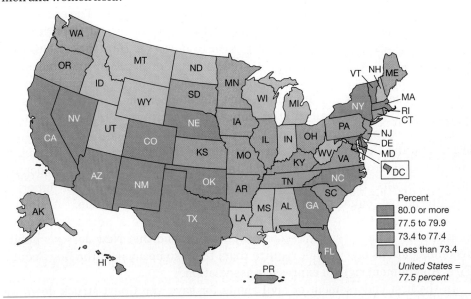

Percent

- 80.0 or more
- 77.5 to 79.9
- 73.4 to 77.4
- Less than 73.4

United States = 77.5 percent

Source: Alemayehu Bishaw and Jessica Semega, "Income, Earnings, and Poverty Data from the 2007 American Community Survey," U.S. Census Bureau, August 2008, www.census.gov/prod/2008pubs/acs-09.pdf (accessed 11/3/12).

denied equal opportunities for advancement. The EEOC has also won large settlements for sexual harassment and pay discrimination in recent years against FedEx, Jack in the Box, Dunkin' Donuts, Ruby Tuesday, IHOP, and dozens of other corporations.[71]

The largest sexual discrimination lawsuit in the nation's history was filed in 2001 against Wal-Mart on behalf of 1.5 million women who worked at Wal-Mart since 1998. Among other things, the plaintiffs allege the following:

▶ Over objections from a female executive, senior management regularly referred to female store employees as "little Janie Qs" and "girls."

▶ A Sam's Club [Wal-Mart's warehouse retail chain] manager in California told another woman that she should "doll-up" to get promoted.

▶ Managers have repeatedly told female employees that men "need to be paid more than women because they have families to support."

▶ A male manager in South Carolina told a female employee that "God made Adam first, so women would always be second to men."

▶ A female personnel manager in Florida was told by her manager that men were paid more than women because "men are here to make a career and women aren't. Retail is for housewives who just need to earn extra money."[72]

However, in 2011 the Court ruled that the class action lawsuit was not valid because there was no "convincing proof of a companywide discriminatory pay and promotion policy." That is, women would have to prove discrimination individually, not as a group. Civil rights experts said this was the "death knell" for class action lawsuits seeking monetary damages for discrimination.[73]

GAY RIGHTS

substantive due process doctrine One interpretation of the due process clause of the Fourteenth Amendment; in this view the Supreme Court has the power to overturn laws that infringe on individual liberties.

The Supreme Court has a similarly mixed record on gay rights. The early cases were not supportive of gay rights. One of the first concerned Georgia's law banning sodomy. The Supreme Court ruled in *Bowers v. Hardwick* (1986) that homosexual behavior was not protected by the Constitution and that state laws banning it could be justified under the most lenient "reasonable basis" test.[74] In other cases the Supreme Court sidestepped the controversial issue of gay rights, choosing alternative constitutional grounds to reach its decisions. For example, in 1995 the Court ruled that the South Boston Allied War Veterans Council did not have to let the Irish-American Gay, Lesbian, and Bisexual Group of Boston march in its St. Patrick's Day parade because of the veterans' First Amendment rights of free expression, thus ignoring the alternative "equal protection" claim made by the gay group.[75] A similar ruling held that the Boy Scouts of America did not have to admit an "avowed homosexual" as an assistant scoutmaster and found that New Jersey's public accommodations law did not require them to do so because of the Boy Scouts' First Amendment right of expressive association.[76]

IN 2011, THE U.S. MILITARY REPEALED its controversial "don't ask, don't tell" policy, which prevented gay men and lesbians from serving openly in the armed forces. At midnight on September 20, 2011, as the repeal formally took effect, Navy Lieutenant Gary Ross (right) married his longtime partner, Dan Swezy.

In the first endorsement of civil rights for gays, the Court struck down an amendment to the Colorado state constitution that would have prevented gays from suing for discrimination in employment or housing. The Court said that the state amendment violated gays' equal protection rights because it "withdrew from homosexuals, but no others, specific legal protection from the injuries caused by discrimination."[77] The Court rejected the state's "reasonable basis" arguments and came close to putting gays in the "suspect classification" that has been restricted to racial and ethnic minorities.

A more important ruling came seven years later in a case involving two Houston men. John Geddes Lawrence and Tyron Garner were prosecuted for same-sex sodomy after police entered Lawrence's apartment—upon receiving a false tip about an armed man in an apartment complex—and found the two having sex. Under Texas law, sodomy was illegal for homosexuals but not for heterosexuals. In a landmark 6–3 ruling, the Supreme Court said that the liberty guaranteed by the Fourteenth Amendment's due process clause allows homosexuals to have sexual relations. "Freedom presumes an autonomy of self that includes freedom of thought, belief, expression, and certain intimate conduct."[78] This reasoning is rooted in the **substantive due process doctrine** that underlies constitutional protections for birth control, abortion, and decisions about how to raise one's children.

The decision overturned *Bowers v. Hardwick*, and the majority opinion had harsh words for that decision, saying it "was not correct when it was decided, and it is not correct today." Five members of the majority signed onto the broad "due process" reasoning of the decision, while Justice O'Connor wrote a concurring opinion in which she agreed that the Texas law was unconstitutional but on narrower grounds: O'Connor's reasoning would have applied only to the four states that treated gays and heterosexuals differently (that is, banning sodomy only for gays). With the broader due process logic, a total of thirteen state laws that banned sodomy were struck down. Justice Scalia wrote a strong dissent, saying that the decision was "the product of a court that has largely signed on to the so-called homosexual agenda" and warned that the ruling "will have far-reaching implications beyond this case." He predicted that the ruling would serve as the basis for constitutional protections for gay marriage.

The Supreme Court has yet to rule on gay marriage, but California may provide the test case. In November 2008, California voters narrowly passed Proposition 8, striking down the state's gay marriage law. In August 2010, a federal district court struck down Proposition 8, and then the state said that it would not defend the Proposition in court. After the state supreme court ruled that proponents of the Proposition had standing to defend the case, the appeal went forward.[79] Gay marriage in California is still on hold until appeals are decided.

This summary of cases demonstrates that the courts can be both a strong advocate of and an impediment to civil rights. In general, however, the courts have a limited *independent* impact on policy. As Alexander Hamilton pointed out in *Federalist 78*, the Supreme Court has "neither the power of the purse nor the sword." That is, it must rely on the other branches of government to carry out its policy decisions, as the school desegregation cases clearly demonstrate.

THE LEGISLATIVE ARENA

Congress has provided the basis for today's protection of civil rights through a series of laws that were enacted, starting in the 1960s. Applying to racial and ethnic minorities and women, these laws attempted to ensure that there is a "level playing field" of equal opportunity.

INITIAL LEGISLATION OF THE 1960S

The bedrock of equal protection that exists today stems from landmark legislation passed by Congress in the 1960s—the 1964 Civil Rights Act, the 1965 Voting Rights Act, and the 1968 Fair Housing Act. President Kennedy was slow to seek civil rights legislation for fear of alienating southern Democrats. The events in Birmingham prompted him to act, but he was assassinated before the legislation was passed. President Lyndon Johnson, a former segregationist, helped push through the Civil Rights Act when he became president. The act barred discrimination in employment based on race, sex, religion, or national origin; banned segregation in public places; and established the EEOC as the enforcement agency for the legislation. One of the southern opponents of the legislation inserted the language referring to sex, thinking that it would defeat the bill (figuring, perhaps, that there would be a majority coalition of male chauvinists and segregationists), but it became law anyway.

The Voting Rights Act of 1965 (VRA) eliminated direct obstacles to minority voting in the South, such as discriminatory literacy tests and other voter registration tests, and also provided the means to enforce the law: federal marshals were charged with overseeing elections in the South. After its passage, President Johnson hailed the VRA as a "triumph for freedom as huge as any ever won on any battlefield."[80] The VRA, which is often cited as one of the most significant pieces of civil rights legislation in our nation's history,[81] precipitated an explosion in black political participation in the South. The most dramatic gains came in Mississippi, where black registration increased from 6.7 percent before the VRA to 59.8 percent in 1967. As one political scientist noted, "The act simply overwhelmed the major bulwarks of the disenfranchising system. In the seven states originally covered, black registration increased from 29.3 percent in March, 1965, to 56.6 percent in 1971–72; the gap between black and white registration rates narrowed from 44.1 percentage points to 11.2."[82]

The last piece of landmark legislation, the Fair Housing Act of 1968, barred discrimination in the rental or sale of a home based on race, sex, religion, and national origin. Important amendments to the law enacted in 1988 added disability and familial status (having children under eighteen), provided new administrative enforcement mechanisms, and expanded Justice Department jurisdiction to bring suit on behalf of victims in federal district courts.[83]

There have been many other amendments to civil rights laws since the 1960s. Most important were the 1975 amendments to the VRA that extended coverage of many of the law's provisions to language minorities; the 1982 VRA amendments, which extended important provisions of the law for twenty-five years and made it easier to bring a lawsuit under the act; the 1991 Civil Rights Act; and the 2006 extension of the VRA for another twenty-five years. The 1991 law overruled or altered parts of twelve Supreme Court decisions that had eroded the intent of Congress when it passed the civil rights legislation. It expanded earlier legislation and increased the costs to employers for intentional, illegal discrimination. Two central debates were over the standard that had to be met in discrimination cases and where the burden of proof should lie: on the employer or on the employee. After vetoing an earlier version of the bill, President George H. W. Bush ultimately agreed that the burden of proof should be on the employer. Thus, the central question was how to define the discriminatory standard.

Democrats in Congress pushed for a relatively tough standard that discrimination be "essential to business practice" in order to be permitted. For example, if a university required all assistant professors to have a Ph.D., and if it could be shown that more white applicants had Ph.D.s than minority applicants, the university would have the burden of proof to demonstrate that the Ph.D. was essential for doing the job. President Bush wanted a less stringent standard of "legitimate business objectives." Congress ended up adopting language that was somewhere in between: the employer must show that the practice is "job related for the position in question and consistent with business necessity."

PROTECTIONS FOR WOMEN

Women have also received extensive protection through legislation. As noted, Title VII of the Civil Rights Act, which barred discrimination based on gender, was almost an accidental part of the bill (it was included by an opponent to the legislation). Indeed, the first executive director of the EEOC would not enforce the gender part of the law because it was a "fluke." In 1966 the National Organization for Women (NOW) was formed to push for enforcement of the law. Its members convinced President Johnson to sign an executive order that eliminated sex discrimination in federal agencies and among federal contractors, but it was difficult to enforce. Finally in 1970 the EEOC started enforcing the law. Before long, one-third of civil rights cases involved sex discrimination, and those numbers have remained high in recent years (see Figure 14.4).

Congress passed the next piece of important legislation for women in 1972: Title IX of the Higher Education Act, which prohibits sex discrimination in institutions that receive federal funds. The law has had the greatest impact in women's sports. In the 1960s and 1970s, opportunities for women to play sports in college or high school were extremely limited. Very few women's scholarships were available at the college level, and budgets for women's sports were tiny compared to the budgets for men's. Though it took nearly thirty years to reach parity between men and women, most universities are now in compliance with Title IX. Nonetheless, the law has its critics. Many men's sports, such as baseball, tennis, wrestling, and gymnastics, were cut at universities that had to bring the number of student athletes into rough parity. Critics argued that such cuts were unfair, especially given that the interest in women's sports was not as high. Defenders of the law argue that the gap in interest in women's and men's sports will not change until there is equal opportunity. There is some evidence to support that claim, as interest is increasing in women's soccer and professional basketball with the WNBA, as well as in well-established women's professional sports such as golf and tennis.

IN NOVEMBER 2006, STUDENTS from James Madison University rallied outside the Department of Education in Washington, D.C., to protest the university's plan to cut ten of its men's athletic teams. The cuts were made to bring the school into compliance with the federal law requiring equity in men's and women's sports.

Another significant effort during this period was the failed Equal Rights Amendment. The amendment passed in 1972 and was sent to the states for ratification. Its wording was simple: "Equality of rights under the law shall not be denied or abridged by the United States or any state on account of sex." Many states passed it within months, but the process lost momentum, and the amendment fell three states short of the required thirty-eight states after the required seven years. The amendment received a three-year extension from Congress but still did not get the additional three states.

In 1994 Congress passed the Violence against Women Act, which allowed women who were the victims of physical abuse and violence to sue in federal court. Part of this law was overturned by the Supreme Court, which ruled that Congress had exceeded its powers under the commerce clause.[84]

PROTECTIONS FOR THE DISABLED AND FOR GAY RIGHTS

Yet another important piece of civil rights legislation was the 1990 Americans with Disabilities Act, which provided strong federal protections for the 45 million disabled Americans in terms of workplace discrimination and access to public facilities. This law produced the curb-cuts in sidewalks, access for wheelchairs to public buses and trains, special seating in sports stadiums, and many other changes that make the daily lives of the disabled a little easier and that provide them an equal opportunity to participate more fully in society. The Supreme Court narrowed the law's scope when it ruled that the law did not apply to state employees.[85]

Congress's track record in protecting gay rights is not quite as strong. In fact, most of the steps taken by Congress have been to restrict rather than expand gay rights. In 1996 Congress reacted to the possibility that some liberal states such as Hawaii would allow gay marriage by passing the Defense of Marriage Act. Its concern was rooted in the "full faith and credit clause" of the Constitution, which says that all states have to respect the laws of other states. Thus, if gay marriages were allowed in one state, all other states would have to recognize that marriage as legal if the couple were to move to another state.

FIGURE » 14.4

DISCRIMINATION CASES IN THE EQUAL EMPLOYMENT OPPORTUNITY COMMISSION, 2009

Discrimination based on race and on sex are the two types that are most frequently reported, but there is a significant amount of discrimination based on age and disability as well. What types of discrimination do you think would be most likely to go unreported?

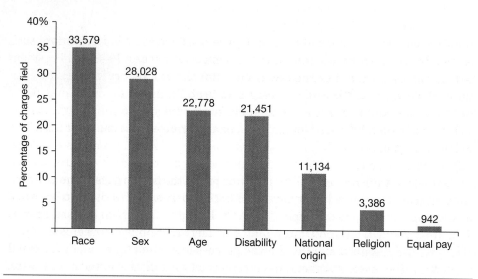

Note: Percentages do not sum to 100 because complaints may be filed in more than one category.

Source: U.S. Equal Employment Opportunity Commission, Charge Statistics, www.eeoc.gov/eeoc/statistics /enforcement/charges.cfm (accessed 11/3/12).

More recently, Congress has proposed an amendment to the Constitution that would ban gay marriage. Acting on the fears expressed by Justice Scalia, members of Congress were concerned that the Supreme Court might strike down the Defense of Marriage Act. President George W. Bush endorsed the amendment, and Democrats have criticized it as a divisive gimmick to appeal to the conservative base of the Republican Party. President Obama opposes the amendment, and while the Democrats are in control of the Senate, any action on the amendment is unlikely.

In what may represent a change of course, in October 2009 Congress passed the Matthew Shepard and James Byrd Jr. Hate Crimes Prevention Act. This legislation expanded the previous hate crime laws based on race, color, religion, or national origin to include attacks based on a victim's sexual orientation, gender identity, or mental or physical disability. The law also lifted a requirement that a victim had to be attacked while engaged in a federally protected activity, such as attending school, for it to be a federal hate crime. In signing the bill, President Obama said, "After more than a decade of opposition and delay, we've passed inclusive hate crimes legislation to help protect our citizens from violence based on what they look like, who they love, how they pray or who they are."[86] The law commemorates the horrific murders of James Byrd Jr. (mentioned earlier) and Matthew Shepard, a gay teenager who in 1998 was beaten by two men, tied to a fence, and left to die. Also, the Employment Non-Discrimination Act, which would prohibit discrimination in employment based on sexual orientation, has been proposed in nearly every Congress since 1994. A version of the bill passed the House in 2007 but died in the Senate. President Obama supports the bill, but today it is unlikely the pass the Republican-controlled House.

THE EXECUTIVE ARENA

The civil rights movement has benefited greatly from presidential action, such as President Truman's integration of the armed services in 1948 and President Eisenhower's use of the National Guard to enforce a court order to integrate Central High School in Little Rock, Arkansas, in 1957. Executive orders by presidents Kennedy and Johnson in 1961 and 1965, respectively, established affirmative action; and in 1969 Richard Nixon expanded the "goals and numerical ranges" for hiring minorities.

The most significant unilateral action taken by a president in the area of civil rights for gays was President Clinton's effort to end the ban on gays in the military. Clinton was surprised by the strength of the opposition to his plan, so he ended up crafting a compromise policy of "don't ask, don't tell," which pleased no one. Under this policy the military would stop actively searching for and discharging gays from the military ranks, and recruits would not need to reveal their sexual orientation. However, if without an investigation the military found out a person was gay, he or she still could be disciplined or discharged.

During the 2008 campaign, President Obama promised to repeal "don't ask, don't tell." After several previous attempts in 2010 were stopped by Republican filibusters, Congress passed the "Don't Ask, Don't Tell Repeal Act of 2010" in December. However, the repeal would not go into effect until sixty days after the Joint Chiefs of Staff and the president filed a report indicating that it would not harm "military readiness and effectiveness, unit cohesion, and military recruiting and retention." That report was filed in July 2011, and the repeal went into effect on September 20, 2011. Minutes after the new policy was in place, Navy Lt. Gary Ross and his long-term partner were married in Vermont to become the first openly gay married person in the military.[87]

The low priority that recent presidential candidates have given to civil rights policy more generally means that it is less likely that significant and dramatic change will come from unilateral action by the president. Instead, attention to civil rights concerns in the executive branch has primarily been in two areas since 1993: racial diversity in presidential appointments and use of the bully pulpit to promote racial concerns and interests.

President Clinton was active on both dimensions. In 1992, as a candidate, Clinton promised a government that "looks like America." His cabinet, subcabinet, and judicial appointments achieved the greatest gender and racial balance of any in history. Fourteen percent of Clinton's first-year presidential appointments were African American (compared to 12 percent of the population in 1992), 6 percent were Hispanic (compared to 9.5 percent of the population), and the percentages of Asian American and Native American appointees were identical to their pro-

THE 2012 SHOOTING OF TRAYVON Martin, an unarmed seventeen-year-old African American man, by a neighborhood watch member raised concerns about racism—both on the part of the shooter, George Zimmerman, and on the part of the local police department, for not immediately arresting Zimmerman. Here, members of Martin's family speak to the media about the shooting.

portions in the population. Clinton delivered an administration that "looked like us" (the proportion of women appointees—27 percent—was well short of their proportion in the population, but it still was a record high). Clinton also used the bully pulpit to advocate a civil rights agenda. Most significant was his effort to promote a "National Conversation on Race," which helped focus national attention on many of the problems faced by minorities.

President George W. Bush did not achieve the same level of diversity in his appointments as Clinton, but his administration was more diverse than that of other Republican presidents. His initial nineteen cabinet and cabinet-rank appointments included fifteen men, four women, and six racial minorities. The rhetoric that surrounded these appointments, however, was not couched in terms of affirmative action, but rather merit. Critics argued that gender and race played a central role in these decisions, just as they did with Clinton, even if the rhetoric had a different tone. Despite the different approach, Bush made serious overtures to minorities, especially Latinos, in his effort to expand the Republican Party base.

Although it is too early to know the impact of the Obama presidency on the civil rights movement, the historical significance of his successful campaign as a minority candidate is clear. At the 2008 Democratic National Convention, some African American delegates openly wept as Obama accepted the party's nomination. Many delegates had not expected that they would live to see an African American become a strong contender for the presidency. Like his predecessors, Obama nominated a diverse cabinet with fourteen men, seven women, and seven racial minorities. Eric Holder is the first African American to serve as attorney general and Sonia Sotomayor is the first Latina on the Supreme Court. Obama also nominated Elena Kagan to the Supreme Court, putting three women on the Court for the first time. But in general, Obama tried to downplay race and diversity concerns. In a few instances race asserted itself onto the agenda, as when Obama publicly rebuked a police officer for arresting an eminent African American scholar, Henry Louis Gates Jr. of Harvard University, as he was trying to get his front door unstuck (the police officer thought Gates was breaking in). That flap died away after Obama hosted a "beer summit" with the officer and Professor Gates at the White House. Racially insensitive comments by Senate Majority Leader Harry Reid caused another brief firestorm that quickly subsided after Obama accepted Reid's apology. Some observers argue that Obama's victory signals the beginning of a "post-racial politics" that places less emphasis on race and devotes more attention to issues that concern all Americans, such as the economy, education, and heath care. However, Obama himself rejects this view.

Race also played a role in the 2012 presidential election. In the Republican primary, Newt Gingrich caused a stir when he called Obama "the greatest food stamp president." When asked whether this label was demeaning to African Americans and to the president, he defended the remark, saying that record numbers of Americans are on food stamps. A brief stir was also caused when Mitt Romney referred to the "birthers" claim that President Obama was not born in the United States by joking that "No one's ever asked to see my birth certificate. They know that this is the place that we were born and raised."[88] However, race did not play a very prominent role in the general election as both candidates focused on the economy.

CONTINUING AND FUTURE CIVIL RIGHTS ISSUES

There is vigorous debate over the likely direction of the civil rights movement in the twenty-first century. There are three main perspectives. The first group, whose views are articulated by such scholars as Stephan Thernstrom of Harvard University and Abigail Thernstrom of the Manhattan Institute, has suggested that our nation must "move beyond race." This group argues that on many social and economic indicators, the gap between blacks and whites has narrowed and that public opposition to race-based policies indicates the need for a new approach. The Supreme Court has largely endorsed this view by implementing a "color-blind jurisprudence" over a broad range of issues. The second group is represented by traditional civil rights activists and groups such as the Congressional Black Caucus and the NAACP; it argues that the civil rights movement must continue to fight for equal opportunity by enforcing existing law and pushing for equality of outcomes by protecting and expanding affirmative action programs and other policies that address racial inequality. These first two groups share the goal of racial equality and integration but differ on how much progress we have made and how to make further progress. A final group does not support the goal of integration; instead, activists such as Louis Farrakhan and the Nation of Islam argue for African American self-sufficiency and separation. They believe that African Americans can never gain equality within what they see as the repressive, white-dominated economic and political system.

Most civil rights advocates endorse the second view. They argue that it would be a mistake to conclude that the work of the civil rights movement is complete. They point to the resegregation of public schools, persistent gaps between whites and racial minorities in health and economic status, racial profiling, hate crimes, a backlash against immigrant groups, and continuing discrimination in employment and housing. At the same time, this group rejects calls for racial separation as short-sighted and self-defeating.

The other two groups would argue that although the traditional civil rights agenda made important contributions to racial equality, further progress will require a different approach. Advocates of the color-blind approach prefer to stop making distinctions between people based on race: they want to use government policies to make sure there is no overt discrimination and provide equal opportunity for all, and then let merit decide outcomes. The segregationists have given up on the civil rights agenda and believe that minorities can achieve success only on their own. Debates among advocates of these three views play out over a broad range of issues, three of which are outlined in the last section of the chapter.

AFFIRMATIVE ACTION

The Civil Rights Act of 1964 ensured that, at least on paper, all Americans would enjoy equality of opportunity. But even after the act was passed, blacks continued to lag behind whites in socioeconomic status; there was still a substantial gap between the equality of opportunity and the equality of outcomes. In an important speech at Howard University in 1965, Johnson outlined his argument for affirmative action, saying, "This is the next and the more profound stage of the battle for civil rights. . . . We seek not just legal equity but human ability, not just equality as a right and a theory but equality as a fact and equality as a result. . . . To this end equal opportunity is essential, but not enough, not enough."[89] Later that year, President Johnson attempted to move closer to equality of outcomes by issuing an executive order requiring all federal agencies and government contractors to submit written proposals to provide an equal opportunity for employment of blacks, women, Asian Americans, and Native Americans within various job categories and to outline programs to achieve those goals. The policy was expanded under President Nixon, and throughout the 1970s and 1980s affirmative action programs grew in the private sector, higher education, and government contracting. Through such programs, employers and universities gave special opportunities to minorities and women, either to make up for past discrimination or to pursue the general goals of diversity.

Affirmative action takes many forms. The most passive type involves extra effort to recruit women and minorities for employment or college admission by placing ads in newspapers and magazines, visiting inner-city schools, or sending out targeted mailings. A more active form involves including race or gender as a "plus factor" in the admissions or hiring decision. That is, from a pool of qualified candidates, a minority applicant may receive an advantage over white applicants. (Women generally do not receive special consideration in admissions decisions, but gender may be a "plus factor" in some employment decisions; in fact, many selective schools have been quietly applying affirmative action for men because more highly qualified women apply than men.) The strongest form of affirmative action is the use of quotas—strict numerical targets to hire or admit a specific number of applicants from underrepresented groups.

Affirmative action has been a controversial policy. Many whites view it as "preferential treatment" and "reverse discrimination." Polls indicate that minorities are much more supportive of the practice than whites. A majority of whites support more passive forms of affirmative action, such as "education programs to assist minorities in competing for college admissions," but draw the line at preferences, even when they are intended to make up for past discrimination.[90] This backlash has spilled over into state politics. California passed Proposition 209 in 1996, which banned the use of "race, sex, color, ethnicity or national origin as a criterion for either discriminating against, or granting preferential treatment to, any individual or group in the operation of the State's system of public employment, public education, or public contracting." Voters in Washington passed a similar resolution in 1999, Florida banned the use of race in college admission decisions in that year, and Michigan passed a broad ban on affirmative action in 2006. Several other state legislatures have considered taking up the issue, but the state and local decisions have been mixed. Voters in Houston, Texas, voted to continue affirmative action in their city in November 1997, perhaps illustrating the importance of the question wording on the resolution. In California the wording of Proposition 209 mentioned the hot-button term "preferential treatment," whereas the Houston resolution simply asked voters if they wanted to retain the city's affirmative action program.[91] Fifty-five percent of voters in California and 58 percent in Michigan voted to eliminate "preferential treatment," while 55 percent of Houston's voters supported keeping the city's affirmative action program.

The Supreme Court has helped define the boundaries of this policy debate. The earliest cases concerning affirmative action in employment upheld preferential treatment and rigid quotas when the policies were necessary to make up for past discrimination. The cases involved a worker training program that set aside 50 percent of the positions for blacks, a labor union that was required to hire enough minorities to get its nonwhite membership to 29.23 percent, and a state police force that was required to promote one black officer for every white even if there was a smaller pool of blacks who were eligible for promotion.[92] In each instance there had been a previous pattern of discrimination and exclusion.

The Supreme Court started moving in a "color-blind" direction in 1989 concerning "set-aside" programs in government contracting. In 1983, Richmond, Virginia, began requiring contractors who had won city construction contracts to subcontract at least 30 percent of the work to minority-owned businesses. The city council noted that 50 percent of Richmond's population was black but only 0.67 percent of the city's prime construction contracts had gone to minority-owned businesses. A white business owner, J. A. Croson, had bid for a city contract and lost to a minority-owned business. Croson sued, saying that his Fourteenth Amendment equal protection rights had been violated. The Court agreed, ruling that set-asides were unconstitutional without evidence of discrimination against minorities and that any such programs had to be "narrowly tailored to meet a compelling state interest." "Generalized assertions" of past discrimination were not adequate to justify such rigid quotas.[93] The same reasoning was applied to federal contracting set-aside programs in 1995.[94]

The Court applied a similar line of analysis to an important reverse-discrimination employment case in 2009. In that case, seventeen white firefighters and one Hispanic firefighter sued the city of New Haven, Connecticut, for throwing out the results of a test that would have been used to promote them. The city tried to ignore the results of the test because no African American firefighters would have qualified for promotion and the city feared a "disparate impact" lawsuit. However, the Court ruled that the exam did appear to be "job related and consistent with business necessity" (as required by Section VII of the Civil Rights Act) and that unless the city could provide a "strong basis in evidence" that it would have been sued, it had to consider the results of the exam.[95]

The landmark decision for affirmative action in higher education is *University of California Regents v. Bakke* (1978).[96] Allan Bakke, a white student, sued when he was denied admission to medical school at the University of California, Davis, in successive years. Bakke's test scores and GPA were significantly higher than those of some minority students who were admitted under the school's affirmative action program. Under that program, sixteen of the 100 slots in the entering class were reserved for minority or disadvantaged students. The Supreme Court agreed with Bakke that rigid racial quotas were unconstitutional but allowed race to be used in admissions decisions as a "plus factor" to promote diversity in the student body. This standard was largely unquestioned until 1996, when the Fifth Circuit Court of Appeals held that it was unconstitutional to consider race in law school admissions at the University of Texas. An appeals court in Washington reached the opposite conclusion in a different case.

In two conflicting cases from the University of Michigan, a district court held that race-conscious undergraduate admissions were acceptable, but a decision a few months later in the same court held that considering race in law school admissions was not constitutional. An appeals court reversed the law school decision, leaving the Supreme Court to issue a definitive ruling. The Court's rulings were consistent with *Bakke*, saying that the law school's "holistic approach" that considered race as one of the factors in the admission decision was acceptable but that the University of Michigan's more rigid approach, which automatically gave minority students twenty of the 100 points needed to guarantee admission, was unacceptable.[97] Though these two decisions affirmed *Bakke*, it was the first time that a majority of the Court clearly stated that "student body diversity is a compelling state interest that can justify the use of race in university admissions."[98]

MULTICULTURAL ISSUES

A host of issues involving the multicultural, multiracial nature of American society will become more important as whites cease to constitute the majority of the population by mid-century. Two key issues are English as the official language and immigration.

Decisions to establish English as the official language in many states have had wide-reaching consequences. For example, the Supreme Court upheld an Alabama state law requiring that the state driver's license test be conducted only in English. A Mexican immigrant, Martha Sandoval, sued under Title VI of the 1964 Civil Rights Act, claiming that the Alabama law had a disparate impact on non-English-speaking residents. However, the Court held in *Alexander v. Sandoval* (2001) that individuals may not sue federally funded state agencies over policies that have a discriminatory effect on minorities under Title VI. This decision has far-reaching consequences for the use of the Civil Rights Act to fight patterns of discrimination. Two areas that have been affected are education policy (for example, civil rights advocates have challenged the use of standardized testing because of its disparate impact on minorities) and environmental policy (lawsuits brought under Title VI have alleged "environmental racism" in decisions to site hazardous waste dumps in predominantly minority areas).

The second prominent issue, immigration, regained center stage in the wake of the September 11 terrorist attacks. At that time, some people saw immigration as a threat that must be curtailed. The government made it clear that it would not engage in racial profiling of Arab Americans—for example, subjecting them to stricter screening at airports—but many commentators argued that such profiling would be justified, and there was at least anecdotal evidence of an increase in discrimination against people of Middle Eastern descent.

Over the past two decades, immigration has been central in many political debates. Some of these debates are nominally about social welfare benefits, but deeper racial issues often are just below the surface. For example, in 1994 voters in California adopted Proposition 187, which denied most public benefits to illegal immigrants but seemed to critics to discriminate against Mexican Americans. Debates over immigration have important political implications. Republicans were strongly in favor of Proposition 187, while Democrats opposed it. When the courts struck down the measure and Democrats won the 1998 gubernatorial race in California with the support of the growing Hispanic population, Republicans softened their position. President George W. Bush was instrumental in trying to move the Republican Party in this direction. He cultivated the Hispanic vote, often presenting part of his speeches in Spanish, and won a record (for Republican presidential candidates) 44 percent of the Latino vote in 2004. Bush pushed for comprehensive immigration reform in 2006. However, anti-immigration Republicans in Congress passed a measure aimed at enforcing existing immigration laws and building a barrier along the border with Mexico. Strong Latino turnout in 2006 is credited, in part, with a return of control of Congress to the Democrats, and Obama won 67 percent of the Latino vote in 2008.

AFFIRMATIVE ACTION AT THE UNIVERSITY OF MICHIGAN

If you were serving on the Supreme Court, how would you have decided the University of Michigan affirmative action cases? In the undergraduate case, Jennifer Gratz had a high school GPA of 3.76 and an ACT score of 25 (eighty-third percentile), and Patrick Hamacher had a GPA of 3.37 and an ACT of 28 (eighty-ninth percentile), but they were denied admission to Michigan. The student in the law school case, Barbara Grutter, was a forty-three-year-old returning student who had an undergraduate GPA of 3.81 at Michigan State University and a 161 on the LSAT. All three students showed that they had higher scores than some of the minority students who were admitted under the university's affirmative action program. The legal question that the Court had to decide was whether the university's affirmative action program violated the equal protection clause of the Fourteenth Amendment and civil rights laws barring discrimination on the basis of race, or if the program could be justified as serving a "compelling state interest" under the strict scrutiny standard.

The crucial point of contention in the debate over the use of race in college admissions decisions is "viewpoint diversity"; the claimed advantage of affirmative action is the diversity that it brings to classroom discussions. Advocates of affirmative action argue that viewpoint diversity is essential to learning and that having racial diversity in the student body is likely to produce more viewpoint diversity than having an all-white student body. Furthermore, proponents argue, the courts are not the proper place to decide these issues. Instead, as with the complex and highly charged topic of racial redistricting, the political branches of government are where these decisions should be made. Advocates also make a very pragmatic argument that getting rid of affirmative action would almost certainly lead to a system that is *less* rooted in merit-based admissions than the current system. This is because states that get rid of race as a factor in admissions often adopt a "10 percent solution," which says that the top 10 percent of any graduating high school class can be admitted to the state university. This means that a student who may be in the top 20 percent of an excellent school might not be admitted even if she had better test scores and grades than a student who was in the top 10 percent of a high school that was not as good.

Opponents reply that supporters of affirmative action have not provided convincing evidence that racial diversity in colleges has any beneficial effects. They also argue that "viewpoint diversity" arguments assume that members of all racial minorities think alike, drawing a comparison to racial profiling in law enforcement. It is just as offensive, they say, that an admissions committee thinks that one black student has the same views as another black student as it is that a police offi-

In 2003, when the University of Michigan affirmative action cases were heard by the Supreme Court, some students demonstrated to show their support for the university's admissions process. Others protested that it was unfair to white students.

cer may pull over a black teenage male just because he fits a certain criminal profile. Opponents also argue that affirmative action amounts to "reverse discrimination" and that any racial classification is harmful.

The Supreme Court has agreed to hear an affirmative action case from Texas in the 2012–13 term. Many are predicting that the Court will endorse a more color-blind approach to college admissions than is allowed by the Michigan precedent.

Critical **Thinking** Questions

1. To what extent should race be used as a "plus factor" to promote racial diversity and viewpoint diversity, if at all?

2. Think of your own experiences in high school and college. Has racial diversity contributed to viewpoint diversity?

The intensity of the immigration debate increased in 2010 when Arizona enacted an anti-immigration law that requires local law enforcement officials to check the immigration status of a person in a "lawful stop, detention, or arrest" if there is a "reasonable suspicion" that the person is an illegal alien. The law also requires immigrants to always carry papers verifying their immigration status and bans people without proper documents from seeking work in public places. States with similar laws include South Carolina, Alabama, Utah, Georgia, and Indiana. Arizona governor Jan Brewer said, "Decades of federal inaction and misguided policy have created a dangerous and unacceptable situation, and states deserve clarity from the court in terms of what role they have in fighting illegal immigration."[99] Opponents of the law argue that it requires illegal racial profiling and that the federal government has the sole responsibility for deciding immigration law.

As noted in Chapter 13, the Supreme Court struck down three of the four main provisions of the law, citing the supremacy clause of the Constitution. This meant that Congress, not the states, decides immigration law when the two laws conflict. The Court upheld the controversial "show me your papers" part of the law, saying that the state was simply enforcing the federal law. However, the Court indicated that the law must be applied in a race-neutral way and could be struck down if there was clear evidence of racial profiling.[100] Several months later a federal district court judge cleared the way for implementation of the "show me your papers" law, saying that the Supreme Court wanted to see actual evidence of discrimination rather than speculation that the law could have a discriminatory effect.[101]

As noted in the introduction, the immigration system is widely viewed as broken and in need of reform. However, both President Bush and President Obama were unable to get their proposals approved by Congress that would have provided a "path to citizenship" for illegal aliens. Americans favor that reform option, but the level of support varies depending on the wording of the question. A CBS News poll showed that 44 percent said that illegal immigrants "should be allowed to stay in their jobs and to eventually apply for U.S. citizenship," and 26 percent said they should be allowed to stay as guest workers, while 26 percent said they should have to leave the United States. But when a Fox News Poll asked if illegals should be allowed to become citizens "only if they meet certain requirements like paying back taxes, learning English, and passing a background check" (which were conditions in both the Bush and Obama proposals) support for the path to citizenship increased to 66 percent (with only 13 percent supporting the guest worker option and 19 percent saying they should be sent back to their home country).[102]

BORDER PATROL AGENTS DETAIN undocumented immigrants apprehended near the Mexican border outside McAllen, Texas. Illegal immigration continues to be a "hot-button" issue in national electoral and legislative politics.

The debates over affirmative action, English as a second language, and immigration reform clearly illustrate the conflictual nature of civil rights policy. However, history as shown that when public opinion strongly supports a given application of civil rights, as with African Americans in the South in the 1960s and more recently the service of gays in the military, public policy soon reflects those views. While it is impossible to say how soon gay marriage will be nationally recognized or comprehensive immigration reform, including a path to citizenship, will become law, given the trends in public opinion, policy appears to be headed in that direction.

CONCLUSION

Enforcing civil rights means providing equal protection of the law to individuals and groups that are discriminated against, which may include noncitizens and illegal immigrants. Figuring out exactly when an individual's civil rights have been violated can be tricky. When does a routine traffic stop by a police officer turn into racial profiling?

To help figure that out, we now can answer the questions about possible civil rights violations that introduced this chapter.

▶ The African American teenagers who were pulled over by the police may or may not have had their civil rights violated, depending on the laws in their state. In Massachusetts, for example, it is prohibited to consider the "race, gender, national or ethnic origin of members of the public in deciding to detain a person or stop a motor vehicle" except in "suspect specific incidents."[103] Pulling over the white teenagers would have been acceptable as long as there was "probable cause" to justify the stop.

▶ The Asian American woman who did not get the job could certainly talk to a lawyer about filing a "disparate impact" discrimination suit. Under the 1991 Civil Rights Act, the employer would have the burden of proof to show that she was not a victim of the "good ol' boy" network.

▶ The gay couple who could not rent the apartment because of their sexual orientation may have a basis for a civil rights lawsuit based on the Fourteenth Amendment; however, this would depend on where they live, given that there is no federal protection against discrimination against gay men and lesbians (and the Supreme Court has not applied the Fourteenth Amendment in this context).

▶ Court decisions concerning affirmative action at the University of Michigan show that the white student who was not admitted to the university of his choice would just have to take his lumps, as long as the affirmative action program considered race as a general "plus factor" rather than assigning more or fewer points for it.

This review of civil rights policy has only highlighted some of the most important issues, but a significant agenda remains. The civil rights movement will continue to use the multiple avenues of the legislative, executive, and judicial branches to secure equal rights for all Americans.

STUDY *guide*

THE CONTEXT OF CIVIL RIGHTS

▶ Describe the historical struggles groups have faced in winning civil rights. **Pages 555–65**

SUMMARY

Civil rights are protections from discrimination both by the government and by individuals and are rooted in laws and the equal protection clause of the Fourteenth Amendment. The concept of equality has evolved over time, with protections now for women, African Americans, Native Americans, Asian Americans, and Latinos. Despite our attempts to live in a color-blind society, awareness of race still influences many people's opinions and behavior.

KEY TERMS

civil rights (p. 555)

Missouri Compromise (p. 558)

disenfranchised (p. 558)

grandfather clause (p. 558)

Jim Crow laws (p. 559)

"separate but equal" (p. 559)

protectionism (p. 562)

PRACTICE QUIZ QUESTIONS

1. The distinction between civil rights and civil liberties is that civil rights _____ while civil liberties _____.

   a) protect against discrimination; are guaranteed in the Bill of Rights

   b) are guaranteed in the Bill of Rights; protect against discrimination

   c) are guaranteed in the Bill of Rights; limit what the government can do to you

   d) limit what the government can do to you; protect against discrimination

   e) limit what the government can do to you; are guaranteed in the Bill of Rights

2. The Missouri Compromise _____.

   a) ruled that people held as slaves are not protected by the Constitution

   b) established that three-fifths of the slaves could count in a state's population

   c) limited the expansion of slavery while maintaining the balance of slave states

   d) gave slaves the right to vote

   e) ended slavery in the South

3. *Plessy v. Ferguson* established _____.

   a) the legitimacy of poll taxes

   b) the "separate but equal" doctrine

   c) that Jim Crow laws were illegal

   d) the process of desegregation in the South

   e) the legality of slavery

4. The principle of _____ was used in many court cases to deny women equal rights.

   a) matriarchy

   b) "separate but equal"

   c) sectionalism

   d) misandry

   e) protectionism

Ⓢ PRACTICE ONLINE

"Big Think" video exercise: *C. Raj Kumar on the Origin of Human Rights*

THE RACIAL DIVIDE TODAY

▶ Analyze inequality among racial, ethnic, and social groups today. **Pages 565–69**

SUMMARY

Beyond the unequal treatment of racial minorities, women, and gays and lesbians, inequalities in political, social, and economic conditions also persist. Whites are able to participate in politics at a higher rate, enjoy a better standard of living, and avoid prejudice in the criminal justice system.

PRACTICE QUIZ QUESTIONS

5. *Most* of the differences in voter turnout among whites relative to racial minorities can be accounted for by

_____.

a) contemporary Jim Crow laws
b) voter purge lists
c) voter ID laws
d) poll taxes
e) education and income

6. The gaps between whites and blacks on health measures are _____ and in many cases _____.

a) large; decreasing
b) large; increasing
c) small; decreasing
d) small; increasing
e) small; staying the same

7. In economic terms, the average Hispanic family is

_____.

a) better off than the average white family from the same area
b) likely to have more assets than the average white family
c) roughly equal with the average white family
d) worse off than the average white family
e) more likely than any other group to be poor

CRITICAL THINKING AND DISCUSSION

Have you ever faced discrimination based on your race, gender, or sexual orientation? If so, what did you learn in this chapter about whether your civil rights were violated?

ⓢ PRACTICE ONLINE

"Critical Thinking" exercise: *Politics Is Everywhere— CensusScope*

THE POLICY-MAKING PROCESS AND CIVIL RIGHTS

▶ Explain the approaches used to bring about change in civil rights policies. **Pages 570–92**

SUMMARY

Depending on the political context, each branch of government has played a role in the expansion of civil rights. Moreover, federalism has played a role in this process: while the state governments often lagged behind the federal government in African Americans' civil rights, they have been on the forefront in protecting the rights of gays and lesbians.

KEY TERMS

de jure (p. 577)
de facto (p. 577)
disparate impact standard (p. 578)
rational basis test (p. 580)
intermediate scrutiny test (p. 580)
strict scrutiny test (p. 582)
substantive due process doctrine (p. 586)

PRACTICE QUIZ QUESTIONS

8. The most successful social movement has been the

_____.

a) women's rights movement
b) gay and lesbian civil rights movement
c) African American civil rights movement
d) United Farm Workers' movement
e) Native American rights movement

9. Early in the civil rights movement, which branch provided most of the successes?
   a) state governments
   b) Congress
   c) the presidency
   d) the bureaucracy
   e) the Supreme Court

10. The difference between de facto segregation and de jure segregation is that de facto segregation _____, while de jure segregation _____.
   a) is the result of circumstances; is mandated by law
   b) is mandated by law; is the result of circumstances
   c) applies to racial minorities; applies to women
   d) applies to women; applies to racial minorities
   e) applies to all groups; applies to racial minorities

11. The strongest protection as the "suspect classification" applies which test?
   a) rational basis
   b) strict scrutiny
   c) intermediate scrutiny
   d) privileged interest
   e) disparate impact

12. The Voting Rights Act of 1965 _____.
   a) established "majority-minority" districts
   b) established compulsory voter registration for African Americans

c) eliminated direct obstacles to minority voting in the South
   d) barred discrimination in the rental or sale of a home
   e) reduced participation by African Americans in the South

13. Relative to the protection of individuals with disabilities, Congress' track record in protecting gay rights is _____.
   a) stronger
   b) about the same
   c) weaker
   d) nonexistent
   e) more focused on job discrimination

CRITICAL THINKING AND DISCUSSION

Which policy-making institution has historically played the most important role in protecting the civil rights of Americans? Does that institution still play that role today?

⑤ PRACTICE ONLINE

"Critical Thinking" exercise: *Process Matters—Little Rock and Desegregation*

CONTINUING AND FUTURE CIVIL RIGHTS ISSUES

▶ Examine affirmative action and other ongoing civil rights issues. **Pages 593–99**

SUMMARY

The public is divided on the appropriateness of civil rights policies, with different groups preferring a "color-blind" or color-conscious approach. Moreover, the debates over issues such as affirmative action, immigration reform, and English as a second language indicate the level of conflict over civil rights policy. Nonetheless, when public opinion does strongly support the application of civil rights in a particular arena, policy makers generally respond to these views.

PRACTICE QUIZ QUESTIONS

14. The Supreme Court's implementation of "color-blind jurisprudence" fits the agenda of those who argue _____.
   a) that the gap between blacks and whites has narrowed
   b) that the civil rights movement needs to continue to fight for equal opportunity

c) that African Americans need to be separate and fully self-sufficient
   d) that equality of outcomes is important
   e) that the gap between blacks and whites has widened

15. What did the case *University of California Regents v. Bakke* establish?
   a) that race could play no role in the college admissions process
   b) that gender could play no role in the college admissions process
   c) that strict racial quotas in the admissions process were legal
   d) that race could be used as a "plus factor" in the admissions process
   e) that gender could be used as a "plus factor" in the admissions process

CRITICAL THINKING AND DISCUSSION

Should government attempt to provide a level playing field by making sure that there is no discrimination, or should it go beyond providing equality of opportunity to also be concerned with the equality of outcomes?

Ⓢ **PRACTICE ONLINE**

"Big Think" video exercise: *Laurence Tribe and the Shifting Supreme Court*

SUGGESTED READING

Canon, David T. *Race, Redistricting, and Representation: The Unintended Consequences of Black-Majority Districts.* Chicago: University of Chicago Press, 1999.

Dawson, Michael C. *Behind the Mule: Race and Class in African-American Politics.* Princeton, NJ: Princeton University Press, 1994.

Gross, Ariela J. *What Blood Won't Tell: A History of Race on Trial in America.* Cambridge, MA: Harvard University Press, 2008.

Hochschild, Jennifer L. *Facing Up to the American Dream: Race, Class, and the Soul of the Nation.* Princeton, NJ: Princeton University Press, 1995.

Katznelson, Ira. *When Affirmative Action Was White: An Untold History of Racial Inequality in Twentieth-Century America.* New York: Norton, 2005.

Kluger, Richard. *Simple Justice: The History of* Brown v. Board of Education *and Black America's Struggle for Equality.* New York: Vintage, 2004.

Kousser, J. Morgan. *Colorblind Injustice: Minority Voting Rights and the Undoing of the Second Reconstruction.* Chapel Hill: University of North Carolina Press, 1999.

Lublin, David. *The Paradox of Representation: Racial Gerrymandering and Minority Interests in Congress.* Princeton, NJ: Princeton University Press, 1997.

Tate, Katherine. *Black Faces in the Mirror: African Americans and Their Representatives in Congress.* Princeton, NJ: Princeton University Press, 2003.

Thernstrom, Stephan, and Abigail Thernstrom. *America in Black and White: One Nation, Indivisible: Race in Modern America.* New York: Simon and Schuster, 1997.

15

Economic Policy

GOVERNMENT SPENDING
(AS PERCENTAGE OF GDP)

PRESIDENT'S BUDGET

25

PERCE 23

18

ECONOMIC POLICIES HAVE GENERATED intense conflict in recent years. Republicans, like Representative Paul Ryan, have argued that the government must cut spending and focus on reducing the national debt and deficit. Both parties have claimed that they have a better plan for helping spur economic growth.

P RESIDENT OBAMA SIGNALED EARLY IN THE 2012 CAMPAIGN that tax policy and income inequality would be important themes in the election. In a speech in December 2011, he argued, "Today, the wealthiest Americans are paying the lowest taxes in over half a century. . . . Today, thanks to loopholes and shelters, a quarter of all millionaires now pay lower tax rates than millions of you, millions of middle-class families. Some billionaires have a tax rate as low as one percent. One percent. That is the height of unfairness. It is wrong."[1] This argument gained political relevance about a month later when the leading Republican candidate for president, Mitt Romney, revealed that he paid only 13.9 percent in federal taxes on the $21.7 million income he earned in 2010. Many people at that level of income pay 25 percent to 30 percent in federal taxes (for example, President Obama paid 26 percent on $1.8 million in 2010, while Newt Gingrich paid 31.6 percent on $3.2 million).[2]

How is it possible that Romney's tax rate was only 13.9 percent? Romney paid every dollar he owed; his taxes were so low because most of his income came from dividends and capital gains that are taxed at only 15 percent, rather than the top marginal rate of 35 percent. Middle-income people who have a marginal rate of 25 percent and pay 7.65 percent of their income in payroll taxes can easily have a total tax burden higher than 13.9 percent. To address this inequity in the tax code, Obama called for a "millionaire's tax" that would set a minimum rate of 30 percent for incomes that reach that level.

CONFLICT & COMPROMISE
in American Politics

Republicans rejected Obama's call for a millionaire's tax, arguing that the problem is not low taxes on the rich, but rather excessive government spending. They argue that low taxes stimulate job creation and that lower taxes on capital gains and dividends encourage investment. Furthermore, taxes on dividends represent double taxation because corporations pay both a corporate income tax that is among the highest in the world and then pay taxes on payouts to shareholders.[3]

Reflecting on the apparent permanency of the Constitution, Benjamin Franklin cautioned, "But in this world nothing can be said to be certain, except death and taxes."[4] Despite the inevitability of taxes, some of the most intense political battles throughout our history have been fought over the appropriate level of taxation. The conflicts during the 2012 national elections are just one recent example of that struggle.

Tax policies are inherently conflictual, due to their redistributive nature: when the government takes money from one group and gives it to another, there will be conflict over those decisions. For example, if tax policy is used to help the poor, the wealthy will obviously pay a larger share of their income in taxes than the poor. But even taxes that do not seem obviously redistributive hit some people harder than others. A 5 percent sales tax is more of a burden for the poor than the nonpoor because poorer people spend a higher proportion of their income. The home mortgage interest deduction on income tax benefits homeowners over renters. The 15 percent tax rate on dividends favors people who invest in stocks over bonds (because interest on bonds is taxed as regular income, usually at a much higher rate than 15 percent). In short, tax policies aimed at helping one segment of the economy come at the expense of another part, which creates political conflict.

Conflict over economic policy goes beyond tax policy. Many of America's political debates concern economic policy: Should we run deficits or have balanced budgets? Have a largely unregulated, free market or regulations for things like pollution and health care? Spend more money to create "green jobs" and promote alternative energy, or subsidize more offshore drilling and build pipelines to maximize the extraction of oil and natural gas? Democrats tend to favor a more activist government that supports a broader range of redistributive programs and regulates the economy to ensure a range of public goods, such as rebuilding the infrastructure. Republicans tend to favor a more limited approach to government that promotes lower taxes and less regulation and allows the free market to determine more social and economic decisions, such as allowing greater development of domestic energy sources.

The conflict over economic policy is clear, but how about compromise? The policy responses to the economic meltdown of 2008–09 were very conflictual, as the public questioned the use of taxpayers' money to support Wall Street and the auto industry. But ultimately, bipartisan majorities agreed on a plan to shore up the banking system and get the economy on sounder footing. The stimulus bill of 2009 was also a compromise package comprising roughly equal parts of tax cuts, federal spending, and support for the states. President Obama has vowed to increase taxes on the wealthy to help reduce the deficits, but House Republicans prefer tax simplification through reducing loopholes and deductions (both sides agree that spending should be cut, but Republicans want more cuts with less tax revenue).

Economic policy also illustrates the other themes of the book. The idea that political process matters is shown by seeing how Congress, the president, and the bureaucracy all have a hand in attempting to promote a healthy economy. The

ways in which politics is everywhere may be less obvious in the area of economic policy, which, one might think, should be determined more by rational economic theories than by rough-and-tumble, partisan politics. We explicitly address this theme in the chapter's conclusion, but the discussion throughout will make it clear that politics is central to the making of economic policy.

This chapter has three main parts. First, we discuss the goals of economic policy making and the trade-offs among those goals. Next, we review the main players in economic policy making—Congress, the president, bureaucratic agencies, and to some extent, the courts. Finally, we talk about the tools and theories of economic policy making, including fiscal policy, monetary policy, regulatory policy, and trade policy.

GOALS OF ECONOMIC POLICY

> EXPLAIN THE MAIN PURPOSES OF GOVERNMENT INVOLVEMENT IN THE ECONOMY

Policy makers have specific goals in mind when they try to influence the economy. Many of these goals seem obvious, such as full employment (it is better to have more people working than not working), but others may be less clear. Also, it is difficult to pursue all the goals simultaneously because there are trade-offs among some of them.

FULL EMPLOYMENT

Employment seems like a good starting point for a healthy economy. If people have jobs, they pay taxes and do not depend on the government for support. Despite this, **full employment** was not an explicit goal of economic policy until 1946, when

full employment The theoretical point at which all citizens who want to be employed have a job.

economic depression A deep, widespread downturn in the economy, like the Great Depression of the 1930s.

Council of Economic Advisers A group of economic advisers, created by the Employment Act of 1946, which provides objective data on the state of the economy and makes economic policy recommendations to the president.

Congress passed the Employment Act. Leaders were concerned that with millions of returning World War II veterans and the wartime economy gearing down, the nation might slide back into the **economic depression** that had created so much hardship in the 1930s. Although the act was largely symbolic (there was no guaranteed right to employment), it did create the **Council of Economic Advisers**, which provides the president with economic information and advice. A more concrete effort to ensure that returning veterans could find jobs was the Servicemen's Readjustment Act (the GI Bill). Enacted in 1944, it had provided low-interest home mortgages for 2.4 million veterans and higher education assistance to 7.8 million veterans by the time the law expired in 1956. Today the government seeks to support the creation of as many jobs as possible through a strong economy. However, despite an unemployment rate hovering around 8 percent through most of 2012, President Obama and Congress were unable to agree on additional job creation measures before the elections, and the prospects for a new jobs bill remained bleak as Congress headed into 2013.

On a more technical level, full employment does not literally mean that everyone is working. There is always a substantial portion of the potential workforce that is not looking for a job. It does not even mean that everyone who is looking for work can get a job, because there is always a certain amount of "frictional unemployment" as people are between jobs. Instead, economists consider a 5 to 5.5 percent unemployment rate to be the level of full employment, or the "natural rate of unemployment."

STABLE PRICES

inflation The increase in the price of consumer goods over time.

The importance of having stable prices is not as obvious as the need for jobs. Why are rising prices—**inflation**—a problem? This is a common question during periods of low inflation. Especially for workers who have automatic raises (cost of living adjustments, or COLAs) as part of their basic pay package, moderate inflation isn't much of a problem. For example, if your rent goes up 4 percent, the price of groceries goes up 3 percent, and the cost of entertainment goes up 3 percent, and you get a 4 percent raise, you will likely be at least as well off as you were in the previous year. However, from 1979 to 1980, inflation was running at 12 percent to 14 percent rather than the 2 to 3 percent that has been typical in recent years (Figure 15.1).

Double-digit inflation can have serious effects on the economy. First, the entire economy is not indexed to inflation, so some people see an erosion of their purchasing power. If your rent goes up 10 percent and groceries are up 15 percent, but your pay goes up by only 4 percent, you are substantially worse off. Second, high inflation penalizes savers and rewards debtors as savings interest rates may be outstripped by inflation (so savings are actually worth less over time), but people who go into debt can repay those debts with cheaper dollars in the future. Finally, long-term economic planning by businesses becomes more difficult when inflation is high, because investors demand high interest rates to compensate for the added risk of future inflation. In 1979 and 1980, short-term interest rates spiked as high as 18 percent. Very few businesses were willing to take on additional debt at that rate of interest as opposed to the more typical 6 to 8 percent, so the economy headed into a recession.

The period of relatively high unemployment and inflation generated two new economic terms: stagflation (a stagnant economy with inflation) and the Misery Index (the sum of the inflation rate and the unemployment rate). Typically,

FIGURE » 15.1

INFLATION AND UNEMPLOYMENT, 1960–2012

The Misery Index is the sum of the unemployment rate and the inflation rate. Which periods have had the highest misery rate since 1960? Were there any external explanations for the high misery rate? How did the government respond to the high levels of unemployment and inflation?

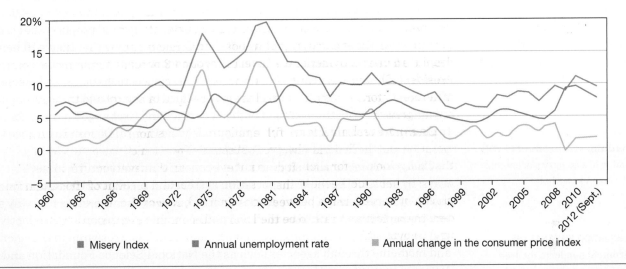

■ Misery Index　　　■ Annual unemployment rate　　　■ Annual change in the consumer price index

Source: Data from the U.S. Department of Labor, Bureau of Labor Statistics. Inflation data from "Consumer Price Index," www.bls.gov/CPI, and unemployment data from "Labor Force Statistics from the Current Population Survey," www.bls.gov/cps (accessed 10/5/12).

unemployment and inflation are not high at the same time, so policy makers were desperate to do something about them. The Misery Index started to creep up in 1970–71 and President Nixon wanted to halt inflation in its tracks, in part to help his reelection chances in 1972. He announced a 90-day wage freeze in 1971, followed by wage and price controls after his reelection. The experiment was abandoned in 1974 when it became obvious that interfering with market forces was not working.[5] From that point on, fighting inflation has largely been left to the Federal Reserve, which raises interest rates to cool down the economy. This process is discussed later in the chapter.

Nixon's concern about inflation reveals another important point about inflation and unemployment. There tend to be basic partisan differences on the goals of full employment and stable prices, with Democrats being more concerned about employment and Republicans more concerned about inflation. This is no surprise, given the Democratic Party's base of support within labor unions and blue-collar workers and the Republican Party's stronger support on Wall Street and with investors whose income is likely to be eroded by high inflation.

PROMOTE THE FREE MARKET AND GROWTH

The American economy is a capitalist system, which means that most economic decisions are voluntarily made between individuals and firms for their mutual benefit. The government generally stays out of most economic activity, except to regulate the market when it produces too much of something that is not in the public's interest, such as pollution or unsafe products. Economists tout the advantage of the free market as promoting the most efficient use of resources. Economic growth is also a central goal. A growing economy provides a better standard of living for each generation.

The government does not get directly involved in most economic transactions, but it can provide the foundation for a strong free market and economic growth. The government protects property rights so that businesses that invest in the growth of their company know that another firm or the government cannot appropriate their property. Property rights also include intellectual property that is protected by patent and copyright laws. If entrepreneurs know that they will benefit from their own discoveries and labor, they are more likely to put in the countless hours required for innovative breakthroughs in science, technology, and medicine. The foundation for the free market is also provided by secure and transparent capital markets through the oversight of the Securities and Exchange Commission, and through a secure banking system, as ensured by the Federal Deposit Insurance Corporation and the Federal Reserve System.

The government also supports the economic infrastructure in several key ways: by subsidizing the transportation system and regulating the telecommunication system; through public works such as building the interstate highway system in the 1950s and 1960s, which boosted economic expansion and productivity; and by promoting economic growth with support of basic research in the sciences and medicine through agencies such as the National Science Foundation and the National Institutes of Health.

Critics of the government's focus on the market and growth claim that the free market often produces inequality and that growth doesn't measure well-being. The "Occupy" movement, with its slogan "we are the 99 percent," has drawn attention to income inequality. But historically, the United States has not focused as much attention on this economic policy goal as many other Western nations. As a consequence, the United States ranks 100th in the world (out of 140 nations in the study) in income equality, just behind nations such as Iran, Uganda, Russia, and China.[6] Other critics of the focus on growth include environmentalists who advocate a "small is beautiful"[7] approach and point out the environmental costs of economic growth, and some economists who question the traditional interpretations of economic growth measurements—in particular, the increase in **gross domestic product (GDP)**, a measure of the nation's overall economic output and activity. These critics argue that a significant part of GDP actually captures a decline in well-being. For example, if we have to spend billions of dollars putting alarms in our homes and cars to warn against intruders, this is not an improvement in the standard of living from the time when such alarms were unnecessary. Yet the purchase of such crime-fighting tools adds to GDP. An ideal measure of economic growth would distinguish between positive and negative forms of economic activity.[8]

The economic meltdown of 2008–09 raised basic questions about the efficiency of economic markets and the need for more regulation of the financial sector. We discuss this more fully later in the chapter, but briefly, Alan Greenspan, chair of the Federal Reserve from 1987 to 2006, testified before a House committee that there had been a "flaw" in his market ideology and that a "once-in-a-century credit tsunami" forced him to rethink some of his free-market policies. Greenspan conceded that the financial industry had not served its shareholders and that more regulation of complex derivatives and the subprime mortgage market might have helped to prevent the economic crisis.[9]

gross domestic product (GDP)
The value of a country's economic output taken as a whole.

ONE IMPORTANT WAY THAT THE government supports the free market and economic growth is by promoting the stability of the banking system. The Federal Deposit Insurance Corporation (FDIC) bolsters confidence in banks by insuring each account holder's deposits in its member banks up to $250,000.

BALANCED BUDGETS

Maintaining a **balanced budget** has been a central economic goal since the 1980s, when **budget deficits** skyrocketed (see Figure 15.2A and Nuts and Bolts 15.1). Large deficits are a concern for several reasons. First, they take a big bite out of current spending. About $258 billion, or 7.3 percent, of the 2012 fiscal year budget went to financing the federal debt. These dollars went to people who own federal bonds and securities; they did not buy a single uniform for a soldier, highway exit ramp, or student loan. Second, the total federal debt is a burden on future generations. Each man, woman, and child in the United States in effect carries more than $51,386 of debt (total debt has grown steadily; see Figure 15.2B). Third, public borrowing "crowds out" private borrowing because there is a finite pool of dollars that people can invest. Let's say you have $1,000 to invest. You could invest it in the stock market or buy corporate bonds that provide businesses the capital they need to expand, or you could buy government bonds to fund the national debt. In the aggregate, this means that if $250 billion is going to fund the federal deficits every year, then that $250 billion is not available for private borrowing that could go directly to creating more jobs and generating economic growth.

balanced budget A spending plan in which the government's expenditures are equal to its revenue.

budget deficit The amount by which a government's spending in a given fiscal year exceeds its revenue.

BALANCE OF PAYMENTS, OR THE CURRENT ACCOUNT

The broadest measure of a nation's balance of payments with the rest of the world is the **current account**: the difference between a nation's receipts (exports and money that Americans earn on foreign investments) and its payments (imports and money that foreigners earn on American investments). The aspect of the current account that gets the most political attention is the **trade deficit**, the difference between imports and exports. The American appetite for foreign goods is huge, and a weaker dollar, which makes foreign goods more expensive, has not corrected the imbalance. The overall current account has also received more attention in recent years as the United States has gone from being the world's largest creditor nation to the world's largest debtor nation.

current account The balance of a country's receipts and its payments in international trade and investment.

trade deficit A measure of how much more a nation imports than it exports.

15.1 **NUTS** *& bolts*

DEFICITS AND DEBT

Budget deficits and the federal debt are related concepts that are easily confused.

► A *budget deficit* occurs when tax revenue is not sufficient to cover government spending in a given year. If tax revenue is higher than spending, then there is a budget surplus.

► The *federal debt* is the total accumulation of all outstanding borrowing by the government.

► The concepts of deficit and debt are related because when the government runs a deficit, it must borrow money to cover the gap. This borrowing then builds up the federal debt.

You can think of this in terms of your own spending habits. Any time you spend more money in a given month than you earn, you are running a deficit. You must borrow money to make up that deficit from a bank, from your parents, or by running up the balance on your credit card. The accumulated sum of your monthly deficits is the total debt that you owe.

FIGURE » 15.2A

FEDERAL BUDGET DEFICITS AND SURPLUSES

The federal deficit is the amount by which the government's spending exceeds its revenue in a given year; the federal debt is the accumulation of these annual deficits. Why do the federal deficits and debt matter? Does the answer depend on the state of the economy?

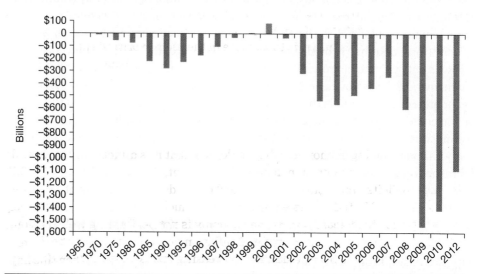

FIGURE » 15.2B

FEDERAL DEBT

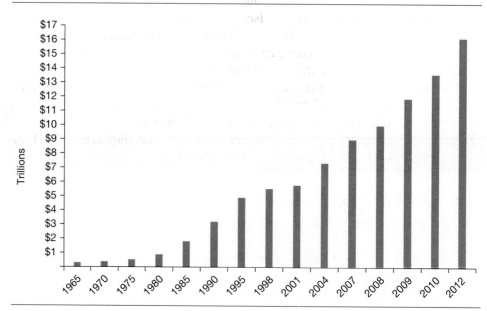

Note: Totals in Figure 15.2A exclude the Social Security Trust Fund and reflect total public debt, including intragovernmental holdings.

Source: Data on budget deficits from the Congressional Budget Office, Historical Budget Data, www.cbo.gov/budget/historical.shtml for budget deficits. Data on federal debt from the U.S. Department of the Treasury, TreasuryDirect, www.treasurydirect.gov/govt/govt.htm (accessed 10/5/12).

There are differences of opinion over whether the United States' debtor status is a problem. Most economists agree that if the current account deficit is driven by a surplus in investments (more foreign investment in America than America has invested overseas), there is no great cause for concern. Though some economists worry about having an increasing share of U.S. businesses and real estate owned by foreign investors, overall this is simply evidence of the strength of the U.S. economy—that is, investors think they can get a greater return on their investments in America than in other countries. However, when the current account deficit is driven by the trade deficit, which is based on consumption rather than investment, this creates longer-term potential problems for the economy that are not sustainable. We discuss this topic more in the section on trade policy.[10]

TRADE-OFFS BETWEEN ECONOMIC GOALS

One challenge facing economic policy makers is that it is difficult to "have it all." The period of economic growth, low unemployment, and low inflation with falling budget deficits (and a surplus by the end of the decade) and a healthy current account that the United States enjoyed through much of the 1990s was relatively unusual. Typically, at least part of the economy is not performing well and some goals are not being met. For example, if inflation starts to increase, the Federal Reserve will attempt to bring it down by increasing interest rates. When this happens, the economy slows because businesses are less willing to expand when the cost of borrowing increases, so unemployment increases. Therefore, there is a trade-off, at least in the short run, between stable prices and full employment and economic growth. But various schools of thought have challenged the strength of this relationship. Indeed, the stagflation of the 1970s that had both high inflation and unemployment powerfully called the trade-off into question.

Steps to address the trade deficit also conflict with other goals. Politicians are often under pressure to protect American jobs and prevent them from going overseas. But if policy makers impose tariffs or other barriers to free trade to protect domestic products and jobs, this action violates the goal of promoting an efficient free market. Tackling trade imbalances through a weaker dollar can undermine the goal of keeping inflation low. When the dollar weakens, imports become more expensive, and this can increase the inflation rate. Policy makers must tread carefully when addressing economic problems to ensure that they are not making some other problem worse. The next section explores who these policy makers are.

THE KEY PLAYERS IN ECONOMIC POLICY MAKING

DESCRIBE THE ROLES PLAYED BY EACH OF THE BRANCHES OF GOVERNMENT IN SHAPING ECONOMIC POLICY

Congress, the president, and the bureaucracy all play important roles in the economic policy making process. Congress, through the "power of the purse," has the constitutional authority to determine the nation's fiscal policy, but the president also has a central role in shaping taxing and spending policy for the nation. The

Federal Reserve and the Treasury implement the nation's monetary policy. The courts play a secondary part by ensuring fair application of economic policy laws and regulations.

CONGRESS

The Constitution places Congress at the center of economic policy making by giving legislators the "power of the purse"—that is, power over the nation's fiscal policy of taxing and spending. In a way, everything Congress does has an impact on the economy, whether it is providing money for an interstate highway or a student loan, regulating the level of air pollutants, or funding the Social Security system. Some committees are more directly related than others to economic policy: budget, appropriations, and tax committees (Ways and Means in the House and Finance in the Senate) direct Congress's **fiscal policy**—taxing and spending; the banking committees have a hand in overseeing aspects of the nation's **monetary policy**—controlling the money supply and interest rates. (However, as we discuss later, monetary policy is primarily the domain of the Federal Reserve System, or the Fed.) The commerce committees, especially in the House, also have their hand in a range of economic policies. Because it is the most important of Congress's economic policy-making responsibilities, we focus our discussion on the budget process and how it has evolved in the past fifty years.

Budget making in Congress was decentralized through much of its history, with various committees and subcommittees serving as the center of the legislative process and no real way to coordinate activity among them. The appropriations committees tried to be the "guardians of the Treasury," but it was difficult to keep the spending requests from other committees in line with overall budgetary expectations because of the two-step process Congress uses to approve any spending: the authorizing committee writes the law that authorizes the spending and then the appropriations committee approves the level of spending.[11] As a result, budgetary power shifted from Congress to the president, starting with the Budget and Accounting Act of 1921. From that point on, presidents have played a central role in the budget process by submitting their budgets to Congress. The president's budget often serves as the starting point for the congressional budget.

The decline in Congress's budgetary power came to a head in the early 1970s with the tension between Congress and President Nixon over the impoundment of appropriated money (that is, the president ordered executive agencies not to spend money that had been authorized by Congress if he believed it was wasteful or unnecessary).[12] Congress responded by passing the Budget and Impoundment Control Act of 1974, which stipulated that unless Congress passed a bill agreeing with the president's impoundment within 45 days, the impoundment was canceled.[13] More important, the act also restored the *institutional* balance between the president and Congress on the budget by creating the Budget Committees in the House and Senate, setting up the budget process outlined in the How It Works box, and establishing the Congressional Budget Office. This office gave Congress independent expertise and advice on budgetary matters so it did not have to rely on the president's numbers. For the first time, Congress had the institutional capacity on budgetary matters to deal with the president on an equal footing.

However, the new process and institutions didn't guarantee smooth sailing. In fact, Congress had a difficult time meeting the various deadlines, and the new

fiscal policy Government decisions about how to influence the economy by taxing and spending.

monetary policy Government decisions about how to influence the economy using control of the money supply and interest rates.

budget making The processes carried out in Congress to determine how government money will be spent and revenue will be raised.

How It Works

THE BUDGET PROCESS

The president submits budget to Congress.

1ST MONDAY IN FEB.

FEB. 15TH

CBO issues budget and economic outlook report.

Other committees with budgetary responsibilities submit "views and estimates" to budget committees.

WITHIN SIX WEEKS OF PRESIDENT'S SUBMISSION

House Budget Committee creates its budget resolution and the House votes on it.

EARLY APRIL

Senate Budget committee creates its budget resolution and the Senate votes on it.

Budget Conference Committee reconciles House and Senate versions of the budget resolution.

House votes on conference version.

BY APRIL 15TH

Senate votes on conference version.

APPROPRIATIONS

After both houses approve the budget resolution, appropriations committees draft legislation authorizing expenditures to the relevant agencies. Each appropriations bill must be passed by both houses and signed into law by the president. If this process is not completed by October 1st, and no temporary measure (a "continuing resolution") is in place, the government will shut down.

Start of the fiscal year.

OCT 1ST

$ POP QUIZ!

1 When does each house of Congress vote on its own version of a budget resolution?

a   the first Monday in February

b   February 15th

c   within 6 weeks of receiving the president's budget proposal

d   early April

e   October 1st

2 If the budget process is not completed by October 1st and no temporary measure is in place

a   the president withdraws his proposal.

b   both houses of Congress vote on the conference version.

c   the government shuts down.

d   the start of the fiscal year is postponed until January.

e   the appropriations committees draft legislation.

process didn't help eliminate the budget deficits. There was a powerful tool in the Budget Act that was ignored for the first five years: **budget reconciliation** was first used in 1980 to bring spending levels into line with the budget resolution (which obviously requires that there *is* a budget resolution—four times since 1974 Congress has failed to adopt the overall budget blueprint).[14] This process requires committees to meet specific spending targets, and then all the changes are combined into one omnibus reconciliation bill. This process has two advantages in terms of adopting budget cuts, which are always difficult because most programs have strong advocates who fight the cuts. First, having everything in a single huge bill makes it much more difficult for members to vote against it because that would mean turning down the entire package, including elements of the bill that individual members of Congress like as well as those that they oppose. Depending on the timing, failure to pass an omnibus spending bill may mean shutting down the government. Second, the Senate treats reconciliation bills differently from other bills or amendments. They cannot be filibustered, and debate is limited to 20 hours, amendments must be germane (they must relate to the bill), and extraneous provisions unrelated to deficit reduction can be struck down. This last point has been an important tool in deficit reduction.[15] Overall, reconciliation has been used in about two-thirds of the budgets since 1980 and has been responsible for cutting hundreds of billions of dollars of spending. As we discuss in Chapter 16, reconciliation was crucial in passing health care reform in 2010 because it allowed Democrats to avoid a Republican filibuster.

Even the powerful tool of reconciliation was inadequate to address the exploding budget deficits of the early to mid-1980s. In 1985 Congress tried to get control of the deficits by passing the Balanced Budget and Emergency Control Act, informally known as Gramm–Rudman–Hollings after its primary sponsors, but it didn't work. When the law was adopted, the budget deficit for the next fiscal year was $221 billion, or 5.4 percent of GDP. The law was supposed to eliminate the deficit within five years, but in 1991 the budget deficit was $269 billion, or 5.5 percent of GDP. Congress was just spinning its wheels.

The budget process changed once again with the Budget Enforcement Act of 1990. Of several important changes, the one that seemed to give Congress the most traction in managing the deficits was a zero-sum, pay-as-you-go (PAYGO) process whereby any new tax cut or spending increase had to be paid for by raising another tax or cutting spending in some other program. The PAYGO procedure, along with the tax increases in President Clinton's 1993 budget, put the nation on the path for the first budget surpluses since the 1960s. There were a few more bumps in the road, including a major budget showdown between Clinton and the Republican Congress in 1995 and 1996 that led to two government shutdowns: one for six days in November 1995, and another for almost a month, from December 1995 to January 1996. Opinion polls suggested Republican leaders were to blame for the shutdown, so Clinton was able to win support for most of his budget priorities. Tensions between Clinton and Congress eased when strong economic growth led to higher revenue than had been forecast, which meant that reducing the deficit became a less contentious process. By 1999, the budget was balanced, and in 2000 there was a substantial surplus ($86.3 billion) for the first time in nearly 50 years.[16]

The surpluses evaporated and massive budget deficits returned in 2002 (the deficit hit $317 billion in 2002 and averaged $475 billion over the next five years). One major contribution to this explosion in the deficits is that PAYGO was allowed to lapse for the 2002 budget—in part to enable funding the war in Iraq and the War on Terror, but also to make it politically easier to pass additional tax cuts. Without the need to pay for tax cuts or spending increases, it is too tempting to let the deficits increase to unsustainable levels. When Democrats regained control of Congress in January 2007, they reinstated the PAYGO rule. However, Congress waived the rule to create a short-term fix for the alternative minimum tax, which was raising taxes for millions of upper-middle-class Amercians,[17] and then again for the Economic Stimulus Act of 2008, which cut taxes for millions of Americans without offsetting the drop in revenue with savings elsewhere in the budget.[18] The PAYGO rule was strengthened further in February 2010, when Congress passed a statute giving it the force of law. However, when the popular payroll tax cut was set to expire early in 2012, Congress simply suspended the PAYGO rule and added $100 billion of additional debt to the nation's tab.[19]

Increased partisan polarization in Congress and differences between Democrats and Republicans in their view of taxing and spending policy makes it difficult to pass a budget in a timely fashion. In recent years Congress has relied on "continuing resolutions," which keep spending at the level of last year's budget, when they cannot agree on a new budget. Even traditionally noncontroversial aspects of fiscal policy, such as increasing the debt ceiling to authorize government borrowing, have become opportunities for partisan politics.

THE PRESIDENT

Once they are in office, presidents quickly realize that the public expects them to promote a healthy economy. Indeed, the state of the economy has a big impact on the public's assessment of presidential performance and also influences election outcomes. President Obama focused on the economy in his first months in office, pushing through a massive stimulus bill; later, in the face of major unemployment, Obama also signed legislation aimed at creating more jobs.

As mentioned in Chapter 11, on the economic front the president is unable to accomplish much single-handedly: Congress, the Fed, and broader domestic and international economic forces all exert an equal or greater influence on the health of the economy. However, the president has a large advising structure to help formulate economic policy. The Office of Management and Budget (OMB), the Council of Economic Advisers (CEA), the Office of the **United States Trade Representative (USTR)**, and the **National Economic Council (NEC)** all provide important economic advice to the president.

The department with the longest track record is the OMB. Its predecessor, the Bureau of the Budget, was created by the 1921 Budget and Accounting Act and was renamed the OMB in 1970. The OMB plays a central role in creating the budget by soliciting spending requests from all federal agencies, suggesting additional cuts, and then coordinating these requests with presidential priorities. It is ultimately responsible for putting together the president's budget, which is then submitted to Congress. The OMB also oversees government reorganization plans and recommends improvements in departmental operations.

Created by the Employment Act of 1946, the CEA's central function is to provide the president with objective data on the state of the economy and expert advice on economic policy. The CEA is responsible for creating the *Annual Economic Report of the President,* which has a wealth of data on various aspects of the economy and an overview of the president's policies. Presidents have varied in how closely they work with the CEA or other

United States Trade Representative (USTR) An agency founded in 1962 to negotiate with foreign governments to create trade agreements, resolve disputes, and participate in global trade policy organizations. Treaties negotiated by the USTR must be ratified by the Senate.

National Economic Council (NEC) A group of economic advisers created in 1993 to work with the president to coordinate economic policy.

THE REMINDER THAT HUNG ON THE wall of Bill Clinton's campaign headquarters in 1992 was just as relevant for President Obama in 2009 when he took office during the deepest economic recession since the 1930s.

parts of their economic team. Some prominent CEA members have been influential in shaping and promoting the administration's tax policy and jobs program. Others have had a more secondary role.

The USTR is responsible for developing and coordinating U.S. international trade, commodity, and direct investment policy and overseeing negotiations on trade policy with other countries.[20] With the increasing importance of globalization, international trade, and Congress's deference to the executive branch on trade issues through the "fast track" procedure, the USTR is an important player in economic policy making.

The NEC was established in 1993 to fulfill a campaign promise by President Clinton to elevate economic policy to the level of national security and foreign policy. The NEC has four principal functions: "to coordinate policy-making for domestic and international economic issues, to coordinate economic policy advice for the President, to ensure that policy decisions and programs are consistent with the President's economic goals, and to monitor implementation of the President's economic policy agenda."[21] The NEC coordinates policy by bringing together cabinet secretaries who work on economic issues, such as the Treasury secretary, budget director, Commerce secretary, CEA chairman, and Labor secretary. As Gene Sperling, head of the NEC in the late 1990s, explained:

> *We drive things, but the policy decisions are made through a team effort. Instead of Treasury just deciding tax policy, or OMB just deciding budget policy, they are instead the lead presenters in an NEC process where the decisions are made as a team, with differences being fairly taken up for decision by the President. . . . The NEC is not a set group of people; it is a fair-process commitment.*[22]

The NEC initially appeared to challenge the CEA's turf, but a division of labor has preserved an important role for each: the NEC is the political arm that coordinates economic policy, and the CEA is the technical arm that provides information about the economy.

These last two sections described the roles of Congress and the president separately, but obviously their interactions are central to understanding economic policy. If the president's party controls Congress, then the president's budget becomes the starting point for congressional negotiations over the budget. If the opposing party controls Congress, then the president's budget is usually considered "dead on arrival" and Congress creates its own document. Of course the president can use the veto threat to try to move Congress closer to his position, but when the budget is contained in one large package that must be signed or vetoed in its entirety, it is difficult to carry out such threats.[23]

THE BUREAUCRACY

Federal Reserve System An independent agency that serves as the central bank of the United States to bring stability to the nation's banking system.

Treasury Department A cabinet-level agency that is responsible for managing the federal government's revenue. It prints currency, collects taxes, and sells government bonds.

All the departments explained so far could be considered part of the larger bureaucracy, but they are included within the Executive Office of the President and therefore are usually considered along with the president. Regular cabinet-level agencies have an impact on fiscal policy by advocating more spending in their policy areas. We will focus on two bureaucratic agencies that are key in creating monetary policy: the **Federal Reserve System**, an independent agency; and the **Treasury Department**, a cabinet-level department.

THE FEDERAL RESERVE SYSTEM

The Federal Reserve Act of 1913 established the Federal Reserve System (commonly known as the Fed), to bring stability and continuity to the nation's banking system. The chair and six other governors serve on the Board of Governors of the Federal Reserve System. The chair has a four-year term and the others have 14-year overlapping terms. All governors are appointed by the president and approved by the Senate. The board is responsible for establishing monetary policy for the nation, which includes influencing interest rates and the money supply and regulating the lending activity of member banks (discussed in more detail later in the chapter). There are 12 regional Federal Reserve banks and more than 2,900 member banks out of the approximately 7,800 banks in the nation.[24] We examine the Fed's operations in the section on monetary policy, but briefly, the regional banks lend money to banks, hold reserves for them, supply currency and coins, buy and sell government securities, and report on the state of the economy in their regions. Equally important, the Federal Reserve is the Open Market Committee, which comprises the seven members of the Board of Governors and the 12 regional bank presidents. However, the bank presidents have only five votes at any given time; therefore, the board controls a majority of the votes.[25]

One crucial characteristic of the Fed is its political independence, which has three primary sources. First, the Fed is an independent agency: its decisions are not subject to presidential or congressional review. Second, the 14-year terms for the six governors and the four-year term for the chair and vice chair purposefully do not overlap with the federal election calendar. One strong indication of the Fed's independence is that presidents typically reappoint chairs who were initially appointed by presidents of the other party: William McChesney Martin, who was appointed by Harry Truman, served through the presidencies of Eisenhower, Kennedy, and Johnson, and part of Nixon's first term. Paul Volcker served under Carter and Reagan, while Alan Greenspan's tenure spanned the presidencies of Reagan, Bush, Clinton, and the second Bush.[26] Ben Bernanke was nominated by

FEDERAL RESERVE CHAIRMAN
Ben Bernanke (left) presents his semiannual report to Congress in February 2010. Although the Fed makes regular reports to Congress and the president, it is an independent agency and its decisions are not subject to presidential and congressional review.

YES, YOU COULD CALL THIS A SLOWDOWN, BUT NOT MUCH ELSE CAN GO WRONG NOW.

THE ECONOMY

BANG!

INFLATION

THE ECONOMY

OOO ANOTHER BUBBLE.

THE 1970S WITNESSED ECONOMIC stagnation along with high inflation, yielding the term "stagflation." As the economy started to recover after the 2008–09 financial crisis, rising prices remained a concern and the possibility of stagflation returned.

Federal Reserve Board The group of seven presidential appointees who govern the Federal Reserve System.

Bush and renominated by Obama. Unlike other presidential appointees in the bureaucracy, members of the **Federal Reserve Board** can be removed only "for cause," the precise definition of which has never been tested. This largely insulates the Fed from the political process.

Third, the Fed does not depend on Congress for its operating budget because it can literally create its own money (see later discussion). Congress's control of the bureaucracy is rooted in the power of the purse (see Chapter 12), but because Congress does not provide the Fed's budget, Congress has much less leverage over it. The Fed's primary source of income is interest on the Treasury securities it owns. After paying for all of its expenses, the Fed returned about $75.4 billion to the Treasury in 2011. Overall, in 2011 the Fed employed 17,120 people with total expenditures of $7.32 billion.[27] The employees are not subject to civil service rules or pay grades; thus the Fed can offer top salaries and hire some of the best people in finance and economics.

Is the Fed's independence a good thing or a bad thing? Supporters point out that the Fed's central goal is shared by nearly all politicians and Americans: a stable economy and slow, steady growth (the Federal Reserve Reform Act of 1977 gives the Fed a dual mandate of pursuing stable prices and maximum employment). Therefore, the argument goes, we should leave the Fed alone, let it do its job, and keep politics out of monetary policy. However, critics argue that its lack of accountability means that it can do things that hurt the economy and voters have no recourse. For example, during Ben Bernanke's confirmation hearings for his second term late in 2009, senators grilled the chair on the Fed's regulatory failures that helped precipitate the financial crisis, its decisions during the bailout of American International Group (AIG), and its inability to spur job growth by encouraging more bank lending.[28] If these failures were indeed the Fed's fault—and that point is debatable—voters can do nothing about it.

But the Fed is not immune to political influence. In fact, one line of research argues that the Fed tries to help presidents during reelection years by encouraging a pro-growth economy.[29] Evidence on this point is mixed, but at a minimum, presidents do have the ability to make it clear when they disagree with the Fed's policies. Presidents also have the opportunity to appoint the chair and vice chair of the Fed, but presidents rarely fire them because they do not want to upset the financial markets. Other research has shown that the Fed is at least somewhat sensitive to the preferences of the president and Congress.[30]

The Fed's ultimate accountability is to Congress, because if things really got out of hand—for example, if the Fed decided to increase interest rates to 20 percent without good reason—Congress could amend the Federal Reserve Act and remove the Fed's responsibility or autonomy in specific areas. The Fed must report to Congress annually on its activities and to the banking committees of Congress twice a year on its plans for monetary policy. The Fed's annual report is subject to an outside audit. Fed officials also frequently testify before Congress on a broad range of issues. And Congress may publicly criticize the Fed when it disagrees with its policies.

THE TREASURY DEPARTMENT

The Treasury Department is another part of the bureaucracy that plays an important role in economic policy making. According to its website, the mission of the Treasury "is to promote the conditions for prosperity and stability in the United States and encourage prosperity and stability in the rest of the world." Specifically, the range of its responsibilities related to economic policy making includes these:

- ▶ Managing federal finances
- ▶ Collecting taxes, duties, and monies paid to and due to the United States and paying all bills of the United States
- ▶ Producing currency and coinage
- ▶ Managing government accounts and the public debt
- ▶ Supervising national banks and thrift institutions
- ▶ Advising on domestic and international financial, monetary, economic, trade, and tax policy
- ▶ Enforcing federal finance and tax laws
- ▶ Investigating and prosecuting tax evaders, counterfeiters, and forgers[31]

Some of these responsibilities overlap with the Fed's, especially supervising banks and managing the public debt. In most instances the responsibilities are complementary rather than competing, such as the management of currency and coins: the Treasury produces currency at the Bureau of Engraving and Printing (about 23.5 million bills are printed every day) and coins at the United States Mint (which makes between 5 and 14 *billion* coins a year), and the Fed distributes them to member banks.[32] Financing federal debt is another matter. The Treasury generally prefers to have lower interest rates to keep down the cost of financing the debt and to promote economic growth, while the Fed is also concerned about keeping rates high enough to avoid inflation. Therefore, the Fed and Treasury must often coordinate their policies to avoid working at cross-purposes.

COOPERATION BETWEEN THE FED AND TREASURY

A dramatic example of cooperation between the Fed and Treasury is the 2008 economic crisis. Problems in the subprime, or high-risk, mortgage market, the collapse of housing prices, and the tightening of credit markets had been putting pressure on the economy through the spring and summer. The first sign of serious trouble came in March when the New York Federal Reserve made a loan of $30 billion to JP Morgan Chase to facilitate the buyout of Bear Stearns, the investment bank that was going bankrupt because of its exposure to mortgage-backed securities. Concerns deepened in September, when the federal government took over the Federal National Mortgage Association and the Federal Home Mortgage Corporation because they were about to go under. These two government-sponsored enterprises, nicknamed "Fannie Mae" and "Freddie Mac," fund most of the home loans in the nation. This federal acquisition, involving a commitment of $200 billion to back up Fannie and Freddie's assets, was "one of the most sweeping government interventions in private financial markets in decades."[33] The takeover calmed the credit markets for a few days, until it became evident that two Wall Street giants, the investment banks Lehman Brothers and Merrill Lynch, were becoming financially unstable because of subprime mortgage exposure and other bad debt. Lehman Brothers went bankrupt, Merrill Lynch was bought by Bank of America, and the markets panicked.

The next day brought more bad news: the world's largest insurance company, AIG, was also deep in the subprime mess and teetering on the edge of bankruptcy, so the Fed stepped in with an $85 billion loan to save it. Despite these dramatic moves, credit markets seized up, and investors started pulling money out of anything remotely related to the financial crisis. A few days later, Washington Mutual, the nation's sixth-largest bank, failed. This series of disasters and near-disasters led to around-the-clock meetings of Fed and Treasury leaders who produced a plan for the government to buy mortgage-related assets from banks and other financial institutions. The three-page proposal was a sweeping request for Congress to grant the Treasury secretary unprecedented, unilateral powers to spend taxpayers' money. Congressional leaders embraced the idea of helping financial institutions deal with their bad debt but questioned the lack of oversight and accountability in the proposal.

Congressional leaders hammered out a compromise bailout bill and then put it up for a vote, assuming that they had enough votes to pass it. In a stunning rebuke to party leaders and President Bush, the House defeated the $700 billion bailout bill by a vote of 205 to 228, with 133 Republicans and 95 Democrats opposing it. The stock market plummeted by 7 percent in the hours after the bill failed. Analysis of the House vote showed that two factors were central: ideology and electoral vulnerability. It was a coalition of the "ends against the middle," with extreme liberals and conservatives voting against it and moderates voting for it. Politically vulnerable members also voted against the unpopular bill, believing their constituents viewed it as an unfair bailout of Wall Street.

Throughout the crisis, which was the worst since the Great Depression, Fed Chair Ben Bernanke and Treasury Secretary Henry Paulson worked together to restore confidence in financial institutions.[34] Secretary Paulson said, "The financial security of all Americans—their retirement savings, their home values, their ability to borrow for college and the opportunities for more and higher-paying jobs—depends on our ability to restore our financial institutions to a sound footing."[35] Congressional leaders picked up this theme, emphasizing the benefits of the plan for "Main Street" rather than just for Wall Street. They emphasized that small businesses were having a hard time getting short-term loans to meet payroll and that individuals were getting turned down for loans to buy cars or pay college tuition. They even started calling the plan a "rescue" rather than a "bailout."

The Senate took the lead on retooling the bill, given the House's earlier inability to act. Wanting to ensure a solid majority behind the bill, leaders added sweeteners (such as increasing the amount of savings insured by the federal government from $100,000 to $250,000 per account to help restore confidence in regular savings accounts) and imposed more accountability (by limiting to $350 billion the amount of mortgage-related assets the Treasury secretary could buy under the Troubled Asset Relief Program [TARP] without congressional permission if he needed more). The Senate passed the bill by a bipartisan 75-to-24 margin.[36] Two days later the House voted for the bill by a 263-to-171 margin, with strong support from both parties.[37] President Bush signed the Emergency Economic Stabilization Act into law on October 3, 2008.

Despite this significant rescue plan, the crisis spiraled out of control in the following weeks. Stock markets plunged worldwide, with the U.S. stock market shedding 35 percent of its value in the two months after the crisis began. Credit markets remained frozen, and it became clear that an alternative approach was needed. The government's purchase of "toxic debt" posed many technical obstacles, and financial markets had no confidence that the plan would work. European leaders swiftly agreed to an approach in which governments would directly invest in banks, providing them with desperately needed capital in return for equity stakes in the banks. The United States followed suit with an initial allocation of $250 billion to directly invest in banks, followed by an announcement that the

Treasury would abandon its plan to buy toxic debt and use all the funds to directly invest in banks. By mid-November, the economic panic had eased, but the situation remained fragile.

When President Obama took office in 2009, things were still very grim. Stocks finally bottomed in March 2009 (down 56 percent from their October 2007 high), shortly after Treasury Secretary Timothy Geithner announced the administration's Financial Stability Plan. The plan focused on four problems: frozen credit markets, weakened bank capital, a backlog of troubled mortgage assets on bank balance sheets, and falling home prices. Working with the Fed to stabilize the financial markets, the Treasury had largely resolved three of those four problems one year later. Credit markets were operating, and banks were in much better shape, having raised more than $140 billion in capital and $60 billion in unsecured debt. Banks used these funds to repay the Treasury, which as of October 2012 had recovered 89 percent of its investments in banks. The Treasury expects to eventually recover all of the TARP expenditures. The housing market, though not fully recovered, has also stabilized, with sales up and prices steady in most markets. Troubled mortgage assets remained on the balance sheets of many banks, but with their stronger base of capital and the strengthened housing market, they were not as great a concern as they had been a year earlier.[38] In September 2012, the Fed announced a new policy to inject money into the economy, promising to buy $40 billion a month of mortgage-backed securities. This was an open-ended commitment, dubbed "QE-infinity" (Quantitive Easing), and was seen as the boldest move yet by the Fed to revive the economy.

Despite the broad success of the financial rescue, it remained a political liability. The rescue was widely perceived as a bailout of Wall Street. Many citizens were outraged over corporate salaries and bonuses, the bailout of the auto industry, and the perception that not enough was being done to help average Americans. The economy lost 8.4 million jobs in 2008–09, millions of Americans were losing their homes, and unemployment remained stuck around 9.5 percent through 2010. Discontent with the bailout contributed to the crushing defeat for Democrats in the

PROTESTERS AT A RALLY AGAINST government bailouts for Wall Street called for the resignation of the chief executive of Goldman Sachs and cancellation of bonuses for all Goldman employees. Huge profits and bonuses on Wall Street in 2009–10 were very controversial, as the unemployment rate remained at nearly 10 percent.

THE INDEPENDENCE OF THE FEDERAL RESERVE

After the economic meltdown of 2008–09 and the Federal Reserve's extraordinary intervention to stabilize the banking system and ease credit markets, critics of the Fed had new ammunition with which to go after their favorite target. Critics questioned why the Fed bailed out some financial institutions, including foreign banks, so they did not have to take losses on billions of dollars of investments guaranteed by the American International Group (AIG) while many other investors and institutions were forced to take a financial haircut. Many members of Congress, most prominently Representative Ron Paul (R-Tex.) and Senator Bernie Sanders (I-Vt.), challenged the independence of the Fed by calling for more transparency in its operations and additional congressional oversight.[a] But after Fed chairman Ben Bernanke warned that giving Congress the power to audit the Fed at any time "would seriously threaten monetary-policy independence, increase inflation fears and market interest rates, and damage economic stability and job creation," the Senate opted for a more modest one-time audit of the central bank's emergency lending program and disclosure of the financial institutions it assisted.

Protesters hold signs in the background as Federal Reserve chairman Ben Bernanke testifies at a congressional hearing about AIG.

Watch a video clip of David Lewis discussing this topic at **wwnorton.com/studyspace**

The question of the independence of the Fed is related to a more general question that is the focus of political science research: When does Congress delegate policy responsibility to an independent agency (such as the Fed), and how does Congress decide how much control to give the president over the agency? One could imagine that Congress and the president would both want to have control over monetary policy and interest rates because they are so important to the functioning of the economy. So why was the Fed given so much independence?

Political scientist David Lewis has studied the conditions under which Congress will delegate power to an agency and insulate it from outside control or allow for more presidential control. Based on a theoretical approach called the New Economics of Organization, Lewis argues that if we can understand the "incentives of the actors, their policy preferences, and the degree of uncertainty, we can predict what the decisions will be."[b] In general, Congress prefers a larger degree of insulation in an agency than the president. This preference for insulation is strong when Congress is controlled by a majority of the party in opposition to the president and when those majorities are relatively large. But under unified government, when the president and Congress are controlled by the same party, larger majorities for the president's party in Congress mean a lower probability of creating insulated agencies (because Congress wants to give the president more control). Lewis tested these hypotheses by examining every agency created between 1946

and 1997, determining whether these agencies are relatively insulated or more open to presidential control. He found strong support for his theory.

It is somewhat surprising then that the creation of the Federal Reserve in 1913 is not consistent with the hypothesis that unified government with large majorities is more likely to create agencies that are subject to presidential control (Democrat Woodrow Wilson was president and the Democrats had a 290-to-127 margin in the House and a 51-to-44 majority in the Senate). This anomaly and the nearly complete independence of the Fed may be explained by the need for a consistent monetary policy: if the Fed were not insulated, Congress and the president would be tempted to influence monetary policy for short-term political gain.

The example of the Fed also runs against Lewis's general preference for a hierarchically structured, functionally organized bureaucracy that is subject to presidential influence in its design. He recognizes that there are some instances in which insulation and independence may be necessary. He says, "Delegating control over interest rates and monetary policy to the Federal Reserve, for example, is probably a case where the loss of efficiency in coordination are outweighed by the potential policy losses from flip-flopping presidential economic policy."[c] Recent efforts by Congress to impose more accountability on the Fed reflect public outrage over the bailouts for Wall Street. But the measured response of a limited audit while preserving the Fed's regulatory power over banks demonstrates that Congress continues to recognize the need for an independent Fed.

2010 midterm elections, despite the fact that it was a bipartisan plan passed at the end of the Bush administration. Exit polls showed that 47 percent of voters in 2010 incorrectly thought that the bailout was passed under Obama, while only 34 percent knew it was under Bush and 19 percent said they didn't know.[39] The financial rescue and the regulation of Wall Street remained issues in the 2012 elections.

THE COURTS

The courts are not directly involved in creating economic policy the way that Congress, the president, and the Fed are. However, the U.S. court system influences economic policy in a way that is often taken for granted but becomes apparent when America's political system is compared to the systems of the developing world. One key difficulty poor nations face in promoting economic development is the lack of an independent, honest legal system. Contract law, patent law, banking and finance law, and property rights are all necessary elements of a legal system that provides the foundation for economic development. If in a given country international corporations cannot count on having their contracts honored or their technological secrets protected, or if they must bribe legal officials at every turn, they are far less likely to consider doing business there.[40] The courts provide this necessary legal foundation. They issue rulings on the regulation of the telecommunications, banking, and energy industries and decisions on environmental law and eminent domain that affect property rights. All these policies have an impact on economic policy.

TOOLS AND THEORIES OF ECONOMIC POLICY

> EXAMINE HOW FISCAL, MONETARY, REGULATORY, AND TRADE POLICIES INFLUENCE THE ECONOMY

This section explores the various tools policy makers have to achieve the goals outlined in the first part of the chapter. We do not want to give the impression that policy makers can pull levers and push buttons to achieve desired outcomes, or that they are immune from external forces that can sink the economy despite their best efforts. However, there are certain things that leaders can do to move the massive U.S. economy in the right direction.

FISCAL POLICY

Fiscal policy is the use of the government's taxing and spending power to influence the direction of the economy. In the 1930s, economist John Maynard Keynes developed the idea of fine-tuning the economy through "countercyclical" taxing and spending policy, usually called **Keynesian economics**. Keynes argued that policy makers can soften the effects of a recession by stimulating the economy when overall demand is low—during a recession, when people aren't spending as much—through tax cuts or increased government spending. Tax cuts put more money in people's pockets, allowing them to spend more than they otherwise

Keynesian economics The theory that governments should use economic policy, like taxing and spending, to maintain stability in the economy.

would, while government spending stimulates the economy through the purchase of various goods, such as highways or military equipment, or direct payments to individuals, such as Social Security checks. From this perspective, it is acceptable to run budget deficits in order to increase employment and national income to give a short-term boost to the economy. Keynes also pointed out that if overall demand is too high, which might result in inflation, policy makers should cool off the economy by cutting spending or raising taxes.[41]

STRATEGIES TO STIMULATE THE ECONOMY

Perhaps the best example of a Keynesian tax cut used to stimulate the economy was the Revenue Act of 1964. The politics of getting the bill passed were tricky: in a reversal of today's partisan politics, liberal Democrats favored the tax cuts to stimulate the economy, and conservative Republicans opposed them because they were afraid of ballooning deficits. But extensive lobbying by President Johnson eventually led to strong bipartisan support.[42] The tax cut, one of the largest in the twentieth century, helped lay the foundation for unprecedented economic expansion in the 1960s.[43]

A more recent version of fiscal policy was the basis for Ronald Reagan's tax cuts in 1981 and has been the centerpiece of economic policy for many Republicans since then. **Supply-side economics** focuses on the ways that tax policy and regulations affect the labor supply rather than on the impact of these policies on overall demand. The primary focus was on how tax rates affect how much people work rather than how they spend. The idea is based on the relationship between the top **marginal tax rate** and total tax revenue as shown in the Laffer curve, named for economist Arthur Laffer. If tax rates are too high, people will work less because a large percentage of their income is going to the government. The basic shape of the curve is intuitive and the endpoints are noncontroversial: if the tax rate is zero, there will be no tax revenue; if the tax rate is 100 percent, nobody will work because they won't get to keep any of their money, so total tax revenue at that end of the curve is also zero.[44] Laffer argued that if tax rates are too high (to the right of the peak in the graph; see Figure 15.3), the government should cut taxes in order to raise total government revenue, which is counterintuitive.[45]

It was too good to be true. When taxes were cut, with the top marginal rate going from 70 to 50 percent, revenue fell and the budget deficits exploded. Supporters of the supply-side theory argue that the problem was on the spending side of the equation rather than on tax revenue. That is, deficits went up because the Democratic Congress spent too much, not because of Reagan's tax cuts. However, taxes and spending as a share of the overall economy both fell during the Reagan presidency: tax revenue fell from 19.6 percent of GDP in 1981, the last year before the tax cuts went into effect, to 18.1 percent of GDP in 1988, the last year of the Reagan presidency. Individual income tax revenue fell from 9.3 percent to 8 percent of GDP over the same period, so most of the decrease in revenue was due to lower individual income taxes. While overall government spending did increase during the 1982–83 recession, spending from the beginning of Reagan's term to the end dropped slightly from 22.2 percent to 21.2 percent of GDP.[46] This suggests that spending was not the source of the budget deficits in the 1980s.

Economists continue to debate the extent to which fiscal policy can influence the economy. Two factors have limited the effectiveness of fiscal policy. First, fiscal policies often cannot be implemented quickly enough to have the intended impact on the **business cycle**—the normal expansion and contraction of the economy. This is especially true when one party controls Congress and the other controls the presidency, but it happens even during unified government.

supply-side economics The theory that lower tax rates will stimulate the economy by encouraging people to save, invest, and produce more goods and services.

marginal tax rate The tax rate paid on income up to some threshold. For example, in 2012 single people paid no tax on their first $8,700 in income, 15 percent on income between $8,700 and $35,350, all the way up to 35 percent on income over $388,350.

business cycle The normal pattern of expansion and contraction of the economy.

FIGURE » 15.3

THE LAFFER CURVE

The Laffer curve shows the theoretical relationship between the tax rate and total tax revenue. How did this curve contribute to the budget deficits of the 1980s?

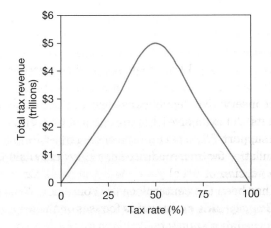

The $787 billion American Recovery and Reinvestment Act of 2009, designed to stimulate the economy and create jobs, ran into problems along these lines. Although the legislation had some immediate impact on the economy, it is impossible to spend that much money (or implement tax cuts) without some time lag. The website that tracks the spending of the stimulus money, Recovery. gov, reports that of the $787 billion, tax cuts comprise $288 billion; contracts, grants, and loans are $275 billion; and entitlements are $224 billion. One year after the recovery bill was enacted, the government reported that nearly 600,000 jobs had been saved but only 34.6 percent of the money had been spent ($272.2 billion). Republicans criticized the Democrats for spending too much money and not enacting policies that would have had a more immediate effect (such as payroll tax cuts), and critics on the left argued that the stimulus wasn't big enough. A payroll tax cut was implemented for 2011–12 that reduced the rate from 6.2 to 4.2 percent, putting an additional $700 in the pocket of the average American worker for each of those years.

Second, on the other side of the Keynesian coin, increasing taxes or cutting spending during good economic times is much more difficult to implement than the more politically popular tax cuts or spending increases. Although the latter is limited by the difficulty of timing the fiscal policy to have a maximum economic impact, the former is limited by politics: politicians do not like to raise taxes or cut spending. Furthermore, even if politicians *wanted* to cut spending, this aspect of fiscal policy is becoming increasingly difficult to use because a growing portion of the federal budget is devoted to **mandatory spending**—that is, entitlements such as Social Security, which must be spent by law, and interest on the federal debt, which must be paid (if the United States defaulted on its debt, there would be an international economic meltdown). So reducing the federal deficit by cutting spending is increasingly difficult.

mandatory spending Expenditures that are required by law, such as the funding for Social Security.

discretionary spending Expenditures that can be cut from the budget without changing the underlying law.

With the 2013 deficit running close to $900 billion, Congress would have to eliminate all nondefense **discretionary spending**—spending that can be cut from the budget without changing the underlying law—which is everything other than defense, entitlements, and interest on the debt ($497 billion), to balance the budget. This would literally mean shutting down the State Department; Homeland Security; the Justice Department, which includes the FBI and all federal law enforcement; and the Interior Department, which includes the national park and forest systems; and eliminating all spending on science, including the National Science Foundation and NASA; transportation; the arts and public broadcasting; student loans; and the food stamps and child nutrition programs. Even shutting down all these parts of the government would still leave a deficit of about $400 billion, which would require more than a 60 percent cut in defense spending to balance the budget. The share of the budget comprised by discretionary spending is projected to fall from 67.6 percent of the budget in 1962 to only 29.9 percent by 2015 (see Figure 15.4). This has clear implications for efforts to balance the budget in the future: it cannot be done through cutting discretionary spending alone but will have to include cuts in mandatory spending (such as Social Security and Medicare) and tax increases.

Given this tenuous relationship between fiscal policy and the state of the economy, critics have suggested an alternative rationale for large budget deficits in relatively good economic times. (Recall that a Keynesian account says that the government should run surpluses during good times, and supply-siders argue that tax cuts should produce surpluses rather than deficits.) Instead of being an effort to stimulate the economy, the large tax cuts and budget deficits of the 1980s and early 2000s were, as Reagan's budget director David Stockman called it, an attempt to "starve the beast."[48] That is, large deficits are the only way to cut down

FIGURE » 15.4

MANDATORY AND DISCRETIONARY SPENDING, 1962–2013

The percentage of the budget allocated for discretionary spending has been shrinking since the 1960s. What implications does this have for members of Congress and the president as they try to reduce the federal deficits?

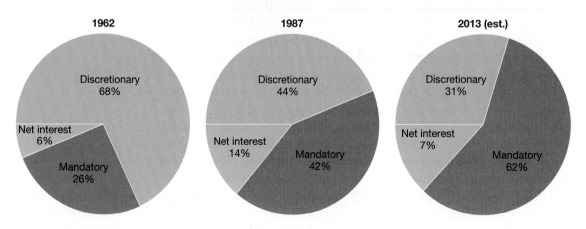

1962
- Discretionary 68%
- Net interest 6%
- Mandatory 26%

1987
- Discretionary 44%
- Net interest 14%
- Mandatory 42%

2013 (est.)
- Discretionary 31%
- Net interest 7%
- Mandatory 62%

Source: The President's Budget for Fiscal Year 2013, Office of Management and Budget, www.Whitehouse.gov/omb/budget (accessed 10/7/12).

TAX RATES AROUND THE WORLD

As we established in our discussion of the size of America's government (Chapter 12), Americans love to complain about their taxes. Ask typical Americans what they think about paying taxes and nobody would rate it high on their list of favorite activities; few would say that they wouldn't mind paying higher taxes. Nonetheless, the United States has one of the lowest overall tax burdens of any developed nation in the world. It is important to examine the overall tax burden because the federal income tax is a relatively small proportion of total taxation for most Americans. In our country, poor to lower-middle-class people pay more in sales taxes and payroll tax than they do in federal income tax. Property taxes and state income taxes also count heavily for many people in figuring out the total tax burden. Overall, the total tax burden in the United States was 34.5 percent of GDP in 2007. Of all the nations listed here, only five countries have a lower tax burden. Most European nations have total tax burdens between 40 and 50 percent, and taxes in Scandinavian countries are more than 50 percent of the size of the economy.

This means that Americans have more disposable income than their counterparts in other countries, but it also means that Americans must pay more for health care and save more for their retirement. The smaller public sector, most significantly in health care and for pensions, also places American companies at a competitive disadvantage with foreign firms that do not have to pay for health care for their employees. For example, General Motors has pointed out for years that they spend more on health care than on steel for the average car they produce. Japanese and German car companies have taken advantage of this situation by grabbing an increasing share of the American market, in part because their national health care plans cover their employees. Health care reform enacted in the United States in 2010 did not alter the basic nature of employer-funded health care, so large corporations such as General Motors are still at a comparative disadvantage.

Therefore, although tax policy is normally considered one of the cornerstones of fiscal policy, it also can play a significant role in helping shape trade policy and trade imbalances between the United States and its trading partners.

COMPARING GLOBAL TAX RATES

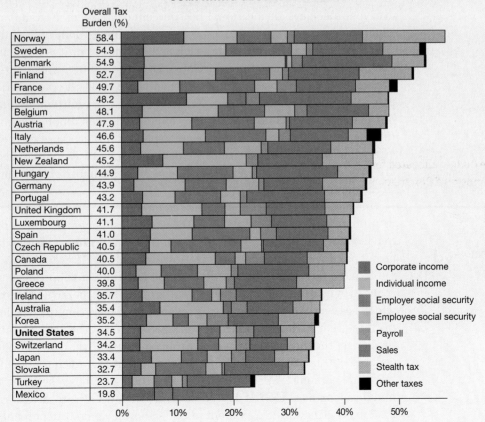

Source: Jack Anderson, "Tax Burden and Spending," Forbes Magazine, *April 13, 2009, www.forbes.com/global/2009/0413/034-tax-burden-spending.html (accessed 5/15/12).*

the size of government. If there is no money available, liberals will not be able to propose new programs and conservatives will be more likely to cut existing programs. The only alternative is raising taxes, which is usually politically unpopular, even though in comparison to other countries our tax bite is relatively small (see the "In Comparison" box). The other possibility, of course, is simply to accept large budget deficits as a permanent part of the economic landscape. While that may be politically tempting, it is not a sustainable strategy in the long run.

REDISTRIBUTIVE IMPLICATIONS OF FISCAL POLICY

Fiscal policy may have a relatively modest impact on the economy, but it determines how the tax burden is distributed and which parts of the economy and policy areas benefit from federal spending—in other words, fiscal policy has *redistributive* implications. There are two ways of thinking about the characteristics of federal taxes: (1) the different types of taxes and (2) their redistributive nature—that is, whether a specific tax is regressive, neutral, or progressive (defined later). There are four major types of federal taxes: personal income taxes, corporate taxes, payroll taxes (for Social Security and Medicare), and excise taxes (such as taxes on cigarettes, alcohol, gasoline, air travel, and telephone lines). The pie charts in Figure 15.5 show how the distribution of tax revenue changed between 1962 and 2010. The proportion of personal income taxes held pretty steady, but excise taxes and corporate taxes fell, and payroll taxes more than doubled.

The increasing share of tax revenue that comes from the payroll tax has important implications for the redistributive nature of taxes. Payroll taxes are **regressive** because everybody pays the same rate of 6.2 percent (with a temporary rate of 4.2 percent in 2011 and 2012) up to a certain income level ($110,100 in 2012; everyone also pays an additional 1.45 percent on all income to support Medicare). Thus someone who earns $110,100 pays the same *amount* of Social Security tax ($6,826) as a wealthy individual such as Bill Gates, but it is a much larger share of that person's income than for Gates. During the 2008 presidential campaign, Barack Obama proposed lifting the earnings cap on the payroll tax to address this inequality and place Social Security on a more secure financial foundation, but the proposal has not been widely supported, even among Democrats. Excise taxes are also regressive—poor people spend a larger share of their income on cigarettes, alcohol, and gas than wealthier people do. Income taxes, in contrast, are **progressive**: upper-income people pay a larger share of their income in taxes than poorer people.

One criticism of President Bush's tax cuts in 2001 and 2002 was that a disproportionate share of the cuts went to the wealthiest people in the country. This may make sense from one perspective, given that the bottom 40 percent of taxpayers do not pay any personal income tax. However, poor and lower-middle-income people do pay a large share of the total payroll tax; thus, that burden could have been reduced by either cutting the payroll tax or increasing the earned income tax credit, which is a way of redistributing tax revenue to poorer people. The effective income tax rate—that is, the total tax a person pays divided by the person's income—for the top fifth of the income distribution dropped from 17.5 percent in 2000 to 13.4 percent in 2009, but their overall share of the income tax revenue collected increased from 81.2 percent to 94.1 percent, because their incomes rose faster than those of middle-income people.[49] If payroll taxes are included, the total average tax rate for the top quintile was 23.2 percent in 2009 and they paid 67.9 percent of all federal taxes. At the same time, the top marginal tax rate is close to the lowest it has been since the 1920s (Figure 15.6).

regressive Taxes that take a larger share of poor people's income than wealthy people's income, such as sales taxes and payroll taxes.

progressive Taxes that require upper-income people to pay a higher tax rate than lower-income people, such as income taxes.

FIGURE » 15.5

FEDERAL REVENUES AND SPENDING, 1962 AND 2013

A much larger share of tax revenue comes from payroll taxes than was true in the 1960s. What implications does this have for the redistributive nature of federal taxes? What have been the biggest changes since the 1960s in the way the federal tax dollar is spent? Are these trends likely to reverse or continue in the next 30 years?

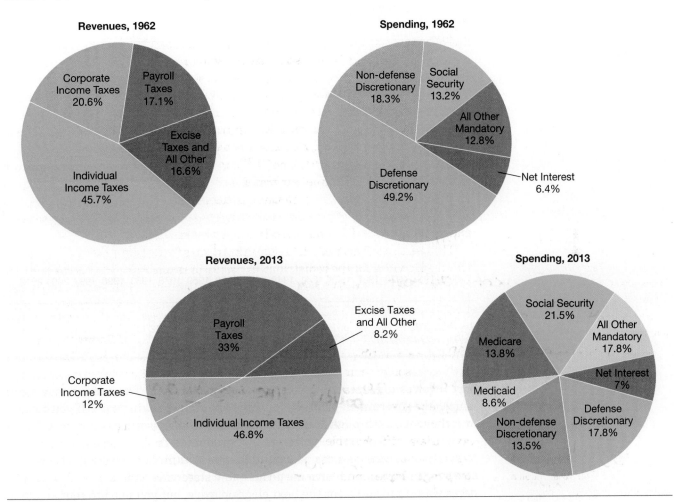

Source: The President's Budget for Fiscal Year 2013, Office of Management and Budget, www.Whitehouse.gov/omb/budget (accessed 10/7/12).

MONETARY POLICY

The starting point of this discussion is to define money. You are probably thinking that you know what the green stuff in your wallet is. You may wish there were more of it, but you know what it is. But if you think about it, money is much more than bills and coins. You probably pay for more things with plastic (debit and credit cards) than coins and currency. Is that money as well? Economists include debit cards in defining money because they represent the money you already have in your checking account, which is the same as cash; but credit cards are not considered money because they are a way of getting a short-term loan. Broader definitions of money also include savings accounts and certificates of deposit. So far, so good. The tricky

FIGURE » 15.6

TOP MARGINAL TAX RATES, 1913–2012

The top marginal tax rate, which is the tax rate paid by the richest Americans on their income above some threshold ($388,350 in 2012), has plummeted in the past 50 years from more than 90 percent to 35 percent. What are the arguments for and against increasing the top marginal tax rate?

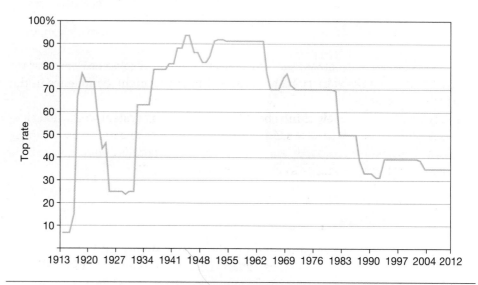

Source: Data from the Internal Revenue Service, "Internal Revenue Bulletin: 2007–45," November 5, 2007, Rev. Proc. 2007-66, www.irs.gov/irb/2007-45_IRB/ar19.html (accessed 5/12/12). 2008–12 rates from www.irs .gov (accessed 11/5/12).

part involves understanding where money comes from. The answer may seem simple: the government prints it. But what about the banking part? If you haven't ever thought this through, it can be confusing or even unsettling.

Consider this example: you have just graduated from college and you want to start your own business as a political consultant. You have volunteered on several campaigns and have even run a few statewide campaigns. Two candidates want to hire you for the next election cycle, but you need to rent an office and buy computers, phones, and other office equipment. This will obviously take some money. So you go to a bank with your business proposal and show them your contracts for the coming election and your plan for repaying the $100,000 loan that you are requesting. To your surprise, the loan officer says yes, and you leave the bank with a checkbook and debit card that have $100,000 behind them! The bank just created $100,000 seemingly out of thin air.[50] How can that be? Doesn't money have to be something more tangible, based on gold or other real assets rather than simply a promise to repay the money? No—at least not in this country since 1933 when the United States abandoned the gold standard. Why doesn't the whole system fall apart? Because it is based on trust and confidence in the banking system. After you get your loan, you could go directly to the computer store and buy $10,000 worth of computers with your new debit card and the sales staff wouldn't ask where the money came from. They would just give you the computers.

The banking system did not always work so smoothly. In fact, it nearly collapsed during the Great Depression in the 1930s. Between 1929 and 1934 nearly 40 percent of banks failed or were closed by the government, and thousands of people lost their life savings because the banks did not have the money to honor all their deposits when everyone wanted to withdraw their money at once. On March 6, 1933, two days after taking the oath of office, Franklin Roosevelt closed all the nation's banks for a full week and only allowed those that were fiscally sound to reopen. In 1933, 4,000 banks were suspended; some of these reopened, but many did not.[51] In order to restore confidence in the banking system, Congress passed the Glass–Steagall Act in 1933, which separated commercial and investment banking and created the Federal Deposit Insurance Corporation, which insured all deposits up to $5,000 (today it is $250,000). Separate legislation also tightened control of the stock market by creating the Securities and Exchange Commission. In 1934, only 61 banks were suspended, and almost overnight, confidence in the system was restored.

Today most people rarely think about how the banking system works and simply assume that their money is safe. But now that we have gotten you thinking about where money comes from, we will provide more details about the banking system by examining the targets and tools of monetary policy.

TARGETS OF MONETARY POLICY

The Fed monitors levels of bank lending, the money supply, and interest rates and tries to meet specific targets set at its monthly meetings. Bank lending is important to monitor and regulate because it is the source of most new money in the economy. This is crucial for economic growth because businesses borrow money to expand, and as they grow, they add jobs. If credit is tight and businesses cannot borrow money, economic growth will suffer, as became painfully evident in late 2008 and 2009. Large public corporations can raise money by selling shares of their company in the stock market, but small businesses do not have this option.

The second target of monetary policy, the money supply, is also central to economic growth and directly related to levels of lending activity. The Fed can influence the amount of money in the system by making it easier or harder for banks to lend money. According to the **monetarist theory** of macroeconomic policy, the amount of money in circulation is the most important determinant of economic activity and inflation. If there is too much money chasing too few goods, there could be inflationary pressure on the economy and prices might rise too quickly.[52] In contrast, if there isn't enough money available, a recession could occur.

Perhaps the most obvious targets of monetary policy are interest rates. Changing interest rates affect the economy by making borrowing money either cheaper or more expensive. Businesses and consumers are more likely to borrow if the interest rate is 6 percent than if it is 12 percent. Consumer purchases of big-ticket items, things that are financed by borrowing rather than purchased with cash, also increase when interest rates are low and dry up when interest rates are high. That is why so many appliance stores and car dealers advertise, "Zero dollars down, and zero percent interest until next January!" Entire sectors of the economy, such as housing, construction, consumer durables, and cars, are very sensitive to interest rates.

THE SACRILEGIOUS CANDIDATE.

UNTIL 1971, EACH U.S. DOLLAR WAS backed by a specific amount of gold. In the late 1800s presidential candidate William Jennings Bryan railed against the burdensome "cross of gold" and argued for a silver-backed currency. But since 1971, the value of the U.S. dollar depends not on gold or silver but on the banking system and international currency markets.

monetarist theory The idea that the amount of money in circulation (the money supply) is the primary influence on economic activity and inflation.

TOOLS OF MONETARY POLICY

reserve requirement The minimum amount of money that a bank is required to have on hand to back up its assets.

discount rate The interest rate that a bank must pay on a short-term loan from the Federal Reserve Bank.

federal funds rate (FFR) The interest rate that a bank must pay on an overnight loan from another bank.

HYPERINFLATION IN GERMANY, Hungary, and other parts of Europe between the world wars was so high that some countries' currency became essentially worthless. In Germany in 1923, it was cheaper to burn money than to buy wood, as this woman demonstrates—using several million deutschemarks as kindling.

What can the Fed do to meet targets it sets on credit availability, the money supply, and interest rates? There are three central tools of monetary policy. The **reserve requirement** is the most obvious and potentially powerful tool for affecting the availability of credit, but it isn't used as often as the other two tools. Banks are required to have a certain amount of money in reserve to make sure they have cash on hand to cover withdrawals. The banking crisis of the early 1930s was created by "runs on the banks" when people panicked and all wanted to withdraw their money at the same time. Even today, if everyone decided to take all their money out at once, the banking system would collapse, because banks are required to have only 10 percent of all deposits on reserve.

By simply changing the amount of money that banks are required to hold for every deposit, the Fed can have a big impact on the amount of money that banks can lend. For example, requiring banks to hold 15 percent of all deposits in reserve instead of 10 percent would contract the amount of money they could lend, whereas dropping the requirement to 5 percent would have the opposite effect. However, because changing the reserve requirement has such a powerful impact on the economy, the Fed has rarely used this tool.[53]

Interest rates are more difficult to manage than the reserve requirement. With the reserve requirement, the Fed simply announces the change in the rate. With interest rates, there is only one rate—the **discount rate**—that the Fed sets directly. This is the rate that the Fed charges to member banks for short-term loans. However, it is far less important as a policy tool than the **federal funds rate (FFR)**, the rate that member banks charge one another on overnight loans, which are the short-term loans that banks use to meet their reserve requirements. Beginning in 1995, the FFR has been the central interest rate target for the Fed.[54] The FFR is set by the demand for overnight loans that are necessary to settle accounts, but the Fed greatly affects those rates.

To make this process clearer, let's go back to our example of the enterprising campaign consultant who got the $100,000 loan. If the bank that gave the loan also had some unexpected withdrawals during that business day, its "vault cash" at the end of the day may have been short of the 10 percent reserve requirement. The bank would have to go to the federal funds market and borrow money from a bank that had excess reserves on that given day. This process of borrowing and lending allows money to flow smoothly throughout the banking system. If reserves are tight all around the country, the price of the short-term loans will be bid up and the FFR will rise. If this happens, the Fed can inject more reserves into the system to keep the FFR at its target (we explain how that happens in the next section). The FFR has a broader impact on the economy because many short-term interest rates track the FFR quite closely.

Despite the Fed's ability to influence short-term interest rates, it has only indirect impact on long-term interest rates, including consumer rates such as mortgages and home equity loans. These rates are set by the market—specifically by the expectations of the bond market for inflation. If an investor thinks that inflation will increase from 3 percent to 6 percent over the next five years, the investor will demand a higher interest rate for lending his money to the government or a corporation than if he thinks inflation will hold steady at about 3 percent. For example, starting in June 2004, the Fed raised the target FFR 17 times in quarter-point increments from 1 percent to 5.25 percent by June 2006. Short-term consumer rates, such as the prime interest rate (the loan rate given to banks' best customers), rose in lockstep with the FFR from 4 percent to 8.25 percent over that period. However, long-term rates, such as the 10-year Treasury note, were all over the place, actually *falling* from May 2004 to June 2005 by three-fourths of a percentage point at the same time the FFR had *increased* by 2.25 percent, much to the surprise of many financial experts.[55] Clearly the bond market felt confident that long-term inflation was being held in check, because it did not demand higher interest rates for long-term loans. Similarly, when the Fed lowered the FFR in 2008 to fight the recession and credit market freeze, the short-term rates followed. Long-term rates also initially dropped but then increased through much of 2009 as inflation fears picked up, only to fall to record lows in 2012 as those concerns dissipated.[56]

The last tool that the Fed uses to meet its monetary targets is **open market operations**—the buying and selling of securities. This is the most important tool because it influences the FFR and the level of bank reserves, and thus the money supply. If the Fed wants to increase the money supply and put downward pressure on the FFR, it will purchase securities such as government bonds from a bank. The bank gives the Fed its bond, and the Fed deposits the appropriate amount of money into the bank's account at the Fed. The bank can use this money to support new loans. Where does the Fed gets its money to buy the bond from the bank? Well, the Fed simply creates the money. You probably have heard the claim that if the government wants to, it could just "print money" to pay for its programs and policies. That claim is literally true, but it would be completely irresponsible. Any government that would run the printing presses to pay for its programs, rather than raising the money through taxes, fees, and borrowing, would soon find itself with hyperinflation as experienced in Germany, Poland, Austria, and Hungary after World War I. (The worst inflation ever recorded was in Hungary after World War II: between July 1945 and August 1946, prices rose by a factor of 30,000,000, 000,000,000,000,000,000!)[57] Our government prints money only to meet the demand for currency from its member banks. However, the Fed's purchase of a government security is like "printing money" and has the same potential inflationary impact, so this powerful tool must be used only when new money is needed in the system. The tool may also be used to contract the money supply or raise interest rates; if this is the desired outcome, the Fed will sell government securities. The member bank will give the Fed money to cover the cost of the bond and therefore take money out of circulation.

The FFR has not always been the target of Fed policy. In the early 1980s, the money supply was the most important target. The focus on the money supply lasted for only a few years, and by 1983 the Fed shifted back to targeting the FFR and the availability of credit more generally. Monetarist theory had fallen out of favor because the money supply became more difficult to measure and control as the banking industry offered an increasing array of types of bank deposits, such as interest-bearing checking accounts. Also, the velocity of money (the number of times money changes hands in a certain period) became much more volatile, which increased the difficulty of predicting the economic impact of a change in the money supply.[58]

In the late 1920s, the Fed took an accommodationist approach of using the discount window (its loans to member banks) to provide additional credit to banks when the economy was expanding and to reduce credit when businesses were not expanding and didn't need loans. At first, this seems to make perfect sense to support the general direction of the economy. But on further reflection it is like

open market operations The process by which the Federal Reserve System buys and sells securities to influence the money supply.

pouring gasoline on a fire that is already burning at the level you like, or like pouring water on a fire that is just getting started. This accommodationist policy contributed to the onset of the Great Depression and the increase in the Depression's severity in the early 1930s by choking off the supply of money just when it was most needed. Critics argued that the Fed should have acted proactively, in a countercyclical way. Rather than simply saying, "Well, there aren't any banks that want to borrow money from us, so there isn't much we can do to stimulate the economy," the Fed should have "flooded the street with money," as the famous banker Benjamin Strong argued in 1928.[59] Starting in 1935, the Fed adopted this countercyclical approach, attempting to stimulate the economy when it started to shrink and cool it down when it grew too fast.

Fed chair Ben Bernanke used this approach to help stop the "credit crunch" that emerged with the meltdown of the subprime mortgage market and related problems in the bond markets in 2008. The Fed increased its balance sheet (its statement of assets and liabilities) from $927 billion on September 10, 2008, to an eye-popping $2.26 trillion by November 11, 2008. About $1.6 trillion of the money injected into the economy came through efforts to stabilize short-term lending, money market funds, and the bailout of AIG (among other things). By October 2012, those loans had been almost entirely repaid as credit markets stabilized. However, overall Fed assets remained at $2.26 trillion, as the securities held by the Fed climbed from $514 billion to $2 trillion from February 2009 to September 2010 (including $1.1 trillion in mortgage-backed securities that the Fed purchased from stressed financial institutions).[60] In the next two years the Fed continued to expand its injection of money into the economy by purchasing an additional $600 billion in securities. This unprecedented intervention in the financial sector clearly prevented a serious crisis, but as noted, critics argue that the Fed has become too powerful and unaccountable a player in economic policy making.

REGULATORY POLICY

Government regulation has a huge impact on the economy. For example, the federal government regulates the quality of food and water, the safety of workplaces and airspaces, and the integrity of the banking and finance system. In general, regulations address market failures such as monopolies, imperfect information, and negative externalities (explained later). There are two main types of regulation: economic and social. Economic regulation sets prices or conditions on entry of firms into an industry, whereas social regulation addresses issues of quality and safety.[61]

ECONOMIC AND SOCIAL REGULATION

A common type of economic regulation concerns price regulation of monopolies. A monopoly occurs when a single firm controls the entire market for a product so it is not subject to competition. When this happens, the monopoly could charge extremely high prices if the government did not regulate it. Sometimes a "natural monopoly" occurs because getting into a specific business is so costly that it only makes sense to have one company. For example, to have more than one water company in a given town or city wouldn't make sense because it costs so much to install water pipes. In this instance there is only one company, but the government regulates the prices that company can charge; alternatively, the water system may be owned by the local government.

When the competitive situation is not a natural monopoly, a large firm may act in a monopolistic way to restrict competition—for example, by slashing prices to drive the competition out of business. As soon as all competitors go out of business, the monopoly is free to raise prices again. Concern about this type of behavior led to the first two significant laws aimed at economic regulation: the Interstate Commerce Act (1887), which created the Interstate Commerce Commission to regulate railroad rates, and the Sherman Antitrust Act (1890), which served to break up Standard Oil in 1910, among other monopolies.

More common than a true monopoly are firms that control most of a market rather than all of it and start acting like a monopoly. For example, Microsoft was sued by the Justice Department and 19 states in 1998 for trying to quash its competition in the rapidly growing area of Internet browsers. Microsoft claimed that Internet Explorer was an integral part of its Windows operating system, while government prosecutors argued that it was a separate piece of software that was being given away for free, putting competitors like Netscape at a huge disadvantage. The district court judge agreed with the Justice Department and ordered that Microsoft be broken up into a Windows-based company and another company that would sell Internet Explorer and other programs. This ruling was overturned on appeal. In the meantime, George W. Bush was elected to his first term as president, and his Justice Department announced that it would not challenge the appeals court ruling. Instead, it proposed a settlement that required Microsoft to share its application programming interfaces with third-party companies.[62] This settlement was challenged by several states but upheld by an appeals court in 2004.

The Microsoft example offers two lessons. First, regulation affects our daily lives in ways that may not be obvious. The extent to which Microsoft dominates the software industry is determined, in part, by the extent to which the government regulates its behavior. Second, politics plays a key role in this process. An important event in the Microsoft case was the election of a president who took a less aggressive stance on regulating potential monopolies than his predecessor had. Recall that Republicans tend to favor a strong role for the free market and a pro-business perspective, which requires a smaller role for government regulation, whereas Democrats generally favor more government regulation to protect the interests of consumers (in the Microsoft case, a broader range of options for Internet browsers), the environment, and workers.

The most common market failures that lead to social regulation are negative externalities: when the costs of a firm's behavior are not entirely borne by the firm but are passed on to other people. When this happens, the firm produces more of an unwanted good than is socially desirable. The classic example is pollution. In a free market, the owners of a coal-fired power plant do not bear the cost of the pollution spewing out of its smokestacks. The people who live downwind from the plant bear the cost. Therefore, the power plant owners have little incentive to curb pollution unless the government regulates it. Other examples of agencies that set social regulations are those that promote safety, such as the National Highway Traffic Safety Administration, the Consumer Product Safety Commission, and the Occupational Safety and Health Administration.

PEAK PERIODS OF REGULATION

Other than the creation of the Interstate Commerce Commission (ICC) and the Federal Trade Commission to regulate monopolies, the federal government has experienced two big spurts of regulation: the mid-1930s and the mid-1960s through the mid-1970s. Most regulation in the first period was economic. In addition to the creation of the Federal Communications Commission (FCC), the Securities and Exchange Commission, the Federal Deposit Insurance Corporation, and the Federal Power Commission, the ICC expanded its regulatory reach into trucking, water barges, oil pipelines, and buses in the 1930s. Other agencies have also expanded the scope of their activities, such as the FCC, which was created to regulate radio but now is also involved in television, cable, and other forms of communication. One type of economic regulation that came to the fore in 2009 and 2010 concerned the financial sector. As noted, Alan Greenspan, among others, attributed the economic meltdown to various market failures, which implies a need for new regulations. Congress followed through in 2010, passing a massive financial sector reform bill that focused on such topics as the "too big to fail" problem, greater protections for consumers in the financial services sector, derivatives trading, and the securitization of subprime mortgages. Others claim that new action was not needed because it was regulators, not regulations, that failed.

Most social regulation came in the 1960s and 1970s as citizens became more concerned about public safety and air and water quality. Public interest groups such as the Sierra Club, Common Cause, the Environmental Defense Fund, Friends of the Earth, Greenpeace, and Public Citizen (the group led by consumer activist Ralph Nader) all pushed for environmental and public safety legislation.[63] Some high-profile reports and events also had an impact on the push for more social regulation. Ralph Nader's 1965 exposé *Unsafe at Any Speed* about the Chevrolet Corvair, and Cleveland's polluted Cuyahoga River catching fire in 1969, increased the pressure on politicians to address these concerns. Congress responded by creating the Environmental Protection Agency and passing the Clean Air Act and Clean Water Act. The range of dangerous chemicals that have been regulated since this time is extensive: the pesticide DDT, asbestos, lead (in both paint and gasoline), chlorofluorocarbons, phosphates, and arsenic, to name a few.[64]

Social regulation has continued to enjoy strong political support, but Congress has pared back economic regulation in the past 30 years, with one exception being the financial sector, for which regulations were strengthened in 2010. The trend toward deregulation started with the airline industry in the mid-1970s. For years economists had argued that the government was keeping the price of airline tickets artificially high by limiting the number of airlines and restricting competition. In 1978 Congress passed the Airline Deregulation Act, which got the federal government out of the business of regulating entry and pricing in the airline industry. The impact of deregulation is mixed. Overall, consumers have benefited from lower ticket prices,[65] more airlines flying more routes to bigger cities, and a rapid expansion in air travel since 1978, which means that flying is now much more common for middle-class Americans. However, many small cities lost air service in the 1980s, despite Congress's promise that this

SOCIAL REGULATIONS HAVE ECONOMIC effects. For example, while most people want a cleaner environment and less pollution, regulations that reduce pollution impose costs on companies.

would not happen, and people who live in cities like Minneapolis, Minnesota, or Charlotte, North Carolina, pay more for their tickets on comparable flights than people who live in Chicago, Atlanta, New York, or other cities that have more competition. Over the past 30 years, Congress passed laws that deregulated many other major industries, including banking, trucking, telephone service, radio, and public utilities. In each instance there have been many advantages for consumers but also some costs.

THE POLITICS OF REGULATION

Regulatory policy also involves interbranch politics between Congress and the bureaucracy. Even when members of Congress agree on some general policy goal—for example, limiting air pollution—they often cannot agree on the precise mechanisms for achieving that goal, so they delegate authority to a regulatory agency. As discussed in Chapter 12, this produces a "principal-agent problem" in which Congress (the principal) cannot be sure that the bureaucracy (the agent) will implement policy according to their goals. A related concern is that the regulatory agency will not be responsive to the wishes of Congress because it has been "captured" by the interests it is supposed to regulate. The Food and Drug Administration, the Federal Aviation Administration, and the U.S. Department of Agriculture, among others, have been accused of serving the industries they are supposed to regulate rather than protecting consumers.[66]

Another area in which regulatory policy has generated some political heat concerns the debate about the trade-off between regulation and economic growth. Regulations impose costs on the free market, which may limit job growth. However, in recent years, two developments in the area of environmental regulation have attempted to address that concern. First, economists have long argued for introducing more market incentives and reducing government regulation to achieve environmental goals. Politicians are starting to listen. In the 2008 presidential campaign, both John McCain and Barack Obama endorsed the idea of "cap and trade" policies as a market approach to reducing carbon emissions (more recently McCain reversed his position, but the approach still has some bipartisan support). Environmentalists have learned that using market principles can work to their advantage, as shown by the example of grazing rights in the West, discussed in the "You Decide" box.

Second, rather than simply regulating old sources of dirtier energy, President Obama has emphasized creating "green jobs." In his 2012 State of the Union message he said, "Transitioning to cleaner sources of energy will enhance our national security, protect the environment and public health, and grow our economy and create new jobs." The White House projects that developing cleaner natural gas to replace other sources of carbon-based energy would create 600,000 jobs over 10 years and tax incentives to promote alternative energy would produce another 100,000 jobs.[67]

So while political debates over regulatory policy may still be quite intense, common ground may be found in pursuing market solutions to regulatory problems. In general, the public interest is often served by regulations that protect the environment, ensure the safety of the food supply, and regulate the dumping of hazardous chemicals, whether it is through traditional economic regulations or more recent market approaches. In each instance, *politics* ends up defining how the public interest is served through regulation.

GRAZING RIGHTS AND FREE MARKET ENVIRONMENTALISM

Imagine you are a Republican U.S. House member who represents a western state. You are a firm believer in the free market, capitalism, and limited government. In other words, whenever possible you would like people to make choices in the free market without government interference or regulation. By the way, this conveniently is a view that is held by a large majority of your constituents. You also are a strong supporter of grazing rights for ranchers in your state. You have often done battle with environmentalists who want to reserve more public lands for recreational uses and conservation than for grazing cattle. On this issue, your constituents are more divided: there is strong support for ranchers, but an increasing proportion of the residents in your district are dependent on tourism.

The scenario that you have to consider here is an actual case that was first publicized in a *New York Times* op-ed piece.[a] The case involves a fifth-generation rancher in southern Utah named Dell LeFevre. He is no friend of environmentalism, saying, "We've got Easterners who don't know the land telling us what to do with it. I am a bitter old cowboy." His bitterness was deepened back in 1991 when he found two dozen of his cows shot to death. He thinks the deed was done by an environmentalist who was trying to get ranchers to leave a scenic part of the Escalante River canyon. So he seems to be a very unlikely candidate to have sat down with an environmentalist named Bill Hedden to accomplish that very goal of ending ranching in the area. Hedden works for a group called the Grand Canyon Trust (GCT) that, as the *Times* article explained, "doesn't use lobbyists or lawsuits (or guns) to drive out ranchers. These environmentalists get land the old-fashioned way. They buy it." Hedden spent about $100,000 to buy and retire the grazing rights from LeFevre for this scenic canyon area. The environmentalists are happy because the vegetation is coming back, and LeFevre is happy because he doesn't have to battle the environmentalists anymore and was able to buy grazing rights in a different area that is better for his cattle. Supporters of "free market environmentalism" say this is a perfect example of allowing the market to determine the best use of the land. If an environmentalist is willing to buy a rancher's grazing rights, this means that the market has determined that hiking and conservation have a greater value than grazing for that piece of land.

If the story ended here, there would be no controversy for you to consider. But as you probably guessed, the story does not end here. Local groups, such as the Canyon Country Rural Alliance, which opposed all limitations on ranchers' grazing rights, lobbied Congress and the Interior Department to disallow such arrangements that remove grazing rights from some public lands. Bowing to pressure, the Interior Department decided that "only Congress may permanently exclude lands from grazing use," so GCT had no guarantee that the Bureau of Land Management wouldn't change its mind and allow grazing. The process of resolving this conflict bounced around the Interior Department and the federal courts for nearly 10 years.

Using free-market forces is an increasingly common way to address a variety of environmental issues, from grazing and water rights to air pollution and global warming.

In the meantime, GCT went to Plan B from the "if you can't lick 'em, join 'em" school of thought: they decided to become ranchers. If the Interior Department wouldn't grant permanent conservation use permits on land designated for grazing, they would buy some cattle. GCT is now one of the largest ranchers in the Colorado Plateau with 1,000 acres of private land and grazing permits that cover 860,000 acres of federal and state lands, including a large part of the Kaibab National Forest adjacent to the North Rim of the Grand Canyon. They are managing the land in an eco-friendly manner with only 800 head of cattle. Though it may seem odd that an environmental group had to take up ranching to get the policy outcome they wanted, it was a compromise that made all sides of the dispute relatively happy. As one opponent of GCT put it, "We turned them from environmentalists into cowboys. I guess what they can do is get their cows and start losing money like the rest of us."[b]

If you were the member of Congress representing this district, what would you decide to do?

Critical **Thinking** Questions

1. Would you support the limitations on permanently removing grazing rights because they are consistent with the desires of many of your constituents? If so, how would you reconcile this with your free market views, and how would you justify the decision to your constituents who support free market environmentalism?

2. Does the compromise position of GCT taking up ranching strike you as a reasonable middle ground? Why or why not?

TRADE POLICY AND THE BALANCE OF PAYMENTS

In many ways, policy aimed at influencing trade is the most difficult area of economic policy making because many factors that shape trade policy are beyond policy makers' control. The strength of the dollar relative to other currencies, consumer tastes, the low cost of labor in developing nations (especially China and India), and economic conditions worldwide all influence the trade balance but are extremely difficult to control.

When the dollar is strong, imports are relatively cheap in the United States and U.S. exports are expensive. Therefore, if the United States is running a trade deficit, it would like the value of the dollar to fall. However, there isn't much it can do about the value of the dollar because that value is determined by international currency markets. How does the value of the dollar affect the trade deficit? Consider the following example. As of October 2012, a euro was worth about $1.30. Therefore, a BMW 135i that would sell for 30,000 euros in Germany would go for about $39,000 in the United States, while a Cadillac CTS that would retail in America for $37,000 would sell for about 28,500 euros in Europe—though this example doesn't factor in shipping costs, dealer incentives, higher taxes in Europe, and so on.

Now see what happens if the dollar falls in value so a euro is worth $1.50. It may seem backward to say that the value of the dollar falls when the value of a euro goes from $1.25 to $1.50, but think of it this way: at the new exchange rate, it takes more dollars to buy the same number of euros, so the dollar is worth less. Now that Cadillac could be purchased in Germany for 24,666 euros and the BMW would still cost 30,000 euros, while the BMW would cost an American consumer $45,000 and the Cadillac is still $37,000. Nothing has changed except the value of the dollar, but suddenly the car buyer's choices have changed dramatically. In both countries the Cadillac has become a much better bargain, and therefore, theoretically, Cadillac sales (and sales of other GM models, as well as those of Chrysler and Ford) should increase and BMW (and Mercedes, Volkswagen, MINI Cooper, etc.) sales should fall.

We say "theoretically" because of the second factor—consumer tastes. If consumers are willing to pay an increasing premium for foreign goods, then a weaker dollar may not help the trade deficit. There isn't much policy makers can do about consumer tastes, despite the ongoing campaign urging citizens to "buy American." The low cost of labor is another factor that policy makers cannot do much to influence. If a foreign firm pays its workers a weekly wage that is equal to what American workers make in an hour for the same job, the foreign firm has a huge competitive advantage. Consequently, the United States has been flooded with cheap consumer goods from nations where labor is very cheap. Low prices are good for American consumers, but they come at the price of large trade deficits and lost American jobs. Furthermore, foreign firms sometimes absorb some currency fluctuations and do not raise the price of their goods in the United States as the dollar falls in value relative to their currency. The final factor—the strength of foreign economies—is also outside the control of American policy makers. If foreign economies are weak, consumers abroad do not have the income to purchase U.S. exports.

Though it is difficult to control trade outcomes, Congress and the president still try by altering trade policies. The main target of trade policy is the trade balance: the difference between the total value of our exports and imports. In recent years the balances reached record deficits exceeding $830 billion a year in 2008 before falling back to $476 billion for the 12-month period ending in June 2012 (Figure 15.7). The

MANY AMERICAN CONSUMER products, including cars, clothing, and electronics, are made overseas because labor is so much cheaper in developing countries. Even people who want to "buy American" have a difficult time, given the increasing globalization of multinational corporations.

FIGURE » 15.7

TRADE DEFICITS, 1974–2011

The trade deficit remains high. Which groups are most likely to support policies aimed at reducing the trade deficit, and which groups would oppose these policies?

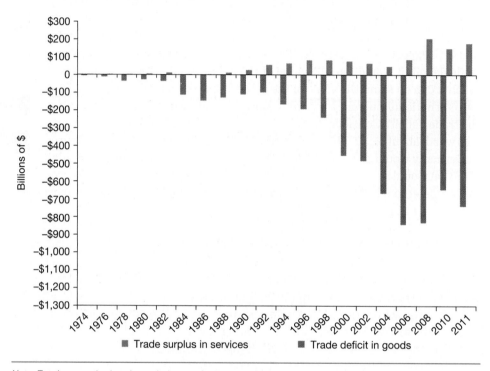

■ Trade surplus in services   ■ Trade deficit in goods

Note: Totals are calculated on a balance of payment basis.

Source: Data from the U.S. Department of Commerce, Bureau of Economic Analysis, International Economic Accounts: Trade in Goods and Services, www.bea.gov/iTable/iTable.cfm?ReqID=681step=1 (accessed 10/8/12).

current account deficit, the broadest measure of the balance of payments including investments, has also been running at record levels. Economists have warned that deficits of this level are not sustainable. There is increasing consensus that something must change—either we need to stop buying as many imports and sell more exports, or the value of the dollar must fall to help make this happen.

The trade deficits have to be financed with borrowing from overseas. In the past, these loans came largely from foreign investment by private individuals who saw greater returns on their investments in the United States than in other countries. The net international investment position at the end of 2011 was –$4.1 trillion (that is, the value of foreign investments in the United States exceeded the value of U.S. investments abroad).[68] Foreign investors now own about 53 percent of publicly owned foreign debt, with Japan and China buying more than any other country in the past 10 years. Why does this matter? If these foreign governments decide to stop investing in American assets or even to start selling them, interest rates will have to rise to attract buyers for our debt, perhaps dramatically.

The types of policies that can be used to reduce the trade deficit are protectionist policies such as trade sanctions, tariffs, and quotas, or attempts to reduce the value of the dollar. Advocates for protectionist policies argue that "free trade" is a myth and we are being taken advantage of by nations that engage in unfair trade practices while selling goods in our open markets. Former senator Ernest F. Hollings once said, "We hear those in the national Congress running around saying, 'Free trade, free trade, I am for free trade,' when they know free trade is like dry water. There is no such thing."[69] It is only fair, they argue, that we set up trade barriers or impose quotas to support our own goods and protect American jobs. Although broadly based protectionist policies have been rare in the past couple of decades, U.S. policy makers have applied protection in selected markets. For example, in 1983 Harley Davidson won special trade protection from the Reagan administration that raised tariffs on imported Japanese motorcycles from 4 percent to 49 percent. In September 2009, President Obama imposed a 35 percent tariff on Chinese tires.

In general, Congress and the president have supported free trade much more than protectionism. Economists have long touted the virtues of exploiting "comparative advantage" through free trade. In 1817 David Ricardo was the first to develop this notion with the example of the production of wine and cloth in Portugal and Britain.[70] According to the argument, Portugal should produce excess wine and export it to Britain because that is where their greatest *relative* advantage lay. Even if it seems counterintuitive, Britain should produce excess cloth and export it, even if Portugal could produce cloth more cheaply than Britain. By focusing on this comparative advantage, free trade maximizes wealth in both countries.[71]

Congress has pursued free trade policies through the North American Free Trade Agreement in 1993, the Uruguay round of the General Agreement on Tariffs and Trade in 1994, fast-track authorization for the U.S. trade representative to negotiate trade agreements with minimal congressional interference (2002), most-favored-nation trading status for China (2000), and the Central American Free Trade Agreement (2005), which reduced barriers and opened markets. Critics of the laws say that they do not provide adequate protections for workers and the environment, promoting a "race to the bottom" to cut costs while putting additional pressure on American jobs and wages.

Current estimates are that the United States could lose 3 million jobs overseas between 2000 and 2015, even in areas thought to be our comparative advantage, such as computer programming. When programmers or computer customer support staff in India earn about one-tenth of what they make in the United States, it is difficult for American firms to compete in international markets unless they employ cheaper labor.[72] The same pressures have led to the virtual extinction of some U.S. industries, such as the manufacturing of consumer electronics, textiles, shoes, and, increasingly, clothing. Thus, while free trade generally enhances worldwide economic growth, there can be significant consequences for specific industries.

With the stakes this high, it is not surprising that politics often plays a central role in trade policy. There are two main explanations for the nature of political influence on trade policy: constituency and ideology.[73] The constituency explanation sees the two major parties representing different groups—Democrats and labor, Republicans and capital—which tends to make the Democrats more protectionist and the Republicans more supportive of free trade. Elaborations of this view agree with the central tendency but note divisions within each constituency. For example, auto- and steelworkers' unions are much more protectionist than dockworkers' unions because any industry with strong exports will support free trade, whereas those that have relatively few exports but are vulnerable to cheap imports are more likely to be protectionist. The ideological explanation focuses on the bipartisan consensus on trade that emerged after the Great Depression, which was seen as having been caused in part by the protective tariffs of the 1930 Smoot-Hawley Act.[74] As with the theories of regulation, both perspectives explain part of the truth. Our political leaders largely support a free trade ideology, but there are divisions along constituency lines on some legislation.

CONCLUSION

There is a common perception that economic policies would work better if we could just take politics out of the economic policy-making process. But that would be like saying "football would be better if we could eliminate the contact," or "poker would be better if we could take out the element of chance." Economic policy making is inherently political. It isn't possible or desirable to have economic policy produced by economists who would deftly push and pull the levers of growth, productivity, and efficiency, implementing their economic theories without interference from politicians. Politics must enter into this process. Economic policy determines who wins and who loses, and elected leaders must be involved in this process if representative democracy is to have any meaning. This is especially true of the budget process because the redistributive implications of taxing and spending are so clear, but as we have discussed, even monetary policy is not insulated from politics. This role for politics is guaranteed by our system of checks and balances: Congress, the president, and to some extent the courts all have a hand in shaping economic policy. The clash between politics and economic theory and the conflicted nature of economic policy making can be illustrated with a few examples.

We discussed earlier the limitation of implementing Keynesian economic theories in fiscal policy. Often, political considerations make it impossible to implement the swift, targeted action called for in the theory. That is because the budget inherently involves debates over some central political questions: How large should the government be? How progressive should the income tax be? Should the millionaires' tax be adopted to reduce income inequality? Should budget deficits be allowed to expand to put pressure on government spending, rather than to stimulate the economy? These are not purely economic questions but also political ones that must be answered through debate and conflict between the opposing parties and branches of government. This is especially true of the debate over tax policy in the 2012 presidential election. President Obama campaigned to raise taxes on the wealthiest 2 percent of Americans, whereas Mitt Romney wanted to reduce tax rates and simplify the tax code by reducing loopholes and deductions. With control of Congress remaining divided through 2013–14, it is likely that fiscal policy will be determined by the politics of compromise more than the purity of economic theory.

Monetary policy is supposed to be more insulated from politics, but even here political pressures are evident. One important example is how fiscal policy (taxing and spending decisions by Congress and the president) can put pressure on monetary policy (the Fed's decisions concerning interest rates and the money supply). With the large budget deficits that the government is currently running, it can become difficult to finance $1.2 trillion a year in new debt. If the demand from private investors, banks, and foreign governments is not sufficient, interest rates may have to rise to attract enough money. This could run counter to Fed policy, which may be concerned that a large increase in long-term interest rates could lead to a recession. However, the alternative would be for the Fed to step in to buy the additional debt, which can create inflationary pressures on the economy. This can put the Fed in a difficult position. The chair of the Fed routinely warns Congress and the president that our budget deficits, debt, and current accounts deficit are not sustainable, but there isn't anything that the chair of the Fed can do to make them change their political decisions about what they think are the best economic policies for the country.

Another useful example of the clash between politics and economic theory is the debate over the proper role for the U.S. government in addressing the 2008 financial meltdown. Many Republicans resisted the active involvement of the government in credit and financial markets because of their belief in the corrective power of markets. Even as the Bush administration responded by bailing out Freddie Mac and Fannie Mae, AIG, and money market funds; buying up bad debt; and directly investing in banks, there was political resistance to telling banks how to use the federal assistance. European leaders, in contrast, insisted that banks use the infusion of government capital to begin making more loans. But in the United States, the Fed and Treasury did not require anything of the banks that were provided with desperately needed funds.

Democrats in Congress fumed that taxpayers' money should not be used for paying stock dividends or bonuses for management. They also argued that banks that took federal money should be required to lend more money to businesses (thus helping solve the central problem of the credit freeze), rather than just holding the cash or using it to acquire other banks. This reveals the fundamental difference between Democrats' and Republicans' approaches to the problem: many Democrats advocated more intervention and government regulation, and Republicans tended to favor less regulation and more reliance on market forces.

The consequences of figuring out the right approach are higher than at any time since the 1930s. The globalization of financial markets means that problems in the United States spread like wildfire through the rest of the world. Within a month of the start of the crisis, emerging capitalist economies such as Hungary, Iceland, Belarus, Poland, Ukraine, and Pakistan teetered on the brink of financial collapse. Greece's debt problems have put pressure on the entire euro zone and concern remains that Spain or Italy might be next. If entire countries start to fail, rather than specific financial institutions, it would be increasingly difficult to contain the damage.[75]

These examples of the budget, financing the debt, and the financial rescue plan are not intended to suggest that politics shouldn't enter into the economic policy-making process. Indeed, just the opposite. They are excellent illustrations of the themes that politics is everywhere and politics is conflictual. It shouldn't be surprising when politics enters the economic policy debate. Elected leaders should be responsive to what their constituents think about the central questions concerning the direction of the economy.

GOALS OF ECONOMIC POLICY

▶ Explain the main purposes of government involvement in the economy. **Pages 607–13**

SUMMARY

Policy makers' pursuit of economic goals—such as full employment, stable prices, or growth—is a complex process. Not only is the government unable to attain these goals on its own, but also the pursuit of one goal often comes at the expense of other economic goals.

KEY TERMS

full employment (p. 607)

economic depression (p. 608)

Council of Economic Advisers (p. 608)

inflation (p. 608)

gross domestic product (GDP) (p. 610)

balanced budget (p. 611)

budget deficit (p. 611)

current account (p. 611)

trade deficit (p. 611)

PRACTICE QUIZ QUESTIONS

1. The Council of Economic Advisors was established _____.

   a) by the Employment Act of 1946
   b) by the Balanced Budget Amendment
   c) in Article I of the Constitution
   d) in Article III of the Constitution
   e) by the Federal Reserve Board

2. Technically, full employment means an unemployment level of about _____.
   a) 0 percent
   b) 2 percent
   c) 5 percent
   d) 8 percent
   e) 10 percent

3. The responsibility of fighting inflation largely falls on _____.

   a) the president
   b) the Office of Management and Budget
   c) the Congress
   d) the Federal Reserve
   e) the private sector

4. When the government attempts to reduce inflation, it typically results in _____.
   a) businesses growing
   b) higher interest rates
   c) lower unemployment
   d) an increase in GDP
   e) lower interest rates

CRITICAL THINKING AND DISCUSSION

Assuming it was politically possible, do you think economic policy should be made by economists and other experts rather than by politicians? Why, or why not?

Ⓢ PRACTICE ONLINE

Critical Thinking exercise: *Political Process Matters— The EU and Monetary Policy*

THE KEY PLAYERS IN ECONOMIC POLICY MAKING

▶ Describe the roles played by each of the branches of government in shaping economic policy. **Pages 613–25**

SUMMARY

The primary actors in making economic policy are Congress, through the "power of the purse"; the president, in shaping taxing and spending policy; and the bureaucracy, in implementing the monetary policy. While they all share the same general goal of a healthy economy, coordinating action across these actors can be difficult.

KEY TERMS

fiscal policy (p. 614)

monetary policy (p. 614)

budget making (p. 614)

budget reconciliation (p. 616)

United States Trade Representative (USTR) (p. 617)

National Economic Council (NEC) (p. 617)

Federal Reserve System (p. 618)

Treasury Department (p. 618)

Federal Reserve Board (p. 620)

PRACTICE QUIZ QUESTIONS

5. The difference between fiscal policy and monetary policy is that fiscal policy is concerned with _____, while monetary policy is concerned with _____.
   a) controlling the money supply and spending; taxing and interest rates
   b) taxing and controlling the money supply; spending and interest rates
   c) taxing and spending; controlling the money supply and interest rates
   d) controlling the money supply and interest rates; taxing and spending
   e) taxing and interest rates; spending and controlling the money supply

6. Budget reconciliation has the advantages of _____ and _____.
   a) decreasing bipartisanship; preventing a Senate filibuster

   b) allowing members to get everything they want; not being subject to a presidential veto
   c) making it difficult for members to vote against the bill; preventing a Senate filibuster
   d) not being subject to a presidential veto; decreasing bipartisanship
   e) making it difficult for members to vote against the bill; not being subject to presidential veto

7. The Federal Reserve Board's actions _____ subject to presidential or congressional review; while the appointment terms of personnel _____ overlap with the federal election calendar.
   a) are; do
   b) are; do not
   c) are sometimes; do
   d) are not; do
   e) are not; do not

8. The Treasury generally prefers _____ interest rates; the Federal Reserve board generally prefers _____ rates.
   a) higher; lower
   b) higher; higher
   c) lower; lower
   d) lower; higher
   e) stable; lower

CRITICAL THINKING AND DISCUSSION

If you were a member of Congress, what would your position be on international trade? Would you support free trade or more protectionist policies? Why?

Ⓢ PRACTICE ONLINE

"What Do Political Scientists Do?" video exercise: *David Lewis on the Executive Branch and the Federal Reserve*

TOOLS AND THEORIES OF ECONOMIC POLICY

▶ Examine how fiscal, monetary, regulatory, and trade policies influence the economy. **Pages 625–44**

SUMMARY

Policy makers have a variety of tools at their disposal to help push the economy in their desired direction. Though there are different theories on the best approach, the use of fiscal policy, monetary policy, and regulation allows the government to influence the country's economic performance.

KEY TERMS

Keynesian economics (p. 625)

supply-side economics (p. 626)

marginal tax rate (p. 626)

business cycle (p. 626)

mandatory spending (p. 627)

discretionary spending (p. 628)

regressive (p. 630)

progressive (p. 630)

monetarist theory (p. 633)

reserve requirement (p. 634)

discount rate (p. 634)

federal funds rate (FFR) (p. 634)

open market operations (p. 635)

PRACTICE QUIZ QUESTIONS

9. Keynesian economics argues that the effects of an economic recession can be reduced by _____.
   a) decreasing government spending
   b) increasing government spending
   c) increasing income taxes
   d) reducing the budget deficit
   e) discouraging consumer spending

10. Reducing the federal deficit by cutting spending is difficult because _____.
   a) the interest rates are too high
   b) a growing portion of the budget is mandatory spending
   c) a growing portion of the budget is discretionary spending
   d) members of Congress put too much pork in budgetary bills
   e) large deficits benefit the economy in the long run

11. Regressive taxes, like the payroll tax, mean that compared to the wealthy, poor people spend _____ of their income on taxes.
   a) none
   b) much less
   c) slightly less
   d) an equal amount
   e) more

12. What does the "reserve requirement" refer to?
   a) the interest rate the Fed charges to member banks
   b) the rate member banks charge one another on overnight loans
   c) the minimum activity level of the Fed's open market operations
   d) the lowest price for government bonds
   e) the minimum level of money banks must always have on hand

13. When the competitive situation is a natural monopoly, the government generally _____.
   a) regulates prices
   b) breaks up the monopoly
   c) stimulates competition
   d) works to reduce negative externalities
   e) does not intervene

14. The government's first regulatory focus was _____ regulation; _____ regulation enjoys strong political support.
   a) social; social
   b) social; environmental
   c) economic; social
   d) economic; economic
   e) environmental; social

15. In general, Congress supports _____; the president supports _____.
   a) protectionism; free trade
   b) protectionism; protectionism
   c) free trade; protectionism
   d) free trade; free trade
   e) tariffs; protectionism

CRITICAL THINKING AND DISCUSSION

Do you support an active role for the government in regulating the economy, or would you prefer the free market to be largely unregulated?

ⓢ **PRACTICE ONLINE**

"Big Think" video exercise: *The Free Market and Politics*

SUGGESTED READING

Friedman, Milton. *Capitalism and Freedom*. 40th anniversary ed. Chicago: University of Chicago Press, 2002.

Friedman, Thomas L. *The World Is Flat: A Brief History of the Twenty-First Century*. New York: Farrar, Straus and Giroux, 2005.

Keynes, John Maynard. *General Theory of Employment, Interest and Money*. New York: Macmillan, 2007; originally published in 1936.

Krugman, Paul. *The Great Unraveling: Losing Our Way in the New Century*. New York: Norton, 2003.

Lewis, Michael. *The Big Short: Inside the Doomsday Machine*. New York: Norton, 2010.

Phillips, Kevin. *Bad Money: Reckless Finance, Failed Politics, and the Global Crisis of American Capitalism*. New York: Viking, 2008.

Soros, George. *The New Paradigm for Financial Markets: The Credit Crash of 2008 and What It Means*. New York: PublicAffairs Books, 2008.

Stiglitz, Joseph E. *Globalization and Its Discontents*. New York: Norton, 2003.

16

Social Policy

HEALTH CARE REFORM HAS BEEN ONE of the most controversial social policies. When the Supreme Court heard arguments for and against the Affordable Care Act in 2012, groups on both sides of the issue demonstrated outside the Court.

PRESIDENT OBAMA SIGNED THE PATIENT PROTECTION and Affordable Care Act into law on March 30, 2010. This comprehensive and historic health care reform legislation was the culmination of a 15-month partisan struggle in Congress. The $1 trillion law (over 10 years) will make health insurance available to an additional 32 million Americans while preventing health insurance companies from dropping sick policyholders or refusing to cover people with preexisting conditions.

President Obama and the Democrats in Congress started working toward this legislation soon after Obama took office in 2009. Many of the lasting images of this political process are related to the deep conflict over the controversial law. Representative Joe Wilson (R-S.C.), for example, shouted, "You lie" when President Obama told a joint session of Congress that his health care plan would not cover illegal immigrants. This breach of decorum was roundly criticized by leaders of both parties, and Wilson later apologized to the president. The broader policy debate often was quite substantive, but it also degenerated into charges of government-run "death panels." House Minority Leader John Boehner (R-Ohio), for example, said the bill "may start us down a treacherous path toward government-encouraged euthanasia."[1] There was nothing in the bill to support the charge, but by the time this and similar comments filtered through conservative talk radio, angry demonstrators around the country were blasting the legislation as socialized medicine and comparing it to Hitler's atrocities during the Holocaust.

CONFLICT & COMPROMISE
in American Politics

Inside Congress, the negotiations were intense. For the first six months of the process, the Senate Finance Committee chair, Max Baucus (D-Mont.), tried to reach out to moderate Republicans to create a bipartisan bill. Early in the fall, as public opposition grew, it became clear that the votes for health care reform would have to come from within the Democratic Party. Needing 60 votes to stop a filibuster meant that Democratic leaders would have to hang onto every Democratic vote, plus the two independents. This gave great power to conservatives in the party, such as Ben Nelson (D-Nebr.), and to independent Joe Lieberman (I-Conn.). Significant conflict also emerged between House and Senate versions of the bill on issues such as federal funding of abortion, how illegal immigrants would be excluded from the policy, and how the programs would be funded.

The House passed its version of the bill in November 2009, and the Senate finally passed its bill on Christmas Eve after an all-night session. Some congressional leaders wanted to push ahead with negotiations between the House and Senate to get the bill done before the end of the year, but Obama convinced them to wait until the new year because everyone was too exhausted.[2] Then came the bombshell of January 19, 2010, when Republican Scott Brown won the Massachusetts Senate seat that had been held by Ted Kennedy for half a century, denying Democrats their filibuster-proof majority. Most pundits and many Democratic leaders thought this would be the end of comprehensive health care reform, but ironically, it provided the impetus to get it passed. Knowing that they no longer had the 60 votes to pass a new bill in the Senate, the House decided to pass the Senate version and amend it with a third bill, the Health Care and Education Reconciliation Act of 2010. The Senate then passed an amended version of the third bill by a 56-to-43 vote (it only required a simple majority because it was passed under a reconciliation process that is typically used to reduce deficits). The amended third bill was then sent back to the House, where it passed 220 to 207, and the president signed it into law.[3] (The "How It Works" box in Chapter 10 shows the unorthodox process used to pass the act.)

Republicans cried foul, saying that Democrats had circumvented the normal legislative process and used reconciliation in an unorthodox manner. Representative Boehner called the legislation "a sloppy mess that the majority of the American people believe should be repealed and replaced."[4] Some opponents turned violent in the week following the passage of health care reform; President Obama and at least 10 members of Congress, including Speaker Pelosi, received death threats, and windows were smashed at Democratic offices in four states.[5]

Although this level of anger is unusual in American politics, trade-offs between social policy and other government priorities often produce political conflict. More money for health insurance subsidies, Social Security, Medicare, food stamps, and welfare means less money for building highways, supporting the military, or developing alternative energy. These trade-offs become especially acute as an aging population requires that an increasing share of federal spending goes to Social Security and Medicare. Resolving these trade-offs must be done through a political process filled with conflict and compromise.

That the political process matters is clearly shown by the importance of the filibuster in the Senate and the reconciliation process that allowed passage of the bill with a majority vote; also, process matters in that decisions made by individual presidents and members of Congress shape social policy. In each instance, policies and their effect on Americans' daily lives could have been very different if alternative procedures had been used or different proposals had passed.

IN 2010, THE PATIENT PROTECTION and Affordable Care Act was signed into law, a victory for supporters, including then-House Speaker Nancy Pelosi.

The politics of social policy is everywhere. Social policy directly affects all Americans at some point in their lives—possibly from the very beginning of life (with programs such as Women, Infants, and Children [WIC] and Head Start), through the middle of life (income support, job training, housing, food stamps, Medicaid, and need-based scholarships), to the end of life (Social Security and Medicare). This chapter discusses the evolution of social policy in the United States, outlines the conditions that create the need for social policies, describes the key players in the social policy-making process, and explains the status of key social policies today and the efforts to reform them. We begin with the historical background of social policy.

THE HISTORY AND BACKGROUND OF SOCIAL POLICY

EXPLAIN WHAT WE MEAN BY SOCIAL POLICY, AND HOW THE NATIONAL GOVERNMENT'S ROLE IN SOCIAL POLICY HAS EVOLVED

Social policy is generally defined in terms of the "social safety net," or **welfare**, which the *American Heritage Dictionary* defines as "regular assistance from the government or a private agency because of need." A broader conception includes government programs aimed at achieving some general social goal, such as support for public education, the income tax deduction for interest paid on home mortgages (to encourage home ownership), or policies aimed at helping job creation and growth. This chapter will address both conceptions of social policies and also discuss how some traditional social welfare programs such as Social Security are not based on need. This section outlines the evolution of social policy in the United States and describes the various types of social policy.

Early in our nation's history, the federal government took little responsibility for social welfare. Private charities, churches, and families largely took care of the poor and disadvantaged. The first significant social policy appeared in the nineteenth century in the form of federal financial support for Civil War veterans and their families. Between 1880 and 1910, the national government spent more than a quarter of

social policy An area of public policy related to maintaining or enhancing the well-being of individuals.

welfare Financial or other assistance provided to individuals by the government, usually based on need.

TYPES OF SOCIAL POLICY

There are two main types of social policy:

▶ *Contributory* (or social insurance) programs include Social Security, Medicare, disability insurance, and unemployment compensation.

  ● similar to insurance programs in that people pay a specified amount of money to cover some future benefit (either expected, as with the programs related to retirement, or unexpected, as with disability and unemployment)

  ● not means-tested; that is, all people may participate in the program regardless of their income

▶ *Noncontributory* (or public assistance) programs include Medicaid, food stamps, housing assistance, welfare, and school lunches.

  ● recipients are not expected to pay for the programs, which are means-tested, meaning that they are aimed at helping poor people

▶ The new health care law (the Affordable Care Act) has elements of both contributory and noncontributory programs. People who are required to buy health insurance are "contributing" to their own insurance. However, those who cannot afford to pay for their insurance receive government subsidies (and thus are participating in a noncontributory program).

BEFORE THE NEW DEAL PROGRAMS in the 1930s, poverty relief was provided mainly by private charities. Here future first lady Eleanor Roosevelt serves meals to unemployed women and their children in a New York restaurant.

its budget on Civil War pensions and support for veterans' widows. This was a larger share of the budget than any other single item other than interest on the debt and a greater percentage of federal spending than today's expenditure on Social Security (today we spend about one-fifth of our budget on Social Security, but of course the overall budget was much smaller then).[6] During the recession of the mid-1890s, populist and progressive reformers sought a national system of unemployment compensation, but such broad-scale policies were several decades ahead of their time.

The stock market crash in 1929 and the ensuing Great Depression created a desperate economic situation for millions of Americans. The value of the stock market shrank by 80 percent, the gross national product decreased by 25 percent, and unemployment climbed to at least 25 percent in the depth of the Depression in 1933. Yet, during the presidential campaign of 1932, the Republican incumbent, Herbert Hoover, upheld the administration's policy of limited government intervention in the economy and in social welfare policies. In contrast, the Democratic candidate, Franklin D. Roosevelt, pledged "a new deal for the American people." FDR won a sweeping victory. Democrats also gained control of both houses of Congress, which provided the platform for enacting FDR's policies.

An immediate concern was to alleviate the suffering caused by unemployment. As FDR argued, "No country, however rich, can afford the waste of its human resources. Demoralization caused by vast unemployment is our greatest extravagance. Morally, it is the greatest menace to our social order."[7] But FDR also wanted to implement a broader "preventative social policy" as outlined by social scientists at the University of Wisconsin, including John R.

Commons, who was a significant force in the creation of unemployment compensation policies, and Edwin Witte, the architect of Social Security.[8] The **New Deal** policies enacted between 1933 and 1935 included the following:

- ▶ The Agricultural Adjustment Administration, which provided farmers with much-needed assistance (farmers were hit hard in the Depression when plummeting commodity prices forced many family farms into bankruptcy)

- ▶ The National Recovery Administration and Public Works Administration, which reinvigorated the business sector

- ▶ The Federal Emergency Relief Administration, which provided $500 million in emergency aid for the poor (about $7 billion in today's dollars)

- ▶ Jobs programs such as the Civil Works Administration and Civilian Conservation Corps, which put more than 2 million people to work, and later the Works Progress Administration, which was a broader program that employed at least one-third of the nation's unemployed

- ▶ Social Security, which included the familiar retirement policy and supported the states for spending on unemployment compensation, disability programs, and support for dependent children of single mothers—the precursor of the central welfare program, Aid to Families with Dependent Children (AFDC), which existed until 1996

- ▶ The National Labor Relations Act, which guaranteed the right to organize a union and set regulations for collective bargaining between management and labor[9]

The role of the federal government in social policy was forever changed. Although some aspects of the New Deal were never repeated on such a broad scale, such as the jobs programs, most of its other programs became the cornerstone of social policy for subsequent generations.

The next major expansion of social policy came during the **Great Society** of President Lyndon Johnson in the mid-1960s. We discussed part of this social agenda in Chapter 14: the civil rights movement, which culminated with the passage of the Civil Rights Act in 1964 and the Voting Rights Act in 1965. The other important aspect of Johnson's Great Society included the War on Poverty and programs concerning health, education, and housing. Johnson's "unconditional" War on Poverty brought economic development and jobs to depressed areas, especially the inner cities, by creating the Office of Economic Opportunity, the Jobs Corps, the Neighborhood Youth Corps, Volunteers in Service to America (VISTA, a domestic counterpart to the Peace Corps), and the Model Cities program. Other programs focused on helping children, including Head Start, which provided preschool education and enrichment for poor children, the Child Nutrition Act of 1966, and an expanded school lunch program. The Food Stamp program was also greatly expanded; urban renewal expanded public housing; a new cabinet-level department, Housing and Urban Development, was created; and the federal government got more involved in an area that typically had been left to the states in the Elementary and Secondary Education Act of 1965. Perhaps the most significant legislation was in health care, with the creation of Medicare, the national program that funds medical care for the elderly, and Medicaid, which funds health care for the poor.[10]

The mounting costs of the Vietnam War created a trade-off: it wasn't possible to continue funding ambitious social programs and the war without creating inflation. Over the following decades there was some conservative backlash

New Deal The set of policies proposed by President Franklin Roosevelt and enacted by Congress between 1933 and 1935 to promote economic recovery and social welfare during the Great Depression.

Great Society The wide-ranging social agenda promoted by President Lyndon Johnson in the mid-1960s that aimed to improve Americans' quality of life through governmental social programs.

PRESIDENT GEORGE W. BUSH
emphasized the idea of an
"ownership society." For example,
Bush proposed privatizing Social
Security to allow people to invest
the money themselves.

ownership society The term
used to describe the social policy
vision of President George W. Bush,
in which citizens take responsibility
for their own social welfare and the
free market plays a greater role in
social policy.

against the "welfare state," especially during the Reagan years (1981–89), as spending on social programs was cut and some programs were eliminated. However, with some exceptions, the Great Society programs remain core components of today's social safety net.

President George W. Bush continued this general direction for social policy, maintaining most existing programs with some cuts and one major expansion, the addition of a prescription benefit to Medicare. Bush attempted to place his stamp on social policy as a "compassionate conservative" with his idea of an **ownership society**, in which people take more responsibility for their own social welfare. Bush proposed privatizing part of Social Security and creating private savings accounts to cover more out-of-pocket medical expenses, in combination with more free market forces and a bigger role for private charity. President Obama has favored an approach that emphasizes the market and community, while preserving an important role for government. As the recent recession and natural disasters such as Hurricane Katrina have demonstrated, crises may overwhelm even the most aggressive and sustained community responses. Market forces cannot adequately address the needs of the unemployed and very poor, especially in times of economic recession. Obama's social policies in his first term have focused on enacting comprehensive health care reform, while maintaining and expanding the social safety net for those devastated by the recession (for example, with the extension of unemployment benefits to cover the long-term unemployed and providing a record number of people with food stamps).

EXAMINE THE PROBLEM OF
POVERTY AS A TARGET OF
SOCIAL POLICIES

POVERTY AND INCOME INEQUALITY

The economic dislocation and poverty of the Great Depression and the desire to eliminate poverty in the 1960s were the two central stimuli for social policy. Although these policies had some success in reducing poverty, the persistence of poverty remains the primary motivator for most social policy. In 2012, the poverty line for a family of four was an annual income of $23,050; for a single person it was $11,170. In 2011, 46.2 million Americans were in poverty—15 percent of the population Even the social programs that do not directly help the poor and disadvantaged, such as Social Security and Medicare, have an impact on poverty. As Figure 16.1 shows, the percentage of the elderly population living in poverty plummeted from more than 35 percent in 1959 to 8.7 percent in 2011. Official statistics on poverty were not collected before 1959, but the rate was certainly much higher in the 1930s before Social Security was established.[11] Given that more than half of the elderly rely on Social Security as their primary income—for the bottom quintile, nearly 80 percent of their income in retirement comes from Social Security—the poverty rate for the elderly would be much higher if Social Security and Medicare did not exist.

Another source of concern for some policy advocates is the growing income and wealth inequality in the United States. Indeed, the top income levels in the nation are benefiting disproportionately from income increases. Since 1980, 80 percent

FIGURE » 16.1

POVERTY RATES BY AGE

Children today are in poverty at nearly twice the rate of the elderly, whereas 45 years ago the poverty rate among the elderly was twice that of children. What changes in social policies in the past 75 years could help explain this change?

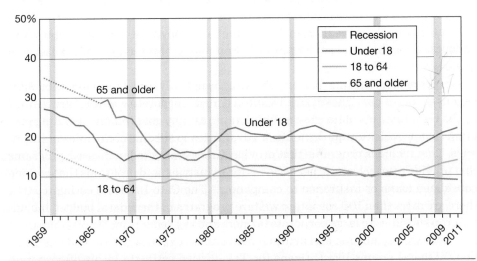

Note: The data points are placed at the midpoints of the respective years. Data for people age 18 and older are not available from 1960 to 1965.

Source: U.S. Census Bureau, *Current Population Survey, 1960 to 2010 Annual Social and Economic Supplements*, available at www.census.gov/prod/2012pubs/p60-243.pdf (accessed 10/9/12).

of the net income gains have gone to the top 1 percent of the income distribution.[12] In 2011, the top 5 percent of households—those earning more than $186,000 a year—earned 21.7 percent of the income, and in 2011, the top quintile earned just over half of the nation's income.[13] From 1979 to 2009, the average income of the top 1 percent grew by $700,000 to $1,220,100 (a 133 percent gain), compared to a $2,600 gain to $18,900 (16 percent) for the bottom fifth of the income levels.[14]

The wealth gap is far greater. The median (meaning that half are above this level and half are below) net worth of U.S. households in 2007 was $120,300, but the median wealth for the top 10 percent was $1.89 million, and this group held 73 percent of the nation's wealth. Even within the top 10 percent, the wealth is concentrated at the top. *Forbes* magazine publishes a list of the wealthiest Americans every year. Bill Gates topped the 2012 list for the nineteenth year in a row, with a net worth of $66 billion, and the person at the bottom of the "*Forbes* 400" was worth $1.1 billion. The collective net worth of the nation's wealthiest 400 people grew $200 billion in the past year to reach $1.7 trillion.[15] In contrast, the total wealth held by the bottom 40 percent of the American public ($532 billion held by *46.7 million* households in 2010) was less than one-third of the total wealth held by the richest 400 people.[16]

According to a study by the nonpartisan Congressional Budget Office (CBO), despite these patterns of inequality, people who earn more than $100,000 receive more benefits from the federal government ($5,690 on average) than people who earn less than $10,000 ($5,560). The study concludes, "Quite simply, if the federal government wanted to flatten the nation's income distribution, it would do better to mail all its checks to random addresses."[17]

How can that be? Consider one big social welfare program: housing. Poor people receive about $35 billion a year from the federal government in direct subsidies for their rent and for public housing. However, this number is dwarfed by the $261 billion spent on tax expenditures for housing in 2011, most of which went to relatively wealthy people through the mortgage interest deduction and capital gains tax exclusions.[18] For example, 68 percent of the tax savings from deducting mortgage interest goes to people in the top fifth of the income ladder.[19] Other government policies that help the wealthy include patent and copyright law, bankruptcy law, bailouts of the financial sector, immigration policy, enforcement of tax law, and monetary policy.[20]

Government programs that help the wealthy not only target individuals but also benefit corporations. These policies, often called "corporate welfare," are defined by the Cato Institute, a libertarian think tank, as "any government spending program that provides unique benefits or advantages to specific companies or industries. That includes programs that provide direct grants to businesses, programs that provide research and other services for industries, and programs that provide subsidized loans or insurance to companies." The Cato Institute estimates that there are more than 100 corporate welfare programs in the federal budget, including crop subsidies to large corporate farmers and tax deductions for oil companies to encourage exploration and drilling, with annual expenditures of about $92 billion.[21] Liberal groups like Citizens for Tax Justice estimate levels of corporate welfare at nearly three times that amount. Clearly there is much more to welfare policies than programs for the poor.

These statistics generate different reactions among politicians and are a good reminder that politics is conflictual. Republicans look at the statistics on poverty and inequality and policies that help the wealthy and argue that the best way to address poverty is to create jobs and have a healthy economy through supply-side tax cuts that promote the creation of capital, investment, and jobs (see Chapter 15). From this perspective, income inequality may in fact be a necessary condition for bringing people out of poverty because wealthy people are the only ones who have enough money to invest to create jobs. Indeed, Rick Santorum argued during the 2012 Republican presidential primaries that "There is income inequality in America. There always has been and, hopefully, and I do say that, there always will be."[22] Democrats argue that making the wealthy pay a larger share of their income in taxes could fund programs to help the poor directly rather than waiting for the trickle-down effect of tax cuts for the wealthy. From this perspective, a direct trade-off exists between inequality and reducing poverty, and progressive taxes are needed to help the poor.

Figure 16.2 shows a significant difference between the performance of Democrats and Republicans in reducing poverty. Between 1960 and 2011, Democrats controlled the White House for 23 years and Republicans for 29 years. During Democratic presidencies the poverty rate fell from the previous year in 18 of those 23 years, and one year remained the same as the previous year. The poverty rate fell during Republican presidencies in only 14 of the 29 years they were in power and remained the same in three years. Overall, the mean change in the poverty rate was –0.41 percent in Democratic years, and it went up by 0.07 percent in Republican years. These differences may not sound like much, but given that each percentage point change in the poverty rate represents more than 3 million people today, the differences are significant. Political scientist Larry Bartels finds that in the past six decades, the inflation-adjusted incomes of working poor families (at the 20th percentile of income) increased six times faster under Democratic presidents than under Republican presidents.[23] This makes some sense given the political base of the two parties: Democrats win large percentages of the votes of poor people, and Republicans usually do better among wealthier voters. Given all the statistics on income inequality and poverty, it is sometimes easy to lose sight of the human face of poverty. Hurricane Katrina, one of our nation's worst natural disasters, serves as a reminder of that human face. The hurricane killed more than 1,800 people, displaced 1.5 million people, and caused more than $100 billion in damage. Middle-class and wealthier people were able to leave New Orleans as the hurricane approached, but 100,000 city residents did not own cars, and there weren't enough buses to handle all the people. A conservative columnist for the *New York Times* delivered a bitter assessment of the government's response: "The first rule of the social fabric—that in times of crisis you protect the vulnerable—was trampled. Leaving the poor in New Orleans was the moral equivalent of leaving the injured on the battlefield. No wonder confidence in civic institutions is plummeting."[24] The media coverage of Hurricane Katrina was shocking to millions of Americans. Images of bodies floating in the water and people standing outside the Louisiana Superdome with their arms outstretched to passing helicopters served as a stark reminder of the costs of poverty. Many Americans believe that such a thing should not be allowed to happen in our country, and national leaders vowed to address the problems exposed by the hurricane. However, despite $33 billion in public and private aid spent in the seven years after the disaster, large parts of the city have still not been rebuilt. Many of the 800,000 people displaced by the storm never returned: the 2010 census shows that the population of New Orleans is 29 percent smaller than it was in 2000.[25]

FIGURE » 16.2

CHANGES IN POVERTY RATES BY PARTY

The poverty rate tends to decrease under Democratic presidents and to go up by about the same margin under Republican presidents. What could explain this difference?

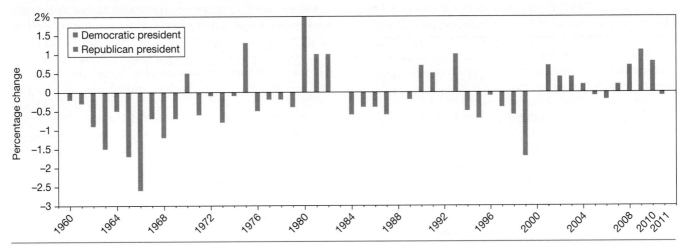

Source: Data from the U.S. Census Bureau, Poverty: Historical Tables, available at www.census.gov/hhes/www/poverty/poverty.html (accessed 10/8/12).

INCOME INEQUALITY AND POLICY

Growing income inequality in the United States has received much attention and debate over the past 10 years. Income inequality is relevant for the subject of social policy because it reveals a continued need for social programs to help the poor. But Larry Bartels, a political scientist at Princeton University, has a different set of questions that drive his research on the topic. After reviewing the economic data showing the dramatic increase in income inequality in the past two generations, Bartels wants to discover whether public policies have created a "New Gilded Age." He concludes that "economic inequality is, in substantial part, a political phenomenon."[a]

Before presenting evidence to support this point, Bartels establishes his credentials as an objective social scientist. Acknowledging that his research could be seen as very partisan (because he concludes that most people fare much better economically under Democratic presidents than under Republican presidents), he says that was not his intention when he started his research. He points out that he is "an unusually apolitical political scientist" and that the last time he voted was in 1984 (for Ronald Reagan). He says that he was surprised by some of his results and that "I have done my best to follow my evidence where it led me."[b]

Watch a video clip of Larry Bartels discussing this topic at **wwnorton.com/studyspace**

Evidence of the partisan basis for income inequality is strong. Using economic data from the post–World War II period, Bartels shows that income inequality increased under Presidents Eisenhower, Nixon, Ford, Reagan, and both Bushes, while it declined during the presidencies of four of the five Democrats during this period (Jimmy Carter was the exception). These differences can be explained by the fact that Democratic presidents tend to pursue policies aimed at creating jobs and economic growth, whereas Republicans are more concerned about keeping inflation low, which has little impact on the income of middle-income and poor Americans but helps those at the top. Tax policies are also consistent with this pattern, with Republican tax cuts that have disproportionately helped the wealthiest Americans. Bartels also concludes that the Republican supply-side theory (or "trickle-down economics," as it has been called by its critics) as a justification for inequality is not valid, concluding that there is "little evidence that large disparities in income and wealth promote growth."[c]

If this is true, why do voters put up with it? That is, if Republican policies are primarily helping people in the top 20 percent income bracket, why don't the other 80 percent consistently vote for Democrats? One theory is that Republican politicians appeal to middle- and low-income voters on social issues, emphasizing the "values divide" on issues such as abortion, stem cell research, and gay marriage. The argument that the poorer classes vote against their own economic interests is

Democratic president Lyndon Johnson immediately after signing the landmark "War on Poverty" bill in August 1964. Since World War II, economic inequality has tended to decrease under Democratic presidents and increase under Republican ones.

advanced by Thomas Frank in a popular book entitled *What's the Matter with Kansas? How Conservatives Won the Heart of America*. However, through the statistical analysis of economic and voting data, Bartels convincingly demonstrates that this is not the case. The working class, especially those without a college education, still vote strongly for the Democratic Party.

Instead, part of the answer appears to be that Republican presidents have had more fortunate timing, being up for election during periods of economic growth. Although Republican presidents have an overall pattern of increasing the gap between rich and poor by primarily helping wealthier Americans, they often have presided over faster economic growth rates in presidential election years, whereas growth rates during Democratic administrations have been spread more evenly over the four-year political cycle. "Myopic voters"—those who consider the recent past more heavily than the full four-year term—rewarded Republican presidents for their relative success during election years. Bartels concludes, "Whether through political skill or pure good luck, Republican presidents have been remarkably successful in targeting income growth to coincide with presidential elections."

Larry Bartels's work on income inequality is an excellent example of political science research that is politically relevant and rigorous, and that addresses questions of central importance to understanding the politics of the policy-making process.

THE KEY PLAYERS IN SOCIAL POLICY MAKING

DESCRIBE THE ROLES PLAYED BY EACH BRANCH OF THE NATIONAL GOVERNMENT AND BY THE STATES IN MAKING AND IMPLEMENTING SOCIAL POLICY

Congress, the president, and bureaucracy all play key roles in shaping social policy. State governments also play a central role in some policy areas such as education and welfare policy, while interest groups are especially important for policies that affect the elderly.

CONGRESS AND THE PRESIDENT

The previous section's argument about differences between Democratic and Republican administrations' performance in lowering the poverty rate ignored one important point: Democratic presidents were more likely than Republican presidents to have a Congress controlled by their party. In 16 of the 24 years of Democratic presidents, Democrats also controlled Congress; Republican presidents enjoyed unified control in only four of the 32 years from 1961 through 2012. This means that Democratic presidents had more opportunity to implement their agendas, while Republican presidents had to do more negotiating with the other party. You might argue that this divided control only prevented Republican presidents from making even deeper cuts in social programs that could have driven the poverty rate even higher, because Democrats in Congress would have been supporting those policies. Although this is a possibility, especially during the Reagan years, divided control may also have prevented Republican presidents from implementing their alternative vision of the best way to address poverty.

This discussion underlies the more basic point: Congress and the president both play central roles in shaping social policy. In some instances the president may take the lead, as with FDR and the New Deal or Lyndon Johnson and the Great Society. In other instances Congress plays a central role, as with health care reform in 2009–10. In all cases the president and Congress must find some common ground. This may be especially difficult under divided government, but even when the president and Congress are of the same party, Congress may be obstructionist: in 1993–94 the Democratic Congress shot down President Clinton's health care proposal, and in 2005 a Republican-controlled Congress ignored President Bush's effort to partially privatize Social Security.

THE BUREAUCRACY

It may seem safe to assume that the bureaucracy makes little difference in social policy and simply implements the policies that are determined by Congress and the president. For some policies, that is fairly close to what happens. For policies such as Social Security that have levels of benefits determined by law, implementing policy largely involves determining that the proper amount of money is going to the right people and mailing out the checks. However, as discussed in Chapter 12, with many social policies, the "on-the-ground" public employees have

WELFARE OFFICES CAN BE ALIENATING places in which it is very difficult to navigate through the bureaucracy. Dozens of women and children wait to speak to counselors in this East Los Angeles welfare office.

a great deal of discretion. One study found that welfare agencies that handed out AFDC benefits had a more "hostile and punitive" attitude toward their clients than those who administered the disability program under Social Security. Welfare offices in general tend not to be very welcoming places. People often have to wait for hours, and welfare office workers are sometimes rude and ask personal questions that are not required by law. Some potential welfare recipients are so alienated by the process that they give up.[26] This is not true of all welfare offices, but there are general differences in how recipients are treated in different types of social welfare programs.

Bureaucratic discretion may also serve more positive ends, though. Political scientist Daniel Carpenter reported that many bureaucratic agencies in the late nineteenth and early twentieth centuries developed political autonomy and strong reputations that allowed them to analyze and solve problems, create new programs, and plan and administer programs efficiently.[27] Many of the same insights apply to agencies that deliver social policies today, such as the Social Security Administration, which has a very strong base of popular and political support.

THE STATES

Social policy has always been strongly influenced by our system of federalism. As long as welfare has existed in the United States, it has been administered at the state and local level, with varying degrees of national control. The 1996 welfare reform bill, Temporary Assistance to Needy Families, gave more power to the states and eliminated all national guarantees. Medicaid is administered at the state level (with federal assistance), and education is almost completely controlled by local and state governments. One sticking point with health care reform in 2009–10 was the extent to which policy would be centered in the states or have a stronger national component. Many Democrats argued for a national "public option," while Republicans favored a more limited approach in which insurance companies would be allowed to compete across state lines. (The stronger national approach failed, but the new law clearly signaled a shift to a more national role in health care.) Education policy is another area where the trend has been toward more involvement of the national government rather than more power returning to the states. But even with the national accountability mechanisms and testing requirements established by President Bush's No Child Left Behind Act, and the incentives provided by President Obama's "Race to the Top" program, education policy remains largely a state and local affair.

INTEREST GROUPS

In general, interest groups that are advocates for social policy are not as influential as groups in other areas, such as business, labor, many other professional associations, or even other public interest groups such as environmental groups or those that focus on specific issues such as gun ownership. A major exception is AARP, one of the most powerful lobbies in the United States (see Chapter 9). AARP has long had a strong voice on behalf of Social Security and Medicare. For example, when President Bush proposed "personal savings accounts" to replace part of the Social Security system, AARP mobilized its significant political muscle to crush the idea before it could receive serious debate in Congress. Similarly, as politicians discussed how to pay for relief efforts following Hurricane Katrina, one proposal was to delay or eliminate the new Medicare prescription drug benefit. AARP was not as vocal on this issue (it is difficult to argue against "everyone chipping in" to pay for hurricane relief), but it worked behind the scenes to make sure that the drug benefit was implemented.

Many interest groups and think tanks work on behalf of the poor, homeless, and other disadvantaged people, but decision makers in Washington generally are less responsive to their concerns because these groups are not politically powerful. The poor tend not to vote, and they do not donate money to political campaigns. Many politicians in Washington care deeply about issues concerning poverty, homelessness, and other social policy problems, but the interest groups and think tanks that try to focus politicians' attention on these issues face a particularly difficult task *because of* the relatively disadvantaged position of the people they represent.

THE POLICY-MAKING PROCESS

TRACE THE STEPS THROUGH WHICH PROBLEMS ARE ADDRESSED BY SOCIAL POLICIES

Another way to understand the role of key players in making policy is to examine the various stages of the process (see the "How It Works" box). The figure shows the stages for Social Security, but all policies go through similar steps. The first stage is to define a problem as an issue that requires the federal government's attention. Of the thousands of possible issues, Congress acts on only a relatively small number. Consider a social policy like food stamps. Poor and hungry people have been part of American society since the arrival of the first settlers, but this was not seen as a problem requiring government intervention until the twentieth century. What causes a society to change its assumptions about whether and how government should address social problems?

Sometimes there is a triggering event: the assassination of President John F. Kennedy led to the passage of gun control legislation, the energy crisis of the early 1970s led to the first comprehensive discussions of energy policy, and Hurricane Katrina led to a reexamination of our readiness for emergencies and our social safety net. Sometimes redefining an issue can move the policy to the next step of the process. For example, the estate tax has been part of our tax system since 1917, but when Republican leaders in Congress redefined it as the "death tax" in the late 1990s, it transformed the politics of the debate and made it a problem that needed a solution. After all, who could support a tax on dead people? (Of course, dead people don't pay taxes—the estate's heirs do—but that nuance was lost in the redefinition of the problem.)

policy agenda The set of desired policies that political leaders view as their top priorities.

Recognizing and defining a problem is just the first step; it still needs to come to the attention of political leaders and get on the **policy agenda**. Political scientists have come up with many colorful terms to describe the process through which this happens, including models based on "garbage cans" or a "policy primeval soup."[28] Whatever the image, the basic idea is that when conditions are right, with the appropriate national political mood and participation from key interest groups and government actors, an issue can reach the agenda. Political scientists Frank Baumgartner and Bryan Jones describe a process of more abrupt change in the policy agenda as issues appear suddenly and then disappear almost as quickly after they are addressed, in a process they call "punctuated equilibrium."[29]

Once the issue is on the active agenda, alternatives are proposed and debated, and the final version of the policy is formulated in Congress (if it is a bill) or the executive branch (if it is an administrative action). Enactment involves a roll call vote in the House and the Senate and then a signature by the president, or a regulatory decision or administrative action by the bureaucracy, or unilateral action by the president (such as an executive order or agreement).

Many factors affect whether or not the policy is implemented successfully. First, the problem has to be solvable and the policy must be clear and consistent in its objectives. It wouldn't make sense for Congress to pass a law telling the Department of Health and Human Services to "eliminate poverty" because such a law could not indicate how this should be done. Second, the policy must be funded adequately and administered by competent bureaucrats who have the required expertise. Finally, external support from the public and relevant interest groups may be critical to the policy's success. For example, AARP's support is critical for the success of any social policy that affects older people. Its support helped pass the prescription drug benefit that was added to Medicare in 2003 and comprehensive health care reform in 2010, and its opposition to the Catastrophic Coverage Act forced Congress to repeal the program one year after it was passed in 1988.[30]

Implementation of a policy is an ongoing process. To ensure that the desires of Congress and the president are being followed, policy evaluation is a critical stage of the process. (See Chapter 12 for a discussion of attempts by Congress and the president to control the bureaucracy.) Policy evaluation has become an increasingly visible part of the policy-making process in the past decade, following passage of the Government Performance and Results Act of 1993. George W. Bush's administration increasingly used this law, which was largely ignored throughout

THE POLICY PROCESS

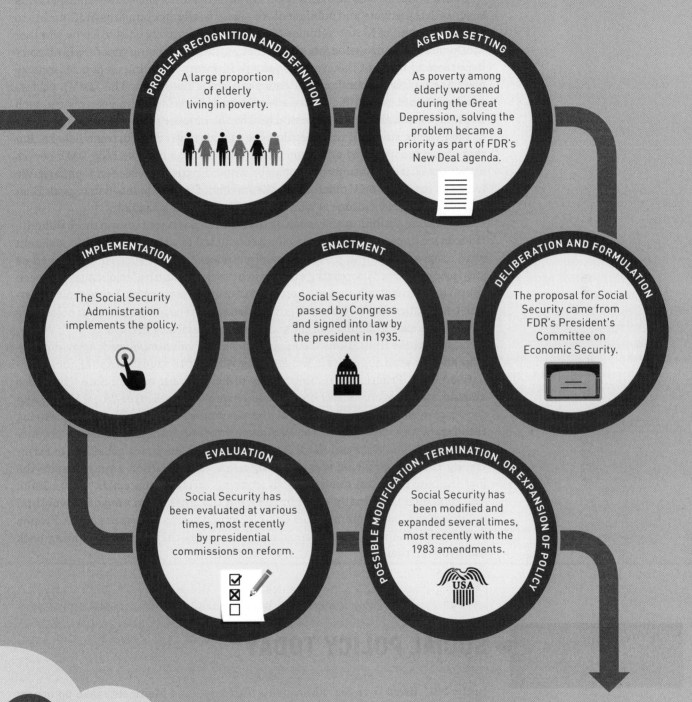

PROBLEM RECOGNITION AND DEFINITION

A large proportion of elderly living in poverty.

AGENDA SETTING

As poverty among elderly worsened during the Great Depression, solving the problem became a priority as part of FDR's New Deal agenda.

IMPLEMENTATION

The Social Security Administration implements the policy.

ENACTMENT

Social Security was passed by Congress and signed into law by the president in 1935.

DELIBERATION AND FORMULATION

The proposal for Social Security came from FDR's President's Committee on Economic Security.

EVALUATION

Social Security has been evaluated at various times, most recently by presidential commissions on reform.

POSSIBLE MODIFICATION, TERMINATION, OR EXPANSION OF POLICY

Social Security has been modified and expanded several times, most recently with the 1983 amendments.

POP QUIZ!

1 Which stage in the policy process means making the problem or issue a priority for government?

  a problem recognition

  b agenda setting

  c deliberation and formulation

  d evaluation

  e none of the above

2 In the case of Social Security, how has the implementation step of policy making occurred?

  a through presidential commissions on reform

  b through the 1983 amendments

  c through the Social Security Administration

  d through the 1935 Social Security Act

  e none of the above

Answers: 1.b; 2.c

much of the 1990s, to impose accountability. Under the law, agencies are required to publish strategic plans and performance measures. Though these efforts sound impressive, it is incredibly difficult to assess whether a government program is achieving its aims.

Political scientist James Q. Wilson explains the difference between measuring success in the private and public sectors—specifically, he compares McDonald's to the Department of Motor Vehicles (DMV).[31] It is relatively easy to know whether McDonald's is doing a good job: simply look at the profits being generated and compare them to those of the previous period. If profits are going up at a reasonable pace, the burger flippers and fry cooks are doing their jobs. The DMV's performance is much more difficult to assess because there is no simple measure, such as profit, to look at. Maybe you could review the number of people served per hour or the average length of time people have to wait to get their driver's license. But that would ignore many other considerations, such as how well the DMV serves disadvantaged populations or people for whom English is a second language. We wouldn't expect a DMV office where 50 percent of its applicants don't speak English to be as efficient as one at which all applicants speak English.

Evaluating a public agency such as the State Department is even more difficult. How do we know if diplomacy is being conducted in a manner that is consistent with congressional and presidential preferences? Would success be defined as staying out of war? Increasing economic activity or cultural exchanges between countries? Strengthening democratic institutions in emerging democracies? Getting cooperation in the War on Terror? Measuring the achievement of objectives like these is very difficult even if those goals can be clearly defined.

Despite these limitations, extensive efforts to evaluate policy do provide decision makers with some basis for deciding whether to modify, expand, or terminate a policy. Programs are notoriously difficult to cut or eliminate. Examples abound, such as wool and mohair subsidies implemented after World War II and the Korean War. More than half of the wool needed to make uniforms during these wars was imported, so the Pentagon wanted to increase domestic production of wool. The National Wool Act in 1954 provided direct subsidies to farmers. By 1994 the program was spending nearly $240 million a year, despite the fact that the Pentagon removed wool from its "strategic materials" list in 1960! The subsidies were finally killed in 1994, but the 2002 Farm Act added wool and mohair to the list of commodities eligible for marketing assistance loans.[32] Some policies are like the zombies in old horror movies—they just keep coming back after you kill them.

ANALYZE THE CURRENT MAJOR AREAS OF SOCIAL POLICY

SOCIAL POLICY TODAY

In the 2013 fiscal year, Social Security, Medicare, and Medicaid make up nearly half of all federal spending. With an aging population and health care costs that continue to grow as a percentage of the economy, these policies will take an even greater share of the budget in the future. Given other spending priorities, political pressure is mounting to put spending on social programs on a more sustainable path. This section will explain the nature of these important programs and discuss recent efforts to reform them.

SOCIAL SECURITY

Social Security is the most popular social program in the United States. Consequently it has developed a reputation as the "third rail" of politics—like the dangerous, power-conducting rail on electrified train tracks—because a politician who dares to touch Social Security risks political death. Despite serious problems concerning its long-term solvency, Social Security has proven remarkably immune to any steps that could be taken to shore up its financial health, such as cutting benefits or raising taxes. The "third rail" quality of the program has been especially evident to those who would like to privatize part of Social Security. President George W. Bush made a serious push for "personal savings accounts" that would replace some Social Security benefits, but Congress rebuffed him when his appeals fell flat with the American public. Why is Social Security so popular, what long-term challenges does it face, and what are the possible solutions to ensure its long-term viability?

One reason that Social Security is so popular is its universal quality—that is, nearly every working American participates in the program, from Bill Gates to the teenager flipping burgers at McDonald's. Once people retire, they are all entitled to Social Security checks without regard to how much income they have from other sources, such as dividends, interest, or other pensions. So, unlike many social programs that develop an "us against them" mentality ("Why should we have to support other people?"), Social Security does not pit citizens from different classes or ethnic groups against each other. Social Security is also popular because it works. It is more efficient than most privately managed pensions, with about 0.8 percent going to administrative expenses, compared with the average mutual fund that spends more than 1 percent. More important, Social Security has accomplished its central goal of helping most Americans have an adequate retirement income: fewer than 10 percent of the elderly are in poverty today, which is a lower rate than the general public (see Figure 16.1) and significantly lower than the 35 percent

Social Security A federal social insurance program that provides cash benefits to retirees based on payroll taxes they have paid over the course of their careers. It is a "pay as you go" program in which working Americans pay taxes to support today's retirees, with a promise that when today's workers retire, their benefits will be paid by the next generation.

16.2 NUTS & bolts

SOCIAL SECURITY

Number of Recipients for Old-Age, Survivors, and Disability Insurance

▶ Old-Age Insurance (the basic retirement program) 39,278,000

▶ Survivors Insurance (retirement program for widows, widowers, and the children of deceased primary wage earners) 6,228,000

▶ Disability Insurance (payments for people and their families who cannot work because of a disability and are not yet retired) 10,787,000

Monthly Retirement Benefits

▶ Individual: Average = $1,235, maximum = $2,513

▶ Couple: Average = $1,847, maximum = $3,437 (if one spouse does not work and the other earns the maximum)

Source: All figures are from the U.S. Social Security Administration Office of Policy, "Monthly Statistical Snapshot, August 2012," available at www.ssa.gov/policy/docs/ quickfacts/stat_snapshot/index.html?9s (accessed 10/8/12).

of the elderly who were in poverty in 1960. Census data also show that nearly half of the elderly (46.2 percent) would be in poverty today without their Social Security payments.[33]

However, Social Security faces long-term problems. President Bush tried to convince the American public that Social Security was in crisis, but they didn't want to hear it. Maybe "crisis" is too strong a word, but unless certain fundamental issues are addressed, the program will be unable to cover its obligations. The longer we wait to address the shortfall, the more difficult solving the problem will be.

The source of the problem is basic changes in the nation's demographic profile. The **Baby Boom generation**, born between 1946 and 1964, is just starting to retire, and between 2000 and 2030 the number of Americans over the age of 65 will more than double, while the number under 65 will grow by only 18 percent.[34] When this happens, there will be fewer workers to support the retirees. In fact, the number of workers per Social Security recipient has fallen from 15 in 1950 to about 3.3 today; by 2034 it will only be 2.[35] See Figure 16.3 for evidence of the aging population.

"Wait a minute," you may be saying. "Why does it matter how many workers there are for each retiree? I thought that Social Security was a pension program that you pay into while you're working and then get the benefits when you retire." Not exactly. Social Security is not a self-funded pension, but a "pay-as-you-go" system in which today's workers support today's retirees. Therefore, the huge increase in the number

Baby Boom generation Americans born between 1946 and 1964, who will be retiring in large numbers over the next 20 years.

FIGURE » 16.3

PEOPLE 65 AND OLDER AS A SHARE OF THE U.S. POPULATION

Elderly people will comprise a much larger share of the population in 2030 than they do today. How might the aging population affect social policy—both in terms of the politics of policy making and in terms of the fiscal implications of this trend?

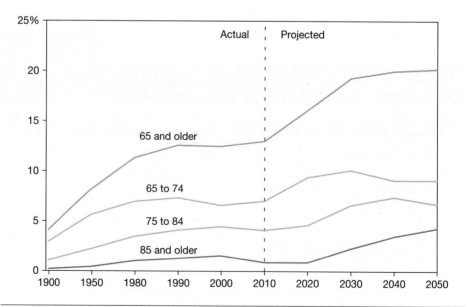

Source: Grayson K. Vincent and Victoria A. Velkoff, "The Next Four Decades, the Older Population in the United States: 2010 to 2050," U.S. Census Bureau, May 2010, p. 10, available at www.census.gov/prod/2010pubs/p25-1138.pdf. Data for 1900–2000 are from The 2012 Statistical Abstract: Historical Data, Table HS-3, www.census.gov/statab/hist/HS-03.pdf (accessed 10/8/12).

of retirees will strain the system because each worker will have to pay higher taxes to maintain the same level of Social Security benefits for retirees. Of course, benefits could be cut, but the "third rail" status of the program has prevented that, at least up to now. This problem was exacerbated by the deep recession and prolonged unemployment starting in 2008, which reduced revenue from the payroll tax. Revenue declined even more in 2011–12 when the payroll tax was cut by 2 percent (about $700 a year for the average worker) to help stimulate the economy. To address the mounting structural deficits, President Obama appointed a bipartisan commission to make recommendations to Congress (which will be discussed below).

Another problem with the pay-as-you-go nature of Social Security is the intergenerational transfer of wealth. The flip side of Social Security's success in reducing the poverty rate for seniors is that more children and working poor are in poverty today. Therefore, some critics have wondered if it makes sense, for example, to have a single mother who is working for the minimum wage pay 6.2 percent of her income in taxes to support the benefits of some people who are living comfortably in retirement. This critique also points out that current retirees will receive far more in benefits than they paid in Social Security taxes, while many current workers won't get back as much as they paid in (if interest on the taxes paid is considered). For example, an average worker who retired in 1990 got back all of his Social Security taxes, plus interest, by 1999. It is difficult to project the rate of return for current workers because we don't know what future benefits or taxes will be.[36] However, it is safe to bet that taxes will be higher and benefits will not keep up the same rate of increase that they have had for the past several decades. Therefore, today's retirees are reaping a windfall that strikes some critics as unfair, especially given that they are better off, on average, than the workers who are currently paying taxes.

Now you can start to see why reforming Social Security is so controversial. Debate over Social Security reform exposes highly charged class-based and intergenerational tensions. Before we examine the various proposals to change Social Security, it is important to explain how the program works and to describe previous reform efforts. Social Security is funded by a payroll tax of 6.2 percent on income up to $110,100 (in 2012) with an equal 6.2 percent that is paid by employers; the self-employed have to pay both halves. The payroll tax also includes 1.45 percent on all income for Medicare (discussed later). This is a regressive tax because poor and middle-income people pay a higher percentage of their income for the Social Security tax than wealthy people pay. The maximum Social Security tax you can pay is $6,826 a year, which is 6.2 percent of $110,100. So a millionaire would pay a little more than 0.5 percent of her income in payroll tax (0.68 percent, to be exact) compared to the 6.2 percent that everyone earning less than $110,100 pays. Although the taxes are regressive, the benefits are progressive; that is, poorer people receive back in benefits a larger share of their lifetime payroll taxes than wealthy people receive. One solution to Social Security's long-term fiscal problem is to increase, or even eliminate, the cap on income that is subjected to the payroll tax. This solution is opposed, however, by those who fear that it would undermine Social Security's popularity among wealthier people.

Policy makers have known about the Baby Boomers since the early 1960s, so why haven't they remedied the Boomers' effect on Social Security? Actually, Social Security faced its first real crisis in the early 1980s, well before the Boomers started retiring. Benefits had increased faster than payroll taxes throughout the 1970s, and the Social Security Administration estimated that it would not be able to meet its obligations as early as 1983. President Reagan and Congress appointed the National Commission on Social Security Reform to make recommendations regarding the program's short-term crisis and long-term problems. The commission issued its report in January 1983, which served as the basis for the 1983 Social Security Amendments. This law solved Social Security's short-term problems and made many other significant changes in the program.

The 1983 law's most significant changes were a gradual increase in the retirement age from 65 to 67, and increases in the payroll tax that generated surpluses for a trust fund to take care of the Boomers' retirement. The first of these changes was relatively straightforward: people born in 1937 or earlier could retire in 2002 at age 65 and receive full benefits. Between 2003 and 2027 the retirement age increases gradually to 67 for full benefits. Early retirement at 62 is an option, if the retiree is willing to accept a permanently reduced benefit level.

The second change, concerning the trust fund, is the source of great confusion and controversy. The idea behind the trust fund was sound: build up a surplus while the Boomers are working and use that money to pay for their retirement. From 1983 to 2008 payroll taxes generated far more revenue than spending on Social Security. The problem is that the money wasn't really saved but spent on general government spending (for example, the war in Afghanistan, food stamps, school loans, and funding the FBI). In turn the government gave the Social Security trust fund an IOU in the form of "special public-debt obligation." These IOUs are not tangible assets that can be traded on the open market; rather, their use is more like an internal bookkeeping mechanism. The government will pay off these IOUs, but the only way it can do so is through increasing taxes, cutting spending in other areas, or additional borrowing.

The best way to understand this is to examine the numbers from the Trustees Report on Social Security. In 2011, Old-Age, Survivors, and Disability Insurance had $805 billion in income ($564 billion from payroll taxes, $103 billion from general Treasury funds to pay for the 2 percent payroll tax holiday, $114 billion from interest on the trust fund, and $24 billion from taxation of Social Security benefits) and $736 billion in expenditures. So even counting the $103 billion that was lost to the tax holiday (which is reasonable because those revenues will return in 2013), taxes fell $45 billion short of covering expenses ([$564 + $103 + $24] – $736). This means that the shortfall had to be made up with general tax revenue. As Figure 16.4 shows, the present value of the trust fund peaked at $2.7 trillion in 2011 and then turned downward when promised benefits exceeded payroll tax revenue.

FIGURE » 16.4

THE SOCIAL SECURITY TRUST FUND

As of 2011, the cost of the Social Security program exceeds Social Security payroll taxes, so taxes will need to be raised to cover the trust fund's obligations and the program's ongoing expenses. What do you think are the best solutions to address the long-term future of Social Security? What are the politically viable solutions?

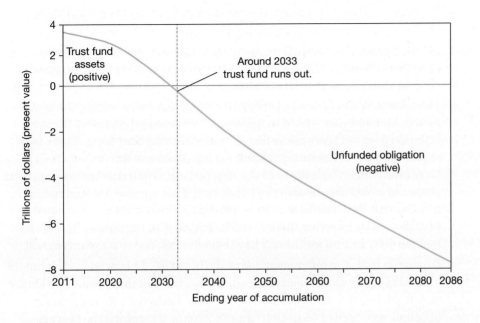

Source: Social Security Administration, 2012 OASDI Trustees Report, Figure II D5, available at www.ssa.gov/OACT/TR/2012/tr2012.pdf (accessed 10/8/12).

The trust fund runs out in 2033, at which point the Social Security system will be able to fund only about 75 percent of its obligations.[37]

Democrats and Republicans alike have misused this issue for political purposes. Democrats criticize Republicans any time they try to reform Social Security, claiming that it is on strong fiscal ground while ignoring that the need for $2.7 trillion from general taxes over a 21-year period will further strain the system and that a huge shortfall remains even after generating that additional money. Republicans note that 2011 is the year in which Social Security started to be in trouble (which is correct) but then use this point to argue that the system is in crisis and that privatization is the only way out. President Bush suggested that Social Security would be "bankrupt" in 2037, which is incorrect given that it would still be able to pay about 75 percent of its obligations. Although both sides have used the issue as demagoguery, both sides make important points as well. Republicans are correct that the sooner we act, the better. The system may not be in crisis today, but it *will* be if we don't do anything about it soon. Democrats are correct that the problems can be solved with relatively small changes to benefits and taxes, but the required changes won't be small if we wait much longer.

SOCIAL SECURITY REFORM

So what is to be done? Dozens of plans to reform Social Security and make it fiscally sound for coming generations have been suggested. There is a surprising amount of agreement among all the serious plans that saving Social Security requires a mixture of benefit cuts and tax increases. The calculations get very complicated in terms of the projected fiscal impact of various reforms, but a mixture of these options would take care of the long-term fiscal problems of Social Security:[38]

▶ Raise payroll taxes by 1 percent and increase the income ceiling that is taxable.

▶ Lower benefits for nonworking spouses. Currently nonworking spouses receive 50 percent of the benefit of their working spouse. Some proposals would cut that benefit to 33 percent.

▶ Index current and future benefits to inflation instead of wages. Currently benefit increases are linked to national average wage increases. Because inflation does not increase as fast as wages, linking benefit increases to inflation would generate significant savings. Because this would mean a large reduction of benefits over the long run, a less extreme version has been proposed called progressive price indexing. This approach would reduce benefits only for those in the top 50 percent or 70 percent of the income distribution by indexing them to inflation (those in the bottom half of the income distribution would still have benefits indexed to wage increases).

▶ Gradually raise the retirement age to 70 (by 2030). This proposed change is viewed by many as fair because it adjusts for the fact that people live longer now than they did in the early years of Social Security. Life expectancy of people who turned 65 in 1940 was 78.7 years. Therefore, the average Social Security recipient would receive about 14 years of benefits. For those who turned 65 in 2005, they could expect to live 18.7 years, and life expectancy is expected to grow about six months per decade. Therefore, by 2030, the average life expectancy for those who reach 65 will be 85. To bring the expected stream of benefits back in line with where it was in 1940, the retirement age would have to be increased to 71.5.[39] Changing the retirement age to 70 would save $620 billion by 2040.

A more controversial proposal is this:

▶ Lower benefits for wealthier recipients—that is, means-test Social Security benefits. The strongest argument in favor of this approach is that Bill Gates doesn't need the measly couple of thousand dollars he will receive each month from Social Security. In fact, he wouldn't even notice if that money was used to reduce Social Security's deficit. More broadly, if benefits are phased out for those in the top third of income levels, it will save billions of dollars a year. The main argument against this proposal is that it would end the universal nature of Social Security and possibly turn it into another welfare program.

Obama's commission on fiscal responsibility endorsed many of these ideas in their report with the dramatic title "The Moment of Truth." They favored increasing the retirement age to keep up with longevity, which would mean increasing it about one month every two years (so it would be at 69 by 2075), increasing the amount of income subject to the payroll tax so that 90 percent of all income is taxed, and making benefits more progressive (which would reduce benefits for wealthier people while actually increasing them for poorer people). The commission said that these changes would place Social Security on a secure long-term foundation.[40] However, despite the bipartisan nature of the recommendations, Congress ignored the report.

The most controversial plans concern partial or full **privatization** of Social Security. This is the main issue that divides Democrats and Republicans: Democrats favor maintaining the basic structure of Social Security's public social insurance system, and Republicans favor moving part or all of the "pay-as-you-go" system to private accounts. The central argument in favor of private accounts is that over the long term, investing in the stock market has historically provided higher returns than the expected returns from Social Security. Also, with private accounts, all assets in the account are owned by the individual and that person's heirs; whereas with Social Security, when an individual dies, that person's heirs do not receive any additional benefits from his or her lifetime contributions to Social Security. Advocates argue that if everyone were able to take their 6.2 percent payroll tax and put that in a retirement account, they would have a modest nest egg by the time they retired that would almost certainly provide a stream of benefits larger than the Social Security check that they would receive under the current system.

Democrats point out the problems with this approach—most important, the transition costs. Because the current system is "pay-as-you-go," if we stopped taking payroll taxes and allowed people to put the money into private accounts, there wouldn't be any money to pay for today's retirees. These transition costs—having to cover the retirement of all current retirees and everyone else who has paid into the system for a substantial number of years—are estimated to be $7 to 8 *trillion*! Some plans, such as President Bush's partial privatization plan, would borrow all of the money to pay the transition costs, but this approach simply shifts the accounting entries and doesn't address long-term financial problems.

A second criticism of these plans is that Social Security should be a part of everyone's retirement plan that they can count on. Investing in the stock market is fine as a supplement to Social Security, but everyone needs that dependable check, and investing in the stock market is too risky (as the collapse of the stock market in 2008–09 reminded us). Although it is true that the stock market outperforms other investments over the long haul, there have been periods as long as 20 years when stock market returns have been flat. So if you happened to retire at the end of one of those slumps, you could find yourself with a much smaller nest egg than you had counted on. Finally, critics point out that the administrative overhead costs of these private accounts would eat up any additional returns that they might earn. Jack Bogle, the founder of Vanguard Investments and one of the leading proponents of low-fee index funds, points out that $1,000 invested in 1950 in a mutual fund that mirrored the returns of the S&P 500 stocks (with reinvesting dividends) would be worth about $500,000 today. However, if the mutual fund charged a relatively modest administrative fee of 2 percent a year, the nest egg would be reduced to $230,000![41]

These issues are not likely to be resolved anytime soon, which illustrates that politics is conflictual. Social Security reform can pit one generation against another or wealthy people against poor people. The stakes in Social Security are extremely high because it is the most popular and visible social program, which makes it all the more difficult to handle.

privatization The process of transferring the management of a government program (like Social Security) from the public sector to the private sector.

HEALTH CARE

Health care policy seemed as difficult to reform as Social Security. Every president since Theodore Roosevelt who attempted comprehensive reform failed until President Obama's success in 2010. In order to understand the new law, we have to understand how health care is provided in the United States and what factors it addresses: the nation's aging population, health care costs that are rising faster than inflation, and the lack of health insurance among more than 46 million Americans.[42] Yet we spend more on health care than any other nation in the world—more than $2.6 trillion, or 17.9 percent of GDP, compared to 9.5 percent for other developed countries (for example, Japan spends 8.5 percent, Germany 11.5 percent, Canada 11.4 percent, and Italy 9.5 percent).[43] All these countries have universal health care; thus we spend almost 90 percent more than they do (in relative terms) but—until the new health care law is implemented—leave more than 46 million people without coverage. This set up a two-tier system in which those who had access to health care got some of the best care in the world and those without access were much less likely to get the health care they needed.

How is health care provided in this country, and how will the new law change it? As Figure 16.5 shows, our current system combines government spending (Medicare and Medicaid), private insurance, charity (donated care), and out-of-pocket payments. **Medicare** is the federal health care program for retired people,

Medicare The federal heath care plan created in 1965 that provides coverage for retired Americans for hospital care (Part A), medical care (Part B), and prescription drugs (Part D).

FIGURE » 16.5

THE HEALTH CARE DOLLAR: WHERE IT CAME FROM AND WHERE IT WENT

Funding for our current health care system comes from a great variety of sources and is spent on many types of care. In trying to slow the increases in health care costs, which areas should receive the most attention?

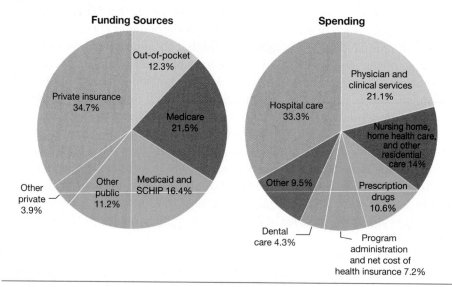

Note: Percentages shown may not add up to 100 percent because of rounding.

Source: Centers for Medicare and Medicaid Services, Office of the Actuary, National Health Statistics Group, available at www.cms.hhs.gov/NationalHealthExpendData/downloads/PieChartSourcesExpenditures2008.pdf (accessed 11/4/12).

and Medicaid is the program that covers poor people. Both programs currently are administered by the Department of Health and Human Services.

Medicare has three main parts. Part A automatically applies to retirees when they qualify for Social Security; it covers inpatient care in hospitals and skilled nursing facilities, hospice care, and some home health care. Medicare Part B helps cover doctors' services, outpatient hospital care, and some other medical services that Part A does not cover, such as some physical and occupational therapy, and other types of home health care. In 2003, Congress passed an important new benefit, the Medicare Prescription Drug Improvement and Modernization Act (Part D). The plan covers about 75 percent of the cost of prescription drugs for anyone who is enrolled in Part A or Part B of Medicare, up to a certain level of expenses (see Nuts and Bolts 16.3). The other government health care program is **Medicaid**, which serves poor people who otherwise would have no health care. Medicaid is administered through the states with substantial funding from the federal government. Although Medicaid is an **entitlement**, states have considerable discretion over the program. As the government's website on Medicaid explains, each state

(1) establishes its own eligibility standards; (2) determines the type, amount, duration, and scope of services; (3) sets the rate of payment for services; and (4) administers its own program. Medicaid policies for eligibility, services, and payment are complex and vary considerably, even among states of similar size or geographic proximity. Thus, a person who is eligible for Medicaid

Medicaid An entitlement program funded by the federal and state governments that provides health care coverage for low-income Americans who would otherwise be unable to afford heath care.

entitlement Any federal government program that provides benefits to Americans who meet requirements specified by law.

16.3 NUTS & bolts

MEDICARE COVERAGE

Medicare Premiums for 2010

Part A (hospital insurance): Most people do not pay Part A premiums because they or a spouse has 40 or more quarters of Medicare-covered employment.

Part B (medical insurance): $110.50 per month.

Part D (prescription drugs): $32.34 per month.

Medicare Deductible and Co-Insurance Amounts for 2010

Part A: Medicare pays all covered costs except a deductible of $1,156 during the first 60 days and co-insurance amounts of $289 per day for days 61 through 90 of a hospital stay and $578 per day for up to 60 "lifetime reserve days" that can be used at any time during one's lifetime. No costs beyond 150 days are covered.

Part B: $140 per year and then a 20 percent co-pay after meeting the $140 deductible.

Part D: $320 per year and then a 25 percent co-pay for the first $2,840 of drugs. The beneficiary then pays 50 percent of the next $2,840 of drug costs. After a $4,550 out-of-pocket annual limit is reached, Medicare pays 95 percent of the costs of drugs.

Note: Part C, known as Medicare Advantage, is not included here because it is not used nearly as widely as Part A or Part B and its provisions get quite complicated.

Source: Health and Human Services, "Strengthening Health and Opportunity for All Americans: Fiscal Year 2013 Budget in Brief," pp. 56–57, available at www.hhs.gov/budget/budget-brief-fy2013.pdf (accessed 11/5/12).

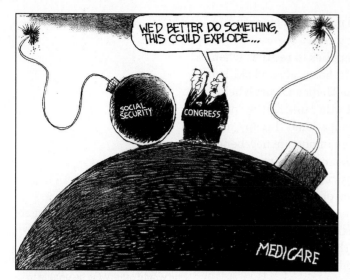

THE UNFUNDED LIABILITIES FOR Medicare are estimated to be about six times as large as the Social Security shortfall. Yet Congress has a very difficult time acting, because any solution involves the politically unpopular combination of tax increases and benefit cuts.

in one state may not be eligible in another state, and the services provided may differ considerably in amount, duration, or scope.[44]

This variation in state coverage means that some states cover virtually all poor people, and others cover as few as one-third of those in need. Overall nearly 40 million Americans receive health care through Medicaid at a cost of $305 billion. The federal government reimburses the states for about 60 percent of the costs ($265 billion in 2011), but this percentage varies by state income level. The federal government paid 75 percent of the Medicaid costs for the poorest state in 2011, Mississippi, and 50 percent of the costs for the 12 wealthiest states, which is the minimum level set by law.[45] Like Medicare, Medicaid faces growing budgetary pressures in the coming years. An increasing share of Medicaid's costs are for long-term nursing home care for the indigent elderly, which continues to grow as the population ages.

The long-term fiscal problems of Medicare and Medicaid are severe. In fact, they dwarf Social Security's problems. The 2010 Medicare Trustees report estimates that Social Security's unfunded liabilities through 2085, or the amount of additional money (beyond the current payroll tax) required to fund all the program's commitments, is $8.6 trillion, while Medicare has unfunded liabilities of $20 trillion (plus another $2.7 trillion to pay for trust fund redemptions).[46] Even though such projections depend on assumptions about future economic performance, demographic trends, and other uncertain variables, the *relative* difference between the two programs is significant. Medicare's troubles are more than two and a half times as serious as Social Security's! While the long-term Medicare deficit is huge, it is less than half the size of the projected unfunded liabilities before health care reform was passed. However, the Trustees noted that their projections assume that cuts in Medicare reimbursements mandated in new health care law will stick. The report expressed skepticism that this would happen.[47]

Another study by the nonpartisan Congressional Budget Office showed that federal spending on health care (including Medicare, Medicaid, and subsidies for the new health insurance exchanges) will continue to grow through 2080 (see Figure 16.6). The CBO estimated that by 2080 federal health care spending would reach about 19 percent of GDP. That is, if the size of the federal government stayed around its historic average of 20 percent of GDP, health care spending would constitute nearly all of noninterest federal spending by 2080. The choices are clear: either everything else must be cut from the budget (defense, education, transportation), health care costs must be reined in, or the size of government will grow. There wouldn't be any money for anything else—defense, Social Security, education— nothing. Clearly the current trends are not sustainable.

HEALTH CARE REFORM

Although comprehensive health care reform had been shot down repeatedly before 2010, several incremental reforms added up to substantial change. In 1996 Congress passed the Health Insurance Portability and Accountability Act, which guaranteed that people could not be denied health care coverage when they switched

FIGURE » 16.6

PROJECTED NATIONAL SPENDING ON HEALTH CARE

If current spending patterns hold, an increasing percentage of federal spending will be devoted to health care, crowding out other programs. Clearly such trends are not sustainable. What changes do you support to reduce health care spending in the long run?

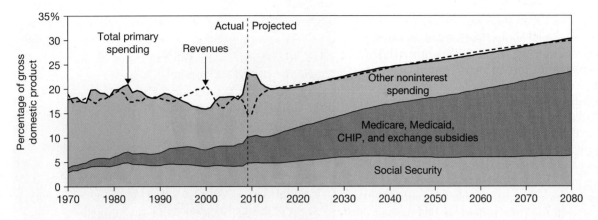

Source: Congressional Budget Office, "The Long-Term Budget Outlook," June 2010 (revised August 2010), Figure A-1, p.68, available at www.cbo.gov/ftpdocs/115xx/doc11579/06-30-LTBO.pdf (accessed 11/4/12).

jobs. The new law also protected the privacy of a patient's health information. Medicaid was expanded in 1997 to provide health care for children in families that make too much to qualify for Medicaid but not enough to buy private insurance for their children (incomes that are no more than double the poverty level). By 2011, more than 7.7 million children were enrolled in the program.[48] The Bush administration pushed for, and Congress passed, limited tax-free health savings accounts that may be used for paying routine out-of-pocket health care expenses or saving for more substantial, unexpected health care costs. Also, Medicare Part D, the prescription drug plan, went into effect in 2006. Despite these incremental reforms, discontent with the system continued to build.

President Obama's primary focus when he took office in January 2009 was to get the economy going. However, he also campaigned on reforming our health care system, and he remained committed to that goal. Yet initially Obama stayed out of the legislative fray in an effort to avoid the centralized micromanaging that had doomed President Clinton's attempt at comprehensive reform in 1993–94. After poll numbers showed the public turning against health care reform, and a series of angry town hall meetings in which members of Congress faced questions about "death panels" and a government takeover of health care, Obama decided he needed to regain control of the debate. In a nationally televised speech before a joint session of Congress, Obama outlined his priorities, answered his critics, and linked the two top priorities of a revitalized economy and health care reform. He vowed to create a health care system

that eases up the pressure on businesses and unleashes the promise of our economy, creating hundreds of thousands of jobs, making take-home wages

THE SOCIAL WELFARE STATE

On many "quality of life" measures, the United States does not stack up very well when compared to the other developed nations. The Organization for Economic Cooperation and Development (OECD) is an organization of 34 of the world's most developed nations, including all of the big European countries, Japan, Canada, Mexico, South Korea, New Zealand, and Australia. OECD data show that among all the OECD's members, the United States is eighth from the bottom in terms of life expectancy (78.2 years compared to 83 years for the top country—Japan—and a median of 80.2 years), fourth from the bottom in infant mortality (6.5 deaths per 1,000 live births compared to a median of 3.3), and dead last in obesity (33.8 percent of Americans are obese compared to a median of 16.9 percent).[a]

How could this be, given that the United States is one of the wealthiest nations in the world? Part of the reason is that our government spends less on social welfare than other OECD countries: we are tenth from the bottom, at 19.5 percent of gross domestic product (GDP) compared to the OECD median of 22 percent. The OECD defines social spending as direct spending and tax expenditures in support of pensions, disability payments, health care, child care, unemployment compensation, housing, cash payments to the poor (welfare), job training, and "other benefits that address one or more social purposes" (education is not included in this definition).[a] Most other OECD countries have publicly funded national health care systems, paid maternity leave (up to two years in some countries), extensive job training programs, and generous retirement benefits. This social welfare state is the product of a long-standing commitment in many European countries to take care of those who are less fortunate. The earliest European health care plan, for example, goes back to 1883 in the Bismarck Republic in Germany. In the last half of the twentieth century, many left-leaning and socialist governments in Europe dramatically increased the size of the social welfare state.

While the *public* social welfare state is definitely much smaller in the United States than in most developed countries, the United States ranks much higher if total social spending—public and private—is measured: we are just above the OECD median of 23.3 percent (at 27.2 percent of GDP). The United States ranks first in the OECD in private spending (10.1 percent of GDP compared to the median of 2.9 percent). The main category driving this difference is health care. The United States spends far more on health care than any other nation in the world: $7,290 per person compared to the second high-

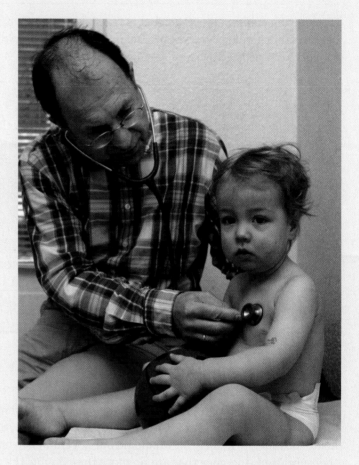

Americans spend far more on health care than any other nation in the world, yet overall health outcomes in the United States are in the bottom third of developed nations. This German doctor is caring for a child as part of a national health care system in which all basic costs are covered by the government.

est spender, Norway, at $4,763; the OECD median is $3,323. Given this average level of overall spending on social welfare and the tremendously high total spending on health care, it is even more puzzling why the United States has such a low ranking on health statistics such as life expectancy, infant mortality, and obesity. The relative performance of the United States to its peers may change after health care reform is fully implemented in 2018.

thousands of dollars higher, and growing our economy by tens of billions more every year. That's how we will stop spending tax dollars to prop up an unsustainable system, and start investing those dollars in innovations and advances that will make our health care system and our economy stronger.[49]

Obama presented several goals: controlling health care costs, providing as close to universal coverage as possible, and paying for the program without adding to the deficit. He then urged Congress to hammer out the details.

In formulating the legislation, Congress sifted through hundreds of options that represent three main types: (1) national single-payer plans, (2) state-regulated health insurance networks combined with public subsidies to help pay for insurance for those who cannot afford it, and (3) **market-based solutions** based on tax credits and flexible spending accounts. The first of these was quickly rejected by Congress and is never likely to be implemented in the United States, despite being the program of choice for nearly all other Western developed nations. Critics dismiss single-payer plans as "socialized medicine" and point to the rationing of care that often occurs under such programs. Similarly, market-based solutions, which most Republicans supported, were rejected by Democratic leaders who believed the approach would leave too many Americans uninsured. This approach has the greatest potential for addressing the inflation of health care costs, but some health care professionals argued that many people would lack the knowledge base necessary to make the appropriate decisions concerning their own health care, because buying health care is much more difficult than shopping for food, clothing, or other consumer goods.

This left the middle ground between a single-payer plan and market-based approaches. The politics of how reform passed was discussed in the introduction to this chapter. Here we summarize the main provisions, as it is impossible to discuss all the details of the voluminous, more than 2,000-page law that one reporter described as "twice as long, and half as intelligible, as Tolstoy's masterwork *War and Peace.*"[50]

The president's first goal—comprehensive coverage—was essential. The problem had to be tackled as a whole. If insurance companies were forced to cover people with preexisting conditions without a mandate that everyone have insurance, people would wait until they were seriously ill to get coverage. Healthy people had to be pooled with sick people to spread the costs of expensive care. This was achieved by requiring businesses with more than 50 employees to provide coverage, and individuals not covered by employers to purchase insurance through new state-regulated private health insurance exchanges (these had to be in place by 2014). Businesses and individuals who do not comply with the mandate will face government fines. However, individuals who cannot afford insurance will receive federal subsidies on a sliding scale (a complicated formula that provides the biggest subsidies to the poorest people and some support all the way up to four times the federal poverty rate). The individual mandate was one of the most controversial parts of the bill, but supporters point out that states already require people to purchase auto insurance if they have a car. People who already have health insurance through their employer and are happy with their current policy do not have to change anything.

Other features of the law include incentives to computerize medical records, which would improve the quality of care, reduce the number of mistakes, and facilitate evaluating quality of care. This is related to one of the law's central cost-control mechanisms: a new nonprofit organization, the Patient-Centered Outcomes Research Institute, will engage in "comparative effectiveness research" to

market-based solutions
Reform options for social policies that are based on tax credits, flexible spending accounts, and other approaches that rely on competition in the free market.

identify the best practices in health care. For example, which health care procedures work to make people healthier, and which are a waste of money? Why do some parts of the country spend more than twice as much on treating the same conditions? Health care providers will be encouraged to adopt these best practices. The law also focuses more resources on preventive care to keep people healthy rather than spend money on them once they get sick.

One other goal was that health care had to pay for itself. Obama vowed that the bill would not "add one dime to the deficit." With a price tag of just under $1 trillion over the first 10 years, paying for the bill was a challenge. However, a combination of higher Medicare taxes, a new investment tax on the wealthy, an excise tax on insurers for expensive health care plans, new fees for drug companies and health insurers, and cuts in Medicare reimbursement meant that the law would actually reduce the federal deficit by $143 billion over the first decade.[51]

Yet the battle over health care reform was not over when Obama signed the bill into law. Opponents promised to repeal the law and featured this pledge in their campaign strategy during the 2010 midterm elections. Despite Republican leaders' interpretation of their decisive midterm victory as a mandate to repeal health care reform, and their vow to do so, it is unlikely they will be successful: Democrats still control the Senate, and Obama would veto any attempt to repeal the law. Furthermore, many popular parts of the law have already gone into effect. These include a temporary high-risk insurance pool for adults with preexisting conditions, since the permanent requirement that insurance companies cover people with preexisting conditions does not go into effect until 2014 (in addition, children under 19 with preexisting conditions could not be dropped from their parents' policies); a fix for the Medicare prescription drug plan "donut hole" (previously, people who spent above a minimal level on drugs but below a high amount were not covered by the law); and coverage for young adults (up to age 26) on their parents' plan. Other popular parts of the law that are already in effect prohibit insurers from charging co-payments or deductibles for preventative care on all new insurance plans, and prevent insurers from dropping policyholders when they get sick.

Republicans have argued for market-based reforms that would introduce more competition into the system to help keep costs down. One proposal that has received a lot of attention is Representative Paul Ryan's (R-Wisc.) "Roadmap for America's Future." His proposal would change Medicare into a voucher system for everyone who is under 55 years old. Instead of the current Medicare system, people would receive a voucher to buy health insurance in exchanges similar to those that are being set up under Obama's health care reform.[52] Critics say that Medicare is more efficient than private insurance, so this will only drive up the overall cost of health care. However, Ryan is correct that Medicare is currently not on a sustainable path, so some change is necessary.

Despite the uncertainty about the legal challenges and efforts by Republicans in Congress to repeal the legislation, the law will likely survive and be strengthened over the years. The legislation is far from perfect: about 10 to 15 million Americans will remain without health insurance when it is fully implemented in 2018, funding for the policy is shaky, and enforcement of the individual mandate is essentially voluntary (through the federal tax code). But if experience with other social legislation is any guide, the law is likely to be amended and improved as problems become evident. As Senator Tom Harkin put it, health care reform is not a mansion, but a "starter home with a solid foundation, a strong roof, and plenty of room for additions and improvements."[53]

Many other issues related to health care will come up in the next decade, including assisted suicide and the "right to die." Voters in Oregon approved a law that went into effect in 1997 allowing the terminally ill to take a fatal dose of medication; the law was upheld by the Supreme Court in 2006.[54] Other issues involve the increasingly high-tech nature of health care: DNA research provides great promise for curing many diseases, while moral and ethical questions arise about cloning, surrogate parenthood, and stem cell research. The coming years will be a challenging period for health care policy.

INCOME SUPPORT AND WELFARE

When most people think of social policy aimed at helping the poor, they think of welfare. The earlier section on the history of social policy outlined the evolution of welfare from a limited policy aimed at helping dependent children of single mothers to a broader policy directed more generally to households headed by one person. Welfare is usually thought of as cash support for people who cannot support themselves. However, **income support** can take many forms, including food stamps, unemployment insurance, Supplemental Security Income, and the Earned Income Tax Credit. We will discuss each and then describe the major reform of welfare in 1996.

The Supplemental Nutrition Assistance Program provides food stamps, which are government-issued coupons that may be used as cash to buy groceries. Anyone who has an income that is less than 130 percent of the poverty level and has resources that do not exceed specific levels may qualify for food stamps. In 2012, the maximum monthly gross income to qualify for food stamps for a family of four was $2,422. As the effects of the economic crisis lingered through 2011, the number of people using food stamps hit a record of nearly 44.7 million, with an average monthly benefit of $133.85 per person.[55]

The Federal-State Unemployment Compensation Program was established in 1935 as part of the Social Security Act. The U.S. Department of Labor oversees the program, but it is administered by the states. The program provides temporary and partial wage replacement for people who have been laid off from their jobs and to help stabilize the economy during recessions. States set a broad range in benefit levels, minimum amount of income earned, and hours worked during the period leading up to unemployment. (For example, you couldn't have worked five hours a week in a minimum wage job and qualify for unemployment insurance.) Also, laid-off workers have to make themselves "available for work." About 97 percent of all workers are covered by unemployment insurance, but only about half of the eligible unemployed make use of the benefit. The regular state programs provide up to 26 weeks of income support, and the Federal-State Extended Benefits Program temporarily provides up to 20 additional weeks in states with relatively high unemployment rates. In January 2012, the average weekly benefit check was $296, which replaced 32.8 percent of the average worker's previous salary. Workers received benefits for an average of 17.5 weeks in 2011.[56]

The Earned Income Tax Credit (EITC) is one of the most successful programs for providing income support for the working poor. Established in 1975, the program aims to help poor people move from welfare to work: it provides tax credits to people who do not earn enough to pay income taxes and are relatively poor. It is intended to offset the burden of social security taxes, which all workers pay as part of payroll

income support Government programs that provide support to low-income Americans, such as welfare, food stamps, unemployment compensation, and the Earned Income Tax Credit.

taxes. In 2011, you could qualify for an EITC if you had two children and earned less than $40,964, one child and earned less than $36,052, or no children and earned less than $13,660; the figures are slightly higher if you are married and filing jointly.[57] The federal government provided $59.5 billion in EITCs in 2010 to 26.8 million recipients, with an average monthly benefit of $185 per recipient; Figure 16.7 shows average monthly figures for other programs.[58] Clearly nobody is getting rich from this program, but it provides added assistance for the working poor.

Another source of income support for poor people is Supplemental Security Income (SSI), a program for aged, blind, and disabled individuals with limited income. The Social Security Administration runs the SSI program, but it is financed through general tax revenues, not Social Security taxes, and it is a means-tested program rather than a contributory program. Many states supplement the maximum monthly federal benefit of $698 for an individual and $1,048 for a couple (in 2012). More than 8.1 million people received SSI benefits in 2011; 85 percent of those recipients were disabled or blind.[59]

FIGURE » 16.7

AVERAGE MONTHLY BENEFITS IN MEANS-TESTED PROGRAMS

Some types of social welfare benefits have increased in the past few decades, while others have decreased and some have remained the same. Identify examples from each category and try to provide a political explanation for why those benefits have increased, decreased, or been funded at about the same level.

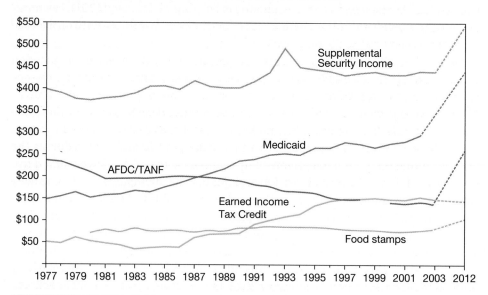

Note: AFDC is Aid to Families with Dependent Children; TANF is Temporary Assistance for Needy Families. Data from AFDC/TANF and the Earned Income Tax Credit cover people of all ages, including the elderly. Data are not available for some programs for certain years, such as TANF in 1999.

Source: Congressional Budget Office, Economic and Budget Issue Brief, "Changes in Participation in Means-Tested Programs," April 20, 2005, p. 5, available at www.cbo.gov/ftpdocs/63xx/ doc6302/04-20-Means-Tested.pdf, for data through 2003 (accessed 10/9/12). Various sources for 2012 (2012 figures are reported in 2003 dollars to allow comparison with the previous study.)

Welfare is straight cash assistance for people who are not working and do not qualify for unemployment compensation. The primary welfare program for the latter half of the twentieth century was **Aid to Families with Dependent Children (AFDC)**. This program became increasingly unpopular through the 1980s, and in 1992 Bill Clinton was the first Democratic presidential nominee to campaign against welfare, promising to "end welfare as we know it."[60] President Clinton did not make this the top priority of his first year in office and instead focused on health care reform and balancing the budget. However, Clinton got the ball rolling on welfare reform in June 1993 by appointing a task force on the issue. Republican leaders offered their own alternatives in the House and Senate late in 1993 and early in 1994. Clinton's commission released its bipartisan plan in January 1994, and the president's plan was submitted to Congress in June. At least a dozen other welfare reform alternatives were proposed in Congress, and some hearings were held, but no action was taken as the midterm elections loomed (it is difficult to get bipartisan compromise on major legislation in the partisan context of election battles).

When the Republicans took over Congress in 1994, the momentum for reform grew. House leaders submitted the Personal Responsibility Act as part of the Republican Contract with America. This bill promised to end welfare as an entitlement, allowing states more flexibility in setting benefit levels and work requirements, creating lifetime limits for the amount of time that people could receive welfare, and attempting to curb out-of-wedlock births by denying benefits. Clinton and Congress haggled over the issue for two years, with the president vetoing three versions of the bill that he believed were too harsh. Finally, in 1996 they agreed on a major reform called **Temporary Assistance for Needy Families (TANF)**. The new law set a five-year lifetime limit on welfare benefits, required single mothers with children above the age of five to find work after two years of receiving benefits, required unmarried mothers who were less than 18 years old to live with an adult and attend school to get full benefits, denied benefits to drug users who were convicted of a felony, and limited people who were not raising children and were between the ages of 18 and 50 to three months of food stamps in any three-year period in which they were not working. Perhaps most important, welfare lost its status as an entitlement and would be administered by the states with the assistance of federal block grants. In February 2006, Congress reauthorized TANF and required that half of a state's caseload participate in work activities for at least 30 hours per week. Welfare reform significantly reduced the number of people on welfare, as Figure 16.8 shows, but it has been criticized for being too hard on the people who need government assistance the most. Critics also point out that TANF block grants have not been adjusted for inflation since they were first created in 1996.[61]

Aid to Families with Dependent Children (AFDC) The federal welfare program in place from 1935 until 1996, when it was replaced by Temporary Assistance for Needy Families (TANF) under President Clinton.

Temporary Assistance for Needy Families (TANF) The welfare program that replaced Aid to Families with Dependent Children (AFDC) in 1996, eliminating the entitlement status of welfare, shifting implementation of the policy to the states, and introducing several new restrictions on receiving aid. These changes led to a significant decrease in the number of welfare recipients.

EDUCATION POLICY

Education policy is largely the domain of state and local governments. For the first century of our nation's history, the national government played virtually no role in education. One important exception was the Morrill Act in 1862, also known as the Land Grant College Act. This law gave land to eligible states to establish colleges that would promote education in the practical professions such as agriculture and mechanical arts. More than 75 colleges and universities today are land grant institutions.

The next major forays by the federal government into education policy came with the GI Bill of Rights in 1944, which provided access to higher education for

FIGURE » 16.8

PARTICIPATION IN MEANS-TESTED PROGRAMS

The social policy "safety net" is supposed to protect poor Americans during periods of economic recession. A deep recession happened in the early 1980s, and the other recession during the time frame depicted here was in the early 1990s. To what extent did the safety net play its intended role?

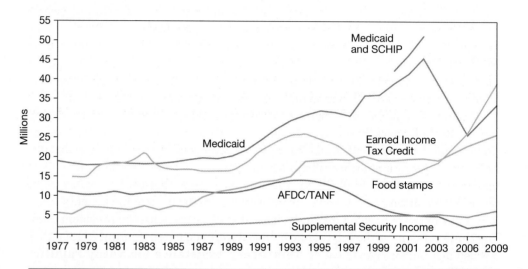

Source: Data for 1977–2003 from Congressional Budget Office, Economic and Budget Issue Brief, "Changes in Partici-pation in Means-Tested Programs," April 20, 2005, p. 3, available at www.cbo.gov/ftpdocs/63xx/ doc6302/04-20-Means-Tested.pdf. Data for 2006 and 2009 from "Dynamics of Economic Well Being: Participation in Government Programs, 2004 to 2007 and 2009; Who Gets Assistance?" Current Population Reports, July 2012, www.census.gov/prod/2012pubs/p70–130.pdf (accessed 10/9/12).

returning World War II veterans, and the Elementary and Secondary Education Act of 1965, which was part of President Johnson's War on Poverty. The Department of Education was created in 1980, signaling the national government's interest in playing an important role in education policy by

▶ establishing and monitoring policies on federal financial aid for education,

▶ collecting data on America's schools and disseminating research,

▶ focusing national attention on key educational issues, and

▶ prohibiting discrimination and ensuring equal access to education.[62]

A more recent debate concerning the national government's role in education policy has focused on standards-based education reform: Should the national government establish standards and impose accountability as a way to improve public schools? The No Child Left Behind Act of 2001 requires yearly statewide standardized testing in math and reading. If the test results show that a school is not meeting annual academic benchmarks, it is labeled a "failing school," which means that it loses some federal funding and its students may transfer to another public school. Critics argue that standardized test results are a poor measurement of progress, as schools "teach to the test" and manipulate other aspects of the evaluation system.

Even with these efforts at imposing a national approach, there is substantial room for variations in state and local implementation of the national law.

President Obama's "Race to the Top" program dedicated $4 billion to competitive grants in 2010 and a proposed $1.35 billion in 2011 to encourage schools to adopt more challenging standards and better tools of assessment, promote better leadership and methods for assessing and rewarding excellent teaching, create better data systems for tracking students' progress, and obtain stronger commitments for improving the worst-performing schools. These grants were aimed at improving the quality of public education while improving accountability.[63] Early in 2012 the Obama administration proposed the RESPECT project (Recognizing Educational Success, Professional Excellence and Collaborative Teaching), which is another set of incentive grants aimed at improving education. The grants would encourage school systems to give teachers more autonomy, make teachers' salaries more competitive with those of other professions while tying compensation to performance, improve teacher education programs while making them more selective, create teacher evaluation systems based on multiple measures, and reform the tenure system.[64]

States and local school districts are also experimenting with various policies aimed at introducing more competition for public schools, including public school choice allowing students to choose which public school they attend and publicly funded vouchers for attending private schools (see "You Decide"). Private foundations have also gotten involved in education policy. The Gates Foundation has contributed more than $2 billion to create smaller schools, reduce class sizes, provide scholarships for higher education (most significantly, $1.5 billion to the United Negro College Fund), improve the use of data, and provide access to technology.[65]

UNDER THE NO CHILD LEFT BEHIND act, schools conduct standardized tests every year. Schools that fail to meet federal goals receive less federal funding. Critics argue that the emphasis on testing distracts from other educational goals.

SCHOOL VOUCHERS

Another important area of social policy is education policy. One of the most controversial areas of education policy over the past 15 years has been school vouchers—the practice of providing taxpayers' money directly to families to allow them to send their children to private schools rather than public schools. The vouchers are similar to a scholarship and are used in several states, including Wisconsin, Florida, Ohio, Pennsylvania, and Utah.[a]

Supporters of the program say that it introduces competition into public education, which suffers from the inefficiencies that are typical of monopolies. They argue that many urban school systems have failed to educate their children and that poor, minority students deserve a better education than they can get in public schools. They say that students who are given the opportunity to leave public schools often improve their academic performance in private schools. Opponents say that private schools engage in "cherry picking," choosing the more motivated students and leaving the more difficult to educate in the public schools, contributing to a downward spiral. Opponents also argue that standardized test scores do not improve for students who participate in voucher programs. Finally, they also say that voucher programs are an unconstitutional violation of the separation between church and state because an overwhelming proportion of the students in these programs attend Catholic parochial schools.

Evidence on opponents' first two points is mixed, but the bulk of the evidence supports their views. The most studied voucher program is the first in the nation, which was established in Milwaukee, Wisconsin, in 1990 using state funding. In the most systematic analysis of that program, John Witte argues that vouchers should be evaluated on a basic question of values, the clash between freedom of choice and equality of opportunity, rather than specific programmatic outcomes, because the effects are small to nonexistent.[b]

The politics of school vouchers has created an unusual alliance between free market conservatives, who are typically Republicans, and inner-city minorities, who normally are strong Democrats. The former believe that school systems can benefit from introducing competitive market forces, and the latter are desperate for anything that will rescue their children from failing public schools. These supporters of vouchers are opposed by teachers' unions, most Democratic politicians, and those who favor strengthening the public schools by investing more money in them and trying new approaches, such as public magnet schools, charter schools, and public school choice.

The Supreme Court has upheld voucher programs while asserting that they did not violate the separation of church and state. However, in a case upholding Cleveland's voucher program, the Court did not give vouchers a green light beyond the narrow facts of the case. Indeed, that 5–4 decision required a voucher program to, among other things,

School vouchers are controversial. Supporters see them as a way to allow poor, inner-city students to escape failing public schools. Critics are concerned that vouchers compound the problems facing public schools, while potentially violating the separation of church and state: most school vouchers go to private, Catholic schools, like the one shown here.

- be a part of a much wider program of multiple educational options, such as magnet schools and after-school tutorial assistance;
- offer parents a real choice between religious and nonreligious education, perhaps even providing incentives for nonreligious education; and
- not only address private schools, but ensure that benefits go to schools regardless of whether they are public or private, religious or not.[c]

Meanwhile, the Arizona state supreme court struck down school voucher programs as a violation of the separation of church and state.

Critical Thinking Questions

1. What do you see as the advantages and disadvantages of providing vouchers to allow students to attend any school they want?

2. Should these programs be expanded, or would they undermine the quality of public schools?

CONCLUSION

The varying successes and failures of efforts to reform Social Security, health care, and welfare reveal a great deal about the role of key players in the policy-making process. The interaction between the president and Congress is central to each story. With Social Security reform, the president initiated a serious reform agenda, but Congress killed the proposal by failing to act. With health care reform, Congress and the president worked together to pass significant legislation. In both instances, interest groups played a key role. Doctors, other health care providers, insurance companies, and drug companies largely supported health care reform, which helped Congress pass the historic but controversial legislation. With Social Security reform, opposition from AARP and a tepid response from the public doomed the idea of private savings accounts, at least for now. But the last chapter on reform is yet to be written. Sooner or later policy makers will have to confront the massive long-term deficits in these programs.

Welfare reform also illustrates the roles of the various players in policy making. As with health care reform, the president and Congress were the most important players in shaping the massive overhaul of the welfare system. However, there were some key differences. First, although the policy-making process in Congress for health care reform was almost entirely partisan, with the Democratic Party dictating the final shape of the bill, welfare reform was shaped by a more bipartisan process between the Republicans in Congress and Democratic President Clinton. Second, those who benefited from welfare were much weaker politically than those who would be directly affected by the reform of health care. As a component of the public, the poor simply do not have much clout because they do not vote, participate in campaigns, or contribute to campaigns as much as the rest of the public. Therefore, they could do little to stop welfare reform. Third, the organized groups opposed to welfare reform and representing the poor do not have the same political power as the health care groups supporting reform. Thus, reform was enacted into law in both instances but with a different mix of players.

The experiences with social policy reform also illustrate the themes of the book. First, health care reform is a perfect example of the conflictual nature of politics. From fictitious "death panels" to health coverage for illegal immigrants and abortion, health care reform ignited many contentious debates. Substantive disagreements about the scope of coverage and how to pay for it also revealed deep fault lines across and within the parties. Despite this conflict, congressional leaders pieced together compromises that created an imperfect but historic law. However, conflict over social policy is far from resolved. The reform of Social Security and Medicare provide fertile ground for intergenerational struggle and class warfare. Clearly, resolving the long-term problems facing social policy in the United States will involve many intense debates.

Social policy, especially the legislative struggles over health care reform, demonstrates that political process matters. The filibuster in the Senate played an important role in the first stages of shaping health care reform, and the decision to use the reconciliation process late in the game ensured passage of the law. Politicians' decisions have a key impact on policy outcomes, and the timing and politics of the policy-making process clearly drive the results. Had congressional leaders made different decisions, it is possible that health care reform would have failed. Finally, politics is everywhere. Social policies touch all Americans at some point in their lives, and the struggles over reforming these policies are at the core of contemporary American politics.

THE HISTORY AND BACKGROUND OF SOCIAL POLICY

▶ Explain what we mean by social policy, and how the national government's role in social policy has evolved. **Pages 653–56**

SUMMARY

Social policy is the catch-all term for government programs that are designed to achieve a general social goal. While the early federal government took little responsibility for social welfare, it has gradually expanded its role since the late nineteenth century. Today, the federal government plays a significant part in ensuring the welfare of its people.

KEY TERMS

social policy (p. 653)

welfare (p. 653)

New Deal (p. 655)

Great Society (p. 655)

ownership society (p. 656)

CRITICAL THINKING AND DISCUSSION

What do you think should be the government's responsibilities in the area of social policy? Do you favor more of an "ownership society" or more of a direct role for the government?

PRACTICE QUIZ QUESTIONS

1. The first significant example of federal involvement in social policy is _____.
   a) the New Deal
   b) aid to Civil War veterans
   c) the Great Society
   d) aid to Mexican-American War veterans
   e) unemployment compensation in the 1890s

2. Social Security was established under the _____; Medicare was established under the _____.
   a) New Deal; Great Society
   b) New Deal; New Deal
   c) Great Society; Great Society
   d) Great Society; New Deal
   e) New Deal; Opportunity Society

3. The principle of the "ownership society" is that _____.
   a) the government has responsibility for the people's social welfare
   b) the government has responsibility for the poor's social welfare
   c) the government has responsibility for health care but not education
   d) the rich have responsibility for the poor's social welfare
   e) people have responsibility for their own welfare

⑤ PRACTICE ONLINE

"Big Think" video exercise: *The Legacy of the New Deal*

POVERTY AND INCOME INEQUALITY

▶ Examine the problem of poverty as a target of social policies. **Pages 656–60**

SUMMARY

Most social programs have an impact on poverty, either directly or indirectly. There is a growing gap between the top income levels and the bottom. Government policies tend to disproportionately favor the wealthy, largely based on the type of social policies the government chooses to implement.

4. The primary motivator for social policy is
_____.

a) economic dislocation
b) poverty
c) the deficit
d) care for the elderly
e) gender inequality

5. Under Democratic presidents, the incomes of working poor families _____ than/as under Republican presidents.
a) increased faster
b) increased slower

c) stayed the same
d) decreased slower
e) decreased faster

> ⓢ **PRACTICE ONLINE**
>
> "What Do Political Scientists Do?" video exercise: *Larry Bartels on Social Policy and Income Inequality*

THE KEY PLAYERS IN SOCIAL POLICY MAKING

▶ Describe the roles played by each branch of the national government and by the states in making and implementing social policy. **Pages 661–63**

SUMMARY

At the federal level, social policy is shaped by Congress, the president, and the bureaucracy. Other groups play a role in social policy as well: policy concerning the elderly is particularly affected by interest groups, while state governments focus on policy concerning welfare and education.

PRACTICE QUIZ QUESTIONS

6. Bureaucratic discretion _____ agency-to-agency consistency of policy provision; it _____ ability to administer policies efficiently.
a) increases; increases
b) increases; decreases
c) decreases; increases
d) decreases; decreases
e) decreases; has no effect on

7. States influence policies on _____; but not _____.
a) Social Security; education
b) Social Security; Medicaid
c) education; Medicaid
d) Medicaid; education
e) Medicaid; Social Security

> ⓢ **PRACTICE ONLINE**
>
> "Critical Thinking" exercise: *Politics Is Everywhere— Welfare Recipients by State*

THE POLICY-MAKING PROCESS

▶ Trace the steps through which problems are addressed by social policies. **Pages 663–66**

SUMMARY

Once an issue is recognized and defined as a problem, and when the conditions are right, the issue reaches the congressional agenda. Once a policy is in place, its effectiveness and implementation are evaluated in an ongoing process, though very few programs are ultimately terminated.

KEY TERM

policy agenda (p. 664)

8. What is the policy agenda?
a) the set of policies political leaders view as priorities
b) the set of issues political leaders view as priorities
c) the set of issues that issue groups view as priorities
d) the set of policies that issue groups view as priorities
e) the set of policies issue groups and political leaders view as priorities

9. Relative to the private sector, public sector programs are _____ to evaluate.
a) easier
b) equally easy
c) harder
d) equally as hard
e) not important

ⓢ PRACTICE ONLINE

"Critical Thinking" exercise: *Politics Is Conflictual—Social Security Reform and Party Platforms*

SOCIAL POLICY TODAY

▶ Analyze the current major areas of social policy. **Pages 666–86**

SUMMARY

The aging population and rising health care costs threaten the future of Social Security and Medicare, which make up half the federal budget. Despite the importance of reforming these programs, politicians are reluctant to enact serious reform for fear of jeopardizing their own political futures.

KEY TERMS

Social Security (p. 667)

Baby Boom generation (p. 668)

privatization (p. 673)

Medicare (p. 674)

Medicaid (p. 675)

entitlement (p. 675)

market-based solutions (p. 679)

income support (p. 681)

Aid to Families with Dependent Children (AFDC) (p. 683)

Temporary Assistance for Needy Families (TANF) (p. 683)

CRITICAL THINKING AND DISCUSSION

Do you support the health care reform law that was enacted in 2010? Or do you think the law was not ambitious enough, or alternatively, an overreach by the national government?

PRACTICE QUIZ QUESTIONS

10. Which group of working Americans is eligible to receive Social Security benefits?
a) those whose income is in the bottom 15%
b) those whose income is in the bottom 25%
c) those whose income is in the bottom 50%
d) income is not a criteria for eligibility
e) only the unemployed are eligible

11. The primary reason Social Security will be financially strained in the coming years is because _____.
a) it is a pay-as-you-go program
b) its stipends are indexed to inflation
c) it is transitioning to privately held accounts
d) compensation to nonworking spouses is equal to benefits for the working spouse
e) most Americans don't approve of Social Security

12. State governments _____ have influence on Medicaid; they _____ have influence on Medicare.
a) do; do
b) do; do not
c) do not; do
d) do not; sometimes
e) do not; do not

13. In President Obama's health care plan, why was it essential to guarantee comprehensive coverage?

   a) to make sure enough people were paying in to the system

   b) to pool risk between sick and healthy people

   c) to reduce the risks of fraud

   d) to prevent individuals from only having one price to pay

   e) to win broad political support

14. The major welfare reform of 1996 instituted the _____ program, which _____ welfare spending relative to its predecessor.

   a) Aid for Families with Dependent Children (AFDC); reduced

   b) AFDC; increased

   c) Temporary Assistance to Needy Families (TANF); reduced

   d) TANF; increased

   e) Medicaid; reduced

15. The long-term fiscal problems of _____ are most severe.

   a) Social Security

   b) Medicare/Medicaid

   c) welfare

   d) federally subsidized student loans

   e) education

ⓢ PRACTICE ONLINE

"Big Think" video exercise: *Paul Krugman on the Retirement Age*

SUGGESTED READING

Altman, Nancy J. *The Battle for Social Security: From FDR's Vision to Bush's Gamble*. New York: Wiley, 2005.

Bartels, Larry M. *Unequal Democracy: The Political Economy of the New Gilded Age*. Princeton, NJ: Princeton University Press, 2008.

King, Ronald F. *Budgeting Entitlements: The Politics of Food Stamps*. Washington, DC: Georgetown University Press, 2000.

Oberlander, Jonathan. *The Political Life of Medicare*. Chicago: University of Chicago Press, 2003.

Skocpol, Theda. *Social Policy in the United States: Future Possibilities in Historical Perspective*. Princeton, NJ: Princeton University Press, 1995.

Soss, Joe. *Unwanted Claims: The Politics of Participation in the U.S. Welfare System*. Ann Arbor: University of Michigan Press, 2000.

Weaver, R. Kent. *Ending Welfare as We Know It*. Washington, DC: Brookings Institution Press, 2000.

17

Foreign Policy

MANY AMERICANS EXPECT FOREIGN POLICY to be an area of agreement and consensus—that as Americans we hold similar goals and similar ideas of what our country should be doing outside our borders. As a result, many Americans agree with Senator Arthur Vandenberg, who in 1945 gave a speech in which he argued, "Politics stops at the water's edge," and tend to see disagreement over foreign policy as somehow unpatriotic and motivated by political factors.

One recent example of these beliefs in action occurred in 2010 when General Stanley McChrystal, then commander of U.S. forces in Afghanistan, was quoted in a *Rolling Stone* article making critical comments about various members of the Obama administration, questioning their knowledge of the situation in Afghanistan and their beliefs about how military action should proceed.[1] McChrystal was soon removed from his position by President Obama. Some responses to the removal echoed Vandenberg's argument that political disagreements over foreign policy are not appropriate—shouldn't Americans defer to the judgments of military leaders, who presumably are in the best position to plan and execute military operations in Afghanistan and elsewhere?

One of the central goals of this chapter is to demonstrate that simple answers are rare in foreign policy. Afghanistan is a good example. After over a decade of military action and efforts to build a stable democracy and a growing economy, Afghanistan remains a dangerous, unstable place. Should the United States be responsible for creating a stable, prosperous Afghan nation? What will happen

CONFLICT & COMPROMISE
in American Politics

if America withdraws its ground forces—can the Afghan government control its borders and aid its citizens? Would terrorist organizations such as Al Qaeda, the group that organized the September 11 attacks, return to using Afghanistan as an organizational haven? These questions are difficult to answer with certainty. Even if we could answer them, reasonable people might arrive at different ideas about what to do in Afghanistan. For example, suppose Afghanistan would develop into a stable, vibrant society if America kept ground forces there for another decade. One person might conclude that staying the course was the best option; another might decide that this outcome was not worth the monetary and human costs.

This example illustrates that we should expect disagreement over America's foreign policy, both in Afghanistan and elsewhere. And we should not be surprised when these disagreements occur in government, even between civilians and military personnel. As we discuss in Chapters 11 and 12, the very fact that bureaucrats are experts, who know a great deal about the policies they administer, means that they will often disagree about the best course of action. McChrystal was removed not because he disagreed with his administration's policy but because that disagreement became public.

This chapter will show that many areas of foreign policy are beset with conflict—and that making and executing policy often requires actors to compromise their differences. This discussion will also highlight how America's foreign and domestic policies are increasingly intertwined. Take the state of America's economy. As discussed in Chapter 15, over the last generation American politicians have approved a series of treaties that reduced tariffs on imports and exports, generating enormous profits for some American companies. American aircraft manufacturers, for example, prospered under trade liberalization, selling passenger and cargo jets to airlines throughout the world. However, trade liberalization has hurt companies that could not respond to increased foreign competition, such as the financially troubled American auto producers that have required substantial federal aid just to stay in business. Many of their workers have been laid off or have taken incentives to quit their jobs or retire early rather than face an uncertain future of layoffs and wage cuts.

Examples of national unity in foreign policy are actually quite rare. Even after the September 11 attacks, the initial surge of unity and common purpose dissolved into debate over the specifics of America's response—from the initial decisions to invade Afghanistan and Iraq to contemporary debates over how best to fight the ongoing threat of terrorist attacks. Again, this conflict is nothing new. Throughout American history there have been many disagreements over foreign policy issues, from whether and how to use military force or form alliances to questions about foreign trade agreements and human rights policies. Although these debates often have political consequences, with positions sometimes taken for political gain, in the main they reflect sincere differences of opinion; in this sense, foreign policy closely resembles domestic policy.

Finally, the political process matters in foreign policy. The president's central role in the making of foreign policy stems in part from constitutional allocations of executive power, such as the president's leadership of the executive branch and his role as commander in chief of the U.S. armed forces. The president also benefits from his ability to act unilaterally, as discussed in Chapter 11. Even so, presidents do not have complete authority to determine America's foreign policy. Factors such as congressional control over federal spending as well as judicial review exercised by federal judges impose significant limits on presidential power in this area.

WHAT IS FOREIGN POLICY?

DESCRIBE THE MAJOR APPROACHES TO UNDERSTANDING FOREIGN POLICY AND TRACE HOW AMERICA'S ROLE IN THE WORLD HAS EVOLVED

Foreign policy refers to government actions involving countries, groups, and corporations that lie outside America's borders. Foreign policy includes military operations, economic interactions, human rights policies, environmental agreements, foreign aid, democracy assistance, interventions in civil wars and other conflicts, and international efforts to limit weapons of mass destruction, including nuclear weapons.

The goals behind many foreign policy actions are complex. For example, some observers argued that America's invasion of Iraq was aimed at securing inexpensive oil for American businesses and consumers. Although this goal may have motivated some politicians to support the war, others might have believed that Iraq possessed weapons of mass destruction or viewed the country as a supporter of terrorist groups. Alternatively, they might have thought that establishing a democratic government in Iraq would serve as a model for other Middle Eastern countries or they might have wanted to end human rights abuses by the Iraqi government.

As these examples illustrate, foreign policy questions are often highly conflictual. Some individuals might have supported the decision to invade Iraq because they placed a high value on building democracy throughout the world. At the same time, others might have opposed the war because they believed that America should not try to export democracy. In the abstract, there is no logical reason to prefer one position over the other; it is a judgment that each of us has to make. Moreover, many of the other arguments for or against invasion, such as the prospects for cheaper oil or the alleged presence of weapons of mass destruction, are controversial because their resolution requires either being able to predict future events or having access to secret information.

Because foreign policy is often complex, debates over what the United States should do in a particular situation are often framed in terms of general principles or rules. These principles essentially summarize the arguments on each side of a foreign policy question, or in some cases, show how seemingly different foreign

foreign policy Government actions that affect countries, corporations, groups, or individuals outside America's borders.

FOREIGN POLICY IS FULL OF controversial questions. For example, should the American military use drones (remote-controlled, unmanned aircraft) to carry out bomb strikes in foreign countries? What if civilians are killed by mistake? What if the target country's government doesn't approve the strike?

policy issues are actually quite similar. This section outlines an important distinction, unilateral versus multilateral action, and two pairs of important concepts: isolationism versus internationalism, and idealism versus realism. An additional concept, constructivism, focuses on how the leaders of a state interpret all of these terms, which are summarized in Nuts and Bolts 17.1. These concepts are more than theoretical guides for decision making; many international relations scholars see them as descriptions of how states actually act.

unilateral action (national) Independent acts of foreign policy undertaken by a nation without the assistance or coordination of other nations.

multilateral action Foreign policy carried out by a nation in coordination with other nations or international organizations.

Unilateral action occurs when one country does something on its own, without coordinating with other countries. For example, some U.S. antiterror operations under both President George W. Bush and President Obama, particularly in Pakistan, have been undertaken without any consultation or notice to U.S. allies—not even to the Pakistanis.[2]

American foreign policy more commonly involves **multilateral action** by the United States alongside other countries or international organizations such as the United Nations. Since early 2008, more than 20 nations, including the United States, have conducted naval patrols off the Gulf of Aden in an attempt to deter pirate attacks against civilian shipping. The United States, in cooperation with the United Nations and several other nations, has sought to force the Syrian government to negotiate with rebel forces and end the civil war in Syria peacefully. Along the same lines, the Quartet on the Middle East is a group comprising the United States, Russia, the European Union, and the United Nations, which is working to facilitate peace negotiations between Israel and the Palestinians. And the so-called Six Powers (the United States, France, Germany, Britain, China, and Russia) negotiated with Iran to place limits on its nuclear programs.

isolationism The idea that a country should refrain from involvement in international affairs.

internationalism The idea that a country should be involved in the affairs of other nations, out of both self-interest and moral obligation.

A second important distinction in foreign policy is between **isolationism** and **internationalism**. Isolationists believe that the United States should avoid making alliances and agreements with other nations, concentrate on defending America's borders, and let the people in other countries work out their problems for themselves. In the case of Syria, an isolationist might argue that U.S. intervention would be futile or potentially counterproductive, too costly, or simply inappropriate.[3]

17.1 NUTS & bolts

THEORIES OF FOREIGN POLICY

Realism	Foreign policy is driven by a state's national interest, as defined by its leaders.
Idealism	Foreign policy reflects the ideals held by a state's leaders, such as protection of human rights.
Internationalism	States should, whenever possible, pursue their foreign policy goals by working together with other nations.
Isolationism	States should, whenever possible, work alone to define and implement their foreign policy, working with other nations only when absolutely necessary.
Constructivism	Foreign policy is not determined by objective factors such as national interest, by ideologies such as idealism, or by admonitions about working alone or with other nations, but by how a state's leaders define these factors.

An internationalist, however, would argue that the United States should establish many agreements with other nations and intervene in international crises whenever it may be able to help, both because of possible economic and security gains and because intervening in civil wars and helping to solve humanitarian crises is morally right. In the case of Syria, internationalists would support U.S. efforts to help and protect the local population, either in concert with other nations or alone if other nations are unwilling to intervene.[4]

The third major distinction in foreign policy making is between **realism** and **idealism**.[5] Realists believe that countries pursue their own interests, seeking to increase their economic and military power and their international influence. In approaching a policy decision, a realist would choose the policy that maximizes American military and economic power relative to other states. Idealists, in contrast, believe that states' concerns extend beyond increasing their power, including principles such as freedom, or democracy. For an idealist, upholding these principles should be a primary goal of U.S. foreign policy. **Constructivists** offer an alternative to both positions, arguing that state actions are shaped by past events rather than ideological beliefs.

To illustrate the differences between these explanations, consider the cases made by each side regarding the invasion of Iraq. Realists John Mearsheimer and Steven Walt argued in February 2003, one month before the U.S. invasion, that there was no need to invade.[6] In their view, the threat of retaliation by America and other countries would deter Saddam Hussein from invading neighboring countries, using weapons of mass destruction, or giving these weapons to terrorists. According to Mearsheimer and Walt, invading Iraq and deposing Hussein was a bad idea because it would not improve America's national security and might harm America's relations with other Middle Eastern countries. In contrast, the idea that America is morally obligated to establish a democratic Iraq is a clear example of idealism, while constructivists would argue that America's actions were driven by past events, such as the decision not to invade Iraq during the first Gulf War in 1991.

These terms are used often in foreign policy debates because they offer convenient ways to summarize the motivations behind policy decisions. That is how we use them in this chapter, but in reality none of these terms provides a fully

realism The idea that a country's foreign policy decisions are motivated by self-interest and the goal of gaining more power.

idealism The idea that a country's foreign policy decisions are based on factors beyond self-interest, including upholding important principles or values.

constructivism The idea that foreign policy is shaped by how a state's leaders define the national interest, ideology, and other factors.

IDEALISTS BELIEVE THAT COUNTRIES' foreign policy goals extend beyond increasing their own power and that countries can work together to further goals such as freedom or democracy. Idealists tend to favor working together through international organizations like the United Nations.

SHOULD AMERICA JOIN THE INTERNATIONAL CRIMINAL COURT?

Foreign policy presents Americans with a fundamental choice: Should America act alone or cooperate with other nations? Unilateral action means that American policy makers can act to further America's self-interest—as these individuals define it, of course. The advantage of multilateral action is that working with other nations may allow the United States to achieve goals that would be unattainable by acting alone. However, multilateral action may sometimes produce policies that are not ideal, or even acceptable, to the United States.

As an example, consider the International Criminal Court (ICC), an agency within the United Nations that was set up in 2002 to prosecute cases of genocide, war crimes, and crimes against humanity.[a] Before the ICC was established, new courts had to be created every time someone was tried for such crimes, such as the International Criminal Tribunal for the Former Yugoslavia, which prosecuted more than 100 political leaders, military leaders, and soldiers. The ICC was created as a permanent international body that would adjudicate these high-profile, international cases.

As of July 2012, over 120 nations have ratified the ICC treaty, which essentially gives the ICC jurisdiction over their citizens.[b] These nations include U.S. allies Great Britain, France, and Germany. However, the United States has not ratified the treaty, nor have allies Israel and Japan. Others who have not ratified include China and Russia.

The United States signed the ICC treaty during President Clinton's administration, but the treaty was never sent to the Senate for a ratification vote. (Clinton expressed doubts about the treaty and faced a Senate in which support for the treaty was weak.) Clinton's successor, George W. Bush, nullified the signature and declared that the United States would not allow its citizens to be prosecuted by the ICC. Bush administration officials even threatened to withhold U.S. forces from UN peacekeeping missions unless they were granted full immunity from ICC prosecution.[c] As of late 2012, this policy remains in place under President Obama, although the United States has sent observers to monitor ICC proceedings.[d]

U.S. criticism of the ICC centers on whether defendants are given full due process rights as they are in American courts, such as the right to see the evidence against them and protection against self-incrimination.[e] However, an analysis by the group Human Rights Watch, which supports the ICC, argued that ICC procedures are similar to those in U.S. courts.[f]

These debates miss a deeper concern. By joining the ICC, United States would lose the ability to protect its citizens prosecution by this court. In theory, the ICC could prosecute merican forces and military leaders for such actions as ion and occupation of Iraq or the interrogation techniques against terror suspects in the detention facility

The International Criminal Court, shown here during a meeting, was set up to allow the prosecution of terrorists and international war criminals, such as individuals involved in genocide. The United States, whose empty seat at the Court is shown here, has refused to join the organization, partly due to concerns that American troops might be tried for their actions during armed conflicts.

at Guantánamo Bay. These concerns are not merely abstract. British soldiers have been prosecuted and convicted by the ICC for abuse of prisoners in Iraq.[g] And American military lawyers expressed concerns that interrogation methods that were commonly used by American forces would put these individuals at risk of ICC prosecution.[h]

The stakes are high on both sides of the question. If the United States joins the ICC, it will pressure other holdout nations to do so, thus increasing the Court's value as a potential deterrent to future cases of genocide, crimes against humanity, and war crimes. But joining the ICC would also put American soldiers and statesmen at risk of prosecution. What would you decide?

Critical **Thinking Questions**

1. The discussion gives several reasons why U.S. leaders might be reluctant to join the ICC. Besides the argument about encouraging holdouts, what are the advantages of joining this organization?

2. When might civilian and military leaders disagree about the decision to join the ICC? Why might military leaders favor joining the organization?

accurate definition of what motivates nations or individuals. No one is a realist or an idealist all the time.

Even President George W. Bush, whom many people have described as an idealist,[7] criticized his opponent, Al Gore, during the 2000 presidential campaign for supporting what Bush called **nation building**—the idea that the United States should intervene to end civil wars in countries such as Bosnia and Kosovo. This criticism is a realist argument; it suggests that because these conflicts did not directly affect the United States, there was no reason to get involved. Yet several years later, when discussing his reasons for going to war in Iraq, Bush said, "I believe we have a duty to free people, to liberate people."[8] Was Bush a realist or an idealist? It depends on the circumstances. His goals motivated him to advocate a realist position in some cases and an idealist one in other situations. The same is true for President Obama. His campaign promise to meet with hostile foreign leaders suggested an idealist perspective, but his increased use of drone aircraft against Al Qaeda in Pakistan and other countries and his decision to assist in NATO operations in Libya but to avoid getting involved with the civil war in Syria are more consistent with realism. For any leader, the realist and idealist labels summarize the motivations behind individual policy decisions and may not necessarily suggest what kinds of policies he or she might prefer in the future.

nation building The use of a country's resources, including the military, to help create democratic institutions abroad and prevent violence in other countries.

HISTORY OF AMERICAN FOREIGN POLICY

This section reviews the evolution of American foreign policy. Its aim is to illustrate what foreign policy is all about, including the types of choices American politicians face, how these policy options have changed over time, and the lack of agreement among American politicians about how to resolve these issues.

THE FOUNDING TO WORLD WAR I

Until America's entry into World War I in 1917, American foreign policy was primarily but not completely isolationist. Most presidents and other elected officials behaved in accordance with George Washington's assertion that the United States should "avoid entangling alliances" with other nations.[9] Isolationism made sense during this period for several reasons. America's distance from Europe reduced the potential for international economic interactions, lowered the level of military threat, and gave early America room to expand without conflicting with European nations.[10] The **Monroe Doctrine**, established by President James Monroe in 1823, stated that America would remain neutral in wars involving European nations and that the United States expected these nations to stop trying to colonize or occupy areas in North and South America.[11] During this time, America expanded by purchasing land from other countries—adding much of the Midwest through the Louisiana Purchase—and by annexing land after military conflicts, such as the large section of the Southwest acquired from Mexico following the Mexican-American War. All of these actions were controversial at the time they were taken—some members of Congress opposed the Louisiana Purchase, for example, believing that then-President Jefferson had exceeded his authority and that America did not need to expand its territory.

America's foreign policy was never completely isolationist, however, even in the early years. The American navy was deployed on many occasions to protect U.S. ships and citizens, and America had several colonies far beyond its borders. America also

Monroe Doctrine The American policy initiated under President James Monroe in 1823 stating that the United States would remain neutral in conflicts between European nations, and that these nations should stop colonizing or occupying areas of North and South America.

built the Panama Canal, leasing land from Panama in the process, and sent troops into conflicts in Nicaragua and other Central American countries. America also maintained significant trading relationships with nations in Europe and elsewhere.

Still, America's involvement in World War I (1914–18) marked a sharp departure in foreign policy, both in the country's participation in an international alliance and in the president's willingness to continue these activities after the conflict.[12] With the war almost over, President Woodrow Wilson offered a peace plan, the Fourteen Points, which proposed reshaping the borders of European countries to mitigate future conflict, creating measures to encourage free trade and democracy, and establishing an international organization that would prevent wars.[13] American diplomats participated in the negotiations that culminated in the Treaty of Versailles, which officially ended the war.[14] The treaty created the League of Nations, an organization similar to the modern United Nations, but the U.S. Senate rejected the treaty, which meant that the United States never joined the League of Nations.[15] (Again, this example illustrates the conflicts that have marked American foreign policy over the last 200 years.)

THE RISE OF INTERNATIONALISM

A great transition in American foreign policy occurred during World War II (1939–45). The United States became directly involved in the conflict only on December 8, 1941, declaring war on Japan the day after Japanese air attacks on Pearl Harbor in Hawaii and American bases in the Philippines. Germany subsequently declared war on the United States on December 11. However, prior to the United States' official involvement, the U.S. military had been supplying Great Britain and its allies with arms, ships, and other supplies, in return for payments and long-term leases on British military bases throughout the world—actions that only narrowly escaped a congressional veto.

During World War II, the Allied Powers—the United States, Great Britain, the Soviet Union, and other countries—fought as a formal alliance, forming joint plans and sharing military hardware and intelligence. After World War II, American politicians and scholars felt that the United States should be a central actor in world affairs. This new policy was justified by realist arguments, such as the need to deter future conflicts and the desire for economic benefits from trading with other nations.[16] Idealists argued for the same policies on grounds that America had a moral obligation to preserve world peace.[17] However, this shift toward internationalism only increased the amount of conflict in American foreign policy, as actors disagreed on where the United States should get involved; what the goals should be; whether intervention should involve military force, foreign aid, diplomacy, or some other policy tool; and whether the country should act alone or in concert with other nations.

Cold War The period of tension and arms competition between the United States and the Soviet Union that lasted from 1945 until 1991.

containment An important feature of American Cold War policy in which the United States used diplomatic, economic, and military strategies in an effort to prevent the Soviet Union from expanding its influence.

THE COLD WAR

Soon after World War II ended, the **Cold War** (1945–91) began as the victorious Allies disagreed over the reconstruction of Germany and the reformation of Eastern European countries that Germany had occupied during the war. In a 1946 speech, former British prime minister Winston Churchill referred to an "iron curtain" that had split Eastern and Western Europe, leaving the East under Soviet domination with few political freedoms.[18] American diplomat George Kennan argued for **containment**, the idea that America should use diplomatic, economic, and military means to prevent the Soviet Union from expanding the set of countries that it controlled or was allied with.[19] This policy constituted the Truman Doctrine, which served as a guiding principle for American foreign policy over the next generation.[20]

During this period the United States implemented several measures to build and strengthen alliances against the Soviet threat. The first was the Marshall Plan, a series of aid and development programs enacted in the late 1940s to restore the economies of Western European countries devastated during World War II.[21] The United States was also instrumental in the formation of the World Bank and the International Monetary Fund, as well as international trade agreements such as the General Agreement on Tariffs and Trade, discussed later in the chapter.

The United States also formed alliances with other countries, including the North Atlantic Treaty Organization (NATO) in 1949. The goal of these organizations was collective security, based on the principle that "an attack against one is an attack against all."[22] The aim was to deter Soviet attacks throughout the world by formalizing America's commitment to defend its allies. The Soviets formed their own alliances, most notably the Warsaw Pact, with nations in Eastern Europe.[23]

The United States was also behind the 1945 creation of the United Nations (UN), an international organization with the aim of preventing wars by facilitating negotiations between combatants, and, if necessary, sending military forces from member states to stop conflicts. Other aspects of the UN's role have included administering relief efforts for refugees, running development efforts, codifying international law, and publicizing and condemning human rights violations.

Clearly, the goal of containment influenced every aspect of American foreign policy after World War II.[24] The Korean War, in which American troops defended South Korea against invasion by North Korea, was motivated largely by containment—North Korea's efforts had the strong support of the Soviet Union and China.[25] America also supported brutal dictators in other countries, such as the Shah of Iran during the 1970s, and overlooked these governments' dismal human rights records on the grounds that their leaders would be valuable allies against the Soviets.[26]

America also maintained large military forces, beginning its first peacetime draft in the 1950s and building a large store of nuclear weapons. These weapons were intended to deter war with the Soviet Union through the threat of **mutually assured destruction**, the idea that even if the Soviet Union unleashed an all-out nuclear assault on U.S. forces, enough American weapons would remain intact to deliver a similarly devastating counterattack. The United States stationed hundreds of thousands of troops in Western Europe and elsewhere to deter the Soviet threat.

War nearly broke out during the Cuban Missile Crisis, when the Soviets attempted to station nuclear missiles in Cuba—within striking range of the United States. However, the issue was defused by a Soviet withdrawal in the face of an American naval blockade of Cuba and a secret American promise to withdraw similar missiles from Turkey in return.

In the early 1960s America became involved in the conflict in Vietnam, believing that North Vietnam's drive to take over South Vietnam was part of the Soviet Union's plan for world domination.[27] The **domino theory** posited that if the United States did not prevent the fall of South Vietnam, the next step would be a Soviet-backed conflict in the Philippines, Australia, or some other American ally. The Vietnam War demonstrated that the domino theory was fundamentally inaccurate; the initial conflict between North and South Vietnam was a civil war rather than an international event.[28] Though the North Vietnamese accepted Soviet support, they did not take orders from the Soviets.

mutually assured destruction The idea that two nations that possess large stores of nuclear weapons—like the United States and the Soviet Union during the Cold War—would both be annihilated in any nuclear exchange, thus making it unlikely that either country would launch a first attack.

domino theory An idea held by American foreign policy makers during the Cold War that the creation of one Soviet-backed communist nation would lead to the spread of communism in that nation's region.

Beginning in the early 1970s, President Richard Nixon and his national security adviser, Henry Kissinger, began a process of **détente** with the Soviet Union. It involved a series of negotiations and cultural exchanges designed to reduce tensions and promote cooperation.[29] These efforts culminated in the 1972 Strategic Arms Limitation Treaty (SALT I), which limited the growth of U.S. and Soviet missile forces.[30]

At the same time, the Arab nations' embargo prohibiting oil shipments to Western countries after the 1973 Arab–Israeli war was a reminder that containment of the Soviet Union could not be America's only foreign policy priority. Tensions over oil increased again when the Organization of the Petroleum Exporting Countries (OPEC) raised prices in 1979. Both events contributed to a recession in America and the electoral defeats of two incumbent presidents, Gerald Ford in 1976 and Jimmy Carter in 1980. Carter's defeat was also, in part, the result of the Iran hostage crisis, in which Iranian students, with government backing, held American embassy staff hostage for more than 14 months.[31]

Tensions increased again with the Soviets' support for the Sandinista rebellion in Nicaragua in the late 1970s and their invasion of Afghanistan in 1980.[32] In response to Soviet military actions in Afghanistan, President Carter withdrew the U.S. Olympic team from the 1980 games in Moscow, suspended sales of wheat to the Soviets, and increased defense spending. These increases steepened under Ronald Reagan, who vowed to put communism "on the ash heap of history." Notwithstanding this rhetoric, Reagan also worked to negotiate arms control agreements with the Soviet Union.[33]

The real change in U.S.–Soviet relations began with the selection of Mikhail Gorbachev as leader of the Soviet Union in 1985 and his policies of *glasnost* ("openness") and *perestroika* ("restructuring"). The Warsaw Pact was dissolved in 1991, with most of its former members becoming democracies. The Soviet Union splintered into 15 countries in 1991, effectively ending the Cold War. Scholars still debate the reasons for these changes. Some argue that the costs of responding to America's military buildup bankrupted the Soviet state, while others point to disaffection with the communist ideology and the inability of the Soviet economy to provide goods and services.[34]

Since the end of the Cold War, the United States and Russia have continued to disagree over many policies, including the enlargement of NATO to include some Warsaw Pact countries, the proposed installation of anti-missile batteries in Poland, the international

IN 1989, THE FALL OF THE BERLIN Wall, which separated West Berlin from communist East Berlin, provided a powerful symbol of the end of the Cold War. With just one superpower—the United States—left, many predicted that democracy would spread and peace would prevail. However, new foreign policy challenges quickly emerged.

response to ethnic cleansing in Bosnia and Kosovo, the U.S. invasion of Iraq in 2003, and the Russian invasion of Georgia in 2008.[35] However, it is important to remember that only 20 years ago, both countries had enough weapons aimed at each other to destroy the entire world. Although differences remain, the two countries have significantly increased commercial and diplomatic ties, to the point that military conflict seems highly unlikely for the foreseeable future.

AFTER THE COLD WAR: HUMAN RIGHTS, TRADE, AND TERRORISM

The end of the Cold War, along with the growing number of democracies worldwide and the development of democratic peace theories (which argue that democracies will not fight other democracies), suggested to some observers that military conflicts would become much rarer, so that other concerns would more strongly influence America's foreign policy.[36] Events early in the post–Cold War era seemed to support this thesis. Human rights became a more important foreign policy topic.[37] The United States became involved in humanitarian relief and nation-building efforts in Somalia, Bosnia, and Kosovo. A series of agreements, including the North American Free Trade Agreement (NAFTA) in 1994 and the formation of the World Trade Organization (WTO) in 1995, lowered tariffs throughout the world. Technological advances in transportation also lowered the cost of shipping goods worldwide, and the industrialization of many third world countries made them low-cost suppliers of manufactured goods to the United States, causing the closing of many domestic factories.

However, new security threats emerged in the form of terrorist groups, most notably Al Qaeda, led by Osama bin Laden. Al Qaeda organized several attacks on Americans, including the bombing of U.S. embassies in Tanzania and Kenya in 1998 and an attack on an American warship in 2000. Then came the Al Qaeda attacks of September 11, 2001. Some analysts and politicians, including President George W. Bush, described these attacks as part of a worldwide "clash of civilizations" or a global War on Terror, pitting the secular, open West against radical Islam.[38] After the attacks, President George W. Bush announced a new U.S. policy, the **Bush Doctrine**, or the doctrine of preemption, whereby the United States would not wait until after an attack to respond but would use military force to eliminate potential threats before they could be put in motion. This policy was behind the decision to invade Iraq in 2003 and the ongoing operations against Al Qaeda, including the attack in August 2011 that resulted in bin Laden's death.

In several important respects, Barack Obama's presidency represents a sharp reversal of many Bush-era policies, with the emphasis now on improving foreign perceptions of America and Americans, and avoiding unilateral action in favor of multilateral coalitions. Obama's 2009 speech in Cairo, in which he acknowledged past American mistakes and called for cooperation around shared interests, as well as many of his policy choices, including intervention in the Libyan civil war, is typical of this new approach.[39] However, as we describe throughout this chapter, many of Obama's policies in regard to the War on Terror and other areas are quite similar to those established by the Bush administration.

The so-called Arab Spring, during which governments in Middle Eastern countries from Tunisia to Yemen were toppled by citizen protests, also creates new challenges for American foreign policy. While the establishment of democratically elected governments

Bush Doctrine The foreign policy of President George W. Bush, under which the United States would use military force preemptively against threats to its national security.

THE AL QAEDA TERRORIST organization headed by Osama bin Laden has been the driving force behind many terrorist attacks on Americans, including the 2001 attacks on the World Trade Center and the Pentagon. In 2011, American forces killed bin Laden, but the group remained a threat.

in these countries would seem to be consistent with American interests, the concern is that citizens in these countries might demand policies that are contrary to stated American goals, including support for the state of Israel. By fall 2012, as these countries held their first free elections, it was not clear what policies will ultimately emerge. What is clear is that the changes initiated by the Arab Spring raise new concerns for American policy makers.

EXPLAIN HOW THE VARIOUS BRANCHES OF GOVERNMENT SHAPE FOREIGN POLICY

FOREIGN POLICY MAKERS

This section focuses on the makers of American foreign policy. Who shapes the United States' relations with other nations, and what is the source of their influence? We begin with the president and the executive branch, then consider Congress, the courts, and finally, other groups and individuals outside the government. Nuts and Bolts 17.2 summarizes the foreign policy powers of the two most important actors: the president and Congress. Our discussion is framed in terms of the book's three themes and our assertion that politics is explainable. Foreign policy often deals with complex global issues, but it can still be analyzed.

This discussion focuses on people and organizations in government whose primary job is foreign policy making, but virtually all executive branch departments and agencies have some responsibility for issues with international reach. For example, the Department of Education administers programs that fund undergraduate, graduate, and scholarly study of the politics, history, and culture of other nations, as well as educational exchanges with universities abroad.[40] Similarly, the Department of Agriculture oversees programs that encourage food exports to other nations and that protect Americans against unsafe imports.[41]

17.2 NUTS & bolts

FOREIGN POLICY POWERS OF THE PRESIDENT AND CONGRESS

President	Congress
Commander in chief of armed forces	Can declare war
Nominates and appoints senior officials in Department of Defense	Senate must approve defense nominees
Negotiates treaties and executive agreements with other nations	Treaties take effect only if approved by Senate
Changes policy with executive orders and findings	Can overturn orders and findings with legislation
Attempts to mobilize public opinion behind foreign policy goals	Makes policy using "Power of the Purse" (annual budget)

THE PRESIDENT AND THE EXECUTIVE BRANCH

The president is the dominant actor in American foreign policy.[42] He and his staff can negotiate treaties or executive agreements with other nations, change policy through executive orders or findings, mobilize public opinion to prompt action by Congress, and shape foreign policy by appointing people to agencies and departments that administer these policies (see Chapter 11). The president also serves as commander in chief of America's armed forces.

Within the Executive Office of the President (EOP), the principal foreign policy agency is the **National Security Council (NSC)**, which develops foreign policy options and presents them to the president. The EOP also includes the Office of the U.S. Trade Representative, which focuses on tariffs and trade disputes; the president's Foreign Intelligence Advisory Board, a group of academics, politicians, and former government officials who advise the president; the Homeland Security Council, which coordinates antiterrorism policies; and the Office of Management and Budget, which prepares the president's annual budget proposals for federal agencies and departments, including those with foreign policy responsibilities.

National Security Council (NSC) Within the Executive Office of the President, a committee that advises the president on matters of foreign policy.

THE DEPARTMENT OF STATE

The principal foreign policy department in the executive branch is the Department of State. Its head, the secretary of state, acts as the official spokesperson for the United States in foreign relations and is an important adviser to the president. State Department officials operate U.S. embassies abroad and interact extensively with the leaders of other countries; they also offer expertise on the politics, economics, and cultures of other nations. Aside from senior staff like the secretary of state, who is nominated by the president and confirmed by the Senate, State Department personnel are generally career civil servants who remain in their positions even after a new president takes office. There are many different

AS OBAMA'S FIRST SECRETARY OF STATE, Hillary Clinton was instrumental in getting Myanmar—widely viewed as having one of the world's most oppressive governments—to introduce economic and political reforms. The United States rewarded Myanmar by lifting sanctions and increasing aid.

offices and working groups in the State Department, from people who deal with treaties to coordinators of international aid, arms control, or assistance for refugees. This wide variation highlights the broad range of issues that are considered foreign policy.

THE DEPARTMENT OF DEFENSE

The Department of Defense carries out military actions as ordered by civilian authorities, ranging from waging full-scale wars such as those in Iraq and Afghanistan, to conducting smaller operations such as the ongoing drone attacks against Al Qaeda forces throughout the Middle East or sending U.S. Navy ships equipped to shoot down ballistic missiles to monitor North Korea's spring 2012 attempt to launch a satellite into orbit.

The military's role in foreign policy is not limited to uses of force. Military personnel also deliver humanitarian aid or help American citizens evacuate from areas of conflict. For example, U.S. Navy ships and helicopters delivered relief aid to Haiti after the 2010 earthquake, and wounded Haitians were airlifted to military ships and facilities in the United States for medical treatment. The American military advises and trains armed forces in other countries. And military personnel may also play a role in foreign policy making, with senior military officials serving as consultants during policy debates and mid-level officers serving in the NSC and on the staff of some congressional committees.

civilian control The idea that military leaders do not formulate military policy, but rather implement directives from civilian leaders.

The overriding principle of America's military is the concept of **civilian control**—the idea that military personnel do not formulate policy but rather implement directives from their civilian leaders in the Executive Branch (the president and senior leaders in the Defense Department) and Congress. Of course, just as in other areas of the executive branch, members of the military are experts who will often know more than their civilian leaders about whether goals are feasible as well as the best ways to achieve them. The question is, what should a president do when military leaders disagree with his or her policy goals? Their disagreement may reflect fundamental problems with his plans or simply indicate that military leaders would prefer a different policy. As we discussed in Chapter 12 (Bureaucracy), these dilemmas are inevitable in all areas of the bureaucracy, including the military, given the reality of bureaucratic expertise.

Most of the time, such disagreements are resolved through dialogue, or by the president and other civilian leaders consulting additional sources to either confirm the military's advice or negate it. In general, the norm is that disagreements between the civilians and the military are accepted as long as they are kept private and if military leaders carry out the orders they are ultimately given without hesitation. However, as in the case of General McChrystal discussed at the beginning of this chapter, when disagreements become public, and when military leaders express a lack of confidence in their civilian leaders, the usual response is to replace these leaders immediately, reflecting the bedrock principle of civilian control.

THE DEPARTMENT OF HOMELAND SECURITY

The Department of Homeland Security was formed after the September 11 attacks by combining the Coast Guard, the Transportation Security Administration, the Border Patrol, and several other agencies. Its responsibilities are to secure America's borders, prevent future terrorist attacks, and coordinate intelligence gathering. Homeland Security's record is mixed. Although there has not been a major terrorist attack on American soil since September 11, 2001, the department has to some extent failed in its mission to facilitate information-sharing and cooperation among various intelligence agencies in government.

INTELLIGENCE AGENCIES

Agencies such as the Central Intelligence Agency (CIA) and National Security Agency (NSA) are primarily responsible for government intelligence-gathering. Most of their work consists of collecting information from public or semipublic sources, such as data on industrial outputs. The director of national intelligence in the EOP leads and coordinates the activities of the various intelligence agencies.

HOW MUCH FOREIGN POLICY POWER DOES THE PRESIDENT HAVE?

Some people argue that the broad powers of the modern presidency have allowed for "imperial presidents" who can implement their preferred policies without the consent of Congress, the American people, or anyone else.[43] Many of the foreign policy actions of President George W. Bush (see Chapter 11) are cited as examples.

Nonetheless, President Bush was typical of recent presidents. As discussed, presidents dominate the making of American foreign policy. Consider the four most recent presidents. George H. W. Bush ordered the invasion of Panama and sent half a million American troops to the Middle East in 1990, asking for congressional authorization only on the eve of battle.[44] During the 1990s President Clinton ordered humanitarian aid for Bosnia and Kosovo and sent troops on peacekeeping missions, all despite opposition from Congress.[45] And during the first two years of his presidency, Barack Obama completed the withdrawal of American ground forces from Iraq and began withdrawing forces from Afghanistan; he also agreed to U.S. participation in a NATO operation to support Libyan rebel forces and expanded drone strikes on terror groups in Pakistan, Yemen, and other countries without explicit congressional approval.

The explanation for presidents' dominance of foreign policy lies in the theory of unilateral presidential power (see Chapter 11).[46] Though the Constitution grants the president several foreign policy powers, it does not set explicit limits on exactly what he can and cannot do. This ambiguity has given presidents the latitude to make foreign policy as they see fit. Members of Congress who disagree with the president must build veto-proof, two-thirds majorities in the House and Senate to overturn presidential foreign policy actions—an especially daunting task when the president's party holds the majority of seats in one or both chambers.

Nonetheless, presidents sometimes pull back from a new foreign policy if they believe congressional support will not be forthcoming. For example, President Clinton never submitted the Kyoto Protocol, an international treaty on combating climate change, for ratification by the Senate because he felt that if the treaty were put to a vote, it would fail.[47] Similarly, no president has ever submitted the 1996 Nuclear Test Ban Treaty for Senate ratification, although Presidents Clinton, Bush, and Obama have implemented a voluntary moratorium on tests.

Clearly, the president dominates foreign policy—but Congress can reverse or thwart presidential initiatives. Thus, in most cases when presidents appear to have acted without constraints, the reality is that members of Congress actually approved of the president's action, were unaware of the action, or were unwilling or unable to organize to overturn the president's policy.

IN 2010, PRESIDENT OBAMA HELD bilateral talks with President Hu Jintao of China in an effort to increase nuclear security. In addition to being the United States' chief diplomat, the president also tends to dominate decisions related to war and security.

CONGRESS

Several groups within Congress participate in making foreign policy. The Committee on Foreign Affairs in the House, and the Foreign Relations Committee in the Senate, are responsible for writing legislation that deals with foreign policy, including setting the annual budget for agencies that carry out those policies. These committees also hold hearings in which they pose questions to foreign policy experts from inside and outside government. The hearings not only educate committee members on foreign policy matters but also draw media and public attention to issues important to the committee.

The House and Senate each have an Intelligence Committee that oversees covert operations and the actions of the CIA, NSA, and similar agencies. Under current law, the president is supposed to give Congress "timely notification" of covert intelligence operations.[48] The intent is to ensure that someone outside the executive branch knows about secret operations and can organize congressional opposition if these actions are deemed illegal, immoral, or unwise.

Congress holds three types of influence over foreign policy, all of which force presidents to compromise with members of Congress when their policy goals are in conflict. The first is the power of the purse. Since members of Congress write annual budgets for every government department and agency, one way for members to shape foreign policy is to forbid expenditures on activities that members want to prevent.

Second, the Senate has the power to approve treaties and confirm the appointments of senior members of the president's foreign policy team, including the secretaries of state and defense, the director of national intelligence, and America's ambassador to the United Nations. Although it is rare for senators to reject a treaty or nominee, sometimes they issue preemptive warnings about what kinds of treaties they will accept or, more commonly, they never put to a vote any treaties that might be voted down.

Third, the Constitution grants Congress the power to declare war on other nations. However, the Constitution does not say that this declaration must occur before hostilities can begin or whether the declaration is necessary at all. In fact, although the United States has been involved in hundreds of military conflicts since the Founding, there have been only five U.S. declarations of war: the War of 1812, the Mexican-American War (declared in 1846), the Spanish-American War (in 1898), and both World Wars (declared in 1917 and 1941, respectively).

In an attempt to codify war-making powers, in 1973 Congress adopted the War Powers Resolution. This legislation was designed to limit the president's war-making powers and to give members of Congress a way to reverse a president's decision to deploy American forces. Although the resolution has been in effect for over 30 years, the question of which branch of the government controls America's armed forces remains controversial.

Of course, members of Congress always have the power to block a president's foreign policy initiatives, but doing so requires enacting a law with enough votes to override a presidential veto, which is often an impossible task. In the debate over funding for the Iraq war, in 2007 the House and Senate passed a funding resolution that included a withdrawal timeline for U.S. troops, but it was approved by a margin of only a few votes in each chamber. After President Bush vetoed the resolution, the two Houses passed a new funding resolution that dropped these restrictions. In more recent cases, such as during the debate over U.S. participation in the NATO operations over Libya, resolutions were offered to cut off funding but did

How It Works

WAR POWERS: WHO CONTROLS THE ARMED FORCES?

THE PRESIDENT

As commander in chief, has the power to deploy troops.

Under the War Powers Resolution, has to notify Congress, and the use of force must be terminated within 60 days if Congress does not approve. However, Congress has never voted to terminate military action, and most presidents have argued that the act is unconstitutional.

Has the power to declare war (but has not used this power since World War II).

CONGRESS

Has the power of the purse: can provide or withhold funding for military action.

ARMED FORCES

POP QUIZ!

1 The Constitution gives _____ the power to declare war.
- **a** the president
- **b** Congress
- **c** the Pentagon
- **d** the State Department
- **e** the ambassador to the target country

2 However, in the past century, almost all military action has been initiated by
- **a** the president.
- **b** Congress.
- **c** the Pentagon.
- **d** the State Department.
- **e** the ambassador to the target country.

not pass either House of Congress. Moreover, concerns over congressional reactions were one reason that Obama administration officials were reluctant to order American forces to intervene in the Syrian civil war.

THE FEDERAL COURTS

The federal courts, including the Supreme Court, weigh in on foreign policy questions through judicial review, determining whether laws, regulations, and presidential actions are consistent with the Constitution. For example, as discussed in Chapter 11, a series of lower court and Supreme Court decisions forced the Bush administration to revise its policies of holding terror suspects indefinitely without charges; the rulings required that the suspects be charged with crimes and tried on those charges. Although this example shows how the courts can reverse presidential actions, two points are key. First, the trials did not give the defendants the same rights as those afforded to American citizens in criminal cases, allowing the presentation of evidence gained through coercion. Second, these trials occurred only after several cases spent years proceeding through the judicial system. During that time, the administration's policy remained in place, and the defendants were imprisoned without trial or any way to contest their imprisonment.[49]

GROUPS OUTSIDE THE FEDERAL GOVERNMENT

Foreign policy choices are also influenced by a variety of individuals and groups outside government, from corporate, citizen, and single-interest groups to the media, public opinion, and international and nongovernmental organizations. Here we explore how these groups participate in the making of foreign policy.

INTEREST GROUPS

Interest groups are organizations that work to convince elected officials and bureaucrats to implement policy changes in line with the group's goals. A diverse set of groups and organizations lobby government over foreign policy, including some foreign corporations and even foreign governments.[50]

One of the most prominent foreign policy interest groups is the American Israel Public Affairs Committee (AIPAC), which seeks "to help make Israel more secure by ensuring that American support remains strong."[51] AIPAC lobbies for increased military aid to Israel and American sanctions against Iran, among other matters, and the group contributes to the campaigns of congressional candidates who share its goals.[52]

Lobbying efforts can even involve foreign governments. In these cases, lobbying efforts center on economic and military aid, trade deals, and more general efforts to improve a country's image among members of Congress and the bureaucracy.

Sometimes interest group lobbying pits business interests against moral concerns. During the debate over granting China more favorable trade terms with U.S. companies in 2007, some groups argued that the legislation should be shelved until the Chinese government guaranteed religious freedoms to its citizens.[53] Other groups favored imposing tariffs on Chinese goods as retaliation for the Chinese government's refusal to revalue its currency—a move that would

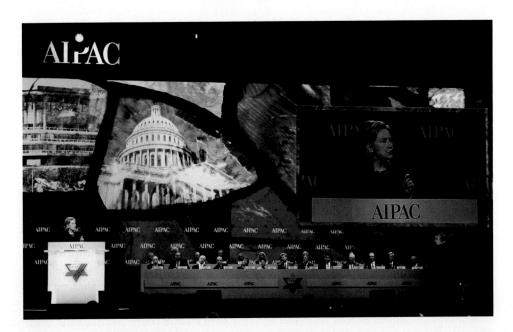

make Chinese goods more expensive and help U.S. manufacturers. Ultimately, members of Congress sympathetic to both groups blocked the trade proposals, although the U.S. government did implement some trade agreements with China that did not require congressional approval.[54] Clearly the political process matters in foreign policy making: the inability to get legislation through Congress meant that the Bush administration had to settle for small steps in liberalizing trade with China—a compromise outcome.

Finally, some groups focus on publicizing international events in the hope of prompting citizens to demand government action. For example, the Stop Kony organization created a video to increase global awareness of Joseph Kony, leader of the Lords Resistance Army, and his alleged use of child soldiers in his fight against the governments of Congo, Central African Republic, and South Sudan.

As mentioned in Chapter 9, the impact of these lobbying efforts is hard to determine. Although AIPAC is a powerful interest group, it is likely that America's foreign policy would largely favor Israel regardless of AIPAC's actions, given the continuing strong support for Israel among the American public and elected officials.[55] Similarly, although by spring 2012 the Kony video had been viewed over 100 million times on various websites and had attracted considerable press attention, it has not resulted in any new international action against Kony. Interest groups' influence over foreign policy depends mainly on the same two factors as their influence over domestic policy: groups hold the most sway when the issue's salience is low (few citizens care about the matter) and the issue is noncontroversial (few citizens or groups oppose the group's objective).

THE MEDIA

Television, radio, print media, and the Internet all inform the public about events in America and elsewhere. As discussed in Chapter 6, although media coverage is a prime source of information about domestic and foreign policy for most Americans, one cannot say that evaluations of America's foreign policy are driven solely by the news media's decisions about what to cover and how to report it. In the case of Afghanistan, there is no doubt that media coverage during 2011 and 2012 was generally negative and that public opinion on the war declined during this period.

However, both trends reflected the facts on the ground during that time: a persistent insurgency, limited reconstruction, political stalemate, and steadily rising American casualties.

PUBLIC OPINION

Foreign policy decisions are also sensitive to public opinion. Congressional attempts in 2007 to make funding for the Iraq conflict conditional on setting troop withdrawal deadlines were driven in part by the shift in public opinion against the war—and by the influence of that shift on the 2006 elections, in which many Republicans who had supported the war were defeated or came close to defeat.[56] Similarly, declines in public support for the war in Afghanistan probably stimulated congressional calls to accelerate withdrawal of American ground forces.

Though elected officials generally consider public opinion when making foreign policy decisions, their judgments must take into account the problems of measuring opinions (see Chapter 5). Public opinion is sensitive to context, including both how and when survey questions are asked. For example, fears of another terrorist attack on the United States increase sharply every time there is an attack elsewhere in the world.

Because public opinion is sensitive to context, Americans may sometimes ignore foreign policy questions (or their representative's positions on these issues) in favor of other concerns. For example, as economic conditions worsened in 2008 and 2009, mentions in mass surveys of the economy as the most important issue facing the country rose sharply, while mentions of Iraq, Afghanistan, fears of a terrorist attack, and other foreign policy issues declined. As long as this decline persists, elected officials can place a low priority on responding to public opinion on foreign policy questions.

A second reason that foreign policy does not always mirror public opinion was discussed in Chapter 10. Most politicians have political goals other than winning re-election, including affecting some aspect of American relations with other nations. For example, President Obama's decision to join in NATO's operations in favor of Libyan rebel forces in March 2012 was taken in spite of strong public opposition—Americans opposed the intervention by a margin of nearly 2:1.[57]

The final reason that American public opinion is not decisive is that many Americans know little about other countries. Table 17.1 provides some sense of what 18- to 24-year-old Americans know about the rest of the world. For example, a majority of young adults surveyed could not locate most other countries on a map.

Americans are more likely to pay attention to foreign policy news or concerns following an important event. Thus, six months after the September 11 attacks, one poll found that Americans rated preventing future attacks a higher priority than any particular domestic policy, even though domestic policy as a general category took priority over foreign policy.[58] However, as the attacks receded into the past, the intensity of public concern about preventing future attacks declined somewhat as well.

INTERGOVERNMENTAL ORGANIZATIONS, NONGOVERNMENTAL ORGANIZATIONS, AND INTERNATIONAL ORGANIZATIONS

America's relationship with the rest of the world is not just about government action. Members of **intergovernmental organizations (IGOs)** and **nongovernmental organizations (NGOs)** provide information and humanitarian

intergovernmental organizations (IGOs) An association of sovereign states that works to protect human rights, increase living standards, and achieve policy goals throughout the world.

nongovernmental organizations (NGOs) Groups operated by private institutions (rather than governments) to promote growth, economic development, and other agendas throughout the world.

TABLE » 17.1

YOUNG AMERICANS' GLOBAL KNOWLEDGE

These data reveal a marked lack of geographic knowledge among 18- to 24-year-old Americans. Most can find the United States, Canada, and Mexico on a world map, but only slightly more than a third can locate Iraq on a map of the Middle East, despite the fact that when the survey was taken, America had been fighting a major war there for nearly three years. Identification rates for the other countries are similarly dismal. What might explain this lack of geographical knowledge?

PERCENTAGE WHO CAN LOCATE ON A WORLD MAP	
United States	94%
Canada	92
Mexico	88
Great Britain	36
ON A MAP OF THE MIDDLE EAST	
Saudi Arabia	37%
Israel	25
Iraq	37
Iran	26

Source: National Geographic–Roper Global Geographic Literacy Survey, 2006, www.nationalgeographic.com/roper2006/findings.html (accessed 8/20/08).

assistance, and carry out other activities that the U.S. government is unable or unwilling to undertake. IGOs are associations of sovereign states, while NGOs are private organizations. Thousands of IGOs and NGOs operate throughout the world.[59]

A primary goal of NGOs is promoting global economic development and growth. One of the largest IGOs, the **World Bank**, funds economic development projects throughout the world. Another IGO, the **International Monetary Fund (IMF)** helps countries manage budget deficits and control the value of their currencies. Many NGOs, such as the Asia Foundation, focus on development in a particular region or on certain activities, such as microlending, in which banks or other institutions provide small loans to citizens in developing nations as a way of stimulating business growth and reducing poverty.

A second role of NGOs is providing humanitarian relief. In the wake of a disaster such as an earthquake or a flood, or during a famine or a war, organizations such as Oxfam International supply populations in crisis with basic necessities. Other groups such as Doctors without Borders provide medical care to populations threatened by violence, epidemics, or natural disasters. Some NGOs also promote human rights. Amnesty International spotlights international cases of people jailed for their political beliefs or held without trial, or the use of cruel punishments such as stoning. Amnesty's campaigns, as well as those of other NGOs,

World Bank A nongovernmental organization established in 1944 that provides financial support for economic development projects in developing nations.

International Monetary Fund (IMF) A nongovernmental organization established in 1944 to help stabilize the international monetary system, improve economic growth, and aid developing nations.

are not always supportive of U.S. policy. For example, Amnesty decries the rendition of terror suspects by the United States.[60]

Finally, NGOs help to build democracies. The Open Society Institute funds efforts to increase mass political participation, strengthen political organizations, and verify the fairness of elections in new democracies throughout the world. The National Democratic Institute and the International Republican Institute conduct similar activities—both organizations, for example, sent groups in 2011 and 2012 to new democracies in the Middle East to assist with building party organizations and developing election rules in the wake of the so-called Arab Spring.[61]

United Nations (UN) An international organization made up of representatives from nearly every nation, with a mission to promote peace and cooperation, uphold international law, and provide humanitarian aid.

The United States is also a member of many international organizations. Best known is the **United Nations (UN)**, an assembly of ambassadors representing almost all of the world's nations that addresses issues of worldwide concern. The UN is involved in economic development, environmental protection, humanitarian relief, and peacekeeping efforts. The United Nations has deployed peacekeeping forces to separate warring parties in Africa, the Middle East, and the former Yugoslavia. As of spring 2012, more than 100,000 UN peacekeeping troops, police, and other personnel were deployed in 16 different areas.

Inside the UN, the Security Council, a group of 15 nations (permanent members Britain, China, France, Russia, and the United States, plus 10 rotating nations) makes the most important UN decisions, particularly those involving its military missions. The UN General Assembly, in which each nation has one vote, debates and votes on other concerns.

EXAMINE THE WAYS AMERICAN FOREIGN POLICY IS IMPLEMENTED

THE TOOLS OF FOREIGN POLICY

This section describes the tools or methods used to implement American foreign policy—most obviously the use of military force, but also changes in trade policy or the provision of foreign or military aid. Although these strategies differ in their costs, and some, such as military force, seem morally questionable to many Americans, all nations use these strategies in pursuit of desired policy outcomes.

MILITARY FORCE

Military force is a fundamental tool of foreign policy. America's military forces serve throughout the world as a deterrent to conflict. For example, the United States stations more than 28,000 troops in South Korea. Many are deployed at the demilitarized zone that separates North Korea from South Korea. Similarly, until the fall of the Soviet Union in 1991, hundreds of thousands of American troops were stationed in Western Europe. Military exercises by U.S. troops, aircraft, and ships serve to remind potential adversaries of America's military power. For example, in early 2012, Iran threatened to close the Strait of Hormuz, a narrow passage that must be traveled by tankers carrying Middle Eastern oil exports. The United States responded by sending a carrier battle group to the strait to conduct flight operations—and to demonstrate that America was ready to keep the passage open by using force if necessary.[62]

MILITARY FORCES AROUND THE WORLD

The U.S. armed forces are considerably more powerful than those of any other nation, but history has shown that American military might is not the universal solution to international problems, even those involving the use of force. Sometimes, in fact, military force is all but useless as a tool of foreign policy.

The table compares the United States' armed forces to those of its major allies and potential adversaries. As the table indicates, America spends vastly more on its military than any of its potential adversaries. America's navy and air force are also much larger than those of any other nation. America's military superiority is also reflected in an extensive network of satellites that are used to photograph foreign sites, eavesdrop on communications, and provide early warning of attacks. America also has the best communications and computer technology, as well as cutting-edge weapons technology such as radar-evading stealth aircraft.

The question is, what advantages does overwhelming military force convey? The American experience in Iraq demonstrates that even a large military force cannot always achieve easy or quick victories. American and coalition forces were able to overrun Iraq quickly in the spring of 2003 and depose its government with minimal casualties, but the same forces, even augmented with additional troops, were unable to prevent subsequent attacks by insurgent groups and violence between different ethnic groups in the country. American and Iraqi forces gradually regained control of the country, but this outcome occurred only after several years of intense violence and thousands of casualties.

In part, the issue in Iraq was that the American military was designed to fight other armies—not to deal with a multipronged insurgency scattered across an entire country. Tanks, artillery, smart bombs, and aircraft carriers are simply useless

Although China's military has more active troops than any other country, its military budget is a fraction of U.S. military spending.

for the kind of small-scale, urban fighting that took place in Iraq after the initial invasion. As time went on, American forces learned how to respond more effectively to the insurgency, using new technologies such as unmanned aircraft, and working with increasing numbers of Iraqi government forces. However, these real successes should not obscure the reality that America's military superiority did not produce an easy or quick victory.

More important, the economic, political, and human costs of military force make this strategy useless in many foreign policy situations. Consider the problem of negotiating trade agreements with other nations: there is no chance that the United States will make military threats against its allies to extract favorable tariffs or quotas—carrying out these threats would end trade entirely, as well as disrupt diplomatic and other connections. Threats are also unlikely to work against adversaries when the costs of carrying them out exceed the potential benefits to the United States. For example, although the U.S. government might prefer that Iran end its nuclear research, the cost of sustained military action against Iran may exceed the benefits of ending this threat.

For all of these reasons, claims about the value of America's military power need to be kept in perspective. Smaller countries and groups have means at their disposal to significantly complicate U.S. military efforts and sometimes even negate our vast military superiority. Thus, while America has the most powerful military in the world, this status does not mean that America can always achieve its foreign policy goals.

COMPARING ARMED FORCES

	MILITARY BUDGET (BILLIONS)	ACTIVE TROOPS	NUCLEAR WEAPONS
United States	$741	1,525,000	2300
China	$106	2,250,000	240
Russia	$83	930,000	3500
France	$54	221,000	350
United Kingdom	$51	195,000	225
Israel	$15	125,000	200
Iran	$21	540,000	0
North Korea	$10	1,075,000	10

tariff A tax levied on imported and exported goods.

World Trade Organization (WTO) An international organization created in 1995 to oversee trade agreements between nations by facilitating negotiations and handling disputes.

most-favored-nation status A standing awarded to countries with which the United States has good trade relations, providing the lowest possible tariff rate. World Trade Organization members must give one another this preferred status.

ONE OF THE MOST CONFLICTUAL issues involving international trade is the enforcement of copyrights on movies, music, and computer software. The Chinese government's refusal to enforce American copyrights has been a source of tension between the two nations.

The United States has also fought wars and lesser conflicts to further its foreign policy goals. Some are all-out military operations, such as the invasion of Iraq. More commonly, these deployments are short-lived operations ranging from the evacuation of American civilians from areas of unrest to the delivery of humanitarian assistance or the use of ship-launched cruise missiles to attack terrorist camps and similar targets.[63]

The size and power of America's military provides numerous options for policy makers. For example, after the September 11 attacks, in an attempt to prevent future terror attacks by Al Qaeda, U.S. forces invaded Afghanistan, which had been used as a base of operations for the organization.[64] It is highly unlikely that any other country could carry out such a large-scale operation so far from home. Nonetheless, military force is not all-powerful. At the end of 2012, American troops were still fighting in Afghanistan, with their mission a long way from being accomplished (see more detail later in the chapter).

TRADE AND ECONOMIC POLICIES

Foreign policy is also aimed at sustaining economic growth in the United States and elsewhere, as well as creating foreign markets for the goods produced by America's domestic industries. Figure 17.1 shows total American trade (imports and exports) with other countries over the last 30 years, expressed as a percentage of U.S. gross domestic product (GDP), which measures the size of the U.S. economy. In recent years, imports and exports have constituted more than 40 percent of GDP. Investment returns (profits from American-owned companies located abroad) are also becoming an ever-larger component of total trade. In dollar terms, the same report estimated that the total value of U.S. trade with other nations was more than $6 trillion per year. Clearly, foreign trade is a critical component of the American economy.

The main tools of trade policy are tariffs and trade agreements. A **tariff** is a tax collected by the government for the import or export of certain commodities, and a trade agreement sets tariff levels or limits the quantities of particular items that can be imported or exported. The United States International Trade Commission maintains a list of all tariffs in effect.[65] By adjusting tariff rates, the government can help or hurt domestic industries. High tariffs on imports help American producers charge lower prices than foreign competitors, and low tariffs on exports help American producers sell to overseas markets.

Over the last two generations, the United States and most other nations have been lowering tariffs and establishing free trade zones, agreements to eliminate tariffs on all imports and exports among specific nations. Examples include the North American Free Trade Agreement (NAFTA), involving the United States, Canada, and Mexico; and the Central American Free Trade Agreement (CAFTA) among the United States, five Central American nations, and the Dominican Republic. Other organizations, such as the **World Trade Organization (WTO),** facilitate negotiations over tariffs and provide a mechanism for adjudicating cases when one nation believes that another is using tariffs unfairly. Finally, the United States has granted many other countries **most-favored-nation status**: tariffs on imports to the United States from these nations are set at the lowest rate placed on any other nation.

Trade is an important part of foreign policy. The United States can use free trade agreements and tariffs to bargain with countries for concessions in other areas.

FIGURE » 17.1

U.S. IMPORTS AND EXPORTS AS A PERCENTAGE OF GROSS DOMESTIC PRODUCT (GDP)

This figure illustrates the importance of trade to the U.S. economy. In recent years, imports and exports have made up more than 40 percent of U.S. economic activity, and the percentage is steadily increasing. Based on these data, what arguments would you make for lowering or increasing barriers to trade?

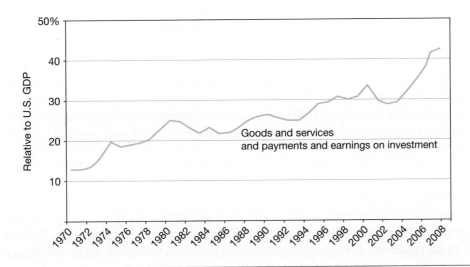

Source: Office of the United States Trade Representative, 2012 Trade Policy Agenda and 2011 Annual Report, available at www.ustr.gov/about-us/press-office/reports-and-publications/2012-0 (accessed 9/22/12).

For example, in the 1990s the Clinton administration used tariffs, most-favored-nation status, and other inducements to force China to moderate its human rights policies and crack down on illegal copying of software and videos.[66] Similarly, among the incentives given to Jordan during peace negotiations with Israel in the 1990s were promises to eliminate tariffs on textile exports to America and to write off $213 million of the $488 million Jordanian debt to the United States.[67]

Economic policies, which may involve the United States acting alone or with other nations, are also used to threaten or sanction countries as a way of inducing them to change their behavior. As noted earlier, in 2007 the UN Security Council authorized sanctions against Iran aimed at forcing the nation to stop enriching uranium, a first step in the production of nuclear weapons.[68] These sanctions included freezing bank accounts held by members of Iran's nuclear team and banning arms sales to the country. Additional sanctions imposed in 2012 cut off Iranian banks from international funds transfer networks, making it difficult for Iranian citizens and corporations to do business outside their nation's borders. If Iran agreed to stop its program, it would receive incentives such as civilian nuclear reactor technology and direct talks with the United States over various issues. At the same time, the United States also discouraged Israel from attacking Iranian nuclear facilities. This combination of carrots and sticks led to ongoing negotiations between the Iranians and a group of nations, including the United States and the European Union. However, as of the end of 2012, no deal had been reached.

DIPLOMACY

The process of diplomacy involves using personal contact and negotiations with national leaders and representatives to work out international agreements or persuade other nations to change their behavior. Sometimes these efforts involve the threat of military action or economic sanctions, or incentives such as economic assistance or other forms of aid. The United States may participate directly in such efforts or mediate between the parties in a dispute. When two countries refuse to meet face-to-face, U.S. diplomats may take part in shuttle diplomacy, in which they meet separately with each country's representatives to convey the other country's proposals and counterproposals.

Diplomacy has often been a useful but limited foreign policy tool. For example, the efforts of American diplomats were instrumental in establishing an international aid fund to help Haiti rebuild after the 2010 earthquake. Similarly, American and Mexican diplomats signed an agreement in 2010 to deter the transportation of illegal drugs across the U.S.–Mexican border. And American diplomats are involved in many behind-the-scenes efforts to help resolve international disputes, such as the ongoing disagreement between Argentina and Great Britain over ownership of the Falkland Islands.

FOREIGN AID

Foreign aid is money, products, or services given to other countries or the citizens of these countries. Sometimes aid reflects the desire to provide basic assistance to satisfy fundamental human needs. For example, the American military is often tasked to deliver food and medical supplies to the victims of earthquakes and other natural disasters. Foreign aid also serves to stimulate economic growth in other nations. Funding from the United States helps to build factories; to advise locals on how to construct and operate water, power, or sewage treatment plants; or to buy hardware to support infrastructure such as Internet access or telephone

THE AMERICAN MILITARY DELIVERED food and medical supplies to Haiti after a devastating earthquake in 2010.

networks. Foreign aid also facilitates international agreements. For example, the peace treaty between Egypt and Israel in 1979 was facilitated by America's agreement to provide substantial military and economic assistance to both countries.[69] Promises of continued American aid to Israel was also one factor in discouraging Israel from attacking Iranian nuclear facilities in 2012.

Figure 17.2 shows the level of American nonmilitary foreign aid in 2010, measured as a percentage of gross national income (GNI, which includes GDP as well as accounting for investment income from other countries), compared to other members of the Organization for Economic Cooperation and Development. Considering the amount of U.S. foreign aid as a percentage of GNI suggests that the United States gives relatively little to other countries. Part of the reason for this perception lies in the size of the U.S. economy: America's foreign aid contributions are the largest of any country when measured in total dollars, but it also has the largest GNI of any country.

ALLIANCES AND TREATIES

A treaty is an agreement between nations to work together on economic or security issues. An alliance is an agreement that commits nations to security guarantees, which are assurances that one country will help another if it

FIGURE » 17.2

U.S. FOREIGN AID IN COMPARATIVE PERSPECTIVE

This figure shows foreign aid contributions expressed as a percentage of gross national income. Do these data imply that America is less generous than other nations in its willingness to donate aid?

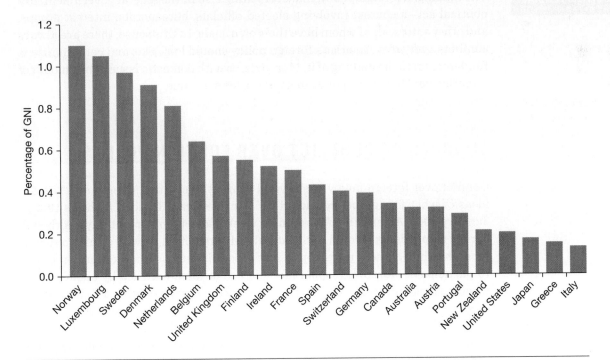

Source: Organization for Economic Cooperation and Development, "Development Cooperation Report 2011," available at www.oecd.org/dac/dcr (accessed 9/22/12).

is attacked. America is a member of many international alliances, most notably the North Atlantic Treaty Organization (NATO); this alliance was formed by the North Atlantic Treaty after World War II to provide collective security against the Soviet Union and Warsaw Pact countries. The organization's mission shifted after the Cold War to focus on coordinating military force toward common goals, with the organization's air strikes in Libya the first instance of operations outside Europe.[70]

The United States is a party to many treaties: bilateral agreements between the United States and one other country, and multilateral agreements involving the United States and several countries.[71] Many of these treaties, such as a series of arms control agreements between the United States and Russia (before 1991, the Soviet Union) implemented significant changes in both U.S. and other military forces, from capping the size of nuclear forces, to restricting the numbers of these forces, to banning some kinds of weapons.

Treaties and alliances enable the United States to commit itself to a course of action or signal its intentions to other nations.[72] By joining NATO and stationing troops in Europe, the United States guaranteed that if Warsaw Pact troops invaded the West, U.S. forces would be part of the resistance. Moreover, if the United States failed to honor its treaty obligations, convincing other nations to enter into future agreements with it would be difficult.

THE POLITICS OF FOREIGN POLICY TODAY

The making of foreign policy, like everything else in the federal government, is a political act—a contest involving elected officials, bureaucrats, interest groups, and other actors, all of whom have their own goals. In this sense, there are always conflicts over what America's foreign policy should look like, and compromise is fundamental to the making of it. Moreover, as with domestic issues, the amount of attention paid to foreign policy matters varies over time.

SOURCES OF CONFLICT OVER FOREIGN POLICY

Conflict over foreign policy has several sources, including Americans' different ideas of what foreign policy should be. Consider Iraq. Table 17.2 shows that in January 2003, American public opinion was divided in important ways. Although survey respondents favored multilateral military action by well over two to one, more than half of these people opposed the conflict unless America's allies agreed to participate. Moreover, support for the use of force declined by about a third when respondents were asked to consider the impending conflict as one in which U.S. forces would suffer thousands of casualties. These data demonstrate the significant divisions in American public opinion at the time of the Iraq invasion.[73] More recently, Americans have been divided on the question of whether the United States should intervene in civil wars in Libya and in Syria.

Where do differences of opinion on foreign policy come from? One source is the realist–idealist distinction discussed earlier: recall that Mearschimer and Walt

TABLE » 17.2

AMERICAN PUBLIC OPINION ON THE INVASION OF IRAQ

These data illustrate the conflict in American public opinion over the decision to go to war in Iraq. A majority supported the decision to invade when this question was asked by itself, but many individuals supported the war only with certain qualifications, such as if America received support from its allies or if casualties were low. Based on these data, to what extent did the decision to invade Iraq reflect public opinion just before the invasion?

FAVOR OR OPPOSE MILITARY ACTION IN IRAQ	JANUARY 2003
Favor	68%
Even if allies won't join	26
Only if allies agree	37
Oppose	25
EVEN IF U.S. SUFFERED THOUSANDS OF CASUALTIES	
Favor	43%
Even if allies won't join	21
Only if allies agree	20
Oppose	48

Source: Pew Research Center, "Public Wants Proof of Iraqi Weapons Programs," January 16, 2003, www.people-press.org/reports/display.php3?ReportID=170 (accessed 9/20/12).

offered a realist argument for staying out of the conflict, and President Bush gave, in part, an idealist argument for invasion. Self-interest is another powerful motive. Several studies found that as National Guard units were mobilized for service in Iraq, support for the war declined in the communities where these units were based.[74]

Disagreements over foreign policy may also reflect citizens' exposure to different information or their disparate ways of understanding the world. Indeed, there are sharp disagreements among citizens over the existence of global warming and its cause—a natural phenomenon or human activity (see Chapter 5).[75] The same study also found that an individual's support for policies designed to combat global warming depends on his or her diagnosis of the problem. Most people who see human activity as the cause favor policies that would alleviate the problem, and most who believe global warming is a natural phenomenon favor the status quo.

Similarly, one of the Bush administration's justifications for invading Iraq in 2003 was the claim that Iraq had or would soon have weapons of mass destruction (WMDs).[76] At the time of the invasion, these beliefs were not unreasonable. Though some experts said that Iraq's weapons programs were defunct or posed no threat, others claimed that Iraq already had WMDs, and still others said that Iraqi scientists were hard at work developing these technologies.[77] Investigations after the war had begun showed that Iraq's WMD programs were years away from producing usable weapons. As one of the leaders of the UN's prewar inspection effort put it, "We were all wrong."[78] But as the comment indicates, at the time of the invasion, many people working for arms control or intelligence agencies throughout the world were sincerely concerned about Iraq's WMDs.

Disagreements may also originate in differing expectations about whether policies will work as intended, as well as the basic facts of a situation. For example, during the debate over whether the United States and its allies should support rebel groups in the Syrian civil war, some members of Congress and Obama administration officials argued that Syria's central geographic and political position in the Middle East made intervention essential—while others used the same arguments as reasons not to get involved.[79] Both sides in these debates were unsure of the size and capabilities of the various rebel groups, whether the groups were willing to work together, whether arming these groups would prolong the conflict or end it, and what kind of political system would result if the rebel groups succeeded in winning control of the country.

Although disagreements over America's foreign policy often occur between members of the Republican and Democratic parties—conflict over the war in Iraq being a prime example—officials from the same party may hold different views about how to resolve foreign policy decisions. For example, in late 2009 many Democratic senators and House members opposed President Obama's plan to expand American combat operations in Afghanistan—not enough to block the plans, especially given widespread support from Republicans, but enough to create some embarrassment for the Obama administration.

Moreover, despite the expectation that senior presidential appointees will be loyal to the president, disagreements are not uncommon even among these individuals. In both the Bush and Obama administrations, for example, there has been considerable conflict among senior advisers on whether to arrest foreign terror suspects, where to hold them, whether to treat them according to the Geneva Conventions, and whether to allow them access to U.S. civilian or military courts. Some senior Obama administration officials opposed the expansion of drone attacks against Al Qaeda groups in Pakistan and elsewhere, as well as America's intervention in the Libyan civil war.

In sum, disagreements about foreign policy are unavoidable, both in government and among the general public. These conflicts will surely continue. For a variety of reasons, citizens and elected officials will disagree on what America's foreign policy should look like, and they will work in elections and in the government to influence their choices.

CONTEMPORARY FOREIGN POLICY ISSUES

This section describes major foreign policy issues facing American citizens and elected officials. From economic crises to weapons of mass destruction, these issues illustrate that foreign policy is everywhere and that the decisions made by people in government will affect the lives of ordinary Americans. They demonstrate the power of the political process in foreign policy making: decisions reflect the people who make them and the rules that structure the debates. And they highlight conflicts over foreign policy, both in government and among the American people.

In addition, this section argues against claims about the decline of American influence throughout the world. Although it is true that other countries such as China and India are increasing their economic and military power and that the United States faces many new and complex issues, it still continues to be an international power, and in many respects is the strongest nation on the globe, with enormous influence over economic, social, and military events worldwide. How the issues described in this section will be resolved remains in question, but there is no doubt that the foreign policy choices of the United States will play a decisive role in their resolution.

GLOBAL WARMING

Decades of scientific research have shown that the Earth is getting warmer, as Figure 17.3 illustrates. Available evidence points to human activity—specifically the burning of fossil fuels, which increases the amount of carbon dioxide in the atmosphere—as a significant cause of global warming.[80]

In some ways, the solution to global warming seems straightforward: the world's nations must reduce carbon dioxide emissions by taxing and otherwise limiting carbon-producing activities and by developing cheaper and more efficient energy sources that produce less carbon. This solution is not easy; research is expensive, and new technologies may carry their own environmental and economic impacts.

Another complication is that efforts to combat global warming require spending money in the present to prevent effects that will only be felt over the next century.

FIGURE » 17.3

THE GLOBAL WARMING TREND

These data show that global temperature levels have increased steadily since the early 1900s. How would a believer in human-caused global warming interpret these data? What would a skeptic say?

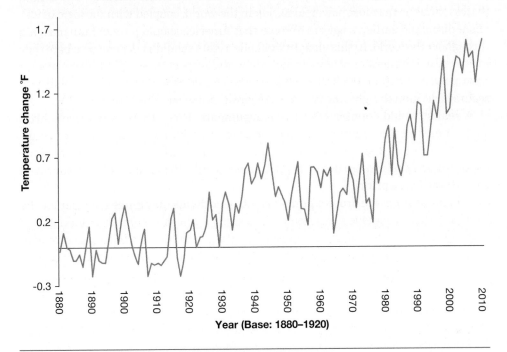

Source: "Global Surface Temperature Trends," available from Center for Climate and Energy Solutions, www.pewclimate.org/facts-figures/trends/surface-temp (accessed 4/29/12).

In effect, one generation must pay the price so that future generations will benefit from the investment. As a result, legislation to reduce carbon emissions may be unpopular with the average American, who is expected to pay for these measures in the form of taxes, higher prices, or lifestyle changes, without necessarily receiving direct benefits.

Addressing global warming also requires a multilateral effort. Even if the United States cuts its carbon emissions, this reduction will have little effect if other nations simultaneously increase their emissions. The problem is particularly acute for developing nations such as China, India, and Brazil. These nations are reluctant to limit their carbon emissions because doing so will make it much harder for them to industrialize and raise their citizens' standard of living.[81] The **Kyoto Protocol**, which set limits on carbon emissions, was signed by developing nations only because the agreement did not significantly limit their future carbon emissions.[82] Subsequent efforts, such as the 2009 Copenhagen climate conference, were unable to devise an international agreement that bridged this gap between developed and developing nations.

Kyoto Protocol An international agreement signed by many nations in 1997 that set limits on carbon emissions in an effort to slow global warming.

HUMAN RIGHTS

In many countries, the freedoms set out in the U.S. Bill of Rights—such as freedom of religion, freedom of speech, freedom of association, freedom of the press, and the rights of the accused—simply do not exist. Many governments routinely use arrests and other forms of repression to silence political opponents or condone violence and ethnic cleansing against minority ethnic or religious groups.

Organizations such as Freedom House and Amnesty International publicize human rights violations, with the goal of alerting citizens worldwide and thereby pressuring governments to end these violations. In 2011, Freedom House's annual survey of political and civil rights in 193 countries found that in many nations, press freedoms, due process rights, and freedom from torture were on the decline.[83] The United States' status as the most powerful nation in the world, coupled with the logic of idealism discussed earlier, suggests to some that America should protect human rights throughout the world. In this view, individuals' rights shouldn't depend on where they live or on their leaders' or neighbors' willingness to respect these rights. As the world's most powerful nation, the argument goes, the United States has a responsibility to secure basic human rights for everyone, regardless of where they live.

A realist would counter with three arguments. First, there is relatively little support among the American people for protecting human rights in other countries. As Table 17.3 shows, defending human rights falls near the bottom of the list of Americans' foreign policy priorities, with only 29 percent of those surveyed identifying it as a priority.

Second, attempts to protect human rights worldwide may make it harder for the United States to achieve other goals. For example, the government of Pakistan is routinely cited for human rights abuses, but Pakistani officials have also provided America with valuable intelligence in the War on Terror and have aided in the capture of Taliban fighters in Afghanistan. If America pressures the Pakistani government to safeguard its citizens' human rights, Pakistan might respond by cutting off U.S. access to its intelligence, disrupting American efforts to stabilize Afghanistan and fight Al Qaeda in other areas. Similarly, while the Arab Spring may have toppled autocratic governments, the United States may not be able to exert too much pressure concerning human rights in these countries, as the newly democratic states have the power to implement new policies that are contrary to American interests.

TABLE » 17.3

AMERICANS' FOREIGN POLICY PRIORITIES

Politicians often cite protecting human rights and promoting democracy as U.S. foreign policy priorities, but these goals find relatively little support among the American public. How might this difference affect America's foreign policy choices?

Protecting against terror attacks	85%
Protecting jobs of American workers	85
Preventing the spread of WMDs	74
Reducing dependence on foreign oil	64
Fighting international drug trafficking	56
Reducing illegal immigration	46
Dealing with global climate change	40
Strengthening the United Nations	37
Defending human rights around the world	29
Improving living standards in the Third World	26
Promoting democracy in other nations	21

Source: Pew Research Center, U.S. Seen as Less Important, China More Powerful, December 3, 2009, www.people-press.org/report/569/ americas-place-in-the-world (accessed 9/15/12).

Third, protecting human rights may strain American military forces. In the case of the mass killings in Darfur, the leaders of Sudan have allowed local militias to attack civilians despite other countries' attempts to encourage Sudanese intervention with offers of economic aid, threats of economic sanctions, and promises to send peacekeeping forces. If the Sudanese leaders continue to ignore these threats and incentives, the only remaining way to stop their abuses is to launch a potentially large-scale military operation. At a minimum, America would provide transportation and logistical support, and such an operation could easily expand to involve American ground forces. Similar arguments were raised against American involvement in the Syrian civil war.

INTERNATIONAL TRADE AND GLOBALIZATION

For the United States, trade is a necessity. America imports an increasing percentage of its oil and natural gas, as well as significant quantities of other resources and manufactured goods. Many economic analyses describe trade in terms of the theory of comparative advantage, which says that nations export items they can produce cheaply, in return for imports that can be produced more efficiently elsewhere. Similarly, outsourcing jobs to foreign countries with lower labor costs makes American companies more efficient. Microsoft, for one, has several large offices throughout the world, and in some of them software developers earn much less than their counterparts in the United States.[84] Even high-level professional jobs can be outsourced: the NightHawk Corporation uses Australian and Swiss radiologists to read X-rays and CAT scans of American patients.[85]

These practices are examples of globalization, reflecting the trend toward increasing interaction and connections among individuals, corporations, and nations (see Chapter 15). New technologies have leveled the global playing field, allowing the cheapest suppliers of goods and services to sell their products throughout the world. Many American companies and their employees profit from this process. More than half the cars that General Motors sells are purchased abroad, and in recent years more Kentucky Fried Chicken restaurants have opened in China than in the United States.

Reflecting all these factors, the last generation of American politics has been marked by international agreements such as NAFTA to reduce or eliminate tariffs among nations, the growth of international organizations such as the WTO to regulate trade and adjudicate trade disputes, and increases in outsourcing of manufacturing jobs and services from developed countries to developing countries.[86] Although these moves toward increased trade and globalization generate significant benefits for many people, the changes do not make everyone better off. Many American manufacturing jobs have been lost as factories that could not compete with cheaper foreign suppliers have either closed or moved to another country, leaving behind unemployed American workers.[87]

Nonetheless, globalization, with all its benefits and challenges, is a reality. This raises two broad questions for American citizens and elected officials. First, how should America respond to nations that close off their markets? For example, in recent years the Chinese government has done many things to restrict imports and expand exports. Though these requirements seem arbitrary and unfair to many American exporters, the American government also imposes restrictions—in 2007, the U.S. Food and Drug Administration blocked American imports of fish farmed in China on the grounds that it contained unapproved drugs and additives, even though these drugs and additives are not illegal in China.[88]

The second question concerns how to help people who are hurt by globalization. The U.S. Department of Labor's Trade Adjustment Assistance Program provides various benefits to American workers who lose their jobs because of new trade agreements: extended unemployment benefits, tax credits for health insurance, and money for retraining programs. However, many workers who have lost their jobs due to globalization (for example, because of outsourcing) are not eligible for these programs, and others are unaware that they exist.[89] Moreover, it is often extremely difficult to retrain people to compete for new jobs that will provide pay and benefits comparable to what they received in their old positions.[90] What should government do to help these victims of globalization? That question will influence debates over exports, imports, and trade agreements for years to come.

AMERICA'S ECONOMY AND THE WORLD

Trade is an example of a more general phenomenon: the state of the American economy is increasingly linked to economic conditions throughout the world. In part, these linkages result from increased imports and exports, giving American companies both new markets and new competitors. But more fundamental, over the last generation global financial markets have become increasingly interconnected. Many investors and hedge funds, for example, buy and sell stocks, bonds, and other financial instruments on a 24-hour basis, trading in American, Asian, and European stock markets whenever they are open. As a result, the impact of gains or declines in one market can be magnified enormously as traders react in whatever stock market happens to be open. For example, when American markets were roiled in 2008 and 2009 by declining stock prices and the collapse of several financial firms, traders worldwide responded by selling holdings in other financial firms, leading to much larger declines in American stock prices than would have occurred without these global connections.

Along the same lines, the interconnectedness of financial markets makes it hard to insulate one country from another's hard times. Many Americans lost wealth due to sharp decreases in home prices in 2008 and 2009, but foreigners who had invested in American banks, financial firms, and real estate also suffered. The same is true for Americans whose overseas holdings lost value as world stock markets declined during this period.

Along with every other country, the United States also faces a situation in which the state of its economy depends to some extent on actions taken elsewhere. For example, China has an enormous trade surplus with America and holds hundreds of billions of dollars in American government bonds. Some observers believe these assets give the Chinese the ability to severely damage the American economy, either by withholding exports or by selling large amounts of American government bonds on international markets, raising the interest rate the United States would have to offer to finance its budget deficit. (Because prospective purchasers of U.S. government bonds could buy them from the Chinese government instead, the U.S. government would have to agree to pay a higher interest rate on the bonds in order to lure these buyers away from the Chinese.) However, the Chinese economy is equally vulnerable. Eliminating the U.S. market for exports would leave Chinese factories without one of their major buyers. And selling bonds at below-market prices to increase American interest rates would likely damage the Chinese economy even more than the American economy.

IRAQ AND AFGHANISTAN

Much of the conflict over American foreign policy in recent years has stemmed from its military operations in Iraq, Afghanistan, and neighboring countries. Though American involvement in Iraq is essentially over, and operations in

AS AMERICAN OPERATIONS IN IRAQ began to wind down in 2009 and 2010, additional forces were sent to Afghanistan in the hope that the "surge" tactic used to good effect in Iraq would be similarly successful in Afghanistan. Here, a group of U.S. Marines participating in the surge listens to a briefing at Camp Dwyer in Helmand Province, Afghanistan.

Afghanistan are gradually winding down, ongoing operations against Al Qaeda forces throughout the region mean that debates over American foreign policy will remain central to American politics.

Currently America's operations in Iraq are limited to training the Iraqi army and helping the government secure its borders. The United States will likely have bases and training operations in Iraq for some time to come. Moreover, although fighting between rival religious groups (Sunni and Shiite Muslim) and ethnic cleansing of neighborhoods and cities by both groups have abated, it remains unclear whether this trend reflects a permanent change. The situation in Afghanistan is much more fluid. American-led forces invaded the country soon after the September 11 attacks, and following initial successes they have struggled to defeat Taliban and Al Qaeda forces and to rebuild both the Afghani government and its civilian infrastructure. Currently the United States is gradually drawing down its ground forces, a process scheduled to end in 2014. However, the success of American efforts to convert insurgents into supporters of the civilian government is very much in doubt. While withdrawal would curb the financial and human costs to America, it could trigger a full-fledged Afghani civil war and result in a government that might aid (or at least tolerate) terrorist groups.

TERRORISM

There have been no major terrorist attacks on the United States since September 11, 2001, but terrorist organizations have carried out bombings in London, Madrid, Bali, and Kenya. Many other terror plots have been stopped before they could be implemented, such as the attempt to detonate a car bomb in New York's Times Square in May 2010.

Much like the solutions to global warming, the proper response to terrorism may seem clear. The United States should deploy its armed forces, law enforcement, intelligence teams, and diplomatic assets, both at home and abroad, to discern what terrorists are planning and disrupt their attacks, and to discourage would-be terrorists from joining radical groups. However, what exactly should be done depends on a number of factors, including the reasons behind the attacks.

Consider American efforts against the Al Qaeda organization, which organized the September 11 attacks. Over the last 11 years, the United States has invaded Afghanistan, where the organization was based at the time of the attacks; destroyed many camps and other centers; and captured or killed many operatives and leaders of the organization, including its founder, Osama Bin Laden, during an attack in Pakistan in August 2011. However, while it is clear that Al Qaeda is far weaker than it was a decade ago, the possibility of an attack on Americans in the United States or abroad remains very real—and it is not clear what more can be done to reduce the danger. (See the "What Do Political Scientists Do?" box.)

American policy makers also remain unsure of the motivation for terrorist attacks. One hypothesis mentioned earlier is that terrorism results from a **"clash of civilizations**."[91] In this view, most terrorists are motivated by hatred of Western religions, culture, ideology, or the West itself—and most of their countrymen agree with their motives, even if many do not condone their methods. If this is the case, then the United States faces a long war, with no room to negotiate or form alliances with Islamic nations—but public opinion data from Islamic countries contradicts this argument. One study found that strong anti-American sentiments are held by a narrow range of organizations and individuals, not an entire region, race, or religion.[92] This finding suggests that in some countries, leaders

"clash of civilizations" The theory that terrorism is motivated by a hatred of Western culture and religion.

and citizens might be willing to work with the United States to end terror attacks and might support positive gestures, such as offers of American development aid.[93] Moreover, it suggests that opposition to U.S. actions might simply reflect disagreement with what these policies are designed to do rather than feelings rooted in cultural or religious differences.

The second big question in the War on Terror involves the rights of terror suspects. The Bush administration, while disavowing torture of suspects and prisoners, authorized aggressive interrogation methods that many believe amount to torture and curtailed suspects' access to lawyers and international observers.[94] (These policies were reversed to some extent by subsequent legislation and by Supreme Court decisions.) The Obama administration has prohibited aggressive interrogation, pledged to close the Guantánamo prison for terror suspects, and announced plans to hold civilian trials for most of those still being held. However, the prison closing and civilian trials have encountered considerable opposition from local governments and members of Congress, and it is not clear when (or whether) they will be implemented.

WEAPONS OF MASS DESTRUCTION

The term **weapons of mass destruction (WMDs)** refers to nuclear bombs, chemical weapons such as nerve gas, and biological weapons such as anthrax. Given the potential for these weapons to inflict mass casualties, the United States and many other nations have placed a high priority on limiting the number of nations that have these weapons and preventing terrorist organizations from obtaining or developing them.

Until recently, very few countries possessed WMDs. Only five countries admitted to having nuclear weapons: the United States, Russia, China, Great Britain, and France—though a sixth nation, Israel, was generally thought to have them as well. Most nations had signed the Nuclear Non-Proliferation Treaty, which prohibited the development of nuclear weapons and mandated inspection of civilian nuclear installations by the International Atomic Energy Agency (IAEA). All signatories were supposed to have destroyed their stockpiles of biological and chemical weapons after the enactment of the Biological Weapons Convention in 1975 and the Chemical Weapons Convention in 1992.

New efforts to develop nuclear weapons put WMDs on the foreign policy agenda. Neither Pakistan nor India signed the nonproliferation treaty; then both countries developed and tested nuclear weapons in the 1990s.[95] North Korea withdrew from the treaty in 2003, banned IAEA inspectors, began reprocessing nuclear reactor fuel into bomb-grade material, and detonated nuclear devices in 2006 and 2009. It has subsequently reneged on several agreements to dismantle its nuclear weapons program. And Iran has begun to reprocess reactor fuel into a form that can be made into weapons-grade material, although Iranian leaders insist that these efforts are not aimed at producing nuclear weapons.

These developments raised two concerns for U.S. decision makers: (1) that an increase in the number of nations with nuclear weapons elevates the chances that such weapons will be used—particularly between nuclear-armed adversaries such as India and Pakistan, or Iran and Israel, and (2) that the proliferation of nuclear weapons, coupled with the availability of nuclear materials and Soviet scientists, might enable terrorist organizations to buy or steal bomb-grade material or a weapon, or hire people to build one. Even nonstate groups have used chemical and biological weapons. For example, the Aum Shinrikyo group released

weapons of mass destruction (WMDs) Weapons that have the potential to cause large-scale loss of life, such as nuclear bombs and chemical or biological weapons.

IRAN'S NUCLEAR PROGRAM IS A CAUSE of concern for U.S. officials and IAEA inspectors. Although Iran claims its program is focused on energy, not weapons, this claim is widely doubted. Here, Iranian president Mahmoud Ahmadinejad tours a nuclear enrichment facility.

sarin nerve gas into the Tokyo subway system in 1995, killing 12 people and injuring hundreds more.[96]

As noted earlier, through multilateral efforts, the United States and other nations have worked to discourage some countries, such as North Korea and Iran, from building nuclear weapons. The approach has emphasized incentives as well as threats—economic and military sanctions serve to pressure nations that continue to develop weapons, while economic aid and even civilian nuclear reactors serve to persuade nations to give up their weapons programs.[97]

The critical question for American citizens and elected officials is what to do if a nation refuses to give up WMDs or if they fall into the hands of a terrorist organization. Responding with force may not eliminate the threat and may even provoke the very attacks it is intended to prevent. In the case of Iran, for example, nuclear facilities have been built underground and hardened against attack. Moreover, Iran might respond to attacks by attacking targets in Israel or by attacking tankers that provide a large fraction of the world's oil supply—in both cases, leading to a larger conflict. Similarly, attacks against North Korean facilities might trigger an all-out North Korean attack against South Korea, whose capital and largest city, Seoul, lies very close to the border between the two nations. Moreover, how should America respond to a WMD attack against its citizens or its allies, particularly if it is unclear which nation or group is responsible for the attack?

OTHER FOREIGN POLICY ISSUES

The issues described in this chapter are just a few of America's most prominent foreign policy questions. Resource availability is another pressing problem. The United States increasingly imports natural resources that are essential to the U.S. economy. Oil and natural gas imports heat homes, generate electricity, and power factories, while other imports such as chromium are essential for manufacturing high-tech equipment, from computers to commercial aircraft. But how can American consumers secure these materials without paying an exorbitant cost or making the U.S. economy overly dependent on foreign suppliers?

An additional concern is that American consumers and corporations compete more intensely for resources than in past decades. Developing countries such as

PREDICTING FUTURE TERROR ATTACKS

In the wake of the September 11 attacks, governments implemented many new policies in an attempt to prevent future attacks—placing cameras in public places, developing lists of possible terror targets, and requiring X-ray scans of shoes at airport security checkpoints. Although these measures have had significant costs in terms of money, lost freedoms, and inconvenience, many would argue that they have worked, in that there have been no major terrorist incidents within the continental United States since 2001.

This conclusion has been strongly challenged by the work of John Mueller, a political scientist at Ohio State University.[a] Mueller's work begins by articulating some simple propositions about who terrorists are and how they pursue their goals, and draws from these propositions a new set of ideas about how to protect America from attack. He begins with the question, What are terrorists trying to do? and then moves to predicting what kinds of targets they will look for and how best to respond to these attacks.

Watch a video clip of political scientist Navin Bapat discussing this topic at **wwnorton.com/studyspace**

Mueller's central proposition is that because terrorists are interested in frightening people, the number of possible targets in America is very large. We normally think of terrorists attacking big, visible targets such as the World Trade Center, or the U.S. Capitol, but in fact there are many public places, from malls to urban centers, where an attack could cause high casualties, and there is an equally large number of bridges, buildings, and dams whose destruction could cause significant loss of life or large monetary damages. Put another way, if attacks are aimed at causing terror, there is a nearly infinite number of places where terrorists can achieve this goal. Even a modest shopping mall in a small town could be a notable target under the right circumstances.

The large number of potential targets, Mueller argues, makes the job of preventing attacks virtually impossible. Attempts to make one target less vulnerable simply makes other targets less safe, for if authorities take steps to secure a target or targets, would-be terrorists can simply switch to another less-guarded one that would be equally attractive given their goals. And given that the number of actual terrorists is quite small, they are extremely difficult to find, regardless of whether they are in other countries or in America.

Mueller's argument has an implication that is chilling at first glance: although we would like to think that we can eliminate the danger of terror attacks, this goal is essentially impossible. As long as people seek to create terror, attacks can happen. However, living with risk is nothing new: virtually all of us accept

Since September 11, 2001, armed security forces have become more common at train stations, malls, and other public places. Is this additional security likely to prevent terrorist attacks?

danger in our everyday lives, from driving cars to the possibility of earthquakes, tornados, or hurricanes. The chances of being involved in a terrorist incident is far lower than these everyday risks. Thus, Mueller argues, though we should think about how to prevent future attacks, we need to place these risks in context and not let fear shape our policy choices.

Mueller also suggests that our antiterrorism policies deemphasize lists of possible terror targets. Even if we identify the 200 most important bridges, or the 100 largest malls, the likelihood of an attack on any of these sites is very small. More important, any efforts we make to protect these targets will be very obvious to potential attackers, who can respond by switching to the 201st bridge, the 101st largest mall, or an entirely different target.

The one exception to this logic, Mueller notes, are targets where the potential damage from an attack is inordinately high, such as civilian nuclear reactors, symbolic targets like the Statue of Liberty, or truly critical infrastructure such as major ports or bridges.

Mueller's final inference is that it may be possible to loosen some precautions against terror attacks. For example, he notes that British authorities have eliminated the requirement that passengers have their shoes x-rayed at airport security checkpoints. Given that this change has not produced any new shoe bombers on flights originating in Britain, Mueller argues, it makes sense for American authorities to consider eliminating this requirement as well.

China, India, and Brazil require increasing amounts of energy and other imports to build factories, improve public services, construct housing, and improve citizens' standard of living. Faced with these growing demands, U.S. policy makers must ensure that American consumers and businesses can obtain the resources they need and decide when and how to encourage Americans to use alternative resources, such as solar or nuclear power, that would reduce dependence on imported sources of energy.

A third question for the makers of American foreign policy is whether and how to mediate between Israel and the Palestinians. Since Israel became a state in 1948, it has fought four major wars and countless minor conflicts with Syria, Jordan, Egypt, Lebanon, and various groups of Palestinians. The United States has been Israel's strongest ally and a major supplier of military hardware and economic aid.[98] However, it has also encouraged the parties to negotiate a peaceful settlement through diplomacy and offers of military and economic aid to both sides. These efforts produced a peace treaty between Egypt and Israel in 1979 and almost yielded a deal between Israel and the Palestinians in 2000.[99] The United States has also worked to limit Israeli settlements in the West Bank and Gaza Strip, as these areas are largely populated by Palestinians and might become part of a new Palestinian state in the event of a peace agreement. (In recent years, the European Union and other nations have also participated in the negotiation process, although no one has been able to broker a comprehensive agreement or persuade the Israelis to stop building new settlements.) The Obama administration has initiated efforts toward both goals, with few signs of success so far.

Over the course of the negotiations, several major issues have persisted, including how to devise an acceptable deal that would establish Israel's borders, force all parties to abandon hostilities, and address the Palestinians' desire for a state of their own. The task is especially difficult because the Palestinians are not a single, uniform group; they are represented by many groups, most notably Fatah and Hamas, each with its own leaders and demands.[100] Negotiations lasting over a generation show no signs of yielding an agreement.

Finally, American citizens and elected officials must decide when America should defer to the judgments of international organizations. It is easy for Americans to support these organizations when their decisions are consistent with American policy, such as when the UN coordinates sanctions against Iran, the WTO enforces American copyrights abroad, or the International Criminal Court tries deposed leaders for crimes committed while in office. The challenge for the United States is deciding what to do when these organizations act against the interests of individual Americans, American businesses, or the country as a whole. For example, the UN withdrew most of its staff from coordinating the reconstruction of Iraq after several attacks on UN staff in 2003 (until expanding its presence in the country again in 2007), and the WTO has forced America to lower trade barriers.

International organizations present a trade-off for American policy makers. These organizations' decisions may be harmful to American interests, but if the United States accepts them—especially when compliance imposes costs—this behavior may increase the chances that other nations will also comply in international efforts that would serve U.S. goals. In this way, international organizations may reduce the extent to which America acts as the world's policeman, protector of human rights, and enforcer of economic policies. The task for U.S. policy makers is to balance these long-term benefits against the real, short-term costs of compliance.

CONCLUSION

Foreign policy matters. National security is a top priority for many Americans. The state of the American economy, from home prices to the unemployment rate, is affected by economic conditions elsewhere. Trade agreements with other nations determine how much American companies are allowed to export and what taxes and fees they must pay to import raw materials and other goods. Solutions to pressing environmental problems such as global warming are inherently international. It is hard to find a domestic issue that does not have a foreign policy component.

Foreign policy is also conflictual. Disagreements among elected officials over what to do in Afghanistan, or over trade agreements or any other question of foreign policy, are not just attempts to attract political support or get media attention. These differences of opinion reflect real dilemmas over what government should do.

In all these respects, the September 11 attacks, the invasions of Iraq and Afghanistan, and the worldwide economic crisis of 2008–09 are not exceptions to the rule; rather, they epitomize just how close to home foreign policy is. Ordinary Americans are finding their lives increasingly affected by actions taken outside U.S. borders.

WHAT IS FOREIGN POLICY?

▶ Describe the major approaches to understanding foreign policy and trace how America's role in the world has evolved. **Pages 695–704**

SUMMARY

Foreign policy is any government action toward a group outside of America's borders. Foreign policy goals are complex, and debates on what America's goals should be are traditionally framed in terms of general principles. The goals of American foreign policy have changed over time and have become increasingly internationalist.

KEY TERMS

foreign policy (p. 695)

unilateral action (national) (p. 696)

multilateral action (p. 696)

isolationism (p. 696)

internationalism (p. 696)

realism (p. 697)

idealism (p. 697)

constructivism (p. 697)

nation building (p. 699)

Monroe Doctrine (p. 699)

Cold War (p. 700)

containment (p. 700)

mutually assured destruction (p. 701)

domino theory (p. 701)

détente (p. 702)

Bush Doctrine (p. 703)

CRITICAL THINKING AND DISCUSSION

Pick one of the foreign policy problems described in this chapter. What policy choices would a realist make? What choices would an idealist make?

PRACTICE QUIZ QUESTIONS

1. When one country does something on its own without coordinating with other countries, it is

   _____.

   a) isolationist
   b) internationalist
   c) acting unilaterally
   d) acting multilaterally
   e) nation building

2. _____ believe that countries pursue their own interests.

   a) Realists
   b) Idealists
   c) Constructivists
   d) Internationalists

3. The Monroe Doctrine stated that in European wars, America would _____.

   a) support Britain
   b) support the attacking country
   c) support the attacked country
   d) provide arms but not troops
   e) remain neutral

4. American foreign policy became increasingly internationalist following _____.

   a) the Civil War
   b) World War I
   c) World War II
   d) the Vietnam War
   e) the Cold War

5. The goal of containment influenced the _____ and _____.
   a) war in Iraq; war in Afghanistan
   b) Korean War; war in Iraq
   c) Vietnam War; war in Iraq
   d) Korean War; Cuban Missile Crisis
   e) Vietnam War; World War II

⑤ **PRACTICE ONLINE**

"Critical Thinking" exercise: *Politics Is Conflictual— The League of Nations*

FOREIGN POLICY MAKERS

▶ Explain how the various branches of government shape foreign policy. **Pages 704–14**

SUMMARY

The major actors in foreign policy are the president and Congress, though the Supreme Court, interest groups, and public opinion all influence foreign policy decisions to a degree. The president's advantage over Congress lies in the ambiguity in the Constitution and the unilateral presidential power.

KEY TERMS

National Security Council (NSC) (p. 705)

civilian control (p. 706)

intergovernmental organizations (IGOs) (p. 712)

nongovernmental organizations (NGOs) (p. 712)

World Bank (p. 713)

International Monetary Fund (IMF) (p. 713)

United Nations (UN) (p. 714)

CRITICAL THINKING AND DISCUSSION

The American president has much more influence over foreign policy than members of Congress do. What are the pros and cons of this allocation of power?

PRACTICE QUIZ QUESTIONS

6. The principal foreign policy department in the executive branch is _____.
   a) the Department of Defense
   b) the Council on Foreign Relations
   c) the Department of International Relations
   d) the Department of State
   e) the Foreign Intelligence Advisory Board

7. The idea that military personnel do not formulate policy, but rather implement directives from civilians is _____.
   a) military deference
   b) civilian control
   c) the Geneva system
   d) civilian-military alliance
   e) the Bush Doctrine

8. Congress holds the _____ and _____, which both influence foreign policy.
   a) power to deploy troops; power of the purse
   b) power to approve treaties; power to deploy troops
   c) power to declare war; power of the purse
   d) power to deploy troops; power to declare war
   e) power to approve appointments; power to deploy troops

9. The War Powers Resolution was designed to _____.
   a) limit the president's war-making powers
   b) limit the Congress' war-making powers
   c) limit the Department of Defense's war-making powers
   d) limit the Pentagon's war-making powers
   e) limit the State Department's war-making powers

⑤ **PRACTICE ONLINE**

"Critical Thinking" exercise: *Political Process Matters— The War Powers Resolution*

THE TOOLS OF FOREIGN POLICY

▶ Examine the ways American foreign policy is implemented. **Pages 714–20**

SUMMARY

American foreign policy is implemented using a variety of tools—beyond the use of military force, other tools include the provision of foreign aid or changes to trade policy. Though all tools can be used in pursuit of desired policy outcomes, the specific tool is selected based on careful consideration of context.

KEY TERMS

tariff (p. 716)

World Trade Organization (WTO) (p. 716)

most-favored-nation status (p. 716)

PRACTICE QUIZ QUESTIONS

10. When a country is given "most-favored-nation" status, it means that the United States _____ any other nation.
   a) gives the country higher levels of foreign aid than
   b) gives the country higher levels of military aid than
   c) sets tariffs on imports to the United States to the lowest rate given to
   d) sets tariffs on exports from the United States to the lowest rate given to
   e) sends that country more troops than

11. The process of _____ involves using personal contact and negotiations with leaders to work out international agreements.
   a) nation building
   b) diplomacy
   c) unilateralism
   d) the Bush Doctrine
   e) the use of force

12. The North American Free Trade Agreement (NAFTA) is an example of _____.
   a) a bilateral agreement
   b) an alliance
   c) a tariff
   d) a multilateral agreement
   e) a sanction

Ⓢ **PRACTICE ONLINE**

"Critical Thinking" exercise: *Politics Is Everywhere—U.S. Military Presence Worldwide*

THE POLITICS OF FOREIGN POLICY TODAY

▶ Analyze several major areas of foreign policy and why they are often controversial. **Pages 720–32**

SUMMARY

Foreign policy is everywhere, and with decisions that are real and meaningful to all Americans. Despite the recent economic rise of China and India, America continues to be an international power, and in many cases, is the strongest nation.

KEY TERMS

Kyoto Protocol (p. 724)

"clash of civilizations" (p. 728)

weapons of mass destruction (WMDs) (p. 729)

CRITICAL THINKING AND DISCUSSION

Using evidence such as international public opinion data from the Pew Research Center or some other source, argue for or against the theory of a contemporary "clash of civilizations."

PRACTICE QUIZ QUESTIONS

13. What factor limits the American response to global warming?
   a) Science is inconclusive that human activity is a significant cause of warming.
   b) The need for reduction in carbon dioxide emissions is not well established.

c) The steps necessary to combat global warming are uncertain.
d) Developing nations' efforts are sufficient.
e) Addressing global warming requires a multilateral effort, which is difficult to coordinate.

14. The American government hesitates to pressure Pakistan on human rights violations most likely because _____.
a) doing so would threaten economic ties with Pakistan
b) attempts to protect human rights may make it harder to achieve goals in Afghanistan
c) evidence of human rights violations in Pakistan is unreliable
d) there is little international condemnation for the Pakistani violations of human rights
e) Pakistan enforces a Bill of Rights

15. The "clash of civilizations" perspective assumes that terrorists are motivated by _____.
a) hatred of the West itself
b) frustration with local economic climate
c) hatred of Christianity
d) refusal to accept secular rule
e) strife in their home country

Ⓢ **PRACTICE ONLINE**

"What Do Political Scientists Do?" video exercise: *Navin Bapat on Terrorism's Effect on Foreign Policy*

SUGGESTED READING

Bueno de Mesquita, Bruce. *Principles of International Politics*. Washington, DC: CQ Press, 2005.

Fisher, Louis. *Presidential War Power*. Lawrence: University Press of Kansas, 2004.

Friedman, Thomas L. *The World Is Flat 3.0: A Brief History of the Twenty-first Century*. New York: Farrar, Straus and Giroux, 2007.

Huntington, Samuel P. *The Clash of Civilizations and the Remaking of World Order*. New York: Free Press, 2002.

Keohane, Robert O. *After Hegemony: Cooperation and Discord in the International System*. Princeton, NJ: Princeton University Press, 2005 (originally published 1984).

Mearsheimer, John J. *The Tragedy of Great Power Politics*. New York: Norton, 2001.

National Commission on Terrorist Attacks upon the United States. *The 9/11 Commission Report: Final Report of the National Commission on Terrorist Attacks upon the United States*. New York: Norton, 2004. Full text also available from the U.S. Government Printing Office at www.gpoaccess .gov/911/index.html.

Ricks, Thomas. *The Gamble: General David Petraeus and the American Military Adventure in Iraq, 2006–2008*. New York: Penguin Press, 2009.

Roach, Stephen. *The Next Asia: Opportunities and Challenges for a New Globalization*. New York: Wiley, 2009.

Sen, Amartya. *Identity and Violence: The Illusion of Destiny*. New York: Norton, 2007.

Simmons, Beth, Frank Dobbin, and Geoffrey Garrett. *The Global Diffusion of Markets and Democracy*. New York: Cambridge University Press, 2008.

Stiglitz, Joseph E. *Making Globalization Work*. New York: Norton, 2007.

APPENDIX

The Declaration of Independence

In Congress, July 4, 1776

The unanimous Declaration of the thirteen united States of America,

When in the Course of human events, it becomes necessary for one people to dissolve the political bands which have connected them with another, and to assume among the powers of the earth, the separate and equal station to which the Laws of Nature and of Nature's God entitle them, a decent respect to the opinions of mankind requires that they should declare the causes which impel them to the separation.

We hold these truths to be self-evident, that all men are created equal, that they are endowed by their Creator with certain unalienable Rights, that among these are Life, Liberty and the pursuit of Happiness.—That to secure these rights, Governments are instituted among Men, deriving their just powers from the consent of the governed. —That whenever any Form of Government becomes destructive of these ends, it is the Right of the People to alter or to abolish it, and to institute new Government, laying its foundation on such principles and organizing its powers in such form, as to them shall seem most likely to effect their Safety and Happiness. Prudence, indeed, will dictate that Governments long established should not be changed for light and transient causes; and accordingly all experience hath shewn, that mankind are more disposed to suffer, while evils are sufferable, than to right themselves by abolishing the forms to which they are accustomed. But when a long train of abuses and usurpations, pursuing invariably the same Object evinces a design to reduce them under absolute Despotism, it is their right, it is their duty, to throw off such Government, and to provide new Guards for their future security.—Such has been the patient sufferance of these Colonies; and such is now the necessity which constrains them to alter their former Systems of Government. The history of the present King of Great Britain is a history of repeated injuries and usurpations, all having in direct object the establishment of an absolute Tyranny over these States. To prove this, let Facts be submitted to a candid world.

He has refused his Assent to Laws, the most wholesome and necessary for the public good.

He has forbidden his Governors to pass Laws of immediate and pressing importance, unless suspended in their operation till his Assent should be obtained; and when so suspended, he has utterly neglected to attend to them.

He has refused to pass other Laws for the accommodation of large districts of people, unless those people would relinquish the right of Representation in the Legislature, a right inestimable to them and formidable to tyrants only.

He has called together legislative bodies at places unusual, uncomfortable, and distant from the depository of their public Records, for the sole purpose of fatiguing them into compliance with his measures.

He has dissolved Representative Houses repeatedly, for opposing with manly firmness his invasions on the rights of the people.

He has refused for a long time, after such dissolutions, to cause others to be elected; whereby the Legislative powers, incapable of Annihilation, have returned to the People at large for their exercise; the State remaining in the mean time exposed to all the dangers of invasion from without, and convulsions within.

He has endeavoured to prevent the population of these States; for that purpose obstructing the Laws for Naturalization of Foreigners; refusing to pass others to encourage their migrations hither, and raising the conditions of new Appropriations of Lands.

He has obstructed the Administration of Justice, by refusing his Assent to Laws for establishing Judiciary powers.

He has made Judges dependent on his Will alone, for the tenure of their offices, and the amount and payment of their salaries.

He has erected a multitude of New Offices, and sent hither swarms of Officers to harrass our people, and eat out their substance.

He has kept among us, in times of peace, Standing Armies without the Consent of our legislatures.

He has affected to render the Military independent of and superior to the Civil power.

He has combined with others to subject us to a jurisdiction foreign to our constitution, and unacknowledged by our laws; giving his Assent to their Acts of pretended Legislation:

For Quartering large bodies of armed troops among us:

For protecting them, by a mock Trial, from punishment for any Murders which they should commit on the Inhabitants of these States:

For cutting off our Trade with all parts of the world:

For imposing Taxes on us without our Consent:

For depriving us in many cases, of the benefits of Trial by Jury:

For transporting us beyond Seas to be tried for pretended offences:

For abolishing the free System of English Laws in a neighboring Province, establishing therein an Arbitrary government, and enlarging its Boundaries so as to render it at once an example and fit instrument for introducing the same absolute rule into these Colonies:

For taking away our Charters, abolishing our most valuable Laws, and altering fundamentally the Forms of our Governments:

For suspending our own Legislatures, and declaring themselves invested with power to legislate for us in all cases whatsoever.

He has abdicated Government here, by declaring us out of his Protection and waging War against us.

He has plundered our seas, ravaged our Coasts, burnt our towns, and destroyed the lives of our people.

He is at this time transporting large Armies of foreign Mercenaries to compleat the works of death, desolation and tyranny, already begun with circumstances of Cruelty & perfidy scarcely paralleled in the most barbarous ages, and totally unworthy the Head of a civilized nation.

He has constrained our fellow Citizens taken Captive on the high Seas to bear Arms against their Country, to become the executioners of their friends and Brethren, or to fall themselves by their Hands.

He has excited domestic insurrections amongst us, and has endeavoured to bring on the inhabitants of our frontiers, the merciless Indian Savages, whose known rule of warfare, is an undistinguished destruction of all ages, sexes and conditions.

In every stage of these Oppressions We have Petitioned for Redress in the most humble terms: Our repeated Petitions have been answered only by repeated injury. A Prince whose character is thus marked by every act which may define a Tyrant, is unfit to be the ruler of a free people.

Nor have We been wanting in attentions to our Brittish brethren. We have warned them from time to time of attempts by their legislature to extend an unwarrantable jurisdiction over us. We have reminded them of the circumstances of our emigration and settlement here. We have appealed to their native justice and magnanimity, and we have conjured them by the ties of our common kindred to disavow these usurpations, which, would inevitably interrupt our connections and correspondence. They too have been deaf to the voice of justice and of consanguinity. We must, therefore, acquiesce in the necessity, which denounces our Separation, and hold them, as we hold the rest of mankind, Enemies in War, in Peace Friends.

We, Therefore, the Representatives of the United States of America, in General Congress, Assembled, appealing to the Supreme Judge of the world for the rectitude of our intentions, do, in the Name, and by Authority of the good People of these Colonies, solemnly publish and declare, That these United Colonies are, and of Right ought to be Free and Independent States; that they are Absolved from all Allegiance to the British Crown, and that all political connection between them and the State of Great Britain, is and ought to be totally dissolved; and that as Free and Independent States, they have full Power to levy War, conclude Peace, contract Alliances, establish Commerce, and to do all other Acts and Things which Independent States may of right do. And for the support of this Declaration, with a firm reliance on the protection of divine Providence, we mutually pledge to each other our Lives, our Fortunes and our sacred Honor.

The foregoing Declaration was, by order of Congress, engrossed, and signed by the following members:

John Hancock

NEW HAMPSHIRE
Josiah Bartlett
William Whipple
Matthew Thornton

MASSACHUSETTS BAY
Samuel Adams
John Adams
Robert Treat Paine
Elbridge Gerry

RHODE ISLAND
Stephen Hopkins
William Ellery

CONNECTICUT
Roger Sherman
Samuel Huntington
William Williams
Oliver Wolcott

NEW YORK
William Floyd
Philip Livingston
Francis Lewis
Lewis Morris

NEW JERSEY
Richard Stockton
John Witherspoon
Francis Hopkinson
John Hart
Abraham Clark

PENNSYLVANIA
Robert Morris
Benjamin Rush
Benjamin Franklin
John Morton
George Clymer
James Smith
George Taylor
James Wilson
George Ross

DELAWARE
Caesar Rodney
George Read
Thomas M'Kean

MARYLAND
Samuel Chase
William Paca
Thomas Stone
Charles Carroll,
*   of Carrollton*

VIRGINIA
George Wythe
Richard Henry Lee
Thomas Jefferson
Benjamin Harrison
Thomas Nelson, Jr.
Francis Lightfoot Lee
Carter Braxton

NORTH CAROLINA
William Hooper
Joseph Hewes
John Penn

SOUTH CAROLINA
Edward Rutledge
Thomas Heyward, Jr.
Thomas Lynch, Jr.
Arthur Middleton

GEORGIA
Button Gwinnett
Lyman Hall
George Walton

Resolved, That copies of the Declaration be sent to the several assemblies, conventions, and committees, or councils of safety, and to the several commanding officers of the continental troops; that it be proclaimed in each of the United States, at the head of the army.

The Articles of Confederation

Agreed to by Congress November 15, 1777;
ratified and in force March 1, 1781

To all whom these Presents shall come, we the undersigned Delegates of the States affixed to our Names, send greeting. Whereas the Delegates of the United States of America, in Congress assembled, did, on the fifteenth day of November, in the Year of Our Lord One thousand Seven Hundred and Seventy seven, and in the Second Year of the Independence of America, agree to certain articles of Confederation and perpetual Union between the States of Newhampshire, Massachusetts-bay, Rhodeisland and Providence Plantations, Connecticut, New-York, New-Jersey, Pennsylvania, Delaware, Maryland, Virginia, North-Carolina, South-Carolina and Georgia in the words following, viz. "Articles of Confederation and perpetual Union between the states of Newhampshire, Massachusettsbay, Rhodeisland and Providence Plantations, Connecticut, New-York, New-Jersey, Pennsylvania, Delaware, Maryland, Virginia, North-Carolina, South-Carolina and Georgia.

Art. I. The Stile of this confederacy shall be "The United States of America."

Art. II. Each state retains its sovereignty, freedom and independence, and every Power, Jurisdiction and right, which is not by this confederation expressly delegated to the United States, in Congress assembled.

Art. III. The said states hereby severally enter into a firm league of friendship with each other, for their common defence, the security of their Liberties, and their mutual and general welfare, binding themselves to assist each other, against all force offered to, or attacks made upon them, or any of them, on account of religion, sovereignty, trade, or any other pretence whatever.

Art. IV. The better to secure and perpetuate mutual friendship and intercourse among the people of the different states in this union, the free inhabitants of each of these states, paupers, vagabonds and fugitives from Justice excepted, shall be entitled to all privileges and immunities of free citizens in the several states; and the people of each state shall have free ingress and regress to and from any other state, and shall enjoy therein all the privileges of trade and commerce, subject to the same duties, impositions and restrictions as the inhabitants thereof respectively, provided that such restriction shall not extend so far as to prevent the removal of property imported into any state, to any other state, of which the Owner is an inhabitant; provided also that no imposition, duties or restriction shall be laid by any state, on the property of the united states, or either of them.

If any Person guilty of, or charged with treason, felony, or other high misdemeanor in any state, shall flee from Justice, and be found in any of the united states, he shall, upon demand of the Governor or executive power, of the state from which he fled, be delivered up and removed to the state having jurisdiction of his offence.

Full faith and credit shall be given in each of these states to the records, acts and judicial proceedings of the courts and magistrates of every other state.

Art. V. For the more convenient management of the general interests of the united states, delegates shall be annually appointed in such manner as the legislature of each state shall direct, to meet in Congress on the first Monday in November, in every year, with a power reserved to each state, to recall its delegates, or any of them, at any time within the year, and to send others in their stead, for the remainder of the Year.

No state shall be represented in Congress by less than two, nor by more than seven Members; and no person shall be capable of being a delegate for more than three years in any term of six years; nor shall any person, being a delegate, be capable of holding any office under the united states, for which he, or another for his benefit receives any salary, fees or emolument of any kind.

Each state shall maintain its own delegates in a meeting of the states, and while they act as members of the committee of the states.

In determining questions in the united states, in Congress assembled, each state shall have one vote.

Freedom of speech and debate in Congress shall not be impeached or questioned in any Court, or place out of Congress, and the members of congress shall be protected in their persons from arrests and imprisonments, during the time of their going to and from, and attendance on congress, except for treason, felony, or breach of the peace.

Art. VI. No state without the Consent of the united states in congress assembled, shall send any embassy to, or receive any embassy from, or enter into any conference, agreement, or alliance or treaty with any King, prince or state; nor shall any person holding any office or profit or trust under the united states, or any of them, accept of any present, emolument, office or title of any kind whatever from any king, prince or foreign state; nor shall the united states in congress assembled, or any of them, grant any title of nobility.

No two or more states shall enter into any treaty, confederation or alliance whatever between them, without the consent of the united states in congress assembled, specifying accurately the purposes for which the same is to be entered into, and how long it shall continue.

No state shall lay any imposts or duties, which may interfere with any stipulations in treaties, entered into by the united states in congress assembled, with any king, prince or state, in pursuance of any treaties already proposed by congress, to the courts of France and Spain.

No vessels of war shall be kept up in time of peace by any state, except such number only, as shall be deemed necessary by the united states in congress assembled, for the defence of such state, or its trade; nor shall any body of forces be kept up by any state, in time of peace, except such number only, as in the judgment of the united states, in congress assembled, shall be deemed requisite to garrison the forts necessary for the defence of such state; but every state shall always keep up a well regulated and disciplined militia, sufficiently armed and accoutred, and shall provide and constantly have ready for use, in public stores, a due number of field pieces and tents, and a proper quantity of arms, ammunition and camp equipage.

No state shall engage in any war without the consent of the united states in congress assembled, unless such state be actually invaded by enemies, or shall have received certain advice of a resolution being formed by some nation of Indians to invade such state, and the danger is so imminent as not to admit of a delay, till the united states in congress asssembled can be consulted; nor shall any state grant commissions to any ships or vessels of war, nor letters of marque or reprisal, except it be after a declaration of war by the united states in congress assembled, and then only against the kingdom or state and the subjects thereof, against which war has been so declared, and under such regulations as shall be established by the united states in congress assembled, unless such state be infested by pirates; in which case vessels of war may be fitted out for that occasion, and kept so long as the danger shall continue, or until the united states in congress assembled shall determine otherwise.

Art. VII. When land-forces are raised by any state for the common defence, all officers of or under the rank of colonel, shall be appointed by the legislature of each state respectively, by whom such forces shall be raised, or in such manner as such state shall direct, and all vacancies shall be filled up by the state which first made the appointment.

Art. VIII. All charges of war, and all other expences that shall be incurred for the common defence or general welfare, and allowed by the united states in congress assembled, shall be defrayed out of a common treasury, which shall be supplied by the several states in proportion to the value of all land within each state, granted to or surveyed for any Person, as such land and the buildings and improvements thereon shall be estimated according to such mode as the united states in congress assembled, shall from time to time direct and appoint.

The taxes for paying that proportion shall be laid and levied by the authority and direction of the legislatures of the several states within the time agreed upon by the united states in congress assembled.

Art. IX. The united states in congress assembled, shall have the sole and exclusive right and power of determining on peace and war, except in the cases mentioned in the sixth article—of sending and receiving ambassadors—entering into treaties and alliances, provided that no treaty of commerce shall be made whereby the legislative power of the respective states shall be restrained from imposing such imposts and duties on foreigners, as their own people are subjected to, or from prohibiting the exportation of any species of goods or commodities whatsoever—of establishing rules for deciding in all cases, what captures on land or water shall be legal, and in what manner prizes taken by land or naval forces in the service of the united states shall be divided or appropriated—of granting letters of marque and reprisal in times of peace—appointing courts for the trial of piracies and felonies committed on the high seas and establishing courts for receiving and determining finally appeals in all cases of captures, provided that no member of congress shall be appointed a judge of any of the said courts.

The united states in congress assembled shall also be the last resort on appeal in all disputes and differences now subsisting or that hereafter may arise between two or more states concerning boundary, jurisdiction or any other cause whatever; which authority shall always be exercised in the manner following. Whenever the legislative or executive authority or lawful agent of any state in controversy with another shall present a petition to congress stating the matter in question and praying for a hearing, notice thereof shall be given by order of congress to the legislative or executive authority of the other state in controversy, and a day assigned for the appearance of the parties by their lawful agents, who shall then be directed to appoint by joint consent, commissioners or judges to constitute a court for hearing and determining the matter in question: but if they cannot agree, congress shall name three persons out of each of the united states, and from the list of such persons each party shall alternately strike out one, the petitioners beginning, until the number shall be reduced to thirteen; and from that number not less than seven, nor more than nine names as congress shall direct, shall in the presence of congress be drawn out by lot, and the persons whose names shall be so drawn or any five of them, shall be commissioners or judges, to hear and finally determine the controversy, so always as a major part of the judges who shall hear the cause shall agree in the determination: and if either party shall neglect to attend at the day appointed, without shewing reasons, which congress shall judge sufficient, or being present shall refuse to strike, the congress shall proceed to nominate three persons out of each state, and the secretary of congress shall strike in behalf of such party absent or refusing; and the judgment and sentence of the court to be appointed, in the manner before prescribed, shall be final and conclusive; and if any of the parties shall refuse to submit to the authority of such court, or to appear to defend their claim or cause, the court shall nevertheless proceed to pronounce sentence, or judgment, which shall in like manner be final and decisive, the judgment or sentence and other proceedings being in either case transmitted to congress, and lodged among the acts of congress for the security of the parties concerned: provided that every commissioner, before he sits in judgment, shall take an oath to be administered by one of the judges of the supreme or superior court of the state, where the cause shall be tried,

"well and truly to hear and determine the matter in question, according to the best of his judgment, without favour, affection or hope of reward:" provided also, that no state shall be deprived of territory for the benefit of the united states.

All controversies concerning the private right of soil claimed under different grants of two or more states, whose jurisdictions as they may respect such lands, and the states which passed such grants are adjusted, the said grants or either of them being at the same time claimed to have originated antecedent to such settlement of jurisdiction, shall on the petition of either party to the congress of the united states, be finally determined as near as may be in the same manner as is before prescribed for deciding disputes respecting territorial jurisdiction between different states.

The united states in congress assembled shall also have the sole and exclusive right and power of regulating the alloy and value of coin struck by their own authority, or by that of the respective states—fixing the standard of weights and measures throughout the united states—regulating the trade and managing all affairs with the Indians, not members of any of the states, provided that the legislative right of any state within its own limits be not infringed or violated—establishing and regulating post-offices from one state to another, throughout all the united states, and exacting such postage on the papers passing thro' the same as may be requisite to defray the expences of the said office—appointing all officers of the land forces, in the service of the united states, excepting regimental officers—appointing all the officers of the naval forces, and commissioning all officers whatever in the service of the united states—making rules for the government and regulation of the said land and naval forces, and directing their operations.

The united states in congress assembled shall have authority to appoint a committee, to sit in the recess of congress, to be denominated "A Committee of the States," and to consist of one delegate from each state; and to appoint such other committees and civil officers as may be necessary for managing the general affairs of the united states under their direction—to appoint one of their number to preside, provided that no person be allowed to serve in the office of president more than one year in any term of three years; to ascertain the necessary sums of Money to be raised for the service of the united states, and to appropriate and apply the same for defraying the public expenses—to borrow money, or emit bills on the credit of the united states, transmitting every half year to the respective states an account of the sums of money so borrowed or emitted,—to build and equip a navy—to agree upon the number of land forces, and to make requisitions from each state for its quota, in proportion to the number of white inhabitants in such state; which requisition shall be binding, and thereupon the legislature of each state shall appoint the regimental officers, raise the men and cloath, arm and equip them in a soldier like manner, at the expense of the united states; and the officers and men so cloathed, armed and equipped shall march to the place appointed, and within the time agreed on by the united states in congress assembled: But if the united states in congress assembled shall, on consideration of circumstances judge proper that any state should not raise men, or should raise a smaller number than its quota, and that any other state should raise a greater number of men than the quota thereof, such extra number shall be raised, officered, cloathed, armed and equipped in the same manner as the quota of such state, unless the legislature of such state shall judge that such extra number cannot be safely spared out of the same, in which case they shall raise officer, cloath, arm and equip as many of such extra number as they judge can be safely spared. And the officers and men so cloathed, armed and equipped, shall march to the place appointed, and within the time agreed on by the united states in congress assembled.

The united states in congress assembled shall never engage in a war, nor grant letters of marque and reprisal in time of peace, nor enter into any treaties or alliances, nor coin money, nor regulate the value thereof, nor ascertain the sums and expenses necessary for the defence and welfare of the united states, or any of them, nor emit bills, nor borrow money on the credit of the united states, nor appropriate money, nor agree upon the number of vessels of war, to be built or purchased, or the number of land or sea forces to be raised, nor appoint a commander in chief of the army or navy, unless nine states assent to the same: nor shall a question on any other point, except for adjourning from day to day be determined, unless by the votes of a majority of the united states in congress assembled.

The congress of the united states shall have power to adjourn to any time within the year, and to any place within the united states, so that no period of adjournment be for a longer duration than the space of six Months, and shall publish the Journal of their proceedings monthly, except such parts thereof relating to treaties, alliances or military operations, as in their judgment require secrecy; and the yeas and nays of the delegates of each state on any question shall be entered on the Journal, when it is desired by any delegate; and the delegates of a state, or any of them, at his or their request shall be furnished with a transcript of the said Journal, except such parts as are above excepted, to lay before the legislatures of the several states.

Art. X. The committee of the states, or any nine of them, shall be authorised to execute, in the recess of congress, such of the powers of congress as the united states in congress assembled, by the consent of nine states, shall from time to time think expedient to vest them with; provided that no power be delegated to the said committee, for the exercise of which, by the articles of confederation, the voice of nine states in the congress of the united states assembled is requisite.

Art. XI. Canada acceding to this confederation, and joining in the measures of the united states, shall be admitted into, and entitled to all the advantages of this union: but no other colony shall be admitted into the same, unless such admission be agreed to by nine states.

Art. XII. All bills of credit emitted, monies borrowed and debts contracted by, or under the authority of congress, before the assembling of the united states, in pursuance of the present confederation, shall be deemed and considered as a charge against the united states, for payment and satisfaction whereof the said united states and the public faith are hereby solemnly pledged.

Art. XIII. Every state shall abide by the determinations of the united states in congress assembled, on all questions which by this confederation are submitted to them. And the Articles of this confederation shall be inviolably observed by every state, and the union shall be perpetual; nor shall any alteration at any time hereafter be made in any of them; unless such alteration be agreed to in a congress of the united states, and be afterwards confirmed by the legislatures of every state.

And Whereas it hath pleased the Great Governor of the World to incline the hearts of the legislatures we respectively represent in congress, to approve of, and to authorize us to ratify the said articles of confederation and perpetual union. Know Ye that we the undersigned delegates, by virtue of the power and authority to us given for that purpose, do by these presents, in the name and in behalf of our respective constituents, fully and entirely ratify and confirm each and every of the said articles of confederation and perpetual union, and all and singular the matters and things therein contained: And we do further solemnly plight and engage the faith of our respective constituents, that they shall abide by the determinations of the united states in congress assembled, on all questions, which by the said confederation are submitted to them. And that the articles thereof shall be inviolably observed by the states we respectively represent, and that the union shall be perpetual. In Witness whereof we have hereunto set our hands in Congress. Done at Philadelphia in the state of Pennsylvania the ninth day of July, in the Year of our Lord one Thousand seven Hundred and Seventy-eight, and in the third year of the independence of America.

The Constitution of the United States of America

We the People of the United States, in Order to form a more perfect Union, establish Justice, insure domestic Tranquility, provide for the common defence, promote the general Welfare, and secure the Blessings of Liberty to ourselves and our Posterity, do ordain and establish this Constitution for the United States of America.

Article I

SECTION 1
[LEGISLATIVE POWERS]

All legislative Powers herein granted shall be vested in a Congress of the United States, which shall consist of a Senate and House of Representatives.

SECTION 2
[HOUSE OF REPRESENTATIVES, HOW CONSTITUTED, POWER OF IMPEACHMENT]

The House of Representatives shall be composed of Members chosen every second Year by the People of the several States, and the Electors in each State shall have the Qualifications requisite for Electors of the most numerous Branch of the State Legislature.

No Person shall be a Representative who shall not have attained to the Age of twenty five Years, and been seven Years a Citizen of the United States, and who shall not, when elected, be an Inhabitant of that State in which he shall be chosen.

Representatives and *direct Taxes*[1] shall be apportioned among the several States which may be included within this Union, according to their respective Numbers, *which shall be determined by adding to the whole Number of free Persons, including those bound to Service for a Term of Years, and excluding Indians not taxed, three fifths of all other Persons.*[2] The actual Enumeration shall be made within three Years after the first Meeting of the Congress of the United States, and within every subsequent Term of ten Years, in such Manner as they shall by Law direct. The Number of Representatives shall not exceed one for every thirty Thousand, but each State shall have at Least one Representative; *and until such enumeration shall be made, the State of New Hampshire shall be entitled to chuse three, Massachusetts eight, Rhode-Island and Providence Plantations one, Connecticut five, New-York six, New Jersey four, Pennsylvania eight, Delaware one, Maryland six, Virginia ten, North Carolina five, South Carolina five, and Georgia three.*[3]

When vacancies happen in the Representation from any State, the Executive Authority thereof shall issue Writs of Election to fill such Vacancies.

The House of Representatives shall chuse their Speaker and other Officers; and shall have the sole Power of Impeachment.

SECTION 3
[THE SENATE, HOW CONSTITUTED, IMPEACHMENT TRIALS]

The Senate of the United States shall be composed of two Senators from each State, *chosen by the Legislature thereof,*[4] for six Years; and each Senator shall have one Vote.

Immediately after they shall be assembled in Consequence of the first Election, they shall be divided as equally as may be into three Classes. The Seats of the Senators of the first Class shall be vacated at the Expiration of the second Year, of the second Class at the Expiration of the fourth Year, and of the third Class at the Expiration of the sixth Year, so that one third may be chosen every second Year; *and if Vacancies happen by Resignation, or otherwise, during the Recess of the Legislature of any State, the Executive thereof may make temporary Appointments until the next Meeting of the Legislature, which shall then fill such Vacancies.*[5]

No Person shall be a Senator who shall not have attained to the Age of thirty Years, and been nine Years a Citizen of the United States, and who shall not, when elected, be an Inhabitant of that State for which he shall be chosen.

The Vice President of the United States shall be President of the Senate, but shall have no Vote, unless they be equally divided.

The Senate shall chuse their other Officers, and also a President pro tempore, in the Absence of the Vice President, or when he shall exercise the Office of President of the United States.

The Senate shall have the sole Power to try all Impeachments. When sitting for that Purpose, they shall be on Oath or Affirmation. When the President of the United States is tried, the Chief Justice shall preside: And no Person shall be convicted without the Concurrence of two thirds of the Members present.

Judgment in Cases of Impeachment shall not extend further than to removal from Office, and disqualification to hold and enjoy any Office of honor, Trust or Profit under the United States: but the Party convicted shall nevertheless be liable and subject to Indictment, Trial, Judgment and Punishment, according to Law.

SECTION 4
[ELECTION OF SENATORS AND REPRESENTATIVES]

The Times, Places and Manner of holding Elections for Senators and Representatives, shall be prescribed in each State by the Legislature thereof; but the Congress may at any time by Law make or alter such Regulations, except as to the Places of chusing Senators.

The Congress shall assemble at least once in every Year, and such Meeting shall be on the first Monday in December, unless they shall by Law appoint a different Day.[6]

SECTION 5
[QUORUM, JOURNALS, MEETINGS, ADJOURNMENTS]

Each House shall be the Judge of the Elections, Returns and Qualifications of its own Members, and a Majority of each shall constitute a Quorum to do Business; but a smaller Number may adjourn from day to day, and may be authorized to compel the Attendance of absent Members, in such Manner, and under such Penalties as each House may provide.

Each House may determine the Rules of its Proceedings, punish its Members for disorderly Behaviour, and, with the Concurrence of two thirds, expel a Member.

Each House shall keep a Journal of its Proceedings, and from time to time publish the same, excepting such Parts as may in their Judgment require Secrecy; and the Yeas and Nays of the Members of either House on any questions shall, at the Desire of one fifth of those Present, be entered on the Journal.

Neither House, during the Session of Congress, shall, without the Consent of the other, adjourn for more than three days, nor to any other Place than that in which the two Houses shall be sitting.

---

[1] Modified by Sixteenth Amendment.
[2] Modified by Fourteenth Amendment.
[3] Temporary provision.
[4] Modified by Seventeenth Amendment.
[5] Modified by Seventeenth Amendment.
[6] Modified by Twentieth Amendment.

SECTION 6

[COMPENSATION, PRIVILEGES, DISABILITIES]

The Senators and Representatives shall receive a Compensation for their Services, to be ascertained by Law, and paid out of the Treasury of the United States. They shall in all Cases, except Treason, Felony and Breach of the Peace, be privileged from Arrest during their Attendance at the Session of their respective Houses, and in going to and returning from the same; and for any Speech or Debate in either House, they shall not be questioned in any other Place.

No Senator or Representative shall, during the Time for which he was elected, be appointed to any civil Office under the Authority of the United States, which shall have been created, or the Emoluments whereof shall have been encreased during such time; and no Person holding any Office under the United States, shall be a Member of either House during his Continuance in Office.

SECTION 7

[PROCEDURE IN PASSING BILLS AND RESOLUTIONS]

All Bills for raising Revenue shall originate in the House of Representatives; but the Senate may propose or concur with Amendments as on other Bills.

Every Bill which shall have passed the House of Representatives and the Senate, shall, before it become a Law, be presented to the President of the United States: If he approve he shall sign it, but if not he shall return it, with his Objections to that House in which it shall have originated, who shall enter the Objections at large on their Journal, and proceed to reconsider it. If after such Reconsideration two thirds of that House shall agree to pass the Bill, it shall be sent, together with the Objections, to the other House, by which it shall likewise be reconsidered, and if approved by two thirds of that House, it shall become a Law. But in all such Cases the Votes of both Houses shall be determined by yeas and Nays, and the Names of the Persons voting for and against the Bill shall be entered on the Journal of each House respectively. If any Bill shall not be returned by the President within ten Days (Sundays excepted) after it shall have been presented to him, the Same shall be a Law, in like Manner as if he had signed it, unless the Congress by their Adjournment prevent its Return, in which Case it shall not be a Law.

Every Order, Resolution, or Vote to which the Concurrence of the Senate and House of Representatives may be necessary (except on a question of Adjournment) shall be presented to the President of the United States; and before the Same shall take Effect, shall be approved by him, or being disapproved by him, shall be repassed by two thirds of the Senate and House of Representatives, according to the Rules and Limitations prescribed in the Case of a Bill.

SECTION 8

[POWERS OF CONGRESS]

The Congress shall have Power

To lay and collect Taxes, Duties, Imposts and Excises, to pay the Debts and provide for the common Defence and general Welfare of the United States; but all Duties, Imposts and Excises shall be uniform throughout the United States;

To borrow Money on the credit of the United States;

To regulate Commerce with foreign Nations, and among the several States, and with the Indian Tribes;

To establish an uniform Rule of Naturalization, and uniform Laws on the subject of Bankruptcies throughout the United States;

To coin Money, regulate the Value thereof, and of foreign Coin, and fix the Standard of Weights and Measures;

To provide for the Punishment of counterfeiting the Securities and current Coin of the United States;

To establish Post Offices and post Roads;

To promote the Progress of Science and useful Arts, by securing for limited Times to Authors and Inventors the exclusive Right to their respective Writings and Discoveries;

To constitute Tribunals inferior to the supreme Court;

To define and punish Piracies and Felonies committed on the high Seas, and Offences against the Law of Nations;

To declare War, grant Letters of Marque and Reprisal, and make Rules concerning Captures on Land and Water;

To raise and support Armies, but no Appropriation of Money to that Use shall be for a longer Term than two Years;

To provide and maintain a Navy;

To make Rules for the Government and Regulation of the land and naval Forces;

To provide for calling forth the Militia to execute the Laws of the Union, suppress Insurrections and repel Invasions;

To provide for organizing, arming, and disciplining, the Militia, and for governing such Part of them as may be employed in the Service of the United States, reserving to the States respectively, the Appointment of the Officers, and the Authority of training the Militia according to the discipline prescribed by Congress;

To exercise exclusive Legislation in all Cases whatsoever, over such District (not exceeding ten Miles square) as may, by Cession of particular States, and the Acceptance of Congress, become the Seat of the Government of the United States, and to exercise like Authority over all Places purchased by the Consent of the Legislature of the State in which the Same shall be, for the Erection of Forts, Magazines, Arsenals, dock-Yards, and other needful Buildings;—And

To make all Laws which shall be necessary and proper for carrying into Execution the foregoing Powers, and all other Powers vested by this Constitution in the Government of the United States, or in any Department or Officer thereof.

SECTION 9

[SOME RESTRICTIONS ON FEDERAL POWER]

The Migration or Importation of such Persons as any of the States now existing shall think proper to admit, shall not be prohibited by the Congress prior to the Year one thousand eight hundred and eight, but a Tax or duty may be imposed on such Importation, not exceeding ten dollars for each Person.[7]

The Privilege of the Writ of Habeas Corpus shall not be suspended, unless when in Cases of Rebellion or Invasion the public Safety may require it.

No Bill of Attainder or ex post facto Law shall be passed.

No Capitation, or other direct, Tax shall be laid, unless in Proportion to the Census or Enumeration herein before directed to be taken.[8]

No Tax or Duty shall be laid on Articles exported from any State.

No Preference shall be given by any Regulation of Commerce or Revenue to the Ports of one State over those of another; nor shall Vessels bound to, or from, one State, be obliged to enter, clear, or pay Duties in another.

No Money shall be drawn from the Treasury, but in Consequence of Appropriations made by Law; and a regular Statement and Account of the Receipts and Expenditures of all public Money shall be published from time to time.

No Title of Nobility shall be granted by the United States: And no Person holding any Office of Profit or Trust under them, shall, without the Consent of the Congress, accept of any present, Emolument, Office, or Title, of any kind whatever, from any King, Prince, or foreign State.

---

[7]Temporary provision.
[8]Modified by Sixteenth Amendment.

SECTION 10

No State shall enter into any Treaty, Alliance, or Confederation; grant Letters of Marque and Reprisal; coin Money; emit Bills of Credit; make any Thing but gold and silver Coin a Tender in Payment of Debts; pass any Bill of Attainder, ex post facto Law, or Law impairing the Obligation of Contracts, or grant any Title of Nobility.

No State shall, without the Consent of the Congress, lay any Imposts or Duties on Imports or Exports, except what may be absolutely necessary for executing its inspection Laws: and the net Produce of all Duties and Imposts, laid by any State on Imports or Exports, shall be for the Use of the Treasury of the United States; and all such Laws shall be subject to the Revision and Control of the Congress.

No State shall, without the Consent of Congress, lay any Duty of Tonnage, keep Troops, or Ships of War in time of Peace, enter into any Agreement or Compact with another State, or with a foreign Power, or engage in War, unless actually invaded, or in such imminent Danger as will not admit of delay.

Article II

SECTION 1

[EXECUTIVE POWER, ELECTION, QUALIFICATIONS OF THE PRESIDENT]

The executive Power shall be vested in a President of the United States of America. *He shall hold his Office during the Term of four Years, and, together with the Vice President, chosen for the same Term, be elected, as follows*[9]

Each State shall appoint, in such Manner as the Legislature thereof may direct, a Number of Electors, equal to the whole Number of Senators and Representatives to which the State may be entitled in the Congress: but no Senator or Representative, or Person holding an Office of Trust or Profit under the United States, shall be appointed an Elector.

The electors shall meet in their respective States, and vote by ballot for two Persons, of whom one at least shall not be an Inhabitant of the same State with themselves. And they shall make a List of all the Persons voted for, and of the Number of Votes for each; which List they shall sign and certify, and transmit sealed to the Seat of the Government of the United States, directed to the President of the Senate. The President of the Senate shall, in the Presence of the Senate and House of Representatives, open all the Certificates, and the Votes shall then be counted. The Person having the greatest Number of Votes shall be the President, if such Number be a Majority of the whole Number of Electors appointed; and if there be more than one who have such Majority, and have an equal Number of Votes, then the House of Representatives shall immediately chuse by Ballot one of them for President; and if no Person have a Majority, then from the five highest on the List the said House shall in like Manner chuse the President. But in chusing the President, the Votes shall be taken by States, the Representation from each State having one Vote; A quorum for this Purpose shall consist of a Member or Members from two thirds of the States, and a Majority of all the States shall be necessary to a Choice. In every Case, after the Choice of the President, the person having the greatest Number of Votes of the Electors shall be the Vice President. But if there should remain two or more who have equal Votes, the Senate shall chuse from them by Ballot the Vice President.[10]

The Congress may determine the Time of chusing the Electors, and the Day on which they shall give their Votes; which Day shall be the same throughout the United States.

---

[9]Number of terms limited to two by Twenty-second Amendment.
[10]Modified by the Twelfth and Twentieth Amendments.

No Person except a natural born Citizen, or a Citizen of the United States, at the time of the Adoption of this Constitution, shall be eligible to the Office of President; neither shall any Person be eligible to that Office who shall not have attained to the Age of thirty five Years, and been fourteen Years a Resident within the United States.

In Case of the Removal of the President from Office, or his Death, Resignation, or Inability to discharge the Powers and Duties of the said Office, the Same shall devolve on the Vice President, and the Congress may by Law provide for the Case of Removal, Death, Resignation or Inability, both of the President and Vice President, declaring what Officer shall then act as President, and such Officer shall act accordingly, until the Disability be removed, or a President shall be elected.

The President shall, at stated Times, receive for his Services, a Compensation, which shall neither be increased nor diminished during the Period for which he shall have been elected, and he shall not receive within that Period any other Emolument from the United States, or any of them.

Before he enter on the Execution of his Office, he shall take the following Oath or Affirmation:—"I do solemnly swear (or affirm) that I will faithfully execute the Office of President of the United States, and will to the best of my Ability, preserve, protect and defend the Constitution of the United States."

SECTION 2

[POWERS OF THE PRESIDENT]

The President shall be Commander in Chief of the Army and Navy of the United States, and of the Militia of the several States, when called into the actual Service of the United States; he may require the Opinion, in writing, of the principal Officer in each of the executive Departments, upon any Subject relating to the Duties of their respective Offices, and he shall have Power to grant Reprieves and Pardons for Offences against the United States, except in Cases of Impeachment.

He shall have Power, by and with the Advice and Consent of the Senate, to make Treaties, provided two thirds of the Senators present concur; and he shall nominate, and by and with the Advice and Consent of the Senate, shall appoint Ambassadors, other public Ministers and Consuls, Judges of the supreme Court, and all other Officers of the United States, whose Appointments are not herein otherwise provided for, and which shall be established by Law: but the Congress may by Law vest the Appointment of such inferior Officers, as they think proper, in the President alone, in the Courts of Law, or in the Heads of Departments.

The President shall have Power to fill up all Vacancies that may happen during the Recess of the Senate, by granting Commissions which shall expire at the End of their next Session.

SECTION 3

[POWERS AND DUTIES OF THE PRESIDENT]

He shall from time to time give to the Congress Information of the State of the Union, and recommend to their Consideration such Measures as he shall judge necessary and expedient; he may, on extraordinary Occasions, convene both Houses, or either of them, and in Case of Disagreement between them, with Respect to the Time of Adjournment, he may adjourn them to such Time as he shall think proper; he shall receive Ambassadors and other public Ministers; he shall take Care that the Laws be faithfully executed, and shall Commission all the Officers of the United States.

SECTION 4

[IMPEACHMENT]

The President, Vice President and all civil Officers of the United States, shall be removed from Office on Impeachment for, and Conviction of, Treason, Bribery, or other high Crimes and Misdemeanors.

Article III

SECTION 1
[JUDICIAL POWER, TENURE OF OFFICE]

The judicial Power of the United States, shall be vested in one supreme Court, and in such inferior Courts as the Congress may from time to time ordain and establish. The Judges, both of the supreme and inferior Courts, shall hold their Offices during good Behaviour, and shall, at stated Times, receive for their Services, a Compensation, which shall not be diminished during their Continuance in Office.

SECTION 2
[JURISDICTION]

The judicial Power shall extend to all Cases, in Law and Equity, arising under this Constitution, the Laws of the United States, and Treaties made, or which shall be made, under their Authority;—to all Cases affecting Ambassadors, other public Ministers and Consuls;—to all Cases of admiralty and maritime Jurisdiction;—to Controversies to which the United States shall be a Party;—to Controversies between two or more States;—*between a State and Citizens of another State;*—between Citizens of different States,—between Citizens of the same State claiming Lands under Grants of different States, *and between a State,* or the Citizens thereof, *and foreign States, Citizens or Subjects.*[11]

In all Cases affecting Ambassadors, other public Ministers and Consuls, and those in which a State shall be Party, the supreme Court shall have original Jurisdiction. In all the other Cases before mentioned, the supreme Court shall have appellate Jurisdiction, both as to Law and Fact, with such Exceptions, and under such Regulations as the Congress shall make.

The Trial of all Crimes, except in Cases of Impeachment, shall be by Jury; and such Trial shall be held in the State where the said Crimes shall have been committed; but when not committed within any State, the Trial shall be at such Place or Places as the Congress may by Law have directed.

SECTION 3
[TREASON, PROOF, AND PUNISHMENT]

Treason against the United States, shall consist only in levying War against them, or in adhering to their Enemies, giving them Aid and Comfort. No Person shall be convicted of Treason unless on the Testimony of two Witnesses to the same overt Act, or on Confession in open Court.

The Congress shall have Power to declare the Punishment of Treason, but no Attainder of Treason shall work Corruption of Blood, or Forfeiture except during the Life of the Person attainted.

Article IV

SECTION 1
[FAITH AND CREDIT AMONG STATES]

Full Faith and Credit shall be given in each State to the public Acts, Records, and judicial Proceedings of every other State. And the Congress may by general Laws prescribe the Manner in which such Acts, Records and Proceedings shall be proved, and the Effect thereof.

SECTION 2
[PRIVILEGES AND IMMUNITIES, FUGITIVES]

The Citizens of each State shall be entitled to all Privileges and Immunities of Citizens in the several States.

A Person charged in any State with Treason, Felony or other Crime, who shall flee from Justice, and be found in another State, shall on Demand of the executive Authority of the State from which he fled, be delivered up, to be removed to the State having Jurisdiction of the Crime.

No person held to Service or Labour in one State, under the Laws thereof, escaping into another, shall, in Consequence of any Law or Regulation therein, be discharged from such Service or Labour, but shall be delivered up on Claim of the Party to whom such Service or Labour may be due.[12]

SECTION 3
[ADMISSION OF NEW STATES]

New States may be admitted by the Congress into this Union; but no new State shall be formed or erected within the Jurisdiction of any other State; nor any State be formed by the Junction of two or more States, or Parts of States, without the Consent of the Legislatures of the States concerned as well as of the Congress.

The Congress shall have Power to dispose of and make all needful Rules and Regulations respecting the Territory or other Property belonging to the United States; and nothing in this Constitution shall be so construed as to Prejudice any Claims of the United States, or of any particular State.

SECTION 4
[GUARANTEE OF REPUBLICAN GOVERNMENT]

The United States shall guarantee to every State in this Union a Republican Form of Government, and shall protect each of them against Invasion; and on Application of the Legislature, or of the Executive (when the Legislature cannot be convened), against domestic Violence.

Article V
[AMENDMENT OF THE CONSTITUTION]

The Congress, whenever two thirds of both Houses shall deem it necessary, shall propose Amendments to this Constitution, or, on the Application of the Legislatures of two thirds of the several States, shall call a Convention for proposing Amendments, which, in either Case, shall be valid to all Intents and Purposes, as Part of this Constitution, when ratified by the Legislatures of three fourths of the several States, or by Conventions in three fourths thereof, as the one or the other Mode of Ratification may be proposed by the Congress; *Provided that no Amendment which may be made prior to the Year One thousand eight hundred and eight shall in any Manner affect the first and fourth Clauses in the Ninth Section of the first Article;* and that no State, without its Consent, shall be deprived of its equal Suffrage in the Senate.

Article VI
[DEBTS, SUPREMACY, OATH]

All Debts contracted and Engagements entered into, before the Adoption of this Constitution, shall be as valid against the United States under this Constitution, as under the Confederation.

---

[11]Modified by the Eleventh Amendment.

[12]Repealed by the Thirteenth Amendment.

This Constitution, and the Laws of the United States which shall be made in Pursuance thereof; and all Treaties made, or which shall be made, under the Authority of the United States, shall be the supreme Law of the Land; and the Judges in every State shall be bound thereby, any Thing in the Constitution or Laws of any State to the Contrary notwithstanding.

The Senators and Representatives before mentioned, and the Members of the several State Legislatures, and all executive and judicial Officers, both of the United States and of the several States, shall be bound by Oath or Affirmation, to support this Constitution; but no religious Test shall be required as a Qualification to any Office or public Trust under the United States.

Article VII

[RATIFICATION AND ESTABLISHMENT]

The Ratification of the Conventions of nine States, shall be sufficient for the Establishment of this Constitution between the States so ratifying the Same.

Done in Convention by the Unanimous Consent of the States present the Seventeenth Day of September in the Year of our Lord one thousand seven hundred and Eighty seven and of the Independence of the United States of America the Twelfth. *In Witness* whereof We have hereunto subscribed our Names,

G:⁰ WASHINGTON—
Presidt. and deputy from Virginia

NEW HAMPSHIRE
John Langdon
Nicholas Gilman

MASSACHUSETTS
Nathaniel Gorham
Rufus King

CONNECTICUT
Wm. Saml. Johnson
Roger Sherman

NEW YORK
Alexander Hamilton

NEW JERSEY
Wil: Livingston
David Brearley
Wm. Paterson
Jona: Dayton

PENNSYLVANIA
B Franklin
Thomas Mifflin
Robt. Morris
Geo. Clymer
Thos. FitzSimons
Jared Ingersoll
James Wilson
Gouv Morris

DELAWARE
Geo: Read
Gunning Bedford jun
John Dickinson
Richard Bassett
Jaco: Broom

MARYLAND
James McHenry
Dan of St Thos. Jenifer
Danl. Carroll

VIRGINIA
John Blair—
James Madison Jr.

NORTH CAROLINA
Wm. Blount
Richd. Dobbs Spaight
Hu Williamson

SOUTH CAROLINA
J. Rutledge
Charles Cotesworth Pinckney
Charles Pinckney
Pierce Butler

GEORGIA
William Few
Abr Baldwin

Amendments to the Constitution

Proposed by Congress and Ratified by the Legislatures of the
Several States, Pursuant to Article V of the Original Constitution.

Amendments I–X, known as the Bill of Rights, were proposed by Congress on September 25, 1789, and ratified on December 15, 1791.

Amendment I
[FREEDOM OF RELIGION, OF SPEECH, AND OF THE PRESS]

Congress shall make no law respecting an establishment of religion, or prohibiting the free exercise thereof; or abridging the freedom of speech, or of the press; or the right of the people peaceably to assemble, and to petition the Government for a redress of grievances.

Amendment II
[RIGHT TO KEEP AND BEAR ARMS]

A well regulated Militia, being necessary to the security of a free State, the right of the people to keep and bear Arms, shall not be infringed.

Amendment III
[QUARTERING OF SOLDIERS]

No Soldier shall, in time of peace be quartered in any house, without the consent of the Owner, nor in time of war, but in a manner to be prescribed by law.

Amendment IV
[SECURITY FROM UNWARRANTABLE SEARCH AND SEIZURE]

The right of the people to be secure in their persons, houses, papers, and effects, against unreasonable searches and seizures, shall not be violated, and no Warrants shall issue, but upon probable cause, supported by Oath or affirmation, and particularly describing the place to be searched, and the persons or things to be seized.

Amendment V
[RIGHTS OF ACCUSED PERSONS IN CRIMINAL PROCEEDINGS]

No person shall be held to answer for a capital, or otherwise infamous crime, unless on a presentment or indictment of a Grand Jury, except in cases arising in the land or naval forces, or in the Militia, when in actual service in time of War or in public danger; nor shall any person be subject for the same offence to be twice put in jeopardy of life or limb; nor shall be compelled in any criminal case to be a witness against himself, nor be deprived of life, liberty, or property, without due process of law; nor shall private property be taken for public use, without just compensation.

Amendment VI
[RIGHT TO SPEEDY TRIAL, WITNESSES, ETC.]

In all criminal prosecutions, the accused shall enjoy the right to a speedy and public trial, by an impartial jury of the State and district wherein the crime shall have been committed, which district shall have been previously ascertained by law, and to be informed of the nature and cause of the accusation; to be confronted with the witnesses against him; to have compulsory process for obtaining witnesses in his favor, and to have the Assistance of Counsel for his defence.

Amendment VII
[TRIAL BY JURY IN CIVIL CASES]

In suits at common law, where the value in controversy shall exceed twenty dollars, the right of trial by jury shall be preserved, and no fact tried by a jury, shall be otherwise reexamined in any Court of the United States, than according to the rules of the common law.

Amendment VIII
[BAILS, FINES, PUNISHMENTS]

Excessive bail shall not be required, nor excessive fines imposed, nor cruel and unusual punishments inflicted.

Amendment IX
[RESERVATION OF RIGHTS OF PEOPLE]

The enumeration in the Constitution, of certain rights, shall not be construed to deny or disparage others retained by the people.

Amendment X
[POWERS RESERVED TO STATES OR PEOPLE]

The powers not delegated to the United States by the Constitution, nor prohibited by it to the States, are reserved to the States respectively, or to the people.

Amendment XI
[*Proposed by Congress on March 4, 1794;
declared ratified on January 8, 1798.*]
[RESTRICTION OF JUDICIAL POWER]

The Judicial power of the United States shall not be construed to extend to any suit in law or equity, commenced or prosecuted against one of the United States by Citizens of another State, or by Citizens or Subjects of any Foreign State.

Amendment XII
[*Proposed by Congress on December 9, 1803;
declared ratified on September 25, 1804.*]
[ELECTION OF PRESIDENT AND VICE PRESIDENT]

The Electors shall meet in their respective states and vote by ballot for President and Vice-President, one of whom, at least, shall not be an inhabitant of the same state with themselves; they shall name in their ballots the person voted for as President, and in distinct ballots the person voted for as Vice-President, and they shall make distinct lists of all persons voted for as President, and of all persons voted for as Vice-President, and of the number of votes for each, which lists they shall sign and certify, and transmit sealed to the seat of the government of the United States, directed to the President of the Senate;—the President of the Senate shall, in presence of the Senate and House of Representatives, open all the certificates and the votes shall then be counted;—The person having the greatest number of votes for President, shall be the President, if such number be a majority of the whole number of Electors appointed; and if no person have such majority, then from the persons having the highest numbers not exceeding three on the list of those voted for as

President, the House of Representatives shall choose immediately, by ballot, the President. But in choosing the President, the votes shall be taken by states, the representation from each state having one vote; a quorum for this purpose shall consist of a member or members from two-thirds of the states, and a majority of all the states shall be necessary to a choice. And if the House of Representatives shall not choose a President whenever the right of choice shall devolve upon them, before the fourth day of March next following, then the Vice-President shall act as President, as in the case of the death or other constitutional disability of the President.—The person having the greatest number of votes as Vice-President, shall be the Vice-President, if such number be a majority of the whole number of Electors appointed, and if no person have a majority, then from the two highest numbers on the list, the Senate shall choose the Vice-President; a quorum for the purpose shall consist of two-thirds of the whole number of Senators, and a majority of the whole number shall be necessary to a choice. But no person constitutionally ineligible to the office of President shall be eligible to that of Vice-President of the United States.

Amendment XIII

[*Proposed by Congress on January 31, 1865;*
declared ratified on December 18, 1865.]

SECTION 1
[ABOLITION OF SLAVERY]

Neither slavery nor involuntary servitude, except as a punishment for crime whereof the party shall have been duly convicted, shall exist within the United States, or any place subject to their jurisdiction.

SECTION 2
[POWER TO ENFORCE THIS ARTICLE]

Congress shall have power to enforce this article by appropriate legislation.

Amendment XIV

[*Proposed by Congress on June 13, 1866;*
declared ratified on July 28, 1868.]

SECTION 1
[CITIZENSHIP RIGHTS NOT TO BE ABRIDGED BY STATES]

All persons born or naturalized in the United States, and subject to the jurisdiction thereof, are citizens of the United States and of the State wherein they reside. No State shall make or enforce any law which shall abridge the privileges or immunities of citizens of the United States; nor shall any State deprive any person of life, liberty, or property, without due process of law; nor deny to any person within its jurisdiction the equal protection of the laws.

SECTION 2
[APPORTIONMENT OF REPRESENTATIVES IN CONGRESS]

Representatives shall be apportioned among the several States according to their respective numbers, counting the whole number of persons in each State, excluding Indians not taxed. But when the right to vote at any election for the choice of electors for President and Vice-President of the United States, Representatives in Congress, the Executive and Judicial officers of a State, or the members of the Legislature thereof, is denied to any of the male inhabitants of such State, being twenty-one years of age, and citizens of the United States, or in any way abridged, except for participation in rebellion, or other crime, the basis of representation therein shall be reduced in the proportion which the number of such male citizens shall bear to the whole number of male citizens twenty-one years of age in such State.

SECTION 3
[PERSONS DISQUALIFIED FROM HOLDING OFFICE]

No person shall be a Senator or Representative in Congress, or elector of President and Vice-President, or hold any office, civil or military, under the United States, or under any State, who, having previously taken an oath, as a member of Congress, or as an officer of the United States, or as a member of any State legislature, or as an executive or judicial officer of any State, to support the Constitution of the United States, shall have engaged in insurrection or rebellion against the same, or given aid or comfort to the enemies thereof. But Congress may by a vote of two-thirds of each House, remove such disability.

SECTION 4
[WHAT PUBLIC DEBTS ARE VALID]

The validity of the public debt of the United States, authorized by law, including debts incurred for payment of pensions and bounties for services in suppressing insurrection or rebellion, shall not be questioned. But neither the United States nor any State shall assume or pay any debt or obligation incurred in aid of insurrection or rebellion against the United States, or any claim for the loss or emancipation of any slave; but all such debts, obligations and claims shall be held illegal and void.

SECTION 5
[POWER TO ENFORCE THIS ARTICLE]

The Congress shall have power to enforce, by appropriate legislation, the provisions of this article.

Amendment XV

[*Proposed by Congress on February 26, 1869;*
declared ratified on March 30, 1870.]

SECTION 1
[NEGRO SUFFRAGE]

The right of citizens of the United States to vote shall not be denied or abridged by the United States or by any State on account of race, color, or previous condition of servitude.

SECTION 2
[POWER TO ENFORCE THIS ARTICLE]

The Congress shall have power to enforce this article by appropriate legislation.

Amendment XVI

[*Proposed by Congress on July 2, 1909; declared*
ratified on February 25, 1913.]
[AUTHORIZING INCOME TAXES]

The Congress shall have power to lay and collect taxes on incomes, from whatever source derived, without apportionment among the several States, and without regard to any census or enumeration.

Amendment XVII

[*Proposed by Congress on May 13, 1912; declared ratified on May 31, 1913.*]
[POPULAR ELECTION OF SENATORS]

The Senate of the United States shall be composed of two Senators from each State, elected by the people thereof, for six years; and each Senator shall have one vote. The electors in each State shall have the qualifications requisite for electors of the most numerous branch of the State legislatures.

When vacancies happen in the representation of any State in the Senate, the executive authority of such State shall issue writs of election to fill such vacancies: *Provided,* That the legislature of any State may empower the executive thereof to make temporary appointments until the people fill the vacancies by election as the legislature may direct.

This amendment shall not be so construed as to affect the election or term of any Senator chosen before it becomes valid as part of the Constitution.

Amendment XVIII

[*Proposed by Congress December 18, 1917; declared ratified on January 29, 1919.*]

SECTION 1
[NATIONAL LIQUOR PROHIBITION]

After one year from the ratification of this article the manufacture, sale, or transportation of intoxicating liquors within, the importation thereof into, or the exportation thereof from the United States and all territory subject to the jurisdiction thereof for beverage purposes is hereby prohibited.

SECTION 2
[POWER TO ENFORCE THIS ARTICLE]

The Congress and the several States shall have concurrent power to enforce this article by appropriate legislation.

SECTION 3
[RATIFICATION WITHIN SEVEN YEARS]

This article shall be inoperative unless it shall have been ratified as an amendment to the Constitution by the legislatures of the several States, as provided in the Constitution, within seven years from the date of the submission hereof to the States by the Congress.[1]

Amendment XIX

[*Proposed by Congress on June 4, 1919; declared ratified on August 26, 1920.*]

[WOMAN SUFFRAGE]

The right of citizens of the United States to vote shall not be denied or abridged by the United States or by any State on account of sex.

Congress shall have power to enforce this article by appropriate legislation.

Amendment XX

[*Proposed by Congress on March 2, 1932; declared ratified on February 6, 1933.*]

SECTION 1
[TERMS OF OFFICE]

The terms of the President and Vice President shall end at noon on the 20th day of January, and the terms of Senators and Representatives at noon on the 3d day of January, of the years in which such terms would have ended if this article had not been ratified; and the terms of their successors shall then begin.

---

[1] Repealed by the Twenty-first Amendment.

SECTION 2
[TIME OF CONVENING CONGRESS]

The Congress shall assemble at least once in every year, and such meeting shall begin at noon on the 3d day of January, unless they shall by law appoint a different day.

SECTION 3
[DEATH OF PRESIDENT-ELECT]

If, at the time fixed for the beginning of the term of the President, the President elect shall have died, the Vice President elect shall become President. If a President shall not have been chosen before the time fixed for the beginning of his term, or if the President elect shall have failed to qualify, then the Vice President elect shall act as President until a President shall have qualified; and the Congress may by law provide for the case wherein neither a President elect nor a Vice President elect shall have qualified, declaring who shall then act as President, or the manner in which one who is to act shall be selected, and such person shall act accordingly until a President or Vice President shall have qualified.

SECTION 4
[ELECTION OF THE PRESIDENT]

The Congress may by law provide for the case of the death of any of the persons from whom the House of Representatives may choose a President whenever the right of choice shall have devolved upon them, and for the case of the death of any of the persons from whom the Senate may choose a Vice President whenever the right of choice shall have devolved upon them.

SECTION 5
[AMENDMENT TAKES EFFECT]

Sections 1 and 2 shall take effect on the 15th day of October following the ratification of this article.

SECTION 6
[RATIFICATION WITHIN SEVEN YEARS]

This article shall be inoperative unless it shall have been ratified as an amendment to the Constitution by the legislatures of three-fourths of the several States within seven years from the date of its submission.

Amendment XXI

[*Proposed by Congress on February 20, 1933; declared ratified on December 5, 1933.*]

SECTION 1
[NATIONAL LIQUOR PROHIBITION REPEALED]

The eighteenth article of amendment to the Constitution of the United States is hereby repealed.

SECTION 2
[TRANSPORTATION OF LIQUOR INTO "DRY" STATES]

The transportation or importation into any State, Territory, or Possession of the United States for delivery or use therein of intoxicating liquors, in violation of the laws thereof, is hereby prohibited.

SECTION 3
[RATIFICATION WITHIN SEVEN YEARS]

This article shall be inoperative unless it shall have been ratified as an amendment to the Constitution by conventions in the several States, as provided in the Constitution, within seven years from the date of the submission hereof to the States by the Congress.

Amendment XXII

[*Proposed by Congress on March 21, 1947;*
declared ratified on February 27, 1951.]

SECTION 1

[TENURE OF PRESIDENT LIMITED]

No person shall be elected to the office of President more than twice, and no person who has held the office of President or acted as President, for more than two years of a term to which some other person was elected President shall be elected to the office of the President more than once. But this Article shall not apply to any person holding the office of President when this Article was proposed by the Congress, and shall not prevent any person who may be holding the office of President, or acting as President, during the term within which this Article becomes operative from holding the office of President or acting as President during the remainder of such term.

SECTION 2

[RATIFICATION WITHIN SEVEN YEARS]

This article shall be inoperative unless it shall have been ratified as an amendment to the Constitution by the legislatures of three-fourths of the several States within seven years from the date of its submission to the States by the Congress.

Amendment XXIII

[*Proposed by Congress on June 16, 1960; declared*
ratified on March 29, 1961.]

SECTION 1

[ELECTORAL COLLEGE VOTES FOR THE DISTRICT OF COLUMBIA]

The District constituting the seat of Government of the United States shall appoint in such manner as the Congress may direct:

A number of electors of President and Vice President equal to the whole number of Senators and Representatives in Congress to which the District would be entitled if it were a State, but in no event more than the least populous State; they shall be in addition to those appointed by the States, but they shall be considered, for the purposes of the election of President and Vice President, to be electors appointed by a State; and they shall meet in the District and perform such duties as provided by the twelfth article of amendment.

SECTION 2

[POWER TO ENFORCE THIS ARTICLE]

The Congress shall have power to enforce this article by appropriate legislation.

Amendment XXIV

[*Proposed by Congress on August 27, 1962;*
declared ratified on January 23, 1964.]

SECTION 1

[ANTI-POLL TAX]

The right of citizens of the United States to vote in any primary or other election for President or Vice President, for electors for President or Vice President, or for Senator or Representative of Congress, shall not be denied or abridged by the United States or any State by reason of failure to pay any poll tax or other tax.

SECTION 2

[POWER TO ENFORCE THIS ARTICLE]

The Congress shall have power to enforce this article by appropriate legislation.

Amendment XXV

[*Proposed by Congress on July 6, 1965; declared*
ratified on February 10, 1967.]

SECTION 1

[VICE PRESIDENT TO BECOME PRESIDENT]

In case of the removal of the President from office or his death or resignation, the Vice President shall become President.

SECTION 2

[CHOICE OF A NEW VICE PRESIDENT]

Whenever there is a vacancy in the office of the Vice President, the President shall nominate a Vice President who shall take the office upon confirmation by a majority vote of both houses of Congress.

SECTION 3

[PRESIDENT MAY DECLARE OWN DISABILITY]

Whenever the President transmits to the President pro tempore of the Senate and the Speaker of the House of Representatives his written declaration that he is unable to discharge the powers and duties of his office, and until he transmits to them a written declaration to the contrary, such powers and duties shall be discharged by the Vice President as Acting President.

SECTION 4

[ALTERNATE PROCEDURES TO DECLARE AND TO END
PRESIDENTIAL DISABILITY]

Whenever the Vice President and a majority of either the principal officers of the executive departments, or of such other body as Congress may by law provide, transmit to the President pro tempore of the Senate and the Speaker of the House of Representatives their written declaration that the President is unable to discharge the powers and duties of his office, the Vice President shall immediately assume the powers and duties of the office as Acting President.

Thereafter, when the President transmits to the President pro tempore of the Senate and the Speaker of the House of Representatives his written declaration that no inability exists, he shall resume the powers and duties of his office unless the Vice President and a majority of either the principal officers of the executive department, or of such other body as Congress may by law provide, transmit within four days to the President pro tempore of the Senate and the Speaker of the House of Representatives their written declaration that the President is unable to discharge the powers and duties of his office. Thereupon Congress shall decide the issue, assembling within forty eight hours for that purpose if not in session. If the Congress, within twenty one days after receipt of the latter written declaration, or, if Congress is not in session, within twenty one days after Congress is required to assemble, determines by two-thirds vote of both Houses that the President is unable to discharge the powers and duties of his office, the Vice President shall continue to discharge the same as Acting President; otherwise, the President shall resume the powers and duties of his office.

Amendment XXVI

[*Proposed by Congress on March 23, 1971; declared ratified on July 1, 1971.*]

SECTION 1

[EIGHTEEN-YEAR-OLD VOTE]

The right of citizens of the United States, who are eighteen years of age or older, to vote shall not be denied or abridged by the United States or by any State on account of age.

SECTION 2

[POWER TO ENFORCE THIS ARTICLE]

The Congress shall have power to enforce this article by appropriate legislation.

Amendment XXVII

[*Proposed by Congress on September 25, 1789; declared ratified on May 8, 1992.*]

[CONGRESS CANNOT RAISE ITS OWN PAY]

No law varying the compensation for the services of the Senators and Representatives, shall take effect, until an election of representatives shall have intervened.

The Federalist Papers

Among the numerous advantages promised by a well constructed Union, none deserves to be more accurately developed than its tendency to break and control the violence of faction. The friend of popular governments never finds himself so much alarmed for their character and fate, as when he contemplates their propensity to this dangerous vice. He will not fail therefore to set a due value on any plan which, without violating the principles to which he is attached, provides a proper cure for it. The instability, injustice, and confusion introduced into the public councils have, in truth, been the mortal diseases under which popular governments have everywhere perished, as they continue to be the favorite and fruitful topics from which the adversaries to liberty derive their most specious declamations. The valuable improvements made by the American constitutions on the popular models, both ancient and modern, cannot certainly be too much admired; but it would be an unwarrantable partiality to contend that they have as effectually obviated the danger on this side, as was wished and expected. Complaints are everywhere heard from our most considerate and virtuous citizens, equally the friends of public and private faith and of public and personal liberty, that our governments are too unstable, that the public good is disregarded in the conflicts of rival parties, and that measures are too often decided, not according to the rules of justice and the rights of the minor party, but by the superior force of an interested and overbearing majority. However anxiously we may wish that these complaints had no foundation, the evidence of known facts will not permit us to deny that they are in some degree true. It will be found, indeed, on a candid review of our situation, that some of the distresses under which we labor have been erroneously charged on the operation of our governments; but it will be found, at the same time, that other causes will not alone account for many of our heaviest misfortunes; and, particularly, for that prevailing and increasing distrust of public engagements and alarm for private rights which are echoed from one end of the continent to the other. These must be chiefly, if not wholly, effects of the unsteadiness and injustice with which a factious spirit has tainted our public administration.

By a faction I understand a number of citizens, whether amounting to a majority or minority of the whole, who are united and actuated by some common impulse of passion, or of interest, adverse to the rights of other citizens, or to the permanent and aggregate interests of the community.

There are two methods of curing the mischiefs of faction: the one, by removing its causes; the other, by controlling its effects.

There are again two methods of removing the causes of faction: the one, by destroying the liberty which is essential to its existence; the other, by giving to every citizen the same opinions, the same passions, and the same interests.

It could never be more truly said than of the first remedy, that it is worse than the disease. Liberty is to faction what air is to fire, an aliment without which it instantly expires. But it could not be a less folly to abolish liberty, which is essential to political life, because it nourishes faction, than it would be to wish the annihilation of air, which is essential to animal life, because it imparts to fire its destructive agency.

The second expedient is as impracticable, as the first would be unwise. As long as the reason of man continues fallible, and he is at liberty to exercise it, different opinions will be formed. As long as the connection subsists between his reason and his self-love, his opinions and his passions will have a reciprocal influence on each other; and the former will be objects to which the latter will attach themselves.

The diversity in the faculties of men, from which the rights of property originate, is not less an insuperable obstacle to a uniformity of interests. The protection of these faculties is the first object of Government. From the protection of different and unequal faculties of acquiring property, the possession of different degrees and kinds of property immediately results; and from the influence of these on the sentiments and views of the respective proprietors, ensues a division of the society into different interests and parties.

The latent causes of faction are thus sown in the nature of man; and we see them everywhere brought into different degrees of activity, according to the different circumstances of civil society. A zeal for different opinions concerning religion, concerning Government, and many other points, as well of speculation as of practice; an attachment to different leaders ambitiously contending for pre-eminence and power; or to persons of other descriptions whose fortunes have been interesting to the human passions, have in turn divided mankind into parties, inflamed them with mutual animosity, and rendered them much more disposed to vex and oppress each other, than to co-operate for their common good. So strong is this propensity of mankind to fall into mutual animosities, that where no substantial occasion presents itself, the most frivolous and fanciful distinctions have been sufficient to kindle their unfriendly passions, and excite their most violent conflicts. But the most common and durable source of factions has been the various and unequal distribution of property. Those who hold and those who are without property have ever formed distinct interests in society. Those who are creditors, and those who are debtors, fall under a like discrimination. A landed interest, a manufacturing interest, a mercantile interest, a moneyed interest, with many lesser interests, grow up of necessity in civilized nations, and divide them into different classes, actuated by different sentiments and views. The regulation of these various and interfering interests forms the principal task of modern Legislation, and involves the spirit of party and faction in the necessary and ordinary operations of Government.

No man is allowed to be judge in his own cause, because his interest would certainly bias his judgment and, not improbably, corrupt his integrity. With equal, nay with greater reason, a body of men are unfit to be both judges and parties at the same time; yet what are many of the most important acts of legislation but so many judicial determinations, not indeed concerning the rights of single persons, but concerning the rights of large bodies of citizens; and what are the different classes of legislators but advocates and parties to the causes which they determine? Is a law proposed concerning private debts? It is a question to which the creditors are parties on one side and the debtors on the other. Justice ought to hold the balance between them. Yet the parties are, and must be, themselves the judges; and the most numerous party, or in other words, the most powerful faction must be expected to prevail. Shall domestic manufacturers be encouraged, and in what degree, by restrictions on foreign manufacturers? are questions which would be differently decided by the landed and the manufacturing classes, and probably by neither with a sole regard to justice and the public good. The apportionment of taxes on the various descriptions of property is an act which seems to require the most exact impartiality; yet there is, perhaps, no legislative act in which greater opportunity and temptation are given to a predominant party to trample on the rules of justice. Every shilling with which they overburden the inferior number is a shilling saved to their own pockets.

It is in vain to say that enlightened statesmen will be able to adjust these clashing interests and render them all subservient to the public good. Enlightened statesmen will not always be at the helm. Nor, in many cases, can such an adjustment be made at all without taking into view indirect and remote considerations, which will rarely prevail over the immediate interest which one party may find in disregarding the rights of another or the good of the whole.

The inference to which we are brought is that the *causes* of faction cannot be removed and that relief is only to be sought in the means of controlling its *effects*.

If a faction consists of less than a majority, relief is supplied by the republican principle, which enables the majority to defeat its sinister views by regular vote. It may clog the administration, it may convulse the society; but it will be unable to execute and mask its violence under the forms of the Constitution. When a majority is included in a faction, the form of popular government, on the other hand, enables it to sacrifice to its ruling passion or interest both the public good and the rights of other citizens. To secure the public good and private rights against the danger of such a faction, and at the same time to preserve the spirit and the form of popular government, is then the great object to which our enquiries are directed. Let me add that it is the great desideratum by which alone this form of government can be rescued from the opprobrium under which it has so long labored and be recommended to the esteem and adoption of mankind.

By what means is this object attainable? Evidently by one of two only. Either the existence of the same passion or interest in a majority at the same time must be prevented, or the majority, having such co-existent passion or interest, must be rendered, by their number and local situation, unable to concert and carry into effect schemes of oppression. If the impulse and the opportunity be suffered to coincide, we well know that neither moral nor religious motives can be relied on as an adequate control. They are not found to be such on the injustice and violence of individuals, and lose their efficacy in proportion to the number combined together, that is, in proportion as their efficacy becomes needful.

From this view of the subject it may be concluded that a pure Democracy, by which I mean a Society consisting of a small number of citizens, who assemble and administer the Government in person, can admit of no cure for the mischiefs of faction. A common passion or interest will, in almost every case, be felt by a majority of the whole; a communication and concert results from the form of Government itself; and there is nothing to check the inducements to sacrifice the weaker party or an obnoxious individual. Hence it is that such Democracies have ever been spectacles of turbulence and contention; have ever been found incompatible with personal security or the rights of property; and have in general been as short in their lives as they have been violent in their deaths. Theoretic politicians, who have patronized this species of Government, have erroneously supposed that by reducing mankind to a perfect equality in their political rights, they would at the same time be perfectly equalized and assimilated in their possessions, their opinions, and their passions.

A Republic, by which I mean a Government in which the scheme of representation takes place, opens a different prospect and promises the cure for which we are seeking. Let us examine the points in which it varies from pure Democracy, and we shall comprehend both the nature of the cure and the efficacy which it must derive from the Union.

The two great points of difference between a Democracy and a Republic are: first, the delegation of the Government, in the latter, to a small number of citizens elected by the rest; secondly, the greater number of citizens and greater sphere of country over which the latter may be extended.

The effect of the first difference is, on the one hand, to refine and enlarge the public views by passing them through the medium of a chosen body of citizens, whose wisdom may best discern the true interest of their country and whose patriotism and love of justice will be least likely to sacrifice it to temporary or partial considerations. Under such a regulation it may well happen that the public voice, pronounced by the representatives of the people, will be more consonant to the public good than if pronounced by the people themselves, convened for the purpose. On the other hand, the effect may be inverted. Men of factious tempers, of local prejudices, or of sinister designs, may, by intrigue, by corruption, or by other means, first obtain the suffrages, and then betray the interests of the people. The question resulting is, whether small or extensive Republics are most favorable to the election of proper guardians of the public weal; and it is clearly decided in favor of the latter by two obvious considerations.

In the first place it is to be remarked that however small the Republic may be, the Representatives must be raised to a certain number in order to guard against the cabals of a few; and that however large it may be they must be limited to a certain number in order to guard against the confusion of a multitude. Hence, the number of Representatives in the two cases not being in proportion to that of the Constituents, and being proportionally greatest in the small Republic, it follows that if the proportion of fit characters be not less in the large than in the small Republic, the former will present a greater option, and consequently a greater probability of a fit choice.

In the next place, as each Representative will be chosen by a greater number of citizens in the large than in the small Republic, it will be more difficult for unworthy candidates to practise with success the vicious arts by which elections are too often carried; and the suffrages of the people being more free, will be more likely to centre on men who possess the most attractive merit and the most diffusive and established characters.

It must be confessed that in this, as in most other cases, there is a mean, on both sides of which inconveniencies will be found to lie. By enlarging too much the number of electors, you render the representative too little acquainted with all their local circumstances and lesser interests; as by reducing it too much, you render him unduly attached to these, and too little fit to comprehend and pursue great and national objects. The Federal Constitution forms a happy combination in this respect; the great and aggregate interests being referred to the national, the local and particular to the State legislatures.

The other point of difference is the greater number of citizens and extent of territory which may be brought within the compass of Republican than of Democratic Government; and it is this circumstance principally which renders factious combinations less to be dreaded in the former than in the latter. The smaller the society, the fewer probably will be the distinct parties and interests composing it; the fewer the distinct parties and interests, the more frequently will a majority be found of the same party; and the smaller the number of individuals composing a majority, and the smaller the compass within which they are placed, the more easily will they concert and execute their plans of oppression. Extend the sphere and you take in a greater variety of parties and interests; you make it less probable that a majority of the whole will have a common motive to invade the rights of other citizens; or if such a common motive exists, it will be more difficult for all who feel it to discover their own strength and to act in unison with each other. Besides other impediments, it may be remarked, that where there is a consciousness of unjust or dishonorable purposes, communication is always checked by distrust in proportion to the number whose concurrence is necessary.

Hence, it clearly appears that the same advantage which a Republic has over a Democracy in controlling the effects of faction is enjoyed by a large over a small republic—is enjoyed by the Union over the States composing it. Does this advantage consist in the substitution of representatives whose enlightened views and virtuous sentiments render them superior to local prejudices and to schemes of injustice? It will not be denied that the representation of the Union will be most likely to possess these requisite endowments. Does it consist in the greater security afforded by a greater variety of parties, against the event of any one party being able to outnumber and oppress the rest? In an equal degree does the increased variety of parties comprised within the Union increase this security? Does it, in fine, consist in the greater obstacles opposed to the concert and accomplishment of the secret wishes of an unjust and interested majority? Here again the extent of the Union gives it the most palpable advantage.

The influence of factious leaders may kindle a flame within their particular States but will be unable to spread a general conflagration through the other States: a religious sect may degenerate into a political faction in a part of the Confederacy; but the variety of sects dispersed over the entire face of it must secure the national Councils against any danger from that source: a rage for paper money, for an abolition of debts, for an equal division of property, or for any other improper or wicked project, will be less apt to pervade the whole body of the Union than a particular member of it; in the same proportion as such a malady is more likely to taint a particular county or district than an entire State.

In the extent and proper structure of the Union, therefore, we behold a republican remedy for the diseases most incident to Republican Government. And according to the degree of pleasure and pride we feel in being republicans ought to be our zeal in cherishing the spirit and supporting the character of federalist.

PUBLIUS

No. 51: Madison

To what expedient, then, shall we finally resort, for maintaining in practice the necessary partition of power among the several departments as laid down in the constitution? The only answer that can be given is that as all these exterior provisions are found to be inadequate the defect must be supplied, by so contriving the interior structure of the government as that its several constituent parts may, by their mutual relations, be the means of keeping each other in their proper places. Without presuming to undertake a full development of this important idea I will hazard a few general observations which may perhaps place it in a clearer light, and enable us to form a more correct judgment of the principles and structure of the government planned by the convention.

In order to lay a due foundation for that separate and distinct exercise of the different powers of government, which to a certain extent is admitted on all hands to be essential to the preservation of liberty, it is evident that each department should have a will of its own; and consequently should be so constituted that the members of each should have as little agency as possible in the appointment of the members of the others. Were this principle rigorously adhered to, it would require that all the appointments for the supreme executive, legislative, and judiciary magistracies should be drawn from the same fountain of authority, the people, through channels having no communication whatever with one another. Perhaps such a plan of constructing the several departments would be less difficult in practice than it may in contemplation appear. Some difficulties, however, and some additional expense would attend the execution of it. Some deviations, therefore, from the principle must be admitted. In the constitution of the judiciary department in particular, it might be inexpedient to insist rigorously on the principle: first, because peculiar qualifications being essential in the members, the primary consideration ought to be to select that mode of choice which best secures these qualifications; second, because the permanent tenure by which the appointments are held in that department must soon destroy all sense of dependence on the authority conferring them.

It is equally evident that the members of each department should be as little dependent as possible on those of the others for the emoluments annexed to their offices. Were the executive magistrate, or the judges, not independent of the legislature in this particular, their independence in every other would be merely nominal.

But the great security against a gradual concentration of the several powers in the same department consists in giving to those who administer each department the necessary constitutional means and personal motives to resist encroachments of the others. The provision for defence must in this, as in all other cases, be made commensurate to the danger of attack. Ambition must be made to counteract ambition. The interest of the man must be connected with the constitutional rights of the place. It may be a reflection on human nature that such devices should be necessary to control the abuses of government. But what is government itself but the greatest of all reflections on human nature? If men were angels, no government would be necessary. If angels were to govern men, neither external nor internal controls on government would be necessary. In framing a government which is to be administered by men over men, the great difficulty lies in this: You must first enable the government to control the governed; and in the next place oblige it to control itself. A dependence on the people is, no doubt, the primary control on the government; but experience has taught mankind the necessity of auxiliary precautions.

This policy of supplying, by opposite and rival interests, the defect of better motives, might be traced through the whole system of human affairs, private as well as public. We see it particularly displayed in all the subordinate distributions of power, where the constant aim is to divide and arrange the several offices in such a manner as that each may be a check on the other; that the private interest of every individual may be a sentinel over the public rights. These inventions of prudence cannot be less requisite in the distribution of the supreme powers of the State.

But it is not possible to give to each department an equal power of self-defense. In republican government, the legislative authority necessarily predominates. The remedy for this inconveniency is to divide the legislature into different branches; and to render them, by different modes of election and different principles of action, as little connected with each other as the nature of their common functions and their common dependence on the society will admit. It may even be necessary to guard against dangerous encroachments by still further precautions. As the weight of the legislative authority requires that it should be thus divided, the weakness of the executive may require, on the other hand, that it should be fortified. An absolute negative on the legislature appears, at first view, to be the natural defense with which the executive magistrate should be armed. But perhaps it would be neither altogether safe nor alone sufficient. On ordinary occasions it might not be exerted with the requisite firmness, and on extraordinary occasions it might be perfidiously abused. May not this defect of an absolute negative be supplied by some qualified connection between this weaker branch of the stronger department, by which the latter may be led to support the constitutional rights of the former, without being too much detached from the rights of its own department?

If the principles on which these observations are founded be just, as I persuade myself they are, and they be applied as a criterion to the several State constitutions, and to the federal Constitution, it will be found that if the latter does not perfectly correspond with them, the former are infinitely less able to bear such a test.

There are, moreover, two considerations particularly applicable to the federal system of America, which place that system in a very interesting point of view.

First. In a single republic, all the power surrendered by the people is submitted to the administration of a single government; and usurpations are guarded against by a division of the government into distinct and separate departments. In the compound republic of America, the power surrendered by the people is first divided between two distinct governments, and then the portion allotted to each subdivided among distinct and separate departments. Hence a double security arises to the rights of the people. The different governments will control each other, at the same time that each will be controlled by itself.

Second. It is of great importance in a republic not only to guard the society against the oppression of its rulers, but to guard one part of the society against the injustice of the other part. Different interests necessarily exist in different classes of citizens. If a majority be united by a common interest, the rights of the minority will be insecure. There are but two methods of providing against this evil: The one by creating a will in the community independent of the majority—that is, of the society itself; the other, by comprehending in the society so many separate descriptions of citizens as will render an unjust combination of a majority of the whole very improbable, if not impracticable. The first method prevails in all governments possessing an hereditary or self-appointed authority. This, at best, is but a precarious security; because a power independent of the society may as well espouse the unjust views of the major as the rightful interests of the minor party, and may possibly be turned against both parties. The second method will be exemplified in the federal republic of the United States. Whilst all authority in it will be derived from and dependent on the society, the society itself will be broken into so many parts, interests and classes of citizens, that the rights of individuals, or of the minority, will be in little danger from interested combinations of the majority. In a free government the security for civil rights must be the same as that for religious rights. It consists in the one case in the multiplicity of interests, and in the other in the multiplicity of sects. The degree of security in both cases will depend on the number of interests and sects; and this may be presumed to depend on the extent of country and number of people comprehended under the same government. This view of the subject must particularly recommend a proper federal system to all the sincere and considerate friends of republican government: Since it shows that in exact proportion as the territory of the Union may be formed into more circumscribed Confederacies, or States, oppressive combinations of a majority will be facilitated; the best security, under the republican form, for the rights of every class of citizens, will be diminished; and consequently the stability and independence of some member of the government, the only other security, must be proportionally increased. Justice is the end of government. It is the end of civil society. It ever has been and ever will be pursued until it be obtained, or until liberty be lost in the pursuit. In a society under the forms of which the stronger faction can readily unite and oppress the weaker, anarchy may as truly be said to reign as in a state of nature, where the weaker individual is not secured against the violence of the stronger: And as, in the latter state, even the stronger individuals are prompted, by the uncertainty of their condition, to submit to a government which may protect the weak as well as themselves: So, in the former state, will the more powerful factions or parties be gradually induced, by a like motive, to wish for a government which will protect all parties, the weaker as well as the more powerful. It can be little doubted that if the State of Rhode Island was separated from the Confederacy and left to itself, the insecurity of rights under the popular form of government within such narrow limits would be displayed by such reiterated oppressions of factious majorities that some power altogether independent of the people would soon be called for by the voice of the very factions whose misrule had proved the necessity of it. In the extended republic of the United States, and among the great variety of interests, parties, and sects which it embraces, a coalition of a majority of the whole society could seldom take place on any other principles than those of justice and the general good; and there being thus less danger to a minor from the will of the major party, there must be less pretext, also, to provide for the security of the former, by introducing into the government a will not dependent on the latter, or, in other words, a will independent of the society itself. It is no less certain than it is important, notwithstanding the contrary opinions which have been entertained, that the larger the society, provided it lie within a practicable sphere, the more duly capable it will be of self-government. And happily for the *republican cause,* practicable sphere may be carried to a very great extent by a judicious modification and mixture of the *federal principle.*

PUBLIUS

No. 78: Hamilton

To the People of the State of New York:

WE PROCEED now to an examination of the judiciary department of the proposed government.

In unfolding the defects of the existing Confederation, the utility and necessity of a federal judicature have been clearly pointed out. It is the less necessary to recapitulate the considerations there urged, as the propriety of the institution in the abstract is not disputed; the only questions which have been raised being relative to the manner of constituting it, and to its extent. To these points, therefore, our observations shall be confined.

The manner of constituting it seems to embrace these several objects: 1st. The mode of appointing the judges. 2d. The tenure by which they are to hold their places. 3d. The partition of the judiciary authority between different courts, and their relations to each other.

First. As to the mode of appointing the judges; this is the same with that of appointing the officers of the Union in general, and has been so fully discussed in the two last numbers, that nothing can be said here which would not be useless repetition.

Second. As to the tenure by which the judges are to hold their places; this chiefly concerns their duration in office; the provisions for their support; the precautions for their responsibility.

According to the plan of the convention, all judges who may be appointed by the United States are to hold their offices DURING GOOD BEHAVIOR; which is conformable to the most approved of the State constitutions and among the rest, to that of this State. Its propriety having been drawn into question by the adversaries of that plan, is no light symptom of the rage for objection, which disorders their imaginations and judgments. The standard of good behavior for the continuance in office of the judicial magistracy, is certainly one of the most valuable of the modern improvements in the practice of government. In a monarchy it is an excellent barrier to the despotism of the prince; in a republic it is a no less excellent barrier to the encroachments and oppressions of the representative body. And it is the best expedient which can be devised in any government, to secure a steady, upright, and impartial administration of the laws.

Whoever attentively considers the different departments of power must perceive, that, in a government in which they are separated from each other, the judiciary, from the nature of its functions, will always be the least dangerous to the political rights of the Constitution; because it will be least in a capacity to annoy or injure them. The Executive not only dispenses the honors, but holds the sword of the community. The legislature not only commands the purse, but prescribes the rules by which the duties and rights of every citizen are to be regulated. The judiciary, on the contrary, has no influence over either the sword or the purse; no direction either of the strength or of the wealth of the society; and can take no active resolution whatever. It may truly be said to have neither FORCE nor WILL, but merely judgment; and must ultimately depend upon the aid of the executive arm even for the efficacy of its judgments.

This simple view of the matter suggests several important consequences. It proves incontestably, that the judiciary is beyond comparison the weakest of the three departments of power; that it can never attack with success either of the other two; and that all possible care is requisite to enable it to defend itself against their attacks. It equally proves, that though individual oppression may now and then proceed from the courts of justice, the general liberty of the people can never be endangered from that quarter; I mean so long as the judiciary remains truly distinct from both the legislature and the Executive. For I agree, that "there is no liberty, if the power of judging be not separated from the legislative and executive powers." And it proves, in the last place, that as liberty can have nothing to fear from the judiciary alone, but would have every thing to fear from its union with either of the other departments; that as all the effects of such a union must ensue from a dependence of the former on the latter, notwithstanding a nominal and apparent separation; that as, from the natural feebleness of the judiciary, it is in continual jeopardy of being overpowered, awed, or influenced by its co-ordinate branches; and that as nothing can contribute so much to its firmness and independence as permanency in office, this quality may therefore be justly regarded as an indispensable ingredient in its constitution, and, in a great measure, as the citadel of the public justice and the public security.

The complete independence of the courts of justice is peculiarly essential in a limited Constitution. By a limited Constitution, I understand one which contains certain specified exceptions to the legislative authority; such, for instance, as that it shall pass no bills of attainder, no ex-post-facto laws, and the like. Limitations of this kind can be preserved in practice no other way than through the medium of courts of justice, whose duty it must be to declare all acts contrary to the manifest tenor of the Constitution void. Without this, all the reservations of particular rights or privileges would amount to nothing.

Some perplexity respecting the rights of the courts to pronounce legislative acts void, because contrary to the Constitution, has arisen from an imagination that the doctrine would imply a superiority of the judiciary to the legislative power. It is urged that the authority which can declare the acts of another void, must necessarily be superior to the one whose acts may be declared void. As this doctrine is of great importance in all the American constitutions, a brief discussion of the ground on which it rests cannot be unacceptable.

There is no position which depends on clearer principles, than that every act of a delegated authority, contrary to the tenor of the commission under which it is exercised, is void. No legislative act, therefore, contrary to the Constitution, can be valid. To deny this, would be to affirm, that the deputy is greater than his principal; that the servant is above his master; that the representatives of the people are superior to the people themselves; that men acting by virtue of powers, may do not only what their powers do not authorize, but what they forbid.

If it be said that the legislative body are themselves the constitutional judges of their own powers, and that the construction they put upon them is conclusive upon the other departments, it may be answered, that this cannot be the natural presumption, where it is not to be collected from any particular provisions in the Constitution. It is not otherwise to be supposed, that the Constitution could intend to enable the representatives of the people to substitute their WILL to that of their constituents. It is far more rational to suppose, that the courts were designed to be an intermediate body between the people and the legislature, in order, among other things, to keep the latter within the limits assigned to their authority. The interpretation of the laws is the proper and peculiar province of the courts. A constitution is, in fact, and must be regarded by the judges, as a fundamental law. It therefore belongs to them to ascertain its meaning, as well as the meaning of any particular act proceeding from the legislative body. If there should happen to be an irreconcilable variance between the two, that which has the superior obligation and validity ought, of course, to be preferred; or, in other words, the Constitution ought to be preferred to the statute, the intention of the people to the intention of their agents.

Nor does this conclusion by any means suppose a superiority of the judicial to the legislative power. It only supposes that the power of the people is superior to both; and that where the will of the legislature, declared in its statutes, stands in opposition to that of the people, declared in the Constitution, the judges ought to be governed by the latter rather than the former. They ought to regulate their decisions by the fundamental laws, rather than by those which are not fundamental.

This exercise of judicial discretion, in determining between two contradictory laws, is exemplified in a familiar instance. It not uncommonly happens, that there are two statutes existing at one time, clashing in whole or in part with each other, and neither of them containing any repealing clause or expression. In such a case, it is the province of the courts to liquidate and fix their meaning and operation. So far as they can, by any fair construction, be reconciled to each other, reason and law conspire to dictate that this should be done; where this is impracticable, it becomes a matter of necessity to give effect to one, in exclusion of the other. The rule which has obtained in the courts for determining their relative validity is, that the last in order of time shall be preferred to the first. But this is a mere rule of construction, not derived from any positive law, but from the nature and reason of the thing. It is a rule not enjoined upon the courts by legislative provision, but adopted by themselves, as consonant to truth and propriety, for the direction of their conduct as interpreters of the law. They thought it reasonable, that between the interfering acts of an EQUAL authority, that which was the last indication of its will should have the preference.

But in regard to the interfering acts of a superior and subordinate authority, of an original and derivative power, the nature and reason of the thing indicate the converse of that rule as proper to be followed. They teach us that the prior act of a superior ought to be preferred to the subsequent act of an inferior and subordinate authority; and that accordingly, whenever a particular statute contravenes the Constitution, it will be the duty of the judicial tribunals to adhere to the latter and disregard the former.

It can be of no weight to say that the courts, on the pretense of a repugnancy, may substitute their own pleasure to the constitutional intentions of the legislature. This might as well happen in the case of two contradictory statutes; or it might as well happen in every adjudication upon any single statute. The courts must declare the sense of the law; and if they should be disposed to exercise WILL instead of JUDGMENT, the consequence would equally be the substitution of their pleasure to that of the legislative body. The observation, if it prove any thing, would prove that there ought to be no judges distinct from that body.

If, then, the courts of justice are to be considered as the bulwarks of a limited Constitution against legislative encroachments, this consideration will afford a strong argument for the permanent tenure of judicial offices, since nothing will contribute so much as this to that independent spirit in the judges which must be essential to the faithful performance of so arduous a duty.

This independence of the judges is equally requisite to guard the Constitution and the rights of individuals from the effects of those ill humors, which the arts of designing men, or the influence of particular conjunctures, sometimes disseminate among the people themselves, and which, though they speedily give place to better information, and more deliberate reflection, have a tendency, in the meantime, to occasion dangerous innovations in the government, and serious oppressions of the minor party in the community. Though I trust the friends of the proposed Constitution will never concur with its enemies, in questioning that fundamental principle of republican government, which admits the right of the people to alter or abolish the established Constitution, whenever they find it inconsistent with their happiness, yet it is not to be inferred from this principle, that the representatives of the people, whenever a momentary inclination happens to lay hold of a majority of their constituents, incompatible with the provisions in the existing Constitution, would, on that account, be justifiable in a violation of those provisions; or that the courts would be under a greater obligation to connive at infractions in this shape, than when they had proceeded wholly from the cabals of the representative body. Until the people have, by some solemn and authoritative act, annulled or changed the established form, it is binding upon themselves collectively, as well as individually; and no presumption, or even knowledge, of their sentiments, can warrant their representatives in a departure from it, prior to such an act. But it is easy to see, that it would require an uncommon portion of fortitude in the judges to do their duty as faithful guardians of the Constitution, where legislative invasions of it had been instigated by the major voice of the community.

But it is not with a view to infractions of the Constitution only, that the independence of the judges may be an essential safeguard against the effects of occasional ill humors in the society. These sometimes extend no farther than to the injury of the private rights of particular classes of citizens, by unjust and partial laws. Here also the firmness of the judicial magistracy is of vast importance in mitigating the severity and confining the operation of such laws. It not only serves to moderate the immediate mischiefs of those which may have been passed, but it operates as a check upon the legislative body in passing them; who, perceiving that obstacles to the success of iniquitous intention are to be expected from the scruples of the courts, are in a manner compelled, by the very motives of the injustice they meditate, to qualify their attempts. This is a circumstance calculated to have more influence upon the character of our governments, than but few may be aware of. The benefits of the integrity and moderation of the judiciary have already been felt in more States than one; and though they may have displeased those whose sinister expectations they may have disappointed, they must have commanded the esteem and applause of all the virtuous and disinterested. Considerate men, of every description, ought to prize whatever will tend to beget or fortify that temper in the courts: as no man can be sure that he may not be to-morrow the victim of a spirit of injustice, by which he may be a gainer to-day. And every man must now feel, that the inevitable tendency of such a spirit is to sap the foundations of public and private confidence, and to introduce in its stead universal distrust and distress.

That inflexible and uniform adherence to the rights of the Constitution, and of individuals, which we perceive to be indispensable in the courts of justice, can certainly not be expected from judges who hold their offices by a temporary commission. Periodical appointments, however regulated, or by whomsoever made, would, in some way or other, be fatal to their necessary independence. If the power of making them was committed either to the Executive or legislature, there would be danger of an improper complaisance to the branch which possessed it; if to both, there would be an unwillingness to hazard the displeasure of either; if to the people, or to persons chosen by them for the special purpose, there would be too great a disposition to consult popularity, to justify a reliance that nothing would be consulted but the Constitution and the laws.

There is yet a further and a weightier reason for the permanency of the judicial offices, which is deducible from the nature of the qualifications they require. It has been frequently remarked, with great propriety, that a voluminous code of laws is one of the inconveniences necessarily connected with the advantages of a free government. To avoid an arbitrary discretion in the courts, it is indispensable that they should be bound down by strict rules and precedents, which serve to define and point out their duty in every particular case that comes before them; and it will readily be conceived from the variety of controversies which grow out of the folly and wickedness of mankind, that the records of those precedents must unavoidably swell to a very considerable bulk, and must demand long and laborious study to acquire a competent knowledge of them. Hence it is, that there can be but few men in the society who will have sufficient skill in the laws to qualify them for the stations of judges. And making the proper deductions for the ordinary depravity of human nature, the number must be still smaller of those who unite the requisite integrity with the requisite knowledge. These considerations apprise us, that the government can have no great option between fit character; and that a temporary duration in office, which would naturally discourage such characters from quitting a lucrative line of practice to accept a seat on the bench, would have a tendency to throw the administration of justice into hands less able, and less well qualified, to conduct it with utility and dignity. In the present circumstances of this country, and in those in which it is likely to be for a long time to come, the disadvantages on this score would be greater than they may at first sight appear; but it must be confessed, that they are far inferior to those which present themselves under the other aspects of the subject.

Upon the whole, there can be no room to doubt that the convention acted wisely in copying from the models of those constitutions which have established GOOD BEHAVIOR as the tenure of their judicial offices, in point of duration; and that so far from being blamable on this account, their plan would have been inexcusably defective, if it had wanted this important feature of good government. The experience of Great Britain affords an illustrious comment on the excellence of the institution.

PUBLIUS

GLOSSARY

Aid to Families with Dependent Children (AFDC) The federal welfare program in place from 1935 until 1996, when it was replaced by Temporary Assistance for Needy Families (TANF) under President Clinton.

amicus curiae Latin for "friend of the court," referring to an interested group or person who shares relevant information about a case to help the Court reach a decision.

Antifederalists Those at the Constitutional Convention who favored strong state governments and feared that a strong national government would be a threat to individual rights.

appeals courts The intermediate level of federal courts that hear appeals from district courts. More generally, an appeals court is any court with appellate jurisdiction.

appellate jurisdiction The authority of a court to hear appeals from lower courts and change or uphold the decision.

apportionment The process of assigning the 435 seats in the House to the states based on increases or decreases in state population.

Articles of Confederation Sent to the states for ratification in 1777, these were the first attempt at a new American government. It was later decided that the Articles restricted national government too much, and they were replaced by the Constitution.

astroturf lobbying Any lobbying method initiated by an interest group that is designed to look like the spontaneous, independent participation of many individuals.

attack journalism A type of increasingly popular media coverage focused on political scandals and controversies, which causes a negative public opinion of political figures.

attitudinalist approach A way of understanding decisions of the Supreme Court based on the political ideologies of the justices.

Baby Boom generation Americans born between 1946 and 1964, who will be retiring in large numbers over the next 20 years.

balanced budget A spending plan in which the government's expenditures are equal to its revenue.

bicameralism The system of having two chambers within one legislative body, like the House and Senate in the U.S. Congress.

Bill of Rights The first 10 amendments to the Constitution; they protect individual rights and liberties.

block grants Federal aid provided to a state government to be spent within a certain policy area, but the state can decide how to spend the money within that area.

broadcast media Communications technologies, such as television and radio, that transmit information over airwaves.

budget deficit The amount by which a government's spending in a given fiscal year exceeds its revenue.

budget making The processes carried out in Congress to determine how government money will be spent and revenue will be raised.

budget maximizers Bureaucrats who seek to increase funding for their agency whether or not that additional spending is worthwhile.

budget reconciliation The process by which congressional committees are held to the spending targets specified in the budget resolution. During this process, the House and Senate Budget Committees combine the budgetary changes from all the legislative committees into an omnibus reconciliation bill to be approved by Congress.

bureaucracy The system of civil servants and political appointees who implement congressional or presidential decisions; also known as the administrative state.

bureaucratic drift Bureaucrats' tendency to implement policies in a way that favors their own political objectives rather than following the original intentions of the legislation.

Bush Doctrine The foreign policy of President George W. Bush, under which the United States would use military force preemptively against threats to its national security.

business cycle The normal pattern of expansion and contraction of the economy.

by-product theory The idea that many Americans acquire political information unintentionally rather than by seeking it out.

Cabinet The group of 15 executive department heads who implement the president's agenda in their respective positions.

casework Assistance provided by members of Congress to their constituents in solving problems with the federal bureaucracy or addressing other specific concerns.

categorical grants Federal aid to state or local governments that is provided for a specific purpose, such as a mass transit program within the transportation budget or a school lunch program within the education budget.

caucus A local meeting in which party members select a party's nominee for the general election.

caucus (congressional) The organization of Democrats within the House and Senate that meets to discuss and debate the party's positions on various issues in order to reach a consensus and to assign leadership positions.

caucus (electoral) A local meeting in which party members select a party's nominee for the general election.

centralized groups Interest groups that have a headquarters, usually in Washington, D.C., as well as members and field offices throughout the country. In general, these groups' lobbying decisions are made at headquarters by the group leaders.

cert pool A system initiated in the Supreme Court in the 1970s in which law clerks screen cases that come to the Supreme Court and recommend to the justices which cases should be heard.

checks and balances A system in which each branch of government has some power over the others.

civilian control The idea that military leaders do not formulate military policy, but rather implement directives from civilian leaders.

civil liberties Basic political freedoms that protect citizens from governmental abuses of power.

civil rights Rights that guarantee individuals freedom from discrimination. These rights are generally grounded in the equal protection clause of the Fourteenth Amendment and more specifically laid out in laws passed by Congress, such as the 1964 Civil Rights Act.

civil servants Employees of bureaucratic agencies within the government.

Civil War Amendments The Thirteenth, Fourteenth, and Fifteenth Amendments to the Constitution, which abolished slavery and granted civil liberties and voting rights to freed slaves after the Civil War.

"clash of civilizations" The theory that terrorism is motivated by a hatred of Western culture and religion.

class-action lawsuit A case brought by a group of individuals on behalf of themselves and others in the general public who are in similar circumstances.

clear and present danger test Established in *Schenk v. United States*, this test allows the government to restrict certain types of speech deemed dangerous.

closed primary A primary election in which only registered members of a particular political party can vote.

closed rules Conditions placed on a legislative debate by the House Rules Committee prohibiting amendments to a bill.

cloture A procedure through which the Senate can limit the amount of time spent debating a bill (cutting off a filibuster), if a supermajority of 60 senators agree.

coattails The idea that a popular president can generate additional support for candidates affiliated with his party. Coattails are weak or nonexistent in most American elections.

coercion A method of eliminating nonparticipation or free riding by potential group members by requiring participation, as in many labor unions.

coercive federalism A form of federalism in which the federal government pressures the states to change their policies by using regulations, mandates, and conditions (often involving threats to withdraw federal funding).

Cold War The period of tension and arms competition between the United States and the Soviet Union that lasted from 1945 until 1991.

collective action problem A situation in which the members of a group would benefit by working together to produce some outcome, but each individual is better off refusing to cooperate and reaping benefits from those who do the work.

commerce clause Part of Article I, Section 8, of the Constitution that gives Congress "the power to regulate Commerce … among the several States." The Supreme Court's interpretation of this clause has varied, but today it serves as the basis for much of Congress's legislation.

commerce clause powers The powers of Congress to regulate the economy granted in Article I, Section 8, of the Constitution.

commercial speech Public expression with the aim of making a profit. It has received greater protection under the First Amendment in recent years but remains less protected than political speech.

common law Law based on the precedent of previous court rulings rather than on legislation. It is used in all federal courts and forty-nine of the fifty state courts.

competitive federalism A form of federalism in which states compete to attract businesses and jobs through the policies they adopt.

concentration The trend toward single-company ownership of several media sources in one area.

concurrent powers Responsibilities for particular policy areas, such as transportation, that are shared by federal, state, and local governments.

conditional party government The theory that lawmakers from the same party will cooperate to develop policy proposals.

confederal government A form of government in which states hold power over a limited national government.

confederations Interest groups made up of several independent, local organizations that provide much of their funding and hold most of the power.

conference The organization of Republicans within the House and Senate that meets to discuss and debate the party's positions on various issues in order to reach a consensus and to assign leadership positions.

conference committees Temporary committees created to negotiate differences between the House and Senate versions of a piece of legislation that has passed through both chambers.

"consent of the governed" The idea that government gains its legitimacy through regular elections in which the people living under that government participate to elect their leaders.

conservative One side of the ideological spectrum defined by support for lower taxes, a free market, and a more limited government; generally associated with Republicans.

consitutional authority Powers derived from the provisions of the Constitution that outline the president's role in government.

constitutional interpretation The process of determining whether a piece of legislation or governmental action is supported by the Constitution.

constitutional revolution A significant change in the Constitution that may be accomplished either through amendments (as after the Civil War) or shifts in the Supreme Court's interpretation of the Constitution (as in the New Deal era).

constructivism The idea that foreign policy is shaped by how a state's leaders define the national interest, ideology, and other factors.

containment An important feature of American Cold War policy in which the United States used diplomatic, economic, and military strategies in an effort to prevent the Soviet Union from expanding its influence.

cooperative federalism A form of federalism in which national and state governments work together to provide services efficiently. This form emerged in the late 1930s, representing a profound shift toward less concrete boundaries of responsibility in national–state relations.

Council of Economic Advisers A group of economic advisers, created by the Employment Act of 1946, which provides objective data on the state of the economy and makes economic policy recommendations to the president.

cross-ownership The trend toward single-company ownership of several kinds of media outlets.

culture wars Political conflict in the United States between "red-state" Americans, who tend to have strong religious beliefs, and "blue-state" Americans, who tend to be more secular.

current account The balance of a country's receipts and its payments in international trade and investment.

de facto Relating to actions or circumstances that occur outside the law or "by fact," such as the segregation of schools that resulted from housing patterns and other factors rather than from laws.

defendant The person or party against whom a case is brought.

de jure Relating to actions or circumstances that occur "by law," such as the legally enforced segregation of schools in the American South before the 1960s.

delegate (congressional role) A member of Congress who loyally represents constituents' direct interests.

descriptive representation When a member of Congress shares the characteristics (such as gender, race, religion, or ethnicity) of his or her constituents.

détente An approach to foreign policy in which cultural exchanges and negotiations are used to reduce tensions between rival nations, such as between the United States and the Soviet Union during the 1970s.

direct incitement test Established in *Brandenberg v. Ohio*, this test protects threatening speech under the First Amendment unless that speech aims to and is likely to cause imminent "lawless action."

direct lobbying Attempts by interest group staff to influence policy by speaking with elected officials or bureaucrats.

discount rate The interest rate that a bank must pay on a short-term loan from the Federal Reserve Bank.

discretionary spending Expenditures that can be cut from the budget without changing the underlying law.

disenfranchised To have been denied the ability to exercise a right, such as the right to vote.

disparate impact standard The idea that discrimination exists if a practice has a negative effect on a specific group, whether or not this effect was intentional.

distributive theory The idea that members of Congress will join committees that best serve the interests of their district and that committee members will support each other's legislation.

district courts Lower-level trial courts of the federal judicial system that handle most U.S. federal cases.

divided government A situation in which the House, Senate, and presidency are not controlled by the same party, such as if Democrats hold the majority of House and Senate seats, and the president is a Republican.

doctrine of interposition The idea that if the national government passes an unconstitutional law, the people of the states (through their state legislatures) can declare the law void. This idea provided the basis for southern secession and the Civil War.

domino theory An idea held by American foreign policy makers during the Cold War that the creation of one Soviet-backed communist nation would lead to the spread of communism in that nation's region.

double jeopardy Being tried twice for the same crime. This is prevented by the Fifth Amendment.

dual federalism The form of federalism favored by Chief Justice Roger Taney in which national and state governments are seen as distinct entities providing separate services. This model limits the power of the national government.

due process clause Part of the Fourteenth Amendment that forbids states from denying "life, liberty, or property" to any person without due process of law. (A nearly identical clause in the Fifth Amendment applies only to the national government.)

due process rights The idea that laws and legal proceedings must be fair. The Constitution guarantees that the government cannot take away a person's "life, liberty, or property, without due process of law." Other specific due process rights are found in the Fourth, Fifth, Sixth, and Eighth Amendments, such as protection from self-incrimination and freedom from illegal searches.

Duverger's law The principle that in a democracy with single-member districts and plurality voting, like the United States, only two parties' candidates will have a realistic chance of winning political office.

earmarks Federally funded local projects attached to bills passed through Congress.

economic depression A deep, widespread downturn in the economy, like the Great Depression of the 1930s.

economic individualism The autonomy of individuals to manage their own financial decisions without government interference.

election cycle The two-year period between general elections.

electoral college The body that votes to select America's president and vice president based on the popular vote in each state. Each candidate nominates a slate of electors who are selected to attend the meeting of the college if their candidate wins the most votes in a state or district.

electoral connection The idea that congressional behavior is centrally motivated by members' desire for re-election.

electoral vote Votes cast by members of the electoral college; after a presidential candidate wins the popular vote in a given state, that candidate's slate of electors cast electoral votes for the candidate on behalf of that state.

entitlement Any federal government program that provides benefits to Americans who meet requirements specified by law.

enumerated powers Powers explicitly granted to Congress, the president, or the Supreme Court in the first three articles of the Constitution. Examples include Congress's power to "raise and support armies" and the president's power as commander in chief.

equal time provision An FCC regulation requiring broadcast media to provide equal airtime on any non-news programming to all candidates running for an office.

establishment clause Part of the First Amendment that states "Congress shall make no law respecting an establishment of religion," which has been interpreted to mean that Congress cannot sponsor or favor any religion.

exclusionary rule The principle that illegally or unconstitutionally acquired evidence cannot be used in a criminal trial.

executive agreement An agreement between the executive branch and a foreign government, which acts as a treaty but does not require Senate approval.

Executive Office of the -President (EOP) The group of policy-related offices that serves as support staff to the president.

executive orders Proclamations made by the president that change government policy without congressional approval.

executive powers clause Part of Article II, Section 1, of the Constitution that states, "The executive Power shall be vested in a President of the United States of America." This broad statement has been used to justify many assertions of presidential power.

executive privilege The right of the president to keep executive branch conversations and correspondence confidential from the legislative and judicial branches.

factions Groups of like-minded people who try to influence the government. American government is set up to avoid domination by any one of these groups.

fairness doctrine An FCC regulation requiring broadcast media to present several points of view to ensure balanced coverage. It was created in the late 1940s and eliminated in 1987.

fast-track authority An expedited system for passing treaties under which support from a simple majority, rather than a two-thirds majority, is needed in both the House and Senate, and no amendments are allowed.

federal civil service A system created by the 1883 Pendleton Civil Service Act in which bureaucrats are hired on the basis of merit rather than political connections.

Federal Communications Commission (FCC) A government agency created in 1934 to regulate American radio stations and later expanded to regulate television, wireless communications technologies, and other broadcast media.

Federal Election Commission The government agency that enforces and regulates election laws; made up of six presidential appointees, of whom no more than three can be members of the same party.

federal funds rate (FFR) The interest rate that a bank must pay on an overnight loan from another bank.

federalism The division of power across the local, state, and national levels of government.

Federalist Papers A series of 85 articles written by Alexander Hamilton, James Madison, and John Jay that sought to sway public opinion toward the Federalists' position.

Federalists Those at the Constitutional Convention who favored a strong national government and a system of separated powers.

federal preemptions Impositions of national priorities on the states through national legislation that is based on the Constitution's supremacy clause.

Federal Reserve Board The group of seven presidential appointees who govern the Federal Reserve System.

Federal Reserve System An independent agency that serves as the central bank of the United States to bring stability to the nation's banking system.

fighting words Forms of expression that "by their very utterance" can incite violence. These can be regulated by the government but are often difficult to define.

filibuster A tactic used by senators to block a bill by continuing to hold the floor and speak—under the Senate rule of unlimited debate—until the bill's supporters back down.

filtering The influence on public opinion that results from journalists' and editors' decisions about which of many potential news stories to report.

fire alarm oversight A method of oversight in which members of Congress respond to complaints about the bureaucracy or problems of implementation only as they arise rather than exercising constant vigilance.

first-mover advantage The president's power to initiate treaty negotiations. Congress cannot initiate treaties and can only consider them once they have been negotiated.

fiscal federalism A form of federalism in which federal funds are allocated to the lower levels of government through transfer payments or grants.

fiscal policy Government decisions about how to influence the economy by taxing and spending.

501(c)(3) organization A tax code classification that applies to most interest groups; this designation makes donations to the group tax-deductible but limits the group's political activities.

527 organization A tax-exempt group formed primarily to influence elections through voter mobilization efforts and issue ads that do not directly endorse or oppose a candidate. Unlike political action committees, they are not subject to contribution limits and spending caps.

foreign policy Government actions that affect countries, corporations, groups, or individuals outside America's borders.

framing The influence on public opinion caused by the way a story is presented or covered, including the details, explanations, and context offered in the report.

free exercise clause Part of the First Amendment that states Congress cannot prohibit or interfere with the practice of religion.

free market An economic system based on competition among businesses without government interference.

free rider problem The incentive to benefit from others' work without making a contribution, which leads individuals in a collective action situation to refuse to work together.

free riding The practice of relying on others to contribute to a collective effort while failing to participate on one's own behalf, yet still benefiting from the group's successes.

full employment The theoretical point at which all citizens who want to be employed have a job.

full faith and credit clause Part of Article IV of the Constitution requiring that each state's laws be honored by the other states. For example, a legal marriage in one state must be recognized across state lines.

gag order An aspect of prior restraint that allows the government to prohibit the media from publishing anything related to an ongoing trial.

general election The election in which voters cast ballots for House members, senators, and (every four years) a president and vice president.

general revenue sharing (GRS) A type of grant used in the 1970s and 1980s in which the federal government provided state governments with funds to be spent at each state's discretion. These grants gave states more control over programs.

gerrymandering Attempting to use the process of redrawing district boundaries to benefit a political party, protect incumbents, or change the proportion of minority voters in a district.

go public A president's use of speeches and other public communications to appeal directly to citizens about issues the president would like the House and Senate to act on.

GOTV ("get out the vote") or the **ground game** A campaign's efforts to "get out the vote" or make sure their supporters vote on Election Day.

government The system for implementing decisions made through the political process.

grandfather clause A type of law enacted in several southern states to allow those who were permitted to vote before the Civil War, and their descendants, to bypass literacy tests and other obstacles to voting, thereby exempting whites from these tests while continuing to disenfranchise African Americans and other people of color.

grassroots lobbying A lobbying strategy that relies on participation by group members, such as a protest or a letter-writing campaign.

Great Compromise A compromise between the large and small states, proposed by Connecticut, in which Congress would have two houses: a Senate with two legislators per state and a House of Representatives in which each state's representation would be based on population (also known as the Connecticut Compromise).

Great Society The wide-ranging social agenda promoted by President Lyndon Johnson in the mid-1960s that aimed to improve Americans' quality of life through governmental social programs.

gridlock An inability to enact legislation because of partisan conflict within Congress or between Congress and the president.

gross domestic product (GDP) The value of a country's economic output taken as a whole.

hard money Donations that are used to help elect or defeat a specific candidate.

hard news Media coverage focused on facts and important issues surrounding a campaign.

hate speech Expression that is offensive or abusive, particularly in terms of race, gender, or sexual orientation. It is currently protected under the First Amendment.

head of government One role of the president, through which he or she has authority over the executive branch.

head of state One role of the president, through which he or she represents the country symbolically and politically.

hold An objection to considering a measure on the Senate floor.

horse race A description of the type of election coverage that focuses more on poll results and speculation about a likely winner than on substantive differences between the candidates.

idealism The idea that a country's foreign policy decisions are based on factors beyond self-interest, including upholding important principles or values.

ideological polarization The effect on public opinion when many citizens move away from moderate positions and toward either end of the political spectrum, identifying themselves as either liberals or conservatives.

ideology A cohesive set of ideas and beliefs used to organize and evaluate the political world.

impeachment A negative or checking power over the other branches that allows Congress to remove the president, vice president, or other "officers of the United States" (including federal judges) for abuses of power.

implied powers Powers supported by the Constitution that are not expressly stated in it.

income support Government programs that provide support to low-income Americans, such as welfare, food stamps, unemployment compensation, and the Earned Income Tax Credit.

incumbency advantage The relative infrequency with which members of Congress are defeated in their attempts for re-election.

incumbent A politician running for re-election to the office he or she currently holds.

independent agencies Government offices or organizations that provide government services and are not part of an executive department.

inflation The increase in the price of consumer goods over time.

informational theory The idea that having committees in Congress made up of experts on specific policy areas helps to ensure well-informed policy decisions.

initiative A direct vote by citizens on a policy change proposed by fellow citizens or organized groups outside government. Getting a question on the ballot typically requires collecting a set number of signatures from registered voters in support of the proposal. There is no mechanism for a national-level initiative.

inside strategies The tactics employed within Washington, D.C., by interest groups seeking to achieve their policy goals.

interest group An organization of people who share common political interests and aim to influence public policy by electioneering and lobbying.

interest group state A government in which most policy decisions are determined by the influence of interest groups.

intergovernmental organizations (IGOs) An association of sovereign states that works to protect human rights, increase living standards, and acheive policy goals throughout the world.

intermediate scrutiny The middle level of scrutiny the courts use when determining whether a law is constitutional. To pass this test, the law or policy must further an important government interest in a way that is "substantially related" to that interest. That is, the law must use means that are a close fit to the government's goal and substantially broader than is necessary to accomplish that goal.

intermediate scrutiny test The middle level of scrutiny the courts use when determining whether unequal treatment is justified by the effect of a law.

internationalism The idea that a country should be involved in the affairs of other nations, out of both self-interest and moral obligation.

International Monetary Fund A nongovernmental organization established in 1944 to help stabilize the international monetary system, improve economic growth, and aid developing nations.

investigative journalists Reporters who dig deeply into a particular topic of public concern, often targeting government failures and inefficiencies.

isolationism The idea that a country should refrain from involvement in international affairs.

issue voters People who are well informed about their own policy preferences and knowledgeable about the candidates, and who use all of this information when they decide how to vote.

Jim Crow laws State and local laws that mandated racial segregation in all public facilities in the South, many border states, and some northern communities between 1876 and 1964.

joint committees Committees that contain members of both the House and Senate but have limited authority.

judicial activism The idea that the Supreme Court should assert its interpretation of the law even if it overrules the elected executive and legislative branches of government.

judicial restraint The idea that the Supreme Court should defer to the democratically elected executive and legislative branches of government rather than contradicting existing laws.

judicial review The Supreme Court's power to strike down a law or executive branch action that it finds unconstitutional.

Judiciary Act of 1789 The law in which Congress laid out the organization of the federal judiciary. The law refined and clarified federal court jurisdiction and set the original number of justices at six. It also created the Office of the Attorney General and established the lower federal courts.

jurisdiction The sphere of a court's legal authority to hear and decide cases.

Keynesian economics The theory that governments should use economic policy, like taxing and spending, to maintain stability in the economy.

Kyoto Protocol An international agreement signed by many nations in 1997 that set limits on carbon emissions in an effort to slow global warming.

latent A group of politically like-minded people that is not represented by any interest group.

latent opinion An opinion formed on the spot, when it is needed (as distinct from a deeply held opinion that is stable over time).

legislative veto A form of oversight in which Congress overturns bureaucratic decisions.

***Lemon* test** The Supreme Court uses this test, established in *Lemon v. Kurtzman*, to determine whether a practice violates the First Amendment's establishment clause.

level of conceptualization The amount of complexity in an individual's beliefs about government and policy, and the extent to which those beliefs are consistent with each other and remain consistent over time.

liberal One side of the ideological spectrum defined by support for stronger government programs and more market regulation; generally associated with Democrats.

liberal–conservative ideology A way of describing political beliefs in terms of a position on the spectrum running from liberal to moderate to conservative.

libertarians Those who prefer very limited government and therefore tend to be conservative on issues such as welfare policy, environmental policy, and public support for education, but liberal on issues of personal liberty such as free speech, abortion, and the legalization of drugs.

limited government A political system in which the powers of the government are restricted to prevent tyranny by protecting property and individual rights.

living Constitution A way of interpreting the Constitution that takes into account evolving national attitudes and circumstances rather than the text alone.

lobbying Efforts to influence public policy through contact with public officials on behalf of an interest group.

mainstream media Media sources that predate the Internet, such as newspapers, magazines, television, and radio.

majority leader The elected head of the party holding the majority of seats in the House or Senate.

majority voting A voting system in which a candidate must win more than 50 percent of votes to win the election. If no candidate wins enough votes to take office, a runoff election is held between the top two vote-getters.

mandatory spending Expenditures that are required by law, such as the funding for Social Security.

marginal tax rate The tax rate paid on income up to some threshold. For example, in 2012 single people paid no tax on their first $8,700 in income, 15 percent on income between $8,700 and $35,350, all the way up to 35 percent on income over $388,350.

market-based solutions Reform options for social policies that are based on tax credits, flexible spending accounts, and other approaches that rely on competition in the free market.

markup One of the steps through which a bill becomes a law, in which the final wording of the bill is determined.

mass associations Interest groups that have a large number of dues-paying individuals as members.

mass media Sources that provide information to the average citizen, such as newspapers, television networks, radio stations, and websites.

mass survey A way to measure public opinion by interviewing a large sample of the population.

media conglomerates Companies that control a large number of media sources across several types of media outlets.

media effects The influence of media coverage on average citizens' opinions and actions.

Medicaid An entitlement program funded by the federal and state governments that provides health care coverage for low-income Americans who would otherwise be unable to afford heath care.

Medicare The federal heath care plan created in 1965 that provides coverage for retired Americans for hospital care (Part A), medical care (Part B), and prescription drugs (Part D).

melting pot The idea that as different racial and ethnic groups come to America, they should assimilate into American culture, leaving their native languages, customs, and traditions behind.

***Miller* test** Established in *Miller v. California*, the Supreme Court uses this three-part test to determine whether speech meets the criteria for obscenity. If so, it can be restricted by the government.

minority leader The elected head of the party holding the minority of seats in the House or Senate.

***Miranda* rights** The list of civil liberties described in the Fifth Amendment that must be read to a suspect before anything the suspect says can be used in a trial.

Missouri Compromise An agreement between pro- and antislavery groups passed by Congress in 1820 in an attempt to ease tensions by limiting the expansion of slavery while also maintaining a balance between slave states and free states.

modified rules Conditions placed on a legislative debate by the House Rules Committee allowing certain amendments to a bill while barring others.

monarchy A form of government in which power is held by a single person, or monarch, who comes to power through inheritance rather than election.

monetarist theory The idea that the amount of money in circulation (the money supply) is the primary influence on economic activity and inflation.

monetary policy Government decisions about how to influence the economy using control of the money supply and interest rates.

Monroe Doctrine The American policy initiated under President James Monroe in 1823 stating that the United States would remain neutral in conflicts between European nations, and that these nations should stop colonizing or occupying areas of North and South America.

mootness The irrelevance of a case by the time it is received by a federal court, causing the court to decline to hear the case.

most-favored-nation status A standing awarded to countries with which the United States has good trade relations, providing the lowest possible tariff rate. World Trade Organization members must give one another this preferred status.

multilateral action Foreign policy carried out by a nation in coordination with other nations or international organizations.

mutually assured destruction The idea that two nations that possess large stores of nuclear weapons—like the United States and the Soviet Union during the Cold War—

would both be annihilated in any nuclear exchange, thus making it unlikely that either country would launch a first attack.

national committee An American political party's principal organization, comprising party representatives from each state.

National Economic Council (NEC) A group of economic advisers created in 1993 to work with the president to coordinate economic policy.

National Security Council (NSC) Within the Executive Office of the President, a committee that advises the president on matters of foreign policy.

national supremacy clause Part of Article VI, Section 2, of the Constitution stating that the Constitution and the laws and treaties of the United States are the "supreme Law of the Land," meaning national laws take precedent over state laws if the two conflict.

nation building The use of a country's resources, including the military, to help create democratic institutions abroad and prevent violence in other countries.

natural rights Also known as "unalienable rights," the Declaration of Independence defines them as "Life, Liberty, and the pursuit of Happiness." The Founders believed that upholding these rights should be the government's central purpose.

necessary and proper clause Part of Article I, Section 8, of the Constitution that grants Congress the power to pass all laws related to one of its expressed powers; also known as the elastic clause.

neutral competence The idea, credited to theorist Max Weber, that suggests bureaucrats should provide expertise without the influence of elected officials, interest groups, or their own political agendas.

New Deal The set of policies proposed by President Franklin Roosevelt and enacted by Congress between 1933 and 1935 to promote economic recovery and social welfare during the Great Depression.

New Deal Coalition The assemblage of groups who aligned with and supported the Democratic Party in support of New Deal policies during the fifth party system, including African Americans, Catholics, Jewish people, union members, and white southerners.

New Jersey Plan In response to the Virginia Plan, smaller states at the Constitutional Convention proposed that each state should receive equal representation in the national legislature, regardless of size.

news cycle The time between the release of information and its publication, like the twenty-four hours between issues of a daily newspaper.

nominating convention A meeting held by each party every four years at which states' delegates select the party's presidential and vice-presidential nominees and approve the party platform.

nongovernmental organizations (NGOs) Groups operated by private institutions (rather than governments) to promote growth, economic development, and other agendas throughout the world.

notice and comment procedure A step in the rule-making process in which proposed rules are published in the Federal Register and made available for debate by the general public.

Office of Management and Budget An office within the Executive Office of the President that is responsible for creating the president's annual budget proposal to Congress, reviewing proposed rules, and other budget-related tasks.

omnibus legislation Large bills that often cover several topics and may contain extraneous, or pork-barrel, projects.

on background or **off the record** Comments a politician makes to the press on the condition that they can be reported only if they are not attributed to that politician.

open market operations The process by which the Federal Reserve System buys and sells securities to influence the money supply.

open primary A primary election in which any registered voter can participate in the contest, regardless of party affiliation.

open rules Conditions placed on a legislative debate by the House Rules Committee allowing relevant amendments to a bill.

open seat An elected position for which there is no incumbent.

oral arguments Spoken presentations made in person by the lawyers of each party to a judge or appellate court outlining the legal reasons their side should prevail.

original intent The theory that justices should surmise the intentions of the Founders when the language of the Constitution is unclear.

original jurisdiction The authority of a court to handle a case first, as in the Supreme Court's authority to initially hear disputes between two states. However, original jurisdiction for the Supreme Court is not exclusive; it may assign such a case to a lower court.

outside strategies The tactics employed outside Washington, D.C., by interest groups seeking to achieve their policy goals.

oversight Congressional efforts to make sure that laws are implemented correctly by the bureaucracy after they have been passed.

ownership society The term used to describe the social policy vision of President George W. Bush, in which citizens take responsibility for their own social welfare and the free market plays a greater role in social policy.

paradox of voting The question of why citizens vote even though their individual votes stand little chance of changing the election outcome.

parliamentary system A system of government in which legislative and executive power are closely joined. The legislature (parliament) selects the chief executive (prime minister) who forms the cabinet from members of the parliament.

party coalitions The groups that identify with a political party, usually described in demographic terms such as African American Democrats or evangelical Republicans.

party identification (party ID) A citizen's loyalty to a specific political party.

party in government The group of office-holders who belong to a specific political party and were elected as candidates of that party.

party in the electorate The group of citizens who identify with a specific political party.

party organization A specific political party's leaders and workers at the national, state, and local levels.

party platform A set of objectives outlining the party's issue positions and priorities. Candidates are not required to support their party's platform.

party principle The idea that a political party exists as an organization distinct from its elected officials or party leaders.

party system A period in which the names of the major political parties, their supporters, and the issues dividing them remain relatively stable.

party unity The extent to which members of Congress in the same party vote together on party votes.

party vote A vote in which the majority of one party opposes the position of the majority of the other party.

peak associations Interest groups whose members are businesses or other organizations rather than individuals.

penny press Newspapers sold for one cent in the 1830s, when more efficient printing presses made reduced-price newspapers available to a larger segment of the population.

picket fence federalism A more refined and realistic form of cooperative federalism in which policy makers within a particular policy area work together across the levels of government.

plaintiff The person or party who brings a case to court.

plea bargain An agreement between a plaintiff and defendant to settle a case before it goes to trial or the verdict is decided. In a civil case this usually involves an admission of guilt and an agreement on monetary damages; in a criminal case it often involves an admission of guilt in return for a reduced charge or sentence.

pluralism The idea that having a variety of parties and interests within a government will strengthen the system, ensuring that no group possesses total control.

plurality voting A voting system in which the candidate who receives the most votes within a geographic area wins the election, regardless of whether that candidate wins a majority (more than half) of the votes.

pocket veto The automatic death of a bill passed by the House and Senate when the president fails to sign the bill in the last ten days of a legislative session.

police patrol oversight A method of oversight in which members of Congress constantly monitor the bureaucracy to make sure that laws are implemented correctly.

police powers The power to enforce laws and provide for public safety.

policy agenda The set of desired policies that political leaders view as their top priorities.

policy mood The level of public support for expanding the government's role in society; whether the public wants government action on a specific issue.

political action committee (PAC) An interest group or a division of an interest group that can raise money to contribute to campaigns or to spend on ads in support of candidates. The amount a PAC can receive from each of its donors and the amount it can spend on federal electioneering are strictly limited.

political appointees People selected by an elected leader, such as the president, to hold a government position.

political business cycle Attempts by elected officials to manipulate the economy before elections by increasing economic growth and reducing unemployment and inflation, with the goal of improving evaluations of their performance in office.

political machine An unofficial patronage system within a political party that seeks to gain political power and government contracts, jobs, and other benefits for party leaders, workers, and supporters.

political socialization The process by which an individual's political opinions are shaped by other people and the surrounding culture.

politico A member of Congress who acts as a delegate on issues that constituents care about (such as immigration reform) and as a trustee on more complex or less salient issues (some foreign policy or regulatory matters).

politics The process that determines what government does.

popular vote The votes cast by citizens in an election.

population The group of people that a researcher or pollster wants to study, such as evangelicals, senior citizens, or Americans.

pork barrel Legislative appropriations that benefit specific constituents, created with the aim of helping local representatives win re-election.

positive externalities Benefits created by a public good that are shared by the primary consumer of the good and by society more generally.

power of the purse The constitutional power of Congress to raise and spend money. Congress can use this as a negative or checking power over the other branches by freezing or cutting their funding.

precedent A legal norm established in court cases that is then applied to future cases dealing with the same legal questions.

presidential approval rating The percentage of Americans who feel that the president is doing a good job in office.

president pro tempore A largely symbolic position usually held by the most senior member of the majority party in the Senate.

press conference An event at which a politician speaks to journalists and, in most cases, answers their questions afterward.

primary A ballot vote in which citizens select a party's nominee for the general election.

primary election A ballot vote in which citizens select a party's nominee for the general election.

prime time Evening hours when television viewership is at its highest and networks often schedule news programs.

priming The influence on the public's general impressions caused by positive or negative coverage of a candidate or issue.

principal–agent game The interaction between a principal (such as the president or Congress), who needs something done, and an agent (such as a bureaucrat), who is responsible for carrying out the principal's orders.

prior restraint A limit on freedom of the press that allows the government to prohibit the media from publishing certain materials.

Prisoner's Dilemma A simple two-person game that illustrates how actions that are in a player's individual self-interest may lead to outcomes that all players consider inferior.

privacy rights Liberties protected by several amendments in the Bill of Rights that shield certain personal aspects of citizens' lives from governmental interference, such as the Fourth Amendment's protection against unreasonable searches and seizures.

privatization The process of transferring the management of a government program (like Social Security) from the public sector to the private sector.

privileges and immunities clause Part of Article IV of the Constitution requiring that states must treat nonstate residents within their borders as they would treat their own residents. This was meant to promote commerce and travel between states.

problem of control A difficulty faced by elected officials in ensuring that when bureaucrats implement policies, they follow these officials' intentions but still have enough discretion to use their expertise.

progressive Taxes that require upper-income people to pay a higher tax rate than lower-income people, such as income taxes.

proportional allocation During the presidential primaries, the practice of determining the number of convention delegates allotted to each candidate based on the percentage of the popular vote cast for each candidate. All Democratic primaries and caucuses use this system, as do some states' Republican primaries and caucuses.

protectionism The idea under which some people have tried to rationalize discriminatory policies by claiming that some groups, like women or African Americans, should be denied certain rights for their own safety or well-being.

public goods Services or actions (such as protecting the environment) that, once provided to one person, become available to everyone. Government is typically needed to provide public goods because they will be under-produced by the free market.

public opinion Citizens' views on politics and government actions.

purposive benefits Satisfaction derived from the experience of working toward a desired policy goal, even if the goal is not achieved.

random sample A subsection of a population chosen to participate in a survey through a selection process in which every member of the population has an equal chance of being chosen. This kind of sampling improves the accuracy of public opinion data.

rational basis test The use of evidence to suggest that differences in the behavior of two groups can rationalize unequal treatment of these groups.

realignment A change in the size or composition of the party coalitions or in the nature of the issues that divide the parties. Realignments typically occur within an election cycle or two, but they can also occur gradually over the course of a decade or longer.

realism The idea that a country's foreign policy decisions are motivated by self-interest and the goal of gaining more power.

recess appointment Selection by the president of a person to be an ambassador or the head of a department while the Senate is not in session, thereby bypassing Senate approval. Unless approved by a subsequent Senate vote, recess appointees serve only to the end of the congressional term.

redistributive tax policies Policies, generally favored by Democratic politicians, that use taxation to attempt to create greater social equality (i.e., higher taxation of the rich to provide programs for the poor).

redistricting Redrawing the geographic boundaries of legislative districts. This happens every ten years to ensure that districts remain roughly equal in population.

red tape Excessive or unnecessarily complex regulations imposed by the bureaucracy.

referendum A direct vote by citizens on a policy change proposed by a legislature or another government body. Referenda are common in state and local elections, but there is no mechanism for a national-level referendum.

regressive Taxes that take a larger share of poor people's income than wealthy people's income, such as sales taxes and payroll taxes.

regulation A rule that allows the government to exercise control over individuals and corporations by restricting certain behaviors.

regulatory capture A situation in which bureaucrats favor the interests of the groups or corporations they are supposed to regulate at the expense of the general public.

remedial legislation National laws that address discriminatory state laws. Authority for such legislation comes from Section 5 of the Fourteenth Amendment.

republican democracy A form of government in which the interests of the people are represented through elected leaders.

republicanism As understood by James Madison and the framers, the belief that a form of government in which the interests of the people are represented through elected leaders is the best form of government.

reserved powers As defined in the Tenth Amendment, powers that are not given to the national government by the Constitution, or not prohibited to the states, are reserved by the states or the people.

reserve requirement The minimum amount of money that a bank is required to have on hand to back up its assets.

revolving door The movement of individuals from government positions to jobs with interest groups or lobbying firms, and vice versa.

ripeness A criterion that federal courts use to decide whether a case is ready to be heard. A case's ripeness is based on whether its central issue or controversy has actually taken place.

roll call vote A recorded vote on legislation; members may vote yes, no, abstain, or present.

runoff election Under a majority voting system, a second election held only if no candidate wins a majority of the votes in the first general election. Only the top two vote-getters in the first election compete in the runoff.

salience The level of familiarity with an interest group's goals among the general population.

sample Within a population, the group of people surveyed in order to gauge the whole population's opinion. Researchers use samples because it would be impossible to interview the entire population.

sampling error A calculation that describes what percentage of the people surveyed may not accurately represent the population being studied. Increasing the number of respondents lowers the sampling error.

select committees Committees in the House or Senate created to address a specific issue for one or two terms.

selective incentives Benefits that can motivate participation in a group effort because they are available only to those who participate, such as member services offered by interest groups.

selective incorporation The process through which the civil liberties granted in the Bill of Rights were applied to the states on a case-by-case basis through the Fourteenth Amendment.

senatorial courtesy A norm in the nomination of district court judges in which the president consults with his party's senators from the relevant state in choosing the nominee.

seniority The informal congressional norm of choosing the member who has served the longest on a particular committee to be the committee chair.

"separate but equal" The idea that racial segregation was acceptable as long as the separate facilities were of equal quality; supported by *Plessy v. Ferguson* and struck down by *Brown v. Board of Education*.

separation of powers The division of government power across the judicial, executive, and legislative branches.

shield laws Legislation, which exists in some states but not at the federal level, that gives reporters the right to refuse to name the sources of their information.

signing statement A document issued by the president when signing a bill into law explaining his interpretation of the law, which often differs from the interpretation of Congress, in an attempt to influence how the law will be implemented.

single-member districts An electoral system in which every elected official represents a geographically defined area, such as a state or congressional district, and each area elects one representative.

slander and **libel** Spoken false statements (slander) and written false statements (libel) that damage a person's reputation. Both can be regulated by the government but are often difficult to distinguish from permissible speech.

slant The imbalance in a story that covers one candidate or policy favorably without providing similar coverage of the other side.

social policy An area of public policy related to maintaining or enhancing the well-being of individuals.

Social Security A federal social insurance program that provides cash benefits to retirees based on payroll taxes they have paid over the course of their careers. It is a "pay as you go" program in which working Americans pay taxes to support today's retirees, with a promise that when today's workers retire, their benefits will be paid by the next generation.

soft money Contributions that can be used for voter mobilization or to promote a policy proposal or point of view as long as these efforts are not tied to supporting or opposing a particular candidate.

soft news Media coverage that aims to entertain or shock, often through sensationalized reporting or by focusing on a candidate or politician's personality.

solicitor general A presidential appointee in the Department of Justice who conducts all litigation on behalf of the federal government before the Supreme Court and supervises litigation in the federal appellate courts.

solidary benefits Satisfaction derived from the experience of working with like-minded people, even if the group's efforts do not achieve the desired impact.

sovereign power The national and state government each have some degree of authority and autonomy.

Speaker of the House The elected leader of the House of Representatives.

split ticket A ballot on which a voter selects candidates from more than one political party.

spoils system The practice of rewarding party supporters with benefits like federal government positions.

standard operating procedures Rules that lower-level bureaucrats must follow when implementing policies.

standing Legitimate justification for bringing a civil case to court.

standing committees Committees that are a permanent part of the House or Senate structure, holding more importance and authority than other committees.

state capacity The knowledge, personnel, and institutions that the government requires to effectively implement policies.

State of the Union An annual speech in which the president addresses Congress to report on the condition of the country and recommend policies.

states' rights The idea that states are entitled to a certain amount of self-government, free of federal government intervention. This became a central issue in the period leading up to the Civil War.

states' sovereign immunity Based on the Eleventh Amendment, immunity that prevents state governments from being sued by private parties in federal court unless the state consents to the suit.

statutory authority (presidential) Powers derived from laws enacted by Congress that add to the powers given to the president in the Constitution.

statutory interpretation The various methods and tests used by the courts for determining the meaning of a law and applying it to specific situations. Congress may overturn the courts' interpretation by writing a new law; thus it also engages in statutory interpretation.

straight ticket A ballot on which a voter selects candidates from only one political party.

street-level bureaucrats Agency employees who directly provide services to the public, such as those who provide job-training services.

strict construction A way of interpreting the Constitution based on its language alone.

strict scrutiny The highest level of scrutiny the courts use when determining whether a law is constitutional. To pass this test, the law or policy must be shown to serve a "compelling state interest" or goal, it must be narrowly tailored to achieve that goal, and it must be the least restrictive means of achieving the goal.

strict scrutiny test The highest level of scrutiny the courts use when determining whether unequal treatment is justified by a "compelling state interest."

substantive due process doctrine One interpretation of the due process clause of the Fourteenth Amendment; in this view the Supreme Court has the power to overturn laws that infringe on individual liberties.

substantive representation When a member of Congress represents constituents' interests and policy concerns.

supply-side economics The theory that lower tax rates will stimulate the economy by encouraging people to save, invest, and produce more goods and services.

suspension of the rules One way of moving a piece of legislation to the top of the agenda in the House: debate on the bill is limited to forty minutes, amendments are not allowed, and the bill must pass by a two-thirds vote.

symbolic speech Nonverbal expression, such as the use of signs or symbols. It benefits from many of the same constitutional protections as verbal speech.

taking the late train An interest group strategy that involves donating money to the winning candidate after an election in hopes of securing a meeting with that person when he or she takes office.

tariff A tax levied on imported and exported goods.

Temporary Assistance for Needy Families (TANF) The welfare program that replaced Aid to Families with Dependent Children (AFDC) in 1996, eliminating the entitlement status of welfare, shifting implementation of the policy to the states, and introducing several new restrictions on receiving aid. These changes led to a significant decrease in the number of welfare recipients.

Three-Fifths Compromise The states' decision during the Constitutional Convention to count each slave as three-fifths of a person in a state's population for the purposes of determining the number of House members and the distribution of taxes.

trade association An interest group composed of companies in the same business or industry (the same "trade") that lobbies for policies that benefit members of the group.

trade deficit A measure of how much more a nation imports than it exports.

Treasury Department A cabinet-level agency that is responsible for managing the federal government's revenue. It prints currency, collects taxes, and sells government bonds.

trustee A member of Congress who represents constituents' interests while also taking into account national, collective, and moral concerns that sometimes cause the member to vote against the preference of a majority of constituents.

"turkey farms" Agencies where campaign workers and donors can be appointed to reward them for their service because it is unlikely that their lack of qualifications will lead to bad policy.

unfunded mandates Federal laws that require the states to do certain things but do not provide state governments with funding to implement these policies.

unified government A situation in which one party holds a majority of seats in the House and Senate and the president is a member of that same party.

unilateral action (national) Independent acts of foreign policy undertaken by a nation without the assistance or coordination of other nations.

unilateral action (presidential) Any policy decision made and acted upon by the president and his staff without the explicit approval or consent of Congress.

unitary executive theory The idea that the vesting clause of the Constitution gives the president the authority to issue orders and policy directives that cannot be undone by Congress.

unitary government A system in which the national, centralized government holds ultimate authority. It is the most common form of government in the world.

United Nations (UN) An international organization made up of representatives from nearly every nation, with a mission to promote peace and cooperation, uphold international law, and provide humanitarian aid.

United States Trade Representative (USTR) An agency founded in 1962 to negotiate with foreign governments to create trade agreements, resolve disputes, and participate in global trade policy organizations. Treaties negotiated by the USTR must be ratified by the Senate.

vesting clause Article II, Section 1, of the Constitution, which states that "executive Power shall be vested in a President of the United States of America," making the president both the head of government and the head of state.

veto The president's rejection of a bill that has been passed by Congress. A veto can be overridden by a two-thirds vote in both the House and Senate.

Virginia Plan A plan proposed by the larger states during the Constitutional Convention that based representation in the national legislature on population. The plan also included a variety of other proposals to strengthen the national government.

voting cues Pieces of information about a candidate that are readily available, easy to interpret, and lead a citizen to decide to vote for a particular candidate.

weapons of mass destruction (WMDs) Weapons that have the potential to cause large-scale loss of life, such as nuclear bombs and chemical or biological weapons.

welfare Financial or other assistance provided to individuals by the government, usually based on need.

whip system An organization of House leaders who work to disseminate information and promote party unity in voting on legislation.

winner-take-all During the presidential primaries, the practice of assigning all of a given state's delegates to the candidate who receives the most popular votes. Some states' Republican primaries and caucuses use this system.

wire service An organization that gathers news and sells it to other media outlets. The invention of the telegraph in the early 1800s made this type of service possible.

World Bank A nongovernmental organization established in 1944 that provides financial support for economic development projects in developing nations.

World Trade Organization (WTO) An international organization created in 1995 to oversee trade agreements between nations by facilitating negotiations and handling disputes.

writ of certiorari The most common way for a case to reach the Supreme Court, in which at least four of the nine justices agree to hear a case that has reached them via an appeal from the losing party in a lower court's ruling.

yellow journalism A style of newspaper popular in the late 1800s that featured sensationalized stories, bold headlines, and illustrations to increase readership.

ENDNOTES

CHAPTER 1

1. Thomas Hobbes, *Leviathan* (1651; repr. Indianapolis, IN: Bobbs, Merrill, 1958).

2. Alexander Hamilton, James Madison, and John Jay, *The Federalist Papers*, ed. Roy P. Fairfield, 2nd ed. (1788; repr. Baltimore, MD: Johns Hopkins University Press, 1981), p. 160.

3. Hamilton, Madison, and Jay, *The Federalist Papers*, p. 18.

4. David Hume, *A Treatise of Human Nature*, ed. T. H. Green and T. H. Grose (New York: Longmans, Green, 1898), p. 301.

5. Examples include E. E. Schattschneider, *The Semisovereign People: A Realist's View of Democracy in America* (New York: Holt, Rinehart, and Winston, 1960); Larry Bartels, *Unequal Democracy: The Politics of the New Gilded Age* (Princeton, NJ: Princeton University Press, 2008); and Jeffrey A. Segal, and Howard Spaeth, *The Supreme Court and the Attitudinal Model Revisited* (New York: Cambridge University Press, 2002).

6. Morris Rosenberg, "Some Determinants of Political Apathy," *Public Opinion Quarterly* 18 (Winter 1954–55): 349–66; Jane Mansbridge, *Beyond Adversary Democracy* (New York: Basic Books, 1980); Nina Eliasoph, *Avoiding Politics: How Americans Produce Apathy in Everyday Life* (New York: Cambridge University Press, 1998); Melanie C. Green, Penny S. Visser, and Philip E. Tetlock, "Coping with Accountability Cross-Pressures: Low-Effort Evasive Tactics and High Effort Quests for Complex Compromises," *Personality and Social Psychology Bulletin* 26:11 (2000): 1380–91.

7. John R. Hibbing and Elizabeth Theiss-Morse, *Stealth Democracy: Americans' Beliefs about How Government Should Work* (New York: Cambridge University Press, 2002), p. 147. See Diana E. Hess, *Controversy in the Classroom: The Democratic Power of Discussion* (New York: Routledge, 2009), for evidence that diverse viewpoints in the classroom have important effects on discussion.

8. Donald Green, Bradley Palmquist, and Eric Schickler, *Partisan Hearts and Minds* (New Haven, CT: Yale University Press, 2004); Christopher Achen, "Political Socialization and Rational Party Identification," *Political Behavior* 24:2 (2002): 151–70.

9. Robert S. Erikson, Michael B. Mackuen, and James A. Stimson, *The Macro Polity* (New York: Cambridge University Press, 2002).

10. Pew Research Center, "Two-in-Three Critical of Bush's Relief Efforts," September 8, 2005, http://people-press.org/reports/display.php3?ReportID=255 (accessed 7/15/12).

11. Congressional Budget Office, "Current Budget Projections," www.cbo.gov/ftpdocs/108xx/doc10871/budgetprojections.pdf; The President's Budget for Fiscal Year 2011, "Total Executive Branch Civilian Full-Time Equivalent (FTE) Employees, 1981–2011," Table 17.1, www.whitehouse.gov/omb/budget/Historicals/; Department of Defense, "Military Personnel Active and Reserve Forces," www.whitehouse.gov/omb/budget/fy2011/assets/mil.pdf; Paul Light, "Fact Sheet on the New True Size of Government," Brookings Institution, September 5, 2003, www.brookings.edu/articles/2003/0905politics_light.aspx; *Federal Register*, www.gpoaccess.gov/fr/. (All accessed 7/15/12.)

12. The ranking varies somewhat from year to year and source to source. See, for example, *The CIA World Factbook*, Country Comparison: Distribution of Family Income—Gini Index: www.cia.gov/library/publications/the-world-factbook/rankorder/2172rank.html (accessed 10/19/12).

13. Linda Feldmann, "How Lines of the Culture War Have Been Redrawn," *Christian Science Monitor*, November 15, 2004, www.csmonitor.com/2004/1115/p01s04=ussc.html (accessed 10/10/07).

14. For details, see Paul R. Abramson, John H. Aldrich, and David W. Rohde, *Change and Continuity in the 2008 and 2010 Elections* (Washington, DC: Congressional Quarterly Press, 2011).

15. Samuel Huntington, *Who Are We? The Challenges to America's National Identity* (New York: Simon and Schuster, 2004); Arthur M. Schlesinger Jr., *The Disuniting of America: Reflections on a Multicultural Society* (New York: Whittle Direct Books, 1991).

16. Charles Taylor, *Multiculturalism: Examining the Politics of Recognition*, ed. Amy Gutmann, with commentary by K. Anthony Appiah, Jürgen Habermas, Steven C. Rockefeller, Michael Walzer, and Susan Wolf (Princeton, NJ: Princeton University Press, 1994); Will Kymlicka, *Multicultural Citizenship: A Liberal Theory of Minority Rights* (New York: Oxford University Press, 1995).

17. Morris P. Fiorina, with Samuel J. Abrams and Jeremy C. Pope, *Culture War: The Myth of a Polarized America*, 2nd ed. (New York: Pearson Longman, 2006), pp. 46–47.

18. Fiorina, *Culture War*.

What Do Political Scientists Do?

a. Fenno's most famous book is *Home Style: U. S. House Members in Their Districts* (Boston: Little, Brown, 1978).

CHAPTER 2

1. Jim DeMint, "Constitution of No," *National Review Online*, June 8, 2010, www.nationalreview.com/articles/229909/constitution-no/jim-demint?pg=2 (accessed 10/16/11).

2. Jennifer Steinhauer, "Constitution Has Its Day (More or Less) in House," *New York Times*, January 6, 2011, www.nytimes.com/2011/01/07/us/politics/07constitution.html (accessed 10/14/11).

3. Mark Trumbull, "On Constitution Day, Tea Party and Foes Duel over Our Founding Document," *Christian Science Monitor*, September 17, 2011, www.csmonitor.com/USA/Politics/2011/0917/On-Constitution-Day-tea-party-and-foes-duel-over-our-founding-document (accessed 10/16/11).

4. For a good overview of the political thought of the American revolution see Gordon S. Wood, *The Radicalism of the American Revolution* (New York: Vintage Books, 1993). For an excellent summary of the history, see Wood's *The American Revolution: A History* (New York: Modern Library, 2003).

5. David McCullough, *John Adams* (New York: Simon and Schuster, 2001), 90.

6. A classic text on the Founding period is Gordon S. Wood, *The Creation of the American Republic* (New York: Norton, 1969).

7. J. W. Peltason, *Corwin and Peltason's Understanding the Constitution*, 7th ed. (Hinsdale, IL: Dryden Press, 1976), p. 12.

8. The pamphlet sold 120,000 copies within a few months of publication, a figure that would leave the Harry Potter books in the dust in terms of the proportion of the literate public that purchased the book.

9. Thomas Hobbes, *Leviathan* (1651; repr. Indianapolis, IN: Bobbs, Merrill, 1958); John Locke, *Second Treatise of Government* (1690; repr. Indianapolis, IN: Bobbs, Merrill, 1952).

10. Richard M. Pious, *The American Presidency* (New York: Basic Books, 1979), p. 18.

11. Charles A. Beard, *An Economic Interpretation of the Constitution of the United States* (New York: Macmillan, 1913).

12. Forrest McDonald, *We the People: The Economic Origins of the Constitution* (Chicago: University of Chicago Press, 1958); Robert E. Brown, *Charles Beard and the Constitution* (New York: Norton, 1956).

13. David Brian Robertson, *The Constitution and America's Destiny* (New York: Cambridge University Press, 2005), p. 4.

14. Robert A. Dahl, *How Democratic Is the American Constitution?* (New Haven, CT: Yale University Press, 2001), p. 12.

15. Alexander Hamilton, John Jay, and James Madison, *The Federalist Papers*, ed. Roy P. Fairfield, 2nd ed. (1788; repr. Baltimore, MD: Johns Hopkins University Press, 1981), p. 22.

16. Many delegates probably assumed that the electors would reflect the wishes of the voters in their states, but there is no clear indication of this in Madison's notes. (Hamilton makes this argument in *The Federalist Papers*.) Until the 1820s, many electors were directly chosen by state legislatures rather than by the people. In the first presidential election, George Washington won the unanimous support of the electors, but in only five states were the electors chosen by the people.

17. Dahl, *How Democratic Is the American Constitution?* p. 67.

18. The actual language of the section avoids the term "slavery." Instead it says, "The Migration or Importation of such Persons as any of the States now existing shall think proper to admit, shall not be prohibited by Congress prior to the Year one thousand eight hundred and eight." The ban on the importation of slaves was implemented on the earliest possible date, January 1, 1808.

19. Patrick Henry, "Shall Liberty or Empire Be Sought?" in *America, 1761–1837*, vol. VIII of *The World's Famous Orations*, ed. William Jennings Bryan (New York: Funk and Wagnalls, 1906), pp. 73, 76.

20. Thomas Jefferson to John Adams, 1787, in *The Writings of Thomas Jefferson*, Memorial Edition, ed. Andrew A. Lipscomb and Albert Ellery Bergh (Washington, DC: Thomas Jefferson Memorial Association of the United States, 1903), vol. 6, p. 370.

21. Louis Fisher, *Constitutional Conflicts between Congress and the President* (Lawrence: University Press of Kansas, 1997), p. 244.

22. This ban prompted the White House to seek covert channels through which to support the Contras, which led to the ill-conceived secret arms deal with Iran (a nation that was under a complete U.S. trade embargo at the time) in which the money from the arms sales was funneled to the Contras.

23. Charlie Savage, "Obama's War on Terror May Resemble Bush's in Some Areas," *New York Times*, February 17, 2009, p. A1.

24. Peter M. Shane, *Madison's Nightmare: How Executive Power Threatens American Democracy* (Chicago: University of Chicago Press, 2009).

25. Deroy Murdock, "Ignorance and American Liberty," *National Review Online*, July 3, 2000, www.nationalreview .com (accessed 11/15/07).

26. Thomas Jefferson to James Madison, in *Thomas Jefferson on Democracy*, ed. Saul Padover (New York: Mentor Books, 1953), p. 153.

27. Cass R. Sunstein, "Making Amends," *The New Republic*, March 3, 1997, p. 42.

28. *Furman v. Georgia*, 408 U.S. 238 (1972).

What Do Political Scientists Do?

a. Philip B. Kurland and Ralph Lerner, eds., *The Founders' Constitution*, vol. 2, Preamble, Document 7 (Chicago: University of Chicago Press, 1987).

b. Bruce Ackerman, "The Living Constitution," p. 1752.

c. Keith E. Whittington, "Originalism within the Living Constitution," American Constitution Society for Law and Policy, July 2007.

d. Akhil Reed Amar, *The Bill of Rights* (New Haven, CT: Yale University Press, 1998).

e. Jeffrey Segal and Harold Spaeth, *The Supreme Court and The Attitudinal Model* (New York: Cambridge University Press, 1993).

In Comparison

a. "EU Voting Row Explained," BBC News, December 13, 2003, http://news.bbc.co.uk/1/hi/world/europe/3309773.stm; "From Jefferson's Brevity to Convolutions of Bureaucrats," *The Observer*, December 14, 2003, www.guardian.co.uk/eu/ story/ 0,7369,1106851,00.html.

You Decide

a. Douglas Linder, "What in the Constitution Cannot Be Amended?" *Arizona Law Review* 23 (1981): 717–33.

b. Kathleen M. Sullivan, "What's Wrong with Constitutional Amendments?" in *New Federalist Papers*, ed. Alan Brinkley, Nelson W. Polsby, and Kathleen M. Sullivan (New York: Norton, 1997), p. 63.

c. Jamin B. Raskin, "A Right to Vote," *The American Prospect*, August 27, 2001, pp. 10–12.

CHAPTER 3

1. The full title of the law is the Patient Protection and Affordable Care Act (PPACA).

2. Ashby Jones, "Conservative Duo Tests Health Law," *Wall Street Journal*, September 13, 2010, http://online.wsj.com/ article/SB10001424052748703897204575487963449135280.html#U301253590305VF (accessed 11/12/11).

3. Tenth Amendment Center, "Ohio Votes to Nullify Insurance Mandates," November 8, 2011. www.tenthamendmentcenter .com/2011/11/08/ohio-votes-to-nullify-insurance -mandates/ (accessed 11/12/11).

4. *State of Florida, et al. v. U.S. Department of Health and Human Services, et al.*, Petition for Writ of Certiorari to the United States Court of Appeals for the Eleventh Circuit, September 27, 2011, www.azgovernor.gov/dms/upload/ PR_092811_Petition.pdf (accessed 10/19/12).

5. State Health Facts.org, Health Care and Coverage, www .statehealthfacts.org/comparecat.jsp?cat=3 (accessed 11/12/11).

6. "Obama's Remarks at the Health Care Bill Signing," *New York Times*, March 23, 2010, www.nytimes.com/2010/03/ 24/us/politics/24health-text.html?pagewanted=3 (accessed 11/10/11).

7. See www.cisstat.com/eng/cis.htm for more information on the Commonwealth of Independent States.

8. Pam Belluck, "Massachusetts Gay Marriage to Remain Legal," *New York Times*, June 14, 2007, www.nytimes .com/2007/06/15/us/15gay.html (accessed 10/18/07). The state supreme court decision that required the state legislature to recognize gay marriage was *Goodridge v. Dept. of Public Health*, 798 N.E.2d 941 (Mass. 2003).

9. *Nancy Wilson and Paula Schoenwether v. Richard Lake and John Ashcroft* (2005) No. 8:04-cv-1680-T-30TBM.

10. "The Supreme Court; Excerpts from Court's Welfare Ruling and Rehnquist's Dissent," *New York Times*, May 18, 1999, p. A20.

11. The Sedition Act was passed within a month of three other laws—the Naturalization Act, the Alien Friends Act, and the Alien Enemies Act—that were all aimed at strengthening the hand of the national government in its naval war against France. Collectively, these four laws are often referred to as the Alien and Sedition Acts. But for our purposes here, the relevant law is the Sedition Act.

12. Stanley Elkins and Eric McKitrick, *The Age of Federalism* (New York: Oxford University Press, 1993).

13. John W. Wright, ed., *New York Times 2000 Almanac* (New York: Penguin Reference, 1999), p. 165. Estimates from various online sources are quite a bit higher, averaging about 620,000 deaths.

14. *Mayor of City of New York v. Miln*, 36 U.S. (11 Pet.) 102 (1837).

15. *Cooley v. Board of Wardens of the Port of Philadelphia*, 53 U.S. 229 (1851).

16. Slaughterhouse Cases, 83 U.S. 36 (1873). See Ronald M. Labbe and Jonathan Lurie, *The Slaughterhouse Cases: Regulation, Reconstruction, and the Fourteenth Amendment* (Lawrence: University Press of Kansas, 2003).

17. Civil Rights Cases, 109 U.S. 3 (1883).

18. *United States v. E.C. Knight Co.*, 156 U.S. 1 (1895).

19. *Hammer v. Dagenhart*, 247 U.S. 251 (1918).

20. *Lochner v. New York*, 198 U.S. 45 (1905).

21. *Schechter Poultry Corporation v. United States* (1935).

22. Four key cases are *West Coast Hotel Company v. Parrish* (1937), *Wright v. Vinton Branch* (1937), *Virginia Railway*

Company v. System Federation (1937), and *National Labor Relations Board v. Jones & Laughlin Steel Corporation* (1937).

23. Martin Grodzins, *The American System* (New York: Rand McNally, 1966).

24. John Shannon, "Middle Class Votes Bring a New Balance to Federalism," February 1, 1997, policy paper 10 from the Urban Institute series "The Future of the Public Sector," www.urban.org/url.cfm?ID=307051 (accessed 1/3/08).

25. Max Sawicky, "An Idea Whose Time Has Returned: Anti-Recession Fiscal Assistance for State and Local Governments," briefing paper (Washington, DC: Economic Policy Institute, October, 2001).

26. This number varies depending on which grants are counted. Tim Conlan finds 15 block grants in this period. See his *From New Federalism to Devolution* (Washington, DC: Brookings Institution, 1998).

27. *Brown v. Board of Education,* 347 U.S. 483 (1954); *Swann v. Charlotte-Mecklenburg Board of Education,* 402 U.S. 1 (1971).

28. *Baker v. Carr,* 369 U.S. 186 (1962); *Reynolds v. Sims,* 377 U.S. 533 (1964); and *Wesberry v. Sanders,* 376 U.S. 1 (1964). Martha Derthick, *Keeping the Compound Republic: Essays in American Federalism* (Washington, DC: Brookings Institution, 2001).

29. *Miranda v. Arizona,* 384 U.S. 436 (1966); *Mapp v. Ohio,* 367 U.S. 643 (1961).

30. "Impact of Unfunded Mandates and Cost Shifts on U.S. Cities," U.S Conference of Mayors, June 2005, www.usmayors.org (accessed 11/13/11).

31. John Kincaid, "Governing the American States," in *Developments in American Politics,* ed. Gillian Peele, Christopher J. Bailey, Bruce Cain, and Guy Peters (Chatham, NJ: Chatham House, 1995), pp. 208–16.

32. Paul Posner, "The Politics of Coercive Federalism in the Bush Era," *Publius* 37:3 (May 2007): 390–412.

33. Barry Rabe, "Environmental Policy and the Bush Era: The Collision between the Administrative Presidency and State Experimentation," *Publius* 37:3 (May 2007): 413–31.

34. Kirk Johnson, "States' Rights Is Rallying Cry for Lawmakers," *New York Times,* March 17, 2010, p. A1. The Supreme Court endorsed this reassertion of state power in an important case concerning immigration policy. In *Chamber of Commerce v. Whiting* 131 S.Ct. 1968 (2011), the Court held that federal immigration law did not preempt an Arizona law that required implementation of federal law in a manner that may have been more aggressive than Congress intended.

35. From a review of Michael S. Greve, *Real Federalism: Why It Matters, How It Could Happen* (Washington, DC: American Enterprise Institute Press, 1999), www.federalismproject.org/publications/books (accessed 10/10/07).

36. Cass Sunstein, *Designing Democracy: What Constitutions Do* (New York: Oxford University Press, 2001), p. 107.

37. J. W. Peltason, *Corwin and Peltason's Understanding the Constitution,* 7th ed. (Hinsdale, IL: Dryden Press, 1976), p. 177.

38. *Garcia v. San Antonio Metropolitan Transit Authority,* 469 U.S. 528 (1985).

39. *Gregory v. Ashcroft,* 501 U.S. 452 (1991).

40. *New York v. United States* (1992) 112 S. Ct. at 2431–32. For a detailed discussion of these issues, see "Constitution of the United States: Analysis and Interpretation" (Washington, DC: Government Printing Office, 2006), www.gpo.gov/fdsys/pkg/GPO-CONAN-2006/pdf/GPO-CONAN-2006.pdf (accessed 10/19/12).

41. *Printz v. United States,* 521 U.S. 898 (1997).

42. *Bond. v. United States,* S.C. 09-1227 (2011).

43. *City of Boerne v. Flores,* 521 U.S. 507 (1997), 520.

44. *Kimel et al. v. Florida Board of Regents,* 528 U.S. 62 (2000).

45. *Alabama v. Garrett,* 531 U.S. 356 (2001).

46. *Tennessee v. Lane,* 541 U.S. 509 (2004).

47. *Nevada Department of Human Resources v. Hibbs,* 538 U.S. 721 (2003).

48. *United States v. Lopez,* 514 U.S. 549 (1995).

49. *United States v. Morrison,* 529 U.S. 598 (2000).

50. *U.S. Term Limits, Inc. v. Thornton,* 514 U.S. 779 (1995).

51. *Romer v. Evans,* 517 U.S. 620 (1996).

52. *Atkins v. Virginia,* 536 U.S. 304 (2002); *Roper v. Simmons,* 543 U.S. 551 (2005).

53. *Gonzales v. Raich,* 545 U.S. 1 (2005).

54. *National Federation of Independent Business et al. v. Sebelius,* 567 U.S. _____ (2012).

55. Ibid., p. 51.

56. Jonathan Turley, "It's Not the Cannabis, It's the Constitution," *Los Angeles Times,* August 5, 2002, Metro section, part 2, p. 11.

57. American Society of Civil Engineers, "Report Card for America's Infrastructure: 2009," www.infrastructurereportcard.org/, accessed November 14, 2011.

58. From a review of Greve, *Real Federalism.*

59. Martha Derthick, *Keeping the Compound Republic: Essays in American Federalism* (Washington, DC: Brookings Institution, 2001), pp. 9–32.

What Do Political Scientists Do?

a. *New State Ice Co. v. Liebmann,* 285 U.S. 262 (1932).

b. Charles R. Shipan and Craig Volden, "The Mechanisms of Policy Diffusion," *American Journal of Political Science* 52:4 (October 2008): 840–57.

In Comparison

a. Jonathan Rodden, "The Dilemma of Fiscal Federalism: Grants and Fiscal Performance around the World," *American Journal of Political Science* 46:3 (July 2002): 670–87.

b. Alfred Stepan, "Federalism and Democracy: Beyond the U.S. Model," *Journal of Democracy* 10:4 (1999): 19–34.

c. Spain has a unitary government, but it is often referred to as a "de facto federation" because it would be politically impossible for the central government to revoke the autonomy of Galicia, Catalonia, or the Basque Country.

d. David Vogel, Michael Toffel, Diahanna Post, and Nazli Uludere Aragon, "Environmental Federalism in the European Union and the United States," in Frank Wijen, Kees Zoeteman, Jan Pieters, Paul van Seters, *A Handbook of Globalisation and Environmental Policy: National Government Interventions in a Global Arena*, 2nd ed. (Northhampton, MA: Edward Elgar, 2012), pp. 321–61.

CHAPTER 4

1. About the Westboro Baptist Church, www.godhatesfags.com/wbcinfo/aboutwbc.html (accessed 12/2/11). The WBC is unaffiliated with the mainstream Baptist Church and has only about 40 members who are mostly relatives of the founder, Fred Phelps. According to the Church's web site, the WBC has held more than 47,000 anti-gay demonstrations since 1991.

2. Timothy J. Nieman, Dean H. Dusinberre, Lawrence M. Maher, "Brief for the Veterans of Foreign Wars as *Amicus Curiae* in Support of Petitioner," U.S. Supreme Court, *Snyder v. Phelps*, May 28, 2010, p. 4.

3. *Snyder v. Phelps*, U.S. Supreme Court slip. op. 09-751 (2011).

4. *Snyder v. Phelps*, Alito dissent.

5. *Arar v. Ashcroft et al.*, 2006 WL 346439 (E.D.N.Y.). The case was also dismissed because Arar, a Canadian citizen, did not have standing to sue the U.S. government. Supporters of this decision (and the practice more generally) say that it is an essential part of the war on terror and that the enemy combatants who are arrested have no legal rights. Opponents say that the practice violates international law and our own standards of decency; furthermore, torture almost never produces useful information because people will say anything to get the torture to stop.

6. *State v. Massey et al.*, Supreme Court of North Carolina, 51 S.E.2d 179 (1949). The case was appealed to the Supreme Court, but the Court declined to hear the case, which means that the state decision stands (*Bunn v. North Carolina*, 336 U.S. 942 [1949]).

7. *Pennsylvania v. Miller*, Pennsylvania Court of Common Pleas, WL 31426193 (2002). However, supreme courts in Minnesota, Wisconsin, and several other states have decided that requiring the Amish to use orange SMV triangles violates their free exercise of religion.

8. *Wisconsin v. Yoder*, 403 U.S. 205 (1972).

9. *Church of Lukumi Babalu Aye v. City of Hialeah*, 508 U.S. 520 (1993).

10. Jeffrey Rosen, "Lemon Law," *New Republic*, March 29, 1993, p. 17.

11. Max Farrand, ed., *The Records of the Federal Convention of 1787*, rev. ed. (New Haven, CT: Yale University Press, 1937), pp. 587–88, 617–18.

12. *The Papers of Thomas Jefferson*, ed. J. Boyd (Princeton, NJ: Princeton University Press, 1958), pp. 557–83, cited in Lester S. Jayson., ed., *The Constitution of the United States of America: Analysis and Interpretation* (Washington, DC: U.S. Government Printing Office, 1973), p. 900.

13. Ralph Ketcham, *The Anti-Federalist Papers and the Constitutional Convention Debates* (New York: Signet Classic, Penguin Putnam, 2003), p. 247.

14. The two that were not ratified by the states were a complicated amendment on congressional apportionment and the pay raise amendment discussed in note 29.

15. 1 Annals of Congress 755 (August 17, 1789), cited in Lester S. Jayson, *The Constitution of the United States of America* (Washington, D.C.: U.S. Government Printing Office, 1973), p. 898.

16. Henry J. Abraham and Barbara A. Perry, *Freedom and the Court: Civil Rights and Civil Liberties in the United States*, 8th ed. (Lawrence: University Press of Kansas, 2003), p. 34.

17. *Barron v. Baltimore*, 32 U.S. 243 (1833), 250.

18. There is an intense scholarly debate on whether the authors of the Fourteenth Amendment intended for it to apply the Bill of Rights to the states. The strongest argument against this position is Raoul Berger's *The Fourteenth Amendment and the Bill of Rights* (1989) and a good book in support is Amar's *The Bill of Rights* (1998).

19. *The Slaughterhouse Cases*, 83 U.S. 36 (1873). The plaintiffs also made a Thirteenth Amendment claim (that the monopoly forced them to work in "involuntary servitude") and a "due process" claim, but both of those were rejected by the Court as well. The Court focused on the "privileges and immunities" argument and the idea of dual citizenship.

20. Abraham and Perry, *Freedom and the Court*, p. 51.

21. *Chicago, Burlington, and Quincy Railroad v. Chicago*, 166 U.S. 226 (1897).

22. *Twining v. New Jersey*, 211 U.S. 78, 98 (1908).

23. The exceptions are the establishment clause of the First Amendment and the Sixth Amendment right to a public trial. *Wolf v. Colorado* also came between the two periods of increased activity, but it only partially applied the Fourth Amendment's prohibition against unreasonable searches and seizures. The Court said that states may not engage in such searches, but then allowed the state to use evidence gathered in an "unreasonable" search. It wasn't until *Mapp v. Ohio* in 1961 that the Court ruled that illegally obtained evidence could not be used in a trial, thus giving the incorporation of the Fourth Amendment some teeth.

24. *Palko v. Connecticut*, 302 U.S. 319 (1937).

25. Abraham and Perry, *Freedom and the Court*, p. 65.

26. *Police Department of Chicago v. Mosley*, 408 U.S. 92 (1972).

27. *United States v. O'Brien,* 391 U.S. 367 (1968); *Ladue v. Gilleo,* 512 U.S. 43 (1994).

28. *Schenk v. United States,* 249 U.S. 47 (1919), 52.

29. Alan Dershowitz, *Shouting Fire: Civil Liberties in a Turbulent Age* (New York: Little, Brown, 2002).

30. *Debs v. United States,* 249 U.S. 211 (1919); *Frohwerk v. United States,* 249 U.S. 204 (1919).

31. *Abrams v. United States,* 250 U.S. 616 (1919), 630–31.

32. *Dennis v. United States,* 341 U.S. 494 (1951).

33. *Brandenburg v. Ohio,* 395 U.S. 444 (1969).

34. *Morse v. Frederick,* 127 S. Ct. 2618 (2007).

35. *Smith v. Goguen,* 415 U.S. 566 (1974).

36. *Tinker v. Des Moines School District,* 393 U.S. 503 (1969).

37. *Spence v. Washington,* 418 U.S. 405 (1974).

38. *Spence v. Washington,* 409–410.

39. *Texas v. Johnson,* 491 U.S. 397 (1989).

40. *United States v. Eichman,* 496 U.S. 310 (1990).

41. *United States v. O'Brien,* 391 U.S. 367, 376 (1968).

42. *Buckley v. Valeo,* 424 U.S. 1 (1976).

43. *Davis v. Federal Election Commission,* 128 S. Ct. 2749 (2008).

44. *McConnell v. Federal Election Commission,* 540 U.S. 93 (2003).

45. *Board of Regents of the University of Wisconsin System et al., Petitioners v. Scott Harold Southworth et al.,* 529 U.S. 217 (2000).

46. Kermit L. Hall, "Free Speech on Public College Campuses: Overview," www.firstamendmentcenter.org/speech/pubcollege/overview.aspx (accessed 2/10/08).

47. Carolyn J. Palmer, Sophie W. Penney, Donald D. Gehring, and Jan A. Neiger, "Hate Speech and Hate Crimes: Campus Conduct Codes and Supreme Court Rulings," *National Association of Student Personnel Administrators Journal* 34:2 (1997), http://publications.naspa.org/naspajournal/vol34/iss2/art4 (accessed 12/18/07).

48. *City of St. Paul v. RAV,* 505 U.S. 377 (1992).

49. *Virginia v. Black,* 538 U.S. 343 (2003).

50. *De Jonge v. State of Oregon,* 299 U.S. 353 (1937).

51. *Edwards v. South Carolina,* 372 U.S. 229 (1963).

52. The Supreme Court declined to review the case in *Smith v. Collin,* 439 U.S. 916 (1978), which meant that the lower court rulings stood (447 F.Supp. 676 [1978], 578 F.2d 1197 [1978]). See Donald A. Downs, *Nazis in Skokie: Freedom, Community and the First Amendment* (Notre Dame, IN: University of Notre Dame Press, 1985), for an excellent analysis of this important case.

53. *Forsyth County v. Nationalist Movement,* 505 U.S. 123 (1992).

54. *Frisby et al. v. Schultz et al.,* 487 U.S. 474 (1988).

55. *Near v. Minnesota,* 283 U.S. 697 (1931), 719–20.

56. *New York Times Co. v. United States,* 403 U.S. 713 (1971).

57. *New York Times v. United States,* 403 U.S. 713 (1971).

58. *Nebraska Press Assn. v. Stuart,* 427 U.S. 539 (1976), 556–62. See Abraham and Perry, *Freedom and the Court,* pp. 209–10, for a discussion of the two cases that reversed and then reinstated the standard of allowing press coverage of trials except in exceptional cases.

59. Douglas Lee, "Gag Orders," www.firstamendmentcenter.org/Press/topic.aspx?topic=gag_orders (accessed 2/10/08).

60. *Chaplinsky v. State of New Hampshire,* 315 U.S. 568 (1942).

61. *Chaplinsky v. State of New Hampshire.*

62. *New York Times v. Sullivan,* 376 U.S. 254 (1964), cited in Abraham and Perry, *Freedom and the Court,* p. 193.

63. Hustler *v. Falwell,* 485 U.S. 46 (1988).

64. *Valentine v. Chrestensen,* 316 U.S. 52 (1942).

65. *Virginia State Board of Pharmacy v. Virginia Citizens Consumer Council, Inc.,* 425 U.S. 748 (1976); *City of Cincinnati v. Discovery Network, Inc. et al.,* 507 U.S. 410 (1993).

66. *Lorillard Tobacco v. Reilly,* 533 U.S. 525 (2001).

67. In 1996, Congress passed the Child Pornography Prevention Act. This law makes the possession, production, or distribution of child pornography a criminal offense punishable with up to 15 years in jail and a fine. However, two parts of the law were struck down by the Court for being "overbroad and unconstitutional." *Ashcroft v. Free Speech Coalition,* 353 U.S. 234 (2002).

68. *Jacobellis v. Ohio,* 378 U.S. 184, 197 (1964).

69. *Miller v. California,* 413 U.S. 15 (1973).

70. *Reno et al. v. American Civil Liberties Union et al.,* 521 U.S. 844 (1997).

71. *Ashcroft v. American Civil Liberties Union,* 535 U.S. 564 (2004).

72. *Federal Communications Commission v. Pacifica Foundation,* 438 U.S. 726 (1978).

73. *Federal Communications Commission et al. v. Fox Television Stations,* 556 U.S. 502 (2009).

74. *Federal Communications Commission and United States v. CBS Corporation,* 556 U.S. 1218 (2009).

75. *Federal Communications Commission v. Fox Television Stations* 567 U.S. ____ (2012), *Federal Communications Commission v. CBS Corporation,* no. 11–1240 (2012), writ of certiorari denied.

76. *United States v. Stevens,* 559 U.S.___, 130 S.Ct. 1577 (2010).

77. James Hudson, " 'A Wall of Separation,' " *Library of Congress Information Bulletin* 57:6 (June 1998), www.loc.gov/loc/lcib/9806/danbury.html (accessed 3/3/08).

78. Abraham and Perry, *Freedom and the Court,* p. 300.

79. *Engle v. Vitale,* 370 U.S. 421 (1962).

80. *Wallace v. Jaffree,* 482 U.S. 38 (1985).

81. *Lee v. Weisman,* 505 U.S. 577 (1992); *Sante Fe Independent School District v. Doe,* 530 U.S. 290 (2000).

82. *Marsh v. Chambers,* 463 U.S. 783 (1983); *Jones v. Clear Creek Independent School,* 61 LW 3819 (1993).

83. *Lemon v. Kurtzman,* 403 U.S. 602 (1971).

84. *Lynch v. Donnelly,* 465 U.S. 668 (1984), 672–73.

85. Jeffrey Rosen, "Big Ten," *New Republic,* March 14, 2004, p. 11.

86. *Van Orden v. Perry*, 03-1500 (2005); *McCreary County et al. v. American Civil Liberties Union of Kentucky*, 03-1693 (2005).

87. *Zelman v. Simmons-Harris*, 536 U.S. 639 (2002).

88. *Arizona Christian School Tuition Organization v. Winn*, U.S. Supreme Court slip. op. 09-987 and 09-991 (2011).

89. *Mitchell v. Helms*, 530 U.S. 793 (2000).

90. *Zobrest v. Catalina School District*, 509 U.S. 1 (1993). A similar decision in 1997 allowed a public school teacher to teach in a special program in a parochial school, *Agostini v. Felton*, 521 U.S. 203 (1997).

91. *Rosenberger v. University of Virginia*, 515 U.S. 819 (1995).

92. *Minersville School District v. Gobitis*, 310 U.S. 586 (1940).

93. *West Virginia Board of Education v. Barnette*, 319 U.S. 624 (1943), 642.

94. We will not cite all the cases here. See Abraham and Perry, *Freedom and the Court*, chap. 6, for a summary of cases on this topic, especially Tables 6.1 and 6.2.

95. *Christian Legal Society v. Martinez*, U.S. Supreme Court, slip. op. 08-1371, p. 6 (2010).

96. *Employment Division, Department of Human Resources of Oregon v. Smith*, 494 U.S. 872 (1990), 878–80. This case is often erroneously reported as having banned the religious use of peyote. In fact, the Court said, "Although it is constitutionally permissible to exempt sacramental peyote use from the operation of drug laws, it is not constitutionally required."

97. *City of Boerne v. Flores*, 521 U.S. 527 (1997).

98. The court case was *Cutter v. Wilkinson*, No. 03-9877 (2005). See Linda Greenhouse, "Supreme Court Rules in Ohio Prison Case," *New York Times*, June 1, 2005, for a discussion of the broader debate.

99. *Gonzales v. O Centro Espirita Beneficiente Uniao Do Vegetal (UDV) et al.*, 546 U.S. 418 (2006). The Sherbert test comes from *Sherbert v. Verner*, 374 U.S. 398 (1963).

100. Edward Walsh, "U.S. Argues for Wider Gun Rights; Supreme Court Filing Reverses Past Policy," *Washington Post*, May 8, 2002, p. A1. For a lengthy memo from the attorney general that explores the individual rights argument, see www.justice.gov/olc/secondamendment2.pdf (accessed 3/22/2012).

101. *District of Columbia v. Heller*, 554 U.S. 290 (2008).

102. *McDonald v. Chicago* 08-1521 (2010).

103. Robert J. Spitzer, *The Politics of Gun Control* (Chatham, NJ: Chatham House, 1995). Also see www.bradycenter.org/cases for a complete list of the cases (accessed 8/21/12). The two cases recognizing the individual right to bear arms were *United States v. Timothy Joe Emerson*, 46 F. Supp. 2d 598 (1999), and the DC Circuit Court case that was appealed in the landmark ruling *Parker v. District of Columbia*, 478 F.3d 370 (DC Cir. 2007).

104. Legal Community against Violence, "Post *Heller* Litigation Summary," November 8, 2011, www.lcav.org/content/post-heller_summary.pdf (accessed 12/5/11).

105. *Safford United School District No. 1 et al. v. Redding*, 557 U.S. 364 (2009).

106. See Abraham and Perry, *Freedom and the Court*, chap. 4, for a discussion of these cases. The most recent case is *Kentucky v. King* 563 U.S. ___ (2011).

107. *Florence v. County of Burlington*, U.S. 10–945 (2012).

108. *United States v. Jones*, 565 U.S. ___ (2012).

109. *Mapp v. Ohio*, 367 U.S. 643 (1961).

110. *United States v. Calandra*, 414 U.S. 338 (1974).

111. *Illinois v. Gates*, 462 U.S. 213 (1983).

112. *Herring v. United States*, 555 U.S. ___ (2009).

113. *Murray v. United States*, 487 U.S. 533 (1988).

114. *Vernonia School District v. Acton*, 515 U.S. 646 (1995); *Board of Education of Pottawatomie County v. Earls*, 536 U.S. 832 (2002).

115. Sharon L. Larson, Joe Eyerman, Misty S. Foster, and Joseph C. Gfroer, "Worker Substance Use and Workplace Policies and Programs," June 2007, Substance Abuse and Mental Health Services Administration, www.oas.samhsa.gov/work2k7/work.pdf (accessed 3/3/08).

116. *Chandler v. Miller*, 520 U.S. 305 (1997).

117. Leslie Cauley, "NSA Has Massive Database of Americans' Phone Calls," *USA Today*, May 11, 2006, p. 1.

118. Lorraine Woellert and Dawn Kopecki, "The Snooping Goes beyond Phone Calls," *Business Week*, May 29, 2006, p. 38; "Data Mining: Federal Efforts Cover a Wide Range of Uses," GAO Report 04-548, May 2004, www.gao.gov/new.items/d04548.pdf (accessed 8/21/12).

119. Eric Lichtblau and James Risen, "Officials Say U.S. Wiretaps Exceeded Law," *New York Times*, April 16, 2009.

120. *Miranda v. Arizona*, 384 U.S. 436 (1966).

121. *New York v. Quarles*, 467 U.S. 649 (1984).

122. *Maryland v. Shatzer*, No. 08-680 (2010).

123. *Berghuis v. Thompkins*, slip op. 08-1470 (2010).

124. *Dickerson v. United States*, 530 U.S. 428 (2000).

125. *Missouri v. Seibert*, 542 U.S. 600 (2004).

126. *Benton v. Maryland*, 395 U.S. 784 (1969).

127. *Lucas v. South Carolina Coastal Council*, 505 U.S. 1003 (1992).

128. The dissenters' argument was that when the plaintiff became the owner, the law was already in effect so the market value of the land would already be lower because the wetlands could not be developed. Therefore, having paid the lower price, the owner should not be able to claim that the land was devalued by the regulation (see the dissent in *Palazzolo v. Rhode Island*, 533 U.S. 606 [2001]). This case gets a little more complicated because Palazzolo indirectly owned the land through shares he bought in a corporation in 1961 before the wetlands

regulations had been passed. He became sole owner of the land after the regulation was enacted in the 1970s. Also, the Court ruled that he was not entitled to compensation because a portion of the land still could be developed and was worth at least $200,000, so he had not been denied "all beneficial use of his property."

129. *Kelo v. City of New London,* 545 U.S. 469 (2005).

130. *Powell v. Alabama,* 287 U.S. 45 (1932).

131. *Gideon v. Wainwright,* 372 U.S. 335 (1963).

132. *Evitts v. Lucy,* 469 U.S. 387 (1985); *Wiggins v. Smith,* 539 U.S. 510 (2003). See Elizabeth Gable and Tyler Green, "*Wiggins v. Smith*: The Ineffective Assistance of Counsel Standard Applied Twenty Years after *Strickland,*" *Georgetown Journal of Legal Ethics* (Summer 2004), for a discussion of many of these issues.

133. *Klopfer v. North Carolina,* 386 U.S. 213 (1967).

134. The law is 18 U.S.C. § 3161(c)(1) and the ruling is *Zedner v. United States,* 05-5992 (2006).

135. The case concerning African Americans is *Batson v. Kentucky,* 106 S. Ct. 1712 (1986); the case about Latinos is *Hernandez v. New York,* 500 U.S. 352 (1991); and the gender case is *J.E.B. v. Alabama ex rel. T.B.,* 511 U.S. 127 (1994). Two recent cases affirming that peremptory challenges could not be used in a racially discriminatory fashion were *Miller-El v. Dretke,* 545 U.S. 231 (2005), and *Snyder v. Louisiana,* 552 U.S. 472 (2008).

136. *Apprendi v. New Jersey,* 530 U.S. 466 (2000); *United States v. Booker,* 543 U.S. 220 (2005); *Blakely v. Washington,* 542 U.S. 296 (2004). For a discussion of these and other relevant cases, see Stephanos Bibas and Susan Klein, "The Sixth Amendment and Criminal Sentencing," *Cardozo Law Review* 30:3 (2008): 775–805.

137. *Furman v. Georgia,* 408 U.S. 238 (1972); *Gregg v. Georgia,* 428 U.S. 513 (1976).

138. See Abraham and Perry, *Freedom and the Court,* pp. 72–73, for a discussion of the earlier cases, and Charles Lane, "5–4 Supreme Court Abolishes Juvenile Executions," *Washington Post,* March 2, 2005, p. A1, for a discussion of the 2002 and 2005 cases. The 2008 case was *Kennedy v. Louisiana,* 554 U.S. ___ (2008).

139. *Weems v. United States,* 217 U.S. 349 (1910).

140. *Trop v. Dulles,* 356 U.S. 86 (1958).

141. *Robinson v. California,* 370 U.S. 660 (1962).

142. *Hudson v. McMillian,* 503 U.S. 1 (1992); *Helling v. McKinney,* 509 U.S. 25 (1993).

143. *Solem v. Helm,* 463 U.S. 277 (1983).

144. *Harmelin v. Michigan,* 501 U.S. 957 (1991).

145. *Ewing v. California,* 538 U.S. 11 (2003); *Lockyer v. Andrade,* 538 U.S. 63 (2003). For a general discussion of these issues, see Editors' Note, "The Eighth Amendment, Proportionality, and the Changing Meaning of 'Punishments,'" *Harvard Law Review* 122:3 (January, 2009): 960–81.

146. *Griswold v. Connecticut,* 381 U.S. 479 (1965), 482–86.

147. *Griswold v. Connecticut,* 512–13.

148. *Roe v. Wade,* 410 U.S. 113 (1973), 129.

149. *Planned Parenthood of Southeastern Pennsylvania v. Casey,* 505 U.S. 833 (1992).

150. Katharine Q. Seeyle, "Mississippi Voters Reject Anti-Abortion Measure," *New York Times,* November 8, 2011, www.nytimes.com/2011/11/09/us/politics/votes-across-the-nation-could-serve-as-a-political-barometer.html (accessed 12/5/11).

151. Department of Human Services, Office of Disease Prevention and Epidemiology, "Annual Report on Oregon's Death with Dignity Act," March 10, 2012, www.public.health.oregon.gov/ProviderPartnerResources/EvaluationResearch/DeathwithDignityAct/Documents/year14.pdf (accessed 8/21/12).

152. *Gonzales v. Oregon,* 546 U.S. 23 (2006).

153. *Lawrence v. Texas,* 539 U.S. 558 (2003).

You Decide

a. Linda Greenhouse, "Justices Decline to Rule on Limits for Drug-Sniffing Dogs," *New York Times,* April 5, 2005, p. A19.

b. *Illinois v. Caballes,* 543 U.S. 405 (2005).

c. Oral arguments in U.S. v. Jones (2012), November 8, 2011, www.supremecourt.gov/oral_arguments/argument_transcripts/10-1259.pdf, p. 44 (accessed 8/20/12).

What Do Political Scientists Do?

a. Bruce Ackerman, *Before the Next Attack: Preserving Civil Liberties in an Age of Terrorism* (New Haven, CT: Yale University Press, 2006); Richard A. Posner, *Not a Suicide Pact: The Constitution in a Time of National Emergency* (New York: Oxford University Press, 2006).

b. Ackerman, *Before the Next Attack,* p. 2.

c. Ackerman, *Before the Next Attack,* p. 4.

d. Posner, *Not a Suicide Pact,* p. 84.

In Comparison

a. *Roper v. Simmons,* 543 U.S. 551 (2005).

b. Charles Lane, "5–4 Supreme Court Abolishes Juvenile Executions," *Washington Post,* March 2, 2005, p. A1.

c. *Roper v. Simmons.*

d. *Roper v. Simmons.*

e. Charles Lane, "Scalia Tells Congress to Mind Its Own Business," *Washington Post,* May 19, 2006, p. A19.

CHAPTER 5

1. "Two-Thirds of Democrats Now Support Gay Marriage," Pew Research Center, July 31, 2012, www.pewforum.org/Politics-and-Elections/2012-opinions-on-for-gay-marriage-unchanged-after-obamas-announcement.aspx (accessed 9/5/12).

2. "No Consensus about Whether Nation Is Divided into Haves and Have Nots," Pew Research Center, September 29, 2011, www.people-press.org/2011/09/29/no-consensus-about-whether-nation-is-divided-into-haves-and-have-nots/ (accessed 9/5/12).

3. For a description of this argument and a dissenting view, see Morris P. Fiorina, Samuel J. Adams, and Jeremy C. Pope, *Culture Wars: The Myth of a Polarized America* (New York: Longman, 2010).

4. For a review, see Arthur Lupia and Mathew D. McCubbins, *The Democratic Dilemma* (New York: Cambridge University Press, 1998).

5. Larry Bartels, "Partisanship and Voting Behavior, 1952–1996," *American Journal of Political Science* 44 (2000): 35–50.

6. Robert S. Erikson, Michael B. Mackuen, and James A. Stimson, *The Macro Polity* (New York: Cambridge University Press, 2002).

7. Angus Campbell, Phillip Converse, Warren Miller, and Donald Stokes, *The American Voter* (New York: Wiley, 1960); Phillip E. Converse, "The Nature of Belief Systems in Mass Publics," in *Ideology and Discontent*, ed. David E. Aptor (Glencoe, IL: Free Press of Glencoe, 1964), pp. 209–61. For more modern versions of these arguments, see Eric R. A. N. Smith, *The Unchanging American Voter* (Berkeley: University of California Press, 1989); Phillip E. Converse and Gregory Markus, "Plus Ça Change . . . : The New CPS Election Study Panel," *American Political Science Review* 73:1 (March, 1979): 32–49.

8. Converse, "The Nature of Belief Systems in Mass Publics," p. 259.

9. Associated Press, "D'oh! More Know Simpsons Than Constitution," March 1, 2006, www.msnbc.msn.com/id/11611015/ (accessed 2/20/08).

10. Ipsos News Center, "Most Americans Can't Name Any Supreme Court Justices, Says FindLaw.com Survey," press release, January 10, 2006, www.ipsos-na.com/news/pressrelease.cfm?id=2933 (accessed 2/20/08).

11. Valerie Strauss, "Despite Lessons on King, Some Unaware of His Dream," *Washington Post*, January 15, 2007, p. B1.

12. Samuel Popkin, *The Reasoning Voter* (Chicago: University of Chicago Press, 1991).

13. John E. Sullivan, James E. Pierson, and Gregory E. Marcus, "Ideological Constraint in the Mass Public: A Methodological Critique and Some New Findings," *American Journal of Political Science* 23 (1978): 244–49.

14. Paul M. Sniderman and Sean M. Theriault, "The Structure of Political Argument and the Logic of Issue Framing," in *Studies in Public Opinion,* ed. Willem Saris and Paul M. Sniderman (Princeton: Princeton University Press, 2004).

15. Norman Nie, Sidney Verba, and John Petrocik, *The Changing American Voter* (Cambridge, MA: Harvard University Press, 1976).

16. Michael X. Delli Carpini and Scott Keeter, *What Americans Know about Politics and Why It Matters* (New Haven, CT: Yale University Press, 1997).

17. For an example focusing on foreign policy opinions, see John Aldrich, John Sullivan, and Eugene Borgida, "Foreign Affairs and Issue Voting: Do Presidential Candidates Waltz before a Blind Audience?" *American Political Science Review* 83 (1989): 125–41.

18. Donald Green, Bradley Palmquist, and Eric Schickler, "Macropartisanship: A Replication and Critique," *American Political Science Review* 92 (1998): 883–99; Robert S. Erikson, Michael B. Mackuen, and James A. Stimson, "What Moves Macropartisanship? A Response to Green, Palmquist, and Schickler," *American Political Science Review* 92 (1998): 901–12.

19. John Zaller, "Coming to Grips with V. O. Key's Concept of Latent Opinion," unpublished paper, University of California, Los Angeles, 1998.

20. Morris Fiorina, *Retrospective Voting in American National Elections* (Cambridge, MA: Harvard University Press, 1981).

21. John Zaller, *The Nature and Origins of Mass Opinion* (New York: Cambridge University Press, 1992).

22. R. Michael Alvarez and John Brehm, *Hard Choices, Easy Answers* (Princeton, NJ: Princeton University Press, 2002).

23. John Zaller and Stanley Feldman, "A Theory of the Survey Response: Revealing Preferences versus Answering Questions," *American Journal of Political Science* 36 (1992): 579–616.

24. Janet M. Box-Steffensmeier and Susan DeBoef, "Macropartisanship and Macroideology in the Sophisticated Electorate," *Journal of Politics* 63:1 (2001): 232–48.

25. Jack Citrin, Donald P. Green, Christopher Muste, and Cara Wong, "Public Opinion toward Immigration Reform: The Role of Economic Motivations," *American Journal of Political Science* 59:3 (1997): 858–82.

26. William G. Jacoby, "Issue Framing and Public Opinion on Government Spending," *American Journal of Political Science* 44:4 (2000): 750–67; L. M. Bartels, "Beyond the Running Tally: Partisan Bias in Political Perceptions," *Political Behavior* 24:2 (2002): 117–50.

27. Donald R. Kinder, "Exploring the Racial Divide: Blacks, Whites, and Opinion on National Policy," *American Journal of Political Science* 45:2 (2001): 439–49; Paul M. Sniderman and Thomas Piazza, *The Scar of Race* (Cambridge, MA: Harvard University Press, 1993).

28. Robert Huckfeldt, Jeffery Levine, William Morgan, and John Sprague, "Accessibility and the Political Utility of Partisan and Ideological Orientations," *American Journal of Political Science* 43:3 (July, 1999): 888–911.

29. George E. Marcus, John L. Sullivan, Elizabeth Theiss-Morse, and Sandra L. Wood, *With Malice toward Some: How People*

Make Civil Liberties Judgments (New York: Cambridge University Press, 1995).

30. Stanley Feldman and Marco R. Steenbergen, "The Humanitarian Foundation of Public Support for Social Welfare,"*American Journal of Political Science* 45:3 (2001): 658–77.

31. R. Michael Alvarez and John Brehm, "American Ambivalence towards Abortion Policy: Development of a Heteroskedastic Probit Model of Competing Values,"*American Journal of Political Science* 39:4 (1995): 1055–82.

32. R. Michael Alvarez and John Brehm, "Are Americans Ambivalent towards Racial Policies?"*American Journal of Political Science* 41 (1997): 345–74.

33. Virginia Sapiro, "Not Your Parents' Political Socialization: Introduction for a New Generation,"*Annual Review of Political Science* 7 (2004): 1–23.

34. Christopher Achen, "Parental Socialization and Rational Party Identification,"*Political Behavior* 24 (2002): 151–70.

35. M. Kent Jennings and Richard G. Niemi, *Generations and Politics: A Panel Study of Young Adults and Their Parents* (Princeton, NJ: Princeton University Press, 1981).

36. J. R. Alford, C. L. Funk, and J. R. Hibbing, "Are Political Orientations Genetically Transmitted?"*American Political Science Review* 99:2 (2005): 153–67.

37. James H. Fowler and Christopher Sawes, "Two Genes Predict Voter Turnout," *Journal of Politics* 70: 3 (July 2008): 579–94.

38. Anal S. Gerbet, Gregory A. Huber, David Doherty, Conor M. Dowling, and Shang E. Ha, "Personality and Political Attitudes: Relationships across Issue Domains and Political Contexts," *American Political Science Review* 104 (February 2010): 111–33.

39. Robert Putnam, *Bowling Alone: The Collapse and Revival of American Community* (New York: Simon and Schuster, 2000).

40. Richard G. Niemi and Mary Hepburn, "The Rebirth of Political Socialization,"*Perspectives on Politics* 24 (1995): 7–16.

41. David Campbell, *Why We Vote: How Schools and Communities Shape Our Civic Life* (Princeton, NJ: Princeton University Press, 2006).

42. Sidney Verba, Kay Schlozman, and Henry Brady, *Voice and Equality:CivicVolunteerisminAmericanPolitics*(Cambridge, MA: Harvard University Press, 1995).

43. Paul Allen Beck and M. Kent Jennings, "Pathways to Participation," *American Political Science Review* 76 (1982): 94–108.

44. Fiorina, *Retrospective Voting in American National Elections.*

45. Edward G. Carmines and James A. Stimson, *Issue Evolution: Race and the Transformation of American Politics* (Princeton, NJ: Princeton University Press, 1990).

46. "United in Remembrance, Divided over Policies: Ten Years after 9/11," Pew Research Center, September 1, 2011, www.people-press.org/2011/09/01/united-in-remembrance-divided-over-policies/1/ (accessed 9/5/12).

47. Pew Research Center, "Public More Optimistic about the Economy, but Still Reluctant to Spend," June 19, 2009, www.people-press.org/report/523/economy-spending (accessed 11/4/09).

48. Robert S. Erikson, Michael B. Mackuen, and James A. Stimson, "Macro-partisanship,"*American Political Science Review* 83 (1989): 1125–42.

49. John Zaller, *The Nature and Origins of Mass Opinion* (New York: Cambridge University Press, 1992).

50. Frank Baumgartner, Suzanna DeBoef, and Amber Bodston, *The Decline of the Death Penalty and the Discovery of Innocence* (New York: Cambridge University Press, 2008).

51. Richard Nadwau et al., "Class, Party, and South-Nonsouth Differences," *American Politics Research* 32 (2004): 52–67.

52. James H. Kuklinski et al., "Racial Prejudice and Attitudes toward Affirmative Action,"*American Journal of Political Science* 41 (1997): 402–19.

53. Donald P. Green, Bradley Palmquist, and Eric Schickler, *Partisan Hearts and Minds* (New Haven, CT: Yale University Press, 2002).

54. Don Balz, "Contests Serve as Warning to Democrats: It's Not 2008 Anymore," *Washington Post*, November 4, 2009, p. A1.

55. For elaboration on this point, see William T. Bianco, Richard G. Niemi, and Harold W. Stanley, "Partisanship and Group Support over Time: A Multivariate Analysis," *American Political Science Review* 80 (September, 1986): 969–76.

56. Arthur Lupia and Mathew D. McCubbins, *The Democratic Dilemma* (New York: Cambridge University Press, 1998).

57. Lawrence R. Jacobs and Robert Y. Shapiro, *Politicians Don't Pander: Political Manipulation and the Loss of Democratic Responsiveness* (Chicago: University of Chicago Press, 2000).

58. Robert Y. Shapiro and Lawrence Jacobs, "Simulating Representation: Elite Mobilization and Political Power in Health Care Reform," *The Forum* 8:1 (2010).

59. Christopher Wlezien and Robert S. Erikson, "The Horse Race: What Polls Reveal as the Election Campaign Unfolds," *International Journal of Public Opinion Research* 19:1 (2007): 74–88.

60. Pollster.com, "IVR and Internet: How Reliable?" September 28, 2006, www.pollster.com/mystery_pollster/ivr_internet _how_reliable.php (accessed 2/21/08).

61. Jason Barabas and Jennifer Jerit, "Are Survey Experiments Externally Valid?" *American Political Science Review* 104 (May 2010): 226–42.

62. For data on reported and actual turnout, see Chapter 8.

63. Anton J. Nederhof, "Methods of Coping with Social Desirability Bias: A Review,"*European Journal of Social Psychology* 15:3 (2006): 263–80.

64. Gary Langer, "Two Years from Election, Looking at Early Polls," *ABC News*, January 18, 2007, http://abcnews.go.com/Politics/story?id=2802742&page=1 (accessed 2/21/08).

65. James H. Kuklinski et al., "Misinformation and the Currency of Democratic Citizenship," *Journal of Politics* 62:3 (2000): 790–816.

66. Pew Research Center, "Health Care Reform Closely Followed, Much Discussed," www.people-press.org/reports/pdf/537.pdf (accessed 11/5/09).

67. George H. Bishop, *The Illusion of Public Opinion: Fact and Artifact in Public Opinion Polls* (Washington, DC: Rowman and Littlefield, 2004).

68. Delli Carpini and Keeter, *What Americans Know about Politics and Why It Matters.*

69. Delli Carpini and Keeter, *What Americans Know about Politics and Why It Matters.*

70. Morris P. Fiorina, Samuel J. Abrams, and Jeremy C. Pope, *Culture War? The Myth of a Polarized America* (New York: Longman, 2002).

71. For data on how responses to these questions changed over time, see "Quick Tables for the GSS 1972–2004 Cumulative Datafile," http://sda.berkeley.edu:8080/quicktables/quickconfig.do?gss04 (accessed 2/13/08).

72. For a review of the literature on trust in government, see Karen Cook, Russell Hardin, and Margaret Levi, *Cooperation without Trust* (New York: Russell Sage Foundation, 2005), as well as Marc J. Hetherington, *Why Trust Matters: Declining Political Trust and the Demise of American Liberalism* (Princeton, NJ: Princeton University Press, 2004).

73. William T. Bianco, *Trust: Representatives and Constituents* (Ann Arbor: University of Michigan Press, 1994).

74. Sean M. Theriault, *The Power of the People: Congressional Competition, Public Attention, and Voter Retribution* (Columbus: Ohio State University Press, 2005).

75. John R. Hibbing and Elizabeth Theiss-Morse, *Congress as Public Enemy: Public Attitudes toward American Political Institutions* (New York: Cambridge University Press, 1995).

76. Thomas Rudolph and Jillian Evans, "Political Trust, Ideology, and Public Support for Government Spending," *American Journal of Political Science* 49 (2005): 660–71.

77. Patricia Moy and Michael Pfau, *With Malice toward All? The Media and Public Confidence in Democratic Institutions* (Boulder, CO: Praeger, 2000).

78. Richard Fenno, *Home Style: U.S. House Members in Their Districts* (Boston: Little, Brown, 1978).

79. William T. Bianco, Daniel Lipinski, and Ryan W. Work, "What Happens when House Members 'Run with Congress'? The Electoral Consequences of Institutional Loyalty," *Legislative Studies Quarterly* 26 (2003): 413–27.

80. Robert S. Erikson, Michael B. Mackuen, and James A. Stimson, *The Macro Polity* (New York: Cambridge University Press, 2002).

81. James A. Stimson, *Public Opinion in America: Moods, Swings, and Cycles* (Boulder, CO: Westview Press, 1999).

82. Robert S. Erikson, Michael B. Mackuen, and James A. Stimson, "American Politics: The Model," unpublished paper, Columbia University, 2000.

83. See, for example, Pew Research Center, "Iraq Looms Large in Nationalized Election," October 5, 2006, www.people-press.org/reports/display.php3?ReportID=290, as well as data at www.pollingreport.com (accessed 9/5/12).

84. Pew Research Center, "Nation's Real Estate Slump Hits Wealthy Areas," October 11, 2007, www.people-press.org/reports/display.php3?ReportID=361 (accessed 5/5/08).

85. Robert Kuttner, "The American Health Care System," *New England Journal of Medicine* 340 (1999): 163–68.

86. Hope Yen, "Frist Wants Immigration Vote This Week," ABC News, September 24, 2006, http://abcnews.go.com/Politics/wireStory?id=2484862 (accessed 2/22/08).

87. Data aggregated from various polls; see Pollingreport.com, "Law and Civil Rights," www.pollingreport.com/civil.htm (accessed 2/25/08).

88. Larry Bartels, "Constituency Opinion and Congressional Policy Making: The Reagan Defense Buildup," *American Political Science Review* 85 (June 1991): 457–74; Jonathan Kastellec, Jeffrey R. Lax, and Justin H. Phillips, "Public Opinion and Senate Confirmation of Supreme Court Nominees," *Journal of Politics* 72 (2010): 767–84.

89. Lawrence R. Jacobs and Robert Y. Shapiro, *Politicians Don't Pander: Political Manipulation and the Loss of Democratic Responsiveness* (Chicago: University of Chicago Press, 2000).

90. Brandice Canes-Wrone, *Who Leads Whom: Presidents, Policy, and the Public* (Chicago: University of Chicago Press, 2005).

91. Thom Shanker and David S. Cloud, "The Reach of War: Bush's Plan for Iraq Runs into Opposition in Congress," *New York Times*, January 12, 2007, p. A1.

What Do Political Scientists Do?

a. James Stimson, *Tides of Consent: How Public Opinion Shapes American Politics* (New York: Cambridge University Press, 2004). See especially Figures 5.7 and 5.8.

CHAPTER 6

1. Jason Barabas, and Jennifer Jerit, "Estimating the Causal Effects of Media Coverage on Policy-Specific Knowledge," *American Journal of Political Sciences* 53 (2008): 73–89.

2. Thomas E. Patterson, *Out of Order* (New York: Alfred A. Knopf, 1993); Robert D. Putnam, *Bowling Alone* (New York: Basic Books, 2000).

3. Thomas Patterson, "Bad News, Period," *Political Science and Politics* 29 (1996): 17–20.

4. Charles E. Clark, *The Public Prints: The Newspaper in Anglo-American Culture, 1665–1740* (New York: Oxford University Press, 1994).

5. William H. Riker, *The Strategy of Rhetoric: Campaigning for the American Constitution* (New Haven, CT: Yale University Press, 1996).

6. Geoffrey R. Stone, *Perilous Times: Free Speech in Wartime from the Sedition Act of 1798 to the War on Terrorism* (New York: Norton, 2004).

7. John D. Stevens, *Sensationalism and the New York Press* (New York: Columbia University Press, 1991).

8. Michael Schudson, *Discovering the News: A Social History of American Newspapers* (New York: Basic Books, 1978).

9. Robert C. Williams, *Horace Greeley: Champion of American Freedom* (New York: New York University Press, 2006).

10. W. Joseph Campbell, *Yellow Journalism: Puncturing the Myths, Defining the Legacies* (Boulder, CO: Praeger, 2003).

11. Lincoln Steffens, *The Shame of the Cities* (New York: McClure, Phillips, 1904); Upton Sinclair, *The Jungle* (New York: Doubleday, Page, 1906).

12. Gay Talese, *The Kingdom and the Power* (New York: Calder and Boyars, 1983).

13. For a detailed history, see United States Early Radio History, www.earlyradiohistory.us (accessed 9/17/12).

14. This discussion draws on the summary "Merging Media: How Relaxing FCC Ownership Rules Has Affected the Media Business," www.pbs.org/newshour/media/conglomeration/fcc2.html (accessed 2/26/08).

15. Peter Braestrup, *Big Story: How the American Press and Television Reported and Interpreted the Crisis of Tet 1968 in Vietnam* (New Haven, CT: Yale University Press, 1983).

16. For an extended discussion of the fairness doctrine and related issues, see "Fairness Doctrine: U.S. Broadcasting Policy," www.museum.tv/eotvsection.php?entrycode=fairnessdoct (accessed 10/17/12).

17. The Project for Excellence in Journalism, "The State of the News Media, 2007: Ownership" (2007), www.stateofthenewsmedia.org/2007/narrative_overview_ownership.asp?cat=5&media=1 (accessed 2/26/08).

18. The FCC website has details of current regulations as well as the agency's strategic goals. See www.fcc.gov (accessed 10/17/12).

19. The *Columbia Journalism Review* maintains a list of holdings for major media companies at Who Owns What, www.cjr.org/tools/owners (accessed 9/17/12).

20. Joanna Glasner, "Tech a Key in Media Rule Change," *Wired*, June 3, 2003, www.wired.com/techbiz/media/news/2003/06/59079 (accessed 2/26/08).

21. Glasner, "Tech a Key in Media Rule Change."

22. See, for example, James J. Cramer, "Newspapers Still Stumble Online," RealMoney.com, May 2, 2005, www.thestreet.com/p/_rms/rmoney/jamesjcramer/10221101.html (accessed 2/26/08).

23. Paul Starr, "Reclaiming the Air," *American Prospect*, March 2004, pp. 57–61.

24. The president's current budget is available at www.whitehouse.gov/omb/budget (accessed 9/17/12). The *Federal Register* can be found at www.gpo.gov/fdsys/browse/collection.action?collectionCode=FR (accessed 9/17/12). and Government Accountability Office reports are available at www.gao.gov (accessed 9/17/12).

25. The Center for Responsive Politics, www.opensecrets.org (accessed 9/17/12).

26. Pollster, www.pollster.com (accessed 9/17/12).

27. Larry Craig Mug Shot, The Smoking Gun, www.thesmokinggun.com/mugshots/larrycraigmug1.html (accessed 11/20/09).

28. National Review Online, www.nationalreview.com (accessed 9/17/12).

29. See www.politico.com/playbook/ (accessed 9/17/12).

30. SCOTUSblog, www.scotusblog.com/ (accessed 9/17/12).

31. See www.themonkeycage.org (accessed 9/17/12).

32. Slate, www.slate.com (accessed 9/17/12).

33. Salon, www.salon.com; The Huffington Post, www.huffingtonpost.com; Power Line, www.powerlineblog.com; Town Hall, www.townhall.com (accessed 9/17/12).

34. A. J. Liebling, "Do You Belong in Journalism?" *The New Yorker*, May 14, 1960, p. 105.

35. See www.milblogging.com/ (accessed 9/17/12).

36. The video "Allen's Listening Tour" is available at http://youtube.com/watch?v=9G7gq7GQ71c (accessed 2/26/08).

37. The *Washington Post* has an archive of previous online discussions at "Post Politics Hour," www.washingtonpost.com/wp-dyn/content/discussion/2010/04/02/D72010/040202897.html (accessed 4/2/10).

38. Geoffrey A. Fowler and Carol Lee, "At Facebook Town Hall, Obama Goes on Offensive," http://online.wsj.com/article/SB10001424052748703838004576275580143706192.html, April 20, 2011 (accessed 9/17/12).

39. For a skeptical introduction to this argument, see the proceedings of "MeetUp, Craigslist, eBay: Has the Web Changed Politics?" a conference at the Harvard School of Law, December 9–11, 2004, http://cyber.law.harvard.edu/is2k4/home (accessed 9/17/12).

40. Bruce Bimber, "Information and Political Engagement in America: The Search for Effects of Information Technology at the Individual Level," *Political Research Quarterly* 54 (2001): 53–67; Caroline J. Tolbert and Ramona S. McNeal, "Unraveling the Effects of the Internet on Political Participation," *Political Research Quarterly* 56 (2003): 175–85.

41. Pew Research Center, "Public Knowledge of Current Affairs Little Changed by News and Information Revolutions," April 15, 2007, www.people-press.org/reports/display.php3?ReportID = 319 (accessed 2/28/08).

42. Shanto Iyengar and Kyu S. Hahn, "Red Media, Blue Media: Evidence of Ideological Selectivity in Media Use," *Journal of Communication* 59 (2009): 19–39.

43. Eric Lawrence, John Sides, and Henry Farrell, "Self-Segregation or Deliberation? Blog Readership, Participation, and Polarization in American Politics," *Perspectives on Politics* 8 (March 2010): 141–57.

44. Markus Prior, *Post-Broadcast Democracy: How Media Choice Increases Inequality in Political Involvement and Polarizes Elections* (New York: Cambridge University Press, 2007).

45. Bill Keller, "Dealing with Assange and the WikiLeaks Secrets," *New York Times Sunday Magazine*, January 26, 2011, pp. 15–21.

46. Michael Calderone, "Obama Calls on HuffPost for Iran Question," June 23, 2009, www.politico.com/michaelcalderone/0609/Obama_calls_on_HuffPost_for_Iran_question.html (accessed 11/20/09).

47. Lance Bennett, *News: The Politics of Illusion* (New York: Pearson, 2012).

48. Samuel Popkin, *The Reasoning Voter* (Chicago: University of Chicago Press, 1991).

49. John Zaller, *The Nature and Origins of Mass Opinion* (New York: Cambridge University Press, 1992).

50. S. H. Chaffee, X. Zhao, and G. Leshner, "Political Knowledge and the Campaign Media of 1992," *Communication Research* 21 (1994): 305–24; Jeffrey J. Mondak, *Nothing to Read: Newspapers and Elections in a Social Experiment* (Ann Arbor: University of Michigan Press, 1995).

51. For a discussion of these concepts, see Paul M. Sniderman and Sean M. Theriault, "The Structure of Political Argument and the Logic of Issue Framing," in *Studies in Public Opinion*, ed. William E. Saris and Paul M. Sniderman (Princeton, NJ: Princeton University Press, 2004); Shanto Iyengar and Donald Kinder, *News That Matters* (Chicago: University of Chicago Press, 1987). See also Maxwell McCombs and Donald L. Shaw, "The Agenda-Setting Functions of Mass Media," *Public Opinion Quarterly* 36 (1972): 176–87; and Amos Tversky and Daniel Kahnemann, "The Framing of Decisions and the Psychology of Choice," *Science* 211 (1981): 453–58.

52. Walter Lippmann, *Public Opinion* (1922; repr. New York: Free Press, 1997).

53. J. T. Klapper, *The Effects of Mass Communication* (New York: Free Press, 1960); see also Paul F. Lazarsfeld, Bernard Berelson, and Hazel Gaudet, *The People's Choice* (New York: Columbia University Press, 1944).

54. Stephen Ansolabehere, Roy Behr, and Shanto Iyengar, "The Evolution of Media Effects Research," in *The Media Game: American Politics in the Television Age*, ed. Stephen Ansolabehere, Roy Behr, and Shanto Iyengar (New York: Macmillan, 1993), 129–38; Steven E. Finkel, "Reexamining the 'Minimal Effects' Model in Recent Presidential Campaigns," *Journal of Politics* 55 (1993): 1–21; Kathleen H. Jamieson, *Everything You Think You Know about Politics . . . And Why You're Wrong* (New York: Basic Books, 2000); Shanto Iyengar and Adam Simon, "New Perspectives and Evidence on Political Communication and Campaign Effects," *Annual Review of Psychology* 51 (2000): 149–69.

55. James N. Druckman and Michael Parkin, "The Impact of Media Bias: How Editorial Slant Affects Voters," *Journal of Politics* 67 (2005): 4, 1030–49; for similar results, see Kim Fridkin Kahn and Patrick J. Kenney, "The Slant of the News," *American Political Science Review* 96 (2002): 381–94.

56. Jon A. Krosnick and Laura Brannon, "The Impact of the Gulf War on the Ingredients of Presidential Evaluations: Multidimensional Effects of Political Involvement," *American Political Science Review* 87 (1993): 963–75.

57. Jon A. Krosnick and Joanne Miller, "News Media Impact on the Ingredients of Presidential Evaluations: Politically Knowledgeable Citizens Are Guided by a Trusted Source," *American Journal of Political Science* 44 (2000): 295–309.

58. The entire list can be found at www.projectcensored.org/top-stories/articles/category/top-stories/top-25-of-2012 (accessed 10/17/12).

59. Pew Research Center, "Cable and Internet Loom Large in a Fragmented Political Universe," January 11, 2004, www.people-press.org/reports/display.php3?ReportID=200 (accessed 2/26/08).

60. See Eric Alterman, *What Liberal Media?* (New York: Basic Books, 2003), and Bernard Goldberg, *Bias* (New York: Regnery, 2001).

61. Pew Research Center, "Press Widely Criticized, but Trusted More than Other Information Sources," September 22, 2011. www.people-press.org/2011/09/22/press-widely-criticized-but-trusted-more-than-other-institutions/ (accessed 9/17/12).

62. Mark Silva, "Fox Rolls Wrong Video, Heads May Roll," November 18, 2009, www.swamppolitics.com/news/politics/ blog/2009/11/fox_rolls_wrong_tape_heads_may.html (accessed 12/1/09).

63. This description runs on the editorial masthead of every issue of *The Nation*.

64. For these and other data, see the Brookings Iraq Index, www.brookings.edu/iraqindex (accessed 9/17/12).

65. Stefano Della Vigna and Ethan Kaplan, "The FOX News Effect: Media Bias and Voting," *Quarterly Journal of Economics* 122 (2007): 1187–1234.

66. Timothy Groseclose, *Left Turn: How Liberal Media Bias Distorts the American Mind* (New York: St. Martin's Press, 2011).

67. Brenden Nyhan, "The Problems with the Groseclose/Milyo Study of Media Bias," www.brendan-nyhan.com/blog/2005/12/the_problems_wi.html, December 22, 2005 (accessed 9/17/12).

68. Andrew Cline, "Media/Political Bias," http://rhetorica.net/bias.htm (accessed 11/02/11).

69. Patterson, "Bad News, Period."

70. Shanto Iyengar, *Is Anyone Responsible?: How Television Frames Political Issues* (Chicago: Chicago University Press, 1991).

71. Regina G. Lawrence, "Game Framing: Tracking the Strategic Frame in Public Policy News," *Political Communication* 17 (2000): 19–43.

72. Thomas Patterson, "Doing Well and Doing Good: How Soft News and Critical Journalism Are Shrinking the News Audience and Weakening Democracy—and What News Outlets Can Do about It" (Cambridge, MA: Joan Shorenstein Center on the Press, Politics, and Public Policy, Harvard University, 2000), www.ksg.harvard.edu/presspol/research_publications/reports/softnews .pdf (accessed 2/29/08).

73. Matthew A. Baum, *Soft News Goes to War: Public Opinion and American Foreign Policy in the New Media Age* (Princeton, NJ: Princeton University Press, 2005).

74. Frank D. Gilliam, Jr., and Shanto Iyengar, "Prime Suspects: The Influence of Local Television News on the Viewing Public," *American Journal of Political Science* 44:3 (2000): 560–73.

75. Thomas E. Patterson, *Out of Order* (New York: Random House, 1994).

76. Pew Research Center, "Self Censorship: How Often and Why: Journalists Avoiding the News," April 30, 2000, www.people -press.org/reports/display .php3?ReportID=39 (accessed 2/29/08).

77. T. E. Patterson, *The Vanishing Voter* (New York: Knopf, 2002); J. N. Cappella and K. H. Jamieson, *Spiral of Cynicism: The Press and the Public Good* (New York: Oxford University Press, 1997).

78. Pippa Norria, *A Virtuous Cycle* (New York: Cambridge University Press, 2003).

79. Quoted in Baum, *Soft News Goes to War*, p. 57.

80. Brent Cunningham, "Across the Great Divide: Class," *Columbia Journalism Review* 3 (May/June, 2004), www .cjrarchives.org/issues/2004/3/cunningham-class.asp (accessed 2/29/08).

81. John R. Hibbing and Elizabeth Theiss-Morse, *Congress as Public Enemy* (New York: Cambridge University Press, 1995); see also John R. Hibbing and Elizabeth Theiss-Morse, "The Media's Role in Public Negativity toward Congress: Distinguishing Emotional Reactions and Cognitive Evaluations," *American Journal of Political Science* 42 (April 1998): 475–98.

82. Shanto Iyengar, Helmut Norpoth, and Kyu S. Hahn, "Consumer Demand for Election News: The Horserace Sells," *Journal of Politics* 66:1 (2004): 157–75.

83. Baum, *Soft News Goes to War*, p. 57.

84. George Lakoff, The Real Issues: Wisconsin Update, February 25, 2011, http://georgelakoff.com/2011/02/25/the-real -issues-a-wisconsin-update/ (accessed 9/17/12).

85. Dennis Chong and James N. Druckman, "Dynamic Public Opinion: Communication Effects over Time," *American Political Science Review* 104 (2010): 663–80.

You Decide

a. Porter Goss, "Loose Lips Sink Spies," *New York Times*, February 10, 2006, p. 25.

What Do Political Scientists Do?

a. Thomas E. Nelson, Rosalee A. Clawson, and Zoe M. Oxley, "Media Framing of a Civil Liberties Conflict and Its Effect on Tolerance," *American Political Science Review* 91 (1997): 567–83.

b. Dennis Chong and James N. Druckman, "A Theory of Framing and Opinion Formation in Competitive Elite Environments," *Journal of Communication* 57 (2007): 99–118.

c. Shanto Iyengar, *Is Anyone Responsible? How Television Frames Political Issues* (Chicago: University of Chicago Press, 1991).

In Comparison

a. Pew Center for Excellence in Journalism, "Swine Flu Coverage around the World," May 28, 2009, www.journalism .org/analysis_report/Swine_Flu_Coverage_around_the _World (accessed 11/18/09).

CHAPTER 7

1. John Aldrich, *Why Parties?* (Chicago: University of Chicago Press, 2005).

2. Joseph Schlesinger, *Political Parties and the Winning of Office* (Ann Arbor: University of Michigan Press, 1994).

3. The three-part description first appeared in V. O. Key, *Politics, Parties, and Pressure Groups* (New York: Crowell, 1956). For a more recent description, see Paul Allen Beck and Marjorie Hershey, *Party Politics in America* (New York: Longman, 2004).

4. William Nesbit Chambers and Walter Dean Burnham, *The American Party Systems: Stages of Political Development* (Oxford, UK: Oxford University Press, 1966).

5. Aldrich, *Why Parties?*

6. Donald H. Hickey, "Federalist Party Unity and the War of 1812," *Journal of American Studies* 12 (April 1978): 23–39; William T. Bianco, David B. Spence, and John D. Wilkerson, "The Electoral Connection in the Early Congress: The Case of the Compensation Act of 1816," *American Journal of Political Science* 40 (February, 1996): 145–71.

7. Aldrich, *Why Parties?*

8. James MacPherson, *Battle Cry of Freedom: The Civil War Era* (New York: Oxford University Press, 1988).

9. Michael F. Holt, *The Rise and Fall of the Whig Party: Jacksonian Politics and the Onset of the Civil War* (New York: Oxford University Press, 1999).

10. Harold W. Stanley, William T. Bianco, and Richard G. Niemi, "Partisanship and Group Support over Time: A Multivariate Analysis," *American Political Science Review* 80 (1986): 969–76.

11. Frank Baumgartner and Bryan D. Jones, *Agendas and Instability in American Politics* (Chicago: University of Chicago Press, 2009).

12. Aldrich, *Why Parties?*

13. James L. Sundquist, *Dynamics of the Party System*, rev. ed. (Washington, DC: Brookings Institution, 1983).

14. Aldrich, *Why Parties?*

15. John H. Aldrich and Richard G. Niemi, "The Sixth American Party System: Electoral Change, 1952–1992," in *Broken Contract: Changing Relationships between Americans and Their Governments*, ed. Steven Craig (Boulder, CO: Westview Press, 1993).

16. Harold W. Stanley and Richard G. Niemi, "Partisanship, Party Coalitions, and Group Support, 1952–2004," *Presidential Studies Quarterly* 36:2 (2006): 172–88.

17. Charles S. Bullock III, Donna R. Hoffman, and Ronald Keith Gaddie, "Regional Variations in the Realignment of American Politics, 1944–2004," *Social Science Quarterly* 87:3 (2006): 494–518.

18. The full list of Democratic constituency groups is available at www.democrats.org/people. A list of Republican coalition groups is available at www.gop.com/coalition-support (accessed 10/18/12).

19. Jon F. Hale, "The Making of the New Democrats," *Political Science Quarterly* 110:2 (1995): 207–32.

20. James Monroe, *The Political Party Matrix* (Albany, NY: SUNY Press, 2001).

21. Gary Cox and Mathew McCubbins, *Legislative Leviathan* (Berkeley: University of California Press, 1993); James M. Snyder and Michael M. Ting, "An Informational Rationale for Political Parties," *American Journal of Political Science* 46 (2002): 90–110.

22. Adam Nagourney and Cassi Feldman, "Early Primary Rush Upends '08 Campaign Plans," *New York Times*, March 12, 2007, p. A1; Linda Feldmann, "An Uproar over '08 Primary Calendar," May 25, 2007, *Christian Science Monitor*, p. 2; Christopher Cooper, "Early Voting May Clip Iowa's Role," *Wall Street Journal*, May 22, 2007, p. A4.

23. Raymond Wolfinger, "Why Political Machines Have Not Withered Away and Other Revisionist Thoughts," *Journal of Politics* 34:2 (1972): 365–98.

24. For details on Tammany Hall, see William L. Riordon, *Plunkitt of Tammany Hall* (1905; repr. New York: Dutton, 1963), www.marxists.org/reference/archive/plunkett-george/tammany-hall (accessed 9/17/12).

25. Riordan, *Plunkitt of Tammany Hall*.

26. David Kirkpatrick, "Pelosi Faces Competing Pressures on Health Care," *New York Times*, November 9, 2009, p. A1.

27. Jason Roberts and Steven Smith, "Procedural Contexts, Party Strategy, and Conditional Party Government," *American Journal of Political Science* 47:2 (2003): 205–317.

28. David Rohde, *Parties and Leaders in the Post-Reform House* (Chicago: University of Chicago Press, 1991).

29. Carl Hulse, 2009, "Advocates of Gun Rights Are Poised for a Victory," *New York Times*, May 20, 2009, p. A16.

30. Catherine Rampell, "Tax Pledge May Scuttle a Deal on Deficit," *New York Times*, November 18, 2011, p. B1.

31. Donald Green, Bradley Palmquist, and Eric Schickler, *Partisan Hearts and Minds* (New Haven, CT: Yale University Press, 2004); Christopher Achen, "Political Socialization and Rational Party Identification," *Political Behavior* 24:2 (2002): 151–70.

32. Morris Fiorina, *Retrospective Voting in American National Elections* (New Haven, CT: Yale University Press, 1981).

33. Michael Meffert, Helmut Norpoth, and Anirudh V. S. Ruhil, "Realignment and Macropartisanship," *American Political Science Review* 95:4 (2001): 953–62.

34. Walter Dean Burnham, "The Reagan Heritage," in *The Election of 1988: Reports and Interpretations*, ed. Gerald M. Pomper et al. (Chatham, NJ: Chatham House, 1989).

35. Martin P. Wattenberg, *The Decline of American Political Parties: 1952–1994* (Cambridge, MA: Harvard University Press, 1996).

36. David S. Broder, *The Party's Over: The Failure of Partisan Politics in America* (New York: Harper and Row, 1971).

37. Donald P. Green and Bradley Palmquist, "Of Artifacts and Partisan Instability," *American Journal of Political Science* 34:3 (August 1990): 872–902.

38. Warren E. Miller and J. Merrill Shanks, *The New American Voter* (Cambridge, MA: Harvard University Press, 1996); Steven J. Rosenstone and John Mark Hansen, *Mobilization, Participation, and Democracy in America* (New York: Macmillan, 1993).

39. D. Sunshine Hillygus and Simon Jackman, "Voter Decision Making in Election 2000: Campaign Effects, Partisan Activation, and the Clinton Legacy," *American Journal of Political Science* 47 (2003): 583–96.

40. Larry M. Bartels, "Partisanship and Voting Behavior, 1952–1996," *American Journal of Political Science* 44:1 (2000): 35–50.

41. Martin P. Wattenberg, *Where Have All the Voters Gone?* (Cambridge, MA: Harvard University Press, 2002).

42. Jill Lawrence, "Party Recruiters Lead Charge for '06 Vote; Choice of Candidates to Run in Fall May Decide Who Controls the House," *USA Today*, May 25, 2006, p. A5.

43. S. A. Miller, "Recruits for 2010 Put Glee in GOP," *Washington Times*, January 6, 2010, p. A1.

44. Compiled from information available at www.ballot-access.org (accessed 12/17/09).

45. www.opensecrets.org/parties/index.php, based on data released by the Federal Election Commission on 11/2/12 (accessed 11/2/12).

46. Patricia Zapor, "Pro-Life Democrats Describe Lonely Role, but See Improvements," *Catholic News Service*, July 28, 2004, www.catholicnews.com/data/stories/cns/0404122.htm (accessed 3/27/08).

47. John Geering, *Party Ideologies in America, 1828–1996* (New York: Cambridge University Press, 2001).

48. John Holusha, "Senate Continues Debate over Immigration Reform," *New York Times*, April 4, 2006, p. A1.

49. E. E. Schattschneider, *Party Government* (New York: McGraw Hill, 1942); Nelson Polsby, *Consequences of Party Reform* (New York: Oxford University Press, 1983).

50. See www.lp.org/our-history (accessed 9/17/12).

51. Steven J. Rosenstone, Roy L. Behr, and Edward Lazarus, *Third Parties in America: Citizen Response to Major Party Failure* (Princeton, NJ: Princeton University Press, 1984).

52. Janet Hook and Peter Wallsten, "GOP Feels Sting of Candidates' Rejection," *Los Angeles Times*, October 10, 2005, p. A1.

53. Gary Cox, *Making Votes Count: Strategic Coordination in the World's Electoral Systems* (Cambridge, UK: Cambridge University Press, 1997).

54. Thomas B. Edsall, "GOP Gains Advantage on Key Issues, Polls Say," *Washington Post*, January 27, 2002, p. A4.

55. John D. McKinnon, "Backing Away from Bush; Some Republican Candidates Avoid Ties with Unpopular President," *Wall Street Journal*, May 23, 2006, p. A4.

What Do Political Scientists Do?

a. David Mayhew, *Congress: The Electoral Connection* (New Haven, CT: Yale University Press, 1974).

b. David W. Rohde, "'Something's Happening Here: What It Is Ain't Exactly Clear': Southern Democrats in the House of Representatives," in *Home Style and Washington Work*, ed. Morris Fiorina and David W. Rhode (Ann Arbor: University of Michigan Press, 1989).

You Decide

a. Nelson Polsby, *Consequences of Party Reform* (New York: Oxford University Press, 1983).

b. Daniel A. Smith and Caroline J. Tolbert, *Educated by Initiative: The Effects of Direct Democracy on Citizens and Political Organizations in the American States* (Ann Arbor: University of Michigan Press, 2004).

In Comparison

a. Michael Gallagher, Michael Laver, and Peter Mair, *Representative Government in Western Europe* (New York: McGraw-Hill, 2000).

CHAPTER 8

1. James Campbell, "The 2002 Midterm Election: A Typical or Atypical Midterm?" *Political Science and Politics* 36 (2003): 203–6.

2. Morris P. Fiorina, *Retrospective Voting in American National Elections* (New Haven, CT: Yale University Press, 1981); V. O. Key, *The Responsible Electorate* (New York: Vintage, 1966).

3. David Mayhew, *Congress: The Electoral Connection* (New Haven, CT: Yale University Press, 1973).

4. For details on early voting, see the Early Voting Information Center site at http://earlyvoting.net/ (accessed 10/19/12).

5. Paul Gronke, "Early Voting Reforms and American Elections," paper presented at the 2004 American Political Science Association Annual Meeting, Chicago, IL. For 2006 data, see Pew Research Center, "Public Cheers Democratic Victory," November 16, 2006, www.people-press.org/reports/display.php3?ReportID=296 (accessed 10/19/12).

6. www.cnn.com/ELECTIONS (accessed 10/19/12).

7. For details, see the Caltech/MIT Voting Technology Project site at www.vote.caltech.edu (accessed 10/19/12).

8. Randall Stross, "The Big Gamble on Electronic Voting," *New York Times*, September 24, 2006, p. 3.

9. An invaluable source for information on election technology, including reports on the use of touch screens in 2006, is the blog Election Updates written by California Institute of Technology professor Michael Alvarez and others at http://electionupdates.caltech.edu/ (accessed 10/19/12).

10. Jonathan N. Wand, Kenneth W. Shotts, Jasjeet S. Sekhon, Walter R. Mebane, Michael C. Herron, and Henry E. Brady, "The Butterfly Ballot Did It: The Aberrant Vote for Buchanan in Palm Beach County, Florida," *American Political Science Review* 95 (2001): 793–809.

11. Robert F. Kennedy, Jr., "Was the 2004 Election Stolen?" *Rolling Stone*, June 1, 2006, www.rollingstone.com/news/story/10432334/was_the_2004_election_stolen (accessed 3/29/08).

12. Farhad Manjoo, "Was the 2004 Election Stolen? No," *Salon*, June 3, 2006, www.salon.com/news/feature/2006/06/03/kennedy (accessed 10/19/12).

13. Minor party candidates are typically selected during party conventions.

14. Barbara Norrander, "Presidential Nomination Politics in the Post-Reform Era," *Political Research Quarterly* 49 (1996): 875–90.

15. Larry Bartels, *Presidential Primaries and the Dynamics of Public Choice* (Princeton, NJ: Princeton University Press, 1988).

16. William G. Mayer, "Forecasting Presidential Nominations or, My Model Worked Just Fine, Thank You," *Political Science and Politics* 36 (2003): 153–59.

17. Marty Cohen, David Karol, Hans Noel, and John Zaller, "Beating Reform: The Resurgence of Parties in Presidential Nominations, 1980 to 2000," paper presented at the 2001 American Political Science Association Annual Meeting, San Francisco, CA.

18. Richard Herrera, "Are 'Superdelegates' Super?" *Political Behavior* 16 (1994): 79–93.

19. For a discussion of the 2004 conventions, see Kennedy School of Government, *Campaigning for President: The Managers Look at 2004* (New York: Rowman and Littlefield, 2005).

20. FairVote, "Maine and Nebraska," www.fairvote.org/e_college/me_ne.htm (accessed 10/19/12).

21. Robert Bennett, "The Problem of the Faithless Elector," *Northwestern University Law Review* 100 (2004): 121–30.

22. James Q. Wilson, "Is the Electoral College Worth Saving?" *Slate*, November 3, 2000, www.slate.com/id/92663 (accessed 10/19/12).

23. Linda Fowler and Robert McClure, *Political Ambition: Who Decides to Run for Congress* (Ann Arbor: University of Michigan Press, 1989).

24. Robin Kolodny, *Pursuing Majorities: Congressional Campaign Committees in American Politics* (Norman: University of Oklahoma Press, 1999).

25. Steven Ansolabehere and Alan Gerber, "Incumbency Advantage and the Persistence of Legislative Majorities," *Legislative Studies Quarterly* 22 (1997): 161–80.

26. For a discussion of Johnson's decision, see Robert A. Caro, *The Path to Power* (New York: Knopf, 1983).

27. Thomas Mann and Norman Ornstein, *The Permanent Campaign and Its Future* (Washington, DC: American Enterprise Institute, 2000).

28. David Mayhew, *Congress: The Electoral Connection* (New Haven, CT: Yale University Press, 1973).

29. Henry Chappell and William Keech, "A New Model of Political Accountability for Economic Performance," *American Political Science Review* 79 (1985): 10–19.

30. Jonathan Krasno and Donald P. Green, "The Dynamics of Campaign Fundraising in House Elections," *Journal of Politics* 56 (1991): 459–74.

31. Michael J. Goff, *The Money Primary: The New Politics of the Early Presidential Nomination Process* (New York: Rowman and Littlefield, 2007).

32. Chris Cillizza, "Consulting Firms Face Conflict in 2008," *Roll Call*, June 20, 2005, p. 1.

33. For details, see Committee on Standards of Official Conduct, "Laws, Rules, and Standards of Conduct Governing Campaign Activity," memorandum April 25, 2008, http://ethics .house.gov/sites/ethics.house.gov/files/m_campaign _activity_2008_o.pdf (accessed 11/6/12).

34. Cherie Maestas, Walter Stone, and L. Sandy Maisel, "Quality Counts: Extending the Strategic Politician Model of Incumbent Deterrence," *American Journal of Political Science* 48 (2004): 479–90.

35. Matt Bai, "Turnout Wins Elections," *New York Times Magazine*, December 14, 2003, p. 100.

36. Christopher Drew, "New Telemarketing Ploy Steers Voters on Republican Path," *New York Times*, November 6, 2006.

37. Donald Green and Alan Gerber, "The Effects of Canvassing, Phone Calls, and Direct Mail on Voter Turnout: A Field Experiment," *American Political Science Review* 94 (2000): 653–69; Lynn Vavreck, Constantine J. Spiliotes, and Linda L. Fowler, "The Effect of Retail Politics in the New Hampshire Primary," *American Journal of Political Science* 46 (2002): 595–610.

38. John Dickerson, "Weak Poll," *Slate*, October 30, 2006, www .slate.com/id/2152529 (accessed 10/19/12).

39. Adam Nagourney and Megan Thee, "With Election Driven by Iraq, Voters Want New Approach," *New York Times*, November 2, 2006, p. A1.

40. For a history of presidential debates, see the Commission on Presidential Debates site at www.debates.org (accessed 10/19/12).

41. See the transcript of the first debate: Commission on Presidential Debates, Debate Transcript, September 30, 2004, www.debates.org/index.php?page=september-30-2004 -debate transcript (accessed 10/19/12).

42. Michael Powell, "Barack Bowl," *New York Times*, March 30, 2008, http://thecaucus.blogs.nytimes.com/2008/03/30/ barack-bowl (accessed 10/19/12).

43. Maureen Dowd, "Eggheads and Cheese Balls," *New York Times*, April 16, 2008.

44. Helen A. S. Popkin and Ree Hines, "MySpace: A Place for Candidates," MSNBC, June 20, 2007, www.msnbc.msn .com/id/19337775 (accessed 10/19/12).

45. Molly Ball, "This Year's Attack Ads Cut Deeper," *Politico*, October 17, 2010, www.politico.com/news/stories/1010/ 43698.html (accessed 10/19/12).

46. For a video library of presidential campaign ads, see Museum of the Moving Image, "The Living Room Candidate: Presidential Campaign Commercials 1952–2012," http://livingroom candidate.org (accessed 10/19/12).

47. Museum of the Moving Image, "The Living Room Candidate: 1964: Johnson vs. Goldwater," http://livingroomcandidate .org/commercials/1964/dowager (accessed 10/19/12).

48. Museum of the Moving Image, "The Living Room Candidate: 1964: Johnson vs. Goldwater."

49. For examples of this argument, see Thomas Patterson, *The Vanishing Voter* (New York: Knopf, 2002), and Jules Witcover, *No Way to Pick a President: How Money and Hired Guns Have Debased American Politics* (London, UK: Routledge, 2001).

50. For examples of these and other campaign ads, see "Most Intriguing Campaign Ads of 2010," ABC News, http:// abcnews.go.com/politics/slideshow/intriguing-political-ads -2010-10887147 (accessed 10/19/12).

51. Paul Freeman, Michael Franz, and Kenneth Goldstein, "Campaign Advertising and Democratic Citizenship," *American Journal of Political Science* 48 (2004): 723–41.

52. Constantine J. Spilotes and Lynn Vavreck, "Campaign Advertising: Partisan Convergence or Divergence," *Journal of Politics* 64 (2002): 249–61.

53. Kathleen Hall Jameson, *Packaging the Presidency: A History and Criticism of Presidential Campaign Advertising* (New York: Oxford University Press, 1996).

54. Steven Ansolabehere and Shanto Iyengar, *Going Negative: How Political Advertisements Shrink and Polarize the Electorate* (New York: Free Press, 1997); Richard Lau, Lee Sigelman, Caroline Heldman, and Paul Babbitt, "The Effects of Negative Political Advertisements: A

Meta-Analytic Analysis," *American Political Science Review* 93 (1999): 851–70.

55. Jonathan Krasno and Frank J. Sorauf, "For the Defense," *Political Science and Politics* 37 (2004): 777–80.

56. Contribution and spending data are available from the Center for Responsive Politics at www.opensecrets.org.

57. Brian Stelter, "The Price of 30 Seconds," *New York Times*, October 1, 2007, http://mediadecoder.blogs.nytimes.com/2007/10/01/the-price-of-30-seconds (accessed 10/19/12).

58. Wal-Mart Stores, Inc., "Annual Report to Shareholders, 2006," March 29, 2006, www.sec.gov/Archives/edgar/data/104169/000119312506066792/dex13.htm (accessed 10/19/12).

59. Data from www.opensecrets.org (accessed 11/1/12).

60. For a review of this literature, see Michael Malbin, *The Election after Reform: Money, Politics, and the Bipartisan Campaign Reform Act* (Washington, DC: Rowman and Littlefield, 2006).

61. For a discussion, see Patterson, *The Vanishing Voter*, especially Chapter 1, "The Incredible Shrinking Electorate," pp. 3–22.

62. William H. Riker and Peter Ordeshook, "A Theory of the Calculus of Voting," *American Political Science Review* 62 (1968): 25–39.

63. Michael McDonald, The United States Elections Project, http://elections.gmu.edu (accessed 10/19/12).

64. Pew Research Center, "Regular Voters, Intermittent Voters, and Those Who Don't," October 18, 2006, available at www.people-press.org/reports/pdf/292.pdf.

65. Raymond Wolfinger and Jonathan Hoffman, "Registering and Voting with Motor Voter," *Political Science and Politics* 34 (2001): 85–92.

66. For a review of the literature on issue voters, see Jon K. Dalager, "Voters, Issues, and Elections: Are Candidates' Messages Getting Through?" *Journal of Politics* 58 (1996): 486–515.

67. Richard P. Lau and David P. Reslawsk, *How Voters Decide: Information Processing during Electoral Campaigns* (New York: Cambridge University Press, 2006).

68. Gary Cox and Jonathan Katz, "Why Did the Incumbency Advantage in U.S. House Elections Grow?" *American Journal of Political Science* 40 (1996): 478–96.

69. Charles Franklin, "Eschewing Obfuscation: Campaigns and the Perceptions of U.S. Senate Incumbents," *American Political Science Review* 85 (December 1991): 1193–214; Wendy M. Rahn, "The Role of Partisan Stereotypes in Information Processing about Political Candidates," *American Journal of Political Science* 37 (May 1993): 472–96.

70. Bruce Cain, John Ferejohn, and Morris Fiorina, *The Personal Vote* (Cambridge, MA: Harvard University Press, 1985).

71. Jeffrey Koch, "Gender Stereotypes and Citizens' Impressions of House Candidates' Ideological Orientations," *American Journal of Political Science* 46 (2002): 453–62; Monica McDermott, "Candidate Occupations and Voter Informa-

tion," *Journal of Politics* 67 (2005): 201–18; Carol Sigelman, Lee Sigelman, Barbara Walkosz, and Michael Nitz, "Black Candidates, White Voters: Understanding Racial Bias in Political Perceptions," *American Journal of Political Science* 39 (February 1995): 243–65.

72. Fiorina, *Retrospective Voting in American National Elections*; Key, *The Responsible Electorate*.

73. Alfred J. Tuchfarber, Stephen E. Bennett, Andrew E. Smith, and Eric W. Rademacher, "The Republican Tidal Wave of 1994: Testing Hypotheses about Realignment, Restructuring, and Rebellion," *Political Science and Politics* 28 (1995): 689–93.

74. Samuel Popkin, *The Reasoning Voter* (Chicago: University of Chicago Press, 1991).

75. Richard R. Lau and David P. Redlawsk, "Advantages and Disadvantages of Cognitive Heuristics in Political Decision Making," *American Journal of Political Science* 45 (2001): 951–71.

76. Morris P. Fiorina, "Keystone Reconsidered," in *Congress Reconsidered*, 8th ed., ed. Lawrence Dodd and Bruce Oppenheimer (Washington, DC: CQ Press, 2004), pp. 159–77.

77. James Campbell and James Garrand, *Forecasting Presidential Elections* (Beverly Hills, CA: Sage, 2000).

78. For 2006 exit poll data, see Pew Research Center, "Public Cheers Democratic Victory," November 16, 2006, www.people-press.org/reports/display.php3?ReportID=296 (accessed 10/19/12).

79. For data on presidential approval and evaluations of Congress in normal and nationalized elections, see Pew Research Center, "Democrats Hold Double-Digit Lead in Competitive Districts," October 6, 2006, www.people-press.org/reports/display.php3?ReportID=293 (accessed 3/31/08).

80. For 2006 exit poll data, see Pew Research Center, "Public Cheers Democratic Victory," November 16, 2006, www.people-press.org/reports/display.php3?ReportID=296 (accessed 10/19/12).

81. Pew Research Center, "Midterm Snapshot: Enthusiasm for Obama Reelection Bid Greater than for Reagan in 1982," October 25, 2010. www.pewresearch.org/pubs/1778/public-split-on-obama-run-in-2012-but-better-than-reagan-outlook-in-1982?src=prc-latest&proj=forum (accessed 10/19/12).

82. Amanda Terkel, "The One-Person Funded Super-PAC: How Wealthy Donors Can Skirt Campaign Finance Restrictions." Huffington Post, October 22, 2010, www.huffingtonpost.com/2010/10/21/super-pac-taxpayers-earmarks-concerned-citizens-campaign-finance_n_772214.html (accessed 10/19/12).

83. Michael Luo and Griff Palmer, "Democrats Retain Edge in Campaign Spending," *New York Times*, October 27, 2010, p. A1.

84. Amy Gardner, "Gauging the Scope of the Tea Party Movement in America," *Washington Post*, October 24, 2010, p. A1.

In Comparison

a. For details on proportional representation in these countries, see Michael Gallagher, Michael Laver, and Peter Mair, *Representation of Government in Modern Europe* (London, UK: McGraw-Hill Europe, 2000).

b. Lani Guinier, "No Two Seats: The Elusive Quest for Political Equality," *Virginia Law Review* 77 (1991): 1414–28.

What Do Political Scientists Do?

a. Sides's post about independent votes, "Three Myths about Political Independents," www.themonkeycage.org/2009/12/three_myths_about_political_in.html (accessed 10/19/12).

CHAPTER 9

1. Capital Eye Blog, "TARP Recipients Paid Out $114 Million for Politicking Last Year," February 4, 2009, www.opensecrets.org/news/2009/02/tarp-recipients-paid-out-114-m.html (accessed 9/18/12).

2. Joe Weisenthal, "Congressmen: Yep, Wall Street Owns Washington," June 4, 2009, www.businessinsider.com/congressman-yep-wall-street-owns-washington-2009-6 (accessed 8/28/09).

3. Robert A. Dahl, *A Preface to Democratic Theory* (Chicago: University of Chicago Press, 1951); and David Truman, *The Governmental Process* (New York: Harper and Row, 1951).

4. Theodore Lowi, *The End of Liberalism: The Second Republic of the United States* (New York: Norton, 1979).

5. Lobbying regulations are often changed; the discussion here is just a general guide. Regular reports on past, current, and proposed lobbying regulations can be found on the website of the Congressional Research Service at www.opencrs.com (accessed 9/19/12).

6. Frank Baumgartner and Beth Leech, *Basic Interests: The Importance of Interest Groups in Politics and in Political Science* (Princeton, NJ: Princeton University Press, 1999), p. 109.

7. Timothy M. LaPira and Nicholas A. Semanko, "Drawing Lobbyists to Washington: Government Activity and the Demand for Advocacy," *Political Research Quarterly* 58: 1 (March 2005): 19–30.

8. Timothy M. LaPira, "The Allure of Reform: The Increasing Demand for Health Care Lobbying from Clinton's Task Force to Obama's Big [Expletive] Deal," in *Interest Group Politics,* 8th ed., ed. Alan Cigler and Burdett Loomis (Washington, DC: CQ Press, 2011).

9. Frances Cairncross, *The Death of Distance: How the Communication Revolution Is Changing Our Lives* (Cambridge, MA: Harvard Business School Press, 2001).

10. Leslie Wayne, "Documents Show Extent of Lobbying by Boeing," *New York Times*, September 3, 2003.

11. Center for Responsive Politics, Lobbying Spending Database, "General Electric Summary, 2006," www.opensecrets.org/lobbyists/clientsum.asp?txtname=General+Electric&year=2006 (accessed 4/7/08).

12. Center for Responsive Politics, "Sierra Club Summary, 2006" (accessed 4/7/08).

13. For more on this argument, see Tim Harford, "There's Not Enough Money in Politics," *Slate*, April 1, 2006, www.slate.com/id/2138874 (accessed 4/8/08); and Stephen Ansolabehere, John M. de Figueiredo, and James M. Snyder, "Why Is There So Little Money in American Politics?" *Journal of Economic Perspectives* 17 (2003): 105–30.

14. John R. Wright, *Interest Groups and Congress: Lobbying, Contributions, and Influence* (New York: Longman, 1995).

15. Scott Ainsworth, *Analyzing Interest Groups: Group Influence on People and Policies* (New York: Norton, 2002).

16. Timothy Egan, "For Thirsty Farmers, Old Friends at Interior," *New York Times*, March 3, 2006, p. A1.

17. Public Citizen Congress Watch, "Congressional Revolving Doors: The Journey from Congress to K Street," July 2005, www.lobbyinginfo.org/documents/RevolveDoor.pdf (accessed 4/9/08).

18. Eric Lipton, "Former Antiterror Officials Find Industry Pays Better," *New York Times*, June 18, 2006, p. A1.

19. Jacob Weisberg, "A Tale of Two Lobbyists," April 19, 2009, www.slate.com/id/2216433/ (accessed 9/19/12).

20. Robert H. Salisbury, John P. Heinz, Edward O. Laumann, and Robert L. Nelson, "Who Works with Whom? Interest Group Alliances and Opposition," *American Political Science Review* 81 (1987): 1217–34.

21. Business-Industry Political Action Committee, "About BIPAC," www.bipac.org/about/about.asp (accessed 4/8/08).

22. One example campaign is MoveOn.org Political Action Committee, "Letter to the Editor: Tell the Media: We Want to End the War. The President Wants Endless War," http://pol.moveon.org/lte/?lte_campaign_id=72 (accessed 4/8/08).

23. Thomas Holyoke, "Choosing Battlegrounds: Interest Group Lobbying across Multiple Venues," *Political Science Quarterly* 56 (2003): 325–36.

24. Scott Ainsworth, "Regulating Lobbyists and Interest Group Influence," *Journal of Politics* 55 (1993): 41–55.

25. AARP, "Policy and Research for Professionals in Aging," www.aarp.org/research/ppi (accessed 4/8/08).

26. James Q. Wilson, *Political Organizations* (New York: Basic Books, 1974).

27. American Automobile Association, Foundation for Traffic Safety, www.aaafoundation.org/home (accessed 4/8/08).

28. Jack Walker, *Mobilizing Interest Groups in America* (Ann Arbor: University of Michigan Press, 1991).

29. Kenneth Kollman, *Outside Lobbying: Public Opinion and Interest Group Strategies* (Princeton, NJ: Princeton University Press, 1998).

30. Robert Salisbury, "An Exchange Theory of Interest Groups," *Midwest Journal of Political Science* 13 (1969): 1–32.

31. Walker, *Mobilizing Interest Groups in America*.

32. Kollman, *Outside Lobbying*.

33. Walker, *Mobilizing Interest Groups in America*.

34. Derived from a search of the congressional lobbying disclosure database at http://disclosures.house.gov/ld/ldsearch.aspx (accessed 1/11/12).

35. John P. Heinz, Edward O. Laumann, and Robert Salisbury, *The Hollow Core: Private Interests in National Policymaking* (Cambridge, MA: Harvard University Press, 1993).

36. Richard L. Hall and Alan V. Deardorff, "Lobbying as Legislative Subsidy," *American Political Science Review* 100 (2006): 69–84.

37. Hall and Deardorff, "Lobbying as Legislative Subsidy."

38. David Austen-Smith and John R. Wright, "Counteractive Lobbying," *American Journal of Political Science* 38:1 (1994): 25–44.

39. Key Lehman Schlozman and John T. Tierney, *Organized Interests and American Democracy* (New York: HarperCollins, 1986).

40. Baumgartner and Leech, *Basic Interests*, p. 152.

41. Christine A. DeGregorio, *Networks of Champions: Leadership, Access, and Advocacy in the U.S. House of Representatives* (Ann Arbor: University of Michigan Press, 1992).

42. Daniel Carpenter, *The Forging of Bureaucratic Autonomy: Reputations, Networks, and Policy Innovation in Executive Agencies, 1862–1928* (Princeton, NJ: Princeton University Press, 2002).

43. Public Citizen Publications, www.citizen.org/publications (accessed 7/25/09).

44. Derived from a search of the NRA Institute for Legislative Action site, www.nraila.org (accessed 9/19/12).

45. Kim Scheppele and Jack L. Walker, "The Litigation Strategies of Interest Groups," in *Mobilizing Interest Groups in America*, ed. Jack Walker (Ann Arbor: University of Michigan Press, 1991).

46. Lauren Cohen Bell, *Warring Factions: Interest Groups, Money, and the New Politics of Senate Confirmation* (Columbus: Ohio State University Press, 2002).

47. Kevin W. Hula, *Lobbying Together: Interest Group Coalitions in Legislative Politics* (Washington, DC: Georgetown University Press, 1999).

48. Jeanne Cummings, "Word Games Could Threaten Climate Bill," June 9, 2009, www.politico.com/news/stories/0609/24059.html (accessed 9/19/12).

49. AARP, "Elected Officials," http://capwiz.com/aarp/dbq/officials (accessed 4/8/08).

50. Dana Milbank, "Obama Is Just Not Their Cup of Tea," *Washington Post*, April 16, 2009; David Espo, " 'Special Interests' on Both Sides in Health Fight," *The Seattle Times*, August 19, 2009, http://seattletimes.com/html/politics/2009692056_apobamahealthspecialinterests.html (accessed 10/26/12).

51. Richard Fenno, *Home Style: U.S. House Members in Their Districts* (Boston: Little, Brown, 1978). See also Brandice Caines-Wrone, David W. Brady, and John F. Cogan, "Out of Step, Out of Office: Electoral Accountability and House Members' Voting," *American Political Science Review* 96 (2002): 127–40.

52. Emily Yoffe, "Am I the Next Jack Abramoff?" April 1, 2006, www.slate.com/id/2137886/ (accessed 8/28/09).

53. Kollman, *Outside Lobbying*.

54. Gregory Calderia, Marie Hojnacki, and John R. Wright, "The Lobbying Activities of Organized Interests in Federal Judicial Nominations," *Journal of Politics* 62 (2000): 51–69.

55. Robert Pear, "Medicare Law Prompts a Rush for Lobbyists," *New York Times*, August 23, 2005.

56. Data from www.opensecrets.org/527s/index.php and based on FEC data (accessed 11/7/12).

57. John R. Wright, "PAC Contributions, Lobbying, and Representation," *Journal of Politics* 51:3 (August 1989): 713–29.

58. John G. Matsusaka, "Direct Democracy and Fiscal Gridlock: Have Voter Initiatives Paralyzed the California Budget?" *State Politics and Policy* 5 (2005): 346–62.

59. Thad Kousser, *Term Limits and the Dismantling of State Legislative Professionalism* (New York: Cambridge University Press, 2004).

60. John G. Matsusaka, *For the Many or the Few: The Initiative, Public Policy, and American Democracy* (Chicago: University of Chicago Press, 2004).

61. Elizabeth R. Gerber, *The Populist Paradox: Interest Group Influence and the Promise of Direct Legislation* (Princeton, NJ: Princeton University Press, 1999).

62. Baumgartner and Leech, *Basic Interests*, Chapter 8, pp. 147–67.

63. Jeffrey Birnbaum, "The Humane Society Becomes a Political Animal," *Washington Post*, January 30, 2007, p. A15.

64. For details, see the blog of the Humane Society's president, Wayne Pacelle, at http://hsus.typepad.com/wayne (accessed 7/25/09).

65. Hayley Tsukayama, "Companies Taking a Stand Against Piracy Caught in SOPA Crosshairs." *The Washington Post* January 13, 2011, p. B1.

66. Jeffrey H. Birnbaum, "The Forces That Set the Agenda," *Washington Post*, April 24, 2005, p. B1.

67. For a review, see Carpenter, *The Forging of Bureaucratic Autonomy*.

68. Baumgartner and Leech, *Basic Interests*, Chapter 7, especially Table 7.1 and Table 7.2, pp. 130 and 132.

69. Baumgartner and Leech, *Basic Interests*, p. 133.

70. Frank Baumgartner, Jeffrey M. Berry, Marie Hojnacki, David C. Kimball, and Beth L. Leech, *Lobbying and Policy Change: Who Wins, Who Loses, and Why* (Chicago: University of Chicago Press, 2009).

71. National Rifle Association Institute for Legislative Action, "Fact Sheet: Right-to-Carry 2007," www.nraila.org/Issues/FactSheets/Read.aspx?ID=18 (accessed 4/9/08).

72. National Rifle Association Institute for Legislative Action, "Fact Sheet: Right-to-Carry: The Stearns/Boucher Right-to-Carry Reciprocity Bill," www.nraila.org/Issues/FactSheets/Read.aspx?id=189&issue=003 (accessed 4/9/08).

73. David Lowery, "Why Do Organized Interests Lobby? A Multi-Goal, Multi-Context Theory of Lobbying," *Polity* 39 (2007): 29–54.

74. Baumgartner and Leech, *Basic Interests*, Chapter 7, pp. 120–46.

75. John M. Berry, *The Interest Group Society* (New York: Harper Collins, 1997); Raymond A. Bauer, Ithiel de Sola Pool, and Lewis Dexter, *American Business and Public Policy* (New York: Atherton Press, 1963).

76. Ken Kollman, *Outside Lobbying* (Princeton, NJ: Princeton University Press, 1998).

77. Frank Baumgartner and Beth Leech, "Interest Niches and Policy Bandwagons: Patterns of Interest Group Involvement in National Politics," *Journal of Politics* 63 (2001): 1191–213.

78. Austen-Smith and Wright, "Counteractive Lobbying"; Frank R. Baumgartner and Beth L. Leech, "The Multiple Ambiguities of 'Counteractive Lobbying,' " *American Journal of Political Science* 40 (1996): 521–42.

In Comparison

a. Mancur Olson, *The Rise and Decline of Nations* (Cambridge, MA: Harvard University Press, 1984).

b. James E. Curtis, Douglas E. Baer, and Edward G. Grubb, "Nations of Joiners: Explaining Voluntary Association Membership in Democratic Societies," *American Sociological Review* 66 (2001): 783–805.

c. Arndt Wonka, Frank R. Baumgartner, Christine Mahoney, and Joost Berkhout, "Measuring the Size and Scope of the EU Interest Group Population," *European Union Politics* 11 (2010): 463–76.

d. Michael Gallagher, Peter Mair, and Michael Laver, *Representative Government in Modern Europe* (New York: McGraw-Hill, 2005).

e. Fritz Plasser and Gunda Plasser, *Global Political Campaigning: A Worldwide Analysis of Campaign Professionals and Their Practices* (New York: Praeger, 2002).

f. Daniel Nelson, "Supplying Trade Reform: Political Institutions and Liberalization in Middle-Income Presidential Democracies," *American Journal of Political Science* 47 (2003): 470–93; Nina Rudra, "Globalization and the Decline of the Welfare State in Less-Developed Countries," *International Organization* 56 (2002): 411–45.

g. Justin Greenwood, *Interest Representation in the European Parliament* (London: Palgrave Macmillan, 2003).

You Decide

a. Jacob Weisberg, "Three Cities, Three Scandals: What Jack Abramoff, Anthony Pellicano, and Jared Paul Stern Have in Common," *Slate*, April 9, 2006, www.slate.com/id/2140238 (accessed 10/25/12).

b. Associated Press, "Others Caught up in Abramoff Scandal," *New York Times*, March 23, 2007, www.nytimes.com/aponline/us/AP-Griles-Abramoff-Glance.htm (accessed 4/5/07). Associated Press, "Former Deputy Interior Secretary to Plead Guilty in Lobbyist Case," *New York Times*, March 23, 2007, www.nytimes.com/aponline/washington/AP-Griles-Abramoff.htm (accessed 4/5/07).

c. For the full text of this proposal, see League of Women Voters et al., "Ethics and Lobbying Reform: Six Benchmarks for Lobbying Reform," January 23, 2006, www.lwv.org (accessed 9/11/12).

What Do Political Scientists Do?

a. Stephen Ansolabehere, John de Figueiredo, and James Snyder, "Why Is There So Little Money in American Politics?" *Journal of Economic Perspectives* 17 (2003): 105–30.

b. Kevin Esterling, "Buying Expertise: Campaign Contributions and Attention to Policy Analysis in Congressional Committees," *American Political Science Review* 101 (2007): 93–109

CHAPTER 10

1. See Paul Gronke, *The Electorate, the Campaign, and the Office: A Unified Approach to Senate and House Elections* (Ann Arbor: University of Michigan Press, 2000), for research showing that the House and Senate elections share many similar characteristics. See Richard F. Fenno, *Senators on the Campaign Trail: The Politics of Representation* (Norman: University of Oklahoma Press, 1996), for a good general discussion of Senate elections.

2. Claudine Gay, "Spirals of Trust? The Effect of Descriptive Representation on the Relationship between Citizens and Their Government," *American Journal of Political Science* 46:4 (October 2002): 717–32; Katherine Tate, *Black Faces in the Mirror: African Americans and Their Representatives in Congress* (Princeton: Princeton University Press, 2003), Chapter 7. However, Tate shows that African Americans who are represented by African Americans in Congress are not any more likely to vote, be involved in politics, or have higher overall approval rates of Congress than African Americans who are not descriptively represented.

3. In addition to those mentioned in the text, there were two other African Americans who were elected by state legislatures to serve in the Senate during the Reconstruction period and one, Roland Burris (D-Ill.), who was appointed to serve the rest of Barack Obama's term.

4. R. Douglas Arnold, *The Logic of Congressional Action* (New Haven, CT: Yale University Press, 1990), pp. 60–71.

5. Richard F. Fenno, *Home Style: House Members in Their Districts* (Boston: Little, Brown, 1978).

6. David R. Mayhew, *Congress: The Electoral Connection* (New Haven, CT: Yale University Press, 1974).

7. Mayhew, *Congress*, p. 17.

8. Mayhew, *Congress*, p. 37.

9. Patrick J. Sellers, "Fiscal Consistency and Federal District Spending in Congressional Elections," *American Journal of Political Science* 41:3 (July 1997): 1024–41.

10. Sean Trende, "In Pennsylvania, the Gerrymander of the Decade?, Real Clear Politics, December 14, 2011, www.realclearpolitics.com/articles/2011/12/14/in_pennsylvania_the_gerrymander_of_the_decade_112404.html (accessed 12/20/11); Dennis Byrne, "GOP Can't Catch a Break on Fairness, *Chicago Tribune*, December 20, 2011, www.chicagotribune.com/news/opinion/ct-oped-1220-byrne-20111220,0,7120320.column (accessed 12/20/11).

11. Dan Eggen, "Justice Staff Saw Texas Districting as Illegal: Voting Rights Finding on Map Pushed by DeLay Was Overruled," *Washington Post*, December 2, 2005, p. A1. The court case is *League of United Latin American Citizens v. Perry*, 547 U.S. (2006).

12. All poll data except the poll comparing Congress to other occupations are from PollingReport.com (www.pollingreport.com). The occupations poll was cited in Karlyn Bowman and Everett Carll Ladd, "Public Opinion toward Congress: A Historical Look," in *Congress, the Press, and the Public*, ed. Thomas E. Mann and Norman J. Ornstein (Washington, DC: Brookings Institution Press, 1994), p. 50.

13. "Check bouncing" is in quotes because the checks did not actually bounce. The scandal involved penalty-free overdrafts permitted in members' accounts in the House bank (which allowed some members to abuse the privilege by using the overdrafts as short-term, interest-free loans). Many voters saw this as another unfair benefit to members of Congress, but others considered it a nonscandal because no taxpayers' money was at stake.

14. Mark J. Rozell, "Press Coverage of Congress, 1946–1992," in *Congress, the Press, and the Public*, ed. Thomas E. Mann and Norman J. Ornstein (Washington, DC: Brookings Institution Press, 1994), p. 110.

15. Burdett A. Loomis, *The Contemporary Congress* (Belmont, CA: Wadsworth, 2000), p. 47.

16. R. Douglas Arnold, *Congress, the Press, and Political Accountability* (Princeton, NJ: Princeton University Press, 2004), p. 80.

17. See Kenneth R. Mayer and David T. Canon, *The Dysfunctional Congress: The Individual Roots of an Institutional Dilemma*, 2nd ed. (New York: Columbia University Press, 2011) for an extended discussion of this argument.

18. Richard F. Fenno, "If as Ralph Nader Says, Congress Is the 'Broken Branch,' How Come We Love Our Congressman So Much?" in *Congress in Change: Evolution and Reform*, ed. Norman J. Ornstein (New York: Praeger, 1975), pp. 277–87.

19. David T. Canon, "History in the Making: The 2nd District in Wisconsin," in *The Battle for Congress: Candidates, Consultants, and Voters*, ed. James A. Thurber (Washington, DC: Brookings Institution Press, 2001), pp. 199–238.

20. Gary C. Jacobson, *The Politics of Congressional Elections*, 5th ed. (New York: Longman, 2001), pp. 24–30.

21. Fenno, *Home Style.*

22. Morris Fiorina, *Congress: Keystone of the Washington Establishment*, rev. ed. (New Haven: Yale University Press, 1989).

23. Mayhew, *Congress: The Electoral Connection*, pp. 82–83.

24. Felicia Sonmez and Joby Warrick, "Congress Sends Defense Bill to Obama after Reworking Detainee Provisions," *Washington Post*, December 15, 2011.

25. John McCain, "Remarks by Senator John McCain on the Conference Report of the FY2012 Omnibus Appropriations Bill, December 16, 2011," http://mccain.senate.gov/public/index.cfm?FuseAction=PressOffice.PressReleases&ContentRecord_id=48f0c068-a39a-0237-fb097faf7546fb90 (accessed 12/19/11).

26. Jonathan Weisman and Jim VandeHei, "Road Bill Reflects the Power of Pork; White House Drops Effort to Rein in Hill," *Washington Post*, August 11, 2005, p. A1.

27. An important qualification to the norm was imposed by Republicans in 1995 when they set a six-year term limit for committee and subcommittee chairs.

28. David W. Rohde, *Parties and Leaders in the Post-reform House* (Chicago: University of Chicago Press, 1991).

29. David Rohde and John Aldrich, "The Transition to Republican Rule in the House: Implications for Theories of Congressional Politics," *Political Science Quarterly* 112:4 (Winter 1997–1998): 541–67.

30. Nelson W. Polsby, *Congress and the Presidency*, 4th ed. (Englewood Cliffs, NJ: Prentice Hall, 1986), p. 111.

31. CBS News, "Obama: Fundraiser-in-chief," August 5, 2010, www.cbsnews.com/video/watch/?id-6747632n (accessed 8/18/10).

32. "James Traficant Hearing; Kick Them in the Crotch," www.youtube.com/watch?v=tQ5Os1400uc&feature=related (accessed 5/7/08).

33. David E. Price, "Congressional Committees in the Policy Process," in *Congress Reconsidered*, 3rd ed., ed. Lawrence C. Dodd and Bruce I. Oppenheimer (Washington, DC: CQ Press, 1985), pp. 161–88.

34. Richard F. Fenno, *Congressmen in Committees* (Boston: Little, Brown, 1973).

35. Richard L. Hall, *Participation in Congress* (New Haven, CT: Yale University Press, 1996).

36. Barbara Sinclair, *Unorthodox Lawmaking* (Washington, DC: CQ Press, 2000), p. xiv.

37. Sinclair, *Unorthodox Lawmaking*, p. 59.

38. Louis Fisher, "The Pocket Veto: Its Current Status," Congressional Research Service Report RL30909, March 30, 2001. The appeals court case was *Barnes v. Kline*, 759 F.2d 21 (D.C. Cir., 1985).

39. Kenneth Chamberlain, "Government Shutdown Scares through the Years," *National Journal*, December 14, 2011, www.nationaljournal.com/congress/government-shutdown-scares-through-the-years-20111214 (accessed 12/19/11).

40. Dafne Eviatar, "Patriot Act Renewal Kicks Off over Party Lines," *Washington Independent*, September 23, 2009, http://

washingtonindependent.com/60575/debate-over-patriot-act-renewal-kicks-off-over-party-lines (accessed 12/19/11).

41. Howard H. Baker Jr., Leaders Lecture Series Address to the Senate (Washington, DC, July 14, 1998) www.senate.gov/artandhistory/history/common/generic/Leaders_Lecture_Series_Baker.htm (accessed 5/7/08).

42. CNN Wire Staff, "Holder to Critics: Have You No Shame?" December 8, 2011, http://articles.cnn.com/2011-12-08/politics/politics_congress-fast-and-furious_1_operation-fast-and-furious-darrell-issa-gop-critics?_s=PM: POLITICS (accessed 12/19/11).

43. Mathew McCubbins and Thomas Schwartz, "Congressional Oversight Overlooked: Police Patrol versus Fire Alarm," *American Journal of Political Science* 28:1 (February 1984): 165–77.

44. *Immigration and Naturalization Service v. Chadha*, 462 U.S. 919 (1983).

45. Louis Fisher, "Legislative Vetoes after *Chadha*," Congressional Research Service Report RS22132, Washington, DC, May 2, 2005, www.loufisher.org/docs/lv/4116.pdf (accessed 12/20/11).

What Do Political Scientists Do?

a. Bill Bishop, *The Big Sort: Why the Clustering of Like-Minded America Is Tearing Us Apart* (Boston: Houghton Mifflin Harcourt, 2008).

b. Sean M. Theriault, *Party Polarization in Congress* (New York: Cambridge University Press, 2008).

c. Sean M. Theriault, "The Procedurally Polarized Congress," unpublished paper, April 6, 2009, http://harrisschool.uchicago.edu/programs/beyond/workshops/ampolpapers/spring09-theriault.pdf (accessed 4/27/11).

You Decide

a. This figure comes from a report by the Citizens against Government Waste, "Pork Alert: Defense Conference Report Loaded with Earmarks,"www.cagw.org/newroom/releases/2009/pork-alert-defense.html (accessed 1/6/10). A lower figure of $4 billion in earmarks was reported in John D. McKinnon and Brody Mullins, "Defense Bill Earmarks Total $4 Billion," *Wall Street Journal*, December 23, 2009, p. A1.

In Comparison

a. Information was drawn from John M. Carey, "Legislative Organization," in *Oxford Handbook of Political Institutions*, ed. Sarah Binder, Rod Rhodes, and Bert Rockman (New York: Oxford University Press, 2005); Gerhard Lowenberg, Peverill Squire, and D. Roderick Kiewiet, eds., *Legislatures: Comparative Perspectives on Representative Assemblies* (Ann Arbor: University of Michigan Press, 2002); and Gary W. Cox, "The Organization of Democratic Legislatures," in *Oxford Handbook of Political Economy*, ed. Barry Weingast and Donald Wittman (New York: Oxford University Press, 2005).

b. Tom Ginsburg, Rosalind Dixon, eds., *Comparative Constitutional Law* (Northhampton, MA: Edward Elgar, 2011), pp. 242–50.

CHAPTER 11

1. John Aldrich, *Why Parties?* (Chicago: University of Chicago Press, 1995).

2. Ernest R. May, *The Making of the Monroe Doctrine* (Cambridge, MA: Harvard University Press, 1975).

3. Arthur M. Schlesinger Jr., *The Age of Jackson* (Boston: Little, Brown, 1945).

4. David Greenberg, "Lincoln's Crackdown," *Slate*, November 30, 2001, www.slate.com/id/2059132 (accessed 4/29/08).

5. Steven Skowronek, *Building a New American State: The Expansion of National Administrative Capacities* (New York: Cambridge University Press, 1982).

6. Theda Skocpol, *Protecting Soldiers and Mothers: The Political Origins of Social Policy in the United States* (Cambridge, MA: Harvard University Press, 1995).

7. Kendrick Clements, *The Presidency of Woodrow Wilson* (Lawrence: University Press of Kansas, 1992).

8. Thomas J. Knock, *To End All Wars: Woodrow Wilson and the Quest for a New World Order* (New York: Oxford University Press, 1992).

9. Arthur M. Schlesinger Jr., *The Crisis of the Old Order, 1919–1933* (Boston: Houghton Mifflin, 1957).

10. William E. Leuchtenburg, *FDR Years: On Roosevelt and His Legacy* (New York: Columbia University Press, 1995).

11. Chester Pach and Elmo Richardson, *The Presidency of Dwight D. Eisenhower* (Lawrence: University Press of Kansas, 1991).

12. Jackie Calmes, "Audit Finds TARP Program Effective," *New York Times*, December 9, 2009, p. D1.

13. Executive Order no. 13425, "Trial of Alien Unlawful Enemy Combatants by Military Commission," February 14, 2007, www.fas.org/irp/offdocs/eo/eo-13425.htm (accessed 4/29/08).

14. Michael D. Shear, "Obama Extends Hospital Visitation Rights to Same-Sex Partners of Gays," *Washington Post*, April 16, 2010, p. A1.

15. Thomas J. Weko, *The Politicizing Presidency: The White House Personnel Office, 1948–1994* (Lawrence: University Press of Kansas, 1995).

16. Walter Dellinger and Dahlia Lithwick, "A Supreme Court Conversation," *Slate*, June 22, 2007, www.slate.com/id/2168856/entry/2168959 (accessed 4/29/08).

17. Jeff Zeleny, "Daschle Ends Bid for Post; Obama Concedes Mistake," *New York Times*, February 3, 2009, p. A1.

18. "Obama Appoints Berwick to Head Medicare and Medicaid during Congressional Recess," *Boston Globe*, July 6, 2010, www.boston.com/news/politics/politicalintelligence/2010/07/obama_appoints_1.html (accessed 11/2/10).

19. Kenneth Mayer, *With the Stroke of a Pen: Executive Orders and Presidential Power* (Princeton, NJ: Princeton University Press, 2001).

20. Kenneth Mayer and Kevin Price, "Unilateral Presidential Powers: Significant Executive Orders, 1949–1999," *Presidential Studies Quarterly* 32 (2002): 367–85.

21. David G. Adler, "The Constitution and Presidential Warmaking: An Enduring Debate," *Political Science Quarterly* 103 (1988): 1–36.

22. Richard F. Grimmett, "The War Powers Resolution: After Thirty Years," Congressional Research Service Report RL32267, March 11, 2004.

23. Lewis Fisher and David G. Adler, "The War Powers Resolution: Time to Say Goodbye," *Political Science Quarterly* 113:1 (1998): 1–20.

24. William G. Howell and Jon C. Pevehouse, *While Dangers Gather: Congressional Checks on Presidential War Powers* (Princeton, NJ: Princeton University Press, 2007).

25. John M. Broder, "The Climate Accord: The Overview; Clinton Adamant on Third World Role in Climate Accord," *New York Times*, December 12, 1997, pp. A1, A16.

26. Jeff Zeleny and Alan Cowell, "Addressing Muslims, Obama Pushes Mideast Peace," *New York Times*, June 4, 2009, p. A1.

27. Richard M. Stevenson, "The Nation; the High-Stakes Politics of Spending the Surplus," *New York Times*, January 7, 2001.

28. Ivo H. Daalder and James M. Lindsay, *America Unbound: The Bush Revolution in American Foreign Policy* (Washington, DC: Brookings Institution Press, 2003).

29. Aaron Wildavsky, "The Two Presidencies," *Trans-Action* 4 (1966): 7–35.

30. Mark A. Peterson, *Legislating Together: The White House and Capitol Hill from Eisenhower to Reagan* (Cambridge, MA: Harvard University Press, 1990).

31. Andrew Rudalevige, *Managing the President's Program: Presidential Leadership and Legislative Policy Formation* (Princeton, NJ: Princeton University Press, 2002).

32. "Campaign 2000: Today—Abortion; The Enduring Battle over Choice," *New York Times*, October 11, 2000.

33. Charles Cameron and Nolan M. McCarty, "Models of Vetoes and Veto Bargaining," *Annual Review of Political Science* 7 (2004): 409–35.

34. Keith Krehbiel, *Pivotal Politics: A Theory of U.S. Lawmaking* (Chicago: University of Chicago Press, 1998).

35. Charles Jones, *The Presidency in a Separated System* (Washington, DC: Brookings Institution Press, 1994).

36. Mark J. Rozell, "The Law: Executive Privilege: Definition and Standards of Application," *Presidential Studies Quarterly* 29:4 (1999): 918–30.

37. Raoul Berger, *Executive Privilege: A Constitutional Myth* (Cambridge, MA: Harvard University Press, 1974). For commentary, see Saikrisha Prakash, "A Comment on the Constitutionality of Executive Privilege," *Minnesota Law Review* 83:5 (May 1999): 1143–89.

38. See Oyez, *United States v. Nixon*, 418 U.S. 683 (1974), www.oyez.org/cases/1970–1979/1974/1974_73_1766 for a summary of the case (accessed 11/1/12).

39. Mark J. Rozell, "Something to Hide: Clinton's Misuse of Executive Privilege," *Political Science and Politics* 32 (1999): 550–53.

40. Mark J. Rozell, *Executive Privilege: The Dilemma of Secrecy and Democratic Accountability* (Baltimore, MD: Johns Hopkins University Press, 1994).

41. Ben Smith and David Paul Kuhn, "Obama Moves Quickly to Reshape DNC," *Politico*, June 13, 2008, www.politico.com/news/stories/0608/11045.html (accessed 7/2/08).

42. John D. McKinnon, "Backing Away from Bush; Some Republican Candidates Avoid Ties with Unpopular President," *Wall Street Journal*, May 23, 2006, p. A4; Carrie Budoff, "Is Bush's Support Worse Than No Support?" *Politico*, July 16, 2007, www.politico.com/news/stories/0707/4960.html (accessed 4/29/08).

43. George C. Edwards III, *The Public Presidency* (New York: St. Martin's Press, 1983); George C. Edwards III, *On Deaf Ears* (New Haven, CT: Yale University Press, 2003).

44. For evidence, see George Edwards, *On Deaf ears: The Limits of the Bully Pulpit* (New Haven, CT: Yale University Press, 2003).

45. For the text of the January 2007 speech, see "Bush: 'We Need to Change Our Strategy in Iraq,'" January 11, 2007, www.cnn.com/2007/POLITICS/01/10/bush.transcript/index.html (accessed 4/29/08).

46. Edwards, *On Deaf Ears.*

47. Samuel Kernell, *Going Public: New Strategies of Presidential Leadership*, 2nd ed. (Washington, DC: Congressional Quarterly Press, 1993).

48. David Carr, "Obama's Social Networking Was the Real Revolution," *New York Times*, November 9, 2008, www.nytimes.com/2008/11/09/technology/09iht-carr.1.17652000.html (accessed 11/2/10).

49. Associated Press, "Bush Regains Power after Colonoscopy," *New York Times*, July 21, 2007, www.nytimes.com/aponline/us/AP-Bush-Colonoscopy.html?hp (accessed 4/29/08).

50. Richard Cohen and Jules Witcover, *A Heartbeat Away: The Investigation and Resignation of Spiro T. Agnew* (New York: Viking, 1974).

51. John Hart, *The Presidential Branch: From Washington to Clinton* (Chatham, NY: Chatham House, 1987).

52. John Hart, "President Clinton and the Politics of Symbolism: Cutting the White House Staff," *Political Science Quarterly* 110 (1995): 385–403.

53. Michael Fletcher, "White House Had Drug Officials Appear with GOP Candidates," *Washington Post*, July 18, 2007, p. A8.

54. See White House, "White House Offices," www.whitehouse.gov/government/off-descrp.html (accessed 4/29/08).

55. Kelly Chang, David Lewis, and Nolan McCarthy, "The Tenure of Political Appointees," paper presented at the 2003 Midwest Political Science Association Annual Meeting, Chicago, April 4.

56. David E. Lewis, "Staffing Alone: Unilateral Action and the Politicization of the Executive Office of the President, 1988–2004," *Presidential Studies Quarterly* 35 (2005): 496–514.

57. Charles E. Walcott and Karen M. Hult, "White House Staff Size: Explanations and Implications," *Presidential Studies Quarterly* 29 (1999): 638–56.

58. Karen M. Hult and Charles E. Walcott, *Empowering the White House: Governance under Nixon, Ford, and Carter* (Lawrence: University Press of Kansas, 2004).

59. David E. Lewis, *The Politics of Presidential Appointments: Political Control and Bureaucratic Performance* (Princeton, NJ: Princeton University Press, 2008).

60. For a series of articles detailing Cheney's role, see "Angler: The Cheney Vice Presidency," *Washington Post,* June 24–27, 2007, www.washingtonpost.com/cheney (accessed 4/29/08).

61. For example, see David Talbot, "Creepier than Nixon," *Salon,* March 31, 2004, http://dir.salon.com/story/news/feature/2004/03/31/dean/index.html (accessed 4/29/08).

62. David Kirkpatrick, "Question of Timing on Bush's Push on Earmarks," *New York Times,* January 29, 2008.

63. John Mueller, *War, Presidents, and Public Opinion* (New York: John Wiley, 1973).

64. Alexander Hamilton and James Madison, *The Pacificus-Helvidius Debates of 1793–1794: Toward the Completion of the American Founding,* ed. Martin J. Frisch (1793; repr. Indianapolis, IN: Liberty Fund, 2007).

65. Richard E. Neustart, *Presidential Power and the Modern Presidents* (New York: Simon and Schuster, 1991).

66. Terry M. Moe and William G. Howell, "The Presidential Power of Unilateral Action," *Journal of Law, Economics, and Organization* 15 (1999): 132–46.

67. James Risen and Eric Lichtblau, "Spying Program Snared U.S. Calls," *New York Times,* December 21, 2005, p. A1; David E. Sanger, "After ABM Treaty: New Freedom for U.S. in Different Kind of Arms Control," *New York Times,* December 15, 2001.

68. For details, see the text of various executive orders at www.whitehouse.gov/briefing-room/presidential-actions/ (accessed 1/27/10).

69. These examples appear throughout Moe and Howell, "The Presidential Power of Unilateral Action"; see also William G. Howell, "Unilateral Powers: A Brief Overview," *Presidential Studies Quarterly* 35:3 (2005): 417–39.

70. David E. Lewis, *Presidents and the Politics of Agency Design* (Palo Alto, CA: Stanford University Press, 2003); William Howell and David Lewis, "Agencies by Presidential Design," *Journal of Politics* 64:4 (2002): 1095–114.

71. Louis Fisher, *Presidential War Power,* 2nd ed. (Lawrence: University Press of Kansas, 2004); James M. Lindsay, "Deference and Defiance: The Shifting Rhythms of Executive–Legislative Relations in Foreign Policy," *Presidential Studies Quarterly* 33:3 (2003): 530–46; Lawrence Margolis, *Executive Agreements and Presidential Power in Foreign Policy* (New York: Praeger, 1985), 209–32.

72. Phillip Cooper, "George W. Bush, Edgar Allan Poe, and the Use and Abuse of Presidential Signing Statements," *Presidential Studies Quarterly* 35:3 (2005): 515–32.

73. Andrew Rudalevige, *The New Imperial Presidency: Renewing Presidential Power after Watergate* (Ann Arbor: University of Michigan Press, 2005).

74. William G. Howell and Kenneth R. Mayer, "The Last One Hundred Days," *Presidential Studies Quarterly* 35:3 (2005): 533–53.

75. Christopher Deering and Forrest Maltzman, "The Politics of Executive Orders: Legislative Constraints on Presidential Power," *Political Research Quarterly* 52:4 (1999): 767–83.

76. David E. Lewis, *Presidents and the Politics of Agency Design: Political Insulation in the United States Government Bureaucracy, 1946–1997* (Palo Alto, CA: Stanford University Press, 2003).

77. David Epstein and Sharyn O'Halloran, *Delegating Powers* (Cambridge, UK: Cambridge University Press, 1999).

78. David G. Adler, "The Steel Seizure Case and Inherent Presidential Power," *Constitutional Commentary* 19 (2002): 155–208.

79. For a discussion of these and related cases, see Dahlia Lithwick and Walter Dellinger, "A Supreme Court Conversation," *Slate,* June 22, 2007, www.slate.com/id/2168856/entry/ 2168959 (accessed 7/4/08); and James Risen, "The Executive Power Awaiting the Next President," *New York Times,* June 22, 2008.

What Do Political Scientists Do?

a. Kenneth R. Mayer and Kevin Price, "Unilateral Presidential Powers: Significant Executive Orders, 1949–99," *Presidential Studies Quarterly* 32:2 (2002): 367–86.

You Decide

a. For details on this example, see http://topics.nytimes.com/top/news/business/companies/solyndra/index.html (accessed 4/11/12).

CHAPTER 12

1. Brad Plumer and Ezra Klein, "Analysis: Little-known Bureaucrat Is Most Powerful Man in Housing Policy," *Washington Post,* August 31, 2011, p. A1.

2. Dwight Waldo, *The Administrative State: A Study of the Political Theory of American Public Administration* (1948; repr. Piscataway, NJ: Transaction Publishers, 2006).

3. Perry Bacon Jr., "House Passes Defense Spending Bill," *Washington Post*, December 16, 2009, http://voices.washingtonpost.com/44/2009/12/house-passes-defense-spending.html (accessed 2/8/10).

4. The original quote is from Robert Dahl and was used in this context in David E. Lewis, *Presidents and the Politics of Agency Design: Political Insulation in the United States Government* (Palo Alto, CA: Stanford University Press, 2003).

5. For a history of the Food and Drug Administration, see John P. Swann, FDA History Office, "History of the FDA," www.fda.gov/oc/history/historyoffda/section2.html (accessed 7/15/08).

6. For details, see Cornelius Kerwin, *Rulemaking: How Government Agencies Write Law and Make Policy* (Washington, DC: CQ Press, 1999).

7. Enterprise Risk Management Initiative, "Costs Associated with Regulatory Risks," www.mgt.ncsu.edu/erm/index.php/articles/entry/regulatory-risk-cost/ (accessed 2/3/10).

8. The full text of the regulations and the rationale for them can be found at Centers for Medicare and Medicaid Services, "Transplants," www.cms.hhs.gov/certificationandcomplianc/20_transplant.asp (accessed 7/20/08).

9. Andrew Pollack, "New Sense of Caution at FDA," *New York Times*, September 29, 2006.

10. There are two exceptions. A patient can enroll in a clinical trial for a new drug during the approval process, but there is a good chance that the patient will get a placebo or a previously approved treatment rather than the drug being tested. The FDA does allow companies to provide some experimental drugs to patients who cannot participate in a trial but only those drugs that have passed early screening trials.

11. Susan Okie, "Access before Approval—A Right to Take Experimental Drugs?" *New England Journal of Medicine* 355 (2004): 437–40.

12. For details, see the U.S. General Services Administration site at www.gsa.gov.

13. Michael Lipsky, *Street Level Bureaucracy* (New York: Russell Sage Foundation, 1983).

14. Stephen Skowronek, *Building a New American State: The Expansion of National Administrative Capacities, 1877–1920* (New York: Cambridge University Press, 1982).

15. PPBS was Program Planning Budget System (Johnson administration), MBO was Management by Objectives (Nixon administration), ZBB was Zero-Based Budgeting (Carter administration), REGO was short for Reinventing Government (Clinton administration), and PBB (Performance Based Budgeting) was President George W. Bush's effort at bureaucratic reorganization. For details, see Cedilia Ferradino, "New Name, Old Challenges: Performance Budgeting's Continuing Struggle to Succeed in Washington," *Rockefeller College Review* 1:2 (2002): 6–23.

16. Terry Moe, "An Assessment of the Positive Theory of Congressional Dominance," *Legislative Studies Quarterly* 4 (1987): 475–98.

17. The survey was conducted by the Council for Excellence in Government. For the full survey results and interpretation, see Council for Excellence in Government, "Attitudes toward Government," www.excelgov.org/index.php?keyword=a432949724f861 (accessed 7/20/08).

18. Jason DeParle, "Minerals Service Had a Mandate to Produce Results," *New York Times*, August 7, 2010, p. A1.

19. Frances E. Rourke, "Responsiveness and Neutral Competence in American Bureaucracy," *Public Administration Review* 52 (1992): 539–46; Max Weber, *Essays on Sociology* (New York: Oxford University Press, 1958).

20. Terry M. Moe, "Power and Political Institutions," *Perspectives on Politics* 3 (2005): 215–33.

21. Karen Orren and Steven Skorownek, "Regimes and Regime Building in American Government: A Review of the Literature on the 1940s," *Political Science Quarterly* 113 (1998): 689–702.

22. Michael Nelson, "A Short, Ironic History of American National Bureaucracy," *Journal of Politics* 44 (1982): 747–78.

23. Nelson, "A Short, Ironic History of American National Bureaucracy."

24. Nelson, "A Short, Ironic History of American National Bureaucracy."

25. John Aldrich, *Why Parties?* (Chicago: University of Chicago Press, 1995).

26. Nelson, "A Short, Ironic History of American National Bureaucracy."

27. Matthew A. Crenson, *The Federal Machine: Beginnings of Bureaucracy in Jacksonian America* (Baltimore, MD: Johns Hopkins University Press, 1975).

28. James Q. Wilson, "The Rise of the Bureaucratic State," in *The American Commonwealth*, ed. Nathan Glazer and Irving Kristol (New York: Basic Books, 1976).

29. Skowronek, *Building a New American State.*

30. Robert Harrison, *Congress, Progressive Reform, and the New American State* (New York: Cambridge University Press, 2004).

31. The U.S. State Department has an excellent summary of the Pendleton Act at http://usinfo.state.gov/usa/infousa/facts/democrac/28.htm.

32. Lawrence C. Dodd and Richard L. Schott, *Congress and the Administrative State* (New York: John Wiley, 1979).

33. Richard F. Bensel, *The Political Economy of American Industrialization, 1877–1900* (New York: Cambridge University Press, 2000).

34. William Riordan, *Plunkitt of Tammany Hall: A Series of Very Plain Talks on Very Practical Politics* (1924; repr. New York: Signet Classics, 1995).

35. Sean Theriault, "Patronage, the Pendleton Act, and the Power of the People," *Journal of Politics* 65 (2003): 50–68.

36. Ira Katznelson and Bruce Pietrykowski, "Rebuilding the American State: Evidence from the 1940s," *Studies in American Political Development* 5:2 (1991) 301–39.

37. David Plotke, *Building a Democratic Political Order: Reshaping American Liberalism in the 1930s and 1940s* (New York: Cambridge University Press, 1996).

38. Theda Skocpol and Kenneth Finegold, "State Capacity and Economic Intervention in the Early New Deal," *Political Science Quarterly* 97 (1999): 255–70.

39. Michael Brown, "State Capacity and Political Choice: Interpreting the Failure of the Third New Deal," *Studies in American Political Development* 9 (1995): 187–212.

40. Ira Katznelson, Kim Geiger, and Daniel Kryder, "Limiting Liberalism: The Southern Veto in Congress, 1933–1950," *Political Science Quarterly* 108 (1993): 283–306.

41. Joseph Califano, "What Was Really Great about the Great Society," *Washington Monthly*, October 1999, www.washingtonmonthly.com/features/1999/9910 .califano.html (accessed 7/16/08).

42. Douglas Arnold, *Congress and the Bureaucracy* (New Haven, CT: Yale University Press, 1978).

43. David T. Canon, *Race, Redistricting, and Representation: The Unintended Consequences of Black Majority Districts* (Chicago: University of Chicago Press, 1999).

44. Charles Murray, *Losing Ground: American Social Policy, 1950–1980* (New York: Basic Books, 1984).

45. Henry J. Aaron, *Politics and the Professors: The Great Society in Perspective* (Washington, DC: Brookings Institution Press, 1978).

46. Michael B. Katz, *In the Shadow of the Poorhouse: A Social History of Welfare in America* (New York: Basic Books, 1996).

47. Stephen Moore, "How the Budget Revolution Was Lost," Cato Policy Analysis no. 281, September 2, 1997, Cato Institute, www.cato.org/pubs/pas/pa-281.html (accessed 7/21/08).

48. Clyde Wayne Crews Jr., "Ten Thousand Commandments," An Annual Snapshot of the Federal Regulatory State," 2003 ed. (Washington, DC: Cato Institute, 2003), www.cato.org/ tech/pubs/10kc_2003.pdf (accessed 7/15/08).

49. Richard P. Nathan, *The Administrative Presidency* (New York: Wiley, 1983).

50. Andrew Rudalevige, "The Structure of Leadership: Presidents, Hierarchies, and Information Flow," *Presidential Studies Quarterly* 35 (2005): 333–60.

51. David E. Lewis, *Presidents and the Policy of Agency Design* (Palo Alto, CA: Stanford University Press, 2003).

52. Terry Moe, "An Assessment of the Positive Theory of Congressional Dominance," *Legislative Studies Quarterly* 4 (1987): 475–98.

53. Mark Hosenball, Michael Isikoff, and Evan Thomas, "Cheney's Long Path to War," *Newsweek*, November 17, 2003, pp. 34–40.

54. Eric Schmitt and Thom Shanker, "A CIA Rival: Pentagon Sets Up Intelligence Unit," *New York Times*, October 24, 2002, p. A1.

55. William A. Niskanen, *Bureaucracy and Public Economics* (Washington, DC: Edward Elgar, 1976); Robert Waples and Jac C. Heckelman, "Public Choice Economics: Where Is There Consensus?" *American Economist* 49 (2005): 66–79.

56. Alan Schick and Felix LoStracco, *The Federal Budget: Politics, Process, Policy* (Washington, DC: Brookings Institution Press, 2000).

57. Joel D. Aberbach, "The Political Significance of the George W. Bush Administration," *Social Policy and Administration* 39:2 (2005): 130–49.

58. David E. Lewis, "The Politics of Agency Termination: Confronting the Myth of Agency Immortality," *Journal of Politics* 64 (2002): 89–107.

59. Ronald A. Wirtz, "Put It on My . . . Er, His Tab: Opinion Polls Show a Big Gap between the Public's Desire for Services and Its Willingness to Pay for These Services," *Fedgazette*, January 2004, www.minneapolisfed.org/pubs/ fedgaz/04-01/tab.cfm (accessed 7/16/08).

60. Paul Light, "Measuring the Health of the Public Service," in *Workways of Governance*, ed. Roger Davidson (Washington, DC: Brookings Institution Press, 2003).

61. John J. Brehm and Scott Gates, *Working, Shirking, and Sabotage* (Ann Arbor: University of Michigan Press, 1998).

62. Paul Light, *A Government Well-Executed: Public Service and Public Performance* (Washington, DC: Brookings Institution Press, 2003).

63. This discussion of the details of the civil service system is based on Bureau of Labor Statistics, "Career Guide to Industries," March 12, 2008, www.bls.gov/oco/cg/cgs041 .htm (accessed 7/16/08).

64. Dennis Cauchon, "Some Federal Workers More Likely to Die Than Lose Jobs," *USA Today* July 19, 2011, p. A1.

65. Ronald N. Johnson and Gary D. Liebcap, *The Federal Civil Service System and the Problem of Bureaucracy* (Chicago: University of Chicago Press, 1993).

66. Eric Lichtblau, "Report Sees Illegal Hiring Practices at Justice Department," *New York Times*, June 25, 2008.

67. For the details of the Hatch Act, see Daniel Engber, "Can Karl Rove Plot Campaign Strategy on the Government's Dime?" *Slate*, April 21, 2006, www.slate.com/id/2140418 (accessed 7/16/08).

68. Samantha Levine, "NASA Denies Chief Made Formal DeLay Endorsement," *Houston Chronicle*, April 1, 2006.

69. Sheryl Gay Stolberg, "Advisers' E-Mail Accounts May Have Mixed Politics and Business, White House Says," *New York Times*, April 12, 2007.

70. Stephen Labaton and Edmund Andrews, "White House Calls Political Briefings Legal," *New York Times*, April 27, 2007.

71. Timothy Noah, "Low Morale at Homeland Security," *Slate*, September 14, 2005, www.slate.com/id/2126313 (accessed 7/17/08).

72. For details on the Senior Executive Service, see the Office of Personnel Management site at www.opm.gov/ses.

73. Christopher Lee, "Ex-Surgeon General Says White House Hushed Him," *Washington Post*, July 11, 2007, p. A1.

74. Andrew C. Revkin, "Climate Expert Says NASA Tried to Silence Him," *New York Times*, January 29, 2006.

75. Andrew C. Revkin, "A Young Bush Appointee Resigns His Post at NASA," *New York Times*, February 8, 2006.

76. Andrew C. Revkin, "NASA's Goals Delete Mention of Home Planet," *New York Times*, July 22, 2006.

77. John D. Huber and Charles R. Shipan, *Deliberate Discretion? The Institutional Foundations of Bureaucratic Autonomy* (New York: Cambridge University Press, 2002).

78. David Epstein and Sharyn O'Halloran, *Delegating Powers: A Transaction Cost Politics Approach to Policy Making under Separate Powers* (New York: Cambridge University Press, 1999).

79. Charles E. Lindbloom, "The Science of 'Muddling Through,'" *Public Administration Review* 19 (1959): 79–88.

80. Mathew D. McCubbins, Roger G. Noll, and Barry R. Weingast, "Structure and Process as Solutions to the Politician's Principal–Agency Problem," *Virginia Law Review* 74 (1989): 431–82.

81. Barry R. Weingast, "Caught in the Middle: The President, Congress, and the Political-Bureaucratic System," in *Institutions of American Democracy: The Executive Branch*, ed. Joel D. Aberbach and Mark A. Peterson (New York: Oxford University Press, 2006).

82. Keith Whittington and Daniel P. Carpenter, "Executive Power in American Institutional Development," *Perspectives on Politics* 1 (2003): 495–513.

83. Dara Cohen, Mariano-Florentino Cuéllar, and Barry R. Weingast, "Crisis Bureaucracy: Homeland Security and the Political Design of Legal Mandates," *Stanford Law Review* 59:3 (2006): 673–760.

84. Federal Communications Commission, "FCC Commissioners," April 1, 2008, www.fcc.gov/commissioners (accessed 7/17/08).

85. Federal Election Commission, "About the FEC: Commissioners," www.fec.gov/members/members.shtml (accessed 7/17/08); Federal Trade Commission, "Commissioners," www.ftc.gov/commissioners/index.shtml (accessed 7/17/08).

86. Charles Shipan, *Designing Judicial Review: Interest Groups, Congress, and Communication Policy* (Ann Arbor: University of Michigan Press, 2000).

87. Roger Noll, Mathew McCubbins, and Barry Weingast, "Administrative Procedures as Instruments of Political Control," *Journal of Law, Economics and Organization* 3 (1987): 243–77.

88. Mathew McCubbins and Thomas Schwartz, "Congressional Oversight Overlooked: Fire Alarms vs. Police Patrols," *American Journal of Political Science* 28 (1984): 165–79.

89. McCubbins and Schwartz, "Congressional Oversight Overlooked."

90. Steven J. Balla and John R. Wright, "Interest Groups, Advisory Committees, and Congressional Control of the Bureaucracy," *American Journal of Political Science* 45 (2001): 799–812.

91. Daniel P. Carpenter, "The Gatekeeper: Organizational Reputation and Pharmaceutical Regulation at the FDA" (unpublished paper, Harvard University, 2006).

92. Terry M. Moe, "Political Control and the Power of the Agent," *Journal of Law, Economics, and Organization* 22 (2006): 1–29.

93. See David Weil, "OSHA: Beyond the Politics," *Frontline*, January 9, 2003, www.pbs.org/wgbh/pages/frontline/shows/workplace/osha/weil.html (accessed 7/17/08).

94. Daniel P. Carpenter, *The Forging of Bureaucratic Autonomy: Reputations, Networks, and Policy Innovation in Executive Agencies, 1862–1928* (Princeton, NJ: Princeton University Press, 2001).

What Do Political Scientists Do?

a. The Yackees' analysis also considers the outcome in which rules lead to no change in government involvement, but we exclude this possibility to simplify the discussion.

CHAPTER 13

1. Ralph Ketcham, *The Anti-Federalist Papers and the Constitutional Convention Debates* (New York: Penguin Putnam, 2003), p. 304.

2. Lester S. Jayson, ed., *The Constitution of the United States of America: Analysis and Interpretation* (Washington, DC: U.S. Government Printing Office, 1973), p. 585.

3. David G. Savage, *Guide to the U.S. Supreme Court*, 4th ed. (Washington, DC: CQ Press, 2004), p. 7.

4. Savage, *Guide to the U.S. Supreme Court*, pp. 5–7.

5. Winfield H. Rose, "*Marbury v. Madison*: How John Marshall Changed History by Misquoting the Constitution," *Political Science and Politics* 36:2 (April 2003): 209–14. Rose argues that in a key quotation in the case, Marshall intentionally left out a clause of the Constitution that suggests that Congress *did* have the power to expand the original jurisdiction of the Court. Other constitutional scholars reject this argument.

6. *Marbury v. Madison*, 1 CR. (5 U.S.) 137 (1803).

7. Revisionist historians, legal scholars, and political scientists have challenged the landmark status of *Marbury v. Madison*. For example, Michael Stokes Paulsen's *Michigan Law Review* article points out that *Marbury* was not cited in subsequent Supreme Court cases as a precedent for judicial review until the late nineteenth century. Legal scholars in the early twentieth century were the first to promote the idea that *Marbury* was a landmark decision. Paulsen also notes that when the opinion was delivered in 1803, it was not controversial. Even the Jeffersonian Democrats, who were at odds with Marshall's Federalists, thought that it was a reasonable decision and not the institutional power-grab that is described in modern accounts. Finally, Marshall made a very narrow case for judicial

review, arguing that the Supreme Court could declare legislation that was contrary to the Court's interpretation of the Constitution null and void only if it concerned judicial powers. Revisionists argue that what appear to be broad claims of judicial power in *Marbury* (e.g., the Court has the power "to say what the law is") are taken out of the context of a much more narrow claim of power. Michael Stokes Paulsen, "Judging Judicial Review: *Marbury* in the Modern Era: The Irrepressible Myth of *Marbury*," *Michigan Law Review* 101 (August, 2003): 2706–43.

8. *Ware v. Hylton*, 3 U.S. 199 (1796).

9. However, in 2011 the Court struck down any class-action claim unless there was "convincing proof of a companywide discriminatory pay and promotion policy"—statistical evidence of pay disparities would not suffice. (David Savage, "Supreme Court Blocks Huge Class-Action Suit against Wal-Mart," *Los Angeles Times*, June 21, 2011).

10. *Lujan v. Defenders of Wildlife*, 504 U.S. 555 (1992).

11. *Campbell v. Clinton*, 99-1843 (this was a District of Columbia appeals court decision; the Supreme Court refused to hear the appeal of the decision), and *Raines v. Byrd*, 956 F. Supp. 25 (1997).

12. U.S. Courts, Federal Court Management Statistics, 2007: District Courts, www.uscourts.gov/cgi-bin/cmsd2007.pl (accessed 3/18/08).

13. Federal Judicial Center, "The Judiciary Act of 1869: An Act to Amend the Judicial System of the United States," www.fjc .gov/history/home.nsf/page/10a_bdy (accessed 7/18/08).

14. Federal Judicial Center, "The U.S. Courts of Appeals and the Federal Judiciary," www.fjc.gov/history/home.nsf/ page/ca_bdy?OpenDocument (accessed 7/18/08).

15. Howard, *Courts of Appeals in the Federal Judicial System* (Princeton: Princeton University Press, 1981), p. 5.

16. U.S. Courts, Federal Judiciary: Frequently Asked Questions, "Federal Judges," www.uscourts.gov/faq.html (accessed 1/17/12).

17. U.S. Courts, Federal Court Management Statistics, 2011: Courts of Appeals, www.uscourts.gov/viewer .aspx?doc=/cgi-bin/cmsa2011Jun.pl (accessed 1/17/12).

18. *Ledbetter v. Goodyear Tire & Rubber Co.*, 550 U.S. 618 (2007).

19. The 11th Amendment does not mention law suits against a state brought in federal court by citizens of that same state. However, in *Alden v. Maine* (1999 527 U.S. 706), the court extended the logic of sovereign immunity to apply to these cases as well.

20. *Pollock v. Farmers' Loan & Trust Company*, 157 U.S. 429 (1895).

21. American Judicature Society, "Judicial Selection in the States: Appellate and General Jurisdiction Courts," 2004, www.ajs.org/js/JudicialSelectionCharts_old.pdf (accessed 9/14/06).

22. The Court ruled that the losing party's due process rights under the Fourteenth Amendment had been violated when the justice who benefited from the campaign spending did not recuse himself from the case. Given the disproportionate and significant spending by Massey and the timing of the spending, the majority ruled, "On these extreme facts the probability of actual bias rises to an unconstitutional level." *Caperton v. A.T. Massey Coal Co.*, 556 U.S. 868 (2009).

23. Paul Brace and Brent D. Boyea, "State Public Opinion, the Death Penalty, and the Practice of Electing Judges," *American Journal of Political Science* 52:2 (April 2008): 360–72.

24. Richard P. Caldarone, Brandice Canes-Wrone, and Tom S. Clark, "Partisan Labels and Democratic Accountability: An Analysis of State Supreme Court Abortion Decisions," *Journal of Politics* 71 (2009): 560–73.

25. Stephen Ware, "The Missouri Plan in National Perspective," *Missouri Law Review* 74 (2009): 751–75.

26. Savage, *Guide to the U.S. Supreme Court*, p. 1003.

27. "President Bush Discusses Judicial Accomplishments and Philosophy, Cincinnati, Ohio, October 6, 2008," georgewbush-whitehouse.archives.gov/news/releases/ 2008/10/20081006-5.html (accessed 12/14/11).

28. Felicia Sonmez, "Senate Republicans Block Obama Appeals Court Nominee," *Washington Post*, December 6, 2011, A1. See http://judicialnominations.org for a comprehensive list of pending nominations and vacancies for federal courts.

29. Supreme Court of the United States *In Re Frederick W. Bauer*, On Petition for a Writ of Mandamus to the United States Court of Appeals for the Seventh Circuit, Brief for the United States in Opposition, No. 90-6351, March 4, 1991, www.usdoj. gov/osg/briefs/1990/sg900418.txt (accessed 7/18/08).

30. Supreme Court of the United States *In Re Frederick W. Bauer*, On Motion for Leave to Proceed in forma pauperis, No. 99-5440, Decided October 18, 1999, per curiam, http:// supreme.lp.findlaw.com/supreme_court/decisions/ 99-5440.html (accessed 7/18/08).

31. John Roberts, U.S. Supreme Court, "2007 Year-End Report on the Federal Judiciary," January 1, 2008, www .supremecourtus.gov/publicinfo/year-end/2007year -endreport.pdf (accessed 3/17/08).

32. For a critical account of the Supreme Court's reduced case load, which dates back to the Rehnquist Court, see Philip Allen Lacovara, "The Incredible Shrinking Court," *American Lawyer*, December 1, 2003, www.judicialaccountability .org/download/shrinkinusgcourt.htm (accessed 7/18/08).

33. *New Jersey v. New York*, No. 120 Orig., 118 S. Ct. 1726 (1998), and *Kansas v. Colorado*, No. 105 Orig., 125 S. Ct. 526 (2004).

34. Abraham, *The Judiciary*, p. 25, says that original jurisdiction has been invoked "about 150 times." A Lexis search revealed an additional twenty-seven original jurisdiction cases between 1987 and December 2004. See U.S. Department

of Justice, Help/Glossary, www.usdoj.gov/osg/briefs/help
.html for a basic discussion of the Supreme Court's original jurisdiction.

35. Amanda L. Tyler, "Setting the Supreme Court's Agenda: Is
    There a Place for Certification?" *George Washington Law
    Review Arguendo* 78 (May 2010): 101–18.

36. Savage, *Guide to the U.S. Supreme Court*, p. 848.

37. See Thomas G. Walker and Lee Epstein, *The Supreme Court
    of the United States: An Introduction* (New York: St. Martin's
    Press, 1993), pp. 80–85, for a more detailed discussion of
    these concepts and citations to the relevant court cases.

38. *Shaw v. Reno*, (1993) 509 *U.S.* 630.

39. *Elk Grove Unified School District v. Newdow* (2004) 542
    U.S. 1.

40. *DeFunis v. Odegaard*, 416 U.S. 312 (1974).

41. The appeals court case is *Byrd v. Raines*, and the case that
    was finally heard by the Court was *Clinton v. City of New
    York*, 524 U.S. 417 (1998).

42. Gregory A. Caldeira and John R. Wright, "The Discuss
    List: Agenda Building in the Supreme Court," *Law and
    Society Review* 24 (1990): 813.

43. Walker and Epstein, *Supreme Court*, p. 89.

44. U.S. Supreme Court, "The Court and Its Procedures," www
    .supremecourtus.gov/about/procedures.pdf (accessed
    3/17/08).

45. *United States v. Nixon*, 418 U.S. 683 (1974).

46. Lee Epstein, Jeffrey A. Segal, Harold J. Spaeth, and
    Thomas G. Walker, *The Supreme Court Compendium:
    Data, Decisions, and Developments*, 3rd ed. (Washington,
    DC: CQ Press, 2003), Table 7-25.

47. Gregory A. Caldeira and John R. Wright, "Amicus Curiae
    before the Supreme Court: Who Participates, When, and
    How Much?" *Journal of Politics* 52 (August 1990): 803.

48. U.S. Supreme Court, Rules of the Supreme Court, adopted
    March 14, 2005, effective May 2, 2005, Rule 28.7, www
    .supremecourtus.gov/ctrules/rulesofthecourt.pdf
    (accessed 7/18/08).

49. Savage, *Guide to the U.S. Supreme Court*, p. 852.

50. U.S. Supreme Court, Argument Transcripts, www.supreme
    courtus.gov/oral_arguments/argument_transcripts
    (accessed 7/18/08).

51. Adam Liptak, "No Argument: Thomas Keeps Five Year
    Silence," *New York Times*, February 12, 2011, www.nytimes
    .com/2011/02/13/us/13thomas.html (accessed 1/18/12).

52. Quoted in Savage, *Guide to the U.S. Supreme Court*, p. 854.

53. Forrest Maltzman, James F. Spriggs II, and Paul J. Wahl-
    beck, *Crafting Law on the Supreme Court: The Collegial
    Game* (New York: Cambridge University Press, 2000),
    p. 33.

54. William H. Rehnquist, "Memorandum to the Conference:
    Policy Regarding Assignments," November 24, 1989,
    papers of Justice Thurgood Marshall, Library of Congress
    Manuscript Division, Washington, DC, quoted in Maltz-
    man, Spriggs, and Wahlbeck, *Crafting Law*, pp. 30–31.

55. *Smith v. Allwright*, 321 U.S. 649 (1944).

56. Walker and Epstein, *Supreme Court*, p. 110.

57. Savage, *Guide to the U.S. Supreme Court*, p. 854.

58. Quoted in Lee Epstein and Thomas G. Walker, *Constitu-
    tional Law for a Changing America*, 5th ed. (Washington,
    DC: CQ Press, 2004), p. 29.

59. *Maryland v. Craig*, 497 U.S. 836 (1990).

60. Epstein and Walker, *Constitutional Law for a Changing
    America*, p. 31.

61. Seth Stern and Stephen Wermiel, *Justice Brennan: Liberal
    Champion* (Boston: Houghton Mifflin Harcourt, 2010).

62. Epstein, Segal, Spaeth, and Walker, *Supreme Court Com-
    pendium*, Table 6-2.

63. Forrest Maltzman and Paul J. Wahlbeck, "Strategic
    Considerations and Vote Fluidity on the Burger Court,"
    American Journal of Political Science 90 (1996): 581–92;
    Maltzman, Spriggs, and Wahlbeck, *Crafting Law*.

64. Thomas R. Marshall, *Public Opinion and the Supreme
    Court* (Boston: Unwin Hyman, 1989), p. 12; as cited in
    Epstein and Walker, *Constitutional Law for a Changing
    America*, p. 92.

65. Thomas M. Keck, *The Most Activist Supreme Court in
    History: The Road to Modern Judicial Conservatism*
    (Chicago: University of Chicago Press, 2004).

66. Marshall, *Public Opinion*, Table 6-8.

67. Jeffrey Rosen, "Has the Supreme Court Gone Too Far?"
    Commentary 116:3 (October 2003).

68. *National Federation of Independent Business v. Sebelius*,
    567 U.S. _____ (2012).

69. Finley Peter Dunne, Paul Green, and Jacques Barzun,
    Mr. Dooley in Peace and in War (1898; repr. Champaign-
    Urbana: University of Illinois Press, 2001).

70. Robert Dahl, "Decision-Making in a Democracy: The
    Supreme Court as a National Policy-Maker," *Journal of
    Public Law* 6 (1957): 279–95, is the classic work on this
    topic. More recent work challenged Dahl's methods but
    largely supports the idea that the Court follows the will of
    the majority.

71. Jeffrey A. Segal, Richard J. Timpone, and Robert M. How-
    ard, "Buyer Beware? Presidential Success through Supreme
    Court Appointments," *Political Research Quarterly* 53:3
    (September 2000): 557–73; Gregory A. Caldeira and Charles
    E. Smith Jr., "Campaigning for the Supreme Court: The
    Dynamics of Public Opinion on the Thomas Nomination,"
    Political Research Quarterly 58:3 (August, 1996): 655–81.

72. William Mishler and Reginald S. Sheehan, "The Supreme
    Court as a Countermajoritarian Institution? The Impact
    of Public Opinion on Supreme Court Decisions," *Ameri-
    can Political Science Review* 87:1 (March 1993): 87–101.

73. David O'Brien, *Storm Center: The Supreme Court in
    American Politics*, 4th ed. (New York: Norton, 1996).

74. Helmut Norpoth and Jeffrey A. Segal, "Popular Influence
    in Supreme Court Decisions," *American Political Science
    Review* 88 (1994): 711–16.

6. Central Intelligence Agency, *World Factbook*, "Country Comparison: Distribution of Family Income, Gini Index," www.cia.gov/library/publications/the-world-factbook/rankorder/2172rank.html (accessed 2/19/12).

7. The phrase comes from environmental economist E. F. Schumacher's influential book, *Small Is Beautiful: Economics as if People Mattered* (New York: Harper and Row, 1973).

8. Jonathan Rowe and Judith Silverstein, "The GDP Myth: Why 'Growth' Isn't Always a Good Thing," *Washington Monthly* 31:3 (March 1999).

9. Scott Lanman and Steve Matthews, "Greenspan Concedes to 'Flaw' in His Market Ideology," Bloomberg.com, October 23, 2008, www.bloomberg.com/apps/news?pid=20601087&sid=ah5qh9Up4rIg (accessed 2/12/10).

10. Juann H. Hung, "Recent Shifts in Financing the U.S. Current-Account Deficit," *CBO Economic and Budget Issue Brief* (Washington, DC: Congressional Budget Office, July 12, 2005), www.cbo.gov (accessed 3/15/08).

11. The classic work on the appropriations process in the prereform era is Richard F. Fenno's *The Power of the Purse: Appropriations Politics in Congress* (Boston: Little, Brown, 1966). D. Roderick Kiewiet and Mathew D. McCubbins reexamine the appropriations process in the postreform era and find that the appropriations committees have maintained much of their power; see *The Logic of Delegation: Congressional Parties and the Appropriations Process* (Chicago: University of Chicago Press, 1991).

12. James Sundquist, *The Decline and Resurgence of Congress* (Washington, DC: Brookings Institution Press, 1981), chap. 8.

13. Action by both houses was required only to restore the more serious "rescissions." For simple deferrals, or postponement of spending, the president's action stood unless either house voted to overrule him (Sundquist, *Decline and Resurgence*, p. 213).

14. Jared Allen, "House Won't Pass Budget in 2010," *The Hill*, June 21, 2010. http://thehill.com/homenews/house/104635-dems-wont-pass-budget (accessed 2/20/12).

15. The specific provision is paragraph (1)(E) of section 313(b)(1) of the Budget Control Act. James Thurber, "Centralization, Devolution, and Turf Protection in the Congressional Budget Process," in *Congress Reconsidered*, 6th ed., ed. Lawrence C. Dodd and Bruce I. Oppenheimer (Washington, DC: CQ Press, 1997), pp. 325–46.

16. These figures exclude the Social Security surplus. Including Social Security, the government had a small surplus in 1969. See the Congressional Budget Office's historical budget data, www.cbo.gov/showdoc.cfm?index=18/21&sequence=0. For data before 1962, see the 1981 *Economic Report of the President* (Washington, DC: Government Printing Office, 1981), p. 316.

17. Howard Gleckman, "Pay Go, Pay Gone: AMT Drives Senate Dems to Blink," Tax Policy Center, December 7, 2007, http://taxvox.taxpolicycenter.org/blog/_archives/2007/12/7/3397043.html (accessed 5/30/08).

18. Internal Revenue Service, "Stimulus Payments—It's Not Too Late," www.irs.gov/newsroom/article/0,,id=177937,00.html(accessed 8/5/08).

19. Lori Montgomery, "House Votes to Revive Pay-as-You-Go Budget Rules," *Washington Post*, February 5, 2010, www.washingtonpost.com/wp-dyn/content/article/2010/02/04/AR2010020400354.html (accessed 2/12/10); and Eric Pianin, "Congress Adds Payroll Tax Cut to Gov't Credit Card," *Fiscal Times*, February 15, 2012, www.thefiscaltimes.com/Articles/2012/02/15/Congress-Adds-Payroll%20Tax-Cut-to-Govt-Credit-Card.aspx#page1 (accessed 2/16/12).

20. Office of the United States Trade Representative, "Who We Are," www.ustr.gov/Who_We_Are/Section_Index.html (accessed 8/5/08).

21. National Economic Council, www.whitehouse.gov/nec (accessed 8/5/08).

22. Bradley H. Patterson, *The White House Staff: Inside the West Wing and Beyond* (Washington, DC: Brookings Institution Press, 2000), pp. 88–95.

23. See Charles M. Cameron, *Veto Bargaining: Presidents and the Politics of Negative Power* (New York: Cambridge University Press, 2000), for a general discussion of the strategic elements of issuing veto threats.

24. Board of Governors of the Federal Reserve System, *The Federal Reserve System: Purposes and Functions*, 9th ed., Washington, DC, June 2005, www.federalreserve.gov/pf/pdf/pf_1.pdf, p. 12.

25. See Donald F. Kettl, *Leadership at the Fed* (New Haven, CT: Yale University Press, 1986), for a good general discussion of the Fed.

26. See Federal Research Board, "Membership of the Board of Governors of the Federal Reserve System, 1914," www.federalreserve.gov/bios/boardmembership.htm, for a list of all Federal Reserve Board members (accessed 8/5/08).

27. Federal Reserve Board, "Annual Report 2011," www.federalreserve.gov/publications/annual-report (accessed 10/5/12).

28. Neil Irwin, "Senators Critical of Bernanke at Hearing," *Washington Post*, December 4, 2009, www.washingtonpost.com/wp-dyn/content/article/2009/12/03/AR2009120301210.html (accessed 2/12/10).

29. Edward R. Tufte, *Political Control of the Economy* (Princeton, NJ: Princeton University Press, 1978); Douglas Hibbs, "The Partisan Model of Macroeconomic Cycles: More Theory and Evidence for the United States," *Economics and Politics* 6 (1994): 1–23.

30. Jim Granato, "The Effect of Policy-Maker Reputation and Credibility on Public Expectations," *Journal of Theoretical Politics* 8 (1996): 449–70; Irwin L. Morris, *Congress, the President, and the Federal Reserve: The Politics of American Monetary Policy-Making* (Ann Arbor: University of Michigan Press, 2000).

31. U.S. Department of the Treasury, "Duties and Functions," www.treasury.gov/education/duties (accessed 8/5/08).

32. U.S. Department of the Treasury, "FAQs: Currency: Production and Circulation," www.treasury.gov/education/faq/currency/production.shtml; United States Mint, "Coin Production Figures," www.usmint.gov/about_the_mint/coin_production/index.cfm?action=production_figures (accessed 8/5/08).

33. Zachary A. Goldfarb, David Cho, and Binyamin Appelbaum, "Treasury to Rescue Fannie and Freddie," *Washington Post*, September 7, 2008, p. A1.

34. Peter Baker, "A Professor and a Banker Bury Old Dogma on Markets," *New York Times*, September 21, 2008, p. A1.

35. Renae Merle, "U.S. Stock Markets Soar on Financial Rescue Plan," *Washington Post*, September 19, 2008; Howard Schneider, Neil Irwin, and Binyamin Appelbaum, "Treasury to Temporarily Guarantee Money Market Funds," *Washington Post*, September 19, 2008.

36. Carl Hulse, "Pressure Builds on House after Senate Backs Bailout," *New York Times*, October 1, 2008, p. A1.

37. David M. Herszenhorn, "Bailout Plan Wins Approval; Democrats Vow Tighter Rules," *New York Times*, October 3, 2008, p. A1.

38. "Department of the Treasury, Financial Stability Plan—One Year Later," February 10, 2010, www.financialstability.gov/latest/pr_02102010.html (accessed 2/12/10).

39. Paul Ried, "Three Laws that Caused Obama Midterm Problems," CBS News, November 3, 2010, www.cbsnews.com/stories/2010/11/03/politics/main7020135.shtml (accessed 11/5/10).

40. For example, in his book *Booty Capitalism: The Politics of Banking in the Philippines* (Ithaca, NY: Cornell University Press, 1998), Paul Hutchcroft cites the culture of cronyism and corruption as the main explanation for lagging economic development in the Philippines.

41. John Maynard Keynes, *General Theory of Employment, Interest and Money* (1936; repr. New York: Macmillan, 2007).

42. Robert Dallek, *Flawed Giant: Lyndon Johnson and His Times, 1961–1973* (New York: Oxford University Press, 1998), pp. 71–74.

43. David Shreve, "President John F. Kennedy and the 1964 Tax Cut," Presidential Recordings Project, www.whitehousetapes.org/news/shreve_taxcut_2001.pdf (accessed 4/26/08).

44. In Laffer's original argument there was only one tax rate. However, to apply the Laffer curve to the real world of tax policy, the theoretical argument must be presented in terms of the top marginal rate, which is the tax rate paid on the last dollars earned (and thus, the rate that influences the marginal decision to work more or fewer hours). The end point of zero tax revenue associated with a 100 percent tax rate would be for Laffer's single tax rate, rather than the top marginal rate (because people would still work as long as they could keep some income in the marginal brackets below the top rate).

45. Arthur B. Laffer, "The Laffer Curve: Past, Present, and Future," Heritage Foundation Backgrounder #1765, June 1, 2004, www.heritage.org/Research/Taxes/bg1765.cfm (accessed 3/27/08).

46. These figures come from the Congressional Budget Office, "Historical Budget Data," www.cbo.gov (accessed 4/18/08).

47. Office of Management and Budget, "Budget of the United States Government, fiscal year 2011," www.whitehouse.gov/omb/budget/Overview/ (accessed 2/16/10).

48. The "starve the beast" line is usually attributed to David Stockman and his book *The Triumph of Politics: The Inside Story of the Reagan Revolution* (New York: Avon Books, 1986). A Web search for "David Stockman" and "starve the beast" produced 566 hits, including a reference in a *National Review* article: Norman B. Ture, "To Cut and To Please," June 10, 2004, www.nationalreview.com/reagan/ture200406101414.asp. However, we have been unable to find the phrase "starve the beast" in Stockman's book. More recently, smaller-government conservatives such as Grover Norquist have embraced the concept.

49. Congressional Budget Office, "The Distribution of Household Income and Federal Taxes, 2008 and 2009," Supplemental Tables 1 and 2, cbo.gov/publication/43373 (accessed 10/7/12).

50. The details get a bit more complicated, but this is essentially how money is created. Banks must hold a reserve of 10 percent of all "demand deposits" (which is what economists call checking accounts), so only $90,000 would actually be put into the money stream because the $10,000 reserve would have to come from money that someone deposited in the bank. Also, the money supply would contract as you pay back your loan. The overall effect on the money supply has to take into account the "multiplier effect"—that is, the money you spend from your loan will get spent many times over. The computer store will take your $10,000 and deposit it in its bank, which allows that bank to make more loans, and so on.

51. *Historical Statistics of the United States: Colonial Times to 1970* (Washington, DC: U.S. Department of Commerce, Bureau of the Census, 1975), Table V 20–30, p. 912.

52. Milton Friedman, "The Quantity Theory of Money: A Restatement," in *The Optimum Quantity of Money and Other Essays* (Chicago: Aldine, 1969), p. 52.

53. These figures are hypothetical. In reality, under the Monetary Control Act (MCA) of 1980, the reserve requirement can range from 8 percent to 14 percent for all demand deposits greater than $25 million. In the original law, banks with demand deposits under $25 million had to have a reserve of only 3 percent. The amount that is subject to the lower reserve requirement is increased every year to reflect overall money supply and currently is about

$71 million. See Board of Governors of the Federal Reserve System, "Reserve Requirement," www.federalreserve.gov/monetarypolicy/reservereq.htm#table1 (accessed 2/7/12).

54. In December 2002, the discount rate was effectively discontinued as an active policy tool and was pegged to 1 percent above the targeted FFR (which means that the "discount rate" is oddly named—it really should be called the "premium rate"). December 2002 *Federal Reserve Bulletin* (pp. 482–83). See Donald D. Hester, "U.S. Monetary Policy in the Greenspan Era: 1987–2003," unpublished paper, University of Wisconsin, Madison, November 14, 2003, http://ideas.repec.org/p/att/wimass/200323.html (accessed 8/10/08), for an extended discussion of this move.

55. Greenspan made the comment in his July 21, 2005, testimony before Congress. For the full text of his remarks, see "Testimony of Chairman Alan Greenspan," Federal Reserve Board's semiannual Monetary Policy Report to the Congress before the Committee on Financial Services, U.S. House of Representatives, July 20, 2005, www.federalreserve.gov/boarddocs/hh/2005/july/testimony.htm (accessed 8/5/08).

56. Between September 2007 and December 2008, the Fed cut the FFR 10 times from 4.75 to nearly zero (the official target rate is 0 to .25), and the prime rate fell from 8.25 to 3.25. Both the FFR and prime have been unchanged since that time (through 2012). The 10-year Treasury, on the other hand, initially fell by two points during the period FFR cuts, but then increased by nearly a point and a half during the first year and a half of the Obama administration, only to settle to record low levels early in 2012 (under 2 percent). See Federal Reserve Bank of New York, Federal Funds Data, for historical interest rates, www.newyorkfed.org/markets/omo/dmm/fedfundsdata.cfm (accessed 2/7/12).

57. Brian W. Cashell, "The Federal Government Debt: Its Size and Economic Significance," Washington, DC: Congressional Research Service, Report RL31590, March 1, 2005, p. 9.

58. William Greider reports that internal debates between Fed members who wanted to emphasize the money supply and those who wanted to emphasize interest rates started as early as 1982. (See *Secrets of the Temple: How the Federal Reserve Runs the Country* [New York: Simon and Schuster, 1987], pp. 479–80.)

59. Greider, *Secrets of the Temple*, pp. 295–98.

60. Board of Governors of the Federal Reserve System, Credit and Liquidity Programs and the Balance Sheet, www.federalreserve.gov/monetarypolicy/bst_recenttrends.htm (accessed 2/16/10).

61. John B. Taylor, *Economics*, 4th ed. (New York: Houghton Mifflin, 2003), chap. 10. Some economics textbooks also define regulation of externalities, such as pollution, as economic regulation.

62. *United States v. Microsoft*, 87 F. Supp. 2d 30 (D.D.C. 2000). See Alan Reynolds, *Microsoft Antitrust Appeal: Judge Jackson's "Findings of Fact" Revisited* (Washington, DC: Hudson Institute, 2002), for a detailed discussion of the case.

63. See *Public Interest Group Profiles: 2004–2005* (Washington, DC: CQ Press, 2004) for information on more than 200 public interest groups.

64. See U.S. Environmental Protection Agency, "Pollutants/Toxins," www.epa.gov/ebtpages/pollutants.html, for a complete list of regulated and banned chemicals.

65. Sam Pelzman and Clifford Winston, "Deregulation of Network Industries: What's Next?" AEI-Brookings Joint Center for Regulatory Studies (Washington, DC: Brookings Institution Press, 2000), p. 2, www.aei.brookings.org/admin/authorpdfs/page.php?id=109 (accessed 6/4/08).

66. Samuel P. Huntington, "The Marasmus of the ICC: The Commission, the Railroads, and the Public Interest," in *Public Administration and Policy: Selected Essays*, ed. Peter Woll (New York: Harper and Row, 1966); Harmon Ziegler, *Interest Groups in American Society* (Englewood Cliffs, NJ: Prentice Hall, 1964).

67. Megan Slack, "Everything You Need to Know: President Obama's Blueprint for American-Made Energy," January 26, 2012, www.whitehouse.gov/blog/2012/01/26/everything-you-need-know-president-obamas-blueprint-american-made-energy?tw_p=twt (accessed 2/19/12).

68. Bureau of Economic Analysis, International Economic Accounts, "U.S. Net International Investment Position at Yearend 2009," June 25, 2010, www.bea.gov/newsreleases/international/intinv/2010/intinv09.htm (accessed 9/13/10).

69. David E. Rosenbloom, "Free Trade Is Like Dry Water, Y'All," *New York Times*, December 19, 2004, Week in Review.

70. David Ricardo, *The Principles of Political Economy and Taxation* (1817). Robert Torrens actually developed the point first in an 1815 essay on the corn trade, but Ricardo usually gets the credit because he explained it more fully.

71. This argument ignores transportation costs and the costs of shifting labor from one industry to another, but its logic is quite powerful. More intuitive, perhaps, is what happens when one nation has a large *absolute* advantage in the cost of production over another. In these situations, if there is free trade, most production of that good will shift to the country that can produce it more cheaply.

72. Suketu Mehta, "A Passage from India," *New York Times*, July 12, 2005, p. A21.

73. See Ronald Rogowski, *Commerce and Coalitions* (Princeton, NJ: Princeton University Press, 1986), for the constituency view. James Shoch, *Trading Blows: Party Competition and U.S. Trade Policy in a Globalizing Era* (Chapel Hill: University of North Carolina Press, 2001), pp. 13–19, reviews both explanations.

74. Judith Goldstein, *Ideas, Interests, and American Trade* (Ithaca, NY: Cornell University Press), 1993.

75. David Smick, "If Entire Countries Go Broke, We'll Go with Them," *Washington Post*, October 26, 2008, p. B3.

What Do Political Scientists Do?

a. Ron Paul, "Why the Fed Likes Independence," Texas Straight Talk Blog, January 11, 2010, www.house.gov/htbin/blog_inc?BLOG,tx14_paul,blog,999,All, Item%20not%20found,ID=100111_3628,TEMPLATE=postingdetail.shtml (accessed 6/25/10).

b. David E. Lewis, *Presidents and the Politics of Agency Design: Political Insulation in the United States Government Bureaucracy, 1946–1997* (Stanford, CA: Stanford University Press, 2003), p. 13.

c. Lewis, *Presidents and the Politics of Agency Design*, p. 161.

You Decide

a. John Tierney, "The Sagebrush Solution," *New York Times*, July 26, 2005, p. A19. Additional information was drawn from www.highcountrynews.org.

b. A very detailed account of this saga may be found in Raymond B. Wrabley Jr., "Managing the Monument: Cows and Conservation in the Grand-Staircase-Escalante National Monument," *Journal of Land, Resources and Environmental Law* 29:2 (2009): 253–80.

CHAPTER 16

1. John Boehner, "Statement by House GOP Leaders Boehner and McCotter on End-of-Life Treatment Counseling in Democrats' Health Care Legislation," press release, July 23, 2009, http://republicanleader.house.gov/news/DocumentSingle.aspx?DocumentID=139131 (accessed 6/18/2010).

2. Jonathan Cohn, "How They Did It: The Inside Account of Health Care Reform's Triumph," *New Republic*, June 10, 2010, pp. 14–25.

3. David M. Herszenhorn and Robert Pear, "Final Votes in Congress Cap Battle on Health Bill," *New York Times*, March 25, 2010, p. A1.

4. Herszenhorn and Pear, "Final Votes in Congress."

5. Sari Horwitz and Ben Pershing, "Anger over Health-Care Reform Spurs Rise in Threats against Congress Members," *Washington Post*, April 9, 2010.

6. Theda Skocpol, *Social Policy in the United States: Future Possibilities in Historical Perspective* (Princeton, NJ: Princeton University Press, 1995), p. 37.

7. Franklin D. Roosevelt's second fireside chat on "Government and Modern Capitalism," Washington, DC, September 30, 1934. For the full text, see "The American Presidency Project," John T. Woolley and Gerhard Peters, University of California, Santa Barbara, www.presidency.ucsb.edu/ws/index.php?pid=14636 (accessed 8/8/08).

8. Skocpol, *Social Policy in the United States*, pp. 145–60.

9. David M. Kennedy, *Freedom from Fear: The American People in Depression and War, 1929–1945* (New York: Oxford University Press, 2001); Byron W. Daynes, William Pederson, and Michael P. Riccards, eds., *The New Deal and Public Policy* (New York: St. Martin's Press, 1998).

10. Robert Dallek, *Flawed Giant: Lyndon Johnson and His Times, 1961–1973* (New York: Oxford University Press, 1998); Irving Berstein, *Guns or Butter: The Presidency of Lyndon Johnson* (New York: Oxford University Press, 1996).

11. Carmen DeNavas-Walt, Bernadette D. Proctor, and Jessica C. Smith, "Income, Poverty, and Health Insurance Coverage in the United States: 2011," September 2010, www.census.gov/prod/2012pubs/p60-243.pdf, p. 14 (accessed 10/9/12).

12. Larry Bartels, "Inequalities," *New York Times*, April 27, 2008, www.nytimes.com/2008/04/27/magazine/27wwln-idealab-t.html?_r=1&oref=slogin&pagewanted=print (accessed 5/10/08).

13. DeNavas-Walt, Proctor, and Smith, "Income, Poverty, and Healthy Insurance Coverage in the United States: 2009," Table 2, A2.

14. Congressional Budget Office, "Distribution of Household Income and Federal Taxes, 2008 and 2009," Supplemental data, August 2012, www.cbo.gov/publication/43373 (accessed 10/9/12).

15. "The Forbes 400: The Richest People in America," Forbes.com, September 19, 2012, www.forbes.com/sites/luisakroll/2012/09/19/the-forbes-400-the-richest-people-in-America/(accessed 10/9/12).

16. "Changes in U.S. Family Finances from 2004 to 2007: Evidence from the Survey of Consumer Finances," Federal Reserve Bulletin, February 2009, www.federalreserve.gov/pubs/bulletin/2009/pdf/scf09.pdf (accessed 10/18/10).

17. Neil Howe and Philip Longman, "The Next New Deal," *Atlantic Monthly*, April, 1992, pp. 88–99. Somewhat surprisingly, it is difficult to measure accurately how much government money goes to different income groups. The most commonly used census data are notoriously unreliable because wealthy people underreport their income. Tax forms would be useful but researchers do not have access to these. The only comprehensive analysis to overcome this data problem that we are aware of is this CBO study from the 1990s.

18. Housing subsidies for poor people may be found in Department of Housing and Urban Development, "Housing Payments, Summary of Assisted Units and Outlays, 2011 Summary Statement and Initiatives," www.hud.gov/offices/cfo/reports/2011/cjs/Housing_Payments_2011.pdf (accessed 2/18/2010). Tax expenditures on the mortgage interest deduction are in the Joint Committee on Taxation, "Estimates of Federal Tax Expenditures for Fiscal Years 2009–2013" (Washington, DC: Government Printing Office, 2010), pp. 34–35.

19. Eric J. Toder, Benjamin H. Harris, and Katherine Lim, "Distributional Effects of Tax Expenditure," Tax Policy Center,

July 21, 2009, www.taxpolicycenter.org/UploadedPDF/411922_expenditures.pdf (accessed 6/17/2010).

20. Dean Baker, *The Conservative Nanny State: How the Wealthy Use the Government to Stay Rich and Get Richer*, May 2006, www.conservative nannystate.org.

21. Chris Edwards and Jeff Patch, "Corporate Welfare," in *Cato Handbook for Policymakers*, 7th ed. (Washington, DC: Cato Institute, 2009), www.cato.org/pubs/handbook/hb111/hb111-26.pdf (accessed 5/12/12).

22. Charles M. Blow, "Santorum's Gospel of Inequality," *New York Times*, 2/17/2012, www.nytimes.com/2012/02/18/opinion/blow-santorum-exalts-inequality.html (accessed 3/1/12).

23. Larry M. Bartels, *Unequal Democracy: The Political Economy of the New Gilded Age* (Princeton, NJ: Princeton University Press, 2008).

24. David Brooks, "The Bursting Point," *New York Times*, September 4, 2005.

25. Bruce Nolan, "6 Years Later, Hurricane Katrina's Scars Linger alongside Robust Recovery," *Times Picayune*, August 28, 2011, www.nola.com/katrina/index.ssf/2011/08/6_years_later_hurricane_katrin.html (accessed 3/1/12).

26. Joe Soss, *Unwanted Claims: The Politics of Participation in the U.S. Welfare System* (Ann Arbor: University of Michigan Press, 2000).

27. Daniel P. Carpenter, *The Forging of Bureaucratic Autonomy: Reputations, Networks, and Policy Innovation in Executive Agencies, 1862–1928* (Princeton, NJ: Princeton University Press, 2001).

28. Michael Cohen, James March, and Johan Olsen, "A Garbage Can Model of Organizational Choice," *Administrative Science Quarterly* 17 (March 1972): 1–25; John W. Kingdon, *Agendas, Alternatives, and Public Policies* (Boston: Little, Brown, 1984).

29. Frank R. Baumgartner and Bryan D. Jones, *Agendas and Instability in American Politics* (Chicago: University of Chicago Press, 1993).

30. See William T. Bianco, *Trust: Representatives and Constituents* (Ann Arbor: University of Michigan Press, 1994), Chapter 6, for a discussion of the repeal of the Catastrophic Coverage Act.

31. James Q. Wilson, *Bureaucracy: What Government Agencies Do and Why They Do It* (New York: Basic Books, 1989).

32. See U.S. Department of Agriculture, "USDA01: End the Wool and Mohair Subsidy," http://govinfo.library.unt.edu/npr/library/reports/ag01.html, for information on the pre-1994 policy; and U.S. Department of Agriculture, "2002 Farm Bill, Title 1: Commodities Programs," www.ers.usda.gov/Features/farmbill/titles/titleIcommodities.htm, for the current law (accessed 8/10/08).

33. Paul N. Van de Water and Arloc Sherman, "Social Security Keeps 20 Million Americans Out of Poverty: A State-by-State Analysis," Center on Budget and Policy Priorities, August 11, 2010, www.cbpp.org/cms/?fa=view&id=3260 (accessed 9/16/10).

34. Social Security Administration, Office of Retirement and Disability Policy, and Office of Research, Evaluation, and Statistics, "Fast Facts & Figures about Social Security, 2009," SSA Publication No. 13–11785, July 2009, http://retirement.gov/policy/docs/chartbooks/fast_facts/2009/fast_facts09.pdf (accessed 2/19/10).

35. See the 2008 OASDI Trustees Report, www.ssa.gov/OACT/TR/TR08/II_project.html#wp105643 (accessed 8/10/08).

36. In general, poorer people get back as much as they paid in plus interest much more quickly than wealthier people because of the progressive nature of the benefits. For a study on projected benefits that retirees will receive, see Dean R. Leimer, "Cohort-Specific Measures of Lifetime Social Security Taxes and Benefits," Social Security Administration, Office of Research, Evaluation, and Statistics, December 2007, www.socialsecurity.gov/policy/docs/workingpapers/wp110.pdf (accessed 8/10/08).

37. Social Security Administration, 2012 OASDI Trustees Report, Figure II D5, www.ssa.gov/OACT/TR/2012/tr2012.pdf (accessed 10/9/12).

38. See Congressional Budget Office, "Menu of Social Security Options," May 25, 2005, www.cbo.gov/ftpdoc.cfm?index=6377&type=1, for a detailed account of the fiscal impact of the various proposals.

39. The life expectancy numbers provided here are for all people. Women have always lived longer than men: in 1940 the difference was 2 years, and in 1990 the difference was 4.3 years. That is, women's life expectancy at age 65 in 1990 was 84.6 and men's was 80.3. Social Security Administration, "Life Expectancy for Social Security," www.ssa.gov/history/lifeexpect.html (accessed 8/10/08).

40. The National Commission on Fiscal Responsibility and Reform, "The Moment of Truth," White House, Washington, DC, December, 2010, www.fiscalcommission.gov/sites/fiscalcommission.gov/files/documents/TheMomentofTruth12_1_2010.pdf (accessed 3/13/12).

41. This figure came from a speech by SEC Commissioner Paul R. Carey, "Social Security Privatization," U.S. Securities and Exchange Commission, Washington, DC, January 31, 2001, www.sec.gov/news/speech/spch459.htm.

42. Carmen DeNavas-Walt, Bernadette D. Proctor, and Jessica C. Smith, "Income, Poverty, and Health Insurance Coverage in the United States: 2008," U.S. Census Bureau, September 2009, www.census.gov/prod/2009pubs/p60-236.pdf (accessed 6/18/2010).

43. The data for Europe come from the Organization for Economic Cooperation and Development, "Health: spending continues to outpace economic growth in most OECD countries," www.oecd.org/newsroom/healthspending continuestoout paceeconomicgrowthinmostoecdcountries

.htm (accessed 10/9/12); the figures for the United States come from Centers for Medicare and Medicaid Services, Office of the Actuary, National Health Statistics Group, www.cms.gov/NationalHealthExpendData/02_ NationalHealthAccountsHistorical.asp#TopOfPage, (accessed 3/1/12).

44. Department of Health and Human Services, Centers for Medicare and Medicaid Services, "Brief Summaries of Medicare and Medicaid," www.cms.hhs.gov/Medicaid GenInfo/ 03_TechnicalSummary.asp (accessed 8/11/08).

45. A complete list of the Federal Medical Assistance Percentages may be found at Department of Health and Human Services, "Federal Financial Participation in State Assistance Expenditures, FY 2009," http://aspe.hhs.gov/ health/fmap09.htm (accessed 8/11/08).

46. 2012 Medicare Trustees Report, Washington, DC, August 2012, p.113, www.cms.gov/Research-Statistics-Data-and -Systems/Statistics-Trends-and-Reports/ReportsTrustFunds/ Downloads/TR2012.pdf (accessed 10/9/12).

47. 2010 Medicare Trustees Report, p. 245.

48. Children's Health Insurance Program, Medicaid.gov, www .medicaid.gov/Medicaid-CHIP-Program-Information/ By-Topics/Childrens-Health-Insurance-Program -CHIP/Childrens-Health-Insurance-Program-CHIP.html (accessed 3/13/12).

49. Barack Obama, "Remarks by the President to a Joint Session of Congress on Health Care," U.S. Capitol, Washington, DC, September 9, 2009, www.whitehouse. gov/the-press-office/remarks-president-a-joint-session -congress-health-care (accessed 5/15/12).

50. Peter Grier, "Health Care Reform Bill 101: Who Must Buy Insurance," *Christian Science Monitor*, March 19, 2010, www.csmonitor.com/USA/Politics/2010/0319/Health -Care-Reform-Bill-101-Who-must-buy-insurance (accessed 5/14/12). This article provides an excellent overview of the essential parts of the bill.

51. Congressional Budget Office, "Cost Estimates for H.R. 4872, Reconciliation Act of 2010 (Final Health Care Legislation)," March 20, 2010, www.cbo.gov/doc.cfm?index=11355 (accessed 5/14/12).

52. Congressman Paul Ryan, "A Roadmap for America's Future: Medicare and Medicaid," www.roadmap.republicans. budget.house.gov/Issues/Issue/?IssueID=8520 (accessed 3/14/12).

53. Tom Harkin, "The Senate's 'Starter Home' Health Reform," Huffington Post, December 30, 2009, www.huffingtonpost. com/sentom-harkin/the-senates-starter-home_b_407155 .html (accessed 6/18/10).

54. *Gonzales v. Oregon*, 546 U.S. 243 (2006).

55. U.S. Department of Agriculture, "Supplementary Assistance Nutrition Program: Program Data, Annual State Data FY 2007 -2011." www.fns.usda.gov/pd/snapmain.htm (accessed 3/1/2012).

56. U.S. Department of Labor, "Unemployment Insurance Data Summary," http://workforcesecurity.doleta.gov/unemploy/ content/data.asp (accessed 3/15/12).

57. Internal Revenue Service, "EITC Awareness Day Fact Sheet," www.irs.gov/pub/irs-utl/eitc_day_fastfacts_011508 .pdf (accessed 8/11/08).

58. Internal Revenue Service, "About EITC," www.eitc.irs.gov/ central/abouteitc/ (accessed 3/15/12).

59. Social Security Administration, Fast Facts about Social Security, 2012, SSI Program, www.ssa.gov/policy/docs/ chartbooks/fast_facts/2012/fast_facts12.html (accessed 10/9/12).

60. R. Kent Weaver, *Ending Welfare as We Know It* (Washington, DC: Brookings Institution Press, 2000).

61. See the analysis of welfare reform by the Center on Budget and Policy Priorities, www.cbpp.org/pubs/tanf.htm, or by the Urban Institute, www.urban.org/toolkit/issues/welfare reform.cfm (accessed 8/18/08).

62. U.S. Department of Education, "Department Overview," www .ed.gov/about/landing.jhtml?src=gu (accessed 11/26/08).

63. U.S. Department of Education, Race to the Top fund, www2.ed.gov/programs/racetothetop/index.html (accessed 2/23/10).

64. Amanda Paulson, "The Next Race to the Top? Arne Duncan Outlines Vision for Teacher Reform," *Christian Science Monitor*, February 15, 2012, www.csmonitor.com/USA/Education/ 2012/0215/The-next-Race-to-the-Top-Arne-Duncan -outlines-vision-for-teacher-reform (accessed 3/14/12).

65. Bill and Melinda Gates Foundation, www.gatesfoundation. org/united-states/Pages/program-overview.aspx (accessed 3/14/12).

What Do Political Scientists Do?

a. Larry Bartels, *Unequal Democracy: The Political Economy of the New Gilded Age* (Princeton, NJ: Princeton University Press, 2008), p. 3. The term "Gilded Age" refers to the period of rapid economic growth in the late nineteenth century, characterized by the "robber barons" of industry and finance. Bartels argues that the recent period of inequality is a New Gilded Age.

b. Bartels, *Unequal Democracy*, p. ix.

c. Bartels, *Unequal Democracy*, p. 14.

In Comparison

a. OECD Directorate for Employment, Labour, and Social Affairs, "Health Data 2011: Frequently Requested Data," www.oecd.org/document/16/0,3746,en_2649_33929 _2085200_1_1_1_1,00.html (accessed 3/14/12).

You Decide

a. *Milwaukee Journal Sentinel*, "Inside Choice Schools: 15 Years of Vouchers," seven-part series, 2005, www2 .jsonline.com/news/choice.

b. John F. Witte, *The Market Approach to Education: An Analysis of America's First Voucher Program* (Princeton, NJ: Princeton University Press, 2001).

c. *Zelman v. Simmons-Harris*, 536 U.S. 639 (2002).

CHAPTER 17

1. Helene Cooper and David Sanger, "Obama Says Afghan Policy Won't Change after Dismissal," *New York Times,* June 23, 2010, p. A1.

2. Mark Mazzeti and Eric Schmitt, "C.I.A. Missile Strike May Have Killed Pakistan's Taliban Leader," *New York Times*, August 6, 2009, p. A7.

3. For an example of the isolationist approach, see Justin Raimondo, "Out of Iraq, into Darfur?" *American Conservative*, June 5, 2006. For a longer exposition of isolationism, see Patrick J. Buchanan, *A Republic, Not an Empire*, updated ed. (Washington, DC: Regnery Publishing, 2002).

4. Robert O. Keohane, *After Hegemony: Cooperation and Discord in the International System* (1984; repr. Princeton, NJ: Princeton University Press, 2005).

5. The distinction was first made in E. H. Carr, *The Twenty Years' Crisis, 1919–1939: An Introduction to the Study of International Relations* (London, UK: Macmillan, 1939). Realism was elaborated as a general theory in Hans Morgenthau, *Politics among Nations: The Struggle for Power and Peace* (New York: Knopf, 1948). For a general overview, see Jonathan Haslam, *No Virtue Like Necessity: Realist Thought in International Relations since Machiavelli* (New Haven, CT: Yale University Press, 2002).

6. John J. Mearsheimer and Stephen Walt, "Keeping Saddam Hussein in a Box," *New York Times*, February 2, 2003. Their argument is developed at greater length in "An Unnecessary War," *Foreign Policy* (January/February 2003). For the theory of offensive realism within the realist paradigm, see John J. Mearsheimer, *The Tragedy of Great Power Politics* (New York: Norton, 2001).

7. See, for example, Lawrence F. Kaplan, "Regime Change," *The New Republic*, 228:8 (March 2003): 21; as well as "Birth of a Bush Doctrine? America's Plans for the Middle East," *The Economist*, March 1, 2003, p. 46.

8. Michelle Sun, "Woodward Calls War in Iraq Idealist," *Cornell Daily Sun*, June 21, 2007.

9. Gilbert Felix, *To the Farewell Address: Ideas in Early American Foreign Policy* (Princeton, NJ: Princeton University Press, 1961).

10. A synoptic account of the United States as a world power, which takes the story up to the 2003 invasion of Iraq, is Niall Ferguson, *Colossus: The Price of America's Empire* (New York: Penguin Press, 2004).

11. Samuel Flagg Bemis, *John Quincy Adams and the Foundations of American Foreign Policy* (New York: Knopf, 1949); Ernest R. May, *The Making of the Monroe Doctrine* (Cambridge, MA: Harvard University Press, 1975). The latter stresses domestic political considerations and argues that the Monroe Doctrine was "actually the by-product of an election campaign."

12. Daniel M. Smith, *The Great Departure: The United States and World War I, 1914–1920* (New York: John Wiley, 1965).

13. Thomas J. Knock, *To End All Wars: Woodrow Wilson and the Quest for a New World Order* (New York: Oxford University Press, 1992).

14. Margaret MacMillan, *Paris 1919: Six Months That Changed the World* (New York: Random House, 2001).

15. John M. Cooper, *Breaking the Heart of the World: Woodrow Wilson and the Fight for the League of Nations* (New York: Cambridge University Press, 2001).

16. John Lewis Gaddis, *Strategies of Containment* (New York: Oxford University Press, 2005).

17. Tony Smith, "Making the World Safe for Democracy in the American Century," *Diplomatic History* 23:2 (1999): 173–88.

18. Winston Churchill, "Sinews of Peace (Iron Curtain)," Westminster College, Fulton, MO, March 5, 1946, available from the Churchill Centre at www.winstonchurchill.org/i4a/pages/index.cfm?pageid=429 (accessed 8/2/08). See also Klaus Larres, *Churchill's Cold War: The Politics of Personal Diplomacy* (New Haven, CT: Yale University Press, 2002).

19. George F. Kennan, "The Sources of Soviet Conduct," *Foreign Affairs* 25:4 (July 1947): 566–82.

20. Robert L. Beisner, *Dean Acheson: A Life in the Cold War* (New York: Oxford University Press, 2006); Dean Acheson, *Present at the Creation* (New York: Norton, 1969).

21. Michael J. Hogan, *The Marshall Plan: America, Britain, and the Reconstruction of Western Europe* (New York: Cambridge University Press, 1987). See also Martin Schain, ed., *The Marshall Plan: Fifty Years Later* (New York: Palgrave, 2001).

22. Marc Trachtenberg, *A Constructed Peace: The Making of the European Settlement, 1945–1963* (Princeton, NJ: Princeton University Press, 1999).

23. The balance of military power between NATO and the Warsaw Pact throughout the Cold War is traced in David Miller, *The Cold War: A Military History* (New York: St. Martin's Press, 1998).

24. Robert A. Packenham, *Liberal America and the Third World* (Princeton, NJ: Princeton University Press, 1973). For an overview, see David P. Forsythe, "Human Rights in U.S. Foreign Policy: Retrospect and Prospect," *Political Science Quarterly* 105:3 (Autumn 1990): 435–54.

25. Sergei N. Goncharov, John W. Lewis, and Xue Litai, *Uncertain Partners: Stalin, Mao, and the Korean War* (Palo Alto, CA: Stanford University Press, 1999).

26. James A. Bill, *The Eagle and the Lion: The Tragedy of American-Iranian Relations* (New Haven, CT: Yale University Press, 1988).

27. Lawrence Freedman, *Kennedy's Wars: Berlin, Cuba, Laos, and Vietnam* (Oxford, UK: Oxford University Press, 2002).

28. William J. Duiker, *Sacred War: Nationalism and Revolution in a Divided Vietnam* (New York: McGraw-Hill, 1995).

29. Henry Kissinger, *Years of Upheaval* (Boston: Little, Brown, 1982); Jussi Hanhimäki, *The Flawed Architect: Henry Kissinger and American Foreign Policy* (New York: Oxford University Press, 2004).

30. Raymond Garthoff, *Détente and Confrontation: American-Soviet Relations from Nixon to Reagan* (Washington, DC: Brookings Institution Press, 1994).

31. Bill, *The Eagle and the Lion.*

32. Odd Arne Westad, ed., *The Fall of Détente: Soviet-American Relations during the Carter Years* (Oslo, Norway: Scandinavian University Press, 1997).

33. Garthoff, *Détente and Confrontation.*

34. Philip Hanson, *The Rise and Fall of the Soviet Economy* (London, UK: Longman, 2003).

35. "Can Russia Ever Be Secured?" *The Economist*, December 7, 1996, p. 45; Peter Finn, "Antimissile Plan by U.S. Strains Ties with Russia," *Washington Post*, February 21, 2007, p. A10; Matthew Kaminski, "NATO's Chill with Russia Isn't Thawing—Diplomatic Rift Hinders Bid to Involve Moscow in Kosovo Peacekeeping," *Wall Street Journal*, July 2, 1999, p. 1.

36. Francis Fukuyama, *The End of History and the Last Man*, updated ed. (New York: Free Press, 2006).

37. For a summary of American human rights policy, see John W. Dietrich, "U.S. Human Rights Policy in the Post–Cold War Era," *Political Science Quarterly* 121:2 (Summer 2006): 269–94.

38. Samuel P. Huntington, *The Clash of Civilizations and the Remaking of World Order* (New York: Free Press, 2002).

39. Scott Wilson, "Obama Calls for Fresh Start with Muslims," *Washington Post*, June 5, 2009, p. A1.

40. For descriptions of some of these cross-cultural programs, see U.S. Department of Education, "Programs by Subject: International Education," www.ed.gov/programs/find/subject/index.html?src=ln (accessed 8/2/08).

41. U.S. Department of Agriculture, Foreign Agricultural Service, "Market Development Programs," www.fas.usda.gov/mos/marketdev.asp, and "Issues and Policies," www.fas.usda.gov/issues_policies.asp (both accessed 8/2/08).

42. Louis Fisher, *Presidential War Power* (Lawrence: University Press of Kansas, 2004).

43. Arthur M. Schlesinger, *The Imperial Presidency* (Boston: Houghton Mifflin, 1973).

44. On Panama, see Stephen Kurkjian, "Bush Used Power as Top Commander for Strike," *Boston Globe*, December 20, 1989, p. 2. On Iraq, see Ronald J. Ostrow, "Legal Experts Split over Bush's Power Policy," *Los Angeles Times*, November 13, 1990, p. 13.

45. Neil A. Lewis, "War Powers: An Old Debate Clinton May Resolve," *New York Times*, May 8, 1993, p. 14; Alison Mitchell, "Deadlocked House Denies Support for Air Campaign," *New York Times*, April 29, 1999, p. A1.

46. Terry Moe and William Howell, "Unilateral Action and Presidential Power: A Theory," *Presidential Studies Quarterly* 29:4 (1999): 850–72.

47. Laurie Goering, "Clinton Signs Pacts on Global Warming: President Acts Despite Strong Opposition to the Treaty in the Senate, Which Must Ratify It," *Chicago Tribune*, November 13, 1998, p. 4.

48. David Hoffman and David B. Ottaway, "Panel Drops Covert-Acts Notification; In Compromise, Bush Pledges to Inform Hill in All but Rare Cases," *Washington Post*, October 27, 1989, p. A1.

49. Dahlia Lithwick, "The Enemy Within," *Slate*, June 12, 2008, www.slate.com/id/2193468 (accessed 8/12/08).

50. Somini Sengupta, "As Musharraf's Woes Grow, Enter an Old Rival, Again," *New York Times*, April 6, 2007, p. A3; Leslie Wayne, "Airbus Seeks a Welcome in Alabama," *New York Times*, June 19, 2007, p. C1.

51. American Israel Public Affairs Committee, "What Is AIPAC?," www.aipac.org/about_AIPAC/default.asp (accessed 8/3/08).

52. American Israel Public Affairs Committee, "Legislation and Policy Update," http://www.aipac.org/Legislation_and_Policy/default.asp (accessed 8/3/08).

53. Andrew Jacobs, "China Angered by U.S. Lobbying on Rights," *New York Times*, August 1, 2008.

54. Steven R. Weisman, "U.S. and China Agree to Ease Foreign Investment," *New York Times*, June 19, 2008.

55. See Pew Research Center, "The U.S. Public's Pro-Israel History," July 19, 2006, www.pewresearch.org/pubs/39/the-u.s.-publics-pro-israel-history (accessed 8/2/08).

56. John Harwood, "War-Weary Public Wants Congress to Lead; Poll Shows Desire for Lawmakers to Set Policy Amid Growing Dismay over Iraq, President Bush," *Wall Street Journal*, December 14, 2006, p. A4; E. J. Dionne, "Slowly Sidling to Iraq's Exit; Many GOP Candidates Part Company with Bush," *Washington Post*, August 29, 2006, p. A15.

57. "Public Wary of Military Intervention in Libya," Pew Research Center, March 14, 2012, www.pewresearch.org/pubs/1927/strong-opposition-us-involvement-libya-military-overcommitted (accessed 9/25/12).

58. Pew Research Center, "Public Opinion Six Months Later," March 7, 2002, www.people-press.org/commentary/display.php3?AnalysisID=44 (accessed 8/2/08).

59. A directory of NGOs can be found at the Department of Public Information site, Nongovernmental Organization Section, www.un.org/dpi/ngosection/asp/form.asp (accessed 8/2/08).

60. See Amnesty International, "The Secretive and Illegal U.S. Programme of Rendition," April 5, 2006, www.amnesty.org/en/news-and-updates/feature-stories/secretive-and-illegal-us-programme-of-rendition-20060405 (accessed 8/12/08).

61. See the National Democratic Institute for International Affairs site at www.ndi.org and the International Republican Institute site at www.iri.org.

62. Elizabeth Bumiller, Eric Schmitt, and Thom Shanker, "U.S. Sends Top Iranian Leader a Warning on Strait Threat," *New York Times,* January 12, 2012, p. A1.

63. Johanna Neuman and Megan K. Stack, "Americans' Beirut Exodus Underway; Hundreds Are Evacuated by Ship and Helicopter," *Los Angeles Times,* July 20, 2006, p. A10. The Clinton administration resorted to cruise missile attacks five times: three against Iraq (1993, 1996, 1998), one in 1995 against Bosnian Serb forces in the former Yugoslavia, and one against targets in Afghanistan and Sudan in 1998. James Mann, "Foreign Policy of the Cruise Missile," *Los Angeles Times,* December 23, 1998, p. 5.

64. A comprehensive account of the Afghanistan invasion and its aftermath is in Barnett R. Rubin, "Saving Afghanistan," *Foreign Affairs* 86:1 (January/February, 2007): 57–78.

65. United States International Trade Commission, Harmonized Tariff Schedule of the United States (2010), Revision 2, www.usitc.gov/docs/tata/hts/bychapter/1002htsa.pdf (accessed 9/14/10).

66. Tyler Marshall, "Clinton to Nudge China on Rights Reform, Officials Say," *Los Angeles Times,* June 17, 1997, p. 7.

67. Elaine Sciolino, "Call It Aid or a Bribe, It's the Price of Peace," *New York Times,* March 26, 1995.

68. Colum Lynch, "U.N. Backs Broader Sanctions on Tehran; Security Council Votes to Freeze Some Assets, Ban Arms Exports," *Washington Post,* March 25, 2007, p. A1.

69. William B. Quandt, *Camp David: Peacemaking and Politics* (Washington, DC: Brookings Institution Press, 1986).

70. John Lewis Gaddis, *The Cold War: A New History* (New York: Penguin Press, 2005).

71. U.S. Department of State, *Treaties in Force,* January 1, 2007, www.state.gov/s/l/treaty/treaties/2007/index.htm (accessed 8/12/08).

72. Lisa L. Martin, "The President and International Commitments: Treaties as Signaling Devices," *Presidential Studies Quarterly* 35:3 (2005): 440–65.

73. Andrew Kohut, "Simply Put, the Public's View Can't Be Put Simply," *Washington Post,* September 29, 2002, p. B5; John B. Judis, "War Resisters," *American Prospect* 13:18 (October 6, 2002), www.prospect.org/cs/articles? article=war_resisters (accessed 9/10/08).

74. P. J. Huffstutter, "A Town Gives until It Hurts," *Los Angeles Times,* November 7, 2003, p. A1.

75. Pew Research Center, "Fewer Americans See Solid Evidence of Global Warming," October 22, 2009, www.people-press.org/report/556/global-warming (accessed 2/17/10).

76. Richard Benedetto, "Poll: Most Support War as a Last Resort," *USA Today,* November 26, 2002, p. A3; Dan Balz and Jim VandeHei, "Democratic Hopefuls Back Bush on Iraq; Gephardt, Lieberman, Edwards Support Launching Preemptive Strike," *Washington Post,* September 14, 2002, p. A4; Jim VandeHei and Juliet Eilperin, "Congress Passes Iraq Resolution; Overwhelming Approval Gives Bush Authority to Attack Unilaterally," *Washington Post,* October 11, 2002, p. A1.

77. Walter Pincus, "U.S. Lacks Specifics on Banned Arms," *Washington Post,* March 16, 2003, p. A17; Michael R. Gordon and Judith Miller, "U.S. Says Hussein Intensifies Quest for A-Bomb Parts," *New York Times,* September 8, 2002.

78. Bob Drogin, "Iraq Weapons Data Flawed, Congress Told," *Los Angeles Times,* January 29, 2004, p. A1.

79. Steven Erlanger, "Syrian Conflict Poses the Risk of Wider Strife," *New York Times,* February 12, 2012, p. A1.

80. For details on the causes, effects, and mitigation of global warming, see the Intergovernmental Panel on Climate Change site at www.ipcc.ch.

81. Thomas C. Schelling, "The Cost of Combating Global Warming," *Foreign Affairs* (November/December 1997).

82. David Victor, *The Collapse of the Kyoto Protocol and the Struggle to Slow Global Warming* (Princeton, NJ: Princeton University Press, 2001).

83. Arch Puddington, "Freedom in the World 2009: Setbacks and Resilience," www.freedomhouse.org/report/countries-crossroads-2011/essay-freedom-world-2009-setbacks.html (accessed 11/5/12).

84. Reuters, "Microsoft, Sun Battle over Indian Programmers," July 8, 2002.

85. See the NightHawk Radiology Services site at www.nighthawkrad.net.

86. For an optimistic review, see Joseph Stiglitz, *Making Globalization Work* (New York: Norton, 2007).

87. Keith Bradsher, "China Finds a Fit with Car Parts: Export Factories Are Gearing Up to Challenge Global Suppliers," *New York Times,* June 7, 2007.

88. Andrew Martin, "FDA Curbs Sale of 5 Seafoods Farmed in China," *New York Times,* June 29, 2007.

89. Joseph Nocera, "The Cufflinks That Went to China," *New York Times,* January 21, 2006; Jodie T. Allen, "NAFTA Math: The Faulty Arithmetic of Job Losses," *Slate,* July 13, 1997, www.slate.com/id/1889 (accessed 8/2/08).

90. Louis Uchitelle, "Retraining, but for What?" *New York Times,* March 26, 2006.

91. Huntington, *The Clash of Civilizations and the Remaking of World Order.*

92. Pew Research Center, "U.S. Image Up Slightly, but Still Negative," June 23, 2005, pewglobal.org/reports/display.php?ReportID=247 (accessed 8/3/08).

94. Amartya Sen, *Identity and Violence: The Illusion of Destiny* (New York: Norton, 2007); see also Bruce Russett, John R. O'Neal, and Michaelene Cox, "Clash of Civilizations, or Realism and Liberalism Déjà Vu? Some Evidence," *Journal of Peace Research* 5 (2000): 583–608.

94. Mark Mazzetti, "CIA Still Awaiting Rules on Interrogating Suspects," *New York Times,* March 25, 2007, p. 14.

95. Anne Applebaum, "Cold War in a Hot Climate," *Slate*, May 28, 2002, www.slate.com/id/2066250 (accessed 8/3/08).

96. Nicholas Kristof, "Japan Arrests More Suspects in Gas Attack," *New York Times*, July 10, 1995, p. 7.

97. Fred Kaplan, "Let's Talk about Nukes," *Slate*, August 16, 2005, www.slate.com/id/2124544 (accessed 8/3/08).

98. John Mearsheimer and Stephen Walt, "The Israel Lobby and U.S. Foreign Policy," *Middle East Policy* 13 (2006): 29–87.

99. For an insider account, see Dennis Ross, *The Missing Peace: The Inside Story of the Fight for Middle East Peace* (New York: Farrar, Straus and Giroux, 2005).

100. Steven Erlanger, "Divide, Yes, but Conquer, Probably Not," *New York Times*, July 8, 2007.

What Do Political Scientists Do?

a. John Mueller, "Assessing Measures Designed to Protect the Homeland," *Policy Studies Journal*, forthcoming; John Mueller, *Overblown: How Politicians, the Terrorism Industry and Others Stoke National Security Fears* (New York: Free Press, 2006).

You Decide

a. See the International Criminal Court site at www.icc-cpi .int/home.html; for background on the ICC, see United Nations, UN News Centre, "The International Criminal Court," www.un.org/News/facts/iccfact.htm.

b. International Criminal Court, "The States Parties to the Rome Statute," June 1, 2008, http://hrw.org/campaigns/icc/ratifications.htm.

c. Thom Shanker and James Dao, "U.S. Might Refuse New Peace Duties without Immunity," *New York Times*, July 3, 2002.

d. David Clark, "U.S to Attend Hague Court Meeting as Observer," Reuters, November 16, 2009, www.reuters.com/article/idUSLG395050 (accessed 2/11/10).

e. Brett D. Schaefer, "Overturning Clinton's Midnight Action on the International Criminal Court," Heritage Foundation Executive Memorandum 708, January 9, 2001, www.heritage.org/Research/InternationalOrganizations/EM708.cfm.

f. Human Rights Watch, "Myths and Facts about the International Criminal Court," http://hrw.org/campaigns/icc/facts.htm.

g. Alan Cowell, "British Soldier Pleads Guilty to War Crime," *New York Times*, September 20, 2006.

h. Michael Lewis, "Military's Opposition to Harsh Interrogation Is Outlined," *New York Times*, July 28, 2005.

ANSWER KEY

CHAPTER 1

1. c
2. b
3. c
4. d
5. d
6. c
7. a
8. e
9. a

CHAPTER 2

1. b
2. e
3. a
4. c
5. c
6. b
7. d
8. b
9. d
10. b
11. d
12. b
13. a
14. b
15. b

CHAPTER 3

1. c
2. b
3. b
4. d
5. c
6. b
7. b
8. b
9. c
10. d
11. b
12. a
13. d
14. c
15. d

CHAPTER 4

1. d
2. b
3. a
4. d
5. b
6. d
7. a
8. d
9. c
10. a
11. a
12. b
13. c
14. c
15. e
16. b

CHAPTER 5

1. d
2. b
3. a
4. d
5. c
6. e
7. a
8. d
9. d
10. a
11. b
12. d
13. a
14. c
15. b

CHAPTER 6

1. a
2. e
3. b
4. b
5. d
6. d
7. d
8. b
9. d
10. c
11. a
12. b
13. e
14. a
15. d

CHAPTER 7

1. c
2. a
3. e
4. b
5. d
6. b
7. e
8. a
9. e
10. a
11. e
12. b
13. c
14. c
15. e

CHAPTER 8

1. a
2. b
3. a
4. d
5. b
6. b
7. b
8. c
9. e
10. a
11. c
12. b
13. a
14. b
15. e

CHAPTER 9

1. e
2. a
3. c
4. b
5. a
6. e
7. a
8. c
9. c
10. a
11. b
12. d
13. d
14. b
15. a

CHAPTER 10

1. d
2. e
3. b
4. b
5. a
6. d
7. d
8. b
9. d
10. a
11. c
12. e
13. b
14. b
15. a

CHAPTER 11

1. c
2. d
3. b
4. d
5. c
6. e
7. b
8. b
9. a
10. c
11. b
12. d
13. a
14. b

CHAPTER 12

1. c
2. a
3. d
4. b
5. e
6. b
7. c
8. b
9. b
10. d
11. b
12. a
13. e
14. a
15. b

CHAPTER 13

1. a
2. d
3. b
4. e
5. a
6. e
7. b
8. c
9. a
10. e
11. b
12. d
13. c
14. a
15. b

CHAPTER 14

1. a
2. c
3. b
4. e
5. e
6. b
7. d
8. c
9. e
10. a
11. b
12. c
13. c
14. a
15. d

CHAPTER 15

1. a
2. c
3. d
4. b
5. c
6. c
7. e
8. d
9. b
10. b
11. e
12. e
13. a
14. c
15. d

CHAPTER 16

1. b
2. a
3. e
4. b
5. a
6. c
7. e
8. a
9. c
10. d
11. a
12. b
13. b
14. c
15. b

CHAPTER 17

1. c
2. a
3. e
4. c
5. d
6. d
7. b
8. c
9. a
10. c
11. b
12. d
13. e
14. b
15. a

CREDITS

TABLES AND FIGURES

Figure 1.2: Map: "2012 Presidential Election, Purple America," by Robert J. Vanderbei, Princeton University. www.princeton .edu/~rvdb/JAVA/election2012/. **Box 5.1**: From "Beyond Red vs. Blue: The 2005 Political Typology." Reprinted by permission of The Pew Research Center for the People & the Press. **Figure 5.1**: Pollster.com, Chart: National Job Approval: President Barack Obama, from http://pollster.com/Obama44JobApprovalr .php. Reprinted with permission. **Table 5.1**: From "American Attitudes Hold Steady in Face of Foreign Crises," August 17, 2006, p. 4. Reprinted by permission of The Pew Research Center for the People & the Press. **Table 5.3**: From "Abortion, the Court, and the Public," Oct. 3, 2005, p. 4. Reprinted by permission of The Pew Research Center for the People & the Press. **Tables 5.4**: From "Beyond Red vs. Blue: The 2005 Political Typology." Reprinted by permission of The Pew Research Center for the People & the Press. **Table 5.7**: From "Support for Health Care Principles, Opposition to Package: Mixed Views of Economic Policies and Health Care Reform Persist," October. 8, 2009, The Pew Research Center For the People & the Press, a project of The Pew Research Center. Reprinted with permission. **Table 6.2**: From "What Americans Know: 1989–2007," April 15, 2007, p. 2. Reprinted by permission of The Pew Research Center for the People & the Press.**Table 6.3**: Mark Blumenthal, Table from "Economic Stimulus and the Many Faces of Public Opinion," www.pollster.com/blogs/economic _stimulus_and_the_many.php. Reprinted with permission. **Chapter 6:** Two tables from "Media Framing of a Civil Liberties Conflict and Its Effect on Tolerance," by Thomas E. Nelson, Rosalee A. Clawson, and Zoe M. Oxley, *American Political Science Review* 91.3 (Sept. 1997): 567–83. © 1997 American Political Science Association. Reprinted with the permission of Cambridge University Press. **Table 6.4**: From "Key News Audiences Now Blend Online and Traditional Sources: Audience Segments in a Changing News Environment," August 17, 2008, The Pew Research Center for the people & the Press, a project of The Pew Research Center. Reprinted with permission. **Figure 7.3**: From "Party Affiliation: What It Is and What It Isn't," September 23, 2004, p. 3. Reprinted by permission of The Pew Research Center for the People & the Press. **Chapter 8**: Two graphs from "Three Myths about Political Independents," by John Sides, www.themonkeycage.org/2009/12/ three_myths_about_political_in.html. Reprinted by permission of the author. **Table 8.8**: Table 5.11 from *The Politics of Congressional Elections, Sixth Edition,* by Gary Jacobson. Copyright © 2004. Reprinted by permission of Pearson Education, Inc. **Figure 10.7**: Graph: "Ideological Distribution of Members" from "Forecasting Polarization in the 113th Senate," September 10, 2012, Voteview. com, http://voteview.com/blog/?p=567. Reprinted by permission of Chris Hare, Keith T. Poole, and Howard Rosenthal. **Chapter 12**: Figure 1 from Jason Webb Yackee and Susan Webb Yackee, "A Bias Toward Business? Assessing Interest Group Influence on the U.S. Bureaucracy," *The Journal of Politics* 68.1 (February 2006): 128–39. Copyright © 2006, Southern Political Science Association. Reprinted with the permission of Cambridge University Press. **Figure 13.5**: Stephen Jessee and Alexander Tahk, "Current Beliefs" from Supreme Court Ideology Project, http://sct.tahk .us/current.html. Reprinted by permission of the authors. **Figure 15.1C**: From "Comparing Ourselves to Others," by Jack Anderson, Chart "Tax Burden and Spending," *Forbes Magazine*, April 13, 2009. Reprinted by permission of Forbes Media LLC © 2009. **Table 17.2:** From "Public Wants Proof of Iraqi Weapons Program," January 16, 2003, p. 4. Reprinted by permission of The Pew Research Center for the People and the Press.

PHOTOGRAPHS

Page iii © Joshua Bickel / Corbis; **Page 3** © White House Photo / Alamy; **5** Jose Luis Magana/AP; **7** (left) U.S. Army Photo by Staff Sgt. Russell Bassett; **7** (right) *Houston Chronicle*, Brett Coomer/AP Photo; **9** Jupiter Images; **11** Orlin Wagner/AP; **12** Charles Dharapak/AP; **13** Joseph Sohm/Visions of America/Corbis; **14** Rick Wilking/AP; **15** Bill Clark/CQ Roll Call/Getty Images; **16** Erin Siegal/Reuters/Landov; **19** © Leigh Vogel/Corbis; **21** Flip Schulke/CORBIS; **22** Sandy Felsenthal/Corbis; **29** © Peter Casolino / Alamy; **31** © North Wind Picture Archives / Alamy; **34** © North Wind Picture Archives / Alamy; **37** Imagno/Getty Images; **38** North Wind Picture Archives; **39** © Bettmann/CORBIS; **44** Leonard de Selva/ CORBIS; **46** Corbis; **49** U.S. Army photo by Staff Sgt. Lynette Hoke, 1st Brigade Combat Team, 34th Infantry Division Public Affairs; **51** KEVIN DIETSCH/UPI/Landov; **52** AP/Wide World Photos; **55** © Porter Gifford/Corbis; **57** (left) © Everett Collection

INDEX

Democratic Party (*continued*)
    Latinos in, 561
    leadership positions in, 446
    limited federal government and, 89
    media and, 225
    party coalitions in, 258, **260**
    party identification in electorate of,
      256, **257, 258**
    party in government of, 251–54
    party organizations of, 247–51
    political machines in, 251
    poverty rates under leadership of,
      659, 660, 661
    presidential platforms of, 265–66
    primaries of, 536, 558
    recruiting and nominating of candidates
      in, 261
    regulation and, 20, 245, 246, 645
    Senate controlled by, 14, 442, 596
    social policy approaches favored by,
      651–53, 654, 660, 661, 671, 673,
      686, 687
    southern, 479, 558, 570, 587
    spending and, 20, 626
    superdelegates in nominating process
      of, 291
    taxes and, 20, 566, 616, 626, 630
    views shaped by identification with, 16
    see also elections, U.S.
Democratic-Republicans, 78, 80, 123, 511, 520
Democratic Senatorial Campaign Committee
    (DSCC), 253
demographics, 170–72
Denmark, 581, 629, **629, 719**
Dennis, James, 569
Department of Motor Vehicles (DMV),
    315, 666
depression, *see* economic depression;
    Great Depression
deregulation:
    of media, 205–7
    negative consequences of, 639
Derthick, Martha, 105
descriptive representation, 381
desegregation, 458, 571–73, 575–78
    of interstate travel, 573
    of schools, *see* school desegregation
    see also segregation
détente, 702
Detroit, Mich., 577
devolution, 89, 100–101
Diallo, Amadou, 569
digital media, *203*
Dingell, John, 15
diplomacy, as foreign policy tool, 718
direct incitement test, 124, 127
direct lobbying, 354–55
disabled people, civil rights of, 557, 589, **590**
discount rate, 634
discretionary spending, 628, **628**
discrimination, 21, 89, 90, 93, 95–97, **96**,
    100, 104, 111, **114**, 119, **181**, 516,
    553–54, 563
    disparate impact standard and, 578
    in employment, 566, 578, 587, 588, 594
    gender, *see* gender discrimination

racial, *see* racial discrimination
    reverse, 531, 595
    sexual, *580*
disparate impact standard, 578
dissents, **537**
distributive theory, 407
district courts, 510, 518–19, 520
District of Columbia, 77, 139, *589*
    courts in, 518, 520
    justices of the peace in, 511
    school desegregation in, 577
districts, 90
diversity, 21, *22*, 591–92
divided government, 68, 269, 626
    social policies impacted by, 661, 687
divorce, *16*, 77, 584
DNA research, 681
Doctors without Borders, 713
Dole, Bob, 287
Dole, Elizabeth, 301, 305, 367
domestic spying, *see* surveillance
Dominican Republic, 716
Dominicans, 561
domino theory, 701
Donaldson, Sam, 231
"don't ask, don't tell," *153, 191, 586,* 591
"donut hole", Medicare, 680
double jeopardy, 120, **122**, 146
Douglas, William O., 151, 530
draft, military, 49–50, 96, *120,* 123, 125
Dream Act, 554
Dred Scott v. Sandford, 80–82, **81**, 118, 512, 558
drinking laws, 72, 90, 98, 580, 582
drones, 429–30, 493, *695,* 699, 722
Druckman, James, 224
Drug-Free Workplace Act (1988), 144
drugs, 21, 125, 153, 469, 471, 473, 528
    advertising of, 130
    employment and, 136, 144
    legalization of, 23
    medical use of illegal, 99, *99,* 100
    possession of, 115, 116, 141–42
    prevention of abuse of, 450
    regulation of, 99, 136, 138, 471
    religion and, 136, 138
    safety of, 469, 471, 473, 474, 498, 499
drug-sniffing dogs, 115, 116, *116*
drug testing, 142–44
dual citizenship, 81, 82, 119
dual federalism, *see* federalism, dual
due process, 48, 52, 62, **73**, 82, 95, **114**, 115,
    119–20, 121, 139–51, *148,* 153,
    556, 698
    gay rights and, 586
Dukes, Betty, *580*
Duncan v. Louisiana, **122**
Dunkin' Donuts, 585
Dunne, Finley Peter, 542
Duverger's law, 271

earmarks, 398, *406*
    see also pork-barrel spending
Earned Income Tax Credit (EITC), 681–83, **684**
economic depression, 608
economic disparity, role of federalism in
    dealing with, 102

economic groups, **340**, 353
economic growth:
    as economic policy goal, 609–10
    in federal systems, 75
economic individualism, 19
economic interests:
    Articles of Confederation and, 34–35
    Constitutional Convention and,
      37–38, 45–46
    Constitution and, 74, 77
    federalism and, 75
    interconnectedness of, 726
    political conflict about, 19–20
    public opinion and, 165, 169, *169, 183,*
      187, 323
    of U.S., 726–27
economic policy, 730
    bureaucracy and role in, 618–23, 644–45
    congressional role in, 614–16, 618, 620,
      622, 633, 639, 644–45
    courts and indirect role in, 625
    financial crisis of 2008 and, 610, 621–23
    fiscal theories and policies in, 625–30,
      627, 644
    goals of, 607–13
    government regulation and impact on,
      636–39
    monetary theories and polices in,
      631–36, 644, 658
    presidential role in, 224–25, 614,
      617–18, *617,* 644, 645
    protectionism and, 643
    on trade and balance of payments,
      641–44, 716, 726
    see also economic stimulus package
Economic Stimulus Act (2008), 617
economic stimulus package, 14, 91, 224–25,
    224, 256, 267, 273, 444, 457,
    617, 627
economy, 74, 76, 83, 87, **88**, 97, **184**, 186–89, **189**
    regulation of, 431
    slavery and, 558
Edison High School, 97
education, 9, 14, 16, 18, 21, 72, 78, 83, 89, 91,
    93–95, 97, 101, 102, 477, 507
    Barack Obama's reform of, 663
    civil liberties and, 126, 133–34, 144
    conflictual issues related to, 21, 115
    desegregation of, *see* school
      desegregation
    government and, 9, 16, 18, 72, 78, 83, 89,
      93–95, 97, 101, 115, 134–35, 378,
      383, 663, 683–85, *685*
    G. W. Bush's reform of, 663, 684
    ideology and, 21, 23
    No Child Left Behind Act and, 480,
      663, 685
    political affiliation and, **260**
    political influence of, 168, 170–71, **171**
    race and, 21, 89, 93
    Race to the Top program and, 663, 685
    sex, 492
    sex discrimination in, 584
    social policies on, 655, 663, 683–85,
      686, *686*
    state differences in, 93, 102

economic policy and, 608, 617, *617*, 625, 643

economic views of, 630

education and, 663

executive orders of, 436

federal campaign funding and, 309, 322–23

foreign policy of, 439, 698, 732

as "Fundraiser-in-Chief," 404

government contracts and, 472

G. W. Bush's policies and, 52, 698

health care reform and, 29, 172, *172*, 176–77, 189, 250, 267, 346, 442, 447, 457, 480, 651–53, 656, 677–79, 680

health care reform of, 455

and Iraq, 439, 457

judges appointed by, 525, 526

millionaire's tax called by, 605–6

as party leader, 446, *447*

Race to the Top program and, 663, 685

2008 campaign platform of, 630, 639

in 2008 Democratic primaries, 264, 290, 303, 309, 322

2008 election results of, 170, **258**, 292, **295**, 322–23, 367

and 2010 elections, *405*, 447

2012 campaign platform of, 301, **302**

in 2012 elections, 290, 292, **295**, 322–31, 592, 605–6

unilateral actions of, 458–59

U.S. Supreme Court and, 545

War on Terror and, 143, 696

Obama administration, 145

Obey, David R., 406

obscenity, 128, 131–32

Occupational Safety and Health Administration (OSHA), 498, 637

Occupy Wall Street, 208, 210, *211*, 337, 347, 357, 575

Ochs, Adolph, 204

O'Connor, Sandra Day, 99, 147, 153

expertise of, 536

Lawrence case and, 586–87

replacement of, 540

O'Donnell, Christine, 264, 303

Office of Civil Rights, 98

Office of Congressional Ethics, 422

Office of Economic Opportunity, 655

Office of Information and Regulatory Affairs, 93

Office of Management and Budget (OMB), 449, 451, 481, 617, 705

Office of National Drug Control Policy (ONDCP), 450

Office of the United States Trade Representative (USTR), 449, 451, 617, 705, 716

"off the record," 216

Ohio, 59, 69, 124, 134, 138, 288, 292, 686

oil, foreign, 702, 725, 730

oil companies, 497, 498

Oklahoma, desegregation in, 576

Old-Age, Survivors, and Disability Insurance (OASDI), **667**, 670

Ollie's Barbeque, 578

Olympics, 125, 702

ombudsman, 421

omnibus legislation, 417

"on background," 216

O'Neill, Thomas "Tip," 318, 395

Open Market Committee, 619

open market operations, 635

open ("crossover") primary, **262**, 284

open rules, 419

open seat, 296

Open Society Institute, 714

opinion writing, in Supreme Court, 535–36, *536*

opposition research, 303

oral argument, in Supreme Court, 534–35, *534*

Oregon, 99, 136, 152–53, 285, 431, 681

Oregon Treaty, 431

O'Reilly, Bill, 208

O'Reilly Factor, The, 208, **220**, 221

Organization for Economic Cooperation and Development (OECD), 486, 678, 719

Organization of the Petroleum Exporting Countries (OPEC), 702

organ transplants, 471

original intent, 55, 538, 540

see also strict construction

originalism, 55

see also original intent

Orwell, George, 145

Outback Steakhouse, 584

outside strategies, 353, 356–65, **366**

oversight, congressional, 483, 495–97

Oversight and Government Reform Committee, 420

ownership society, 656, *656*

Oxfam International, 713

Oxley, Zoe, 223

PACs, *see* political action committees

Paine, Thomas, **32**, 36, 39

Pakistan, 429, *514*, 542, 581, 645, 696, 699, 722, 724, 728, 729

Palestinians, 439

Israeli conflict with, *222*, 696, 732

Palin, Sarah, 226, *227*, 317, 322

Palm Beach County, Fla., 286–87

Palmquist, Bradley, 170

Panama, 545, 700, 707

Panama Canal, 699–700

paradox of voting, 313–14

pardons, 42, 50, 80, 123, 443

Paris, Treaty of, 513

Parkin, Michael, 224

parks, national, 9

Parks, Rosa, 572

Parliament, British, 440, 514

parliamentary system, 6, 43, 73, 341, 440, **440**, 514

parties in service, 246

partisanship cues, 317

party coalitions, 258, **259, 260**

party identification (party ID), 256, **257, 258**

party in government, 242, 251–54

developing agendas and, 267

party in the electorate, 242, 256–58

party organization, 242, 247–51, 274

in other countries, 252

party platforms, 265–66, 291

party principle, 244

party systems, 243–46

realignment in, 246–47

party unity, loyalty, 256, 402

patents, 49, 610, 626

Patient-Centered Outcomes Research Institute, 679–80

Patriot Act 415; USA PATRIOT Act

Patriot Guard Riders, 111

patronage, 251

Patterson, Thomas, 228

Paul, Rand, *168*

Paul, Ron, *168, 297*, 624

Paulson, Henry, 622

Pawtucket, R.I., 134

pay-as-you-go (PAYGO), 616–17

payroll taxes, 629, 630

Social Security funded by, 669–70, **671**, 672, 673, 676

Peace Corps, 432, 459, 655

peak associations, 348

Pearl Harbor, Hawaii, 51, 700

Pelosi, Nancy, *241*, 400, 405, 421, 652, *653*

Pendleton Civil Service Act (1883), 478

Penn, Sean, 130

Pennsylvania, 35, 47, 117, 265, 292, 303, 388, 686

Pennsylvania Gazette, 203

penny press, 203

Pentagon Papers, 129

per curiam opinions, **537**

permanent campaign, 297–98, *298*

Perot, Ross, 270, 287, 295, 309

Persian Gulf, 545

Persian Gulf War, 224, 433, 438, 456

personal information, 116, 144–45

Personal Responsibility and Work Opportunity Act (1996), 88, 683

personal vote, 252

Pew Center for Excellence in Journalism, 230

Pew Charitable Trusts, 220

Pew Research Center, *165*, 166, 176, 188, 189

Pew Trust poll, 159

Philadelphia, Pa., **33**, 35, 36, 81, 581

Philippines, 700, 701

Phoenix, Ariz., 553

phone banks, 299, 300

photography, Internet and, *211*, 212

Pierce, Franklin, 431

Pig Book, 406

Pinckney, Charles, 41, 117

plaintiff, 515

Plame, Valerie, 443

Planned Parenthood, 151

Plato, 514

plea bargaining, 515

Pledge of Allegiance, **60**, 61, 135, 531

Plessy v. Ferguson, 559, 577

Plunkitt, George Washington, 251, 478

pluralism, 40, 340, 581

plurality opinions, **537**

plurality voting, 271, 286

pocket vetoes, 441

Pointer v. Texas, **122**

Poland, 41, **486**, 581, **629**, 635, 645, 702–3

Robinson, Jackie, 559
Robinson v. California, **122**
robo-polls, 174
Rockefeller, Nelson, 448
Rock Hill, S.C., 573
Rodriguez, Alex, 144
Roe v. Wade, 151–52, 536, 541, 543–44
Rohde, David, 255, 401
roll call votes, 402
Rolling Stone, 693
Romania, 41
Romney, Mitt, 176, 201, *257*, 281, 282, **295**,
    300, 323, 592, 605
    2012 campaign platform of, 301
    2012 election and, 322–31
Roosevelt, Eleanor, *654*
Roosevelt, Franklin D., 52, 245, *245*, 432, *432*,
    456, 479, 507, 633, 654, 661
    court-packing plan of, 523, 545
    Supreme Court switch and, 542
Roosevelt, Theodore, 29, 432, 674
Rosenberg, Gerald, 544
Ross, Gary, *586*
Rothman, Steven R., 411
Rove, Karl, 360–61, 491
rubber stamping, 50
Ruby Tuesday, 585
rules, influence on political process of, 10, 15, 30
rules and regulations, bureaucracy and, 500
"running scared," 385
runoff elections, 286
Rush Limbaugh Show, The, **220**, 221
Russia, 124, 696, 698, 714
    military size of, **715**
    nuclear weapons of, 702, 729
Rutledge, Justice, 510
Rwanda, 433, 581
Ryan, Paul, *605*, 680

St. Patrick's Day parade, 586
St. Paul, Minn., 127
salience, 368–69, 370
Salon, 210
Salt Lake City, Utah, 125
same-sex marriage, 159–60, 563
Samoa, 581
samples:
    random, 173, **173**, 174, 178
    survey, 173, **173**
sampling error, **173**
Sam's Club, 585
San Antonio, Tex., 97
sanctions, 725
Sandanistas, 51, 702
Sanders, Bernard, *418*
Sanders, Bernie, 624
San Diego, Calif., 216
Sandoval, Martha, 596
Santeria, 114
Santorum, Rick, 282, 658
Sarbanes-Oxley Act (2002), 480
satellite television, 205
Saudi Arabia, 150, 542
Scalia, Antonin, 99, 150, 508, 513, *534*, 535,
    538, 540, *540*, 590
    Lawrence dissent of, 587

Schattschneider, E. E., 12, 104
Schenk, Charles, *120*, 123–24
Schiavo, Michael, 152
Schiavo, Terri, 152
Schickler, Eric, 170
Schilb v. Kuebel, **122**
school desegregation, 55, 542, 543, 570, 571,
    575–78, 591
    Brown I and, 542, 543, 544, 559, 571,
       576–77
    Brown II and, 559, 577
    busing and, 543, 577, *577*
school lunches, 518, 655
school prayer, 21, 61, 115, 133–34, 543, *545*
school vouchers, 21, 23, 686, *686*
Schultz, Debbie Wasserman, *241*
Scotland, 73
Scott, Dred, 82
SCOTUSblog (Supreme Court blog), 210
scrutiny, 123
searches and seizures, 90, 115, 116, **122**,
    140–45, *141*, 153
Seattle, Wash., 578
secession, 80, *379*, 431, 558
Second Amendment, **118**, 121, **122**, 138
Second Continental Congress, 32–33, *32*, 33
second party system, **242**, 243–44, 246
Securities and Exchange Commission (SEC),
    610, 633, 638
security, 7, 74, 76, 89, 114, 115, 128–29, 138,
    143, 144–45, 153, 732
    civil liberties versus, 143
    collective, 701
    foreign policy treaties and, 703, 720
    post-9/11 measures in, 731, *731*
    see also defense
Sedition Act (1918), 79–80, 124
Segal, Jeffrey, 55
segregation, 82, *83*, 89, 93, 181, 559, 563, 570
    de jure vs. de facto, 577
    separate but equal doctrine and, 559,
       575–77
select committees, 407
selective incentives, 352
selective incorporation, 118–21, **122**
self-incrimination, 90, 120, **122**, 139,
    145–47, 148
self-rule:
    constitutional importance of, 36
    Locke's view on, 37
Seminole Tribe v. Florida, **96**
Senate, U.S., 222, 240, 253, 590, 683, 698,
    700, 707, 708
    "advice and consent" of, 50, *51*, 62
    Agriculture Committee of, 407
    appointments confirmed by, 435, 436,
       477, 483, 491, 511, 520, 522, 523,
       525, 526–28, 708
    Appropriations Committee of, 415
    approval ratings of, 187
    bailout bill of 2008 retooled and passed
       in, 622
    Banking, Housing and Urban Affairs
       Committee, *420*
    Bill of Rights creation in, 117
    bills in, 418

    Budget Committee of, 415–17
    constituencies in elections for, 285–86
    Constitutional Convention and,
       35, 41, **45**
    constitutional requirements of
       candidates for, **289**
    creation of laws in, 97, 125, 129, 161
    Democratic control of, 321, 323, 442, 596
    in economic policy making, 614, 616, 619,
       619, 620, 624
    election to, 49, 59, 284, 286
    equal apportionment of states' votes
       in, 61
    filibuster in, 527
    Finance Committee in, 614
    Foreign Relations Committee in, 708
    House vs., 379
    impeachment and, 460–61
    incumbents in, **394**
    Intelligence Committee of, 708
    Iraq War and, 708, 712, 722
    Judiciary Committee of, *51*, 415, 527
    League of Nations and, 432
    majority in, 281
    party ideological differences and
       polarization in, 251–54
    president pro tempore of, 400, 448
    public knowledge of, 176
    reelection to, 385–87
    Republican control of, 92, **185**, 268, 433,
       441, 450, 479, 480, 661
    roll call votes in, 402
    rules and procedures in, 15
    Rules Committee of, 417, 419
    treaties approved by, 439
    veto overridden by, 437, 441
    vice president's presiding over, 451
    see also Congress, U.S.; House of
       Representatives, U.S.
senatorial courtesy, 526
Seneca Falls Convention (1848), 22, 571
senior citizens, 248
Senior Executive Service (SES), 492
seniority, 399
"separate but equal" doctrine, 162, 245, 480,
    559, 575–77
separation of church and state, **122**, 133–35
    school vouchers issue and, 686, *686*
separation of powers, 8, 63, 136, 150, 581
    Articles of Confederation structuring
       of, 33–34
    conflict over, 72, 78–79
    constitutional framework for, 49–54
    issue at Constitutional Convention of,
       39, *39*, 42, 43–44, 47–48
    James Madison's view on, 37, 39–40, 43
    other democracies shunning of, 514
    Supreme Court in, 540, 545
separatism, racial, 21
September 11, 2001 terrorist attacks, 89,
    104, 141, 143, *143*, 144–45, *165*, 166,
    169, **184**, 303, 406, 694, *703*, 712,
    716, 728
    foreign policy impacted by, 703, 706–7,
       731, 733

public opinion on, 91, 161, 165, 176, 485–87, **487**
on social policies, 653–54, 657–58, **674**, 675–76, 681–83
on social welfare, 678
state and local, 88, **88**, 89, 104
U.S. compared with other nations for, 486, **486**
Sperling, Gene, 618
Spirit of the Laws, The (Montesquieu), 37
split tickets, casting of, 318–19
spoils system, 244, 477, *477*, 478
sports, 144
spying:
domestic, 116, 129, 140–41, 143, 144–45, 153; *see also* surveillance
foreign, 144
Sri Lanka, 581
stagflation, 608, 613, *620*
Stamp Act (1765), 31
standardized tests, 686
standard of proof, 515
Standard Oil, 637
standard operating procedures, 473
standing, 518
standing committees, 407
Stanton, Cady, 571
state capacity, 473, 479
State Children's Health Program (SCHIP), **674, 684**
State Department, U.S., 214, 477, **481**, 493, *493*, 628, 666
foreign policy and role of, 705–6
number of employees in, **484**
state laws, judicial review of, 513
State of the Union address, 441, 447, 448
media coverage of, 217
states:
economic differences among, 102, **103**
income assistance and welfare administered by, 681, 682
Medicaid and discretionary power of, 675–76
policy diffusion among, 94, *94*
political differences among, 20, **20**, 23, 138
social policy formation and role of, 662–63, 682
states' rights, 80–81, 86, 87–88, 92–98, 99, 100–101, 117–18, 119, 120–21, 123, 127, 138, 152–53, 513
states' sovereign immunity, 96
statistical analysis, research and, 11
statutory interpretation, 513
Steffens, Lincoln, 204
stem cell research, 21, 23, 92, 492, 660, 681
Stevens, John Paul, 523, 540
Stewart, Jon, 217, 218, 221
Stewart, Potter, 131
Stimson, James, 187
stimulus package, *see* economic stimulus package
Stockman, David, 628
stock markets, 633, 634, 654, 727
in financial crisis of 2008, 621–23, 727
Stone, Harlan Fiske, 536
Stonewall Rebellion, 563

Stop Online Piracy Act (SOPA), 365
straight tickets, casting of, 318–19
Strategic Arms Limitation Treaty (SALT I), 702
street-level bureaucrats, 472
strict construction, 538, 539, 542
see also original intent
strict scrutiny, 123, 129, 582, **582**, 597
strip searches, 140–41
Strong, Benjamin, 636
student activity fees, 126, 134–35
Student Nonviolent Coordinating Committee (SNCC), 573
Stupak, Bart, 268
substantive due process doctrine, 153, 586
substantive representation, 382
Sudan, 150, 581
Darfur conflict in, 725
suicides, assisted, 72, 99
Sullivan, Kathleen, 61
"sunshine reforms," 421
Sunstein, Cass, 93
superdelegates, 291
supermajorities, 46
Supplemental Nutrition Assistance Program, 681
Supplemental Security Income (SSI), 681–82
supply-side economics, 626, 660
Supreme Court, U.S., *51*, 63, 210, 358, 390, *509*, 520–22, *523*, 528–47, 681, 729
ACA and, 70
access to, 528–33, **529**
as agent of change, 544
allocation of power to, 8, **35**, 50, 54, 77
amicus curiae and, 533–34
appellate jurisdiction of, 510, **512**, 520
appointments to, *51*, 54, 79, 95
attitudinalist approach and, 537
briefs for, 533–34
campaign finance reforms and, 125–26, 310
case criteria of, 530–33
chief justices of, 80–81, 117, 510–11
civil liberties and, 117–53
civil rights issues and, 558, 559, 562, 572, 573, 575–87, 589, 593, 594–95, 596
color-blind jurisprudence of, 579–80, 593, 595
constitutional amendments to overturn decisions of, 59, 61, 77, 125
constitutional interpretation by, 44, 55, 60, 62, *62*, 63, 77, 79, 80–81, 95–98, **96**, *97*, 99, 100, **116**, 117–53, 430, 438–39, 458, 512–13, 521, 538, 540, 542, 598
decision making of, 537–42, *543*
docket of, 528, 530
executive privilege ruling of, 443
FDR's court-packing plan for, 523, 545
federalism and, 77, 79, **81**, 82–84, *83*, 89, *90*, 93–98, **96**, 99, 100, 104, 117–18, 120–21, 136, 138, 144, 512
G. W. Bush's appointments to, 435–36
hearing cases before, 533–36, *534*
interpretation of laws by, 8, 13, 50, 54, 79, 83, 93, 95–96, 99, 100, 131–32, 512–13

judicial activism of, 540, 578–80
judicial restraint of, 540
judicial review by, 50, 54, 510–15, *511*, 546
justices' conference in, 535
legislative vetos and, 420
living Constitution and, 55
opinion writing in, 535–36, *536*
oral argument in, 534–35, *534*
original intent, 55, 538, 540
original jurisdiction of, 511, **512**, 529, *530*
pocket vetos and, 415
policy implications of composition of, 52, 54, 79, 95, 100
as policy-making institution, 508, 543–47
as political institution, 508, 532, 537–42
precedent overruled by, 516–17, **517**
public knowledge of, *161*, 162
public opinion and, 536, *536*, 540, 541–42
"riding circuit" by justices of, 510
Rule 10 of, 532, *532*
rules of access for, 529–30
on school voucher programs, 686
separation of powers and, 540, 545
"special master" hearings, and, 530
speech protected by, 112
strategic approach to, 540
strict construction and, 55, 538, 539, 542
2012 elections and, 507
unilateral presidential actions and, 460
War Powers Resolution and, 438–39
workload of, 528–29, **529**
writ of certification and, 530
writ of certiorari and, 530
writ of mandamus issued by, 511
see also judicial branch; *specific cases*
surge, in troops, *see* troop surge
surveillance, 129, 141, 143, 144–45, 458
see also spying
surveys, 163, 191
interpretation of, 178, 180–81, 187
mass, 172, **173**
problems with, 161–64, 176–77, **181**, 712
research and, 11
techniques of, 174–75
wording of, 165, *175*, 180, 184
see also polls
suspension of rules, 417
Sweden, 73, **719**
government spending in, 486, **486**
tax rates in, 629, **629**
Swezy, Dan, *586*
Swift Vets and POWs for Truth, **306**
swine flu, 230, **230**
swing states, 292, **294**
Switzerland, 74, 75, **486, 629, 719**
Syria, 150, 696–97, 699, 722, 725, 732

Taiwan, 581
Taliban, 186, 215, 218, 303, 724, 728
talk radio, 208, 226
Tammany Hall, 251, *251*
Taney, Roger, 80–81
Tanzania, 703
Target, 312
tariffs, 39, 47, 80, 643, 703, 710, 715, 726
definition of, 716